Merriam-Webster's
Notebook
Spanish-English
Dictionary

Merriam-Webster, Incorporated
Springfield, Massachusetts, U.S.A.

Preface

MERRIAM-WEBSTER'S NOTEBOOK SPANISH-ENGLISH DICTIONARY is a concise reference to the core vocabulary of Spanish and English. Its 40,000 entries and over 50,000 translations provide up-to-date coverage of the basic vocabulary and idioms in both languages. In addition, the book includes many specifically Latin-American words and phrases.

IPA (International Phonetic Alphabet) pronunciations are given for all English words. Included as well are tables of irregular verbs in both languages and the most common Spanish and English abbreviations.

This book shares many details of presentation with our larger *Merriam-Webster's Spanish-English Dictionary,* but for reasons of conciseness it also has a number of features uniquely its own. Users need to be familiar with the following major features of this dictionary.

Main entries follow one another in strict alphabetical order, without regard to intervening spaces or hyphens. The Spanish letter combinations *ch* and *ll* are alphabetized within the letters *C* and *L;* however, the Spanish letter *ñ* is alphabetized separately between *N* and *O.*

Homographs (words spelled the same but having different meanings or parts of speech) are run on at a single main entry if they are closely related. Run-on homograph entries are replaced in the text by a boldfaced swung dash (as **haber** . . . *v aux* . . . — ∼ *nm* . . .). Homographs of distinctly different origin (as **date**[1] and **date**[2]) are given separate entries.

Run-on entries for related words that are not homographs may also follow the main entry. Thus we have the main entry **calcular** *vt* followed by run-on entries for — **calculador, -dora** *adj* . . . — **calculadora** *nf* . . . and — **cálculo** *nm.* However, if a related word falls later in the alphabet than a following unrelated main entry, it will be entered at its own place. Thus **ear** and its run-on — **eardrum** precede the main entry **earl** which is followed by the main entry **earlobe.**

Variant spellings appear at the main entry separated by *or* (as **judgment** *or* **judgement, paralyze** *or Brit* **paralyse,** or **cacahuate** *or* **cacahuete**).

Inflected forms of English verbs, adjectives, adverbs, and nouns are shown when they are irregular (as **wage** . . . **waged, waging; ride** . . . **rode, ridden; good** . . . **better, best;** or **fly** . . . *n, pl* **flies**) or when there might be doubt about their spelling (as **ego** . . . *n, pl* **egos**). Inflected forms of Spanish irregular verbs are shown in the section Conjugation of Spanish Verbs on page 3a; numerical references to this table are included at the main entry (as **poseer** {20} *vt*). Irregular plurals of Spanish nouns or adjectives are shown at the main entry (as **ladrón, -drona** *n, mpl* **-drones**).

Cross-references are provided to lead the user to the appropriate main entry (as **mice** → **mouse** or **sobrestimar** → **sobreestimar**).

Pronunciation information is either given explicitly or implied for all English words. Pronunciation of Spanish words is assumed to be regular and is generally omitted; it is included, however, for certain foreign borrowings (as **pizza** ['pitsa, 'pisa]). A full list of the pronunciation symbols used appears on page 6a.

The grammatical function of entry words is indicated by an italic **functional label** (as *vt, adj,* or *nm*). Italic **usage labels** may be added at the entry or sense as well (as **timbre** *nm* . . . **4** *Lat* **:** postage stamp, **center** *or Brit* **centre** . . . *n* . . ., or **garra** *nf* . . . **2** *fam* **:** hand, paw). These labels are also included in the translations (**bag** *n* . . . **2** HANDBAG **:** bolso *m,* cartera *f Lat*).

Usage notes are occasionally placed before a translation to clarify meaning or use (as **que** *conj* . . . **2** (*in comparisons*) **:** than).

Synonyms may appear before the translation word(s) in order to provide context for the meaning of an entry word or sense (as **sitio** *nm* . . . **2** ESPACIO **:** room, space; or **meet** . . . *vt* . . . **2** SATISFY **:** satisfacer).

Bold notes are sometimes used before a translation to introduce a plural sense or a common phrase using the main entry word (as **mueble** *nm* . . . **2** ∼**s** *nmpl* **:** furniture, furnishings, or **call** . . . *vt* . . . **2** ∼ **off :** cancelar). Note that when an entry word is repeated in a bold note, it is replaced by a swung dash.

Contents

A GENUINE MERRIAM-WEBSTER

The name *Webster* alone is no guarantee of excellence. It is used by a number of publishers and may serve mainly to mislead an unwary buyer.

Merriam-Webster™ is the name you should look for when you consider the purchase of dictionaries or other fine reference books. It carries the reputation of a company that has been publishing since 1831 and is your assurance of quality and authority.

Copyright © 2004 by Merriam-Webster, Incorporated
ISBN 978-0-87779-672-5

Made in the United States of America
10TH PTG. HPS OH DECEMBER, 2018

Conjugation of Spanish Verbs

Simple Tenses

Tense	Regular Verbs Ending in -AR hablar		Regular Verbs Ending in -ER comer		Regular Verbs Ending in -IR vivir	
PRESENT INDICATIVE	hablo	hablamos	como	comemos	vivo	vivimos
	hablas	habláis	comes	coméis	vives	vivís
	habla	hablan	come	comen	vive	viven
PRESENT SUBJUNCTIVE	hable	hablemos	coma	comamos	viva	vivamos
	hables	habléis	comas	comáis	vivas	viváis
	hable	hablen	coma	coman	viva	vivan
PRETERIT INDICATIVE	hablé	hablamos	comí	comimos	viví	vivimos
	hablaste	hablasteis	comiste	comisteis	viviste	vivisteis
	habló	hablaron	comió	comieron	vivió	vivieron
IMPERFECT INDICATIVE	hablaba	hablábamos	comía	comíamos	vivía	vivíamos
	hablabas	hablabais	comías	comíais	vivías	vivíais
	hablaba	hablaban	comía	comían	vivía	vivían
IMPERFECT SUBJUNCTIVE	hablara	habláramos	comiera	comiéramos	viviera	viviéramos
	hablaras	hablarais	comieras	comierais	vivieras	vivierais
	hablara	hablaran	comiera	comieran	viviera	vivieran
	or		*or*		*or*	
	hablase	hablásemos	comiese	comiésemos	viviese	viviésemos
	hablases	hablaseis	comieses	comieseis	vivieses	vivieseis
	hablase	hablasen	comiese	comiesen	viviese	viviesen
FUTURE INDICATIVE	hablaré	hablaremos	comeré	comeremos	viviré	viviremos
	hablarás	hablaréis	comerás	comeréis	vivirás	viviréis
	hablará	hablarán	comerá	comerán	vivirá	vivirán
FUTURE SUBJUNCTIVE	hablare	habláremos	comiere	comiéremos	viviere	viviéremos
	hablares	hablareis	comieres	comiereis	vivieres	viviereis
	hablare	hablaren	comiere	comieren	viviere	vivieren
CONDITIONAL	hablaría	hablaríamos	comería	comeríamos	viviría	viviríamos
	hablarías	hablaríais	comerías	comeríais	vivirías	viviríais
	hablaría	hablarían	comería	comerían	viviría	vivirían
IMPERATIVE		hablemos		comamos		vivamos
	habla	hablad	come	comed	vive	vivid
	hable	hablen	coma	coman	viva	vivan
PRESENT PARTICIPLE (GERUND)	hablando		comiendo		viviendo	
PAST PARTICIPLE	hablado		comido		vivido	

Compound Tenses

1. Perfect Tenses

The perfect tenses are formed with *haber* and the past participle:

PRESENT PERFECT
    he hablado, etc. (*indicative*);
    haya hablado, etc. (*subjunctive*)

PAST PERFECT
    había hablado, etc. (*indicative*);
    hubiera hablado, etc. (*subjunctive*)
    or
    hubiese hablado, etc. (*subjunctive*)

PRETERIT PERFECT
    hube hablado, etc. (*indicative*)

FUTURE PERFECT
    habré hablado, etc. (*indicative*)

CONDITIONAL PERFECT
    habría hablado, etc. (*indicative*)

2. Progressive Tenses

The progressive tenses are formed with *estar* and the present participle:

PRESENT PROGRESSIVE
    estoy llamando, etc. (*indicative*);
    esté llamando, etc. (*subjunctive*)

IMPERFECT PROGRESSIVE
    estaba llamando, etc. (*indicative*);
    estuviera llamando, etc. (*subjunctive*)
    or
    estuviese llamando, etc. (*subjunctive*)

PRETERIT PROGRESSIVE
    estuve llamando, etc. (*indicative*)

FUTURE PROGRESSIVE
    estaré llamando, etc. (*indicative*)

CONDITIONAL PROGRESSIVE
    estaría llamando, etc. (*indicative*)

PRESENT PERFECT PROGRESSIVE
    he estado llamando, etc. (*indicative*);
    haya estado llamando, etc. (*subjunctive*)

PAST PERFECT PROGRESSIVE
    había estado llamando, etc. (*indicative*);
    hubiera estado llamando, etc. (*subjunctive*)
    or
    hubiese estado llamando, etc. (*subjunctive*)

Irregular Verbs

The *imperfect subjunctive*, the *future subjunctive*, the *conditional*, and most forms of the *imperative* are not included in the model conjugations, but can be derived as follows:

The *imperfect subjunctive* and the *future subjunctive* are formed from the third person plural form of the preterit tense by removing the last syllable (*-ron*) and adding the appropriate suffix:

PRETERIT INDICATIVE, THIRD PERSON PLURAL (querer)	quisieron
IMPERFECT SUBJUNCTIVE (querer)	quisiera, quisieras, etc. *or* quisiese, quisieses, etc.
FUTURE SUBJUNCTIVE (querer)	quisiere, quisieres, etc.

The *conditional* uses the same stem as the future indicative:

FUTURE INDICATIVE (poner)	pondré, pondrás, etc.
CONDITIONAL (poner)	pondría, pondrías, etc.

The third person singular, first person plural, and third person plural forms of the *imperative* are the same as the corresponding forms of the present subjunctive.

The second person singular form of the *imperative* is generally the same as the third person singular of the present indicative. Exceptions are noted in the model conjugations list.

The second person plural (*vosotros*) form of the *imperative* is formed by removing the final *-r* of the infinitive form and adding a *-d* (ex.: *oír* → *oíd*).

Model Conjugations of Irregular Verbs

The model conjugations below include the following simple tenses: the *present indicative* (*IND*), the *present subjunctive* (*SUBJ*), the *preterit indicative* (*PRET*), the *imperfect indicative* (*IMPF*), the *future indicative* (*FUT*), the second person singular form of the *imperative* (*IMPER*) when it differs from the third person singular of the present indicative, the *gerund* or *present participle* (*PRP*), and the *past participle* (*PP*). Each set of conjugations is preceded by the corresponding infinitive form of the verb, shown in bold type. Only tenses containing irregularities are listed, and the irregular verb forms within each tense are displayed in bold type.

Each irregular verb entry in the Spanish-English section of this dictionary is cross-referenced by number to one or of the following model conjugations. These cross-reference numbers are shown in curly braces { } immediately following the entry's functional label.

1 **abolir** (*defective verb*) : *IND* abolimos, abolís (*other forms not used*); *SUBJ* (*not used*); *IMPER* (*only second person plural is used*)

2 **abrir** : *PP* **abierto**

3 **actuar** : *IND* **actúo, actúas, actúa**, actuamos, actuáis, **actúan**; *SUBJ* **actúe, actúes, actúe**, actuemos, actuéis, **actúen**; *IMPER* **actúa**

4 **adquirir** : *IND* **adquiero, adquieres, adquiere**, adquirimos, adquirís, **adquieren**; *SUBJ* **adquiera, adquieras, adquiera**, adquiramos, adquiráis, **adquieran**; *IMPER* **adquiere**

5 **airar** : *IND* **aíro, aíras, aíra**, airamos, airáis, **aíran**; *SUBJ* **aíre, aíres, aíre**, airemos, airéis, **aíren**; *IMPER* **aíra**

6 **andar** : *PRET* **anduve, anduviste, anduvo, anduvimos, anduvisteis, anduvieron**

7 **asir** : *IND* **asgo**, ases, ase, asimos, asís, asen; *SUBJ* **asga, asgas, asga, asgamos, asgáis, asgan**

8 **aunar** : *IND* **aúno, aúnas, aúna**, aunamos, aunáis, **aúnan**; *SUBJ* **aúne, aúnes, aúne**, aunemos, aunéis, **aúnen**; *IMPER* **aúna**

9 **avergonzar** : *IND* **avergüenzo, avergüenzas, avergüenza**, avergonzamos, avergonzáis, **avergüenzan**; *SUBJ* **avergüence, avergüences, avergüence**, avergoncemos, avergoncéis, **avergüencen**; *PRET* **avergoncé**; *IMPER* **avergüenza**

10 **averiguar** : *SUBJ* **averigüe, averigües, averigüe, averigüemos, averigüéis, averigüen**; *PRET* **averigüé**, averiguaste, averiguó, averiguamos, averiguasteis, averiguaron

11 **bendecir** : *IND* **bendigo**, bendices, bendice, bendecimos, bendecís, **bendicen**; *SUBJ* **bendiga, bendigas, bendiga, bendigamos, bendigáis, bendigan**; *PRET* **bendije, bendijiste, bendijo, bendijimos, bendijisteis, bendijeron**; *IMPER* **bendice**

12 **caber** : *IND* **quepo**, cabes, cabe, cabemos, cabéis, caben; *SUBJ* **quepa, quepas, quepa, quepamos, quepáis, quepan**; *PRET* **cupe, cupiste, cupo, cupimos, cupisteis, cupieron**; *FUT* **cabré, cabrás, cabrá, cabremos, cabréis, cabrán**

13 **caer** : *IND* **caigo**, caes, cae, caemos, caéis, caen; *SUBJ* **caiga, caigas, caiga, caigamos, caigáis, caigan**; *PRET* caí, **caíste, cayó, caímos, caísteis, cayeron**; *PRP* **cayendo**; *PP* **caído**

14 **cocer** : *IND* **cuezo, cueces, cuece**, cocemos, cocéis, **cuecen**; *SUBJ* **cueza, cuezas, cueza**, cozamos, cozáis, **cuezan**; *IMPER* **cuece**

15 **coger** : *IND* **cojo**, coges, coge, cogemos, cogéis, cogen; *SUBJ* **coja, cojas, coja, cojamos, cojáis, cojan**

16 **colgar** : *IND* **cuelgo, cuelgas, cuelga**, colgamos, colgáis, **cuelgan**; *SUBJ* **cuelgue, cuelgues, cuelgue**, colguemos, colguéis, **cuelguen**; *PRET* **colgué**, colgaste, colgó, colgamos, colgasteis, colgaron; *IMPER* **cuelga**

17 **concernir** (*defective verb; used only in the third person singular and plural of the present indicative, present subjunctive, and imperfect subjunctive) see 25* **discernir**

18 **conocer** : *IND* **conozco**, conoces, conoce, conocemos, conocéis, conocen; *SUBJ* **conozca, conozcas, conozca, conozcamos, conozcáis, conozcan**

19 **contar** : *IND* **cuento, cuentas, cuenta**, contamos, contáis, **cuentan**; *SUBJ* **cuente, cuentes, cuente**, contemos, contéis, **cuenten**; *IMPER* **cuenta**

20 **creer** : *PRET* creí, **creíste, creyó, creímos, creísteis, creyeron**; *PRP* **creyendo**; *PP* **creído**

21 **cruzar** : *SUBJ* **cruce, cruces, cruce, crucemos, crucéis, crucen**; *PRET* **crucé**, cruzaste, cruzó, cruzamos, cruzasteis, cruzaron

22 **dar** : *IND* **doy**, das, da, damos, **dais**, dan; *SUBJ* **dé**, des, **dé**, demos, deis, den; *PRET* **di, diste, dio, dimos, disteis, dieron**

23 **decir** : *IND* **digo, dices, dice**, decimos, decís, **dicen**; *SUBJ* **diga, digas, diga, digamos, digáis, digan**; *PRET* **dije, dijiste, dijo, dijimos, dijisteis, dijeron**; *FUT* **diré, dirás, dirá, diremos, diréis, dirán**; *IMPER* **di**; *PRP* **diciendo**; *PP* **dicho**

24 **delinquir** : *IND* **delinco**, delinques, delinque, delinquimos, delinquís, delinquen; *SUBJ* **delinca, delincas, delinca, delincamos, delincáis, delincan**

25 **discernir** : *IND* **discierno, disciernes, discierne**, discernimos, discernís, **disciernen**; *SUBJ* **discierna, disciernas, discierna**, discernamos, discernáis, **disciernan**; *IMPER* **discierne**

26 **distinguir** : *IND* **distingo**, distingues, distingue, distinguimos, distinguís, distinguen; *SUBJ* **distinga, distingas, distinga, distingamos, distingáis, distingan**

27 **dormir** : *IND* **duermo, duermes, duerme**, dormimos, dormís, **duermen**; *SUBJ* **duerma, duermas, duerma, durmamos, durmáis, duerman**; *PRET* dormí, dormiste, **durmió**, dormimos, dormisteis, **durmieron**; *IMPER* **duerme**; *PRP* **durmiendo**

28 **elegir** : *IND* **elijo, eliges, elige**, elegimos, elegís, **eligen**; *SUBJ* **elija, elijas, elija, elijamos, elijáis, elijan**; *PRET* elegí, elegiste, **eligió**, elegimos, elegisteis, **eligieron**; *IMPER* **elige**; *PRP* **eligiendo**

29 **empezar** : *IND* **empiezo, empiezas, empieza**, empezamos, empezáis, **empiezan**; *SUBJ* **empiece, empieces, empiece, empecemos, empecéis, empiecen**; *PRET* **empecé**, empezaste, empezó, empezamos, empezasteis, empezaron; *IMPER* **empieza**

30 **enraizar** : *IND* **enraízo, enraízas, enraíza**, enraizamos, enraizáis, **enraízan**; *SUBJ* **enraíce, enraíces, enraíce**, enraicemos, enraicéis, **enraícen**; *PRET* **enraicé**, enraizaste, enraizó, enraizamos, enraizasteis, enraizaron; *IMPER* **enraíza**

31 **erguir** : *IND* **irgo** or **yergo, irgues** or **yergues, irgue** or **yergue**, erguimos, erguís, **irguen** or **yerguen**; *SUBJ* **irga** or **yerga, irgas** or **yergas, irga** or **yerga, irgamos, irgáis, irgan** or **yergan**; *PRET* erguí, erguiste, **irguió**, erguimos, erguisteis, **irguieron**; *IMPER* **irgue** or **yergue**; *PRP* **irguiendo**

32 **errar** : *IND* **yerro, yerras, yerra**, erramos, erráis, **yerran**; *SUBJ* **yerre, yerres, yerre**, erremos, erréis, **yerren**; *IMPER* **yerra**

33 **escribir** : *PP* **escrito**

34 **estar** : *IND* **estoy, estás, está**, estamos, estáis, **están**; *SUBJ* **esté, estés, esté**, estemos, estéis, **estén**; *PRET* **estuve, estuviste, estuvo, estuvimos, estuvisteis, estuvieron**; *IMPER* **está**

35 **exigir** : *IND* **exijo**, exiges, exige, exigimos, exigís, exigen; *SUBJ* **exija, exijas, exija, exijamos, exijáis, exijan**

36 **forzar** : *IND* **fuerzo, fuerzas, fuerza**, forzamos, forzáis, **fuerzan**; *SUBJ* **fuerce, fuerces, fuerce**, forcemos, forcéis, **fuercen**; *PRET* **forcé**, forzaste, forzó, forzamos, forzasteis, forzaron; *IMPER* **fuerza**

37 **freír** : *IND* **frío, fríes, fríe**, freímos, freís, **fríen**; *SUBJ* **fría, frías, fría, friamos, friáis, frían**; *PRET* freí, **freíste, frió, freímos, freísteis, frieron**; *IMPER* **fríe**; *PRP* **friendo**; *PP* **frito**

38 **gruñir** : *PRET* gruñí, gruñiste, **gruñó**, gruñimos, gruñisteis, **gruñeron**; *PRP* **gruñendo**

39 **haber** : *IND* **he, has, ha, hemos**, habéis, **han**; *SUBJ* **haya, hayas, haya, hayamos, hayáis, hayan**; *PRET* **hube, hubiste, hubo, hubimos, hubisteis, hubieron**; *FUT* **habré, habrás, habrá, habremos, habréis, habrán**; *IMPER* **he**

40 **hacer** : *IND* **hago**, haces, hace, hacemos, hacéis, hacen; *SUBJ* **haga, hagas, haga, hagamos, hagáis, hagan**; *PRET* **hice, hiciste, hizo, hicimos, hicisteis, hicieron**; *FUT* **haré, harás, hará, haremos, haréis, harán**; *IMPER* **haz**; *PP* **hecho**

41 **huir** : *IND* **huyo, huyes, huye**, huimos, huís, **huyen**; *SUBJ* **huya, huyas, huya, huyamos, huyáis, huyan**; *PRET* huí, huiste, **huyó**, huimos, huisteis, **huyeron**; *IMPER* **huye**; *PRP* **huyendo**

42 **imprimir** : *PP* **impreso**

43 **ir** : *IND* **voy, vas, va, vamos, vais, van**; *SUBJ* **vaya, vayas, vaya, vayamos, vayáis, vayan**; *PRET* **fui, fuiste, fue, fuimos, fuisteis, fueron**; *IMPF* **iba, ibas, iba, íbamos, ibais, iban**; *IMPER* **ve**; *PRP* **yendo**; *PP* **ido**

44 **jugar** : *IND* **juego, juegas, juega**, jugamos, jugáis, **juegan**; *SUBJ* **juegue, juegues, juegue, juguemos, juguéis, jueguen**; *PRET* **jugué**, jugaste, jugó, jugamos, jugasteis, jugaron; *IMPER* **juega**

45 **lucir** : *IND* **luzco**, luces, luce, lucimos, lucís, lucen; *SUBJ* **luzca, luzcas, luzca, luzcamos, luzcáis, luzcan**

46 **morir** : *IND* **muero, mueres, muere**, morimos, morís, **mueren**; *SUBJ* **muera, mueras, muera, muramos, muráis, mueran**; *PRET* morí, moriste, **murió**, morimos, moristeis, **murieron**; *IMPER* **muere**; *PRP* **muriendo**; *PP* **muerto**

47 **mover** : *IND* **muevo, mueves, mueve**, movemos, movéis, **mueven**; *SUBJ* **mueva, muevas, mueva**, movamos, mováis, **muevan**; *IMPER* **mueve**

48 **nacer** : *IND* **nazco**, naces, nace, nacemos, nacéis, nacen; *SUBJ* **nazca, nazcas, nazca, nazcamos, nazcáis, nazcan**

49 **negar** : *IND* **niego, niegas, niega**, negamos, negáis, **niegan**; *SUBJ* **niegue, niegues, niegue, neguemos, neguéis, nieguen**; *PRET* **negué**, negaste, negó, negamos, negasteis, negaron; *IMPER* **niega**

50 **oír** : *IND* **oigo, oyes, oye, oímos**, oís, **oyen**; *SUBJ* **oiga, oigas, oiga, oigamos, oigáis, oigan**; *PRET* oí, **oíste, oyó, oímos, oísteis, oyeron**; *IMPER* **oye**; *PRP* **oyendo**; *PP* **oído**

51 **oler** : *IND* **huelo, hueles, huele**, olemos, oléis, **huelen**; *SUBJ* **huela, huelas, huela**, olamos, oláis, **huelan**; *IMPER* **huele**

52 **pagar** : *SUBJ* **pague, pagues, pague, paguemos, paguéis, paguen**; *PRET* **pagué**, pagaste, pagó, pagamos, pagasteis, pagaron

53 **parecer** : *IND* **parezco**, pareces, parece, parecemos, parecéis, parecen; *SUBJ* **parezca, parezcas, parezca, parezcamos, parezcáis, parezcan**

54 **pedir** : *IND* **pido, pides, pide**, pedimos, pedís, **piden**; *SUBJ* **pida, pidas, pida, pidamos, pidáis, pidan**; *PRET* pedí, pediste, **pidió**, pedimos, pedisteis, **pidieron**; *IMPER* **pide**; *PRP* **pidiendo**

55 **pensar** : *IND* **pienso, piensas, piensa**, pensamos, pensáis, **piensan**; *SUBJ* **piense, pienses, piense**, pensemos, penséis, **piensen**; *IMPER* **piensa**

56 **perder** : *IND* **pierdo, pierdes, pierde**, perdemos, perdéis, **pierden**; *SUBJ* **pierda, pierdas, pierda**, perdamos, perdáis, **pierdan**; *IMPER* **pierde**

57 **placer** : *IND* **plazco**, places, place, placemos, placéis, placen; *SUBJ* **plazca, plazcas, plazca, plazcamos, plazcáis, plazcan**; *PRET* plací, placiste, plació *or* **plugo**, placimos, placisteis, placieron *or* **pluguieron**

58 **poder** : *IND* **puedo, puedes, puede**, podemos, podéis, **pueden**; *SUBJ* **pueda, puedas, pueda**, podamos, podáis, **puedan**; *PRET* **pude, pudiste, pudo**, pudimos, pudisteis, **pudieron**; *FUT* **podré, podrás, podrá, podremos, podréis, podrán**; *IMPER* **puede**; *PRP* **pudiendo**

59 **podrir** *or* **pudrir** : *PP* **podrido** *(all other forms based on* pudrir*)*

60 **poner** : *IND* **pongo**, pones, pone, ponemos, ponéis, ponen; *SUBJ* **ponga, pongas, ponga, pongamos, pongáis, pongan**; *PRET* **puse, pusiste, puso**, pusimos, pusisteis, **pusieron**; *FUT* **pondré, pondrás, pondrá, pondremos, pondréis, pondrán**; *IMPER* **pon**; *PP* **puesto**

61 **producir** : *IND* **produzco**, produces, produce, producimos, producís, producen; *SUBJ* **produzca, produzcas, produzca, produzcáis, produzcan**; *PRET* **produje, produjiste, produjo, produjimos, produjisteis, produjeron**

62 **prohibir** : *IND* **prohíbo, prohíbes, prohíbe**, prohibimos, prohibís, **prohíben**; *SUBJ* **prohíba, prohíbas, prohíba**, prohibamos, prohibáis, **prohíban**; *IMPER* **prohíbe**

63 **proveer** : *PRET* proveí, **proveíste, proveyó, proveímos, proveísteis, proveyeron**; *PRP* **proveyendo**; *PP* **provisto**

64 **querer** : *IND* **quiero, quieres, quiere**, queremos, queréis, **quieren**; *SUBJ* **quiera, quieras, quiera**, queramos, queráis, **quieran**; *PRET* **quise, quisiste, quiso**, quisimos, quisisteis, **quisieron**; *FUT* **querré, querrás, querrá, querremos, querréis, querrán**; *IMPER* **quiere**

65 **raer** : *IND* rao *or* **raigo** *or* **rayo**, raes, rae, raemos, raéis, raen; *SUBJ* **raiga** *or* **raya, raigas** *or* **rayas, raiga** *or* **raya, raigamos** *or* **rayamos, raigáis** *or* **rayáis, raigan** *or* **rayan**; *PRET* raí, raíste, rayó, raímos, raísteis, rayeron; *PRP* rayendo; *PP* raído

66 **reír** : *IND* **río, ríes, ríe, reímos**, reís, **ríen**; *SUBJ* **ría, rías, ría, riamos, riáis, rían**; *PRET* reí, **reíste, rió, reímos, reísteis, rieron**; *IMPER* **ríe**; *PRP* **riendo**; *PP* **reído**

67 **reñir** : *IND* **riño, riñes, riñe**, reñimos, reñís, **riñen**; *SUBJ* **riña, riñas, riña, riñamos, riñáis, riñan**; *PRET* reñí, reñiste, **riñó**, reñimos, reñisteis, **riñeron**; *PRP* **riñendo**

68 **reunir** : *IND* **reúno, reúnes, reúne**, reunimos, reunís, **reúnen**; *SUBJ* **reúna, reúnas, reúna**, reunamos, reunáis, **reúnan**; *IMPER* **reúne**

69 **roer** : *IND* roo *or* **roigo** *or* **royo**, roes, roe, roemos, roéis, roen; *SUBJ* roa *or* **roiga** *or* **roya**, roas *or* **roigas** *or* **royas**, roa *or* **roiga** *or* **roya**, roamos *or* **roigamos** *or* **royamos**, roáis *or* **roigáis** *or* **royáis**, roan *or* **roigan** *or* **royan**; *PRET* roí, roíste, royó, roímos, roísteis, royeron; *PRP* royendo; *PP* roído

70 **romper** : *PP* **roto**

71 **saber** : *IND* **sé**, sabes, sabe, sabemos, sabéis, saben; *SUBJ* **sepa, sepas, sepa, sepamos, sepáis, sepan**; *PRET* **supe, supiste, supo**, supimos, supisteis, supieron; *FUT* sabré, sabrás, sabrá, sabremos, sabréis, sabrán

72 **sacar** : *SUBJ* **saque, saques, saque, saquemos, saquéis, saquen**; *PRET* **saqué**, sacaste, sacó, sacamos, sacasteis, sacaron

73 **salir** : *IND* **salgo**, sales, sale, salimos, salís, salen; *SUBJ* **salga, salgas, salga, salgamos, salgáis, salgan**; *FUT* **saldré, saldrás, saldrá, saldremos, saldréis, saldrán**; *IMPER* **sal**

74 **satisfacer** : *IND* **satisfago**, satisfaces, satisface, satisfacemos, satisfacéis, satisfacen; *SUBJ* **satisfaga, satisfagas, satisfaga, satisfagamos, satisfagáis, satisfagan**; *PRET* **satisfice, satisficiste, satisfizo, satisficimos, satisficisteis, satisficieron**; *FUT* **satisfaré, satisfarás, satisfará, satisfaremos, satisfaréis, satisfarán**; *IMPER* **satisfaz** *or* **satisface**; *PP* **satisfecho**

75 **seguir** : *IND* **sigo, sigues, sigue**, seguimos, seguís, **siguen**; *SUBJ* **siga, sigas, siga, sigamos, sigáis, sigan**; *PRET* seguí, seguiste, **siguió**, seguimos, seguisteis, **siguieron**; *IMPER* **sigue**; *PRP* **siguiendo**

76 **sentir** : *IND* **siento, sientes, siente**, sentimos, sentís, **sienten**; *SUBJ* **sienta, sientas, sienta, sintamos, sintáis, sientan**; *PRET* sentí, sentiste, **sintió**, sentimos, sentisteis, **sintieron**; *IMPER* **siente**; *PRP* **sintiendo**

77 **ser** : *IND* **soy, eres, es, somos, sois, son**; *SUBJ* **sea, seas, sea, seamos, seáis, sean**; *PRET* **fui, fuiste, fue, fuimos, fuisteis, fueron**; *IMPF* **era, eras, era, éramos, erais, eran**; *IMPER* **sé**; *PRP* **siendo**; *PP* **sido**

78 **soler** *(defective verb; used only in the present, preterit, and imperfect indicative, and the present and imperfect subjunctive) see* 47 **mover**

79 **tañer** : *PRET* tañí, tañiste, **tañó**, tañimos, tañisteis, **tañeron**; *PRP* **tañendo**

80 **tener** : *IND* **tengo, tienes, tiene**, tenemos, tenéis, **tienen**; *SUBJ* **tenga, tengas, tenga, tengamos, tengáis, tengan**; *PRET* **tuve, tuviste, tuvo, tuvimos, tuvisteis, tuvieron**; *FUT* **tendré, tendrás, tendrá, tendremos, tendréis, tendrán**; *IMPER* **ten**

81 **traer** : *IND* **traigo**, traes, trae, traemos, traéis, traen; *SUBJ* **traiga, traigas, traiga, traigamos, traigáis, traigan**; *PRET* **traje, trajiste, trajo, trajimos, trajisteis, trajeron**; *PRP* **trayendo**; *PP* **traído**

82 **trocar** : *IND* **trueco, truecas, trueca**, trocamos, trocáis, **truecan**; *SUBJ* **trueque, trueques, trueque**, troquemos, troquéis, **truequen**; *PRET* **troqué**, trocaste, trocó, trocamos, trocasteis, trocaron; *IMPER* **trueca**

83 **uncir** : *IND* **unzo**, unces, unce, uncimos, uncís, uncen; *SUBJ* **unza, unzas, unza, unzamos, unzáis, unzan**

84 **valer** : *IND* **valgo**, vales, vale, valemos, valéis, valen; *SUBJ* **valga, valgas, valga, valgamos, valgáis, valgan**; *FUT* **valdré, valdrás, valdrá, valdremos, valdréis, valdrán**

85 **variar** : *IND* **varío, varías, varía**, variamos, variáis, **varían**; *SUBJ* **varíe, varíes, varíe**, variemos, variéis, **varíen**; *IMPER* **varía**

86 **vencer** : *IND* **venzo**, vences, vence, vencemos, vencéis, vencen; *SUBJ* **venza, venzas, venza, venzamos, venzáis, venzan**

87 **venir** : *IND* **vengo, vienes, viene**, venimos, venís, **vienen**; *SUBJ* **venga, vengas, venga, vengamos, vengáis, vengan**; *PRET* **vine, viniste, vino, vinimos, vinisteis, vinieron**; *FUT* **vendré, vendrás, vendrá, vendremos, vendréis, vendrán**; *IMPER* **ven**; *PRP* **viniendo**

88 **ver** : *IND* **veo**, ves, ve, vemos, veis, ven; *PRET* **vi, viste, vio**, vimos, visteis, vieron; *IMPER* **ve**; *PRP* **viendo**; *PP* **visto**

89 **volver** : *IND* **vuelvo, vuelves, vuelve**, volvemos, volvéis, **vuelven**; *SUBJ* **vuelva, vuelvas, vuelva**, volvamos, volváis, **vuelvan**; *IMPER* **vuelve**; *PP* **vuelto**

90 **yacer** : *IND* **yazco** *or* **yazgo** *or* **yago**, yaces, yace, yacemos, yacéis, yacen; *SUBJ* **yazca** *or* **yazga** *or* **yaga, yazcas** *or* **yazgas** *or* **yagas, yazca** *or* **yazga** *or* **yaga, yazcamos** *or* **yazgamos** *or* **yagamos, yazcáis** *or* **yazgáis** *or* **yagáis, yazcan** *or* **yazgan** *or* **yagan**; *IMPER* **yace** *or* **yaz**

Abbreviations in This Work

adj	adjective	*interj*	interjection	*nmfpl*	plural noun invariable for gender	*prep phr*	prepositional phrase
adv	adverb	*Lat*	Latin America			*pron*	pronoun
adv	adverbial phrase	*m*	masculine	*nmfs & pl*	noun invariable for both gender and number	*s.o.*	someone
algn	alguien (someone)	*mf*	masculine or feminine			*sth*	something
art	article	*mpl*	masculine plural	*nmpl*	masculine plural noun	*usu*	usually
Brit	Great Britain	*n*	noun	*nms & pl*	invariable singular or plural masculine noun	*v*	verb
conj	conjunction	*nf*	feminine noun			*v aux*	auxiliary verb
conj phr	conjunctive phrase	*nfpl*	feminine plural noun	*npl*	plural noun	*vi*	intransitive verb
esp	especially	*nfs & pl*	invariable singular or plural feminine noun	*ns & pl*	noun invariable for plural	*v impers*	impersonal verb
etc	et cetera					*vr*	reflexive verb
f	feminine	*nm*	masculine noun	*pl*	plural	*vt*	transitive verb
fam	familiar or colloquial	*nmf*	masculine or feminine noun	*pp*	past participle		
fpl	feminine plural			*prep*	preposition		

Pronunciation Symbols

VOWELS

æ ask, bat, glad
ɑ cot, bomb
a *New England* aunt, *British* ask, glass, *Spanish* casa
e *Spanish* peso, jefe
ɛ egg, bet, fed
ə about, javelin, Alabama
ə when italicized as in əl, əm, ən, indicates a syllabic pronunciation of the consonant as in bottle, prism, button
ər further, stir
i very, any, thirty, *Spanish* piña

iː eat, bead, bee
ɪ id, bid, pit
o Ohio, yellower, potato, *Spanish* óvalo
oː oats, own, zone, blow
ɔ awl, maul, caught, paw
ʊ sure, should, could
uː boot, few, coo
ʌ under, putt, bud
eɪ eight, wade, bay
aɪ ice, bite, tie
aʊ out, gown, plow
ɔɪ oyster, coil, boy
ː indicates the preceding vowel is long. Long vowels are almost always diph-

thongs in English, but not in Spanish.

CONSONANTS

b baby, labor, cab
β *Spanish* cabo, óvalo
d day, ready, kid
dʒ just, badger, fudge
ð then, either, bathe
f foe, tough, buff
g go, bigger, bag
ɣ *Spanish* tragara, daga
h hot, aha
j yes, vineyard
k cat, keep, lacquer, flock
l law, hollow, boil
m mat, hemp, hammer, rim

n new, tent, tenor, run
ɲ *Spanish* cabaña, piña
ŋ rung, hang, swinger
p pay, lapse, top
r rope, burn, tar
s sad, mist, kiss
ʃ shoe, mission, slush
t toe, button, mat
ţ indicates that some speakers of English pronounce this sound as a voiced alveolar flap [ɾ], as in later, catty, battle
tʃ choose, batch
θ thin, ether, bath
v vat, never, cave
w wet, software
z zoo, easy, buzz

ʒ azure, beige
h, k, when italicized indi-
p, t cate sounds which are present in the pronunciation of some speakers of English but absent in the pronunciation of others, so that *whence* ['hwɛnts] can be pronounced as ['hwɛns], ['hwɛnts], ['wɛnts], or ['wɛns]

STRESS MARKS
ˈ high stress **pen**manship
ˌ low stress penman**ship**

Spanish Spelling-to-Sound Correspondences

VOWELS
a [a]
e [e] in open syllables (syllables ending with a vowel); [ɛ] in closed syllables (syllables ending with a consonant)
i [i]; before another vowel in the same syllable pronounced as [j] ([ʒ] or [ʃ] in Argentina and Uruguay; [dʒ] when at the beginning of a word in the Caribbean)
o [o] in open syllables (syllables ending with a vowel); [ɔ] in closed syllables (syllables ending with a consonant)
u [u]; before another vowel in the same syllable pronounced as [w]
y [i]; before another vowel in the same syllable pronounced

as [j] ([ʒ] or [ʃ] in Argentina and Uruguay; [dʒ] when at the beginning of a word in the Caribbean)

CONSONANTS
b [b] at the beginning of a word or after *m* or *n*; [β] elsewhere
c [s] before *i* or *e* in Latin America and parts of southern Spain, [θ] in northern Spain; [k] elsewhere
ch [tʃ]; frequently [ʃ] in Chile and Panama; sometimes [ts] in Chile
d [d] at the beginning of a word or after *n* or *l*; [ð] elsewhere, frequently silent between vowels
f [f]; [Φ] in Honduras (no English equivalent for this sound; like [f] but made with both lips)

g [x] before *i* or *e* ([h] in the Caribbean and Central America); [g] at the beginning of a word or after *n* and not before *i* or *e*; [ɣ] elsewhere, frequently silent between vowels
gu [gw] at the beginning of a word before *a, o;* [ɣw] elsewhere before *a, o;* frequently just [w] between vowels; [g] at the beginning of a word before *i, e;* [ɣ] elsewhere before *i, e;* frequently silent between vowels
gü [gw] at the beginning of a word, [ɣw] elsewhere; frequently just [w] between vowels
h silent
j [x] ([h] in the Caribbean and Central America)
k [k]
l [l]

ll [j]; [ʒ] or [ʃ] in Argentina and Uruguay; [dʒ] when at the beginning of a word in the Caribbean, [lʲ] in Bolivia, Paraguay, Peru, and parts of northern Spain (no English equivalent; like "lli" in million)
m [m]
n [n]; frequently [ŋ] at the end of a word when next word begins with a vowel
ñ [ɲ]
p [p]
qu [k]
r [r] (no English equivalent; a trilled sound) at the beginning of words; [ţ]/[ɾ] elsewhere
rr [r] (no English equivalent; a trilled sound)
s [s]; frequently [z] before *b, d, g, m, n, l, r;* at the end of a word [h] or silent in many parts of Latin Ameri-

ca and some parts of Spain
t [t]
v [b] at the beginning of a word or after *m* or *n;* [β] elsewhere
x [ks] or [gz] between vowels; [s] before consonants
z [s] in Latin America and parts of southern Spain, [θ] in northern Spain; at the end of a word [h] or silent in many parts of Latin America and some parts of Spain

For example words for the phonetic symbols, see Pronunciation Symbols above.

Spanish-English

A

a[1] *nf* : a, first letter of the Spanish alphabet
a[2] *prep* **1** : to **2 ~ las dos** : at two o'clock **3 al día siguiente** : (on) the following day **4 ~ pied** : on foot **5 de lunes ~ viernes** : from Monday until Friday **6 tres veces ~ la semana** : three times per week **7 ~ la** : in the manner of, like
abadía *nf* : abbey
abajo *adv* **1** : down, below, downstairs **2 ~ de** *Lat* : under, beneath **3 de ~** : (at the) bottom **4 hacia ~** : downwards
abalanzarse {21} *vr* : hurl oneself, rush
abandonar *vt* **1** : abandon, leave **2** RENUNCIAR A : give up — **abandonarse** *vr* **1** : neglect oneself **2 ~ a** : give oneself over to — **abandonado, -da** *adj* **1** : abandoned, deserted **2** DESCUIDADO : neglected **3** DESALIÑADO : slovenly — **abandono** *nm* **1** : abandonment, neglect **2 por ~** : by default
abanico *nm* : fan — **abanicar** {72} *vt* : fan
abaratar *vt* : lower the price of — **abaratarse** *vr* : become cheaper
abarcar {72} *vt* **1** : cover, embrace **2** *Lat* : monopolize
abarrotar *vt* : pack, cram — **abarrotes** *nmpl Lat* **1** : groceries **2 tienda de ~** : grocery store
abastecer {53} *vt* : supply, stock — **abastecimiento** *nm* : supply, provisions — **abasto** *nm* **1** : supply **2 no dar ~ a** : be unable to cope with
abatir *vt* **1** : knock down, shoot down **2** DEPRIMIR : depress — **abatirse** *vr* **1** : get depressed **2 ~ sobre** : swoop down on — **abatido, -da** *adj* : dejected, depressed — **abatimiento** *nm* : depression, dejection
abdicar {72} *v* : abdicate — **abdicación** *nf, pl* **-ciones** : abdication
abdomen *nm, pl* **-dómenes** : abdomen — **abdominal** *adj* : abdominal
abecé *nm* : ABC — **abecedario** *nm* : alphabet
abedul *nm* : birch
abeja *nf* : bee — **abejorro** *nm* : bumblebee
aberración *nf, pl* **-ciones** : aberration
abertura *nf* : opening
abeto *nm* : fir (tree)
abierto, -ta *adj* : open
abigarrado, -da *adj* : multicolored
abismo *nm* : abyss, chasm — **abismal** *adj* : vast, enormous
abjurar *vi* **~ de** : abjure
ablandar *vt* : soften (up) — **ablandarse** *vr* : soften
abnegarse {49} *vr* : deny oneself — **abnegado, -da** *adj* : self-sacrificing — **abnegación** *nf, pl* **-ciones** : self-denial
abochornar *vt* : embarrass — **abochornarse** *vr* : get embarrassed
abofetear *vt* : slap
abogado, -da *n* : lawyer — **abogacía** *nf* : legal profession — **abogar** {52} *vi* **~ por** : plead for, defend
abolengo *nm* : lineage
abolir {1} *vt* : abolish — **abolición** *nf, pl* **-ciones** : abolition
abollar *vt* : dent — **abolladura** *nf* : dent
abominar *vt* : abominate — **abominable** *adj* : abominable — **abominación** *nf, pl* **-ciones** : abomination
abonar *vt* **1** : pay (a bill, etc.) **2** : fertilize (the soil) — **abonarse** *vr* : subscribe — **abonado, -da** *n* : subscriber — **abono** *nm* **1** : payment, installment **2** FERTILIZANTE : fertilizer **3** : season ticket (to the theater, etc.)
abordar *vt* **1** : tackle (a problem) **2** : accost, approach (a person) **3** *Lat* : board — **abordaje** *nm* : boarding
aborigen *nmf, pl* **-rígenes** : aborigine — **~** *adj* : aboriginal, native
aborrecer {53} *vt* : abhor, detest — **aborrecible** *adj* : hateful — **aborrecimiento** *nm* : loathing
abortar *vi* : have a miscarriage — *vt* : abort — **aborto** *nm* : abortion, miscarriage
abotonar *vt* : button — **abotonarse** *vr* : button up
abovedado, -da *adj* : vaulted
abrasar *vt* : burn, scorch — **abrasarse** *vr* : burn up — **abrasador, -dora** *adj* : burning
abrasivo, -va *adj* : abrasive — **abrasivo** *nm* : abrasive
abrazar {21} *vt* : hug, embrace — **abrazarse** *vr* : embrace — **abrazadera** *nf* : clamp — **abrazo** *nm* : hug, embrace
abrebotellas *nms & pl* : bottle opener — **abrelatas** *nms & pl* : can opener
abrevadero *nm* : watering trough
abreviar *vt* **1** : shorten, abridge **2** : abbreviate (a word) — **abreviación** *nf, pl* **-ciones** : shortening — **abreviatura** *nf* : abbreviation
abridor *nm* : bottle opener, can opener
abrigar {52} *vt* **1** : wrap up (in clothing) **2** ALBERGAR : cherish, harbor — **abrigarse** *vr* : dress warmly — **abrigado, -da** *adj* **1** : sheltered **2** : warm, wrapped up (of persons) — **abrigo** *nm* **1** : coat, overcoat **2** REFUGIO : shelter, refuge
abril *nm* : April
abrillantar *vt* : polish, shine
abrir {2} *vt* **1** : open **2** : unlock, undo — *vi* : open up — **abrirse** *vr* **1** : open up **2** : clear up (of weather)
abrochar *vt* : button, fasten — **abrocharse** *vr* : fasten, do up
abrogar {52} *vt* : annul, repeal
abrumar *vt* : overwhelm — **abrumador, -dora** *adj* : overwhelming, oppressive
abrupto, -ta *adj* **1** ESCARPADO : steep **2** ÁSPERO : rugged, harsh **3** REPENTINO : abrupt
absceso *nm* : abscess
absolución *nf, pl* **-ciones 1** : absolution **2** : acquittal (in law)
absoluto, -ta *adj* **1** : absolute, unconditional **2 en absoluto** : not at all — **absolutamente** *adv* : absolutely
absolver {89} *vt* **1** : absolve **2** : acquit (in law)
absorber *vt* **1** : absorb **2** : take up (time, energy, etc.) — **absorbente** *adj* **1** : absorbent **2** INTERESANTE : absorbing — **absorción** *nf, pl* **-ciones** : absorption — **absorto, -ta** *adj* : absorbed, engrossed
abstemio, -mia *adj* : abstemious — **~** *n* : teetotaler
abstenerse {80} *vr* : abstain, refrain — **abstención** *nf, pl* **-ciones** : abstention — **abstinencia** *nf* : abstinence
abstracción *nf, pl* **-ciones** : abstraction — **abstracto, -ta** *adj* : abstract — **abstraer** {81} *vt* : abstract — **abstraerse** *vr* : lose oneself in thought — **abstraído, -da** *adj* : preoccupied
absurdo, -da *adj* : absurd, ridiculous — **absurdo** *nm* : absurdity
abuchear *vt* : boo, jeer — **abucheo** *nm* : booing
abuelo, -la *n* **1** : grandfather, grandmother **2 abuelos** *nmpl* : grandparents
abulia *nf* : apathy, lethargy
abultar *vi* : bulge, be bulky — *vt* : enlarge, expand — **abultado, -da** *adj* : bulky
abundar *vi* : abound, be plentiful — **abundancia** *nf* : abundance — **abundante** *adj* : abundant
aburrir *vt* : bore — **aburrirse** *vr* : get bored — **aburrido, -da** *adj* **1** : bored **2** TEDIOSO : boring — **aburrimiento** *nm* : boredom
abusar *vi* **1** : go too far **2 ~ de** : abuse — **abusivo, -va** *adj* : outrageous, excessive — **abuso** *nm* : abuse
abyecto, -ta *adj* : abject, wretched
acá *adv* : here, over here
acabar *vi* **1** : finish, end **2 ~ de** : have just (done something) **3 ~ con** : put an end to **4 ~ por** : end up (doing sth) — *vt* : finish — **acabarse** *vr* : come to an end — **acabado, -da** *adj* **1** : finished, perfect **2** AGOTADO : old, worn-out — **acabado** *nm* : finish
academia *nf* : academy — **académico, -ca** *adj* : academic
acaecer {53} *vi* : happen, occur
acallar *vt* : quiet, silence
acalorar *vt* : stir up, excite — **acalorarse** *vr* : get worked up — **acalorado, -da** *adj* : emotional, heated
acampar *vi* : camp — **acampada** *nf* **ir de ~** : go camping
acanalado, -da *adj* **1** : grooved **2** : corrugated (of iron, etc.)
acantilado *nm* : cliff
acaparar *vt* **1** : hoard **2** MONOPOLIZAR : monopolize
acápite *nm Lat* : paragraph
acariciar *vt* **1** : caress **2** : cherish (hopes, ideas, etc.)
ácaro *nm* : mite
acarrear *vt* **1** : haul, carry **2** OCASIONAR : give rise to — **acarreo** *nm* : transport
acaso *adv* **1** : perhaps, maybe **2 por si ~** : just in case
acatar *vt* : comply with, respect — **acatamiento** *nm* : compliance, respect
acatarrarse *vr* : catch a cold
acaudalado, -da *adj* : wealthy, rich
acaudillar *vt* : lead
acceder *vi* **1** : agree **2 ~ a** : gain access to, enter
acceso *nm* **1** : access **2** ENTRADA : entrance **3** : attack, bout (of an illness) — **accesible** *adj* : accessible
accesorio *nm* : accessory — **accesorio, -ria** *adj* : incidental
accidentado, -da *adj* **1** : eventful, turbulent **2** : rough, uneven (of land, etc.) **3** HERIDO : injured — **~** *n* : accident victim
accidental *adj* : accidental — **accidentarse** *vr* : have an accident — **accidente** *nm* **1** : accident **2** : unevenness (of land)
acción *nf, pl* **-ciones 1** : action **2** ACTO : act, deed **3** : share, stock (in finance) — **accionar** *vt* : activate — *vi* : gesticulate — **accionista** *nmf* : stockholder
acebo *nm* : holly
acechar *vt* : watch, stalk — **acecho** *nm* **estar al ~ por** : be on the lookout for
aceite *nm* : oil — **aceitar** *vt* : oil — **aceitera** *nf* **1** : oilcan **2** : cruet (in cookery) **3** *Lat* : oil refinery — **aceitoso, -sa** *adj* : oily
aceituna *nf* : olive
acelerar *v* : accelerate — **acelerarse** *vr* : hurry up — **aceleración** *nf, pl* **-ciones** : acceleration — **acelerador** *nm* : accelerator
acelga *nf* : (Swiss) chard
acentuar {3} *vt* **1** : accent **2** ENFATIZAR : emphasize, stress — **acentuarse** *vr* : stand out — **acento** *nm* **1** : accent **2** ÉNFASIS : stress, emphasis
acepción *nf, pl* **-ciones** : sense, meaning
aceptar *vt* : accept — **aceptable** *adj* : acceptable — **aceptación** *nf, pl* **-ciones 1** : acceptance **2** ÉXITO : success
acequia *nf* : irrigation ditch
acera *nf* : sidewalk
acerbo, -ba *adj* : harsh, caustic
acerca *prep* **~ de** : about, concerning
acercar {72} *vt* : bring near or closer — **acercarse** *vr* : approach, draw near
acero *nm* **1** : steel **2 ~ inoxidable** : stainless steel
acérrimo, -ma *adj* **1** : staunch, steadfast **2** : bitter (of an enemy)
acertar {55} *vt* : guess correctly — *vi* **1** ATINAR : be accurate **2 ~ a** : manage to — **acertado, -da** *adj* : correct, accurate
acertijo *nm* : riddle
acervo *nm* : heritage
acetona *nf* : acetone, nail-polish remover
achacar {72} *vt* : attribute, impute
achacoso, -sa *adj* : sickly
achaparrado, -da *adj* : squat, stocky
achaque *nm* : aches and pains
achatar *vt* : flatten
achicar {72} *vt* **1** : make smaller **2** ACOBARDAR : intimidate **3** : bail out (water) — **achicarse** *vr* : become intimidated
achicharrar *vt* : scorch, burn to a crisp
achicoria *nf* : chicory
aciago, -ga *adj* : fateful, unlucky
acicalar *vt* : dress up, adorn — **acicalarse** *vr* : get dressed up
acicate *nm* **1** : spur **2** INCENTIVO : incentive
ácido, -da *adj* : acid, sour — **acidez** *nf, pl* **-deces** : acidity — **ácido** *nm* : acid
acierto *nm* **1** : correct answer **2** HABILIDAD : skill, sound judgment
aclamar *vt* : acclaim — **aclamación** *nf, pl* **-ciones** : acclaim, applause
aclarar *vt* **1** CLARIFICAR : clarify, explain **2** : rinse (clothing) **3 ~ la voz** : clear one's throat — *vi* : clear up — **aclararse** *vr* : become clear — **aclaración** *nf, pl* **-ciones** : explanation — **aclaratorio, -ria** *adj* : explanatory
aclimatar *vt* : acclimatize — **aclimatarse** *vr* **~ a** : get used to — **aclimatación** *nf, pl* **-ciones** : acclimatization
acné *nm* : acne
acobardar *vt* : intimidate — **acobardarse** *vr* : become frightened
acodarse *vr* **~ en** : lean (one's elbows) on
acoger {15} *vt* **1** REFUGIAR : shelter **2** RECIBIR : receive, welcome — **acogerse** *vr* **1** : take refuge **2 ~ a** : resort to — **acogedor, -dora** *adj* : cozy, welcoming — **acogida** *nf* **1** : welcome **2** REFUGIO : refuge
acolchar *vt* : pad
acólito *nm* MONAGUILLO : altar boy
acometer *vt* **1** : attack **2** EMPRENDER : undertake — *vi* **~ contra** : rush against — **acometida** *nf* : attack, assault
acomodar *vt* **1** ADAPTAR : adjust **2** COLOCAR : put, make a place for — **acomodarse** *vr* **1** : settle in **2 ~ a** : adapt to — **acomodado, -da** *adj* : well-to-do — **acomodaticio, -cia** *adj* : accommodating, obliging — **acomodo** *nm* : job, position
acompañar *vt* **1** : accompany **2** ADJUNTAR : enclose — **acompañamiento** *nm* : accompaniment — **acompañante** *nmf* **1** COMPAÑERO : companion **2** : accompanist (in music)
acompasado, -da *adj* : rhythmic, measured
acondicionar *vt* : fit out, equip — **acondicionado, -da** *adj* : equipped
acongojar *vt* : distress, upset — **acongojarse** *vr* : get upset
aconsejar *vt* : advise — **aconsejable** *adj* : advisable
acontecer {53} *vi* : occur, happen — **acontecimiento** *nm* : event
acopiar *vt* : gather, collect — **acopio** *nm* : collection, stock
acoplar *vt* : couple, connect — **acoplarse** *vr* : fit together — **acoplamiento** *nm* : connection, coupling
acorazado, -da *adj* : armored — **acorazado** *nm* : battleship
acordar {19} *vt* **1** : agree (on) **2** *Lat* : award — **acordarse** *vr* : remember
acorde *adj* **1** : in agreement **2 ~ con** : in keeping with — **~** *nm* : chord (in music)
acordeón *nm, pl* **-deones** : accordion
acordonar *vt* **1** : cordon off **2** : lace up (shoes)
acorralar *vt* : corner, corral
acortar *vt* : shorten, cut short — **acortarse** *vr* : get shorter
acosar *vt* : hound, harass — **acoso** *nm* : harassment
acostar {19} *vt* : put to bed — **acostarse** *vr* **1** : go to bed **2** TUMBARSE : lie down
acostumbrar *vt* : accustom — *vi* **~ a** : be in the habit of — **acostumbrarse** *vr* **~ a** : get used to — **acostumbrado, -da** *adj* **1** HABITUADO : accustomed **2** HABITUAL : usual
acotar *vt* **1** ANOTAR : annotate **2** DELIMITAR : mark off (land) — **acotación** *nf, pl* **-ciones** : marginal note — **acotado, -da** *adj* : enclosed
acre *adj* **1** : pungent **2** MORDAZ : harsh, biting
acrecentar {55} *vt* : increase — **acrecentamiento** *nm* : growth, increase
acreditar *vt* **1** : accredit, authorize **2** PROBAR : prove — **acreditarse** *vr* : prove oneself — **acreditado, -da** *adj* **1** : reputable **2** : accredited (in politics, etc.)
acreedor, -dora *adj* : worthy — **~** *n* : creditor
acribillar *vt* **1** : riddle, pepper **2 ~ a** : harass with
acrílico *nm* : acrylic
acrimonia *nf* or **acritud** *nf* **1** : pungency **2** RESENTIMIENTO : bitterness, acrimony
acrobacia *nf* : acrobatics — **acróbata** *nmf* : acrobat — **acrobático, -ca** *adj* : acrobatic
acta *nf* **1** : certificate **2** : minutes *pl* (of a meeting)
actitud *nf* **1** : attitude **2** POSTURA : posture, position
activar *vt* **1** : activate **2** ESTIMULAR : stimulate, speed up — **actividad** *nf* : activity — **activo, -va** *adj* : active — **activo** *nm* : assets *pl*
acto *nm* **1** ACCIÓN : act, deed **2** : act (in theater) **3 en el ~** : right away
actor *nm* : actor — **actriz** *nf, pl* **-trices** : actress
actual *adj* : present, current — **actualidad** *nf* **1** : present time **2 ~es** *nfpl* : current affairs — **actualizar** {21} *vt* : modernize — **actualización** *nf, pl* **-ciones** : modernization — **actualmente** *adv* : at present, nowadays

actuar {3} *vi* **1** : act, perform **2 ~ de** : act as
acuarela *nf* : watercolor
acuario *nm* : aquarium
acuartelar *vt* : quarter (troops)
acuático, -ca *adj* : aquatic, water
acuchillar *vt* : knife, stab
acudir *vi* **1** : go, come **2 ~ a** : be present at, attend **3 ~ a** : turn to
acueducto *nm* : aqueduct
acuerdo *nm* **1** : agreement **2 de ~** : OK, all right **3 de ~ con** : in accordance with **4 estar de ~** : agree
acumular *vt* : accumulate — **acumularse** *vr* : pile up — **acumulación** *nf, pl* **-ciones** : accumulation — **acumulador** *nm* : storage battery — **acumulativo, -va** *adj* : cumulative
acunar *vt* : rock
acuñar *vt* **1** : mint (money) **2** : coin (a word)
acuoso, -sa *adj* : watery
acupuntura *nf* : acupuncture
acurrucarse {72} *vr* : curl up, nestle
acusar *vt* **1** : accuse **2** MOSTRAR : reveal, show — **acusación** *nf, pl* **-ciones** : accusation, charge — **acusado, -da** *adj* : prominent, marked — **~** *n* : defendant
acuse *nm* **~ de recibo** : acknowledgment of receipt
acústica *nf* : acoustics — **acústico, -ca** *adj* : acoustic
adagio *nm* **1** REFRÁN : adage, proverb **2** : adagio (in music)
adaptar *vt* **1** : adapt **2** AJUSTAR : adjust, fit — **adaptarse** *vr* **~ a** : adapt to — **adaptable** *adj* : adaptable — **adaptación** *nf, pl* **-ciones** : adaptation — **adaptador** *nm* : adapter (in electricity)
adecuar {8} *vt* : adapt, make suitable — **adecuarse** *vr* **~ a** : be appropriate for — **adecuado, -da** *adj* : suitable, appropriate
adelantar *vt* **1** : advance, move forward **2** PASAR : overtake **3** : pay in advance — **adelantarse** *vr* **1** : move forward, get ahead **2** : be fast (of a clock) — **adelantado, -da** *adj* **1** : advanced, ahead **2** : fast (of a clock) **3 por ~** : in advance — **adelante** *adv* **1** : ahead, forward **2 ¡~!** : come in! **3 más ~** : later on, further on — **adelanto** *nm* **1** : advance **2** *or* **~ de dinero** : advance payment
adelgazar {21} *vt* : make thin — *vi* : lose weight
ademán *nm, pl* **-manes 1** GESTO : gesture **2 ~es** *nmpl* : manners **3 en ~ de** : as if to
además *adv* **1** : besides, furthermore **2 ~ de** : in addition to, as well as
adentro *adv* : inside, within — **adentrarse** *vr* **~ en** : go into, get inside of
adepto, -ta *n* : follower, supporter
aderezar {21} *vt* : season, dress — **aderezo** *nm* : dressing, seasoning
adeudar *vt* **1** : debit **2** DEBER : owe — **adeudo** *nm* **1** DÉBITO : debit **2** *Lat* : debt
adherirse {76} *vr* : adhere, stick — **adherencia** *nf* : adherence — **adhesión** *nf, pl* **-siones 1** : adhesion **2** APOYO : support — **adhesivo, -va** *adj* : adhesive — **adhesivo** *nm* : adhesive
adición *nf, pl* **-ciones** : addition — **adicional** *adj* : additional
adicto, -ta *adj* : addicted — **~** *n* : addict
adiestrar *vt* : train
adinerado, -da *adj* : wealthy
adiós *nm, pl* **adioses 1** : farewell **2 ¡~!** : good-bye!
aditamento *nm* : attachment, accessory
aditivo *nm* : additive
adivinar *vt* **1** : guess **2** PREDECIR : foretell — **adivinación** *nf, pl* **-ciones** : guessing, prediction — **adivinanza** *nf* : riddle — **adivino, -na** *n* : fortune-teller
adjetivo *nm* : adjective
adjudicar {72} *vt* : award — **adjudicarse** *vr* : appropriate — **adjudicación** *nf, pl* **-ciones** : awarding
adjuntar *vt* : enclose (with a letter, etc.) — **adjunto, -ta** *adj* : enclosed, attached — **~** *n* : assistant
administración *nf, pl* **-ciones 1** : administration **2** : administering (of a drug, etc.) **3** DIRECCIÓN : management — **administrador, -dora** *n* : administrator, manager — **administrar** *vt* **1** : manage, run **2** : administer (a drug, etc.) — **administrativo, -va** *adj* : administrative
admirar *vt* : admire — **admirarse** *vr* : be amazed — **admirable** *adj* : admirable — **admiración** *nf, pl* **-ciones 1** : admiration **2** ASOMBRO : amazement — **admirador, -dora** *n* : admirer
admitir *vt* **1** : admit **2** ACEPTAR : accept — **admisible** *adj* : admissible, acceptable — **admisión** *nf, pl* **-siones 1** : admission **2** ACEPTACIÓN : acceptance
ADN *nm* : DNA
adobe *nm* : adobe
adobo *nm* : marinade
adoctrinar *vt* : indoctrinate — **adoctrinamiento** *nm* : indoctrination
adolecer {53} *vi* **~ de** : suffer from
adolescente *adj & nmf* : adolescent — **adolescencia** *nf* : adolescence
adonde *conj* : where
adónde *adv* : where
adoptar *vt* : adopt (a child), take (a decision) — **adopción** *nf, pl* **-ciones** : adoption — **adoptivo, -va** *adj* : adopted, adoptive
adoquín *nm, pl* **-quines** : cobblestone
adorar *vt* : adore, worship — **adorable** *adj* : adorable — **adoración** *nf, pl* **-ciones** : adoration, worship
adormecer {53} *vt* **1** : make sleepy **2** ENTUMECER : numb — **adormecerse** *vr* : doze off — **adormecimiento** *nm* : drowsiness — **adormilarse** *vr* : doze
adornar *vt* : decorate, adorn — **adorno** *nm* : ornament, decoration
adquirir {4} *vt* **1** : acquire **2** COMPRAR : purchase — **adquisición** *nf, pl* **-ciones 1** : acquisition **2** COMPRA : purchase
adrede *adv* : intentionally, on purpose
adscribir {33} *vt* : assign, appoint
aduana *nf* : customs (office) — **aduanero, -ra** *adj* : customs — **~** *n* : customs officer
aducir {61} *vt* : cite, put forward
adueñarse *vr* **~ de** : take possession of
adular *vt* : flatter — **adulación** *nf, pl* **-ciones** : adulation, flattery — **adulador, -dora** *adj* : flattering — **~** *n* : flatterer
adulterar *vt* : adulterate
adulterio *nm* : adultery — **adúltero, -ra** *n* : adulterer
adulto, -ta *adj & n* : adult
adusto, -ta *adj* : stern, severe
advenedizo, -za *n* : upstart
advenimiento *nm* : advent, arrival
adverbio *nm* : adverb — **adverbial** *adj* : adverbial
adversario, -ria *n* : adversary, opponent — **adverso, -sa** *adj* : adverse — **adversidad** *nf* : adversity
advertir {76} *vt* **1** AVISAR : warn **2** NOTAR : notice — **advertencia** *nf* : warning
adviento *nm* : Advent
adyacente *adj* : adjacent
aéreo, -rea *adj* : aerial, air
aerobic *nm* : aerobics *pl*
aerodinámico, -ca *adj* : aerodynamic
aeródromo *nm* : airfield
aerolínea *nf* : airline
aeromozo, -za *n* : flight attendant, steward *m*, stewardess *f*
aeronave *nf* : aircraft
aeropuerto *nm* : airport
aerosol *nm* : aerosol, spray
afable *adj* : affable — **afabilidad** *nf* : affability
afán *nm, pl* **afanes 1** ANHELO : eagerness **2** EMPEÑO : effort, hard work — **afanarse** *vr* : toil — **afanosamente** *adv* : industriously, busily — **afanoso, -sa** *adj* **1** : eager **2** TRABAJOSO : arduous
afear *vt* : make ugly, disfigure
afección *nf, pl* **-ciones** : ailment, complaint
afectar *vt* : affect — **afectación** *nf, pl* **-ciones** : affectation — **afectado, -da** *adj* : affected
afectivo, -va *adj* : emotional
afecto *nm* : affection — **afecto, -ta** *adj* **~ a** : fond of — **afectuoso, -sa** *adj* : affectionate, caring
afeitar *vt* : shave — **afeitarse** *vr* : shave — **afeitada** *nf* : shave
afeminado, -da *adj* : effeminate
aferrarse {55} *vr* : cling, hold on
afianzar {21} *vt* : secure, strengthen — **afianzarse** *vr* : become established
afiche *nm Lat* : poster
afición *nf, pl* **-ciones 1** : penchant, fondness **2** PASATIEMPO : hobby — **aficionado, -da** *n* **1** ENTUSIASTA : enthusiast, fan **2** AMATEUR : amateur — **aficionarse** *vr* **~ a** : become interested in
afilar *vt* : sharpen — **afilado, -da** *adj* : sharp — **afilador** *nm* : sharpener
afiliarse *vr* **~ a** : join, become a member of — **afiliación** *nf, pl* **-ciones** : affiliation — **afiliado, -da** *adj* : affiliated
afín *adj, pl* **afines** : related, similar — **afinidad** *nf* : affinity, similarity
afinar *vt* **1** : tune **2** PULIR : perfect, refine
afirmar *vt* **1** : state, affirm **2** REFORZAR : strengthen — **afirmación** *nf, pl* **-ciones** : statement, affirmation — **afirmativo, -va** *adj* : affirmative
afligir {35} *vt* **1** : afflict **2** APENAR : distress — **afligirse** *vr* : grieve — **aflicción** *nf, pl* **-ciones** : grief, sorrow — **afligido -da** *adj* : sorrowful, distressed
aflojar *vt* : loosen, slacken — *vi* : ease up — **aflojarse** *vr* : become loose, slacken
aflorar *vi* : come to the surface, emerge — **afloramiento** *nm* : outcrop
afluencia *nf* : influx — **afluente** *nm* : tributary
afortunado, -da *adj* : fortunate, lucky — **afortunadamente** *adv* : fortunately
afrentar *vt* : insult — **afrenta** *nf* : affront, insult
africano, -na *adj* : African
afrontar *vt* : confront, face
afuera *adv* **1** : out **2** : outside, outdoors — **afueras** *nfpl* : outskirts
agachar *vt* : lower — **agacharse** *vr* : crouch, stoop
agalla *nf* **1** BRANQUIA : gill **2 tener ~s** *fam* : have guts
agarrar *vt* **1** ASIR : grasp **2** *Lat* : catch — **agarrarse** *vr* : hold on, cling — **agarradera** *nf Lat* : handle — **agarrado, -da** *adj fam* : stingy — **agarre** *nm* : grip, grasp — **agarrón** *nm, pl* **-rones** : tug, pull
agasajar *vt* : fête, wine and dine — **agasajo** *nm* : lavish attention
agave *nm* : agave
agazaparse *vr* : crouch down
agencia *nf* : agency, office — **agente** *nmf* : agent, officer
agenda *nf* **1** : agenda **2** LIBRETA : notebook
ágil *adj* : agile — **agilidad** *nf* : agility
agitar *vt* **1** : agitate, shake **2** : wave, flap (wings, etc.) **3** PERTURBAR : stir up — **agitarse** *vr* **1** : toss about **2** INQUIETARSE : get upset — **agitación** *nf, pl* **-ciones 1** : agitation, shaking **2** INTRANQUILIDAD : restlessness — **agitado, -da** *adj* **1** : agitated, excited **2** : choppy, rough (of the sea)
aglomerar *vt* : amass — **aglomerarse** *vr* : crowd together
agnóstico, -ca *adj & n* : agnostic
agobiar *vt* **1** : oppress **2** ABRUMAR : overwhelm — **agobiado, -da** *adj* : weary, weighed down — **agobiante** *adj* : oppressing, oppressive
agonizar {21} *vi* : be dying — **agonía** *nf* **1** : death throes **2** PENA : agony — **agonizante** *adj* : dying
agorero, -ra *adj* : ominous
agostar *vt* : wither
agosto *nm* : August
agotar *vt* **1** : deplete, use up **2** CANSAR : exhaust, weary — **agotarse** *vr* **1** : run out, give out **2** CANSARSE : get tired — **agotado, -da** *adj* **1** CANSADO : exhausted **2** : sold out — **agotador, -dora** *adj* : exhausting — **agotamiento** *nm* : exhaustion
agraciado, -da *adj* **1** : attractive **2** AFORTUNADO : fortunate
agradar *vi* : be pleasing — **agradable** *adj* : pleasant, agreeable — **agrado** *nm* **1** : taste, liking **2 con ~** : with pleasure
agradecer {53} *vt* : be grateful for, thank — **agradecido, -da** *adj* : grateful — **agradecimiento** *nm* : gratitude
agrandar *vt* : enlarge — **agrandarse** *vr* : grow larger
agrario, -ria *adj* : agrarian, agricultural
agravar *vt* **1** : make heavier **2** EMPEORAR : aggravate, worsen — **agravarse** *vr* : get worse
agraviar *vt* : insult — **agravio** *nm* : insult
agredir {1} *vt* : attack
agregar {52} *vt* : add, attach — **agregado, -da** *n* : attaché — **agregado** *nm* : aggregate
agresión *nf, pl* **-siones** : aggression, attack — **agresividad** *nf* : aggressiveness — **agresivo, -va** *adj* : aggressive — **agresor, -sora** *n* : aggressor, attacker
agreste *adj* : rugged, wild
agriar *vt* : sour — **agriarse** *vr* **1** : turn sour (of milk, etc.) **2** : become embittered
agrícola *adj* : agricultural — **agricultura** *nf* : agriculture, farming — **agricultor, -tora** *n* : farmer
agridulce *adj* **1** : bittersweet **2** : sweet-and-sour (in cooking)
agrietar *vt* : crack — **agrietarse** *vr* **1** : crack **2** : chap
agrimensor, -sora *n* : surveyor
agrio, agria *adj* : sour
agrupar *vt* : group together — **agruparse** *vr* : form a group — **agrupación** *nf, pl* **-ciones** : group, association — **agrupamiento** *nm* : grouping
agua *nf* **1** : water **2 ~ oxigenada** : hydrogen peroxide **3 ~s negras** *or* **~s residuales** : sewage
aguacate *nm* : avocado
aguacero *nm* : downpour
aguado, -da *adj* **1** : watery **2** *Lat fam* : soft, flabby — **aguar** {10} *vt* **1** : water down, dilute **2 ~ la fiesta** *fam* : spoil the party
aguafuerte *nm* : etching
aguanieve *nf* : sleet
aguantar *vt* **1** SOPORTAR : bear, withstand **2** SOSTENER : hold — *vi* : hold out, last — **aguantarse** *vr* **1** : resign oneself **2** CONTENERSE : restrain oneself — **aguante** *nm* **1** : patience **2** RESISTENCIA : endurance
aguardar *vt* : await
aguardiente *nm* : clear brandy
aguarrás *nm* : turpentine
agudo, -da *adj* **1** : acute, sharp **2** : shrill, high-pitched (in music) — **agudeza** *nf* **1** : sharpness **2** : witticism
agüero *nm* : augury, omen
aguijón *nm, pl* **-jones 1** : stinger (of an insect) **2** ESTÍMULO : goad, stimulus — **aguijonear** *vt* : goad
águila *nf* : eagle
aguja *nf* **1** : needle **2** : hand (of a clock) **3** : spire (of a church)
agujero *nm* : hole
agujeta *nf* **1** *Lat* : shoelace **2 ~s** *nfpl* : (muscular) stiffness
aguzar {21} *vt* **1** : sharpen **2 ~ el oído** : prick up one's ears
ahí *adv* **1** : there **2 por ~** : somewhere, thereabouts
ahijado, -da *n* : godchild, godson *m*, goddaughter *f*
ahínco *nm* : eagerness, zeal
ahogar {52} *vt* **1** : drown **2** ASFIXIAR : smother — **ahogarse** *vr* : drown — **ahogo** *nm* : breathlessness
ahondar *vt* : deepen — *vi* : elaborate, go into detail
ahora *adv* **1** : now **2 ~ mismo** : right now
ahorcar {72} *vt* : hang, kill by hanging — **ahorcarse** *vr* : hang oneself
ahorita *adv Lat fam* : right now
ahorrar *vt* : save, spare — *vi* : save up — **ahorrarse** *vr* : spare oneself — **ahorro** *nm* : saving
ahuecar {72} *vt* **1** : hollow out **2** : cup (one's hands)
ahumar {8} *vt* : smoke, cure — **ahumado, -da** *adj* : smoked
ahuyentar *vt* : scare away, chase away
airado, -da *adj* : irate, angry
aire *nm* **1** : air **2 ~ acondicionado** : air-conditioning **3 al ~ libre** : in the open air, outdoors — **airear** *vt* : air, air out
aislar {5} *vt* **1** : isolate **2** : insulate (in electricity) — **aislamiento** *nm* **1** : isolation **2** : (electrical) insulation
ajar *vt* **1** : crumple, wrinkle **2** ESTROPEAR : spoil
ajedrez *nm* : chess
ajeno, -na *adj* **1** : someone else's **2** EXTRAÑO : alien **3 ~ a** : foreign to
ajetreado, -da *adj* : hectic, busy — **ajetrearse** *vr* : bustle about — **ajetreo** *nm* : hustle and bustle
ají *nm, pl* **ajíes** *Lat* : chili pepper
ajo *nm* : garlic
ajustar *vt* **1** : adjust, adapt **2** ACORDAR : agree on **3** SALDAR : settle — **ajustarse** *vr* : fit, conform — **ajustable** *adj* : adjustable — **ajustado, -da** *adj* **1** : close, tight **2** CEÑIDO : tight-fitting — **ajuste** *nm* : adjustment
ajusticiar *vt* : execute, put to death
al (*contraction of* **a** *and* **el**) → **a**[2]
ala *nf* **1** : wing **2** : brim (of a hat)
alabanza *nf* : praise — **alabar** *vt* : praise
alacena *nf* : cupboard, larder
alacrán *nm, pl* **-cranes** : scorpion
alado, -da *adj* : winged
alambre *nm* : wire
alameda *nf* **1** : poplar grove **2** : tree-lined avenue — **álamo** *nm* : poplar
alarde *nm* : show, display — **alardear** *vi* : boast
alargar {52} *vt* **1** : extend, lengthen **2** PROLONGAR : prolong — **alargarse** *vr* : become longer — **alargador** *nm* : extension cord
alarido *nm* : howl, shriek
alarmar *vt* : alarm — **alarma** *nf* : alarm — **alarmante** *adj* : alarming
alba *nf* : dawn
albahaca *nf* : basil
albañil *nm* : bricklayer, mason
albaricoque *nm* : apricot
albedrío *nm* **libre ~** : free will
alberca *nf* **1** : reservoir, tank **2** *Lat* : swimming pool
albergar {52} *vt* : house, lodge — **albergue** *nm* **1** : lodging **2** REFUGIO : shelter **3 ~ juvenil** : youth hostel
albóndiga *nf* : meatball
alborear *v impers* : dawn — **albor** *nm* : dawning — **alborada** *nf* : dawn
alborotar *vt* : excite, stir up — *vi* : make a racket — **alborotarse** *vr* : get excited — **alborotado, -da** *adj* : excited, agitated — **alborotador, -dora** *n* : agitator, rioter — **alboroto** *nm* : ruckus
alborozar {21} *vt* : gladden — **alborozo** *nm* : joy
álbum *nm* : album
alcachofa *nf* : artichoke
alcalde, -desa *n* : mayor
alcance *nm* **1** : reach **2** ÁMBITO : range, scope
alcancía *nf* : money box
alcantarilla *nf* : sewer, drain
alcanzar {21} *vt* **1** : reach **2** LLEGAR A : catch up with **3** LOGRAR : achieve, attain — *vi* **1** : suffice, be enough **2 ~ a** : manage to
alcaparra *nf* : caper
alcázar *nm* : fortress, castle
alce *nm* : moose, European elk
alcoba *nf* : bedroom
alcohol *nm* : alcohol — **alcohólico, -ca** *adj & n* : alcoholic — **alcoholismo** *nm* : alcoholism
aldaba *nf* : door knocker
aldea *nf* : village — **aldeano, -na** *n* : villager
aleación *nf, pl* **-ciones** : alloy
aleatorio, -ria *adj* : random
aleccionar *vt* : instruct, teach
aledaño, -ña *adj* : bordering — **aledaños** *nmpl* : outskirts
alegar {52} *vt* : assert, allege — *vi Lat* : argue — **alegato** *nm* **1** : allegation (in law) **2** *Lat* : argument
alegoría *nf* : allegory — **alegórico, -ca** *adj* : allegorical
alegrar *vt* : make happy, cheer up — **alegrarse** *vr* : be glad — **alegre** *adj* **1** CONTENTO : glad, happy **2** : colorful, bright — **alegremente** *adv* : happily — **alegría** *nf* : joy, cheer
alejar *vt* **1** : remove, move away **2** ENAJE-

NAR : estrange — **alejarse** *vr* : move away, drift apart — **alejado, -da** *adj* : remote — **alejamiento** *nm* **1** : removal **2** : estrangement (of persons)
alemán, -mana *adj, mpl* **-manes** : German — **alemán** *nm* : German (language)
alentar {55} *vt* : encourage — **alentador, -dora** *adj* : encouraging
alergia *nf* : allergy — **alérgico, -ca** *adj* : allergic
alero *nm* : eaves *pl*
alertar *vt* : alert — **alerta** *adv* : on the alert — **alerta** *adj & nf* : alert
aleta *nf* **1** : fin, flipper **2** : small wing
alevosía *nf* : treachery — **alevoso, -sa** *adj* : treacherous
alfabeto *nm* : alphabet — **alfabético, -ca** *adj* : alphabetical — **alfabetismo** *nm* : literacy — **alfabetizar** {21} *vt* **1** : teach literacy **2** : alphabetize
alfalfa *nf* : alfalfa
alfarería *nf* : pottery
alféizar *nm* : sill, windowsill
alfil *nm* : bishop (in chess)
alfiler *nm* **1** : pin **2** BROCHE : brooch — **alfiletero** *nm* : pincushion
alfombra *nf* : carpet, rug — **alfombrilla** *nf* : small rug, mat
alga *nf* : seaweed
álgebra *nf* : algebra
algo *pron* **1** : something **2 ~ de** : some, a little — **~** *adv* : somewhat, rather
algodón *nm, pl* **-dones** : cotton
alguacil *nm* : constable, bailiff
alguien *pron* : somebody, someone
alguno, -na *adj* (**algún** *before masculine singular nouns*) **1** : some, any **2** (*in negative constructions*) : not any, not at all **3 algunas veces** : sometimes — **~** *pron* **1** : one, someone, somebody **2 algunos, -nas** *pron pl* : some, a few
alhaja *nf* : jewel
alharaca *nf* : fuss
aliado, -da *n* : ally — **~** *adj* : allied — **alianza** *nf* : alliance — **aliarse** {85} *vr* : form an alliance
alias *adv & nm* : alias
alicaído, -da *adj* : depressed
alicates *nmpl* : pliers
aliciente *nm* **1** : incentive **2** : attraction (to a place)
alienar *vt* : alienate — **alienación** *nf, pl* **-ciones** : alienation
aliento *nm* **1** : breath **2** ÁNIMO : encouragement, strength
aligerar *vt* **1** : lighten **2** APRESURAR : hasten, quicken
alimaña *nf* : pest, vermin
alimentar *vt* : feed, nourish — **alimentarse** *vr* **~ con** : live on — **alimentación** *nf, pl* **-ciones 1** : feeding **2** NUTRICIÓN : nourishment — **alimenticio, -cia** *adj* : nourishing — **alimento** *nm* : food, nourishment
alinear *vt* : align, line up — **alinearse** *vr* **~ con** : align oneself with — **alineación** *nf, pl* **-ciones 1** : alignment **2** : lineup (in sports)
aliño *nm* : dressing, seasoning — **aliñar** *vt* : season, dress
alisar *vt* : smooth
alistarse *vr* : join up, enlist — **alistamiento** *nm* : enlistment
aliviar *vt* : relieve, soothe — **aliviarse** *vr* : recover, get better — **alivio** *nm* : relief
aljibe *nm* : cistern, tank
allá *adv* **1** : there, over there **2 más ~** : farther away **3 más ~ de** : beyond
allanar *vt* **1** : smooth, level out **2** *Spain* : break into (a house) **3** *Lat* : raid — **allanamiento** *nm* **1** *Spain* : breaking and entering **2** *Lat* : raid
allegado, -da *n* : close friend, relation
allí *adv* : there, over there
alma *nf* : soul
almacén *nm, pl* **-cenes 1** : warehouse **2** *Lat* : shop, store **3 grandes almacenes** : department store — **almacenamiento** *or* **almacenaje** *nm* : storage — **almacenar** *vt* : store
almádena *nf* : sledgehammer
almanaque *nm* : almanac
almeja *nf* : clam
almendra *nf* **1** : almond **2** : kernel (of nuts, fruit, etc.)
almiar *nm* : haystack
almíbar *nm* : syrup
almidón *nm, pl* **-dones** : starch — **almidonar** *vt* : starch
almirante *nm* : admiral
almohada *nf* : pillow — **almohadilla** *nf* : small pillow, pad — **almohadón** *nm, pl* **-dones** : bolster, large cushion
almorranas *nfpl* : hemorrhoids, piles
almorzar {36} *vi* : have lunch — *vt* : have for lunch — **almuerzo** *nm* : lunch
alocado, -da *adj* : crazy, wild
áloe *or* **aloe** *nm* : aloe
alojar *vt* : house, lodge — **alojarse** *vr* : lodge, room — **alojamiento** *nm* : lodging, accommodations *pl*
alondra *nf* : lark
alpaca *nf* : alpaca
alpinismo *nm* : mountain climbing — **alpinista** *nmf* : mountain climber
alpiste *nm* : birdseed
alquilar *vt* : rent, lease — **alquilarse** *vr* : be for rent — **alquiler** *nm* : rent, rental
alquitrán *nm, pl* **-tranes** : tar
alrededor *adv* **1** : around, about **2 ~ de** : approximately — **alrededor de** *prep phr* : around — **alrededores** *nmpl* : outskirts
alta *nf* : discharge (of a patient)
altanería *nf* : haughtiness — **altanero, -ra** *adj* : haughty
altar *nm* : altar
altavoz *nm, pl* **-voces** : loudspeaker
alterar *vt* **1** : alter, modify **2** PERTURBAR : disturb — **alterarse** *vr* : get upset — **alteración** *nf, pl* **-ciones 1** : alteration **2** ALBOROTO : disturbance — **alterado, -da** *adj* : upset
altercado *nm* : altercation, argument
alternar *vi* **1** : alternate **2 ~ con** : socialize with — *vt* : alternate — **alternarse** *vr* : take turns — **alternativa** *nf* : alternative — **alternativo, -va** *adj* : alternating, alternative — **alterno, -na** *adj* : alternate
Alteza *nf* : Highness
altiplano *nm* : high plateau
altitud *nf* : altitude
altivez *nf, pl* **-veces** : haughtiness — **altivo, -va** *adj* : haughty
alto, -ta *adj* **1** : tall, high **2** RUIDOSO : loud — **alto** *adv* **1** ARRIBA : high **2** : loud, loudly — **~** *nm* **1** ALTURA : height, elevation **2** : stop, halt — **~** *interj* : halt!, stop! — **altoparlante** *nm Lat* : loudspeaker
altruista *adj* : altruistic — **altruismo** *nm* : altruism
altura *nf* **1** : height **2** ALTITUD : altitude **3 a la ~ de** : near, up by
alubia *nf* : kidney bean
alucinar *vi* : hallucinate — **alucinación** *nf, pl* **-ciones** : hallucination
alud *nm* : avalanche
aludir *vi* : allude, refer — **aludido, -da** *adj* **darse por ~** : take it personally
alumbrar *vt* **1** : light, illuminate **2** PARIR : give birth to — **alumbrado** *nm* : (electric) lighting — **alumbramiento** *nm* : childbirth
aluminio *nm* : aluminum
alumno, -na *n* : pupil, student
alusión *nf, pl* **-siones** : allusion
aluvión *nm, pl* **-viones** : flood, barrage
alzar {21} *vt* : lift, raise — **alzarse** *vr* : rise (up) — **alza** *nf* : rise — **alzamiento** *nm* : uprising
ama → **amo**
amabilidad *nf* : kindness — **amable** *adj* : kind, nice
amaestrar *vt* : train
amagar {52} *vt* **1** : show signs of **2** AMENAZAR : threaten — *vi* : be imminent — **amago** *nm* **1** INDICIO : sign **2** AMENAZA : threat
amainar *vi* : abate
amamantar *v* : breast-feed, nurse
amanecer {53} *v impers* : dawn — *vi* : wake up — **~** *nm* : dawn, daybreak
amanerado *adj* : affected, mannered
amansar *vt* **1** : tame **2** APACIGUAR : soothe — **amansarse** *vr* : calm down
amante *adj* **~ de** : fond of — **~** *nmf* : lover
amañar *vt* : rig, tamper with
amapola *nf* : poppy
amar *vt* : love
amargar {52} *vt* : make bitter — **amargado, -da** *adj* : embittered — **amargo, -ga** *adj* : bitter — **amargo** *nm* : bitterness — **amargura** *nf* : bitterness, grief
amarillo, -lla *adj* : yellow — **amarillo** *nm* : yellow
amarrar *vt* **1** : moor **2** ATAR : tie up
amasar *vt* **1** : knead **2** : amass (a fortune, etc.)
amateur *adj & nmf* : amateur
amatista *nf* : amethyst
ambages *nmpl* **sin ~** : without hesitation, straight to the point
ámbar *nm* : amber
ambición *nf, pl* **-ciones** : ambition — **ambicionar** *vt* : aspire to — **ambicioso, -sa** *adj* : ambitious
ambiente *nm* **1** AIRE : atmosphere **2** MEDIO : environment, surroundings *pl* — **ambiental** *adj* : environmental
ambigüedad *nf* : ambiguity — **ambiguo, -gua** *adj* : ambiguous
ámbito *nm* : domain, sphere
ambos, -bas *adj & pron* : both
ambulancia *nf* : ambulance
ambulante *adj* : traveling, itinerant
ameba *nf* : amoeba
amedrentar *vt* : intimidate
amén *nm* **1** : amen **2 ~ de** : in addition to
amenazar {21} *vt* : threaten — **amenaza** *nf* : threat, menace
amenizar {21} *vt* : make pleasant, enliven — **ameno, -na** *adj* : pleasant
americano, -na *adj* : American
ameritar *vt Lat* : deserve
ametralladora *nf* : machine gun
amianto *nm* : asbestos
amiba → **ameba**
amígdala *nf* : tonsil — **amigdalitis** *nf* : tonsilitis
amigo, -ga *adj* : friendly, close — **~** *n* : friend — **amigable** *adj* : friendly
amilanar *vt* : daunt — **amilanarse** *vr* : lose heart
aminorar *vt* : diminish
amistad *nf* : friendship — **amistoso, -sa** *adj* : friendly
amnesia *nf* : amnesia
amnistía *nf* : amnesty
amo, ama *n* **1** : master *m*, mistress *f* **2 ama de casa** : homemaker, housewife **3 ama de llaves** : housekeeper
amodorrado, -da *adj* : drowsy
amolar {19} *vt* **1** : grind, sharpen **2** MOLESTAR : annoy
amoldar *vt* : adapt, adjust — **amoldarse** *vr* **~ a** : adapt to
amonestar *vt* : admonish, warn — **amonestación** *nf, pl* **-ciones** : admonition, warning
amoníaco *or* **amoniaco** *nm* : ammonia
amontonar *vt* : pile up — **amontonarse** *vr* : pile up (of things), form a crowd (of persons)
amor *nm* : love
amordazar {21} *vt* : gag
amorío *nm* : love affair — **amoroso, -sa** *adj* **1** : loving **2** *Lat* : sweet, lovable
amortado, -da *adj* : black-and-blue
amortiguar {10} *vt* : muffle, soften, tone down — **amortiguador** *nm* : shock absorber
amortizar {21} *vt* : pay off — **amortización** *nf* : repayment
amotinar *vt* : incite (to riot) — **amotinarse** *vr* : riot, rebel
amparar *vt* : shelter, protect — **ampararse** *vr* **1 ~ de** : take shelter from **2 ~ en** : have recourse to — **amparo** *nm* : refuge, protection
ampliar {85} *vt* **1** : expand **2** : enlarge (a photograph) — **ampliación** *nf, pl* **-ciones 1** : expansion, enlargement **2** : extension (of a building)
amplificar {72} *vt* : amplify — **amplificador** *nm* : amplifier
amplio, -plia *adj* : broad, wide, ample — **amplitud** *nf* **1** : breadth, extent **2** ESPACIOSIDAD : spaciousness
ampolla *nf* **1** : blister **2** : vial, ampoule — **ampollarse** *vr* : blister
ampuloso, -sa *adj* : pompous
amputar *vt* : amputate — **amputación** *nf, pl* **-ciones** : amputation
amueblar *vt* : furnish (a house, etc.)
amurallar *vt* : wall in
anacardo *nm* : cashew nut
anaconda *nf* : anaconda
anacrónico, -ca *adj* : anachronistic — **anacronismo** *nm* : anachronism
ánade *nmf* : duck
anagrama *nm* : anagram
anales *nmpl* : annals
analfabeto, -ta *adj & n* : illiterate — **analfabetismo** *nm* : illiteracy
analgésico *nm* : painkiller, analgesic
analizar {21} *vt* : analyze — **análisis** *nm* : analysis — **analítico, -ca** *adj* : analytical, analytic
analogía *nf* : analogy — **análogo, -ga** *adj* : analogous
ananá *or* **ananás** *nm, pl* **-nás** : pineapple
anaquel *nm* : shelf
anaranjado, -da *adj* : orange-colored
anarquía *nf* : anarchy — **anarquista** *adj & nmf* : anarchist
anatomía *nf* : anatomy — **anatómico, -ca** *adj* : anatomic, anatomical
anca *nf* **1** : haunch **2 ~s de rana** : frogs' legs
ancestral *adj* : ancestral
ancho, -cha *adj* : wide, broad, ample — **ancho** *nm* : width
anchoa *nf* : anchovy
anchura *nf* : width, breadth
anciano, -na *adj* : aged, elderly — **~** *n* : elderly person
ancla *nf* : anchor — **anclar** *v* : anchor
andadas *nfpl* **1** : tracks **2 volver a las ~** : go back to one's old ways
andadura *nf* : walking, journey
andaluz, -luza *adj & n, mpl* **-luces** : Andalusian
andamio *nm* : scaffold
andanada *nf* **1** : volley **2 soltar una ~** : reprimand
andanzas *nfpl* : adventures
andar {6} *vi* **1** CAMINAR : walk **2** IR : go, travel **3** FUNCIONAR : run, work **4 ~ en** : rummage around in **5 ~ por** : be approximately — *vt* : cover, travel — **~** *nm* : gait, walk
andén *nm, pl* **-denes 1** : (train) platform **2** *Lat* : sidewalk
andino, -na *adj* : Andean
andorrano, -na *adj* : Andorran
andrajos *nmpl* : tatters — **andrajoso, -sa** *adj* : ragged
anécdota *nf* : anecdote
anegar {52} *vt* : flood — **anegarse** *vr* **1** : be flooded **2** AHOGARSE : drown
anemia *nf* : anemia — **anémico, -ca** *adj* : anemic
anestesia *nf* : anesthesia — **anestésico, -ca** *adj* : anesthetic — **anestésico** *nm* : anesthetic
anexar *vt* : annex, attach — **anexo, -xa** *adj* : attached — **anexo** *nm* : annex
anfibio, -bia *adj* : amphibious — **anfibio** *nm* : amphibian
anfiteatro *nm* : amphitheater
anfitrión, -triona *n, mpl* **-triones** : host, hostess *f*
ángel *nm* : angel — **angelical** *adj* : angelic, angelical
angloparlante *adj* : English-speaking
anglosajón, -jona *adj, mpl* **-jones** : Anglo-Saxon
angosto, -ta *adj* : narrow
anguila *nf* : eel
ángulo *nm* **1** : angle **2** ESQUINA : corner — **angular** *adj* : angular — **anguloso, -sa** *adj* : angular
angustiar *vt* **1** : anguish, distress **2** INQUIETAR : worry — **angustiarse** *vr* : get upset — **angustia** *nf* **1** : anguish **2** INQUIETUD : worry — **angustioso, -sa** *adj* **1** : anguished **2** INQUIETANTE : distressing
anhelar *vt* : yearn for, crave — **anhelante** *adj* : yearning, longing — **anhelo** *nm* : longing
anidar *vi* : nest
anillo *nm* : ring
ánima *n* : soul
animación *nf, pl* **-ciones 1** VIVEZA : liveliness **2** BULLICIO : hustle and bustle — **animado, -da** *adj* : cheerful, animated — **animador, -dora** *n* **1** : (television) host **2** : cheerleader
animadversión *nf, pl* **-siones** : animosity
animal *nm* : animal — **~** *nmf* : brute, beast — **~** *adj* : brutish
animar *vt* **1** ALENTAR : encourage **2** ALEGRAR : cheer up — **animarse** *vr* **1** : liven up **2 ~ a** : get up the nerve to
ánimo *nm* **1** : spirit, soul **2** HUMOR : mood, spirits *pl* **3** ALIENTO : encouragement
animosidad *nf* : animosity, ill will
animoso, -sa *adj* : spirited, brave
aniquilar *vt* : annihilate — **aniquilación** *n, pl* **-ciones** : annihilation
anís *nm* : anise
aniversario *nm* : anniversary
ano *nm* : anus
anoche *adv* : last night
anochecer {53} *vi* : get dark — **~** *nm* : dusk, nightfall
anodino, -na *adj* : insipid, dull
anomalía *nf* : anomaly
anonadado, -da *adj* : dumbfounded
anónimo, -ma *adj* : anonymous — **anonimato** *nm* : anonymity
anorexia *nf* : anorexia
anormal *adj* : abnormal — **anormalidad** *nf* : abnormality
anotar *vt* **1** : annotate **2** APUNTAR : jot down — **anotación** *nf, pl* **-ciones** : annotation, note
anquilosarse *vr* **1** : become paralyzed **2** ESTANCARSE : stagnate — **anquilosamiento** *nm* **1** : paralysis **2** ESTANCAMIENTO : stagnation
ansiar {85} *vt* : long for — **ansia** *nf* **1** INQUIETUD : uneasiness **2** ANGUSTIA : anguish **3** ANHELO : longing — **ansiedad** *nf* : anxiety — **ansioso, -sa** *adj* **1** : anxious **2** DESEOSO : eager
antagónico, -ca *adj* : antagonistic — **antagonismo** *nm* : antagonism — **antagonista** *nmf* : antagonist
antaño *adv* : yesteryear, long ago
antártico, -ca *adj* : antarctic
ante[1] *nm* **1** : elk, moose **2** GAMUZA : suede
ante[2] *prep* **1** : before, in front of **2** : in view of **3 ~ todo** : above all
anteanoche *adv* : the night before last
anteayer *adv* : the day before yesterday
antebrazo *nm* : forearm
anteceder *vt* : precede — **antecedente** *adj* : previous, prior — **~** *nm* : precedent — **antecesor, -sora** *n* **1** : ancestor **2** PREDECESOR : predecessor
antedicho, -cha *adj* : aforesaid
antelación *nf, pl* **-ciones 1** : advance notice **2 con ~** : in advance
antemano *adv* **de ~** : beforehand
antena *nf* : antenna
antenoche → **anteanoche**
anteojos *nmpl* **1** : glasses, eyeglasses **2 ~ bifocales** : bifocals
antepasado, -da *n* : ancestor
antepecho *nm* : ledge
antepenúltimo, -ma *adj* : third from last
anteponer {60} *vt* **1** : place before **2** PREFERIR : prefer
anterior *adj* **1** : previous, earlier **2** DELANTERO : front — **anterioridad** *nf* **con ~** : beforehand, in advance — **anteriormente** *adv* : previously
antes *adv* **1** : before, earlier **2** ANTERIORMENTE : previously **3** PRIMERO : first **4** MEJOR : rather **5 ~ de** : before, previous to **6 ~ que** : before
antesala *nf* : waiting room
antiaéreo, -rea *adj* : antiaircraft
antibiótico *nm* : antibiotic
anticipar *vt* **1** : move up (a date, etc.) **2** : pay in advance — **anticiparse** *vr* **1** : be early **2** ADELANTARSE : get ahead — **anticipación** *nf, pl* **-ciones 1** : anticipation **2 con ~** : in advance — **anticipado, -da** *adj* **1** : ad-

vance, early **2 por ~** : in advance — **anticipo** *nm* **1** : advance (payment) **2** : foretaste

anticoncepción *nf, pl* **-ciones** : contraception — **anticonceptivo, -va** *adj* : contraceptive — **anticonceptivo** *nm* : contraceptive

anticongelante *nm* : antifreeze

anticuado, -da *adj* : antiquated, outdated

anticuario, -ria *n* : antique dealer — **anticuario** *nm* : antique shop

anticuerpo *nm* : antibody

antídoto *nm* : antidote

antier → **anteayer**

antiestético, -ca *adj* : unsightly

antifaz *nm, pl* **-faces** : mask

antífona *nf* : anthem

antigualla *nf* : relic, old thing

antiguo, -gua *adj* **1** : ancient, old **2** ANTERIOR : former **3** ANTICUADO : old-fashioned **4 muebles antiguos** : antique furniture — **antiguamente** *adv* **1** : long ago **2** ANTES : formerly — **antigüedad** *nf* **1** : antiquity **2** : seniority (in the workplace) **3 ~es** *nfpl* : antiques

antihigiénico, -ca *adj* : unsanitary

antihistamínico *nm* : antihistamine

antiinflamatorio, -ria *adj* : anti-inflammatory

antílope *nm* : antelope

antinatural *adj* : unnatural

antipatía *nf* : aversion, dislike — **antipático, -ca** *adj* : unpleasant

antirreglamentario, -ria *adj* : unlawful

antirrobo, -ba *adj* : antitheft

antisemita *adj* : anti-Semitic — **antisemitismo** *nm* : anti-Semitism

antiséptico, -ca *adj* : antiseptic — **antiséptico** *nm* : antiseptic

antisocial *adj* : antisocial

antítesis *nf* : antithesis

antojarse *vr* **1** APETECER : crave **2** PARECER : seem, appear — **antojadizo, -za** *adj* : capricious — **antojo** *nm* : whim, craving

antología *nf* : anthology

antorcha *nf* : torch

antro *nm* : dive, den

antropófago, -ga *nmf* : cannibal

antropología *nf* : anthropology

anual *adj* : annual, yearly — **anualidad** *nf* : annuity — **anuario** *nm* : yearbook, annual

anudar *vt* : knot — **anudarse** *vr* : tie, knot

anular *vt* : annul, cancel — **anulación** *nf, pl* **-ciones** : annulment, cancellation

anunciar *vt* **1** : announce **2** : advertise (products) — **anunciante** *nmf* : advertiser — **anuncio** *nm* **1** : announcement **2** *or* **~ publicitario** : advertisement

anzuelo *nm* **1** : fishhook **2 morder el ~** : take the bait

añadir *vt* : add — **añadidura** *nf* **1** : additive, addition **2 por ~** : in addition, furthermore

añejo, -ja *adj* : aged, vintage

añicos *nmpl* **hacer(se) ~** : smash to pieces

añil *adj & nm* : indigo (color)

año *nm* **1** : year **2 Año Nuevo** : New Year

añorar *vt* : long for, miss — **añoranza** *nf* : nostalgia

añoso, -sa *adj* : aged, old

aorta *nf* : aorta

apabullar *vt* : overwhelm

apacentar {55} *vt* : pasture, graze

apachurrar *vt Lat* : crush

apacible *adj* : gentle, mild

apaciguar {10} *vt* : appease, pacify — **apaciguarse** *vr* : calm down

apadrinar *vt* **1** : be a godparent to **2** : sponsor (an artist, etc.)

apagar {52} *vt* **1** : turn or switch off **2** EXTINGUIR : extinguish, put out — **apagarse** *vr* **1** EXTINGUIRSE : go out **2** : die down — **apagado, -da** *adj* **1** : off, out **2** : dull, subdued (of colors, sounds, etc.) — **apagador** *nm Lat* : (light) switch — **apagón** *nm, pl* **-gones** : blackout

apalancar {72} *vt* **1** LEVANTAR : jack up **2** ABRIR : pry open — **apalancamiento** *nm* : leverage

apalear *vt* : beat up, thrash

aparador *nm* **1** : sideboard **2** *Lat* : shop window

aparato *nm* **1** : machine, appliance, apparatus **2** : system (in anatomy) **3** OSTENTACIÓN : ostentation — **aparatoso, -sa** *adj* **1** : ostentatious **2** ESPECTACULAR : spectacular

aparcar {72} *v Spain* : park — **aparcamiento** *nm Spain* **1** : parking **2** : parking lot

aparcero, -ra *n* : sharecropper

aparear *vt* : mate, pair up — **aparearse** *vr* : mate

aparecer {53} *vi* **1** : appear **2** PRESENTARSE : show up — **aparecerse** *vr* : appear

aparejar *vt* **1** : rig (a ship) **2** : harness (an animal) — **aparejado, -da** *adj* **llevar ~** : entail — **aparejo** *nm* **1** : equipment, gear **2** : harness (for an animal) **3** : rigging (for a ship)

aparentar *vt* **1** : seem **2** FINGIR : feign — **aparente** *adj* : apparent, seeming

aparición *nf, pl* **-ciones 1** : appearance **2** FANTASMA : apparition — **apariencia** *nf* **1** : appearance, look **2 en ~** : apparently

apartado *nm* **1** : section, paragraph **2 ~ postal** : post office box

apartamento *nm* : apartment

apartar *vt* **1** ALEJAR : move away **2** SEPARAR : set aside, separate — **apartarse** *vr* **1** : move away **2** DESVIARSE : stray — **aparte** *adv* **1** : apart, separately **2** ADEMÁS : besides

apasionar *vt* : excite, fascinate — **apasionarse** *vr* : get excited — **apasionado, -da** *adj* : passionate, excited — **apasionante** *adj* : exciting

apatía *nf* : apathy — **apático, -ca** *adj* : apathetic

apearse *vr* **1** : dismount **2** : get out of or off (a vehicle)

apedrear *vt* : stone

apegarse {52} *vr* **~ a** : become attached to, grow fond of — **apegado, -da** *adj* : devoted — **apego** *nm* : fondness

apelar *vi* **1** : appeal **2 ~ a** : resort to — **apelación** *nf, pl* **-ciones** : appeal

apellido *nm* : last name, surname — **apellidarse** *vr* : have for a last name

apenar *vt* : sadden — **apenarse** *vr* **1** : grieve **2** *Lat* : become embarrassed

apenas *adv* : hardly, scarcely — **~** *conj* : as soon as

apéndice *nm* : appendix — **apendicitis** *nf* : appendicitis

apercibir *vt* **1** : warn **2** *Lat* : notice — **apercibirse** *vr* **~ de** : notice — **apercibimiento** *nm* : warning

aperitivo *nm* **1** : appetizer **2** : aperitif

apero *nm* : tool, implement

apertura *nf* : opening

apesadumbrar *vt* : sadden — **apesadumbrarse** *vr* : be weighed down

apestar *vi* : stink — **apestoso, -sa** *adj* : stinking, foul

apetecer {53} *vt* : crave, long for — **apetecible** *adj* : appealing

apetito *nm* : appetite — **apetitoso, -sa** *adj* : appetizing

ápice *nm* **1** : apex, summit **2** PIZCA : bit, smidgen

apilar *vt* : pile up — **apilarse** *vr* : pile up

apiñar *vt* : pack, cram — **apiñarse** *vr* : crowd together

apio *nm* : celery

apisonadora *nf* : steamroller

aplacar {72} *vt* : appease, placate — **aplacarse** *vr* : calm down

aplanar *vt* : flatten, level

aplastar *vt* : crush — **aplastante** *adj* : overwhelming

aplaudir *v* : applaud — **aplauso** *nm* **1** : applause **2** : acclaim

aplazar {21} *vt* : postpone, defer — **aplazamiento** *nm* : postponement

aplicar {72} *vt* : apply — **aplicarse** *vr* : apply oneself — **aplicable** *adj* : applicable — **aplicación** *nf, pl* **-ciones** : application — **aplicado, -da** *adj* : diligent

aplomo *nm* : aplomb

apocarse {72} *vr* : belittle oneself — **apocado, -da** *adj* : timid — **apocamiento** *nm* : timidity

apodar *vt* : nickname

apoderar *vt* : empower — **apoderarse** *vr* **~ de** : seize — **apoderado, -da** *n* : agent, proxy

apodo *nm* : nickname

apogeo *nm* : peak, height

apología *nf* : defense, apology

apoplejía *nf* : stroke, apoplexy

aporrear *vt* : bang on, beat

aportar *vt* : contribute — **aportación** *nf, pl* **-ciones** : contribution

apostar[1] {19} *v* : bet, wager

apostar[2] *vt* : station, post

apostillar *vt* : annotate — **apostilla** *nf* : note

apóstol *nm* : apostle

apóstrofo *nm* : apostrophe

apostura *nf* : elegance, grace

apoyar *vt* **1** : support **2** INCLINAR : lean, rest — **apoyarse** *vr* **~ en** : lean on, rest on — **apoyo** *nm* : support

apreciar *vt* **1** ESTIMAR : appreciate **2** EVALUAR : appraise — **apreciable** *adj* : considerable — **apreciación** *nf, pl* **-ciones 1** : appreciation **2** VALORACIÓN : appraisal — **aprecio** *nm* **1** : appraisal **2** ESTIMA : esteem

aprehender *vt* : apprehend — **aprehensión** *nf, pl* **-siones** : apprehension, capture

apremiar *vt* : urge — *vi* : be urgent — **apremiante** *adj* : pressing, urgent — **apremio** *nm* : urgency

aprender *v* : learn — **aprenderse** *vr* : memorize

aprendiz, -diza *n, mpl* **-dices** : apprentice, trainee — **aprendizaje** *nm* : apprenticeship

aprensión *nf, pl* **-siones** : apprehension, dread — **aprensivo, -va** *adj* : apprehensive

apresar *vt* : capture, seize — **apresamiento** *nm* : seizure, capture

aprestar *vt* : make ready — **aprestarse** *vr* : get ready

apresurar *vt* : speed up — **apresurarse** *vr* : hurry — **apresuradamente** *adv* : hurriedly, hastily — **apresurado, -da** *adj* : in a rush

apretar {55} *vt* **1** : press, push (a button) **2** : tighten (a knot, etc.) **3** ESTRECHAR : squeeze — *vi* **1** : press (down) **2** : fit too tightly — **apretón** *nm, pl* **-tones 1** : squeeze **2 ~ de manos** : handshake — **apretado, -da** *adj* **1** : tight **2** *fam* : tightfisted

aprieto *nm* : predicament, jam

aprisa *adv* : quickly

aprisionar *vt* : imprison

aprobar {19} *vt* **1** : approve of **2** : pass (an exam, etc.) — *vi* : pass — **aprobación** *nf, pl* **-ciones** : approval

apropiarse *vr* **~ de** : take possession of, appropriate — **apropiación** *nf, pl* **-ciones** : appropriation — **apropiado, -da** *adj* : appropriate

aprovechar *vt* : take advantage of, make good use of — *vi* : be of use — **aprovecharse** *vr* **~ de** : take advantage of — **aprovechado, -da** *adj* **1** : diligent **2** OPORTUNISTA : opportunistic

aproximar *vt* : bring closer — **aproximarse** *vr* : approach — **aproximación** *nf, pl* **-ciones** : approximation — **aproximadamente** *adv* : approximately — **aproximado, -da** *adj* : approximate

apto, -ta *adj* **1** : suitable **2** CAPAZ : capable — **aptitud** *nf* : aptitude, capability

apuesta *nf* : bet, wager

apuesto, -ta *adj* : elegant, good-looking

apuntalar *vt* : prop up, shore up

apuntar *vt* **1** : aim, point **2** ANOTAR : jot down **3** SEÑALAR : point at **4** : prompt (in theater) — **apuntarse** *vr* **1** : sign up **2** : score, chalk up (a victory, etc.) — **apunte** *nm* : note

apuñalar *vt* : stab

apurar *vt* **1** : hurry, rush **2** AGOTAR : use up **3** PREOCUPAR : trouble — **apurarse** *vr* **1** : worry **2** *Lat* : hurry up — **apuradamente** *adv* : with difficulty — **apurado, -da** *adj* **1** : needy **2** DIFÍCIL : difficult **3** *Lat* : rushed — **apuro** *nm* **1** : predicament, jam **2** *Lat* : hurry

aquejar *vt* : afflict

aquel, aquella *adj, mpl* **aquellos** : that, those

aquél, aquélla *pron, mpl* **aquéllos 1** : that (one), those (ones) **2** : the former

aquello *pron* : that, that matter

aquí *adv* **1** : here **2** AHORA : now **3 por ~** : hereabouts

aquietar *vt* : calm — **aquietarse** *vr* : calm down

ara *nf* **1** : altar **2 en ~s de** : for the sake of

árabe *adj* : Arab, Arabic — **~** *nm* : Arabic (language)

arado *nm* : plow

arancel *nm* : tariff

arándano *nm* : blueberry

araña *nf* **1** : spider **2** LÁMPARA : chandelier

arañar *v* : scratch, claw — **arañazo** *nm* : scratch

arar *v* : plow

arbitrar *v* **1** : arbitrate **2** : referee, umpire (in sports) — **arbitraje** *nm* : arbitration — **arbitrario, -ria** *adj* : arbitrary — **arbitrio** *nm* **1** : (free) will **2** JUICIO : judgment — **árbitro, -tra** *n* **1** : arbitrator **2** : referee, umpire (in sports)

árbol *nm* : tree — **arboleda** *nf* : grove

arbusto *nm* : shrub, bush

arca *nf* **1** : ark **2** COFRE : chest

arcada *nf* **1** : arcade **2 ~s** *nfpl* : retching

arcaico, -ca *adj* : archaic

arcano, -na *adj* : arcane, secret

arce *nm* : maple tree

archipiélago *nm* : archipelago

archivar *vt* : file — **archivador** *nm* : filing cabinet — **archivo** *nm* **1** : file **2** : archives *pl*

arcilla *nf* : clay

arco *nm* **1** : arch **2** : bow (in sports, music, etc.) **3** : arc (in geometry) **4 ~ iris** : rainbow

arder *vi* : burn

ardid *nm* : scheme, ruse

ardiente *adj* **1** : burning **2** FOGOSO : ardent

ardilla *nf* **1** : squirrel **2 ~ listada** : chipmunk

ardor *nm* **1** : burning **2** ENTUSIASMO : passion, ardor

arduo, -dua *adj* : arduous

área *nf* : area

arena *nf* **1** : sand **2** PALESTRA : arena — **arenoso, -sa** *adj* : sandy, gritty

arenque *nm* : herring

arete *nm Lat* : earring

argamasa *nf* : mortar

argentino, -na *adj* : Argentinian, Argentine

argolla *nf* : hoop, ring

argot *nm* : slang

argüir {41} *vt* **1** : argue **2** DEMOSTRAR : prove, show — *vi* : argue

argumentar *vt* : argue, contend — **argumentación** *nf, pl* **-ciones** : (line of) argument — **argumento** *nm* **1** : argument, reasoning **2** TRAMA : plot, story line

árido, -da *adj* : dry, arid — **aridez** *nf, pl* **-deces** : aridity

arisco, -ca *adj* : surly

aristocracia *nf* : aristocracy — **aristócrata** *nmf* : aristocrat — **aristocrático, -ca** *adj* : aristocratic

aritmética *nf* : arithmetic — **aritmético, -ca** *adj* : arithmetic, arithmetical

armar *vt* **1** : arm **2** MONTAR : assemble — **arma** *nf* **1** : arm, weapon **2 ~ de fuego** : firearm — **armada** *nf* : navy — **armado, -da** *adj* : armed — **armadura** *nf* **1** : armor **2** ARMAZÓN : framework — **armamento** *nm* : armament, arms *pl*

armario *nm* **1** : (clothes) closet **2** : cupboard, cabinet

armazón *nmf, pl* **-zones** : frame, framework

armisticio *nm* : armistice

armonizar {21} *vt* **1** : harmonize **2** : reconcile (differences, etc.) — *vi* : harmonize, go together — **armonía** *nf* : harmony — **armónica** *nf* : harmonica — **armónico, -ca** *adj* : harmonic — **armonioso, -sa** *adj* : harmonious

arnés *nm, pl* **-neses** : harness

aro *nm* **1** : hoop, ring **2** *Lat* : earring

aroma *nm* : aroma, scent — **aromático, -ca** *adj* : aromatic

arpa *nf* : harp

arpón *nm, pl* **-pones** : harpoon

arquear *vt* : arch, bend — **arquearse** *vr* : bend, bow

arqueología *nf* : archaeology — **arqueológico, -ca** *adj* : archaeological — **arqueólogo, -ga** *n* : archaeologist

arquero, -ra *n* **1** : archer **2** PORTERO : goalkeeper, goalie

arquetipo *nm* : archetype

arquitectura *nf* : architecture — **arquitecto, -ta** *n* : architect — **arquitectónico, -ca** *adj* : architectural

arrabal *nm* **1** : slum **2 ~es** *nmpl* : outskirts

arracimarse *vr* : cluster together

arraigar {52} *vi* : take root, become established — **arraigarse** *vr* : settle down — **arraigado, -da** *adj* : deeply rooted, well established — **arraigo** *nm* : roots *pl*

arrancar {72} *vt* **1** : pull out, tear off **2** : start (an engine), boot (a computer) — *vi* **1** : start an engine **2** : get going — **arranque** *nm* **1** : starter (of a car) **2** ARREBATO : outburst **3 punto de ~** : starting point

arrasar *vt* **1** : destroy, devastate **2** LLENAR : fill to the brim

arrastrar *vt* **1** : drag **2** ATRAER : draw, attract — *vi* : hang down, trail — **arrastrarse** *vr* **1** : crawl, creep **2** HUMILLARSE : grovel — **arrastre** *nm* **1** : dragging **2** : trawling (for fish)

arrear *vt* : urge on

arrebatar *vt* **1** : snatch, seize **2** CAUTIVAR : captivate — **arrebatarse** *vr* : get carried away — **arrebatado, -da** *adj* : hotheaded, rash — **arrebato** *nm* : outburst

arreciar *vi* : intensify, worsen

arrecife *nm* : reef

arreglar *vt* **1** COMPONER : fix **2** ORDENAR : tidy up **3** SOLUCIONAR : solve, work out — **arreglarse** *vr* **1** : get dressed (up) **2 arreglárselas** *fam* : get by, manage — **arreglado, -da** *adj* **1** : fixed, repaired **2** ORDENADO : tidy **3** SOLUCIONADO : settled, sorted out **4** ATAVIADO : smart, dressed-up — **arreglo** *nm* **1** : arrangement **2** REPARACIÓN : repair **3** ACUERDO : agreement

arremangarse {52} *vr* : roll up one's sleeves

arremeter *vi* : attack, charge — **arremetida** *nf* : attack, onslaught

arremolinarse *vr* **1** : crowd around, mill about **2** : swirl (about)

arrendar {55} *vt* : rent, lease — **arrendador, -dora** *n* : landlord, landlady *f* — **arrendamiento** *nm* : rent, rental — **arrendatario, -ria** *n* : tenant, renter

arrepentirse {76} *vr* **1** : regret, be sorry **2** : repent (for one's sins) — **arrepentido, -da** *adj* : repentant — **arrepentimiento** *nm* : regret, repentance

arrestar *vt* : arrest, detain — **arresto** *nm* : arrest

arriar *vt* : lower

arriba *adv* **1** (*indicating position*) : above, overhead **2** (*indicating direction*) : up, upwards **3** : upstairs (of a house) **4 ~ de** : more than **5 de ~ abajo** : from top to bottom

arribar *vi* **1** : arrive **2** : dock, put into port — **arribista** *nmf* : parvenu, upstart — **arribo** *nm* : arrival

arriendo → **arrendimiento**

arriesgar {52} *vt* : risk, venture — **arriesgarse** *vr* : take a chance — **arriesgado, -da** *adj* : risky

arrimar *vt* : bring closer, draw near — **arrimarse** *vr* : approach

arrinconar *vt* **1** : corner, box in **2** ABANDONAR : push aside

arrobar *vt* : entrance — **arrobarse** *vr* : be enraptured — **arrobamiento** *nm* : rapture, ecstasy

arrodillarse *vr* : kneel (down)

arrogancia *nf* : arrogance — **arrogante** *adj* : arrogant

arrojar *vt* **1** : hurl, cast **2** EMITIR : give off, spew out **3** PRODUCIR : yield — **arrojarse** *vr* : throw oneself — **arrojado, -da** *adj* : daring — **arrojo** *nm* : boldness, courage

arrollar *vt* **1** : sweep away **2** DERROTAR : crush, overwhelm **3** : run over (with a vehicle) — **arrollador, -dora** *adj* : overwhelming

arropar *vt* : clothe, cover (up) — **arroparse** *vr* : wrap oneself up

arroyo *nm* **1** RIACHUELO : stream **2** : gutter (in a street)
arroz *nm, pl* **arroces** : rice
arrugar {52} *vt* : wrinkle, crease — **arrugarse** *vr* : get wrinkled — **arruga** *nf* : wrinkle, crease
arruinar *vt* : ruin, wreck — **arruinarse** *vr* **1** : be ruined **2** EMPOBRECERSE : go bankrupt
arrullar *vt* : lull to sleep — *vi* : coo — **arrullo** *nm* **1** : lullaby **2** : cooing (of doves)
arrumbar *vt* : lay aside
arsenal *nm* : arsenal
arsénico *nm* : arsenic
arte *nmf (usually m in singular, f in plural)* **1** : art **2** HABILIDAD : skill **3** ASTUCIA : cunning, cleverness **4** → **bello**
artefacto *nm* : artifact, device
arteria *nf* : artery
artesanía *nm* **1** : craftsmanship **2** : handicrafts *pl* — **artesanal** *adj* : handmade — **artesano, -na** *n* : artisan, craftsman
ártico, -ca *adj* : arctic
articular *vt* : articulate — **articulación** *nf, pl* **-ciones 1** : articulation, pronunciation **2** COYUNTURA : joint
artículo *nm* **1** : article **2 ~s de primera necesidad** : essentials **3 ~s de tocador** : toiletries
artífice *nmf* : artisan, craftsman
artificial *adj* : artificial
artificio *nm* **1** HABILIDAD : skill **2** APARATO : device **3** ARDID : artifice, ruse — **artificioso, -sa** *adj* : cunning, deceptive
artillería *nf* : artillery
artilugio *nm* : gadget
artimaña *nf* : ruse, trick
artista *nmf* **1** : artist **2** ACTOR : actor, actress *f* — **artístico, -ca** *adj* : artistic
artritis *nms & pl* : arthritis — **artrítico, -ca** *adj* : arthritic
arveja *nf Lat* : pea
arzobispo *nm* : archbishop
as *nm* : ace
asa *nf* : handle
asado, -da *adj* : roasted, grilled — **asado** *nm* : roast — **asador** *nm* : spit — **asaduras** *nfpl* : offal, entrails
asalariado, -da *n* : wage earner — **~** *adj* : salaried
asaltar *vt* **1** : assault **2** ROBAR : mug, rob — **asaltante** *nmf* **1** : assailant **2** ATRACADOR : mugger, robber — **asalto** *nm* **1** : assault **2** ROBO : mugging, robbery
asamblea *nf* : assembly, meeting
asar *vt* : roast, grill — **asarse** *vr fam* : roast, feel the heat
asbesto *nm* : asbestos
ascender {56} *vi* **1** : ascend, rise up **2** : be promoted (in a job) **3 ~ a** : amount to — *vt* : promote — **ascendencia** *nf* : ancestry, descent — **ascendiente** *nmf* : ancestor — **~** *nm* : influence — **ascensión** *nf, pl* **-siones** : ascent — **ascenso** *nm* **1** : ascent, rise **2** : promotion (in a job) — **ascensor** *nm* : elevator
asco *nm* **1** : disgust **2 hacer ~s de** : turn up one's nose at **3 me da ~** : it makes me sick
ascua *nf* **1** : ember **2 estar en ~s** *fam* : be on edge
asear *vt* : clean, tidy up — **asearse** *vr* : get cleaned up — **aseado, -da** *adj* : clean, tidy
asediar *vt* **1** : besiege **2** ACOSAR : harass — **asedio** *nm* **1** : siege **2** ACOSO : harassment
asegurar *vt* **1** : assure **2** FIJAR : secure **3** : insure (a car, house, etc.) — **asegurarse** *vr* : make sure
asemejarse *vr* **1** : be similar **2 ~ a** : look like, resemble
asentar {55} *vt* **1** : set down **2** INSTALAR : set up, establish **3** *Lat* : state — **asentarse** *vr* **1** : settle **2** ESTABLECERSE : settle down — **asentado, -da** *adj* : settled, established
asentir {76} *vi* : assent, agree — **asentimiento** *nm* : assent
aseo *nm* : cleanliness
asequible *adj* : accessible, attainable
aserrar {55} *vt* : saw — **aserradero** *nm* : sawmill — **aserrín** *nm, pl* **-rrines** : sawdust
asesinar *vt* **1** : murder **2** : assassinate — **asesinato** *nm* **1** : murder **2** : assassination — **asesino, -na** *n* **1** : murderer, killer **2** : assassin
asesorar *vt* : advise, counsel — **asesorarse** *vr* **~ de** : consult — **asesor, -sora** *n* : advisor, consultant — **asesoramiento** *nm* : advice, counsel
asestar {55} *vt* **1** : aim (a weapon) **2** : deal (a blow)
aseverar *vt* : assert — **aseveración** *nf, pl* **-ciones** : assertion
asfalto *nm* : asphalt
asfixiar *vt* : asphyxiate, suffocate — **asfixiarse** *vr* : suffocate — **asfixia** *nf* : asphyxiation, suffocation
así *adv* **1** : like this, like that, thus **2 ~ de** : so, that (much) **3 ~ que** : so, therefore **4 ~ que** : as soon as **5 ~ como** : as well as — **~** *adj* : such, like that — **~** *conj* AUNQUE : even though
asiático, -ca *adj* : Asian, Asiatic
asidero *nm* : handle
asiduo, -dua *adj* : frequent, regular
asiento *nm* : seat
asignar *vt* **1** : assign, allocate **2** DESTINAR : appoint — **asignación** *nf, pl* **-ciones 1** : assignment **2** SUELDO : salary, pay — **asignatura** *nf* : subject, course
asilo *nm* **1** : asylum, home **2** REFUGIO : refuge, shelter — **asilado, -da** *n* : inmate
asimilar *vt* : assimilate — **asimilarse** *vr* **~ a** : resemble
asimismo *adv* **1** : similarly, likewise **2** TAMBIÉN : as well, also
asir {7} *vt* : seize, grasp — **asirse** *vr* **~ a** : cling to
asistir *vi* **~ a** : attend, be present at — *vt* : assist — **asistencia** *nf* **1** : attendance **2** AYUDA : assistance — **asistente** *nmf* **1** : assistant **2 los ~s** : those present
asma *nf* : asthma — **asmático, -ca** *adj* : asthmatic
asno *nm* : ass, donkey
asociar *vt* : associate — **asociarse** *vr* **1** : form a partnership **2 ~ a** : join, become a member of — **asociación** *nf, pl* **-ciones** : association — **asociado, -da** *adj* : associate, associated — **~** *n* : associate, partner
asolar {19} *vt* : devastate
asomar *vt* : show, stick out — *vi* : appear, show — **asomarse** *vr* **1** : appear **2** : stick one's head out (of a window)
asombrar *vt* : amaze, astonish — **asombrarse** *vr* : be amazed — **asombro** *nm* : amazement, astonishment — **asombroso, -sa** *adj* : amazing, astonishing
asomo *nm* **1** : hint, trace **2 ni por ~** : by no means
aspaviento *nm* : exaggerated gestures, fuss
aspecto *nm* **1** : aspect **2** APARIENCIA : appearance, look
áspero, -ra *adj* : rough, harsh — **aspereza** *nf* : roughness, harshness
aspersión *nf, pl* **-siones** : sprinkling — **aspersor** *nm* : sprinkler
aspiración *nf, pl* **-ciones 1** : breathing in **2** ANHELO : aspiration
aspiradora *nf* : vacuum cleaner
aspirar *vi* **~ a** : aspire to — *vt* : inhale, breathe in — **aspirante** *nmf* : applicant, candidate
aspirina *nf* : aspirin
asquear *vt* : sicken, disgust
asquerosidad *nf* : filth, foulness — **asqueroso, -sa** *adj* : disgusting, sickening
asta *nf* **1** : flagpole **2** CUERNO : antler, horn **3** : shaft (of a spear) — **astado, -da** *adj* : horned
asterisco *nm* : asterisk
asteroide *nm* : asteroid
astigmatismo *nm* : astigmatism
astillar *vt* : splinter — **astilla** *nf* : splinter, chip
astillero *nm* : shipyard
astral *adj* : astral
astringente *adj & nm* : astringent
astro *nm* **1** : heavenly body **2** : star (of movies, etc.)
astrología *nf* : astrology
astronauta *nmf* : astronaut — **astronáutica** *nf* : astronautics
astronave *nf* : spaceship
astronomía *nf* : astronomy — **astronómico, -ca** *adj* : astronomical — **astrónomo, -ma** *n* : astronomer
astucia *nf* **1** : astuteness **2** ARDID : cunning, guile — **astuto, -ta** *adj* **1** : astute **2** TAIMADO : crafty
asueto *nm* : time off, break
asumir *vt* : assume — **asunción** *nf, pl* **-ciones** : assumption
asunto *nm* **1** : matter, affair **2** NEGOCIO : business
asustar *vt* : scare, frighten — **asustarse** *vr* **~ de** : be frightened of — **asustadizo, -za** *adj* : jumpy, skittish — **asustado, -da** *adj* : frightened, afraid
atacar {72} *v* : attack — **atacante** *nmf* : attacker
atado *nm* : bundle
atadura *nf* : tie, bond
atajar *vt* : block, cut off — *vi* **~ por** : take a shortcut through — **atajo** *nm* : shortcut
atañer {79} *vi* **~ a** : concern, have to do with
ataque *nm* **1** : attack, assault **2** ACCESO : fit **3 ~ de nervios** : nervous breakdown
atar *vt* : tie up, tie down — **atarse** *vr* : tie (up)
atardecer {53} *v impers* : get dark — **~** *nm* : late afternoon, dusk
atareado, -da *adj* : busy
atascar {72} *vt* **1** : block, clog **2** ESTORBAR : hinder — **atascarse** *vr* **1** OBSTRUIRSE : become obstructed **2** : get bogged down — **atasco** *nm* **1** : blockage **2** EMBOTELLAMIENTO : traffic jam
ataúd *nm* : coffin
ataviar {85} *vt* : dress (up) — **ataviarse** *vr* : dress up — **atavío** *nm* : attire
atemorizar {21} *vt* : frighten — **atemorizarse** *vr* : get scared
atención *nf, pl* **-ciones 1** : attention **2 prestar ~** : pay attention **3 llamar la ~** : attract attention — **~** *interj* : attention!, watch out!
atender {56} *vt* **1** : attend to **2** CUIDAR : look after **3** : heed (advice, etc.) — *vi* : pay attention
atenerse {80} *vr* **~ a** : abide by
atentamente *adv* **1** : attentively **2 le saluda ~** : sincerely yours
atentar {55} *vi* **~ contra** : make an attempt on — **atentado** *nm* : attack
atento, -ta *adj* **1** : attentive, mindful **2** CORTÉS : courteous
atenuar {3} *vt* **1** : dim (lights), tone down (colors, etc.) **2** DISMINUIR : lessen — **atenuante** *nmf* : extenuating circumstances
ateo, atea *adj* : atheistic — **~** *n* : atheist
aterciopelado, -da *adj* : velvety, downy
aterido, -da *adj* : frozen stiff
aterrar {55} *vt* : terrify — **aterrador, -dora** *adj* : terrifying
aterrizar {21} *vi* : land — **aterrizaje** *nm* : landing
aterrorizar {21} *vt* : terrify
atesorar *vt* : hoard, amass
atestar {55} *vt* **1** : crowd, pack **2** : testify to (in law) — **atestado, -da** *adj* : stuffed, packed
atestiguar {10} *vt* : testify to
atiborrar *vt* : stuff, cram — **atiborrarse** *vr* : stuff oneself
ático *nm* **1** : penthouse **2** DESVÁN : attic
atildado, -da *adj* : smart, neat
atinar *vi* : be on target
atípico, -ca *adj* : atypical
atirantar *vt* : tighten
atisbar *vt* **1** : spy on **2** VISLUMBRAR : catch a glimpse of — **atisbo** *nm* : sign, hint
atizar {21} *vt* **1** : poke (a fire) **2** : rouse, stir up (passions, etc.) — **atizador** *nm* : poker
atlántico, -ca *adj* : Atlantic
atlas *nm* : atlas
atleta *nmf* : athlete — **atlético, -ca** *adj* : athletic — **atletismo** *nm* : athletics
atmósfera *nf* : atmosphere — **atmosférico, -ca** *adj* : atmospheric
atolondrado, -da *adj* **1** : scatterbrained **2** ATURDIDO : bewildered, dazed
átomo *nm* : atom — **atómico, -ca** *adj* : atomic — **atomizador** *nm* : atomizer
atónito, -ta *adj* : astonished, amazed
atontar *vt* : stun, daze
atorar *vt* : block — **atorarse** *vr* : get stuck
atormentar *vt* : torment, torture — **atormentarse** *vr* : torment oneself, agonize — **atormentador, -dora** *n* : tormenter
atornillar *vt* : screw
atorrante *nmf Lat* : bum, loafer
atosigar {52} *vt* : harass, annoy
atracar {72} *vi* : dock, land — *vt* : hold up, mug — **atracarse** *vr fam* **~ de** : gorge oneself with — **atracadero** *nm* : dock, pier — **atracador, -dora** *n* : robber, mugger
atracción *nf, pl* **-ciones** : attraction
atraco *nm* : holdup, robbery
atractivo, -va *adj* : attractive — **atractivo** *nm* : attraction, appeal
atraer {81} *vt* : attract
atragantarse *vr* : choke
atrancar {72} *vt* : block, bar — **atrancarse** *vr* : get blocked, get stuck
atrapar *vt* : trap, capture
atrás *adv* **1** DETRÁS : back, behind **2** ANTES : before, earlier **3 para ~** *or* **hacia ~** : backwards
atrasar *vt* **1** : put back (a clock) **2** DEMORAR : delay — *vi* : lose time — **atrasarse** *vr* : fall behind — **atrasado, -da** *adj* **1** : late, overdue **2** : backward (of countries, etc.) **3** : slow (of a clock) — **atraso** *nm* **1** RETRASO : delay **2** : backwardness **3 ~s** *nmpl* : arrears
atravesar {55} *vt* **1** CRUZAR : cross **2** TRASPASAR : pierce **3** : lay across (a road, etc.) **4** : go through (a situation) — **atravesarse** *vr* : be in the way
atrayente *adj* : attractive
atreverse *vr* : dare — **atrevido, -da** *adj* **1** : bold **2** INSOLENTE : insolent — **atrevimiento** *nm* **1** : boldness **2** DESCARO : insolence
atribuir {41} *vt* **1** : attribute **2** : confer (powers, etc.) — **atribuirse** *vr* : take credit for
atribular *vt* : afflict, trouble
atributo *nm* : attribute
atrincherar *vt* : entrench — **atrincherarse** *vr* : dig oneself in
atrocidad *nf* : atrocity
atronador, -dora *adj* : thunderous
atropellar *vt* **1** : run over **2** : violate, abuse (a person) — **atropellarse** *vr* : rush — **atropellado, -da** *adj* : hasty — **atropello** *nm* : abuse, outrage
atroz *adj, pl* **atroces** : atrocious
atuendo *nm* : attire
atufar *vt* : vex — **atufarse** *vr* : get angry
atún *nm, pl* **atunes** : tuna
aturdir *vt* **1** : stun, shock **2** CONFUNDIR : bewilder — **aturdido, -da** *adj* : dazed, bewildered
audaz *adj, pl* **-daces** : bold, daring — **audacia** *nf* : boldness, audacity
audible *adj* : audible
audición *nf, pl* **-ciones 1** : hearing **2** : audition (in theater, etc.)
audiencia *nf* : audience
audífono *nm* **1** : hearing aid **2 ~s** *nmpl Lat* : headphones, earphones
audiovisual *adj* : audiovisual
auditar *vt* : audit — **auditor, -tora** *n* : auditor
auditorio *nm* **1** : auditorium **2** PÚBLICO : audience
auge *nm* **1** : peak **2** : (economic) boom
augurar *vt* : predict, foretell — **augurio** *nm* : omen
augusto, -ta *adj* : august
aula *nf* : classroom
aullar {8} *vi* : howl — **aullido** *nm* : howl
aumentar *vt* : increase, raise — *vi* : increase, grow — **aumento** *nm* : increase, rise
aun *adv* **1** : even **2 ~ así** : even so
aún *adv* **1** : still, yet **2 más ~** : furthermore
aunar {8} *vt* : join, combine — **aunarse** *vr* : unite
aunque *conj* **1** : though, although, even if **2 ~ sea** : at least
aureola *nf* **1** : halo **2** FAMA : aura
auricular *nm* **1** : telephone receiver **2 ~es** *nmpl* : headphones
aurora *nf* : dawn
ausentarse *vr* : leave, go away — **ausencia** *nf* : absence — **ausente** *adj* : absent — **~** *nmf* **1** : absentee **2** : missing person (in law)
auspicios *nmpl* : sponsorship, auspices
austero, -ra *adj* : austere — **austeridad** *nf* : austerity
austral *adj* : southern
australiano, -na *adj* : Australian
austriaco *or* **austríaco, -ca** *adj* : Austrian
auténtico, -ca *adj* : authentic, genuine — **autenticidad** *nf* : authenticity
auto *nm* : auto, car
autoayuda *nf* : self-help
autobiografía *nf* : autobiography — **autobiográfico, -ca** *adj* : autobiographical
autobús *nm, pl* **-buses** : bus
autocompasión *nf* : self-pity
autocontrol *nm* : self-control
autocracia *nf* : autocracy
autóctono, -na *adj* : indigenous, native
autodefensa *nf* : self-defense
autodidacta *adj* : self-taught
autodisciplina *nf* : self-discipline
autoestop → **autostop**
autografiar *vt* : autograph — **autógrafo** *nm* : autograph
autómata *nm* : automaton
automático, -ca *adj* : automatic — **automatización** *nf, pl* **-ciones** : automation — **automatizar** {21} *vt* : automate
automotor, -triz *adj, fpl* **-trices** : self-propelled
automóvil *nm* : automobile — **automovilista** *nmf* : motorist — **automovilístico, -ca** *adj* : automobile, car
autonomía *nf* : autonomy — **autónomo, -ma** *adj* : autonomous
autopista *nf* : expressway, highway
autopropulsado, -da *adj* : self-propelled
autopsia *nf* : autopsy
autor, -tora *n* **1** : author **2** : perpetrator (of a crime)
autoridad *nf* : authority — **autoritario, -ria** *adj* : authoritarian
autorizar {21} *vt* : authorize, approve — **autorización** *nf, pl* **-ciones** : authorization — **autorizado, -da** *adj* **1** PERMITIDO : authorized **2** : authoritative
autorretrato *nm* : self-portrait
autoservicio *nm* **1** : self-service restaurant **2** SUPERMERCADO : supermarket
autostop *nm* **1** : hitchhiking **2 hacer ~** : hitchhike — **autostopista** *nmf* : hitchhiker
autosuficiente *adj* : self-sufficient
auxiliar *vt* : aid, assist — **~** *adj* : auxiliary — **~** *nmf* **1** : assistant, helper **2 ~ de vuelo** : flight attendant — **auxilio** *nm* **1** : aid, assistance **2 primeros ~s** : first aid
avalancha *nf* : avalanche
avalar *vt* : guarantee, endorse — **aval** *nm* : guarantee, endorsement
avanzar {21} *v* : advance, move forward — **avance** *nm* : advance — **avanzado, -da** *adj* : advanced
avaricia *nf* : greed, avarice — **avaricioso, -sa** *adj* : avaricious, greedy — **avaro, -ra** *adj* : miserly — **~** *n* : miser
avasallar *vt* : overpower, subjugate — **avasallador, -dora** *adj* : overwhelming
ave *nf* : bird
avecinarse *vr* : approach
avecindarse *vr* : settle, take up residence
avellana *nf* : hazelnut
avena *nf* **1** : oats *pl* **2** *or* **harina de ~** : oatmeal
avenida *nf* : avenue
avenir {87} *vt* : reconcile, harmonize — **avenirse** *vr* : agree, come to terms
aventajar *vt* : be ahead of, surpass
aventar {55} *vt* **1** : fan **2** : winnow (grain) **3** *Lat* : throw, toss
aventurar *vt* : venture, risk — **aventurarse** *vr* : take a risk — **aventura** *nf* **1** : adventure **2** RIESGO : risk **3** AMORÍO : love affair — **aventurado, -da** *adj* : risky — **aventurero, -ra** *adj* : adventurous — **~** *n* : adventurer
avergonzar {9} *vt* : shame, embarrass — **avergonzarse** *vr* : be ashamed, be embarrassed
averiar {85} *vt* : damage — **averiarse** *vr* : break down — **avería** *nf* **1** : damage **2**

: breakdown (of an automobile) — **averiado, -da** adj **1** : damaged, faulty **2** : broken down (of an automobile)
averiguar {10} vt **1** : find out **2** INVESTIGAR : investigate — **averiguación** nf, pl **-ciones** : investigation, inquiry
aversión nf, pl **-siones** : aversion, dislike
avestruz nm, pl **-truces** : ostrich
aviación nf, pl **-ciones** : aviation — **aviador, -dora** n : aviator
aviar {85} vt : prepare, make ready
ávido, -da adj : eager, avid — **avidez** nf, pl **-deces** : eagerness
avío nm **1** : preparation, provision **2 ∼s** nmpl : gear, equipment
avión nm, pl **aviones** : airplane — **avioneta** nf : light airplane
avisar vt **1** : notify **2** ADVERTIR : warn — **aviso** nm **1** : notice **2** ADVERTENCIA : warning **3** Lat : advertisement, ad **4 estar sobre ∼** : be on the alert
avispa nf : wasp — **avispón** nm, pl **-pones** : hornet
avispado, -da adj fam : clever, sharp
avistar vt : catch sight of
avivar vt **1** : enliven, brighten **2** : arouse (desire, etc.) **3** : intensify (pain)
axila nf : underarm, armpit
axioma nm : axiom
ay interj **1** : oh! **2** : ouch!, ow!
ayer adv : yesterday — **∼** nm : yesteryear, days gone by
ayote nm Lat : pumpkin
ayudar vt : help, assist — **ayudarse** vr **∼ de** : make use of — **ayuda** nf : help, assistance — **ayudante** nmf : helper, assistant
ayunar vi : fast — **ayunas** nfpl **en ∼** : fasting — **ayuno** nm : fast
ayuntamiento nm **1** : town hall, city hall (building) **2** : town or city council
azabache nm : jet
azada nf : hoe — **azadonar** vt : hoe
azafata nf : stewardess f
azafrán nm, pl **-franes** : saffron
azalea nf : azalea
azar nm **1** : chance **2 al ∼** : at random — **azaroso, -sa** adj : hazardous (of a journey, etc.), eventful (of a life)
azorar vt **1** : alarm **2** DESCONCERTAR : embarrass — **azorarse** vr : get embarrassed
azotar vt : beat, whip — **azote** nm **1** LÁTIGO : whip, lash **2** CALAMIDAD : scourge
azotea nf : flat or terraced roof
azteca adj : Aztec
azúcar nmf : sugar — **azucarado, -da** adj : sugary — **azucarera** nf : sugar bowl — **azucarero, -ra** adj : sugar
azufre nm : sulphur
azul adj & nm : blue — **azulado, -da** adj : bluish
azulejo nm **1** : ceramic tile **2** Lat : bluebird
azur n : azure, sky blue
azuzar {21} vt : incite, urge on

B

b nf : b, second letter of the Spanish alphabet
babear vi : drool, slobber — **baba** nf : saliva, drool
babel nmf : bedlam
babero nm : bib
babor nm : port (side)
babosa nf : slug — **baboso, -sa** adj **1** : slimy **2** Lat fam : silly
babucha nf : slipper
babuino nm : baboon
bacalao nm : cod
bache nm **1** : pothole, rut **2** DIFICULTADES : bad time
bachiller nmf : high school graduate — **bachillerato** nm : high school diploma
bacon nm Spain : bacon
bacteria nf : bacterium
bagaje nm : baggage, luggage
bagatela nf : trinket
bagre nm : catfish
bahía nf : bay
bailar v : dance — **bailarín, -rina** n, mpl **-rines** : dancer — **baile** nm **1** : dance **2** FIESTA : dance party, ball
bajar vt **1** : bring down, lower **2** DESCENDER : go down, come down — vi : descend, drop — **bajarse** vr **∼ de** : get out of, get off — **baja** nf **1** : fall, drop **2** CESE : dismissal **3** PERMISO : sick leave **4** : (military) casualty — **bajada** nf **1** : descent, drop **2** PENDIENTE : slope
bajeza nf : lowness, meanness
bajío nm : sandbank, shoal
bajo, -ja adj **1** : low, lower **2** : short (in stature) **3** : soft, faint (of sounds) **4** VIL : base, vile — **bajo** adv **1** : low **2 habla más ∼** : speak more softly — **∼** nm **1** : ground floor **2** DOBLADILLO : hem **3** : bass (in music) — **∼** prep : under, below — **bajón** nm, pl **-jones** : sharp drop, slump
bala nf **1** : bullet **2** : bale (of cotton, etc.)
balada nf : ballad
balancear vt **1** : balance **2** : swing (one's arms, etc.), rock (a boat) — **balancearse** vr : swing, sway — **balance** nm **1** : balance **2** : balance sheet — **balanceo** nm : swaying, rocking
balancín nm, pl **-cines 1** : seesaw **2** MECEDORA : rocking chair
balanza nf : scales pl, balance
balar vi : bleat
balaustrada nf : balustrade, banister
balazo nm **1** DISPARO : shot **2** : bullet wound
balbucear vi **1** : stammer, stutter **2** : babble (of a baby) — **balbuceo** nm : stammering, muttering, babbling
balcón nm, pl **-cones** : balcony
balde nm **1** : bucket, pail **2 en ∼** : in vain
baldío, -día adj **1** : uncultivated **2** INÚTIL : useless — **baldío** nm : wasteland
baldosa nf : floor tile
balear vt Lat : shoot (at) — **baleo** nm Lat : shot, shooting
balido nm : bleat
balín nm, pl **-lines** : pellet
balística nf : ballistics — **balístico, -ca** adj : ballistic
baliza nf **1** : buoy **2** : beacon (for aircraft)
ballena nf : whale
ballesta nf **1** : crossbow **2** : spring (of an automobile)
ballet nm : ballet
balneario nm : spa
balompié nm : soccer
balón nm, pl **-lones** : ball — **baloncesto** nm : basketball — **balonvolea** nm : volleyball
balsa nf **1** : raft **2** ESTANQUE : pond, pool
bálsamo nm : balsam, balm — **balsámico, -ca** adj : soothing
baluarte nm : bulwark, bastion
bambolear vi : sway, swing — **bambolearse** vr : sway, rock
bambú nm, pl **-búes** or **-bús** : bamboo
banal adj : banal
banana nf Lat : banana — **banano** nm Lat : banana
banca nf **1** : banking **2** BANCO : bench — **bancario, -ria** adj : bank, banking — **bancarrota** nf : bankruptcy — **banco** nm **1** : bank **2** BANCA : stool, bench, pew **3** : school (of fish)
banda nf **1** : band, strip **2** : band (in music) **3** PANDILLA : gang **4** : flock (of birds) **5 ∼ sonora** : sound track — **bandada** nf : flock (of birds), school (of fish)
bandazo nm : lurch
bandeja nf : tray, platter
bandera nf : flag, banner
banderilla nf : banderilla
banderín nm, pl **-rines** : pennant, small flag
bandido, -da n : bandit
bando nm **1** : proclamation, edict **2** PARTIDO : faction, side
bandolero, -ra n : bandit
banjo nm : banjo
banquero, -ra n : banker
banqueta nf **1** : stool, footstool **2** Lat : sidewalk
banquete nm : banquet
bañar vt **1** : bathe, wash **2** SUMERGIR : immerse **3** CUBRIR : coat, cover — **bañarse** vr **1** : take a bath **2** : go swimming — **bañera** nf : bathtub — **bañista** nmf : bather — **baño** nm **1** : bath, swim **2** BAÑERA : bathtub **3 ¿dónde está el ∼?** : where is the bathroom? **4 ∼ María** : double boiler
baqueta nf **1** : ramrod **2 ∼s** nfpl : drumsticks
bar nm : bar, tavern
barajar vt **1** : shuffle (cards) **2** CONSIDERAR : consider — **baraja** nf : deck of cards
baranda nf : rail, railing — **barandal** nm : handrail, banister
barato, -ta adj : cheap — **barato** adv : cheap, cheaply — **barata** nf Lat : sale, bargain — **baratija** nf : trinket — **baratillo** nm : secondhand store, flea market
barba nf **1** : beard, stubble **2** BARBILLA : chin
barbacoa nf : barbecue
barbaridad nf **1** : barbarity, cruelty **2 ¡qué ∼!** : that's outrageous! — **barbarie** nf : barbarism, savagery — **bárbaro, -ra** adj : barbaric
barbecho nm : fallow land
barbero, -ra n : barber — **barbería** nf : barbershop
barbilla nf : chin
barbudo, -da adj : bearded
barca nf **1** : boat **2 ∼ de pasaje** : ferryboat — **barcaza** nf : barge — **barco** nm : boat, ship
barítono nm : baritone
barman nm : bartender
barnizar {21} vt **1** : varnish **2** : glaze (ceramics) — **barniz** nm, pl **-nices 1** : varnish **2** : glaze (on ceramics)
barómetro nm : barometer
barón nm, pl **-rones** : baron — **baronesa** nf : baroness
barquero nm : boatman
barquillo nm : wafer, cone
barra nf **1** : bar, rod, stick **2** : counter (of a bar, etc.)
barraca nf **1** : hut, cabin **2** CASETA : booth, stall
barranco nm or **barranca** nf : ravine, gorge, gully
barredera nf : street-sweeping machine
barrenar vt : drill — **barrena** nf : drill, auger
barrer v : sweep
barrera nf : barrier
barreta nf : crowbar
barriada nf : district, quarter
barrica nf : cask, keg
barricada nf : barricade
barrido nm : sweep, sweeping
barriga nf : belly
barril nm **1** : barrel, keg **2 de ∼** : draft
barrio nm **1** : neighborhood **2 ∼ bajo** : slums pl
barro nm **1** : mud **2** ARCILLA : clay **3** GRANO : pimple, blackhead — **barroso, -sa** adj : muddy
barrote nm : bar (on a window)
barrunto nm **1** : suspicion **2** INDICIO : sign, indication
bártulos nmpl : things, belongings
barullo nm : racket, ruckus
basa nf : base, pedestal — **basar** vt : base — **basarse** vr **∼ en** : be based on
báscula nf : scales pl
base nf **1** : base **2** FUNDAMENTO : basis, foundation **3 ∼ de datos** : database — **básico, -ca** adj : basic
basquetbol or **básquetbol** nm Lat : basketball
bastar vi : be enough, suffice — **bastante** adv **1** : fairly, rather **2** SUFICIENTE : enough — **∼** adj : enough, sufficient — **∼** pron : enough
bastardo, -da adj & n : bastard
bastidor nm **1** : frame **2** : wing (in theater) **3 entre ∼es** : behind the scenes, backstage
bastilla nf : hem
bastión nf, pl **-tiones** : bastion, stronghold
basto, -ta adj : coarse, rough
bastón nm, pl **-tones 1** : cane, walking stick **2** : baton (in parades)
basura nf : garbage, rubbish — **basurero, -ra** n : garbage collector
bata nf **1** : bathrobe, housecoat **2** : smock (of a doctor, laboratory worker, etc.)
batallar vi : battle, fight — **batalla** nf **1** : battle, fight, struggle **2 de ∼** : ordinary, everyday — **batallón** nm, pl **-llones** : battalion
batata nf : yam, sweet potato
batear v : bat, hit — **bate** nm : baseball bat — **bateador, -dora** n : batter, hitter
batería nf **1** : battery **2** : drums pl **3 ∼ de cocina** : kitchen utensils pl
batir vt **1** : beat, whip **2** DERRIBAR : knock down — **batirse** vr : fight — **batido** nm : milk shake — **batidor** nm : eggbeater, whisk — **batidora** nf : electric mixer
batuta nf : baton
baúl nm : trunk, chest
bautismo nm : baptism — **bautismal** adj : baptismal — **bautizar** {21} vt : baptize — **bautizo** nm : baptism, christening
baya nf : berry
bayeta nf : cleaning cloth
bayoneta nf : bayonet
bazar nm : bazaar
bazo nm : spleen
bazofia nf fam : rubbish, hogwash
beato, -ta adj : blessed
bebé nm : baby
beber v : drink — **bebedero** nm : watering trough — **bebedor, -dora** n : (heavy) drinker — **bebida** nf : drink, beverage — **bebido, -da** adj : drunk
beca nf : grant, scholarship
becerro, -rra n : calf
befa nf : jeer, taunt
beige adj & nm : beige
beisbol or **béisbol** nm : baseball — **beisbolista** nmf : baseball player
beldad nf : beauty
belén nf, pl **-lenes** : Nativity scene
belga adj : Belgian
beliceño, -ña adj : Belizean
bélico, -ca adj : military, war — **belicoso, -sa** adj : warlike
beligerancia nf : belligerence — **beligerante** adj & nmf : belligerent
belleza nf : beauty — **bello, -lla** adj **1** : beautiful **2 bellas artes** : fine arts
bellota nf : acorn
bemol adj & nm : flat (in music)
bendecir {11} vt **1** : bless **2 ∼ la mesa** : say grace — **bendición** nf, pl **-ciones** : benediction, blessing — **bendito, -ta** adj **1** : blessed, holy **2** DICHOSO : fortunate **3 ¡bendito sea Dios!** : thank goodness!
benefactor, -tora n : benefactor
beneficiar vt : benefit, assist — **beneficiarse** vr : benefit, profit — **beneficiario, -ria** n : beneficiary — **beneficio** nm **1** : gain, profit **2** BIEN : benefit — **beneficioso, -sa** adj : beneficial — **benéfico, -ca** adj : charitable
benemérito, -ta adj : worthy
beneplácito nm : approval, consent
benévolo, -la adj : benevolent, kind — **benevolencia** nf : benevolence, kindness
bengala nf or **luz de ∼** : flare
benigno, -na adj **1** : mild **2** : benign (in medicine) — **benignidad** nf : mildness, kindness
benjamín, -mina n, mpl **-mines** : youngest child
beodo, -da adj & n : drunk
berenjena nf : eggplant
berrear vi **1** : bellow, low **2** : bawl, howl (of a person) — **berrido** nm **1** : bellowing **2** : howl, scream (of a person)
berro nm : watercress
berza nf : cabbage
besar vt : kiss — **besarse** vr : kiss (each other) — **beso** nm : kiss
bestia nf : beast, animal — **bestial** adj : bestial, brutal — **bestialidad** nf : brutality
betabel nm Lat : beet
betún nm, pl **-tunes** : shoe polish
bianual adj : biannual
biberón nm, pl **-rones** : baby's bottle
Biblia nf : Bible — **bíblico, -ca** adj : biblical
bibliografía nf : bibliography — **bibliográfico, -ca** adj : bibliographic, bibliographical
biblioteca nf : library — **bibliotecario, -ria** n : librarian
bicarbonato nm **∼ de soda** : baking soda
bicentenario nm : bicentennial
bíceps nms & pl : biceps
bicho nm : small animal, bug
bicicleta nf : bicycle — **bici** nf fam : bike
bicolor adj : two-tone
bidón nm, pl **-dones** : large can, drum
bien adv **1** : well, good **2** CORRECTAMENTE : correctly, right **3** MUY : very, quite **4** DE BUENA GANA : willingly **5 ∼ que** : although **6 más ∼** : rather — **bien** adj **1** : all right, well **2** AGRADABLE : pleasant, nice **3** SATISFACTORIO : satisfactory **4** CORRECTO : correct, right — **bien** nm **1** : good **2 ∼es** nmpl : property, goods
bienal adj & nf : biennial
bienaventurado, -da adj : blessed, fortunate
bienestar nm : welfare, well-being
bienhechor, -chora n : benefactor
bienintencionado, -da adj : well-meaning
bienvenido, -da adj : welcome — **bienvenida** nf **1** : welcome **2 dar la ∼ a** : welcome (s.o.)
bife nm Lat : steak
bifocales nmpl : bifocals
bifurcarse {72} vr : fork — **bifurcación** nf, pl **-ciones** : fork, branch
bigamia nf : bigamy
bigote nm **1** : mustache **2 ∼s** nmpl : whiskers (of an animal)
bikini nm : bikini
bilingüe adj : bilingual
bilis nf : bile
billar nm : pool, billiards
billete nm **1** : bill, banknote **2** BOLETO : ticket — **billetera** nf : billfold, wallet
billón nm, pl **-llones** : trillion
bimensual, -suale adj : twice a month — **bimestral** adj : bimonthly
binario, -ria adj : binary
bingo nm : bingo
binoculares nmpl : binoculars
biodegradable adj : biodegradable
biofísica nf : biophysics
biografía nf : biography — **biográfico, -ca** adj : biographical — **biógrafo, -fa** n : biographer
biología nf : biology — **biológico, -ca** adj : biological, biologic — **biólogo, -ga** n : biologist
biombo nm : folding screen
biomecánica nf : biomechanics
biopsia nf : biopsy
bioquímica nf : biochemistry — **bioquímico, -ca** adj : biochemical
biotecnología nf : biotechnology
bipartidista adj : bipartisan
bípedo nm : biped
biquini → bikini
birlar vt fam : swipe, pinch
bis adv **1** : twice (in music) **2** : A (in an address) — **∼** nm : encore
bisabuelo, -la n : great-grandfather m, great-grandmother f
bisagra nf : hinge
bisecar {72} vt : bisect
biselar vt : bevel
bisexual adj : bisexual
bisiesto adj **año ∼** : leap year
bisnieto, -ta n : great-grandson m, great-granddaughter f
bisonte nm : bison, buffalo
bisoño, -ña n : novice
bistec nm : steak
bisturí nm : scalpel
bisutería nf : costume jewelry
bit nm : bit (unit of information)
bizco, -ca adj : cross-eyed
bizcocho nm : sponge cake
bizquear vi : squint — **bizquera** nf : squint
blanco, -ca adj : white — **blanco, -ca** n : white person — **blanco** nm **1** : white **2** DIANA : target, bull's-eye **3** : blank (space) — **blancura** nf : whiteness
blandir {1} vt : wave, brandish
blando, -da adj **1** : soft, tender **2** DÉBIL : weak-willed **3** INDULGENTE : lenient — **blandura** nf **1** : softness, tenderness **2** DE-

BILIDAD : weakness 3 INDULGENCIA : leniency
blanquear *vt* 1 : whiten, bleach 2 : launder (money) — *vi* : turn white — **blanqueador** *nm Lat* : bleach
blasfemar *vi* : blaspheme — **blasfemia** *nf* : blasphemy — **blasfemo, -ma** *adj* : blasphemous
bledo *nm* **no me importa un ~** *fam* : I couldn't care less
blindaje *nm* : armor, armor plating — **blindado, -da** *adj* : armored
bloc *nm, pl* **blocs** : (writing) pad
bloquear *vt* 1 OBSTRUIR : block, obstruct 2 : blockade — **bloque** *nm* 1 : block 2 : bloc (in politics) — **bloqueo** *nm* 1 OBSTRUCCIÓN : blockage 2 : blockade
blusa *nf* : blouse — **blusón** *nm, pl* **-sones** : smock
boato *nm* : showiness
bobina *nf* : bobbin, reel
bobo, -ba *adj* : silly, stupid — ~ *n* : fool, simpleton
boca *nf* 1 : mouth 2 ENTRADA : entrance 3 **~ arriba** : faceup 4 **~ abajo** : facedown, prone 5 **~ de riego** : hydrant
bocacalle *nf* : entrance (to a street)
bocado *nm* 1 : bite, mouthful 2 : bit (of a bridle) — **bocadillo** *nm Spain* : sandwich
bocajarro *nm* **a ~** : point-blank
bocallave *nf* : keyhole
bocanada *nf* 1 : swallow, swig 2 : puff, gust (of smoke, wind, etc.)
boceto *nm* : sketch, outline
bochorno *nm* 1 VERGÜENZA : embarrassment 2 : muggy weather — **bochornoso, -sa** *adj* 1 VERGONZOSO : embarrassing 2 : muggy, sultry
bocina *nf* 1 : horn 2 : mouthpiece (of a telephone) — **bocinazo** *nm* : honk, toot
boda *nf* : wedding
bodega *nf* 1 : wine cellar 2 : warehouse 3 : hold (of a ship or airplane) 4 *Lat* : grocery store
bofetear *vt* : slap — **bofetada** *nf or* **bofetón** *nm* : slap (in the face)
boga *nf* : fashion, vogue
bohemio, -mia *adj & n* : bohemian
boicotear *vt* : boycott — **boicot** *nm, pl* **-cots** : boycott
boina *nf* : beret
bola *nf* 1 : ball 2 *fam* : fib
bolera *nf* : bowling alley
boleta *nf Lat* : ticket — **boletería** *nf Lat* : ticket office
boletín *nm, pl* **-tines** 1 : bulletin 2 **~ de noticias** : news release
boleto *nm* : ticket
boliche *nm* 1 : bowling 2 BOLERA : bowling alley
bolígrafo *nm* : ballpoint pen
bolillo *nm* : bobbin
boliviano, -na *adj* : Bolivian
bollo *nm* : bun, sweet roll
bolo *nm* 1 : bowling pin 2 **~s** *nmpl* : bowling
bolsa *nf* 1 : bag 2 *Lat* : pocketbook, purse 3 **la Bolsa** : the stock market — **bolsillo** *nm* : pocket — **bolso** *nm Spain* : pocketbook, handbag
bomba *nf* 1 : bomb 2 **~ de gasolina** : gas pump
bombachos *nmpl* : baggy trousers
bombardear *vt* : bomb, bombard — **bombardeo** *nm* : bombing, bombardment — **bombardero** *nm* : bomber (airplane)
bombear *vt* : pump — **bombero, -ra** *n* : firefighter
bombilla *nf* : lightbulb — **bombillo** *nm Lat* : lightbulb
bombo *nm* 1 : bass drum 2 **a ~s y platillos** : with a great fanfare
bombón *nm, pl* **-bones** : candy, chocolate
bonachón, -chona *adj, mpl* **-chones** *fam* : good-natured
bonanza *nf* 1 : fair weather (at sea) 2 PROSPERIDAD : prosperity
bondad *nf* : goodness, kindness — **bondadoso, -sa** *adj* : kind, good
boniato *nm* : sweet potato
bonificación *nf, pl* **-ciones** 1 : bonus, extra 2 DESCUENTO : discount
bonito, -ta *adj* : pretty, lovely
bono *nm* 1 : bond 2 VALE : voucher
boquear *vi* : gasp — **boqueada** *nf* : gasp
boquerón *nm, pl* **-rones** : anchovy
boquete *nm* : gap, opening
boquiabierto, -ta *adj* : open-mouthed, speechless
boquilla *nf* : mouthpiece (of a musical instrument)
borbollar *vi* : bubble
borbotar *or* **borbotear** *vi* : boil, bubble, gurgle — **borbotón** *nm, pl* **-tones** 1 : spurt 2 **salir a borbotones** : gush out
bordar *v* : embroider — **bordado** *nm* : embroidery, needlework
borde *nm* 1 : border, edge 2 **al ~ de** : on the verge of — **bordear** *vt* : border — **bordillo** *nm* : curb
bordo *nm* **a ~** : aboard, on board
borla *nf* 1 : pom-pom, tassel 2 : powder puff
borracho, -cha *adj & n* : drunk — **borrachera** *nf* : drunkenness
borrar *vt* : erase, blot out — **borrador** *nm* 1 : rough draft 2 : eraser (for a blackboard)
borrascoso, -sa *adj* : stormy
borrego, -ga *n* : lamb, sheep — **borrego** *nm Lat* : false rumor, hoax
borrón *nm, pl* **-rrones** 1 : smudge, blot 2 **~ y cuenta nueva** : let's forget about it — **borroso, -sa** *adj* 1 : blurry, smudgy 2 INDISTINTO : vague, hazy
bosque *nm* : woods, forest — **boscoso, -sa** *adj* : wooded
bosquejar *vt* : sketch (out) — **bosquejo** *nm* : outline, sketch
bostezar {21} *vi* : yawn — **bostezo** *nm* : yawn
bota *nf* : boot
botánica *nf* : botany — **botánico, -ca** *adj* : botanical
botar *vt* 1 : throw, hurl 2 *Lat* : throw away 3 : launch (a ship) — *vi* : bounce
bote *nm* 1 : small boat 2 *Spain* : can 3 TARRO : jar 4 SALTO : bounce, jump
botella *nf* : bottle
botín *nm, pl* **-tines** 1 : ankle boot 2 DESPOJOS : booty, plunder
botiquín *nm, pl* **-quines** 1 : medicine cabinet 2 : first-aid kit
botón *nm, pl* **-tones** 1 : button 2 YEMA : bud — **botones** *nmfs & pl* : bellhop
botulismo *nm* : botulism
boutique *nf* : boutique
bóveda *nf* : vault
boxear *vi* : box — **boxeador, -dora** *n* : boxer — **boxeo** *nm* : boxing
boya *nf* : buoy — **boyante** *adj* 1 : buoyant 2 PRÓSPERO : prosperous, thriving
bozal *nm* 1 : muzzle 2 : halter (for a horse)
bracear *vi* 1 : wave one's arms 2 NADAR : swim, crawl
bracero, -ra *n* : day laborer
bragas *nf Spain* : panties
bragueta *nf* : fly, pants zipper
braille *adj & nm* : braille
bramante *nm* : twine, string
bramar *vi* 1 : bellow, roar 2 : howl (of the wind) — **bramido** *nm* : bellow, roar
brandy *nm* : brandy
branquia *nf* : gill
brasa *nf* : ember
brasier *nm Lat* : brassiere
brasileño, -ña *adj* : Brazilian
bravata *nf* 1 : boast, bravado 2 AMENAZO : threat
bravo, -va *adj* 1 : fierce, savage 2 : rough (of the sea) 3 *Lat* : angry — ~ *interj* : bravo!, well done! — **bravura** *nf* 1 FEROCIDAD : fierceness 2 VALENTÍA : bravery
braza *nf* 1 : breaststroke 2 : fathom (measurement) — **brazada** *nf* : stroke (in swimming)
brazalete *nm* 1 : bracelet 2 : (cloth) armband
brazo *nm* 1 : arm 2 : branch (of a river, etc.) 3 **~ derecho** : right-hand man 4 **~s** *nmpl* : hands, laborers
brea *nf* : tar
brebaje *nm* : concoction
brecha *nf* : breach, gap
brécol *nm* : broccoli
bregar {52} *vi* 1 LUCHAR : struggle 2 TRABAJAR : work hard — **brega** *nf* **andar a la ~** : struggle
breña *nf or* **breñal** *nm* : scrubland, brush
breve *adj* 1 : brief, short 2 **en ~** : shortly, in short — **brevedad** *nf* : brevity, shortness — **brevemente** *adv* : briefly
brezal *nm* : moor, heath — **brezo** *nm* : heather
bricolaje *or* **bricolage** *nm* : do-it-yourself
brida *nf* : bridle
brigada *nf* 1 : brigade 2 EQUIPO : gang, team, squad
brillar *vi* : shine, sparkle — **brillante** *adj* : brilliant, shiny — ~ *nm* : diamond — **brillantez** *nf* : brilliance — **brillo** *nm* 1 : luster, shine 2 ESPLENDOR : splendor — **brilloso, -sa** *adj* : shiny
brincar {72} *vi* : jump about, frolic — **brinco** *nm* : jump, skip
brindar *vi* : drink a toast — *vt* : offer, provide — **brindarse** *vr* : offer one's assistance — **brindis** *nm* : drink, toast
brío *nm* 1 : force, determination 2 ÁNIMO : spirit, verve — **brioso, -sa** *adj* : spirited, lively
brisa *nf* : breeze
británico, -ca *adj* : British
brizna *nf* 1 : strand, thread 2 : blade (of grass)
brocado *nm* : brocade
brocha *nf* : paintbrush
broche *nm* 1 : fastener, clasp 2 ALFILER : brooch
brocheta *nf* : skewer
brócoli *nm* : broccoli
bromear *vi* : joke, fool around — **broma** *nf* : joke, prank — **bromista** *adj* : fun-loving, joking — ~ *nmf* : joker, prankster
bronca *nf fam* : fight, row
bronce *nm* : bronze — **bronceado, -da** *adj* : suntanned — **bronceado** *nm* : tan — **broncearse** *vr* : get a suntan
bronco, -ca *adj* 1 : harsh, rough 2 : untamed, wild (of a horse)
bronquitis *nf* : bronchitis
broqueta *nf* : skewer
brotar *vi* 1 : bud, sprout 2 : stream, gush (of a river, tears, etc.) 3 : arise (of feelings, etc.) 4 : break out (in medicine) — **brote** *nm* 1 : outbreak 2 : sprout, bud, shoot (of plants)
brujería *nf* : witchcraft — **bruja** *nf* 1 : witch 2 *fam* : old hag — **brujo** *nm* : warlock, sorcerer — **brujo, -ja** *adj* : bewitching
brújula *nf* : compass
bruma *nf* : haze, mist — **brumoso, -sa** *adj* : hazy, misty
bruñir {38} *vt* : burnish, polish
brusco, -ca *adj* 1 SÚBITO : sudden, abrupt 2 TOSCO : brusque, rough — **brusquedad** *nf* : abruptness, brusqueness
brutal *adj* : brutal — **brutalidad** *nf* : brutality
bruto, -ta *adj* 1 : brutish, stupid 2 : crude (of petroleum, etc.), uncut (of diamonds) 3 **peso ~** : gross weight — ~ *n* : brute
bucal *adj* : oral
bucear *vi* 1 : dive, swim underwater 2 **~ en** : delve into — **buceo** *nm* : (underwater) diving
bucle *nm* : curl
budín *nm, pl* **-dines** : pudding
budismo *nm* : Buddhism — **budista** *adj & nmf* : Buddhist
buenamente *adv* 1 : easily 2 VOLUNTARIAMENTE : willingly
buenaventura *nf* 1 : good luck 2 **decir la ~ a uno** : tell s.o.'s fortune
bueno, -na *adj* (**buen** *before masculine singular nouns*) 1 : good 2 AMABLE : kind 3 APROPIADO : appropriate 4 SALUDABLE : well, healthy 5 : nice, fine (of weather) 6 **buenos días** : hello, good day 7 **buenas noches** : good night 8 **buenas tardes** : good afternoon, good evening — **bueno** *interj* : OK!, all right!
buey *nm* : ox, steer
búfalo *nm* : buffalo
bufanda *nf* : scarf
bufar *vi* : snort — **bufido** *nm* : snort
bufet *or* **bufé** *nm* : buffet-style meal
bufete *nm* 1 : law practice 2 MESA : writing desk
bufo, -fa *adj* : comic — **bufón, -fona** *n, mpl* **-fones** : buffoon, jester — **bufonada** *nf* : wisecrack
buhardilla *nf* : attic, garret
búho *nm* : owl
buitre *nm* : vulture
bujía *nf* : spark plug
bulbo *nm* : bulb (of a plant)
bulevar *nm* : boulevard
búlgaro, -ra *adj* : Bulgarian
bulla *nf* : uproar, racket
bulldozer *nm* : bulldozer
bullicio *nm* 1 : uproar 2 AJETREO : hustle and bustle — **bullicioso, -sa** *adj* : noisy, boisterous
bullir {38} *vi* 1 : boil 2 AJETREARSE : bustle, stir
bulto *nm* 1 : package, bundle 2 VOLUMEN : bulk, size 3 FORMA : form, shape 4 PROTUBERANCIA : lump, swelling
bumerán *nm, pl* **-ranes** : boomerang
buñuelo *nm* : fried pastry
buque *nm* : ship
burbujear *vi* : bubble — **burbuja** *nf* : bubble
burdel *nm* : brothel
burdo, -da *adj* : coarse, rough
burgués, -guesa *adj & n, mpl* **-gueses** : bourgeois — **burguesía** *nf* : bourgeoisie
burlar *vt* : trick, deceive — **burlarse** *vr* **~ de** : make fun of — **burla** *nf* 1 MOFA : mockery, ridicule 2 BROMA : joke, trick
burlesco, -ca *adj* : comic, funny
burlón, -lona *adj, mpl* **-lones** : mocking
burocracia *nf* : bureaucracy — **burócrata** *nmf* : bureaucrat — **burocrático, -ca** *adj* : bureaucratic
burro, -rra *n* 1 : donkey 2 *fam* : dunce — ~ *adj* : stupid — **burro** *nm* 1 : sawhorse 2 *Lat* : stepladder
bus *nm* : bus
buscar {72} *vt* 1 : look for, seek 2 **ir a ~ a uno** : fetch s.o. — *vi* : search — **busca** *nf* : search — **búsqueda** *nf* : search
busto *nm* : bust (in sculpture)
butaca *nf* 1 : armchair 2 : seat (in a theater)
butano *nm* : butane
buzo *nm* : diver
buzón *nm, pl* **-zones** : mailbox
byte ['bait] *nm* : byte

C

c *nf* : c, third letter of the Spanish alphabet
cabal *adj* 1 : exact 2 COMPLETO : complete — **cabales** *nmpl* **no estar en sus ~** : not be in one's right mind
cabalgar {52} *vi* : ride — **cabalgata** *nf* : cavalcade
caballa *nf* : mackerel
caballería *nf* 1 : cavalry 2 CABALLO : horse, mount — **caballeriza** *nf* : stable
caballero *nm* 1 : gentleman 2 : knight (rank) — **caballerosidad** *nf* : chivalry — **caballeroso, -sa** *adj* : chivalrous
caballete *nm* 1 : ridge (of a roof) 2 : easel (for a canvas) 3 : bridge (of the nose)
caballito *nm* 1 : rocking horse 2 **~s** *nmpl* : merry-go-round
caballo *nm* 1 : horse 2 : knight (in chess) 3 **~ de fuerza** : horsepower
cabaña *nf* : cabin, hut
cabaret *nm, pl* **-rets** : nightclub, cabaret
cabecear *vi* 1 : shake one's head, nod 2 : pitch, lurch (of a boat)
cabecera *nf* 1 : head (of a bed, etc.) 2 : heading (in a text) 3 **médico de ~** : family doctor
cabecilla *nmf* : ringleader
cabello *nm* : hair — **cabelludo, -da** *adj* : hairy
caber {12} *vi* 1 : fit, go (into) 2 **no cabe duda** : there's no doubt
cabestro *nm* : halter
cabeza *nf* 1 : head 2 **de ~** : head first — **cabezada** *nf* 1 : butt (of the head) 2 **dar ~s** : nod off
cabezal *nm* : bolster, headrest
cabida *nf* 1 : room, capacity 2 **dar ~ a** : accommodate, find room for
cabina *nf* 1 : booth 2 : cab (of a truck, etc.) 3 : cabin, cockpit (of an airplane)
cabizbajo, -ja *adj* : downcast
cable *nm* : cable
cabo *nm* 1 : end, stub 2 TROZO : bit 3 : corporal (in the military) 4 : cape (in geography) 5 **al fin y al ~** : after all 6 **llevar a ~** : carry out, do
cabra *nf* : goat
cabriola *nf* 1 : leap, skip 2 **hacer ~s** : prance around
cabrito *nm* : kid (goat)
cacahuate *or* **cacahuete** *nm* : peanut
cacao *nm* 1 : cacao (tree) 2 : cocoa (drink)
cacarear *vi* : crow, cackle — *vt fam* : boast about
cacería *nf* : hunt
cacerola *nf* : pan, saucepan
cacharro *nm* 1 *fam* : thing, piece of junk 2 *fam* : jalopy 3 **~s** *nmpl* : pots and pans
cachear *vt* : search, frisk
cachemir *nm or* **cachemira** *nf* : cashmere
cachete *nm Lat* : cheek — **cachetada** *nf Lat* : slap
cacho *nm* 1 *fam* : piece, bit 2 *Lat* : horn
cachorro, -rra *n* 1 : cub 2 PERRITO : puppy
cactus *or* **cacto** *nm* : cactus
cada *adj* : each, every
cadalso *nm* : scaffold
cadáver *nm* : corpse
cadena *nf* 1 : chain 2 : (television) channel 3 **~ de montaje** : assembly line
cadencia *nf* : cadence
cadera *nf* : hip
cadete *nmf* : cadet
caducar {72} *vi* : expire — **caducidad** *nf* : expiration
caer {13} *vi* 1 : fall, drop 2 **~ bien a uno** : be to one's liking 3 **dejar ~** : drop 4 **me cae bien** : I like her, I like him — **caerse** *vr* : drop, fall (down)
café *nm* 1 : coffee 2 : café — ~ *adj Lat* : brown — **cafetera** *nf* : coffeepot — **cafetería** *nf* : coffee shop, cafeteria — **cafeína** *nf* : caffeine
caída *nf* 1 : fall, drop 2 PENDIENTE : slope
caimán *nm, pl* **-manes** : alligator
caja *nf* 1 : box, case 2 : checkout counter, cashier's desk (in a store) 3 **~ fuerte** : safe 4 **~ registradora** : cash register — **cajero, -ra** *n* 1 : cashier 2 : (bank) teller — **cajetilla** *nf* : pack (of cigarettes) — **cajón** *nm, pl* **-jones** 1 : drawer (in furniture) 2 : large box, crate
cajuela *nf Lat* : trunk (of a car)
cal *nf* : lime
cala *nf* : cove
calabaza *nf* 1 : pumpkin, squash, gourd 2 **dar ~s a** *fam* : give the brush-off to — **calabacín** *nm, pl* **-cines** *or* **calabacita** *nf Lat* : zucchini
calabozo *nm* 1 : prison 2 CELDA : cell
calamar *nm* : squid
calambre *nm* 1 ESPASMO : cramp 2 : (electric) shock
calamidad *nf* : calamity
calar *vt* 1 : soak (through) 2 PERFORAR : pierce — **calarse** *vr* : get drenched
calavera *nf* : skull
calcar {72} *vt* 1 : trace 2 IMITAR : copy, imitate
calcetín *nm, pl* **-tines** : sock
calcinar *vt* : char
calcio *nm* : calcium
calcomanía *nf* : decal
calcular *vt* : calculate, estimate — **calculador, -dora** *adj* : calculating — **calculadora** *nf* : calculator — **cálculo** *nm* 1 : calculation 2 : calculus (in mathematics and medicine) 3 **~ biliar** : gallstone
caldera *nf* 1 : cauldron 2 : boiler (for heating, etc.) — **caldo** *nm* : broth, stock
calefacción *nf, pl* **-ciones** : heating, heat
calendario *nm* : calendar

calentar {55} *vt* : heat (up), warm (up) — **calentarse** *vr* : get warm, heat up — **calentador** *nm* : heater — **calentura** *nf* : temperature, fever
calibre *nm* **1** : caliber **2** DIÁMETRO : bore, diameter — **calibrar** *vt* : calibrate
calidad *nf* **1** : quality **2 en ~ de** : as, in the capacity of
cálido, -da *adj* : hot, warm
calidoscopio *nm* : kaleidoscope
caliente *adj* **1** : hot **2** ACALORADO : heated, fiery
calificar {72} *vt* **1** : qualify **2** EVALUAR : rate **3** : grade (an exam, etc.) — **calificación** *nf, pl* **-ciones 1** : qualification **2** EVALUACIÓN : rating **3** NOTA : grade — **calificativo, -va** *adj* : qualifying — **calificativo** *nm* : qualifier, epithet
caligrafía *nf* : penmanship
calistenia *nf* : calisthenics
cáliz *nm, pl* **-lices** : chalice
caliza *nf* : limestone
callar *vi* : keep quiet, be silent — *vt* **1** : silence, hush **2** OCULTAR : keep secret — **callarse** *vr* : remain silent — **callado, -da** *adj* : quiet, silent
calle *nf* : street, road — **callejear** *vi* : wander about the streets — **callejero, -ra** *adj* **1** : street **2 perro callejero** : stray dog — **callejón** *nm, pl* **-jones 1** : alley **2 ~ sin salida** : dead-end street
callo *nm* : callus, corn
calma *nf* : calm, quiet — **calmante** *adj* : soothing — **~** *nm* : tranquilizer — **calmar** *vt* : calm, soothe — **calmarse** *vr* : calm down — **calmo, -ma** *adj Lat* : calm — **calmoso, -sa** *adj* **1** : calm **2** LENTO : slow
calor *nm* **1** : heat, warmth **2 tener ~** : be hot — **caloría** *nf* : calorie
calumnia *nf* : slander, libel — **calumniar** *vt* : slander, libel
caluroso, -sa *adj* **1** : hot **2** : warm, enthusiastic (of applause, etc.)
calvo, -va *adj* : bald — **calvicie** *nf* : baldness
calza *nf* : wedge
calzada *nf* : roadway
calzado *nm* : footwear — **calzar** {21} *vt* **1** : wear (shoes) **2** : put shoes on (s.o.)
calzones *nmpl Lat* : panties — **calzoncillos** *nmpl* : underpants, briefs
cama *nf* : bed
camada *nf* : litter, brood
camafeo *nm* : cameo
cámara *nf* **1** : chamber **2** *or* **~ fotográfica** : camera **3** : house (in government)
camarada *nmf* : comrade — **camaradería** *nf* : camaraderie
camarero, -ra *n* **1** : waiter, waitress *f* **2** : steward *m*, stewardess *f* (on a ship, etc.) — **camarera** *nf* : chambermaid *f*
camarón *nm, pl* **-rones** : shrimp
camarote *nm* : cabin, stateroom
cambiar *vt* **1** : change **2** CANJEAR : exchange — *vi* **1** : change **2** : shift gears (of an automobile) — **cambiarse** *vr* **1** : change (clothing) **2** : move (to a new address) — **cambiable** *adj* : changeable — **cambio** *nm* **1** : change **2** CANJE : exchange **3 en ~** : on the other hand
camello *nm* : camel
camilla *nf* : stretcher — **camillero** *nm* : orderly (in a hospital)
caminar *vi* : walk — *vt* : cover (a distance) — **caminata** *nf* : hike
camino *nm* **1** : road, path **2** RUTA : way **3 a medio ~** : halfway (there) **4 ponerse en ~** : set out
camión *nm, pl* **-miones 1** : truck **2** *Lat* : bus — **camionero, -ra** *n* **1** : truck driver **2** *Lat* : bus driver — **camioneta** *nm* : light truck, van
camisa *nf* **1** : shirt **2 ~ de fuerza** : straitjacket — **camiseta** *nf* : T-shirt, undershirt — **camisón** *nm, pl* **-sones** : nightshirt, nightgown
camorra *nf fam* : fight, trouble
camote *nm Lat* : sweet potato
campamento *nm* : camp
campana *nf* : bell — **campanada** *nf* : stroke (of a bell), peal — **campanario** *nm* : bell tower — **campanilla** *nf* : (small) bell
campaña *nf* **1** : countryside **2** : (military or political) campaign
campeón, -peona *n, mpl* **-peones** : champion — **campeonato** *nm* : championship
campesino, -na *n* : peasant, farm laborer — **campestre** *adj* : rural, rustic
camping *nm* **1** : campsite **2 hacer ~** : go camping
campiña *nf* : countryside
campo *nm* **1** : field **2** CAMPIÑA : countryside, country **3** CAMPAMENTO : camp
camuflaje *nm* : camouflage — **camuflar** *vt* : camouflage
cana *nf* : gray hair
canadiense *adj* : Canadian
canal *nm* **1** : canal **2** MEDIO : channel **3** : (radio or television) channel — **canalizar** {21} *vt* : channel
canalete *nm* : paddle (of a canoe)
canalla *nf* : rabble — **~** *nmf fam* : swine, bastard
canapé *nm* **1** : canapé **2** SOFÁ : sofa, couch
canario *nm* : canary
canasta *nf* : basket — **canasto** *nm* : large basket
cancelar *vt* **1** : cancel **2** : pay off, settle (a debt) — **cancelación** *nf, pl* **-ciones 1** : cancellation **2** : payment in full (of a debt)
cáncer *nm* : cancer — **canceroso, -sa** *adj* : cancerous
cancha *nf* : court, field (for sports)
canciller *nm* : chancellor
canción *nf, pl* **-ciones 1** : song **2 ~ de cuna** : lullaby — **cancionero** *nm* : songbook
candado *nm* : padlock
candela *nf* : candle — **candelabro** *nm* : candelabra — **candelero** *nm* **1** : candlestick **2 estar en el ~** : be in the limelight
candente *adj* : red hot
candidato, -ta *n* : candidate — **candidatura** *nf* : candidacy
cándido, -da *adj* : naïve — **candidez** *nf* **1** : simplicity **2** INGENUIDAD : naïveté
candil *nm* : oil lamp — **candilejas** *nfpl* : footlights
candor *nm* : naïveté, innocence
canela *nf* : cinnamon
cangrejo *nm* : crab
canguro *nm* : kangaroo
caníbal *nmf* : cannibal — **canibalismo** *nm* : cannibalism
canicas *nfpl* : (game of) marbles
canino, -na *adj* : canine — **canino** *nm* : canine (tooth)
canjear *vt* : exchange — **canje** *nm* : exchange, trade
cano, -na *adj* : gray, gray-haired
canoa *nf* : canoe
canon *nm, pl* **cánones** : canon
canonizar {21} *vt* : canonize
canoso, -sa *adj* : gray, gray-haired
cansar *vt* : tire (out) — *vi* : be tiring — **cansarse** *vr* : get tired — **cansado, -da** *adj* **1** : tired **2** PESADO : tiresome — **cansancio** *nm* : fatigue, weariness
cantalupo *nm* : cantaloupe
cantar *v* : sing — **~** *nm* : song — **cantante** *nmf* : singer
cántaro *nm* **1** : pitcher, jug **2 llover a ~s** *fam* : rain cats and dogs
cantera *nf* : quarry (excavation)
cantidad *nf* **1** : quantity, amount **2 una ~ de** : lots of
cantimplora *nf* : canteen, water bottle
cantina *nf* **1** : canteen, cafeteria **2** *Lat* : tavern, bar
canto *nm* **1** : singing, song **2** BORDE, LADO : edge **3 de ~** : on end, sideways **4 ~ rodado** : boulder — **cantor, -tora** *adj* **1** : singing **2 pájaro ~** : songbird — **~** *n* : singer
caña *nf* **1** : cane, reed **2 ~ de pescar** : fishing pole
cáñamo *nm* : hemp
cañería *nf* : pipes, piping — **caño** *nm* **1** : pipe **2** : spout (of a fountain) — **cañón** *nm, pl* **-ñones 1** : cannon **2** : barrel (of a gun) **3** : canyon (in geography)
caoba *nf* : mahogany
caos *nm* : chaos — **caótico, -ca** *adj* : chaotic
capa *nf* **1** : cape, cloak **2** : coat (of paint, etc.), coating (in cooking) **3** ESTRATO : layer, stratum **4** : (social) class
capacidad *nf* **1** : capacity **2** APTITUD : ability
capacitar *vt* : train, qualify — **capacitación** *nf, pl* **-ciones** : training
caparazón *nm, pl* **-zones** : shell
capataz *nmf, pl* **-taces** : foreman
capaz *adj, pl* **-paces 1** : capable, able **2** ESPACIOSO : spacious
capellán *nm, pl* **-llanes** : chaplain
capilla *nf* : chapel
capital *adj* **1** : capital **2** PRINCIPAL : chief, principal — **~** *nm* : capital (assets) — **~** *nf* : capital (city) — **capitalismo** *nm* : capitalism — **capitalista** *nmf* capitalist — **~** *adj* : capitalistic — **capitalizar** {21} *vt* : capitalize
capitán, -tana *n, mpl* **-tanes** : captain
capitolio *nm* : capitol
capitular *vi* : capitulate, surrender — **capitulación** *nf, pl* **-ciones** : surrender
capítulo *nm* : chapter
capó *nm* : hood (of a car)
capote *nm* : cloak, cape
capricho *nm* : whim, caprice — **caprichoso, -sa** *adj* : whimsical, capricious
cápsula *nf* : capsule
captar *vt* **1** : grasp **2** ATRAER : gain, attract (interest, etc.) **3** : harness (waters)
capturar *vt* : capture, seize — **captura** *nf* : capture, seizure
capucha *nf* : hood (of clothing)
capullo *nm* **1** : cocoon **2** : (flower) bud
caqui *adj & nm* : khaki
cara *nf* **1** : face **2** ASPECTO : appearance **3** *fam* : nerve, gall **4 ~ a** *or* **de ~ a** : facing
carabina *nf* : carbine
caracol *nm* **1** : snail **2** *Lat* : conch **3** RIZO : curl
carácter *nm, pl* **-racteres 1** : character **2** ÍNDOLE : nature — **característica** *nf* : characteristic — **característico, -ca** *adj* : characteristic — **caracterizar** {21} *vt* : characterize
caramba *interj* : oh my!, good grief!
carámbano *nm* : icicle
caramelo *nm* **1** : caramel **2** DULCE : candy
carátula *nf* **1** CARETA : mask **2** : jacket (of a record, etc.) **3** *Lat* : face (of a watch)
caravana *nf* **1** : caravan **2** REMOLQUE : trailer
caray → **caramba**
carbohidrato *nm* : carbohydrate
carbón *nm, pl* **-bones 1** : coal **2** : charcoal (for drawing) — **carboncillo** *nm* : charcoal — **carbonero, -ra** *adj* : coal — **carbonizar** {21} *vt* : char — **carbono** *nm* : carbon — **carburador** *nm* : carburetor — **carburante** *nm* : fuel
carcajada *nf* : loud laugh, guffaw
cárcel *nf* : jail, prison — **carcelero, -ra** *n* : jailer
carcinógeno *nm* : carcinogen
carcomer *vt* : eat away at — **carcomido, -da** *adj* : worm-eaten
cardenal *nm* **1** : cardinal **2** CONTUSIÓN : bruise
cardíaco *or* **cardiaco, -ca** *adj* : cardiac, heart
cárdigan *nm, pl* **-gans** : cardigan
cardinal *adj* : cardinal
cardiólogo, -ga *n* : cardiologist
cardo *nm* : thistle
carear *vt* : bring face-to-face
carecer {53} *vi* **~ de** : lack — **carencia** *nf* : lack, want — **carente** *adj* **~ de** : lacking (in)
carestía *nf* **1** : high cost **2** ESCASEZ : dearth, scarcity
careta *nf* : mask
cargar {52} *vt* **1** : load **2** : charge (a battery, a purchase, etc.) **3** LLEVAR : carry **4 ~ de** : burden with — *vi* **1** : load **2 ~ con** : pick up, carry away — **carga** *nf* **1** : load **2** CARGAMENTO : freight, cargo **3** RESPONSABILIDAD : burden **4** : charge (in electricity, etc.) — **cargado, -da** *adj* **1** : loaded, burdened **2** PESADO : heavy, stuffy **3** : charged (of a battery) **4** FUERTE : strong, concentrated — **cargamento** *nm* : cargo, load — **cargo** *nm* **1** : charge **2** PUESTO : position, office
cariarse *vr* : decay (of teeth)
caribe *adj* : Caribbean
caricatura *nf* **1** : caricature **2** : (political) cartoon — **caricaturizar** *vt* : caricature
caricia *nf* : caress
caridad *nf* **1** : charity **2** LIMOSNA : alms *pl*
caries *nfs & pl* : cavity (in a tooth)
cariño *nm* : affection, love — **cariñoso, -sa** *adj* : affectionate, loving
carisma *nf* : charisma — **carismático, -ca** *adj* : charismatic
caritativo, -va *adj* : charitable
cariz *nm, pl* **-rices** : appearance, aspect
carmesí *adj & nm* : crimson
carmín *nm, pl* **-mines** *or* **~ de labios** : lipstick
carnada *nf* : bait
carnal *adj* **1** : carnal **2 primo ~** : first cousin
carnaval *nm* : carnival
carne *nf* **1** : meat **2** : flesh (of persons or fruits) **3 ~ de cerdo** : pork **4 ~ de gallina** : goose bumps **5 ~ de ternera** : veal
carné *nm* → **carnet**
carnero *nm* **1** : ram, sheep **2** : mutton (in cooking)
carnet *nm* **1 ~ de conducir** : driver's license **2 ~ de identidad** : identification card, ID
carnicería *nf* **1** : butcher shop **2** MATANZA : slaughter — **carnicero, -ra** *n* : butcher
carnívoro, -ra *adj* : carnivorous — **carnívoro** *nm* : carnivore
carnoso, -sa *adj* : fleshy
caro, -ra *adj* **1** : expensive **2** QUERIDO : dear — **caro** *adv* : dearly
carpa *nf* **1** : carp **2** TIENDA : tent
carpeta *nf* : folder
carpintería *nf* : carpentry — **carpintero, -ra** *n* : carpenter
carraspear *vi* : clear one's throat — **carraspera** *nf* **1** : hoarseness **2 tener ~** : have a frog in one's throat
carrera *nf* **1** : running, run **2** COMPETICIÓN : race **3** : course (of studies) **4** PROFESIÓN : career, profession
carreta *nf* : cart, wagon
carrete *nm* : reel, spool
carretera *nf* : highway, road
carretilla *nf* : wheelbarrow
carril *nm* **1** : lane (of a road) **2** : rail (for a railroad)
carrillo *nm* : cheek
carrito *nm* : cart, trolley
carrizo *nm* : reed
carro *nm* **1** : wagon, cart **2** *Lat* : automobile, car — **carrocería** *nf* : body (of an automobile)
carroña *nf* : carrion
carroza *nf* **1** : carriage **2** : float (in a parade)
carruaje *nm* : carriage
carrusel *nm* : merry-go-round, carousel
carta *nf* **1** : letter **2** NAIPE : playing card **3** : charter (of an organization, etc.) **4** MENÚ : menu **5** MAPA : map, chart
cartel *nm* : poster, bill — **cartelera** *nf* : billboard
cartera *nf* **1** : briefcase **2** BILLETERA : wallet **3** *Lat* : pocketbook, handbag — **carterista** *nmf* : pickpocket
cartero, -ra *nm* : mail carrier, mailman *m*
cartílago *nm* : cartilage
cartilla *nf* **1** : primer, reader **2** : booklet, record (of a savings account, etc.)
cartón *nm, pl* **-tones 1** : cardboard **2** : carton (of cigarettes, etc.)
cartucho *nm* : cartridge
casa *nf* **1** : house **2** HOGAR : home **3** EMPRESA : company, firm **4 ~ flotante** : houseboat
casar *vt* : marry — *vi* : go together, match up — **casarse** *vr* **1** : get married **2 ~ con** : marry — **casado, -da** *adj* : married — **casamiento** *nm* **1** : marriage **2** BODA : wedding
cascabel *nm* : small bell
cascada *nf* : waterfall
cascanueces *nms & pl* : nutcracker
cascar {72} *vt* : crack (a shell, etc.) — **cascarse** *vr* : crack, chip — **cáscara** *nf* : skin, peel, shell — **cascarón** *nm, pl* **-rones** : eggshell
casco *nm* **1** : helmet **2** : hull (of a boat) **3** : hoof (of a horse) **4** : fragment (of ceramics, etc.) **5** : center (of a town) **6** ENVASE : empty bottle
caserío *nm* **1** *Spain* : country house **2** POBLADO : hamlet
casero, -ra *adj* **1** : homemade **2** DOMÉSTICO : domestic, household — **~** *n* : landlord, landlady *f*
caseta *nf* : booth, stall
casete → **cassette**
casi *adv* **1** : almost, nearly **2** (*in negative phrases*) : hardly
casilla *nf* **1** : compartment, pigeonhole **2** CASETA : booth **3** : box (on a form)
casino *nm* **1** : casino **2** : (social) club
caso *nm* **1** : case **2 en ~ de** : in the event of **3 hacer ~** : pay attention **4 no venir al ~** : be beside the point
caspa *nf* : dandruff
cassette *nmf* : cassette
casta *nf* **1** : lineage, descent **2** : breed (of animals) **3** : caste (in India)
castaña *nf* : chestnut
castañetear *vi* : chatter (of teeth)
castaño, -ña *adj* : chestnut (color)
castañuela *nf* : castanet
castellano *nm* : Spanish, Castilian (language)
castidad *nf* : chastity
castigar {52} *vt* **1** : punish **2** : penalize (in sports) — **castigo** *nm* **1** : punishment **2** : penalty (in sports)
castillo *nm* : castle
casto, -ta *adj* : chaste, pure — **castizo, -za** *adj* : pure, traditional (in style)
castor *nm* : beaver
castrar *vt* : castrate
castrense *adj* : military
casual *adj* : chance, accidental — **casualidad** *nf* **1** : coincidence **2 por ~** *or* **de ~** : by chance — **casualmente** *adv* : by chance
cataclismo *nm* : cataclysm
catalán, -lana *adj, mpl* **-lanes** : Catalan — **catalán** *nm* : Catalan (language)
catalizador *nm* : catalyst
catalogar {52} *vt* : catalog, classify — **catálogo** *nm* : catalog
catapulta *nf* : catapult
catar *vt* : taste, sample
catarata *nf* **1** : waterfall **2** : cataract (in medicine)
catarro *nm* RESFRIADO : cold
catástrofe *nf* : catastrophe, disaster — **catastrófico, -ca** *adj* : catastrophic, disastrous
catecismo *nm* : catechism
cátedra *nf* : chair (at a university)
catedral *nf* : cathedral
catedrático, -ca *n* : professor
categoría *nf* **1** : category **2** RANGO : rank **3 de ~** : first-rate — **categórico, -ca** *adj* : categorical
católico, -ca *adj & n* : Catholic — **catolicismo** *nm* : Catholicism
catorce *adj & nm* : fourteen — **catorceavo** *nm* : fourteenth
catre *nm* : cot
cauce *nm* **1** : riverbed **2** VÍA : channel, means *pl*
caucho *nm* : rubber
caución *nf, pl* **-ciones** : security, guarantee
caudal *nm* **1** : volume of water, flow **2** RIQUEZA : wealth
caudillo *nm* : leader, commander
causar *vt* : cause, provoke — **causa** *nf* **1** : cause **2** RAZÓN : reason **3** : case (in law) **4 a ~ de** : because of
cáustico, -ca *adj* : caustic
cautela *nf* : caution — **cauteloso, -sa** *adj* : cautious — **cautelosamente** *adv* : cautiously, warily
cautivar *vt* **1** : capture **2** ENCANTAR : captivate — **cautiverio** *nm* : captivity — **cautivo, -va** *adj & n* : captive
cauto, -ta *adj* : cautious
cavar *v* : dig
caverna *nf* : cavern, cave

cavidad *nf* : cavity
cavilar *vi* : ponder
cayado *nm* : crook, staff
cazar {21} *vt* **1** : hunt **2** ATRAPAR : catch, bag — *vi* : go hunting — **caza** *nf* **1** : hunt, hunting **2** : game (animals) — **cazador, -dora** *n* : hunter
cazo *nm* **1** : saucepan **2** CUCHARÓN : ladle — **cazuela** *nf* : casserole
CD *nm* : CD, compact disc
cebada *nf* : barley
cebar *vt* **1** : bait **2** : feed, fatten (animals) **3** : prime (a firearm, etc.) — **cebo** *nm* **1** CARNADA : bait **2** : charge (of a firearm)
cebolla *nf* : onion — **cebolleta** *nf* : scallion, green onion — **cebollino** *nm* : chive
cebra *nf* : zebra
cecear *vi* : lisp — **ceceo** *nm* : lisp
cedazo *nm* : sieve
ceder *vi* **1** : yield, give way **2** DISMINUIR : diminish, abate — *vt* : cede, hand over
cedro *nm* : cedar
cédula *nf* : document, certificate
cegar {49} *vt* **1** : blind **2** TAPAR : block, stop up — *vi* : be blinded, go blind — **ceguera** *nf* : blindness
ceja *nf* : eyebrow
cejar *vi* : give in, back down
celada *nf* : trap, ambush
celador, -dora *n* : guard, warden
celda *nf* : cell (of a jail)
celebrar *vt* **1** : celebrate **2** : hold (a meeting), say (Mass) **3** ALEGRARSE DE : be happy about — **celebrarse** *vr* : take place — **celebración** *nf, pl* **-ciones** : celebration — **célebre** *adj* : famous, celebrated — **celebridad** *nf* : celebrity
celeridad *nf* : swiftness, speed
celeste *adj* **1** : celestial, heavenly **2** *or* **azul ~** : sky blue — **celestial** *adj* : celestial, heavenly
celibato *nm* : celibacy — **célibe** *adj* : celibate
celo *nm* **1** : zeal **2 en ~** : in heat **3 ~s** *nmpl* : jealousy **4 tener ~s** : be jealous
celofán *nm, pl* **-fanes** : cellophane
celoso, -sa *adj* **1** : jealous **2** DILIGENTE : zealous
célula *nf* : cell — **celular** *adj* : cellular
celulosa *nf* : cellulose
cementerio *nm* : cemetery
cemento *nm* **1** : cement **2 ~ armado** : reinforced concrete
cena *nf* : supper, dinner
cenagal *nm* : bog, quagmire — **cenagoso** *adj* : swampy
cenar *vi* : have dinner, have supper — *vt* : have for dinner or supper
cenicero *nm* : ashtray
cenit *nm* : zenith
ceniza *nf* : ash
censo *nm* : census
censurar *vt* **1** : censor **2** REPROBAR : censure, criticize — **censura** *nf* **1** : censorship **2** REPROBACIÓN : censure, criticism
centavo *nm* **1** : cent **2** : centavo (unit of currency)
centellear *vi* : sparkle, twinkle — **centella** *nf* **1** : flash **2** CHISPA : spark — **centelleo** *nm* : twinkling, sparkle
centenar *nm* : hundred — **centenario** *nm* : centennial
centeno *nm* : rye
centésimo, -ma *adj* : hundredth
centígrado *adj* : centigrade, Celsius
centigramo *nm* : centigram
centímetro *nm* : centimeter
centinela *nmf* : sentinel, sentry
central *adj* : central — **~** *nf* : main office, headquarters — **centralita** *nf* : switchboard — **centralizar** {21} *vt* : centralize
centrar *vt* : center — **centrarse** *vr* **~ en** : focus on — **céntrico, -ca** *adj* : central — **centro** *nm* **1** : center **2** : downtown (of a city) **3 ~ de mesa** : centerpiece
centroamericano, -na *adj* : Central American
ceñir {67} *vt* **1** : encircle **2** : fit (s.o.) tightly — **ceñirse** *vr* **~ a** : limit oneself to — **ceñido, -da** *adj* : tight
ceño *nm* **1** : frown **2 fruncir el ~** : knit one's brow, frown
cepillo *nm* **1** : brush **2** : (carpenter's) plane **3 ~ de dientes** : toothbrush — **cepillar** *vt* **1** : brush **2** : plane (wood)
cera *nf* **1** : wax, beeswax **2** : floor wax, furniture wax
cerámica *nf* **1** : ceramics *pl* **2** : (piece of) pottery
cerca[1] *nf* : fence — **cercado** *nm* : enclosure
cerca[2] *adv* **1** : close, near **2 ~ de** : near, close to **3 ~ de** : nearly, almost — **cercano, -na** *adj* : near, close — **cercanía** *nf* **1** : proximity **2 ~s** *nfpl* : outskirts
cercar {72} *vt* **1** : fence in **2** RODEAR : surround
cerciorarse *vr* **~ de** : make sure of
cerco *nm* **1** : circle, ring **2** ASEDIO : siege **3** *Lat* : fence
cerda *nf* : bristle
cerdo *nm* **1** : pig, hog **2 ~ macho** : boar
cereal *adj & nm* : cereal
cerebro *nm* : brain — **cerebral** *adj* : cerebral
ceremonia *nf* : ceremony — **ceremonial** *adj* : ceremonial — **ceremonioso, -sa** *adj* : ceremonious
cereza *nf* : cherry
cerilla *nf* : match — **cerillo** *nm Lat* : match
cerner {56} *or* **cernir** *vt* : sift — **cernerse** *vr* **1** : hover **2 ~ sobre** : loom over — **cernidor** *nm* : sieve
cero *nm* : zero
cerrar {55} *vt* **1** : close, shut **2** : turn off (a faucet, etc.) **3** : bring to an end — *vi* **1** : close up, lock up **2** : close down (a business, etc.) — **cerrarse** *vr* **1** : close, shut **2** TERMINAR : come to a close, end — **cerrado, -da** *adj* **1** : closed, shut, locked **2** : overcast (of weather) **3** : sharp (of a curve) **4** : thick, broad (of an accent) — **cerradura** *nf* : lock — **cerrajero, -ra** *n* : locksmith
cerro *nm* : hill
cerrojo *nm* : bolt, latch
certamen *nm, pl* **-támenes** : competition, contest
certero, -ra *adj* : accurate, precise
certeza *nf* : certainty — **certidumbre** *nf* : certainty
certificar {72} *vt* **1** : certify **2** : register (mail) — **certificado, -da** *adj* : certified, registered — **certificado** *nm* : certificate
cervato *nm* : fawn
cerveza *nf* **1** : beer **2 ~ de barril** : draft beer — **cervecería** *nf* **1** : brewery **2** BAR : beer hall, bar
cesar *vi* : cease, stop — *vt* : dismiss, lay off — **cesación** *nf, pl* **-ciones** : cessation, suspension — **cesante** *adj* **1** : laid off **2** *Lat* : unemployed — **cesantía** *nf Lat* : unemployment
cesárea *nf* : cesarean (section)
cese *nm* **1** : cessation, stop **2** DESTITUCIÓN : dismissal
césped *nm* : lawn, grass
cesta *nf* : basket — **cesto** *nm* **1** : (large) basket **2 ~ de basura** : wastebasket
cetro *nm* : scepter
chabacano *nm Lat* : apricot
chabola *nf Spain* : shack, shanty
chacal *nm* : jackal
cháchara *nf fam* : gabbing, chatter
chacra *nf Lat* : (small) farm
chafar *vt fam* : flatten, crush
chal *nm* : shawl
chaleco *nm* : vest
chalet *nm Spain* : house
chalupa *nf* **1** : small boat **2** *Lat* : small stuffed tortilla
chamarra *nf* : jacket
chamba *nf Lat fam* : job
champaña *or* **champán** *nm* : champagne
champiñón *nm, pl* **-ñones** : mushroom
champú *nm, pl* **-pús** *or* **-púes** : shampoo
chamuscar {72} *vt* : scorch
chance *nm Lat* : chance, opportunity
chancho *nm Lat* : pig
chanclos *nmpl* : galoshes
chantaje *nm* : blackmail — **chantajear** *vt* : blackmail
chanza *nf* : joke, jest
chapa *nf* **1** : sheet, plate **2** INSIGNIA : badge — **chapado, -da** *adj* **1** : plated **2 chapado a la antigua** : old-fashioned
chaparrón *nm, pl* **-rrones** : downpour
chapotear *vi* : splash
chapucero, -ra *adj* : shoddy, sloppy — **chapuza** *nf* : botched job
chapuzón *nm, pl* **-zones** : dip, short swim
chaqueta *nf* : jacket
charca *nf* : pond — **charco** *nm* : puddle
charlar *vi* : chat — **charla** *nf* : chat, talk — **charlatán, -tana** *adj, mpl* **-tanes** : talkative — **~** *n* **1** : chatterbox **2** FARSANTE : charlatan
charol *nm* **1** : patent leather **2** BARNIZ : varnish
chasco *nm* **1** : trick, joke **2** DECEPCIÓN : disappointment
chasis *nms & pl* : chassis
chasquear *vt* **1** : click (the tongue), snap (one's fingers) **2** : crack (a whip) — **chasquido** *nm* **1** : click, snap **2** : crack (of a whip)
chatarra *nf* : scrap (metal)
chato, -ta *adj* **1** : pug-nosed **2** APLANADO : flat
chauvinismo *nm* : chauvinism — **chauvinista** *adj* : chauvinist, chauvinistic
chaval, -vala *n fam* : kid, boy *m*, girl *f*
checo, -ca *adj* : Czech — **checo** *nm* : Czech (language)
chef *nm* : chef
cheque *nm* : check — **chequera** *nf* : checkbook
chequear *vt Lat* **1** : check, inspect, verify **2** : check in (baggage) — **chequeo** *nm* **1** : (medical) checkup **2** *Lat* : check, inspection
chica → chico
chicano, -na *adj* : Chicano, Mexican-American
chícharo *nm Lat* : pea
chicharrón *nm, pl* **-rrones** : pork rind
chichón *nm, pl* **-chones** : bump
chicle *nm* : chewing gum
chico, -ca *adj* : little, small — **~** *n* : child, boy *m*, girl *f*
chiflar *vt* : whistle at, boo — *vi Lat* : whistle — **chiflado, -da** *adj fam* : crazy, nuts — **chiflido** *nm* : whistling
chile *nm* : chili pepper
chileno, -na *adj* : Chilean
chillar *vi* **1** : shriek, scream **2** CHIRRIAR : screech, squeal — **chillido** *nm* **1** : scream **2** CHIRRIDO : screech, squeal — **chillón, -llona** *adj, mpl* **-llones** : shrill, loud
chimenea *nf* **1** : chimney **2** HOGAR : fireplace
chimpancé *nm* : chimpanzee
chinche *nf* : bedbug
chino, -na *adj* : Chinese — **chino** *nm* : Chinese (language)
chiquillo, -lla *n* : kid, child
chiquito, -ta *adj* : tiny — **~** *n* : little child, tot
chiribita *nf* : spark
chiripa *nf* **1** : fluke **2 de ~** : by sheer luck
chirivía *nf* : parsnip
chirriar {85} *vi* **1** : squeak, creak **2** : screech (of brakes, etc.) — **chirrido** *nm* **1** : squeak, creak **2** : screech (of brakes)
chisme *nm* : (piece of) gossip — **chismear** *vi* : gossip — **chismoso, -sa** *adj* : gossipy — **~** *n* : gossip
chispear *vi* : spark — **chispa** *nf* : spark
chisporrotear *vi* : crackle, sizzle — **chisporroteo** *nm* : crackle
chiste *nm* : joke, funny story — **chistoso, -sa** *adj* : funny, witty
chivo, -va *n* : kid, young goat
chocar {72} *vi* **1** : crash, collide **2** ENFRENTARSE : clash — **chocante** *adj* **1** : striking, shocking **2** *Lat* : unpleasant, rude
choclo *nm Lat* : ear of corn, corncob
chocolate *nm* : chocolate
chofer *or* **chófer** *nm* **1** : chauffeur **2** CONDUCTOR : driver
choque *nm* **1** : shock **2** : crash, collision (of vehicles) **3** CONFLICTO : clash
chorizo *nm* : chorizo, sausage
chorrear *vi* **1** : drip **2** BROTAR : pour out, gush — **chorro** *nm* **1** : stream, jet **2** HILO : trickle
chovinismo → chauvinismo
choza *nf* : hut, shack
chubasco *nm* : downpour, squall
chuchería *nf* **1** : knickknack, trinket **2** DULCE : sweet
chueco, -ca *adj Lat* : crooked
chuleta *nf* : cutlet, chop
chulo, -la *adj fam* : cute, pretty
chupar *vt* **1** : suck **2** ABSORBER : absorb **3** *fam* : guzzle — *vi* : suckle — **chupada** *nf* : suck, sucking — **chupete** *nm* **1** : pacifier **2** *Lat* : lollipop
churro *nm* **1** : fried dough **2** *fam* : botch, mess
chusco, -ca *adj* : funny
chusma *nf* : riffraff, rabble
chutar *vi* : shoot (in soccer)
cianuro *nm* : cyanide
cicatriz *nf, pl* **-trices** : scar — **cicatrizar** {21} *vi* : form a scar, heal
cíclico, -ca *adj* : cyclical
ciclismo *nm* : cycling — **ciclista** *nmf* : cyclist
ciclo *nm* : cycle
ciclón *nm, pl* **-clones** : cyclone
ciego, -ga *adj* : blind — **ciegamente** *adv* : blindly
cielo *nm* **1** : sky **2** : heaven (in religion)
ciempiés *nms & pl* : centipede
cien *adj* : a hundred, hundred — **~** *nm* : one hundred
ciénaga *nf* : swamp, bog
ciencia *nf* **1** : science **2 a ~ cierta** : for a fact
cieno *nm* : mire, mud, silt
científico, -ca *adj* : scientific — **~** *n* : scientist
ciento *adj* (*used in compound numbers*) : one hundred — **~** *nm* **1** : hundred, group of a hundred **2 por ~** : percent
cierre *nm* **1** : closing, closure **2** BROCHE : fastener, clasp
cierto, -ta *adj* **1** : true **2** SEGURO : certain **3 por ~** : as a matter of fact
ciervo, -va *n* : deer, stag *m*, hind *f*
cifra *nf* **1** : number, figure **2** : sum (of money, etc.) **3** CLAVE : code, cipher — **cifrar** *vt* **1** : write in code **2 ~ la esperanza en** : pin all one's hopes on
cigarrillo *nm* : cigarette — **cigarro** *nm* **1** : cigarette **2** PURO : cigar
cigüeña *nf* : stork
cilantro *nm* : cilantro, coriander
cilindro *nm* : cylinder — **cilíndrico, -ca** *adj* : cylindrical
cima *nf* : peak, summit
címbalo *nm* : cymbal
cimbrar *or* **cimbrear** *vt* : shake, rock — **cimbrarse** *or* **cimbrearse** *vr* : sway
cimentar {55} *vt* **1** : lay the foundation of **2** : cement, strengthen (relations, etc.) — **cimientos** *nmpl* : base, foundation(s)
cinc *nm* : zinc
cincel *nm* : chisel — **cincelar** *vt* : chisel
cinco *adj & nm* : five
cincuenta *adj & nm* : fifty — **cincuentavo, -va** *adj* : fiftieth — **cincuentavo** *nm* : fiftieth
cine *nm* : cinema, movies *pl* — **cinematográfico, -ca** *adj* : movie, film
cínico, -ca *adj* : cynical — **~** *n* : cynic — **cinismo** *nm* : cynicism
cinta *nf* **1** : ribbon, band **2 ~ adhesiva** : adhesive tape **3 ~ métrica** : tape measure **4 ~ magnetofónica** : magnetic tape
cinto *nm* : belt, girdle — **cintura** *nf* : waist — **cinturón** *nm, pl* **-rones** **1** : belt **2 ~ de seguridad** : seat belt
ciprés *nm, pl* **-preses** : cypress
circo *nm* : circus
circuito *nm* : circuit
circulación *nf, pl* **-ciones** **1** : circulation **2** TRÁFICO : traffic — **circular** *vi* **1** : circulate **2** : drive (a vehicle) — **~** *adj* : circular
círculo *nm* : circle
circuncidar *vt* : circumcise — **circuncisión** *nf, pl* **-siones** : circumcision
circundar *vt* : surround
circunferencia *nf* : circumference
circunscribir {33} *vt* : confine, limit — **circunscribirse** *vr* **~ a** : limit oneself to — **circunscripción** *nf, pl* **-ciones** : district, constituency
circunspecto, -ta *adj* : circumspect, cautious
circunstancia *nf* : circumstance — **circunstancial** *adj* : chance — **circunstante** *nmf* **1** : bystander **2 los ~s** : those present
circunvalación *nf, pl* **-ciones** **1** : encircling **2 carretera de ~** : bypass
cirio *nm* : candle
ciruela *nf* **1** : plum **2 ~ pasa** : prune
cirugía *nf* : surgery — **cirujano, -na** *n* : surgeon
cisma *nf* : schism
cisne *nm* : swan
cisterna *nf* : cistern
cita *nf* **1** : appointment, date **2** REFERENCIA : quote, quotation — **citación** *nf, pl* **-ciones** : summons — **citar** *vt* **1** : quote, cite **2** CONVOCAR : make an appointment with **3** : summon (in law) — **citarse** *vr* **~ con** : arrange to meet
cítrico *nm* : citrus (fruit)
ciudad *nf* : city, town — **ciudadano, -na** *n* **1** : citizen **2** HABITANTE : resident — **ciudadanía** *nf* : citizenship
cívico, -ca *adj* : civic
civil *adj* : civil — **~** *nmf* : civilian — **civilidad** *nf* : civility — **civilización** *nf, pl* **-ciones** : civilization — **civilizar** {21} *vt* : civilize
cizaña *nf* : discord, rift
clamar *vi* : clamor, cry out — **clamor** *nm* : clamor, outcry — **clamoroso, -sa** *adj* : clamorous, loud
clan *nm* : clan
clandestino, -na *adj* : clandestine, secret
clara *nf* : egg white
claraboya *nf* : skylight
claramente *adv* : clearly
clarear *v impers* **1** : dawn **2** ACLARAR : clear up — *vi* : be transparent
claridad *nf* **1** : clarity, clearness **2** LUZ : light
clarificar {72} *vt* : clarify — **clarificación** *nf, pl* **-ciones** : clarification
clarín *nm, pl* **-rines** : bugle
clarinete *nm* : clarinet
clarividente *adj* **1** : clairvoyant **2** PERSPICAZ : perspicacious — **clarividencia** *nf* **1** : clairvoyance **2** PERSPICACIA : farsightedness
claro *adv* **1** : clearly **2** POR SUPUESTO : of course, surely — **~** *nm* **1** : clearing, glade **2 ~ de luna** : moonlight — **claro, -ra** *adj* **1** : clear, bright **2** : light (of colors) **3** EVIDENTE : clear, evident
clase *nf* **1** : class **2** TIPO : sort, kind
clásico, -ca *adj* : classic, classical — **clásico** *nm* : classic
clasificar {72} *vt* **1** : classify, sort out **2** : rate, rank (a hotel, a team, etc.) — **clasificarse** *vr* : qualify (in competitions) — **clasificación** *nf, pl* **-ciones** **1** : classification **2** : league (in sports)
claudicar {72} *vi* : back down
claustro *nm* : cloister
claustrofobia *nf* : claustrophobia — **claustrofóbico, -ca** *adj* : claustrophobic
cláusula *nf* : clause
clausurar *vt* : close (down) — **clausura** *nf* : closure, closing
clavado *nm Lat* : dive
clavar *vt* **1** : nail, hammer **2** HINCAR : drive in, plunge
clave *nf* **1** CIFRA : code **2** SOLUCIÓN : key **3** : clef (in music) — **~** *adj* : key
clavel *nm* : carnation
clavicémbalo *nm* : harpsichord
clavícula *nf* : collarbone
clavija *nf* **1** : peg, pin **2** : (electric) plug
clavo *nm* **1** : nail **2** : clove (spice)
claxon *nm, pl* **cláxones** : horn (of an automobile)
clemencia *nf* : clemency, mercy — **clemente** *adj* : merciful
clerical *adj* : clerical — **clérigo, -ga** *n* : clergyman, cleric — **clero** *nm* : clergy
cliché *nm* **1** : cliché **2** : negative (of a photograph)
cliente, -ta *n* : customer, client — **clientela** *nf* : clientele, customers *pl*
clima *nm* **1** : climate **2** AMBIENTE : atmosphere — **climático, -ca** *adj* : climatic

climatizar {21} *vt* : air-condition — **climatizado, -da** *adj* : air-conditioned
clímax *nm* : climax
clínica *nf* : clinic — **clínico, -ca** *adj* : clinical
clip *nm, pl* **clips** : (paper) clip
cloaca *nf* : sewer
cloquear *vi* : cluck — **cloqueo** *nm* : cluck, clucking
cloro *nm* : chlorine
clóset *nm Lat, pl* **clósets** : (built-in) closet, cupboard
club *nm* : club
coacción *nf, pl* **-ciones** : coercion — **coaccionar** *vt* : coerce
coagular *v* : clot, coagulate — **coagularse** *vr* : coagulate — **coágulo** *nm* : clot
coalición *nf, pl* **-ciones** : coalition
coartada *nf* : alibi
coartar *vt* : restrict, limit
cobarde *nmf* : coward — ~ *adj* : cowardly — **cobardía** *nf* : cowardice
cobaya *nf* : guinea pig
cobertizo *nm* : shelter, shed
cobertor *nm* : bedspread
cobertura *nf* **1** : cover **2** : coverage (of news, etc.)
cobijar *vt* : shelter — **cobijarse** *vr* : take shelter — **cobija** *nf Lat* : blanket — **cobijo** *nm* : shelter
cobra *nf* : cobra
cobrar *vt* **1** : charge, collect **2** : earn (a salary, etc.) **3** ADQUERIR : acquire, gain **4** : cash (a check) — *vi* : be paid — **cobrador, -dora** *n* **1** : collector **2** : conductor (of a bus, etc.)
cobre *nm* : copper
cobro *nm* : collection (of money), cashing (of a check)
cocaína *nf* : cocaine
cocción *nf, pl* **-ciones** : cooking
cocear *vi* : kick
cocer {14} *vt* **1** : cook **2** HERVIR : boil
coche *nm* **1** : car, automobile **2** : coach (of a train) **3** *or* ~ **de caballos** : carriage **4** ~ **fúnebre** : hearse — **cochecito** *nm* : baby carriage, stroller — **cochera** *nf* : garage, carport
cochino, -na *n* : pig, hog — ~ *adj fam* : dirty, filthy — **cochinada** *nf fam* : dirty thing — **cochinillo** *nm* : piglet
cocido, -da *adj* **1** : boiled, cooked **2 bien** ~ : well-done — **cocido** *nm* : stew
cociente *nm* : quotient
cocina *nf* **1** : kitchen **2** : (kitchen) stove **3** : (art of) cooking, cuisine — **cocinar** *v* : cook — **cocinero, -ra** *n* : cook, chef
coco *nm* : coconut
cocodrilo *nm* : crocodile
coctel *or* **cóctel** *nm* **1** : cocktail **2** FIESTA : cocktail party
codazo *nm* **1** : nudge **2 dar un** ~ **a** : elbow, nudge
codicia *nf* : greed — **codiciar** *vt* : covet — **codicioso, -sa** *adj* : covetous, greedy
código *nm* **1** : code **2** ~ **postal** : zip code **3** ~ **morse** : Morse code
codo *nm* : elbow
codorniz *nf, pl* **-nices** : quail
coexistir *vi* : coexist
cofre *nm* : chest, coffer
coger {15} *vt* **1** : take (hold of) **2** ATRAPAR : catch **3** : pick up (from the ground) **4** : pick (fruit, etc.) — **cogerse** *vr* : hold on
cohechar *vt* : bribe — **cohecho** *nm* : bribe, bribery
coherencia *nf* : coherence — **coherente** *adj* : coherent — **cohesión** *nf, pl* **-siones** : cohesion
cohete *nm* : rocket
cohibir {62} *vt* **1** : restrict **2** : inhibit (a person) — **cohibirse** *vr* : feel inhibited — **cohibido, -da** *adj* : inhibited, shy
coincidir *vi* **1** : coincide **2** ~ **con** : agree with — **coincidencia** *nf* : coincidence
cojear *vi* **1** : limp **2** : wobble (of furniture, etc.) — **cojera** *nf* : limp
cojín *nm, pl* **-jines** : cushion — **cojinete** *nm* **1** : pad, cushion **2** : bearing (of a machine)
cojo, -ja *adj* **1** : lame **2** : wobbly (of furniture) — ~ *n* : lame person
col *nf* **1** : cabbage **2** ~ **de Bruselas** : Brussels sprout
cola *nf* **1** : tail **2** FILA : line (of people) **3** : end (of a line) **4** PEGAMENTO : glue **5** ~ **de caballo** : ponytail
colaborar *vi* : collaborate — **colaboración** *nf, pl* **-ciones** : collaboration — **colaborador, -dora** *n* **1** : collaborator **2** : contributor (to a periodical)
colada *nf Spain* **1** : laundry **2 hacer la** ~ : do the washing
colador *nm* : colander, strainer
colapso *nm* : collapse
colar {19} *vt* : strain, filter — **colarse** *vr* : sneak in, gate-crash
colcha *nf* : bedspread, quilt — **colchón** *nm, pl* **-chones** : mattress — **colchoneta** *nf* : mat
colear *vi* : wag its tail
colección *nf, pl* **-ciones** : collection — **coleccionar** *vt* : collect — **coleccionista** *nmf* : collector — **colecta** *nf* : collection (of donations)
colectividad *nf* : community — **colectivo, -va** *adj* : collective — **colectivo** *nm* **1** : collective **2** *Lat* : city bus
colector *nm* : sewer
colega *nmf* : colleague
colegio *nm* **1** : school **2** : (professional) college — **colegial, -giala** *n* : schoolboy *m*, schoolgirl *f*
colegir {28} *vt* : gather
cólera *nm* : cholera — ~ *nf* : anger, rage — **colérico, -ca** *adj* **1** : bad-tempered **2** FURIOSO : angry
colesterol *nm* : cholesterol
coleta *nf* : pigtail
colgar {16} *vt* **1** : hang **2** : hang up (a telephone) **3** : hang out (laundry) — *vi* : hang up — **colgante** *adj* : hanging — ~ *nm* : pendant
colibrí *nm* : hummingbird
cólico *nm* : colic
coliflor *nf* : cauliflower
colilla *nf* : (cigarette) butt
colina *nf* : hill
colindar *vi* ~ **con** : be adjacent to — **colindante** *adj* : adjacent
coliseo *nm* : coliseum
colisión *nf, pl* **-siones** : collision — **colisionar** *vi* ~ **contra** : collide with
collar *nm* **1** : necklace **2** : collar (for pets)
colmar *vt* **1** : fill to the brim **2** : fulfill (a wish, etc.) **3** ~ **de** : shower with — **colmado, -da** *adj* : heaping
colmena *nf* : beehive
colmillo *nm* **1** : canine (tooth) **2** : fang (of a dog, etc.), tusk (of an elephant)
colmo *nm* **1** : height, limit **2 ¡eso es el** ~**!** : that's the last straw!
colocar {72} *vt* **1** PONER : place, put **2** : find a job for — **colocarse** *vr* **1** SITUARSE : position oneself **2** : get a job — **colocación** *nf, pl* **-ciones** **1** : placement, placing **2** EMPLEO : position, job
colombiano, -na *adj* : Colombian
colon *nm* : (intestinal) colon
colonia *nf* **1** : colony **2** PERFUME : cologne **3** *Lat* : residential area — **colonial** *adj* : colonial — **colonizar** {21} *vt* : colonize — **colonización** *nf, pl* **-ciones** : colonization — **colono, -na** *n* : settler, colonist
coloquial *adj* : colloquial — **coloquio** *nm* **1** : talk, discussion **2** CONGRESO : conference
color *nm* : color — **colorado, -da** *adj* : red — **colorear** *vt* : color — **colorete** *nm* : rouge — **colorido** *nm* : colors *pl*, coloring
colosal *adj* : colossal
columna *nf* **1** : column **2** ~ **vertebral** : spine, backbone — **columnista** *nmf* : columnist
columpiar *vt* : push (on a swing) — **columpiarse** *vr* : swing — **columpio** *nm* : swing
coma[1] *nm* : coma
coma[2] *nf* : comma
comadre *nf* **1** : godmother of one's child, mother of one's godchild **2** *fam* : (female) friend — **comadrear** *vi fam* : gossip
comadreja *nf* : weasel
comadrona *nf* : midwife
comandancia *nf* : command headquarters, command — **comandante** *nmf* **1** : commander **2** : major (in the military) — **comando** *nm* **1** : commando **2** *Lat* : command
comarca *nf* : region, area
combar *vt* : bend, curve
combatir *vt* : combat, fight against — *vi* : fight — **combate** *nm* **1** : combat **2** : fight (in boxing) — **combatiente** *nmf* : combatant, fighter
combinar *vt* **1** : combine **2** : put together, match (colors, etc.) — **combinarse** *vr* : get together — **combinación** *nf, pl* **-ciones** **1** : combination **2** : connection (in travel)
combustible *nm* : fuel — ~ *adj* : combustible — **combustión** *nf, pl* **-tiones** : combustion
comedia *nf* : comedy
comedido, -da *adj* : moderate
comedor *nm* : dining room
comensal *nmf* : diner, dinner guest
comentar *vt* **1** : comment on, discuss **2** MENCIONAR : mention — **comentario** *nm* **1** : comment, remark **2** ANÁLISIS : commentary — **comentarista** *nmf* : commentator
comenzar {29} *v* : begin, start
comer *vt* **1** : eat **2** *fam* : eat up, eat into — *vi* **1** : eat **2** CENAR : have a meal **3 dar de** ~ : feed — **comerse** *vr* : eat up
comercio *nm* **1** : commerce, trade **2** NEGOCIO : business — **comercial** *adj* : commercial — **comercializar** {21} *vt* : market — **comerciante** *nmf* : merchant, dealer — **comerciar** *vi* : do business, trade
comestible *adj* : edible — **comestibles** *nmpl* : groceries, food
cometa *nm* : comet — ~ *nf* : kite
cometer *vt* **1** : commit **2** ~ **un error** : make a mistake — **cometido** *nm* : assignment, task
comezón *nf, pl* **-zones** : itchiness, itching
comicios *nmpl* : elections
cómico, -ca *adj* : comic, comical — ~ *n* : comic, comedian
comida *nf* **1** ALIMENTO : food **2** *Spain* : lunch **3** *Lat* : dinner **4 tres** ~**s al día** : three meals a day
comienzo *nm* : beginning
comillas *nfpl* : quotation marks
comino *nm* : cumin
comisario, -ria *n* : commissioner — **comisaría** *nf* : police station
comisión *nf, pl* **-siones** **1** : commission **2** COMITÉ : committee
comité *nm* : committee
como *conj* **1** : as, since **2** SÍ : if — ~ *prep* **1** : like, as **2 así** ~ : as well as — ~ *adv* **1** : as **2** APROXIMADAMENTE : around, about
cómo *adv* **1** : how **2** ~ **no** : by all means **3 ¿**~ **te llamas?** : what's your name?
cómoda *nf* : chest of drawers
comodidad *nf* : comfort, convenience
comodín *nm, pl* **-dines** : joker (in playing cards)
cómodo, -da *adj* **1** : comfortable **2** ÚTIL : handy, convenient
comoquiera *adv* **1** : in any way **2** ~ **que** : however
compacto, -ta *adj* : compact
compadecer {53} *vt* : feel sorry for — **compadecerse** *vr* ~ **de** : take pity on
compadre *nm* **1** : godfather of one's child, father of one's godchild **2** *fam* : buddy
compañero, -ra *n* : companion, partner — **compañerismo** *nm* : companionship
compañía *nf* : company
comparar *vt* : compare — **comparable** *adj* : comparable — **comparación** *nf, pl* **-ciones** : comparison — **comparativo, -va** *adj* : comparative
comparecer *vt* : appear (before a court, etc.)
compartimiento *or* **compartimento** *nm* : compartment
compartir *vt* : share
compás *nm, pl* **-pases** **1** : compass **2** : rhythm, time (in music)
compasión *nf, pl* **-siones** : compassion, pity — **compasivo, -va** *adj* : compassionate
compatible *adj* : compatible — **compatibilidad** *nf* : compatibility
compatriota *nmf* : compatriot, fellow countryman
compeler *vt* : compel
compendiar *vt* : summarize — **compendio** *nm* : summary
compensar *vt* : compensate for — **compensación** *nf, pl* **-ciones** : compensation
competir {54} *vi* : compete — **competencia** *nf* **1** : competition, rivalry **2** CAPACIDAD : competence — **competente** *adj* : competent — **competición** *nf, pl* **-ciones** : competition — **competidor, -dora** *n* : competitor
compilar *vt* : compile
compinche *nmf fam* : friend, chum
complacer {57} *vt* : please — **complacerse** *vr* ~ **en** : take pleasure in — **complaciente** *adj* : obliging, helpful
complejidad *nf* : complexity — **complejo, -ja** *adj* : complex — **complejo** *nm* : complex
complementar *vt* : complement — **complementario, -ria** *adj* : complementary — **complemento** *nm* **1** : complement **2** : object (in grammar)
completar *vt* : complete — **completo, -ta** *adj* **1** : complete **2** PERFECTO : perfect **3** LLENO : full — **completamente** *adv* : completely
complexión *nf, pl* **-xiones** : constitution, build
complicar {72} *vt* **1** : complicate **2** IMPLICAR : involve — **complicación** *nf, pl* **-ciones** : complication — **complicado, -da** *adj* : complicated, complex
cómplice *nmf* : accomplice — ~ *adj* : conspiratorial, knowing
complot *nm, pl* **-plots** : conspiracy, plot
componer {60} *vt* **1** : make up, compose **2** : compose, write (a song) **3** ARREGLAR : fix, repair — **componerse** *vr* ~ **de** : consist of — **componente** *adj* & *nm* : component, constituent
comportarse *vr* : behave — **comportamiento** *nm* : behavior
composición *nf, pl* **-ciones** : composition — **compositor, -tora** *n* : composer, songwriter
compostura *nf* **1** : composure **2** REPARACIÓN : repair
comprar *vt* : buy, purchase — **compra** *nf* **1** : purchase **2 ir de** ~**s** : go shopping — **comprador, -dora** *n* : buyer, shopper
comprender *vt* **1** : comprehend, understand **2** ABARCAR : cover, include — **comprensible** *adj* : understandable — **comprensión** *nf, pl* **-siones** : understanding — **comprensivo, -va** *adj* : understanding
compresa *nf* **1** : compress **2** *or* ~ **higiénica** : sanitary napkin
compresión *nf, pl* **-siones** : compression — **comprimido** *nm* : pill, tablet — **comprimir** *vt* : compress
comprobar {19} *vt* **1** VERIFICAR : check **2** DEMOSTRAR : prove — **comprobación** *nf, pl* **-ciones** : verification, check — **comprobante** *nm* **1** : proof **2** RECIBO : receipt, voucher
comprometer *vt* **1** : compromise **2** ARRIESGAR : jeopardize **3** OBLIGAR : commit, put under obligation — **comprometerse** *vr* **1** : commit oneself **2** ~ **con** : get engaged to — **comprometedor, -dora** *adj* : compromising — **comprometido, -da** *adj* **1** : compromising, awkward **2** : engaged (to be married) — **compromiso** *nm* **1** : obligation, commitment **2** : (marriage) engagement **3** ACUERDO : agreement **4** APURO : awkward situation
compuesto, -ta *adj* **1** : compound **2** ~ **de** : made up of, consisting of — **compuesto** *nm* : compound
compulsivo, -va *adj* : compelling, urgent
computar *vt* : compute, calculate — **computadora** *nf or* **computador** *nm* **1** : computer **2** ~ **portátil** : laptop computer — **computo** *nm* : calculation
comulgar {52} *vi* : receive Communion
común *adj, pl* **-munes** **1** : common **2** ~ **y corriente** : ordinary **3 por lo** ~ : generally
comuna *nf* : commune — **comunal** *adj* : communal
comunicar {72} *vt* : communicate — **comunicarse** *vr* **1** : communicate **2** ~ **con** : get in touch with — **comunicación** *nf, pl* **-ciones** : communication — **comunicado** *nm* : communiqué — **comunicativo, -va** *adj* : communicative
comunidad *nf* : community
comunión *nf, pl* **-niones** : communion, Communion
comunismo *nm* : Communism — **comunista** *adj* & *nmf* : Communist
con *prep* **1** : with **2** A PESAR DE : in spite of **3** (*before an infinitive*) : by **4** ~ **(tal) que** : so long as
cóncavo, -va *adj* : concave
concebir {54} *v* : conceive — **concebible** *adj* : conceivable
conceder *vt* **1** : grant, bestow **2** ADMITIR : concede
concejal, -jala *n* : councilman, alderman
concentrar *vt* : concentrate — **concentrarse** *vr* : concentrate — **concentración** *nf, pl* **-ciones** : concentration
concepción *nf, pl* **-ciones** : conception — **concepto** *nm* **1** : concept **2** OPINIÓN : opinion
concernir {17} *vi* ~ **a** : concern — **concerniente** *adj* ~ **a** : concerning
concertar {55} *vt* **1** : arrange, coordinate **2** (*used before an infinitive*) : agree **3** : harmonize (in music) — *vi* : be in harmony
concesión *nf, pl* **-siones** **1** : concession **2** : awarding (of prizes, etc.)
concha *nf* : shell
conciencia *nf* **1** : conscience **2** CONOCIMIENTO : consciousness, awareness — **concientizar** {21} *vt Lat* : make aware — **concientizarse** *vr Lat* ~ **de** : realize
concienzudo, -da *adj* : conscientious
concierto *nm* **1** : concert **2** : concerto (musical composition)
conciliar *vt* : reconcile — **conciliación** *nf, pl* **-ciones** : reconciliation
concilio *nm* : council
conciso, -sa *adj* : concise
conciudadano, -na *n* : fellow citizen
concluir {41} *vt* : conclude — *vi* : come to an end — **conclusión** *nf, pl* **-siones** : conclusion — **concluyente** *adj* : conclusive
concordar {19} *vi* : agree — *vt* : reconcile — **concordancia** *nf* : agreement — **concordia** *nf* : harmony, concord
concretar *vt* : make concrete, specify — **concretarse** *vr* : become definite, take shape — **concreto, -ta** *adj* **1** : concrete **2** DETERMINADO : specific **3 en** ~ : specifically — **concreto** *nm Lat* : concrete
concurrir *vi* **1** : come together, meet **2** ~ **a** : take part in — **concurrencia** *nf* : audience, turnout — **concurrido, -da** *adj* : busy, crowded
concursar *vi* : compete, participate — **concursante** *nmf* : competitor — **concurso** *nm* **1** : competition **2** CONCURRENCIA : gathering **3** AYUDA : help, cooperation
condado *nm* : county
conde, -desa *n* : count *m*, countess *f*
condenar *vt* **1** : condemn, damn **2** : sentence (a criminal) — **condena** *nf* **1** : condemnation **2** SENTENCIA : sentence — **condenación** *nf, pl* **-ciones** : condemnation, damnation
condensar *vt* : condense — **condensación** *nf, pl* **-ciones** : condensation
condesa *nf* → **conde**
condescender {56} *vi* **1** : acquiesce, agree **2** ~ **a** : condescend to — **condescendiente** *adj* : condescending
condición *nf, pl* **-ciones** **1** : condition, state **2** CALIDAD : capacity, position — **condicional** *adj* : conditional
condimento *nm* : condiment, seasoning
condolerse {47} *vr* : sympathize — **condolencia** *nf* : condolence
condominio *nm* **1** : joint ownership **2** *Lat* : condominium
condón *nm, pl* **-dones** : condom
conducir {61} *vt* **1** DIRIGIR : direct, lead **2** MANEJAR : drive — *vi* **1** : drive **2** ~ **a** : lead to — **conducirse** *vr* : behave
conducta *nf* : behavior, conduct

conducto *nm* : conduit, duct

conductor, -tora *n* : driver

conectar *vt* **1** : connect **2** ENCHUFAR : plug in — *vi* : connect

conejo, -ja *n* : rabbit — **conejera** *nf* : (rabbit) hutch

conexión *nf, pl* **-xiones** : connection — **conexo, -xa** *adj* : connected

confabularse *vr* : conspire, plot

confeccionar *vt* : make (up), prepare — **confección** *nf, pl* **-ciones 1** : making, preparation **2** : tailoring, dressmaking

confederación *nf, pl* **-ciones** : confederation

conferencia *nf* **1** : lecture **2** REUNIÓN : conference

conferir {76} *vt* : confer, bestow

confesar {55} *v* : confess — **confesarse** *vr* : go to confession — **confesión** *nf, pl* **-siones 1** : confession **2** CREDO : religion, creed

confeti *nm* : confetti

confiar {85} *vi* : trust — *vt* : entrust — **confiable** *adj* : trustworthy, reliable — **confiado, -da** *adj* **1** : confident **2** CRÉDULO : trusting — **confianza** *nf* **1** : trust **2** : confidence (in oneself)

confidencia *nf* : confidence, secret — **confidencial** *adj* : confidential — **confidencialidad** *nf* : confidentiality — **confidente** *nmf* **1** : confidant, confidante *f* **2** : (police) informer

configuración *nf, pl* **-ciones** : configuration, shape

confín *nm, pl* **-fines** : boundary, limit — **confinar** *vt* **1** : confine **2** DESTERRER : exile

confirmar *vt* : confirm — **confirmación** *nf, pl* **-ciones** : confirmation

confiscar {72} *vt* : confiscate

confitería *nm* : candy store

confitura *nf* : jam

conflagración *nf, pl* **-ciones 1** : war, conflict **2** INCENDIO : fire

conflicto *nm* : conflict

confluencia *nf* : junction, confluence

conformar *vt* : shape, make up — **conformarse** *vr* **1** RESIGNARSE : resign oneself **2** ~ **con** : content oneself with — **conforme** *adj* **1** : content, satisfied **2** ~ **a** : in accordance with — ~ *conj* : as — **conformidad** *nf* **1** : agreement **2** RESIGNACIÓN : resignation

confortar *vt* : comfort — **confortable** *adj* : comfortable

confrontar *vt* **1** : confront **2** COMPARAR : compare — *vi* : border — **confrontarse** *vr* ~ **con** : face up to — **confrontación** *nf, pl* **-ciones** : confrontation

confundir *vt* : confuse, mix up — **confundirse** *vr* : make a mistake, be confused — **confusión** *nf, pl* **-siones** : confusion — **confuso, -sa** *adj* **1** : confused **2** INDISTINTO : hazy, indistinct — **congelar** *vt* : freeze — **congelarse** *vr* : freeze — **congelación** *nf, pl* **-ciones** : freezing — **congelado, -da** *adj* : frozen — **congelador** *nm* : freezer

congeniar *vi* : get along

congestión *nf, pl* **-tiones** : congestion — **congestionado, -da** *adj* : congested

congoja *nf* : anguish, grief

congraciarse *vr* : ingratiate oneself

congratular *vt* : congratulate

congregar {52} *vt* : bring together — **congregarse** *vr* : congregate — **congregación** *nf, pl* **-ciones** : congregation, gathering

congreso *nm* : congress — **congresista** *nmf* : member of congress

conjeturar *vt* : guess, conjecture — **conjetura** *nf* : guess, conjecture

conjugar {52} *vt* : conjugate — **conjugación** *nf, pl* **-ciones** : conjugation

conjunción *nf, pl* **-ciones** : conjunction

conjunto, -ta *adj* : joint — **conjunto** *nm* **1** : collection **2** : outfit (of clothing) **3** GRUPO : band **4 en** ~ : as a whole

conjurar *vt* : ward off — *vi* : conspire, plot

conllevar *vt* : entail

conmemorar *vt* : commemorate — **conmemoración** *nf, pl* **-ciones** : commemoration — **conmemorativo, -va** *adj* : commemorative

conmigo *pron* : with me

conminar *vt* : threaten

conmiseración *nf, pl* **-ciones** : pity, commiseration

conmocionar *vt* : shock — **conmoción** *nf, pl* **-ciones 1** : shock, upheaval **2** *or* ~ **cerebral** : concussion

conmover {47} *vt* **1** : move, touch **2** SACUDIR : shake (up) — **conmoverse** *vr* : be moved — **conmovedor, -dora** *adj* : moving, touching

conmutador *nm* **1** : (electric) switch **2** *Lat* : switchboard

cono *nm* : cone

conocer {18} *vt* **1** : know **2** : meet (a person), get to know (a city, etc.) **3** RECONOCER : recognize — **conocerse** *vr* **1** : meet, get to know each other **2** : know oneself — **conocedor, -dora** *adj & n* : expert — **conocido, -da** *adj* : well-known — ~ *n* : acquaintance — **conocimiento** *nm* **1** : knowledge **2** SENTIDO : consciousness

conque *conj* : so

conquistar *vt* : conquer — **conquista** *nf* : conquest — **conquistador, -dora** *adj* : conquering — **conquistador** *nm* : conqueror

consabido, -da *adj* **1** : well-known **2** HABITUEL : usual

consagrar *vt* **1** : consecrate **2** DEDICAR : devote — **consagración** *nf, pl* **-ciones** : consecration

consciencia *nf* → **conciencia** — **consciente** *adj* : conscious, aware

consecución *nf, pl* **-ciones** : attainment

consecuencia *nf* **1** : consequence **2 en** ~ : accordingly — **consecuente** *adj* : consistent

consecutivo, -va *adj* : consecutive

conseguir {75} *vt* **1** : get, obtain **2** ~ **hacer algo** : manage to do sth

consejo *nm* **1** : advice, counsel **2** : council (assembly) — **consejero, -ra** *n* : adviser, counselor

consenso *nm* : consensus

consentir {76} *vt* **1** : allow, permit **2** MIMAR : pamper, spoil — *vi* : consent — **consentimiento** *nm* : consent, permission

conserje *nmf* : caretaker, janitor

conservar *vt* **1** : preserve **2** GUARDAR : keep, conserve — **conservarse** *vr* : keep — **conserva** *nf* **1** : preserve(s) **2** ~**s** *nfpl* : canned goods — **conservación** *nf, pl* **-ciones** : conservation, preservation — **conservador, -dora** *adj & n* : conservative — **conservatorio** *nm* : conservatory

considerar *vt* **1** : consider **2** RESPETAR : respect — **considerable** *adj* : considerable — **consideración** *nf, pl* **-ciones 1** : consideration **2** RESPETO : respect — **considerado, -da** *adj* **1** : considerate **2** RESPETADO : respected

consigna *nf* **1** ESLOGAN : slogan **2** ORDEN : orders **3** : checkroom (for baggage)

consigo *pron* : with her, with him, with you, with oneself

consiguiente *adj* **1** : consequent **2 por** ~ : consequently

consistir *vi* ~ **en 1** : consist of **2** : lie in, consist in — **consistencia** *nf* : consistency — **consistente** *adj* **1** : firm, solid **2** ~ **en** : consisting of

consolar {19} *vt* : console, comfort — **consolarse** *vr* : console oneself — **consolación** *nf, pl* **-ciones** : consolation

consolidar *vt* : consolidate — **consolidación** *nf, pl* **-ciones** : consolidation

consomé *nm* : consommé

consonante *adj* : consonant, harmonious — ~ *nf* : consonant

consorcio *nm* : consortium

conspirar *vi* : conspire, plot — **conspiración** *nf, pl* **-ciones** : conspiracy — **conspirador, -dora** *n* : conspirator

constancia *nf* **1** : record, evidence **2** PERSEVERANCIA : perseverance — **constante** *adj* : constant — **constantemente** *adv* : constantly, continually

constar *vi* **1** : be evident, be clear **2** ~ **de** : consist of

constatar *vt* **1** : verify **2** AFIRMAR : state, affirm

constelación *nf, pl* **-ciones** : constellation

consternación *nf, pl* **-ciones** : consternation

constipado, -da *adj* **estar** ~ : have a cold — **constipado** *nm* : cold — **constiparse** *vr* : catch a cold

constituir {41} *vt* **1** FORMAR : constitute, form **2** FUNDAR : establish, set up — **constituirse** *vr* ~ **en** : set oneself up as — **constitución** *nf, pl* **-ciones** : constitution — **constitucional** *adj* : constitutional — **constitutivo, -va** *adj* : constituent — **constituyente** *adj & nm* : constituent

constreñir {67} *vt* **1** : force, compel **2** RESTRINGIR : restrict, limit

construir {41} *vt* : build, construct — **construcción** *nf, pl* **-ciones** : construction, building — **constructivo, -va** *adj* : constructive — **constructor, -tora** *n* : builder

consuelo *nm* : consolation, comfort

consuetudinario, -ria *adj* : customary

cónsul *nmf* : consul — **consulado** *nm* : consulate

consultar *vt* : consult — **consulta** *nf* : consultation — **consultor, -tora** *n* : consultant — **consultorio** *nm* : office (of a doctor or dentist)

consumar *vt* **1** : consummate, complete **2** : commit (a crime)

consumir *vt* : consume — **consumirse** *vr* : waste away — **consumición** *nf, pl* **-ciones 1** : consumption **2** : drink (in a restaurant) — **consumido, -da** *adj* : thin, emaciated — **consumidor, -dora** *n* : consumer — **consumo** *nm* : consumption

contabilidad *nf* **1** : accounting, bookkeeping **2** : accountancy (profession) — **contable** *nmf Spain* : accountant, bookkeeper

contactar *vi* ~ **con** : get in touch with, contact — **contacto** *nm* : contact

contado, -da *adj* : numbered, few — **contado** *nm* **al** ~ : (in) cash

contador, -dora *n Lat* : accountant — **contador** *nm* : meter

contagiar *vt* **1** : infect **2** : transmit (a disease) — **contagiarse** *vr* **1** : be contagious **2** : become infected (with a disease) — **contagio** *nm* : contagion, infection — **contagioso, -sa** *adj* : contagious, infectious

contaminar *vt* : contaminate, pollute — **contaminación** *nf, pl* **-ciones** : contamination, pollution

contar {19} *vt* **1** : count **2** NARRAR : tell — *vi* **1** : count **2** ~ **con** : rely on, count on

contemplar *vt* **1** MIRAR : look at, behold **2** CONSIDERAR : contemplate — **contemplación** *nf, pl* **-ciones** : contemplation

contemporáneo, -nea *adj & n* : contemporary

contender {56} *vi* : contend, compete — **contendiente** *nmf* : competitor

contener {80} *vt* **1** : contain **2** RESTRINGIR : restrain, hold back — **contenerse** *vr* : restrain oneself — **contenedor** *nm* : container — **contenido, -da** *adj* : restrained — **contenido** *nm* : contents *pl*

contentar *vt* : please, make happy — **contentarse** *vr* ~ **con** : be satisfied with — **contento, -ta** *adj* : glad, happy, contented

contestar *vt* : answer — *vi* : reply, answer back — **contestación** *nf, pl* **-ciones** : answer, reply

contexto *nm* : context

contienda *nf* **1** COMBATE : dispute, fight **2** COMPETICIÓN : contest

contigo *pron* : with you

contiguo, -gua *adj* : adjacent

continente *nm* : continent — **continental** *adj* : continental

contingencia *nf* : contingency — **contingente** *adj & nm* : contingent

continuar {3} *v* : continue — **continuación** *nf, pl* **-ciones 1** : continuation **2 a** ~ : next, then — **continuidad** *nf* : continuity — **continuo, -nua** *adj* **1** : continuous, steady **2** FRECUENTE : continual

contorno *nm* **1** : outline **2** ~**s** *nmpl* : surrounding area

contorsión *nf, pl* **-siones** : contortion

contra *prep* **1** : against **2 en** ~ : against — ~ *nm* **los pros y los** ~**s** : the pros and cons

contraatacar {72} *v* : counterattack — **contraataque** *nm* : counterattack

contrabajo *nm* : double bass

contrabalancear *vt* : counterbalance

contrabandista *nmf* : smuggler — **contrabando** *nm* **1** : smuggling **2** : contraband (goods)

contracción *nf, pl* **-ciones** : contraction

contrachapado *nm* : plywood

contradecir {11} *vt* : contradict — **contradicción** *nf, pl* **-ciones** : contradiction — **contradictorio, -ria** *adj* : contradictory

contraer {81} *vt* **1** : contract **2** ~ **matrimonio** : get married — **contraerse** *vr* : contract, tighten up

contrafuerte *nm* : buttress

contragolpe *nm* : backlash

contralto *nmf* : contralto

contrapartida *nf* : compensation

contrapelo: **a** ~ *adv phr* : the wrong way

contrapeso *nm* : counterbalance

contraponer {60} *vt* **1** : counter, oppose **2** COMPARAR : compare

contraproducente *adj* : counterproductive

contrariar {85} *vt* **1** : oppose **2** MOLESTAR : vex, annoy — **contrariedad** *nf* **1** : obstacle **2** DISGUSTO : annoyance — **contrario, -ria** *adj* **1** OPUESTO : opposite **2 al contrario** : on the contrary **3 ser** ~ **a** : be opposed to

contrarrestar *vt* : counteract

contrasentido *nm* : contradiction (in terms)

contraseña *nf* : password

contrastar *vt* **1** : check, verify **2** RESISTIR : resist — *vi* : contrast — **contraste** *nm* : contrast

contratar *vt* **1** : contract for **2** : hire, engage (workers)

contratiempo *nm* **1** : mishap **2** DIFICULTAD : setback

contrato *nm* : contract — **contratista** *nmf* : contractor

contraventana *nf* : shutter

contribuir {41} *vi* **1** : contribute **2** : pay taxes — **contribución** *nf, pl* **-ciones 1** : contribution **2** IMPUESTO : tax — **contribuyente** *nmf* **1** : contributor **2** : taxpayer

contrincante *nmf* : opponent

contrito, -ta *adj* : contrite

controlar *vt* **1** : control **2** COMPROBAR : monitor, check — **control** *nm* **1** : control **2** VERIFICACIÓN : inspection, check — **controlador, -dora** *n* : controller

controversia *nf* : controversy

contundente *adj* **1** : blunt **2** : forceful, convincing (of arguments, etc.)

contusión *nf, pl* **-siones** : bruise

convalecencia *nf* : convalescence — **convaleciente** *adj & nmf* : convalescent

convencer {86} *vt* : convince, persuade — **convencerse** *vr* : be convinced — **convencimiento** *nm* : conviction, belief

convención *nf, pl* **-ciones** : convention — **convencional** *adj* : conventional

convenir {87} *vi* **1** : be suitable, be advisable **2** ~ **en** : agree on — **conveniencia** *nf* **1** : convenience **2** : suitability (of an action, etc.) — **conveniente** *adj* **1** : convenient **2** ACONSEJABLE : suitable, advisable **3** PROVECHOSO : useful — **convenio** *nm* : agreement, pact

convento *nm* : convent, monastery

converger {15} *or* **convergir** *vi* : converge

conversar *vi* : converse, talk — **conversación** *nf, pl* **-ciones** : conversation

conversión *nf, pl* **-siones** : conversion — **converso, -sa** *n* : convert

convertir {76} *vt* : convert — **convertirse** *vr* ~ **en** : turn into — **convertible** *adj & nm* : convertible

convexo, -xa *adj* : convex

convicción *nf, pl* **-ciones** : conviction — **convicto, -ta** *adj* : convicted

convidar *vt* : invite — **convidado, -da** *n* : guest

convincente *adj* : convincing

convite *nm* **1** : invitation **2** : banquet

convivir *vi* : live together — **convivencia** *nf* : coexistence, living together

convocar {72} *vt* : convoke, call together

convulsión *nf, pl* **-siones 1** : convulsion **2** TRASTORNO : upheaval — **convulsivo, -va** *adj* : convulsive

conyugal *adj* : conjugal — **cónyuge** *nmf* : spouse, partner

coñac *nm* : cognac, brandy

cooperar *vi* : cooperate — **cooperación** *nf, pl* **-ciones** : cooperation — **cooperativa** *nf* : cooperative, co-op — **cooperativo, -va** *adj* : cooperative

coordenada *nf* : coordinate

coordinar *vt* : coordinate — **coordinación** *nf, pl* **-ciones** : coordination — **coordinador, -dora** *n* : coordinator

copa *nf* **1** : glass, goblet **2** : cup (in sports) **3 tomar una** ~ : have a drink

copia *nf* : copy — **copiar** *vt* : copy

copioso, -sa *adj* : copious, abundant

copla *nf* **1** : (popular) song **2** ESTROFA : verse, stanza

copo *nm* **1** : flake **2** *or* ~ **de nieve** : snowflake

coquetear *vi* : flirt — **coqueteo** *nm* : flirting, flirtation — **coqueto, -ta** *adj* : flirtatious — ~ *n* : flirt

coraje *nm* **1** : valor, courage **2** IRA : anger

coral[1] *nm* : coral

coral[2] *adj* : choral — ~ *nf* : choir, chorale

Corán *nm* **el** ~ : the Koran

coraza *nf* **1** : armor plating **2** : shell

corazón *nm, pl* **-zones 1** : heart **2** : core (of fruit) **3 mi** ~ : my darling — **corazonada** *nf* **1** : hunch **2** IMPULSO : impulse

corbata *nf* : tie, necktie

corchete *nm* **1** : hook and eye, clasp **2** : square bracket (punctuation mark)

corcho *nm* : cork

cordel *nm* : cord, string

cordero *nm* : lamb

cordial *adj* : cordial — **cordialidad** *nf* : cordiality

cordillera *nf* : mountain range

córdoba *nf* : córdoba (Nicaraguan unit of currency)

cordón *nm, pl* **-dones 1** : cord **2** ~ **policial** : (police) cordon **3 cordones** *nmpl* : shoelaces

cordura *nf* : sanity

corear *vt* : chant

coreografía *nf* : choreography

cornamenta *nf* : antlers *pl*

corneta *nf* : bugle

coro *nm* **1** : chorus **2** : (church) choir

corona *nf* **1** : crown **2** : wreath, garland (of flowers) — **coronación** *nf, pl* **-ciones** : coronation — **coronar** *vt* : crown

coronel *nm* : colonel

coronilla *nf* **1** : crown (of the head) **2 estar hasta la** ~ : be fed up

corporación *nf, pl* **-ciones** : corporation

corporal *adj* : corporal, bodily

corporativo, -va *adj* : corporate

corpulento, -ta *adj* : stout

corral *nm* **1** : farmyard **2** : pen, corral (for animals) **3** *or* **corralito** : playpen

correa *nf* **1** : strap, belt **2** : leash (for a dog, etc.)

corrección *nf, pl* **-ciones 1** : correction **2** : correctness, propriety (of manners) — **correccional** *nm* : reformatory — **correctivo, -va** *adj* : corrective — **correcto, -ta** *adj* **1** : correct, right **2** CORTÉS : polite

corredizo, -za *adj* : sliding

corredor, -dora *n* **1** : runner, racer **2** AGENTE : agent, broker — **corredor** *nm* : corridor, hallway

corregir {28} *vt* : correct — **corregirse** *vr* : mend one's ways

correlación *nf, pl* **-ciones** : correlation

correo *nm* **1** : mail **2** ~ **aéreo** : airmail

correr *vi* **1** : run, race **2** : flow (of a river, etc.) **3** : pass (of time) — *vt* **1** : run **2** RECORRER : travel over, cover **3** : draw (curtains) — **correrse** *vr* **1** : move along **2** : run (of colors)

corresponder *vi* **1** : correspond **2** PERTENECER : belong **3** ENCAJAR : fit **4** ~ **a** : reciprocate, repay — **corresponderse** *vr* : write to each other — **correspondencia** *nf* **1** : correspondence **2** : connection (of a train, etc.) — **correspondiente** *adj* : cor-

responding, respective — **corresponsal** *nmf* : correspondent
corretear *vi* : run about, scamper
corrida *nf* **1** : run **2** *or* **~ de toros** : bullfight — **corrido, -da** *adj* **1** : straight, continuous **2** *fam* : worldly
corriente *adj* **1** : current **2** NORMAL : common, ordinary **3** : running (of water, etc.) — **~** *nf* **1** : current (of water, electricity, etc.), draft (of air) **2** TENDENCIA : tendency, trend — **~** *nm* **al ~ 1** : up-to-date **2** ENTERADO : aware, informed
corrillo *nm* : clique, circle — **corro** *nm* : ring, circle (of people)
corroborar *vt* : corroborate
corroer {69} *vt* **1** : corrode (of metals) **2** : erode, wear away — **corroerse** *vr* : corrode
corromper *vt* **1** : corrupt **2** PUDRIR : rot — **corrompido, -da** *adj* : corrupt
corrosión *nf, pl* **-siones** : corrosion — **corrosivo, -va** *adj* : corrosive
corrupción *nf, pl* **-ciones 1** : corruption **2** DESCOMPOSICIÓN : decay, rot — **corrupto, -ta** *adj* : corrupt
corsé *nm* : corset
cortar *vt* **1** : cut **2** RECORTAR : cut out **3** QUITAR : cut off — *vi* : cut — **cortarse** *vr* **1** : cut oneself **2** : be cut off (on the telephone) **3** : curdle (of milk) **4 ~ el pelo** : have one's hair cut — **cortada** *nf Lat* : cut — **cortante** *adj* : cutting, sharp
cortaúñas *nms & pl* : nail clippers
corte[1] *nm* **1** : cutting **2** ESTILO : cut, style **3 ~ de pelo** : haircut
corte[2] *nf* **1** : court **2 hacer la ~ a** : court, woo — **cortejar** *vt* : court, woo
cortejo *nm* **1** : entourage **2** NOVIAZGO : courtship **3 ~ fúnebre** : funeral procession
cortés *adj* : courteous, polite — **cortesía** *nf* : courtesy, politeness
corteza *nf* **1** : bark **2** : crust (of bread) **3** : rind, peel (of fruit)
cortina *nm* : curtain
corto, -ta *adj* **1** : short **2** ESCASO : scarce **3** *fam* : timid, shy **4 ~ de vista** : nearsighted — **cortocircuito** *nm* : short circuit
corvo, -va *adj* : curved, bent
cosa *nf* **1** : thing **2** ASUNTO : matter, affair **3 ~ de** : about **4 poca ~** : nothing much
cosechar *v* : harvest, reap — **cosecha** *nf* **1** : harvest, crop **2** : vintage (of wine)
coser *v* : sew
cosmético, -ca *adj* : cosmetic — **cosmético** *nm* : cosmetic
cósmico, -ca *adj* : cosmic
cosmopolita *adj* : cosmopolitan
cosmos *nm* : cosmos
cosquillas *nfpl* **1** : tickling **2 hacer ~** : tickle — **cosquilleo** *nm* : tickling sensation, tingle
costa *nf* **1** : coast, shore **2 a toda ~** : at any cost
costado *nm* **1** : side **2 al ~** : alongside
costar {19} *v* : cost
costarricense *or* **costarriqueño, -ña** *adj* : Costa Rican
coste *nm* → **costo** — **costear** *vt* : pay for
costero, -ra *adj* : coastal
costilla *nf* **1** : rib **2** CHULETA : chop, cutlet
costo *nm* : cost, price — **costoso, -sa** *adj* : costly
costra *nf* : scab
costumbre *nf* **1** : custom, habit **2 de ~** : usual
costura *nf* **1** : sewing, dressmaking **2** PUNTADAS : seam — **costurera** *nf* : dressmaker
cotejar *vt* : compare
cotidiano, -na *adj* : daily
cotizar {21} *vt* : quote, set a price on — **cotización** *nf, pl* **-ciones** : quotation, price — **cotizado, -da** *adj* : in demand
coto *nm* : enclosure, reserve
cotorra *nf* **1** : small parrot **2** *fam* : chatterbox — **cotorrear** *vi fam* : chatter, gab
coyote *nm* : coyote
coyuntura *nf* **1** : joint **2** SITUACIÓN : situation, moment
coz *nm, pl* **coces** : kick (of an animal)
cráneo *nf* : cranium, skull
cráter *nm* : crater
crear *vt* : create — **creación** *nf, pl* **-ciones** : creation — **creativo, -va** *adj* : creative — **creador, -dora** *n* : creator
crecer {53} *vi* **1** : grow **2** AUMENTAR : increase — **crecido, -da** *adj* **1** : full-grown **2** : large (of numbers) — **creciente** *adj* **1** : growing, increasing **2** : crescent (of the moon) — **crecimiento** *nm* **1** : growth **2** AUMENTO : increase
credenciales *nfpl* : credentials
credibilidad *nf* : credibility
crédito *nm* : credit
credo *nm* : creed
crédulo, -la *adj* : credulous, gullible
creer {20} *v* **1** : believe **2** SUPONER : suppose, think — **creerse** *vr* : regard oneself as — **creencia** *nf* : belief — **creíble** *adj* : believable, credible — **creído, -da** *adj fam* : conceited
crema *nf* : cream
cremación *nf, pl* **-ciones** : cremation
cremallera *nf* : zipper
cremoso, -sa *adj* : creamy
crepe *nmf* : crepe, pancake
crepitar *vi* : crackle
crepúsculo *nm* : twilight, dusk
crespo, -pa *adj* : curly, frizzy
crespón *nm, pl* **-pones** : crepe (fabric)
cresta *nf* **1** : crest **2** : comb (of a rooster)
cretino, -na *n* : cretin
creyente *nmf* : believer
criar {85} *vt* **1** : nurse (a baby) **2** EDUCAR : bring up, rear **3** : raise, breed (animals) — **cría** *nf* **1** : breeding, rearing **2** : young animal — **criadero** *nm* : farm, hatchery — **criado, -da** *n* : servant, maid *f* — **criador, -dora** *n* : breeder — **crianza** *nf* : upbringing, rearing
criatura *nf* **1** : creature **2** NIÑO : baby, child
crimen *nm, pl* **crímenes** : crime — **criminal** *adj & nmf* : criminal
críquet *nm* : cricket (game)
crin *nf* : mane
criollo, -lla *adj & n* : Creole
cripta *nf* : crypt
crisantemo *nm* : chrysanthemum
crisis *nf* **1** : crisis **2 ~ nerviosa** : nervous breakdown
crispar *vt* **1** : tense (muscles), clench (one's fist) **2** IRRITAR : irritate, set on edge — **crisparse** *vr* : tense up
cristal *nm* **1** : crystal **2** VIDRIO : glass, piece of glass — **cristalería** *nf* : glassware — **cristalino, -na** *adj* : crystalline — **cristalino** *nm* : lens (of the eye) — **cristalizar** {21} *vi* : crystallize
cristiano, -na *adj & n* : Christian — **cristianismo** *nm* : Christianity — **Cristo** *nm* : Christ
criterio *nm* **1** : criterion **2** JUICIO : judgment, opinion
criticar {72} *vt* : criticize — **crítica** *nf* **1** : criticism **2** RESEÑA : review, critique — **crítico, -ca** *adj* : critical — **~** *n* : critic, reviewer
croar *vi* : croak
cromo *nm* : chromium, chrome
cromosoma *nm* : chromosome
crónica *nf* **1** : chronicle **2** : (news) report
crónico, -ca *adj* : chronic
cronista *nmf* : reporter, newscaster
cronología *nf* : chronology — **cronológico, -ca** *adj* : chronological
cronometrar *vt* : time, clock — **cronómetro** *nm* : chronometer, stopwatch
croqueta *nf* : croquette
croquis *nms & pl* : (rough) sketch
cruce *nm* **1** : crossing **2** : crossroads, intersection **3 ~ peatonal** : crosswalk
crucero *nm* **1** : cruise **2** : cruiser (ship)
crucial *adj* : crucial
crucificar {72} *vt* : crucify — **crucifijo** *nm* : crucifix — **crucifixión** *nf, pl* **-fixiones** : crucifixion
crucigrama *nm* : crossword puzzle
crudo, -da *adj* **1** : harsh, crude **2** : raw (of food) — **crudo** *nm* : crude oil
cruel *adj* : cruel — **crueldad** *nf* : cruelty
crujir *vi* : rustle, creak, crackle, crunch — **crujido** *nm* : rustle, creak, crackle, crunch — **crujiente** *adj* : crunchy, crisp
cruzar {21} *vt* **1** : cross **2** : exchange (words) — **cruzarse** *vr* **1** : intersect **2** : pass each other — **cruz** *nf, pl* **cruces** : cross — **cruzada** *nf* : crusade — **cruzado, -da** *adj* : crossed — **cruzado** *nm* : crusader
cuaderno *nm* : notebook
cuadra *nf* **1** : stable **2** *Lat* : (city) block
cuadrado, -da *adj* : square — **cuadrado** *nm* : square
cuadragésimo, -ma *adj* : fortieth, forty- — **~** *n* : fortieth, forty- (in a series)
cuadrar *vi* **1** : conform, agree **2** : add up, tally (numbers) — *vt* : square — **cuadrarse** *vr* : stand at attention
cuadrilátero *nm* **1** : quadrilateral **2** : ring (in sports)
cuadrilla *nf* : gang, group
cuadro *nm* **1** : square **2** PINTURA : painting **3** DESCRIPCIÓN : picture, description **4** : staff, management (of an organization) **5** CUADRADO : check, square **6** : (baseball) diamond
cuadrúpedo *nm* : quadruped
cuadruple *adj* : quadruple — **cuadruplicar** {72} *vt* : quadruple
cuajar *vi* **1** : curdle **2** COAGULAR : clot, coagulate **3** : set (of pudding, etc.) **4** AFIANZARSE : catch on — *vt* **1** : curdle **2 ~ de** : fill with
cual *pron* **1 el ~, la ~, los ~es, las ~es** : who, whom, which **2 lo ~** : which **3 cada ~** : everyone, everybody — **~** *prep* : like, as
cuál *pron* : which (one), what (one) — **~** *adj* : which, what
cualidad *nf* : quality, trait
cualquiera (**cualquier** *before nouns*) *adj, pl* **cualesquiera** : any, whatever — **~** *pron, pl* **cualesquiera** : anyone, whatever
cuán *adv* : how
cuando *conj* **1** : when **2** SI : since, if **3 ~ más** : at the most **4 de vez en ~** : from time to time — **~** *prep* : during, at the time of
cuándo *adv* **1** : when **2 ¿desde ~?** : since when?
cuantía *nf* **1** : quantity, extent **2** IMPORTANCIA : importance — **cuantioso, -sa** *adj* : abundant, considerable
cuanto *adv* **1** : as much as **2 ~ antes** : as soon as possible **3 en ~** : as soon as **4 en ~ a** : as for, as regards — **cuanto, -ta** *adj* : as many, whatever — **~** *pron* **1** : as much as, all that, everything **2 unos cuantos, unas cuantas** : a few
cuánto *adv* : how much, how many — **cuánto, -ta** *adj* : how much, how many — **~** *pron* : how much, how many
cuarenta *adj & nm* : forty — **cuarentavo, -va** *adj* : fortieth — **cuarentavo** *nm* : fortieth
cuarentena *nf* : quarantine
Cuaresma *nf* : Lent
cuartear *vt* : quarter, divide up — **cuartearse** *vr* : crack, split
cuartel *nm* **1** : barracks *pl* **2 ~ general** : headquarters **3 no dar ~** : show no mercy
cuarteto *nm* : quartet
cuarto, -ta *adj* : fourth — **~** *n* : fourth (in a series) — **cuarto** *nm* **1** : quarter, fourth **2** HABITACIÓN : room
cuarzo *nm* : quartz
cuatro *adj & nm* : four — **cuatrocientos, -tas** *adj* : four hundred — **cuatrocientos** *nms & pl* : four hundred
cuba *nf* : cask, barrel
cubano, -na *adj* : Cuban
cubeta *nf* **1** : keg, cask **2** *Lat* : pail, bucket
cúbico, -ca *adj* : cubic, cubed — **cubículo** *nm* : cubicle
cubierta *nf* **1** : cover, covering **2** : (automobile) tire **3** : deck (of a ship) — **cubierto** *nm* **1** : cutlery, place setting **2 a ~** : under cover
cubo *nm* **1** : cube **2** *Spain* : pail, bucket **3** : hub (of a wheel)
cubrecama *nm* : bedspread
cubrir {2} *vt* : cover — **cubrirse** *vr* **1** : cover oneself **2** : cloud over
cucaracha *nf* : cockroach
cuchara *nf* : spoon — **cucharada** *nf* : spoonful — **cucharilla** *or* **cucharita** *nf* : teaspoon — **cucharón** *nm, pl* **-rones** : ladle
cuchichear *vi* : whisper — **cuchicheo** *nm* : whisper
cuchilla *nf* **1** : (kitchen) knife **2 ~ de afeitar** : razor blade — **cuchillada** *nf* : stab, knife wound — **cuchillo** *nm* : knife
cuclillas *nfpl* **en ~** : squatting, crouching
cuco *nm* : cuckoo — **cuco, -ca** *adj fam* : pretty, cute
cucurucho *nm* : ice-cream cone
cuello *nm* **1** : neck **2** : collar (of clothing)
cuenca *nf* **1** : river basin **2** : (eye) socket — **cuenco** *nm* **1** : bowl **2** CONCAVIDAD : hollow
cuenta *nf* **1** : calculation, count **2** : (bank) account **3** FACTURA : check, bill **4** : bead (for a necklace, etc.) **5 darse ~** : realize **6 tener en ~** : bear in mind
cuento *nm* **1** : story, tale **2 ~ de hadas** : fairy tale
cuerda *nf* **1** : cord, rope, string **2 ~s vocales** : vocal cords **3 dar ~ a** : wind up
cuerdo, -da *adj* : sane, sensible
cuerno *nm* **1** : horn **2** : antlers *pl* (of a deer)
cuero *nm* **1** : leather, hide **2 ~ cabelludo** : scalp
cuerpo *nm* **1** : body **2** : corps (in the military, etc.)
cuervo *nm* : crow
cuesta *nf* **1** : slope **2 a ~s** : on one's back **3 ~ abajo** : downhill **4 ~ arriba** : uphill
cuestión *nf, pl* **-tiones** : matter, affair — **cuestionar** *vt* : question — **cuestionario** *nm* **1** : questionnaire **2** : quiz (in school)
cueva *nf* : cave
cuidar *vt* **1** : take care of, look after **2** : pay attention to (details, etc.) — *vi* **1 ~ de** : look after **2 ~ de que** : make sure that — **cuidarse** *vr* : take care of oneself — **cuidado** *nm* **1** : care **2** PREOCUPACIÓN : worry, concern **3 tener ~** : be careful **4 ¡cuidado!** : watch out!, careful! — **cuidadoso, -sa** *adj* : careful — **cuidadosamente** *adv* : carefully
culata *nf* : butt (of a gun) — **culatazo** *nf* : kick, recoil
culebra *nf* : snake
culinario, -ria *adj* : culinary
culminar *vi* : culminate — **culminación** *nf, pl* **-ciones** : culmination
culo *nm fam* : backside, bottom
culpa *nf* **1** : fault, blame **2** PECADO : sin **3 echar la ~ a** : blame **4 tener la ~** : be at fault — **culpabilidad** *nf* : guilt — **culpable** *adj* : guilty — **~** *nmf* : culprit, guilty party — **culpar** *vt* : blame
cultivar *vt* : cultivate — **cultivo** *nm* **1** : farming, cultivation **2 ~s** : crops
culto, -ta *adj* : cultured, educated — **culto** *nm* **1** : worship **2** : (religious) cult — **cultura** *nf* : culture — **cultural** *adj* : cultural
cumbre *nf* : summit, top
cumpleaños *nms & pl* : birthday
cumplido, -da *adj* **1** : complete, full **2** CORTÉS : courteous — **cumplido** *nm* : compliment, courtesy
cumplimentar *vt* **1** : congratulate **2** CUMPLIR : carry out — **cumplimiento** *nm* : carrying out, performance
cumplir *vt* **1** : accomplish, carry out **2** : keep (a promise), observe (a law, etc.) **3** : reach (a given age) — *vi* **1** : expire, fall due **2 ~ con el deber** : do one's duty — **cumplirse** *vr* **1** : expire **2** REALIZARSE : come true
cúmulo *nm* **1** : heap, pile **2** : cumulus (cloud)
cuna *nf* **1** : cradle **2** ORIGEN : birthplace
cundir *vi* **1** PROPAGARSE : spread, propagate **2** : go a long way
cuneta *nf* : ditch (in a road), gutter (in a street)
cuña *nf* : wedge
cuñado, -da *n* : brother-in-law *m*, sister-in-law *f*
cuota *nf* **1** : fee, dues **2** CUPO : quota **3** *Lat* : installment, payment
cupo *nm* **1** : quota, share **2** *Lat* : capacity, room
cupón *nm, pl* **-pones** : coupon
cúpula *nf* : dome, cupola
cura *nf* : cure, treatment — **~** *nm* : priest — **curación** *nf, pl* **-ciones** : healing — **curar** *vt* **1** : cure **2** : dress (a wound) **3** CURTIR : tan (hides) — **curarse** *vr* : get well
curiosear *vi* **1** : snoop, pry **2** : browse (in a store) — *vt* : look over — **curiosidad** *nf* : curiosity — **curioso, -sa** *adj* **1** : curious, inquisitive **2** RARO : unusual, strange
currículum *nm, pl* **-lums** *or* **currículo** *nm* : résumé, curriculum vitae
cursar *vt* **1** : take (a course), study **2** ENVIAR : send, pass on
cursi *adj fam* : affected, pretentious
cursiva *nf* : italics *pl*
curso *nm* **1** : course **2** : (school) year **3 en ~** : under way **4 en ~** : current
curtir *vt* **1** : tan **2** : harden (skin, features, etc.) — **curtiduría** *nf* : tannery
curva *nf* **1** : curve, bend **2 ~ de nivel** : contour — **curvo, -va** *adj* : curved, bent
cúspide *nf* : apex, peak
custodia *nf* : custody — **custodiar** *vt* : guard, look after — **custodio, -dia** *n* : guardian
cutáneo, -nea *adj* : skin
cutícula *nf* : cuticle
cutis *nms & pl* : skin, complexion
cuyo, -ya *adj* **1** : whose, of whom, of which **2 en cuyo caso** : in which case

D

d *nf* : d, fourth letter of the Spanish alphabet
dádiva *nf* : gift, handout — **dadivoso, -sa** *adj* : generous
dado, -da *adj* **1** : given **2 dado que** : provided that, since — **dados** *nmpl* : dice
daga *nf* : dagger
daltónico, -ca *adj* : color-blind
dama *nf* **1** : lady **2 ~s** *nfpl* : checkers
damnificar {72} *vt* : damage, injure
danés, -nesa *adj* : Danish — **danés** *nm* : Danish (language)
danzar {21} *v* : dance — **danza** *nf* : dance, dancing
dañar *vt* : damage, harm — **dañarse** *vr* **1** : be damaged **2** : hurt oneself — **dañino, -na** *adj* : harmful — **daño** *nm* **1** : damage, harm **2 ~s y perjuicios** : damages
dar {22} *vt* **1** : give **2** PRODUCIR : yield, produce **3** : strike (the hour) **4** MOSTRAR : show — *vi* **1 ~ como** : consider, regard as **2 ~ con** : run into, meet **3 ~ contra** : knock against **4 ~ para** : be enough for — **darse** *vr* **1** : happen **2 ~ contra** : bump into **3 ~ por** : consider oneself **4 dárselas de** : pose as
dardo *nm* : dart
dársena *nf* : dock
datar *vt* : date — *vi* **~ de** : date from
dátil *nm* : date (fruit)
dato *nm* **1** : fact **2 ~s** *nmpl* : data
de *prep* **1** : of **2 ~ Managua** : from Managua **3 ~ niño** : as a child **4 ~ noche** : at night **5 las tres ~ la mañana** : three o'clock in the morning **6 más ~ 10** : more than 10
deambular *vi* : wander about, stroll
debajo *adv* **1** : underneath **2 ~ de** : under, underneath **3 por ~** : below, beneath
debatir *vt* : debate — **debatirse** *vr* : struggle — **debate** *nm* : debate
deber *vt* : owe — *v aux* **1** : have to, should **2** (*expressing probability*) : must — **deberse** *vr* **~ a** : be due to — **~** *nm* **1** : duty **2 ~es** *nmpl* : homework — **debido, -da** *adj* **~ a** : due to, owing to
débil *adj* : weak, feeble — **debilidad** *nf* : weakness — **debilitar** *vt* : weaken — **debilitarse** *vr* : get weak — **débilmente** *adv* : weakly, faintly
débito *nm* **1** : debit **2** DEUDA : debt

debutar vi : debut — **debut** nm, pl **~s** : debut — **debutante** nf : debutante f
década nf : decade
decadencia nf : decadence — **decadente** adj : decadent
decaer {13} vi : decline, weaken
decano, -na n : dean
decapitar vt : behead
decena nf : ten, about ten
decencia nf : decency
decenio nm : decade
decente adj : decent
decepcionar vt : disappoint — **decepción** nf, pl **-ciones** : disappointment
decibelio or **decibel** nm : decibel
decidir vt : decide, determine — vi : decide — **decidirse** vr : make up one's mind — **decididamente** adv : definitely, decidedly — **decidido, -da** adj : determined, resolute
decimal adj : decimal
décimo, -ma adj & n : tenth
decimoctavo, -va adj : eighteenth — **~** n : eighteenth (in a series)
decimocuarto, -ta adj : fourteenth — **~** n : fourteenth (in a series)
decimonoveno, -na or **decimonono, -na** adj : nineteenth — **~** n : nineteenth (in a series)
decimoquinto, -ta adj : fifteenth — **~** n : fifteenth (in a series)
decimoséptimo, -ma adj : seventeenth — **~** n : seventeenth (in a series)
decimosexto, -ta adj : sixteenth — **~** n : sixteenth (in a series)
decimotercero, -ra adj : thirteenth — **~** n : thirteenth (in a series)
decir {23} vt **1** : say **2** CONTAR : tell **3 es ~** : that is to say **4 querer ~** : mean — **decirse** vr **1** : tell oneself **2¿cómo se dice...en español?** : how do you say...in Spanish? — **~** nm : saying, expression
decisión nf, pl **-siones** : decision — **decisivo, -va** adj : decisive
declarar vt : declare — vi : testify — **declararse** vr **1** : declare oneself **2** : break out (of a fire, an epidemic, etc.) — **declaración** nf, pl **-ciones** : statement
declinar v : decline
declive nm **1** : decline **2** PENDIENTE : slope
decolorar vt : bleach — **decolorarse** vr : fade
decoración nf, pl **-ciones** : decoration — **decorado** nm : stage set — **decorar** vt : decorate — **decorativo, -va** adj : decorative
decoro nm : decency, decorum — **decoroso, -sa** adj : decent, proper
decrecer {53} vi : decrease
decrépito, -ta adj : decrepit
decretar vt : decree — **decreto** nm : decree
dedal nm : thimble
dedicar {72} vt : dedicate — **dedicarse** vr **~ a** : devote oneself to — **dedicación** nf, pl **-ciones** : dedication — **dedicatoria** nf : dedication, inscription
dedo nm **1** : finger **2 ~ del pie** : toe
deducir {61} vt **1** INFERIR : deduce **2** DESCONTAR : deduct — **deducción** nf, pl **-ciones** : deduction
defecar {72} vi : defecate
defecto nm : defect — **defectuoso, -sa** adj : defective, faulty
defender {56} vt : defend — **defenderse** vr : defend oneself — **defensa** nf : defense — **defensiva** nf : defensive — **defensivo, -va** adj : defensive — **defensor, -sora** n **1** : defender **2** or **abogado defensor** : defense counsel
deferencia nf : deference — **deferente** adj : deferential
deficiencia nf : deficiency — **deficiente** adj : deficient
déficit nm, pl **-cits** : deficit
definir vt : define — **definición** nf, pl **-ciones** : definition — **definitivo, -va** adj **1** : definitive **2 en definitiva** : in short
deformar vt **1** : deform **2** : distort (the truth, etc.) — **deformación** nf, pl **-ciones** : distortion — **deforme** adj : deformed — **deformidad** nf : deformity
defraudar vt **1** : defraud **2** DECEPCIONAR : disappoint
degenerar vi : degenerate — **degenerado, -da** adj : degenerate
degradar vt **1** : degrade **2** : demote (in the military)
degustar vt : taste
dehesa nf : pasture
deidad nf : deity
dejar vt **1** : leave **2** ABANDONAR : abandon **3** PERMITIR : allow — vi **~ de** : quit — **dejado, -da** adj : slovenly, careless
dejo nm **1** : aftertaste **2** : (regional) accent
delantal nm : apron
delante adv **1** : ahead **2 ~ de** : in front of
delantera nf **1** : front **2 tomar la ~** : take the lead — **delantero, -ra** adj : front, forward — **~** n : forward (in sports)
delatar vt : denounce, inform against
delegar {52} vt : delegate — **delegación** nf, pl **-ciones** : delegation — **delegado, -da** n : delegate, representative
deleitar vt : delight, please — **deleite** nm : delight
deletrear vi : spell (out)
delfín nm, pl **-fines** : dolphin
delgado, -da adj : thin
deliberar vi : deliberate — **deliberación** nf, pl **-ciones** : deliberation — **deliberado, -da** adj : deliberate, intentional
delicadeza nf **1** : delicacy, daintiness **2** SUAVIDAD : gentleness **3** TACTO : tact — **delicado, -da** adj **1** : delicate **2** SENSIBLE : sensible **3** DISCRETO : tactful
delicia nf : delight — **delicioso, -sa** adj **1** : delightful **2** RICO : delicious
delictivo, -va adj : criminal
delimitar vt : define, set the boundaries of
delincuencia nf : delinquency, crime — **delincuente** adj & nmf : delinquent, criminal — **delinquir** {24} vi : break the law
delirante adj : delirious — **delirar** vi **1** : be delirious **2 ~ por** fam : rave about — **delirio** nm **1** : delirium **2 ~ de grandeza** : delusions of grandeur
delito nm : crime
delta nm : delta
demacrado, -da adj : emaciated
demandar vt **1** : sue **2** PEDIR : demand **3** Lat : require — **demanda** nf **1** : lawsuit **2** PETICIÓN : request **3 la oferta y la ~** : supply and demand — **demandante** nmf : plaintiff
demás adj : rest of the, other — **~** pron **1 lo (la, los, las) ~** : the rest, others **2 por ~** : extremely **3 por lo ~** : otherwise **4 y ~** : and so on
demasiado adv **1** : too **2** : too much — **~** adj : too much, too many
demencia nf : madness — **demente** adj : insane, mad
democracia nf : democracy — **demócrata** nmf : democrat — **democrático, -ca** adj : democratic
demoler {47} vt : demolish — **demolición** nf, pl **-ciones** : demolition
demonio nm : devil, demon
demorar v : delay — **demorarse** vr : take a long time — **demora** nf : delay
demostrar {19} vt **1** : demonstrate **2** MOSTRAR : show — **demostración** nf, pl **-ciones** : demonstration
demudar vt : change, alter
denegar {49} vt : deny, refuse — **denegación** nf, pl **-ciones** : denial, refusal
denigrar vt **1** : denigrate **2** INJURIAR : insult
denominador nm : denominator
denotar vt : denote, show
densidad nf : density — **denso, -sa** adj : dense
dental adj : dental — **dentado, -da** adj : toothed, notched — **dentadura** nf **~ postiza** : dentures pl — **dentífrico** nm : toothpaste — **dentista** nmf : dentist
dentro adv **1** : in, inside **2 ~ de poco** : soon, shortly **3 por ~** : inside
denuedo nm : courage
denunciar vt **1** : denounce **2** : report (a crime) — **denuncia** nf **1** : accusation **2** : (police) report
departamento nm **1** : department **2** Lat : apartment
depender vi **1** : depend **2 ~ de** : depend on — **dependencia** nf **1** : dependence, dependency **2** SUCURSAL : branch office — **dependiente** adj : dependent — **dependiente, -ta** n : clerk, salesperson
deplorar vt : deplore, regret
deponer {60} vt : remove from office, depose
deportar vt : deport — **deportación** nf, pl **-ciones** : deportation
deporte nm : sport, sports pl — **deportista** nmf : sportsman m, sportswoman f — **deportivo, -va** adj **1** : sporty **2 artículos deportivos** : sporting goods
depositar vt **1** : put, place **2** : deposit (in a bank, etc.) — **depósito** nm **1** : deposit **2** ALMACÉN : warehouse
depravado, -da adj : depraved
depreciarse vr : depreciate — **depreciación** nf : depreciation
depredador nm : predator
deprimir vt : depress — **deprimirse** vr : get depressed — **depresión** nf, pl **-siones** : depression
derecha nf **1** : right side **2** : right wing (in politics) — **derechista** adj : right-wing — **derecho** nm **1** : right **2** LEY : law — **~** adv : straight — **derecho, -cha** adj **1** : right, right-hand **2** VERTICAL : upright **3** RECTO : straight
deriva nf **1** : drift **2 a la ~** : adrift — **derivación** nf, pl **-ciones** : derivation — **derivar** vi **1** : drift **2 ~ de** : derive from
derramamiento nm **~ de sangre** : bloodshed
derramar vt **1** : spill **2** : shed (tears, blood) — **derramarse** vr : overflow — **derrame** nm **1** : spilling **2** : discharge, hemorrhage
derrapar vi : skid — **derrape** nm : skid
derretir {54} vt : melt, thaw — **derretirse** vr **1** : melt, thaw **2 ~ por** fam : be crazy about
derribar vt **1** : demolish **2** : bring down (a plane, a tree, etc.) **3** : overthrow (a government, etc.)
derrocar {72} vt : overthrow
derrochar vt : waste, squander — **derrochador, -dora** n : spendthrift — **derroche** nm : extravagance, waste
derrotar vt : defeat — **derrota** nf : defeat
derruir {41} vt : demolish, tear down
derrumbar vt : demolish, knock down — **derrumbarse** vr : collapse, break down — **derrumbamiento** nm : collapse — **derrumbe** nm : collapse
desabotonar vt : unbutton, undo
desabrido, -da adj : bland
desabrochar vt : unbutton, undo — **desabrocharse** vr : come undone
desacato nm **1** : disrespect **2** : contempt (of court) — **desacatar** vt : defy, disobey
desacertado, -da adj : mistaken, wrong — **desacertar** {55} vi : be mistaken — **desacierto** nm : mistake, error
desaconsejar vt : advise against — **desaconsejable** adj : inadvisable
desacreditar vt : discredit
desactivar vt : deactivate
desacuerdo nm : disagreement
desafiar {85} vt : defy, challenge — **desafiante** adj : defiant
desafilado, -da adj : blunt
desafinado, -da adj : out-of-tune, off-key
desafío nm : challenge, defiance
desafortunado, -da adj : unfortunate — **desafortunadamente** adv : unfortunately
desagradar vt : displease — **desagradable** adj : disagreeable, unpleasant
desagradecido, -da adj : ungrateful
desagrado nm **1** : displeasure **2 con ~** : reluctantly
desagravio nm : amends, reparation
desagregarse {52} vr : disintegrate
desaguar {10} vi : drain, empty — **desagüe** nm **1** : drainage **2** : drain (of a sink, etc.)
desahogar {52} vt **1** : relieve **2** : give vent to (anger, etc.) — **desahogarse** vr : let off steam, unburden oneself — **desahogado, -da** adj **1** : roomy **2** ADINERADO : comfortable, well-off — **desahogo** nm **1** : relief **2 con ~** : comfortably
desahuciar vt **1** : deprive of hope **2** DESALOJAR : evict — **desahucio** nm : eviction
desaire nm : snub, rebuff — **desairar** vt : snub, slight
desalentar {55} vt : discourage — **desaliento** nm : discouragement
desaliñado, -da adj : slovenly
desalmado, -da adj : heartless, cruel
desalojar vt **1** : evacuate **2** DESAHUCIAR : evict
desamparar vt : abandon — **desamparo** nm : abandonment, desertion
desamueblado, -da adj : unfurnished
desangrarse vr : lose blood, bleed to death
desanimar vt : discourage — **desanimarse** vr : get discouraged — **desanimado, -da** adj : downhearted, despondent — **desánimo** nm : discouragement
desanudar vt : untie
desaparecer {53} vi : disappear — **desaparecido, -da** n : missing person — **desaparición** nf, pl **-ciones** : disappearance
desapasionado, -da adj : dispassionate
desapego nm : indifference
desapercebido, -da adj : unnoticed
desaprobar {19} vt : disapprove of — **desaprobación** nf, pl **-ciones** : disapproval
desaprovechar vt : waste
desarmar vt **1** : disarm **2** DESMONTAR : dismantle, take apart — **desarme** nm : disarmament
desarraigar {52} vt : uproot, root out
desarreglar vt **1** : mess up **2** : disrupt (plans, etc.) — **desarreglado, -da** adj : disorganized — **desarreglo** nm : untidiness, disorder
desarrollar vt : develop — **desarrollarse** vr : take place — **desarrollo** nm : development
desarticular vt **1** : break up, dismantle **2** : dislocate (a bone)
desaseado, -da adj **1** : dirty **2** DESORDENADO : messy
desastre nm : disaster — **desastroso, -sa** adj : disastrous
desatar vt **1** : undo, untie **2** : unleash (passions) — **desatarse** vr **1** : come undone **2** DESENCADENARSE : break out, erupt
desatascar {72} vt : unclog
desatender {56} vt **1** : disregard **2** : neglect (an obligation, etc.) — **desatento, -ta** adj : inattentive
desatinado, -da adj : foolish, silly
desautorizado, -da adj : unauthorized
desavenencia nf : disagreement
desayunar vi : have breakfast — vt : have for breakfast — **desayuno** nm : breakfast
desbancar {72} vt : oust
desbarajuste nm : disorder, confusion
desbaratar vt : ruin, destroy — **desbaratarse** vr : fall apart
desbocarse {72} vr : run away, bolt
desbordar vt **1** : overflow **2** : exceed (limits) — **desbordarse** vr : overflow — **desbordamiento** nm : overflow
descabellado, -da adj : crazy
descafeinado, -da adj : decaffeinated
descalabrar vt : hit on the head — **descalabro** nm : misfortune, setback
descalificar {72} vt : disqualify — **descalificación** nf, pl **-ciones** : disqualification
descalzarse {21} vr : take off one's shoes — **descalzo, -za** adj : barefoot
descaminar vt : mislead, lead astray
descansar v : rest — **descanso** nm **1** : rest **2** : landing (of a staircase) **3** : intermission (in theater), halftime (in sports)
descapotable adj & nm : convertible
descarado, -da adj : insolent, shameless
descargar {52} vt **1** : unload **2** : discharge (a firearm, etc.) — **descarga** nf **1** : unloading **2** : discharge (of a firearm, of electricity, etc.) — **descargo** nm **1** : unloading **2** : discharge (of a duty, etc.) **3** : defense (in law)
descarnado, -da adj : scrawny, gaunt
descaro nm : insolence, nerve
descarrilar vi : derail — **descarrilarse** vr : be derailed
descartar vt : reject — **descartarse** vr : discard
descascarar vt : peel, shell, husk
descender {56} vt **1** : go down **2** BAJAR : lower — vi **1** : descend **2 ~ de** : be descended from — **descendiencia** nf **1** : descendants pl **2** LINAJE : lineage, descent — **descendiente** nmf : descendant — **descenso** nm **1** : descent **2** : drop, fall (in level, in temperature, etc.)
descifrar vt : decipher, decode
descolgar {16} vt **1** : take down **2** : pick up, answer (the telephone)
descolorarse vr : fade — **descolorido, -da** adj : faded, discolored
descomponer {60} vt : break down — **descomponerse** vr **1** : rot, decompose **2** Lat : break down — **descompuesto, -ta** adj Lat : out of order
descomunal adj : enormous
desconcertar {55} vt : disconcert, confuse — **desconcertante** adj : confusing — **desconcierto** nm : confusion, bewilderment
desconectar vt : disconnect
desconfiar {85} vi **~ de** : distrust — **desconfiado, -da** adj : distrustful — **desconfianza** nf : distrust
descongelar vt **1** : thaw, defrost **2** : unfreeze (assets)
descongestionante nm : decongestant
desconocer {18} vt : not know, fail to recognize — **desconocido, -da** adj : unknown — **~** n : stranger
desconsiderado, -da adj : inconsiderate
desconsolar vt : distress — **desconsolado, -da** adj : heartbroken — **desconsuelo** nm : grief, sorrow
descontar {19} vt : discount
descontento, -ta adj : dissatisfied — **descontento** nm : discontent
descontinuar vt : discontinue
descorazonado, -da adj : discouraged
descorrer vt : draw back
descortés adj, pl **-teses** : rude — **descortesía** nf : discourtesy, rudeness
descoyuntar vt : dislocate
descrédito nm : discredit
descremado, -da adj : nonfat, skim
describir {33} vt : describe — **descripción** nf, pl **-ciones** : description — **descriptivo, -va** adj : descriptive
descubierto, -ta adj **1** : exposed, uncovered **2 al descubierto** : in the open — **descubierto** nm : deficit, overdraft
descubrir {2} vt **1** : discover **2** REVELAR : reveal — **descubrimiento** nm : discovery
descuento nm : discount
descuidar vt : neglect — **descuidarse** vr **1** : be careless **2** ABANDONARSE : let oneself go — **descuidado, -da** adj **1** : careless, sloppy **2** DESATENDIDO : neglected — **descuido** nm : neglect, carelessness
desde prep **1** : from (a place), since (a time) **2 ~ luego** : of course
desdén nm : scorn, disdain — **desdeñar** vt : scorn — **desdeñoso, -sa** adj : disdainful
desdicha nf **1** : misery **2** DESGRACIA : misfortune — **desdichado, -da** adj : unfortunate, unhappy
desear vt : wish, want — **deseable** adj : desirable
desecar vt : dry up
desechar vt **1** : throw away **2** RECHAZAR : reject — **desechable** adj : disposable — **desechos** nmpl : rubbish
desembarazarse {21} vr **~ de** : get rid of
desembarcar {72} vi : disembark — vt : unload — **desembarcadero** nm : jetty, landing pier — **desembarco** nm : landing
desembocar {72} vi **~ en 1** : flow into **2** : lead to (a result) — **desembocadura** nf **1** : mouth (of a river) **2** : opening, end (of a street)
desembolsar vt : pay out — **desembolso** nm : payment, outlay
desembragar vi : disengage the clutch
desempacar {72} v Lat : unpack
desempate nm : tiebreaker
desempeñar vt **1** : play (a role) **2** : redeem (from a pawnshop) — **desempeñarse** vr : get out of debt
desempleo nm : unemployment — **desempleado, -da** adj : unemployed
desempolvar vt : dust

desencadenar *vt* 1 : unchain 2 : trigger, unleash (protests, crises, etc.) — **desencadenarse** *vr* : break loose
desencajar *vt* 1 : dislocate 2 DESCONECTAR : disconnect
desencanto *nm* : disillusionment
desenchufar *vt* : disconnect, unplug
desenfadado, -da *adj* : carefree, confident — **desenfado** *nm* : confidence, ease
desenfrenado, -da *adj* : unrestrained — **desenfreno** *nm* : abandon, lack of restraint
desenganchar *vt* : unhook
desengañar *vt* : disillusion — **desengaño** *nm* : disappointment
desenlace *nm* : ending, outcome
desenmarañar *vt* : disentangle
desenmascarar *vt* : unmask
desenredar *vt* : untangle — **desenredarse** *vr* ~ **de** : extricate oneself from
desenrollar *vt* : unroll, unwind
desentenderse {56} *vr* ~ **de** : want nothing to do with
desenterrar {55} *vt* : dig up, disinter
desentonar *vi* 1 : be out of tune 2 : clash (of colors, etc.)
desenvoltura *nf* : confidence, ease
desenvolver {89} *vt* : unfold, unwrap — **desenvolverse** *vr* : unfold, develop
desenvuelto, -ta *adj* : confident, self-assured
deseo *nm* : desire — **deseoso, -sa** *adj* : eager, anxious
desequilibrar *vt* : throw off balance — **desequilibrado, -da** *adj* : unbalanced — **desequilibrio** *nm* : imbalance
desertar *vt* : desert — **deserción** *nf, pl* **-ciones** : desertion — **desertor, -tora** *n* : deserter
desesperar *vt* : exasperate — *vi* : despair — **desesperarse** *vr* : become exasperated — **desesperación** *nf, pl* **-ciones** : desperation, despair — **desesperado, -da** *adj* : desperate, hopeless
desestimar *vt* : reject
desfalcar {72} *vt* : embezzle — **desfalco** *nm* : embezzlement
desfallecer {53} *vi* 1 : weaken 2 DESMAYARSE : faint
desfavorable *adj* : unfavorable
desfigurar *vt* 1 : disfigure, mar 2 : distort (the truth)
desfiladero *nm* : mountain pass, gorge
desfilar *vi* : march, parade — **desfile** *nm* : parade, procession
desfogar {52} *vt* : vent — **desfogarse** *vr* : let off steam
desgajar *vt* : tear off, break apart — **desgajarse** *vr* : come off
desgana *nf* 1 : lack of appetite 2 : lack of enthusiasm, reluctance
desgarbado, -da *adj* : gawky, ungainly
desgarrar *vt* : tear, rip — **desgarrador, -dora** *adj* : heartbreaking — **desgarro** *nm* : tear
desgastar *vt* : wear away, wear down — **desgaste** *nm* : deterioration, wear and tear
desgracia *nf* 1 : misfortune 2 **caer en** ~ : fall into disgrace 3 **por** ~ : unfortunately — **desgraciadamente** *adv* : unfortunately — **desgraciado, -da** *adj* : unfortunate
deshabitado, -da *adj* : uninhabited
deshacer {40} *vt* 1 : undo 2 DESTRUIR : destroy, ruin 3 DISOLVER : dissolve 4 : break (an agreement), cancel (plans, etc.) — **deshacerse** *vr* 1 : come undone 2 ~ **de** : get rid of 3 ~ **en** : lavish, heap (praise, etc.) — **deshecho, -cha** *adj* 1 : undone 2 DESTROZADO : destroyed, ruined
desheredar *vt* : disinherit
deshidratar *vt* : dehydrate
deshielo *nm* : thaw
deshilachar *vt* : unravel — **deshilacharse** *vr* : fray
deshonesto, -ta *adj* : dishonest
deshonrar *vt* : dishonor, disgrace — **deshonra** *nf* : dishonor — **deshonroso, -sa** *adj* : dishonorable
deshuesar *vt* 1 : pit (a fruit) 2 : bone, debone (meat)
desidia *nf* 1 : indolence 2 DESASEO : sloppiness
desierto, -ta *adj* : deserted, uninhabited — **desierto** *nm* : desert
designar *vt* : designate — **designación** *nf, pl* **-ciones** : appointment (to an office, etc.)
designio *nm* : plan
desigual *adj* 1 : unequal 2 DISPAREJO : uneven — **desigualdad** *nf* : inequality
desilusionar *vt* : disappoint, disillusion — **desilusión** *nf, pl* **-siones** : disappointment, disillusionment
desinfectar *vt* : disinfect — **desinfectante** *adj & nm* : disinfectant
desinflar *vt* : deflate — **desinflarse** *vr* : deflate, go flat
desinhibido, -da *adj* : uninhibited
desintegrar *vt* : disintegrate — **desintegrarse** *vr* : disintegrate — **desintegración** *nf, pl* **-ciones** : disintegration
desinteresado, -da *adj* : unselfish, generous — **desinterés** *nm* : unselfishness
desistir *vi* ~ **de** : give up
desleal *adj* : disloyal — **deslealtad** *nf* : disloyalty
desleír {66} *vt* : dilute, dissolve
desligar {52} *vt* 1 : untie 2 SEPARAR : separate — **desligarse** *vr* : extricate oneself
desliz *nm, pl* **-lices** : slip, mistake — **deslizar** {21} *vt* : slide, slip — **deslizarse** *vr* : slide, glide
deslucido, -da *adj* : dingy, tarnished
deslumbrar *vt* : dazzle — **deslumbrante** *adj* : dazzling, blinding
deslustrar *vt* : tarnish, dull
desmán *nm, pl* **-manes** : outrage, excess
desmandarse *vr* : get out of hand
desmantelar *vt* : dismantle
desmañado, -da *adj* : clumsy
desmayar *vi* : lose heart — **desmayarse** *vr* : faint — **desmayo** *nm* : faint
desmedido, -da *adj* : excessive
desmejorar *vt* : impair — *vi* : deteriorate
desmemoriado, -da *adj* : forgetful
desmentir {76} *vt* : deny — **desmentido** *nm* : denial
desmenuzar {21} *vt* 1 : crumble 2 EXAMINAR : scrutinize — **desmenuzarse** *vr* : crumble
desmerecer {53} *vt* : be unworthy of — *vi* : decline in value
desmesurado, -da *adj* : excessive
desmigajar *vt* : crumble
desmontar *vt* 1 : dismantle, take apart 2 ALLANAR : level — *vi* : dismount
desmoralizar {21} *vt* : demoralize
desmoronarse *vr* : crumble
desnivel *nm* : unevenness
desnudar *vt* : undress, strip — **desnudarse** *vr* : get undressed — **desnudez** *nf, pl* **-deces** : nudity, nakedness — **desnudo, -da** *adj* : nude, naked — **desnudo** *nm* : nude
desnutrición *nf, pl* **-ciones** : malnutrition
desobedecer {53} *v* : disobey — **desobediencia** *nf* : disobedience — **desobediente** *adj* : disobedient
desocupar *vt* : empty, vacate — **desocupado, -da** *adj* 1 : vacant 2 DESEMPLEADO : unemployed
desodorante *adj & nm* : deodorant
desolado, -da *adj* 1 : desolate 2 DESCONSOLADO : devastated, distressed — **desolación** *nf, pl* **-ciones** : desolation
desorden *nm, pl* **desórdenes** : disorder, mess — **desordenado, -da** *adj* : untidy — **desordenadamente** *adv* : in a disorderly way
desorganizar {21} *vt* : disorganize — **desorganización** *nf, pl* **-ciones** : disorganization
desorientar *vt* : disorient, confuse — **desorientarse** *vr* : lose one's way
desovar *vi* : spawn
despachar *vt* 1 : deal with (a task, etc.) 2 ENVIAR : dispatch, send 3 : wait on, serve (customers) — **despacho** *nm* 1 : dispatch, shipment 2 OFICINA : office
despacio *adv* : slowly
desparramar *vt* : spill, scatter, spread
despavorido, -da *adj* : terrified
despecho *nm* 1 : spite 2 **a** ~ **de** : despite, in spite of
despectivo, -va *adj* 1 : pejorative 2 DESPRECIATIVO : contemptuous
despedazar {21} *vt* : tear apart
despedir {54} *vt* 1 : see off 2 DESTITUIR : dismiss, fire 3 DESPRENDER : emit — **despedirse** *vr* : say good-bye — **despedida** *nf* : farewell, good-bye
despegar {52} *vt* : detach, unstick — *vi* : take off — **despegado, -da** *adj* : cold, distant — **despegue** *nm* : takeoff
despeinar *vt* : ruffle (hair) — **despeinado, -da** *adj* : disheveled, unkempt
despejar *vt* : clear, free — *vi* : clear up — **despejado, -da** *adj* 1 : clear, fair 2 LÚCIDO : clear-headed
despellejar *vt* : skin (an animal)
despensa *nf* : pantry, larder
despeñadero *nm* : precipice
desperdiciar *vt* : waste — **desperdicio** *nm* 1 : waste 2 ~**s** *nmpl* : scraps
desperfecto *nm* : flaw, defect
despertar {55} *vi* : awaken, wake up — *vt* : wake, rouse — **despertador** *nm* : alarm clock
despiadado, -da *adj* : pitiless, merciless
despido *nm* : dismissal, layoff
despierto, -ta *adj* : awake
despilfarrar *vt* : squander — **despilfarrador, -dora** *n* : spendthrift — **despilfarro** *nm* : extravagance, wastefulness
despistar *vt* : throw off the track, confuse — **despistarse** *vr* : lose one's way — **despistado, -da** *adj* 1 : absentminded 2 DESORIENTADO : confused — **despiste** *nm* 1 : absentmindedness 2 ERROR : mistake
desplazar {21} *vt* : displace — **desplazarse** *vr* : travel
desplegar {49} *vt* : unfold, spread out — **despliegue** *nm* : display
desplomarse *vr* : collapse
desplumar *vt* 1 : pluck 2 *fam* : fleece
despoblado, -da *adj* : uninhabited, deserted — **despoblado** *nm* : deserted area
despojar *vt* : strip, deprive — **despojos** *nmpl* 1 : plunder 2 RESTOS : remains, scraps
desportillar *vt* : chip — **desportillarse** *vr* : chip — **desportilladura** *nf* : chip, nick
déspota *nmf* : despot
despotricar *vi* : rant (and rave)
despreciar *vt* : despise, scorn — **despreciable** *adj* 1 : despicable 2 **una cantidad** ~ : a negligible amount — **desprecio** *nm* : disdain, scorn
desprender *vt* 1 : detach, remove 2 EMITIR : give off — **desprenderse** *vr* 1 : come off 2 DEDUCIRSE : be inferred, follow — **desprendimiento** *nm* ~ **de tierras** : landslide
despreocupado, -da *adj* : carefree, unconcerned
desprestigiar *vt* : discredit — **desprestigiarse** *vr* : lose face
desprevenido, -da *adj* : unprepared
desproporcionado, -da : out of proportion
despropósito *nm* : (piece of) nonsense, absurdity
desprovisto, -ta *adj* ~ **de** : lacking in
después *adv* 1 : afterward 2 ENTONCES : then, next 3 ~ **de** : after 4 **después (de) que** : after 5 ~ **de todo** : after all
despuntado, -da *adj* : blunt, dull
desquiciar *vt* : drive crazy
desquitarse *vr* 1 : retaliate 2 ~ **con** : take it out on, get back at — **desquite** *nm* : revenge
destacar {72} *vt* : emphasize — *vi* : stand out — **destacado, -da** *adj* : outstanding
destapar *vt* : open, uncover — **destapador** *nm Lat* : bottle opener
destartalado, -da *adj* : dilapidated
destellar *vi* : flash, sparkle — **destello** *nm* : sparkle, twinkle, flash
destemplado, -da *adj* 1 : out of tune 2 MAL : out of sorts 3 : unpleasant (of weather)
desteñir {67} *vt* : fade, bleach — *vi* : run, fade — **desteñirse** *vr* : fade
desterrar {55} *vt* : banish, exile — **desterrado, -da** *n* : exile
destetar *vt* : wean
destiempo *adv* **a** ~ : at the wrong time
destierro *nm* : exile
destilar *vt* : distill — **destilería** *nf* : distillery
destinar *vt* 1 : assign, allocate 2 NOMBRAR : appoint — **destinado, -da** *adj* : destined — **destinatario, -ria** *n* : addressee — **destino** *nm* 1 : destiny 2 RUMBO : destination
destituir {41} *vt* : dismiss — **destitución** *nf, pl* **-ciones** : dismissal
destornillar *vt* : unscrew — **destornillador** *nm* : screwdriver
destreza *nf* : skill, dexterity
destrozar {21} *vt* : destroy, wreck — **destrozos** *nmpl* : damage, destruction
destrucción *nf, pl* **-ciones** : destruction — **destructivo, -va** *adj* : destructive — **destruir** {41} *vt* : destroy
desunir *vt* : split, divide
desusado, -da *adj* 1 : obsolete 2 INSÓLITO : unusual — **desuso** *nm* **caer en** ~ : fall into disuse
desvaído, -da *adj* 1 : pale, washed-out 2 BORROSO : vague, blurred
desvalido, -da *adj* : destitute, needy
desvalijar *vt* : rob
desván *nm, pl* **-vanes** : attic
desvanecer {53} *vt* : make disappear — **desvanecerse** *vr* 1 : vanish 2 DESMAYARSE : faint
desvariar {85} *vi* : be delirious — **desvarío** *nm* : delirium
desvelar *vt* : keep awake — **desvelarse** *vr* : stay awake — **desvelo** *nm* 1 : sleeplessness 2 ~**s** *nmpl* : efforts
desvencijado, -da *adj* : dilapidated, rickety
desventaja *nf* : disadvantage
desventura *nf* : misfortune
desvergonzado, -da *adj* : shameless — **desvergüenza** *nf* : shamelessness
desvestir {54} *vt* : undress — **desvestirse** *vr* : get undressed
desviación *nf, pl* **-ciones** 1 : deviation 2 : detour (in a road) — **desviar** {85} *vt* : divert, deflect — **desviarse** *vr* 1 : branch off 2 APARTARSE : stray — **desvío** *nm* : diversion, detour
detallar *vt* : detail — **detallado, -da** *adj* : detailed, thorough — **detalle** *nm* 1 : detail 2 **al** ~ : retail — **detallista** *adj* : retail — ~ *nmf* : retailer
detectar *vt* : detect — **detective** *nmf* : detective
detener {80} *vt* 1 : arrest, detain 2 PARAR : stop 3 RETRASAR : delay — **detenerse** *vr* 1 : stop 2 DEMORARSE : linger — **detención** *nf, pl* **-ciones** : arrest, detention
detergente *nm* : detergent
deteriorar *vt* : damage — **deteriorarse** *vr* : wear out, deteriorate — **deteriorado, -da** *adj* : damaged, worn — **deterioro** *nm* : deterioration, damage
determinar *vt* 1 : determine 2 MOTIVAR : bring about 3 DECIDIR : decide — **determinarse** *vr* : decide — **determinación** *nf, pl* **-ciones** 1 : determination 2 **tomar una** ~ : make a decision — **determinado, -da** *adj* 1 : determined 2 ESPECÍFICO : specific
detestar *vt* : detest
detonar *vi* : explode, detonate — **detonación** *nf, pl* **-ciones** : detonation
detrás *adv* 1 : behind 2 ~ **de** : in back of 3 **por** ~ : from behind
detrimento *nm* **en** ~ **de** : to the detriment of
deuda *nf* : debt — **deudor, -dora** *n* : debtor
devaluar {3} *vt* : devalue — **devaluarse** *vr* : depreciate
devastar *vt* : devastate — **devastador, -dora** *adj* : devastating
devenir {87} *vi* 1 : come about 2 ~ **en** : become, turn into
devoción *nf, pl* **-ciones** : devotion
devolución *nf, pl* **-ciones** : return
devolver {89} *vt* 1 RESTITUIR : give back 2 : refund, pay back — *vi* : vomit — **devolverse** *vr Lat* : return, come back
devorar *vt* : devour
devoto, -ta *adj* : devout — ~ *n* : devotee
día *nm* 1 : day 2 : daytime 3 **al** ~ : up-to-date 4 **en pleno** ~ : in broad daylight
diabetes *nf* : diabetes — **diabético, -ca** *adj & n* : diabetic
diablo *nm* : devil — **diablillo** *nm* : imp, rascal — **diablura** *nf* : prank — **diabólico, -ca** *adj* : diabolic, diabolical
diafragma *nm* : diaphragm
diagnosticar {72} *vt* : diagnose — **diagnóstico, -ca** *adj* : diagnostic — **diagnóstico** *nm* : diagnosis
diagonal *adj & nf* : diagonal
diagrama *nm* : diagram
dial *nm* : dial (of a radio, etc.)
dialecto *nm* : dialect
dialogar {52} *vi* : have a talk — **diálogo** *nm* : dialogue
diamante *nm* : diamond
diámetro *nm* : diameter
diana *nf* 1 : reveille 2 BLANCO : target, bull's-eye
diario, -ria *adj* : daily — **diario** *nm* 1 : diary 2 PERIÓDICO : newspaper — **diariamente** *adv* : daily
diarrea *nf* : diarrhea
dibujar *vt* 1 : draw 2 DESCRIBIR : portray — **dibujante** *nmf* : draftsman *m*, draftswoman *f* — **dibujo** *nm* 1 : drawing 2 ~**s animados** : (animated) cartoons
diccionario *nm* : dictionary
dicha *nf* 1 ALEGRÍA : happiness 2 SUERTE : good luck — **dicho** *nm* : saying, proverb — **dichoso, -sa** *adj* 1 : happy 2 AFORTUNADO : lucky
diciembre *nm* : December
dictar *vt* 1 : dictate 2 : pronounce (a sentence), deliver (a speech) — **dictado** *nm* : dictation — **dictador, -dora** *n* : dictator — **dictadura** *nf* : dictatorship
diecinueve *adj & nm* : nineteen — **diecinueveavo, -va** *adj* : nineteenth
dieciocho *adj & nm* : eighteen — **dieciochoavo, -va** *or* **dieciochavo, -va** *adj* : eighteenth
dieciséis *adj & nm* : sixteen — **dieciseisavo, -va** *adj* : sixteenth
diecisiete *adj & nm* : seventeen — **diecisieteavo, -va** *adj* : seventeenth
diente *nm* 1 : tooth 2 : prong, tine (of a fork, etc.) 3 ~ **de ajo** : clove of garlic 4 ~ **de león** : dandelion
diesel ['disel] *adj & nm* : diesel
diestra *nf* : right hand — **diestro, -tra** *adj* 1 : right 2 HÁBIL : skillful
dieta *nf* : diet — **dietético, -ca** *adj* : dietetic, dietary
diez *adj & nm, pl* **dieces** : ten
difamar *vt* : slander, libel — **difamación** *nf, pl* **-ciones** : slander, libel
diferencia *nf* : difference — **diferenciar** *vt* : distinguish between — **diferenciarse** *vr* : differ — **diferente** *adj* : different
diferir {76} *vt* : postpone — *vi* : differ
difícil *adj* : difficult — **dificultad** *nf* : difficulty — **dificultar** *vt* : hinder, obstruct
difteria *nf* : diphtheria
difundir *vt* 1 : spread (out) 2 : broadcast (television, etc.)
difunto, -ta *adj & n* : deceased
difusión *nf, pl* **-siones** : spreading
digerir {76} *vt* : digest — **digerible** *adj* : digestible — **digestión** *nf, pl* **-tiones** : digestion — **digestivo, -va** *adj* : digestive
dígito *nm* : digit — **digital** *adj* : digital
dignarse *vr* ~ **a** : deign to
dignatario, -ria *n* : dignitary — **dignidad** *nf* : dignity — **digno, -na** *adj* : worthy
digresión *nf, pl* **-ciones** : digression
dilapidar *vt* : waste, squander
dilatar *vt* 1 : expand, dilate 2 PROLONGAR : prolong 3 POSPONER : postpone
dilema *nm* : dilemma
diligencia *nf* 1 : diligence 2 TRÁMITE : procedure, task — **diligente** *adj* : diligent
diluir {41} *vt* : dilute
diluvio *nm* 1 : flood 2 LLUVIA : downpour
dimensión *nf, pl* **-siones** : dimension
diminuto, -ta *adj* : minute, tiny
dimitir *vi* : resign — **dimisión** *nf, pl* **-siones** : resignation
dinámico, -ca *adj* : dynamic
dinamita *nf* : dynamite
dínamo *or* **dinamo** *nmf* : dynamo
dinastía *nf* : dynasty
dineral *nm* : large sum, fortune
dinero *nm* : money
dinosaurio *nm* : dinosaur

diócesis *nfs & pl* : diocese
dios, diosa *n* : god, goddess *f* — **Dios** *nm* : God
diploma *nm* : diploma — **diplomado, -da** *adj* : qualified, trained
diplomacia *nf* : diplomacy — **diplomático, -ca** *adj* : diplomatic — ~ *n* : diplomat
diputación *nf, pl* **-ciones** : delegation — **diputado, -da** *n* : delegate
dique *nm* : dike
dirección *nf, pl* **-ciones 1** : address **2** SENTIDO : direction **3** GESTIÓN : management **4** : steering (of an automobile) — **direccional** *nf Lat* : turn signal, blinker — **directa** *nf* : high gear — **directiva** *nf* : board of directors — **directivo, -va** *adj* : managerial — ~ *n* : manager, director — **directo, -ta** *adj* **1** : direct **2** DERECHO : straight — **director, -tora** *n* **1** : director, manager **2** : conductor (of an orchestra) — **directorio** *nm* : directory — **directriz** *nf, pl* **-trices** : guideline
dirigencia *nf* : leaders *pl*, leadership — **dirigente** *nmf* : director, leader
dirigible *nm* : dirigible, blimp
dirigir {35} *vt* **1** : direct, lead **2** : address (a letter, etc.) **3** ENCAMINAR : aim **4** : conduct (music) — **dirigirse** *vr* **1 ~ a** : go towards **2 ~ a algn** : speak to s.o., write to s.o.
discernir {25} *vt* : discern, distinguish — **discernimiento** *nm* : discernment
disciplinar *vt* : discipline — **disciplina** *nf* : discipline
discípulo, -la *n* : disciple, follower
disco *nm* **1** : disc, disk **2** : discus (in sports) **3 ~ compacto** : compact disc
discordante *adj* : discordant — **discordia** *nf* : discord
discoteca *nf* : disco, discotheque
discreción *nf, pl* **-ciones** : discretion
discrepancia *nf* **1** : discrepancy **2** DESACUERDO : disagreement — **discrepar** *vi* : differ, disagree
discreto, -ta *adj* : discreet
discriminar *vt* **1** : discriminate against **2** DISTINGUIR : distinguish — **discriminación** *nf, pl* **-ciones** : discrimination
disculpar *vt* : excuse, pardon — **disculparse** *vr* : apologize — **disculpa** *nf* **1** : apology **2** EXCUSA : excuse
discurrir *vi* **1** : pass, go by **2** REFLEXIONAR : ponder, reflect
discurso *nm* : speech, discourse
discutir *vt* **1** : discuss **2** CUESTIONAR : dispute — *vi* : argue — **discusión** *nf, pl* **-siones 1** : discussion **2** DISPUTA : argument — **discutible** *adj* : debatable
disecar {72} *vt* : dissect — **disección** *nf, pl* **-ciones** : dissection
diseminar *vt* : disseminate, spread
disentería *nf* : dysentery
disentir {76} *vi* **~ de** : disagree with — **disentimiento** *nm* : disagreement, dissent
diseñar *vt* : design — **diseñador, -dora** *n* : designer — **diseño** *nm* : design
disertación *nf, pl* **-ciones 1** : lecture **2** : (written) dissertation
disfrazar {21} *vt* : disguise — **disfrazarse** *vr* **~ de** : disguise oneself as — **disfraz** *nm, pl* **-fraces 1** : disguise **2** : costume (for a party, etc.)
disfrutar *vt* : enjoy — *vi* : enjoy oneself
disgustar *vt* : upset, annoy — **disgustarse** *vr* **1** : get annoyed **2** ENEMISTARSE : fall out (with s.o.) — **disgusto** *nm* **1** : annoyance, displeasure **2** RIÑA : quarrel
disidente *adj & nmf* : dissident
disimular *vt* : conceal, hide — *vi* : pretend — **disimulo** *nm* : pretense
disipar *vt* **1** : dispel **2** DERROCHAR : squander
diskette [di'sket] *nm* : floppy disk, diskette
dislexia *nf* : dyslexia — **disléxico, -ca** *adj* : dyslexic
dislocar {72} *vt* : dislocate — **dislocarse** *vr* : become dislocated
disminuir {41} *vt* : reduce — *vi* : decrease, drop — **disminución** *nf, pl* **-ciones** : decrease
disociar *vt* : dissociate
disolver {89} *vt* : dissolve — **disolverse** *vr* : dissolve
disparar *vi* : shoot, fire — *vt* : shoot — **dispararse** *vr* : shoot up, skyrocket
disparatado, -da *adj* : absurd — **disparate** *nm* : nonsense, silly thing
disparejo, -ja *adj* : uneven — **disparidad** *nf* : difference, disparity
disparo *nm* : shot
dispensar *vt* **1** : dispense, distribute **2** DISCULPAR : excuse
dispersar *vt* : disperse, scatter — **dispersarse** *vr* : disperse — **dispersión** *nf, pl* **-siones** : scattering
disponer {60} *vt* **1** : arrange, lay out **2** ORDENAR : decide, stipulate — *vi* **~ de** : have at one's disposal — **disponerse** *vr* **~ a** : be ready to — **disponibilidad** *nf* : availability — **disponible** *adj* : available
disposición *nf, pl* **-ciones 1** : arrangement **2** APTITUD : aptitude **3** : order, provision (in law) **4 a ~ de** : at the disposal of
dispositivo *nm* : device, mechanism
dispuesto, -ta *adj* : prepared, ready
disputar *vi* **1** : argue **2** COMPETIR : compete — *vt* : dispute — **disputa** *nf* : dispute, argument
disquete → **diskette**
distanciar *vt* : space out — **distanciarse** *vr* : grow apart — **distancia** *nf* : distance — **distante** *adj* : distant
distinguir {26} *vt* : distinguish — **distinguirse** *vr* : distinguish oneself, stand out — **distinción** *nf, pl* **-ciones** : distinction — **distintivo, -va** *adj* : distinctive — **distinto, -ta** *adj* **1** : different **2** CLARO : distinct, clear
distorsión *nf, pl* **-siones** : distortion
distraer {81} *vt* **1** : distract **2** DIVERTIR : entertain — **distraerse** *vr* **1** : get distracted **2** ENTRETENERSE : amuse oneself — **distracción** *nf, pl* **-ciones 1** : amusement **2** DESPISTE : absentmindedness — **distraído, -da** *adj* : distracted, absentminded
distribuir {41} *vt* : distribute — **distribución** *nf, pl* **-ciones** : distribution — **distribuidor, -dora** *n* : distributor
distrito *nm* : district
disturbio *nm* : disturbance
disuadir *vt* : dissuade, discourage — **disuasivo, -va** *adj* : deterrent
diurno, -na *adj* : day, daytime
divagar {52} *vi* : digress
diván *nm, pl* **-vanes** : divan, couch
divergir {35} *vi* **1** : diverge **2 ~ en** : differ on
diversidad *nf* : diversity
diversificar {72} *vt* : diversify
diversión *nf, pl* **-siones** : fun, entertainment
diverso, -sa *adj* : diverse
divertir {76} *vt* : entertain — **divertirse** *vr* : enjoy oneself, have fun — **divertido, -da** *adj* : entertaining
dividendo *nm* : dividend
dividir *vt* **1** : divide **2** REPARTIR : distribute
divinidad *nf* : divinity — **divino, -na** *adj* : divine
divisa *nf* **1** : currency **2** EMBLEMA : emblem
divisar *vt* : discern, make out
división *nf, pl* **-siones** : division — **divisor** *nm* : denominator
divorciar *vt* : divorce — **divorciarse** *vr* : get a divorce — **divorciado, -da** *n* : divorcé *m*, divorcée *f* — **divorcio** *nm* : divorce
divulgar {52} *vt* **1** : divulge, reveal **2** PROPAGAR : spread, circulate
dizque *adv Lat* : supposedly, apparently
doblar *vt* **1** : double **2** PLEGAR : fold **3** : turn (a corner) **4** : dub (a film) — *vi* : turn — **doblarse** *vr* **1** : double over **2 ~ a** : give in to — **dobladillo** *nm* : hem — **doble** *adj & nm* : double — ~ *nmf* : stand-in, double — **doblemente** *adv* : doubly — **doblegar** {52} *vt* : force to yield — **doblegarse** *vr* : give in — **doblez** *nm, pl* **-bleces** : fold, crease
doce *adj & nm* : twelve — **doceavo, -va** *adj* : twelfth — **docena** *nf* : dozen
docente *adj* : teaching
dócil *adj* : docile
doctor, -tora *n* : doctor — **doctorado** *nm* : doctorate
doctrina *nf* : doctrine
documentar *vt* : document — **documentación** *nf, pl* **-ciones** : documentation — **documental** *adj & nm* : documentary — **documento** *nm* : document
dogma *nm* : dogma — **dogmático, -ca** *adj* : dogmatic
dólar *nm* : dollar
doler {47} *vi* **1** : hurt **2 me duelen los pies** : my feet hurt — **dolerse** *vr* **~ de** : complain about — **dolor** *nm* **1** : pain **2** PENA : grief **3 ~ de cabeza** : headache **4 ~ de estómago** : stomachache — **dolorido, -da 1** : sore **2** AFLIGIDO : hurt — **doloroso, -sa** *adj* : painful
domar *vt* : tame, break in
domesticar {72} *vt* : domesticate, tame — **doméstico, -ca** *adj* : domestic
domicilio *nm* : home, residence
dominar *vt* **1** : dominate, control **2** : master (a subject, a language, etc.) — **dominarse** *vr* : control oneself — **dominación** *nf, pl* **-ciones** : domination — **dominante** *adj* : dominant
domingo *nm* : Sunday — **dominical** *adj* **periódico ~** : Sunday newspaper
dominio *nm* **1** : authority **2** : mastery (of a subject) **3** TERRITORIO : domain
dominó *nm, pl* **-nós** : dominoes *pl* (game)
don[1] *nm* : courtesy title preceding a man's first name
don[2] *nm* **1** : gift **2** TALENTO : talent — **donación** *nf, pl* **-ciones** : donation — **donador, -dora** *n* : donor
donaire *nm* : grace, charm
donar *vt* : donate — **donante** *nmf* : donor — **donativo** *nm* : donation
donde *conj* : where — ~ *prep Lat* : over by
dónde *adv* **1** : where **2 ¿de ~ eres?** : where are you from? **3 ¿por ~?** : whereabouts?
dondequiera *adv* **1** : anywhere **2 ~ que** : wherever, everywhere
doña *nf* : courtesy title preceding a woman's first name
doquier *adv* **por ~** : everywhere
dorar *vt* **1** : gild **2** : brown (food) — **dorado, -da** *adj* : gold, golden
dormir {27} *vt* : put to sleep — *vi* : sleep — **dormirse** *vr* : fall asleep — **dormido, -da** *adj* **1** : asleep **2** ENTUMECIDO : numb — **dormilón, -lona** *n* : sleepyhead, late riser — **dormitar** *vi* : doze — **dormitorio** *nm* **1** : bedroom **2** : dormitory (in a college)
dorso *nm* : back
dos *adj & nm* : two — **doscientos, -tas** *adj* : two hundred — **doscientos** *nms & pl* : two hundred
dosel *nm* : canopy
dosis *nfs & pl* : dose, dosage
dotar *vt* **1** : provide, equip **2 ~ de** : endow with — **dotación** *nf, pl* **-ciones 1** : endowment, funding **2** PERSONAL : personnel — **dote** *nf* **1** : dowry **2 ~s** *nfpl* : gift, talent
dragar {52} *vt* : dredge — **draga** *nf* : dredge
dragón *nm, pl* **-gones** : dragon
drama *nm* : drama — **dramático, -ca** *adj* : dramatic — **dramatizar** {21} *vt* : dramatize — **dramaturgo, -ga** *n* : dramatist, playwright
drástico, -ca *adj* : drastic
drenar *vt* : drain — **drenaje** *nm* : drainage
droga *nf* : drug — **drogadicto, -ta** *n* : drug addict — **drogar** {52} *vt* : drug — **drogarse** *vr* : take drugs — **droguería** *nf* : drugstore
dromedario *nm* : dromedary
dual *adj* : dual
ducha *nf* : shower — **ducharse** *vr* : take a shower
ducho, -cha *adj* : experienced, skilled
duda *nf* : doubt — **dudar** *vt* : doubt — *vi* **~ en** : hesitate to — **dudoso, -sa** *adj* **1** : doubtful **2** SOSPECHOSO : questionable
duelo *nm* **1** : duel **2** LUTO : mourning
duende *nm* : elf, imp
dueño, -na *n* **1** : owner **2** : landlord, landlady *f*
dulce *adj* **1** : sweet **2** : fresh (of water) **3** SUAVE : mild, gentle — ~ *nm* : candy, sweet — **dulzura** *nf* : sweetness
duna *nf* : dune
dúo *nm* : duo, duet
duodécimo, -ma *adj* : twelfth — ~ *n* : twelfth (in a series)
dúplex *nms & pl* : duplex (apartment)
duplicar {72} *vt* **1** : double **2** : duplicate, copy (a document, etc.) — **duplicado, -da** *adj* : duplicate — **duplicado** *nm* : copy
duqe *nm* : duke — **duquesa** *nf* : duchess
durabilidad *nf* : durability
duración *nf, pl* **-ciones** : duration, length
duradero, -ra *adj* : durable, lasting
durante *prep* **1** : during **2 ~ una hora** : for an hour
durar *vi* : endure, last
durazno *nm Lat* : peach
duro *adv* : hard — **duro, -ra** *adj* **1** : hard **2** SEVERO : harsh — **dureza** *nf* **1** : hardness **2** SEVERIDAD : harshness

E

e[1] *nf* : e, fifth letter of the Spanish alphabet
e[2] *conj (used instead of* **y** *before words beginning with i or hi)* : and
ebanista *nmf* : cabinetmaker
ébano *nm* : ebony
ebrio, -bria *adj* : drunk
ebullición *nf, pl* **-ciones** : boiling
echar *vt* **1** : throw, cast **2** EXPULSAR : expel, dismiss **3** : give off, emit (smoke, sparks, etc.) **4** BROTAR : sprout **5** PONER : put (on) **6 ~ a perder** : spoil, ruin **7 ~ de menos** : miss — **echarse** *vr* **1** : throw oneself **2** ACOSTARSE : lie down **3 ~ a** : start (to)
eclesiástico, -ca *adj* : ecclesiastic — ~ *nm* : clergyman
eclipse *nm* : eclipse — **eclipsar** *vi* : eclipse
eco *nm* : echo
ecología *nf* : ecology — **ecológico, -ca** *adj* : ecological — **ecologista** *nmf* : ecologist
economía *nf* **1** : economy **2** : economics (science) — **economico, -ca** *adj* **1** : economic, economical **2** BARATO : inexpensive — **economista** *nmf* : economist — **economizar** {21} *v* : save
ecosistema *nm* : ecosystem
ecuación *nf, pl* **-ciones** : equation
ecuador *nm* : equator
ecuánime *adj* **1** : even-tempered **2** : impartial (in law)
ecuatoriano, -na *adj* : Ecuadorian, Ecuadorean, Ecuadoran
ecuestre *adj* : equestrian
edad *nf* **1** : age **2 Edad Media** : Middle Ages *pl* **3 ¿qué ~ tienes?** : how old are you?
edición *nf, pl* **-ciones 1** : publishing, publication **2** : edition (of a book, etc.)
edicto *nm* : edict
edificar {72} *vt* : build — **edificio** *nm* : building
editar *vt* **1** : publish **2** : edit (a film, a text, etc.) — **editor, -tora** *n* **1** : publisher **2** : editor — **editorial** *adj* : publishing — ~ *nm* : editorial — ~ *nf* : publishing house
edredón *nm, pl* **-dones** : (down) comforter, duvet
educar {72} *vt* **1** : educate **2** CRIAR : bring up, raise **3** : train (the body, the voice, etc.) — **educación** *nf, pl* **-ciones 1** : education **2** MODALES : (good) manners *pl* — **educado, -da** *adj* : polite — **educador, -dora** *n* : educator — **educativo, -va** *adj* : educational
efectivo, -va *adj* **1** : effective **2** REAL : real — **efectivo** *nm* : cash — **efectivamente** *adv* **1** : really **2** POR SUPUESTO : yes, indeed — **efecto** *nm* **1** : effect **2 en ~** : in fact **3 ~s** *nmpl* : goods, property — **efectuar** {3} *vt* : bring about, carry out
efervescente *adj* : effervescent — **efervescencia** *nf* : effervescence
eficaz *adj, pl* **-caces 1** : effective **2** EFICIENTE : efficient — **eficacia** *nf* **1** : effectiveness **2** EFICIENCIA : efficiency
eficiente *adj* : efficient — **eficiencia** *nf* : efficiency
efímero, -ra *adj* : ephemeral
efusivo, -va *adj* : effusive
egipcio, -cia *adj* : Egyptian
ego *nm* : ego — **egocéntrico, -ca** *adj* : egocentric — **egoísmo** *nm* : egoism — **egoísta** *adj* : egoistic — ~ *nmf* : egoist
egresar *vi* : graduate — **egresado, -da** *n* : graduate — **egreso** *nm* : graduation, commencement
eje *nm* **1** : axis **2** : axle (of a wheel, etc.)
ejecutar *vt* **1** : execute, put to death **2** REALIZAR : carry out — **ejecución** *nf, pl* **-ciones** : execution
ejecutivo, -va *adj & n* : executive
ejemplar *adj* : exemplary — ~ *nm* **1** : copy, issue **2** EJEMPLO : example — **ejemplificar** {72} *vt* : exemplify — **ejemplo** *nm* **1** : example **2 por ~** : for example
ejercer {86} *vt* **1** : practice (a profession) **2** : exercise (a right, etc.) — *vi* **~ de** : practice as, work as — **ejercicio** *nm* **1** : exercise **2** : practice (of a profession, etc.)
ejército *nm* : army
el, la *art, pl* **los, las** : the — **el** *pron (referring to masculine nouns)* **1** : the one **2 ~ que** : he who, whoever, the one that
él *pron* : he, him
elaborar *vt* **1** : manufacture, produce **2** : draw up (a plan, etc.)
elástico, -ca *adj* : elastic — **elástico** *nm* : elastic — **elasticidad** *nf* : elasticity
elección *nf, pl* **-ciones 1** : election **2** SELECCIÓN : choice — **elector, -tora** *n* : voter — **electorado** *nm* : electorate — **electoral** *adj* : electoral
electricidad *nf* : electricity — **eléctrico, -ca** *adj* : electric, electrical — **electricista** *nmf* : electrician — **electrificar** {72} *vt* : electrify — **electrizar** {21} *vt* : electrify, thrill — **electrocutar** *vt* : electrocute
electrodo *nm* : electrode
electrodoméstico *nm* : electric appliance
electromagnético, -ca *adj* : electromagnetic
electrón *nm, pl* **-trones** : electron — **electrónico, -ca** *adj* : electronic — **electrónica** *nf* : electronics
elefante, -ta *n* : elephant
elegante *adj* : elegant — **elegancia** *nf* : elegance
elegía *nf* : elegy
elegir {28} *vt* **1** : elect **2** ESCOGER : choose, select — **elegible** *adj* : eligible
elemento *nm* : element — **elemental** *adj* **1** : elementary, basic **2** ESENCIAL : fundamental
elenco *nm* : cast (of actors)
elevar *vt* **1** : raise, lift **2** ASCENDER : elevate (in a hierarchy), promote — **elevarse** *vr* : rise — **elevación** *nf, pl* **-ciones** : elevation — **elevador** *nm* **1** : hoist **2** *Lat* : elevator
eliminar *vt* : eliminate — **eliminación** *nf, pl* **-ciones** : elimination
elipse *nf* : ellipse — **elíptico, -ca** *adj* : elliptical, elliptic
elite *or* **élite** *nf* : elite
elixir *or* **elíxir** *nm* : elixir
ella *pron* : she, her — **ello** *pron* : it — **ellos, ellas** *pron pl* **1** : they, them **2 de ellos, de ellas** : theirs
elocuente *adj* : eloquent — **elocuencia** *nf* : eloquence
elogiar *vt* : praise — **elogio** *nm* : praise
eludir *vt* : avoid, elude
emanar *vi* **~ de** : emanate from
emancipar *vt* : emancipate — **emanciparse** *vr* : free oneself — **emancipación** *nf, pl* **-ciones** : emancipation
embadurnar *vt* : smear, daub
embajada *nf* : embassy — **embajador, -dora** *n* : ambassador
embalar *vt* : wrap up, pack — **embalaje** *nm* : packing
embaldosar *vt* : pave with tiles
embalsamar *vt* : embalm
embalse *nm* : dam, reservoir
embarazar {21} *vt* **1** : make pregnant **2** IMPEDIR : restrict, hamper — **embarazada** *adj* : pregnant — **embarazo** *nm* **1** : pregnancy **2** IMPEDIMENTO : hindrance, obsta-

cle — **embarazoso, -sa** adj : embarrassing

embarcar {72} vt : load — **embarcarse** vr : embark, board — **embarcación** nf, pl **-ciones** : boat, craft — **embarcadero** nm : pier, jetty — **embarco** nm : embarkation

embargar {52} vt **1** : seize, impound **2** : overwhelm (with emotion, etc.) — **embargo** nm **1** : embargo **2** : seizure (in law) **3 sin ~** : nevertheless

embarque nm : loading (of goods), boarding (of passengers)

embarrancar {72} vi : run aground

embarullarse vr fam : get mixed up

embaucar {72} vt : trick, swindle — **embaucador, -dora** n : swindler

embeber vt : absorb — vi : shrink — **embeberse** vr : become absorbed

embelesar vt : enchant, delight — **embelesado, -da** adj : spellbound

embellecer {53} vt : embellish, beautify

embestir {54} vt : attack, charge at — vi : charge, attack — **embestida** nf **1** : attack **2** : charge (of a bull)

emblema nm : emblem

embobar vt : amaze, fascinate

embocadura nf **1** : mouth (of a river, etc.) **2** : mouthpiece (of an instrument)

émbolo nm : piston

embolsarse vr : put in one's pocket

emborracharse vr : get drunk

emborronar vt **1** : smudge, blot **2** GARABATEAR : scribble

emboscar {72} vt : ambush — **emboscada** nf : ambush

embotar vt : dull, blunt

embotellar vt : bottle (up) — **embotellamiento** nm : traffic jam

embrague nm : clutch — **embragar** {52} vi : engage the clutch

embriagarse {52} vr : get drunk — **embriagado, -da** adj : intoxicated, drunk — **embriagador, -dora** adj : intoxicating — **embriaguez** nf : drunkenness

embrión nm, pl **-briones** : embryo

embrollo nm : tangle, confusion

embrujar vt : bewitch — **embrujo** nm : spell, curse

embrutecer vt : brutalize

embudo nm : funnel

embuste nm : lie — **embustero, -ra** adj : lying — **~** n : liar, cheat

embutir vt : stuff — **embutido** nm : sausage, cold meat

emergencia nf : emergency

emerger {15} vi : emerge, appear

emigrar vi **1** : emigrate **2** : migrate (of animals) — **emigración** nf, pl **-ciones 1** : emigration **2** : migration (of animals) — **emigrante** adj & nmf : emigrant

eminente adj : eminent — **eminencia** nf : eminence

emitir vt **1** : emit **2** EXPRESAR : express (an opinion, etc.) **3** : broadcast (on radio or television) **4** : issue (money, stamps, etc.) — **emisión** nf, pl **-siones 1** : emission **2** : broadcast (on radio or television) **3** : issue (of money, etc.) — **emisora** nf : radio station

emoción nf, pl **-ciones** : emotion — **emocional** adj : emotional — **emocionante** adj **1** : moving, touching **2** APASIONANTE : exciting, thrilling — **emocionar** vt **1** : move, touch **2** APASIONAR : excite, thrill — **emocionarse** vr **1** : be moved **2** APASIONARSE : get excited — **emotivo, -va** adj **1** : emotional **2** CONMOVEDOR : moving

empacar {72} vt Lat : pack

empachar vt : give indigestion to — **empacharse** vr : get indigestion — **empacho** nm : indigestion

empadronarse vr : register to vote

empalagoso, -sa adj : excessively sweet, cloying

empalizada nf : palisade (fence)

empalmar vt : connect, link — vi : meet, converge — **empalme** nm **1** : connection, link **2** : junction (of a railroad, etc.)

empanada nf : pie, turnover — **empanadilla** nf : meat or seafood pie

empanar vt : bread (in cooking)

empantanar vt : flood — **empantanarse** vr **1** : become flooded **2** : get bogged down

empañar vt **1** : steam (up) **2** : tarnish (one's reputation, etc.) — **empañarse** vr : fog up

empapar vt : soak — **empaparse** vr : get soaking wet

empapelar vt : wallpaper

empaquetar vt : pack, package

emparedado, -da adj : walled in, confined — **emparedado** nm : sandwich

emparejar vt : match up, pair — **emparejarse** vr : pair off

emparentado, -da adj : related, kindred

empastar vt : fill (a tooth) — **empaste** nm : filling

empatar vi : result in a draw, be tied — **empate** nm : draw, tie

empedernido, -da adj : inveterate, hardened

empedrar {55} vt : pave (with stones) — **empedrado** nm : paving, pavement

empeine nm : instep

empeñar vt : pawn — **empeñarse** vr **1** : insist, persist **2** ENDEUDARSE : go into debt **3 ~ en** : make an effort to — **empeñado, -da** adj **1** : determined, committed **2** ENDEUDADO : in debt — **empeño** nm **1** : determination, effort **2 casa de ~s** : pawnshop

empeorar vi : get worse — vt : make worse

empequeñecer {53} vt : diminish, make smaller

emperador nm : emperor — **emperatriz** nf, pl **-trices** : empress

empezar {29} v : start, begin

empinar vt : raise — **empinarse** vr : stand on tiptoe — **empinado, -da** adj : steep

empírico, -ca adj : empirical

emplasto nm : poultice

emplazar {21} vt **1** : summon, subpoena **2** SITUAR : place, locate — **emplazamiento** nm **1** : location, site **2** CITACIÓN : summons, subpoena

emplear vt **1** : employ **2** USAR : use — **emplearse** vr **1** : get a job **2** USARSE : be used — **empleado, -da** n : employee — **empleador, -dora** n : employer — **empleo** nm **1** : occupation, job **2** USO : use

empobrecer {53} vt : impoverish — **empobrecerse** vr : become poor

empollar vi : brood (eggs) — vt : incubate

empolvarse vr : powder one's face

empotrar vt : fit, build into — **empotrado, -da** adj : built-in

emprender vt : undertake, begin — **emprendedor, -dora** adj : enterprising

empresa nf **1** COMPAÑÍA : company, firm **2** TAREA : undertaking — **empresarial** adj : business, managerial — **empresario, -ria** n **1** : businessman m, businesswoman f **2** : impresario (in theater), promoter (in sports)

empujar v : push — **empuje** nm : impetus, drive — **empujón** nm, pl **-jones** : push, shove

empuñar vt : grasp, take hold of

emular vt : emulate

en prep **1** : in **2** DENTRO DE : into, inside (of) **3** SOBRE : on **4 ~ avión** : by plane **5 ~ casa** : at home

enajenar vt : alienate — **enajenación** nf, pl **-ciones** : alienation

enagua nf : slip, petticoat

enaltecer {53} vt : praise, extol

enamorar vt : win the love of — **enamorarse** vr : fall in love — **enamorado, -da** adj : in love — **~** n : lover, sweetheart

enano, -na adj & n : dwarf

enarbolar vt **1** : hoist, raise **2** : brandish (arms, etc.)

enardecer {53} vt : stir up, excite

encabezar {21} vt **1** : head, lead **2** : put a heading on (an article, a list, etc.) — **encabezamiento** nm **1** : heading **2** : headline (in a newspaper)

encabritarse vr : rear up

encadenar vt **1** : chain, tie (up) **2** ENLAZAR : connect, link

encajar vt : fit (together) — vi **1** : fit **2** CUADRAR : conform, tally — **encaje** nm : lace

encalar vt : whitewash

encallar vi : run aground

encaminar vt : direct, aim — **encaminarse** vr **~ a** : head for — **encaminado, -da** adj **~ a** : aimed at, designed to

encandilar vt : dazzle

encanecer {53} vi : turn gray

encantar vt : enchant, bewitch — vi **me encanta esta canción** : I love this song — **encantado, -da** adj **1** : delighted **2** HECHIZADO : bewitched — **encantador, -dora** adj : charming, delightful — **encantamiento** nm : enchantment, spell — **encanto** nm **1** : charm, fascination **2** HECHIZO : spell

encapotarse vr : cloud over — **encapotado, -da** adj : overcast

encapricharse vr **~ con** : be infatuated with

encapuchado, -da adj : hooded

encaramar vt : lift up — **encaramarse** vr **~ a** : climb up on

encarar vt : face, confront

encarcelar vt : imprison — **encarcelamiento** nm : imprisonment

encarecer {53} vt : increase, raise (price, value, etc.) — **encarecerse** vr : become more expensive

encargar {52} vt **1** : put in charge of **2** PEDIR : order — **encargarse** vr **~ de** : take charge of — **encargado, -da** adj : in charge — **~** n : manager, person in charge — **encargo** nm **1** : errand **2** TAREA : assignment, task **3** PEDIDO : order

encariñarse vr **~ con** : become fond of

encarnar vt : embody — **encarnación** nf, pl **-ciones** : embodiment — **encarnado, -da** adj **1** : incarnate **2** ROJO : red

encarnizarse {21} vr **~ con** : attack viciously — **encarnizado, -da** adj : bitter, bloody

encarrilar vt : put on the right track

encasillar vt : pigeonhole

encauzar {21} vt : channel

encender {56} vt **1** : light, set fire to **2** PRENDER : switch on, start **3** AVIVAR : arouse (passions, etc.) — **encenderse** vr **1** : get excited **2** RUBORIZARSE : blush — **encendedor** nm : lighter — **encendido, -da** adj : lit, on — **encendido** nm : ignition (switch)

encerar vt : wax, polish — **encerado, -da** adj : waxed — **encerado** nm : blackboard

encerrar {55} vt **1** : lock up, shut away **2** CONTENER : contain

encestar vi : score (in basketball)

enchilada nf : enchilada

enchufar vt : plug in, connect — **enchufe** nm : plug, socket

encía nf : gum (tissue)

encíclica nf : encyclical

enciclopedia nf : encyclopedia — **enciclopédico, -ca** adj : encyclopedic

encierro nm **1** : confinement **2** : sit-in (at a university, etc.)

encima adv **1** : on top **2** ADEMÁS : as well, besides **3 ~ de** : on, over, on top of **4 por ~ de** : above, beyond

encinta adj : pregnant

enclenque adj : weak, sickly

encoger {15} v : shrink — **encogerse** vr **1** : shrink **2** : cower, cringe **3 ~ de hombros** : shrug (one's shoulders) — **encogido, -da** adj **1** : shrunken **2** TÍMIDO : shy

encolar vt : glue, stick

encolerizar {21} vt : enrage, infuriate — **encolerizarse** vr : get angry

encomendar {55} vt : entrust

encomienda nf **1** : charge, mission **2** Lat : parcel

encono nm : rancor, animosity

encontrar {19} vt **1** : find **2** : meet, encounter (difficulties, etc.) — **encontrarse** vr **1** : meet **2** HALLARSE : find oneself, be — **encontrado, -da** adj : contrary, opposing

encorvar vt : bend, curve — **encorvarse** vr : bend over, stoop

encrespar vt **1** : curl **2** IRRITAR : irritate — **encresparse** vr **1** : curl one's hair **2** IRRITARSE : get annoyed **3** : become choppy (of the sea)

encrucijada nf : crossroads

encuadernar vt : bind (a book) — **encuadernación** nf, pl **-ciones** : bookbinding

encuadrar vt **1** : frame **2** ENCAJAR : fit **3** COMPRENDER : contain, include

encubrir {2} vt : conceal, cover (up) — **encubierto, -ta** adj : covert — **encubrimiento** nm : cover-up

encuentro nm : meeting, encounter

encuestar vt : poll, take a survey of — **encuesta** nf **1** : investigation, inquiry **2** SONDEO : survey — **encuestador, -dora** n : pollster

encumbrado, -da adj : eminent, distinguished

encurtir vt : pickle

endeble adj : weak, feeble — **endeblez** nf : weakness, frailty

endemoniado, -da adj : wicked

enderezar {21} vt **1** : straighten (out) **2** : put upright, stand on end

endeudarse vr : go into debt — **endeudado, -da** adj : indebted, in debt — **endeudamiento** nm : debt

endiablado, -da adj **1** : wicked, diabolical **2** : complicated, difficult

endibia or **endivia** nf : endive

endosar vt : endorse — **endoso** nm : endorsement

endulzar {21} vt **1** : sweeten **2** : soften, mellow (a tone, a response, etc.) — **endulzante** nm : sweetener

endurecer {53} vt : harden — **endurecerse** vr : become hardened

enema nm : enema

enemigo, -ga adj : hostile — **~** n : enemy — **enemistad** nf : enmity — **enemistar** vt : make enemies of — **enemistarse** vr **~ con** : fall out with

energía nf : energy — **enérgico, -ca** adj : energetic, vigorous, forceful

enero nm : January

enervar vt **1** : enervate, weaken **2** fam : get on one's nerves

enésimo, -ma adj **por enésima vez** : for the umpteenth time

enfadar vt : annoy, make angry — **enfadarse** vr : get annoyed — **enfado** nm : anger, annoyance — **enfadoso, -sa** adj : annoying

enfatizar {21} vt : emphasize — **énfasis** nms & pl : emphasis — **enfático, -ca** adj : emphatic

enfermar vt : make sick — vi : get sick — **enfermedad** nf : sickness, disease — **enfermería** nf : infirmary — **enfermero, -ra** n : nurse — **enfermizo, -za** adj : sickly — **enfermo, -ma** adj : sick — **~** n : sick person, patient

enflaquecer {53} vi : lose weight

enfocar {72} vt **1** : focus (on) **2** : consider (a problem, etc.) — **enfoque** nm : focus

enfrascarse {72} vr **~ en** : immerse oneself in, get caught up in

enfrentar vt **1** : confront, face **2** : bring face to face — **enfrentarse** vr **~ con** : confront, clash with — **enfrente** adv **1** : opposite **2 ~ de** : in front of

enfriar {85} vt : chill, cool — **enfriarse** vr **1** : get cold **2** RESFRIARSE : catch a cold — **enfriamiento** nm **1** : cooling off **2** CATARRO : cold

enfurecer {53} vt : infuriate — **enfurecerse** vr : fly into a rage

enfurruñarse vr fam : sulk

engalanar vt : decorate — **engalanarse** vr : dress up

enganchar vt : hook, snag, catch — **engancharse** vr **1** : get caught **2** ALISTARSE : enlist

engañar vt **1** EMBAUCAR : trick, deceive **2** : cheat on, be unfaithful to — **engañarse** vr **1** : deceive oneself **2** EQUIVOCARSE : be mistaken — **engaño** nm : deception, deceit — **engañoso, -sa** adj : deceptive, deceitful

engatusar vt : coax, cajole

engendrar vt **1** : beget **2** : engender, give rise to (suspicions, etc.)

englobar vt : include, embrace

engomar vt : glue

engordar vt : fatten — vi : gain weight

engorroso, -sa adj : bothersome

engranar v : mesh, engage — **engranaje** nm : gears pl

engrandecer {53} vt **1** : enlarge **2** ENALTECER : exalt

engrapar vt Lat : staple — **engrapadora** nf Lat : stapler

engrasar vt : lubricate, grease — **engrase** nm : lubrication

engreído, -da adj : conceited

engrosar {19} vt : swell — vi : gain weight

engrudo nm : paste

engullir {38} vt : gulp down, gobble up

enhebrar vt : thread

enhorabuena nf : congratulations pl

enigma nm : enigma — **enigmático, -ca** adj : enigmatic

enjabonar vt : soap (up), lather

enjaezar {21} vt : harness

enjalbegar {52} vt : whitewash

enjambrar vi : swarm — **enjambre** nm : swarm

enjaular vt **1** : cage **2** fam : jail

enjuagar {52} vt : rinse — **enjuague** nm **1** : rinse **2 ~ bucal** : mouthwash

enjugar {52} vt **1** : wipe away (tears) **2** : wipe out (debt)

enjuiciar vt **1** : prosecute **2** JUZGAR : try

enjuto, -ta adj : gaunt, lean

enlace nm **1** : bond, link **2** : junction (of a highway, etc.)

enlatar vt : can

enlazar {21} vt : join, link — vi **~ con** : link up with

enlistarse vr Lat : enlist

enlodar vt : cover with mud

enloquecer {53} vt : drive crazy — **enloquecerse** vr : go crazy

enlosar vt : pave, tile

enlutarse vr : go into mourning

enmarañar vt **1** : tangle **2** COMPLICAR : complicate **3** CONFUNDIR : confuse — **enmarañarse** vr **1** : get tangled up **2** CONFUNDIRSE : become confused

enmarcar {72} vt : frame

enmascarar vt : mask

enmendar {55} vt **1** : amend **2** CORREGIR : emend, correct — **enmendarse** vr : mend one's ways — **enmienda** nf **1** : amendment **2** CORRECCIÓN : correction

enmohecerse {53} vr **1** : become moldy **2** OXIDARSE : rust

enmudecer {53} vt : silence — vi : fall silent

ennegrecer {53} vt : blacken

ennoblecer {53} vt : ennoble, dignify

enojar vt **1** : anger **2** MOLESTAR : annoy — **enojarse** vr **~ con** : get upset with — **enojo** nm **1** : anger **2** MOLESTIA : annoyance — **enojoso, -sa** adj : annoying

enorgullecer {53} vt : make proud — **enorgullecerse** vr **~ de** : pride oneself on

enorme adj : enormous — **enormemente** adv : enormously, extremely — **enormidad** nf : enormity

enraizar {30} vi : take root

enredadera nf : climbing plant, vine

enredar vt **1** : tangle up, entangle **2** CONFUNDIR : confuse **3** IMPLICAR : involve — **enredarse** vr **1** : become entangled **2 ~ en** : get mixed up in — **enredo** nm **1** : tangle **2** EMBROLLO : confusion, mess — **enredoso, -sa** adj : tangled up, complicated

enrejado nm **1** : railing **2** REJILLA : grating, grille **3** : trellis (for plants)

enrevesado, -da adj : complicated

enriquecer {53} vt : enrich — **enriquecerse** vr : get rich

enrojecer {53} vt : redden — **enrojecerse** vr : blush

enrolar vt : enlist — **enrolarse** vr **~ en** : enlist in

enrollar vt : roll up, coil

enroscar {72} vt **1** : roll up **2** ATORNILLAR : screw in

ensalada nf : salad

ensalzar {21} vt : praise

ensamblar vt : assemble, fit together

ensanchar vt **1** : widen **2** AMPLIAR : expand — **ensanche** nm **1** : widening **2** : (urban) expansion, development

ensangrentado, -da *adj* : bloody, bloodstained
ensañarse *vr* : act cruelly
ensartar *vt* : string, thread
ensayar *vi* : rehearse — *vt* : try out, test — **ensayo** *nm* **1** : essay **2** PRUEBA : trial, test **3** : rehearsal (in theater, etc.)
enseguida *adv* : right away, immediately
ensenada *nf* : inlet, cove
enseñar *vt* **1** : teach **2** MOSTRAR : show — **enseñanza** *nf* **1** EDUCACIÓN : education **2** INSTRUCCIÓN : teaching
enseres *nmpl* **1** : equipment **2 ~ domésticos** : household goods
ensillar *vt* : saddle (up)
ensimismarse *vr* : lose oneself in thought
ensombrecer {53} *vt* : cast a shadow over, darken
ensoñación *nf, pl* **-ciones** : fantasy, daydream
ensordecer {53} *vt* : deafen — *vi* : go deaf — **ensordecedor, -dora** *adj* : deafening
ensortijar *vt* : curl
ensuciar *vt* : soil — **ensuciarse** *vr* : get dirty
ensueño *nm* : daydream, fantasy
entablar *vt* : initiate, start
entallar *vt* : tailor, fit (clothing) — *vi* : fit
entarimado *nm* : floorboards, flooring
ente *nm* **1** : being **2** ORGANISMO : body, organization
entender {56} *vt* **1** : understand **2** OPINAR : think, believe — *vi* **1** : understand **2 ~ de** : know about, be good at — **entenderse** *vr* **1** : understand each other **2** LLEVARSE BIEN : get along well — **~** *nm* **a mi ~** : in my opinion — **entendido, -da** *adj* **1** : understood **2 eso se da por ~** : that goes without saying **3 tener ~** : be under the impression — **entendimiento** *nm* **1** : understanding **2** INTELIGENCIA : intellect
enterar *vt* : inform — **enterarse** *vr* : find out, learn — **enterado, -da** *adj* : well-informed
entereza *nf* **1** HONRADEZ : integrity **2** FORTALEZA : fortitude **3** FIRMEZA : resolve
enternecer {53} *vt* : move, touch
entero, -ra *adj* **1** : whole **2** TOTAL : absolute, total **3** INTACTO : intact — **entero** *nm* : integer, whole number
enterrar {55} *vt* : bury
entibiar *vt* : cool (down) — **entibiarse** *vr* : become lukewarm
entidad *nf* **1** : entity **2** ORGANIZACIÓN : body, organization
entierro *nm* **1** : burial **2** : funeral (ceremony)
entomología *nf* : entomology — **entomólogo, -ga** *n* : entomologist
entonar *vt* : sing, intone — *vi* : be in tune
entonces *adv* **1** : then **2 desde ~** : since then
entornado, -da *adj* : half-closed, ajar
entorno *nm* : surroundings *pl*, environment
entorpecer {53} *vt* **1** : hinder, obstruct **2** : numb, dull (wits, reactions, etc.)
entrada *nf* **1** : entrance, entry **2** BILLETE : ticket **3** COMIENZO : beginning **4** : inning (in baseball) **5 ~s** *nfpl* : income **6 tener ~s** : have a receding hairline
entraña *nf* **1** : core, heart **2 ~s** *nfpl* VÍSCERAS : entrails, innards — **entrañable** *adj* : close, intimate — **entrañar** *vt* : involve
entrar *vi* **1** : enter **2** EMPEZAR : begin — *vt* : introduce, bring in
entre *prep* **1** : between **2** : among
entreabrir {2} *vt* : leave ajar — **entreabierto, -ta** *adj* : half-open, ajar
entreacto *nm* : intermission
entrecejo *nm* **fruncir el ~** : knit one's brows, frown
entrecortado, -da *adj* : faltering (of the voice), labored (of breathing)
entrecruzar {21} *vi* : intertwine
entredicho *nm* : doubt, question
entregar {52} *vt* : deliver, hand over — **entregarse** *vr* : surrender — **entrega** *nf* **1** : delivery **2** DEDICACIÓN : dedication, devotion **3 ~ inicial** : down payment
entrelazar {21} *vt* : intertwine — **entrelazarse** *vr* : become intertwined
entremés *nm, pl* **-meses 1** : hors d'oeuvre **2** : short play (in theater)
entremeterse → **entrometerse**
entremezclar *vt* : mix (up)
entrenar *vt* : train, drill — **entrenarse** *vr* : train — **entrenador, -dora** *n* : trainer, coach — **entranamiento** *nm* : training
entrepierna *nf* : crotch
entresacar {72} *vt* : pick out, select
entresuelo *nm* : mezzanine
entretanto *adv* : meanwhile — **~** *nm* **en el ~** : in the meantime
entretener {80} *vt* **1** : entertain **2** DESPISTAR : distract **3** RETRASAR : delay, hold up — **entretenerse** *vr* **1** : amuse oneself **2** DEMORARSE : dawdle — **entretenido, -da** *adj* : entertaining — **entretenimiento** *nm* **1** : entertainment, amusement **2** PASATIEMPO : pastime
entrever {88} *vt* : catch a glimpse of, make out
entrevistar *vt* : interview — **entrevista** *nf* : interview — **entrevistador, -dora** *n* : interviewer
entristecer {53} *vt* : sadden
entrometerse *vr* : interfere — **entrometido, -da** *adj* : meddling, nosy — *n* : meddler
entroncar {72} *vi* : be related, be connected
entumecer {53} *vt* : make numb — **entumecerse** *vr* : go numb — **entumecido, -da** *adj* **1** : numb **2** : stiff (of muscles, etc.)
enturbiar *vt* : cloud — **enturbiarse** *vr* : become cloudy
entusiasmar *vt* : fill with enthusiasm — **entusiasmarse** *vr* : get excited — **entusiasmo** *nm* : enthusiasm — **entusiasta** *adj* : enthusiastic — **~** *nmf* : enthusiast
enumerar *vt* : enumerate, list — **enumeración** *nf, pl* **-ciones** : enumeration, count
enunciar *vt* : enunciate — **enunciación** *nf, pl* **-ciones** : enunciation
envalentonar *vt* : make bold, encourage — **envalentonarse** *vr* : be brave
envanecerse {53} *vr* : become vain
envasar *vt* **1** : package **2** : bottle, can — **envase** *nm* **1** : packaging **2** RECIPIENTE : container **3** : jar, bottle, can
envejecer {53} *v* : age — **envejecido, -da** *adj* : aged, old — **envejecimiento** *nm* : aging
envenenar *vt* : poison — **envenenamiento** *nm* : poisoning
envergadura *nf* **1** ALCANCE : scope **2** : span (of wings, etc.)
envés *nm, pl* **-veses** : reverse side
enviar {85} *vt* : send — **enviado, -da** *n* : envoy, correspondent
envidiar *vt* : envy — **envidia** *nf* : envy, jealousy — **envidioso, -sa** *adj* : jealous, envious
envilecer {53} *vt* : degrade, debase — **envilecimiento** *nm* : degradation
envío *nm* **1** : sending, shipment **2** : remittance (of funds)
enviudar *vi* : be widowed
envolver {89} *vt* **1** : wrap **2** RODEAR : surround **3** IMPLICAR : involve — **envoltorio** *nm or* **envoltura** *nf* : wrapping, wrapper
enyesar *vt* **1** : plaster **2** ESCAYOLAR : put in a plaster cast
enzima *nf* : enzyme
épico, -ca *adj* : epic — **épica** *nf* : epic
epidemia *nf* : epidemic — **epidémico, -ca** *adj* : epidemic
epilepsia *nf* : epilepsy — **epiléptico, -ca** *adj & n* : epileptic
epílogo *nm* : epilogue
episodio *nm* : episode
epitafio *nm* : epitaph
epíteto *nm* : epithet
época *nf* **1** : epoch, period **2** ESTACIÓN : season
epopeya *nf* : epic poem
equidad *nf* : equity, justice
equilátero, -ra *adj* : equilateral
equilibrar *vt* : balance — **equilibrado, -da** *adj* : well-balanced — **equilibrio** *nm* **1** : balance, equilibrium **2** JUICIO : good sense
equinoccio *nm* : equinox
equipaje *nm* : baggage, luggage
equipar *vt* : equip
equiparar *vt* **1** IGUALAR : make equal **2** COMPARAR : compare — **equiparable** *adj* : comparable
equipo *nm* **1** : equipment **2** : team, crew (in sports, etc.)
equitación *nf, pl* **-ciones** : horseback riding
equitativo, -va *adj* : equitable, fair, just
equivaler {84} *vi* : be equivalent — **equivalencia** *nf* : equivalence — **equivalente** *adj & nm* : equivalent
equivocar {72} *vt* : mistake, confuse — **equivocarse** *vr* : make a mistake — **equivocación** *nf, pl* **-ciones** : error, mistake — **equivocado, -da** *adj* : mistaken, wrong
equívoco, -ca *adj* : ambiguous — **equívoco** *nm* : misunderstanding
era *nf* : era
erario *nm* : public treasury, funds *pl*
erección *nf, pl* **-ciones** : erection
erguir {31} *vt* : raise, lift — **erguirse** *vr* : rise (up) — **erguido, -da** *adj* : erect, upright
erigir {35} *vt* : build, erect — **erigirse** *vr* **~ en** : set oneself up as
erizarse {21} *vr* : bristle, stand on end — **erizado, -da** *adj* : bristly
erizo *nm* **1** : hedgehog **2 ~ de mar** : sea urchin
ermitaño, -ña *n* : hermit
erosionar *vt* : erode — **erosión** *nf, pl* **-siones** : erosion
erótico, -ca *adj* : erotic
erradicar {72} *vt* : eradicate
errar {32} *vt* : miss — *vi* **1** : be wrong, be mistaken **2** VAGAR : wander — **errado, -da** *adj Lat* : wrong, mistaken
errata *nf* : misprint
errático, -ca *adj* : erratic
error *nm* : error — **erróneo, -nea** *adj* : erroneous, mistaken
eructar *vi* : belch, burp — **eructo** *nm* : belch, burp
erudito, -ta *adj* : erudite, learned
erupción *nf, pl* **-ciones 1** : eruption **2** SARPULLIDO : rash
esa, ésa → **ese, ése**
esbelto, -ta *adj* : slender, slim
esbozar {21} *vt* : sketch, outline — **esbozo** *nm* : sketch, outline
escabechar *vt* : pickle — **escabeche** *nm* : brine (for pickling)
escabel *nm* : footstool
escabroso, -sa *adj* **1** : rugged, rough **2** ESPINOSO : thorny, difficult **3** ATREVIDO : shocking, risqué
escabullirse {38} *vr* : slip away, escape
escalar *vt* : climb, scale — *vi* : escalate — **escala** *nf* **1** : scale **2** ESCALERA : ladder **3** : stopover (of an airplane, etc.) — **escalada** *nf* : ascent, climb — **escalador, -dora** *n* ALPINISTA : mountain climber
escaldar *vt* : scald
escalera *nf* **1** : stairs *pl*, staircase **2** ESCALA : ladder **3 ~ mecánica** : escalator
escalfar *vt* : poach
escalinata *nf* : flight of stairs
escalofrío *nm* : shiver, chill — **escalofriante** *adj* : chilling, horrifying
escalonar *vt* **1** : stagger, spread out **2** : terrace (land) — **escalón** *nm, pl* **-lones** : step, rung
escama *nf* **1** : scale (of fish or reptiles) **2** : flake (of skin) — **escamoso, -sa** *adj* : scaly
escamotear *vt* **1** : conceal **2 ~ algo a algn** : rob s.o. of sth
escandalizar {21} *vt* : scandalize — **escandalizarse** *vr* : be shocked — **escándalo** *nm* **1** : scandal **2** ALBOROTO : scene, commotion — **escandaloso, -sa** *adj* **1** : shocking, scandalous **2** RUIDOSO : noisy
escandinavo, -va *adj* : Scandinavian
escáner *nm* : scanner
escaño *nm* **1** : seat (in a legislative body) **2** BANCO : bench
escapar *vi* : escape, run away — **escaparse** *vr* **1** : escape **2** : leak out (of gas, water, etc.) — **escapada** *nf* : escape
escaparate *nm* : store window
escapatoria *nf* : loophole, way out
escape *nm* **1** : leak (of gas, water, etc.) **2** : exhaust (from a vehicle)
escarabajo *nm* : beetle
escarbar *vt* **1** : dig, scratch, poke **2 ~ en** : pry into
escarcha *nf* : frost (on a surface)
escarlata *adj & nf* : scarlet — **escarlatina** *nf* : scarlet fever
escarmentar {55} *vi* : learn one's lesson — **escarmiento** *nm* : lesson, punishment
escarnecer {53} *vt* : ridicule, mock — **escarnio** *nm* : ridicule, mockery
escarola *nf* : escarole, endive
escarpa *nf* : steep slope — **escarpado, -da** *adj* : steep
escasear *vi* : be scarce — **escasez** *nf, pl* **-seces** : shortage, scarcity — **escaso, -sa** *adj* **1** : scarce **2 ~ de** : short of
escatimar *vt* : be sparing with, skimp on
escayolar *vt* : put in a plaster cast — **escayola** *nf* **1** : plaster (for casts) **2** : plaster cast
escena *nf* **1** : scene **2** ESCENARIO : stage — **escenario** *nm* **1** : setting, scene **2** ESCENA : stage — **escénico, -ca** *adj* : scenic
escepticismo *nm* : skepticism — **escéptico, -ca** *adj* : skeptical — **~** *n* : skeptic
esclarecer {53} *vt* : shed light on, clarify
esclavo, -va *n* : slave — **esclavitud** *nf* : slavery — **esclavizar** {21} *vt* : enslave
esclerosis *nf* **~ múltiple** : multiple sclerosis
esclusa *nf* : floodgate, lock (of a canal)
escoba *nf* : broom
escocer {14} *vi* : sting
escocés, -cesa *adj, mpl* **-ceses 1** : Scottish **2** : tartan, plaid — **escocés** *nm, pl* **-ceses** : Scotch (whiskey)
escoger {15} *vt* : choose — **escogido, -da** *adj* : choice, select
escolar *adj* : school — **~** *nmf* : student, pupil
escolta *nmf* : escort — **escoltar** *vt* : escort, accompany
escombros *nmpl* : ruins, rubble
esconder *vt* : hide, conceal — **esconderse** *vr* : hide — **escondidas** *nfpl* **1** *Lat* : hide-and-seek **2 a ~** : secretly, in secret — **escondite** *nm* **1** : hiding place **2** : hide-and-seek (game) — **escondrijo** *nm* : hiding place
escopeta *nf* : shotgun
escoplo *nm* : chisel
escoria *nf* **1** : slag **2** : dregs *pl* (of society, etc.)
escorpión *nm, pl* **-piones** : scorpion
escote *nm* **1** : (low) neckline **2 pagar a ~** : go Dutch
escotilla *nf* : hatchway
escribir {33} *v* : write — **escribirse** *vr* **1** : write to one another, correspond **2** : be spelled — **escribiente** *nmf* : clerk — **escrito, -ta** *adj* : written — **escritos** *nmpl* : writings — **escritor, -tora** *n* : writer — **escritorio** *nm* : desk — **escritura** *nf* **1** : handwriting **2** : deed (in law)
escroto *nm* : scrotum
escrúpulo *nm* : scruple — **escrupuloso, -sa** *adj* : scrupulous
escrutar *vt* **1** : scrutinize **2** : count (votes) — **escrutinio** *nm* **1** : scrutiny **2** : count (of votes)
escuadra *nf* **1** : square (instrument) **2** : fleet (of ships), squad (in the military) — **escuadrón** *nm, pl* **-drones** : squadron
escuálido, -da *adj* **1** : skinny **2** SUCIO : squalid
escuchar *vt* **1** : listen to **2** *Lat* : hear — *vi* : listen
escudo *nm* **1** : shield **2** *or* **~ de armas** : coat of arms
escudriñar *vt* : scrutinize, examine
escuela *nf* : school
escueto, -ta *adj* : plain, simple
esculpir *v* : sculpt — **escultor, -tora** *n* : sculptor — **escultura** *nf* : sculpture
escupir *v* : spit
escurrir *vt* **1** : drain **2** : wring out (clothes) — *vi* **1** : drain **2** : drip-dry (of clothes) — **escurrirse** *vr* **1** : drain **2** *fam* : slip away — **escurridizo, -da** *adj* : slippery, evasive — **escurridor** *nm* **1** : dish drainer **2** COLADOR : colander
ese, esa *adj, mpl* **esos** : that, those
ése, ésa *pron, mpl* **ésos** : that one, those ones *pl*
esencia *nf* : essence — **esencial** *adj* : essential
esfera *nf* **1** : sphere **2** : dial (of a watch) — **esférico, -ca** *adj* : spherical
esfinge *nf* : sphinx
esforzar {36} *vt* : strain — **esforzarse** *vr* : make an effort — **esfuerzo** *nm* : effort
esfumarse *vr* : fade away, vanish
esgrimir *vt* **1** : brandish, wield **2** : make use of (an argument, etc.) — **esgrima** *nf* **1** : fencing **2 hacer ~** : fence
esguince *nm* : sprain, strain
eslabonar *vt* : link, connect — **eslabón** *nm, pl* **-bones** : link
eslavo, -va *adj* : Slavic
eslogan *nm, pl* **-lóganes** : slogan
esmaltar *vt* : enamel — **esmalte** *nm* **1** : enamel **2 ~ de uñas** : nail polish
esmerado, -da *adj* : careful
esmeralda *nf* : emerald
esmerarse *vr* : take great care
esmeril *nm* : emery
esmoquin *nm, pl* **-móquines** : tuxedo
esnob *nmf, pl* **esnobs** : snob — **~** *adj* : snobbish
eso *pron (neuter)* **1** : that **2 ¡~ es!** : that's it!, that's right! **3 en ~** : at that point, then
esófago *nm* : esophagus
esos, ésos → **ese, ése**
espabilarse *vr* **1** : wake up **2** DARSE PRISA : get moving — **espabilado, -da** *adj* **1** : awake **2** LISTO : bright, clever
espaciar *vt* : space out, spread out — **espacial** *adj* : space — **espacio** *nm* **1** : space **2 ~ exterior** : outer space — **espacioso, -sa** *adj* : spacious
espada *nf* **1** : sword **2 ~s** *nfpl* : spades (in playing cards)
espagueti *nm or* **espaguetis** *nmpl* : spaghetti
espalda *nf* **1** : back **2 ~s** *nfpl* : shoulders, back
espantar *vt* : scare, frighten — **espantarse** *vr* : become frightened — **espantajo** *nm or* **espantapájaros** *nms & pl* : scarecrow — **espanto** *nm* : fright, fear — **espantoso, -sa** *adj* **1** : frightening, horrific **2** TERRIBLE : awful, terrible
español, -ñola *adj* : Spanish — **español** *nm* : Spanish (language)
esparadrapo *nm* : adhesive bandage
esparcir {83} *vt* : scatter, spread — **esparcirse** *vr* **1** : be scattered, spread out **2** DIVERTIRSE : enjoy oneself
espárrago *nm* : asparagus
espasmo *nm* : spasm — **espasmódico, -ca** *adj* : spasmodic
espátula *nf* : spatula
especia *nf* : spice
especial *adj & nm* : special — **especialidad** *nf* : specialty — **especialista** *nmf* : specialist — **especializarse** {21} *vr* **~ en** : specialize in — **especialmente** *adv* : especially
especie *nf* **1** : species **2** CLASE : type, kind
especificar {72} *vt* : specify — **especificación** *nf, pl* **-ciones** : specification — **específico, -ca** *adj* : specific
espécimen *nm, pl* **especímenes** : specimen
espectáculo *nm* **1** : show, performance **2** VISIÓN : spectacle, view — **espectacular** *adj* : spectacular — **espectador, -dora** *n* : spectator
espectro *nm* **1** : spectrum **2** FANTASMA : ghost
especulación *nf, pl* **-ciones** : speculation
espejo *nm* : mirror — **espejismo** *nm* **1** : mirage **2** ILUSIÓN : illusion
espeluznante *adj* : terrifying, hair-raising
esperar *vt* **1** : wait for **2** CONTAR CON : expect **3 ~ que** : hope (that) — *vi* : wait — **espera** *nf* : wait — **esperanza** *nf* : hope, expectation — **esperanzado, -da** *adj* : hopeful — **esperanzar** {21} *vt* : give hope to
esperma *nmf* **1** : sperm **2 ~ de ballena** : blubber
esperpento *nm* : (grotesque) sight, fright

espesar *vt* : thicken — **espesarse** *vr* : thicken — **espeso, -sa** *adj* : thick, heavy — **espesor** *nm* : thickness, density — **espesura** *nf* **1** ESPESOR : thickness **2** : thicket

espetar *vt* : blurt (out)

espiar {85} *vt* : spy on — *vi* : spy — **espía** *nmf* : spy

espiga *nf* : ear (of wheat, etc.)

espina *nf* **1** : thorn **2** : (fish) bone **3 ~ dorsal** : spine, backbone

espinaca *nf* **1** : spinach (plant) **2 ~s** *nfpl* : spinach (food)

espinazo *nm* : spine, backbone

espinilla *nf* **1** : shin **2** GRANO : blackhead, pimple

espinoso, -sa *adj* **1** : prickly **2** : bony (of fish) **3** : difficult, thorny (of problems, etc.)

espionaje *nm* : espionage

espiral *adj & nf* : spiral

espirar *v* : breathe out, exhale

espíritu *nm* **1** : spirit **2 Espíritu Santo** : Holy Spirit — **espiritual** *adj* : spiritual — **espiritualidad** *nf* : spirituality

espita *nf* : spigot, faucet

espléndido, -da *adj* **1** : splendid **2** GENEROSO : lavish — **esplendor** *nm* : splendor

espliego *nm* : lavender

espolear *vt* : spur on

espoleta *nf* : fuse

espolvorear *vt* : sprinkle, dust

esponja *nf* **1** : sponge **2 tirar la ~** : throw in the towel — **esponjoso, -sa** *adj* : spongy

espontaneidad *nf* : spontaneity — **espontáneo, -nea** *adj* : spontaneous

espora *nf* : spore

esporádico, -ca *adj* : sporadic

esposo, -sa *n* : spouse, wife *f*, husband *m* — **esposar** *vt* : handcuff — **esposas** *nfpl* : handcuffs

esprintar *vi* : sprint (in sports) — **esprint** *nm* : sprint

espuela *nf* : spur

espumar *vt* : skim — **espuma** *nf* **1** : foam, froth **2** : (soap) lather **3** : head (on beer) — **espumoso, -sa** *adj* **1** : foamy, frothy **2** : sparkling (of wine)

esqueleto *nm* : skeleton

esquema *nf* : outline, sketch

esquí *nm* **1** : ski **2** : skiing (sport) **3 ~ acuático** : waterskiing — **esquiador, -dora** *n* : skier — **esquiar** {85} *vi* : ski

esquilar *vt* : shear

esquimal *adj* : Eskimo

esquina *nf* : corner

esquirol *nm* : strikebreaker, scab

esquivar *vt* **1** : evade, dodge (a blow) **2** EVITAR : avoid — **esquivo, -va** *adj* : shy, elusive

esquizofrenia *nf* : schizophrenia — **esquizofrénico, -ca** *adj & n* : schizophrenic

esta, ésta → **este**[1], **éste**

estable *adj* : stable — **estabilidad** *nf* : stability — **estabilizar** {21} *vt* : stabilize

establecer {53} *vt* : establish — **establecerse** *vr* : establish oneself, settle — **establecimiento** *nm* : establishment

establo *nm* : stable

estaca *nf* : stake — **estacada** *nf* **1** : (picket) fence **2 dejar en la ~** : leave in a lurch

estación *nf, pl* **-ciones 1** : season **2 ~ de servicio** : gas station — **estacionar** *v* : park — **estacionamiento** *nm* : parking — **estacionario, -ria** *adj* : stationary

estadía *nf Lat* : stay

estadio *nm* **1** : stadium **2** FASE : phase, stage

estadista *nmf* : statesman

estadística *nf* : statistics — **estadístico, -ca** *adj* : statistical

estado *nm* **1** : state **2 ~ civil** : marital status

estadounidense *adj & nmf* : American (from the United States)

estafar *vt* : swindle, defraud — **estafa** *nf* : swindle, fraud — **estafador, -dora** *n* : cheat, swindler

estallar *vi* **1** : explode **2** : break out (of war, an epidemic, etc.) **3 ~ en llamas** : burst into flames — **estallido** *nm* **1** : explosion **2** : report (of a gun) **3** : outbreak (of war, etc.)

estampar *vt* : stamp, print — **estampa** *nf* **1** : print, illustration **2** ASPECTO : appearance — **estampado, -da** *adj* : printed

estampida *nf* : stampede

estampilla *nf* : stamp

estancarse {72} *vr* **1** : stagnate **2** : come to a halt — **estancado, -da** *adj* : stagnant

estancia *nf* **1** : stay **2** HABITACIÓN : (large) room **3** *Lat* : (cattle) ranch

estanco, -ca *adj* : watertight

estándar *adj & nm* : standard — **estandarizar** {21} *vt* : standardize

estandarte *nm* : standard, banner

estanque *nm* **1** : pool, pond **2** : reservoir (for irrigation)

estante *nm* : shelf — **estantería** *nf* : shelves *pl*, bookcase

estaño *nm* : tin

estar {34} *v aux* : be — *vi* **1** : be **2** : be at home **3** QUEDARSE : stay, remain **4 ¿cómo estás?** : how are you? **5 ~ a** : cost **6 ~ bien (mal)** : be well (sick) **7 ~ para** : be in the mood for **8 ~ por** : be in favor of **9 ~ por** : be about to — **estarse** *vr* : stay, remain

estarcir {83} *vt* : stencil

estárter *nm* : choke (of an automobile)

estatal *adj* : state, national

estático, -ca *adj* **1** : static **2** INMÓVIL : unmoving, still — **estática** *nf* : static

estatua *nf* : statue

estatura *nf* : height

estatus *nm* : status, prestige

estatuto *nm* : statute — **estatutario, -ria** *adj* : statutory

este[1], **esta** *adj, mpl* **estos** : this, these

este[2] *adj* : eastern, east — **este** *nm* **1** : east **2** : east wind **3 el Este** : the Orient

éste, ésta *pron, mpl* **éstos 1** : this one, these ones *pl* **2** : the latter

estela *nf* **1** : wake (of a ship) **2** : trail (of smoke, etc.)

estera *nf* : mat

estéreo *adj & nm* : stereo — **estereofónico, -ca** *adj* : stereophonic

estereotipo *nm* : stereotype

estéril *adj* **1** : sterile **2** : infertile — **esterilidad** *nf* **1** : sterility **2** : infertility — **esterilizar** {21} *vt* : sterilize

estética *nf* : aesthetics — **estético, -ca** *adj* : aesthetic

estiércol *nm* : dung, manure

estigma *nm* : stigma — **estigmatizar** {21} *vt* : stigmatize

estilarse {21} *vr* : be in fashion

estilo *nm* **1** : style **2** MANERA : fashion, manner — **estilista** *nmf* : stylist

estima *nf* : esteem, regard — **estimación** *nf, pl* **-ciones 1** : esteem **2** VALORACIÓN : estimate — **estimado, -da** *adj* **Estimado señor** : Dear Sir — **estimar** *vt* **1** : esteem, respect **2** VALORAR : value, estimate **3** CONSIDERAR : consider

estimular *vt* **1** : stimulate **2** ALENTAR : encourage — **estimulante** *adj* : stimulating — ~ *nm* : stimulant — **estímulo** *nm* : stimulus

estío *nm* : summertime

estipular *vt* : stipulate

estirar *vt* : stretch (out), extend — **estirado, -da** *adj* **1** : stretched, extended **2** ALTANERO : stuck-up, haughty — **estiramiento** *nm* **~ facial** : face-lift — **estirón** *nm, pl* **-rones** : pull, tug

estirpe *nf* : lineage, stock

estival *adj* : summer

esto *pron (neuter)* **1** : this **2 en ~** : at this point **3 por ~** : for this reason

estofa *nf* **1** : class, quality **2 de baja ~** : low-class

estofar *vt* : stew — **estofado** *nm* : stew

estoicismo *nm* : stoicism — **estoico, -ca** *adj* : stoic, stoical — **~** *n* : stoic

estómago *nm* : stomach — **estomacal** *adj* : stomach

estorbar *vt* : obstruct — *vi* : get in the way — **estorbo** *nm* **1** : obstacle **2** MOLESTIA : nuisance

estornino *nm* : starling

estornudar *vi* : sneeze — **estornudo** *nm* : sneeze

estos, éstos → **este, éste**

estrabismo *nm* : squint

estrado *nm* : platform, stage

estrafalario, -ria *adj* : eccentric, bizarre

estragar {52} *vt* : devastate — **estragos** *nmpl* **1** : ravages **2 hacer ~ en** *or* **causar ~ entre** : wreak havoc with

estragón *nm* : tarragon

estrangular *vt* : strangle — **estrangulación** *nf* : strangulation

estratagema *nf* : stratagem

estrategia *nf* : strategy — **estratégico, -ca** *adj* : strategic

estrato *nm* : stratum

estratosfera *nf* : stratosphere

estrechar *vt* **1** : narrow **2** : strengthen (a bond) **3** ABRAZAR : embrace **4 ~ la mano a uno** : shake s.o.'s hand — **estrecharse** *vr* : narrow — **estrechez** *nf, pl* **-checes 1** : narrowness **2 estrecheces** *nfpl* : financial problems — **estrecho, -cha** *adj* **1** : tight, narrow **2** ÍNTIMO : close — **estrecho** *nm* : strait

estrella *nf* **1** : star **2** DESTINO : destiny **3 ~ de mar** : starfish — **estrellado, -da** *adj* **1** : starry **2** : star-shaped

estrellar *v* : crash — **estrellarse** *vr* **~ contre** : smash into

estremecer {53} *vt* : cause to shudder — *vi* : tremble, shake — **estremecerse** *vr* : shudder, shiver (with emotion) — **estremecimiento** *nm* : shaking, shivering

estrenar *vt* **1** : use for the first time **2** : premiere, open (a film, etc.) — **estrenarse** *vr* : make one's debut — **estreno** *nm* : debut, premiere

estreñirse {67} *vr* : be constipated — **estreñimiento** *nm* : constipation

estrépito *nm* : clamor, din — **estrepitoso, -sa** *adj* : noisy, clamorous

estrés *nm, pl* **estreses** : stress — **estresante** *adj* : stressful — **estresar** *vt* : stress (out)

estría *nf* : groove

estribaciones *nfpl* : foothills

estribar *vi* **~ en** : stem from, lie in

estribillo *nm* : refrain, chorus

estribo *nm* **1** : stirrup **2** : running board (of a vehicle) **3** CONTRAFUERTE : buttress **4 perder los ~s** : lose one's temper

estribor *nm* : starboard

estricto, -ta *adj* : strict

estridente *adj* : strident, shrill

estrofa *nf* : stanza, verse

estropajo *nm* : scouring pad

estropear *vt* **1** : ruin, spoil **2** DAÑAR : damage — **estropearse** *vr* **1** : go bad **2** AVERIARSE : break down — **estropicio** *nm* : damage, havoc

estructura *nf* : structure — **estructural** *adj* : structural

estruendo *nm* : din, roar — **estruendoso, -sa** *adj* : thunderous

estrujar *vt* : squeeze

estuario *nm* : estuary

estuche *nm* : kit, case

estuco *nm* : stucco

estudiar *v* : study — **estudiante** *nmf* : student — **estudiantil** *adj* : student — **estudio** *nm* **1** : study **2** OFICINA : studio, office **3 ~s** *nmpl* : studies, education — **estudioso, -sa** *adj* : studious

estufa *nf* : stove, heater

estupefaciente *adj & nm* : narcotic — **estupefacto, -ta** *adj* : astonished

estupendo, -da *adj* : stupendous, marvelous

estúpido, -da *adj* : stupid — **estupidez** *nf, pl* **-deces** : stupidity

estupor *nm* **1** : stupor **2** ASOMBRO : amazement

etapa *nf* : stage, phase

etcétera : et cetera, and so on

éter *nm* : ether

etéreo, -rea *adj* : ethereal

eterno, -na *adj* : eternal — **eternidad** *nf* : eternity — **eternizarse** {21} *vr* : take forever

ética *nf* : ethics — **ético, -ca** *adj* : ethical

etimología *nf* : etymology

etíope *adj* : Ethiopian

etiqueta *nf* **1** : tag, label **2** PROTOCOLO : etiquette **3 de ~** : formal, dressy — **etiquetar** *vt* : label

étnico, -ca *adj* : ethnic

eucalipto *nm* : eucalyptus

Eucaristía *nf* : Eucharist, communion

eufemismo *nm* : euphemism — **eufemístico, -ca** *adj* : euphemistic

euforia *nf* : euphoria — **eufórico, -ca** *adj* : euphoric

europeo, -pea *adj* : European

eutanasia *nf* : euthanasia

evacuar *vt* : evacuate, vacate — *vi* : have a bowel movement — **evacuación** *nf, pl* **-ciones** : evacuation

evadir *vt* : evade, avoid — **evadirse** *vr* : escape

evaluar {3} *vt* : evaluate — **evaluación** *nf, pl* **-ciones** : evaluation

evangelio *nm* : gospel — **evangélico, -ca** *adj* : evangelical — **evangelismo** *nm* : evangelism

evaporar *vt* : evaporate — **evaporarse** *vr* : evaporate, disappear — **evaporación** *nf, pl* **-ciones** : evaporation

evasión *nf, pl* **-siones 1** : evasion **2** FUGA : escape — **evasiva** *nf* : excuse, pretext — **evasivo, -va** *adj* : evasive

evento *nm* : event

eventual *adj* **1** : temporary **2** POSIBLE : possible — **eventualidad** *nf* : possibility, eventuality

evidencia *nf* **1** : evidence, proof **2 poner en ~** : demonstrate — **evidenciar** *vt* : demonstrate, show — **evidente** *adj* : evident — **evidentemente** *adj* : evidently, apparently

evitar *vt* **1** : avoid **2** IMPEDIR : prevent — **evitable** *adj* : avoidable

evocar {72} *vt* : evoke

evolución *nf, pl* **-ciones** : evolution — **evolucionar** *vi* : evolve

exacerbar *vt* **1** : exacerbate **2** IRRITAR : irritate

exacto, -ta *adj* : precise, exact — **exactamente** *adv* : exactly — **exactitud** *nf* : precision, accuracy

exagerar *v* : exaggerate — **exageración** *nf, pl* **-ciones** : exaggeration — **exagerado, -da** *adj* : exaggerated

exaltar *vt* **1** : exalt, extol **2** EXCITAR : excite, arouse — **exaltarse** *vr* : get worked-up — **exaltado, -da** *adj* : worked up, hotheaded

examen *nm, pl* **exámenes 1** : examination, test **2** ANÁLISIS : investigation — **examinar** *vt* **1** : examine **2** ESTUDIAR : study, inspect — **examinarse** *vr* : take an exam

exánime *adj* : lifeless

exasperar *vt* : exasperate, irritate — **exasperación** *nf, pl* **-ciones** : exasperation

excavar *v* : excavate — **excavación** *nf, pl* **-ciones** : excavation

exceder *vt* : exceed, surpass — **excederse** *vr* : go too far — **excedente** *adj & nm* : surplus, excess

excelente *adj* : excellent — **excelencia** *nf* **1** : excellence **2 Su Excelencia** : His/Her Excellency

excéntrico, -ca *adj & n* : eccentric — **excentricidad** *nf* : eccentricity

excepción *nf, pl* **-ciones** : exception — **excepcional** *adj* : exceptional

excepto *prep* : except (for) — **exceptuar** {3} *vt* : exclude, except

exceso *nm* **1** : excess **2 ~ de velocidad** : speeding — **excesivo, -va** *adj* : excessive

excitar *vt* : excite, arouse — **excitarse** *vr* : get excited — **excitable** *adj* : excitable — **excitación** *nf, pl* **-ciones** : excitement, agitation, arousal — **excitante** *adj* : exciting

exclamar *v* : exclaim — **exclamación** *nf, pl* **-ciones** : exclamation

excluir {41} *vt* : exclude — **exclusión** *nf, pl* **-siones** : exclusion — **exclusivo, -va** *adj* : exclusive

excomulgar {52} *vt* : excommunicate — **excomunión** *nf, pl* **-niones** : excommunication

excremento *nm* : excrement

exculpar *vt* : exonerate

excursión *nf, pl* **-siones** : excursion — **excursionista** *nmf* **1** : tourist, sightseer **2** : hiker

excusar *vt* **1** : excuse **2** EXIMIR : exempt — **excusarse** *vr* : apologize — **excusa** *nf* **1** : excuse **2** DISCULPA : apology

exento, -ta *adj* : exempt

exequias *nfpl* : funeral rites

exhalar *vt* **1** : exhale **2** : give off (an odor, etc.)

exhaustivo, -va *adj* : exhaustive — **exhausto, -ta** *adj* : exhausted, worn-out

exhibir *vt* : exhibit, show — **exhibición** *nf, pl* **-ciones** : exhibition

exhortar *vt* : exhort, admonish

exigir {35} *vt* : demand, require — **exigencia** *nf* : demand, requirement — **exigente** *adj* : demanding

exiguo, -gua *adj* : meager

exiliar *vt* : exile — **exiliarse** *vr* : go into exile — **exiliado, -da** *adj* : exiled, in exile — **~** *n* : exile — **exilio** *nm* : exile

eximir *vt* : exempt

existir *vi* : exist — **existencia** *nf* **1** : existence **2 ~s** *nfpl* MERCANCÍA : goods, stock — **existente** *adj* : existing

éxito *nm* **1** : success, hit **2 tener ~** : be successful — **exitoso, -sa** *adj Lat* : successful

éxodo *nm* : exodus

exorbitante *adj* : exorbitant

exorcizar {21} *vt* : exorcize — **exorcismo** *nm* : exorcism

exótico, -ca *adj* : exotic

expandir *vt* : expand — **expandirse** *vr* : spread — **expansión** *nf, pl* **-siones** : expansion — **expansivo, -va** *adj* : expansive

expatriarse {85} *vr* **1** : emigrate **2** EXILIARSE : go into exile — **expatriado, -da** *adj & n* : expatriate

expectativa *nf* **1** : expectation, hope **2 ~s** *nfpl* : prospects

expedición *nf, pl* **-ciones** : expedition

expediente *nm* **1** : expedient **2** DOCUMENTOS : file, record **3** INVESTIGACIÓN : inquiry, proceedings

expedir {54} *vt* **1** : issue **2** ENVIAR : dispatch — **expedito, -ta** *adj* : free, clear

expeler *vt* : expel, eject

expendedor, -dora *n* : dealer, seller

expensas *nfpl* **1** : expenses **2 a ~ de** : at the expense of

experiencia *nf* : experience

experimentar *vi* : experiment — *vt* **1** : experiment with, test out **2** SENTIR : experience, feel — **experimentado, -da** *adj* : experienced — **experimental** *adj* : experimental — **experimento** *nm* : experiment

experto, -ta *adj & n* : expert

expiar {85} *vt* : atone for

expirar *vi* **1** : expire **2** MORIR : die

explayar *vt* : extend — **explayarse** *vr* **1** : spread out **2** HABLAR : speak at length

explicar {72} *vt* : explain — **explicarse** *vr* : understand — **explicación** *nf, pl* **-ciones** : explanation — **explicativo, -va** *adj* : explanatory

explícito, -ta *adj* : explicit

explorar *vt* : explore — **exploración** *nf, pl* **-ciones** : exploration — **explorador, -dora** *n* : explorer, scout — **exploratorio, -ria** *adj* : exploratory

explosión *nf, pl* **-siones 1** : explosion **2** : outburst (of anger, laughter, etc.) — **explosivo, -va** *adj* : explosive — **explosivo** *nm* : explosive

explotar *vt* **1** : exploit **2** : operate, run (a factory, etc.), work (a mine) — *vi* : explode — **explotación** *nf, pl* **-ciones 1** : exploitation **2** : running (of a business), working (of a mine)

exponer {60} *vt* **1** : expose **2** : explain, set out (ideas, theories, etc.) **3** EXHIBIR : exhibit, display — *vi* : exhibit — **exponerse** *vr* **~ a** : expose oneself to

exportar *vt* : export — **exportaciones** *nfpl* : exports — **exportador, -dora** *n* : exporter

exposición *nf, pl* **-ciones 1** : exposure **2** : exhibition (of objects, art, etc.) **3** : exposition, setting out (of ideas, etc.) — **expositor, -tora** *n* **1** : exhibitor **2** : exponent (of a theory, etc.)

exprés *nms & pl* **1** : express (train) **2** *or* **café ~** : espresso

expresamente *adv* : expressly, on purpose

expresar *vt* : express — **expresarse** *vr* : ex-

press oneself — **expresión** *nf, pl* **-siones** : expression — **expresivo, -va** *adj* **1** : expressive **2** CARIÑOSO : affectionate
expreso, -sa *adj* : express — **expreso** *nm* : express train, express
exprimir *vt* **1** : squeeze **2** EXPLOTAR : exploit — **exprimidor** *nm* : squeezer, juicer
expuesto, -ta *adj* **1** : exposed **2** PELIGROSO : risky, dangerous
expulsar *vt* : expel, eject — **expulsión** *nf, pl* **-siones** : expulsion
exquisito, -ta *adj* **1** : exquisite **2** RICO : delicious — **exquisitez** *nf* **1** : exquisiteness **2** : delicacy, special dish
éxtasis *nms & pl* : ecstasy — **extático, -ta** *adj* : ecstatic
extender {56} *vt* **1** : spread out **2** : draw up (a document), write out (a check) — **extenderse** *vr* **1** : extend, spread **2** DURAR : last — **extendido, -da** *adj* **1** : widespread **2** : outstretched (of arms, wings, etc.)
extensamente *adv* : extensively
extensión *nf, pl* **-siones 1** : extension **2** AMPLITUD : expanse **3** ALCANCE : range, extent — **extenso, -sa** *adj* : extensive
extenuar {3} *vt* : exhaust, tire out
exterior *adj* **1** : exterior, external **2** EXTRANJERO : foreign — ~ *nm* **1** : outside **2 en el ~** : abroad — **exteriorizar** {21} *vt* : show, reveal — **exteriormente** *adv* : outwardly, externally
exterminar *vt* : exterminate — **exterminación** *nf, pl* **-ciones** : extermination — **exterminio** *nm* : extermination
externo, -na *adj* : external
extinguir {26} *vt* **1** : extinguish (a fire) **2** : put an end to, wipe out — **extinguirse** *vr* **1** : go out (of fire, light, etc.) **2** : become extinct — **extinción** *nf, pl* **-ciones** : extinction — **extinguidor** *nm Lat* : fire extinguisher — **extinto, -ta** *adj* : extinct — **extintor** *nm* : fire extinguisher
extirpar *vt* : remove, eradicate
extorsión *nf, pl* **-siones 1** : extortion **2** MOLESTIA : trouble
extra *adv* : extra — ~ *adj* **1** ADICIONAL : additional **2** : top-quality — ~ *nmf* : extra (in movies) — ~ *nm* : extra (expense)
extraditar *vt* : extradite
extraer {81} *vt* : extract — **extracción** *nf, pl* **-ciones** : extraction — **extracto** *nm* **1** : extract **2** RESUMEN : abstract, summary
extranjero, -ra *adj* : foreign — ~ *n* : foreigner — **extranjero** *nm* : foreign countries *pl*
extrañar *vt* : miss (someone) — **extrañarse** *vr* : be surprised — **extrañeza** *nf* : surprise — **extraño, -ña** *adj* **1** : foreign **2** RARO : strange, odd — ~ *n* : stranger
extraoficial *adj* : unofficial
extraordinario, -ria *adj* : extraordinary
extrasensorial *adj* : extrasensory
extraterrestre *adj & nmf* : extraterrestrial
extravagante *adj* : extravagant, outrageous — **extravagancia** *nf* : extravagance, outlandishness
extraviar {85} *vt* : lose, misplace — **extraviarse** *vr* : get lost — **extravío** *nm* : loss
extremar *vt* : carry to extremes — **extremarse** *vr* : do one's utmost — **extremadamente** *adv* : extremely — **extremado, -da** *adj* : extreme — **extremidad** *nf* **1** : tip, end **2 ~es** *nfpl* : extremities — **extremista** *adj & nmf* : extremist — **extremo, -ma** *adj* **1** : extreme **2 en caso ~** : as a last resort — **extremo** *nm* **1** : end **2 en ~** : in the extreme, extremely **3 en último ~** : as a last resort
extrovertido -da *adj* : extroverted — ~ *n* : extrovert
exuberante *adj* : exuberant — **exuberancia** *nf* : exuberance
exudar *vt* : exude
eyacular *vi* : ejaculate — **eyaculación** *nf, pl* **-ciones** : ejaculation

F

f *nf* : f, sixth letter of the Spanish alphabet
fabricar {72} *vt* **1** : manufacture **2** CONSTRUIR : build, construct **3** INVENTAR : fabricate — **fábrica** *nf* : factory — **fabricación** *nf, pl* **-ciones** : manufacture — **fabricante** *nmf* : manufacturer
fábula *nf* **1** : fable **2** MENTIRA : story, lie
fabuloso, -sa *adj* : fabulous
facción *nf, pl* **-ciones 1** : faction **2 ~es** *nfpl* RASGOS : features
faceta *nf* : facet
facha *nf* : appearance, look
fachada *nf* : façade
facial *adj* : facial
fácil *adj* **1** : easy **2** PROBABLE : likely — **fácilmente** *adv* : easily, readily — **facilidad** *nf* **1** : facility, ease **2 ~es** *nfpl* : facilities, services — **facilitar** *vt* **1** : facilitate **2** PROPORCIONAR : provide, supply
facsímil *or* **facsímile** *nm* **1** COPIA : facsimile, copy **2** : fax
factible *adj* : feasible
factor *nm* : factor
factoría *nf* : factory
factura *nf* **1** : bill, invoice **2** HECHURA : making, manufacture — **facturar** *vt* **1** : bill for **2** : check in (baggage, etc.)
facultad *nf* **1** : faculty, ability **2** AUTORIDAD : authority **3** : school (of a university) — **facultativo, -va** *adj* : optional
faena *nf* **1** : task, job **2 ~s domésticas** : housework
fagot *nm* : bassoon
faisán *nm, pl* **-sanes** : pheasant
faja *nf* **1** : sash **2** : girdle, corset **3** : strip (of land)
fajo *nm* : bundle, sheaf
falda *nf* **1** : skirt **2** : side, slope (of a mountain)
falible *adj* : fallible
fálico, -ca *adj* : phallic
fallar *vi* : fail, go wrong — *vt* **1** : pronounce judgment on **2** ERRAR : miss — **falla** *nf* **1** : flaw, defect **2** : (geological) fault
fallecer {53} *vi* : pass away, die — **fallecimiento** *nm* : demise, death
fallido, -da *adj* : failed, unsuccessful
fallo *nm* **1** : error **2** SENTENCIA : sentence, verdict
falo *nm* : phallus, penis
falsear *vt* : falsify, distort — **falsedad** *nf* **1** : falseness **2** MENTIRA : falsehood, lie — **falsificación** *nf, pl* **-ciones** : forgery, fake — **falsificador, -dora** *n* : forger — **falsificar** {72} *vt* **1** : counterfeit, forge **2** ALTERAR : falsify — **falso, -sa** *adj* **1** : false, untrue **2** FALSIFICADO : counterfeit, forged
falta *nf* **1** CARENCIA : lack **2** DEFECTO : defect, fault, error **3** AUSENCIA : absence **4** : offense, misdemeanor (in law) **5** : foul (in sports) **6 hacer ~** : be lacking, be needed **7 sin ~** : without fail — **faltar** *vi* **1** : be lacking, be needed **2** : be missing **3** QUEDAR : remain, be left **4 ¡no faltaba más!** : don't mention it! — **falto, -ta** *adj* **~ de** : lacking (in)
fama *nf* **1** : fame **2** REPUTACIÓN : reputation
famélico, -ca *adj* : starving
familia *nf* : family — **familiar** *adj* **1** : familial, family **2** CONOCIDO : familiar **3** : informal (of language, etc.) — ~ *nmf* : relation, relative — **familiaridad** *nf* : familiarity — **familiarizarse** {21} *vr* **~ con** : familiarize oneself with
famoso, -sa *adj* : famous
fanático, -ca *adj* : fanatic, fanatical — ~ *n* : fanatic — **fanatismo** *nm* : fanaticism
fanfarria *nf* : fanfare
fanfarrón, -rrona *adj, mpl* **-rrones** *fam* : boastful — ~ *n fam* : braggart — **fanfarronear** *vi* : boast, brag
fango *nm* : mud, mire — **fangoso, -sa** *adj* : muddy
fantasear *vi* : fantasize, daydream — **fantasía** *nf* **1** : fantasy **2** IMAGINACIÓN : imagination
fantasma *nm* : ghost, phantom — **fantasmal** *adj* : ghostly
fantástico, -ca *adj* : fantastic
fardo *nm* : bundle
farfullar *v* : jabber, gabble
farmacéutico, -ca *adj* : pharmaceutical — ~ *n* : pharmacist — **farmacia** *nf* : drugstore, pharmacy
faro *nm* **1** : lighthouse **2** : headlight (of an automobile) — **farol** *nm* **1** LINTERNA : lantern **2** FAROLA : streetlight — **farola** *nf* **1** : lamppost **2** FAROL : streetlight
farsa *nf* : farce — **farsante** *nmf* : charlatan, fraud
fascículo *nm* : installment, part (of a publication)
fascinar *vt* : fascinate — **fascinación** *nf, pl* **-ciones** : fascination — **fascinante** *adj* : fascinating
fascismo *nm* : fascism — **fascista** *adj & nmf* : fascist
fase *nf* : phase
fastidiar *vt* : annoy, bother — *vi* : be annoying or bothersome — **fastidio** *nm* : annoyance — **fastidioso, -sa** *adj* : annoying, bothersome
fatal *adj* **1** : fateful **2** MORTAL : fatal **3** *fam* : awful, terrible — **fatalidad** *nf* **1** : fate, destiny **2** DESGRACIA : misfortune
fatídico, -ca *adj* : fateful, momentous
fatiga *nf* : fatigue — **fatigado, -da** *adj* : weary, tired — **fatigar** {52} *vt* : tire — **fatigarse** *vr* : get tired — **fatigoso, -sa** *adj* : fatiguing, tiring
fatuo, -tua *adj* **1** : fatuous **2** PRESUMIDO : conceited
fauna *nf* : fauna
favor *nm* **1** : favor **2 a ~ de** : in favor of **3 por ~** : please — **favorable** *adj* **1** : favorable **2 ser ~ a** : be in favor of — **favorecedor, -dora** *adj* : flattering — **favorecer** {53} *vt* **1** AYUDAR : favor **2** : look well on, suit — **favoritismo** *nm* : favoritism — **favorito, -ta** *adj & n* : favorite
fax *nm* : fax — **faxear** *vt* : fax
faz *nf, pl* **faces** : face, countenance
fe *nf* **1** : faith **2 dar ~ de** : bear witness to **3 de buena ~** : in good faith
fealdad *nf* : ugliness
febrero *nm* : February
febril *adj* : feverish
fecha *nf* **1** : date **2 ~ de caducidad** *or* **~ de vencimiento** : expiration date **3 ~ límite** : deadline — **fechar** *vt* : date, put a date on
fechoría *nf* : misdeed
fécula *nf* : starch (in food)
fecundar *vt* **1** : fertilize (an egg) **2** : make fertile — **fecundo, -da** *adj* : fertile
federación *nf, pl* **-ciones** : federation — **federal** *adj* : federal
felicidad *nf* **1** : happiness **2 ¡~es!** : best wishes!, congratulations!, happy birthday! — **felicitación** *nf, pl* **-ciones** : congratulation — **felicitar** *vt* : congratulate — **felicitarse** *vr* **~ de** : be glad about
feligrés, -gresa *n, mpl* **-greses** : parishioner
felino, -na *adj & n* : feline
feliz *adj, pl* **-lices 1** : happy **2** AFORTUNADO : fortunate **3 Feliz Navidad** : Merry Christmas
felpa *nf* **1** : plush **2** : terry cloth (for towels, etc.)
felpudo *nm* : doormat
femenino, -na *adj* **1** : feminine **2** : female (in biology) — **femenino** *nm* : feminine (in grammar) — **femineidad** *nf* : femininity — **feminismo** *nm* : feminism — **feminista** *adj & nmf* : feminist
fenómeno *nm* : phenomenon — **fenomenal** *adj* **1** : phenomenal **2** *fam* : fantastic, terrific
feo, fea *adj* **1** : ugly **2** DESAGRADABLE : unpleasant, nasty
féretro *nm* : coffin
feria *nf* **1** : fair, market **2** FIESTA : festival, holiday **3** *Lat fam* : small change — **feriado, -da** *adj* **día feriado** : public holiday
fermentar *v* : ferment — **fermentación** *nf, pl* **-ciones** : fermentation — **fermento** *nm* : ferment
feroz *adj, pl* **-roces** : ferocious, fierce — **ferocidad** *nf* : ferocity, fierceness
férreo, -rrea *adj* **1** : iron **2 vía férrea** : railroad track
ferretería *nf* : hardware store
ferrocarril *nm* : railroad, railway — **ferroviario, -ria** *adj* : rail, railroad
ferry *nm, pl* **ferrys** : ferry
fértil *adj* : fertile, fruitful — **fertilidad** *nf* : fertility — **fertilizante** *nm* : fertilizer — **fertilizar** *vt* : fertilize
fervor *nm* : fervor, zeal — **ferviente** *adj* : fervent
festejar *vt* **1** : celebrate **2** AGASAJAR : entertain, wine and dine — **festejo** *nm* : celebration, festivity
festín *nm, pl* **-tines** : banquet, feast
festival *nm* : festival — **festividad** *nf* : festivity — **festivo, -va** *adj* **1** : festive **2 día festivo** : holiday
fetiche *nm* : fetish
fétido, -da *adj* : foul-smelling, fetid
feto *nm* : fetus — **fetal** *adj* : fetal
feudal *adj* : feudal
fiable *adj* : reliable — **fiabilidad** *nf* : reliability
fiado, -da *adj* : on credit — **fiador, -dora** *n* : bondsman, guarantor
fiambres *nfpl* : cold cuts
fianza *nf* **1** : bail, bond **2 dar ~** : pay a deposit
fiar {85} *vt* **1** : guarantee **2** : sell on credit — *vi* **ser de ~** : be trustworthy — **fiarse** *vr* **~ de** : place trust in
fiasco *nm* : fiasco
fibra *nf* **1** : fiber **2 ~ de vidrio** : fiberglass
ficción *nf, pl* **-ciones** : fiction
ficha *nf* **1** : token **2** TARJETA : index card **3** : counter, chip (in games) — **fichar** *vt* : file, index — **fichero** *nm* **1** : card file **2** : filing cabinet
ficticio, -cia *adj* : fictitious
fidedigno, -na *adj* : reliable, trustworthy
fidelidad *nf* : fidelity, faithfulness
fideo *nm* : noodle
fiebre *nf* **1** : fever **2 ~ del heno** : hay fever **3 ~ palúdica** : malaria
fiel *adj* **1** : faithful, loyal **2** PRECISO : accurate, reliable — ~ *nm* **1** : pointer (of a scale) **2 los ~es** : the faithful — **fielmente** *adv* : faithfully
fieltro *nm* : felt
fiero, -ra *adj* : fierce, ferocious — **fiera** *nf* : wild animal, beast
fierro *nm Lat* : iron (bar)
fiesta *nf* **1** : party **2** DIA FESTIVO : holiday, feast day
figura *nf* **1** : figure **2** FORMA : shape, form — **figurar** *vi* **1** : figure (in), be included (among) **2** DESTACAR : stand out — *vt* : represent — **figurarse** *vr* : imagine
fijar *vt* **1** : fasten, affix **2** CONCRETAR : set, fix — **fijarse** *vr* **1** : settle **2 ~ en** : notice, pay attention to — **fijo, -ja** *adj* **1** : fixed, firm **2** PERMANENTE : permanent
fila *nf* **1** : line, file, row **2 ponerse en ~** : line up
filantropía *nf* : philanthropy — **filantrópico, -ca** *adj* : philanthropic — **filántropo, -pa** *n* : philanthropist
filatelia *nf* : philately, stamp collecting
filete *nm* : fillet
filial *adj* : filial — ~ *nf* : affiliate, subsidiary
filigrana *nf* **1** : filigree **2** : watermark (on paper)
filipino, -na *adj* : Filipino
filmar *vt* : film, shoot — **filme** *or* **film** *nm* : film, movie
filo *nm* **1** : edge **2 dar ~ a** : sharpen
filón *nm, pl* **-lones 1** : vein (of minerals) **2** *fam* : gold mine
filoso, -sa *adj Lat* : sharp
filosofía *nf* : philosophy — **filosófico, -ca** *adj* : philosophical — **filósofo, -fa** *n* : philosopher
filtrar *v* : filter — **filtrarse** *vr* : leak out, seep through — **filtro** *nm* : filter
fin *nm* **1** : end **2** OBJETIVO : purpose, aim **3 en ~** : well, in short **4 ~ de semana** : weekend **5 por ~** : finally, at last
final *adj* : final — ~ *nm* : end, conclusion — ~ *nf* : final (in sports) — **finalidad** *nf* : purpose, aim — **finalista** *nmf* : finalist — **finalizar** {21} *v* : finish, end — **finalmente** *adv* : finally
financiar *vt* : finance, fund — **financiero, -ra** *adj* : financial — ~ *n* : financier — **finanzas** *nfpl* : finance
finca *nf* **1** : farm, ranch **2** *Lat* : country house
fingir {35} *v* : feign, pretend — **fingido, -da** *adj* : false, feigned
finito, -ta *adj* : finite
finlandés, -desa *adj* : Finnish
fino, -na *adj* **1** : fine **2** DELGADO : slender **3** REFINADO : refined **4** AGUDO : sharp, keen — **finura** *nf* **1** : fineness **2** REFINAMIENTO : refinement
firma *nf* **1** : signature **2** : (act of) signing **3** EMPRESA : firm, company
firmamento *nm* : firmament, sky
firmar *v* : sign
firme *adj* **1** : firm, resolute **2** ESTABLE : steady, stable — **firmeza** *nf* **1** : strength, resolve **2** ESTABILIDAD : firmness, stability
fiscal *adj* : fiscal — ~ *nmf* : district attorney — **fisco** *nm* : (national) treasury
fisgar {52} *vt* : pry into — *vi* : pry — **fisgón, -gona** *n, mpl* **-gones** : snoop, busybody
física *nf* : physics — **físico, -ca** *adj* : physical — ~ *n* : physicist — **físico** *nm* : physique
fisiología *nf* : physiology — **fisiológico, -ca** *adj* : physiological — **fisiólogo, -ga** *n* : physiologist
fisioterapia *nf* : physical therapy — **fisioterapeuta** *nmf* : physical therapist
fisonomía *nf* : features *pl*, appearance
fisura *nf* : fissure
fláccido, -da *or* **flácido, -da** *adj* : flaccid, flabby
flaco, -ca *adj* **1** : thin, skinny **2** DÉBIL : weak
flagrante *adj* : flagrant
flamante *adj* **1** : bright, brilliant **2** NUEVO : brand-new
flamenco, -ca *adj* **1** : flamenco (of music or dance) **2** : Flemish — **flamenco** *nm* **1** : flamingo **2** : flamenco (music or dance)
flaquear *vi* : weaken, flag — **flaqueza** *nf* **1** : thinness **2** DEBILIDAD : weakness
flash *nm* : flash
flatulencia *nf* : flatulence
flauta *nf* **1** : flute **2 ~ dulce** : recorder — **flautín** *nm, pl* **-tines** : piccolo — **flautista** *nmf* : flutist
flecha *nf* : arrow
fleco *nm* **1** : fringe **2** *Lat* : bangs *pl*
flema *nf* : phlegm — **flemático, -ca** *adj* : phlegmatic
flequillo *nm* : bangs *pl*
fletar *vt* **1** : charter, rent **2** *Lat* : transport — **flete** *nm* **1** : charter **2** : shipping (charges) **3** *Lat* : transport, freight
flexible *adj* : flexible — **flexibilidad** *nf* : flexibility
flirtear *vi* : flirt
flojo, -ja *adj* **1** SUELTO : loose, slack **2** DÉBIL : weak **3** PEREZOSO : lazy — **flojera** *nf fam* : lethargy
flor *nf* : flower — **flora** *nf* : flora — **floral** *adj* : floral — **floreado, -da** *adj* : flowered — **florear** *vi Lat* : flower, bloom — **florecer** {53} *vi* **1** : bloom, blossom **2** PROSPERAR : flourish — **floreciente** *adj* : flourishing — **florero** *nm* : vase — **florido, -da** *adj* : flowery — **florista** *nmf* : florist — **floritura** *nf* : frill, flourish
flota *nf* : fleet
flotar *vi* : float — **flotador** *nm* **1** : float **2** : life preserver (for a swimmer) — **flotante** *adj* : floating, buoyant — **flote: a ~** *adv phr* : afloat
flotilla *nf* : flotilla, fleet
fluctuar {3} *vi* : fluctuate — **fluctuación** *nf, pl* **-ciones** : fluctuation
fluir {41} *vi* : flow — **fluidez** *nf* **1** : fluidity **2** : fluency (of language, etc.) — **fluido, -da** *adj* **1** : fluid **2** : fluent (of language) — **fluido** *nm* : fluid — **flujo** *nm* : flow
fluorescente *adj* : fluorescent
fluoruro *nm* : fluoride
fluvial *adj* : river
fobia *nf* : phobia
foca *nf* : seal (animal)

foco nm 1 : focus 2 : spotlight, floodlight (in theater, etc.) 3 Lat : lightbulb
fofo, -fa adj : flabby
fogata nf : bonfire
fogón nm, pl -gones : burner
fogoso, -sa adj : ardent
folklore nm : folklore — **folklórico, -ca** adj : folk, traditional
follaje nm : foliage
folleto nm : pamphlet, leaflet
fomentar vt : promote, encourage — **fomento** nm : promotion, encouragement
fonda nf : boarding house
fondear vt : sound out, examine — vi : anchor
fondillos nmpl : seat (of pants, etc.)
fondo nm 1 : bottom 2 : rear, back, end 3 PROFUNDIDAD : depth 4 : background (of a painting, etc.) 5 Lat : slip, petticoat 6 ~s nmpl : funds, resources 7 a ~ : thoroughly, in depth 8 en el ~ : deep down
fonético, -ca adj : phonetic — **fonética** nf : phonetics
fontanería nf Spain : plumbing — **fontanero, -ra** n Spain : plumber
footing ['fu,tɪŋ] nm 1 : jogging 2 hacer ~ : jog
forajido, -da n : bandit, outlaw
foráneo, -nea adj : foreign, strange
forastero, -ra n : stranger, outsider
forcejear vi : struggle — **forcejeo** nm : struggle
forense adj : forensic
forja nf : forge — **forjar** vt 1 : forge 2 CREAR, FORMAR : build up, create
forma nf 1 : form, shape 2 MANERA : manner, way 3 en ~ : fit, healthy 4 ~s nfpl : appearances, conventions — **formación** nf, pl -ciones 1 : formation 2 EDUCACIÓN : training
formal adj 1 : formal 2 SERIO : serious 3 FIABLE : dependable, reliable — **formalidad** nf 1 : formality 2 SERIEDAD : seriousness 3 FIABILIDAD : reliability
formar vt 1 : form, shape 2 CONSTITUIR : constitute 3 EDUCAR : train, educate — **formarse** vr 1 DESARROLLARSE : develop, take shape 2 EDUCARSE : be educated
formato nm : format
formidable adj 1 : tremendous 2 fam : fantastic, terrific
fórmula nf : formula
formular vt 1 : formulate, draw up 2 : make, lodge (a complaint, etc.)
formulario nm : form
fornido, -da adj : well-built, burly
foro nm : forum
forraje nm : forage, fodder — **forrajear** vi : forage
forrar vt 1 : line (a garment) 2 : cover (a book) — **forro** nm 1 : lining 2 CUBIERTA : book cover
fortalecer {53} vt : strengthen — **fortaleza** nf 1 : fortress 2 FUERZA : strength 3 : (moral) fortitude
fortificar {72} vt : fortify — **fortificación** nf, pl -ciones : fortification
fortuito, -ta adj : fortuitous, chance
fortuna nf 1 SUERTE : fortune, luck 2 RIQUEZA : wealth, fortune 3 por ~ : fortunately
forzar {36} vt 1 : force 2 : strain (one's eyes) — **forzosamente** adv : necessarily — **forzoso, -sa** adj : necessary, inevitable
fosa nf 1 : pit, ditch 2 TUMBA : grave 3 ~s nasales : nostrils
fósforo nm 1 : phosphorus 2 CERILLA : match — **fosforescente** adj : phosphorescent
fósil nm : fossil
foso nm 1 : ditch 2 : pit (of a theater) 3 : moat (of a castle)
foto nf : photo
fotocopia nf : photocopy — **fotocopiadora** nf : photocopier — **fotocopiar** vt : photocopy
fotogénico, -ca adj : photogenic
fotografía nf 1 : photography 2 : photograph, picture — **fotografiar** {85} vt : photograph — **fotográfico, -ca** adj : photographic — **fotógrafo, -fa** n : photographer
fotosíntesis nf : photosynthesis
fracasar vi : fail — **fracaso** nm : failure
fracción nf, pl -ciones 1 : fraction 2 : faction (in politics) — **fraccionamiento** nm Lat : housing development
fractura nf : fracture — **fracturarse** vr : fracture, break (a bone)
fragancia nf : fragrance, scent — **fragante** adj : fragrant
fragata nf : frigate
frágil adj 1 : fragile 2 DÉBIL : frail, delicate — **fragilidad** nf 1 : fragility 2 DEBILIDAD : frailty
fragmento nm : fragment
fragor nm : clamor, din
fragoso, -sa adj : rough, rugged
fragua nf : forge — **fraguar** {10} vt 1 : forge 2 IDEAR : concoct — vi : harden, solidify
fraile nm : friar, monk
frambuesa nf : raspberry
francés, -cesa adj, mpl -ceses : French — **francés** nm : French (language)
franco, -ca adj 1 : frank, candid 2 : free (in commerce) — **franco** nm : franc
francotirador, -dora n : sniper
franela nf : flannel
franja nf 1 : stripe, band 2 FLECO : fringe
franquear vt 1 : clear (a path, etc.) 2 : cross over (a doorstep, etc.) 3 : pay postage on (mail) — **franqueo** nm : postage
franqueza nf : frankness
frasco nm : small bottle, vial, flask
frase nf 1 : phrase 2 ORACIÓN : sentence
fraternal adj : brotherly, fraternal — **fraternidad** nf : brotherhood, fraternity — **fraternizar** {21} vi : fraternize — **fraterno, -na** adj : brotherly, fraternal
fraude nm : fraud — **fraudulento, -ta** adj : fraudulent
fray nm (used in titles) : brother, friar
frazada nf Lat : blanket
frecuencia nf 1 : frequency 2 con ~ : often, frequently — **frecuentar** vt : frequent, haunt — **frecuente** adj : frequent
fregadero nm : kitchen sink
fregar {49} vt 1 : scrub, wash 2 Lat fam : annoy — vi Lat fam : be a pest
freír {37} vt : fry
fregona nf Spain : mop
frenar vt 1 : brake 2 RESTRINGIR : curb, check
frenesí nm : frenzy — **frenético, -ca** adj : frantic, frenzied
freno nm 1 : brake 2 : bit (of a bridle) 3 CONTROL : check, restraint
frente nm 1 : front 2 : facade (of a building) 3 al ~ de : at the head of 4 ~ a : opposite 5 de ~ : (facing) forward 6 hacer ~ a : face up to, brave — ~ nf : forehead
fresa nf : strawberry
fresco, -ca adj 1 : fresh 2 FRÍO : cool 3 fam : insolent, nervy — **fresco** nm 1 : fresh air 2 FRESCOR : coolness 3 : fresco (art or painting) — **frescor** nm : coolness, cool air — **frescura** nf 1 : freshness 2 FRÍO : coolness 3 fam : nerve, insolence
fresno nm : ash (tree)
frialdad nf 1 : coldness 2 INDIFERENCIA : indifference
fricción nf, pl -ciones 1 : friction 2 MASAJE : rubbing, massage — **friccionar** vt : rub
frigidez nf : frigidity
frigorífico nm Spain : refrigerator
frijol nm Lat : bean
frío, fría adj 1 : cold 2 INDIFERENTE : cool, indifferent — **frío** nm 1 : cold 2 INDIFERENCIA : coldness, indifference 3 hacer ~ : be cold (outside) 4 tener ~ : be cold, feel cold
frito, -ta adj 1 : fried 2 fam : fed up
frívolo, -la adj : frivolous — **frivolidad** nf : frivolity
fronda nf 1 : frond 2 or ~s nfpl : foliage — **frondoso, -sa** adj : leafy
frontera nf : border, frontier — **fronterizo, -za** adj : border, on the border — **frontero, -ra** adj : facing, opposite
frotar vt : rub — **frotarse** vr ~ las manos : rub one's hands
fructífero, -ra adj : fruitful
frugal adj : frugal, thrifty — **frugalidad** nf : frugality
fruncir {83} vt 1 : gather (in pleats) 2 ~ el ceño : frown 3 ~ la boca : purse one's lips
frustrar vt : frustrate — **frustrarse** vr : fail — **frustración** nf, pl -ciones : frustration — **frustrado, -da** adj 1 : frustrated 2 FRACASADO : failed, unsuccessful — **frustrante** adj : frustrating
fruta nf : fruit — **frutilla** nf Lat : strawberry — **fruto** nm 1 : fruit 2 RESULTADO : result, consequence
fucsia adj & nm : fuchsia
fuego nm 1 : fire 2 : flame, burner (on a stove) 3 ~s artificiales nmpl : fireworks 4 ¿tienes fuego? : have you got a light?
fuelle nm : bellows
fuente nf 1 : fountain 2 MANANTIAL : spring 3 ORIGEN : source 4 PLATO : platter, serving dish
fuera adv 1 : outside, out 2 : abroad, away 3 ~ de : outside of, beyond 4 ~ de : aside from, in addition to
fuerte adj 1 : strong 2 : bright (of colors), loud (of sounds) 3 EXTREMO : intense 4 DURO : hard — ~ adv 1 : strongly, hard 2 : loudly 3 MUCHO : abundantly, a lot — ~ nm 1 : fort 2 ESPECIALIDAD : strong point
fuerza nf 1 : strength 2 VIOLENCIA : force 3 PODER : power, might 4 ~s armadas nfpl : armed forces 5 a ~ de : by dint of 6 a la ~ : necessarily
fuga nf 1 : flight, escape 2 : fugue (in music) 3 ESCAPE : leak — **fugarse** {52} vr : flee, run away — **fugaz** adj, pl -gaces : fleeting — **fugitivo, -va** adj & n : fugitive
fulano, -na n : so-and-so, what's-his-name, what's-her-name
fulgor nm : brilliance, splendor
fulminar vt 1 : strike with lightning 2 : strike down (with an illness, etc.) — **fulminante** adj : devastating
fumar v : smoke — **fumarse** vr 1 : smoke 2 fam : squander — **fumador, -dora** n : smoker
funámbulo, -la n : tightrope walker
función nf, pl -ciones 1 : function 2 TRABAJOS : duties pl 3 : performance, show (in theater) — **funcional** adj : functional — **funcionamiento** nm 1 : functioning 2 en ~ : in operation — **funcionar** vi 1 : function, run, work 2 no funciona : out of order — **funcionario, -ria** n : civil servant, official
funda nf 1 : cover, sheath 2 or ~ de almohada : pillowcase
fundar vt 1 ESTABLECER : found, establish 2 BASAR : base — **fundarse** vr ~ en : be based on — **fundación** nf, pl -ciones : foundation — **fundador, -dora** n : founder — **fundamental** adj : fundamental, basic — **fundamentalmente** adv : basically — **fundamentar** vt 1 : lay the foundations for 2 BASAR : base — **fundamento** nm 1 : foundation 2 ~s nmpl : fundamentals
fundir vt 1 : melt down, smelt 2 FUSIONAR : fuse, merge — **fundirse** vr 1 : blend, merge 2 DERRETIRSE : melt 3 : burn out (of a lightbulb) — **fundición** nf, pl -ciones 1 : smelting 2 : foundry
fúnebre adj 1 : funeral 2 LÚGUBRE : gloomy
funeral adj : funeral, funerary — ~ nm 1 : funeral 2 ~es nmpl EXEQUIAS : funeral (rites) — **funeraria** nf : funeral home
funesto, ta adj : terrible, disastrous
fungir {35} vi Lat : act, function
furgón nm, pl -gones 1 : van, truck 2 : freight car (of a train) 3 ~ de cola : caboose — **furgoneta** nf : van
furia nf 1 CÓLERA : fury, rage 2 VIOLENCIA : violence — **furibundo, -da** adj : furious — **furioso, -sa** adj 1 : furious, irate 2 INTENSO : intense, violent — **furor** nm : fury
furtivo, -va adj : furtive
furúnculo nm : boil
fuselaje nm : fuselage
fusible nm : fuse
fusil nm : rifle — **fusilar** vt : shoot (by firing squad)
fusión nf, pl -siones 1 : fusion 2 UNIÓN : union, merger — **fusionar** vt 1 : fuse 2 UNIR : merge — **fusionarse** vr : merge
futbol or **fútbol** nm 1 : soccer 2 ~ americano : football — **futbolista** nmf : soccer player, football player
fútil adj : trifling, trivial
futuro, -ra adj : future — **futuro** nm : future

G

g nf : g, seventh letter of the Spanish alphabet
gabán nm, pl -banes : topcoat, overcoat
gabardina nf 1 : trench coat, raincoat 2 : gabardine (fabric)
gabinete nm 1 : cabinet (in government) 2 : (professional) office
gacela nf : gazelle
gaceta nf : gazette
gachas nfpl : porridge
gacho, -cha adj : drooping
gaélico, -ca adj : Gaelic
gafas nfpl 1 : eyeglasses 2 ~ de sol : sunglasses
gaita nf : bagpipes pl
gajo nm : segment (of fruit)
gala nf 1 : gala 2 de ~ : formal 3 hacer ~ de : display, show off 4 ~s nfpl : finery
galáctico, -ca adj : galactic
galán nm, pl -lanes 1 : leading man (in theater) 2 fam : boyfriend
galante adj : gallant — **galantear** vt : court, woo — **galantería** nf 1 : gallantry 2 CUMPLIDO : compliment
galápago nm : (aquatic) turtle
galardón nm, pl -dones : reward
galaxia nf : galaxy
galera nf : galley
galería nf 1 : corridor 2 : gallery, balcony (in a theater)
galés, -lesa adj, mpl -leses : Welsh
galgo nm : greyhound
galimatías nms & pl : gibberish
gallardía nf 1 : bravery 2 ELEGANCIA : elegance — **gallardo, -da** adj 1 : brave 2 APUESTO : elegant, good-looking
gallego, -ga adj : Galician
galleta nf 1 : (sweet) cookie 2 : (salted) cracker
gallina nf 1 : hen 2 ~ de Guinea : guinea fowl — **gallinero** nm : henhouse, (chicken) coop — **gallo** nm : rooster, cock
galón nm, pl -lones 1 : gallon 2 : stripe (military insignia)
galopar vi : gallop — **galope** nm : gallop
galvanizar {21} vt : galvanize
gama nf 1 : range, spectrum 2 : scale (in music)
gamba nf : large shrimp, prawn
gamuza nf 1 : chamois (animal) 2 : chamois (leather), suede
gana nf 1 : desire, wish 2 APETITO : appetite 3 de buena ~ : willingly, heartily 4 de mala ~ : unwillingly 5 no me da la ~ : I don't feel like it 6 tener ~s de : feel like, be in the mood for
ganado nm 1 : cattle pl, livestock 2 ~ ovino : sheep pl 3 ~ porcino : swine pl — **ganadería** nf 1 : cattle raising 2 GANADO : livestock
ganador, -dora adj : winning — ~ n : winner
ganancia nf : profit
ganar vt 1 : earn 2 : win (in games, etc.) 3 CONSEGUIR : gain 4 ADQUERIR : get, obtain 5 ~ a algn : win over s.o., beat s.o. — vi : win — **ganarse** vr 1 : win, gain 2 ~ la vida : make a living
gancho nm 1 : hook 2 HORQUILLA : hairpin 3 Lat : (clothes) hanger
gandul, -dula adj & n fam : good-for-nothing — **gandul** nm Lat : pigeon pea
ganga nf : bargain
gangrena nf : gangrene
gángster nmf : gangster
ganso, -sa n : goose, gander m — **gansada** nf : silly thing, nonsense
gañir {38} vi : yelp — **gañido** nm : yelp
garabatear v : scribble — **garabato** nm : scribble
garaje nm : garage
garantizar {21} vt : guarantee — **garante** nmf : guarantor — **garantía** nf 1 : guarantee, warranty 2 FIANZA : surety
garapiñar vt : candy (fruits, etc.)
garbanzo nm : chickpea, garbanzo
garbo nm : grace, elegance — **garboso, -sa** adj : graceful, elegant
gardenia nf : gardenia
garfio nm : hook, gaff
garganta nf 1 : throat 2 CUELLO : neck 3 DESFILADERO : ravine, gorge — **gargantilla** nf : necklace
gárgara nf 1 : gargling, gargle 2 hacer ~s : gargle
gárgola nf : gargoyle
garita nf 1 : sentry box 2 CABAÑA : cabin, hut
garito nm : gambling den
garra nf 1 : claw, talon 2 fam : hand, paw
garrafa nf : decanter, carafe — **garrafón** nm, pl -fones : large decanter or bottle
garrapata nf : tick
garrocha nf 1 : lance, pike 2 Lat : pole (in sports)
garrote nm : club, cudgel
garúa nf Lat : drizzle
garza nf : heron
gas nm 1 : gas 2 ~ lacrimógeno : tear gas
gasa nf : gauze
gaseosa nf : soda, soft drink
gasolina nf : gasoline, gas — **gasoil** or **gasóleo** nm : diesel fuel — **gasolinera** nf : gas station, service station
gastar vt 1 : spend 2 CONSUMIR : consume, use up 3 DESPERDICIAR : squander, waste — **gastarse** vr 1 : spend 2 DETERIORARSE : wear out — **gastado, -da** adj 1 : spent 2 : worn-out (of clothing, etc.) — **gastador, -dora** n : spendthrift — **gasto** nm 1 : expense, expenditure 2 ~s generales : overhead
gástrico, -ca adj : gastric
gastronomía nf : gastronomy — **gastrónomo, -ma** n : gourmet
gatas: a ~ adv phr : on all fours
gatear vi : crawl, creep
gatillo nm : trigger — **gatillero** nm Mex : gunman
gato, -ta n : cat — **gatito, -ta** n : kitten — **gato** nm : jack (for an automobile)
gaucho nm : gaucho
gaveta nf : drawer
gavilla nf 1 : sheaf 2 PANDILLA : gang
gaviota nf : gull, seagull
gay ['ge, 'gai] adj : gay (homosexual)
gaza nf : loop
gazpacho nm : gazpacho
géiser nm : geyser
gelatina nf : gelatin
gema nf : gem
gemelo, -la adj & n : twin — **gemelo** nm 1 : cuff link 2 ~s nmpl : binoculars
gemir {54} vi : moan, groan, whine — **gemido** nm : moan, groan, whine
gen or **gene** nm : gene
genealogía nf : genealogy — **genealógico, -ca** adj : genealogical
generación nf, pl -ciones : generation
generador nm : generator
general adj 1 : general 2 en ~ or por lo ~ : in general, generally — ~ nmf : general — **generalidad** nf 1 : generalization 2 MAYORÍA : majority — **generalizar** {21} vi : generalize — vt : spread (out) — **generalizarse** vr : become widespread — **generalmente** adv : usually, generally
generar vt : generate
género nm 1 : kind, sort 2 : gender (in grammar) 3 ~ humano : human race — **genérico, -ca** adj : generic
generoso, -sa adj 1 : generous, unselfish 2 : ample (in quantity) — **generosidad** nf : generosity
génesis nfs & pl : genesis
genética nf : genetics — **genético, -ca** adj : genetic

genial *adj* 1 : brilliant 2 ESTUPENDO : great, terrific

genio *nm* 1 : genius 2 CARÁCTER : temper, disposition 3 : genie (in mythology)

genital *adj* : genital — **genitales** *nmpl* : genitals

genocidio *nm* : genocide

gente *nf* 1 : people 2 *fam* : relatives *pl*, folks *pl* 3 **ser buena ~** : be nice, be kind

gentil *adj* 1 AMABLE : kind 2 : gentile (in religion) — **gentileza** *nf* : kindness, courtesy

gentío *nm* : crowd, mob

gentuza *nf* : riffraff, rabble

genuflexión *nf, pl* **-xiones** : genuflection

genuino, -na *adj* : genuine

geografía *nf* : geography — **geográfico, -ca** *adj* : geographic, geographical

geología *nf* : geology — **geológico, -ca** *adj* : geologic, geological

geometría *nf* : geometry — **geométrico, -ca** *adj* : geometric, geometrical

geranio *nm* : geranium

gerencia *nf* : management — **gerente** *nmf* : manager

geriatría *nf* : geriatrics — **geriátrico, -ca** *adj* : geriatric

germen *nm, pl* **gérmenes** : germ

germinar *vi* : germinate, sprout

gestación *nf, pl* **-ciones** : gestation

gesticular *vi* : gesticulate, gesture — **gesticulación** *nf, pl* **-ciones** : gesticulation

gestión *nf, pl* **-tiones** 1 : procedure, step 2 ADMINISTRACIÓN : management — **gestionar** *vt* 1 : negotiate, work towards 2 ADMINISTRAR : manage, handle

gesto *nm* 1 : gesture 2 : (facial) expression 3 MUECA : grimace

gigante *adj & nm* : giant — **gigantesco, -ca** *adj* : gigantic

gimnasia *nf* : gymnastics — **gimnasio** *nm* : gymnasium, gym — **gimnasta** *nmf* : gymnast

gimotear *vi* : whine, whimper

ginebra *nf* : gin

ginecología *nf* : gynecology — **ginecólogo, -ga** *n* : gynecologist

gira *nf* : tour

girar *vi* : turn (around), revolve — *vt* 1 : turn, twist, rotate 2 : draft (checks) 3 : transfer (funds)

girasol *nm* : sunflower

giratorio, -ria *adj* : revolving

giro *nm* 1 : turn, rotation 2 LOCUCIÓN : expression 3 **~ bancario** : bank draft 4 **~ postal** : money order

giroscopio *nm* : gyroscope

gis *nm Lat* : chalk

gitano, -na *adj & n* : Gypsy

glaciar *nm* : glacier — **glacial** *adj* : glacial, icy

gladiador *nm* : gladiator

glándula *nf* : gland

glasear *vt* : glaze, ice (cake, etc.) — **glaseado** *nm* : icing

glicerina *nf* : glycerin

globo *nm* 1 : globe 2 : balloon 3 **~ ocular** : eyeball — **global** *adj* 1 : global 2 TOTAL : total, overall

glóbulo *nm* : blood cell, corpuscle

gloria *nf* : glory

glorieta *nf* 1 : bower, arbor 2 *Spain* : rotary, traffic circle

glorificar {72} *vt* : glorify

glorioso, -sa *adj* : glorious

glosario *nm* : glossary

glotón, -tona *adj, mpl* **-tones** : gluttonous — **~** *n* : glutton — **glotonería** *nf* : gluttony

glucosa *nf* : glucose

gnomo ['nomo] *nm* : gnome

gobernar {55} *v* 1 : govern, rule 2 DIRIGIR : direct, manage 3 : steer (a boat, etc.) — **gobernación** *nf, pl* **-ciones** : governing, government — **gobernador, -dora** *n* : governor — **gobernante** *adj* : ruling, governing — **~** *n* : ruler, leader — **gobierno** *nm* : government

goce *nm* : enjoyment

gol *nm* : goal (in sports)

golf *nm* : golf — **golfista** *nmf* : golfer

golfo *nm* : gulf

golondrina *nf* 1 : swallow 2 **~ de mar** : tern

golosina *nf* : sweet, candy — **goloso, -sa** *adj* : fond of sweets

golpe *nm* 1 : blow 2 PUÑETAZO : punch 3 : knock (on a door, etc.) 4 **de ~** : suddenly 5 **de un ~** : all at once 6 **~ de estado** : coup d'etat — **golpear** *vt* 1 : hit, punch 2 : slam, bang (a door, etc.) — *vi* : knock (at a door)

goma *nf* 1 CAUCHO : rubber 2 PEGAMENTO : glue 3 *or* **~ elástica** : rubber band 4 **~ de mascar** : chewing gum 5 **~ de borrar** : eraser

gong *nm* : gong

gordo, -da *adj* 1 : fat, plump 2 GRUESO : thick 3 : fatty (of meat) 4 *fam* : big, serious — **~** *n* : fat person — **gorda** *nf Lat* : thick corn tortilla — **gordo** *nm* 1 GRASA : fat 2 : jackpot (in a lottery) — **gordura** *nf* : fatness, flab

gorgotear *vi* : gurgle, bubble

gorila *nm* : gorilla

gorjear *vi* 1 : chirp, tweet 2 : gurgle (of a baby) — **gorjeo** *nm* : chirping

gorra *nf* 1 : cap, bonnet 2 **de ~** *fam* : for free

gorrear *vt fam* : bum, scrounge

gorrión *nm, pl* **-rriones** : sparrow

gorro *nm* 1 : cap, bonnet 2 **de ~** *fam* : for free

gota *nf* 1 : drop 2 : gout (in medicine) — **gotear** *vi* : drip, leak — **goteo** *nm* : drip, dripping — **gotera** *nf* : leak

gótico, -ca *adj* : Gothic

gozar {21} *vi* 1 : enjoy oneself 2 **~ de algo** : enjoy sth

gozne *nm* : hinge

gozo *nm* 1 : joy 2 PLACER : enjoyment, pleasure — **gozoso, -sa** *adj* : joyful, glad

grabar *vt* 1 : engrave 2 : record, tape — **grabación** *nf, pl* **-ciones** : recording — **grabado** *nm* : engraving — **grabadora** *nf* : tape recorder

gracia *nf* 1 : grace 2 FAVOR : favor, kindness 3 HUMOR : humor, wit 4 **~s** *nfpl* : thanks 5 **¡(muchas) ~s!** : thank you (very much)! — **gracioso, -sa** *adj* : funny, amusing

grada *nf* 1 : step, stair 2 : row (in a theater, etc.) 3 **~s** *nfpl* : bleachers, grandstand — **gradación** *nf, pl* **-ciones** : gradation, scale — **gradería** *nf* : rows *pl*, stands *pl* — **grado** *nm* 1 : degree 2 : grade (in school) 3 **de buen ~** : willingly

graduar {3} *vt* 1 : regulate, adjust 2 MARCAR : calibrate 3 : confer a degree on (in education) — **graduarse** *vr* : graduate (from a school) — **graduación** *nf, pl* **-ciones** 1 : graduation 2 : alcohol content, proof — **graduado, -da** *n* : graduate — **gradual** *adj* : gradual — **gradualmente** *adv* : little by little, gradually

gráfico, -ca *adj* : graphic — **gráfica** *nf* : graph — **gráfico** *nm* 1 : graph 2 : graphic (in computers)

gragea *nf* : pill, tablet

grajo *nm* : rook (bird)

gramática *nf* : grammar — **gramatical** *adj* : grammatical

gramo *nm* : gram

gran → **grande**

grana *nf* : scarlet

granada *nf* 1 : pomegranate 2 : grenade (in the military)

granate *nm* : garnet

grande *adj* (**gran** *before singular nouns*) 1 : large, big 2 ALTO : tall 3 : great (in quality, intensity, etc.) 4 *Lat* : grown-up — **grandeza** *nf* 1 : greatness 2 NOBLEZA : nobility — **grandiosidad** *nf* : grandeur — **grandioso, -sa** *adj* : grand, magnificent

granel: **a ~** *adv phr* 1 : in bulk 2 : in abundance

granero *nm* : barn, granary

granito *nm* : granite

granizar {21} *v impers* : hail — **granizada** *nf* : hailstorm — **granizado** *nm* : iced drink — **granizo** *nm* : hail

granja *nf* : farm — **granjero, -ra** *n* : farmer

grano *nm* 1 : grain 2 SEMILLA : seed 3 : (coffee) bean 4 BARRO : pimple

granuja *nmf* : rascal

grapa *nf* : staple — **grapadora** *nf* : stapler — **grapar** *vt* : staple

grasa *nf* 1 : grease 2 : fat (in cooking, etc.) — **grasiento, -ta** *adj* : greasy, oily — **graso, -sa** *adj* : fatty, greasy, oily — **grasoso, -sa** *adj Lat* : greasy, oily

gratificar {72} *vt* 1 : give a tip or bonus to 2 SATISFACER : gratify, satisfy — **gratificación** *nf, pl* **-ciones** 1 : bonus, tip, reward 2 SATISFACCIÓN : gratification

gratis *adv & adj* : free

gratitud *nf* : gratitude

grato, -ta *adj* : pleasant, agreeable

gratuito, -ta *adj* 1 : gratuitous, unwarranted 2 GRATIS : free

grava *nf* : gravel

gravar *vt* 1 : tax 2 CARGAR : burden — **gravamen** *nm, pl* **-vámenes** 1 : burden, obligation 2 IMPUESTO : tax

grave *adj* 1 : grave, serious 2 : deep, low (of a voice, etc.) — **gravedad** *nf* : gravity

gravilla *nf* : gravel

gravitar *vi* 1 : gravitate 2 **~ sobre** : weigh on — **gravitación** *nf, pl* **-ciones** : gravitation

gravoso, -sa *adj* : costly, burdensome

graznar *vi* : caw, quack, honk — **graznido** *nm* : caw, quack, honk

gregario, -ria *adj* : gregarious

gremio *nm* : guild, (trade) union

greñas *nfpl* : shaggy hair, mop

griego, -ga *adj* : Greek — **griego** *nm* : Greek (language)

grieta *nf* : crack, crevice

grifo *nm Spain* : faucet, tap

grillete *nm* : shackle

grillo *nm* 1 : cricket 2 **~s** *nmpl* : fetters, shackles

grima *nf* **dar ~** : annoy, irritate

gringo, -ga *adj & n Lat fam* : Yankee, gringo

gripe *nf or* **gripa** *nf Lat* : flu, influenza

gris *adj & nm* : gray

gritar *v* : shout, scream, cry — **grito** *nm* 1 : shout, scream, cry 2 **dar ~s** : shout

grosella *nf* : currant

grosería *nf* 1 : vulgar remark 2 DESCORTESÍA : rudeness — **grosero, -ra** *adj* 1 : coarse, vulgar 2 DESCORTÉS : rude

grosor *nm* : thickness

grotesco, -ca *adj* : grotesque, hideous

grúa *nf* : crane, derrick

grueso, -sa *adj* 1 : thick 2 CORPULENTO : stout, heavy — **gruesa** *nf* : gross — **grueso** *nm* 1 GROSOR : thickness 2 : main body, mass 3 **en ~** : wholesale

grulla *nf* : crane (bird)

grumo *nm* : lump, clot — **grumoso, -sa** *adj* : lumpy

gruñir {38} *vi* 1 : growl, grunt 2 *fam* : grumble — **gruñido** *nm* 1 : growl, grunt 2 *fam* : grumble — **gruñón, -ñona** *adj, mpl* **-ñones** *fam* : grumpy, grouchy — **~** *n fam* : grouch

grupa *nf* : rump, hindquarters *pl*

grupo *nm* : group

gruta *nf* : grotto

guacamayo *nm or* **guacamaya** *nf Lat* : macaw

guacamole *nm* : guacamole

guadaña *nf* : scythe

guagua *nf Lat* 1 : baby 2 AUTOBÚS : bus

guajalote, -ta *or* **guajolote, -ta** *n Lat* : turkey

guante *nm* : glove

guapo, -pa *adj* : handsome, good-looking

guaraní *nm* : Guarani (language of Paraguay)

guarda *nmf* 1 : keeper, custodian 2 GUARDIÁN : security guard — **guardabarros** *nms & pl* : fender — **guardabosque** *nmf* : forest ranger — **guardacostas** *nmfs & pl* : coast guard vessel — **guardaespaldas** *nmfs & pl* : bodyguard — **guardameta** *nmf* : goalkeeper — **guardapolvo** *nm* : overalls *pl* — **guardar** *vt* 1 : keep 2 PROTEGER : guard, protect 3 RESERVAR : save — **guardarse** *vr* **~ de** 1 : refrain from 2 : guard against — **guardarropa** *nm* 1 : cloakroom, checkroom 2 ARMARIO : wardrobe

guardería *nf* : nursery, day-care center

guardia *nf* 1 : guard, vigilence 2 TURNO : duty, watch — **~** *nmf* 1 : guard 2 *or* **~ municipal** : police officer — **guardián, -diana** *n, mpl* **-dianes** 1 : guardian, keeper 2 GUARDA : security guard

guarecer {53} *vt* : shelter, protect — **guarecerse** *vr* : take shelter

guarida *nf* 1 : den, lair (of animals) 2 : hideout (of persons)

guarnecer {53} *vt* 1 : adorn, garnish 2 : garrison (an area) — **guarnición** *nf, pl* **-ciones** 1 : garnish, trimming 2 : (military) garrison

guasa *nf fam* 1 : joke 2 **de ~** : in jest — **guasón, -sona** *adj, mpl* **-sones** *fam* : joking, witty — **~** *n fam* : joker

guatemalteco, -ca *adj* : Guatemalan

guayaba *nf* : guava

gubernamental *or* **gubernativo, -va** *adj* : governmental

guepardo *nm* : cheetah

güero, -ra *adj Lat* : blond, fair

guerra *nf* 1 : war, warfare 2 LUCHA : conflict, struggle — **guerrear** *vi* : wage war — **guerrero, -ra** *adj* 1 : war, fighting 2 BELICOSO : warlike — **~** *n* : warrior — **guerrilla** *nf* : guerrilla warfare — **guerrillero, -ra** *adj & n* : guerrilla

gueto *nm* : ghetto

guiar {85} *vt* 1 : guide, lead 2 ACONSEJAR : advise — **guiarse** *vr* : be guided by, go by — **guía** *nf* 1 : guidebook 2 ORIENTACIÓN : guidance — **~** *nmf* : guide, leader

guijarro *nm* : pebble

guillotina *nf* : guillotine

guinda *nf* : morello (cherry)

guiñar *vi* : wink — **guiño** *nm* : wink

guión *nm, pl* **guiones** 1 : script, screenplay 2 : hyphen, dash (in punctuation) — **guionista** *nmf* : scriptwriter, screenwriter

guirnalda *nf* : garland

guisa *nf* 1 : manner, fashion 2 **a ~ de** : by way of 3 **de tal ~** : in such a way

guisado *nm* : stew

guisante *nm* : pea

guisar *vt* : cook — **guiso** *nm* : stew, casserole

guitarra *nf* : guitar — **guitarrista** *nmf* : guitarist

gula *nf* : gluttony

gusano *nm* 1 : worm 2 : maggot (larva)

gustar *vt* 1 : taste 2 *Lat* : like — *vi* 1 : be pleasing 2 **como guste** : as you like 3 **me gustan los dulces** : I like sweets — **gusto** *nm* 1 : taste 2 PLACER : pleasure, liking 3 **a ~** : comfortable, at ease 4 **al ~** : to taste 5 **mucho ~** : pleased to meet you — **gustoso, -sa** *adj* 1 : tasty 2 AGRADABLE : pleasant 3 **hacer algo ~** : do sth willingly

gutural *adj* : guttural

H

h *nf* : h, eighth letter of the Spanish alphabet

haba *nf* : broad bean

habanero, -ra *adj* : Havanan — **habano** *nm* : Havana cigar

haber {39} *v aux* 1 : have, has 2 **~ de** : must — *v impers* 1 **hay** : there is, there are 2 **hay que** : it is necessary (to) 3 **¿qué hay?** *or* **¿qué hubo?** : how's it going? — **~** *nm* 1 : assets *pl* 2 : credit side (in accounting) 3 **~es** *nmpl* : income, earnings

habichuela *nf* 1 : bean 2 **~ verde** : string bean

hábil *adj* 1 : able, skillful 2 LISTO : clever 3 **horas ~es** : business hours — **habilidad** *nf* : ability, skill

habilitar *vt* 1 : equip, furnish 2 AUTORIZAR : authorize

habitar *vt* : inhabit — *vi* : reside, dwell — **habitable** *adj* : habitable, inhabitable — **habitación** *nf, pl* **-ciones** 1 : room, bedroom 2 MORADA : dwelling, abode 3 : habitat (in biology) — **habitante** *nmf* : inhabitant, resident — **hábitat** *nm* : habitat

hábito *nm* : habit — **habitual** *adj* : habitual, usual — **habituar** {3} *vt* : accustom, habituate — **habituarse** *vr* **~ a** : get used to

hablar *vi* 1 : speak, talk 2 **~ de** : mention, talk about 3 **~ con** : talk to, speak with — *vt* 1 : speak (a language) 2 DISCUTIR : discuss — **hablarse** *vr* 1 : speak to each other 2 **se habla inglés** : English spoken — **habla** *nf* 1 : speech 2 IDIOMA : language, dialect 3 **de ~ inglesa** : English-speaking — **hablador, -dora** *adj* : talkative — **~** *n* : chatterbox — **habladuría** *nf* 1 : rumor 2 **~s** *nfpl* : gossip — **hablante** *nmf* : speaker

hacedor, -dora *n* : creator, maker

hacendado, -da *n* : landowner, rancher

hacer {40} *vt* 1 : do, perform 2 CONSTRUIR, CREAR : make 3 OBLIGAR : force, oblige — *vi* : act — *v impers* 1 **~ calor/viento** : be hot/be windy 2 **~ falta** : be necessary 3 **hace mucho tiempo** : a long time ago 4 **no lo hace** : it doesn't matter — **hacerse** *vr* 1 VOLVERSE : become 2 : pretend (to be) 3 **~ a** : get used to 4 **se hace tarde** : it's getting late

hacha *nf* 1 : hatchet, ax 2 ANTORCHA : torch

hachís *nm* : hashish

hacia *prep* 1 : toward, towards 2 CERCA DE : near, around, about 3 **~ abajo** : downward 4 **~ adelante** : forward

hacienda *nf* 1 : estate, ranch 2 BIENES : property 3 *Lat* : livestock 4 **Hacienda** : department of revenue

hacinar *vt* : stack

hada *nf* : fairy

hado *nm* : fate

halagar {52} *vt* : flatter — **halagador, -dora** *adj* : flattering — **halago** *nm* : flattery — **halagüeño, -ña** *adj* 1 : flattering 2 PROMETEDOR : promising

halcón *nm, pl* **-cones** : hawk, falcon

halibut *nm, pl* **-buts** : halibut

hálito *nm* : breath

hallar *vt* 1 : find 2 DESCUBRIR : discover, find out — **hallarse** *vr* : be, find oneself — **hallazgo** *nm* : discovery, find

halo *nm* : halo

hamaca *nf* : hammock

hambre *nf* 1 : hunger 2 INANICIÓN : starvation, famine 3 **tener ~** : be hungry — **hambriento, -ta** *adj* : hungry, starving — **hambruna** *nf* : famine

hamburguesa *nf* : hamburger

hampa *nf* : underworld — **hampón, -pona** *n, mpl* **-pones** : criminal, thug

hámster *nm* : hamster

hándicap *nm* : handicap (in sports)

hangar *nm* : hangar

haragán, -gana *adj, mpl* **-ganes** : lazy, idle — **~** *n* : slacker, idler — **haraganear** : be lazy, loaf

harapiento, -ta *adj* : ragged, in rags — **harapos** *nmpl* : rags, tatters

harina *nf* : flour

hartar *vt* 1 : glut, satiate 2 FASTIDIAR : annoy — **hartarse** *vr* 1 : gorge oneself 2 CANSARSE : get fed up — **harto, -ta** *adj* 1 : full, satiated 2 CANSADO : tired, fed up — **harto** *adv* : extremely, very — **hartura** *nf* 1 : surfeit 2 ABUNDANCIA : abundance, plenty

hasta *prep* 1 : until, up until (in time) 2 : as far as, up to (in space) 3 **¡~ luego!** : see you later! 4 **~ que** : until — **~** *adv* : even

hastiar {85} *vt* 1 : make weary, bore 2 ASQUEAR : sicken — **hastiarse** *vr* **~ de** : get tired of — **hastío** *nm* 1 : weariness, tedium 2 REPUGNANCIA : disgust

hato *nm* 1 : flock, herd 2 : bundle (of possessions)

haya *nf* : beech

haz *nm, pl* **haces** 1 : bundle, sheaf 2 : beam (of light)

hazaña *nf* : feat, exploit

hazmerreír *nm fam* : laughingstock
he {39} *v impers* **~ aquí** : here is, here are, behold
hebilla *nf* : buckle
hebra *nf* : strand, thread
hebreo, -brea *adj* : Hebrew — **hebreo** *nm* : Hebrew (language)
hecatombe *nm* : disaster
hechizo *nm* **1** : spell **2** ENCANTO : charm, fascination — **hechicería** *nf* : sorcery, witchcraft — **hechicero, -ra** *n* : sorcerer, sorceress *f* — **hechizar** {21} *vt* **1** : bewitch **2** CAUTIVAR : charm
hecho, -cha *adj* **1** : made, done **2** : ready-to-wear (of clothing) **3 ~ y derecho** : full-fledged, mature — **hecho** *nm* **1** : fact **2** SUCESO : event **3** ACTO : act, deed **4 de ~** : in fact — **hechura** *nf* **1** : making, creation **2** FORMA : shape, form **3** : build (of the body) **4** ARTESANÍA : workmanship
heder {56} *vi* : stink, reek — **hediondez** *nf, pl* **-deces** : stench — **hediondo, -da** *adj* : stinking — **hedor** *nm* : stench
helar {55} *v* : freeze — **helarse** *vr* : freeze up, freeze over — **helado, -da** *adj* **1** : freezing cold **2** CONGELADO : frozen — **helada** *nf* : frost — **heladería** *nf* : ice-cream parlor — **helado** *nm* : ice cream — **heladora** *nf* : freezer
helecho *nm* : fern
hélice *nf* **1** : propeller **2** ESPIRAL : spiral, helix
helicóptero *nm* : helicopter
helio *nm* : helium
hembra *nf* **1** : female **2** MUJER : woman
hemisferio *nm* : hemisphere
hemorragia *nf* **1** : hemorrhage **2 ~ nasal** : nosebleed
hemorroides *nfpl* : hemorrhoids, piles
henchir {54} *vt* : stuff, fill
hender {56} *vt* : cleave, split — **hendidura** *nf* : crevice, fissure
henequén *nm, pl* **-quenes** : sisal
heno *nm* : hay
hepatitis *nf* : hepatitis
heraldo *nm* : herald
herbolario, -ria *n* : herbalist
heredar *vt* : inherit — **heredad** *nm* : rural property, estate — **heredero, -ra** *n* : heir, heiress *f* — **hereditario, -ria** *adj* : hereditary
hereje *nmf* : heretic — **herejía** *nf* : heresy
herencia *nf* **1** : inheritance **2** : heredity (in biology)
herir {76} *vt* **1** : injure, wound **2** : hurt (feelings, pride, etc.) — **herida** *nf* : injury, wound — **herido, -da** *adj* **1** : injured, wounded **2** : hurt (of feelings, pride, etc.) — **~** *n* : injured person, casualty
hermano, -na *n* : brother *m*, sister *f* — **hermanastro, -tra** *n* : half brother *m*, half sister *f* — **hermandad** *nf* : brotherhood
hermético, -ca *adj* : hermetic, watertight
hermoso, -sa *adj* : beautiful, lovely — **hermosura** *nf* : beauty
hernia *nf* : hernia
héroe *nm* : hero — **heroico, -ca** *adj* : heroic — **heroína** *nf* **1** : heroine **2** : heroin (narcotic) — **heroísmo** *nm* : heroism
herradura *nf* : horseshoe
herramienta *nf* : tool
herrero, -ra *n* : blacksmith
herrumbre *nf* : rust
hervir {76} *v* : boil — **hervidero** *nm* **1** : mass, swarm **2** : hotbed (of intrigue, etc.) — **hervidor** *nm* : kettle — **hervor** *nm* **1** : boiling **2** ENTUSIASMO : fervor, ardor
heterogéneo, -nea *adj* : heterogeneous
heterosexual *adj & nmf* : heterosexual
hexágono *nm* : hexagon — **hexagonal** *adj* : hexagonal
hez *nf, pl* **heces** : dregs *pl*, scum
hiato *nm* : hiatus
hibernar *vi* : hibernate — **hibernación** *nf, pl* **-ciones** : hibernation
híbrido, -da *adj* : hybrid — **híbrido** *nm* : hybrid
hidalgo, -ga *n* : nobleman *m*, noblewoman *f*
hidratante *adj* : moisturizing
hidrato *nm* **~ de carbono** : carbohydrate
hidráulico, -ca *adj* : hydraulic
hidroavión *nm, pl* **-aviones** : seaplane
hidroeléctrico, -ca *adj* : hydroelectric
hidrofobia *nf* : rabies
hidrógeno *nm* : hydrogen
hidroplano *nm* : hydroplane
hiedra *nf* **1** : ivy **2 ~ venenosa** : poison ivy
hiel *nm* **1** : bile **2** AMARGURA : bitterness
hielo *nm* **1** : ice **2** FRIALDAD : coldness **3 romper el ~** : break the ice
hiena *nf* : hyena
hierba *nf* **1** : herb **2** CÉSPED : grass **3 mala ~** : weed — **hierbabuena** *nf* : mint
hierro *nm* **1** : iron **2 ~ fundido** : cast iron
hígado *nm* : liver
higiene *nf* : hygiene — **higiénico, -ca** *adj* : hygienic
higo *nm* : fig
hijo, -ja *n* **1** : son *m*, daughter *f* **2 hijos** *nmpl* : children, offspring — **hijastro, -tra** *n* : stepson *m*, stepdaughter *f*
hilar *v* **1** : spin **2 ~ delgado** : split hairs — **hilado** *nm* : yarn, thread
hilaridad *nf* : hilarity
hilera *nf* : file, row
hilo *nm* **1** : thread **2** LINO : linen **3** ALAMBRE : wire **4** : trickle (of water, etc.) **5 ~ dental** : dental floss
hilvanar *vt* **1** : baste, tack **2** : put together (ideas, etc.)
himno *nm* **1** : hymn **2 ~ nacional** : national anthem
hincapié *nm* **hacer ~ en** : emphasize, stress
hincar {72} *vt* : drive in, plunge — **hincarse** *vr* **~ de rodillas** : kneel (down)
hinchar *vt Spain* : inflate, blow up — **hincharse** *vr* **1** : swell (up) **2** *Spain fam* : stuff oneself — **hinchado, -da** *adj* **1** : swollen **2** POMPOSO : pompous — **hinchazón** *nf, pl* **-zones** : swelling
hindú *adj & nmf* : Hindu — **hinduismo** *nm* : Hinduism
hinojo *nm* : fennel
hiperactivo, -va *adj* : hyperactive
hipersensible *adj* : oversensitive
hipertensión *nf, pl* **-siones** : hypertension, high blood pressure
hípico, -ca *adj* : equestrian, horse
hipil → **huipil**
hipnosis *nfs & pl* : hypnosis — **hipnótico, -ca** *adj* : hypnotic — **hipnotismo** *nm* : hypnotism — **hipnotizador, -dora** *n* : hypnotist — **hipnotizar** {21} *vt* : hypnotize
hipo *nm* **1** : hiccup, hiccups *pl* **2 tener ~** : have hiccups
hipocondríaco, -ca *adj* : hypochondriacal — **~** *n* : hypochondriac
hipocresía *nf* : hypocrisy — **hipócrita** *adj* : hypocritical — **~** *nmf* : hypocrite
hipodérmico, -ca *adj* : hypodermic
hipódromo *nm* : racetrack
hipopótamo *nm* : hippopotamus
hipoteca *nf* : mortgage — **hipotecar** {72} *vt* : mortgage
hipótesis *nfs & pl* : hypothesis — **hipotético, -ca** *adj* : hypothetical
hiriente *adj* : hurtful, offensive
hirsuto, -ta *adj* **1** : hairy **2** : bristly, wiry (of hair)
hirviente *adj* : boiling
hispano, -na *or* **hispánico, -ca** *adj & n* : Hispanic — **hispanoamericano, -na** *adj* : Latin-American — **~** *n* : Latin American — **hispanohablante** *or* **hispanoparlante** *adj* : Spanish-speaking
histeria *nf* : hysteria — **histérico, -ca** *adj* : hysterical — **histerismo** *nm* : hysteria
historia *nf* **1** : history **2** CUENTO : story — **historiador, -dora** *n* : historian — **historial** *nm* : record, background — **histórico, -ca** *adj* **1** : historical **2** IMPORTANTE : historic, important — **historieta** *nf* : comic strip
hito *nm* : milestone, landmark
hocico *nm* : snout, muzzle
hockey ['hoke, -ki] *nm* : hockey
hogar *nm* **1** : home **2** CHIMENEA : hearth, fireplace — **hogareño, -ña** *adj* **1** : home-loving **2** DOMÉSTICO : home, domestic
hoguera *nf* : bonfire
hoja *nf* **1** : leaf **2** : sheet (of paper) **3 ~ de afeitar** : razor blade — **hojalata** *nf* : tinplate — **hojaldre** *nm* : puff pastry — **hojear** *vt* : leaf through — **hojuela** *nf Lat* : flake
hola *interj* : hello!, hi!
holandés, -desa *adj, mpl* **-deses** : Dutch
holgado, -da *adj* **1** : loose, baggy **2** : comfortable (of an economic situation, a victory, etc.) — **holgazán, -zana** *adj, mpl* **-zanes** : lazy — **~** *n* : slacker, idler — **holgazanear** *vi* : laze about, loaf — **holgura** *nf* **1** : looseness **2** BIENESTAR : comfort, ease
hollín *nm, pl* **-llines** : soot
holocausto *nm* : holocaust
hombre *nm* **1** : man **2 el ~** : mankind **3 ~ de estado** : statesman **4 ~ de negocios** : businessman
hombrera *nf* **1** : shoulder pad **2** : epaulet (of a uniform)
hombría *nf* : manliness
hombro *nm* : shoulder
hombruno, -na *adj* : mannish
homenaje *nm* **1** : homage **2 rendir ~ a** : pay tribute to
homeopatía *nf* : homeopathy
homicidio *nm* : homicide, murder — **homicida** *adj* : homicidal, murderous — **~** *nmf* : murderer
homogéneo, -nea *adj* : homogeneous
homólogo, -ga *adj* : equivalent — **~** *n* : counterpart
homosexual *adj & nmf* : homosexual — **homosexualidad** *nf* : homosexuality
hondo, -da *adj* : deep — **hondo** *adv* : deeply — **hondonada** *nf* : hollow — **hondura** *nf* : depth
hondureño, -ña *adj* : Honduran
honesto, -ta *adj* : decent, honorable — **honestidad** *nf* : honesty, integrity
hongo *nm* **1** : mushroom **2** : fungus (in botany and medicine)
honor *nm* : honor — **honorable** *adj* : honorable — **honorario, -ria** *adj* : honorary — **honorarios** *nmpl* : payment, fee — **honra** *nf* : honor — **honradez** *nf, pl* **-deces** : honesty, integrity — **honrado, -da** *adj* : honest, upright — **honrar** *vt* : honor — **honrarse** *vr* : be honored — **honroso, -sa** *adj* : honorable
hora *nf* **1** : hour **2** : (specific) time **3** CITA : appointment **4 a la última ~** : at the last minute **5 ~ punta** : rush hour **6 media ~** : half an hour **7 ¿qué ~ es?** : what time is it? **8 ~s de oficina** : office hours **9 ~s extraordinarias** : overtime
horario *nm* : schedule, timetable
horca *nf* **1** : gallows *pl* **2** : pitchfork (in agriculture)
horcajadas: **a ~** *adv phr* : astride
horda *nf* : horde
horizonte *nm* : horizon — **horizontal** *adj* : horizontal
horma *nf* **1** : form, mold, last **2** : shoe tree
hormiga *nf* : ant
hormigón *nm, pl* **-gones** : concrete
hormigueo *nm* : tingling, pins and needles
hormiguero *nm* **1** : anthill **2** : swarm (of people)
hormona *nf* : hormone
horno *nm* **1** : oven (for cooking) **2** : small furnace, kiln — **hornada** *nf* : batch — **hornear** *vt* : bake — **hornillo** *nf* : portable stove
horóscopo *nm* : horoscope
horquilla *nf* **1** : hairpin, bobby pin **2** HORCA : pitchfork
horrendo, -da *adj* : horrendous, awful — **horrible** *adj* : horrible — **horripilante** *adj* : horrifying — **horror** *nm* **1** : horror, dread **2** ATROCIDAD : atrocity — **horrorizar** {21} *vt* : horrify, terrify — **horrorizarse** *vr* : be horrified — **horroroso, -sa** *adj* : horrifying, dreadful
hortaliza *nf* : (garden) vegetable — **hortelano, -na** *n* : truck farmer — **horticultura** *nf* : horticulture
hosco, -ca *adj* : sullen, gloomy
hospedar *vt* : put up, lodge — **hospedarse** *vr* : stay, lodge — **hospedaje** *nm* : lodging
hospital *nm* : hospital — **hospitalario, -ria** *adj* : hospitable — **hospitalidad** *nf* : hospitality — **hospitalizar** {21} *vt* : hospitalize
hostería *nf* : small hotel, inn
hostia *nf* : host (in religion)
hostigar {52} *vt* **1** : whip **2** ACOSAR : harass, pester
hostil *adj* : hostile — **hostilidad** *nf* : hostility
hotel *nm* : hotel — **hotelero, -ra** *adj* : hotel — **~** *n* : hotel manager, hotelier
hoy *adv* **1** : today **2 de ~ en adelante** : from now on **3 ~ (en) día** : nowadays **4 ~ mismo** : this very day
hoyo *nm* : hole — **hoyuelo** *nm* : dimple
hoz *nf, pl* **hoces** : sickle
huarache *nm* : huarache (sandal)
hueco, -ca *adj* **1** : hollow, empty **2** ESPONJOSO : soft, spongy **3** RESONANTE : resonant — **hueco** *nm* **1** : hollow, cavity **2** : recess (in a wall, etc.) **3 ~ de escalera** : stairwell
huelga *nf* **1** : strike **2 declararse en ~** : go on strike — **huelguista** *nmf* : striker
huella *nf* **1** : footprint **2** VESTIGIO : track, mark **3 ~ digital** *or* **~ dactilar** : fingerprint
huérfano, -na *n* : orphan — **~** *adj* : orphaned
huerta *nf* : truck farm — **huerto** *nm* **1** : vegetable garden **2** : (fruit) orchard
hueso *nm* **1** : bone **2** : pit, stone (of a fruit)
huésped, -peda *n* : guest — **huésped** *nm* : host (organism)
huesudo, -da *adj* : bony
huevo *nm* **1** : egg **2 ~s estrellados** : fried eggs **3 ~s revueltos** : scrambled eggs — **hueva** *nf* : roe
huida *nf* : flight, escape — **huidizo, -za** *adj* **1** : shy **2** FUGAZ : fleeting
huipil *nm Lat* : traditional embroidered blouse or dress
huir {41} *vi* **1** : escape, flee **2 ~ de** : shun, avoid
hule *nm* **1** : oilcloth **2** *Lat* : rubber
humano, -na *adj* **1** : human **2** COMPASIVO : humane — **humano** *nm* : human (being) — **humanidad** *nf* **1** : humanity, mankind **2** BENEVOLENCIA : humaneness **3 ~es** *nfpl* : humanities — **humanismo** *nm* : humanism — **humanista** *nmf* : humanist — **humanitario, -ria** *adj & n* : humanitarian
humear *vi* : smoke, steam — **humareda** *nf* : cloud of smoke
humedad *nf* **1** : dampness **2** : humidity (in meteorology) — **humedecer** {53} *vt* : moisten, dampen — **humedecerse** *vr* : become moist — **húmedo, -da** *adj* **1** : moist, damp **2** : humid (in meteorology)
humildad *nf* : humility — **humilde** *adj* : humble — **humillación** *nf, pl* **-ciones** : humiliation — **humillante** *adj* : humiliating — **humillar** *vt* : humiliate — **humillarse** *vr* : humble oneself
humo *nm* **1** : smoke, steam, fumes **2 ~s** *nmpl* : airs, conceit
humor *nm* **1** : mood, temper **2** GRACIA : humor **3 de buen ~** : in a good mood — **humorismo** *nm* : humor, wit — **humorista** *nmf* : humorist, comedian — **humorístico, -ca** *adj* : humorous
hundir *vt* **1** : sink **2** : destroy, ruin (a building, plans, etc.) — **hundirse** *vr* **1** : sink **2** DERRUMBARSE : collapse — **hundido, -da** *adj* : sunken — **hundimiento** *nm* **1** : sinking **2** DERRUMBE : collapse
húngaro, -ra *adj* : Hungarian
huracán *nm, pl* **-canes** : hurricane
huraño, -ña *adj* : unsociable
hurgar {52} *vi* **~ en** : rummage around in
hurón *nm, pl* **-rones** : ferret
hurra *interj* : hurrah!, hooray!
hurtadillas: **a ~** *adv phr* : stealthily, on the sly
hurtar *vt* : steal — **hurto** *nm* **1** ROBO : theft **2** : stolen property
husmear *vt* : sniff out, pry into — *vi* : nose around
huy *interj* : ow!, ouch!

I

i *nf* : i, ninth letter of the Spanish alphabet
ibérico, -ca *adj* : Iberian — **íbero, -ra** *or* **íbero, -ra** *adj* : Iberian
iceberg *nm, pl* **-bergs** : iceberg
icono *nm* : icon
ictericia *nf* : jaundice
ida *nf* **1** : outward journey **2 ~ y vuelta** : round-trip **3 ~s y venidas** : comings and goings
idea *nf* **1** : idea **2** OPINIÓN : opinion
ideal *adj & nm* : ideal — **idealismo** *nm* : idealism — **idealista** *adj* : idealistic — **~** *nmf* : idealist — **idealizar** {21} *vt* : idealize
idear *vt* : devise, think up
ídem *nm* : the same, ditto
identidad *nf* : identity — **idéntico, -ca** *adj* : identical — **identificar** {72} *vt* : identify — **identificarse** *vr* **1** : identify oneself **2 ~ con** : identify with — **identificación** *nf, pl* **-ciones** : identification
ideología *nf* : ideology — **ideológico, -ca** *adj* : ideological
idílico, -ca *adj* : idyllic
idioma *nm* : language — **idiomático, -ca** *adj* : idiomatic
idiosincrasia *nf* : idiosyncrasy — **idiosincrásico, -ca** *adj* : idiosyncratic
idiota *adj* : idiotic — **~** *nmf* : idiot — **idiotez** *nf* : idiocy
ídolo *nm* : idol — **idolatrar** *vt* : idolize — **idolatría** *nf* : idolatry
idóneo, -nea *adj* : suitable, fitting — **idoneidad** *nf* : fitness, suitability
iglesia *nf* : church
iglú *nm* : igloo
ignición *nf, pl* **-ciones** : ignition
ignífugo, -ga *adj* : fire-resistant, fireproof
ignorar *vt* **1** : ignore **2** DESCONOCER : be unaware of — **ignorancia** *nf* : ignorance — **ignorante** *adj* : ignorant — **~** *nmf* : ignorant person
igual *adv* **1** : in the same way **2 por ~** : equally — **~** *adj* **1** : equal **2** IDÉNTICO : the same **3** LISO : smooth, even **4** SEMEJANTE : similar — **~** *nmf* : equal, peer — **igualar** *vt* **1** : make equal **2** : be equal to **3** NIVELAR : level (off) — **igualdad** *nf* **1** : equality **2** UNIFORMIDAD : uniformity — **igualmente** *adv* : likewise
iguana *nf* : iguana
ijada *nf* : flank
ilegal *adj* : illegal
ilegible *adj* : illegible
ilegítimo, -ma *adj* : illegitimate — **ilegitimidad** *nf* : illegitimacy
ileso, -sa *adj* : unharmed
ilícito, -ta *adj* : illicit
ilimitado, -da *adj* : unlimited
ilógico, -ca *adj* : illogical
iluminar *vt* : illuminate — **iluminarse** *vr* : light up — **iluminación** *nf, pl* **-ciones 1** : illumination **2** ALUMBRADO : lighting
ilusionar *vt* : excite — **ilusionarse** *vr* : get one's hopes up — **ilusión** *nf, pl* **-siones 1** : illusion **2** ESPERANZA : hope — **ilusionado, -da** *adj* : excited
iluso -sa *adj* : naïve, gullible — **~** *n* : dreamer, visionary — **ilusorio, -ria** *adj* : illusory
ilustrar *vt* **1** : illustrate **2** ACLARAR : explain — **ilustración** *nf, pl* **-ciones 1** : illustration **2** SABER : learning **3 la Ilustración** : the Enlightenment — **ilustrado, -da** *adj* **1** : illustrated **2** ERUDITO : learned — **ilustrador, -dora** *n* : illustrator
ilustre *adj* : illustrious
imagen *nf, pl* **imágenes** : image, picture
imaginar *vt* : imagine — **imaginarse** *vr* : imagine — **imaginación** *nf, pl* **-ciones** : imagination — **imaginario, -ria** *adj* : imaginary — **imaginativo, -va** *adj* : imaginative
imán *nm, pl* **imanes** : magnet — **imantar** *vt* : magnetize

imbécil *adj* : stupid, idiotic — ~ *nmf* : idiot
imborrable *adj* : indelible
imbuir {41} *vt* ~ **de** : imbue with
imitar *vt* **1** COPIAR : imitate, copy **2** : impersonate — **imitación** *nf, pl* **-ciones 1** COPIA : imitation, copy **2** : impersonation — **imitador, -dora** *n* : impersonator
impaciencia *nf* : impatience — **impacientar** *vt* : make impatient, exasperate —**impacientarse** *vr* : grow impatient — **impaciente** *adj* : impatient
impacto *nm* : impact
impar *adj* : odd — ~ *nm* : odd number
imparcial *adj* : impartial — **imparcialidad** *nf* : impartiality
impartir *vt* : impart, give
impasible *adj* : impassive
impasse *nm* : impasse
impávido, -da *adj* : fearless
impecable *adj* : impeccable, spotless
impedir {54} *vt* **1** : prevent **2** DIFICULTAR : impede, hinder — **impedido, -da** *adj* : disabled — **impedimento** *nm* : obstacle, impediment
impeler *vt* : drive, propel
impenetrable *adj* : impenetrable
impenitente *adj* : unrepentant
impensable *adj* : unthinkable — **impensado, -da** *adj* : unexpected
imperar *vi* **1** : reign, rule **2** PREDOMINAR : prevail — **imperante** *adj* : prevailing
imperativo, -va *adj* : imperative — **imperativo** *nm* : imperative
imperceptible *adj* : imperceptible
imperdible *nm* : safety pin
imperdonable *adj* : unforgivable
imperfección *nf, pl* **-ciones** : imperfection — **imperfecto, -ta** *adj* : imperfect — **imperfecto** *nm* : imperfect (tense)
imperial *adj* : imperial — **imperialismo** *nm* : imperialism — **imperialista** *adj & nmf* : imperialist
impericia *nf* : lack of skill
imperio *nm* **1** : empire **2** DOMINIO : rule — **imperioso, -sa** *adj* **1** : imperious **2** URGENTE : pressing, urgent
impermeable *adj* **1** : waterproof **2** ~ **a** : impervious to — ~ *nm* : raincoat
impersonal *adj* : impersonal
impertinente *adj* : impertinent — **impertinencia** *nf* : impertinence
ímpetu *nm* **1** : impetus **2** ENERGÍA : energy, vigor **3** VIOLENCIA : force — **impetuoso, -sa** *adj* : impetuous — **impetuosidad** *nf* : impetuosity
impío, -pía *adj* : impious, ungodly
implacable *adj* : implacable
implantar *vt* **1** : implant **2** ESTABLECER : establish, introduce
implemento *nm Lat* : implement, tool
implicar {72} *vt* **1** : involve, implicate **2** SIGNIFICAR : imply — **implicación** *nf, pl* **-ciones** : implication
implícito, -ta *adj* : implicit
implorar *vt* : implore
imponer {60} *vt* **1** : impose **2** : command (respect, etc.) — *vi* : be imposing — **imponerse** *vr* **1** : assert oneself, command respect **2** PREVALECER : prevail — **imponente** *adj* : imposing, impressive — **imponible** *adj* : taxable
impopular *adj* : unpopular — **impopularidad** *nf* : unpopularity
importación *nf, pl* **-ciones 1** : importation **2** **importaciones** *nfpl* : imports — **importado, -da** *adj* : imported — **importador, -dora** *adj* : importing — ~ *n* : importer
importancia *nf* : importance — **importante** *adj* : important — **importar** *vi* **1** : matter, be important **2** **no me importa** : I don't care — *vt* **1** : import **2** ASCENDER A : amount to, cost
importe *nm* **1** : price **2** CANTIDAD : sum, amount
importunar *vt* : bother — **importuno, -na** *adj* **1** : inopportune **2** MOLESTO : bothersome
imposible *adj* : impossible — **imposibilidad** *nf* : impossibility
imposición *nf, pl* **-ciones 1** : imposition **2** IMPUESTO : tax
impostor, -tora *n* : impostor
impotente *adj* : powerless, impotent — **impotencia** *nf* : impotence
impracticable *adj* **1** : impracticable **2** INTRANSITABLE : impassable
impreciso, -sa *adj* : vague, imprecise — **imprecisión** *nf, pl* **-siones 1** : vagueness **2** ERROR : inaccuracy
impredecible *adj* : unpredictable
impregnar *vt* : impregnate
imprenta *nf* **1** : printing **2** : printing shop, press
imprescindible *adj* : essential, indispensable
impresión *nf, pl* **-siones 1** : impression **2** IMPRENTA : printing — **impresionable** *adj* : impressionable — **impresionante** *adj* : impressive — **impresionar** *vt* **1** : impress **2** CONMOVER : affect, move — *vi* : make an impression — **impresionarse** *vr* **1** : be impressed **2** CONMOVERSE : be affected
impreso, -sa *adj* : printed — **impreso** *nm* **1** FORMULARIO : form **2** **~s** *nmpl* : printed matter — **impresor, -sora** *n* : printer — **impresora** *nf* : (computer) printer
imprevisible *adj* : unforeseeable — **imprevisto, -ta** *adj* : unexpected, unforeseen
imprimir {42} *vt* **1** : print **2** DAR : impart, give
improbable *adj* : improbable — **improbabilidad** *nf* : improbability
improcedente *adj* : inappropriate
improductivo, -va *adj* : unproductive
improperio *nm* : insult
impropio, -pia *adj* **1** : inappropriate **2** INCORRECTO : incorrect
improvisar *v* : improvise — **improvisado, -da** *adj* : improvised, impromptu — **improvisación** *nf, pl* **-ciones** : improvisation — **improviso**: **de** ~ *adv phr* : suddenly
imprudente *adj* : imprudent, rash — **imprudencia** *nf* : imprudence, carelessness
impúdico, -ca *adj* : shameless, indecent
impuesto *nm* **1** : tax **2** ~ **sobre la renta** : income tax
impugnar *vt* : challenge, contest
impulsar *vt* : propel, drive — **impulsividad** *nf* : impulsiveness — **impulsivo, -va** *adj* : impulsive — **impulso** *nm* **1** : drive, thrust **2** MOTIVACIÓN : impulse
impune *adj* : unpunished — **impunidad** *nf* : impunity
impuro, -ra *adj* : impure — **impureza** *nf* : impurity
imputar *vt* : impute, attribute
inacabable *adj* : interminable, endless
inaccesible *adj* : inaccessible
inaceptable *adj* : unacceptable
inactivo, -va *adj* : inactive — **inactividad** *nf* : inactivity
inadaptado, -da *adj* : maladjusted — ~ *n* : misfit
inadecuado, -da *adj* **1** : inadequate **2** INAPROPIADO : inappropriate
inadmisible *adj* : inadmissible
inadvertido, -da *adj* **1** : unnoticed **2** DISTRAÍDO : distracted — **inadvertencia** *nf* : oversight
inagotable *adj* : inexhaustible
inaguantable *adj* : unbearable
inalámbrico, -ca *adj* : wireless, cordless
inalcanzable *adj* : unreachable, unattainable
inalterable *adj* **1** : unchangeable **2** : impassive (of character) **3** : fast (of colors)
inanición *nf, pl* **-ciones** : starvation, famine
inanimado, -da *adj* : inanimate
inaplicable *adj* : inapplicable
inapreciable *adj* : imperceptible
inapropiado, -da *adj* : inappropriate
inarticulado, -da *adj* : inarticulate
inasequible *adj* : unattainable
inaudito, -ta *adj* : unheard-of, unprecedented
inaugurar *vt* : inaugurate — **inauguración** *nf, pl* **-ciones** : inauguration — **inaugural** *adj* : inaugural
inca *adj* : Inca, Incan
incalculable *adj* : incalculable
incandescencia *nf* : incandescence — **incandescente** *adj* : incandescent
incansable *adj* : tireless
incapacitar *vt* : incapacitate, disable — **incapacidad** *nf* : incapacity, inability — **incapaz** *adj, pl* **-paces** : incapable
incautar *vt* : confiscate, seize
incendiar *vt* : set fire to, burn (down) — **incendiarse** *vr* : catch fire — **incendiario, -ria** *adj* : incendiary — ~ *n* : arsonist — **incendio** *nm* **1** : fire **2** ~ **premeditado** : arson
incentivo *nm* : incentive
incertidumbre *nf* : uncertainty
incesante *adj* : incessant
incesto *nm* : incest — **incestuoso, -sa** *adj* : incestuous
incidencia *nf* **1** : impact **2** SUCESO : incident — **incidental** *adj* : incidental — **incidente** *nm* : incident
incidir *vi* ~ **en 1** : fall into (a habit, mistake, etc.) **2** INFLUIR EN : affect, influence
incienso *nm* : incense
incierto, -ta *adj* : uncertain
incinerar *vt* **1** : incinerate **2** : cremate (a corpse) — **incineración** *nf, pl* **-ciones 1** : incineration **2** : cremation (of a corpse) — **incinerador** *nm* : incinerator
incipiente *adj* : incipient
incisión *nf, pl* **-siones** : incision
incisivo, -va *adj* : incisive — **incisivo** *nm* : incisor
incitar *vt* : incite, rouse
incivilizado, -da *adj* : uncivilized
inclinar *vt* : tilt, lean — **inclinarse** *vr* **1** : lean (over) **2** ~ **a** : be inclined to — **inclinación** *nf, pl* **-ciones 1** : inclination **2** LADEAR : incline, tilt
incluir {41} *vt* **1** : include **2** ADJUNTAR : enclose — **inclusión** *nf, pl* **-siones** : inclusion — **inclusive** *adv* : up to and including — **inclusivo, -va** *adj* : inclusive — **incluso** *adv* : even, in fact — **incluso, -sa** *adj* : enclosed
incógnito, -ta *adj* **1** : unknown **2 de** ~ : incognito
incoherente *adj* : incoherent — **incoherencia** *nf* : incoherence
incoloro, -ra *adj* : colorless
incombustible *adj* : fireproof
incomible *adj* : inedible
incomodar *vt* **1** : inconvenience **2** ENFADAR : bother, annoy — **incomodarse** *vr* **1** : take the trouble **2** ENFADARSE : get annoyed — **incomodidad** *nf* : discomfort — **incómodo, -da** *adj* **1** : uncomfortable **2** INCONVENIENTE : inconvenient, awkward
incomparable *adj* : incomparable
incompatible *adj* : incompatible — **incompatibilidad** *nf* : incompatibility
incompetente *adj* : incompetent — **incompetencia** *nf* : incompetence
incompleto, -ta *adj* : incomplete
incomprendido, -da *adj* : misunderstood — **incomprensible** *adj* : incomprehensible — **incomprensión** *nf, pl* **-siones** : lack of understanding
incomunicado, -da *adj* **1** : isolated **2** : in solitary confinement
inconcebible *adj* : inconceivable
inconcluso, -sa *adj* : unfinished
incondicional *adj* : unconditional
inconformista *adj & nmf* : nonconformist
inconfundible *adj* : unmistakable
incongruente *adj* : incongruous
inconmensurable *adj* : vast, immeasurable
inconsciente *adj* **1** : unconscious, unaware **2** IRREFLEXIVO : reckless — ~ *nm* **el** ~ : the unconscious — **inconsciencia** *nf* **1** : unconsciousness **2** INSENSATEZ : thoughtlessness
inconsecuente *adj* : inconsistent — **inconsecuencia** *nf* : inconsistency
inconsiderado, -da *adj* : inconsiderate
inconsistente *adj* **1** : flimsy **2** : watery (of a sauce, etc.) **3** : inconsistent (of an argument) — **inconsistencia** *nf* : inconsistency
inconsolable *adj* : inconsolable
inconstante *adj* : changeable, unreliable — **inconstancia** *nf* : inconstancy
inconstitucional *adj* : unconstitutional
incontable *adj* : countless
incontenible *adj* : irrepressible
incontestable *adj* : indisputable
incontinente *adj* : incontinent — **incontinencia** *nf* : incontinence
inconveniente *adj* **1** : inconvenient **2** INAPROPIADO : inappropriate — ~ *nm* : obstacle, problem — **inconveniencia** *nf* **1** : inconvenience **2** : tactless remark
incorporar *vt* **1** AGREGAR : incorporate, add **2** : mix (in cooking) — **incorporarse** *vr* **1** : sit up **2** ~ **a** : join — **incorporación** *nf, pl* **-ciones** : incorporation
incorrecto, -ta *adj* **1** : incorrect **2** DESCORTÉS : impolite
incorregible *adj* : incorrigible
incrédulo, -la *adj* : incredulous — **incredulidad** *nf* : incredulity, disbelief
increíble *adj* : incredible, unbelievable
incrementar *vt* : increase — **incremento** *nm* : increase
incriminar *vt* **1** : incriminate **2** ACUSAR : accuse
incrustar *vt* : set, inlay — **incrustarse** *vr* : become embedded
incubar *vt* : incubate — **incubadora** *nf* : incubator
incuestionable *adj* : unquestionable
inculcar {72} *vt* : instill
inculpar *vt* : accuse, charge
inculto, -ta *adj* **1** : uneducated **2** : uncultivated (of land)
incumplimiento *nm* **1** : noncompliance **2** ~ **de contrato** : breach of contract
incurable *adj* : incurable
incurrir *vi* ~ **en 1** : incur (expenses, etc.) **2** : fall into, commit (crimes)
incursión *nf, pl* **-siones** : raid
indagar {52} *vt* : investigate — **indagación** *nf, pl* **-ciones** : investigation
indebido, -da *adj* : undue
indecente *adj* : indecent, obscene — **indecencia** *nf* : indecency, obscenity
indecible *adj* : inexpressible
indecisión *nf, pl* **-siones** : indecision — **indeciso, -sa** *adj* **1** : undecided **2** IRRESOLUTO : indecisive
indefenso, -sa *adj* : defenseless, helpless
indefinido, -da *adj* : indefinite — **indefinidamente** *adv* : indefinitely
indeleble *adj* : indelible
indemnizar {21} *vt* : indemnify, compensate — **indemnización** *nf, pl* **-ciones** : compensation
independiente *adj* : independent — **independencia** *nf* : independence — **independizarse** {21} *vr* : become independent
indescifrable *adj* : indecipherable
indescriptible *adj* : indescribable
indeseable *adj* : undesirable
indestructible *adj* : indestructible
indeterminado, -da *adj* : indeterminate
indicar {72} *vt* **1** : indicate **2** MOSTRAR : show — **indicación** *nf, pl* **-ciones 1** : sign, indication **2** **indicaciones** *nfpl* : directions — **indicador** *nm* **1** : sign, signal **2** : gauge, dial, meter — **indicativo, -va** *adj* : indicative — **indicativo** *nm* : indicative (mood)
índice *nm* **1** : indication **2** : index (of a book, etc.) **3** : index finger **4** ~ **de natalidad** : birth rate
indicio *nm* : indication, sign
indiferente *adj* **1** : indifferent **2** **me es** ~ : it doesn't matter to me — **indiferencia** *nf* : indifference
indígena *adj* : indigenous, native — ~ *nmf* : native
indigente *adj & nmf* : indigent — **indigencia** *nf* : poverty
indigestión *nf, pl* **-tiones** : indigestion — **indigesto, -ta** *adj* : indigestible
indignar *vt* : outrage, infuriate — **indignarse** *vr* : become indignant — **indignación** *nf, pl* **-ciones** : indignation — **indignado, -da** *adj* : indignant — **indignidad** *nf* : indignity — **indigno, -na** *adj* : unworthy
indio, -dia *adj* **1** : American Indian **2** : Indian (from India)
indirecta *nf* **1** : hint **2** **lanzar una** ~ : drop a hint — **indirecto, -ta** *adj* : indirect
indisciplina *nf* : lack of discipline — **indisciplinado, -da** *adj* : undisciplined
indiscreto, -ta *adj* : indiscreet — **indiscreción** *nf, pl* **-ciones 1** : indiscretion **2** : tactless remark
indiscriminado, -da *adj* : indiscriminate
indiscutible *adj* : indisputable
indispensable *adj* : indispensable
indisponer {60} *vt* **1** : upset, make ill **2** ENEMISTAR : set against, set at odds — **indisponerse** *vr* **1** : become ill **2** ~ **con** : fall out with — **indisposición** *nf, pl* **-ciones** : indisposition, illness — **indispuesto, -ta** *adj* : unwell, indisposed
indistinto, -ta *adj* : indistinct
individual *adj* : individual — **individualidad** *nf* : individuality — **individualizar** {21} *vt* : individualize — **individuo** *nm* : individual
indivisible *adj* : indivisible
índole *nf* **1** : nature, character **2** TIPO : type, kind
indolente *adj* : indolent, lazy — **indolencia** *nf* : indolence, laziness
indoloro, -ra *adj* : painless
indómito, -ta *adj* : indomitable
indonesio, -sia *adj* : Indonesian
inducir {61} *vt* **1** : induce **2** DEDUCIR : infer
indudable *adj* : beyond doubt — **indudablemente** *adv* : undoubtedly
indulgente *adj* : indulgent — **indulgencia** *nf* : indulgence
indultar *vt* : pardon, reprieve — **indulto** *nm* : pardon, reprieve
industria *nf* : industry — **industrial** *adj* : industrial — ~ *nmf* : industrialist, manufacturer — **industrialización** *nf, pl* **-ciones** : industrialization — **industrializar** {21} *vt* : industrialize — **industrioso, -sa** *adj* : industrious
inédito, -ta *adj* : unpublished
inefable *adj* : inexpressible
ineficaz *adj, pl* **-caces 1** : ineffective **2** INEFICIENTE : inefficient
ineficiente *adj* : inefficient — **ineficiencia** *nf* : inefficiency
ineligible *adj* : ineligible
ineludible *adj* : unavoidable, inescapable
inepto, -ta *adj* : inept — **ineptitud** *nf* : ineptitude
inequívoco, -ca *adj* : unequivocal
inercia *nf* : inertia
inerme *adj* : unarmed, defenseless
inerte *adj* : inert
inesperado, -da *adj* : unexpected
inestable *adj* : unstable — **inestabilidad** *nf* : instability
inevitable *adj* : inevitable
inexacto, -ta *adj* **1** : inexact **2** INCORRECTO : incorrect, wrong
inexistente *adj* : nonexistent
inexorable *adj* : inexorable
inexperiencia *nf* : inexperience — **inexperto, -ta** *adj* : inexperienced, unskilled
inexplicable *adj* : inexplicable
infalible *adj* : infallible
infame *adj* **1** : infamous, vile **2** *fam* : horrible — **infamia** *nf* : infamy, disgrace
infancia *nf* : infancy — **infanta** *nf* : infanta, princess — **infante** *nm* **1** : infante, prince **2** : infantryman (in the military) — **infantería** *nf* : infantry — **infantil** *adj* **1** : child's, children's **2** INMADURO : childish
infarto *nm* : heart attack
infatigable *adj* : tireless
infectar *vt* : infect — **infectarse** *vr* : become infected — **infección** *nf, pl* **-ciones** : infection — **infeccioso, -sa** *adj* : infectious — **infecto, -ta** *adj* **1** : infected **2** : foul, sickening
infecundo, -da *adj* : infertile
infeliz *adj, pl* **-lices** : unhappy — **infelicidad** *nf* : unhappiness
inferior *adj & nmf* : inferior — **inferioridad** *nf* : inferiority
inferir {76} *vt* **1** DEDUCIR : infer **2** : cause (harm or injury)
infernal *adj* : infernal, hellish
infestar *vt* : infest
infiel *adj* : unfaithful — **infidelidad** *nf* : infidelity
infierno *nm* **1** : hell **2** **el quinto** ~ *fam* : the middle of nowhere
infiltrar *vt* : infiltrate — **infiltrarse** *vr* : infiltrate

infinidad *nf* **1** : infinity **2 una ~ de** : countless — **infinitivo** *nm* : infinitive — **infinito, -ta** *adj* : infinite — **infinito** *nm* : infinity

inflación *nf, pl* **-ciones** : inflation — **inflacionario, -ria** *or* **inflacionista** *adj* : inflationary

inflamar *vt* : inflame — **inflamable** *adj* : flammable, inflammable — **inflamación** *nf, pl* **-ciones** : inflammation — **inflamatorio, -ria** *adj* : inflammatory

inflar *vt* **1** : inflate **2** EXAGERAR : exaggerate — **inflarse** *vr* **~ de** : swell (up) with

inflexible *adj* : inflexible — **inflexión** *nf, pl* **-xiones** : inflection

infligir {35} *vt* : inflict

influencia *nf* : influence — **influenciar** → **influir**

influenza *nf* : influenza

influir {41} *vt* : influence — *vi* **~ en** *or* **~ sobre** : have an influence on — **influjo** *nm* : influence — **influyente** *adj* : influential

información *nf, pl* **-ciones 1** : information **2** NOTICIAS : news **3** : directory assistance (on the telephone)

informal *adj* **1** : informal **2** IRRESPONSABLE : unreliable

informar *v* : inform — **informarse** *vr* : get information, find out — **informante** *nmf* : informant — **informática** *nf* : information technology — **informativo, -va** *adj* : informative — **informatizar** {21} *vt* : computerize

informe *adj* : shapeless — **~** *nm* **1** : report **2 ~s** *nmpl* : information, data **3 ~s** *nmpl* : references (for employment)

infortunado, -da *adj* : unfortunate — **infortunio** *nm* : misfortune

infracción *nf, pl* **-ciones** : violation, infraction

infraestructura *nf* : infrastructure

infrahumano, -na *adj* : subhuman

infranqueable *adj* **1** : impassable **2** INSUPERABLE : insurmountable

infrarrojo, -ja *adj* : infrared

infrecuente *adj* : infrequent

infringir {35} *vt* : infringe

infructuoso, -sa *adj* : fruitless

infundado, -da *adj* : unfounded, baseless

infundir *vt* : instill, infuse — **infusión** *nf, pl* **-siones** : infusion

ingeniar *vt* : invent, think up

ingeniería *nf* : engineering — **ingeniero, -ra** *n* : engineer

ingenio *nm* **1** : ingenuity **2** AGUDEZA : wit **3** MÁQUINA : device, apparatus **4 ~ azucarero** *Lat* : sugar refinery — **ingenioso, -sa** *adj* **1** : ingenious **2** AGUDO : clever, witty — **ingeniosamente** *adv* : cleverly

ingenuidad *nf* : naïveté, ingenuousness — **ingenuo, -nua** *adj* : naive

ingerir {76} *vt* : ingest, consume

ingle *nf* : groin

inglés, -glesa *adj, mpl* **-gleses** : English — **inglés** *nm* : English (language)

ingrato, -ta *adj* **1** : ungrateful **2 un trabajo ingrato** : a thankless task — **ingratitud** *nf* : ingratitude

ingrediente *nm* : ingredient

ingresar *vt* : deposit — *vi* **~ en** : enter, be admitted into, join — **ingreso** *nm* **1** : entrance, entry **2** : admission (into a hospital, etc.) **3 ~s** *nmpl* : income, earnings

inhábil *adj* **1** : unskillful, clumsy **2 ~ para** : unsuited for — **inhabilidad** *nf* : unskillfulness

inhabitable *adj* : uninhabitable — **inhabitado, -da** *adj* : uninhabited

inhalar *vt* : inhale — **inhalación** *nf* : inhalation

inherente *adj* : inherent

inhibir *vt* : inhibit — **inhibición** *nf, pl* **-ciones** : inhibition

inhóspito, -ta *adj* : inhospitable

inhumano, -na *adj* : inhuman, inhumane — **inhumanidad** *nf* : inhumanity

iniciar *vt* : initiate, begin — **iniciación** *nf, pl* **-ciones 1** : initiation **2** COMIENZO : beginning — **inicial** *adj & nf* : initial — **iniciativa** *nf* : initiative — **inicio** *nm* : start, beginning

inigualado, -da *adj* : unequaled

ininterrumpido, -da *adj* : uninterrupted

injerirse {76} *vr* : interfere — **injerencia** *nf* : interference

injertar *vt* : graft — **injerto** *nm* : graft

injuriar *vt* : insult — **injuria** *nf* : insult — **injurioso, -sa** *adj* : insulting, abusive

injusticia *nf* : injustice, unfairness — **injusto, -ta** *adj* : unfair, unjust

inmaculado, -da *adj* : immaculate

inmaduro, -ra *adj* **1** : immature **2** : unripe (of fruit) — **inmadurez** *nf* : immaturity

inmediaciones *nfpl* : surrounding area

inmediato, -ta *adj* **1** : immediate **2** CONTIGUO : adjoining **3 de ~** : immediately, right away **4 ~ a** : next to, close to — **inmediatamente** *adv* : immediately

inmejorable *adj* : excellent

inmenso, -sa *adj* : immense, vast — **inmensidad** *nf* : immensity

inmerecido, -da *adj* : undeserved

inmersión *nf, pl* **-siones** : immersion

inmigrar *vi* : immigrate — **inmigración** *nf, pl* **-ciones** : immigration — **inmigrante** *adj & nmf* : immigrant

inminente *adj* : imminent, impending — **inminencia** *nf* : imminence

inmiscuirse {41} *vr* : interfere

inmobiliario, -ria *adj* : real estate, property

inmodesto, -ta *adj* : immodest

inmoral *adj* : immoral — **inmoralidad** *nf* : immorality

inmortal *adj & nmf* : immortal — **inmortalidad** *nf* : immortality

inmóvil *adj* : motionless, still — **inmovilizar** {21} *vt* : immobilize

inmueble *nm* : building, property

inmundicia *nf* : filth, trash — **inmundo, -da** *adj* : dirty, filthy

inmunizar {21} *vt* : immunize — **inmune** *adj* : immune — **inmunidad** *nf* : immunity — **inmunización** *nf, pl* **-ciones** : immunization

inmutable *adj* : unchangeable

innato, -ta *adj* : innate

innecesario, -ria *adj* : unnecessary, needless

innegable *adj* : undeniable

innoble *adj* : ignoble

innovar *vt* : introduce — *vi* : innovate — **innovación** *nf, pl* **-ciones** : innovation — **innovador, -dora** *adj* : innovative — **~** *n* : innovator

innumerable *adj* : innumerable

inocencia *nf* : innocence — **inocente** *adj & nmf* : innocent — **inocentón, -tona** *adj, mpl* **-tones** : naive — **~** *n* : simpleton, dupe

inocular *vt* : inoculate — **inoculación** *nf, pl* **-ciones** : inoculation

inocuo, -cua *adj* : innocuous

inodoro, -ra *adj* : odorless — **inodoro** *nm* : toilet

inofensivo, -va *adj* : inoffensive, harmless

inolvidable *adj* : unforgettable

inoperable *adj* : inoperable

inoperante *adj* : ineffective

inopinado, -da *adj* : unexpected

inoportuno, -na *adj* : untimely, inopportune

inorgánico, -ca *adj* : inorganic

inoxidable *adj* **1** : rustproof **2 acero ~** : stainless steel

inquebrantable *adj* : unwavering

inquietar *vt* : disturb, worry — **inquietarse** *vr* : worry — **inquietante** *adj* : disturbing, worrisome — **inquieto, -ta** *adj* : anxious, worried — **inquietud** *nf* : anxiety, worry

inquilino, -na *n* : tenant

inquirir {4} *vi* : make inquiries — *vt* : investigate

insaciable *adj* : insatiable

insalubre *adj* : unhealthy

insatisfecho, -cha *adj* **1** : unsatisfied **2** DESCONTENTO : dissatisfied

inscribir {33} *vt* **1** : enroll, register **2** GRABAR : inscribe, engrave — **inscribirse** *vr* : register — **inscripción** *nf, pl* **-ciones 1** : inscription **2** REGISTRO : registration

insecto *nm* : insect — **insecticida** *nm* : insecticide

inseguro, -ra *adj* **1** : insecure **2** PELIGROSO : unsafe **3** DUDOSO : uncertain — **inseguridad** *nf* **1** : insecurity **2** PELIGRO : lack of safety **3** DUDA : uncertainty

inseminar *vt* : inseminate — **inseminación** *nf, pl* **-ciones** : insemination

insensato, -ta *adj* : senseless, foolish — **insensatez** *nf* : foolishness, thoughtlessness

insensible *adj* **1** : insensitive, unfeeling **2** : numb (in medicine) **3** IMPERCEPTIBLE : imperceptible — **insensibilidad** *nf* : insensitivity

inseparable *adj* : inseparable

insertar *vt* : insert

insidia *nf* : snare, trap — **insidioso, -sa** *adj* : insidious

insigne *adj* : noted, famous

insignia *nf* **1** : insignia, badge **2** BANDERA : flag

insignificante *adj* : insignificant, negligible

insincero, -ra *adj* : insincere

insinuar {3} *vt* : insinuate — **insinuarse** *vr* **~ en** : worm one's way into — **insinuación** *nf, pl* **-ciones** : insinuation — **insinuante** *adj* : insinuating, suggestive

insípido, -da *adj* : insipid

insistir *v* : insist — **insistencia** *nf* : insistence — **insistente** *adj* : insistent

insociable *adj* : unsociable

insolación *nf, pl* **-ciones** : sunstroke

insolencia *nf* : insolence — **insolente** *adj* : insolent

insólito, -ta *adj* : rare, unusual

insoluble *adj* : insoluble

insolvencia *nf* : insolvency, bankruptcy — **insolvente** *adj* : insolvent, bankrupt

insomnio *nm* : insomnia — **insomne** *nmf* : insomniac

insondable *adj* : unfathomable

insonorizado, -da *adj* : soundproof

insoportable *adj* : unbearable

insospechado, -da *adj* : unexpected

insostenible *adj* : untenable

inspeccionar *vt* : inspect — **inspección** *nf, pl* **-ciones** : inspection — **inspector, -tora** *n* : inspector

inspirar *vt* : inspire — *vi* : inhale — **inspirarse** *vr* : be inspired — **inspiración** *nf, pl* **-ciones 1** : inspiration **2** RESPIRACIÓN : inhalation — **inspirador, -dora** *adj* : inspirational

instalar *vt* : install — **instalarse** *vr* : settle — **instalación** *nf, pl* **-ciones** : installation

instancia *nf* **1** : request **2 en última ~** : ultimately, as a last resort

instantáneo, -nea *adj* : instantaneous, instant — **instantánea** *nf* : snapshot — **instante** *nm* **1** : instant **2 a cada ~** : frequently, all the time **3 al ~** : immediately

instar *vt* : urge, press

instaurar *vt* : establish — **instauración** *nf, pl* **-ciones** : establishment

instigar {52} *vt* : incite, instigate — **instigador, -dora** *n* : instigator

instinto *nm* : instinct — **instintivo, -va** *adj* : instinctive

institución *nf, pl* **-ciones** : institution — **institucional** *adj* : institutional — **institucionalizar** {21} *vt* : institutionalize — **instituir** {41} *vt* : institute, establish — **instituto** *nm* : institute — **institutriz** *nf, pl* **-trices** : governess

instruir {41} *vt* : instruct — **instrucción** *nf, pl* **-ciones 1** : instruction **2 instrucciones** *nfpl* : instructions, directions — **instructivo, -va** *adj* : instructive — **instructor, -tora** *n* : instructor

instrumento *nm* : instrument — **instrumental** *adj* : instrumental

insubordinarse *vr* : rebel — **insubordinado, -da** *adj* : insubordinate — **insubordinación** *nf, pl* **-ciones** : insubordination

insuficiente *adj* : insufficient, inadequate — **insuficiencia** *nf* **1** : insufficiency, inadequacy **2 ~ cardíaca** : heart failure

insufrible *adj* : insufferable

insular *adj* : insular, island

insulina *nf* : insulin

insulso, -sa *adj* **1** : insipid, bland **2** SOSO : dull

insultar *vt* : insult — **insultante** *adj* : insulting — **insulto** *nm* : insult

insuperable *adj* : insurmountable

insurgente *adj & nmf* : insurgent

insurrección *nf, pl* **-ciones** : insurrection, uprising

intachable *adj* : irreproachable

intacto, -ta *adj* : intact

intangible *adj* : intangible

integrar *vt* : integrate — **integrarse** *vr* : become integrated — **integración** *nf, pl* **-ciones** : integration — **integral** *adj* **1** : integral **2 pan ~** : whole grain bread — **íntegro, -gra** *adj* **1** : honest, upright **2** ENTERO : whole, complete — **integridad** *nf* **1** RECTITUD : integrity **2** TOTALIDAD : wholeness

intelecto *nm* : intellect — **intelectual** *adj & nmf* : intellectual

inteligencia *nf* : intelligence — **inteligente** *adj* : intelligent — **inteligible** *adj* : intelligible

intemperie *nf* **a la ~** : in the open air, outside

intempestivo, -va *adj* : untimely, inopportune

intención *nf, pl* **-ciones** : intention, intent — **intencionado, -da** *adj* **1** : intended **2 bien ~** : well-meaning **3 mal ~** : malicious — **intencional** *adj* : intentional

intensidad *nf* : intensity — **intensificar** {72} *vt* : intensify — **intensificarse** *vr* : intensify — **intensivo, -va** *adj* : intensive — **intenso, -sa** *adj* : intense

intentar *vt* : attempt, try — **intento** *nm* **1** : intention **2** TENTATIVA : attempt

interactuar {3} *vi* : interact — **interacción** *nf, pl* **-ciones** : interaction — **interactivo, -va** *adj* : interactive

intercalar *vt* : insert, intersperse

intercambio *nm* : exchange — **intercambiable** *adj* : interchangeable — **intercambiar** *vt* : exchange, trade

interceder *vi* : intercede

interceptar *vt* : intercept — **intercepción** *nf, pl* **-ciones** : interception

intercesión *nf, pl* **-siones** : intercession

interés *nm, pl* **-reses** : interest — **interesado, -da** *adj* **1** : interested **2** EGOISTA : selfish — **interesante** *adj* : interesting — **interesar** *vt* : interest — *vi* : be of interest — **interesarse** *vr* : take an interest

interfaz *nf, pl* **-faces** : interface

interferir {76} *vi* : interfere — *vt* : interfere with — **interferencia** *nf* : interference

interino, -na *adj* : temporary, interim — **interiormente** *adv* : inwardly

interior *adj* : interior, inner — **~** *nm* : interior, inside — **interiormente** *adv* : inwardly

interjección *nf, pl* **-ciones** : interjection

interlocutor, -tora *n* : speaker

intermediario, -ria *adj & n* : intermediary

intermedio, -dia *adj* : intermediate — **intermedio** *nm* : intermission

interminable *adj* : interminable, endless

intermisión *nf, pl* **-siones** : intermission, pause

intermitente *adj* : intermittent — **~** *nm* : blinker, turn signal

internacional *adj* : international

internar *vt* : commit, confine — **internarse** *vr* : penetrate — **internado** *nm* : boarding school — **interno, -na** *adj* : internal — **~** *n* **1** : boarder **2** : inmate (in a jail, etc.)

interponer {60} *vt* : interpose — **interponerse** *vr* : intervene

interpretar *vt* **1** : interpret **2** : play, perform (in theater, etc.) — **interpretación** *nf, pl* **-ciones** : interpretation — **intérprete** *nmf* **1** TRADUCTOR : interpreter **2** : performer (of music)

interrogar {52} *vt* : interrogate, question — **interrogación** *nf, pl* **-ciones 1** : interrogation **2 signo de ~** : question mark — **interrogativo, -va** *adj* : interrogative — **interrogatorio** *nm* : interrogation, questioning

interrumpir *v* : interrupt — **interrupción** *nf, pl* **-ciones** : interruption — **interruptor** *nm* : (electrical) switch

intersección *nf, pl* **-ciones** : intersection

intervalo *nm* : interval

intervenir {87} *vi* **1** : take part **2** MEDIAR : intervene — *vt* **1** : tap (a telephone) **2** INSPECCIONAR : audit **3** OPERAR : operate on — **intervención** *nf, pl* **-ciones 1** : intervention **2** : audit (in business) **3** *or* **~ quirúrgica** : operation — **interventor, -tora** *n* : inspector, auditor

intestino *nm* : intestine — **intestinal** *adj* : intestinal

intimar *vi* **~ con** : become friendly with — **intimidad** *nf* **1** : private life **2** AMISTAD : intimacy

intimidar *vt* : intimidate

íntimo, -ma *adj* **1** : intimate, close **2** PRIVADO : private

intolerable *adj* : intolerable — **intolerancia** *nf* : intolerance — **intolerante** *adj* : intolerant

intoxicar {72} *vt* : poison — **intoxicación** *nf, pl* **-ciones** : poisoning

intranquilizar {21} *vt* : make uneasy — **intranquilizarse** *vr* : be anxious — **intranquilidad** *nf* : uneasiness, anxiety — **intranquilo, -la** *adj* : uneasy, worried

intransigente *adj* : unyielding, intransigent

intransitable *adj* : impassable

intransitivo, -va *adj* : intransitive

intrascendente *adj* : unimportant, insignificant

intravenoso, -sa *adj* : intravenous

intrépido, -da *adj* : intrepid, fearless

intrigar {52} *v* : intrigue — **intriga** *nf* : intrigue — **intrigante** *adj* : intriguing

intrincado, -da *adj* : intricate, involved

intrínseco, -ca *adj* : intrinsic — **intrínsecamente** *adv* : intrinsically, inherently

introducción *nf, pl* **-ciones** : introduction — **introducir** {61} *vt* **1** : introduce **2** METER : insert — **introducirse** *vr* **~ en** : penetrate, get into — **introductorio, -ria** *adj* : introductory

intromisión *nf, pl* **-siones** : interference

introvertido, -da *adj* : introverted — **~** *n* : introvert

intrusión *nf, pl* **-siones** : intrusion — **intruso, -sa** *adj* : intrusive — **~** *n* : intruder

intuir {41} *vt* : sense — **intuición** *nf, pl* **-ciones** : intuition — **intuitivo, -va** *adj* : intuitive

inundar *vt* : flood — **inundarse** *vr* **~ de** : be inundated with — **inundación** *nf, pl* **-ciones** : flood

inusitado, -da *adj* : unusual, uncommon

inútil *adj* **1** : useless **2** INVÁLIDO : disabled — **inutilidad** *nf* : uselessness — **inutilizar** {21} *vt* **1** : make useless **2** INCAPACITAR : disable

invadir *vt* : invade

invalidez *nf, pl* **-deces 1** : invalidity **2** : disability (in medicine) — **inválido, -da** *adj & n* : invalid

invalorable *adj Lat* : invaluable

invariable *adj* : invariable

invasión *nf, pl* **-siones** : invasion — **invasor, -sora** *adj* : invading — **~** *n* : invader

invencible *adj* : invincible

inventar *vt* **1** : invent **2** : fabricate, make up (a word, an excuse, etc.) — **invención** *nf, pl* **-ciones 1** : invention **2** MENTIRA : lie, fabrication

inventario *nm* : inventory

inventiva *nf* : inventiveness — **inventivo, -va** *adj* : inventive — **inventor, -tora** *n* : inventor

invernadero *nm* : greenhouse

invernal *adj* : winter

inverosímil *adj* : unlikely

inversión *nf, pl* **-siones 1** : inversion, reversal **2** : investment (of money, time, etc.)

inverso, -sa *adj* **1** : inverse **2** CONTRARIO : opposite **3 a la inversa** : the other way around, inversely

inversor, -sora *n* : investor

invertebrado, -da *adj* : invertebrate — **invertebrado** *nm* : invertebrate

invertir {76} *vt* **1** : invert, reverse **2** : invest (money, time, etc.) — *vi* : make an investment

investidura *nf* : investiture

investigar {52} *vt* **1** : investigate **2** ESTUDIAR : research — *vi* **~ sobre** : do research into — **investigación** *nf, pl* **-ciones 1** : investigation **2** ESTUDIO : research — **investigador, -dora** *n* : investigator, researcher

investir {54} *vt* : invest

inveterado, -da *adj* : deep-seated, inveterate
invicto, -ta *adj* : undefeated
invierno *nm* : winter
invisible *adj* : invisible — **invisibilidad** *nf* : invisibility
invitar *vt* : invite — **invitación** *nf, pl* **-ciones** : invitation — **invitado, -da** *n* : guest
invocar {72} *vt* : invoke — **invocación** *nf, pl* **-ciones** : invocation
involuntario, -ria *adj* : involuntary
invulnerable *adj* : invulnerable
inyectar *vt* : inject — **inyección** *nf, pl* **-ciones** : injection, shot — **inyectado, -da** *adj* **ojos inyectados** : bloodshot eyes
ion *nm* : ion — **ionizar** {21} *vt* : ionize
ir {43} *vi* **1** : go **2** FUNCIONAR : work, function **3** CONVENIR : suit **4 ¿cómo te va?** : how are you? **5 ~ con prisa** : be in a hurry **6 ~ por** : follow, go along **7 vamos** : let's go — *v aux* **1 ~ a** : be going to, be about to **2 ~ caminando** : take a walk **3 vamos a ver** : we shall see — **irse** *vr* : go away, be gone
ira *nf* : rage, anger — **iracundo, -da** *adj* : irate, angry
iraní *adj* : Iranian
iraquí *adj* : Iraqi
iris *nms & pl* **1** : iris (of the eye) **2 arco ~** : rainbow
irlandés, -desa *adj, mpl* **-deses** : Irish
ironía *nf* : irony — **irónico, -ca** *adj* : ironic, ironical
irracional *adj* : irrational
irradiar *vt* : radiate, irradiate
irrazonable *adj* : unreasonable
irreal *adj* : unreal
irreconciliable *adj* : irreconcilable
irreconocible *adj* : unrecognizable
irrecuperable *adj* : irretrievable
irreductible *adj* : unyielding
irreemplazable *adj* : irreplaceable
irreflexivo, -va *adj* : rash, unthinking
irrefutable *adj* : irrefutable
irregular *adj* : irregular — **irregularidad** *nf* : irregularity
irrelevante *adj* : irrelevant
irreparable *adj* : irreparable
irreprimible *adj* : irrepressible
irreprochable *adj* : irreproachable
irresistible *adj* : irresistible
irresoluto, -ta *adj* : indecisive, irresolute
irrespetuoso, -sa *adj* : disrespectful
irresponsable *adj* : irresponsible — **irresponsabilidad** *nf* : irresponsibility
irreverente *adj* : irreverent
irreversible *adj* : irreversible
irrevocable *adj* : irrevocable
irrigar {52} *vt* : irrigate — **irrigación** *nf, pl* **-ciones** : irrigation
irrisorio, -ria *adj* : laughable, ridiculous
irritar *vt* : irritate — **irritarse** *vr* : get annoyed — **irritable** *adj* : irritable — **irritación** *nf, pl* **-ciones** : irritation — **irritante** *adj* : irritating
irrompible *adj* : unbreakable
irrumpir *vi* **~ en** : burst into
isla *nf* : island
islámico, -ca *adj* : Islamic, Muslim
islandés, -desa *adj, mpl* **-deses** : Icelandic
isleño, -ña *n* : islander
israelí *adj* : Israeli
istmo *nm* : isthmus
italiano, -na *adj* : Italian — **italiano** *nm* : Italian (language)
itinerario *nm* : itinerary
izar {21} *vt* : hoist, raise
izquierda *nf* : left — **izquierdista** *adj & nmf* : leftist — **izquierdo, -da** *adj* : left

J

j *nf* : j, tenth letter of the Spanish alphabet
jabalí *nm, pl* **-líes** : wild boar
jabalina *nf* : javelin
jabón *nm, pl* **-bones** : soap — **jabonar** *vt* : soap (up) — **jabonera** *nf* : soap dish — **jabonoso, -sa** *adj* : soapy
jaca *nf* : pony
jacinto *nm* : hyacinth
jactarse *vr* : boast, brag — **jactancia** *nf* : boastfulness, bragging — **jactancioso, -sa** *adj* : boastful
jadear *vi* : pant, gasp — **jadeante** *adj* : panting, breathless — **jadeo** *nm* : gasp, panting
jaez *nm, pl* **jaeces 1** : harness **2 jaeces** *nmpl* : trappings
jaguar *nm* : jaguar
jaiba *nf Lat* : crab
jalapeño *nm Lat* : jalapeño pepper
jalar *v Lat* : pull, tug
jalea *nf* : jelly
jaleo *nm fam* **1** : uproar, racket **2 armar un ~** : raise a ruckus
jalón *nm, pl* **-lones** *Lat* : pull, tug
jamaicano, -na *or* **jamaiquino, -na** *adj* : Jamaican
jamás *adv* **1** : never **2 para siempre ~** : for ever and ever
jamelgo *nm* : nag (horse)
jamón *nm, pl* **-mones 1** : ham **2 ~ serrano** : cured ham
Janucá *nmf* : Hanukkah
japonés, -nesa *adj, mpl* **-neses** : Japanese — **japonés** *nm* : Japanese (language)
jaque *nm* **1** : check (in chess) **2 ~ mate** : checkmate
jaqueca *nf* : headache, migraine
jarabe *nm* : syrup
jardín *nm, pl* **-dines 1** : garden **2 ~ infantil** *or* **~ de niños** *Lat* : kindergarten — **jardinería** *nf* : gardening — **jardinero, -ra** *n* : gardener
jarra *nf* : pitcher, jug — **jarro** *nm* : pitcher — **jarrón** *nm, pl* **-rrones** : vase
jaula *nf* : cage
jauría *nf* : pack of hounds
jazmín *nm, pl* **-mines** : jasmine
jazz ['jas, 'dʒas] *nm* : jazz
jeans ['jins, 'dʒins] *nmpl* : jeans
jefe, -fa *n* **1** : chief, leader **2** PATRÓN : boss **3 ~ de cocina** : chef — **jefatura** *nf* **1** : leadership **2** SEDE : headquarters
jengibre *nm* : ginger
jeque *nm* : sheikh, sheik
jerarquía *nf* **1** : hierarchy **2** RANGO : rank — **jerárquico, -ca** *adj* : hierarchical
jerez *nm, pl* **-reces** : sherry
jerga *nf* **1** : coarse cloth **2** ARGOT : jargon, slang
jerigonza *nf* **1** : jargon **2** GALIMATÍAS : gibberish
jeringa *or* **jeringuilla** *nf* : syringe — **jeringar** {52} *vt fam* : annoy, pester
jeroglífico *nm* : hieroglyphic
jersey *nm, pl* **-seys** : jersey
jesuita *adj & nm* : Jesuit
Jesús *nm* : Jesus
jilguero *nm* : goldfinch
jinete *nmf* : horseman, horsewoman *f*, rider
jirafa *nf* : giraffe
jirón *nm, pl* **-rones** : shred, tatter
jitomate *nm Lat* : tomato
jockey ['jɔki, 'dʒɔ-] *nmf, pl* **-keys** [-kis] : jockey
jocoso, -sa *adj* : humorous, jocular
jofaina *nf* : washbowl
jolgorio *nm* : merrymaking
jornada *nf* **1** : day's journey **2** : working day — **jornal** *nm* : day's pay — **jornalero, -ra** *n* : day laborer
joroba *nf* : hump — **jorobado, -da** *adj* : hunchbacked, humpbacked — **~** *n* : hunchback — **jorobar** *vt fam* : annoy
jota *nf* **1** : iota, jot **2 no veo ni ~** : I can't see a thing
joven *adj, pl* **jóvenes** : young — **~** *nmf* : young man *m*, young woman *f*, youth
jovial *adj* : jovial, cheerful
joya *nf* : jewel — **joyería** *nf* : jewelry store — **joyero, -ra** *n* : jeweler — **joyero** *nm* : jewelry box
juanete *nm* : bunion
jubilación *nf, pl* **-ciones** : retirement — **jubilado, -da** *adj* : retired — **~** *nmf* : retiree — **jubilar** *vt* : retire, pension off — **jubilarse** *vr* : retire — **jubileo** *nm* : jubilee
júbilo *nm* : joy, jubilation — **jubiloso, -sa** *adj* : joyous, jubilant
judaísmo *nm* : Judaism
judía *nf* **1** : bean **2** *or* **~ verde** : green bean, string bean
judicial *adj* : judicial
judío, -día *adj* : Jewish — **~** *n* : Jew
judo ['juðo, 'dʒu-] *nm* : judo
juego *nm* **1** : game **2** : playing (of children, etc.) **3** *or* **~s de azar** : gambling **4** CONJUNTO : set **5 estar en ~** : be at stake **6 fuera de ~** : offside (in sports) **7 hacer ~** : go together, match **8 ~ de manos** : conjuring trick **9 poner en ~** : bring into play
juerga *nf fam* : spree, binge
jueves *nms & pl* : Thursday
juez *nmf, pl* **jueces 1** : judge **2** ÁRBITRO : umpire, referee
jugar {44} *vi* **1** : play **2** : gamble (in a casino, etc.) **3** APOSTAR : bet **4 ~ (al) tenis** : play tennis — *vt* : play — **jugarse** *vr* : risk, gamble (away) — **jugada** *nf* **1** : play, move **2** TRETA : (dirty) trick — **jugador, -dora** *n* **1** : player **2** : gambler
juglar *nm* : minstrel
jugo *nm* **1** : juice **2** SUSTANCIA : substance, essence — **jugoso, -sa** *adj* **1** : juicy **2** SUSTANCIAL : substantial, important
juguete *nm* : toy — **juguetear** *vi* : play — **juguetería** *nf* : toy store — **juguetón, -tona** *adj, mpl* **-tones** : playful
juicio *nm* **1** : judgment **2** RAZÓN : reason, sense **3 a mi ~** : in my opinion — **juicioso, -sa** *adj* : wise, sensible
julio *nm* : July
junco *nm* : reed, rush
jungla *nf* : jungle
junio *nm* : June
juntar *vt* **1** UNIR : join, unite **2** REUNIR : collect — **juntarse** *vr* **1** : join (together) **2** REUNIRSE : meet, get together — **junta** *nf* **1** : board, committee **2** REUNIÓN : meeting **3** : (political) junta **4** : joint, gasket — **junto, -ta** *adj* **1** : joined **2** PRÓXIMO : close, adjacent **3** (*used adverbially*) : together **4 ~ a** : next to **5 ~ con** : together with — **juntura** *nf* : joint
Júpiter *nm* : Jupiter
jurar *v* **1** : swear **2 ~ en falso** : commit perjury — **jurado** *nm* **1** : jury **2** : juror, member of a jury — **juramento** *nm* : oath
jurídico, -ca *adj* : legal
jurisdicción *nf, pl* **-ciones** : jurisdiction
jurisprudencia *nf* : jurisprudence
justamente *adv* **1** : fairly, justly **2** PRECISAMENTE : precisely, exactly
justicia *nf* : justice, fairness
justificar {72} *vt* **1** : justify **2** DISCULPAR : excuse, vindicate — **justificación** *nf, pl* **-ciones** : justification
justo, -ta *adj* **1** : just, fair **2** EXACTO : exact **3** APRETADO : tight — **justo** *adv* **1** : just, exactly **2 ~ a tiempo** : just in time
juvenil *adj* : youthful — **juventud** *nf* **1** : youth **2** JÓVENES : young people
juzgar {52} *vt* **1** : try (a case in court) **2** ESTIMAR : judge, consider **3 a ~ por** : judging by — **juzgado** *nm* : court, tribunal

K

k *nf* : k, eleventh letter of the Spanish alphabet
kaki → **caqui**
karate *or* **kárate** *nm* : karate
kilo *nm* : kilo — **kilogramo** *nm* : kilogram
kilómetro *nm* : kilometer — **kilometraje** *nm* : distance in kilometers, mileage — **kilométrico, -ca** *adj fam* : endless
kilovatio *nm* : kilowatt
kiosco *nm* → **quiosco**

L

l *nf* : l, twelfth letter of the Spanish alphabet
la *pron* **1** : her, it **2** (*formal*) : you **3 ~ que** : the one who — **~** *art* → **el**
laberinto *nm* : labyrinth, maze
labia *nf fam* : gift of gab
labio *nm* : lip
labor *nf* **1** : work, labor **2** TAREA : task **3 ~es domésticas** : housework — **laborable** *adj* **día ~** : business day — **laborar** *vi* : work — **laboratorio** *nm* : laboratory, lab — **laborioso, -sa** *adj* : laborious
labrar *vt* **1** : cultivate, till **2** : work (metals), carve (stone, wood) **3** CAUSAR : cause, bring about — **labrado, -da** *adj* **1** : cultivated, tilled **2** : carved, wrought — **labrador, -dora** *n* : farmer — **labranza** *nf* : farming
laca *nf* **1** : lacquer **2** : hair spray
lacayo *nm* : lackey
lacerar *vt* : lacerate
lacio, -cia *adj* **1** : limp **2** : straight (of hair)
lacónico, -ca *adj* : laconic
lacra *nf* : scar
lacrar *vt* : seal — **lacre** *nm* : sealing wax
lacrimógeno, -na *adj* **gas lacrimógeno** : tear gas — **lacrimoso, -sa** *adj* : tearful
lácteo, -tea *adj* **1** : dairy **2 Vía Láctea** : Milky Way
ladear *vt* : tilt — **ladearse** *vr* : lean
ladera *nf* : slope, hillside
ladino, -na *adj* : crafty
lado *nm* **1** : side **2 al ~** : next door, nearby **3 al ~ de** : beside, next to **4 de ~** : sideways **5 por otro ~** : on the other hand **6 por todos ~s** : everywhere, all around
ladrar *vi* : bark — **ladrido** *nm* : bark
ladrillo *nm* : brick
ladrón, -drona *n, mpl* **-drones** : thief
lagarto *nm* : lizard — **lagartija** *nf* : (small) lizard
lago *nm* : lake
lágrima *nf* : tear
laguna *nf* **1** : lagoon **2** VACÍO : gap
laico, -ca *adj* : lay, secular — **~** *n* : layman *m*, layperson
lamentar *vt* **1** : regret, be sorry about **2 lo lamento** : I'm sorry — **lamentarse** *vr* : lament — **lamentable** *adj* **1** : deplorable **2** TRISTE : sad, pitiful — **lamento** *nm* : lament, moan
lamer *vt* **1** : lick **2** : lap (against) — **lamida** *nf* : lick
lámina *nf* **1** PLANCHA : sheet **2** DIBUJO : plate, illustration — **laminar** *vt* : laminate
lámpara *nf* : lamp
lampiño, -ña *adj* : beardless, hairless
lana *nf* **1** : wool **2 de ~** : woolen
lance *nm* **1** : event, incident **2** : throw (of dice, etc.) **3** RIÑA : quarrel
lanceta *nf* : lancet
lancha *nf* **1** : boat, launch **2 ~ motora** : motorboat
langosta *nf* **1** : lobster **2** : locust (insect) — **langostino** *nm* : prawn, crayfish
languidecer {53} *vi* : languish — **languidez** *nf, pl* **-deces** : languor — **lánguido, -da** *adj* : languid, listless
lanilla *nf* : nap (of fabric)
lanudo, -da *adj* : woolly
lanza *nf* : spear, lance
lanzar {21} *vt* **1** : throw **2** : shoot (a glance), give (a sigh, etc.) **3** : launch (a missile, a project) — **lanzarse** *vr* : throw oneself — **lanzamiento** *nm* : throwing, launching
lapicero *nm* : (mechanical) pencil
lápida *nf* : tombstone
lapidar *vt* : stone
lápiz *nm, pl* **-pices 1** : pencil **2 ~ de labios** : lipstick
lapso *nm* : lapse (of time) — **lapsus** *nms & pl* : lapse, slip (of the tongue)
largar {52} *vt* **1** AFLOJAR : loosen, slacken **2** *fam* : give — **largarse** *vr fam* : go away, beat it — **largo, -ga** *adj* **1** : long **2 a la larga** : in the long run **3 a lo largo** : lengthwise **4 a lo largo de** : along — **largo** *nm* : length — **largometraje** *nm* : feature film — **largueza** *nf* : generosity
laringe *nf* : larynx — **laringitis** *nfs & pl* : laryngitis
larva *nf* : larva
las → **el**
lascivo, -va *adj* : lascivious, lewd
láser *nm* : laser
lastimar *vt* : hurt — **lastimarse** *vr* : hurt oneself — **lástima** *nf* **1** : pity **2 dar ~** : be pitiful **3 me dan ~** : I feel sorry for them **4 ¡qué ~!** : what a shame! — **lastimero, -ra** *adj* : pitiful, wretched — **lastimoso, -sa** *adj* : pitiful, terrible
lastre *nm* : ballast
lata *nf* **1** : tinplate **2** : (tin) can **3** *fam* : nuisance, bore **4 dar (la) ~ a** *fam* : bother, annoy
latente *adj* : latent
lateral *adj* : side, lateral
latido *nm* **1** : beat, throb **2 ~ del corazón** : heartbeat
latifundio *nm* : large estate
látigo *nm* : whip — **latigazo** *nm* : lash
latín *nm* : Latin (language)
latino, -na *adj* **1** : Latin **2** : Latin-American — **~** *n* : Latin American — **latinoamericano, -na** *adj* : Latin-American — **~** *n* : Latin American
latir *vi* : beat, throb
latitud *nf* : latitude
latón *nm, pl* **-tones** : brass
latoso, -sa *adj fam* : annoying
laúd *nm* : lute
laudable *adj* : laudable
laureado, -da *adj* : prize-winning
laurel *nm* **1** : laurel **2** : bay leaf (in cooking)
lava *nf* : lava
lavar *vt* : wash — **lavarse** *vr* **1** : wash oneself **2 ~ las manos** : wash one's hands — **lavable** *adj* : washable — **lavabo** *nm* **1** : sink **2** RETRETE : lavatory, toilet — **lavadero** *nm* : laundry room — **lavado** *nm* : wash, washing — **lavadora** *nf* : washing machine — **lavamanos** *nms & pl* : washbowl — **lavandería** *nf* : laundry (service) — **lavaplatos** *nms & pl* **1** : dishwasher **2** *Lat* : kitchen sink — **lavativa** *nf* : enema — **lavatorio** *nm* : lavatory, washroom — **lavavajillas** *nms & pl* : dishwasher
laxante *adj & nm* : laxative — **laxo, -xa** *adj* : loose
lazo *nm* **1** VÍNCULO : link, bond **2** LAZADA : bow **3** : lasso, lariat — **lazada** *nf* : bow, loop
le *pron* **1** : (to) her, (to) him, (to) it **2** (*formal*) : (to) you **3** (*as direct object*) : him, you
leal *adj* : loyal, faithful — **lealtad** *nf* : loyalty, allegiance
lebrel *nm* : hound
lección *nf, pl* **-ciones 1** : lesson **2** : lecture (in a classroom)
leche *nf* **1** : milk **2 ~ descremada** *or* **~ desnatada** : skim milk **3 ~ en polvo** : powdered milk — **lechera** *nf* : milk jug — **lechería** *nf* : dairy store — **lechero, -ra** *adj* : dairy — **~** *n* : milkman *m*, milk dealer
lecho *nm* : bed
lechón, -chona *n, mpl* **-chones** : suckling pig
lechoso, -sa *adj* : milky
lechuga *nf* : lettuce
lechuza *nf* : owl
lector, -tora *n* : reader — **lectura** *nf* **1** : reading **2** ESCRITOS : reading matter
leer {20} *v* : read
legación *nf, pl* **-ciones** : legation
legado *nm* **1** : legacy **2** ENVIADO : legate, emissary
legajo *nm* : dossier, file
legal *adj* : legal — **legalidad** *nf* : legality — **legalizar** {21} *vt* : legalize — **legalización** *nf, pl* **-ciones** : legalization
legar {52} *vt* : bequeath

legendario, -ria *adj* : legendary
legible *adj* : legible
legión *nf, pl* **-giones** : legion — **legionario, -ria** *n* : legionnaire
legislar *vi* : legislate — **legislación** *nf, pl* **-ciones** : legislation — **legislador, -dora** *n* : legislator — **legislatura** *nf* : legislature
legítimo, -ma *adj* **1** : legitimate **2** GENUINO : authentic — **legitimidad** *nf* : legitimacy
lego, -ga *adj* **1** : secular, lay **2** IGNORANTE : ignorant — **~** *n* : layman *m,* layperson
legua *nf* : league
legumbre *nf* : vegetable
leído, -da *adj* : well-read
lejano, -na *adj* : distant, far away — **lejanía** *nf* : distance
lejía *nf* : bleach
lejos *adv* **1** : far (away) **2 a lo ~** : in the distance **3 de ~** *or* **desde ~** : from afar **4 ~ de** : far from
lelo, -la *adj* : silly, stupid
lema *nm* : motto
lencería *nf* **1** : linen **2** : (women's) lingerie
lengua *nf* **1** : tongue **2** IDIOMA : language **3 morderse la ~** : hold one's tongue
lenguado *nm* : sole, flounder
lenguaje *nm* : language
lengüeta *nf* **1** : tongue (of a shoe) **2** : reed (of a musical instrument)
lengüetada *nf* **beber a ~s** : lap (up)
lente *nmf* **1** : lens **2 ~s** *nmpl* : eyeglasses **3 ~s de contacto** : contact lenses
lenteja *nf* : lentil — **lentejuela** *nf* : sequin
lento, -ta *adj* : slow — **lento** *adv* : slowly — **lentitud** *nf* : slowness
leña *nf* : firewood — **leñador, -dora** *n* : lumberjack, woodcutter — **leño** *nm* : log
león, -ona *n, mpl* **leones** : lion, lioness *f*
leopardo *nm* : leopard
leotardo *nm* : leotard, tights *pl*
lepra *nf* : leprosy — **leproso, -sa** *n* : leper
lerdo, -da *adj* **1** TORPE : clumsy **2** TONTO : slow-witted
les *pron* **1** : (to) them, (to) you **2** (*as direct object*) : them, you
lesbiano, -na *adj* : lesbian — **lesbiana** *nf* : lesbian — **lesbianismo** *nm* : lesbianism
lesión *nf, pl* **-siones** : lesion, wound — **lesionado, -da** *adj* : injured, wounded — **lesionar** *vt* **1** : injure, wound **2** DAÑAR : damage
letal *adj* : lethal
letanía *nf* : litany
letárgico, -ca *adj* : lethargic — **letargo** *nm* : lethargy
letra *nf* **1** : letter **2** ESCRITURA : handwriting **3** : lyrics *pl* (of a song) **4 ~ de cambio** : bill of exchange **5 ~s** *nfpl* : arts — **letrado, -da** *adj* : learned — **letrero** *nm* : sign, notice
letrina *nf* : latrine
leucemia *nf* : leukemia
levadizo, -za *adj* **puente levadizo** : drawbridge
levadura *nf* **1** : yeast **2 ~ en polvo** : baking powder
levantar *vt* **1** : lift, raise **2** RECOGER : pick up **3** CONSTRUIR : erect, put up **4** ENCENDER : rouse, stir up **5 ~ la mesa** *Lat* : clear the table — **levantarse** *vr* **1** : rise, stand up **2** : get out of bed **3** SUBLEVARSE : rise up — **levantamiento** *nm* **1** : raising, lifting **2** SUBLEVACIÓN : uprising
levante *nm* **1** : east **2** : east wind
levar *vt* **~ anclas** : weigh anchor
leve *adj* **1** : light, slight **2** : minor, trivial (of wounds, sins, etc.) — **levedad** *nf* : lightness — **levemente** *adv* : lightly, slightly
léxico *nm* : vocabulary, lexicon
ley *nf* **1** : law **2 de (buena) ~** : genuine, pure (of metals)
leyenda *nf* **1** : legend **2** : caption (of an illustration, etc.)
liar {85} *vt* **1** : bind, tie (up) **2** : roll (a cigarette) **3** CONFUNDIR : confuse, muddle — **liarse** *vr* : get mixed up
libanés, -nesa *adj, mpl* **-neses** : Lebanese
libelo *nm* **1** : libel **2** : petition (in court)
libélula *nf* : dragonfly
liberación *nf, pl* **-ciones** : liberation, deliverance
liberal *adj & nmf* : liberal — **liberalidad** *nf* : generosity, liberality
liberar *vt* : liberate, free — **libertad** *nf* **1** : freedom, liberty **2 ~ bajo fianza** : bail **3 ~ condicional** : parole **4 en ~** : free — **libertar** *vt* : set free
libertinaje *nm* : licentiousness — **libertino, -na** *n* : libertine
libido *nf* : libido
libio, -bia *adj* : Libyan
libra *nf* **1** : pound **2 ~ esterlina** : pound sterling
librar *vt* **1** : free, save **2** : wage, fight (a battle) **3** : draw, issue (a check, etc.) — **librarse** *vr* **~ de** : free oneself from, get rid of
libre *adj* **1** : free **2** : unoccupied (of space), spare (of time) **3 al aire ~** : in the open air **4 ~ de impuestos** : tax-free
librea *nf* : livery
libro *nm* **1** : book **2 ~ de bolsillo** : paperback — **librería** *nf* : bookstore — **librero, -ra** *n* : bookseller — **librero** *nm Lat* : bookcase — **libreta** *nf* : notebook
licencia *nf* **1** : license, permit **2** PERMISO : permission **3** : (military) leave — **licenciado, -da** *n* **1** : graduate **2** *Lat* : lawyer — **licenciar** *vt* : dismiss, discharge — **licenciarse** *vr* : graduate — **licenciatura** *nf* : degree
licencioso, -sa *adj* : licentious
liceo *nm* : high school
licitar *vt* : bid for
lícito, -ta *adj* **1** : lawful, legal **2** JUSTO : just, fair
licor *nm* **1** : liquor **2** : liqueur — **licorera** *nf* : decanter
licuadora *nf* : blender — **licuado** *nm* : milk shake — **licuar** {3} *vt* : liquefy
lid *nf* **1** : fight **2 en buena ~** : fair and square
líder *adj* : leading — **~** *nmf* : leader — **liderato** *or* **liderazgo** *nm* : leadership
lidia *nf* : bullfight — **lidiar** *v* : fight
liebre *nf* : hare
lienzo *nm* **1** : cotton or linen cloth **2** : canvas (for a painting) **3** PARED : wall
liga *nf* **1** : league **2** *Lat* : rubber band **3** : garter (for stockings) — **ligadura** *nf* **1** ATADURA : tie, bond **2** : ligature (in medicine or music) — **ligamento** *nm* : ligament — **ligar** {52} *vt* : bind, tie (up)
ligero, -ra *adj* **1** : light, lightweight **2** LEVE : slight **3** ÁGIL : agile **4** FRÍVOLO : lighthearted, superficial — **ligeramente** *adv* : lightly, slightly — **ligereza** *nf* **1** : lightness **2** : flippancy (of character), thoughtlessness (of actions) **3** AGILIDAD : agility
lija *nf* : sandpaper — **lijar** *vt* : sand
lila *nf* : lilac
lima *nf* **1** : file **2** : lime (fruit) **3 ~ para uñas** : nail file — **limar** *vt* : file
limbo *nm* : limbo
limitar *vt* : limit — *vi* **~ con** : border on — **limitación** *nf, pl* **-ciones** : limitation, limit — **límite** *nm* **1** : limit **2** CONFÍN : boundary, border **3 ~ de velocidad** : speed limit **4 fecha ~** : deadline — **limítrofe** *adj* : bordering
limo *nm* : slime, mud
limón *nm, pl* **-mones 1** : lemon **2 ~ verde** *Lat* : lime — **limonada** *nf* : lemonade
limosna *nf* **1** : alms **2 pedir ~** : beg — **limosnero, -ra** *n* : beggar
limpiabotas *nmfs & pl* : bootblack
limpiaparabrisas *nms & pl* : windshield wiper
limpiar *vt* **1** : clean, wipe (away) **2 ~ en seco** : dry-clean — **limpieza** *nf* **1** : cleanliness **2** : (act of) cleaning — **limpio** *adv* : cleanly, fairly — **limpio, -pia** *adj* **1** : clean, neat **2** HONRADO : honest **3** NETO : net, clear
limusina *nf* : limousine
linaje *nm* : lineage, ancestry
linaza *nf* : linseed
lince *nm* : lynx
linchar *vt* : lynch
lindar *vi* **~ con** : border on — **lindante** *adj* : bordering — **linde** *nmf* *or* **lindero** *nm* : boundary
lindo, -da *adj* **1** : pretty, lovely **2 de lo lindo** *fam* : a lot
línea *nf* **1** : line **2 ~ de conducta** : course of action **3 en ~** : on-line **4 guardar la ~** : watch one's figure — **lineal** *adj* : linear
lingote *nm* : ingot
lingüista *nmf* : linguist — **lingüística** *nf* : linguistics — **lingüístico, -ca** *adj* : linguistic
linimento *nm* : liniment
lino *nm* **1** : flax (plant) **2** : linen (fabric)
linóleo *nm* : linoleum
linterna *nf* **1** FAROL : lantern **2** : flashlight
lío *nm* **1** : bundle **2** *fam* : mess, trouble **3** *fam* : (love) affair
liofilizar {21} *vt* : freeze-dry
liquen *nm* : lichen
liquidar *vt* **1** : liquefy **2** : liquidate (merchandise, etc.) **3** : settle, pay off (a debt, etc.) — **liquidación** *nf, pl* **-ciones 1** : liquidation **2** REBAJA : clearance sale — **líquido, -da** *adj* **1** : liquid **2** NETO : net — **líquido** *nm* : liquid
lira *nf* : lyre
lírico, -ca *adj* : lyric, lyrical — **lírica** *nf* : lyric poetry
lirio *nm* : iris
lisiado, -da *adj* : disabled — **~** *n* : disabled person — **lisiar** *vt* : disable, cripple
liso, -sa *adj* **1** : smooth **2** PLANO : flat **3** SENCILLO : plain **4 pelo ~** : straight hair
lisonjear *vt* : flatter — **lisonja** *nf* : flattery
lista *nf* **1** : stripe **2** ENUMERACIÓN : list **3** : menu (in a restaurant) — **listado, -da** *adj* : striped
listo, -ta *adj* **1** : clever, smart **2** PREPARADO : ready
listón *nm, pl* **-tones 1** : ribbon **2** : strip (of wood)
lisura *nf* : smoothness
litera *nf* : bunk bed, berth
literal *adj* : literal
literatura *nf* : literature — **literario, -ria** *adj* : literary
litigar {52} *vi* : litigate — **litigio** *nm* **1** : litigation **2 en ~** : in dispute
litografía *nf* **1** : lithography **2** : lithograph (picture)
litoral *adj* : coastal — **~** *nm* : shore, seaboard
litro *nm* : liter
liturgia *nf* : liturgy — **litúrgico, -ca** *adj* : liturgical
liviano, -na *adj* **1** LIGERO : light **2** INCONSTANTE : fickle
lívido, -da *adj* : livid
llaga *nf* : sore, wound
llama *nf* **1** : flame **2** : llama (animal)
llamar *vt* **1** : call **2** : call up (on the telephone) — *vi* **1** : phone, call **2** : knock, ring (at the door) — **llamarse** *vr* **1** : be called **2 ¿cómo te llamas?** : what's your name? — **llamada** *nf* : call — **llamado, -da** *adj* : named, called — **llamamiento** *nm* : call, appeal
llamarada *nf* **1** : blaze **2** : flushing (of the face)
llamativo, -va *adj* : flashy, showy
llamear *vi* : flame, blaze
llano, -na *adj* **1** : flat **2** : straightforward (of a person, a message, etc.) **3** SENCILLO : plain, simple — **llano** *nm* : plain — **llaneza** *nf* : simplicity
llanta *nf* **1** : rim (of a wheel) **2** *Lat* : tire
llanto *nm* : crying, weeping
llanura *nf* : plain
llave *nf* **1** : key **2** *Lat* : faucet **3** INTERRUPTOR : switch **4 cerrar con ~** : lock **5 ~ inglesa** : monkey wrench — **llavero** *nm* : key chain
llegar {52} *vi* **1** : arrive, come **2** ALCANZAR : reach **3** BASTAR : be enough **4 ~ a** : manage to **5 ~ a ser** : become — **llegada** *nf* : arrival
llenar *vt* : fill (up), fill in — **lleno, -na** *adj* **1** : full **2 de lleno** : completely — **lleno** *nm* : full house
llevar *vt* **1** : take, carry **2** CONDUCIR : lead **3** : wear (clothing, etc.) **4** TENER : have **5 llevo una hora aquí** : I've been here for an hour — **llevarse** *vr* **1** : take (away) **2 ~ bien** : get along well — **llevadero, -ra** *adj* : bearable
llorar *vi* : cry, weep — **lloriquear** *vi* : whimper, whine — **lloro** *nm* : crying — **llorón, -rona** *n, mpl* **-rones** : crybaby, whiner — **lloroso, -sa** *adj* : tearful
llover {47} *v impers* : rain — **llovizna** *nf* : drizzle — **lloviznar** *v impers* : drizzle
lluvia *nf* : rain — **lluvioso, -sa** *adj* : rainy
lo *pron* **1** : him, it **2** (*formal, masculine*) : you **3 ~ que** : what, that which — **~** *art* **1** : the **2 ~ mejor** : the best (part) **3 sé ~ bueno que eres** : I know how good you are
loa *nf* : praise — **loable** *adj* : praiseworthy — **loar** *vt* : praise
lobo, -ba *n* : wolf
lóbrego, -ga *adj* : gloomy
lóbulo *nm* : lobe
local *adj* : local — **~** *nm* : premises *pl* — **localidad** *nf* : town, locality — **localizar** {21} *vt* **1** : localize **2** ENCONTRAR : locate — **localizarse** *vr* : be located
loción *nf, pl* **-ciones** : lotion
loco, -ca *adj* **1** : crazy, insane **2 a lo loco** : wildly, recklessly **3 volverse ~** : go mad — **~** *n* **1** : crazy person, lunatic **2 hacerse el loco** : act the fool
locomoción *nf, pl* **-ciones** : locomotion — **locomotora** *nf* : engine, locomotive
locuaz *adj, pl* **-cuaces** : talkative, loquacious
locución *nf, pl* **-ciones** : expression, phrase
locura *nf* **1** : insanity, madness **2** INSENSATEZ : crazy act, folly
locutor, -tora *n* : announcer
locutorio *nm* : phone booth
lodo *nm* : mud — **lodazal** *nm* : quagmire
logaritmo *nm* : logarithm
lógica *nf* : logic — **lógico, -ca** *adj* : logical — **logística** *nf* : logistics *pl*
logotipo *nm* : logo
lograr *vt* **1** : achieve, attain **2** CONSEGUIR : get, obtain **3 ~ hacer** : manage to do — **logro** *nm* : achievement, success
loma *nf* : hill, hillock
lombriz *nf, pl* **-brices** : worm
lomo *nm* **1** : back (of an animal) **2** : spine (of a book) **3 ~ de cerdo** : pork loin
lona *nf* : canvas
loncha *nf* : slice (of bacon, etc.)
lonche *nm Lat* : lunch — **lonchería** *nf Lat* : luncheonette
longaniza *nf* : sausage
longevidad *nf* : longevity — **longevo, -va** *adj* : long-lived
longitud *nf* **1** : longitude **2** LARGO : length
lonja → **loncha**
loro *nm* : parrot
los, las *pron* **1** : them **2** : you **3 los que, las que** : those who, the ones who — **los** *art* → **el**
losa *nf* **1** : flagstone **2** *or* **~ sepulcral** : tombstone
lote *nm* **1** : batch, lot **2** *Lat* : plot of land
lotería *nf* : lottery
loto *nm* : lotus
loza *nf* : crockery, earthenware
lozano, -na *adj* **1** : healthy-looking, vigorous **2** : luxuriant (of plants) — **lozanía** *nf* **1** : (youthful) vigor **2** : luxuriance (of plants)
lubricar {72} *vt* : lubricate — **lubricante** *adj* : lubricating — **~** *nm* : lubricant
lucero *nm* : bright star
luchar *vi* **1** : fight, struggle **2** : wrestle (in sports) — **lucha** *nf* **1** : struggle, fight **2** : wrestling (sport) — **luchador, -dora** *n* : fighter, wrestler
lucidez *nf, pl* **-deces** : lucidity — **lúcido, -da** *adj* : lucid
lucido, -da *adj* : magnificent, splendid
luciérnaga *nf* : firefly, glowworm
lucir {45} *vi* **1** : shine **2** *Lat* : appear, seem — *vt* **1** : wear, sport **2** OSTENTAR : show off — **lucirse** *vr* **1** : shine, excel **2** PRESUMIR : show off — **lucimiento** *nm* **1** : brilliance **2** ÉXITO : brilliant performance, success
lucrativo, -va *adj* : lucrative — **lucro** *nm* : profit
luego *adv* **1** : then **2** : later (on) **3 desde ~** : of course **4 ¡hasta ~!** : see you later! **5 ~ que** : as soon as — **~** *conj* : therefore
lugar *nm* **1** : place **2** ESPACIO : space, room **3 dar ~ a** : give rise to **4 en ~ de** : instead of **5 tener ~** : take place
lugarteniente *nmf* : deputy
lúgubre *adj* : gloomy
lujo *nm* **1** : luxury **2 de ~** : deluxe — **lujoso, -sa** *adj* : luxurious
lujuria *nf* : lust
lumbre *nf* **1** : fire **2 poner en la ~** : put on the stove
luminoso, -sa *adj* : shining, luminous
luna *nf* **1** : moon **2** : (window) glass **3** ESPEJO : mirror **4 ~ de miel** : honeymoon — **lunar** *adj* : lunar — **~** *nm* : mole, beauty spot
lunes *nms & pl* : Monday
lupa *nf* : magnifying glass
lúpulo *nm* : hops
lustrar *vt* : shine, polish — **lustre** *nm* **1** BRILLO : luster, shine **2** ESPLENDOR : glory — **lustroso, -sa** *adj* : lustrous, shiny
luto *nm* **1** : mourning **2 estar de ~** : be in mourning
luxación *nf, pl* **-ciones** : dislocation
luz *nf, pl* **luces 1** : light **2** : lighting (in a room, etc.) **3** *fam* : electricity **4 a la ~ de** : in light of **5 dar a ~** : give birth **6 sacar a la ~** : bring to light

M

m *nf* : m, 13th letter of the Spanish alphabet
macabro, -bra *adj* : macabre
macarrón *nm, pl* **-rrones 1** : macaroon **2 macarrones** *nmpl* : macaroni
maceta *nf* : flowerpot
machacar {72} *vt* : crush, grind — *vi* **~ sobre** : go on about — **machacón, -cona** *adj, mpl* **-cones** : tiresome, boring
machete *nm* : machete — **machetear** *vt* : hack with a machete
macho *adj* **1** : male **2** *fam* : macho — **~** *nm* **1** : male **2** *fam* : he-man — **machista** *nm* : male chauvinist
machucar {72} *vt* **1** : beat, crush **2** : bruise (fruit)
macizo, -za *adj* : solid — **macizo** *nm* **~ de flores** : flower bed
mácula *nf* : stain
madeja *nf* : skein, hank
madera *nf* **1** : wood **2** : lumber (for construction) **3 ~ dura** : hardwood — **madero** *nm* : piece of lumber, plank
madre *nf* **1** : mother **2 ~ política** : mother-in-law — **madrastra** *nf* : stepmother
madreselva *nf* : honeysuckle
madriguera *nf* : burrow, den
madrileño, -ña *adj* : of or from Madrid
madrina *nf* **1** : godmother **2** : bridesmaid (at a wedding)
madrugada *nf* : dawn, daybreak — **madrugador, -dora** *n* : early riser
madurar *v* **1** : mature **2** : ripen (of fruit) — **madurez** *nf, pl* **-reces 1** : maturity **2** : ripeness (of fruit) — **maduro, -ra** *adj* **1** : mature **2** : ripe (of fruit)
maestría *nf* : mastery, skill — **maestro, -tra** *adj* : masterly, skilled — **~** *n* **1** : teacher (in grammar school) **2** EXPERTO : expert, master
Mafia *nf* : Mafia
magia *nf* : magic — **mágico, -ca** *adj* : magic, magical
magisterio *nm* : teachers *pl,* teaching profession
magistrado, -da *n* : magistrate, judge
magistral *adj* **1** : masterful **2** : magisterial (of an attitude, etc.)
magnánimo, -ma *adj* : magnanimous — **magnanimidad** *nf* : magnanimity
magnate *nmf* : magnate, tycoon
magnesia *nf* : magnesia — **magnesio** *nm* : magnesium
magnético, -ca *adj* : magnetic — **magnetismo** *nm* : magnetism — **magnetizar** {21} *vt* : magnetize
magnetófono *nm* : tape recorder

magnificencia *nf* : magnificence — **magnífico, -ca** *adj* : magnificent
magnitud *nf* : magnitude
magnolia *nf* : magnolia
mago, -ga *n* **1** : magician **2 los Reyes Magos** : the Magi
magro, -gra *adj* **1** : lean **2** MEZQUINO : poor, meager
magullar *vt* : bruise — **magulladura** *nf* : bruise
mahometano, -na *adj* : Islamic, Muslim — ~ *n* : Muslim
maicena *nf* : cornstarch
maíz *nm* : corn
maja *nf* : pestle
majadero, -ra *adj* : foolish, silly — ~ *n* : fool
majar *vt* : crush
majestad *nf* **1** : majesty **2 Su Majestad** : His/Her Majesty — **majestuoso, -sa** *adj* : majestic
majo, -ja *adj* **1** : nice **2** GUAPO : good-looking
mal *adv* **1** : badly, poorly **2** INCORRECTAMENTE : incorrectly **3** DIFÍCILMENTE : with difficulty, hardly **4 de ~ en peor** : from bad to worse **5 menos ~** : it's just as well — ~ *nm* **1** : evil **2** DAÑO : harm, damage **3** ENFERMEDAD : illness — ~ *adj* → **malo**
malabarismo *nm* : juggling — **malabarista** *nmf* : juggler
malacostumbrar *vt* : spoil, pamper — **malacostumbrado, -da** *adj* : spoiled
malaria *nf* : malaria
malasio, -sia *adj* : Malaysian
malaventura *nf* : misfortune — **malaventurado, -da** *adj* : unfortunate
malayo, -ya *adj* : Malay, Malayan
malcriado, -da *adj* : bad-mannered, spoiled
maldad *nf* **1** : evil **2** : evil deed
maldecir {11} *vt* : curse, damn — *vi* **1** : curse, swear **2 ~ de** : speak ill of — **maldición** *nf, pl* **-ciones** : curse — **maldito, -ta** *adj fam* : damned
maleable *adj* : malleable
maleante *nmf* : crook
malecón *nm, pl* **-cones** : jetty
maleducado, -da *adj* : rude
maleficio *nm* : curse — **maléfico, -ca** *adj* : evil, harmful
malentendido *nm* : misunderstanding
malestar *nm* **1** : discomfort **2** INQUIETUD : uneasiness
maleta *nf* **1** : suitcase **2 hacer la ~** : pack one's bags — **maletero, -ra** *n* : porter — **maletero** *nm* : trunk (of an automobile) — **maletín** *nm, pl* **-tines 1** PORTAFOLIO : briefcase **2** : overnight bag
malévolo, -la *adj* : malevolent — **malevolencia** *nf* : malevolence
maleza *nf* **1** : underbrush **2** MALAS HIERBAS : weeds *pl*
malgastar *vt* : waste, squander
malhablado, -da *adj* : foul-mouthed
malhechor, -chora *n* : criminal, delinquent
malhumorado, -da *adj* : bad-tempered, cross
malicia *nf* : malice — **malicioso, -sa** *adj* : malicious
maligno, -na *adj* **1** : malignant **2** PERNICIOSO : harmful, evil
malla *nf* **1** : mesh **2 ~s** *nfpl* : tights
malo, -la *adj* (**mal** *before masculine singular nouns*) **1** : bad **2** : poor (in quality) **3** ENFERMO : unwell **4 estar de malas** : be in a bad mood — ~ *n* : villain, bad guy (in movies, etc.)
malograr *vt* : waste — **malograrse** *vr* **1** FRACASAR : fail **2** : die young — **malogro** *nm* : failure
maloliente *adj* : smelly
malpensado, -da *adj* : malicious, nasty
malsano, -na *adj* : unhealthy
malsonante *adj* : rude
malta *nf* : malt
maltratar *vt* : mistreat
maltrecho, -cha *adj* : battered
malvado, -da *adj* : evil, wicked
malvavisco *nm* : marshmallow
malversar *vt* : embezzle — **malversación** *nf, pl* **-ciones** : embezzlement
mama *nf* : teat (of an animal), breast (of a woman)
mamá *nf fam* : mom, mama
mamar *vi* **1** : suckle **2 dar de ~ a** : breast-feed — *vt* **1** : suckle, nurse **2** : learn from childhood, grow up with — **mamario, -ria** *adj* : mammary
mamarracho *nm fam* : mess, sight
mambo *nm* : mambo
mamífero, -ra *adj* : mammalian — **mamífero** *nm* : mammal
mamografía *nf* : mammogram
mampara *nf* : screen, room divider
mampostería *nf* : masonry
manada *nf* **1** : flock, herd, pack **2 en ~** : in droves
manar *vi* **1** : flow **2 ~ en** : be rich in — **manantial** *nm* **1** : spring **2** ORIGEN : source
manchar *vt* **1** : stain, spot, mark **2** : tarnish (a reputation, etc.) — **mancharse** *vr* : get dirty — **mancha** *nf* : stain
mancillar *vt* : sully, stain
manco, -ca *adj* : one-armed, one-handed
mancomunar *vt* : combine, join — **mancomunarse** *vr* : unite — **mancomunidad** *nf* : union
mandar *vt* **1** : command, order **2** ENVIAR : send **3** *Lat* : hurl, throw — *vi* **1** : be in charge **2 ¿mande?** *Lat* : yes?, pardon? — **mandadero, -ra** *nm* : messenger — **mandado** *nm* : errand — **mandamiento** *nm* **1** : order, warrant **2** : commandment (in religion)
mandarina *nf* : mandarin orange, tangerine
mandato *nm* **1** : term of office **2** ORDEN : mandate — **mandatario, -ria** *n* **1** : leader (in politics) **2** : agent (in law)
mandíbula *nf* : jaw, jawbone
mandil *nm* : apron
mando *nm* **1** : command, leadership **2 al ~ de** : in charge of **3 ~ a distancia** : remote control
mandolina *nf* : mandolin
mandón, -dona *adj, mpl* **-dones** : bossy
manecilla *nf* : hand (of a clock), pointer
manejar *vt* **1** : handle, operate **2** : manage (a business, etc.) **3** : manipulate (a person) **4** *Lat* : drive (a car) — **manejarse** *vr* **1** : manage, get by **2** *Lat* : behave — **manejo** *nm* **1** : handling, use **2** : management (of a business, etc.)
manera *nf* **1** : way, manner **2 de ~ que** : so that **3 de ninguna ~** : by no means **4 de todas ~s** : anyway
manga *nf* **1** : sleeve **2** MANGUERA : hose
mango *nm* **1** : hilt, handle **2** : mango (fruit)
mangonear *vt fam* : boss around — *vi* **1** : be bossy **2** HOLGAZANEAR : loaf, fool around
manguera *nf* : hose
maní *nm, pl* **-níes** *Lat* : peanut
manía *nf* **1** : mania, obsession **2** MODA PASAJERA : craze, fad **3** ANTIPATÍA : dislike — **maníaco, -ca** *adj* : maniacal — ~ *n* : maniac
maniatar *vt* : tie the hands of
maniático, -ca *adj* : obsessive, fussy — ~ *n* : fussy person, fanatic
manicomio *nm* : insane asylum
manicura *nf* : manicure — **manicuro, -ra** *n* : manicurist
manido, -da *adj* : stale, hackneyed
manifestar {55} *vt* **1** : demonstrate, show **2** DECLARAR : express, declare — **manifestarse** *vr* **1** : become evident **2** : demonstrate (in politics) — **manifestación** *nf, pl* **-ciones 1** : manifestation, sign **2** : demonstration (in politics) — **manifestante** *nmf* : protester, demonstrator — **manifiesto, -ta** *adj* : manifest, evident — **manifiesto** *nm* : manifesto
manija *nf* : handle
manillar *nm* : handlebars *pl*
maniobra *nf* : maneuver — **maniobrar** *v* : maneuver
manipular *vt* **1** : manipulate **2** MANEJAR : handle — **manipulación** *nf, pl* **-ciones** : manipulation
maniquí *nmf, pl* **-quíes** : mannequin, model — ~ *nm* : mannequin, dummy
manirroto, -ta *adj* : extravagant — ~ *n* : spendthrift
manivela *nf* : crank
manjar *nm* : delicacy, special dish
mano *nf* **1** : hand **2** : coat (of paint, etc.) **3 a ~** *or* **a la ~** : at hand, nearby **4 dar la ~** : shake hands **5 de segunda ~** : second-hand **6 ~ de obra** : labor, manpower
manojo *nm* : bunch
manopla *nf* : mitten
manosear *vt* **1** : handle excessively **2** : fondle (a person)
manotazo *nm* : slap
mansalva : **a ~** *adv phr* : at close range, without risk
mansarda *nf* : attic
mansedumbre *nf* **1** : gentleness **2** : tameness (of an animal)
mansión *nf, pl* **-siones** : mansion
manso, -sa *adj* **1** : gentle **2** : tame (of an animal)
manta *nf* **1** : blanket **2** *Lat* : poncho
manteca *nf* : lard, fat — **mantecoso, -sa** *adj* : greasy
mantel *nm* : tablecloth — **mantelería** *nf* : table linen
mantener {80} *vt* **1** : support **2** CONSERVAR : preserve **3** : keep up, maintain (relations, correspondence, etc.) **4** AFIRMAR : affirm — **mantenerse** *vr* **1** : support oneself **2 ~ firme** : hold one's ground — **mantenimiento** *nm* **1** : maintenance **2** SUSTENTO : sustenance
mantequilla *nf* : butter — **mantequera** *nf* : churn — **mantequería** *nf* : dairy
mantilla *nf* : mantilla
manto *nm* : cloak
mantón *nm, pl* **-tones** : shawl
manual *adj* : manual — ~ *nm* : manual, handbook
manubrio *nm* **1** : handle, crank **2** *Lat* : handlebars *pl*
manufactura *nf* **1** : manufacture **2** FÁBRICA : factory
manuscrito *nm* : manuscript — **manuscrito, -ta** *adj* : handwritten
manutención *nf, pl* **-ciones** : maintenance
manzana *nf* **1** : apple **2** : (city) block — **manzanar** *nm* : apple orchard — **manzano** *nm* : apple tree
maña *nf* **1** : skill **2** ASTUCIA : cunning, guile
mañana *adv* : tomorrow — ~ *nm* **el ~** : the future — ~ *nf* : morning
mañoso, -sa *adj* **1** : skillful **2** *Lat* : finicky
mapa *nm* : map — **mapamundi** *nm* : map of the world
mapache *nm* : raccoon
maqueta *nf* : model, mock-up
maquillaje *nm* : makeup — **maquillarse** *vr* : put on makeup
máquina *nf* **1** : machine **2** LOCOMOTORA : locomotive **3 a toda ~** : at full speed **4 ~ de escribir** : typewriter — **maquinación** *nf, pl* **-ciones** : machination — **maquinal** *adj* : mechanical — **maquinaria** *nf* **1** : machinery **2** : mechanism, works *pl* (of a watch, etc.) — **maquinilla** *nf* : small machine — **maquinista** *nmf* **1** : machinist **2** : (railroad) engineer
mar *nmf* **1** : sea **2 alta ~** : high seas *pl*
maraca *nf* : maraca
maraña *nf* **1** : thicket **2** ENREDO : tangle, mess
maratón *nm, pl* **-tones** : marathon
maravilla *nf* **1** : wonder, marvel **2** : marigold (flower) — **maravillar** *vt* : astonish — **maravillarse** *vr* : be amazed — **maravilloso, -sa** *adj* : marvelous
marca *nf* **1** : mark **2** : brand (on livestock) **3** *or* **~ de fábrica** : trademark **4** : record (in sports) — **marcado, -da** *adj* : marked — **marcador** *nm* **1** : scoreboard **2** *Lat* : marker, felt-tipped pen
marcapasos *nms & pl* : pacemaker
marcar {72} *vt* **1** : mark **2** : brand (livestock) **3** INDICAR : indicate, show **4** : dial (a telephone, etc.) **5** : score (in sports) — *vi* **1** : score **2** : dial (on the telephone, etc.)
marchar *vi* **1** : go **2** CAMINAR : walk **3** FUNCIONAR : work, run — **marcharse** *vr* : leave, go — **marcha** *nf* **1** : march **2** PASO : pace, speed **3** : gear (of an automobile) **4 poner en ~** : put in motion
marchitarse *vr* : wither, wilt — **marchito, -ta** *adj* : withered
marcial *adj* : martial, military
marco *nm* **1** : frame **2** : goalposts *pl* (in sports) **3** ENTORNO : setting, framework
marea *nf* : tide — **marear** *vt* **1** : make nauseous or dizzy **2** CONFUNDIR : confuse — **marearse** *vr* **1** : become nauseated or dizzy **2** CONFUNDIRSE : get confused — **mareado, -da** *adj* **1** : sick, nauseous **2** ATURDIDO : dazed, dizzy
maremoto *nm* : tidal wave
mareo *nm* **1** : nausea, seasickness **2** VÉRTIGO : dizziness
marfil *nm* : ivory
margarina *nf* : margarine
margarita *nf* : daisy
margen *nm, pl* **márgenes 1** : edge, border **2** : margin (of a page, etc.) — **marginado, -da** *adj* **1** : alienated **2 clases marginadas** : underclass — ~ *n* : outcast — **marginal** *adj* : marginal — **marginar** *vt* : ostracize, exclude
mariachi *nm* : mariachi musician or band
maridaje *nm* : marriage, union — **marido** *nm* : husband
marihuana *or* **mariguana** *or* **marijuana** *nf* : marijuana
marimba *nf* : marimba
marina *nf* **1** : coast **2** *or* **~ de guerra** : navy, fleet
marinada *nf* : marinade — **marinar** *vt* : marinate
marinero, -ra *adj* **1** : sea, marine **2** : seaworthy (of a ship) — **marinero** *nm* : sailor — **marino, -na** *adj* : marine — **marino** *nm* : seaman, sailor
marioneta *nf* : puppet, marionette
mariposa *nf* **1** : butterfly **2 ~ nocturna** : moth
mariquita *nf* : ladybug
marisco *nm* **1** : shellfish **2 ~s** *nmpl* : seafood
marisma *nf* : salt marsh
marítimo, -ma *adj* : maritime, shipping
mármol *nm* : marble
marmota *nf* **~ de América** : groundhog
marquesina *nf* : marquee, (glass) canopy
marrano, -na *n* **1** : pig, hog **2** *fam* : slob
marrar *vt* : miss (a target) — *vi* : fail
marrón *adj & nm, pl* **-rrones** : brown
marroquí *adj* : Moroccan
marsopa *nf* : porpoise
marsupial *nm* : marsupial
Marte *nm* : Mars
martes *nms & pl* : Tuesday
martillo *nm* **1** : hammer **2 ~ neumático** : jackhammer — **martillar** *or* **martillear** *v* : hammer
mártir *nmf* : martyr — **martirio** *nm* : martyrdom — **martirizar** {21} *vt* **1** : martyr **2** ATORMENTAR : torment
marxismo *nm* : Marxism — **marxista** *adj & nmf* : Marxist
marzo *nm* : March
mas *conj* : but
más *adv* **1** : more **2 el/la/lo ~** : (the) most **3** (*in negative constructions*) : (any) longer **4 ¡qué día ~ bonito!** : what a beautiful day! — ~ *adj* **1** : more **2** : most **3 ¿quién ~?** : who else? — ~ *prep* : plus — ~ *pron* **1 a lo ~** : at most **2 de ~** : extra, spare **3 ~ o menos** : more or less **4 ¿tienes ~?** : do you have more?
masa *nf* **1** : mass, volume **2** : dough (in cooking) **3 ~s** *nfpl* : people, masses
masacre *nf* : massacre
masaje *nm* : massage — **masajear** *vt* : massage
mascar {72} *v* : chew
máscara *nf* : mask — **mascarada** *nf* : masquerade — **mascarilla** *nf* : mask (in medecine, etc.)
mascota *nf* : mascot
masculino, -na *adj* **1** : masculine, male **2** VARONIL : manly **3** : masculine (in grammar) — **masculinidad** *nf* : masculinity
mascullar *v* : mumble
masilla *nf* : putty
masivo, -va *adj* : mass, large-scale
masón *nm, pl* **-sones** : Mason, Freemason — **masónico, -ca** *adj* : Masonic
masoquismo *nm* : masochism — **masoquista** *adj* : masochistic — ~ *nmf* : masochist
masticar {72} *v* : chew
mástil *nm* **1** : mast **2** ASTA : flagpole **3** : neck (of a stringed instrument)
mastín *nm, pl* **-tines** : mastiff
masturbarse *vr* : masturbate — **masturbación** *nf, pl* **-ciones** : masturbation
mata *nf* : bush, shrub
matadero *nm* : slaughterhouse
matador *nm* : matador, bullfighter
matamoscas *nms & pl* : flyswatter
matar *vt* **1** : kill **2** : slaughter (animals) — **matarse** *vr* **1** : be killed **2** SUICIDARSE : commit suicide — **matanza** *nf* : slaughter, killing
matasanos *nms & pl fam* : quack
matasellos *nms & pl* : postmark
mate *adj* : matte, dull — ~ *nm* **1** : maté **2 jaque ~** : checkmate
matemáticas *nfpl* : mathematics — **matemático, -ca** *adj* : mathematical — ~ *n* : mathematician
materia *nf* **1** ASUNTO : matter **2** MATERIAL : material — **material** *adj* **1** : material **2 daños ~es** : property damage — ~ *nm* **1** : material **2** EQUIPO : equipment, gear — **materialismo** *nm* : materialism — **materialista** *adj* : materialistic — **materializar** {21} *vt* : bring to fruition — **materializarse** *vr* : materialize — **materialmente** *adv* : absolutely
maternal *adj* : maternal — **maternidad** *nf* **1** : motherhood **2** : maternity hospital — **materno, -na** *adj* **1** : maternal **2 lengua materna** : mother tongue
matinal *adj* : morning
matinée *or* **matiné** *nf* : matinee
matiz *nm, pl* **-tices 1** : nuance **2** : hue, shade (of colors) — **matizar** {21} *vt* **1** : blend (colors) **2** : qualify (a statement, etc.) **3 ~ de** : tinge with
matón *nm, pl* **-tones 1** : bully **2** CRIMINAL : gangster, hoodlum
matorral *nm* : thicket
matraca *nf* **1** : rattle, noisemaker **2 dar la ~ a** : pester
matriarcado *nm* : matriarchy
matrícula *nf* **1** : list, roll, register **2** INSCRIPCIÓN : registration **3** : license plate (of an automobile) — **matricular** *vt* : register — **matricularse** *vr* : register, matriculate
matrimonio *nm* **1** : marriage **2** PAREJA : (married) couple — **matrimonial** *adj* : marital
matriz *nf, pl* **-trices 1** : matrix **2** : uterus, womb (in anatomy)
matrona *nf* : matron
matutino, -na *adj* : morning
maullar {8} *vi* : meow — **maullido** *nm* : meow
maxilar *nm* : jaw, jawbone
máxima *nf* : maxim
máxime *adv* : especially
máximo, -ma *adj* : maximum, highest — **máximo** *nm* **1** : maximum **2 al ~** : to the full
maya *adj*: Mayan
mayo *nm* : May
mayonesa *nf* : mayonnaise
mayor *adj* **1** (*comparative of* **grande**) : bigger, larger, greater, older **2** (*superlative of* **grande**) : biggest, largest, greatest, oldest **3 al por ~** : wholesale **4 ~ de edad** : of (legal) age — ~ *nmf* **1** : major (in the military) **2** ADULTO : adult **3 ~es** *nmfpl* : grown-ups — **mayoral** *nm* : foreman
mayordomo *nm* : butler
mayoreo *nm Lat* : wholesale
mayoría *nf* : majority
mayorista *adj* : wholesale — ~ *nmf* : wholesaler
mayormente *adv* : primarily
mayúscula *nf* : capital letter — **mayúsculo, -la** *adj* **1** : capital, uppercase **2 un fallo mayúsculo** : a terrible mistake
maza *nf* : mace (weapon)
mazapán *nm, pl* **-panes** : marzipan
mazmorra *nf* : dungeon
mazo *nm* **1** : mallet **2** MAJA : pestle
mazorca *nf* **~ de maíz** : corncob
me *pron* **1** (*direct object*) : me **2** (*indirect object*) : to me, for me, from me **3** (*reflexive*) : myself, to myself, for myself, from myself

mecánica *nf* : mechanics — **mecánico, -ca** *adj* : mechanical — **~** *n* : mechanic
mecanismo *nm* : mechanism — **mecanización** *nf, pl* **-ciones** : mechanization — **mecanizar** {21} *vt* : mechanize
mecanografiar {85} *vt* : type — **mecanografía** *nf* : typing — **mecanógrafo, -fa** *n* : typist
mecate *nm Lat* : rope
mecedora *nf* : rocking chair
mecenas *nmfs & pl* : patron, sponsor — **mecenazgo** *nm* : patronage, sponsorship
mecer {86} *vt* **1** : rock **2** : push (on a swing) — **mecerse** *vr* : rock, swing
mecha *nf* **1** : fuse (of a bomb, etc.) **2** : wick (of a candle)
mechero *nm* **1** : burner **2** *Spain* : cigarette lighter
mechón *nm, pl* **-chones** : lock (of hair)
medalla *nf* : medal — **medallón** *nm, pl* **-llones 1** : medallion **2** : locket (jewelry)
media *nf* **1** : average **2 ~s** *nfpl* : stockings **3 a ~s** : by halves, halfway
mediación *nf, pl* **-ciones** : mediation
mediado, -da *adj* **1** : half full, half empty, half over **2** : halfway through — **mediados** *nmpl* **a ~ de** : halfway through, in the middle of
mediador, -dora *n* : mediator
medialuna *nf* **1** : crescent **2** : croissant (pastry)
medianamente *adv* : fairly
medianero, -ra *adj* **pared medianera** : dividing wall
mediano, -na *adj* **1** : medium, average **2** MEDIOCRE : mediocre
medianoche *nf* : midnight
mediante *prep* : through, by means of
mediar *vi* **1** : be in the middle **2** INTERVENIR : mediate **3 ~ entre** : be between
medicación *nf, pl* **-ciones** : medication — **medicamento** *nm* : medicine — **medicar** {72} *vt* : medicate — **medicarse** *vr* : take medicine — **medicina** *nf* : medicine — **medicinal** *adj* : medicinal
medición *nf, pl* **-ciones** : measurement
médico, -ca *adj* : medical — **~** *n* : doctor, physician
medida *nf* **1** : measurement, measure **2** MODERACIÓN : moderation **3** GRADO : extent, degree **4 tomar ~s** : take steps — **medidor** *nm Lat* : meter, gauge
medieval *adj* : medieval
medio, -dia *adj* **1** : half **2** MEDIANO : average **3 una media hora** : half an hour **4 la clase media** : the middle class — **medio** *adv* : half — **~** *nm* **1** : half **2** MANERA : means *pl*, way **3 en ~ de** : in the middle of **4 ~ ambiente** : environment **5 ~s** *nmpl* : means, resources
mediocre *adj* : mediocre, average — **mediocridad** *nf* : mediocrity
mediodía *nm* : noon, midday
medioevo *nm* : Middle Ages
medir {54} *vt* **1** : measure **2** CONSIDERAR : weigh, consider — **medirse** *vr* : be moderate
meditar *vi* : meditate, contemplate — *vt* **1** : think over, consider **2** PLANEAR : plan, work out — **meditación** *nf, pl* **-ciones** : meditation
mediterráneo, -nea *adj* : Mediterranean
medrar *vt* : flourish, thrive
medroso, -sa *adj* : fearful
médula *nf* **1** : marrow **2 ~ espinal** : spinal cord
medusa *nf* : jellyfish
megabyte *nm* : megabyte
megáfono *nm* : megaphone
mejicano → **mexicano**
mejilla *nf* : cheek
mejillón *nm, pl* **-llones** : mussel
mejor *adv* **1** (*comparative*) : better **2** (*superlative*) : best **3 a lo ~** : maybe, perhaps — **~** *adj* **1** (*comparative of* **bueno** *or* **bien**) : better **2** (*superlative of* **bueno** *or* **bien**) : best **3 lo ~** : the best thing **4 tanto ~** : so much the better — **mejora** *nf* : improvement
mejorana *nf* : marjoram
mejorar *vt* : improve — *vi* : improve, get better
mejunje *nm* : concoction, brew
melancolía *nf* : melancholy — **melancólico, -ca** *adj* : melancholic, melancholy
melaza *nf* : molasses
melena *nf* **1** : long hair **2** : mane (of a lion)
melindroso, -sa *adj* **1** : affected **2** *Lat* : finicky
mella *nf* : chip, nick — **mellado, -da** *adj* : chipped, jagged
mellizo, -za *adj & n* : twin
melocotón *nm, pl* **-tones** : peach
melodía *nf* : melody — **melódico, -ca** *adj* : melodic
melodrama *nm* : melodrama — **melodramático, -ca** *adj* : melodramatic
melón *nm, pl* **-lones** : melon
meloso, -sa *adj* **1** : sweet, honeyed **2** EMPALAGOSO : cloying
membrana *nf* : membrane
membrete *nm* : letterhead, heading
membrillo *nm* : quince
membrudo, -da *adj* : muscular, burly
memorable *adj* : memorable
memorándum *or* **memorando** *nm, pl* **-dums** *or* **-dos 1** : memorandum **2** AGENDA : notebook
memoria *nf* **1** : memory **2** RECUERDO : remembrance **3** INFORME : report **4 de ~** : by heart **5 ~s** *nfpl* : memoirs — **memorizar** {21} *vt* : memorize
mena *nf* : ore
menaje *nm* : household goods *pl*, furnishings *pl*
mencionar *vt* : mention, refer to — **mención** *nf, pl* **-ciones** : mention
mendaz *adj, pl* **-daces** : lying
mendigar {52} *vi* : beg — *vt* : beg for — **mendicidad** *nf* : begging — **mendigo, -ga** *n* : beggar
mendrugo *nm* : crust (of bread)
menear *vt* **1** : move, shake **2** : sway (one's hips) **3** : wag (a tail) — **menearse** *vr* **1** : sway, shake, move **2** *fam* : hurry up
menester *nm* **ser ~** : be necessary — **menestroso, -sa** *adj* : needy
menguar *vt* : diminish, lessen — *vi* **1** : decline, decrease **2** : wane (of the moon) — **mengua** *nf* : decrease, decline
menopausia *nf* : menopause
menor *adj* **1** (*comparative of* **pequeño**) : smaller, lesser, younger **2** (*superlative of* **pequeño**) : smallest, least, youngest **3** : minor (in music) **4 al por ~** : retail — **~** *nmf* : minor, juvenile
menos *adv* **1** (*comparative*) : less **2** (*superlative*) : least **3 ~ de** : fewer than — **~** *adj* **1** (*comparative*) : less, fewer **2** (*superlative*) : least, fewest — **~** *prep* **1** : minus **2** EXCEPTO : except — **~** *pron* **1** : less, fewer **2 al ~** *or* **por lo ~** : at least **3 a ~ que** : unless — **menoscabar** *vt* **1** : lessen **2** ESTROPEAR : harm, damage — **menospreciar** *vt* **1** DESPRECIAR : scorn **2** SUBESTIMAR : undervalue — **menosprecio** *nm* : contempt
mensaje *nm* : message — **mensajero, -ra** *n* : messenger
menso, -sa *adj Lat fam* : foolish, stupid
menstruar {3} *vi* : menstruate — **menstruación** *nf* : menstruation
mensual *adj* : monthly — **mensualidad** *nf* **1** : monthly payment **2** : monthly salary
mensurable *adj* : measurable
menta *nf* **1** : mint, peppermint **2 ~ verde** : spearmint
mental *adj* : mental — **mentalidad** *nf* : mentality
mentar {55} *vt* : mention, name
mente *nf* : mind
mentir {76} *vi* : lie — **mentira** *nf* : lie — **mentirilla** *nf* : fib — **mentiroso, -sa** *adj* : lying — **~** *n* : liar
mentís *nms & pl* : denial
mentol *nm* : menthol
mentón *nm, pl* **-tones** : chin
menú *nm, pl* **-nús** : menu
menudear *vi* : occur frequently — **menudeo** *nm Lat* : retail, retailing
menudillos *nmpl* : giblets
menudo, -da *adj* **1** : small, insignificant **2 a ~** : often
meñique *nm or* **dedo ~** : little finger, pinkie
meollo *nm* **1** : marrow **2** ESENCIA : essence, core
mercado *nm* **1** : market **2 ~ de valores** : stock market — **mercadería** *nf* : merchandise, goods *pl*
mercancía *nf* : merchandise, goods *pl* — **mercante** *nmf* : merchant, dealer — **mercantil** *adj* : commercial
mercenario, -ria *adj & n* : mercenary
mercería *nf* : notions store
mercurio *nm* : mercury
Mercurio *nm* : Mercury (planet)
merecer {53} *vt* : deserve — *vi* : be worthy — **merecedor, -dora** *adj* : deserving, worthy — **merecido** *nm* **recibir su ~** : get one's just deserts
merendar {55} *vi* : have an afternoon snack — *vt* : have as an afternoon snack — **merendero** *nm* **1** : snack bar **2** : picnic area
merengue *nm* **1** : meringue **2** : merengue (dance)
meridiano, -na *adj* **1** : midday **2** CLARO : crystal-clear — **meridiano** *nm* : meridian — **meridional** *adj* : southern
merienda *nf* : afternoon snack, tea
mérito *nm* : merit, worth — **meritorio, -ria** *adj* : deserving — **~** *n* : intern, trainee
mermar *vi* : decrease — *vt* : reduce, cut down — **merma** *nf* : decrease
mermelada *nf* : marmalade, jam
mero, -ra *adj* **1** : mere, simple **2** *Lat fam* (*used as an intensifier*) : very, real — **mero** *adv Lat fam* **1** : nearly, almost **2 aquí ~** : right here
merodear *vi* **1** : maraud **2 ~ por** : prowl about (a place)
mes *nm* : month
mesa *nf* **1** : table **2** COMITÉ : committee, board
mesarse *vr* **~ los cabellos** : tear one's hair
meseta *nf* : plateau
Mesías *nm* : Messiah
mesilla *nf* : small table
mesón *nm, pl* **-sones** : inn — **mesonero, -ra** *n* : innkeeper
mestizo, -za *adj* **1** : of mixed ancestry **2** HÍBRIDO : hybrid — **~** *n* : person of mixed ancestry
mesura *nf* : moderation — **mesurado, -da** *adj* : moderate, restrained
meta *nf* : goal, objective
metabolismo *nm* : metabolism
metafísica *nf* : metaphysics — **metafísico, -ca** *adj* : metaphysical
metáfora *nf* : metaphor — **metafórico, -ca** *adj* : metaphoric, metaphorical
metal *nm* **1** : metal **2** : brass section (in an orchestra) — **metálico, -ca** *adj* : metallic, metal — **metalurgia** *nf* : metallurgy
metamorfosis *nfs & pl* : metamorphosis
metano *nm* : methane
metedura *nf* **~ de pata** *fam* : blunder
meteoro *nm* : meteor — **meteórico, -ca** *adj* : meteoric — **meteorito** *nm* : meteorite — **meteorología** *nf* : meteorology — **meteorólogo, -ga** *adj* : meteorological, meteorologic — **~** *n* : meteorologist
meter *vt* **1** : put (in) **2** : place (in a job, etc.) **3** ENREDAR : involve **4** CAUSAR : make, cause **5** : spread (a rumor) **6** *Lat* : strike (a blow) — **meterse** *vr* **1** : get in, enter **2 ~ en** : get involved in, meddle in **3 ~ con** *fam* : pick a fight with
meticuloso, -sa *adj* : meticulous
método *nm* : method — **metódico, -ca** *adj* : methodical — **metodología** *nf* : methodology
metomentodo *nmf fam* : busybody
metralla *nf* : shrapnel — **metralleta** *nf* : submachine gun
métrico, -ca *adj* : metric, metrical
metro *nm* **1** : meter **2** : subway (train)
metrópoli *nf or* **metrópolis** *nfs & pl* : metropolis — **metropolitano, -na** *adj* : metropolitan
mexicano, -na *adj* : Mexican — **mexicoamericano, -na** *adj* : Mexican-American
mezcla *nf* **1** : mixture **2** ARGAMASA : mortar — **mezclar** *vt* **1** : mix, blend **2** CONFUNDIR : mix up, muddle **3** INVOLUCRAR : involve — **mezclarse** *vr* **1** : get mixed up **2** : mingle (socially) — **mezcolanza** *nf* : mixture
mezclilla *nf Lat* : denim
mezquino, -na *adj* **1** : mean, petty **2** ESCASO : meager — **mezquindad** *nf* : meanness, stinginess
mezquita *nf* : mosque
mezquite *nm* : mesquite
mi *adj* : my
mí *pron* **1** : me **2** *or* **~ mismo, ~ misma** : myself **3 a ~ no me importa** : it doesn't matter to me
miajas → **migajas**
miau *nm* : meow
mica *nf* : mica
mico *nm* : (long-tailed) monkey
microbio *nm* : microbe, germ — **microbiología** *nf* : microbiology
microbús *nm, pl* **-buses** : minibus
microcosmos *nms & pl* : microcosm
microfilm *nm, pl* **-films** : microfilm
micrófono *nm* : microphone
microondas *nms & pl* : microwave (oven)
microorganismo *nm* : microorganism
microscopio *nm* : microscope — **microscópico, -ca** *adj* : microscopic
miedo *nm* **1** : fear **2 dar ~** : be frightening — **miedoso, -sa** *adj* : fearful
miel *nf* : honey
miembro *nm* **1** : member **2** EXTREMIDAD : limb, extremity
mientras *adv or* **~ tanto** : meanwhile, in the meantime — **~** *conj* **1** : while, as **2 ~ que** : while, whereas **3 ~ viva** : as long as I live
miércoles *nms & pl* : Wednesday
mies *nf* : (ripe) corn, grain
miga *nf* : crumb — **migajas** *nfpl* **1** : breadcrumbs **2** SOBRAS : leftovers
migración *nf, pl* **-ciones** : migration
migraña *nf* : migraine
migrar *vi* : migrate
mijo *nm* : millet
mil *adj & nm* : thousand
milagro *nm* : miracle — **milagroso, -sa** *adj* : miraculous
milenio *nm* : millennium
milésimo, -ma *adj* : thousandth
milicia *nf* **1** : militia **2** : military (service)
miligramo *nm* : milligram
mililitro *nm* : milliliter
milímetro *nm* : millimeter
militante *adj & nmf* : militant
militar *adj* : military — **~** *nmf* : soldier — **militarizar** {21} *vt* : militarize
milla *nf* : mile
millar *nm* : thousand
millón *nm, pl* **-llones 1** : million **2 mil millones** : billion — **millonario, -ria** *n* : millionaire — **millonésimo, -ma** *adj* : millionth
mimar *vt* : pamper, spoil
mimbre *nm* : wicker
mímica *nf* **1** : mime, sign language **2** IMITACIÓN : mimicry
mimo *nm* : pampering — **~** *nmf* : mime
mina *nf* **1** : mine **2** : lead (for pencils) — **minar** *vt* **1** : mine **2** DEBILITAR : undermine
mineral *adj* : mineral — **~** *nm* **1** : mineral **2** : ore (of a metal)
minería *nf* : mining — **minero, -ra** *adj* : mining — **~** *n* : miner
miniatura *nf* : miniature
minifalda *nf* : miniskirt
minifundio *nm* : small farm
minimizar {21} *vt* : minimize
mínimo, -ma *adj* **1** : minimum **2** MINÚSCULO : minute **3 en lo más ~** : in the slightest — **mínimo** *nm* : minimum
minino, -na *n fam* : pussycat
ministerio *nm* : ministry — **ministro, -tra** *n* **1** : minister, secretary **2 primer ministro** : prime minister
minoría *nf* : minority
minorista *adj* : retail — **~** *nmf* : retailer
minoritario, -ria *adj* : minority
minucia *nf* : trifle, small detail — **minucioso, -sa** *adj* **1** : detailed **2** METICULOSO : thorough
minué *nm* : minuet
minúsculo, -la *adj* : minuscule, tiny
minusvalía *nf* : handicap, disability — **minusválido, -da** *adj* : disabled
minuta *nf* **1** : bill, fee **2** BORRADOR : rough draft
minuto *nm* : minute — **minutero** *nm* : minute hand
mío, mía *adj* **1** : mine **2 una amiga mía** : a friend of mine — **~** *pron* **el mío, la mía** : mine, my own
miope *adj* : nearsighted
mirar *vt* **1** : look at **2** OBSERVAR : watch **3** CONSIDERAR : consider — *vi* **1** : look **2 ~ a** : face, overlook **3 ~ por** : look after — **mirarse** *vr* **1** : look at oneself **2** : look at each other — **mira** *nf* **1** : sight (of a firearm or instrument) **2** INTENCIÓN : aim, objective — **mirada** *nf* : look — **mirado, -da** *adj* **1** : careful **2** CONSIDERADO : considerate **3 bien ~** : well thought of — **mirador** *nm* **1** BALCÓN : balcony **2** : lookout, vantage point — **miramiento** *nm* : consideration
mirlo *nm* : blackbird
misa *nf* : Mass
miscelánea *nf* : miscellany
miserable *adj* **1** : poor **2** LASTIMOSO : miserable, wretched — **miseria** *nf* **1** : poverty **2** DESGRACIA : misfortune, misery
misericordia *nf* : mercy — **misericordioso, -sa** *adj* : merciful
mísero, -ra *adj* : wretched, miserable
misil *nm* : missile
misión *nf, pl* **-siones** : mission — **misionero, -ra** *adj & n* : missionary
mismo *adv* (*used for emphasis*) : right, exactly — **mismo, -ma** *adj* **1** : same **2** (*used for emphasis*) : very **3** : -self **4 por lo ~** : for that reason
misoginia *nf* : misogyny — **misógino** *nm* : misogynist
misterio *nm* : mystery — **misterioso, -sa** *adj* : mysterious
mística *nf* : mysticism — **místico, -ca** *adj* : mystic, mystical — **~** *n* : mystic
mitad *nf* **1** : half **2** MEDIO : middle
mítico, -ca *adj* : mythical, mythic
mitigar {52} *vt* : mitigate
mitin *nm, pl* **mítines** : (political) meeting
mito *nm* : myth — **mitología** *nm* : mythology — **mitológico, -ca** *adj* : mythological
mixto, -ta *adj* **1** : mixed, joint **2** : coeducational (of a school)
mnemónico, -ca *adj* : mnemonic
mobiliario *nm* : furniture
mocasín *nm, pl* **-sines** : moccasin
mochila *nf* : backpack, knapsack
moción *nf, pl* **-ciones** : motion
moco *nm* **1** : mucus **2 limpiarse los ~s** : wipe one's nose — **mocoso, -sa** *n fam* : kid, brat
moda *nf* **1** : fashion, style **2 a la ~** *or* **de ~** : in style, fashionable **3 ~ pasajera** : fad — **modal** *adj* : modal — **modales** *nmpl* : manners — **modalidad** *nf* : type, kind
modelar *vt* : model, mold — **modelo** *adj* : model — **~** *nm* : model, pattern — **~** *nmf* : model, mannequin
módem *or* **modem** [ˈmoðɛm] *nm* : modem
moderar *vt* **1** : moderate **2** : reduce (speed, etc.) **3** PRESIDIR : chair (a meeting) — **moderarse** *vr* : restrain oneself — **moderación** *nf, pl* **-ciones** : moderation — **moderado, -da** *adj & n* : moderate — **moderador, -dora** *n* : moderator, chairperson
moderno, -na *adj* : modern — **modernismo** *nm* : modernism — **modernizar** {21} *vt* : modernize
modesto, -ta *adj* : modest — **modestia** *nf* : modesty
modificar {72} *vt* : modify, alter — **modificación** *nf, pl* **-ciones** : alteration
modismo *nm* : idiom
modista *nmf* **1** : dressmaker **2** : (fashion) designer
modo *nm* **1** : way, manner **2** : mood (in grammar) **3** : mode (in music) **4 a ~ de** : by way of **5 de ~ que** : so (that) **6 de todos ~s** : in any case, anyway
modorra *nf* : drowsiness
modular *vt* : modulate — **modulación** *nf, pl* **-ciones** : modulation

módulo *nm* : module, unit

mofa *nf* : ridicule, mockery — **mofarse** *vr* **~ de** : make fun of

mofeta *nf* : skunk

moflete *nm fam* : fat cheek — **mofletudo, -da** *adj fam* : fat-cheeked, chubby

mohín *nm, pl* **-hines** : grimace — **mohino, -na** *adj* : sulky

moho *nm* **1** : mold, mildew **2** ÓXIDO : rust — **mohoso, -sa** *adj* **1** : moldy **2** OXIDADO : rusty

moisés *nm, pl* **-seses** : bassinet, cradle

mojar *vt* **1** : wet, moisten **2** : dunk (food) — **mojarse** *vr* : get wet — **mojado, -da** *adj* : wet, damp

mojigato, -ta *adj* : prudish — **~** *n* : prude

mojón *nm, pl* **-jones** : boundary stone, marker

molar *nm* : molar

moldear *vt* : mold, shape — **molde** *nm* : mold, form — **moldura** *nf* : molding

mole[1] *nf* : mass, bulk

mole[2] *nm* **1** : Mexican chili sauce **2** : meat served with mole

molécula *nf* : molecule — **molecular** *adj* : molecular

moler {47} *vt* : grind, crush

molestar *vt* **1** : annoy, bother **2 no ~** : do not disturb — *vi* : be a nuisance — **molestarse** *vr* **1** : bother **2** OFENDERSE : take offense — **molestia** *nf* **1** : annoyance, nuisance **2** MALESTAR : discomfort — **molesto, -ta** *adj* **1** : annoyed **2** FASTIDIOSO : annoying **3** INCÓMODO : in discomfort — **molestoso, -sa** *adj* : bothersome, annoying

molido, -da *adj* **1** : ground (of meat, etc.) **2** *fam* : worn out, exhausted

molino *nm* **1** : mill **2 ~ de viento** : windmill — **molinero, -ra** *n* : miller — **molinillo** *nm* : grinder, mill

mollera *nf* **1** : crown (of the head) **2** *fam* : brains *pl*

molusco *nm* : mollusk

momento *nm* **1** : moment, instant **2** : (period of) time **3** : momentum (in physics) **4 de ~** : for the moment **5 de un ~ a otro** : any time now — **momentáneamente** *adv* : momentarily — **momentáneo, -nea** *adj* **1** : momentary **2** PASAJERO : temporary

momia *nf* : mummy

monaguillo *nm* : altar boy

monarca *nmf* : monarch — **monarquía** *nf* : monarchy

monasterio *nm* : monastery — **monástico, -ca** *adj* : monastic

mondadientes *nms & pl* : toothpick

mondar *vt* : peel

mondongo *nm* : innards *pl*, guts *pl*

moneda *nf* **1** : coin **2** : currency (of a country) — **monedero** *nm* : change purse

monetario, -ria *adj* : monetary

monitor *nm* : monitor

monja *nf* : nun — **monje** *nm* : monk

mono, -na *n* : monkey — **~** *adj fam* : lovely, cute

monogamia *nf* : monogamy — **monógamo -ma** *adj* : monogamous

monografía *nf* : monograph

monograma *nm* : monogram

monolingüe *adj* : monolingual

monólogo *nm* : monologue

monopatín *nm, pl* **-tines** : scooter, skateboard

monopolio *nm* : monopoly — **monopolizar** {21} *vt* : monopolize

monosílabo *nm* : monosyllable — **monosilábico, -ca** *adj* : monosyllabic

monoteísmo *nm* : monotheism — **monoteísta** *adj* : monotheistic

monotonía *nf* : monotony — **monótono, -na** *adj* : monotonous

monóxido *nm* **~ de carbono** : carbon monoxide

monstruo *nm* : monster — **monstruosidad** *nf* : monstrosity — **monstruoso, -sa** *adj* : monstrous

monta *nf* : importance, value

montaje *nm* **1** : assembly **2** : staging (in theater), editing (of films)

montaña *nf* **1** : mountain **2 ~ rusa** : roller coaster — **montañero, -ra** *n* : mountain climber — **montañoso, -sa** *adj* : mountainous

montar *vt* **1** : mount **2** ESTABLECER : establish **3** ENSAMBLAR : assemble, put together **4** : stage (a performance) **5** : cock (a gun) — *vi* **1 ~ a caballo** : ride horseback **2 ~ en bicicleta** : get on a bicycle

monte *nm* **1** : mountain **2** BOSQUE : woodland **3** *or* **~ bajo** : scrubland **4 ~ de piedad** : pawnshop

montés *adj, pl* **-teses** : wild (of animals or plants)

montículo *nm* : mound, hillock

montón *nm, pl* **-tones 1** : heap, pile **2 un ~ de** *fam* : lots of

montura *nf* **1** : mount (horse) **2** SILLA : saddle **3** : frame (of glasses)

monumento *nm* : monument — **monumental** *adj fam* : monumental, huge

monzón *nm, pl* **-zones** : monsoon

moño *nm* **1** : bun (of hair) **2** *Lat* : bow (knot)

mora *nf* **1** : mulberry **2** ZARZAMORA : blackberry

morada *nf* : residence, dwelling

morado, -da *adj* : purple — **morado** *nm* : purple

moral *adj* : moral — **~** *nf* **1** : ethics, morals *pl* **2** ÁNIMO : morale — **moraleja** *nf* : moral (of a story) — **moralidad** *nf* : morality — **moralista** *adj* : moralistic — **~** *nmf* : moralist

morar *vi* : live, reside

morboso, -sa *adj* : morbid

mordaz *adj* : caustic, scathing — **mordacidad** *nf* : bite, sharpness

mordaza *nf* : gag

morder {47} *v* : bite — **mordedura** *nf* : bite (of an animal)

mordisquear *vt* : nibble (on) — **mordisco** *nm* : nibble, bite

moreno, -na *adj* **1** : dark-haired, brunette **2** : dark-skinned — **~** *n* **1** : brunette **2** : dark-skinned person

moretón *nm, pl* **-tones** : bruise

morfina *nf* : morphine

morir {46} *vi* **1** : die **2** APAGARSE : die out, go out — **morirse** *vr* **1 ~ de** : die of **2 ~ por** : be dying for — **moribundo, -da** *adj* : dying

moro, -ra *adj* : Moorish — **~** *n* : Moor

moroso, -sa *adj* : delinquent, in arrears — **morosidad** *nf* : delinquency (in payment)

morral *nm* : backpack

morriña *nf* : homesickness

morro *nm* : snout

morsa *nf* : walrus

morse *nm* : Morse code

mortaja *nf* : shroud

mortal *adj* **1** : mortal **2** : deadly (of a wound, an enemy, etc.) — **~** *nmf* : mortal — **mortalidad** *nf* : mortality — **mortandad** *nf* : death toll

mortero *nm* : mortar

mortífero, -ra *adj* : deadly, lethal

mortificar {72} *vt* **1** : mortify **2** ATORMENTAR : torment — **mortificarse** *vr* : be distressed

mosaico *nm* : mosaic

mosca *nf* : fly

moscada *adj* → **nuez**

mosquearse *vr fam* **1** : become suspicious **2** ENFADARSE : get annoyed

mosquito *nm* : mosquito — **mosquitero** *nm* **1** : (window) screen **2** : mosquito net

mostachón *nm, pl* **-chones** : macaroon

mostaza *nf* : mustard

mostrador *nm* : counter (in a store)

mostrar {19} *vt* : show — **mostrarse** *vr* : show oneself, appear

mota *nf* : spot, speck — **moteado, -da** *adj* : speckled, spotted

mote *nm* : nickname

motel *nm* : motel

motín *nm, pl* **-tines 1** : riot, uprising **2** : mutiny (of troops)

motivo *nm* **1** : motive, cause **2** : motif (in art, music, etc.) — **motivación** *nf, pl* **-ciones** : motivation — **motivar** *vt* **1** : cause **2** IMPULSAR : motivate

moto *nf* : motorcycle, motorbike — **motocicleta** *nf* : motorcycle — **motociclista** *nmf* : motorcyclist

motor, -triz *or* **-tora** *adj* : motor — **motor** *nm* : motor, engine — **motorista** *nmf* **1** : motorcyclist **2** *Lat* : motorist

mover {47} *vt* **1** : move, shift **2** : shake (the head) **3** PROVOCAR : provoke — **moverse** *vr* **1** : move (over) **2** APRESURARSE : get a move on — **movedizo, -za** *adj* : movable, shifting — **movible** *adj* : movable

móvil *adj* : mobile — **~** *nm* **1** MOTIVO : motive **2** : mobile — **movilidad** *nf* : mobility — **movilizar** {21} *vt* : mobilize

movimiento *nm* **1** : movement, motion **2 ~ sindicalista** : labor movement

mozo, -za *adj* : young — **~** *n* **1** : young man *m*, young woman *f* **2** *Lat* : waiter *m*, waitress *f*

muchacho, -cha *n* : kid, boy *m*, girl *f*

muchedumbre *nf* : crowd

mucho *adv* **1** : very much, a lot **2** : long, a long time — **mucho, -cha** *adj* **1** : a lot of, many, much **2 muchas veces** : often — **~** *pron* : a lot, many, much

mucosidad *nf* : mucus

muda *nf* **1** : molting (of animals) **2** : change (of clothing) — **mudanza** *nf* **1** : change **2** TRASLADO : move, change of residence — **mudar** *v* **1** : molt, shed **2** CAMBIAR : change — **mudarse** *vr* **1** : change (one's clothes) **2** TRASLADARSE : move (one's residence)

mudo, -da *adj* **1** : mute **2** SILENCIOSO : silent

mueble *nm* **1** : piece of furniture **2 ~s** *nmpl* : furniture, furnishings

mueca *nf* **1** : grimace, face **2 hacer ~s** : makes faces

muela *nf* **1** : tooth, molar **2 ~ de juicio** : wisdom tooth

muelle *adj* : soft — **~** *nm* **1** : wharf, jetty **2** RESORTE : spring

muérdago *nm* : mistletoe

muerte *nf* : death — **muerto, -ta** *adj* **1** : dead **2** : dull (of colors, etc.) — **~** *nm* : dead person, deceased

muesca *nf* : nick, notch

muestra *nf* **1** : sample **2** SEÑAL : sign, show

mugir {35} *vi* : moo, bellow — **mugido** *nm* : mooing, bellowing

mugre *nf* : grime, filth — **mugriento, -ta** *adj* : filthy, grimy

muguete *nm* : lily of the valley

mujer *nf* **1** : woman **2** ESPOSA : wife **3 ~ de negocios** : businesswoman

mulato, -ta *adj & n* : mulatto

muleta *nf* **1** : crutch **2** APOYO : prop, support

mullido, -da *adj* : soft, spongy

mulo, -la *n* : mule

multa *nf* : fine — **multar** *vt* : fine

multicolor *adj* : multicolored

multicultural *adj* : multicultural

multimedia *adj* : multimedia

multinacional *adj* : multinational

multiplicar {72} *v* : multiply — **multiplicarse** *vr* : multiply, reproduce — **múltiple** *adj* : multiple — **multiplicación** *nf, pl* **-ciones** : multiplication — **múltiplo** *nm* : multiple

multitud *nf* : crowd, multitude

mundo *nm* **1** : world **2 todo el ~** : everyone, everybody — **mundanal** *adj* : worldly — **mundano, -na** *adj* **1** : worldly, earthly **2 la vida mundana** : high society — **mundial** *adj* : world, worldwide

municiones *nfpl* : ammunition

municipal *adj* : municipal — **municipio** *nm* **1** : municipality **2** AYUNTAMIENTO : town council

muñeca *nf* **1** : doll **2** : wrist (in anatomy) — **muñeco** *nm* **1** : boy doll **2** MANIQUÍ : dummy, puppet

muñon *nm, pl* **-ñones** : stump (of an arm or leg)

mural *adj & nm* : mural — **muralla** *nf* : wall, rampart

murciélago *nm* : bat (animal)

murmullo *nm* **1** : murmur, murmuring **2** : rustling (of leaves, etc.)

murmurar *vi* **1** : murmur, whisper **2** CRITICAR : gossip

muro *nm* : wall

musa *nf* : muse

musaraña *nf* : shrew

músculo *nm* : muscle — **muscular** *adj* : muscular — **musculatura** *nf* : muscles *pl* — **musculoso, -sa** *adj* : muscular

muselina *nf* : muslin

museo *nm* : museum

musgo *nm* : moss — **musgoso, -sa** *adj* : mossy

música *nf* : music — **musical** *adj* : musical — **músico, -ca** *adj* : musical — **~** *n* : musician

musitar *vt* : mumble

muslo *nm* : thigh

musulmán, -mana *adj & n, mpl* **-manes** : Muslim

mutar *v* : mutate — **mutación** *nf, pl* **-ciones** : mutation — **mutante** *adj & nmf* : mutant

mutilar *vt* : mutilate — **mutilación** *nf, pl* **-ciones** : mutilation

mutuo, -tua *adj* : mutual

muy *adv* **1** : very, quite **2** DEMASIADO : too

N

n *nf* : n, 14th letter of the Spanish alphabet

nabo *nm* : turnip

nácar *nm* : mother-of-pearl

nacer {48} *vi* **1** : be born **2** : hatch (of an egg), sprout (of a plant) **3** SURGIR : arise, spring up — **nacido, -da** *adj & n* **recién ~** : newborn — **naciente** *adj* **1** : new, growing **2** : rising (of the sun) — **nacimiento** *nm* **1** : birth **2** : source (of a river) **3** ORIGEN : beginning **4** BELÉN : Nativity scene

nación *nf, pl* **-ciones** : nation, country — **nacional** *adj* : national — **~** *nmf* : national, citizen — **nacionalidad** *nf* : nationality — **nacionalismo** *nm* : nationalism — **nacionalista** *adj & nmf* : nationalist — **nacionalizar** {21} *vt* **1** : nationalize **2** : naturalize (as a citizen) — **nacionalizarse** *vr* : become naturalized

nada *pron* **1** : nothing **2 de ~** : you're welcome **3 ~ más** : nothing else, nothing more — **~** *adv* : not at all — **~** *nf* **la ~** : nothingness

nadar *v* : swim — **nadador, -dora** *n* : swimmer

nadería *nf* : small thing, trifle

nadie *pron* : nobody, no one

nado: **a ~** *adv phr* : swimming

nafta *nf Lat* : gasoline

naipe *nm* : playing card

nalgas *nfpl* : buttocks, bottom

nana *nf* : lullaby

naranja *adj & nm* : orange (color) — **~** *nf* : orange (fruit) — **naranjal** *nm* : orange grove — **naranjo** *nm* : orange tree

narciso *nm* : narcissus, daffodil

narcótico, -ca *adj* : narcotic — **narcótico** *nm* : narcotic — **narcotizar** {21} *vt* : drug — **narcotraficante** *nmf* : drug trafficker — **narcotráfico** *nm* : drug trafficking

nariz *nf, pl* **-rices 1** : nose **2** OLFATO : sense of smell **3 narices** *nfpl* : nostrils

narrar *vt* : narrate, tell — **narración** *nf, pl* **-ciones** : narration — **narrador, -dora** *n* : narrator — **narrativa** *nf* : narrative, storytelling

nasal *adj* : nasal

nata *nf Spain* : cream

natación *nf, pl* **-ciones** : swimming

natal *adj* : native, birth — **natalicio** *nm* : birthday — **natalidad** *nf* : birthrate

natillas *nfpl* : custard

natividad *nf* : birth, nativity

nativo, -va *adj & n* : native

natural *adj* **1** : natural **2** NORMAL : normal **3 ~ de** : native of, from — **~** *nm* **1** : temperament **2** NATIVO : native — **naturaleza** *nf* : nature — **naturalidad** *nf* : naturalness — **naturalista** *adj* : naturalistic — **naturalización** *nf, pl* **-ciones** : naturalization — **naturalizar** {21} *vt* : naturalize — **naturalizarse** *vr* : become naturalized — **naturalmente** *adv* **1** : naturally **2** POR SUPUESTO : of course

naufragar {52} *vi* **1** : be shipwrecked **2** FRACASAR : fail — **naufragio** *nm* : shipwreck — **náufrago, -ga** *adj* : shipwrecked — **~** *n* : castaway

náusea *nf* **1** : nausea **2 dar ~s** : nauseate **3 ~s matutinas** : morning sickness — **nauseabundo, -da** *adj* : nauseating

náutico, -ca *adj* : nautical

navaja *nf* : pocketknife, penknife

naval *adj* : naval

nave *nf* **1** : ship **2** : nave (of a church) **3 ~ espacial** : spaceship

navegar {52} *v* : navigate, sail — **navegable** *adj* : navigable — **navegación** *nf, pl* **-ciones** : navigation — **navegante** *adj* : sailing, seafaring — **~** *nmf* : navigator

Navidad *nf* **1** : Christmas **2 feliz ~** : Merry Christmas — **navideño, -ña** *adj* : Christmas

naviero, -ra *adj* : shipping

nazi *adj & nmf* : Nazi — **nazismo** *nm* : Nazism

neblina *nf* : mist

nebuloso, -sa *adj* **1** : hazy, misty, foggy **2** VAGO : vague, nebulous

necedad *nf* **1** : stupidity **2 decir ~es** : talk nonsense

necesario, -ria *adj* : necessary — **necesariamente** *adv* : necessarily — **necesidad** *nf* **1** : need, necessity **2** POBREZA : poverty **3 ~es** *nfpl* : hardships — **necesitado, -da** *adj* : needy — **necesitar** *vt* : need — *vi* **~ de** : have need of

necio, -cia *adj* : silly, dumb

necrología *nf* : obituary

néctar *nm* : nectar

nectarina *nf* : nectarine

neerlandés, -desa *adj, mpl* **-deses** : Dutch — **neerlandés** *nm* : Dutch (language)

nefasto, -ta *adj* **1** : ill-fated **2** *fam* : terrible, awful

negar {49} *vt* **1** : deny **2** REHUSAR : refuse **3** : disown (a person) — **negarse** *vr* : refuse — **negación** *nf, pl* **-ciones 1** : denial **2** : negative (in grammar) — **negativa** *nf* **1** : denial **2** RECHAZO : refusal — **negativo, -va** *adj* : negative — **negativo** *nm* : negative (of a photograph)

negligente *adj* : negligent — **negligencia** *nf* : negligence

negociar *vt* : negotiate — *vi* : deal, do business — **negociable** *adj* : negotiable — **negociación** *nf, pl* **-ciones** : negotiation — **negociante** *nmf* : businessman *m*, businesswoman *f* — **negocio** *nm* **1** : business **2** TRANSACCIÓN : deal **3 ~s** : business, commerce

negro, -gra *adj* : black, dark — **~** *n* : dark-skinned person — **negro** *nm* : black (color) — **negrura** *nf* : blackness — **negruzco, -ca** *adj* : blackish

nene, -na *n fam* : baby, small child

nenúfar *nm* : water lily

neón *nm* : neon

neoyorquino, -na *adj* : of or from New York

nepotismo *nm* : nepotism

Neptuno *nm* : Neptune

nervio *nm* **1** : nerve **2** : sinew (in meat) **3** VIGOR : vigor, energy **4 tener ~s** : be nervous — **nerviosismo** *nf* : nervousness — **nervioso, -sa** *adj* **1** : nervous, anxious **2 sistema nervioso** : nervous system

nervudo, -da *adj* : sinewy

neto, -ta *adj* **1** : clear, distinct **2** : net (of weight, salaries, etc.)

neumático *nm* : tire

neumonía *nf* : pneumonia

neurología *nf* : neurology — **neurológico, -ca** *adj* : neurological, neurologic — **neurólogo, -ga** *n* : neurologist

neurosis *nfs & pl* : neurosis — **neurótico, -ca** *adj & n* : neurotic

neutral *adj* : neutral — **neutralidad** *nf* : neutrality — **neutralizar** {21} *vt* : neutralize — **neutro, -tra** *adj* **1** : neutral **2** : neuter (in biology and grammar)

neutrón *nm, pl* **-trones** : neutron

nevar {55} *v impers* : snow — **nevada** *nf* : snowfall — **nevado, -da** *adj* **1** : snow-

covered, snowy 2 : snow-white — nevasca nf : snowstorm
nevera nf : refrigerator
nevisca nf : light snowfall, flurry
nexo nm : link, connection
ni conj 1 : neither, nor 2 ~ que : as if 3 ~ siquiera : not even
nicaragüense adj : Nicaraguan
nicho nm : niche
nicotina nf : nicotine
nidada nf : brood (of chicks, etc.)
nido nm 1 : nest 2 GUARIDA : hiding place, den
niebla nf : fog, mist
nieto, -ta n 1 : grandson m, granddaughter f 2 nietos nmpl : grandchildren
nieve nf : snow
nigeriano, -na adj : Nigerian
nilón or nilon nm, pl -lones : nylon
nimio, -mia adj : insignificant, trivial — nimiedad nf 1 : trifle 2 INSIGNIFICANCIA : triviality
ninfa nf : nymph
ninguno, -na (ningún before masculine singular nouns) adj : no, not any — ~ pron 1 : neither, none 2 : no one, nobody
niña nf 1 : pupil (of the eye) 2 la ~ de los ojos : the apple of one's eye
niño, -ña n : child, boy m, girl f — ~ adj 1 : young 2 INFANTIL : immature, childish — niñero, -ra n : baby-sitter, nanny — niñez nf, pl -ñeces : childhood
nipón, -pona adj : Japanese
níquel nm : nickel
nítido, -da adj : clear, sharp — nitidez nf, pl -deces : clarity, sharpness
nitrato nm : nitrate
nitrógeno nm : nitrogen
nivel nm 1 : level, height 2 ~ de vida : standard of living — nivelar vt : level (out)
no adv 1 : not 2 (in answer to a question) : no 3 ¡como ~! : of course! 4 ~ bien : as soon as 5 ~ fumador : non-smoker — ~ nm : no
noble adj & nmf : noble — nobleza nf : nobility
noche nf 1 : night, evening 2 buenas ~s : good evening, good night 3 de ~ or por la ~ : at night 4 hacerse de ~ : get dark — Nochebuena nf : Christmas Eve — nochecita nf : dusk — Nochevieja nf : New Year's Eve
noción nf, pl -ciones 1 : notion, concept 2 nociones nfpl : rudiments
nocivo, -va adj : harmful, noxious
nocturno, -na adj 1 : night 2 : nocturnal (of animals, etc.) — nocturno nm : nocturne
nogal nm 1 : walnut tree 2 ~ americano : hickory
nómada nmf : nomad — ~ adj : nomadic
nomás adv Lat : only, just
nombrar vt 1 : appoint 2 CITAR : mention — nombrado, -da adj : famous, well-known — nombramiento nm : appointment, nomination — nombre nm 1 : name 2 SUSTANTIVO : noun 3 FAMA : fame, renown 4 ~ de pila : first name
nómina nf : payroll
nominal adj : nominal
nominar vt : nominate — nominación nf, pl -ciones : nomination
nomo nm : gnome
non adj : odd, not even — ~ nm : odd number
nonagésimo, -ma adj & n : ninetieth
nopal nm : nopal, prickly pear
nordeste or noreste adj 1 : northeastern 2 : northeasterly (of wind, etc.) — ~ nm : northeast
nórdico, -ca adj : Scandinavian
noreste → nordeste
noria nf 1 : waterwheel 2 : Ferris wheel (at a fair, etc.)
norma nf : rule, norm, standard — normal adj 1 : normal 2 escuela ~ : teacher-training college — normalidad nf : normality — normalizar {21} vt 1 : normalize 2 ESTANDARIZAR : standardize — normalizarse vr : return to normal — normalmente adv : ordinarily, generally
noroeste adj 1 : northwestern 2 : northwesterly (of wind, etc.) — ~ nm : northwest
norte adj : north, northern — ~ nm 1 : north 2 : north wind
norteamericano, -na adj : North American
norteño, -ña adj : northern
noruego, -ga adj : Norwegian — noruego nm : Norwegian (language)
nos pron 1 (direct object) : us 2 (indirect object) : to us, for us, from us 3 (reflexive) : ourselves 4 : each other, one another
nosotros, -tras pron 1 (subject) : we 2 (object) : us 3 or ~ mismos : ourselves
nostalgia nf 1 : nostalgia 2 sentir ~ por : be homesick for — nostálgico, -ca adj : nostalgic
nota nf 1 : note 2 : grade, mark (in school) 3 CUENTA : bill, check — notable adj : noteworthy, notable — notar vt : notice — notarse vr : be evident, seem
notario, -ria n : notary (public)
noticia nf 1 : news item, piece of news 2 ~s nfpl : news — noticiario nm : newscast — noticiero nm Lat : newscast
notificar {72} vt : notify — notificación nf, pl -ciones : notification
notorio, -ria adj 1 : obvious 2 CONOCIDO : well-known — notoriedad nf : fame, notoriety
novato, -ta adj : inexperienced — ~ n : beginner, novice
novecientos, -tas adj : nine hundred — novecientos nms & pl : nine hundred
novedad nf 1 : newness, innovation 2 NOTICIAS : news 3 ~es : novelties, latest news — novedoso, -sa adj : original, novel
novela nf 1 : novel 2 : soap opera (on television) — novelesco, -ca adj 1 : fictional 2 FANTÁSTICO : fabulous — novelista nmf : novelist
noveno, -na adj : ninth — noveno nm : ninth
noventa adj & nm : ninety — noventavo, -va adj : ninetieth — noventavo nm : ninetieth
novia → novio
noviazgo nm : engagement
novicio, -cia n : novice
noviembre nm : November
novillo, -lla n : young bull m, heifer f
novio, -via n 1 : boyfriend m, girlfriend f 2 PROMETIDO : fiancé m, fiancée f 3 : bridegroom m, bride f (at a wedding)
novocaína nf : novocaine
nube nf : cloud — nubarrón nm, pl -rrones : storm cloud — nublado, -da adj 1 : cloudy 2 ENTURBIADO : clouded, dim — nublado nm : storm cloud — nublar vt 1 : cloud 2 OSCURECER : obscure — nublarse vr : get cloudy — nuboso, -sa adj : cloudy
nuca nf : nape, back of the neck
núcleo nm 1 : nucleus 2 CENTRO : center, core — nuclear adj : nuclear
nudillo nm : knuckle
nudismo nm : nudism — nudista adj & nmf : nudist
nudo nm 1 : knot 2 : crux, heart (of a problem, etc.) — nudoso, -sa adj : knotty, gnarled
nuera nf : daughter-in-law
nuestro, -tra adj : our — ~ pron (with definite article) : ours, our own
nuevamente adv : again, anew
nueve adj & nm : nine
nuevo, -va adj 1 : new 2 de nuevo : again, once more
nuez nf, pl nueces 1 : nut 2 or ~ de nogal : walnut 3 ~ de Adán : Adam's apple 4 ~ moscada : nutmeg
nulo, -la adj 1 or ~ y sin efecto : null and void 2 INCAPAZ : useless, inept — nulidad nf 1 : nullity 2 es una ~ fam : he's a total loss
numerar vt : number — numeración nf, pl -ciones 1 : numbering 2 NÚMEROS : numbers pl, numerals pl — numeral adj : numeral — número nm 1 : number, numeral 2 : issue (of a publication) 3 sin ~ : countless —numérico, -ca adj : numerical — numeroso, -sa adj : numerous
nunca adv 1 : never, ever 2 ~ más : never again 3 ~ jamás : never ever
nupcial adj : nuptial, wedding — nupcias nfpl : nuptials, wedding
nutria nf : otter
nutrir vt 1 ALIMENTAR : feed, nourish 2 FOMENTAR : fuel, foster — nutrición nf, pl -ciones : nutrition — nutrido, -da adj 1 : nourished 2 ABUNDANTE : considerable, abundant — nutriente nm : nutrient — nutritivo, -va adj : nourishing, nutritious
ñ nf : fifteenth letter of the Spanish alphabet

O

o[1] nf : o, 16th letter of the Spanish alphabet
o[2] conj (u before words beginning with o- or ho-) 1 : or, either 2 ~ sea : in other words
oasis nms & pl : oasis
obcecar {72} vt : blind (by emotions) — obcecarse vr : become stubborn
obedecer {53} vt : obey — vi 1 : obey 2 ~ a : respond to 3 ~ a : be due to — obediencia nf : obedience — obediente adj : obedient
obertura nf : overture
obeso, -sa adj : obese — obesidad nf : obesity
obispo nm : bishop
objetar v : object — objeción nf, pl -ciones : objection
objeto nm : object — objetivo, -va adj : objective — objetivo nm 1 : objective, goal 2 : lens (in photography, etc.)
objetor, -tora n ~ de conciencia : conscientious objector
oblicuo, -cua adj : oblique
obligar {52} vt : require, oblige — obligarse vr : commit oneself (to do something) — obligación nf, pl -ciones : obligation — obligado, -da adj 1 : obliged 2 FORZOSO : obligatory — obligatorio, -ria adj : mandatory
oblongo, -ga adj : oblong
oboe nm : oboe — ~ nmf : oboist
obra nf 1 : work, deed 2 : work (of art, literature, etc.) 3 CONSTRUCCIÓN : construction work 4 ~ maestra : masterpiece 5 ~s públicas : public works — obrar vt : work, produce — vi : act, behave — obrero, -ra adj la clase obrera : the working class — ~ n : worker, laborer
obsceno, -na adj : obscene — obscenidad nf : obscenity
obsequiar vt : give, present — obsequio nm : gift, present
observar vt 1 : observe, watch 2 ADVERTIR : notice 3 ACATAR : observe, obey 4 COMENTAR : remark — observación nf, pl -ciones : observation — observador, -dora adj : observant — ~ n : observer — observancia nf : observance — observatorio nm : observatory
obsesionar vt : obsess — obsesionarse vr : be obsessed — obsesión nf, pl -siones : obsession — obsesivo, -va adj : obsessive — obseso, -sa adj : obsessed
obsoleto, -ta adj : obsolete
obstaculizar {21} vt : hinder — obstáculo nm : obstacle
obstante: no ~ conj phr : nevertheless, however — ~ prep phr : in spite of, despite
obstar {21} vi ~ a or ~ para : stop, prevent
obstetricia nf : obstetrics — obstetra nmf : obstetrician
obstinarse vr : be stubborn — obstinado, -da adj 1 : obstinate, stubborn 2 TENAZ : persistent
obstruir {41} vt : obstruct — obstrucción nf, pl -ciones : obstruction
obtener {80} vt : obtain, get
obtuso, -sa adj : obtuse
obviar vt : get around, avoid
obvio, -via adj : obvious — obviamente adv : obviously, clearly
oca nf : goose
ocasión nf, pl -siones 1 : occasion 2 OPORTUNIDAD : opportunity 3 GANGA : bargain — ocasional adj 1 : occasional 2 ACCIDENTAL : accidental, chance — ocasionar vt : cause
ocaso nm 1 : sunset 2 DECADENCIA : decline
occidente nm 1 : west 2 el Occidente : the West — occidental adj : western, Western
océano nm : ocean — oceanografía nf : oceanography
ochenta adj & nm : eighty
ocho adj & nm : eight — ochocientos, -tas adj : eight hundred — ochocientos nms & pl : eight hundred
ocio nm 1 : free time, leisure 2 INACTIVIDAD : idleness — ociosidad nf : idleness, inactivity — ocioso, -sa adj 1 : idle, inactive 2 INÚTIL : useless
ocre adj & nm : ocher
octágono nm : octagon — octagonal adj : octagonal
octava nf : octave
octavo, -va adj & n : eighth
octeto nm : byte
octogésimo, -ma adj & n : eightieth
octubre nm : October
ocular adj : ocular, eye — oculista nmf : ophthalmologist
ocultar vt : conceal, hide — ocultarse vr : hide — oculto, -ta adj : hidden, occult
ocupar vt 1 : occupy 2 : hold (a position, etc.) 3 : provide work for — ocuparse vr 1 ~ de : concern oneself with 2 ~ de : take care of (children, etc.) — ocupación nf, pl -ciones 1 : occupation 2 EMPLEO : job — ocupado, -da adj 1 : busy 2 : occupied (of a place) 3 señal de occupado : busy signal — ocupante nmf : occupant
ocurrir vi : occur, happen — ocurrirse vr ~ a : occur to — occurrencia nf 1 : occurrence, event 2 SALIDA : witty remark, quip
oda nf : ode
odiar vt : hate — odio nm : hatred — odioso, -sa adj : hateful
odisea nf : odyssey
odontología nf : dentistry, dental surgery — odontólogo, -ga n : dentist, dental surgeon
oeste adj : west, western — ~ nm 1 : west 2 el Oeste : the West
ofender vt : offend — ofenderse vr : take offense — ofensa nf : offense, insult — ofensiva nf : offensive — ofensivo, -va adj : offensive
oferta nf 1 : offer 2 de ~ : on sale 3 ~ y demanda : supply and demand
oficial adj : official — ~ nmf 1 : skilled worker 2 : officer (in the military)
oficina nf : office — oficinista nmf : office worker
oficio nm : trade, profession — oficioso, -sa adj : unofficial
ofrecer {53} vt 1 : offer 2 : provide, present (an opportunity, etc.) — ofrecerse vr : volunteer — ofrecimiento nm : offer
ofrenda nf : offering
oftalmología nf : ophthalmology — oftalmólogo, -ga n : ophthalmologist
ofuscar {72} vt 1 : blind, dazzle 2 CONFUNDIR : confuse — ofuscarse vr ~ con : be blinded by — ofuscación nf, pl -ciones 1 : blindness 2 CONFUSIÓN : confusion
ogro nm : ogre
oír {50} vi : hear — vt 1 : hear 2 ESCUCHAR : listen to 3 ¡oiga! or ¡oye! : excuse me!, listen! — oídas: de ~ adv phr : by hearsay — oído nm 1 : ear 2 : (sense of) hearing 3 duro de ~ : hard of hearing
ojal nm : buttonhole
ojalá interj : I hope so!, if only!
ojear vt : eye, look at — ojeada nf : glimpse, glance
ojeriza nf 1 : ill will 2 tener ~ a : have a grudge against
ojo nm 1 : eye 2 PERSPICACIA : shrewdness 3 : span (of a bridge) 4 ¡~! : look out!, pay attention!
ola nf : wave — oleada nf : wave, surge — oleaje nm : swell (of the sea)
olé interj : bravo!
oleada nf : wave, swell — oleaje nm : waves pl, surf
óleo nm 1 : oil 2 CUADRO : oil painting — oleoducto nm : oil pipeline
oler {51} vt : smell — vi 1 : smell 2 ~ a : smell of — olerse vr fam : have a hunch about
olfatear vt 1 : sniff 2 OLER : sense, sniff out — olfato nm 1 : sense of smell 2 PERSPICACIA : nose, instinct
Olimpiada or Olimpíada nf : Olympics pl, Olympic Games pl — olímpico, -ca adj : Olympic
oliva nf : olive — olivo nm : olive tree
olla nf 1 : pot 2 ~ podrida : (Spanish) stew
olmo nm : elm
olor nm : smell — oloroso, -sa adj : fragrant
olvidar vt 1 : forget 2 DEJAR : leave (behind) — olvidarse vr : forget — olvidadizo, -za adj : forgetful — olvido nm 1 : forgetfulness 2 DESCUIDO : oversight
ombligo nm : navel
omelette nmf Lat : omelet
ominoso, -sa adj : ominous
omitir vt : omit — omisión nf, pl -siones : omission
ómnibus nm, pl -bus or -buses : bus
omnipotente adj : omnipotent
omóplato or omoplato nm : shoulder blade
once adj & nm : eleven — onceavo, -va adj & n : eleventh
onda nf : wave — ondear vi : ripple — ondulación nf, pl -ciones : undulation — ondulado, -da adj : wavy — ondular vt : wave (hair) — vi : undulate, ripple
ónice nmf or ónix nm : onyx
onza nf : ounce
opaco, -ca adj 1 : opaque 2 DESLUSTRADO : dull
ópalo nm : opal
opción nf, pl -ciones : option — opcional adj : optional
ópera nf : opera
operar vt 1 : operate on 2 Lat : operate, run (a machine) — vi 1 : operate 2 NEGOCIAR : deal, do business — operarse vr 1 : have an operation 2 OCURRIR : take place — operación nf, pl -ciones 1 : operation 2 TRANSACCIÓN : transaction, deal — operacional adj : operational — operador, -dora n 1 : operator 2 : cameraman (for television, etc.)
opereta nf : operetta
opinar vt : think — vi : express an opinion — opinión nf, pl -niones : opinion
opio nm : opium
oponer {60} vt 1 : raise, put forward (arguments, etc.) 2 ~ resistencia : put up a fight — oponerse vr ~ a : oppose, be against — oponente nmf : opponent
oporto nm : port (wine)
oportunidad nf : opportunity — oportunista nmf : opportunist — oportuno, -na adj 1 : opportune, timely 2 APROPIADO : suitable
opositor, -tora n 1 : opponent 2 : candidate (for a position) — oposición nf, pl -ciones : opposition
oprimir vt 1 : press, squeeze 2 TIRANIZAR : oppress — opresión nf, pl -siones 1 : oppression 2 ~ de pecho : tightness in the chest — opresivo, -va adj : oppressive — opresor, -sora n : oppressor
optar vi 1 ~ a : apply for 2 ~ por : choose, opt for
óptica nf 1 : optics 2 : optician's (shop) — óptico, -ca adj : optical — ~ n : optician
optimismo nm : optimism — optimista adj : optimistic — ~ nmf : optimist
optometría nf : optometry — optometrista nmf : optometrist
opuesto adj 1 : opposite 2 CONTRADICTORIO : opposed, conflicting
opulencia nf : opulence — opulento, -ta adj : opulent
oración nf, pl -ciones 1 : prayer 2 FRASE : sentence, clause
oráculo nm : oracle

orador, -dora *n* : speaker

oral *adj* : oral

orar *vi* : pray

órbita *nf* **1** : orbit (in astronomy) **2** : eye socket — **orbitar** *vi* : orbit

orden *nm, pl* **órdenes 1** : order **2 ~ del día** : agenda (at a meeting) **3 ~ público** : law and order — **~** *nf, pl* **órdenes 1** : order (of food) **2 ~ religiosa** : religious order **3 ~ de compra** : purchase order

ordenador *nm Spain* : computer

ordenar *vt* **1** : order, command **2** ARREGLAR : put in order **3** : ordain (a priest) — **ordenanza** *nm* : orderly (in the armed forces) — **~** *nf* : ordinance, regulation

ordeñar *vt* : milk

ordinal *adj & nm* : ordinal

ordinario, -ria *adj* **1** : ordinary **2** GROSERO : common, vulgar

orear *vt* : air

orégano *nm* : oregano

oreja *nf* : ear

orfanato *or* **orfelinato** *nm* : orphanage

orfebre *nmf* : goldsmith, silversmith

orgánico, -ca *adj* : organic

organigrama *nm* : flowchart

organismo *nm* **1** : organism **2** ORGANIZACIÓN : agency, organization

organista *nmf* : organist

organizar {21} *vt* : organize — **organizarse** *vr* : get organized — **organización** *nf, pl* **-ciones** : organization — **organizador, -dora** *n* : organizer

órgano *nm* : organ

orgasmo *nm* : orgasm

orgía *nf* : orgy

orgullo *nm* : pride — **orgulloso, -sa** *adj* : proud

orientación *nf, pl* **-ciones 1** : orientation **2** DIRECCIÓN : direction **3** CONSEJO : guidance

oriental *adj* **1** : eastern **2** : oriental — **~** *nmf* : Oriental

orientar *vt* **1** : orient, position **2** GUIAR : guide, direct — **orientarse** *vr* **1** : orient oneself **2 ~ hacia** : turn towards

oriente *nm* **1** : east, East **2 el Oriente** : the Orient

orificio *nm* : orifice, opening

origen *nm, pl* **orígenes** : origin — **original** *adj & nm* : original — **originalidad** *nf* : originality — **originar** *vt* : give rise to — **originarse** *vr* : originate, arise — **originario, -ria** *adj* **~ de** : native of

orilla *nf* **1** : border, edge **2** : bank (of a river), shore (of the sea)

orinar *vi* : urinate — **orina** *nf* : urine

oriol *nm* : oriole

oriundo, -da *adj* **~ de** : native of

orla *nf* : border

ornamental *adj* : ornamental — **ornamento** *nm* : ornament

ornar *vt* : adorn

ornitología *nf* : ornithology

oro *nm* : gold

orquesta *nf* : orchestra — **orquestar** *vt* : orchestrate

orquídea *nf* : orchid

ortiga *nf* : nettle

ortodoxia *nf* : orthodoxy — **ortodoxo, -xa** *adj* : orthodox

ortografía *nf* : spelling

ortopedia *nf* : orthopedics — **ortopédico, -ca** *adj* : orthopedic

oruga *nf* : caterpillar

orzuelo *nm* : sty (in the eye)

os *pron pl Spain* **1** (*direct or indirect object*) : you, to you **2** (*reflexive*) : yourselves, to yourselves **3** : each other, to each other

osado, -da *adj* : bold, daring — **osadía** *nf* **1** : boldness, daring **2** DESCARO : audacity, nerve

osamenta *nf* : skeleton

osar *vi* : dare

oscilar *vi* **1** : swing, sway **2** FLUCTUAR : fluctuate — **oscilación** *nf, pl* **-ciones 1** : swinging **2** FLUCTUACIÓN : fluctuation

oscuro, -ra *adj* **1** : dark **2** : obscure (of ideas, persons, etc.) **3 a oscuras** : in the dark — **oscurecer** {53} *vt* **1** : darken **2** : confuse, cloud (the mind) **3 al ~** : at nightfall — *v impers* : get dark — **oscurecerse** *vr* : grow dark — **oscuridad** *nf* **1** : darkness **2** : obscurity (of ideas, persons, etc.)

óseo, ósea *adj* : skeletal, bony

oso, osa *n* **1** : bear **2 ~ de peluche** *or* **~ de felpa** : teddy bear

ostensible *adj* : evident, obvious

ostentar *vt* **1** : flaunt, display **2** POSEER : have, hold — **ostentación** *nf, pl* **-ciones** : ostentation — **ostentoso, -sa** *adj* : ostentatious, showy

osteopatía *n* : osteopathy — **osteópata** *nmf* : osteopath

osteoporosis *nf* : osteoporosis

ostra *nf* : oyster

ostracismo *nm* : ostracism

otear *vt* : scan, survey

otoño *nm* : autumn, fall — **otoñal** *adj* : autumn, fall

otorgar {52} *vt* **1** : grant, award **2** : draw up (a legal document)

otro, otra *adj* **1** : another, other **2 otra vez** : again — **~** *pron* **1** : another (one), other (one) **2 los otros, las otras** : the others, the rest

ovación *nf, pl* **-ciones** : ovation

óvalo *nm* : oval — **oval** *or* **ovalado, -da** *adj* : oval

ovario *nm* : ovary

oveja *nf* **1** : sheep, ewe **2 ~ negra** : black sheep

overol *nm Lat* : overalls *pl*

ovillo *nm* **1** : ball (of yarn) **2 hacerse un ~** : curl up (into a ball)

ovni *or* **OVNI** *nm* (*objeto volador no identificado*) : UFO

ovular *vi* : ovulate — **ovulación** *nf, pl* **-ciones** : ovulation

oxidar *vi* : rust — **oxidarse** *vr* : get rusty — **oxidación** *nf, pl* **-ciones** : rusting — **oxidado, -da** *adj* : rusty — **óxido** *nm* : rust

oxígeno *nm* : oxygen

oye → **oír**

oyente *nmf* **1** : listener **2** : auditor (student)

ozono *nm* : ozone

P

p *nf* : p, 17th letter of the Spanish alphabet

pabellón *nm, pl* **-llones 1** : pavilion **2** : block, building (in a hospital complex, etc.) **3** : summerhouse (in a garden, etc.) **4** BANDERA : flag

pabilo *nm* : wick

pacer {48} *v* : graze

paces → **paz**

paciencia *nf* : patience — **paciente** *adj & nmf* : patient

pacificar {72} *vt* : pacify, calm — **pacificarse** *vr* : calm down — **pacífico, -ca** *adj* : peaceful, pacific — **pacifismo** *nm* : pacifism — **pacifista** *adj & nmf* : pacifist

pacotilla *nf* **de ~** : second-rate, trashy

pacto *nm* : pact, agreement — **pactar** *vt* : agree on — *vi* : come to an agreement

padecer {53} *vt* : suffer, endure — *vi* **~ de** : suffer from — **padecimiento** *nm* : suffering

padre *nm* **1** : father **2 ~s** *nmpl* : parents — **~** *adj Lat fam* : great, fantastic — **padrastro** *nm* : stepfather — **padrino** *nm* **1** : godfather **2** : best man (at a wedding)

padrón *nm, pl* **-drones** : register, roll

paella *nf* : paella

paga *nf* : pay, wages *pl* — **pagadero, -ra** *adj* : payable

pagano, -na *adj & n* : pagan, heathen

pagar {52} *vt* : pay, pay for — *vi* : pay — **pagaré** *nm* : IOU

página *nf* : page

pago *nm* : payment

país *nm* **1** : country, nation **2** REGIÓN : region, land — **paisaje** *nm* : scenery, landscape — **paisano, -na** *n* : compatriot

paja *nf* **1** : straw **2** *fam* : nonsense

pájaro *nm* **1** : bird **2 ~ carpintero** : woodpecker — **pajarera** *nf* : aviary

pajita *nf* : (drinking) straw

pala *nf* **1** : shovel, spade **2** : blade (of an oar or a rotor) **3** : paddle, racket (in sports)

palabra *nf* **1** : word **2** HABLA : speech **3 tener la ~** : have the floor — **palabrota** *nf* : swearword

palacio *nm* **1** : palace, mansion **2 ~ de justicia** : courthouse

paladar *nm* : palate — **paladear** *vt* : savor

palanca *nf* **1** : lever, crowbar **2** *fam* : leverage, influence **3 ~ de cambio** *or* **~ de velocidades** : gearshift

palangana *nf* : washbowl

palco *nm* : box (in a theater)

palestino, -na *adj* : Palestinian

paleta *nf* **1** : small shovel, trowel **2** : palette (in art) **3** : paddle (in sports, etc.)

paletilla *nf* : shoulder blade

paliar *vt* : alleviate, ease — **paliativo, -va** *adj* : palliative

pálido, -da *adj* : pale — **palidecer** {53} *vi* : turn pale — **palidez** *nf, pl* **-deces** : paleness, pallor

palillo *nm* **1** : small stick **2** *or* **~ de dientes** : toothpick

paliza *nf* : beating

palma *nf* **1** : palm (of the hand) **2** : palm (tree or leaf) **3 batir ~s** : clap, applaud — **palmada** *nf* **1** : pat, slap **2 ~s** *nfpl* : clapping

palmera *nf* : palm tree

palmo *nm* **1** : span, small amount **2 ~ a ~** : bit by bit

palmotear *vi* : applaud — **palmoteo** *nm* : clapping, applause

palo *nm* **1** : stick **2** MANGO : shaft, handle **3** MÁSTIL : mast **4** POSTE : pole **5** GOLPE : blow **6** : suit (of cards)

paloma *nf* : pigeon, dove — **palomilla** *nf* : moth — **palomitas** *nfpl* : popcorn

palpar *vt* : feel, touch — **palpable** *adj* : palpable

palpitar *vi* : palpitate, throb — **palpitación** *nf, pl* **-ciones** : palpitation

palta *nf Lat* : avocado

paludismo *nm* : malaria

pampa *nf* : pampa

pan *nm* **1** : bread **2** : loaf (of bread, etc.) **3 ~ tostado** : toast

pana *nf* : corduroy

panacea *nf* : panacea

panadería *nf* : bakery, bread shop — **panadero, -ra** *n* : baker

panal *nm* : honeycomb

panameño, -ña *adj* : Panamanian

pancarta *nf* : placard, banner

pancito *nm Lat* : (bread) roll

páncreas *nms & pl* : pancreas

panda *nmf* : panda

pandemonio *nm* : pandemonium

pandero *nm* : tambourine — **pandereta** *nf* : (small) tambourine

pandilla *nf* : gang

panecillo *nm Spain* : (bread) roll

panel *nm* : panel

panfleto *nm* : pamphlet

pánico *nm* : panic

panorama *nm* : panorama — **panorámico, -ca** *adj* : panoramic

panqueque *nm Lat* : pancake

pantaletas *nfpl Lat* : panties

pantalla *nf* **1** : screen **2** : lampshade

pantalón *nm, pl* **-lones 1** *or* **pantalones** *nmpl* : pants *pl*, trousers *pl* **2 pantalones vaqueros** : jeans

pantano *nm* **1** : swamp, marsh **2** EMBALSE : reservoir — **pantanoso, -sa** *adj* : marshy, swampy

pantera *nf* : panther

pantimedias *nfpl Lat* : panty hose

pantomima *nf* : pantomime

pantorrilla *nf* : calf (of the leg)

pantufla *nf* : slipper

panza *nf* : belly, paunch — **panzón, -zona** *adj, mpl* **-zones** : potbellied

pañal *nm* : diaper

paño *nm* **1** : cloth **2** TRAPO : rag, dust cloth **3 ~ de cocina** : dishcloth **4 ~ higiénico** : sanitary napkin **5 ~s menores** : underwear

pañuelo *nm* **1** : handkerchief **2** : scarf, kerchief

papa[1] *nm* : pope

papa[2] *nf Lat* **1** : potato **2 ~s fritas** : potato chips, french fries

papá *nm fam* **1** : dad, pop **2 ~s** *nmpl* : parents, folks

papada *nf* : double chin

papagayo *nm* : parrot

papal *adj* : papal

papalote *nm Lat* : kite

papanatas *nmfs & pl fam* : simpleton

papaya *nf* : papaya

papel *nm* **1** : paper, sheet of paper **2** : role, part (in theater, etc.) **3 ~ de aluminio** : aluminum foil **4 ~ higiénico** *or* **~ de baño** : toilet paper **5 ~ de lija** : sandpaper **6 ~ pintado** : wallpaper — **papeleo** *nm* : paperwork, red tape — **papelera** *nf* : wastebasket — **papelería** *nf* : stationery store — **papeleta** *nf* **1** : ticket, slip **2** : ballot (paper)

paperas *nfpl* : mumps

papilla *nf* **1** : baby food, pap **2 hacer ~** : smash to bits

paquete *nm* **1** : package, parcel **2** : pack (of cigarettes, etc.)

paquistaní *adj* : Pakistani

par *nm* **1** : pair, couple **2** : par (in golf) **3** NOBLE : peer **4 abierto de ~ en ~** : wide open **5 sin ~** : without equal — **~** *adj* : even (in number) — **~** *nf* **1** : par **2 a la ~ que** : at the same time as

para *prep* **1** : for **2** HACIA : towards **3** : (in order) to **4** : around, by (a time) **5 ~ adelante** : forwards **6 ~ atrás** : backwards **7 ~ que** : so (that), in order that

parabienes *nmpl* : congratulations

parábola *nf* : parable

parabrisas *nms & pl* : windshield

paracaídas *nms & pl* : parachute — **paracaidista** *nmf* **1** : parachutist **2** : paratrooper (in the military)

parachoques *nms & pl* : bumper

parada *nf* **1** : stop **2** : (act of) stopping **3** DESFILE : parade — **paradero** *nm* **1** : whereabouts **2** *Lat* : bus stop — **parado, -da** *adj* **1** : idle, stopped **2** *Lat* : standing (up) **3 bien (mal) parado** : in good (bad) shape

paradoja *nf* : paradox

parafernalia *nf* : paraphernalia

parafina *nf* : paraffin

parafrasear *vt* : paraphrase — **paráfrasis** *nfs & pl* : paraphrase

paraguas *nms & pl* : umbrella

paraguayo, -ya *adj* : Paraguayan

paraíso *nm* : paradise

paralelo, -la *adj* : parallel — **paralelo** *nm* : parallel — **paralelismo** *nm* : similarity

parálisis *nfs & pl* : paralysis — **paralítico, -ca** *adj* : paralytic — **paralizar** {21} *vt* : paralyze

parámetro *nm* : parameter

páramo *nm* : barren plateau

parangón *nm, pl* **-gones 1** : comparison **2 sin ~** : matchless

paraninfo *nm* : auditorium, hall

paranoia *nf* : paranoia — **paranoico, -ca** *adj & n* : paranoid

parapeto *nm* : parapet, rampart

parapléjico, -ca *adj & n* : paraplegic

parar *vt* **1** : stop **2** *Lat* : stand, prop — *vi* **1** : stop **2 ir a ~** : end up, wind up — **pararse** *vr* **1** : stop **2** *Lat* : stand up

pararrayos *nms & pl* : lightning rod

parásito, -ta *adj* : parasitic — **parásito** *nm* : parasite

parasol *nm* : parasol

parcela *nf* : parcel, tract (of land) — **parcelar** *vt* : parcel (up)

parche *nm* : patch

parcial *adj* **1** : partial **2 a tiempo ~** : part-time — **parcialidad** *nf* : partiality, bias

parco, -ca *adj* : sparing, frugal

pardo, -da *adj* : brownish grey

parear *vt* : pair (up)

parecer {53} *vi* **1** : seem, look **2** ASEMEJARSE A : look like, seem like **3 me parece que** : I think that, in my opinion **4 ¿qué te parece?** : what do you think? **5 según parece** : apparently — **parecerse** *vr* **~ a** : resemble — **~** *nm* **1** : opinion **2** ASPECTO : appearance **3 al ~** : apparently — **parecido, -da** *adj* **1** : similar **2 bien parecido** : good-looking — **parecido** *nm* : resemblance, similarity

pared *nf* : wall

parejo, -ja *adj* **1** : even, smooth **2** SEMEJANTE : similar — **pareja** *nf* **1** : couple, pair **2** : partner (person)

parentela *nf* : relatives *pl*, kin — **parentesco** *nm* : relationship, kinship

paréntesis *nms & pl* **1** : parenthesis **2** DIGRESIÓN : digression **3 entre ~** : by the way

paria *nmf* : outcast

paridad *nf* : equality

pariente *nmf* : relative, relation

parir *vi* : give birth, have a baby — *vt* : give birth to

parking *nm* : parking lot

parlamentar *vi* : discuss — **parlamentario, -ria** *adj* : parliamentary — **~** *n* : member of parliament — **parlamento** *nm* : parliament

parlanchín, -china *adj, mpl* **-chines** : talkative, chatty — **~** *n* : chatterbox

parlotear *vi fam* : chatter — **parloteo** *nm fam* : chatter

paro *nm* **1** : stoppage, shutdown **2** DESEMPLEO : unemployment **3** *Lat* : strike **4 ~ cardíaco** : cardiac arrest

parodia *nf* : parody — **parodiar** *vt* : parody

párpado *nm* : eyelid — **parpadear** *vi* **1** : blink **2** : flicker (of light), twinkle (of stars) — **parpadeo** *nm* **1** : blink **2** : flicker (of light), twinkling (of stars)

parque *nm* **1** : park **2 ~ de atracciones** : amusement park

parqué *nm* : parquet

parquear *vt Lat* : park

parquedad *nf* : frugality, moderation

parquímetro *nm* : parking meter

parra *nf* : grapevine

párrafo *nm* : paragraph

parranda *nf fam* : party, spree

parrilla *nf* **1** : broiler, grill **2** : grate (of a chimney, etc.) — **parrillada** *nf* : barbecue

párroco *nm* : parish priest — **parroquia** *nf* **1** : parish **2** : parish church — **parroquial** *adj* : parochial — **parroquiano, -na** *nm* **1** : parishioner **2** CLIENTE : customer

parsimonia *nf* **1** : calm **2** FRUGALIDAD : thrift — **parsimonioso, -sa** *adj* **1** : calm, unhurried **2** FRUGAL : thrifty

parte *nf* **1** : part **2** PORCIÓN : share **3** LADO : side **4** : party (in negotiations, etc.) **5 de ~ de** : on behalf of **6 ¿de ~ de quién?** : who is speaking? **7 en alguna ~** : somewhere **8 en todas ~s** : everywhere **9 tomar ~** : take part — **~** *nm* **1** : report **2 ~ meteorológico** : weather forecast

partero, -ra *n* : midwife

partición *nf, pl* **-ciones** : division, sharing

participar *vi* **1** : participate, take part **2 ~ en** : have a share in — *vt* : notify — **participación** *nf, pl* **-ciones 1** : participation **2** : share, interest (in a fund, etc.) **3** NOTICIA : notice — **participante** *adj* : participating — **~** *nmf* : participant — **partícipe** *nmf* : participant

participio *nm* : participle

partícula *nf* : particle

particular *adj* **1** : particular **2** PRIVADO : private — **~** *nm* **1** : matter **2** PERSONA : individual — **particularidad** *nf* : peculiarity — **particularizar** {21} *vt* : distinguish, characterize — *vi* : go into details

partir *vt* **1** : split, divide **2** ROMPER : break, crack **3** REPARTIR : share (out) — *vi* **1** : depart **2 ~ de** : start from **3 a ~ de** : as of, from — **partirse** *vr* **1** : split (open) **2** RAJARSE : crack — **partida** *nf* **1** : departure **2** : entry, item (in a register, etc.) **3** JUEGO : game **4** : group (of persons) **5 mala ~** : dirty trick **6 ~ de nacimiento** : birth certificate — **partidario, -ria** *n* : follower, supporter — **partido** *nm* **1** : (political) party **2** : game, match (in sports) **3** PARTIDARIOS : following **4 sacar ~ de** : make the most of

partitura *nf* : (musical) score

parto *nm* **1** : childbirth **2 estar de ~** : be in labor

parvulario *nm* : nursery school

pasa *nf* **1** : raisin **2 ~ de Corinto** : currant

pasable *adj* : passable

pasada *nf* **1** : pass, wipe, coat (of paint, etc.) **2 de ~** : in passing **3 mala ~** : dirty trick — **pasadizo** *nm* : corridor — **pasado, -da** *adj* **1** : past **2** PODRIDO : bad, spoiled **3** ANTICUADO : out-of-date **4 el año pasado** : last year — **pasado** *nm* : past

pasador *nm* **1** CERROJO : bolt **2** : barrette (for the hair)

pasaje *nm* **1** : passage **2** BILLETE : ticket, fare **3** PASILLO : passageway **4** PASAJEROS : passengers *pl* — **pasajero, -ra** *adj* : passing — **~** *n* : passenger

pasamanos *nms & pl* : handrail, banister

pasaporte *nm* : passport

pasar *vi* **1** : pass, go (by) **2** ENTRAR : come in **3** SUCEDER : happen **4** TERMINARSE : be over, end **5 ~ de** : exceed **6 ¿qué pasa?** : what's the matter? — *vt* **1** : pass **2** : spend (time) **3** CRUZAR : cross **4** TOLERAR : tolerate **5** SUFRIR : go through, suffer **6** : show (a movie, etc.) **7 pasarlo bien** : have a good time **8 ~ por alto** : overlook, omit — **pasarse** *vr* **1** : pass, go away **2** ESTROPEARSE : spoil, go bad **3** OLVIDARSE : slip one's mind **4** EXCEDERSE : go too far

pasarela *nf* **1** : footbridge **2** : gangway (on a ship)

pasatiempo *nm* : pastime, hobby

Pascua *nf* **1** : Easter (Christian feast) **2** : Passover (Jewish feast) **3** NAVIDAD : Christmas

pase *nm* : pass

pasear *vi* : take a walk, go for a ride — *vt* **1** : take for a walk **2** EXHIBIR : parade, show off — **pasearse** *vr* : go for a walk, go for a ride — **paseo** *nm* **1** : walk, ride **2** *Lat* : outing

pasillo *nm* : passage, corridor

pasión *nf, pl* **-siones** : passion

pasivo, -va *adj* : passive — **pasivo** *nm* : liabilities *pl*

pasmar *vt* : astonish, amaze — **pasmarse** *vr* : be astonished — **pasmado, -da** *adj* : stunned, flabbergasted — **pasmo** *nm* : astonishment — **pasmoso, -sa** *adj* : astonishing

paso[1]**, -sa** *adj* : dried (of fruit)

paso[2] *nm* **1** : step **2** HUELLA : footprint **3** RITMO : pace **4** CRUCE : crossing **5** PASAJE : passage, way through **6** : (mountain) pass **7 de ~** : in passing

pasta *nf* **1** : paste **2** MASA : dough **3** *or* **~s** : pasta **4 ~ de dientes** *or* **~ dentífrica** : toothpaste

pastar *v* : graze

pastel *nm* **1** : cake **2** EMPANADA : pie **3** : pastel (crayon) — **pastelería** *nf* : pastry shop

pasteurizar {21} *vt* : pasteurize

pastilla *nf* **1** : pill, tablet **2** : bar (of chocolate, soap, etc.) **3 ~ para la tos** : lozenge, cough drop

pasto *nm* **1** : pasture **2** *Lat* : grass, lawn — **pastor, -tora** *n* **1** : shepherd **2** : pastor (in religion) — **pastoral** *adj* : pastoral

pata *nf* **1** : paw, leg (of an animal) **2** : foot, leg (of furniture) **3 meter la ~** *fam* : put one's foot in it — **patada** *nf* **1** : kick **2** : stamp (of the foot) — **patalear** *vi* **1** : kick **2** : stamp (one's feet)

patata *nf Spain* : potato

patear *vt* : kick — *vi* **1** : kick **2** : stamp (one's feet)

patentar *vt* : patent — **patente** *adj* : obvious, patent — **~** *nf* : patent

paternal *adj* : fatherly, paternal — **paternidad** *nf* **1** : fatherhood **2** : paternity (in law) — **paterno, -na** *adj* : paternal

patético, -ca *adj* : pathetic, moving

patillas *nfpl* : sideburns

patinar *vi* **1** : skate **2** RESBALAR : slip, slide — **patín** *nm, pl* **-tines** : skate — **patinador, -dora** *n* : skater — **patinaje** *nm* : skating — **patinazo** *nm* **1** : skid **2** *fam* : blunder — **patinete** *nm* : scooter

patio *nm* **1** : courtyard, patio **2** *or* **~ de recreo** : playground

pato, -ta *n* **1** : duck **2 pagar el pato** *fam* : take the blame — **patito, -ta** *n* : duckling

patología *nf* : pathology — **patológico, -ca** *adj* : pathological

patraña *nf* : hoax

patria *nf* : native land

patriarca *nm* : patriarch

patrimonio *nm* **1** : inheritance **2** : (historical or cultural) heritage

patriota *adj* : patriotic — **~** *nmf* : patriot — **patriótico, -ca** *adj* : patriotic — **patriotismo** *nm* : patriotism

patrocinador, -dora *n* : sponsor — **patrocinar** *vt* : sponsor — **patrocinio** *nm* : sponsorship

patrón, -trona *n, mpl* **-trones 1** : patron **2** JEFE : boss **3** : landlord, landlady *f* (of a boarding house, etc.) — **patrón** *nm, pl* **-trones** : pattern (in sewing) — **patronato** *nm* **1** : patronage **2** FUNDACIÓN : foundation, trust

patrulla *nf* **1** : patrol **2** : (police) cruiser — **patrullar** *v* : patrol

paulatino, -na *adj* : gradual

pausa *nf* : pause, break — **pausado, -da** *adj* : slow, deliberate

pauta *nf* : guideline

pavimento *nm* : pavement — **pavimentar** *vt* : pave

pavo, -va *n* **1** : turkey **2 pavo real** : peacock

pavonearse *vr* : strut, swagger

pavor *nm* : dread, terror — **pavoroso, -sa** *adj* : terrifying

payaso, -sa *n* : clown — **payasada** *nf* : antic, buffoonery — **payasear** *vi Lat fam* : clown (around)

paz *nf, pl* **paces 1** : peace **2 dejar en ~** : leave alone **3 hacer las paces** : make up, reconcile

peaje *nm* : toll

peatón *nm, pl* **-tones** : pedestrian

peca *nf* : freckle

pecado *nm* : sin — **pecador, -dora** *adj* : sinful — **~** *n* : sinner — **pecaminoso, -sa** *adj* : sinful — **pecar** {72} *vi* : sin

pecera *nf* : fishbowl, fish tank

pecho *nm* **1** : chest **2** MAMA : breast **3** CORAZÓN : heart, courage **4 dar el ~** : breast-feed **5 tomar a ~** : take to heart — **pechuga** *nf* : breast (of fowl)

pecoso, -sa *adj* : freckled

pectoral *adj* : pectoral

peculiar *adj* **1** : particular **2** RARO : peculiar, odd — **peculiaridad** *nf* : peculiarity

pedagogía *nf* : education, pedagogy — **pedagogo, -ga** *n* : educator, teacher

pedal *nm* : pedal — **pedalear** *vi* : pedal

pedante *adj* : pedantic, pompous

pedazo *nm* **1** : piece, bit **2 hacerse ~s** : fall to pieces

pedernal *nm* : flint

pedestal *nm* : pedestal

pediatra *nmf* : pediatrician

pedigrí *nm* : pedigree

pedir {54} *vt* **1** : ask for, request **2** : order (food, merchandise, etc.) — *vi* **1** : ask **2 ~ prestado** : borrow — **pedido** *nm* **1** : order **2 hacer un ~** : place an order

pedregoso, -sa *adj* : rocky, stony

pedrería *nf* : precious stones *pl*

pegar {52} *vt* **1** : stick, glue, paste **2** : sew on (a button, etc.) **3** JUNTAR : bring together **4** GOLPEAR : hit, strike **5** PROPINAR : deal (a blow, etc.) **6** : transmit (an illness) **7 ~ un grito** : let out a scream — *vi* **1** : adhere, stick **2** GOLPEAR : hit — **pegarse** *vr* **1** : hit oneself, hit each other **2** ADHERIRSE : stick, adhere **3** CONTAGIARSE : be transmitted — **pegadizo, -za** *adj* **1** : catchy **2** CONTAGIOSO : contagious — **pegajoso, -sa** *adj* **1** : sticky **2** *Lat* : catchy — **pegamento** *nm* : glue

peinar *vt* : comb — **peinarse** *vr* : comb one's hair — **peinado** *nm* : hairstyle, hairdo — **peine** *nm* : comb — **peineta** *nf* : ornamental comb

pelado, -da *adj* **1** : shorn, hairless **2** : peeled (of fruit, etc.) **3** *fam* : bare **4** *fam* : broke, penniless

pelaje *nm* : coat (of an animal), fur

pelar *vt* **1** : cut the hair of (a person) **2** MONDAR : peel (fruit) **3** : pluck (a chicken, etc.), skin (an animal) — **pelarse** *vr* **1** : peel **2** *fam* : get a haircut

peldaño *nm* **1** : step (of stairs) **2** : rung (of a ladder)

pelear *vi* **1** : fight **2** DISCUTIR : quarrel — **pelearse** *vr* : have a fight — **pelea** *nf* **1** : fight **2** DISCUSIÓN : quarrel

peletería *nf* : fur shop

peliagudo, -da *adj* : tricky, difficult

pelícano *nm* : pelican

película *nf* : movie, film

peligro *nm* **1** : danger **2** RIESGO : risk — **peligroso, -sa** *adj* : dangerous

pelirrojo, -ja *adj* : red-haired — **~** *n* : redhead

pellejo *nm* : skin, hide

pellizcar {72} *vt* : pinch — **pellizco** *nm* : pinch

pelo *nm* **1** : hair **2** : coat, fur (of an animal) **3** : pile, nap (of fabric) **4 con ~s y señales** : in great detail **5 no tener ~ en la lengua** *fam* : not to mince words **6 tomar el ~ a algn** *fam* : pull someone's leg — **pelón, -lona** *adj fam, mpl* **-lones** : bald

pelota *nf* : ball

pelotón *nm, pl* **-tones** : squad, detachment

peltre *nm* : pewter

peluca *nf* : wig

peluche *nm* **1** : plush **2 oso de ~** : teddy bear

peludo, -da *adj* : hairy, furry

peluquería *nf* : hairdresser's, barber shop — **peluquero, -ra** *n* : barber, hairdresser

pelusa *nf* : fuzz, lint

pelvis *nfs & pl* : pelvis

pena *nf* **1** : penalty **2** TRISTEZA : sorrow **3** DOLOR : suffering, pain **4** *Lat* : embarrassment **5 a duras ~s** : with great difficulty **6 ¡qué ~!** : what a shame! **7 valer la ~** : be worthwhile

penacho *nm* **1** : crest, tuft **2** : plume (ornament)

penal *adj* : penal — **~** *nm* : prison, penitentiary — **penalidad** *nf* **1** : hardship **2** : penalty (in law) — **penalizar** {21} *vt* : penalize

penalty *nm* : penalty (in sports)

penar *vt* : punish — *vi* : suffer

pendenciero, -ra *adj* : quarrelsome

pender *vi* : hang — **pendiente** *adj* **1** : pending **2 estar ~ de** : be watching out for — **~** *nf* : slope — **~** *nm Spain* : earring

pendón *nm, pl* **-dones** : banner

péndulo *nm* : pendulum

pene *nm* : penis

penetrar *vi* **1** : penetrate **2 ~ en** : go into — *vt* **1** : penetrate **2** : pierce (one's heart, etc.) **3** ENTENDER : fathom, grasp — **penetración** *nf, pl* **-ciones 1** : penetration **2** PERSPICACIA : insight — **penetrante** *adj* **1** : penetrating **2** : sharp (of odors, etc.), piercing (of sounds) **3** : deep (of a wound, etc.)

penicilina *nf* : penicillin

península *nf* : peninsula — **peninsular** *adj* : peninsular

penitencia *nf* **1** : penitence **2** CASTIGO : penance — **penitenciaría** *nf* : penitentiary — **penitente** *adj & nmf* : penitent

penoso, -sa *adj* **1** : painful, distressing **2** TRABAJOSO : difficult **3** *Lat* : shy

pensar {55} *vi* **1** : think **2 ~ en** : think about — *vt* **1** : think **2** CONSIDERAR : think about **3 ~ hacer algo** : intend to do sth — **pensador, -dora** *n* : thinker — **pensamiento** *nm* **1** : thought **2** : pansy (flower) — **pensativo, -va** *adj* : pensive, thoughtful

pensión *nf, pl* **-siones 1** : boarding house **2** : (retirement) pension **3 ~ alimenticia** : alimony — **pensionista** *nmf* **1** : lodger **2** JUBILADO : retiree

pentágono *nm* : pentagon

pentagrama *nm* : staff (in music)

penúltimo, -ma *adj* : next to last, penultimate

penumbra *nf* : half-light

penuria *nf* : dearth, shortage

peña *nf* : rock, crag — **peñasco** *nm* : crag, large rock — **peñón** *nm, pl* **-ñones** : craggy rock

peón *nm, pl* **peones 1** : laborer, peon **2** : pawn (in chess)

peonía *nf* : peony

peor *adv* **1** (*comparative of* **mal**) : worse **2** (*superlative of* **mal**) : worst — **~** *adj* **1** (*comparative of* **malo**) : worse **2** (*superlative of* **malo**) : worst

pepino *nm* : cucumber — **pepinillo** *nm* : pickle, gherkin

pepita *nf* **1** : seed, pip **2** : nugget (of gold, etc.)

pequeño, -ña *adj* : small, little — **pequeñez** *nf, pl* **-ñeces 1** : smallness **2** NIMIEDAD : trifle

pera *nf* : pear — **peral** *nm* : pear tree

percance *nm* : mishap, setback

percatarse *vr* **~ de** : notice

percepción *nf, pl* **-ciones** : perception — **perceptible** *adj* : perceptible

percha *nf* **1** : perch (for birds) **2** : (coat) hanger **3** : coatrack (on a wall)

percibir *vt* **1** : perceive **2** : receive (a salary, etc.)

percusión *nf, pl* **-siones** : percussion

perder {56} *vt* **1** : lose **2** : miss (an opportunity, etc.) **3** DESPERDICIAR : waste (time) — *vi* : lose — **perderse** *vr* **1** : get lost **2** DESAPARECER : disappear **3** DESPERDICIARSE : be wasted — **perdedor, -dora** *n* : loser — **pérdida** *nf* **1** : loss **2** ESCAPE : leak **3 ~ de tiempo** : waste of time — **perdido, -da** *adj* **1** : lost **2 un caso perdido** *fam* : a hopeless case

perdigón *nm, pl* **-gones** : shot, pellet

perdiz *nf, pl* **-dices** : partridge

perdón *nm, pl* **-dones** : forgiveness, pardon — **perdón** *interj* : sorry! — **perdonar** *vt* **1** DISCULPAR : forgive **2** : pardon (in law)

perdurar *vi* : last, endure — **perdurable** *adj* : lasting

perecer {53} *vi* : perish, die — **perecedero, -ra** *adj* : perishable

peregrinación *nf, pl* **-ciones** *or* **peregrinaje** *nm* : pilgrimage — **peregrino, -na** *adj* **1** : migratory **2** RARO : unusual, odd — **~** *n* : pilgrim

perejil *nm* : parsley

perenne *adj & nm* : perennial

pereza *nf* : laziness — **perezoso, -sa** *adj* : lazy

perfección *nf, pl* **-ciones** : perfection — **perfeccionar** *vt* **1** : perfect **2** MEJORAR : improve — **perfeccionista** *nmf* : perfectionist — **perfecto, -ta** *adj* : perfect

perfidia *nf* : treachery — **pérfido, -da** *adj* : treacherous

perfil *nm* **1** : profile **2** CONTORNO : outline **3 ~es** *nmpl* RASGOS : features — **perfilar** *vt* : outline — **perfilarse** *vr* **1** : be outlined **2** CONCRETARSE : take shape

perforar *vt* **1** : perforate **2** : drill, bore (a hole) — **perforación** *nf, pl* **-ciones** : perforation — **perforadora** *nf* : (paper) punch

perfume *nm* : perfume, scent — **perfumar** *vt* : perfume — **perfumarse** *vr* : put perfume on

pergamino *nm* : parchment

pericia *nf* : skill

periferia *nf* : periphery, outskirts (of a city, etc.) — **periférico, -ca** *adj* : peripheral

perilla *nf* **1** : goatee **2** *Lat* : knob **3 venir de ~s** *fam* : come in handy

perímetro *nm* : perimeter

periódico, -ca *adj* : periodic — **periódico** *nm* : newspaper — **periodismo** *nm* : journalism — **periodista** *nmf* : journalist

período *or* **periodo** *nm* : period

periquito *nm* : parakeet

periscopio *nm* : periscope

perito, -ta *adj & n* : expert

perjudicar {72} *vt* : harm, damage — **perjudicial** *adj* : harmful — **perjuicio** *nm* **1** : harm, damage **2 en ~ de** : to the detriment of

perjurar *vi* : perjure oneself — **perjurio** *nm* : perjury

perla *nf* **1** : pearl **2 de ~s** *fam* : great, just fine

permanecer {53} *vi* : remain — **permanencia** *nf* **1** : permanence **2** : stay, staying (in a place) — **permanente** *adj* : permanent — **~** *nf* : permanent (wave)

permeable *adj* : permeable

permitir *vt* **1** : permit, allow **2 ¿me permite?** : may I? — **permitirse** *vr* : allow oneself — **permisible** *adj* : permissible, allowable — **permisivo, -va** *adj* : permissive — **permiso** *nm* **1** : permission **2** : permit, license (document) **3** : leave (in the military) **4 con ~** : excuse me

permuta *nf* : exchange

pernicioso, -sa *adj* : pernicious, destructive

pero *conj* : but — **~** *nm* **1** : fault **2** REPARO : objection

perorar *vi* : make a speech — **perorata** *nf* : (long-winded) speech

perpendicular *adj & nf* : perpendicular

perpetrar *vt* : perpetrate

perpetuar {3} *vt* : perpetuate — **perpetuo, -tua** *adj* : perpetual

perplejo, -ja *adj* : perplexed — **perplejidad** *nf* : perplexity

perro, -rra *n* **1** : dog, bitch *f* **2 perro caliente** : hot dog — **perrera** *nf* : kennel

perseguir {75} *vt* **1** : pursue, chase **2** ACOSAR : persecute — **persecución** *nf, pl* **-ciones 1** : pursuit, chase **2** ACOSO : persecution

perseverar *vi* : persevere — **perseverancia** *nf* : perseverance

persiana *nf* : (venetian) blind

persistir *vi* : persist — **persistencia** *nf* : persistence — **persistente** *adj* : persistent

persona *nf* : person — **personaje** *nm* **1** : character (in literature, etc.) **2** : important person, celebrity — **personal** *adj* : personal — **~** *nm* : personnel, staff — **personalidad** *nf* : personality — **personificar** {72} *vi* : personify

perspectiva *nf* **1** : perspective **2** VISTA : view **3** POSIBILIDAD : prospect, outlook

perspicacia *nf* : shrewdness, insight — **perspicaz** *adj, pl* **-caces** : shrewd, discerning

persuadir *vt* : persuade — **persuadirse** *vr* : become convinced — **persuasión** *nf, pl* **-siones** : persuasion — **persuasivo, -va** *adj* : persuasive

pertenecer {53} *vi* **~ a** : belong to — **perteneciente** *adj* **~ a** : belonging to — **pertenencia** *nf* **1** : ownership **2 ~s** *nfpl* : belongings

pertinaz *adj, pl* **-naces 1** OBSTINADO : obstinate **2** PERSISTENTE : persistent

pertinente *adj* : pertinent, relevant — **pertinencia** *nf* : relevance

perturbar *vt* : disturb — **perturbación** *nf, pl* **-ciones** : disturbance

peruano, -na *adj* : Peruvian

pervertir {76} *vt* : pervert — **perversión** *nf, pl* **-siones** : perversion — **perverso, -sa** *adj* : perverse — **pervertido, -da** *adj* : perverted, depraved — **~** *n* : pervert

pesa *nf* **1** : weight **2 ~s** : weights (in sports) — **pesadez** *nf, pl* **-deces 1** : heaviness **2** *fam* : tediousness, drag

pesadilla *nf* : nightmare

pesado, -da *adj* **1** : heavy **2** LENTO : sluggish **3** MOLESTO : annoying **4** ABURRIDO : tedious **5** DURO : tough, difficult — **~** *n fam* : bore, pest — **pesadumbre** *nf* : grief, sorrow

pésame *nm* : condolences *pl*

pesar *vt* : weigh — *vi* **1** : weigh, be heavy **2** INFLUIR : carry weight **3 pese a** : despite — **~** *nm* **1** : sorrow, grief **2** REMORDIMIENTO : remorse **3 a ~ de** : in spite of

pescado *nm* : fish — **pesca** *nf* **1** : fishing **2** PECES : fish *pl*, catch **3 ir de ~** : go fishing — **pescadería** *nf* : fish market — **pescador, -dora** *n, mpl* **-dores** : fisherman — **pescar** {72} *vt* **1** : fish for **2** *fam* : catch (a cold, etc.) **3** *fam* : catch hold of, nab — *vi* : fish

pescuezo *nm* : neck (of an animal)

pese a → **pesar**

pesebre *nm* : manger

pesero *nm Lat* : minibus

peseta *nf* : peseta

pesimismo *nm* : pessimism — **pesimista** *adj* : pessimistic — ~ *nmf* : pessimist
pésimo, -ma *adj* : awful
peso *nm* **1** : weight **2** CARGA : burden **3** : peso (currency) **4** ~ **pesado** : heavyweight
pesquero, -ra *adj* : fishing
pesquisa *nf* : inquiry
pestaña *nf* : eyelash — **pestañear** *vi* : blink — **pestañeo** *nm* : blink
peste *nm* **1** : plague **2** *fam* : stench, stink **3** *Lat fam* : cold, bug — **pesticida** *nm* : pesticide — **pestilencia** *nf* **1** : stench **2** PLAGA : pestilence
pestillo *nm* : bolt, latch
petaca *nf Lat* : suitcase
pétalo *nm* : petal
petardo *nm* : firecracker
petición *nf, pl* **-ciones** : petition, request
petirrojo *nm* : robin
petrificar {72} *vt* : petrify
petróleo *nm* : oil, petroleum — **petrolero, -ra** *adj* : oil — **petrolero** *nm* : oil tanker
petulante *adj* : insolent, arrogant
peyorativo, -va *adj* : pejorative
pez *nm, pl* **peces 1** : fish **2** ~ **de colores** : goldfish **3** ~ **espada** : swordfish **4** ~ **gordo** *fam* : big shot
pezón *nm, pl* **-zones** : nipple
pezuña *nf* : hoof
piadoso, -sa *adj* **1** : compassionate **2** DEVOTO : pious, devout
piano *nm* : piano — **pianista** *nmf* : pianist, piano player
piar {85} *vi* : chirp, tweet
pibe, -ba *n Lat fam* : kid, child
pica *nf* **1** : pike, lance **2** : spade (in playing cards)
picado, -da *adj* **1** : perforated **2** : minced, chopped (of meat, etc.) **3** : decayed (of teeth) **4** : choppy (of the sea) **5** *fam* : annoyed — **picada** *nf* **1** : bite, sting **2** *Lat* : sharp descent — **picadillo** *nm* : minced meat — **picadura** *nf* **1** : sting, bite **2** : (moth) hole
picante *adj* : hot, spicy
picaporte *nm* **1** : door handle **2** ALDABA : door knocker **3** PESTILLO : latch
picar {72} *vt* **1** : sting, bite **2** : peck at, nibble on (food) **3** PERFORAR : prick, puncture **4** TRITURAR : chop, mince — *vi* **1** : bite, take the bait **2** ESCOCER : sting, itch **3** COMER : nibble **4** : be spicy (of food) — **picarse** *vr* **1** : get a cavity **2** ENFADARSE : take offense
picardía *nf* **1** : craftiness **2** TRAVESURA : prank — **picaresco, -ca** *adj* **1** : picaresque **2** TRAVIESO : roguish — **pícaro, -ra** *adj* **1** : mischievous **2** MALICIOSO : villainous — ~ *n* : rascal, scoundrel
picazón *nf, pl* **-zones** : itch
pichón, -chona *n, mpl* **-chones** : (young) pigeon
picnic *nm, pl* **-nics** : picnic
pico *nm* **1** : beak **2** CIMA : peak **3** PUNTA : (sharp) point **4** : pick, pickax (tool) **5 las siete y** ~ : a little after seven — **picotazo** *nm* : peck — **picotear** *vt* : peck — *vi fam* : nibble, pick — **picudo, -da** *adj* : pointy
pie *nm* **1** : foot (in anatomy) **2** : base, bottom, stem **3 al** ~ **de la letra** : word for word **4 dar** ~ **a** : give rise to **5 de** ~ : standing (up) **6 de** ~**s a cabeza** : from top to bottom
piedad *nf* **1** : pity, mercy **2** DEVOCIÓN : piety
piedra *nf* **1** : stone **2** : flint (of a lighter) **3** GRANIZO : hailstone **4** ~ **angular** : cornerstone **5** → **pómez**
piel *nf* **1** : skin **2** CUERO : leather **3** PELO : fur, pelt
pienso *nm* : feed, fodder
pierna *nf* : leg
pieza *nf* **1** : piece, part **2** *or* ~ **de teatro** : play **3** HABITACIÓN : room
pigmento *nm* : pigment — **pigmentación** *nf, pl* **-ciones** : pigmentation
pigmeo, -mea *adj* : pygmy
pijama *nm* : pajamas *pl*
pila *nf* **1** : battery **2** MONTÓN : pile **3** FREGADERO : sink **4** : basin (of a fountain, etc.)
pilar *nm* : pillar
píldora *nf* : pill
pillar *vt* **1** : catch **2** : get (a joke, etc.) — **pillaje** *nm* : pillage — **pillo, -lla** *adj* : crafty — ~ *n* : rascal, scoundrel
piloto *nmf* : pilot — **pilotar** *vt* : pilot
pimienta *nf* : pepper (condiment) — **pimiento** *nm* : pepper (fruit) — **pimentero** *nm* : pepper shaker — **pimentón** *nm, pl* **-tones 1** : paprika **2** : cayenne pepper
pináculo *nm* : pinnacle
pincel *nm* : paintbrush
pinchar *vt* **1** : pierce, prick **2** : puncture (a tire, etc.) **3** INCITAR : goad — **pinchazo** *nm* **1** : prick **2** : puncture (of a tire, etc.)
pingüino *nm* : penguin
pino *nm* : pine (tree)
pintar *v* : paint — **pintarse** *vr* : put on makeup — **pinta** *nf* **1** : spot **2** : pint (measure) **3** *fam* : appearance — **pintada** *nf* : graffiti — **pinto, -ta** *adj* : speckled, spotted — **pintor, -tora** *n, mpl* **-tores** : painter — **pintoresco, -ca** *adj* : picturesque, quaint — **pintura** *nf* **1** : paint **2** CUADRO : painting
pinza *nf* **1** : clothespin **2** : claw, pincer (of a crab, etc.) **3** ~**s** *nfpl* : tweezers
pinzón *nm, pl* **-zones** : finch
piña *nf* **1** : pine cone **2** ANANÁS : pineapple
piñata *nf* : piñata
piñón *nm, pl* **-ñones** : pine nut
pío[1]**, pía** *adj* **1** : pious **2** : piebald (of a horse)
pío[2] *nm* : peep, chirp
piojo *nm* : louse
pionero, -ra *n* : pioneer
pipa *nf* **1** : pipe (for smoking) **2** *Spain* : seed, pip
pique *nm* **1** : grudge **2** RIVALIDAD : rivalry **3 irse a** ~ : sink, founder
piqueta *nf* : pickax
piquete *nm* : picket (line) — **piquetear** *v* : picket
piragua *nf* : canoe
pirámide *nf* : pyramid
piraña *nf* : piranha
pirata *adj* : bootleg, pirated — ~ *nmf* : pirate — **piratear** *vt* **1** : bootleg, pirate **2** : hack into (a computer)
piropo *nm* : (flirtatious) compliment
pirueta *nf* : pirouette
pirulí *nm* : (cone-shaped) lollipop
pisada *nf* **1** : footstep **2** HUELLA : footprint
pisapapeles *nms & pl* : paperweight
pisar *vt* **1** : step on **2** HUMILLAR : walk all over, abuse — *vi* : step, tread
piscina *nf* **1** : swimming pool **2** : (fish) pond
piso *nm* **1** : floor, story **2** *Lat* : floor (of a room) **3** *Spain* : apartment
pisotear *vt* : trample (on)
pista *nf* **1** : trail, track **2** INDICIO : clue **3** ~ **de aterrizaje** : runway, airstrip **4** ~ **de baile** : dance floor **5** ~ **de hielo** : ice-skating rink
pistacho *nm* : pistachio
pistola *nf* **1** : pistol, gun **2** PULVERIZADOR : spray gun — **pistolera** *nf* : holster — **pistolero** *nm* : gunman
pistón *nm, pl* **-tones** : piston
pito *nm* **1** SILBATO : whistle **2** CLAXON : horn — **pitar** *vi* **1** : blow a whistle **2** : beep, honk (of a horn) — *vt* : whistle at — **pitido** *nm* **1** : whistle, whistling **2** : beep (of a horn) — **pitillo** *nm fam* : cigarette
pitón *nm, pl* **-tones** *nm* : python
pitorro *nm* : spout
pivote *nm* : pivot
piyama *nmf Lat* : pajamas *pl*
pizarra *nf* **1** : slate **2** ENCERADO : blackboard — **pizarrón** *nm, pl* **-rrones** *Lat* : blackboard
pizca *nf* **1** : pinch (of salt) **2** ÁPICE : speck, tiny bit **3** *Lat* : harvest
pizza ['pitsa, 'pisa] *nf* : pizza — **pizzería** *nf* : pizzeria
placa *nf* **1** : sheet, plate **2** INSCRIPCIÓN : plaque **3** : (police) badge
placenta *nf* : placenta
placer {57} *vt* : please — ~ *nm* : pleasure — **placentero, -ra** *adj* : pleasant, agreeable
plácido, -da *adj* : placid, calm
plaga *nf* **1** : plague **2** CALAMIDAD : disaster — **plagar** {52} *vt* : plague, infest
plagiar *vt* : plagiarize — **plagio** *nm* : plagiarism
plan *nm* **1** : plan **2 en** ~ **de** : as **3 no te pongas en ese** ~ *fam* : don't be that way
plana *nf* **1** : page **2 en primera** ~ : on the front page
plancha *nf* **1** : iron (for ironing) **2** : grill (for cooking) **3** LÁMINA : sheet, plate — **planchar** *v* : iron — **planchado** *nm* : ironing
planear *vt* : plan — *vi* : glide — **planeador** *nm* : glider
planeta *nm* : planet
planicie *nf* : plain
planificar {72} *vt* : plan — **planificación** *nf, pl* **-ciones** : planning
planilla *nf Lat* : list, roster
plano, -na *adj* : flat — **plano** *nm* **1** : map, plan **2** : plane (surface) **3** NIVEL : level **4 de** ~ : flatly, outright **5 primer** ~ : foreground, close-up (in photography)
planta *nf* **1** : plant **2** PISO : floor, story **3** : sole (of the foot) — **plantación** *nf, pl* **-ciones 1** : plantation **2** : (action of) planting — **plantar** *vt* **1** : plant **2** *fam* : deal, land — **plantarse** *vr* : stand firm
plantear *vt* **1** : expound, set forth **2** : raise (a question) **3** CAUSAR : create, pose (a problem) — **plantearse** *vr* : think about, consider
plantel *nm* **1** : staff, team **2** *Lat* : educational institution
plantilla *nf* **1** : insole **2** PATRÓN : pattern, template **3** : staff (of a business, etc.)
plasma *nm* : plasma
plástico, -ca *adj* : plastic — **plástico** *nm* : plastic
plata *nf* **1** : silver **2** *Lat fam* : money **3** ~ **de ley** : sterling silver
plataforma *nf* **1** : platform **2** ~ **petrolífera** : oil rig **3** ~ **de lanzamiento** : launching pad
plátano *nm* **1** : banana **2** : plantain
platea *nf* : orchestra, pit (in a theater)
plateado, -da *adj* **1** : silver, silvery (color) **2** : silver-plated
platicar {72} *vi* : talk, chat — **plática** *nf* : chat, conversation
platija *nf* : flatfish, flounder
platillo *nm* **1** : saucer **2** CÍMBALO : cymbal **3** *Lat* : dish, course
platino *nm* : platinum
plato *nm* **1** : plate, dish **2** : course (of a meal) **3** ~ **principal** : entrée
platónico, -ca *adj* : platonic
playa *nf* **1** : beach, seashore **2** ~ **de estacionamiento** *Lat* : parking lot
plaza *nf* **1** : square, plaza **2** : seat (in transportation) **3** PUESTO : post, position **4** MERCADO : market, marketplace **5** ~ **de toros** : bullring
plazo *nm* **1** : period, term **2** PAGO : installment **3 a largo** ~ : long-term
plazoleta *or* **plazuela** *nf* : small square
pleamar *nf* : high tide
plebe *nf* : common people — **plebeyo, -ya** *adj & nm* : plebeian
plegar {49} *vt* : fold, bend — **plegarse** *vr* **1** : give in, yield **2** : jackknife (of a truck) — **plegable** *or* **plegadizo, -za** *adj* : folding, collapsible
plegaria *nf* : prayer
pleito *nm* **1** : lawsuit **2** *Lat* : dispute, fight
plenilunio *nm* : full moon
pleno, -na *adj* **1** : full, complete **2 en plena forma** : in top form **3 en pleno día** : in broad daylight — **plenitud** *nf* : fullness, abundance
pleuresía *nf* : pleurisy
pliego *nm* : sheet (of paper) — **pliegue** *nm* **1** : crease, fold **2** : pleat (in fabric)
plisar *vt* : pleat
plomería *nf Lat* : plumbing — **plomero, -ra** *n Lat* : plumber
plomo *nm* **1** : lead **2** FUSIBLE : fuse
pluma *nf* **1** : feather **2** : (fountain) pen — **plumaje** *nm* : plumage — **plumero** *nm* : feather duster — **plumilla** *nf* : nib — **plumón** *nm, pl* **-mones** : down
plural *adj & nm* : plural — **pluralidad** *nf* : plurality
pluriempleo *nm* **hacer** ~ : have more than one job
plus *nm* : bonus
plusvalía *nf* : appreciation, capital gain
plutocracia *nf* : plutocracy
Plutón *nm* : Pluto
plutonio *nm* : plutonium
pluvial *adj* : rain
poblar {19} *vt* **1** : settle, colonize **2** HABITAR : inhabit — **poblarse** *vr* : become crowded — **población** *nf, pl* **-ciones 1** : city, town, village **2** HABITANTES : population — **poblado, -da** *adj* **1** : populated **2** : thick, bushy (of a beard, eyebrows, etc.) — **poblado** *nm* : village
pobre *adj* **1** : poor **2 ¡**~ **de mí!** : poor me! — ~ *nmf* **1** : poor person **2 los** ~**s** : the poor **3 ¡pobre!** : poor thing! — **pobreza** *nf* : poverty
pocilga *nf* : pigsty
poción *nf, pl* **-ciones** *or* **pócima** *nf* : potion
poco, -ca *adj* **1** : little, not much, (a) few **2 pocas veces** : rarely — ~ *pron* **1** : little, few **2 hace poco** : not long ago **3 poco a poco** : bit by bit, gradually **4 por poco** : nearly, just about **5 un poco** : a little, a bit — **poco** *adv* : little, not much
podar *vt* : prune
poder {58} *v aux* **1** : be able to, can **2** (*expressing possibility*) : might, may **3** (*expressing permission*) : can, may **4 ¿cómo puede ser?** : how can it be? **5 ¿puedo pasar?** : may I come in? — *vi* **1** : be possible **2** ~ **con** : cope with, manage **3 no puedo más** : I've had enough — ~ *nm* **1** : power **2** POSESIÓN : possession — **poderío** *nm* : power — **poderoso, -sa** *adj* : powerful
podólogo, -ga *n* : chiropodist
podrido, -da *adj* : rotten
poema *nm* : poem — **poesía** *nf* **1** : poetry **2** POEMA : poem — **poeta** *nmf* : poet — **poético, -ca** *adj* : poetic
póker *nm* → **póquer**
polaco, -ca *adj* : Polish
polar *adj* : polar — **polarizar** {21} *vt* : polarize
polea *nf* : pulley
polémica *nf* : controversy — **polémico, -ca** *adj* : controversial — **polemizar** *vt* : argue
polen *nm, pl* **pólenes** : pollen
policía *nf* : police — ~ *nmf* : police officer, policeman *m*, policewoman *f* — **policíaco, -ca** *adj* **1** : police **2 novela policíaca** : detective story
poliéster *nm* : polyester
poligamia *nf* : polygamy — **polígamo, -ma** *n* : polygamist
polígono *nm* : polygon
polilla *nf* : moth
polio *or* **poliomielitis** *nf* : polio, poliomyelitis
politécnico, -ca *adj* : polytechnic
política *nf* **1** : politics **2** POSTURA : policy — **político, -ca** *adj* **1** : political **2 hermano político** : brother-in-law — ~ *n* : politician
póliza *nf or* ~ **de seguros** : insurance policy
polizón *nm, pl* **-zones** : stowaway
pollo, -lla *n* **1** : chicken, chick **2** : chicken (for cooking) — **pollera** *nf Lat* : skirt — **pollería** *nf* : poultry shop — **pollito, -ta** *n* : chick
polo *nm* **1** : pole **2** : polo (sport) **3** ~ **norte** : North Pole
poltrona *nf* : easy chair
polución *nf, pl* **-ciones** : pollution
polvo *nm* **1** : powder **2** SUCIEDAD : dust **3** ~**s** *nmpl* : face powder **4 hacer** ~ *fam* : crush, shatter — **polvareda** *nf* : cloud of dust — **polvera** *nf* : compact (for powder) — **pólvora** *nf* : gunpowder — **polvoriento, -ta** *adj* : dusty
pomada *nf* : ointment
pomelo *nm* : grapefruit
pómez *nm or* **piedra** ~ *nf* : pumice
pomo *nm* : knob, doorknob
pompa *nf* **1** : (soap) bubble **2** ESPLENDOR : pomp **3** ~**s fúnebres** : funeral — **pomposo, -sa** *adj* **1** : pompous **2** ESPLÉNDIDO : splendid
pómulo *nm* : cheekbone
ponchar *vt Lat* : puncture — **ponchadura** *nf Lat* : puncture
ponche *nm* : punch (drink)
poncho *nm* : poncho
ponderar *vt* **1** : consider **2** ALABAR : speak highly of
poner {60} *vt* **1** : put **2** AGREGAR : add **3** CONTRIBUIR : contribute **4** SUPONER : suppose **5** DISPONER : arrange, set out **6** : give (a name), call **7** ENCENDER : turn on **8** ESTABLECER : set up, establish **9** : lay (eggs) — *vi* : lay eggs — **ponerse** *vr* **1** : move (into a position) **2** : put on (clothing, etc.) **3** : set (of the sun) **4** ~ **furioso** : become angry
poniente *nm* **1** OCCIDENTE : west **2** : west wind
pontífice *nm* : pontiff
pontón *nm, pl* **-tones** : pontoon
ponzoña *nf* : poison, venom
popa *nf* **1** : stern **2 a** ~ : astern
popelín *nm, pl* **-lines** : poplin
popote *nm Lat* : (drinking) straw
populacho *nm* : rabble, masses *pl*
popular *adj* **1** : popular **2** : colloquial (of language) — **popularidad** *nf* : popularity — **popularizar** {21} *vt* : popularize — **populoso, -sa** *adj* : populous
póquer *nm* : poker (card game)
por *prep* **1** : for **2** (*indicating an approximate time*) : around, during **3** (*indicating an approximate place*) : around, about **4** A TRAVÉS DE : through, along **5** A CAUSA DE : because of **6** (*indicating rate or ratio*) : per **7** *or* ~ **medio de** : by means of **8** : times (in mathematics) **9** SEGÚN : as for, according to **10 estar** ~ : be about to **11** ~ **ciento** : percent **12** ~ **favor** : please **13** ~ **lo tanto** : therefore **14 ¿por qué?** : why?
porcelana *nf* : porcelain, china
porcentaje *nm* : percentage
porción *nf, pl* **-ciones** : portion, piece
pordiosero, -ra *n* : beggar
porfiar {85} *vi* : insist — **porfiado, -da** *adj* : obstinate, persistent
pormenor *nm* : detail
pornografía *nf* : pornography — **pornográfico, -ca** *adj* : pornographic
poro *nm* : pore — **poroso, -sa** *adj* : porous
poroto *nm Lat* : bean
porque *conj* **1** : because **2** *or* **por que** : in order that — **porqué** *nm* : reason
porquería *nf* **1** SUCIEDAD : filth **2** : shoddy thing, junk
porra *nf* : nightstick, club — **porrazo** *nm* : blow, whack
portaaviones *nms & pl* : aircraft carrier
portada *nf* **1** : facade **2** : title page (of a book), cover (of a magazine)
portador, -dora *n* : bearer
portaequipajes *nms & pl* : luggage rack
portafolio *or* **portafolios** *nm, pl* **-lios 1** : portfolio **2** MALETÍN : briefcase
portal *nm* **1** : doorway **2** VESTÍBULO : hall, vestibule
portamonedas *nms & pl* : purse
portar *vt* : carry, bear — **portarse** *vr* : behave
portátil *adj* : portable
portaviones *nm* → **portaaviones**
portavoz *nmf, pl* **-voces** : spokesperson, spokesman *m*, spokeswoman *f*
portazo *nm* **dar un** ~ : slam the door
porte *nm* **1** : transport, freight **2** ASPECTO : bearing, appearance **3** ~ **pagado** : postage paid
portento *nm* : marvel, wonder — **portentoso, -sa** *adj* : marvelous
porteño, -ña *adj* : of or from Buenos Aires
portería *nf* **1** : superintendent's office **2** : goal, goalposts *pl* (in sports) — **portero, -ra** *n* **1** : goalkeeper, goalie **2** CONSERJE : janitor, superintendent
portezuela *nf* : door (of an automobile)
pórtico *nm* : portico
portilla *nf* : porthole
portugués, -guesa *adj, mpl* **-gueses** : Portuguese — **portugués** *nm* : Portuguese (language)
porvenir *nm* : future
pos: en ~ **de** *adv phr* : in pursuit of
posada *nf* : inn
posaderas *nfpl fam* : backside, bottom

posar *vi* : pose — *vt* : place, lay — **posarse** *vr* : settle, rest

posavasos *nms & pl* : coaster

posdata *nf* : postscript

pose *nf* : pose

poseer {20} *vt* : possess, own — **poseedor, -dora** *n* : possessor, owner — **poseído, -da** *adj* : possessed — **posesión** *nf, pl* **-siones** : possession — **posesionarse** *vr* ~ **de** : take possession of, take over — **posesivo, -va** *adj* : possessive

posguerra *nf* : postwar period

posibilidad *nf* : possibility — **posibilitar** *vt* : make possible — **posible** *adj* **1** : possible **2 de ser** ~ : if possible

posición *nf, pl* **-ciones** : position — **posicionar** *vt* : position — **posicionarse** *vr* : take a stand

positivo, -va *adj* : positive

poso *nm* : sediment, (coffee) grounds

posponer {60} *vt* **1** : postpone **2** RELEGAR : put behind, subordinate

postal *adj* : postal — ~ *nf* : postcard

postdata → **posdata**

poste *nm* : post, pole

póster *nm, pl* **-ters** : poster

postergar {52} *vt* **1** : pass over **2** APLAZAR : postpone

posteridad *nf* : posterity — **posterior** *adj* **1** : later, subsequent **2** TRASERO : back, rear — **posteriormente** *adv* : subsequently, later

postigo *nm* **1** : small door **2** CONTRAVENTANA : shutter

postizo, -za *adj* : artificial, false

postrarse *vr* : prostrate oneself — **postrado, -da** *adj* : prostrate

postre *nm* : dessert

postular *vt* **1** : advance, propose **2** *Lat* : nominate — **postulado** *nm* : postulate

póstumo, -ma *adj* : posthumous

postura *nf* : position, stance

potable *adj* : drinkable, potable

potaje *nm* : thick vegetable soup

potasio *nm* : potassium

pote *nm* : jar

potencia *nf* : power — **potencial** *adj & nm* : potential — **potente** *adj* : powerful

potro, -tra *n* : colt *m*, filly *f* — **potro** *nm* : horse (in gymnastics)

pozo *nm* **1** : well **2** : shaft (in a mine)

práctica *nf* **1** : practice **2 en la** ~ : in practice — **practicable** *adj* : practicable, feasible — **practicante** *adj* : practicing — ~ *nmf* : practitioner — **practicar** {72} *vt* **1** : practice **2** REALIZAR : perform, carry out — *vi* : practice — **práctico, -ca** *adj* : practical

pradera *nf* : grassland, prairie — **prado** *nm* : meadow

pragmático, -ca *adj* : pragmatic

preámbulo *nm* : preamble

precario, -ria *adj* : precarious

precaución *nf, pl* **-ciones 1** : precaution **2** PRUDENCIA : caution, care **3 con** ~ : cautiously

precaver *vt* : guard against — **precavido, -da** *adj* : prudent, cautious

preceder *v* : precede — **precedencia** *nf* : precedence, priority — **precedente** *adj* : preceding, previous — ~ *nm* : precedent

precepto *nm* : precept

preciado, -da *adj* : prized, valuable — **preciarse** *vr* ~ **de** : pride oneself on, boast about

precinto *nm* : seal

precio *nm* : price, cost — **preciosidad** *nf* **1** VALOR : value **2** : beautiful thing — **precioso, -sa** *adj* **1** HERMOSO : beautiful **2** VALIOSO : precious

precipicio *nm* : precipice

precipitar *vt* **1** : hasten, speed up **2** ARROJAR : hurl — **precipitarse** *vr* **1** APRESURARSE : rush **2** : act rashly **3** ARROJARSE : throw oneself — **precipitación** *nf, pl* **-ciones 1** : precipitation **2** PRISA : haste — **precipitadamente** *adv* : in a rush, hastily — **precipitado, -da** *adj* : hasty

preciso, -sa *adj* **1** : precise **2** NECESARIO : necessary — **precisamente** *adv* : precisely, exactly — **precisar** *vt* **1** : specify, determine **2** NECESITAR : require — **precisión** *nf, pl* **-siones 1** : precision **2** NECESIDAD : necessity

preconcebido *adj* : preconceived

precoz *adj, pl* **-coces 1** : early **2** : precocious (of children)

precursor, -sora *n* : forerunner

predecesor, -sora *n* : predecessor

predecir {11} *vt* : foretell, predict

predestinado, -da *adj* : predestined

predeterminar *vt* : predetermine

prédica *nf* : sermon

predicado *nm* : predicate

predicar {72} *v* : preach — **predicador, -dora** *n* : preacher

predicción *nf, pl* **-ciones 1** : prediction **2** PRONÓSTICO : forecast

predilección *nf, pl* **-ciones** : preference — **predilecto, -ta** *adj* : favorite

predisponer {60} *vt* : predispose — **predisposición** *nf, pl* **-ciones** : predisposition

predominar *vi* : predominate — **predominante** *adj* : predominant, prevailing — **predominio** *nm* : predominance

preeminente *adj* : preeminent

prefabricado, -da *adj* : prefabricated

prefacio *nm* : preface

preferir {76} *vt* : prefer — **preferencia** *nf* **1** : preference **2 de** ~ : preferably — **preferente** *adj* : preferential — **preferible** *adj* : preferable — **preferido, -da** *adj* : favorite

prefijo *nm* **1** : prefix **2** *Spain* : area code

pregonar *vt* : proclaim, announce

pregunta *nf* **1** : question **2 hacer** ~**s** : ask questions — **preguntar** *v* : ask — **preguntarse** *vr* : wonder

prehistórico, -ca *adj* : prehistoric

prejuicio *nm* : prejudice

preliminar *adj & nm* : preliminary

preludio *nm* : prelude

prematrimonial *adj* : premarital

prematuro, -ra *adj* : premature

premeditar *vt* : premeditate — **premeditación** *nf, pl* **-ciones** : premeditation

premenstrual *adj* : premenstrual

premio *nm* **1** : prize **2** RECOMPENSA : reward **3** ~ **gordo** : jackpot — **premiado, -da** *adj* : prizewinning — **premiar** *vt* **1** : award a prize to **2** RECOMPENSAR : reward

premisa *nf* : premise

premonición *nf, pl* **-ciones** : premonition

premura *nf* : haste, urgency

prenatal *adj* : prenatal

prenda *nf* **1** : piece of clothing **2** GARANTÍA : pledge **3** : forfeit (in a game) — **prendar** *vt* : captivate — **prendarse** *vr* ~ **de** : fall in love with

prender *vt* **1** SUJETAR : pin, fasten **2** APRESAR : capture **3** : light (a match, etc.) **4** *Lat* : turn on (a light, etc.) — *vi* **1** : take root **2** ARDER : catch, burn (of fire) — **prenderse** *vr* : catch fire — **prendedor** *nm Lat* : brooch, pin

prensa *nf* : press — **prensar** *vt* : press

preñado, -da *adj* **1** : pregnant **2** ~ **de** : filled with

preocupar *vt* : worry — **preocuparse** *vr* **1** : worry **2** ~ **de** : take care of — **preocupación** *nf, pl* **-ciones** : worry

preparar *vt* : prepare — **prepararse** *vr* : get ready — **preparación** *nf, pl* **-ciones** : preparation — **preparado, -da** *adj* : prepared, ready — **preparado** *nm* : preparation — **preparativo, -va** *adj* : preparatory, preliminary — **preparativos** *nmpl* : preparations —**preparatorio, -ria** *adj* : preparatory

preposición *nf, pl* **-ciones** : preposition

prepotente *adj* : arrogant, domineering

prerrogativa *nf* : prerogative

presa *nf* **1** : catch, prey **2** DIQUE : dam **3 hacer** ~ **en** : seize

presagiar *vt* : presage, forebode — **presagio** *nm* **1** : omen **2** PREMONICIÓN : premonition

presbítero *nm* : presbyter, priest

prescindir *vi* ~ **de 1** : do without **2** OMITIR : dispense with

prescribir {33} *vt* : prescribe — **prescripción** *nf, pl* **-ciones** : prescription

presencia *nf* **1** : presence **2** ASPECTO : appearance — **presenciar** *vt* : be present at, witness

presentar *vt* **1** : present **2** OFRECER : offer, give **3** MOSTRAR : show **4** : introduce (persons) — **presentarse** *vr* **1** : show up **2** : arise, come up (of a problem, etc.) **3** : introduce oneself — **presentación** *nf, pl* **-ciones 1** : presentation **2** : introduction (of persons) **3** ASPECTO : appearance — **presentador, -dora** *n* : presenter, host (of a television program, etc.)

presente *adj* **1** : present **2 tener** ~ : keep in mind — ~ *nm* **1** : present **2 entre los** ~**s** : among those present

presentir {76} *vt* : have a presentiment of — **presentimiento** *nm* : premonition

preservar *vt* : preserve, protect — **preservación** *nf, pl* **-ciones** : preservation — **preservativo** *nm* : condom

presidente, -ta *n* **1** : president **2** : chair, chairperson (of a meeting) — **presidencia** *nf* **1** : presidency **2** : chairmanship (of a meeting) — **presidencial** *adj* : presidential

presidio *nm* : prison — **presidiario, -ria** *n* : convict

presidir *vt* **1** : preside over, chair **2** PREDOMINAR : dominate

presión *nf, pl* **-siones 1** : pressure **2** ~ **arterial** : blood pressure **3 hacer** ~ : press — **presionar** *vt* **1** : press **2** COACCIONAR : put pressure on

preso, -sa *adj* : imprisoned — ~ *n* : prisoner

prestar *vt* **1** : lend, loan **2** : give (aid) **3** ~ **atención** : pay attention — **prestado, -da** *adj* **1** : borrowed, on loan **2 pedir** ~ : borrow — **prestamista** *nmf* : moneylender — **préstamo** *nm* : loan

prestidigitación *nf, pl* **-ciones** : sleight of hand — **prestidigitador, -dora** *n* : magician

prestigio *nm* : prestige — **prestigioso, -sa** *adj* : prestigious

presto, -ta *adj* : prompt, ready — **presto** *adv* : promptly, right away

presumir *vt* : presume — *vi* : boast, show off — **presumido, -da** *adj* : conceited, vain — **presunción** *nf, pl* **-ciones 1** : presumption **2** VANIDAD : vanity — **presunto, -ta** *adj* : presumed, alleged — **presuntuoso, -sa** *adj* : conceited

presuponer {60} *vt* : presuppose — **presupuesto** *nm* **1** : budget, estimate **2** SUPUESTO : assumption

presuroso, -sa *adj* : hasty, quick

pretender *vt* **1** : try to **2** AFIRMAR : claim **3** CORTEJAR : court, woo **4** ~ **que** : expect — **pretencioso, -sa** *adj* : pretentious — **pretendido** *adj* : supposed — **pretendiente** *nmf* **1** : candidate **2** : pretender (to a throne) — ~ *nm* : suitor — **pretensión** *nf, pl* **-siones 1** INTENCIÓN : intention, aspiration **2** : claim (to a throne, etc.) **3 pretensiones** *nfpl* : pretensions

pretérito *nm* : past (in grammar)

pretexto *nm* : pretext, excuse

prevalecer {53} *vi* : prevail — **prevaleciente** *adj* : prevailing, prevalent

prevenir {87} *vt* **1** : prevent **2** AVISAR : warn — **prevenirse** {87} *vr* ~ **contra** *or* ~ **de** : take precautions against — **prevención** *nf, pl* **-ciones 1** : prevention **2** PRECAUCIÓN : precaution **3** PREJUICIO : prejudice — **prevenido, -da** *adj* **1** : prepared, ready **2** PRECAVIDO : cautious — **preventivo, -va** *adj* : preventive

prever {88} *vt* **1** : foresee **2** PLANEAR : plan

previo, -via *adj* : previous, prior

previsible *adj* : foreseeable — **previsión** *nf, pl* **-siones 1** : foresight **2** PREDICCIÓN : prediction, forecast — **previsor, -sora** *adj* : farsighted, prudent

prieto, -ta *adj* **1** CEÑIDO : tight **2** *Lat fam* : dark-skinned

prima *nf* **1** : bonus **2** : (insurance) premium **3** → **primo**

primario, -ria *adj* **1** : primary **2 escuela primaria** : elementary school

primate *nm* : primate

primavera *nf* **1** : spring (season) **2** : primrose (flower) — **primaveral** *adj* : spring

primero, -ra *adj* (**primer** *before masculine singular nouns*) **1** : first **2** MEJOR : top, leading **3** PRINCIPAL : main, basic **4 de primera** : first-rate — ~ *n* : first (person or thing) — **primero** *adv* **1** : first **2** MÁS BIEN : rather, sooner

primitivo, -va *adj* : primitive

primo, -ma *n* : cousin

primogénito, -ta *adj & n* : firstborn

primor *nm* : beautiful thing

primordial *adj* : basic, fundamental

primoroso, -sa *adj* **1** : exquisite, fine **2** HÁBIL : skillful

princesa *nf* : princess

principado *nm* : principality

principal *adj* : main, principal

príncipe *nm* : prince

principio *nm* **1** : principle **2** COMIENZO : beginning, start **3** ORIGEN : origin **4 al** ~ : at first **5 a** ~**s de** : at the beginning of — **principiante** *nmf* : beginner

pringar {52} *vt* : spatter (with grease) — **pringoso, -sa** *adj* : greasy

prioridad *nf* : priority

prisa *nf* **1** : hurry, rush **2 a** ~ *or* **de** ~ : quickly **3 a toda** ~ : as fast as possible **4 darse** ~ : hurry **5 tener** ~ : be in a hurry

prisión *nf, pl* **-siones 1** : prison **2** ENCARCELAMIENTO : imprisonment — **prisionero, -ra** *n* : prisoner

prisma *nm* : prism — **prismáticos** *nmpl* : binoculars

privar *vt* **1** : deprive **2** PROHIBIR : forbid **3** *Lat* : knock out — **privarse** *vr* : deprive oneself — **privación** *nf, pl* **-ciones** : deprivation — **privado, -da** *adj* : private — **privativo, -va** *adj* : exclusive

privilegio *nm* : privilege — **privilegiado, -da** *adj* : privileged

pro *prep* : for, in favor of — ~ *nm* **1** : pro, advantage **2 en** ~ **de** : for, in support of **3 los pros y los contras** : the pros and cons

proa *nf* : bow, prow

probabilidad *nf* : probability — **probable** *adj* : probable, likely — **probablemente** *adv* : probably

probar {19} *vt* **1** : try, test **2** : try on (clothing) **3** DEMOSTRAR : prove **4** DEGUSTAR : taste — *vi* : try — **probarse** *vr* : try on (clothing) — **probeta** *nf* : test tube

problema *nm* : problem — **problemático, -ca** *adj* : problematic

proceder *vi* **1** : proceed, act **2** : be appropriate **3** ~ **de** : come from — **procedencia** *nf* : origin — **procedente** *adj* ~ **de** : coming from, originating in — **procedimiento** *nm* **1** : procedure, method **2** : proceedings *pl* (in law)

procesar *vt* **1** : prosecute **2** : process (data) — **procesador** *nm* ~ **de textos** : word processor — **procesamiento** *nm* : processing — **procesión** *nf, pl* **-siones** : procession — **proceso** *nm* **1** : process **2** : trial, proceedings *pl* (in law)

proclamar *vt* : proclaim — **proclama** *nf* : proclamation — **proclamación** *nf, pl* **-ciones** : proclamation

procrear *vi* : procreate — **procreación** *nf, pl* **-ciones** : procreation

procurar *vt* **1** : try, endeavor **2** CONSEGUIR : obtain, procure — **procurador, -dora** *n* : attorney

prodigar {52} *vt* : lavish — **prodigio** *nm* : wonder, prodigy — **prodigioso, -sa** *adj* : prodigious

pródigo, -ga *adj* : extravagant, prodigal

producir {61} *vt* **1** : produce **2** CAUSAR : cause **3** : yield, bear (interest, fruit, etc.) — **producirse** *vr* : take place — **producción** *nf, pl* **-ciones** : production — **productividad** *nf* : productivity — **productivo, -va** *adj* : productive — **producto** *nm* : product — **productor, -tora** *n* : producer

proeza *nf* : exploit

profanar *vt* : profane, desecrate — **profanación** *nf, pl* **-ciones** : desecration — **profano, -na** *adj* : profane

profecía *nf* : prophecy

proferir {76} *vt* **1** : utter **2** : hurl (insults)

profesar *vt* **1** : profess **2** : practice (a profession, etc.) — **profesión** *nf, pl* **-siones** : profession — **profesional** *adj & nmf* : professional — **profesor, -sora** *n* **1** : teacher **2** : professor (at a university, etc.) — **profesorado** *nm* **1** : teaching profession **2** PROFESORES : faculty

profeta *nm* : prophet — **profético, -ca** *adj* : prophetic — **profetisa** *nf* : (female) prophet — **profetizar** {21} *vt* : prophesy

prófugo, -ga *adj & n* : fugitive

profundo, -da *adj* **1** HONDO : deep **2** : profound (of thoughts, etc.) — **profundamente** *adv* : deeply, profoundly — **profundidad** *nf* : depth — **profundizar** {21} *vt* : study in depth

profuso, -sa *adj* : profuse — **profusión** *nf, pl* **-siones** : profusion

progenie *nf* : progeny, offspring

programa *nm* **1** : program **2** : curriculum (in education) — **programación** *nf, pl* **-ciones** : programming — **programador, -dora** *n* : programmer — **programar** *vt* **1** : schedule **2** : program (a computer, etc.)

progreso *nm* : progress — **progresar** *vi* : (make) progress — **progresión** *nf, pl* **-ciones** : progression — **progresista** *adj & nmf* : progressive — **progresivo, -va** *adj* : progressive, gradual

prohibir {62} *vt* : prohibit, forbid — **prohibición** *nf, pl* **-ciones** : ban, prohibition — **prohibido, -da** *adj* : forbidden — **prohibitivo, -va** *adj* : prohibitive

prójimo *nm* : neighbor, fellow man

prole *nf* : offspring

proletariado *nm* : proletariat — **proletario, -ria** *adj & n* : proletarian

proliferar *vi* : proliferate — **proliferación** *nf, pl* **-ciones** : proliferation — **prolífico, -ca** *adj* : prolific

prolijo, -ja *adj* : wordy, long-winded

prólogo *nm* : prologue, foreword

prolongar {52} *vt* **1** : prolong **2** ALARGAR : lengthen — **prolongarse** *vr* : last, continue — **prolongación** *nf, pl* **-ciones** : extension

promedio *nm* : average

promesa *nf* : promise — **prometedor, -dora** *adj* : promising, hopeful — **prometer** *vt* : promise — *vi* : show promise — **prometerse** *vr* : get engaged — **prometido, -da** *adj* : engaged — ~ *n* : fiancé *m*, fiancée *f*

prominente *adj* : prominent — **prominencia** *nf* : prominence

promiscuo, -cua *adj* : promiscuous — **promiscuidad** *nf* : promiscuity

promocionar *vt* : promote — **promoción** *nf, pl* **-ciones** : promotion

promontorio *nm* : promontory

promover {47} *vt* **1** : promote **2** CAUSAR : cause — **promotor, -tora** *n* : promoter

promulgar {52} *vt* **1** : proclaim **2** : enact (a law)

pronombre *nm* : pronoun

pronosticar {72} *vt* : predict, forecast — **pronóstico** *nm* **1** : prediction, forecast **2** : (medical) prognosis

pronto, -ta *adj* **1** : quick, prompt **2** PREPARADO : ready — **pronto** *adv* **1** : soon **2** RAPIDAMENTE : quickly, promptly **3 de** ~ : suddenly **4 por lo** ~ : for the time being **5 tan** ~ **como** : as soon as

pronunciar *vt* **1** : pronounce **2** : give, deliver (a speech) — **pronunciarse** *vr* **1** : declare oneself **2** SUBLEVARSE : revolt — **pronunciación** *nf, pl* **-ciones** : pronunciation

propagación *nf, pl* **-ciones** : propagation

propaganda *nf* **1** : propaganda **2** PUBLICIDAD : advertising

propagar {52} *vt* : propagate, spread — **propagarse** *vr* : propagate

propano *nm* : propane

propasarse *vr* : go too far

propensión *nf, pl* **-siones** : inclination, propensity — **propenso, -sa** *adj* : prone, inclined

propiamente *adv* : exactly

propicio, -cia *adj* : favorable, propitious

propiedad *nf* **1** : property **2** PERTINENCIA : ownership, possession — **propietario, -ria** *n* : owner, proprietor

propina *nf* : tip

propinar *vt* : give, deal (a blow, etc.)

propio, -pia *adj* **1** : own **2** APROPIADO : proper, appropriate **3** CARACTERÍSTICO

: characteristic, typical **4** MISMO : himself, herself, oneself

proponer {60} *vt* **1** : propose **2** : nominate (a person) — **proponerse** *vr* : propose, intend

proporción *nf, pl* **-ciones** : proportion — **proporcionado, -da** *adj* : proportionate — **proporcional** *adj* : proportional — **proporcionar** *vt* **1** : provide **2** AJUSTAR : adapt, proportion

proposición *nf, pl* **-ciones** : proposal, proposition

propósito *nm* **1** : purpose, intention **2 a ~** : incidentally, by the way **3 a ~** : on purpose, intentionally

propuesta *nf* **1** : proposal **2** : offer (of employment, etc.)

propulsar *vt* **1** : propel, drive **2** PROMOVER : promote — **propulsión** *nf, pl* **-siones** : propulsion

prorrogar {52} *vt* **1** : extend **2** APLAZAR : postpone — **prórroga** *nf* **1** : extension, deferment **2** : overtime (in sports)

prorrumpir *vi* : burst forth, break out

prosa *nf* : prose

proscribir {33} *vt* **1** : prohibit, ban **2** DESTERRAR : exile — **proscripción** *nf, pl* **-ciones 1** : ban **2** DESTIERRO : banishment — **proscrito, -ta** *adj* : banned — **~** *n* : exile, outlaw

proseguir {75} *v* : continue — **prosecución** *nf, pl* **-ciones** : continuation

prospección *nf, pl* **-ciones** : prospecting, exploration

prospecto *nm* : prospectus

prosperar *vi* : prosper, thrive — **prosperidad** *nf* : prosperity — **próspero, -ra** *adj* : prosperous, flourishing

prostituir {41} *vt* : prostitute — **prostitución** *nf, pl* **-ciones** : prostitution — **prostituta** *nf* : prostitute

protagonista *nmf* : protagonist — **protagonizar** *vt* : star in

proteger {15} *vt* : protect — **protegerse** *vr* : protect oneself — **protección** *nf, pl* **-ciones** : protection — **protector, -tora** *adj* : protective — **~** *n* : protector — **protegido, -da** *n* : protégé

proteína *nf* : protein

protestar *v* : protest — **protesta** *nf* : protest — **protestante** *adj & nmf* : Protestant

protocolo *nm* : protocol

prototipo *nm* : prototype

protuberancia *nf* : protuberance — **protuberante** *adj* : protuberant

provecho *nm* **1** : benefit, advantage **2 ¡buen ~!** : enjoy your meal! — **provechoso, -sa** *adj* : profitable, beneficial

proveer {63} *vt* : provide, supply — **proveedor, -dora** *n* : supplier

provenir {87} *vi* **~ de** : come from

proverbio *nm* : proverb — **proverbial** *adj* : proverbial

providencia *nf* **1** : providence **2** PRECAUCIÓN : precaution — **providencial** *adj* : providential

provincia *nf* : province — **provincial** *adj* : provincial — **provinciano, -na** *adj* : provincial, parochial

provisión *nf, pl* **-siones** : provision — **provisional** *adj* : provisional

provocar {72} *vt* **1** : provoke, cause **2** IRRITAR : irritate — **provocación** *nf, pl* **-ciones** : provocation — **provocativo, -va** *adj* : provocative

próximo, -ma *adj* **1** CERCANO : near **2** SIGUIENTE : next — **próximamente** *adv* : shortly, soon — **proximidad** *nf* **1** : proximity **2 ~es** *nfpl* : vicinity

proyectar *vt* **1** : plan **2** LANZAR : throw, hurl **3** : cast (light) **4** : show (a film) — **proyección** *nf, pl* **-ciones** : projection — **proyectil** *nm* : missile — **proyecto** *nm* : plan, project — **proyector** *nm* : projector

prudencia *nf* : prudence, care — **prudente** *adj* : prudent, sensible

prueba *nf* **1** : proof, evidence **2** : test (in education, medicine, etc.) **3** : event (in sports) **4 a ~ de agua** : waterproof

psicoanálisis *nm* : psychoanalysis — **psicoanalista** *nmf* : psychoanalyst — **psicoanalizar** {21} *vt* : psychoanalyze

psicología *nf* : psychology — **psicológico, -ca** *adj* : psychological — **psicólogo, -ga** *n* : psychologist

psicópata *nmf* : psychopath

psicosis *nfs & pl* : psychosis

psicoterapia *nf* : psychotherapy — **psicoterapeuta** *nmf* : psychotherapist

psicótico, -ca *adj & n* : psychotic

psiquiatría *nf* : psychiatry — **psiquiatra** *nmf* : psychiatrist — **psiquiátrico, -ca** *adj* : psychiatric

psíquico, -ca *adj* : psychic

púa *nf* **1** : sharp point **2** : tooth (of a comb) **3** : thorn (of a plant), quill (of a porcupine, etc.) **4** : (guitar) pick

pubertad *nf* : puberty

publicar {72} *vt* **1** : publish **2** DIVULGAR : divulge, disclose — **publicación** *nf, pl* **-ciones** : publication

publicidad *nf* **1** : publicity **2** : advertising (in marketing) — **publicista** *nmf* : publicist — **publicitar** *vt* **1** : publicize **2** : advertise (a product, etc.) — **publicitario, -ria** *adj* : advertising

público, -ca *adj* : public — **público** *nm* **1** : public **2** : audience (of theater, etc.), spectators *pl* (of sports)

puchero *nm* **1** : (cooking) pot **2** GUISADO : stew **3 hacer ~s** : pout

púdico, -ca *adj* : modest

pudiente *adj* : wealthy

pudín *nm, pl* **-dines** : pudding

pudor *nm* : modesty — **pudoroso, -sa** *adj* : modest

pudrir {59} *vt* **1** : rot **2** *fam* : annoy — **pudrirse** *vr* : rot

pueblo *nm* **1** : town, village **2** NACIÓN : people, nation

puente *nm* **1** : bridge **2 hacer ~** : have a long weekend **3 ~ levadizo** : drawbridge

puerco, -ca *n* **1** : pig **2 puerco espín** : porcupine — **~** *adj* : dirty, filthy

pueril *adj* : childish

puerro *nm* : leek

puerta *nf* **1** : door, gate **2 a ~ cerrada** : behind closed doors

puerto *nm* **1** : port **2** : (mountain) pass **3** REFUGIO : haven

puertorriqueño, -ña *adj* : Puerto Rican

pues *conj* **1** : since, because **2** POR LO TANTO : so, therefore **3** (*used interjectionally*) : well, then

puesta *nf* **1 ~ a punto** : tune-up **2 ~ de sol** : sunset **3 ~ en marcha** : starting up — **puesto, -ta** *adj* **1** : put, set **2** VESTIDO : dressed — **puesto** *nm* **1** : place **2** EMPLEO : position, job **3** : stand, stall (in a market) **4 ~ avanzado** : outpost — **~ que** *conj* : since, given that

púgil *nm* : boxer

pugnar *vi* : fight — **pugna** *nf* : fight, battle

pulcro, -cra *adj* : tidy, neat

pulga *nf* **1** : flea **2 tener malas ~s** : have a bad temper

pulgada *nf* : inch — **pulgar** *nm* **1** : thumb **2** : big toe

pulir *vt* **1** : polish **2** REFINAR : touch up, perfect

pulla *nf* : cutting remark, gibe

pulmón *nm, pl* **-mones** : lung — **pulmonar** *adj* : pulmonary — **pulmonía** *nf* : pneumonia

pulpa *nf* : pulp

pulpería *nf Lat* : grocery store

púlpito *nm* : pulpit

pulpo *nm* : octopus

pulsar *vt* **1** : press (a button), strike (a key) **2** : play (music) — **pulsación** *nf, pl* **-ciones 1** : beat, throb **2** : keystroke (on a typewriter, etc.)

pulsera *nf* : bracelet

pulso *nm* **1** : pulse **2** : steadiness (of hand)

pulular *vi* : swarm

pulverizar {21} *vt* **1** : pulverize, crush **2** : spray (a liquid) — **pulverizador** *nm* : atomizer, spray

puma *nf* : puma

punitivo, -va *adj* : punitive

punta *nf* **1** : tip, end **2** : point (of a needle, etc.) **3 ~ del dedo** : fingertip **4 sacar ~ a** : sharpen

puntada *nf* **1** : stitch **2 ~s** *nfpl* : seam

puntal *nm* : prop, support

puntapié *nm* : kick

puntear *vt* : pluck (a guitar)

puntería *nf* : aim, marksmanship

puntiagudo, -da *adj* : sharp, pointed

puntilla *nf* **1** : lace edging **2 de ~s** : on tiptoe

punto *nm* **1** : dot, point **2** : period (in punctuation) **3** ASUNTO : item, question **4** LUGAR : spot, place **5** MOMENTO : moment **6** : point (in a score) **7** PUNTADA : stitch **8 a las dos en ~** : at two o'clock sharp **9 dos ~s** : colon **10 hasta cierto ~** : up to a point **11 ~ de partida** : starting point **12 ~ muerto** : deadlock **13 ~ y coma** : semicolon

puntuación *nf, pl* **-ciones 1** : punctuation **2** : scoring, score (in sports)

puntual *adj* **1** : prompt, punctual **2** EXACTO : accurate, detailed — **puntualidad** *nf* **1** : punctuality **2** EXACTITUD : accuracy

puntuar {3} *vt* : punctuate — *vi* : score (in sports)

punzar {21} *vt* : prick, puncture — **punzada** *nf* **1** PINCHAZO : prick **2** : sharp pain — **punzante** *adj* **1** : sharp **2** MORDAZ : biting, caustic

puñado *nm* **1** : handful **2 a ~s** : by the handful

puñal *nm* : dagger — **puñalada** *nf* : stab

puño *nm* **1** : fist **2** : cuff (of a shirt) **3** : handle, hilt (of a sword, etc.) — **puñetazo** *nm* : punch (with the fist)

pupila *nf* : pupil (of the eye)

pupitre *nm* : desk

puré *nm* **1** : purée **2 ~ de papas** *or* **~ de patatas** *Spain* : mashed potatoes

pureza *nf* : purity

purga *nf* : purge — **purgar** {52} *vt* : purge — **purgatorio** *nm* : purgatory

purificar {72} *vt* : purify — **purificación** *nf, pl* **-ciones** : purification

puritano, -na *adj* : puritanical — **~** *n* : puritan

puro, -ra *adj* **1** : pure **2** SIMPLE : plain, simple **3** *Lat fam* : only, just — **puro** *nm* : cigar

púrpura *nf* : purple — **purpúreo, -rea** *adj* : purple

pus *nm* : pus

pusilánime *adj* : cowardly

puta *nf* : whore

putrefacción *nf, pl* **-ciones** : putrefaction, rot — **pútrido, -da** *adj* : putrid, rotten

Q

q *nf* : q, 18th letter of the Spanish alphabet

que *conj* **1** : that **2** (*in comparisons*) : than **3** (*introducing a reason or cause*) : so that, or else **4 es ~** : the thing is that **5 yo ~ tú** : if I were you — **~** *pron* **1** (*referring to persons*) : who, whom **2** (*referring to things*) : that, which **3 el (la, lo, las, los) ~** : he (she, it, they) who, whoever, the one(s) that

qué *adv* **1** : how, what **2 ¡~ lindo!** : how lovely! — **~** *adj* : what, which — **~** *pron* **1** : what **2 ¿~ crees?** : what do you think?

quebrar {55} *vt* : break — *vi* : go bankrupt — **quebrarse** *vr* : break — **quebrada** *nf* : ravine, gorge — **quebradizo, -za** *adj* : breakable, fragile — **quebrado, -da** *adj* **1** : bankrupt **2** : rough, uneven (of land, etc.) **3** ROTO : broken — **quebrado** *nm* : fraction — **quebradura** *nf* : crack, fissure — **quebrantar** *vt* **1** : break **2** DEBILITAR : weaken — **quebranto** *nm* **1** : harm, damage **2** AFLICCIÓN : grief, pain

queda *nf* → **toque**

quedar *vi* **1** PERMANECER : remain, stay **2** ESTAR : be **3** FALTAR : be left **4** : fit, look (of clothing, etc.) **5 no queda lejos** : it's not far **6 ~ en** : agree to, agree on — **quedarse** *vr* **1** : stay **2 ~ con** : keep

quedo, -da *adj* : quiet, still — **quedo** *adv* : softly, quietly

quehacer *nm* **1** : task **2 ~es** *nmpl* : chores

queja *nf* : complaint — **quejarse** *vr* **1** : complain **2** GEMIR : moan, groan — **quejido** *nm* : moan, whimper — **quejoso, -sa** *adj* : complaining, whining

quemar *vt* **1** : burn **2** MALGASTAR : squander — *vi* : burn — **quemarse** *vr* **1** : burn oneself **2** : burn (up) **3** : get sunburned — **quemado, -da** *adj* **1** : burned **2** AGOTADO : burned-out **3 estar ~** : be fed up — **quemador** *nm* : burner — **quemadura** *nf* : burn — **quemarropa: a ~** *adj & adv phr* : point-blank

querella *nf* **1** : dispute, quarrel **2** : charge (in law)

querer {64} *vt* **1** : want **2** AMAR : love **3 ~ decir** : mean **4 ¿quieres pasarme la leche?** : please pass the milk **5 sin ~** : unintentionally — **~** *nm* : love — **querido, -da** *adj* : dear, beloved — **~** *n* **1** : darling **2** AMANTE : lover

queroseno *nm* : kerosene

querubín *nm, pl* **-bines** : cherub

queso *nm* : cheese — **quesadilla** *nf Lat* : quesadilla

quicio *nm* **1 estar fuera de ~** : be beside oneself **2 sacar de ~** : drive crazy

quiebra *nf* **1** : break **2** BANCARROTA : bankruptcy

quien *pron, pl* **quienes 1** (*subject*) : who **2** (*object*) : whom **3** (*indefinite*) : whoever, anyone, some people

quién *pron, pl* **quiénes 1** (*subject*) : who **2** (*object*) : whom **3 ¿de ~ es este lápiz?** : whose pencil is this?

quienquiera *pron, pl* **quienesquiera** : whoever, whomever

quieto, -ta *adj* **1** : calm, quiet **2** INMÓVIL : still — **quietud** *nf* : stillness

quijada *nf* : jaw, jawbone (of an animal)

quilate *nm* : carat, karat

quilla *nf* : keel

quimera *nf* : illusion — **quimérico, -ca** *adj* : fanciful

química *nf* : chemistry — **químico, -ca** *adj* : chemical — **~** *n* : chemist

quince *adj & nm* : fifteen — **quinceañero, -ra** *n* : fifteen-year-old, teenager — **quincena** *nf* : two-week period, fortnight — **quincenal** *adj* : semimonthly, twice a month

quincuagésimo, -ma *adj & n* : fiftieth

quinientos, -tas *adj* : five hundred — **quinientos** *nms & pl* : five hundred

quinina *nf* : quinine

quinqué *nm* : oil lamp

quinta *nf* : country house, villa

quintaesencia *nf* : quintessence

quinteto *nm* : quintet

quinto, -ta *adj & n* : fifth — **quinto** *nm* : fifth

quiosco *nm* : kiosk, newsstand

quiropráctico, -ca *n* : chiropractor

quirúrgico, -ca *adj* : surgical

quisquilloso, -sa *adj* : fastidious, fussy

quiste *nm* : cyst

quitar *vt* **1** : remove, take away **2** : take off (clothes) **3** : get rid of, relieve (pain, etc.) — **quitarse** *vr* **1** : withdraw, leave **2** : take off (one's clothes) **3 ~ de** : give up (a habit) **4 ~ de encima** : get rid of — **quitaesmalte** *nm* : nail-polish remover — **quitamanchas** *nms & pl* : stain remover — **quitanieves** *nm* : snowplow — **quitasol** *nm* : parasol

quizá *or* **quizás** *adv* : maybe, perhaps

R

r *nf* : r, 19th letter of the Spanish alphabet

rábano *nm* **1** : radish **2 ~ picante** : horseradish

rabí *nmf, pl* **-bíes** : rabbi

rabia *nf* **1** : rage, anger **2** : rabies (disease) — **rabiar** *vi* **1** : be furious **2** : be in great pain **3 ~ por** : be dying for — **rabioso, -sa** *adj* **1** : enraged, furious **2** : rabid, having rabies

rabino, -na *n* : rabbi

rabo *nm* **1** : tail **2 el ~ del ojo** : the corner of one's eye

racha *nf* **1** : gust of wind **2** SERIE : series, string — **racheado, -da** *adj* : gusty

racial *adj* : racial

racimo *nm* : bunch, cluster

raciocinio *nm* : reason, reasoning

ración *nf, pl* **-ciones 1** : share, ration **2** : helping (of food)

racional *adj* : rational — **racionalizar** {21} *vt* : rationalize

racionar *vt* : ration — **racionamiento** *nm* : rationing

racismo *nm* : racism — **racista** *adj & nmf* : racist

radar *nm* : radar

radiación *nf, pl* **-ciones** : radiation

radiactivo, -va *adj* : radioactive — **radiactividad** *nf* : radioactivity

radiador *nm* : radiator

radiante *adj* : radiant

radical *adj & nmf* : radical

radicar {72} *vi* **~ en** : lie in, be rooted in

radio *nm* **1** : radius **2** : spoke (of a wheel) **3** : radium (element) — **~** *nmf* : radio

radioactivo, -va *adj* : radioactive — **radioactividad** *nf* : radioactivity

radiodifusión *nf, pl* **-siones** : broadcasting — **radioemisora** *nf* : radio station — **radioescucha** *nmf* : listener — **radiofónico, -ca** *adj* : radio

radiografía *nf* : X ray — **radiografiar** {85} *vt* : x-ray

radiología *nf* : radiology — **radiólogo, -ga** *n* : radiologist

raer {65} *vt* : scrape off

ráfaga *nf* **1** : gust (of wind) **2** : flash (of light)

raído, -da *adj* : worn, shabby

raíz *nf, pl* **raíces 1** : root **2** ORIGEN : origin, source **3 echar raíces** : take root

raja *nf* **1** : crack, slit **2** RODAJA : slice — **rajar** *vt* : crack, split — **rajarse** *vr* **1** : crack, split open **2** *fam* : back out

rajatabla: a ~ *adv phr* : strictly, to the letter

ralea *nf* : sort, kind

ralentí *nm* : neutral (gear)

rallar *vt* : grate — **rallador** *nm* : grater

rama *nf* : branch — **ramaje** *nm* : branches *pl* — **ramal** *nm* : branch (of a railroad, etc.) — **ramificarse** {72} *vr* : branch (off) — **ramillete** *nm* **1** : bouquet **2** GRUPO : cluster, bunch — **ramo** *nm* **1** : branch **2** RAMILLETE : bouquet

rampa *nf* : ramp, incline

rana *nf* **1** : frog **2 ~ toro** : bullfrog

rancho *nm* : ranch, farm — **ranchero, -ra** *n* : rancher, farmer

rancio, -cia *adj* **1** : rancid **2** : aged (of wine)

rango *nm* **1** : rank **2** : (social) standing

ranúnculo *nm* : buttercup

ranura *nf* : groove, slot

rapar *vt* **1** : shave **2** : crop (hair)

rapaz *adj, pl* **-paces** : rapacious, predatory

rápido, -da *adj* : rapid, quick — **rápidamente** *adv* : rapidly, fast — **rapidez** *nf* : speed — **rápido** *adv* : quickly, fast — **~** *nm* **1** : express train **2 ~s** *nmpl* : rapids

rapiña *nf* **1** : plunder **2 ave de ~** : bird of prey

rapsodia *nf* : rhapsody

raptar *vt* : kidnap — **rapto** *nm* : kidnapping — **raptor, -tora** *n* : kidnapper

raqueta *nf* : racket (in sports)

raro, -ra *adj* **1** : rare **2** EXTRAÑO : odd, strange — **raramente** *adv* : rarely, infrequently — **rareza** *nf* : rarity

ras *nm* **a ~ de** : level with

rascacielos *nms & pl* : skyscraper

rascar {72} *vt* **1** : scratch **2** RASPAR : scrape — **rascarse** *vr* : scratch oneself

rasgar {52} *vt* : rip, tear — **rasgarse** *vr* : rip

rasgo *nm* **1** : stroke (of a pen) **2** CARACTERÍSTICA : trait, characteristic **3 ~s** *nmpl* FACCIONES : features

rasguear *vt* : strum

rasguñar *vt* : scratch — **rasguño** *nm* : scratch

raso, -sa *adj* **1** : level, flat **2** : low (of a flight) **3 soldado raso** : private (in the army) — **raso** *nm* : satin

raspar *vt* **1** : scrape **2** LIMAR : file down, smooth — *vi* : be rough — **raspadura** *nf* **1** : scratch **2 ~s** *nfpl* : scrapings

rastra *nf* **1** : rake **2 a ~s** : unwillingly — **rastrear** *vt* : track, trace — **rastrero, -ra** *adj* **1** : creeping **2** DESPRECIABLE : despicable — **rastrillar** *vt* : rake — **rastrillo** *nm* : rake — **rastro** *nm* **1** : trail, track **2** SEÑAL : sign

rasurar *vt Lat* : shave — **rasurarse** *vr Lat* : shave

rata *nf* : rat

ratear *vt* : steal — **ratero, -ra** *n* : thief

ratificar {72} *vt* : ratify — **ratificación** *nf, pl* **-ciones** : ratification

rato *nm* **1** : while **2 al poco ~** : shortly after **3 pasar el ~** : pass the time

ratón *nm, pl* **-tones** : mouse — **ratonera** *nf* : mousetrap

raudal *nm* **1** : torrent **2 a ~es** : in abundance — **raudo, -da** *adj* : swift

raya *nf* **1** : line **2** LISTA : stripe **3** : part (in the hair) — **rayar** *vt* : scratch — *vi* **1 al ~ el día** : at daybreak **2 ~ en** : border on — **rayarse** *vr* : get scratched

rayo *nm* **1** : ray, beam **2** : bolt of lightning **3 ~s X** : X rays

rayón *nm* : rayon

raza *nf* **1** : (human) race **2** : breed (of animals) **3 de ~** : thoroughbred, pedigreed

razón *nf, pl* **-zones 1** : reason **2 dar ~** : inform **3 en ~ de** : because of **4 tener ~** : be right — **razonable** *adj* : reasonable — **razonamiento** *nm* : reasoning — **razonar** *v* : reason, think

reacción *nf, pl* **-ciones** : reaction — **reaccionar** *vi* : react — **reaccionario, -ria** *adj & n* : reactionary

reacio, -cia *adj* : resistant, stubborn

reactivar *vt* : reactivate, revive

reactor *nm* **1** : jet (airplane) **2 ~ nuclear** : nuclear reactor

reajustar *vt* : readjust — **reajuste** *nm* : readjustment

real *adj* **1** : royal **2** VERDADERO : real, true

realce *nm* **1** : relief **2 dar ~** : highlight

realeza *nf* : royalty

realidad *nf* **1** : reality **2 en ~** : actually, in fact

realismo *nm* : realism — **realista** *adj* : realistic — **~** *nmf* : realist

realizar {21} *vt* **1** : carry out **2** : achieve (a goal) **3** : produce (a film or play) **4** : realize (a profit) — **realizarse** *vr* **1** : fulfill oneself **2** : come true (of a dream, etc.) — **realización** *nf, pl* **-ciones** : execution, realization

realmente *adv* : really, actually

realzar {21} *vt* : highlight, enhance

reanimar *vt* : revive

reanudar *vt* : resume, renew — **reanudarse** *vr* : resume

reaparecer {53} *vi* : reappear — **reaparición** *nf, pl* **-ciones** : reappearance

reavivar *vt* : revive

rebajar *vt* **1** : lower, reduce **2** HUMILLAR : humiliate — **rebajarse** *vr* **1** : humble oneself **2 ~ a** : stoop to — **rebaja** *nf* **1** : reduction **2** DESCUENTO : discount **3 ~s** *nfpl* : sales

rebanada *nf* : slice

rebaño *nm* **1** : herd **2** : flock (of sheep)

rebasar *vt* : surpass, exceed

rebatir *vt* : refute

rebelarse *vr* : rebel — **rebelde** *adj* : rebellious — **~** *nmf* : rebel — **rebeldía** *nf* : rebelliousness — **rebelión** *nf, pl* **-liones** : rebellion

reblandecer *vt* : soften

rebobinar *vt* : rewind

rebosar *vi* **1** : overflow **2 ~ de** : be bursting with — *vt* : overflow with

rebotar *vi* : bounce, rebound — **rebote** *nm* **1** : bounce **2 de ~** : on the rebound

rebozar {21} *vt* : coat in batter

rebuscado, -da *adj* : pretentious

rebuznar *vi* : bray

recabar *vt* **1** : obtain, collect **2 ~ fondos** : raise money

recado *nm* **1** MENSAJE : message **2** *Spain* : errand

recaer {13} *vi* **1** : relapse **2 ~ sobre** : fall on — **recaída** *nf* : relapse

recalcar {72} *vt* : emphasize, stress

recalcitrante *adj* : recalcitrant

recalentar {55} *vt* **1** : overheat **2** : reheat, warm up (food) — **recalentarse** *vr* : overheat

recámara *nf* **1** : chamber (of a firearm) **2** *Lat* : bedroom

recambio *nm* **1** : spare part **2** : refill (for a pen, etc.)

recapitular *vt* : recapitulate, sum up — **recapitulación** *nf, pl* **-ciones** : recapitulation

recargar {52} *vt* **1** : overload **2** : recharge (a battery), reload (a firearm, etc.) — **recargado, -da** *adj* : overly elaborate — **recargo** *nm* : surcharge

recato *nm* : modesty — **recatado, -da** *adj* : modest, demure

recaudar *vt* : collect — **recaudación** *nf, pl* **-ciones** : collection — **recaudador, -dora** *n* **~ de impuestos** : tax collector

recelar *vt* : distrust, fear — **recelo** *nm* : distrust, suspicion — **receloso, -sa** *adj* : distrustful, suspicious

recepción *nf, pl* **-ciones** : reception — **recepcionista** *nmf* : receptionist

receptáculo *nm* : receptacle

receptivo, -va *adj* : receptive — **receptor, -tora** *n* : recipient — **receptor** *nm* : receiver (of a radio, etc.)

recesión *nf, pl* **-siones** : recession

receso *nm Lat* : recess, adjournment

receta *nf* **1** : recipe **2** : prescription (in medicine)

rechazar {21} *vt* **1** : reject, refuse **2** REPELER : repel **3** : reflect (light) — **rechazo** *nm* : rejection

rechinar *vi* **1** : squeak, creak **2** : grind, gnash (one's teeth)

rechoncho, -cha *adj fam* : chubby

recibir *vt* **1** : receive **2** ACOGER : welcome — *vi* : receive visitors — **recibidor** *nm* : vestibule, entrance hall — **recibimiento** *nm* : reception, welcome — **recibo** *nm* : receipt

reciclar *vt* **1** : recycle **2** : retrain (workers) — **reciclaje** *nm* : recycling

recién *adv* **1** : newly, recently **2 ~ casados** : newlyweds — **reciente** *adj* : recent — **recientemente** *adv* : recently

recinto *nm* **1** : enclosure **2** ÁREA : area, site

recio, -cia *adj* : tough, strong

recipiente *nm* : container, receptacle — **~** *nmf* : recipient

recíproco, -ca *adj* : reciprocal, mutual

recitar *vt* : recite — **recital** *nm* : recital

reclamar *vt* : demand, ask for — *vi* : complain — **reclamación** *nf, pl* **-ciones 1** : claim, demand **2** QUEJA : complaint — **reclamo** *nm* **1** : lure (in hunting) **2** *Lat* : inducement, attraction

reclinar *vt* : rest, lean — **reclinarse** *vr* : recline, lean back

recluir {41} *vt* : confine, lock up — **recluirse** *vr* : shut oneself away — **reclusión** *nf, pl* **-siones** : imprisonment — **recluso, -sa** *n* : prisoner

recluta *nmf* : recruit — **reclutamiento** *nm* : recruitment — **reclutar** *vt* : recruit, enlist

recobrar *vt* : recover, regain — **recobrarse** *vr* **~ de** : recover from

recodo *nm* : bend

recoger {15} *vt* **1** : collect, gather **2** COGER : pick up **3** LIMPIAR, ORDENAR : clean up, tidy (up) — **recogerse** *vr* : retire, withdraw — **recogedor** *nm* : dustpan — **recogido, -da** *adj* : quiet, secluded

recolección *nf, pl* **-ciones 1** : collection **2** COSECHA : harvest

recomendar {55} *vt* : recommend — **recomendación** *nf, pl* **-ciones** : recommendation

recompensar *vt* : reward — **recompensa** *nf* : reward

reconciliar *vt* : reconcile — **reconciliarse** *vr* : be reconciled — **reconciliación** *nf, pl* **-ciones** : reconciliation

recóndito, -ta *adj* : hidden

reconfortar *vt* : comfort

reconocer {18} *vt* **1** : recognize **2** ADMITIR : admit **3** EXAMINAR : examine — **reconocible** *adj* : recognizable — **reconocido, -da** *adj* **1** : recognized, accepted **2** AGRADECIDO : grateful — **reconocimiento** *nm* **1** : recognition **2** AGRADECIMIENTO : gratitude **3** : (medical) examination

reconsiderar *vt* : reconsider

reconstruir {41} *vt* : reconstruct — **reconstrucción** *nf, pl* **-ciones** : reconstruction

recopilar *vt* **1** RECOGER : collect, gather **2** : compile — **recopilación** *nf, pl* **-ciones** : collection, compilation

récord *nm, pl* **-cords** : record

recordar {19} *vt* **1** ACORDARSE DE : remember **2** : remind — *vi* : remember — **recordatorio** *nm* : reminder

recorrer *vt* **1** : travel through **2** : cover (a distance) — **recorrido** *nm* **1** : journey, trip **2** TRAYECTO : route, course

recortar *vt* **1** : reduce **2** CORTAR : cut (out) **3** : trim (hair) — **recortarse** *vr* : stand out — **recorte** *nm* **1** : cut, cutting **2 ~s de periódicos** : newspaper clippings

recostar {19} *vt* : lean, rest — **recostarse** *vr* : lie down

recoveco *nm* **1** : bend **2** RINCÓN : nook, corner

recrear *vt* **1** : recreate **2** ENTRETENER : entertain — **recrearse** *vr* : to enjoy oneself — **recreativo, -va** *adj* : recreational — **recreo** *nm* **1** : recreation, amusement **2** : recess, break (at school)

recriminar *vt* : reproach

recrudecer {53} *vi* : worsen — **recrudecerse** *vr* : intensify, get worse

rectángulo *nm* : rectangle — **rectangular** *adj* : rectangular

rectificar {72} *vt* **1** : rectify, correct **2** AJUSTAR : straighten (out) — **rectitud** *nf* **1** : straightness **2** : (moral) rectitude — **recto, -ta** *adj* **1** : straight **2** INTEGRO : upright, honorable — **recto** *nm* : rectum

rector, -tora *adj* : governing, managing — **~** *n* : rector — **rectoría** *nf* : rectory

recubrir {2} *vt* : cover, coat

recuento *nm* : count, recount

recuerdo *nm* **1** : memory **2** : souvenir, remembrance (of a journey, etc.) **3 ~s** *nmpl* SALUDOS : regards

recuperar *vt* **1** : recover, retrieve **2 ~ el tiempo perdido** : make up for lost time — **recuperarse** *vr* **~ de** : recover from — **recuperación** *nf, pl* **-ciones 1** : recovery **2 ~ de datos** : data retrieval

recurrir *vi* **~ a** : turn to (a person), resort to (force, etc.) — **recurso** *nm* **1** : recourse, resort **2** : appeal (in law) **3 ~s** *nmpl* : resources

red *nf* **1** : net **2** SISTEMA : network, system **3 la Red** : the Internet

redactar *vt* : write (up), draft — **redacción** *nf, pl* **-ciones 1** : writing, drafting **2** : editing (of a newspaper, etc.) — **redactor, -tora** *n* : editor

redada *nf* **1** : (police) raid **2** : catch (in fishing)

redescubrir {2} *vt* : rediscover

redención *nf, pl* **-ciones** : redemption — **redentor, -tora** *adj* : redeeming

redil *nm* : fold, pen

rédito *nm* : interest, yield

redoblar *vt* : redouble

redomado, -da *adj* : out-and-out

redondear *vt* **1** : make round **2** : round off (a number, etc.) — **redonda** *nf* **1** : whole note (in music) **2 a la ~** : in the surrounding area — **redondel** *nm* **1** : ring, circle **2** : bullring — **redondo, -da** *adj* **1** : round **2** PERFECTO : excellent

reducir {61} *vt* : reduce — **reducirse** *vr* **~ a** : come down to, amount to — **reducción** *nf, pl* **-ciones** : reduction — **reducido, -da** *adj* **1** : reduced, limited **2** PEQUEÑO : small

redundante *adj* : redundant — **redundancia** *nf* : redundancy

reedición *nf, pl* **-ciones** : reprint

reembolsar *vt* : refund, reimburse, repay — **reembolso** *nm* : refund, reimbursement

reemplazar {21} *vt* : replace — **reemplazo** *nm* : replacement

reencarnación *nf, pl* **-ciones** : reincarnation

reencuentro *nm* : reunion

reestructurar *vt* : restructure

refaccionar *vt Lat* : repair, renovate — **refacciones** *nfpl Lat* : repairs, renovations

referir {76} *vt* **1** : tell **2** REMITIR : refer — **referirse** *vr* **~ a** : refer to — **referencia** *nf* **1** : reference **2 hacer ~ a** : refer to — **referéndum** *nm, pl* **-dums** : referendum — **referente** *adj* **~ a** : concerning

refinar *vt* : refine — **refinado, -da** *adj* : refined — **refinamiento** *nm* : refinement — **refinería** *nf* : refinery

reflector *nm* **1** : reflector **2** : spotlight, searchlight, floodlight

reflejar *vt* : reflect — **reflejarse** *vr* : be reflected — **reflejo** *nm* **1** : reflection **2** : (physical) reflex **3 ~s** *nmpl* : highlights (in hair)

reflexionar *vi* : reflect, think — **reflexión** *nf, pl* **-xiones** : reflection, thought — **reflexivo, -va** *adj* **1** : reflective, thoughtful **2** : reflexive (in grammar)

reflujo *nm* : ebb (tide)

reforma *nf* **1** : reform **2 ~s** *nfpl* : renovations — **reformador, -dora** *n* : reformer — **reformar** *vt* **1** : reform **2** : renovate, repair (a house, etc.) — **reformarse** *vr* : mend one's ways — **reformatorio** *nm* : reformatory

reforzar {36} *vt* : reinforce

refrán *nm, pl* **-franes** : proverb, saying

refregar {49} *vt* : scrub

refrenar *vt* **1** : rein in (a horse) **2** CONTENER : restrain — **refrenarse** *vr* : restrain oneself

refrendar *vt* : approve, endorse

refrescar {72} *vt* **1** : refresh, cool **2** : brush up on (knowledge) — *vi* : turn cooler — **refrescante** *adj* : refreshing — **refresco** *nm* : soft drink

refriega *nf* : scuffle, skirmish

refrigerar *vt* **1** : refrigerate **2** CLIMATIZAR : air-condition — **refrigeración** *nf, pl* **-ciones 1** : refrigeration **2** AIRE ACONDICIONADO : air-conditioning — **refrigerador** *nmf Lat* : refrigerator — **refrigerio** *nm* : refreshments *pl*

refrito, -ta *adj* : refried — **refrito** *nm* : rehash

refuerzo *nm* : reinforcement

refugiar *vt* : shelter — **refugiarse** *vr* : take refuge — **refugiado, -da** *n* : refugee — **refugio** *nm* : refuge, shelter

refulgir {35} *vi* : shine brightly

refunfuñar *vi* : grumble, groan

refutar *vt* : refute

regadera *nf* **1** : watering can **2** *Lat* : shower head, shower

regalar *vt* : give (as a gift) — **regalarse** *vr* **~ con** : treat oneself to

regaliz *nm, pl* **-lices** : licorice

regalo *nm* **1** : gift, present **2** PLACER : pleasure, delight

regañadientes: **a ~** *adv phr* : reluctantly, unwillingly

regañar *vt* : scold — *vi* **1** QUEJARSE : grumble **2** *Spain* : quarrel — **regañon, -ñona** *adj, mpl* **-ñones** *fam* : grumpy, irritable

regar {49} *vt* **1** : irrigate, water **2** ESPARCIR : scatter

regatear *vt* **1** : haggle over **2** ESCATIMAR : skimp on — *vi* : bargain, haggle

regazo *nm* : lap (of a person)

regenerar *vt* : regenerate

regentar *vt* : run, manage

régimen *nm, pl* **regímenes 1** : regime **2** DIETA : diet **3 ~ de vida** : lifestyle

regimiento *nm* : regiment

regio, -gia *adj* : royal, regal

región *nf, pl* **-giones** : region, area — **regional** *adj* : regional

regir {28} *vt* **1** : rule **2** ADMINISTRAR : manage, run **3** DETERMINAR : govern, determine — *vi* : apply, be in force — **regirse** *vr* **~ por** : be guided by

registrar *vt* **1** : register **2** GRABAR : record, tape **3** : search (a house, etc.), frisk (a person) — **registrarse** *vr* **1** : register **2** : be recorded (of temperatures, etc.) — **registrador, -dora** *adj* **caja registradora** : cash register — **~** *n* : registrar — **registro** *nm* **1** : registration **2** : register (book) **3** : registry (office) **4** : range (of a voice, etc.) **5** INSPECCIÓN : search

regla *nf* **1** : rule, regulation **2** : ruler (for measuring) **3** MENSTRUACIÓN : period — **reglamentación** *nf, pl* **-ciones 1** : regulation **2** REGLAS : rules *pl* — **reglamentar** *vt* : regulate — **reglamentario, -ria** *adj* : regulation, official — **reglamento** *nm* : regulations *pl*, rules *pl*

regocijar *vt* : gladden, delight — **regocijarse** *vr* : rejoice — **regocijo** *nm* : delight, rejoicing

regodearse *vr* : be delighted — **regodeo** *nm* : delight

regordete *adj fam* : chubby

regresar *vi* : return, come back, go back — *vt Lat* : give back — **regresión** *nf, pl* **-siones** : regression — **regresivo, -va** *adj* : regressive — **regreso** *nm* **1** : return **2 estar de ~** : be back, be home again

reguero *nm* **1** : irrigation ditch **2** SEÑAL : trail, trace **3 correr como un ~ de pólvora** : spread like wildfire

regular *adj* **1** : regular **2** MEDIANO : medium, average **3 por lo ~** : in general — **~** *vt* : regulate, control — **regulación** *nf, pl* **-ciones** : regulation, control — **regularidad** *nf* : regularity — **regularizar** {21} *vt* : normalize, make regular

rehabilitar *vt* **1** : rehabilitate **2** : reinstate (s.o. in a position) **3** : renovate (a building, etc.) — **rehabilitación** *nf* **1** : rehabilitation **2** : reinstatement (in a position) **3** : renovation (of a building, etc.)

rehacer {40} *vt* **1** : redo **2** REPARAR : repair — **rehacerse** *vr* **1** : recover **2 ~ de** : get over

rehén *nm, pl* **-henes** : hostage

rehuir {41} *vt* : avoid, shun

rehusar {8} *v* : refuse

reimprimir *vt* : reprint — **reimpresión** *nf, pl* **-siones** : reprinting, reprint

reina *nf* : queen — **reinado** *nm* : reign — **reinante** *adj* : reigning — **reinar** *vi* **1** : reign **2** PREVALECER : prevail

reincidir *vi* : backslide, relapse

reino *nm* : kingdom, realm

reintegrar *vt* **1** : reinstate **2** : refund (money), reimburse (expenses, etc.) — **reintegrarse** *vr* **~ a** : return to — **reintegro** *nm* : reimbursement

reír {66} *vi* : laugh — *vt* : laugh at — **reírse** *vr* : laugh

reiterar *vt* : repeat, reiterate

reivindicar {72} *vt* **1** : claim **2** RESTAURAR : restore

reja *nf* : grille, grating — **rejilla** *nf* : grille, grate, screen

rejuvenecer {53} *vt* : rejuvenate — **rejuvenecerse** *vr* : be rejuvenated

relación *nf, pl* **-ciones 1** : relation, connection **2** COMUNICACIÓN : relationship, relations *pl* **3** RELATO : account **4** LISTA : list **5 con ~ a** *or* **en ~ a** : in relation to — **relacionar** *vt* : relate, connect — **relacionarse** *vr* **~ con** : be connected to, interact with

relajar *vt* : relax — **relajarse** *vr* : relax — **relajación** *nf, pl* **-ciones** : relaxation — **relajado, -da** *adj* **1** : relaxed **2** : dissolute, lax (in behavior)

relamerse *vr* : smack one's lips, lick its chops

relámpago *nm* : flash of lightning — **relampaguear** *vi* : flash

relatar *vt* : relate, tell

relativo, -va *adj* **1** : relative **2 en lo relativo a** : with regard to — **relatividad** *nf* : relativity

relato *nm* **1** : account, report **2** CUENTO : story, tale

releer {20} *vt* : reread

relegar {52} *vt* : relegate

relevante *adj* : outstanding, important
relevar *vt* **1** : relieve, take over from **2 ~ de** : exempt from — **relevo** *nm* **1** : relief, replacement **2 carrera de ~s** : relay race
relieve *nm* **1** : relief (in art, etc.) **2** IMPORTANCIA : prominence, importance **3 poner en ~** : emphasize
religión *nf, pl* **-giones** : religion — **religioso, -sa** *adj* : religious — **~** *n* : monk *m*, nun *f*
relinchar *vi* : neigh, whinny — **relincho** *nm* : neigh, whinny
reliquia *nf* **1** : relic **2 ~ de familia** : family heirloom
rellenar *vt* **1** : refill **2** : stuff, fill (in cooking) — **relleno, -na** *adj* : stuffed, filled — **relleno** *nm* : stuffing, filling
reloj *nm* **1** : clock **2** *or* **~ de pulsera** : wristwatch **3 ~ de arena** : hourglass **4 como un ~** : like clockwork
relucir {45} *vi* **1** : glitter, shine **2 sacar a ~** : bring up, mention — **reluciente** *adj* : brilliant, shining
relumbrar *vi* : shine brightly
remachar *vt* **1** : rivet **2** RECALAR : stress, drive home — **remache** *nm* : rivet
remanente *nm* : remainder, surplus
remanso *nm* : pool
remar *vi* : row
rematar *vt* **1** : conclude, finish up **2** MATAR : finish off **3** LIQUIDAR : sell off cheaply **4** *Lat* : auction — *vi* **1** : shoot (in sports) **2** TERMINAR : end — **rematado, -da** *adj* : utter, complete — **remate** *nm* **1** : shot (in sports) **2** FIN : end
remedar *vt* : imitate, mimic
remediar *vt* **1** : remedy, repair **2** : solve (a problem) **3** EVITAR : avoid — **remedio** *nm* **1** : remedy, cure **2** SOLUCIÓN : solution **3 sin ~** : hopeless
rememorar *vi* : recall
remendar {55} *vt* : mend
remesa *nf* **1** : remittance **2** : shipment (of merchandise)
remezón *nm, pl* **-zones** *Lat* : mild earthquake, tremor
remiendo *nm* : mend, patch
remilgado, -da *adj* **1** : prudish **2** AFECTADO : affected — **remilgo** *nm* : primness, affectation
reminiscencia *nf* : reminiscence
remisión *nf, pl* **-siones** : remission
remiso, -sa *adj* **1** : reluctant **2** NEGLIGENTE : remiss
remitir *vt* **1** : send, remit **2 ~ a** : refer to, direct to — *vi* : subside, let up — **remite** *nm* : return address — **remitente** *nmf* : sender (of a letter, etc.)
remo *nm* : paddle, oar
remodelar *vt* **1** : remodel **2** : restructure (an organization)
remojar *vt* : soak, steep — **remojo** *nm* **poner en ~** : soak
remolacha *nf* : beet
remolcar {72} *vt* : tow, tug — **remolcador** *nm* : tugboat
remolino *nm* **1** : whirlwind, whirlpool **2** : crowd (of people) **3** : cowlick (of hair)
remolque *nm* **1** : towing, tow **2** : trailer (vehicle)
remontar *vt* **1** : overcome **2** SUBIR : go up — **remontarse** *vr* **1** : soar **2 ~ a** : date from, go back to
rémora *nf* : hindrance
remorder {47} *vt* : trouble, worry — **remordimiento** *nm* : remorse
remoto, -ta *adj* : remote — **remotamente** *adv* : remotely, slightly
remover {47} *vt* **1** : stir **2** : move around, turn over (earth, embers, etc.) **3** REAVIVIR : bring up again **4** DESPEDIR : fire, dismiss
remunerar *vt* : remunerate
renacer {48} *vi* : be reborn, revive — **renacimiento** *nm* **1** : rebirth, revival **2 el Renacimiento** : the Renaissance
renacuajo *nm* : tadpole, pollywog
rencilla *nf* : quarrel
renco, -ca *adj Lat* : lame
rencor *nm* **1** : rancor, hostility **2 guardar ~** : hold a grudge — **rencoroso, -sa** *adj* : resentful
rendición *nf, pl* **-ciones** : surrender — **rendido, -da** *adj* **1** : submissive **2** AGOTADO : exhausted
rendija *nf* : crack, split
rendir {54} *vt* **1** : render, give **2** PRODUCIR : yield, produce **3** CANSAR : exhaust — *vi* : make progress, go a long way — **rendirse** *vr* : surrender, give up — **rendimiento** *nm* **1** : performance **2** : yield, return (in finance, etc.)
renegar {49} *vt* : deny — *vi* **1** QUEJARSE : grumble **2 ~ de** ABJURAR : renounce, disown — **renegado, -da** *n* : renegade
renglón *nm, pl* **-glones 1** : line (of writing) **2** *Lat* : line (of products)
reno *nm* : reindeer
renombre *nm* : renown — **renombrado, -da** *adj* : famous, renowned
renovar {19} *vt* **1** : renew, restore **2** : renovate (a building, etc.) — **renovación** *nf, pl* **-ciones 1** : renewal **2** : renovation (of a building, etc.)
renquear *vi* : limp, hobble
rentar *vt* **1** : produce, yield **2** *Lat* : rent —
renta *nf* **1** : income **2** ALQUILER : rent **3 impuesto sobre la ~** : income tax — **rentable** *adj* : profitable
renunciar *vi* **1** : resign **2 ~ a** : renounce, relinquish — **renuncia** *nf* **1** : renunciation **2** DIMISIÓN : resignation
reñir {67} *vi* **~ con** : argue with, fall out with — *vt* **1** : scold **2** DISPUTAR : fight — **reñido, -da** *adj* **1** : hard-fought **2 ~ con** : on bad terms with
reo, rea *n* **1** : accused, defendant **2** CULPABLE : culprit
reojo *nm* **de ~** : out of the corner of one's eye
reorganizar {21} *vt* : reorganize
repantigarse {52} *vr* : sprawl out
reparar *vt* **1** : repair, fix **2** : make amends for (an offense, etc.) — *vi* **1 ~ en** ADVERTIR : take notice of **2 ~ en** CONSIDERAR : consider — **reparación** *nf, pl* **-ciones 1** : reparation, amends **2** ARREGLO : repair — **reparo** *nm* **1** : reservation, objection **2 poner ~s a** : object to
repartir *vt* **1** : allocate **2** DISTRIBUIR : distribute **3** ESPARCIR : spread — **repartición** *nf, pl* **-ciones** : distribution — **repartidor, -dora** *n* : delivery person, distributor — **reparto** *nm* **1** : allocation **2** DISTRIBUCIÓN : delivery **3** : cast (of characters)
repasar *vt* **1** : review, go over **2** ZURCIR : mend — **repaso** *nm* **1** : review **2** : mending (of clothes)
repeler *vt* **1** : repel **2** REPUGNAR : disgust — **repelente** *adj* : repellent, repulsive
repente *nm* **1** : fit, outburst **2 de ~** : suddenly — **repentino, -na** *adj* : sudden
repercutir *vi* **1** : reverberate **2 ~ en** : have repercussions on — **repercusión** *nf, pl* **-siones** : repercussion
repertorio *nm* : repertoire
repetir {54} *vt* **1** : repeat **2** : have a second helping of (food) — **repetirse** *vr* **1** : repeat oneself **2** : recur (of an event, etc.) — **repetición** *nf, pl* **-ciones 1** : repetition **2** : rerun, repeat (of a program, etc.) — **repetido, -da** *adj* **1** : repeated **2 repetidas veces** : repeatedly, time and again — **repetitivo, -va** *adj* : repetitive, repetitious
repicar {72} *vt* : ring — *vi* : ring out, peal — **repique** *nm* : ringing, pealing
repisa *nf* **1** : shelf, ledge **2 ~ de ventana** : windowsill
replegar {49} *vt* : fold — **replegarse** *vr* : retreat, withdraw
repleto, -ta *adj* **1** : replete, full **2 ~ de** : packed with
replicar {72} *vt* : reply, retort — *vi* : answer back — **réplica** *nf* **1** RESPUESTA : reply **2** COPIA : replica, reproduction
repliegue *nm* **1** : fold **2** : (military) withdrawal
repollo *nm* : cabbage
reponer {60} *vt* **1** : replace **2** REPLICAR : reply — **reponerse** *vr* : recover
reportar *vt* **1** : yield, bring **2** *Lat* : report — **reportaje** *nm* : article, (news) report — **reporte** *nm Lat* : report — **reportero, -ra** *n* : reporter
reposar *vi* **1** DESCANSAR : rest **2** : stand, settle (of liquids, dough, etc.) — **reposado, -da** *adj* : calm, relaxed — **reposición** *nf, pl* **-ciones 1** : replacement **2** : rerun, repeat (of a program, etc.) — **reposo** *nm* : rest
repostar *vi* **1** : stock up on **2** : refuel (an airplane, etc.) — *vi* : fill up, refuel
reprender *vt* : reprimand, scold — **reprensible** *adj* : reprehensible
represalia *nf* **1** : reprisal **2 tomar ~s** : retaliate
represar *vt* : dam
representar *vt* **1** : represent **2** : perform (a play, etc.) **3** APARENTAR : look, appear as — **representación** *nf, pl* **-ciones 1** : representation **2** : performance (of a play, etc.) **3 en ~ de** : on behalf of — **representante** *nmf* **1** : representative **2** ACTOR : performer — **representativo, -va** *adj* : representative
represión *nf, pl* **-siones** : repression
reprimenda *nf* : reprimand
reprimir *vt* **1** : repress **2** : suppress (a rebellion, etc.)
reprobar {19} *vt* **1** : reprove, condemn **2** *Lat* : fail (an exam, etc.)
reprochar *vt* : reproach — **reprocharse** *vr* : reproach oneself — **reproche** *nm* : reproach
reproducir {61} *vt* : reproduce — **reproducirse** *vr* **1** : breed, reproduce **2** : recur (of an event, etc.) — **reproducción** *nf, pl* **-ciones** : reproduction — **reproductor, -tora** *adj* : reproductive
reptil *nm* : reptile
república *nf* : republic — **republicano, -na** *adj & n* : republican
repudiar *vt* : repudiate
repuesto *nm* : spare (auto) part
repugnar *vt* : disgust — **repugnancia** *nf* : disgust — **repugnante** *adj* : disgusting
repujar *vt* : emboss
repulsivo, -va *adj* : repulsive
reputar *vt* : consider, deem — **reputación** *nf, pl* **-ciones** : reputation
requerir {76} *vt* **1** : require **2** : summon, send for (a person)
requesón *nm, pl* **-sones** : cottage cheese
réquiem *nm* : requiem
requisito *nm* **1** : requirement **2 ~ previo** : prerequisite
res *nf* **1** : beast, animal **2** *Lat or* **carne de ~** : beef
resabio *nm* **1** VICIO : bad habit, vice **2** DEJO : aftertaste
resaca *nf* **1** : undertow **2 tener ~** : have a hangover
resaltar *vi* **1** : stand out **2 hacer ~** : bring out, highlight — *vt* : emphasize
resarcir {83} *vt* : compensate, repay — **resarcirse** *vr* **~ de** : make up for
resbalar *vi* **1** : slip, slide **2** : skid (of an automobile) — **resbalarse** *vr* : slip, skid — **resbaladizo, -za** *adj* : slippery — **resbalón** *nm, pl* **-lones** : slip — **resbaloso, -sa** *adj Lat* : slippery
rescatar *vt* **1** : rescue, ransom **2** RECUPERAR : recover, get back — **rescate** *nm* **1** : rescue **2** : ransom (money) **3** RECUPERACIÓN : recovery
rescindir *vt* : cancel — **rescisión** *nf, pl* **-siones** : cancellation
rescoldo *nm* : embers *pl*
resecar {72} *vt* : dry (out) — **resecarse** *vr* : dry up — **reseco, -ca** *adj* : dry, dried-up
resentirse {76} *vr* **1** : suffer, be weakened **2** OFENDERSE : be offended **3 ~ de** : feel the effects of — **resentido, -da** *adj* : resentful — **resentimiento** *nm* : resentment
reseñar *vt* **1** : review **2** DESCRIBIR : describe — **reseña** *nf* **1** : review, report **2** DESCRIPCIÓN : description
reservar *vt* **1** : reserve **2** GUARDAR : keep, save — **reservarse** *vr* **1** : save oneself **2** : keep for oneself — **reserva** *nf* **1** : reservation **2** PROVISIÓN : reserve **3 de ~** : spare, in reserve — **reservación** *nf, pl* **-ciones** : reservation — **reservado, -da** *adj* **1** : reserved **2** : confidential (of a document, etc.)
resfriar {85} *vt* : cool — **resfriarse** *vr* **1** : cool off **2** CONSTIPARSE : catch a cold — **resfriado** *nm* CATARRO : cold — **resfrío** *nm Lat* : cold
resguardar *vt* : protect — **resguardarse** *vr* : protect oneself — **resguardo** *nm* **1** : protection **2** RECIBO : receipt
residir *vi* **1** : reside, live **2 ~ en** : lie in — **residencia** *nf* **1** : residence **2** *or* **~ universitaria** : dormitory — **residencial** *adj* : residential — **residente** *adj & nmf* : resident
residuo *nm* **1** : residue **2 ~s** *nmpl* : waste — **residual** *adj* : residual
resignar *vt* : resign — **resignarse** *vr* **~ a** : resign oneself to — **resignación** *nf, pl* **-ciones** : resignation
resina *nf* **1** : resin **2 ~ epoxídica** : epoxy
resistir *vt* **1** AGUANTAR : stand, bear **2** : withstand (temptation, etc.) — *vi* : resist — **resistirse** *vr* **~ a** : be resistant to — **resistencia** *nf* **1** : resistance **2** AGUANTE : endurance, stamina — **resistente** *adj* : resistant, strong, tough
resma *nf* : ream
resollar {19} *vi* : breathe heavily, pant
resolver {89} *vt* **1** : resolve **2** DECIDIR : decide — **resolverse** *vr* : make up one's mind — **resolución** *nf, pl* **-ciones 1** : resolution **2** DECISIÓN : decision **3** FIRMEZA : determination, resolve
resonar {19} *vi* : resound — **resonancia** *nf* **1** : resonance **2** CONSECUENCIAS : impact, repercussions *pl* — **resonante** *adj* : resonant, resounding
resoplar *vi* **1** : puff, pant **2** : snort (with annoyance)
resorte *nm* **1** MUELLE : spring **2 tocar ~s** : pull strings
respaldar *vt* : back, endorse — **respaldarse** *vr* : lean back — **respaldo** *nm* **1** : back (of a chair, etc.) **2** APOYO : support, backing
respectar *vt* : concern, relate to — **respectivo, -va** *adj* : respective — **respecto** *nm* **1 al ~** : in this respect **2 ~ a** : in regard to, concerning
respetar *vt* : respect — **respetable** *adj* : respectable — **respeto** *nm* **1** : respect **2 presentar sus ~s** : pay one's respects — **respetuoso, -sa** *adj* : respectful
respingo *nm* : start, jump
respirar *v* : breathe — **respiración** *nf, pl* **-ciones** : respiration, breathing — **respiratorio, -ria** *adj* : respiratory — **respiro** *nm* **1** : breath **2** DESCANSO : respite, break
resplandecer {53} *vi* : shine — **resplandeciente** *adj* : shining, gleaming — **resplandor** *nm* **1** : brilliance, gleam **2** : flash (of lightning, etc.)
responder *vt* : answer, reply — *vi* **1** : answer **2** REPLICAR : answer back **3 ~ a** : respond to **4 ~ de** : answer for (something)
responsable *adj* : responsible — **responsabilidad** *nf* : responsibility
respuesta *nf* **1** : answer, reply **2** REACCIÓN : response
resquebrajar *vt* : split, crack — **resquebrajarse** *vr* : crack
resquicio *nm* **1** : crack, crevice **2** VESTIGIO : trace, glimmer
resta *nf* : subtraction
restablecer {53} *vt* : reestablish, restore — **restablecerse** *vr* : recover — **restablecimiento** *nm* : restoration, recovery
restallar *vi* : crack, crackle
restar *vt* **1** : deduct, subtract **2** DISMINUIR : minimize — *vi* : be left — **restante** *adj* **1** : remaining **2 lo ~** : the rest
restauración *nf, pl* **-ciones** : restoration
restaurante *nm* : restaurant
restaurar *vt* : restore
restituir {41} *vt* : return, restore — **restitución** *nf, pl* **-ciones** : restitution
resto *nm* **1** : rest, remainder **2 ~s** *nmpl* : leftovers **3** *or* **~s mortales** : mortal remains
restregar {49} *vt* : rub, scrub — **restregarse** *vr* : rub
restringir {35} *vt* : restrict, limit — **restricción** *nf, pl* **-ciones** : restriction, limitation — **restrictivo, -va** *adj* : restrictive
resucitar *vt* : resuscitate, revive — *vi* : come back to life
resuelto, -ta *adj* : determined, resolved
resuello *nm* : heavy breathing, panting
resultar *vi* **1** : succeed, work out **2** SALIR : turn out (to be) **3 ~ de** : be the result of **4 ~ en** : result in — **resultado** *nm* : result, outcome
resumir *v* : summarize, sum up — **resumen** *nm, pl* **-súmenes 1** : summary **2 en ~** : in short
resurgir {35} *vi* : reappear, revive — **resurgimiento** *nm* : resurgence — **resurrección** *nf, pl* **-ciones** : resurrection
retahíla *nf* : string, series
retal *nm* : remnant
retardar *vt* **1** RETRASAR : delay **2** POSPONER : postpone
retazo *nm* **1** : remnant, scrap **2** : fragment (of a text, etc.)
retener {80} *vt* **1** : retain, keep **2** : withhold (funds, etc.) **3** DETENER : detain — **retención** *nf, pl* **-ciones 1** : retention **2** : deduction, withholding (of funds)
reticente *adj* : reluctant — **reticencia** *nf* : reluctance
retina *nf* : retina
retintín *nm, pl* **-tines 1** : tinkling, jingle **2 con ~** : sarcastically
retirar *vt* **1** : remove, take away **2** : withdraw (funds, statements, etc.) — **retirarse** *vr* **1** : retreat, withdraw **2** JUBILARSE : retire — **retirada** *nf* **1** : withdrawal **2 batirse en ~** : beat a retreat — **retirado, -da** *adj* **1** : remote, secluded **2** JUBILADO : retired — **retiro** *nm* **1** : retreat **2** JUBILACIÓN : retirement **3** *Lat* : withdrawal
reto *nm* : challenge, dare
retocar {72} *vt* : touch up
retoño *nm* : sprout, shoot
retoque *nm* **1** : retouching **2 el último ~** : the finishing touch
retorcer {14} *vt* **1** : twist, contort **2** : wring out (clothes, etc.) — **retorcerse** *vr* **1** : get twisted up **2** : squirm, writhe (in pain) — **retorcijón** *nm, pl* **-jones** : cramp, spasm — **retorcimiento** *nm* : twisting, wringing out
retórica *nf* : rhetoric — **retórico, -ca** *adj* : rhetorical
retornar *v* : return — **retorno** *nm* : return
retozar {21} *vi* : frolic, romp — **retozón, -zona** *adj* : playful, frisky
retractarse *vr* **1** : withdraw, back down **2 ~ de** : take back, retract
retraer {81} *vt* : retract — **retraerse** *vr* : withdraw — **retraído, -da** *adj* : withdrawn, shy
retrasar *vt* **1** : delay, hold up **2** APLAZAR : postpone **3** : set back (a clock) — **retrasarse** *vr* **1** : be late **2** : fall behind (in work, etc.) — **retrasado, -da** *adj* **1** : retarded **2** : in arrears (of payments) **3** : backward (of a country) **4** : slow (of a clock) — **retraso** *nm* **1** : delay **2** SUBDESARROLLO : backwardness **3 ~ mental** : mental retardation
retratar *vt* **1** : portray **2** FOTOGRAFIAR : photograph **3** DIBUJAR : paint a portrait of — **retrato** *nm* **1** : portrayal **2** DIBUJO : portrait **3** FOTOGRAFÍA : photograph
retrete *nm* : restroom, toilet
retribuir {41} *vt* **1** : pay **2** RECOMPENSAR : reward — **retribución** *nf, pl* **-ciones 1** : payment **2** RECOMPENSA : reward
retroactivo, -va *adj* : retroactive
retroceder *vi* **1** : go back, turn back **2** CEDER : back down — **retroceso** *nm* **1** : backward movement **2** : backing down
retrógrado, -da *adj & nmf* : reactionary
retrospectiva *nf* : hindsight — **retrospectivo, -va** *adj* : retrospective
retrovisor *nm* : rearview mirror
retumbar *vi* : resound, reverberate, rumble
reumatismo *nm* : rheumatism
reunir {68} *vt* **1** : unite, join **2** TENER : have, possess **3** RECOGER : gather, collect — **reunirse** *vr* : meet, gather — **reunión** *nf, pl* **-niones 1** : meeting **2** : (social) gathering, reunion
revalidar *vt* : confirm, ratify
revancha *nf* **1** : revenge **2** : rematch (in sports)
revelar *vt* **1** : reveal, disclose **2** : develop (film) — **revelación** *nf, pl* **-ciones** : revelation — **revelado** *nm* : developing (of film) — **revelador, -dora** *adj* : revealing

reventar {55} *v* : burst, blow up — **reventarse** *vr* : burst — **reventón** *nm, pl* **-tones** : blowout, flat tire
reverberar *vi* : reverberate — **reverberación** *nf, pl* **-ciones** : reverberation
reverenciar *vt* : revere — **reverencia** *nf* **1** : bow, curtsy **2** VENERACIÓN : reverence — **reverendo, -da** *adj & nmf* : reverend — **reverente** *adj* : reverent
reversa *nf Lat* : reverse (gear)
reverso *nm* **1** : back, reverse **2 el ~ de la medalla** : the complete opposite — **reversible** *adj* : reversible
revertir {76} *vi* **1** : revert **2 ~ en** : result in
revés *nm, pl* **-veses 1** : back, wrong side **2** CONTRATIEMPO : setback **3** BOFETADA : slap **4** : backhand (in sports) **5 al ~** : the other way around, upside down, inside out
revestir {54} *vt* **1** : coat, cover **2** ASUMIR : take on, assume — **revestimiento** *nm* : covering, coating
revisar *vt* **1** : examine, inspect **2** : check over, overhaul (machinery, etc.) **3** MODIFICAR : revise — **revisión** *nf, pl* **-siones 1** : revision **2** INSPECCIÓN : inspection, check — **revisor, -sora** *n* : inspector
revistar *vt* : review, inspect (troops, etc.) — **revista** *nf* **1** : magazine, journal **2** : revue (in theater) **3 pasar ~** : review, inspect
revivir *vi* : revive, come alive again — *vt* : relive
revocar {72} *vt* : revoke
revolcar {82} *vt* : knock over, knock down — **revolcarse** *vr* : roll around
revolotear *vi* : flutter, flit — **revoloteo** *nm* : fluttering, flitting
revoltijo *nm* : mess, jumble
revoltoso, -sa *adj* : rebellious
revolución *nf, pl* **-ciones** : revolution — **revolucionar** *vt* : revolutionize — **revolucionario, -ria** *adj & n* : revolutionary
revolver {89} *vt* **1** : mix, stir **2** : upset (one's stomach) **3** DESORGANIZAR : mess up — **revolverse** *vr* **1** : toss and turn **2** VOLVERSE : turn around
revólver *nm* : revolver
revuelo *nm* : commotion
revuelta *nf* : uprising, revolt — **revuelto, -ta** *adj* **1** : choppy, rough **2** DESORDENADO : messed up **3 huevos revueltos** : scrambled eggs
rey *nm* : king
reyerta *nf* : brawl, fight
rezagarse {52} *vr* : fall behind, lag
rezar {21} *vi* **1** : pray **2** DECIR : say — *vt* : say, recite — **rezo** *nm* : prayer
rezongar {52} *vi* : gripe, grumble
rezumar *v* : ooze
ría *nf* : estuary
riachuelo *nm* : brook, stream
riada *nf* : flood
ribera *nf* : bank, shore
ribetear *vt* : border, trim — **ribete** *nm* **1** : border, trim **2** : embellishment
rico, -ca *adj* **1** : rich, wealthy **2** ABUNDANTE : abundant **3** SABROSO : rich, tasty — **~** *n* : rich person
ridiculizar {21} *vt* : ridicule — **ridículo, -la** *adj* : ridiculous — **ridículo** *nm* **1 hacer el ~** : make a fool of oneself **2 poner en ~** : ridicule
riego *nm* : irrigation
riel *nm* : rail
rienda *nf* **1** : rein **2 dar ~ suelta a** : give free rein to
riesgo *nm* : risk
rifa *nf* : raffle — **rifar** *vt* : raffle (off) — **rifarse** *vr fam* : fight over
rifle *nm* : rifle
rígido, -da *adj* **1** : rigid, stiff **2** SEVERO : harsh, strict — **rigidez** *nf, pl* **-deces 1** : rigidity, stiffness **2** SEVERIDAD : harshness, strictness
rigor *nm* **1** : rigor, harshness **2** EXACTITUD : precision **3 de ~** : essential, obligatory — **riguroso, -sa** *adj* : rigorous
rima *nf* **1** : rhyme **2 ~s** *nfpl* : verse, poetry — **rimar** *vi* : rhyme
rimbombante *adj* : showy, pompous
rímel *nm* : mascara
rincón *nm, pl* **-cones** : corner, nook
rinoceronte *nm* : rhinoceros
riña *nf* **1** : fight, brawl **2** DISPUTA : dispute, quarrel
riñón *nm, pl* **-ñones** : kidney
río *nm* **1** : river **2** TORRENTE : torrent, stream
riqueza *nf* **1** : wealth **2** ABUNDANCIA : richness **3 ~s naturales** : natural resources
risa *nf* **1** : laughter, laugh **2 dar ~ a algn** : make s.o. laugh **3 morirse de la ~** *fam* : die laughing
risco *nm* : crag, cliff
risible *adj* : laughable
ristra *nf* : string, series
risueño, -ña *adj* : cheerful, smiling
ritmo *nm* **1** : rhythm **2** VELOCIDAD : pace, speed — **rítmico, -ca** *adj* : rhythmical
rito *nm* : rite, ritual — **ritual** *adj & nm* : ritual
rival *adj & nmf* : rival — **rivalidad** *nf* : rivalry, competition — **rivalizar** {21} *vi* **~ con** : rival, compete with
rizar {21} *vt* **1** : curl **2** : ripple (a surface) — **rizarse** *vr* : curl — **rizado, -da** *adj* **1** : curly **2** : choppy (of water) — **rizo** *nm* **1** : curl **2** : ripple (in water) **3** : loop (in aviation)
róbalo *nm* : bass (fish)
robar *vt* **1** : steal **2** : burglarize (a house, etc.) **3** SECUESTRAR : kidnap — **robo** *nm* : robbery, theft
roble *nm* : oak
robot *nm, pl* **-bots** : robot — **robótica** *nf* : robotics
robustecer {53} *vt* : make stronger, strengthen — **robusto, -ta** *adj* : robust, sturdy
roca *nf* : rock, boulder
roce *nm* **1** : rubbing, chafing **2** RASGUÑO : graze, scratch **3 tener un ~ con** : have a brush with
rociar {85} *vt* : spray, sprinkle — **rocío** *nm* : dew
rocoso, -sa *adj* : rocky
rodaja *nf* : slice
rodar {19} *vi* **1** : roll, roll down, roll along **2** GIRAR : turn, go around **3** : travel (of a vehicle) **4** : film (of movies, etc.) — *vt* **1** : film, shoot **2** : break in (a vehicle) — **rodaje** *nm* **1** : filming, shooting **2** : breaking in (of a vehicle)
rodear *vt* **1** : surround, encircle **2** *Lat* : round up (cattle) — **rodearse** *vr* **~ de** : surround oneself with — **rodeo** *nm* **1** : rodeo, roundup **2** DESVÍO : detour **3 andar con ~s** : beat around the bush
rodilla *nf* : knee
rodillo *nm* **1** : roller **2** : rolling pin (for pastry)
roer {69} *vt* **1** : gnaw **2** ATORMENTAR : eat away at, torment — **roedor** *nm* : rodent
rogar {16} *vt* : beg, request — *vi* : pray
rojo, -ja *adj* **1** : red **2 ponerse ~** : blush — **rojo** *nm* : red — **rojez** *nf* : redness — **rojizo, -za** *adj* : reddish
rollizo, -za *adj* : plump, chubby
rollo *nm* **1** : roll, coil **2** *fam* : boring speech, lecture
romance *nm* **1** : romance **2** : Romance (language)
romano, -na *adj & n* : Roman
romántico, -ca *adj* : romantic — **romanticismo** *nm* : romanticism
romería *nf* : pilgrimage, procession
romero *nm* : rosemary
romo, -ma *adj* : blunt, dull
rompecabezas *nms & pl* : puzzle
romper {70} *vt* **1** : break **2** RASGAR : rip, tear **3** : break off (relations), break (a contract) — *vi* **1** : break (of the day, waves, etc.) **2 ~ a** : begin to, burst out with **3 ~ con** : break off with — **romperse** *vr* : break
ron *nm* : rum
roncar {72} *vi* : snore — **ronco, -ca** *adj* : hoarse
ronda *nf* **1** : rounds *pl*, patrol **2** : round (of drinks, etc.) — **rondar** *vt* **1** : patrol **2** : hang around (a place) **3** : be approximately (an age, a number, etc.) — *vi* **1** : be on patrol **2** MERODEAR : prowl about
ronquera *nf* : hoarseness
ronquido *nm* : snore
ronronear *vi* : purr — **ronroneo** *nm* : purr, purring
ronzar {21} *vt* : munch, crunch
roña *nf* **1** : mange **2** SUCIEDAD : dirt, filth — **roñoso, -sa** *adj* **1** : mangy **2** SUCIO : dirty **3** *fam* : stingy
ropa *nf* **1** : clothes *pl*, clothing **2 ~ interior** : underwear — **ropaje** *nm* : robes *pl*, regalia — **ropero** *nm* : wardrobe, closet
rosa *nf* : rose (flower) — **~** *adj* : rose-colored — **~** *nm* : rose (color) — **rosado, -da** *adj* **1** : pink **2 vino rosado** : rosé — **rosado** *nm* : pink (color) — **rosal** *nm* : rosebush
rosario *nm* : rosary
rosbif *nm* : roast beef
rosca *nf* **1** : thread (of a screw) **2** ESPIRAL : ring, coil
roseta *nf* : rosette
rosquilla *nf* : doughnut
rostro *nm* : face
rotación *nf, pl* **-ciones** : rotation — **rotativo, -va** *adj* : rotary, revolving
roto, -ta *adj* : broken, torn
rotonda *nf* : traffic circle, rotary
rótula *nf* : kneecap
rótulo *nm* **1** : heading, title **2** ETIQUETA : label, sign
rotundo, -da *adj* : categorical, absolute
rotura *nf* : break, tear, fracture
rozar {21} *vt* **1** : graze, touch lightly **2** APROXIMARSE DE : touch on, border on — *vi* : scrape, rub — **rozarse** *vr* **1** : rub, chafe **2 ~ con** *fam* : rub elbows with — **rozadura** *nf* : scratch
rubí *nm, pl* **rubíes** : ruby
rubicundo, -da *adj* : ruddy
rubio, -bia *adj & n* : blond
rubor *nm* : flush, blush — **ruborizarse** {21} *vr* : blush
rubrica *nf* **1** : flourish (in writing) **2** TÍTULO : title, heading
rudeza *nf* : roughness, coarseness
rudimentos *nmpl* : rudiments, basics — **rudimentario, -ria** *adj* : rudimentary
rudo, -da *adj* **1** : rough, harsh **2** GROSERO : coarse, unpolished
rueda *nf* **1** : wheel **2** CORRO : circle, ring **3** RODAJA : (round) slice **4 ir sobre ~s** : go smoothly — **ruedo** *nm* : bullring
ruego *nm* : request
rugir {35} *vi* : roar — **rugido** *nm* : roar
rugoso, -sa *adj* **1** : rough **2** ARRUGADO : wrinkled
ruibarbo *nm* : rhubarb
ruido *nm* : noise — **ruidoso, -sa** *adj* : loud, noisy
ruina *nf* **1** : ruin, destruction **2** COLAPSO : collapse **3 ~s** *nfpl* : ruins, remains — **ruinoso, -sa** *adj* : run-down, dilapidated
ruiseñor *nm* : nightingale
ruleta *nf* : roulette
rulo *nm* : curler, roller
rumano, -na *adj* : Romanian, Rumanian
rumba *nf* : rumba
rumbo *nm* **1** : direction, course **2** ESPLENDIDEZ : lavishness **3 con ~ a** : bound for, heading for **4 perder el ~** : go off course
rumiar *vt* : mull over — *vi* : chew the cud — **rumiante** *adj & nm* : ruminant
rumor *nm* **1** : rumor **2** MURMULLO : murmur — **rumorearse** *or* **rumorarse** *vr* : be rumored — **rumoroso, -sa** *adj* : murmuring, babbling
ruptura *nf* **1** : break, rupture **2** : breach (of a contract) **3** : breaking off (of relations)
rural *adj* : rural
ruso, -sa *adj* : Russian — **ruso** *nm* : Russian (language)
rústico, -ca *adj* **1** : rural, rustic **2 en rústica** : in paperback
ruta *nf* : route
rutina *nf* : routine — **rutinario, -ria** *adj* : routine

S

s *nf* : s, 20th letter of the Spanish alphabet
sábado *nm* : Saturday
sábana *nf* : sheet
sabandija *nf* : bug
saber {71} *vt* **1** : know **2** SER CAPAZ DE : know how to, be able to **3** ENTERARSE : learn, find out **4 a ~** : namely — *vi* **1** : taste **2 ~ de** : know about — **~** *nm* : knowledge — **sabelotodo** *nmf fam* : know-it-all — **sabido, -da** *adj* : well-known — **sabiduría** *nf* **1** : wisdom **2** CONOCIMIENTO : learning, knowledge — **sabiendas**: **a ~** *adv phr* : knowingly — **sabio, -bia** *adj* **1** : learned **2** PRUDENTE : wise, sensible
sabor *nm* : flavor, taste — **saborear** *vt* : savor
sabotaje *nm* : sabotage — **saboteador, -dora** *n* : saboteur — **sabotear** *vt* : sabotage
sabroso, -sa *adj* : delicious, tasty
sabueso *nm* **1** : bloodhound **2** *fam* : sleuth
sacacorchos *nms & pl* : corkscrew
sacapuntas *nms & pl* : pencil sharpener
sacar {72} *vt* **1** : take out **2** OBTENER : get, obtain **3** EXTRAER : extract, withdraw **4** : bring out (a book, a product, etc.) **5** : take (photos), make (copies) **6** QUITAR : remove **7 ~ adelante** : bring up (children), carry out (a project, etc.) **8 ~ la lengua** : stick out one's tongue — *vi* : serve (in sports)
sacarina *nf* : saccharin
sacerdote, -tisa *n* : priest *m*, priestess *f* — **sacerdocio** *nm* : priesthood — **sacerdotal** *adj* : priestly
saciar *vt* : satisfy
saco *nm* **1** : bag, sack **2** : sac (in anatomy) **3** *Lat* : jacket
sacramento *nm* : sacrament — **sacramental** *adj* : sacramental
sacrificar {72} *vt* : sacrifice — **sacrificarse** *vr* : sacrifice oneself — **sacrificio** *nm* : sacrifice
sacrilegio *nm* : sacrilege — **sacrílego, -ga** *adj* : sacrilegious
sacro, -cra *adj* : sacred — **sacrosanto, -ta** *adj* : sacrosanct
sacudir *vt* **1** : shake **2** GOLPEAR : beat **3** CONMOVER : shake up, shock — **sacudirse** *vr* : shake off — **sacudida** *nf* **1** : shaking **2** : jolt (of a train, etc.), tremor (of an earthquake) **3** : (emotional) shock
sádico, -ca *adj* : sadistic — **~** *n* : sadist — **sadismo** *nm* : sadism
saeta *nf* : arrow
safari *nm* : safari
sagaz *adj, pl* **-gaces** : shrewd, sagacious — **sagacidad** *nf* : shrewdness
sagrado, -da *adj* : sacred, holy
sal *nf* : salt
sala *nf* **1** : room, hall **2** : living room (of a house) **3 ~ de espera** : waiting room
salar *vt* : salt — **salado, -da** *adj* **1** : salty **2** GRACIOSO : witty **3 agua salada** : salt water
salario *nm* : salary, wage
salchicha *nf* : sausage — **salchichón** *nf, pl* **-chones** : salami-like cold cut
saldar *vt* **1** : settle, pay off **2** VENDER : sell off — **saldo** *nm* **1** : balance (of an account) **2 ~s** *nmpl* : remainders, sale items
salero *nm* : saltshaker
salir {73} *vi* **1** : go out, come out **2** PARTIR : leave **3** APARECER : appear **4** RESULTAR : turn out **5** : rise (of the sun) **6 ~ adelante** : get by **7 ~ con** : go out with, date **8 ~ de** : come from — **salirse** *vr* **1** : leave **2** ESCAPARSE : leak out, escape **3** SOLTARSE : come off **4 ~ con la suya** : get one's own way — **salida** *nf* **1** : exit **2** : (action of) leaving, departure **3** SOLUCIÓN : way out **4** : leak (of gas, liquid, etc.) **5** OCURRENCIA : witty remark **6 ~ de emergencia** : emergency exit **7 ~ del sol** : sunrise — **saliente** *adj* **1** : departing, outgoing **2** DESTACADO : outstanding
saliva *nf* : saliva
salmo *nm* : psalm
salmón *nm, pl* **-mones** : salmon
salmuera *nf* : brine
salón *nm, pl* **-lones 1** : lounge, sitting room **2 ~ de belleza** : beauty salon **3 ~ de clase** : classroom
salpicar {72} *vt* **1** : splash, spatter **2 ~ de** : pepper with — **salpicadera** *nf Lat* : fender — **salpicadura** *nf* : splash
salsa *nf* **1** : sauce **2** : (meat) gravy **3** : salsa (music)
saltamontes *nms & pl* : grasshopper
saltar *vi* **1** : jump, leap **2** REBOTAR : bounce **3** : come off (of a button, etc.) **4** ROMPERSE : shatter **5** ESTALLAR : explode, blow up — *vt* **1** : jump (over) **2** OMITIR : skip, miss — **saltarse** *vr* **1** : come off **2** OMITIR : skip, miss
saltear *vt* : sauté
saltimbanqui *nmf* : acrobat
salto *nm* **1** : jump, leap **2** : dive (into water) **3 ~ de agua** : waterfall — **saltón, -tona** *adj, mpl* **-tones** : bulging, protruding
salud *nf* **1** : health **2 ¡salud!** : here's to your health! **3 ¡salud!** *Lat* : bless you! (when someone sneezes) — **saludable** *adj* : healthy
saludar *vt* **1** : greet, say hello to **2** : salute (in the military) — **saludo** *nm* **1** : greeting **2** : (military) salute **3 ~s** : best wishes, regards
salva *nf* **~ de aplausos** : round of applause
salvación *nf, pl* **-ciones** : salvation
salvado *nm* : bran
salvador, -dora *n* : savior, rescuer
salvadoreño, -ña *adj* : (El) Salvadoran
salvaguardar *vt* : safeguard
salvaje *adj* **1** : wild **2** PRIMITIVO : savage, primitive — **~** *nmf* : savage
salvar *vt* **1** : save, rescue **2** RECORRER : cover, travel **3** SUPERAR : overcome — **salvarse** *vr* : save oneself — **salvavidas** *nms & pl* **1** : life preserver **2 bote ~** : lifeboat
salvia *nf* : sage (plant)
salvo, -va *adj* : safe — **salvo** *prep* **1** : except (for), save **2 ~ que** : unless
samba *nf* : samba
San → **santo**
sanar *vt* : heal, cure — *vi* : recover — **sanatorio** *nm* **1** : sanatorium **2** HOSPITAL : clinic, hospital
sanción *nf, pl* **-ciones** : sanction — **sancionar** *vt* : sanction
sandalia *nf* : sandal
sándalo *nm* : sandalwood
sandía *nf* : watermelon
sandwich ['sandwitʃ, 'saŋgwitʃ] *nm, pl* **-wiches** [-dwitʃes, -gwi-] : sandwich
saneamiento *nm* : sanitation
sangrar *vt* **1** : bleed **2** : indent (a paragraph) — *vi* : bleed — **sangrante** *adj* : bleeding — **sangre** *nf* **1** : blood **2 a ~ fría** : in cold blood — **sangriento, -ta** *adj* : bloody
sanguijuela *nf* : leech
sanguinario, -ria *adj* : bloodthirsty — **sanguíneo, -nea** *adj* : blood
sano, -na *adj* **1** : healthy **2** : (morally) wholesome **3** ENTERO : intact **4 sano y salvo** : safe and sound — **sanidad** *nf* **1** : health **2** : public health, sanitation — **sanitario, -ria** *adj* : sanitary, health — **sanitario** *nm Lat* : toilet
santiamén *nm* **en un ~** : in no time at all
santo, -ta *adj* **1** : holy **2 Santo, Santa** (**San** *before masculine names except those beginning with D or T*) : Saint — **~** *n* : saint — **santo** *nm* **1** : saint's day **2** *Lat* : birthday — **santidad** *nf* : holiness, sanctity — **santiguarse** {10} *vr* : cross oneself — **santuario** *nm* : sanctuary
saña *nf* **1** : fury **2** BRUTALIDAD : viciousness
sapo *nm* : toad
saque *nm* : serve (in tennis, etc.), throw-in (in soccer)
saquear *vt* : sack, loot — **saqueador, -dora** *n* : looter — **saqueo** *nm* : sacking, looting
sarampión *nm* : measles *pl*
sarape *nm Lat* : serape
sarcasmo *nm* : sarcasm — **sarcástico, -ca** *adj* : sarcastic
sardina *nf* : sardine
sardónico, -ca *adj* : sardonic

sargento nmf : sergeant
sarpullido nm : rash
sartén nmf, pl -tenes : frying pan
sastre, -tra n : tailor — sastrería nf 1 : tailoring 2 : tailor's shop
Satanás nm : Satan — satánico, -ca adj : satanic
satélite nm : satellite
sátira nf : satire — satírico, -ca adj : satirical
satisfacer {74} vt 1 : satisfy 2 CUMPLIR : fulfill, meet 3 PAGAR : pay — satisfacerse vr 1 : be satisfied 2 VENGARSE : take revenge — satisfacción nf, pl -ciones : satisfaction — satisfactorio, -ria adj : satisfactory — satisfecho, -cha adj : satisfied
saturar vt : saturate — saturación nf, pl -ciones : saturation
Saturno nm : Saturn
sauce nm : willow
sauna nmf : sauna
savia nf : sap
saxofón nm, pl -fones : saxophone
sazón nf, pl -zones 1 : seasoning 2 MADUREZ : ripeness 3 a la ~ : at that time, then 4 en ~ : ripe, in season — sazonar vt : season
se pron 1 (reflexive) : himself, herself, itself, oneself, yourself, yourselves, themselves 2 (indirect object) : (to) him, (to) her, (to) you, (to) them 3 : each other, one another 4 ~ dice que : it is said that 5 ~ habla inglés : English spoken
sebo nm 1 : fat 2 : tallow (for candles, etc.) 3 : suet (for cooking)
secar {72} v : dry — secarse vr : dry (up) — secador nm : hair dryer — secadora nf : (clothes) dryer
sección nf, pl -ciones : section
seco, -ca adj 1 : dry 2 : dried (of fruits, etc.) 3 TAJANTE : sharp, brusque 4 fam : thin, skinny 5 a secas : simply, just 6 en seco : suddenly
secretar vt : secrete — secreción nf, pl -ciones : secretion
secretario, -ria n : secretary — secretaría nf : secretariat
secreto, -ta adj : secret — secreto nm 1 : secret 2 en ~ : in confidence
secta nf : sect
sector nm : sector
secuaz nmf, pl -cuaces : follower, henchman
secuela nf : consequence
secuencia nf : sequence
secuestrar vt 1 : kidnap 2 : hijack (an airplane, etc.) 3 EMBARGAR : confiscate, seize — secuestrador, -dora n 1 : kidnapper 2 : hijacker (of an airplane, etc.) — secuestro nm 1 : kidnapping 2 : hijacking (of an airplane, etc.) 3 : seizure (of goods)
secular adj : secular
secundar vt : support, second — secundario, -ria adj : secondary
sed nf 1 : thirst 2 tener ~ : be thirsty
seda nf : silk
sedal nm : fishing line
sedar vt : sedate — sedante adj & nm : sedative
sede nf 1 : seat, headquarters 2 Santa Sede : Holy See
sedentario, -ria adj : sedentary
sedición nf, pl -ciones : sedition — sedicioso, -sa adj : seditious
sediento, -ta adj : thirsty
sedimento nm : sediment
sedoso, -sa adj : silky, silken
seducir {61} vt 1 : seduce 2 ATRAER : captivate, charm — seducción nf, pl -ciones : seduction — seductor, -tora adj 1 : seductive 2 ENCANTADOR : charming — ~ n : seducer
segar {49} vt : reap — segador, -dora n : reaper, harvester
seglar adj : lay, secular — ~ nm : layperson, layman m, laywoman f
segmento nm : segment
segregar {52} vt : segregate — segregación nf, pl -ciones : segregation
seguir {75} vt : follow — vi : go on, continue — seguida: en ~ adv phr : right away — seguido adv 1 : straight (ahead) 2 Lat : often — seguido, -da adj 1 : continuous 2 CONSECUTIVO : consecutive — seguidor, -dora n : follower
según prep : according to — ~ adv : it depends — ~ conj : as, just as
segundo, -da adj : second — ~ n : second (one) — segundo nm : second (unit of time)
seguro, -ra adj 1 : safe 2 FIRME : secure 3 CIERTO : sure, certain 4 FIABLE : reliable — seguramente adv : for sure, surely — seguridad nf 1 : safety 2 GARANTÍA : security 3 CERTEZA : certainty 4 CONFIANZA : confidence — seguro adv : certainly — ~ nm 1 : insurance 2 : safety (device)
seis adj & nm : six — seiscientos, -tas adj : six hundred — seiscientos nms & pl : six hundred
seísmo nm : earthquake
selección nf, pl -ciones : selection — seleccionar vt : select, choose — selectivo, -va adj : selective — selecto, -ta adj : choice, select
sellar vt 1 : seal 2 TIMBRAR : stamp — sello nm 1 : seal 2 TIMBRE : stamp 3 or ~ distintivo : hallmark
selva nf 1 : jungle 2 BOSQUE : forest
semáforo nm : traffic light
semana nf : week — semanal adj : weekly — semanario nm : weekly
semántica nf : semantics — semántico, -ca adj : semantic
semblante nm 1 : countenance, face 2 APARIENCIA : look
sembrar {55} vt 1 : sow 2 ~ de : strew with
semejar vi : resemble — semejarse vr : look alike — semejante adj 1 : similar 2 TAL : such — ~ nm : fellowman — semejanza nf : similarity
semen nm : semen — semental nm 1 : stud 2 caballo ~ : stallion
semestre nm : semester
semiconductor nm : semiconductor
semifinal nf : semifinal
semilla nf : seed — semillero nm 1 : nursery (for plants) 2 HERVIDERO : hotbed, breeding ground
seminario nm 1 : seminary 2 CURSO : seminar, course
sémola nf : semolina
senado nm : senate — senador, -dora n : senator
sencillo, -lla adj 1 : simple 2 ÚNICO : single — sencillez nf : simplicity
senda nf or sendero nm : path, way
sendos, -das adj pl : each, both
senil adj : senile
seno nm 1 : breast, bosom 2 : sinus (in anatomy) 3 ~ materno : womb
sensación nf, pl -ciones : feeling, sensation — sensacional adj : sensational — sensacionalista adj : sensationalistic, lurid
sensato, -ta adj : sensible — sensatez nf : good sense
sensible adj 1 : sensitive 2 APRECIABLE : considerable, significant — sensibilidad nf : sensitivity — sensitivo, -va or sensorial adj : sense, sensory
sensual adj : sensual, sensuous — sensualidad nf : sensuality
sentar {55} vt 1 : seat, sit 2 ESTABLECER : establish, set — vi 1 : suit 2 ~ bien a : agree with (of food or drink) — sentarse vr : sit (down) — sentado, -da adj 1 : sitting, seated 2 dar por sentado : take for granted
sentencia nf 1 FALLO : sentence, judgment 2 MÁXIMA : saying — sentenciar vt : sentence
sentido, -da adj 1 : heartfelt, sincere 2 SENSIBLE : touchy, sensitive — sentido nm 1 : sense 2 CONOCIMIENTO : consciousness 3 DIRECCIÓN : direction 4 doble ~ : double entendre 5 ~ común : common sense 6 ~ del humor : sense of humor 7 ~ único : one-way
sentimiento nm 1 : feeling, emotion 2 PESAR : regret — sentimental adj : sentimental — sentimentalismo nm : sentimentality
sentir {76} vt 1 : feel 2 OÍR : hear 3 LAMENTAR : be sorry for 4 lo siento : I'm sorry — vi : feel — sentirse vr : feel
seña nf 1 : sign 2 ~s nfpl DIRECCIÓN : address 3 ~s particulares : distinguishing marks
señal nf 1 : signal 2 AVISO, INDICIO : sign 3 DEPÓSITO : deposit 4 dar ~es de : show signs of 5 en ~ de : as a token of — señalado, -da adj : notable — señalar vt 1 INDICAR : indicate, point out 2 MARCAR : mark 3 FIJAR : fix, set — señalarse vr : distinguish oneself
señor, -ñora n 1 : gentleman m, man m, lady f, woman f 2 : Sir m, Madam f 3 : Mr. m, Mrs. f 4 señora : wife f 5 el Señor : the Lord — señorial adj : stately — señorita nf 1 : young lady, young woman 2 : Miss
señuelo nm 1 : decoy 2 TRAMPA : bait, lure
separar vt 1 : separate 2 QUITAR : detach, remove 3 APARTAR : move away 4 DESTITUIR : dismiss — separarse vr 1 APARTARSE : separate 2 : part company — separación nf, pl -ciones : separation — separado, -da adj 1 : separate 2 : separated (of persons) 3 por separado : separately
septentrional adj : northern
séptico, -ca adj : septic
septiembre nm : September
séptimo, -ma adj : seventh — ~ n : seventh
sepulcro nm : tomb, sepulchre — sepultar vt : bury — sepultura nf 1 : burial 2 TUMBA : grave
sequedad nf : dryness — sequía nf : drought
séquito nm : retinue, entourage
ser {77} vi 1 : be 2 a no ~ que : unless 3 ¿cuánto es? : how much is it? 4 es más : what's more 5 ~ de : belong to 6 ~ de : come from 7 son las diez : it's ten o'clock — ~ nm 1 ENTE : being 2 ~ humano : human being
serbio, -bia adj : Serb, Serbian
serenar vt : calm — serenarse vr : calm down — serenata nf : serenade — serenidad nf : serenity — sereno, -na adj 1 : serene, calm 2 : fair, clear (of weather) — sereno nm : night watchman
serie nf 1 : series 2 fabricación en ~ : mass production 3 fuera de ~ : extraordinary — serial nm : serial
serio, -ria adj 1 : serious 2 RESPONSABLE : reliable 3 en serio : seriously — seriedad nf : seriousness
sermón nm, pl -mones : sermon — sermonear vt : lecture, reprimand
serpentear vi : twist, wind — serpiente nf 1 : serpent, snake 2 ~ de cascabel : rattlesnake
serrado, -da adj : serrated
serrano, -na adj 1 : mountain 2 jamón serrano : cured ham
serrar {55} vt : saw — serrín nm, pl -rrines : sawdust — serrucho nm : saw, handsaw
servicio nm 1 : service 2 ~s nmpl : restroom — servicial adj : obliging, helpful — servidor, -dora n 1 : servant 2 su seguro servidor : yours truly — servidumbre nf 1 : servitude 2 CRIADOS : help, servants pl — servil adj : servile
servilleta nf : napkin
servir {54} vt : serve — vi 1 : work, function 2 VALER : be of use — servirse vr 1 : help oneself 2 sírvase sentarse : please have a seat
sesenta adj & nm : sixty
sesgo nm : bias, slant
sesión nf, pl -siones 1 : session 2 : showing (of a film), performance (of a play)
seso nm : brain — sesudo, -da adj 1 : sensible 2 fam : brainy
seta nf : mushroom
setecientos, -tas adj : seven hundred — setecientos nms & pl : seven hundred
setenta adj & nm : seventy
setiembre nm → septiembre
seto nm 1 : fence 2 ~ vivo : hedge
seudónimo nm : pseudonym
severo, -ra adj 1 : harsh, severe 2 : strict (of a teacher, etc.) — severidad nf : severity
sexagésimo, -ma adj & n : sixtieth
sexo nm : sex — sexismo nm : sexism — sexista adj & nmf : sexist
sexteto nm : sextet
sexto, -ta adj & n : sixth
sexual adj : sexual — sexualidad nf : sexuality
sexy adj, pl sexy or sexys : sexy
si conj 1 : if 2 (in indirect questions) : whether 3 ~ bien : although 4 ~ no : otherwise, or else
sí[1] adv 1 : yes 2 creo que ~ : I think so 3 porque ~ fam : (just) because — ~ nm : consent
sí[2] pron 1 de por ~ or en ~ : by itself, in itself, per se 2 fuera de ~ : beside oneself 3 para ~ (mismo) : to himself, to herself, for himself, for herself 4 entre ~ : among themselves
sico- → psico-
SIDA or **sida** nm : AIDS
siderurgia nf : iron and steel industry
sidra nf : (hard) cider
siega nf 1 : harvesting 2 : harvest (time)
siembra nf 1 : sowing 2 : sowing season
siempre adv 1 : always 2 Lat : still 3 para ~ : forever, for good 4 ~ que : whenever, every time 5 ~ que or ~ y cuando : provided that
sien nf : temple
sierra nf 1 : saw 2 CORDILLERA : mountain range 3 la ~ : the mountains pl
siervo, -va n : slave
siesta nf : nap, siesta
siete adj & nm : seven
sífilis nf : syphilis
sifón nm, pl -fones : siphon
sigilo nm : secrecy
sigla nf : acronym, abbreviation
siglo nm 1 : century 2 hace ~s : for ages
significar {72} vt 1 : mean, signify 2 EXPRESAR : express — significación nf, pl -ciones 1 : significance, importance 2 : meaning (of a word, etc.) — significado, -da adj : well-known — significado nm : meaning — significativo, -va adj : significant
signo nm 1 : sign 2 ~ de admiración : exclamation point 3 ~ de interrogación : question mark
siguiente adj : next, following
sílaba nf : syllable
silbar v 1 : whistle 2 ABUCHEAR : hiss, boo — silbato nm : whistle — silbido nm 1 : whistle, whistling 2 ABUCHEO : hiss, booing
silenciar vt : silence — silenciador nm : muffler — silencio nm : silence — silencioso, -sa adj : silent, quiet
silicio nm : silicon
silla nf 1 : chair 2 or ~ de montar : saddle 3 ~ de ruedas : wheelchair — sillón nm, pl -llones : armchair, easy chair
silo nm : silo
silueta nf 1 : silhouette 2 CONTORNO : outline, shape
silvestre adj : wild
silvicultura nf : forestry
símbolo nm : symbol — simbólico, -ca adj : symbolic — simbolismo nm : symbolism — simbolizar {21} vt : symbolize
simetría nf : symmetry — simétrico, -ca adj : symmetrical, symmetric
simiente nf : seed
símil nm 1 : simile 2 COMPARACIÓN : comparison — similar adj : similar, alike
simio nm : ape
simpatía nf 1 : liking, affection 2 AMABILIDAD : friendliness — simpático, -ca adj 1 : nice, likeable 2 AMABLE : pleasant, kind — simpatizante nmf : sympathizer — simpatizar {21} vi 1 : get along, hit it off 2 ~ con : sympathize with
simple adj 1 SENCILLO : simple 2 MERO : pure, sheer 3 TONTO : simpleminded — ~ n : fool, simpleton — simpleza nf 1 : simpleness 2 TONTERÍA : silly thing — simplicidad nf : simplicity — simplificar {72} vt : simplify
simposio or **simposium** nm : symposium
simular vt 1 : simulate 2 FINGIR : feign — simulacro nm : simulation, drill
simultáneo, -nea adj : simultaneous
sin prep 1 : without 2 ~ que : without
sinagoga nf : synagogue
sincero, -ra adj : sincere — sinceramente adv : sincerely — sinceridad nf : sincerity
síncopa nf : syncopation
sincronizar {21} vt : synchronize
sindicato nm : (labor) union — sindical adj : union, labor
síndrome nm : syndrome
sinfín nm 1 : endless number 2 un ~ de : no end of
sinfonía nf : symphony — sinfónico, -ca adj : symphonic
singular adj 1 : exceptional, outstanding 2 PECULIAR : peculiar 3 : singular (in grammar) — ~ nm : singular — singularizar {21} vt : single out — singularizarse vr : stand out
siniestro, -tra adj 1 : sinister 2 IZQUIERDO : left — siniestro nm : disaster
sinnúmero nm → sinfín
sino conj 1 : but, rather 2 EXCEPTO : except, save
sinónimo, -ma adj : synonymous — sinónimo nm : synonym
sinopsis nfs & pl : synopsis
sinrazón nf, pl -zones : wrong
sintaxis nfs & pl : syntax
síntesis nfs & pl : synthesis — sintético, -ca adj : synthetic — sintetizar {21} vt 1 : synthesize 2 RESUMIR : summarize
síntoma nm : symptom — sintomático, -ca adj : symptomatic
sintonía nf 1 : tuning in (of a radio) 2 en ~ con : in tune with — sintonizar {21} vt : tune (in) to
sinuoso, -sa adj : winding
sinvergüenza nmf : scoundrel
sionismo nm : Zionism
siquiera adv 1 : at least 2 ni ~ : not even — ~ conj : even if
sirena nf 1 : mermaid 2 : siren (of an ambulance, etc.)
sirio, -ria adj : Syrian
sirviente, -ta n : servant, maid f
sisear vi : hiss — siseo nm : hiss
sismo nm : earthquake — sísmico, -ca adj : seismic
sistema nm 1 : system 2 por ~ : systematically — sistemático, -ca adj : systematic
sitiar vt : besiege
sitio nm 1 : place, site 2 ESPACIO : room, space 3 CERCO : siege 4 en cualquier ~ : anywhere
situar {3} vt : situate, place — situarse vr 1 : be located 2 ESTABLECERSE : get oneself established — situación nf, pl -ciones : situation, position — situado, -da adj : situated, placed
slip nm : briefs pl, underpants pl
smoking nm : tuxedo
so prep : under
sobaco nm : armpit
sobar vt 1 : finger, handle 2 : knead (dough) — sobado, -da adj : worn, shabby
soberanía nf : sovereignty — soberano, -na adj & n : sovereign
soberbia nf : pride, arrogance — soberbio, -bia adj : proud, arrogant
sobornar vt : bribe — soborno nm 1 : bribe 2 : (action of) bribery
sobrar vi 1 : be more than enough 2 RESTAR : be left over — sobra nf 1 : surplus 2 de ~ : to spare 3 ~s nfpl : leftovers — sobrado, -da adj : more than enough — sobrante adj : remaining
sobre[1] nm : envelope
sobre[2] prep 1 : on, on top of 2 POR ENCIMA DE : over, above 3 ACERCA DE : about 4 ~ todo : especially, above all
sobrecama nmf Lat : bedspread
sobrecargar {52} vt : overload, overburden
sobrecoger {15} vt : startle — sobrecogerse vr : be startled
sobrecubierta nf : dust jacket
sobredosis nfs & pl : overdose
sobreentender {56} vt : infer, understand — sobreentenderse vr : be understood
sobreestimar vt : overestimate
sobregiro nm : overdraft

sobrellevar *vt* : endure, bear
sobremesa *nf* **de ~** : after-dinner
sobrenatural *adj* : supernatural
sobrenombre *nm* : nickname
sobrentender → **sobreentender**
sobrepasar *vt* : exceed
sobreponer {60} *vt* **1** : superimpose **2** ANTEPONER : put before — **sobreponerse** *vr* **~ a** : overcome
sobresalir {73} *vi* **1** : protrude **2** DESTACARSE : stand out — **sobresaliente** *adj* : outstanding
sobresaltar *vt* : startle — **sobresaltarse** *vr* : start, jump up — **sobresalto** *nm* : fright
sobrestimar → **sobreestimar**
sobretodo *nm* : overcoat
sobrevenir {87} *vi* : happen, ensue
sobrevivencia *nf* → **supervivencia**
sobreviviente *adj & nmf* → **superviviente**
sobrevivir *vi* : survive — *vt* : outlive
sobrevolar {19} *vt* : fly over
sobriedad *nf* **1** : sobriety **2** MODERACIÓN : restraint
sobrino, -na *n* : nephew *m*, niece *f*
sobrio, -bria *adj* : sober
socarrón, -rrona *adj, mpl* **-rrones** : sarcastic
socavar *vt* : undermine
sociable *adj* : sociable — **social** *adj* : social — **socialismo** *nm* : socialism — **socialista** *adj & nmf* : socialist — **sociedad** *nf* **1** : society **2** EMPRESA : company **3 ~ anónima** : incorporated company — **socio, -cia** *n* **1** : partner **2** MIEMBRO : member — **sociología** *nf* : sociology — **sociólogo, -ga** *n* : sociologist
socorrer *vt* : help — **socorrista** *nmf* : lifeguard — **socorro** *nm* : help
soda *nf* : soda (water)
sodio *nf* : sodium
sofá *nm* : couch, sofa
sofisticación *nf, pl* **-ciones** : sophistication — **sofisticado, -da** *adj* : sophisticated
sofocar {72} *vt* **1** : suffocate, smother **2** : put out (a fire), stifle (a rebellion, etc.) — **sofocarse** *vr* **1** : suffocate **2** *fam* : get upset — **sofocante** *adj* : suffocating, stifling
sofreír {66} *vt* : sauté
soga *nf* : rope
soja *nf* → **soya**
sojuzgar *vt* : subdue, subjugate
sol *nm* **1** : sun **2 hacer ~** : be sunny
solamente *adv* : only, just
solapa *nf* **1** : lapel (of a jacket) **2** : flap (of an envelope) — **solapado, -da** *adj* : secret, underhanded
solar[1] *adj* : solar, sun
solar[2] *nm* : lot, site
solariego, -ga *adj* : ancestral
solaz *nm, pl* **-laces 1** : solace **2** DESCANSO : relaxation — **solazarse** {21} *vr* : relax
soldado *nm* **1** : soldier **2 ~ raso** : private
soldar {19} *vt* : weld, solder — **soldador** *nm* : soldering iron — **soldador, -dora** *n* : welder
soleado, -da *adj* : sunny
soledad *nf* : loneliness, solitude
solemne *adj* : solemn — **solemnidad** *nf* : solemnity
soler {78} *vi* **1** : be in the habit of **2 suele llegar tarde** : he usually arrives late
solicitar *vt* **1** : request, solicit **2** : apply for (a job, etc.) — **solicitante** *nmf* : applicant — **solícito, -ta** *adj* : solicitous, obliging — **solicitud** *nf* **1** : concern **2** PETICIÓN : request **3** : application (for a job, etc.)
solidaridad *nf* : solidarity
sólido, -da *adj* **1** : solid **2** : sound (of an argument, etc.) — **sólido** *nm* : solid — **solidez** *nf* : solidity — **solidificar** {72} *vt* : solidify — **solidificarse** *vr* : solidify, harden
soliloquio *nm* : soliloquy
solista *nmf* : soloist
solitario, -ria *adj* **1** : solitary **2** AISLADO : lonely, deserted — **~** *n* : recluse — **solitaria** *nf* : tapeworm — **solitario** *nm* : solitaire
sollozar {21} *vi* : sob — **sollozo** *nm* : sob
solo, -la *adj* **1** : alone **2** AISLADO : lonely **3 a solas** : alone, by oneself — **solo** *nm* : solo
sólo *adv* : just, only
solomillo *nm* : sirloin
solsticio *nm* : solstice
soltar {19} *vt* **1** : release **2** DEJAR CAER : let go of, drop **3** DESATAR : unfasten, undo — **soltarse** *vr* **1** : break free **2** DESATARSE : come undone
soltero, -ra *adj* : single, unmarried — **~** *n* **1** : bachelor *m*, single woman *f* **2 apellido de soltera** : maiden name
soltura *nf* **1** : looseness **2** : fluency (in language) **3** AGILIDAD : agility, ease
soluble *adj* : soluble
solución *nf, pl* **-ciones** : solution — **solucionar** *vt* : solve, resolve
solventar *vt* **1** : settle, pay **2** RESOLVER : resolve — **solvente** *adj & nm* : solvent
sombra *nf* **1** : shadow **2** : shade (of a tree, etc.) **3 ~s** *nfpl* : darkness, shadows — **sombreado, -da** *adj* : shady
sombrero *nm* : hat
sombrilla *nf* : parasol, umbrella
sombrío, -bría *adj* : dark, somber, gloomy
somero, -ra *adj* : superficial
someter *vt* **1** : subjugate **2** SUBORDINAR : subordinate **3** : subject (to treatment, etc.) **4** PRESENTAR : submit, present — **someterse** *vr* **1** : submit, yield **2 ~ a** : undergo
somnífero, -ra *adj* : soporific — **somnífero** *nm* : sleeping pill — **somnoliento, -ta** *adj* : drowsy, sleepy
somos → **ser**
son[1] → **ser**
son[2] *nm* **1** : sound **2 en ~ de** : as, in the manner of
sonajero *nm* : (baby's) rattle
sonámbulo, -la *n* : sleepwalker
sonar {19} *vi* **1** : sound **2** : ring (as a bell) **3** : look or sound familiar **4 ~ a** : sound like — **sonarse** *vr or* **~ las narices** : blow one's nose
sonata *nf* : sonata
sondear *vt* **1** : sound, probe **2** : survey, sound out (opinions, etc.) — **sondeo** *nm* **1** : sounding, probing **2** ENCUESTA : survey, poll
soneto *nm* : sonnet
sónico, -ca *adj* : sonic
sonido *nm* : sound
sonoro, -ra *adj* **1** : resonant, sonorous **2** RUIDOSO : loud
sonreír {66} *vi* : smile — **sonreírse** *vr* : smile — **sonriente** *adj* : smiling — **sonrisa** *nf* : smile
sonrojar *vt* : cause to blush — **sonrojarse** *vr* : blush — **sonrojo** *nm* : blush
sonrosado, -da *adj* : rosy, pink
sonsacar {72} *vt* : wheedle (out)
soñar {19} *v* **1** : dream **2 ~ con** : dream about **3 ~ despierto** : daydream — **soñador, -dora** *adj* : dreamy — **~** *n* : dreamer — **soñoliento, -ta** *adj* : sleepy, drowsy
sopa *nf* : soup
sopesar *vt* : weigh, consider
soplar *vi* : blow — *vt* : blow out, blow off, blow up — **soplete** *nm* : blowtorch — **soplo** *nm* : puff, gust
soplón, -plona *n, pl* **-plones** *fam* : sneak
sopor *nm* : drowsiness — **soporífero, -ra** *adj* : soporific
soportar *vt* **1** SOSTENER : support **2** AGUANTAR : bear — **soporte** *nm* : support
soprano *nmf* : soprano
sor *nf* : Sister (in religion)
sorber *vt* **1** : sip **2** ABSORBER : absorb **3** CHUPAR : suck up — **sorbete** *nm* : sherbet — **sorbo** *nm* **1** : sip, swallow **2 beber a ~s** : sip
sordera *nf* : deafness
sórdido, -da *adj* : sordid, squalid
sordo, -da *adj* **1** : deaf **2** : muted (of a sound) — **sordomudo, -da** *n* : deaf-mute
sorna *nf* : sarcasm
sorprender *vt* : surprise — **sorprenderse** *vr* : be surprised — **sorprendente** *adj* : surprising — **sorpresa** *nf* : surprise
sortear *vt* **1** : raffle off, draw lots for **2** ESQUIVAR : dodge — **sorteo** *nm* : drawing, raffle
sortija *nf* **1** : ring **2** : ringlet (of hair)
sortilegio *nm* **1** HECHIZO : spell **2** HECHICERÍA : sorcery
sosegar {49} *vt* : calm, pacify — **sosegarse** *vr* : calm down — **sosegado, -da** *adj* : calm, tranquil — **sosiego** *nm* : calm
soslayo: de ~ *adv phr* : obliquely, sideways
soso, -sa *adj* **1** : insipid, tasteless **2** ABURRIDO : dull
sospechar *vt* : suspect — **sospecha** *nf* : suspicion — **sospechoso, -sa** *adj* : suspicious — **~** *n* : suspect
sostener {80} *vt* **1** : support **2** SUJETAR : hold **3** MANTENER : sustain, maintain — **sostenerse** *vr* **1** : stand (up) **2** CONTINUAR : remain **3** SUSTENTARSE : support oneself — **sostén** *nm, pl* **-tenes 1** APOYO : support **2** SUSTENTO : sustenance **3** : brassiere, bra — **sostenido, -da** *adj* **1** : sustained **2** : sharp (in music) — **sostenido** *nm* : sharp
sótano *nm* : basement
soterrar {55} *vt* **1** : bury **2** ESCONDER : hide
soto *nm* : grove
soviético, -ca *adj* : Soviet
soy → **ser**
soya *nf* : soy
Sr. *nm* : Mr. — **Sra.** *nf* : Mrs., Ms. — **Srta.** *or* **Srita.** *nf* : Miss, Ms.
su *adj* **1** : his, her, its, their, one's **2** (*formal*) : your
suave *adj* **1** : soft **2** LISO : smooth **3** APACIBLE : gentle, mild — **suavidad** *nf* **1** : softness, smoothness **2** APACIBILIDAD : mildness, gentleness — **suavizar** {21} *vt* : soften, smooth
subalimentado, -da *adj* : undernourished, underfed
subalterno, -na *adj* **1** SUBORDINADO : subordinate **2** SECUNDARIO : secondary — **~** *n* : subordinate
subarrendar {55} *vt* : sublet
subasta *nf* : auction — **subastar** *vt* : auction (off)
subcampeón, -peona *n, mpl* **-peones** : runner-up
subcomité *nm* : subcommittee
subconsciente *adj & nm* : subconscious
subdesarrollado, -da *adj* : underdeveloped
subdirector, -tora *n* : assistant manager
súbdito, -ta *n* : subject
subdividir *vt* : subdivide — **subdivisión** *nf, pl* **-siones** : subdivision
subestimar *vt* : underestimate
subir *vt* **1** : climb, go up **2** LLEVAR : bring up, take up **3** AUMENTAR : raise — *vi* **1** : go up, come up **2 ~ a** : get in (a car), get on (a bus, etc.) — **subirse** *vr* **1** : climb (up) **2 ~ a** : get in (a car), get on (a bus, etc.) **3 ~ a la cabeza** : go to one's head — **subida** *nf* **1** : ascent, climb **2** AUMENTO : rise **3** PENDIENTE : slope — **subido, -da** *adj* **1** : bright, strong **2 ~ de tono** : risqué
súbito, -ta *adj* **1** : sudden **2 de súbito** : all of a sudden, suddenly
subjetivo, -va *adj* : subjective
subjuntivo, -va *adj* : subjunctive — **subjuntivo** *nm* : subjunctive (case)
sublevar *vt* : stir up, incite to rebellion — **sublevarse** *vr* : rebel — **sublevación** *nf, pl* **-ciones** : uprising, rebellion
sublime *adj* : sublime
submarino, -na *adj* : underwater — **submarino** *nm* : submarine — **submarinismo** *nm* : scuba diving
subordinar *vt* : subordinate — **subordinado, -da** *adj & n* : subordinate
subproducto *nm* : by-product
subrayar *vt* **1** : underline **2** ENFATIZAR : emphasize, stress
subrepticio, -cia *adj* : surreptitious
subsanar *vt* **1** : rectify, correct **2** : make up for (a deficiency), overcome (an obstacle)
subscribir → **suscribir**
subsidio *nm* : subsidy, benefit
subsiguiente *adj* : subsequent
subsistir *vi* **1** : live, subsist **2** SOBREVIVIR : survive — **subsistencia** *nf* : subsistence
substancia *nf* → **sustancia**
subterfugio *nm* : subterfuge
subterráneo, -nea *adj* : underground, subterranean — **subterráneo** *nm* : underground passage
subtítulo *nm* : subtitle
suburbio *nm* **1** : suburb **2** : slum (outside a city) — **suburbano, -na** *adj* : suburban
subvencionar *vt* : subsidize — **subvención** *nf, pl* **-ciones** : subsidy, grant
subvertir {76} *vt* : subvert — **subversión** *nf, pl* **-siones** : subversion — **subversivo, -va** *adj & n* : subversive
subyacente *adj* : underlying
subyugar {52} *vt* : subjugate, subdue
succión *nf, pl* **-ciones** : suction — **succionar** *vt* : suck up, draw in
sucedáneo *nm* : substitute
suceder *vi* **1** : happen, occur **2 ~ a** : follow **3 suceda lo que suceda** : come what may — **sucesión** *nf, pl* **-siones** : succession — **sucesivo, -va** *adj* : successive — **suceso** *nm* **1** : event **2** INCIDENTE : incident — **sucesor, -sora** *n* : successor
suciedad *nf* **1** : dirtiness **2** MUGRE : dirt, filth
sucinto, -ta *adj* : succinct, concise
sucio, -cia *adj* : dirty, filthy
suculento, -ta *adj* : succulent
sucumbir *vi* : succumb
sucursal *nf* : branch (of a business)
sudadera *nf* : sweatshirt — **sudado, -da** *adj* : sweaty
sudafricano, -na *adj* : South African
sudamericano, -na *adj* : South American
sudar *vi* : sweat
sudeste → **sureste**
sudoeste → **suroeste**
sudor *nm* : sweat — **sudoroso, -sa** *adj* : sweaty
sueco, -ca *adj* : Swedish — **sueco** *nm* : Swedish (language)
suegro, -gra *n* **1** : father-in-law *m*, mother-in-law *f* **2 suegros** *nmpl* : in-laws
suela *nf* : sole (of a shoe)
sueldo *nm* : salary, wage
suelo *nm* **1** : ground **2** : floor (in a house) **3** TIERRA : soil, land
suelto, -ta *adj* : loose, free — **suelto** *nm* : loose change
sueño *nm* **1** : dream **2 coger el ~** : get to sleep **3 tener ~** : be sleepy
suero *nm* **1** : whey **2** : serum (in medicine)
suerte *nf* **1** : luck, fortune **2** AZAR : chance **3** DESTINO : fate **4** CLASE : sort, kind **5 por ~** : luckily **6 tener ~** : be lucky
suéter *nm* : sweater
suficiencia *nf* **1** CAPACIDAD : competence, proficiency **2** PRESUNCIÓN : smugness — **suficiente** *adj* **1** : enough, sufficient **2** PRESUNTUOSO : smug — **suficientemente** *adv* : enough
sufijo *nm* : suffix
sufragio *nm* : suffrage, vote
sufrir *vt* **1** : suffer **2** SOPORTAR : bear, stand — *vi* : suffer — **sufrido, -da** *adj* **1** : long-suffering **2** : sturdy, serviceable (of clothing) — **sufrimiento** *nm* : suffering
sugerir {76} *vt* : suggest — **sugerencia** *nf* : suggestion — **sugestión** *nf, pl* **-tiones** : suggestion — **sugestionable** *adj* : impressionable — **sugestionar** *vt* : influence — **sugestivo, -va** *adj* **1** : suggestive **2** ESTIMULANTE : interesting, stimulating
suicidio *nm* : suicide — **suicida** *adj* : suicidal — **~** *nmf* : suicide (victim) — **suicidarse** *vr* : commit suicide
suite *nf* : suite
suizo, -za *adj* : Swiss
sujetar *vt* **1** : hold (on to) **2** FIJAR : fasten **3** DOMINAR : subdue — **sujetarse** *vr* **1 ~ a** : hold on to, cling to **2 ~ a** : abide by — **sujeción** *nf, pl* **-ciones 1** : fastening **2** DOMINACIÓN : subjection — **sujetador** *nm* *Spain* : brassiere, bra — **sujetapapeles** *nms & pl* : paper clip — **sujeto, -ta** *adj* **1** : fastened **2 ~ a** : subject to — **sujeto** *nm* **1** : individual **2** : subject (in grammar)
sulfuro *nm* : sulfur — **sulfúrico, -ca** *adj* : sulfuric
sultán *nm, pl* **-tanes** : sultan
suma *nf* **1** : sum, total **2** : addition (in mathematics) **3 en ~** : in short — **sumamente** *adv* : extremely — **sumar** *vt* **1** : add (up) **2** TOTALIZAR : add up to, total — *vi* : add up — **sumarse** *vr* **~ a** : join
sumario, -ria *adj* : concise — **sumario** *nm* **1** : summary **2** : indictment (in law)
sumergir {35} *vt* : submerge, plunge — **sumergirse** *vr* : be submerged — **sumergible** *adj* : waterproof (of a watch, etc.)
sumidero *nm* : drain
suministrar *vt* : supply, provide — **suministro** *nm* : supply, provision
sumir *vt* : plunge, immerse — **sumirse** *vr* **~ en** : sink into
sumisión *nf, pl* **-siones** : submission — **sumiso, -sa** *adj* : submissive
sumo, -ma *adj* **1** : highest, supreme **2 de suma importancia** : of great importance
suntuoso, -sa *adj* : sumptuous, lavish
super *or* **súper** *nm fam* : supermarket
superabundancia *nf* : overabundance
superar *vt* **1** : surpass, outdo **2** VENCER : overcome — **superarse** *vr* : improve oneself
superávit *nm* : surplus
superestructura *nf* : superstructure
superficie *nf* **1** : surface **2** ÁREA : area — **superficial** *adj* : superficial
superfluo, -flua *adj* : superfluous
superintendente *nmf* : supervisor, superintendent
superior *adj* **1** : superior **2** : upper (of a floor, etc.) **3 ~ a** : above, higher than — **~** *nm* : superior — **superioridad** *nf* : superiority
superlativo, -va *adj* : superlative — **superlativo** *nm* : superlative
supermercado *nm* : supermarket
superpoblado, -da *adj* : overpopulated
supersónico, -ca *adj* : supersonic
superstición *nf, pl* **-ciones** : superstition — **supersticioso, -sa** *adj* : superstitious
supervisar *vt* : supervise, oversee — **supervisión** *nf, pl* **-siones** : supervision — **supervisor, -sora** *n* : supervisor
supervivencia *nf* : survival — **superviviente** *adj* : surviving — **~** *nmf* : survivor
suplantar *vt* : supplant, replace
suplemento *nm* : supplement — **suplementario, -ria** *adj* : supplementary
suplente *adj & nmf* : substitute
suplicar {72} *vt* : beg, entreat — **súplica** *nf* : plea, entreaty
suplicio *nm* : ordeal, torture
suplir *vt* **1** : make up for **2** REEMPLAZAR : replace
supo, etc. → **saber**
suponer {60} *vt* **1** : suppose, assume **2** SIGNIFICAR : mean **3** IMPLICAR : involve, entail — **suposición** *nf, pl* **-ciones** : supposition
supositorio *nm* : suppository
supremo, -ma *adj* : supreme — **supremacía** *nf* : supremacy
suprimir *vt* **1** : suppress, eliminate **2** : delete (text) — **supresión** *nf, pl* **-siones 1** : suppression, elimination **2** : deletion (of text)
supuesto, -ta *adj* **1** : supposed, alleged **2 por supuesto** : of course — **supuesto** *nm* : assumption — **supuestamente** *adv* : allegedly
sur *nm* **1** : south, South **2** : south wind **3 del ~** : south, southerly
surafricano, -na → **sudafricano**
suramericano, -na → **sudamericano**
surcar {72} *vt* **1** : plow (earth) **2** : cut through (air, water, etc.) — **surco** *nm* : groove, furrow, rut
sureño, -ña *adj* : southern, Southern — **~** *n* : Southerner
sureste *adj* **1** : southeast, southeastern **2** : southeasterly (of wind, etc.) — **~** *nm* : southeast, Southeast
surf *or* **surfing** *nm* : surfing
surgir {35} *vi* **1** : arise **2** APARECER : appear — **surgimiento** *nm* : rise, emergence
suroeste *adj* **1** : southwest, southwestern **2** : southwesterly (of wind, etc.) — **~** *nm* : southwest, Southwest
surtir *vt* **1** : supply, provide **2 ~ efecto** : have an effect — **surtirse** *vr* **~ de** : stock up on — **surtido, -da** *adj* **1** : assorted, varied **2** : stocked (with merchandise) — **surtido** *nm* : assortment, selection — **surtidor** *nm* : gas pump
susceptible *adj* **1** : susceptible, sensitive **2**

~ **de** : capable of — **susceptibilidad** nf : sensitivity
suscitar vt : provoke, arouse
suscribir {33} vt 1 : sign (a formal document) 2 RATIFICAR : endorse — **suscribirse** vr ~ **a** : subscribe to — **suscripción** nf, pl **-ciones** : subscription — **suscriptor, -tora** n : subscriber
susodicho, -cha adj : aforementioned
suspender vt 1 : suspend 2 COLGAR : hang 3 Spain : fail (an exam, etc.) — **suspensión** nf, pl **-siones** : suspension — **suspenso** nm 1 Spain : failure (in an exam, etc.) 2 Lat : suspense
suspicaz adj, pl **-caces** : suspicious
suspirar vi : sigh — **suspiro** nm : sigh
sustancia nf 1 : substance 2 **sin** ~ : shallow, lacking substance — **sustancial** adj : substantial, significant — **sustancioso, -sa** adj : substantial, solid
sustantivo nm : noun
sustentar vt 1 : support 2 ALIMENTAR : sustain, nourish 3 MANTENER : maintain — **sustentarse** vr : support oneself — **sustentación** nf, pl **-ciones** : support — **sustento** nm 1 : means of support, livelihood 2 ALIMENTO : sustenance
sustituir {41} vt : replace, substitute — **sustitución** nf, pl **-ciones** : replacement, substitution — **sustituto, -ta** n : substitute
susto nm : fright, scare
sustraer {81} vt 1 : remove, take away 2 : subtract (in mathematics) — **sustraerse** vr ~ **a** : avoid, evade — **sustracción** nf, pl **-ciones** : subtraction
susurrar vi 1 : whisper 2 : murmur (of water) 3 : rustle (of leaves, etc.) — vt : whisper — **susurro** nm 1 : whisper 2 : murmur (of water) 3 : rustle, rustling (of leaves, etc.)
sutil adj 1 : delicate, fine 2 : subtle (of fragrances, differences, etc.) — **sutileza** nf : subtlety
sutura nf : suture
suyo, -ya adj 1 : his, her, its, one's, theirs 2 (formal) : yours 3 **un primo suyo** : a cousin of his/hers — ~ pron 1 : his, hers, its (own), one's own, theirs 2 (formal) : yours
switch nm Lat : switch

T

t nf : t, 21st letter of the Spanish alphabet
taba nf : anklebone
tabaco nm : tobacco — **tabacalero, -ra** adj : tobacco
tábano nm : horsefly
taberna nf : tavern
tabicar {72} vt : wall up — **tabique** nm : thin wall, partition
tabla nf 1 : board, plank 2 LISTA : table, list 3 ~ **de planchar** : ironing board 4 ~**s** nfpl : stage, boards pl — **tablado** nm 1 : flooring 2 PLATAFORMA : platform 3 : (theater) stage — **tablero** nm 1 : bulletin board 2 : board (in games) 3 PIZARRA : blackboard 4 ~ **de instrumentos** : dashboard, instrument panel
tableta nf 1 : tablet, pill 2 : bar (of chocolate)
tablilla nf : slat — **tablón** nm, pl **-lones** 1 : plank, beam 2 ~ **de anuncios** : bulletin board
tabú adj : taboo — **tabú** nm, pl **-búes** or **-bús** : taboo
tabular vt : tabulate
taburete nm : stool
tacaño, -na adj : stingy, miserly
tacha nf 1 : flaw, defect 2 **sin** ~ : flawless
tachar vt 1 : cross out, delete 2 ~ **de** : accuse of, label as
tachón nm, pl **-chones** : stud, hobnail — **tachuela** nf : tack, hobnail
tácito, -ta adj : tacit
taciturno, -na adj : taciturn
taco nm 1 : stopper, plug 2 Lat : heel (of a shoe) 3 : cue (in billiards) 4 : taco (in cooking)
tacón nm, pl **-cones** 1 : heel (of a shoe) 2 **de** ~ **alto** : high-heeled
táctica nf : tactic, tactics pl — **táctico, -ca** adj : tactical
tacto nm 1 : (sense of) touch, feel 2 DELICADEZA : tact
tafetán nm, pl **-tanes** : taffeta
tailandés, -desa adj : Thai
taimado, -da adj : crafty, sly
tajar vt : cut, slice — **tajada** nf 1 : slice 2 **sacar** ~ fam : get one's share — **tajante** adj : categorical — **tajo** nm 1 : cut, gash 2 ESCARPA : steep cliff
tal adv 1 : so, in such a way 2 **con** ~ **que** : provided that, as long as 3 **¿qué** ~**?** : how are you?, how's it going? — ~ adj 1 : such, such a 2 ~ **vez** : maybe, perhaps — ~ pron 1 : such a one, such a thing 2 ~ **para cual** : two of a kind
taladrar vt : drill — **taladro** nm : drill
talante nm 1 HUMOR : mood 2 VOLUNTAD : willingness
talar vt : cut down, fell
talco nm : talcum powder
talego nm : sack
talento nm : talent — **talentoso, -sa** adj : talented
talismán nm, pl **-manes** : talisman, charm
talla nf 1 : sculpture, carving 2 ESTATURA : height 3 : size (in clothing) — **tallar** vt 1 : sculpt, carve 2 : measure (someone's height)
tallarín nf, pl **-rines** : noodle
talle nm 1 : waist, waistline 2 FIGURA : figure 3 : measurements pl (of clothing)
taller nm 1 : workshop 2 : studio (of an artist)
tallo nm : stalk, stem
talón nm, pl **-lones** 1 : heel (of the foot) 2 : stub (of a check) — **talonario** nm : checkbook
taltuza nf : gopher
tamal nm : tamale
tamaño, -ña adj : such a, such a big — **tamaño** nm 1 : size 2 **de** ~ **natural** : life-size
tambalearse vr 1 : teeter, wobble 2 : stagger, totter (of persons)
también adv : too, as well, also
tambor nm : drum — **tamborilear** vi : drum
tamiz nm : sieve — **tamizar** {21} vt : sift
tampoco adv : neither, not either
tampón nm, pl **-pones** 1 : tampon 2 : ink pad (for stamping)
tan adv 1 : so, so very 2 ~ **pronto como** : as soon as 3 ~ **sólo** : only, merely
tanda nf 1 TURNO : turn, shift 2 GRUPO : batch, lot, series
tangente nf : tangent
tangible adj : tangible
tango nm : tango
tanque nm : tank
tantear vt 1 : feel, grope 2 SOPESAR : size up, weigh — vi : feel one's way — **tanteador** nm : scoreboard — **tanteo** nm 1 : weighing, sizing up 2 PUNTUACIÓN : scoring (in sports)
tanto adv 1 : so much 2 (in expressions of time) : so long — ~ nm 1 : certain amount 2 : goal, point (in sports) 3 **un** ~ : somewhat, rather — **tanto, -ta** adj 1 : so much, so many 2 (in comparisons) : as much, as many 3 fam : however many — ~ pron 1 : so much, so many 2 **entre** ~ : meanwhile 3 **por lo** ~ : therefore
tañer {79} vt 1 : ring (a bell) 2 : play (a musical instrument)
tapa nf 1 : cover, top, lid 2 Spain : snack
tapacubos nms & pl : hubcap
tapar vt 1 : cover, put a lid on 2 OCULTAR : block out 3 ENCUBRIR : cover up — **tapadera** nf 1 : cover, lid 2 : front (to hide a deception)
tapete nm 1 : small rug, mat 2 : cover (for a table)
tapia nf : (adobe) wall, garden wall — **tapiar** vt 1 : wall in 2 : block off (a door, etc.)
tapicería nf 1 : upholstery 2 TAPIZ : tapestry — **tapicero, -ra** n : upholsterer
tapioca nf : tapioca
tapiz nm, pl **-pices** : tapestry — **tapizar** {21} vt : upholster
tapón nm, pl **-pones** 1 : cork 2 : cap (for a bottle, etc.) 3 : plug, stopper (for a sink)
tapujo nm **sin** ~**s** : openly, outright
taquigrafía nf : stenography, shorthand — **taquígrafo, -fa** n : stenographer
taquilla nf 1 : box office 2 RECAUDACIÓN : earnings pl, take — **taquillero, -ra** adj **un éxito taquillero** : a box-office hit
tarántula nf : tarantula
tararear vt : hum
tardar vi 1 : take a long time, be late 2 **a más** ~ : at the latest — vt : take (time) — **tardanza** nf : lateness, delay — **tarde** adv 1 : late 2 ~ **o temprano** : sooner or later — ~ nf 1 : afternoon, evening 2 **¡buenas** ~**s!** : good afternoon!, good evening! 3 **en la** ~ or **por la** ~ : in the afternoon, in the evening — **tardío, -día** adj : late, tardy — **tardo, -da** adj : slow
tarea nf 1 : task, job 2 : homework (in education)
tarifa nf 1 : fare, rate 2 LISTA : price list 3 ARANCEL : duty, tariff
tarima nf : platform, stage
tarjeta nf 1 : card 2 ~ **de crédito** : credit card 3 ~ **postal** : postcard
tarro nm : jar, pot
tarta nf 1 : cake 2 TORTA : tart
tartamudear vi : stammer, stutter — **tartamudeo** nm : stutter, stammer
tartán nm, pl **-tanes** : tartan, plaid
tártaro nm : tartar
tarugo nm 1 : block (of wood) 2 fam : blockhead, dunce
tasa nf 1 : rate 2 IMPUESTO : tax 3 VALORACIÓN : appraisal — **tasación** nf, pl **-ciones** : appraisal — **tasar** vt 1 : set the price of 2 VALORAR : appraise, value
tasca nf : cheap bar, dive
tatuar {3} vt : tattoo — **tatuaje** nm : tattoo, tattooing
taurino, -na adj : bull, bullfighting — **tauromaquia** nf : (art of) bullfighting
taxi nm, pl **taxis** : taxi, taxicab — **taxista** nmf : taxi driver
taza nf 1 : cup 2 : (toilet) bowl — **tazón** nm, pl **-zones** : bowl
te pron 1 (direct object) : you 2 (indirect object) : for you, to you, from you 3 (reflexive) : yourself, for yourself, to yourself, from yourself
té nm : tea
teatro nm : theater — **teatral** adj : theatrical
techo nm 1 : roof 2 : ceiling (of a room) 3 LÍMITE : upper limit, ceiling — **techumbre** nf : roofing
tecla nf : key (of a musical instrument or a machine) — **teclado** nm : keyboard — **teclear** vt : type in, enter
técnica nf 1 : technique, skill 2 TECNOLOGÍA : technology — **técnico, -ca** adj : technical — ~ n : technician
tecnología nf : technology — **tecnológico, -ca** adj : technological
tecolote nm Lat : owl
tedio nm : boredom — **tedioso, -sa** adj : tedious, boring
teja nf : tile — **tejado** nm : roof
tejer v 1 : knit, crochet 2 : weave (on a loom)
tejido nm 1 : fabric, cloth 2 : tissue (of the body)
tejón nm, pl **-jones** : badger
tela nf 1 : fabric, material 2 ~ **de araña** : spiderweb — **telar** nm : loom — **telaraña** nf : spiderweb, cobweb
tele nf fam : TV, television
telecomunicación nf, pl **-ciones** : telecommunication
teledifusión nf, pl **-siones** : television broadcasting
teledirigido, -da adj : remote-controlled
telefonear v : telephone, call — **telefónico, -ca** adj : telephone — **telefonista** nmf : telephone operator — **teléfono** nm 1 : telephone 2 **llamar por** ~ : make a phone call
telegrafiar {85} v : telegraph — **telegráfico, -ca** adj : telegraphic — **telégrafo** nm : telegraph
telegrama nm : telegram
telenovela nf : soap opera
telepatía nf : telepathy — **telepático, -ca** adj : telepathic
telescopio nm : telescope — **telescópico, -ca** adj : telescopic
telespectador, -dora n : (television) viewer
telesquí nm, pl **-squís** : ski lift
televidente nmf : (television) viewer
televisión nf, pl **-siones** : television, TV — **televisar** vt : televise — **televisor** nm : television set
telón nm, pl **-lones** 1 : curtain (in theater) 2 ~ **de fondo** : backdrop, background
tema nm : theme
temblar {55} vi 1 : tremble, shiver 2 : shake (of a building, the ground, etc.) — **temblor** nm 1 : shaking, trembling 2 or ~ **de tierra** : tremor, earthquake — **tembloroso, -sa** adj : trembling, shaky
temer vt : fear, dread — vi : be afraid — **temerario, -ria** adj : reckless — **temeridad** nf 1 : recklessness 2 : rash act — **temeroso, -sa** adj : fearful — **temor** nm : fear, dread
temperamento nm : temperament — **temperamental** adj : temperamental
temperatura nf : temperature
tempestad nf : storm — **tempestuoso, -sa** adj : stormy
templar vt 1 : temper (steel) 2 : moderate (temperature) 3 : tune (a musical instrument) — **templarse** vr : warm up, cool down — **templado, -da** adj 1 : temperate, mild 2 TIBIO : lukewarm 3 VALIENTE : courageous — **templanza** nf 1 : moderation 2 : mildness (of weather)
templo nm : temple, synagogue
tempo nm : tempo
temporada nf 1 : season, time 2 PERÍODO : period, spell — **temporal** adj 1 : temporal 2 PROVISIONAL : temporary — ~ nm : storm — **temporero, -ra** n : temporary or seasonal worker
temporizador nm : timer
temprano, -na adj : early — **temprano** adv : early
tenaz adj, pl **-naces** : tenacious — **tenaza** nf or **tenazas** nfpl 1 : pliers 2 : tongs (for the fireplace, etc.) 3 : claw (of a crustacean)
tendedero nm : clothesline
tendencia nf : tendency, trend
tender {56} vt 1 : spread out, stretch out 2 : hang out (clothes) 3 : lay (cables, etc.) 4 : set (a trap) — vi ~ **a** : have a tendency towards — **tenderse** vr : stretch out, lie down
tendero, -ra n : shopkeeper
tendido nm 1 : laying (of cables, etc.) 2 : seats pl, stand (at a bullfight)
tendón nm, pl **-dones** : tendon
tenebroso, -sa adj 1 : gloomy, dark 2 SINIESTRO : sinister
tenedor, -dora n 1 : holder 2 ~ **de libros** : bookkeeper — **tenedor** nm : table fork — **teneduría** nf ~ **de libros** : bookkeeping
tener {80} vt 1 : have, possess 2 SUJETAR : hold 3 TOMAR : take 4 ~ **frío (hambre, etc.)** : be cold (hungry, etc.) 5 ~ **... años** : be ... years old 6 ~ **por** : think, consider — v aux 1 ~ **que** : have to, ought to 2 **tenía pensado escribirte** : I've been thinking of writing to you — **tenerse** vr 1 : stand up 2 ~ **por** : consider oneself
tenería nf : tannery
tengo → **tener**
tenia nf : tapeworm
teniente nmf : lieutenant
tenis nms & pl 1 : tennis 2 ~ nmpl : sneakers — **tenista** nmf : tennis player
tenor nm 1 : tenor 2 : tone, sense (in style)
tensar vt 1 : tense, make taut 2 : draw (a bow) — **tensarse** vr : become tense — **tensión** nf, pl **-siones** 1 : tension 2 ~ **arterial** : blood pressure — **tenso, -sa** adj : tense
tentación nf, pl **-ciones** : temptation
tentáculo nm : tentacle
tentar {55} vt 1 : feel, touch 2 ATRAER : tempt — **tentador, -dora** adj : tempting
tentativa nf : attempt
tentempié nm fam : snack
tenue adj 1 : tenuous 2 : faint, weak (of sounds) 3 : light, fine (of thread, rain, etc.)
teñir {67} vt 1 : dye 2 ~ **de** : tinge with
teología nf : theology — **teólogo, -ga** n : theologian
teorema nm : theorem
teoría nf : theory — **teórico, -ca** adj : theoretical
tequila nm : tequila
terapia nf 1 : therapy 2 ~ **ocupacional** : occupational therapy — **terapeuta** nmf : therapist — **terapéutico, -ca** adj : therapeutic
tercermundista adj : third-world
tercero, -ra adj (**tercer** before masculine singular nouns) 1 : third 2 **el Tercer Mundo** : the Third World — ~ n : third (in a series)
terciar vt : sling (sth over one's shoulders), tilt (a hat) — vi 1 : intervene 2 ~ **en** : take part in
tercio nm : third
terciopelo nm : velvet
terco, -ca adj : obstinate, stubborn
tergiversar vt : distort, twist
termal adj : thermal, hot — **termas** nfpl : hot springs
terminar vt : conclude, finish — vi 1 : finish 2 ACABARSE : come to an end — **terminarse** vr 1 : run out 2 ACABARSE : come to an end — **terminación** nf, pl **-ciones** : termination, conclusion — **terminal** adj : terminal, final — ~ nm (in some regions f) : (electric or electronic) terminal — ~ nf (in some regions m) : terminal, station — **término** nm 1 : end 2 PLAZO : period, term 3 ~ **medio** : happy medium 4 ~**s** nmpl : terms — **terminología** nf : terminology
termita nf : termite
termo nm : thermos
termómetro nm : thermometer
termóstato nm : thermostat
ternero, -ra n : calf — **ternera** nf : veal
ternura nf : tenderness
terquedad nf : obstinacy, stubbornness
terracota nf : terra-cotta
terraplén nm, pl **-plenes** : embankment
terráqueo, -quea adj : earth, terrestrial
terrateniente nmf : landowner
terraza nf 1 : terrace 2 BALCÓN : balcony
terremoto nm : earthquake
terreno nm 1 : terrain 2 SUELO : earth, ground 3 SOLAR : plot, tract of land — **terreno, -na** adj : earthly — **terrestre** adj : terrestrial
terrible adj : terrible
terrier nmf : terrier
territorio nm : territory — **territorial** adj : territorial
terrón nm, pl **-rones** 1 : clod (of earth) 2 ~ **de azúcar** : lump of sugar
terror nm : terror — **terrorífico, -ca** adj : terrifying — **terrorismo** nm : terrorism — **terrorista** adj & nmf : terrorist
terroso, -sa adj : earthy
terso, -sa adj 1 : smooth 2 : polished, flowing (of a style) — **tersura** nf : smoothness
tertulia nf : gathering, group
tesis nfs & pl : thesis
tesón nm : persistence, tenacity
tesoro nm 1 : treasure 2 : thesaurus (book) 3 **el Tesoro** : the Treasury — **tesorero, -ra** n : treasurer
testaferro nm : figurehead
testamento nm : testament, will — **testamentario, -ria** n : executor, executrix f — **testar** vi : draw up a will
testarudo, -da adj : stubborn
testículo nm : testicle
testificar {72} v : testify — **testigo** nmf 1 : witness 2 ~ **ocular** : eyewitness — **testimoniar** vi : testify — **testimonio** nm : testimony
tétano or **tétanos** nm : tetanus
tetera nf : teapot
tetilla nf 1 : teat, nipple (of a man) 2 : nipple

(of a baby bottle) — **tetina** *nf* : nipple (of a baby bottle)

tétrico, -ca *adj* : somber, gloomy

textil *adj & nm* : textile

texto *nm* : text — **textual** *adj* **1** : textual **2** EXACTO : literal, exact

textura *nf* : texture

tez *nf, pl* **teces** : complexion

ti *pron* **1** : you **2 ~ mismo, ~ misma** : yourself

tía → **tío**

tianguis *nms & pl Lat* : open-air market

tibio, -bia *adj* : lukewarm

tiburón *nm, pl* **-rones** : shark

tic *nm* : tic

tiempo *nm* **1** : time **2** ÉPOCA : age, period **3** : weather (in meteorology) **4** : halftime (in sports) **5** : tempo (in music) **6** : tense (in grammar)

tienda *nf* **1** : store, shop **2** *or* **~ de campaña** : tent

tiene → **tener**

tienta *nf* **andar a ~s** : feel one's way, grope around

tierno, -na *adj* **1** : tender, fresh, young **2** CARIÑOSO : affectionate

tierra *nf* **1** : land **2** SUELO : ground, earth **3** *or* **~ natal** : native land **4 la Tierra** : the Earth **5 por ~** : overland **6 ~ adentro** : inland

tieso, -sa *adj* **1** : stiff, rigid **2** ERGUIDO : erect **3** ENGREÍDO : haughty

tiesto *nm* : flowerpot

tifoideo, -dea *adj* **fiebre tifoidea** : typhoid fever

tifón *nm, pl* **-fones** : typhoon

tifus *nm* : typhus

tigre, -gresa *n* **1** : tiger, tigress *f* **2** *Lat* : jaguar

tijera *nf or* **tijeras** *nfpl* : scissors — **tijeretada** *nf* : cut, snip

tildar *vt* **~ de** : brand as, call

tilde *nf* **1** : tilde **2** ACENTO : accent mark

tilo *nm* : linden (tree)

timar *vt* : swindle, cheat

timbre *nm* **1** : bell **2** : tone, timbre (of a voice, etc.) **3** SELLO : seal, stamp **4** *Lat* : postage stamp — **timbrar** *vt* : stamp

tímido, -da *adj* : timid, shy — **timidez** *nf* : timidity, shyness

timo *nm fam* : swindle, hoax

timón *nm, pl* **-mones 1** : rudder **2 coger el ~** : take the helm, take charge

tímpano *nm* **1** : eardrum **2 ~s** *nmpl* : timpani, kettledrums

tina *nf* **1** : vat **2** BAÑERA : bathtub

tinieblas *nfpl* **1** : darkness **2 estar en ~ sobre** : be in the dark about

tino *nm* **1** : good judgment, sense **2** TACTO : tact

tinta *nf* **1** : ink **2 saberlo de buena ~** : have it on good authority — **tinte** *nm* **1** : dye, coloring **2** MATIZ : overtone — **tintero** *nm* : inkwell

tintinear *vi* : jingle, tinkle, clink — **tintineo** *nm* : jingle, tinkle, clink

tinto, -ta *adj* **1** : dyed, stained **2** : red (of wine)

tintorería *nf* : dry cleaner (service)

tintura *nf* **1** : dye, tint **2 ~ de yodo** : tincture of iodine

tiña *nf* : ringworm

tío, tía *n* : uncle *m*, aunt *f*

tiovivo *nm* : merry-go-round

típico, -ca *adj* : typical

tiple *nm* : soprano

tipo *nm* **1** : type, kind **2** FIGURA : figure (of a woman), build (of a man) **3** : rate (of interest, etc.) **4** : (printing) type, typeface — **tipo, -pa** *n fam* : guy *m*, gal *f*

tipografía *nf* : typography, printing — **tipográfico, -ca** *adj* : typographical — **tipógrafo, -fa** *n* : printer

tique *or* **tíquet** *nm* : ticket — **tiquete** *nm Lat* : ticket

tira *nf* **1** : strip, strap **2 ~ cómica** : comic strip

tirabuzón *nf, pl* **-zones 1** : corkscrew **2** RIZO : curl, coil

tirada *nf* **1** : throw **2** DISTANCIA : distance **3** IMPRESIÓN : printing, issue — **tirador** *nm* : handle, knob — **tirador, -dora** *n* : marksman *m*, markswoman *f*

tiranía *nf* : tyranny — **tiránico, -ca** *adj* : tyrannical — **tiranizar** {21} *vt* : tyrannize — **tirano, -na** *adj* : tyrannical — **~** *n* : tyrant

tirante *adj* **1** : taut, tight **2** : tense (of a situation, etc.) — **~** *nm* **1** : (shoulder) strap **2 ~s** *nmpl* : suspenders

tirar *vt* **1** : throw **2** DESECHAR : throw away **3** DERRIBAR : knock down **4** DISPARAR : shoot, fire **5** IMPRIMIR : print — *vi* **1** : pull **2** DISPARAR : shoot **3** ATRAER : attract **4** *fam* : get by, manage **5 ~ a** : tend towards — **tirarse** *vr* **1** : throw oneself **2** *fam* : spend (time)

tiritar *vi* : shiver

tiro *nm* **1** : shot, gunshot **2** : shot, kick (in sports) **3** : team (of horses, etc.) **4 a ~** : within range

tiroides *nmf* : thyroid (gland)

tirón *nm, pl* **-rones 1** : pull, yank **2 de un ~** : in one go

tirotear *vt* : shoot at — **tiroteo** *nm* : shooting

tisis *nfs & pl* : tuberculosis

títere *nm* : puppet

titilar *vi* : flicker

titiritero, -ra *n* **1** : puppeteer **2** ACRÓBATA : acrobat

titubear *vi* **1** : hesitate **2** BALBUCEAR : stutter, stammer — **titubeante** *adj* : hesitant, faltering — **titubeo** *nm* : hesitation

titular *vt* : title, call — **titularse** *vr* **1** : be called, be titled **2** LICENCIARSE : receive a degree — **~** *adj* : titular, official — **~** *nm* : headline — **~** *nmf* : holder, incumbent — **título** *nm* **1** : title **2** : degree, qualification (in education)

tiza *nf* : chalk

tiznar *vt* : blacken (with soot, etc.) — **tizne** *nm* : soot

toalla *nf* : towel — **toallero** *nm* : towel rack

tobillo *nm* : ankle

tobogán *nm, pl* **-ganes 1** : toboggan, sled **2** : slide (in a playground, etc.)

tocadiscos *nms & pl* : record player

tocado, -da *adj fam* : touched, not all there — **tocado** *nm* : headgear, headdress

tocador *nm* : dressing table

tocar {72} *vt* **1** : touch, feel **2** MENCIONAR : touch on, refer to **3** : play (a musical instrument) — *vi* **1** : knock, ring **2 ~ en** : touch on, border on

tocayo, -ya *n* : namesake

tocino *nm* **1** : bacon **2** : salt pork (for cooking) — **tocineta** *nf Lat* : bacon

tocólogo, -ga *n* : obstetrician

tocón *nm, pl* **-cones** : stump (of a tree)

todavía *adv* **1** AÚN : still **2** (*in comparisons*) : even **3 ~ no** : not yet

todo, -da *adj* **1** : all **2** CADA, CUALQUIER : every, each **3 a toda velocidad** : at top speed **4 todo el mundo** : everyone, everybody — **~** *pron* **1** : everything, all **2 todos, -das** *pl* : everybody, everyone, all — **todo** *nm* : whole — **todopoderoso, -sa** *adj* : almighty, all-powerful

toga *nf* **1** : toga **2** : gown, robe (of a judge, etc.)

toldo *nm* : awning, canopy

tolerar *vt* : tolerate — **tolerancia** *nf* : tolerance — **tolerante** *adj* : tolerant

toma *nf* **1** : capture **2** DOSIS : dose **3** : take (in film) **4 ~ de corriente** : wall socket, outlet **5 ~ y daca** : give-and-take — **tomar** *vt* **1** : take **2** : have (food or drink) **3** CAPTURAR : capture, seize **4 ~ el sol** : sunbathe **5 ~ tierra** : land — *vi* : drink (alcohol) — **tomarse** *vr* **1** : take (time, etc.) **2** : drink, eat, have (food, drink)

tomate *nm* : tomato

tomillo *nm* : thyme

tomo *nm* : volume

ton *nm* **sin ~ ni son** : without rhyme or reason

tonada *nf* : tune

tonel *nm* : barrel, cask

tonelada *nf* : ton — **tonelaje** *nm* : tonnage

tónica *nf* **1** : tonic (water) **2** TENDENCIA : trend, tone — **tónico, -ca** *adj* : tonic — **tónico** *nm* : tonic (in medicine)

tono *nm* **1** : tone **2** : shade (of colors) **3** : key (in music)

tontería *nf* **1** : silly thing or remark **2** ESTUPIDEZ : foolishness **3 decir ~s** : talk nonsense — **tonto, -ta** *adj* **1** : stupid, silly **2 a tontas y a locas** : haphazardly — **~** *n* : fool, idiot

topacio *nm* : topaz

toparse *vr* **~ con** : run into, come across

tope *nm* **1** : limit, end **2** *or* **~ de puerta** : doorstop **3** *Lat* : bump — **~** *adj* : maximum

tópico, -ca *adj* **1** : topical, external **2** MANIDO : trite — **tópico** *nm* : cliché

topo *nm* : mole (animal)

toque *nm* **1** : (light) touch **2** : ringing, peal (of a bell) **3 ~ de queda** : curfew **4 ~ de diana** : reveille — **toquetear** *vt* : finger, handle

tórax *nms & pl* : thorax

torbellino *nm* : whirlwind

torcer {14} *vt* **1** : twist, bend **2** : turn (a corner) **3** : wring (out) — *vi* : turn — **torcerse** *vr* **1** : twist, sprain **2** FRUSTRARSE : go wrong **3** DESVIARSE : go astray — **torcedura** *nf* **1** : twisting **2** ESGUINCE : sprain — **torcido, -da** *adj* : twisted, crooked

tordo, -da *adj* : dappled — **tordo** *nm* : thrush (bird)

torear *vt* **1** : fight (bulls) **2** ELUDIR : dodge, sidestep — *vi* : fight bulls — **toreo** *nm* : bullfighting — **torero, -ra** *n* : bullfighter

tormenta *nf* : storm — **tormento** *nm* **1** : torture **2** ANGUSTIA : torment, anguish — **tormentoso, -sa** *adj* : stormy

tornado *nm* : tornado

tornar *vt* CONVERTIR : render, turn — *vi* : go back, return — **tornarse** *vr* : become, turn into

torneo *nm* : tournament

tornillo *nm* : screw

torniquete *nm* **1** : turnstile **2** : tourniquet (in medicine)

torno *nm* **1** : winch **2** : (carpenter's) lathe **3 ~ de alfarero** : (potter's) wheel **4 ~ de banco** : vise **5 en ~ a** : around, about

toro *nm* **1** : bull **2 ~s** *nmpl* : bullfight

toronja *nf* : grapefruit

torpe *adj* **1** : clumsy, awkward **2** ESTÚPIDO : stupid, dull

torpedear *vt* : torpedo — **torpedo** *nm* : torpedo

torpeza *nf* **1** : clumsiness, awkwardness **2** ESTUPIDEZ : slowness, stupidity

torre *nf* **1** : tower **2** : turret (on a ship, etc.) **3** : rook, castle (in chess)

torrente *nm* **1** : torrent **2 ~ sanguíneo** : bloodstream — **torrencial** *adj* : torrential

tórrido, -da *adj* : torrid

torsión *nf, pl* **-siones** : twisting

torta *nf* **1** : torte, cake **2** *Lat* : sandwich

tortazo *nm fam* : blow, wallop

tortícolis *nfs & pl* : stiff neck

tortilla *nf* **1** : tortilla **2** *or* **~ de huevo** : omelet

tórtola *nf* : turtledove

tortuga *nf* **1** : turtle, tortoise **2 ~ de agua dulce** : terrapin

tortuoso, -sa *adj* : tortuous, winding

tortura *nf* : torture — **torturar** *vt* : torture

tos *nf* **1** : cough **2 ~ ferina** : whooping cough

tosco, -ca *adj* : rough, coarse

toser *vi* : cough

tosquedad *nf* : coarseness

tostar {19} *vt* **1** : toast **2** BRONCEAR : tan — **tostarse** *vr* : get a tan — **tostada** *nf* **1** : piece of toast **2** *Lat* : tostada — **tostador** *nm* : toaster

tostón *nm, pl* **-tones** *Lat* : fried plantain chip

total *adj & nm* : total — **~** *adv* : so, after all — **totalidad** *nf* : whole — **totalitario, -ria** *adj & n* : totalitarian — **totalitarismo** *nm* : totalitarianism — **totalizar** {21} *vt* : total, add up to

tóxico, -ca *adj* : toxic, poisonous — **tóxico** *nm* : poison — **toxicomanía** *nf* : drug addiction — **toxicómano, -na** *n* : drug addict — **toxina** *nf* : toxin

tozudo, -da *adj* : stubborn

traba *nf* : obstacle, hindrance

trabajar *vi* **1** : work **2** : act, perform (in theater, etc.) — *vt* **1** : work (metal) **2** : knead (dough) **3** MEJORAR : work on, work at — **trabajador, -dora** *adj* : hard-working — **~** *n* : worker — **trabajo** *nm* **1** : work **2** EMPLEO : job **3** TAREA : task **4** ESFUERZO : effort **5 costar ~** : be difficult **6 ~ en equipo** : teamwork **7 ~s** *nmpl* : hardships, difficulties — **trabajoso, -sa** *adj* : hard, laborious

trabalenguas *nms & pl* : tongue twister

trabar *vt* **1** : join, connect **2** OBSTACULIZAR : impede **3** : strike up (a conversation, etc.) **4** : thicken (sauces) — **trabarse** *vr* **1** : jam **2** ENREDARSE : become entangled **3 se le traba la lengua** : he gets tongue-tied

trabucar {72} *vt* : mix up

tracción *nf* : traction

tractor *nm* : tractor

tradición *nf, pl* **-ciones** : tradition — **tradicional** *adj* : traditional

traducir {61} *vt* : translate — **traducción** *nf, pl* **-ciones** : translation — **traductor, -tora** *n* : translator

traer {81} *vt* **1** : bring **2** CAUSAR : cause, bring about **3** CONTENER : carry, have **4** LLEVAR : wear — **traerse** *vr* **1** : bring along **2 traérselas** : be difficult

traficar {72} *vi* **~ en** : traffic in — **traficante** *nmf* : dealer, trafficker — **tráfico** *nm* **1** : trade (of merchandise) **2** : traffic (of vehicles)

tragaluz *nf, pl* **-luces** : skylight

tragar {52} *vt* **1** : swallow **2** *fam* : put up with — *vi* : swallow — **tragarse** *vr* **1** : swallow **2** ABSORBER : absorb, swallow up

tragedia *nf* : tragedy — **trágico, -ca** *adj* : tragic

trago *nm* **1** : swallow, swig **2** *fam* : drink, liquor — **tragón, -gona** *adj fam* : greedy — **~** *nmf fam* : glutton

traicionar *vt* : betray — **traición** *nf, pl* **-ciones 1** : betrayal **2** : treason (in law) — **traidor, -dora** *adj* : traitorous, treacherous — **~** *n* : traitor

trailer *nm* : trailer

traje *nm* **1** : dress, costume **2** : (man's) suit **3 ~ de baño** : bathing suit

trajinar *vi fam* : rush around — **trajín** *nm, pl* **-jines** *fam* : hustle and bustle

trama *nf* **1** : plot **2** : weave, weft (of fabric) — **tramar** *vt* **1** : plot, plan **2** : weave (fabric)

tramitar *vt* : negotiate — **trámite** *nm* : procedure, step

tramo *nm* **1** : stretch, section **2** : flight (of stairs)

trampa *nf* **1** : trap **2 hacer ~s** : cheat — **trampear** *vt* : cheat

trampilla *nf* : trapdoor

trampolín *nm, pl* **-lines 1** : diving board **2** : trampoline (in a gymnasium, etc.)

tramposo, -sa *adj* : crooked, cheating — **~** *n* : cheat, swindler

tranca *nf* **1** : cudgel, club **2** : bar (for a door or window)

trance *nm* **1** : critical juncture **2** : (hypnotic) trance **3 en ~ de** : in the process of

tranquilo, -la *adj* : calm, tranquil — **tranquilidad** *nf* : tranquility, peace — **tranquilizante** *nm* : tranquilizer — **tranquilizar** {21} *vt* : calm, soothe — **tranquilizarse** *vr* : calm down

trans- *see also* **tras-**

transacción *nf, pl* **-ciones** : transaction

transatlántico, -ca *adj* : transatlantic — **transatlántico** *nm* : ocean liner

transbordador *nm* **1** : ferry **2 ~ espacial** : space shuttle — **transbordar** *vt* : transfer — *vi* : change (of trains, etc.) — **transbordo** *nm* **hacer ~** : change (trains, etc.)

transcribir {33} *vt* : transcribe — **transcripción** *nf, pl* **-ciones** : transcription

transcurrir *vi* : elapse, pass — **transcurso** *nm* : course, progression

transeúnte *nmf* : passerby

transferir {76} *vt* : transfer — **transferencia** *nf* : transfer, transference

transformar *vt* **1** : transform, change **2** CONVERTIR : convert — **transformarse** *vr* : be transformed — **transformación** *nf, pl* **-ciones** : transformation — **transformador** *nm* : transformer

transfusión *nf, pl* **-siones** : transfusion

transgredir {1} *vt* : transgress — **transgresión** *nf* : transgression

transición *nf, pl* **-ciones** : transition

transido, -da *adj* : overcome, stricken

transigir {35} *vi* : give in, compromise

transistor *nm* : transistor

transitar *vi* : go, travel — **transitable** *adj* : passable

transitivo, -va *adj* : transitive

tránsito *nm* **1** : transit **2** TRÁFICO : traffic **3 hora de máximo ~** : rush hour — **transitorio, -ria** *adj* : transitory

transmitir *vt* **1** : transmit **2** : broadcast (radio, TV, etc.) **3** CEDER : pass on — **transmisión** *nf, pl* **-siones 1** : broadcast **2** TRANSFERENCIA : transfer **3** : transmission (of an automobile) — **transmisor** *nm* : transmitter

transparentarse *vr* : be transparent — **transparente** *adj* : transparent

transpirar *vi* : perspire, sweat — **transpiración** *nf, pl* **-ciones** : perspiration, sweat

transponer {60} *vt* : transpose, move — **transponerse** *vr* **1** : set (of the sun, etc.) **2** DORMITAR : doze off

transportar *vt* : transport, carry — **transportarse** *vr* : get carried away — **transporte** *nm* : transport, transportation

transversal *adj* **corte ~** : cross section

tranvía *nm* : streetcar, trolley

trapear *vt Lat* : mop

trapecio *nm* : trapeze

trapisonda *nf* : scheme, plot

trapo *nm* **1** : cloth, rag **2 ~s** *nmpl fam* : clothes

tráquea *nf* : trachea, windpipe

traquetear *vi* : rattle around, shake — **traqueteo** *nm* : rattling

tras *prep* **1** DESPUÉS DE : after **2** DÉTRAS DE : behind

tras- *see also* **trans-**

trascender {56} *vi* **1** : leak out, become known **2** EXTENDERSE : spread **3 ~ de** : transcend — **trascendencia** *nf* : importance — **trascendental** *adj* **1** : transcendental **2** IMPORTANTE : important

trasegar *vt* : move around

trasero, -ra *adj* : rear, back — **trasero** *nm* : buttocks *pl*

trasfondo *nm* **1** : background **2** : undercurrent (of suspicion, etc.)

trasladar *vt* **1** : transfer, move **2** POSPONER : postpone — **trasladarse** *vr* : move, relocate — **traslado** *nm* **1** : transfer, move **2** COPIA : copy

traslapar *vt* : overlap — **traslaparse** *vr* : overlap

traslucirse {45} *vr* **1** : be translucent **2** REVELARSE : be revealed — **traslúcido, -da** : translucent

trasnochar *vi* : stay up all night

traspasar *vt* **1** : pierce, go through **2** EXCEDER : go beyond **3** ATRAVESAR : cross, go across **4** : transfer (a business, etc.) — **traspaso** *nm* : transfer, sale

traspié *nm* **1** : stumble, trip **2** ERROR : blunder

trasplantar *vt* : transplant — **trasplante** *nm* : transplant

trasquilar *vt* : shear

traste *nm* **1** : fret (on a guitar, etc.) **2** *Lat* : (kitchen) utensil **3 dar al ~ con** : ruin **4 irse al ~** : fall through

trastos *nmpl fam* : pieces of junk, stuff

trastornar *vt* **1** : disturb, disrupt **2** VOLVER LOCO : drive crazy — **trastornarse** *vr* : go crazy — **trastornado, -da** *adj* : disturbed, deranged — **trastorno** *nm* **1** : disturbance, disruption **2** : (medical or psychological) disorder

trastrocar *vt* : change, switch around

tratable *adj* : friendly, sociable

tratar *vi* **1 ~ con** : deal with **2 ~ de** : try to **3 ~ de** *or* **~ sobre** : be about, concern **4 ~ en** : deal in — *vt* **1** : treat **2** MANEJAR : deal with, handle — **tratarse** *vr* **~ de** : be about, concern — **tratado** *nm* **1** : treatise **2** CONVENIO : treaty — **tratamiento** *nm* : treatment — **trato** *nm* **1** : treatment **2** ACUERDO : deal, agreement **3 ~s** *nmpl* : dealings

trauma *nm* : trauma — **traumático, -ca** *adj* : traumatic
través *nm* **1 a ~ de** : across, through **2 de ~** : sideways
travesaño *nm* : crosspiece
travesía *nf* : voyage, crossing (of the sea)
travesura *nf* **1** : prank **2 ~s** *nfpl* : mischief — **travieso, -sa** *adj* : mischievous, naughty
trayecto *nm* **1** : trajectory, path **2** VIAJE : journey **3** RUTA : route — **trayectoria** *nf* : path, trajectory
traza *nf* **1** : design, plan **2** ASPECTO : appearance — **trazado** *nm* **1** : outline, sketch **2** DISEÑO : plan, layout — **trazar** {21} *vt* **1** : trace, outline **2** : draw up (a plan, etc.) — **trazo** *nm* : stroke, line
trébol *nm* **1** : clover, shamrock **2 ~es** *nmpl* : clubs (in playing cards)
trece *adj & nm* : thirteen — **treceavo, -va** *adj* : thirteenth — **treceavo** *nm* : thirteenth (fraction)
trecho *nm* **1** : stretch, period **2** DISTANCIA : distance **3 de ~ a ~** : at intervals
tregua *nf* **1** : truce **2 sin ~** : without respite
treinta *adj & nm* : thirty — **treintavo, -va** *adj* : thirtieth — **treintavo** *nm* : thirtieth (fraction)
tremendo, -da *adj* : tremendous, enormous
trementina *nf* : turpentine
trémulo, -la *adj* : trembling, flickering
tren *nm* **1** : train **2 ~ de aterrizaje** : landing gear
trenza *nf* : braid, pigtail — **trenzar** {21} *vt* : braid — **trenzarse** *vr Lat* : get involved
trepar *vi* **1** : climb **2** : creep, spread (of a plant) — **treparse** *vr* : climb (up) — **trepador, -dora** *adj* : climbing — **trepadora** *nf* **1** : climbing plant **2** *fam* : social climber
trepidar *vi* : shake, vibrate
tres *adj & nm* : three — **trescientos, -tas** *adj* : three hundred — **trescientos** *nms & pl* : three hundred
treta *nf* : trick
triángulo *nm* : triangle — **triangular** *adj* : triangular
tribu *nf* : tribe — **tribal** *adj* : tribal
tribulación *nf, pl* **-ciones** : tribulation
tribuna *nf* **1** : dais, platform **2** : grandstand, bleachers *pl* (in a stadium)
tribunal *nm* : court, tribunal
tributar *vt* : pay, render — *vi* : pay taxes — **tributo** *nm* **1** : tribute **2** IMPUESTO : tax
triciclo *nm* : tricycle
tricolor *adj* : tricolored
tridimensional *adj* : three-dimensional
trigésimo, -ma *adj & n* : thirtieth
trigo *nm* : wheat
trigonometría *nf* : trigonometry
trillado, -da *adj* : trite
trillar *vt* : thresh — **trilladora** *nf* : threshing machine
trillizo, -za *n* : triplet
trilogía *nf* : trilogy
trimestral *adj* : quarterly
trinar *vi* : warble
trinchar *vt* : carve
trinchera *nf* **1** : trench, ditch **2** IMPERMEABLE : trench coat
trineo *nm* : sled, sleigh
trinidad *nf* : trinity
trino *nm* : trill, warble
trío *nm* : trio
tripa *nf* **1** : gut, intestine **2 ~s** *nfpl fam* : belly, tummy
triple *adj & nm* : triple — **triplicar** {72} *vt* : triple
trípode *nm* : tripod
tripular *vt* : man — **tripulación** *nf, pl* **-ciones** : crew — **tripulante** *nmf* : crew member
tris *nm* **estar en un ~ de** : be within an inch of
triste *adj* **1** : sad **2** SOMBRÍO : dismal, gloomy **3** MISERABLE : sorry, miserable — **tristeza** *nf* : sadness, grief
tritón *nm, pl* **-tones** : newt
triturar *vt* : crush, grind
triunfar *vi* : triumph, win — **triunfal** *adj* : triumphal — **triunfante** *adj* : triumphant — **triunfo** *nm* : triumph, victory
trivial *adj* : trivial
triza *nf* **1** : shred, bit **2 hacer ~s** : smash to pieces
trocar {82} *vt* **1** CONVERTIR : change **2** INTERCAMBIAR : exchange
trocha *nf* : path, trail
trofeo *nm* : trophy
trombón *nm, pl* **-bones 1** : trombone **2** : trombonist (musician)
trombosis *nf* : thrombosis
trompa *nf* **1** : trunk (of an elephant), snout **2** : horn (musical instrument) **3** : tube (in anatomy)
trompeta *nf* : trumpet — **trompetista** *nmf* : trumpet player
trompo *nm* : top (toy)
tronada *nf* : thunderstorm — **tronar** {19} *vi* : thunder, rage — *vt Lat fam* : shoot — *v impers* : thunder
tronchar *vt* **1** : snap **2** TRUNCAR : cut short
tronco *nm* **1** : trunk (of a tree) **2** : torso (of a person) **3 dormir como un ~** : sleep like a log
trono *nm* : throne
tropa *nf* : troops *pl*, soldiers *pl*
tropel *nm* : mob
tropezar {29} *vi* **1** : trip, stumble **2 ~ con** : come up against, run into — **tropezón** *nm, pl* **-zones 1** : stumble **2** EQUIVOCACIÓN : mistake, slip
trópico *nm* : tropic — **tropical** *adj* : tropical
tropiezo *nm* **1** CONTRATIEMPO : snag, setback **2** EQUIVOCACIÓN : mistake, slip
trotar *vi* **1** : trot **2** *fam* : rush about — **trote** *nm* **1** : trot **2** *fam* : rush, bustle **3 al ~** : at a trot, quickly
trozo *nm* : piece, bit, chunk
trucha *nf* : trout
truco *nm* **1** : knack **2** ARDID : trick
trueno *nm* : thunder
trueque *nm* : barter, exchange
trufa *nf* : truffle
truncar {72} *vt* **1** : cut short **2** : thwart, spoil (plans, etc.)
tu *adj* : your
tú *pron* : you
tuba *nf* : tuba
tuberculosis *nf* : tuberculosis
tubo *nm* **1** : tube, pipe **2 ~ de escape** : exhaust pipe (of a vehicle) **3 ~ de desagüe** : drainpipe — **tubería** *nf* : pipes *pl*, tubing
tuerca *nf* : nut (for a screw)
tuerto, -ta *adj* : one-eyed, blind in one eye
tuétano *nm* : marrow
tufo *nm* **1** : vapor **2** *fam* : stench, stink
tugurio *nm* : hovel
tulipán *nm, pl* **-panes** : tulip
tullido, -da *adj* : crippled, paralyzed
tumba *nf* : tomb, grave
tumbar *vt* : knock down, knock over — **tumbarse** *vr* : lie down — **tumbo** *nm* **dar ~s** : jolt, bump around
tumor *nm* : tumor
tumulto *nm* **1** : commotion, tumult **2** MOTÍN : riot — **tumultuoso, -sa** *adj* : tumultuous
tuna *nf* : prickly pear
túnel *nm* : tunnel
túnica *nf* : tunic
tupé *nm* : toupee
tupido, -da *adj* : dense, thick
turba *nf* **1** : peat **2** MUCHEDUMBRE : mob, throng
turbación *nf, pl* **-ciones 1** : disturbance **2** CONFUSIÓN : confusion
turbante *nm* : turban
turbar *vt* **1** : disturb, upset **2** CONFUNDIR : confuse, bewilder
turbina *nf* : turbine
turbio, -bia *adj* **1** : cloudy, murky **2** : blurred (of vision, etc.) — **turbión** *nm, pl* **-biones** : squall
turbulencia *nf* : turbulence — **turbulento, -ta** *adj* : turbulent
turco, -ca *adj* : Turkish — **turco** *nm* : Turkish (language)
turista *nmf* : tourist — **turismo** *nm* : tourism, tourist industry — **turístico, -ca** *adj* : tourist, travel
turnarse *vr* : take turns, alternate — **turno** *nm* **1** : turn **2 ~ de noche** : night shift
turquesa *nf* : turquoise
turrón *nm, pl* **-rrones** : nougat
tutear *vt* : address as *tú*
tutela *nf* **1** : guardianship (in law) **2 bajo la ~ de** : under the protection of
tuteo *nm* : addressing as *tú*
tutor, -tora *n* **1** : guardian **2** : tutor (in education)
tuyo, -ya *adj* : yours, of yours — **~** *pron* **1 el tuyo, la tuya, lo tuyo, los tuyos, las tuyas** : yours **2 los tuyos** : your family, your friends

U

u[1] *nf* : u, 22d letter of the Spanish alphabet
u[2] *conj* (*used before words beginning with o- or ho-*) : or
uapití *nm* : American elk, wapiti
ubicar {72} *vt Lat* **1** COLOCAR : place, position **2** LOCALIZAR : find — **ubicarse** *vr* : be located
ubre *nf* : udder
Ud., Uds. → **usted**
ufanarse *vr* **~ de** : boast about — **ufano, -na** *adj* **1** : proud **2** ENGREÍDO : self-satisfied
ujier *nm* : usher
úlcera *nf* : ulcer
ulterior *adj* : later, subsequent — **ulteriormente** *adv* : subsequently
últimamente *adv* : lately, recently
ultimar *vt* **1** : complete, finish **2** *Lat* : kill — **ultimátum** *nm, pl* **-tums** : ultimatum
último, -ma *adj* **1** : last **2** : latest, most recent (in time) **3** : farthest (in space) **4 por último** : finally
ultrajar *vt* : outrage, insult — **ultraje** *nm* : outrage, insult
ultramar *nm* **de ~** *or* **en ~** : overseas — **ultramarino, -na** *adj* : overseas — **ultramarinos** *nmpl* **tienda de ~** : grocery store
ultranza: **a ~** *adv phr* : to the extreme — **a ~** *adj phr* : out-and-out, complete
ultrasonido *nm* : ultrasound
ultravioleta *adj* : ultraviolet
ulular *vi* **1** : hoot (of an owl) **2** : howl (of a wolf, the wind, etc.) — **ululato** *nm* : hoot (of an owl)
umbilical *adj* : umbilical
umbral *nm* : threshold
un, una *art, mpl* **unos 1** : a, an **2 unos** *or* **unas** *pl* : some, a few **3 unos** *or* **unas** *pl* : about, approximately — **un** *adj* → **uno**
unánime *adj* : unanimous — **unanimidad** *nf* : unanimity
uncir {83} *vt* : yoke
undécimo, -ma *adj & n* : eleventh
ungir {35} *vt* : anoint — **ungüento** *nm* : ointment
único, -ca *adj* **1** : only, sole **2** EXCEPCIONAL : unique — **~** *n* : only one — **únicamente** *adv* : only
unicornio *nm* : unicorn
unidad *nf* **1** : unit **2** ARMONÍA : unity — **unido, -da** *adj* **1** : united **2** : close (of friends, etc.)
unificar {72} *vt* : unify — **unificación** *nf, pl* **-ciones** : unification
uniformar *vt* **1** : standardize **2** : put into uniform — **uniformado, -da** *adj* : uniformed — **uniforme** *adj & nm* : uniform — **uniformidad** *nf* : uniformity
unilateral *adj* : unilateral
unir *vt* **1** : unite, join **2** COMBINAR : combine, mix together — **unirse** *vr* **1** : join together **2 ~ a** : join — **unión** *nf, pl* **uniones 1** : union **2** JUNTURA : joint, coupling
unísono *nm* **al ~** : in unison
unitario, -ria *adj* : unitary
universal *adj* : universal
universidad *nf* : university, college — **universitario, -ria** *adj* : university, college
universo *nm* : universe
uno, una (**un** *before masculine singular nouns*) *adj* : one — **~** *pron* **1** : one **2 unos, unas** *pl* : some **3 uno(s) a otro(s)** : one another, each other **4 uno y otro** : both — **uno** *nm* : one (number)
untar *vt* **1** : smear, grease **2** *fam* : bribe — **untuoso, -sa** *adj* : greasy, sticky
uña *nf* **1** : nail, fingernail **2** : claw (of a cat, etc.), hoof (of a horse, etc.)
uranio *nm* : uranium
Urano *nm* : Uranus
urbano, -na *adj* : urban, city — **urbanidad** *nf* : politeness, courtesy — **urbanización** *nf, pl* **-ciones** : housing development — **urbanizar** *vt* : develop, urbanize — **urbe** *nf* : large city
urdir *vt* **1** : warp **2** PLANEAR : plot — **urdimbre** *nf* : warp (of a fabric)
urgir {35} *v impers* : be urgent, be pressing — **urgencia** *nf* **1** : urgency **2** EMERGENCIA : emergency — **urgente** *adj* : urgent
urinario, -ria *adj* : urinary — **urinario** *nm* : urinal (place)
urna *nf* **1** : urn **2** : ballot box (for voting)
urraca *nf* : magpie
uruguayo, -ya *adj* : Uruguayan
usar *vt* **1** : use **2** LLEVAR : wear — **usarse 1** EMPLEARSE : be used **2** : be worn, be in fashion — **usado, -da** *adj* **1** : used **2** GASTADO : worn, worn-out — **usanza** *nf* : custom, usage — **uso** *nm* **1** : use **2** DESGASTE : wear and tear **3** USANZA : custom, usage
usted *pron* **1** (*used in formal address; often written as* **Ud.** *or* **Vd.**) : you **2 ~es** *pl* (*often written as* **Uds.** *or* **Vds.**) : you (all)
usual *adj* : usual
usuario, -ria *n* : user
usura *nf* : usury — **usurero, -ra** *n* : usurer
usurpar *vt* : usurp
utensilio *nm* : utensil, tool
útero *nm* : uterus, womb
utilizar {21} *vt* : use, utilize — **útil** *adj* : useful — **útiles** *nmpl* : implements, tools — **utilidad** *nf* : utility, usefulness — **utilitario, -ria** *adj* : utilitarian — **utilización** *nf, pl* **-ciones** : utilization, use
uva *nf* : grape

V

v *nf* : v, 23d letter of the Spanish alphabet
va → **ir**
vaca *nf* : cow
vacaciones *nfpl* **1** : vacation **2 estar de ~** : be on vacation **3 irse de ~** : go on vacation
vacante *adj* : vacant — **~** *nf* : vacancy
vaciar {85} *vt* **1** : empty (out) **2** AHUECAR : hollow out **3** : cast, mold (a statue, etc.)
vacilar *vi* **1** : hesitate, waver **2** : flicker (of light) **3** TAMBALEARSE : be unsteady, wobble **4** *fam* : joke, fool around — **vacilación** *nf, pl* **-ciones** : hesitation — **vacilante** *adj* **1** : hesitant **2** OSCILANTE : unsteady
vacío, -cía *adj* : empty — **vacío** *nm* **1** : void **2** : vacuum (in physics) **3** HUECO : space, gap
vacuna *nf* : vaccine — **vacunación** *nf, pl* **-ciones** : vaccination — **vacunar** *vt* : vaccinate
vacuno, -na *adj* : bovine
vadear *vt* : ford — **vado** *nm* : ford
vagabundear *vi* : wander — **vagabundo, -da** *adj* **1** : vagrant **2** : stray (of a dog, etc.) — **~** *n* : hobo, bum — **vagancia** *nf* **1** : vagrancy **2** PEREZA : laziness, idleness — **vagar** {52} *vi* : roam, wander
vagina *nf* : vagina
vago, -ga *adj* **1** : vague **2** PEREZOSO : lazy, idle — **~** *n* : idler, loafer
vagón *nm, pl* **-gones** : car (of a train)
vahído *nm* : dizzy spell
vaho *nm* **1** : breath **2** VAPOR : vapor, steam
vaina *nf* **1** : sheath, scabbard **2** : pod (in botany) **3** *Lat fam* : bother, pain
vainilla *nf* : vanilla
vaivén *nm, pl* **-venes 1** : swinging, swaying **2** : coming and going (of people, etc.) **3 vaivenes** *nmpl* : ups and downs
vajilla *nf* : dishes *pl*
vale *nm* **1** : voucher **2** PAGARÉ : IOU — **valedero, -ra** *adj* : valid
valentía *nf* : courage, bravery
valer {84} *vt* **1** : be worth **2** COSTAR : cost **3** GANAR : gain, earn **4** EQUIVALER A : be equal to — *vi* **1** : have value, cost **2** SER VÁLIDO : be valid, count **3** SERVIR : be of use **4 hacerse ~** : assert oneself **5 más vale** : it's better — **valerse** *vr* **1 ~ de** : take advantage of **2 ~ solo** *or* **~ por sí mismo** : look after oneself
valeroso, -sa *adj* : courageous
valga, etc. → **valer**
valía *nf* : worth
validar *vt* : validate — **validez** *nf* : validity — **válido, -da** *adj* : valid
valiente *adj* **1** : brave **2** (*used ironically*) : fine, great
valija *nf* : case, valise
valioso, -sa *adj* : valuable
valla *nf* **1** : fence **2** : hurdle (in sports) — **vallar** *vt* : put a fence around
valle *nm* : valley
valor *nm* **1** : value, worth **2** VALENTÍA : courage, valor **3 objetos de ~** : valuables **4 sin ~** : worthless **5 ~es** *nmpl* : values, principles **6 ~es** *nmpl* : securities, bonds — **valoración** *nf, pl* **-ciones** : valuation — **valorar** *vt* : evaluate, assess
vals *nm* : waltz
válvula *nf* : valve
vamos → **ir**
vampiro *nm* : vampire
van → **ir**
vanagloriarse *vr* : boast, brag
vándalo *nm* : vandal — **vandalismo** : vandalism
vanguardia *nf* **1** : vanguard **2** : avant-garde (in art, music, etc.) **3 a la ~** : at/in the forefront
vanidad *nf* : vanity — **vanidoso, -sa** *adj* : vain, conceited
vano, -na *adj* **1** INÚTIL : vain, useless **2** SUPERFICIAL : empty, hollow **3 en vano** : in vain
vapor *nm* **1** : steam, vapor **2 al ~** : steamed — **vaporizador** *nm* : vaporizer — **vaporizar** {21} *vt* : vaporize
vaquero, -ra *n* : cowboy *m*, cowgirl *f* — **vaqueros** *nmpl* : jeans
vara *nf* **1** : stick, rod **2** : staff (of office)
varado, -da *adj* : stranded
variar {85} *vt* **1** : vary **2** CAMBIAR : change, alter — *vi* : vary, change — **variable** *adj & nf* : variable — **variación** *nf, pl* **-ciones** : variation — **variado, -da** *adj* : varied — **variante** *nf* : variant
varicela *nf* : chicken pox
varicoso, -sa *adj* : varicose
variedad *nf* : variety
varilla *nf* : rod, stick
vario, -ria *adj* **1** : varied **2 ~s** *pl* : several
varita *nf* : wand
variz *nf, pl* **-rices** *or* **várices** : varicose vein
varón *nm, pl* **-rones 1** : man, male **2** NIÑO : boy — **varonil** *adj* : manly
vas → **ir**
vasco, -ca *adj* : Basque — **vasco** *nm* : Basque (language)
vasija *nf* : container, vessel
vaso *nm* **1** : glass **2** : vessel (in anatomy)
vástago *nm* **1** : offspring, descendent **2** BROTE : shoot **3** VARILLA : rod
vasto, -ta *adj* : vast
vaticinar *vt* : prophesy, predict — **vaticinio** *nm* : prophecy
vatio *nm* : watt
vaya, etc. → **ir**
Vd., Vds. → **usted**
ve, etc. → **ir, ver**
vecinal *adj* : local
vecino, -na *n* **1** : neighbor **2** HABITANTE : resident, inhabitant — **~** *adj* : neighboring — **vecindad** *nf* : neighborhood, vicini-

ty — **vecindario** *nm* **1** : neighborhood **2** VECINOS : community, residents *pl*

vedar *vt* : prohibit — **veda** *nf* **1** : prohibition, ban **2** : closed season (for hunting and fishing) — **vedado** *nm* : preserve (for game, etc.)

vega *nf* : fertile lowland

vegetal *nm* : vegetable, plant — ~ *adj* : vegetable — **vegetación** *nf, pl* **-ciones** : vegetation — **vegetar** *vi* : vegetate — **vegetariano, -na** *adj & n* : vegetarian

vehemente *adj* : vehement

vehículo *nm* : vehicle

veinte *adj & nm* : twenty — **veinteavo, -va** *adj* : twentieth — **veinteavo** *nm* : twentieth — **veintena** *nf* : group of twenty, score

vejar *vt* : mistreat, humiliate — **vejación** *nf, pl* **-ciones** : humiliation

vejez *nf* : old age

vejiga *nf* **1** : bladder **2** AMPOLLA : blister

vela *nf* **1** : candle **2** : sail (of a ship) **3** VIGILIA : vigil **4 pasar la noche en ~** : have a sleepless night

velada *nf* : evening (party)

velar *vt* **1** : hold a wake over **2** CUIDAR : watch over **3** : blur (a photograph) **4** OCULTAR : veil, mask — *vi* **1** : stay awake **2 ~ por** : watch over — **velado, -da** *adj* **1** : veiled, hidden **2** : blurred (of a photograph)

velero *nm* : sailing ship

veleta *nf* : weather vane

vello *nm* **1** : body hair **2** PELUSA : down, fuzz — **vellón** *nm, pl* **-llones** : fleece — **velloso, -sa** *adj* : downy, fluffy — **velludo, -da** *adj* : hairy

velo *nm* : veil

veloz *adj, pl* **-loces** : fast, quick — **velocidad** *nf* **1** : speed, velocity **2** MARCHA : gear (of an automobile) — **velocímetro** *nm* : speedometer

vena *nf* **1** : vein **2** : grain (of wood) **3** DISPOSICIÓN : mood **4 tener ~ de** : have a talent for

venado *nm* **1** : deer **2** : venison (in cooking)

vencer {86} *vt* **1** : beat, defeat **2** SUPERAR : overcome — *vi* **1** : win **2** CADUCAR : expire — **vencerse** *vr* : collapse, give way — **vencedor, -dora** *adj* : winning — ~ *n* : winner — **vencido, -da** *adj* **1** : beaten, defeated **2** CADUCADO : expired **3** : due, payable (in finance) **4 darse por ~** : give up — **vencimiento** *nm* **1** : expiration **2** : maturity (of a loan)

venda *nf* : bandage — **vendaje** *nm* : bandage, dressing — **vendar** *vt* **1** : bandage **2 ~ los ojos** : blindfold

vendaval *nm* : gale

vender *vt* : sell — **venderse** *vr* **1** : be sold **2 se vende** : for sale — **vendedor, -dora** *n* **1** : seller **2** : salesman *m*, saleswoman *f* (in a store)

vendimia *nf* : grape harvest

vendrá, etc. → **venir**

veneno *nm* **1** : poison **2** : venom (of a snake, etc.) — **venenoso, -sa** *adj* : poisonous

venerar *vt* : venerate, revere — **venerable** *adj* : venerable — **veneración** *nf, pl* **-ciones** : veneration, reverence

venéreo, -rea *adj* : venereal

venezolano, -na *adj* : Venezuelan

venga → **venir**

vengar {52} *vt* : avenge — **vengarse** *vr* : get even, take revenge — **venganza** *nf* : vengeance, revenge — **vengativo, -va** *adj* : vindictive, vengeful

venia *nf* **1** : permission **2** : pardon (in law)

venial *adj* : venial, petty

venir {87} *vi* **1** : come **2** LLEGAR : arrive **3** HALLARSE : be, appear **4** QUEDAR : fit **5 que viene** : coming, next **6 ~ a ser** : turn out to be **7 ~ bien** : be suitable — **venirse** *vr* **1** : come **2 ~ abajo** : fall apart, collapse — **venida** *nf* **1** : arrival, coming **2** REGRESO : return — **venidero, -ra** *adj* : coming

venta *nf* **1** : sale, selling **2 en ~** : for sale

ventaja *nf* : advantage — **ventajoso, -sa** *adj* : advantageous

ventana *nf* **1** : window **2 ~ de la nariz** : nostril — **ventanilla** *nf* **1** : window (of a vehicle or airplane) **2** : ticket window, box office (of a theater, etc.)

ventilar *vt* : ventilate, air (out) — **ventilación** *nf, pl* **-ciones** : ventilation — **ventilador** *nm* : fan, ventilator

ventisca *nf* : blizzard — **ventisquero** *nm* : snowdrift

ventoso, -sa *adj* : windy — **ventosidad** *nf* : wind, flatulence

ventrílocuo, -cua *n* : ventriloquist

ventura *nf* **1** : fortune, luck **2** SATISFACCIÓN : happiness **3 a la ~** : at random — **venturoso, -sa** *adj* : fortunate, happy

ver {88} *vt* **1** : see **2** : watch (television, etc.) — *vi* **1** : see **2 a ~** *or* **vamos a ~** : let's see **3 no tener nada que ~ con** : have nothing to do with **4 ya veremos** : we'll see — **verse** *vr* **1** : see oneself **2** HALLARSE : find oneself **3** ENCONTRARSE : see each other, meet

vera *nf* **1** : side, edge **2** : bank (of a river)

veracidad *nf* : truthfulness

verano *nm* : summer — **veraneante** *nmf* : summer vacationer — **veranear** *vi* : spend the summer — **veraniego, -ga** *adj* : summer

veras *nfpl* **de ~** : really

veraz *adj, pl* **-races** : truthful

verbal *adj* : verbal

verbena *nf* : festival, fair

verbo *nm* : verb — **verboso, -sa** *adj* : verbose

verdad *nf* **1** : truth **2 de ~** : really, truly **3 ¿verdad?** : right?, isn't that so? — **verdaderamente** *adv* : really, truly — **verdadero, -dera** *adj* : true, real

verde *adj* **1** : green **2** : dirty, risqué (of a joke, etc.) — ~ *nm* : green — **verdor** *nm* : greenness

verdugo *nm* **1** : executioner, hangman **2** : cruel person, tyrant

verdura *nf* : vegetable(s), green(s)

vereda *nf* **1** : path, trail **2** *Lat* : sidewalk

veredicto *nm* : verdict

vergüenza *nf* **1** : shame **2** TIMIDEZ : bashfulness, shyness — **vergonzoso, -sa** *adj* **1** : shameful **2** TÍMIDO : bashful, shy

verídico, -ca *adj* : true, truthful

verificar {72} *vt* **1** : verify, confirm **2** EXAMINAR : test, check out — **verificarse** *vr* **1** : take place **2** : come true (of a prophecy, etc.) — **verificación** *nf, pl* **-ciones** : verification

verja *nf* **1** : (iron) gate **2** : rails *pl* (of a fence) **3** ENREJADO : grating, grille

vermut *nm, pl* **-muts** : vermouth

vernáculo, -la *adj* : vernacular

verosímil *adj* **1** : probable, likely **2** CREÍBLE : credible

verraco *nm* : boar

verruga *nf* : wart

versar *vi* **~ sobre** : deal with, be about — **versado, -da** *adj* **~ en** : versed in

versátil *adj* **1** : versatile **2** VOLUBLE : fickle

versión *nf, pl* **-siones 1** : version **2** TRADUCCIÓN : translation

verso *nm* **1** : poem, verse **2** : line (of poetry)

vértebra *nf* : vertebra

verter {56} *vt* **1** : pour (out) **2** DERRAMAR : spill **3** TIRAR : dump — *vi* : flow — **vertedero** *nm* **1** : dump, landfill **2** DESAGÜE : drain, outlet

vertical *adj & nf* : vertical

vértice *nm* : vertex, apex

vertiente *nf* : slope

vértigo *nm* : vertigo, dizziness — **vertiginoso, -sa** *adj* : dizzy

vesícula *nf* **1** : blister **2 ~ biliar** : gallbladder

vestíbulo *nm* : vestibule, hall, foyer

vestido *nm* **1** : dress **2** ROPA : clothing, clothes *pl*

vestigio *nm* : vestige, trace

vestir {54} *vt* **1** : dress, clothe **2** LLEVAR : wear — *vi* : dress — **vestirse** *vr* : get dressed — **vestimenta** *nf* : clothing — **vestuario** *nm* **1** : wardrobe, clothes *pl* **2** : dressing room (in a theater), locker room (in sports)

veta *nf* **1** : vein, seam **2** : grain (of wood)

vetar *vt* : veto

veteado, -da *adj* : streaked, veined

veterano, -na *adj & n* : veteran

veterinaria *nf* : veterinary medicine — **veterinario, -ria** *adj* : veterinary — ~ *n* : veterinarian

veto *nm* : veto

vetusto, -ta *adj* : ancient

vez *nf, pl* **veces 1** : time **2** TURNO : turn **3 a la ~** : at the same time **4 a veces** : sometimes **5 de una ~** : all at once **6 de una ~ para siempre** : once and for all **7 de ~ en cuando** : from time to time **8 dos veces** : twice **9 en ~ de** : instead of **10 una ~** : once

vía *nf* **1** : way, road, route **2** MEDIO : means **3** : track, line (of a railroad) **4** : (anatomical) tract **5 en ~ de** : in the process of — ~ *prep* : via

viable *adj* : viable, feasible — **viabilidad** *nf* : viability

viaducto *nm* : viaduct

viajar *vi* : travel — **viajante** *nmf* : traveling salesperson — **viaje** *nm* : trip, journey — **viajero, -ra** *adj* : traveling — ~ *n* **1** : traveler **2** PASAJERO : passenger

vial *adj* : road, traffic

víbora *nf* : viper

vibrar *vi* : vibrate — **vibración** *nf, pl* **-ciones** : vibration — **vibrante** *adj* : vibrant

vicario, -ria *n* : vicar

vicepresidente, -ta *n* : vice president

viceversa *adv* : vice versa

vicio *nm* **1** : vice **2** MALA COSTUMBRE : bad habit **3** DEFECTO : defect — **viciado, -da** *adj* **1** : corrupt **2** : stuffy, stale (of air, etc.) — **viciar** *vt* **1** : corrupt **2** ESTROPEAR : spoil, pollute — **vicioso, -sa** *adj* : depraved, corrupt

vicisitud *nf* : vicissitude

víctima *nf* : victim

victoria *nf* : victory — **victorioso, -sa** *adj* : victorious

vid *nf* : vine, grapevine

vida *nf* **1** : life **2** DURACIÓN : lifetime **3 de por ~** : for life **4 estar con ~** : be alive

video *or* **vídeo** *nm* **1** : video **2** : VCR, videocassette recorder

vidrio *nm* : glass — **vidriado** *nm* : glaze — **vidriar** *vt* : glaze — **vidriera** *nf* **1** : stained-glass window **2** : glass door **3** *Lat* : shopwindow — **vidrioso, -sa** *adj* **1** : delicate (of a subject, etc.) **2 ojos vidriosos** : glassy eyes

vieira *nf* : scallop

viejo, -ja *adj* : old — ~ *n* **1** : old man *m*, old woman *f* **2 hacerse ~** : get old

viene, etc. → **venir**

viento *nm* : wind

vientre *nm* **1** : abdomen, belly **2** MATRIZ : womb **3** INTESTINO : bowels *pl*

viernes *nms & pl* **1** : Friday **2 Viernes Santo** : Good Friday

vietnamita *adj & nm* : Vietnamese

viga *nf* : beam, girder

vigencia *nf* **1** : validity **2 entrar en ~** : go into effect — **vigente** *adj* : valid, in force

vigésimo, -ma *adj & n* : twentieth

vigía *nmf* : lookout

vigilar *vt* : look after, watch over — *vi* : keep watch — **vigilancia** *nf* **1** : vigilance **2 bajo ~** : under surveillance — **vigilante** *adj* : vigilant — ~ *nmf* : watchman, guard — **vigilia** *nf* **1** : wakefulness **2** : vigil (in religion)

vigor *nm* **1** : vigor **2 entrar en ~** : go into effect — **vigorizante** *adj* : invigorating — **vigoroso, -sa** *adj* : vigorous

VIH *nm* : HIV

vil *adj* : vile, despicable — **vileza** *nf* **1** : vileness **2** : despicable act — **vilipendiar** *vt* : revile

villa *nf* **1** : town, village **2** : villa (house)

villancico *nm* : (Christmas) carol

villano, -na *n* : villain

vilo *nm* **en ~** : suspended, in the air

vinagre *nm* : vinegar — **vinagrera** *nf* : cruet — **vinagreta** *nf* : vinaigrette

vincular *vt* : tie, link — **vínculo** *nm* : link, tie, bond

vindicar *vt* **1** : vindicate **2** VENGAR : avenge

vino[1], **etc.** → **venir**

vino[2] *nm* : wine

viña *nf or* **viñedo** *nm* : vineyard

vio, etc. → **ver**

viola *nf* : viola

violar *vt* **1** : violate (a law, etc.) **2** : rape (a person) — **violación** *nf, pl* **-ciones 1** : violation, offense **2** : rape (of a person)

violencia *nf* : violence, force — **violentar** *vt* **1** : force **2** : break into (a house, etc.) — **violentarse** *vr* **1** : force oneself **2** AVERGONZARSE : be embarrassed — **violento, -ta** *adj* **1** : violent **2** INCÓMODO : awkward, embarrassing

violeta *adj & nm* : violet (color) — ~ *nf* : violet (flower)

violín *nm, pl* **-lines** : violin — **violinista** *nmf* : violinist — **violoncelista** *or* **violonchelista** *nmf* : cellist — **violoncelo** *or* **violonchelo** *nm* : cello, violoncello

virar *vi* : turn, change direction — **viraje** *nm* **1** : turn, swerve **2** CAMBIO : change

virgen *adj & nmf, pl* **vírgenes** : virgin — **virginal** *adj* : virginal — **virginidad** *nf* : virginity

viril *adj* : virile — **virilidad** *nf* : virility

virtual *adj* : virtual

virtud *nf* **1** : virtue **2 en ~ de** : by virtue of — **virtuoso, -sa** *adj* : virtuous — ~ *n* : virtuoso

viruela *nf* **1** : smallpox **2 picado de ~s** : pockmarked

virulento, -ta *adj* : virulent

virus *nms & pl* : virus

visa *nf Lat* : visa — **visado** *nm Spain* : visa

vísceras *nfpl* : entrails — **visceral** *adj* : visceral

viscoso, -sa *adj* : viscous — **viscosidad** *nf* : viscosity

visera *nf* : visor

visible *adj* : visible — **visibilidad** *nf* : visibility

visión *nf, pl* **-siones 1** : eyesight **2** APARICIÓN : vision, illusion **3** PUNTO DE VISTA : view, perspective — **visionario, -ria** *adj & n* : visionary

visitar *vt* : visit — **visita** *nf* **1** : visit **2 tener ~** : have company — **visitante** *adj* : visiting — ~ *nmf* : visitor

vislumbrar *vt* : make out, discern — **vislumbre** *nf* **1** : glimpse, sign **2** RESPLANDOR : glimmer, gleam

viso *nm* **1** : sheen **2 tener ~s de** : seem, show signs of

visón *nm, pl* **-sones** : mink

víspera *nf* : eve, day before

vista *nf* **1** : vision, eyesight **2** MIRADA : look, gaze **3** PANORAMA : view, vista **4** : hearing (in court) **5 a primera ~** *or* **a simple ~** : at first sight **6 hacer la ~ gorda** : turn a blind eye **7 perder de ~** : lose sight of — **vistazo** *nm* **1** : glance **2 echar un ~** : have a look

visto, -ta *adj* **1** : clear, obvious **2** COMÚN : commonly seen **3 estar bien ~** : be approved of **4 estar mal ~** : be frowned upon **5 nunca ~** : unheard-of **6 por lo visto** : apparently **7 visto que** : since, given that — **visto** *nm* **~ bueno** : approval — ~ *pp* → **ver**

vistoso, -sa *adj* : colorful, bright

visual *adj* : visual — **visualizar** {21} *vt* : visualize

vital *adj* : vital — **vitalicio, -cia** *adj* : life, for life — **vitalidad** *nf* : vitality

vitamina *nf* : vitamin

viticultor, -tora *n* : winegrower — **viticultura** *nf* : wine growing

vitorear *vt* : cheer, acclaim

vítreo, -trea *adj* : glassy

vitrina *nf* **1** : showcase, display case **2** *Lat* : shopwindow

vituperar *vt* : censure — **vituperio** *nm* : censure

viudo, -da *n* : widower *m*, widow *f* — ~ *adj* : widowed — **viudez** *nf* : widowerhood, widowhood

viva *nm* **dar ~s** : cheer

vivacidad *nf* : vivacity, liveliness

vivamente *adv* **1** : vividly **2** PROFUNDAMENTE : deeply, acutely

vivaz *adj, pl* **-vaces 1** : lively, vivacious **2** AGUDO : vivid, sharp

víveres *nmpl* : provisions, supplies

vivero *nm* **1** : nursery (for plants) **2** : (fish) hatchery, (oyster) bed

viveza *nf* **1** : liveliness **2** : vividness (of colors, descriptions, etc.) **3** ASTUCIA : sharpness (of mind) — **vívido, -da** *adj* : vivid

vividor, -dora *n* : freeloader

vivienda *nf* **1** : housing **2** MORADA : dwelling

viviente *adj* : living

vivificar {72} *vt* : enliven

vivir *vi* **1** : live, be alive **2 ~ de** : live on — *vt* : experience, live (through) — ~ *nm* **1** : life, lifestyle **2 de mal ~** : disreputable — **vivo, -va** *adj* **1** : alive **2** INTENSO : intense, bright **3** ANIMADO : lively **4** ASTUTO : sharp, quick **5 en vivo** : live

vocablo *nm* : word — **vocabulario** *nm* : vocabulary

vocación *nf, pl* **-ciones** : vocation — **vocacional** *adj* : vocational

vocal *adj* : vocal — ~ *nmf* : member (of a committee, etc.) — ~ *nf* : vowel — **vocalista** *nmf* : singer, vocalist

vocear *v* : shout — **vocerío** *nm* : shouting

vociferar *vi* : shout

vodka *nmf* : vodka

volar {19} *vi* **1** : fly **2** : blow away (of papers, etc.) **3** *fam* : disappear **4 irse volando** : rush off — *vt* : blow up — **volador, -dora** *adj* : flying — **volandas: en ~** *adv phr* : in the air — **volante** *adj* : flying — ~ *nm* **1** : steering wheel **2** : shuttlecock (in badminton) **3** : flounce (of fabric) **4** *Lat* : flier, circular

volátil *adj* : volatile

volcán *nm, pl* **-canes** : volcano — **volcánico, -ca** *adj* : volcanic

volcar {82} *vt* **1** : upset, knock over **2** VACIAR : empty out — *vi* : overturn — **volcarse** *vr* **1** : overturn, tip over **2 ~ en** : throw oneself into

voleibol *nm* : volleyball

voltaje *nm* : voltage

voltear *vt* : turn over, turn upside down — **voltearse** *vr Lat* : turn (around) — **voltereta** *nf* : somersault

voltio *nm* : volt

voluble *adj* : fickle

volumen *nm, pl* **-lúmenes** : volume — **voluminoso, -sa** *adj* : voluminous

voluntad *nf* **1** : will **2** DESEO : wish **3** INTENCIÓN : intention **4 a ~** : at will **5 buena ~** : goodwill **6 mala ~** : ill will **7 fuerza de ~** : willpower — **voluntario, -ria** *adj* : voluntary — ~ *n* : volunteer — **voluntarioso, -sa** *adj* **1** : willing **2** TERCO : stubborn, willful

voluptuoso, -sa *adj* : voluptuous

volver {89} *vi* **1** : return, come or go back **2 ~ a** : return to, do again **3 ~ en sí** : come to — *vt* **1** : turn, turn over, turn inside out **2** CONVERTIR EN : turn (into) **3 ~ loco** : drive crazy — **volverse** *vr* **1** : turn (around) **2** HACERSE : become

vomitar *vi* : vomit — *vt* **1** : vomit **2** : spew (out) — **vómito** *nm* **1** : (action of) vomiting **2** : vomit

voraz *adj, pl* **-races** : voracious

vos *pron Lat* : you

vosotros, -tras *pron Spain* : you, yourselves

votar *vi* : vote — *vt* : vote for — **votación** *nf, pl* **-ciones** : vote, voting — **votante** *nmf* : voter — **voto** *nm* **1** : vote **2** : vow (in religion)

voy → **ir**

voz *nf, pl* **voces 1** : voice **2** GRITO : shout, yell **3** VOCABLO : word, term **4** RUMOR : rumor **5 dar voces** : shout **6 en ~ alta** : loudly **7 en ~ baja** : softly

vuelco *nm* : upset, overturning

vuelo *nm* **1** : flight **2** : (action of) flying **3** : flare (of clothing) **4 al ~** : on the wing

vuelta *nf* **1** : turn **2** REVOLUCIÓN : circle, revolution **3** CURVA : bend, curve **4** REGRESO : return **5** : round, lap (in sports) **6** PASEO : walk, drive, ride **7** REVÉS : back, other side **8** *Spain* : change **9 dar ~s** : spin **10 estar de ~** : be back — **vuelto** *nm Lat* : change

vuestro, -tra *adj Spain* : your, of yours — ~ *pron Spain* (*with definite article*) : yours

vulgar *adj* **1** : vulgar **2** CORRIENTE : com-

mon — **vulgaridad** *nf* **1** : vulgarity **2** BANALIDAD : banality — **vulgo** *nm* el ~ : the masses, common people
vulnerable *adj* : vulnerable — **vulnerabilidad** *nf* : vulnerability

WXYZ

w *nf* : w, 24th letter of the Spanish alphabet
wáter *nm Spain* : toilet
whisky *nm, pl* **-skys** *or* **-skies** : whiskey
x *nf* : x, 25th letter of the Spanish alphabet
xenofobia *nf* : xenophobia
xilófono *nm* : xylophone
y[1] *nf* : y, 26th letter of the Spanish alphabet
y[2] *conj* : and
ya *adv* **1** : already **2** AHORA : (right) now **3** MÁS TARDE : later, soon **4** ~ **no** : no longer **5** ~ **que** : now that, since, inasmuch as
yacer {90} *vi* : lie (on or in the ground) — **yacimiento** *nm* : bed, deposit
yanqui *adj & nmf* : Yankee

yate *nm* : yacht
yegua *nf* : mare
yelmo *nm* : helmet
yema *nf* **1** : bud, shoot **2** : yolk (of an egg) **3** *or* ~ **del dedo** : fingertip
yerba *nf* **1** *or* ~ **mate** : maté **2** → **hierba**
yermo, -ma *adj* : barren, deserted — **yermo** *nm* : wasteland
yerno *nm* : son-in-law
yerro *nm* : blunder, mistake
yerto, -ta *adj* : stiff
yesca *nf* : tinder
yeso *nm* **1** : gypsum **2** : plaster (for art, construction)
yo *pron* **1** (*subject*) : I **2** (*object*) : me **3 soy** ~ : it is I, it's me — ~ *nm* : ego, self
yodo *nm* : iodine
yoga *nm* : yoga
yogurt *or* **yogur** *nm* : yogurt
yuca *nf* : yucca
yugo *nm* : yoke (of oxen)
yugoslavo, -va *adj* : Yugoslavian
yugular *adj* : jugular
yunque *nm* : anvil
yunta *nf* : yoke
yuxtaponer {60} *vt* : juxtapose — **yuxtaposición** *nf, pl* **-ciones** : juxtaposition
z *nf* : z, 27th letter of the Spanish alphabet
zacate *nm Lat* : grass
zafar *vt Lat* : loosen, untie — **zafarse** *vr* **1** : come undone **2** : get free of (an obligation, etc.)

zafio, -fia *adj* : coarse
zafiro *nm* : sapphire
zaga *nf* a la ~ *or* en ~ : behind, in the rear
zaguán *nm, pl* **-guanes** : (entrance) hall
zaherir {76} *vt* : hurt (s.o.'s feelings)
zaino, -na *adj* : chestnut (color)
zalamería *nf* : flattery — **zalamero, -ra** *adj* : flattering — ~ *n* : flatterer
zambullirse {38} *vr* : dive, plunge — **zambullida** *nf* : dive, plunge
zanahoria *nf* : carrot
zancada *nf* : stride, step — **zancadilla** *nf* **1** : trip, stumble **2 hacer una** ~ **a algn** : trip s.o. up
zancos *nmpl* : stilts
zancudo *nm Lat* : mosquito
zángano, -na *n fam* : lazy person, slacker — **zángano** *nm* : drone (bee)
zanja *nf* : ditch, trench — **zanjar** *vt* : settle, resolve
zapallo *nm Lat* : pumpkin — **zapallito** *nm Lat* : zucchini
zapapico *nm* : pickax
zapato *nm* : shoe — **zapatería** *nf* : shoe store — **zapatero, -ra** *n* : shoemaker, cobbler — **zapatilla** *nf* **1** : slipper **2** : sneaker (for sports, etc.)
zar *nm* : czar
zarandear *vt* **1** : sift **2** SACUDIR : shake
zarcillo *nm* : earring
zarpa *nf* : paw

zarpar *vi* : set sail, raise anchor
zarza *nf* : bramble — **zarzamora** *nf* : blackberry
zigzag *nm, pl* **-zags** *or* **-zagues** : zigzag — **zigzaguear** *vi* : zigzag
zinc *nm* : zinc
zíper *nm Lat* : zipper
zircón *nm, pl* **-cones** : zircon
zócalo *nm* **1** : base (of a column, etc.) **2** : baseboard (of a wall) **3** *Lat* : main square, plaza
zodíaco *nm* : zodiac
zona *nf* : zone, area
zoo *nm* : zoo — **zoología** *nf* : zoology — **zoológico, -ca** *adj* : zoological — **zoológico** *nm* : zoo — **zoólogo, -ga** *n* : zoologist
zopilote *nm Lat* : buzzard
zoquete *nmf fam* : oaf, blockhead
zorrillo *nm Lat* : skunk
zorro, -rra *n* : fox, vixen *f* — ~ *adj* : foxy, sly
zozobra *nf* : anxiety, worry — **zozobrar** *vi* : capsize
zueco *nm* : clog (shoe)
zumbar *vi* : buzz — *vt fam* : hit, beat — **zumbido** *nm* : buzzing
zumo *nf* : juice
zurcir {83} *vt* : darn, mend
zurdo, -da *adj* : left-handed — ~ *n* : left-handed person — **zurda** *nf* : left hand
zutano, -na → **fulano**

English-Spanish

A

a[1] ['eɪ] *n, pl* **a's** *or* **as** ['eɪz] : a *f*, primera letra del alfabeto inglés

a[2] [ə, 'eɪ] *art* (**an** [ən, 'æn] *before vowel or silent h*) **1** : un *m*, una *f* **2** PER : por, a la, al

aback [ə'bæk] *adv* **be taken ~** : quedarse desconcertado

abacus ['æbəkəs] *n, pl* **abaci** ['æbəˌsaɪ, -ˌki:] *or* **abacuses** : ábaco *m*

abandon [ə'bændən] *vt* **1** DESERT : abandonar **2** GIVE UP : renunciar a — **~** *n* : desenfreno *m* — **abandonment** [ə'bændənmənt] *n* : abandono *m*

abashed [ə'bæʃt] *adj* : avergonzado

abate [ə'beɪt] *vi* **abated; abating** : amainar, disminuir

abattoir ['æbəˌtwɑr] *n* : matadero *m*

abbey ['æbi] *n, pl* **-beys** : abadía *f* — **abbot** ['æbət] *n* : abad *m*

abbreviate [ə'bri:viˌeɪt] *vt* **-ated; -ating** : abreviar — **abbreviation** [əˌbri:vi'eɪʃən] *n* : abreviatura *f*, abreviación *f*

abdicate ['æbdɪˌkeɪt] *v* **-cated; -cating** : abdicar — **abdication** [ˌæbdɪ'keɪæən] *n* : abdicación *f*

abdomen ['æbdəmən, æb'do:mən] *n* : abdomen *m*, vientre *m* — **abdominal** [æb'dɑmənəl] *adj* : abdominal

abduct [æb'dʌkt] *vt* : secuestrar — **abduction** [æb'dʌkʃən] *n* : secuestro *m*

aberration [ˌæbə'reɪʃən] *n* : aberración *f*

abet [ə'bɛt] *vt* **abetted; abetting** *or* **aid and ~** : ser cómplice de

abeyance [ə'beɪənts] *n* : desuso *m*

abhor [əb'hɔr, æb-] *vt* **-horred; -horring** : aborrecer

abide [ə'baɪd] *v* **abode** [ə'bo:d] *or* **abided; abiding** *vt* : soportar, tolerar — *vi* **1** DWELL : morar **2 ~ by** : atenerse a

ability [ə'bɪləti] *n, pl* **-ties 1** CAPABILITY : aptitud *f*, capacidad *f* **2** SKILL : habilidad *f*

abject ['æbˌdʒɛkt, æb'-] *adj* : miserable, desdichado

ablaze [ə'bleɪz] *adj* : en llamas

able ['eɪbəl] *adj* **abler; ablest 1** CAPABLE : capaz, hábil **2** COMPETENT : competente

abnormal [æb'nɔrməl] *adj* : anormal — **abnormality** [ˌæbnər'mæləti, -nɔr-] *n, pl* **-ties** : anormalidad *f*

aboard [ə'bord] *adv* : a bordo — **~** *prep* : a bordo de

abode *n* : morada *f*, domicilio *m*

abolish [ə'bɑlɪʃ] *vt* : abolir, suprimir — **abolition** [ˌæbə'lɪʃən] *n* : abolición *f*

abominable [ə'bɑmənəbəl] *adj* : abominable, aborrecible — **abomination** [əˌbɑmə'neɪʃən] *n* : abominación *f*

aborigine [ˌæbə'rɪdʒəni] *n* : aborigen *mf*

abort [ə'bɔrt] *vt* : abortar — **abortion** [ə'bɔrʃən] *n* : aborto *m* — **abortive** [ə'bɔrtɪv] *adj* UNSUCCESSFUL : malogrado

abound [ə'baʊnd] *vi* **~ in** : abundar en

about [ə'baʊt] *adv* **1** APPROXIMATELY : aproximadamente, más o menos **2** AROUND : alrededor **3 be ~ to** : estar a punto de **4 be up and ~** : estar levantado — **~** *prep* **1** AROUND : alrededor de **2** CONCERNING : acerca de, sobre

above [ə'bʌv] *adv* : arriba — **~** *prep* **1** : encima de **2 ~ all** : sobre todo — **aboveboard** *adj* : honrado

abrasive [ə'breɪsɪv] *adj* **1** : abrasivo **2** BRUSQUE : brusco, mordaz

abreast [ə'brɛst] *adv* **1** : al lado **2 keep ~ of** : mantenerse al corriente de

abridge [ə'brɪdʒ] *vt* **abridged; abridging** : abreviar

abroad [ə'brɔd] *adv* **1** : en el extranjero **2** WIDELY : por todas partes **3 go ~** : ir al extranjero

abrupt [ə'brʌpt] *adj* **1** SUDDEN : repentino **2** BRUSQUE : brusco

abscess ['æbˌsɛs] *n* : absceso *m*

absence ['æbsənts] *n* **1** : ausencia *f* **2** LACK : falta *f*, carencia *f* — **absent** ['æbsənt] *adj* : ausente — **absentee** [ˌæbsən'ti:] *n* : ausente *mf* — **absentminded** [ˌæbsənt'maɪndəd] *adj* : distraído, despistado

absolute ['æbsəˌlu:t, ˌæbsə'lu:t] *adj* : absoluto — **absolutely** [ˌæbsə'lu:tli] *adv* : absolutamente

absolve [əb'zɑlv, æb-, -'sɑlv] *vt* **-solved; -solving** : absolver

absorb [əb'zɔrb, æb-, -'sɔrb] *vt* : absorber — **absorbent** [əb'zɔrbənt, æb-, -'sɔr-] *adj* : absorbente — **absorption** [əb'zɔrpʃən, æb-, -'sɔrp-] *n* : absorción *f*

abstain [əb'steɪn, æb-] *vi* **~ from** : abstenerse de — **abstinence** ['æbstənənts] *n* : abstinencia *f*

abstract [æb'strækt, 'æbˌ-] *adj* : abstracto — **~** *vt* : extraer — **~** ['æbˌstrækt] *n* : resumen *m* — **abstraction** [æb'strækʃən] *n* : abstracción *f*

absurd [əb'sərd, -'zərd] *adj* : absurdo — **absurdity** [əb'sərdəti, -'zərdəti] *n, pl* **-ties** : absurdo *m*

abundant [ə'bʌndənt] *adj* : abundante — **abundance** [ə'bʌndənts] *n* : abundancia *f*

abuse [ə'bju:z] *vt* **abused; abusing 1** MISUSE : abusar de **2** MISTREAT : maltratar **3** REVILE : insultar — **~** [ə'bju:s] *n* **1** : abuso *m* **2** INSULTS : insultos *mpl* — **abusive** [ə'bju:sɪv] *adj* : injurioso

abut [ə'bʌt] *vi* **abutted; abutting ~ on** : colindar con

abyss [ə'bɪs, 'æbɪs] *n* : abismo *m* — **abysmal** [ə'bɪzməl] *adj* : atroz, pésimo

academy [ə'kædəmi] *n, pl* **-mies** : academia *f* — **academic** [ˌækə'dɛmɪk] *adj* **1** : académico **2** THEORETICAL : teórico

accelerate [ɪk'sɛləˌreɪt, æk-] *v* **-ated; -ating** : acelerar — **acceleration** [ɪkˌsɛlə'reɪʃən, æk-] *n* : aceleración *f*

accent ['ækˌsɛnt, æk'sɛnt] *vt* : acentuar — **~** ['ækˌsɛnt, sənt] *n* : acento *m* — **accentuate** [ɪk'sɛntʃʊˌeɪt, æk-] *vt* **-ated; -ating** : acentuar, subrayar

accept [ɪk'sɛpt, æk-] *vt* : aceptar — **acceptable** [ɪk'sɛptəbəl, æk-] *adj* : aceptable — **acceptance** [ɪk'sɛptənts, æk-] *n* **1** : aceptación *f* **2** APPROVAL : aprobación *f*

access ['ækˌsɛs] *n* : acceso *m* — **accessible** [ɪk'sɛsəbəl, æk-] *adj* : accesible, asequible

accessory *n, pl* **-ries 1** : accesorio *m* **2** ACCOMPLICE : cómplice *mf*

accident ['æksədənt] *n* **1** MISHAP : accidente *m* **2** CHANCE : casualidad *f* — **accidental** [ˌæksə'dɛntəl] *adj* : accidental — **accidentally** [ˌæksə'dɛntəli, -'dɛntli] *adv* **1** BY CHANCE : por casualidad **2** UNINTENTIONALLY : sin querer

acclaim [ə'kleɪm] *vt* : aclamar — **~** *n* : aclamación *f*

acclimatize [ə'klaɪməˌtaɪz] *vt* **-tized; -tizing** : aclimatar

accommodate [ə'kɑməˌdeɪt] *vt* **-dated; -dating 1** ADAPT : acomodar, adaptar **2** SATISFY : complacer, satisfacer **3** HOLD : tener cabida para — **accomodation** [əˌkɑmə'deɪʃən] *n* **1** : adaptación *f* **2 ~s** *npl* LODGING : alojamiento *m*

accompany [ə'kʌmpəni, -'kɑm-] *vt* **-nied; -nying** : acompañar

accomplice [ə'kɑmpləs, -'kʌm-] *n* : cómplice *mf*

accomplish [ə'kɑmplɪʃ, -'kʌm-] *vt* : realizar, llevar a cabo — **accomplishment** [ə'kɑmplɪʃmənt, -'kʌm-] *n* **1** COMPLETION : realización *f* **2** ACHIEVEMENT : logro *m*, éxito *m*

accord *n* **1** AGREEMENT : acuerdo *m* **2 of one's own ~** : voluntariamente — **accordance** [ə'kɔrdənts] *n* **in ~ with** : conforme a, de acuerdo con — **accordingly** [ə'kɔrdɪŋli] *adv* : en consecuencia — **according to** [ə'kɔrdɪŋ] *prep* : según

accordion [ə'kɔrdiən] *n* : acordeón *m*

accost [ə'kɔst] *vt* : abordar

account [ə'kaʊnt] *n* **1** : cuenta *f* **2** REPORT : relato *m*, informe *m* **3** WORTH : importancia *f* **4 on ~ of** : a causa de, debido a **5 on no ~** : de ninguna manera — **~** *vi* **~ for** : dar cuenta de, explicar — **accountable** [ə'kaʊntəbəl] *adj* : responsable — **accountant** [ə'kaʊntənt] *n* : contador *m*, -dora *f Lat*; contable *mf Spain* — **accounting** [ə'kaʊntɪŋ] *n* : contabilidad *f*

accrue [ə'kru:] *vi* **-crued; -cruing** : acumularse

accumulate [ə'kju:mjəˌleɪt] *v* **-lated; -lating** *vt* : acumular — *vi* : acumularse — **accumulation** [əˌkju:mjə'leɪʃən] *n* : acumulación *f*

accurate ['ækjərət] *adj* : exacto, preciso — **accuracy** ['ækjərəsi] *n* : exactitud *f*, precisión *f*

accuse [ə'kju:z] *vt* **-cused; -cusing** : acusar — **accusation** [ˌækjə'zeɪʃən] *n* : acusación *f*

accustomed [ə'kʌstəmd] *adj* **1** : acostumbrado **2 become ~ to** : acostumbrarse a

ace ['eɪs] *n* : as *m*

ache ['eɪk] *vi* **ached; aching** : doler — **~** *n* : dolor *m*

achieve [ə'tʃi:v] *vt* **achieved; achieving** : lograr, realizar — **achievement** [ə'tʃi:vmənt] *n* : logro *m*, éxito *m*

acid ['æsəd] *adj* : ácido — **~** *n* : ácido *m*

acknowledge [ɪk'nɑlɪdʒ, æk-] *vt* **-edged; -edging 1** ADMIT : admitir **2** RECOGNIZE : reconocer **3 ~ receipt of** : acusar recibo de — **acknowledgment** [ɪk'nɑlɪdʒmənt, æk-] *n* **1** : reconocimiento *m* **2** THANKS : agradecimiento *m* **3 ~ of receipt** : acuse *m* de recibo

acne ['ækni] *n* : acné *m*

acorn ['eɪˌkɔrn, -kərn] *n* : bellota *f*

acoustic [ə'ku:stɪk] *or* **acoustical** [-stɪkəl] *adj* : acústico — **acoustics** [ə'ku:stɪks] *ns & pl* : acústica *f*

acquaint [ə'kweɪnt] *vt* **1 ~ s.o. with** : poner a algn al corriente de **2 be ~ed with** : conocer a (una persona), saber (un hecho) — **acquaintance** [ə'kweɪntənts] *n* **1** : conocimiento *m* **2** : conocido *m*, -da *f* (persona)

acquire [ə'kwaɪr] *vt* **-quired; -quiring** : adquirir — **acquisition** [ˌækwə'zɪʃən] *n* : adquisición *f*

acquit [ə'kwɪt] *vt* **-quitted; -quitting** : absolver

acre ['eɪkər] *n* : acre *m* — **acreage** ['eɪkərɪdʒ] *n* : superficie *f* en acres

acrid ['ækrəd] *adj* : acre

acrobat ['ækrəˌbæt] *n* : acróbata *mf* — **acrobatic** [ˌækrə'bætɪk] *adj* : acrobático

acronym ['ækrəˌnɪm] *n* : siglas *fpl*

across [ə'krɔs] *adv* **1** : de un lado a otro **2** CROSSWISE : a través **3 go ~** : atravesar — **~** *prep* **1** : a través de **2 ~ the street** : al otro lado de la calle

acrylic [ə'krɪlɪk] *n* : acrílico *m*

act ['ækt] *vi* **1** : actuar **2** PRETEND : fingir **3** FUNCTION : funcionar **4 ~ as** : servir de — *vt* : interpretar (un papel) — **~** *n* **1** ACTION : acto *m*, acción *f* **2** DECREE : ley *f* **3** : acto *m* (en una obra de teatro), número *m* (en un espectáculo) — **acting** *adj* : interino

action ['ækʃən] *n* **1** : acción *f* **2** LAWSUIT : demanda *f* **3 take ~** : tomar medidas

activate ['æktəˌveɪt] *vt* **-vated; -vating** : activar

active ['æktɪv] *adj* **1** : activo **2** LIVELY : enérgico **3 ~ volcano** : volcán *m* en actividad — **activity** [æk'tɪvəti] *n, pl* **-ties** : actividad *f*

actor ['æktər] *n* : actor *m* — **actress** ['æktrəs] *n* : actriz *f*

actual ['æktʃʊəl] *adj* : real, verdadero — **actually** ['æktʃʊəli, -əəli] *adv* : realmente, en realidad

acupuncture ['ækjʊˌpʌŋktʃər] *n* : acupuntura *f*

acute [ə'kju:t] *adj* **acuter; acutest 1** : agudo **2** PERCEPTIVE : perspicaz

ad ['æd] → **advertisement**

adamant ['ædəmənt, -ˌmænt] *adj* : inflexible

adapt [ə'dæpt] *vt* : adaptar — *vi* : adaptarse — **adaptable** [ə'dæptəbəl] *adj* : adaptable — **adaptation** [ˌæˌdæp'teɪʃən, -dəp-] *n* : adaptación *f* — **adapter** [ə'dæptər] *n* : adaptador *m*

add ['æd] *vt* **1** : añadir **2** *or* **~ up** : sumar — *vi* : sumar

addict ['ædɪkt] *n* **1** : adicto *m*, -ta *f* **2** *or* **drug ~** : drogadicto *m*, -ta *f*; toxicómano *m*, -na *f* — **addiction** [ə'dɪkʃən] *n* : dependencia *f*

addition [ə'dɪʃən] *n* **1** : suma *f* (en matemáticas) **2** ADDING : adición *f* **3 in ~** : además — **additional** [ə'dɪʃənəl] *adj* : adicional — **additive** ['ædətɪv] *n* : aditivo *m*

address [ə'drɛs] *vt* **1** : dirigirse a (una persona) **2** : ponerle la dirección a (una carta) **3** : tratar (un asunto) — **~** [ə'drɛs, 'æˌdrɛs] *n* **1** : dirección *f*, domicilio *m* **2** SPEECH : discurso *m*

adept [ə'dɛpt] *adj* : experto, hábil

adequate ['ædɪkwət] *adj* : adecuado, suficiente

adhere [æd'hɪr, əd-] *vi* **-hered; -hering 1** STICK : adherirse **2 ~ to** : observar — **adherence** [æd'hɪrənts, əd-] *n* **1** : adhesión *f* **2** : observancia *f* (de una ley, etc.) — **adhesive** [æd'hi:sɪv, əd-, -zɪv] *adj* : adhesivo — **~** *n* : adhesivo *m*

adjacent [ə'dʒeɪsənt] *adj* : adyacente, contiguo

adjective ['ædʒɪktɪv] *n* : adjetivo *m*

adjoining [ə'dʒɔɪnɪŋ] *adj* : contiguo, vecino

adjourn [ə'dʒərn] *vt* : aplazar, suspender — *vi* : suspenderse

adjust [ə'dʒʌst] *vt* : ajustar, arreglar — *vi* : adaptarse — **adjustable** [ə'dʒʌstəbəl] *adj* : ajustable — **adjustment** [ə'dʒʌstmənt] *n* : ajuste *m* (a una máquina, etc.), adaptación *f* (de una persona)

ad–lib ['æd'lɪb] *v* **-libbed; -libbing** : improvisar

administer [æd'mɪnəstər, əd-] *vt* : administrar — **administration** [ædˌmɪnə'streɪʃən, əd-] *n* : administración *f* — **administrative** [æd'mɪnəˌstreɪtɪv, əd-] *adj* : administrativo — **administrator** [æd'mɪnəˌstreɪtər, əd-] *n* : administrador *m*, -dora *f*

admirable ['ædmərəbəl] *adj* : admirable

admiral ['ædmərəl] *n* : almirante *m*

admire [æd'maɪr] *vt* **-mired; -miring** : admirar — **admiration** [ˌædmə'reɪʃən] *n* : admiración *f* — **admirer** [æd'maɪrər] *n* : admirador *m*, -dora *f*

admit [æd'mɪt, əd-] *vt* **-mitted; -mitting 1** : admitir, dejar entrar **2** ACKNOWLEDGE : reconocer — **admission** [æd'mɪʃən] *n* **1** ADMITTANCE : entrada *f*, admisión *f* **2** ACKNOWLEDGMENT : reconocimiento *m* — **admittance** [æd'mɪtənts, əd-] *n* : admisión *f*, entrada *f*

admonish [æd'mɑnɪʃ, əd-] *vt* : amonestar, reprender

ado [ə'du:] *n* **1** : alboroto *m*, bulla *f* **2 without further ~** : sin más (preámbulos)

adolescent [ˌædəl'ɛsənt] *n* : adolescente *mf* — **adolescence** [ˌædəl'ɛsənts] *n* : adolescencia *f*

adopt [ə'dɑpt] *vt* : adoptar — **adoption** [ə'dɑpʃən] *n* : adopción *f*

adore [ə'dor] *vt* **adored; adoring 1** : adorar **2** LIKE, LOVE : encantarle (algo a uno) — **adorable** [ə'dorəbəl] *adj* : adorable — **adoration** [ˌædə'reɪæən] *n* : adoración *f*

adorn [ə'dɔrn] *vt* : adornar — **adornment** [ə'dɔrnmənt] *n* : adorno *m*

adrift [ə'drɪft] *adj & adv* : a la deriva

adroit [ə'drɔɪt] *adj* : diestro, hábil

adult [ə'dʌlt, 'æˌdʌlt] *adj* : adulto — **~** *n* : adulto *m*, -ta *f*

adultery [ə'dʌltəri] *n, pl* **-teries** : adulterio *m*

advance [əd'vænts, əd-] *v* **-vanced; -vancing** *vt* : adelantar — *vi* : avanzar, adelantarse — **~** *n* **1** : avance *m* **2** PROGRESS : adelanto *m* **3 in ~** : por adelantado — **advancement** [æd'væntsmənt, əd-] *n* : adelanto *m*, progreso *m*

advantage [əd'væntɪdʒ, æd-] *n* **1** : ventaja *f* **2 take ~ of** : aprovecharse de — **advantageous** [ˌædˌvæn'teɪdʒəs, -vən-] *adj* : ventajoso

advent ['ædˌvɛnt] *n* **1** ARRIVAL : llegada *f* **2 Advent** : Adviento *m*

adventure [æd'vɛntʃər, əd-] *n* : aventura *f* — **adventurous** [æd'vɛntʃərəs, əd-] *adj* **1** : intrépido **2** RISKY : arriesgado

adverb ['ædˌvərb] *n* : adverbio *m*

adversary ['ædvərˌsɛri] *n, pl* **-saries** : adversario *m*, -ria *f*

adverse [æd'vərs, 'æd-ˌ] *adj* : adverso, desfavorable — **adversity** [æd'vərsəti, əd-] *n, pl* **-ties** : adversidad *f*

advertise ['ædvərˌtaɪz] *v* **-tised; -tising** *vt* : anunciar — *vi* : hacer publicidad — **advertisement** ['ædvərˌtaɪzmənt] *n* : anuncio *m* — **advertiser** ['ædvərˌtaɪzər] *n* : anunciante *mf* — **advertising** ['ædvərˌtaɪzɪŋ] *n* : publicidad *f*

advice [æd'vaɪs] *n* : consejo *m*

advise [æd'vaɪz, əd-] *vt* **-vised; -vising 1** COUNSEL : aconsejar, asesorar **2** RECOMMEND : recomendar **3** INFORM : informar — **advisable** [æd'vaɪzəbəl, əd-] *adj* : aconsejable — **adviser** [æd'vaɪzər, əd-] *n* : consejero *m*, -ra *f*; asesor *m*, -sora *f* — **advisory** [æd'vaɪzəri, əd-] *adj* : consultivo

advocate ['ædvəˌkeɪt] *vt* **-cated; -cating** : recomendar — **~** ['ædvəkət] *n* : defensor *m*, -sora *f*

aerial ['æriəl] *adj* : aéreo — **~** *n* : antena *f*

aerobics [ˌær'o:bɪks] *ns & pl* : aeróbic *m*

aerodynamic [ˌæro:daɪ'næmɪk] *adj* : aerodinámico

aerosol ['ærəˌsɔl] *n* : aerosol *m*
aesthetic [ɛs'θɛt̬ɪk] *adj* : estético
afar [ə'fɑr] *adv* : lejos
affable ['æfəbəl] *adj* : afable
affair [ə'fær] *n* **1** : asunto *m*, cuestión *f* **2** *or* **love ~** : amorío *m*, aventura *f*
affect [ə'fɛkt, æ-] *vt* **1** : afectar **2** FEIGN : fingir — **affection** [ə'fɛkʃən] *n* : afecto *m*, cariño *m* — **affectionate** [ə'fɛkʃənət] *adj* : afectuoso, cariñoso
affinity [ə'fɪnət̬i] *n, pl* **-ties** : afinidad *f*
affirm [ə'fərm] *vt* : afirmar — **affirmative** [ə'fərmət̬ɪv] *adj* : afirmativo
affix [ə'fɪks] *vt* : fijar, pegar
afflict [ə'flɪkt] *vt* : afligir — **affliction** [ə'flɪkʃən] *n* : aflicción *f*
affluent ['æˌflu:ənt; æ'flu:-, ə-] *adj* : próspero, adinerado
afford [ə'ford] *vt* **1** : tener los recursos para, permitirse (el lujo de) **2** PROVIDE : brindar
affront [ə'frʌnt] *n* : afrenta *f*
afloat [ə'flo:t] *adv & adj* : a flote
afoot [ə'fʊt] *adj* : en marcha
afraid [ə'freɪd] *adj* **1 be ~** : tener miedo **2 I'm ~ not** : me temo que no
African ['æfrɪkən] *adj* : africano
after ['æftər] *adv* **1** AFTERWARD : después **2** BEHIND : detrás, atrás — **~** *conj* : después de (que) — **~** *prep* **1** : después de **2 ~ all** : después de todo **3 it's ten ~ five** : son las cinco y diez
aftereffect ['æftərəˌfɛkt] *n* : efecto *m* secundario
aftermath ['æftərˌmæθ] *n* : consecuencias *fpl*
afternoon [ˌæftər'nu:n] *n* : tarde *f*
afterward ['æftərwərd] *or* **afterwards** [-wərdz] *adv* : después, más tarde
again [ə'gɛn, -'gɪn] *adv* **1** : otra vez, de nuevo **2 ~ and ~** : una y otra vez **3 then ~** : por otra parte
against [ə'gɛntst, -'gɪntst] *prep* : contra, en contra de
age ['eɪdʒ] *n* **1** : edad *f* **2** ERA : era *f*, época *f* **3 be of ~** : ser mayor de edad **4 for ~s** : hace siglos **5 old ~** : vejez *f* — **~** *vi* **aged; aging** : envejecer — **aged** *adj* **1** ['eɪdʒəd, 'eɪdʒd] OLD : anciano, viejo **2** ['eɪdʒd] **children ~ 10 to 17** : niños de 10 a 17 años
agency ['eɪdʒəntsi] *n, pl* **-cies** : agencia *f*
agenda [ə'dʒɛndə] *n* : orden *m* del día
agent ['eɪdʒənt] *n* : agente *mf*, representante *mf*
aggravate ['ægrəˌveɪt] *vt* **-vated; -vating 1** WORSEN : agravar, empeorar **2** ANNOY : irritar
aggregate ['ægrɪgət] *adj* : total, global — **~** *n* : total *m*
aggression [ə'grɛʃən] *n* : agresión *f* — **aggressive** [ə'grɛsɪv] *adj* : agresivo — **aggressor** [ə'grɛsər] *n* : agresor *m*, -sora *f*
aghast [ə'gæst] *adj* : horrorizado
agile ['ædʒəl] *adj* : ágil — **agility** [ə'dʒɪlət̬i] *n, pl* **-ties** : agilidad *f*
agitate ['ædʒəˌteɪt] *v* **-tated; -tating** *vt* **1** SHAKE : agitar **2** TROUBLE : inquietar — **agitation** [ˌædʒə'teɪʃən] *n* : agitación *f*, inquietud *f*
agnostic [æg'nɑstɪk] *n* : agnóstico *m*, -ca *f*
ago [ə'go:] *adv* **1** : hace **2 long ~** : hace mucho tiempo
agony ['ægəni] *n, pl* **-nies 1** PAIN : dolor *m* **2** ANGUISH : angustia *f* — **agonize** ['ægəˌnaɪz] *vi* **-nized; -nizing** : atormentarse — **agonizing** ['ægəˌnaɪzɪŋ] *adj* : angustioso
agree [ə'gri:] *v* **agreed; agreeing** *vt* **1** : acordar **2 ~ that** : estar de acuerdo de que — *vi* **1** : estar de acuerdo **2** CORRESPOND : concordar **3 ~ to** : acceder a **4 this climate ~s with me** : este clima me sienta bien — **agreeable** [ə'gri:əbəl] *adj* **1** PLEASING : agradable **2** WILLING : dispuesto — **agreement** [ə'gri:mənt] *n* : acuerdo *m*
agriculture ['ægrɪˌkʌltʃər] *n* : agricultura *f* — **agricultural** [ˌægrɪ'kʌltʃərəl] *adj* : agrícola
aground [ə'graʊnd] *adv* **run ~** : encallar
ahead [ə'hɛd] *adv* **1** IN FRONT : por delante, adelante **2** BEFOREHAND : por adelantado **3** LEADING : a la delantera **4 get ~** : adelantar — **ahead of** *prep* **1** : delante de, antes de **2 get ~ of** : adelantarse a
aid ['eɪd] *vt* : ayudar — **~** *n* : ayuda *f*, asistencia *f*
AIDS ['eɪdz] *n* : SIDA *m*, sida *m*
ail ['eɪl] *vi* : estar enfermo — **ailment** ['eɪlmənt] *n* : enfermedad *f*
aim ['eɪm] *vt* : apuntar (un arma), dirigir (una observación) — *vi* **1** : apuntar **2** ASPIRE : aspirar — **~** *n* **1** : puntería *f* **2** GOAL : propósito *m*, objetivo *m* — **aimless** ['eɪmləs] *adj* : sin objetivo
air ['ær] *vt or* **~ out** : airear **2** EXPRESS : expresar **3** BROADCAST : emitir — **~** *n* **1** : aire *m* **2 be on the ~** : estar en el aire — **air–conditioning** [ˌærkən'dɪʃənɪŋ] *n* : aire *m* acondicionado — **air conditioned** ['ærkənˌdɪʃənd] *n* : climatizado — **aircraft** ['ærˌkræft] *ns & pl* **1** : avión *m*, aeronave *f* **2 ~ carrier** : portaaviones *m* — **air force** *n* : fuerza *f* aérea — **airline** ['ærˌlaɪn] *n* : aerolínea *f*, línea *f* aérea — **airliner** ['ærˌlaɪnər] *n* : avión *m* de pasajeros — **airmail** *n* : correo *m* aéreo — **airplane** ['ærˌpleɪn] *n* : avión *m* — **airport** ['ærˌport] *n* : aeropuerto *m* — **airstrip** ['ærˌstrɪp] *n* : pista *f* de aterrizaje — **airtight** ['ærˌtaɪt] *adj* : hermético — **airy** ['æri] *adj* **airier** [-iər]; **-est** : aireado, bien ventilado
aisle ['aɪl] *n* **1** : pasillo *m* **2** : nave *f* lateral (de una iglesia)
ajar [ə'dʒɑr] *adj* : entreabierto
akin [ə'kɪn] *adj* **~ to** : semejante a
alarm [ə'lɑrm] *n* **1** : alarma *f* **2** ANXIETY : inquietud *f* — *vt* : alarmar, asustar — **alarm clock** *n* : despertador *m*
alas [ə'læs] *interj* : ¡ay!
album ['ælbəm] *n* : álbum *m*
alcohol ['ælkəˌhɔl] *n* : alcohol *m* — **alcoholic** [ˌælkə'hɔlɪk] *adj* : alcohólico — **~** *n* : alcohólico *m*, -ca *f* — **alcoholism** ['ælkəhɔˌlɪzəm] *n* : alcoholismo *m*
alcove ['ælˌko:v] *n* : nicho *m*, hueco *m*
ale ['eɪl] *n* : cerveza *f*
alert [ə'lərt] *adj* **1** WATCHFUL : alerta, atento **2** LIVELY : vivo — **~** *n* : alerta *f* — **~** *vt* : alertar, poner sobre aviso
alfalfa [æl'fælfə] *n* : alfalfa *f*
alga ['ælgə] *n, pl* **-gae** ['ælˌdʒi:] : alga *f*
algebra ['ældʒəbrə] *n* : álgebra *f*
alias ['eɪliəs] *adv* : alias — **~** *n* : alias *m*
alibi ['æləˌbaɪ] *n* : coartada *f*
alien ['eɪliən] *adj* : extranjero — **~** *n* **1** FOREIGNER : extranjero *m*, -ra *f* **2** EXTRATERRESTRIAL : extraterrestre *mf*
alienate ['eɪliəˌneɪt] *vt* **-ated; -ating** : enajenar — **alienation** [ˌeɪliə'neɪʃən] *n* : enajenación *f*
alight [ə'laɪt] *vi* **1** LAND : posarse **2 ~ from** : apearse de
align [ə'laɪn] *vt* : alinear — **alignment** [ə'laɪnmənt] *n* : alineación *f*
alike [ə'laɪk] *adv* : igual, del mismo modo — **~** *adj* : parecido
alimony ['æləˌmo:ni] *n, pl* **-nies** : pensión *f* alimenticia
alive [ə'laɪv] *adj* **1** LIVING : vivo, viviente **2** LIVELY : animado, activo
all ['ɔl] *adv* **1** COMPLETELY : todo, completamente **2 ~ the better** : tanto mejor **3 ~ the more** : aún más, todavía más — **~** *adj* : todo — **~** *pron* **1** : todo, -da **2 ~ in ~** : en general **3 not at ~** : de ninguna manera — **all–around** [ˌɔlə'raʊnd] *adj* VERSATILE : completo
allay [ə'leɪ] *vt* **1** ALLEVIATE : aliviar **2** CALM : aquietar
allege [ə'lɛdʒ] *vt* **-leged; -leging** : alegar — **allegation** [ˌælɪ'geɪʃən] *n* : alegato *m*, acusación *f* — **alleged** [ə'lɛdʒd, ə'lɛdʒəd] *adj* : presunto — **allegedly** [ə'lɛdʒədli] *adv* : supuestamente
allegiance [ə'li:dʒənts] *n* : lealtad *f*
allegory ['æləˌgori] *n, pl* **-ries** : alegoría *f* — **allegorical** [ˌælə'gɔrɪkəl] *adj* : alegórico
allergy ['ælərdʒi] *n, pl* **-gies** : alergia *f* — **allergic** [ə'lərdʒɪk] *adj* : alérgico
alleviate [ə'li:viˌeɪt] *vt* **-ated; -ating** : aliviar
alley ['æli] *n, pl* **-leys** : callejón *m*
alliance [ə'laɪənts] *n* : alianza *f*
alligator ['æləˌgeɪt̬ər] *n* : caimán *m*
allocate ['æləˌkeɪt] *vt* **-cated; -cating** : asignar — **allocation** [ˌælə'keɪʃən] *n* : asignación *f*, reparto *m*
allot [ə'lɑt] *vt* **-lotted; -lotting** : asignar — **allotment** [ə'lɑtmənt] *n* : reparto *m*, asignación *f*
allow [ə'laʊ] *vt* **1** PERMIT : permitir **2** GRANT : dar, conceder **3** ADMIT : admitir **4** CONCEDE : reconocer — *vi* **~ for** : tener en cuenta — **allowance** [ə'laʊənts] *n* **1** : pensión *f*, subsidio *m* **2 make ~s for** : tener en cuenta, disculpar
alloy ['æˌlɔɪ, ə'lɔɪ] *n* : aleación *f*
all right *adv* **1** YES : sí, de acuerdo **2** WELL : bien **3** DEFINITELY : bien, sin duda — **~** *adj* : bien, bueno
allude [ə'lu:d] *vi* **-luded; -luding** : aludir
allure [ə'lʊr] *vt* **-lured; -luring** : atraer — **alluring** [ə'lʊrɪŋ] *adj* : atrayente, seductor
allusion [ə'lu:ʒən] *n* : alusión *f*
ally [ə'laɪ, 'æˌlaɪ] *vi* **-lied; -lying ~ oneself with** : aliarse con — **~** ['æˌlaɪ, ə'laɪ] *n* : aliado *m*, -da *f*
almanac ['ɔlməˌnæk, 'æl-] *n* : almanaque *m*
almighty [ɔl'maɪt̬i] *adj* : omnipotente, todopoderoso
almond ['ɑmənd, 'ɑl-, 'æ-, 'æl-] *n* : almendra *f*
almost ['ɔlˌmo:st, ɔl'mo:st] *adv* : casi
alms ['ɑmz, 'ɑlmz, 'ælmz] *ns & pl* : limosna *f*
alone [ə'lo:n] *adv* : sólo, solamente, únicamente — **~** *adj* : solo
along [ə'lɔŋ] *adv* **1** FORWARD : adelante **2 ~ with** : con, junto con **3 all ~** : desde el principio — **~** *prep* : por, a lo largo de — **alongside** [əˌlɔŋ'saɪd] *adv* : al costado — **~** *or* **~ of** *prep* : al lado de
aloof [ə'lu:f] *adj* : distante, reservado
aloud [ə'laʊd] *adv* : en voz alta
alphabet ['ælfəˌbɛt] *n* : alfabeto *m* — **alphabetical** [ˌælfə'bɛt̬ɪkəl] *or* **alphabetic** [-'bɛt̬ɪk] *adj* : alfabético
already [ɔl'rɛdi] *adv* : ya
also ['ɔlˌso:] *adv* : también, además
altar ['ɔltər] *n* : altar *m*
alter ['ɔltər] *vt* : alterar, modificar — **alteration** [ˌɔltə'reɪʃən] *n* : alteración *f*, modificación *f*
alternate ['ɔltərnət] *adj* : alterno — **~** ['ɔltərˌneɪt] *v* **-nated; -nating** : alternar — **alternating current** *n* : corriente *f* alterna — **alternative** [ɔl'tərnət̬ɪv] *adj* : alternativo — **~** *n* : alternativa *f*
although [ɔl'ðo:] *conj* : aunque
altitude ['æltəˌtu:d, -ˌtju:d] *n* : altitud *f*
altogether [ˌɔltə'gɛðər] *adv* **1** COMPLETELY : completamente, del todo **2** ON THE WHOLE : en suma, en general
aluminum [ə'lu:mənəm] *n* : aluminio *m*
always ['ɔlwiz, -ˌweɪz] *adv* **1** : siempre **2** FOREVER : para siempre
am → **be**
amass [ə'mæs] *vt* : amasar, acumular
amateur ['æmətʃər, -tər, -ˌtʊr, -ˌtjʊr] *adj* : amateur — **~** *n* : amateur *mf*; aficionado *m*, -da *f*
amaze [ə'meɪz] *vt* **amazed; amazing** : asombrar — **amazement** [ə'meɪzmənt] *n* : asombro *m* — **amazing** [ə'meɪzɪŋ] *adj* : asombroso
ambassador [æm'bæsədər] *n* : embajador *m*, -dora *f*
amber ['æmbər] *n* : ámbar *m*
ambiguous [æm'bɪgjʊəs] *adj* : ambiguo — **ambiguity** [ˌæmbə'gju:ət̬i] *n, pl* **-ties** : ambigüedad *f*
ambition [æm'bɪʃən] *n* : ambición *f* — **ambitious** [æm'bɪʃəs] *adj* : ambicioso
ambivalence [æm'bɪvələnts] *n* : ambivalencia *f* — **ambivalent** [æm'bɪvələnt] *adj* : ambivalente
amble ['æmbəl] *vi or* **~ along** : andar sin prisa
ambulance ['æmbjələnts] *n* : ambulancia *f*
ambush ['æmˌbʊʃ] *vt* : emboscar — **~** *n* : emboscada *f*
amen ['eɪ'mɛn, 'ɑ-] *interj* : amén
amenable [ə'mi:nəbəl, -'mɛ-] *adj* **~ to** : receptivo a
amend [ə'mɛnd] *vt* : enmendar — **amendment** [ə'mɛndmənt] *n* : enmienda *f* — **amends** [ə'mɛndz] *ns & pl* **make ~ for** : reparar
amenities [ə'mɛnət̬iz, -'mi:-] *npl* : servicios *mpl*, comodidades *fpl*
American [ə'mɛrɪkən] *adj* : americano
amethyst ['æməθəst] *n* : amatista *f*
amiable ['eɪmi:əbəl] *adj* : amable, agradable
amicable ['æmɪkəbəl] *adj* : amigable, amistoso
amid [ə'mɪd] *or* **amidst** [ə'mɪdst] *prep* : en medio de, entre
amiss [ə'mɪs] *adv* **1** : mal **2 take sth ~** : tomar algo a mal — **~** *adj* **1** WRONG : malo **2 something is ~** : algo anda mal
ammonia [ə'mo:njə] *n* : amoníaco *m*
ammunition [ˌæmjə'nɪʃən] *n* : municiones *fpl*
amnesia [æm'ni:ʒə] *n* : amnesia *f*
amnesty ['æmnəsti] *n, pl* **-ties** : amnistía *f*
among [ə'mʌŋ] *prep* : entre
amorous ['æmərəs] *adj* : amoroso
amount [ə'maʊnt] *vi* **1 ~ to** : equivaler a **2 ~ to** TOTAL : sumar, ascender a — **~** *n* : cantidad *f*
amphibian [æm'fɪbiən] *n* : anfibio *m* — **amphibious** [æm'fɪbiəs] *adj* : anfibio
amphitheater ['æmfəˌθi:ət̬ər] *n* : anfiteatro *m*
ample ['æmpəl] *adj* **-pler; -plest 1** SPACIOUS : amplio, extenso **2** ABUNDANT : abundante
amplify ['æmpləˌfaɪ] *vt* **-fied; -fying** : amplificar — **amplifier** ['æmpləˌfaɪər] *n* : amplificador *m*
amputate ['æmpjəˌteɪt] *vt* **-tated; -tating** : amputar — **amputation** [ˌæmpjə'teɪʃən] *n* : amputación *f*
amuse [ə'mju:z] *vt* **amused; amusing 1** : hacer reír, divertir **2** ENTERTAIN : entretener — **amusement** [ə'mju:zmənt] *n* : diversión *f* — **amusing** *adj* : divertido
an → **a**[2]
analogy [ə'nælədʒi] *n, pl* **-gies** : analogía *f* — **analogous** [ə'næləgəs] *adj* : análogo
analysis [ə'næləsəs] *n, pl* **-yses** [-ˌsi:z] : análisis *m* — **analytic** [ˌænə'lɪt̬ɪk] *or* **analytical** [-t̬ɪkəl] *adj* : analítico — **analyze** ['ænəˌlaɪz] *vt* **-lyzed; -lyzing** : analizar
anarchy ['ænərki, -ˌnɑr-] *n* : anarquía *f*
anatomy [ə'næt̬əmi] *n, pl* **-mies** : anatomía *f* — **anatomic** [ˌænə'tɑmɪk] *or* **anatomical** [-mɪkəl] *adj* : anatómico
ancestor ['ænˌsɛstər] *n* : antepasado *m*, -da *f* — **ancestral** [æn'sɛstrəl] *adj* : ancestral — **ancestry** ['ænˌsɛstri] *n* **1** DESCENT : linaje *m*, abolengo *m* **2** ANCESTORS : antepasados *mpl*, -das *fpl*
anchor ['æŋkər] *n* **1** : ancla *f* **2** : presentador *m*, -dora *f* (en televisión) — **~** *vt* **1** : anclar **2** FASTEN : sujetar — *vi* : anclar
anchovy ['ænˌtʃo:vi, æn'tʃo:-] *n, pl* **-vies** *or* **-vy** : anchoa *f*
ancient ['eɪntʃənt] *adj* : antiguo, viejo
and ['ænd] *conj* **1** : y (*e before words beginning with i- or hi-*) **2 come ~ see** : ven a ver **3 more ~ more** : cada vez más **4 try ~ finish it soon** : trata de terminarlo pronto
anecdote ['ænɪkˌdo:t] *n* : anécdota *f*
anemia [ə'ni:miə] *n* : anemia *f* — **anemic** [ə'ni:mɪk] *adj* : anémico
anesthesia [ˌænəs'θi:ʒə] *n* : anestesia *f* — **anesthetic** [ˌænəs'θɛt̬ɪk] *adj* : anestésico — **~** *n* : anestésico *m*
anew [ə'nu:, -'nju:] *adv* : de nuevo, nuevamente
angel ['eɪndʒəl] *n* : ángel *m* — **angelic** [æn'dʒɛlɪk] *or* **angelical** [-lɪkəl] *adj* : angélico
anger ['æŋgər] *vt* : enojar, enfadar — **~** *n* : ira *f*, enojo *m*, enfado *m*
angle *n* **1** : ángulo *m* **2** POINT OF VIEW : perspectiva *f*, punto *m* de vista — **angler** ['æŋglər] *n* : pescador *m*, -dora *f*
Anglo–Saxon [ˌæŋglo'sæksən] *adj* : anglosajón
angry ['æŋgri] *adj* **-grier; -est** : enojado, enfadado
anguish ['æŋgwɪʃ] *n* : angustia *f*
angular ['æŋgjələr] *adj* **1** : angular **2 ~ features** : rasgos *mpl* angulosos
animal ['ænəməl] *n* : animal *m*
animate ['ænəmət] *adj* : animado — **~** ['ænəˌmeɪt] *vt* **-mated; -mating** : animar — **animated** *adj* **1** : animado **2 ~ cartoon** : dibujos *mpl* animados — **animation** [ˌænə'meɪʃən] *n* : animación *f*
animosity [ˌænə'mɑsət̬i] *n, pl* **-ties** : animosidad *f*
anise ['ænəs] *n* : anís *m*
ankle ['æŋkəl] *n* : tobillo *m*
annals ['ænəlz] *npl* : anales *mpl*
annex [ə'nɛks, 'æˌnɛks] *vt* : anexar — **~** ['æˌnɛks, -nɪks] *n* : anexo *m*
annihilate [ə'naɪəˌleɪt] *vt* **-lated; -lating** : aniquilar — **annihilation** [əˌnaɪə'leɪʃən] *n* : aniquilación *f*
anniversary [ˌænə'vərsəri] *n, pl* **-ries** : aniversario *m*
annotate ['ænəˌteɪt] *vt* **-tated; -tating** : anotar — **annotation** [ˌænə'teɪʃən] *n* : anotación *f*
announce [ə'naʊnts] *vt* **-nounced; -nouncing** : anunciar — **announcement** [ə'naʊntsmənt] *n* : anuncio *m* — **announcer** [ə'naʊntsər] *n* : locutor *m*, -tora *f*
annoy [ə'nɔɪ] *vt* : fastidiar, molestar — **annoyance** [ə'nɔɪənts] *n* : fastidio *m*, molestia *f* — **annoying** [ə'nɔɪɪŋ] *adj* : molesto, fastidioso
annual ['ænjʊəl] *adj* : anual — **~** *n* : anuario *m*
annuity [ə'nu:ət̬i] *n, pl* **-ties** : anualidad *f*
annul [ə'nʌl] *vt* **annulled; annulling** : anular — **annulment** [ə'nʌlmənt] *n* : anulación *f*
anoint [ə'nɔɪnt] *vt* : ungir
anomaly [ə'nɑməli] *n, pl* **-lies** : anomalía *f*
anonymous [ə'nɑnəməs] *adj* : anónimo — **anonymity** [ˌænə'nɪmət̬i] *n* : anonimato *m*
another [ə'nʌðər] *adj* **1** : otro **2 in ~ minute** : en un minuto más — **~** *pron* : otro, otra
answer ['æntsər] *n* **1** REPLY : respuesta *f*, contestación *f* **2** SOLUTION : solución *f* — **~** *vt* **1** : contestar a, responder a **2 ~ the door** : abrir la puerta — *vi* : contestar, responder
ant ['ænt] *n* : hormiga *f*
antagonize [æn'tægəˌnaɪz] *vt* **-nized; -nizing** : provocar la enemistad de — **antagonism** [æn'tægəˌnɪzəm] *n* : antagonismo *m*
antarctic [ænt'ɑrktɪk, -'ɑrt̬ɪk] *adj* : antártico
antelope ['æntəlˌo:p] *n, pl* **-lope** *or* **-lopes** : antílope *m*
antenna [æn'tɛnə] *n, pl* **-nae** [-ˌni:, -ˌnaɪ] *or* **-nas** : antena *f*
anthem ['ænθəm] *n* : himno *m*
anthology [æn'θɑlədʒi] *n, pl* **-gies** : antología *f*
anthropology [ˌænθrə'pɑlədʒi] *n* : antropología *f*
antibiotic [ˌæntibaɪ'ɑt̬ɪk, ˌæntaɪ-, -bi-] *adj* : antibiótico — **~** *n* : antibiótico *m*
antibody ['æntiˌbɑdi] *n, pl* **-bodies** : anticuerpo *m*
anticipate [æn'tɪsəˌpeɪt] *vt* **-pated; -pating 1** FORESEE : anticipar, prever **2** EXPECT : esperar — **anticipation** [ænˌtɪsə'peɪʃən] *n* : anticipación *f*, expectación *f*
antics ['æntɪks] *npl* : payasadas *fpl*
antidote ['æntɪˌdo:t] *n* : antídoto *m*
antifreeze ['æntiˌfri:z] *n* : anticongelante *m*
antipathy [æn'tɪpəθi] *n, pl* **-thies** : antipatía *f*
antiquated ['æntəˌkweɪt̬əd] *adj* : anticuado
antique [æn'ti:k] *adj* : antiguo — **~** *n* : antigüedad *f* — **antiquity** [æn'tɪkwət̬i] *n, pl* **-ties** : antigüedad *f*
anti–Semitic [ˌæntisə'mɪt̬ɪk, ˌæntaɪ-] *adj* : antisemita
antiseptic [ˌæntə'sɛptɪk] *adj* : antiséptico — **~** *n* : antiséptico *m*
antisocial [ˌænti'so:ʃəl, ˌæntaɪ-] *adj* **1** : antisocial **2** UNSOCIABLE : poco sociable
antithesis [æn'tɪθəsɪs] *n, pl* **-eses** [-ˌsi:z] : antítesis *f*
antlers ['æntlərz] *npl* : cornamenta *f*
antonym ['æntəˌnɪm] *n* : antónimo *m*
anus ['eɪnəs] *n* : ano *m*
anvil ['ænvəl, -vɪl] *n* : yunque *m*
anxiety [æŋk'zaɪət̬i] *n, pl* **-eties 1** APPREHENSION : inquietud *f*, ansiedad *f* **2** EAGERNESS : anhelo *m* — **anxious** ['æŋkʃəs] *adj* **1** WORRIED : inquieto, preocupado **2** EAGER : ansioso — **anxiously** ['æŋkʃəsli] *adv* : con ansiedad
any ['ɛni] *adv* **1** SOMEWHAT : algo, un poco **2 it's not ~ good** : no sirve para nada **3 we can't wait ~ longer** : no podemos espe-

rar más — ~ *adj* **1 :** alguno **2** (*in negative constructions*) **:** ningún **3** WHATEVER **:** cualquier **4 in ~ case :** en todo caso — ~ *pron* **1 :** alguno, **-na 2 :** ninguno, **-na 3 do you want ~ more rice? :** ¿quieres más arroz?

anybody ['ɛni,bʌdi, -,bɑ-] → **anyone**

anyhow ['ɛni,haʊ] *adv* **1 :** de todas formas **2** HAPHAZARDLY **:** de cualquier modo

anymore [,ɛni'mor] *adv* **not ~ :** ya no

anyone ['ɛni,wʌn] *pron* **1** SOMEONE **:** alguien **2** WHOEVER **:** quienquiera **3 I don't see ~ :** no veo a nadie

anyplace ['ɛni,pleɪs] → **anywhere**

anything ['ɛni,θɪŋ] *pron* **1** SOMETHING **:** algo, alguna cosa **2** (*in negative constructions*) **:** nada **3** WHATEVER **:** cualquier cosa, lo que sea

anytime ['ɛni,taɪm] *adv* **:** en cualquier momento

anyway ['ɛni,weɪ] → **anyhow**

anywhere ['ɛni,*h*wɛr] *adv* **1 :** en cualquier parte, dondequiera **2** (*used in questions*) **:** en algún sitio **3 I can't find it ~ :** no lo encuentro por ninguna parte

apart [ə'pɑrt] *adv* **1 :** aparte **2 ~ from :** excepto, aparte de **3 fall ~ :** deshacerse, hacerse pedazos **4 live ~ :** vivir separados **5 take ~ :** desmontar, desmantelar

apartment [ə'pɑrtmənt] *n* **:** apartamento *m*

apathy ['æpəθi] *n* **:** apatía *f* — **apathetic** [,æpə'θɛt̬ɪk] *adj* **:** apático, indiferente

ape *n* **:** simio *m*

aperture ['æpərtʃər, -,tʃʊr] *n* **:** abertura *f*

apex ['eɪ,pɛks] *n, pl* **apexes** *or* **apices** ['eɪpə,si:z, 'æ-] **:** ápice *m,* cumbre *f*

apiece [ə'pi:s] *adv* **:** cada uno

aplomb [ə'plɑm, -'plʌm] *n* **:** aplomo *m*

apology [ə'pɑlədʒi] *n, pl* **-gies :** disculpa *f* — **apologetic** [ə,pɑlə'dʒɛt̬ɪk] *adj* **:** lleno de disculpas — **apologize** [ə'pɑlə,dʒaɪz] *vi* **-gized; -gizing :** disculparse, pedir perdón

apostle [ə'pɑsəl] *n* **:** apóstol *m*

apostrophe [ə'pɑstrə,fi:] *n* **:** apóstrofo *m*

appall [ə'pɔl] *vt* **:** horrorizar — **appalling** [ə'pɔlɪŋ] *adj* **:** horroroso

apparatus [,æpə'ræt̬əs, -'reɪ-] *n, pl* **-tuses** *or* **-tus :** aparato *m*

apparel [ə'pærəl] *n* **:** ropa *f*

apparent [ə'pærənt] *adj* **1** OBVIOUS **:** claro, evidente **2** SEEMING **:** aparente — **apparently** [ə'pærəntli] *adv* **:** al parecer, por lo visto

apparition [,æpə'rɪʃən] *n* **:** aparición *f*

appeal [ə'pi:l] *vi* **1 ~ for :** solicitar **2 ~ to :** apelar a (la bondad de algn, etc.) **3 ~ to** ATTRACT **:** atraer a — ~ *n* **1 :** apelación *f* (en derecho) **2** REQUEST **:** llamamiento *m* **3** ATTRACTION **:** atractivo *m* — **appealing** [ə'pi:lɪŋ] *adj* **:** atractivo

appear [ə'pɪr] *vi* **1 :** aparecer **2 :** comparecer (ante un tribunal), actuar (en el teatro) **3** SEEM **:** parecer — **appearance** [ə'pɪrən*t*s] *n* **1 :** aparición *f* **2** LOOK **:** apariencia *f,* aspecto *m*

appease [ə'pi:z] *vt* **-peased; -peasing :** apaciguar, aplacar

appendix [ə'pɛndɪks] *n, pl* **-dixes** *or* **-dices** [-də,si:z] **:** apéndice *m* — **appendicitis** [ə,pɛndə'saɪt̬əs] *n* **:** apendicitis *f*

appetite ['æpə,taɪt] *n* **:** apetito *m* — **appetizer** ['æpə,taɪzər] *n* **:** aperitivo *m* — **appetizing** ['æpə,taɪzɪŋ] *adj* **:** apetitoso

applaud [ə'plɔd] *v* **:** aplaudir — **applause** [ə'plɔz] *n* **:** aplauso *m*

apple ['æpəl] *n* **:** manzana *f*

appliance [ə'plaɪən*t*s] *n* **:** aparato *m*

apply [ə'plaɪ] *v* **-plied; -plying** *vt* **1 :** aplicar **2 ~ oneself :** aplicarse — *vi* **1 :** aplicarse **2 ~ for :** solicitar, pedir — **applicable** ['æplɪkəbəl, ə'plɪkə-] *adj* **:** aplicable — **applicant** ['æplɪkənt] *n* **:** solicitante *mf;* candidato *m,* **-ta** *f* — **application** [,æplə'keɪʃən] *n* **1 :** aplicación *f* **2 :** solicitud *f* (para un empleo, etc.)

appoint [ə'pɔɪnt] *vt* **1** NAME **:** nombrar **2** FIX, SET **:** fijar, señalar — **appointment** [ə'pɔɪntmənt] *n* **1** APPOINTING **:** nombramiento *m* **2** ENGAGEMENT **:** cita *f*

apportion [ə'porʃən] *vt* **:** distribuir, repartir

appraise [ə'preɪz] *vt* **-praised; -praising :** evaluar, valorar — **appraisal** [ə'preɪzəl] *n* **:** evaluación *f*

appreciate [ə'pri:ʃi,eɪt, -'prɪ-] *v* **-ated; -ating** *vt* **1** VALUE **:** apreciar **2** UNDERSTAND **:** darse cuenta de **3 I ~ your help :** te agradezco tu ayuda — *vi* **:** aumentar en valor — **appreciation** [ə,pri:ʃi'eɪʃən, -,prɪ-] *n* **1** GRATITUDE **:** agradecimiento *m* **2** VALUING **:** apreciación *f,* valoración *f* — **appreciative** [ə'pri:ʃət̬ɪv, -'prɪ-; ə'pri:ʃi,eɪ-] *adj* **1 :** apreciativo **2** GRATEFUL **:** agradecido

apprehend [,æprɪ'hɛnd] *vt* **1** ARREST **:** aprehender, detener **2** DREAD **:** temer **3** COMPREHEND **:** comprender — **apprehension** [,æprɪ'hɛntʃən] *n* **1** ARREST **:** detención *f,* aprehensión *f* **2** ANXIETY **:** aprensión *f,* temor *m* — **apprehensive** [,æprɪ'hɛn*t*sɪv] *adj* **:** aprensivo, inquieto

apprentice [ə'prɛntɪs] *n* **:** aprendiz *m,* **-diza** *f*

approach [ə'pro:tʃ] *vt* **1** NEAR **:** acercarse a **2 :** dirigirse a (algn), abordar (un problema, etc.) — *vi* **:** acercarse — ~ *n* **1** NEARING **:** acercamiento *m* **2** POSITION **:** enfoque *m* **3** ACCESS **:** acceso *m* — **approachable** [ə'pro:tʃəbəl] *adj* **:** accesible, asequible

appropriate [ə'pro:pri,eɪt] *vt* **-ated; -ating :** apropiarse de — ~ [ə'pro:priət] *adj* **:** apropiado

approve [ə'pru:v] *vt* **-proved; -proving :** aprobar — **approval** [ə'pru:vəl] *n* **:** aprobación *f*

approximate [ə'prɑksəmət] *adj* **:** aproximado — ~ [ə'prɑksə,meɪt] *vt* **-mated; -mating :** aproximarse a — **approximately** [ə'prɑksəmətli] *adv* **:** aproximadamente

apricot ['æprə,kɑt, 'eɪ-] *n* **:** albaricoque *m,* chabacano *m Lat*

April ['eɪprəl] *n* **:** abril *m*

apron ['eɪprən] *n* **:** delantal *m*

apropos [,æprə'po:, 'æprə,po:] *adv* **:** a propósito

apt ['æpt] *adj* **1** FITTING **:** apto, apropiado **2** LIABLE **:** propenso — **aptitude** ['æptə,tu:d, -,tju:d] *n* **:** aptitud *f*

aquarium [ə'kwæriəm] *n, pl* **-iums** *or* **-ia** [-iə] **:** acuario *m*

aquatic [ə'kwɑt̬ɪk, -'kwæ-] *adj* **:** acuático

aqueduct ['ækwə,dʌkt] *n* **:** acueducto *m*

Arab ['ærəb] *adj* **:** árabe — **Arabic** ['ærəbɪk] *adj* **:** árabe — ~ *n* **:** árabe *m* (idioma)

arbitrary ['ɑrbə,trɛri] *adj* **:** arbitrario

arbitrate ['ɑrbə,treɪt] *v* **-trated; -trating :** arbitrar — **arbitration** [,ɑrbə'treɪʃən] *n* **:** arbitraje *m*

arc ['ɑrk] *n* **:** arco *m*

arcade [ɑr'keɪd] *n* **1 :** arcada *f* **2 shopping ~ :** galería *f* comercial

arch ['ɑrtʃ] *n* **:** arco *m* — ~ *vt* **:** arquear — *vi* **:** arquearse

archaeology *or* **archeology** [,ɑrki'ɑlədʒi] *n* **:** arqueología *f* — **archaeological** [,ɑrkiə'lɑdʒɪkəl] *adj* **:** arqueológico — **archaeologist** [,ɑrki'ɑlədʒɪst] *n* **:** arqueólogo *m,* **-ga** *f*

archaic [ɑr'keɪɪk] *adj* **:** arcaico

archbishop [ɑrtæ'bɪʃəp] *n* **:** arzobispo *m*

archery ['ɑrtʃəri] *n* **:** tiro *m* al arco

archipelago [,ɑrkə'pɛlə,go:, ,ɑrtʃə-] *n, pl* **-goes** *or* **-gos** [-go:z] **:** archipiélago *m*

architecture ['ɑrkə,tɛk*t*ʃər] *n* **:** arquitectura *f* — **architect** ['ɑrkə,tɛkt] *n* **:** arquitecto *m,* **-ta** *f* — **architectural** [,ɑrkə'tɛk*t*ʃərəl] *adj* **:** arquitectónico

archives ['ɑr,kaɪvz] *npl* **:** archivo *m*

archway ['ɑrtʃ,weɪ] *n* **:** arco *m* (de entrada)

arctic ['ɑrktɪk, 'ɑrt̬-] *adj* **:** ártico

ardent ['ɑrdənt] *adj* **:** ardiente, fervoroso — **ardor** ['ɑrdər] *n* **:** ardor *m,* fervor *m*

arduous ['ɑrdʒʊəs] *adj* **:** arduo

are → **be**

area ['æriə] *n* **1** REGION **:** área *f,* zona *f* **2** FIELD **:** campo *m* **3 ~ code :** código *m* de la zona *Lat,* prefijo *m Spain*

arena [ə'ri:nə] *n* **:** arena *f,* ruedo *m*

aren't ['ɑrnt, 'ɑrənt] (*contraction of* **are not**) → **be**

Argentine ['ɑrdʒən,taɪn, -,ti:n] *or* **Argentinean** *or* **Argentinian** [,ɑrdʒən'tɪniən] *adj* **:** argentino

argue ['ɑr,gju:] *v* **-gued; -guing** *vi* **1** QUARREL **:** discutir **2 ~ against :** argumentar contra — *vt* **:** argumentar, sostener — **argument** ['ɑrgjəmənt] *n* **1** QUARREL **:** disputa *f,* discusión *f* **2** REASONING **:** argumentos *mpl*

arid ['ærəd] *adj* **:** árido — **aridity** [ə'rɪdət̬i, æ-] *n* **:** aridez *f*

arise [ə'raɪz] *vi* **arose** [ə'ro:z]; **arisen** [ə'rɪzən]; **arising 1 :** levantarse **2 ~ from :** surgir de

aristocracy [,ærə'stɑkrəsi] *n, pl* **-cies :** aristocracia *f* — **aristocrat** [ə'rɪstə,kræt] *n* **:** aristócrata *mf* — **aristocratic** [ə,rɪstə'kræt̬ɪk] *adj* **:** aristocrático

arithmetic [ə'rɪθmə,tɪk] *n* **:** aritmética *f*

ark ['ɑrk] *n* **:** arca *f*

arm ['ɑrm] *n* **1 :** brazo *m* **2** WEAPON **:** arma *f* — ~ *vt* **:** armar — **armament** ['ɑrməmənt] *n* **:** armamento *m* — **armchair** ['ɑrm,tʃɛr] *n* **:** sillón *m* — **armed** ['ɑrmd] *adj* **1 ~ forces :** fuerzas *fpl* armadas **2 ~ robbery :** robo *m* a mano armada

armistice ['ɑrməstɪs] *n* **:** armisticio *m*

armor *or Brit* **armour** ['ɑrmər] *n* **:** armadura *f* — **armored** *or Brit* **armoured** ['ɑrmərd] *adj* **:** blindado, acorazado — **armory** *or Brit* **armoury** ['ɑrmri, 'ɑrməri] **:** arsenal *m*

armpit ['ɑrm,pɪt] *n* **:** axila *f,* sobaco *m*

army ['ɑrmi] *n, pl* **-mies :** ejército *m*

aroma [ə'ro:mə] *n* **:** aroma *m* — **aromatic** [,ærə'mæt̬ɪk] *adj* **:** aromático

around [ə'raʊnd] *adv* **1 :** de circunferencia **2** NEARBY **:** por ahí **3** APPROXIMATELY **:** más o menos, aproximadamente **4 all ~ :** por todos lados, todo alrededor **5 turn ~ :** voltearse — ~ *prep* **1** SURROUNDING **:** alrededor de **2** THROUGHOUT **:** por **3** NEAR **:** cerca de **4 ~ the corner :** a la vuelta de la esquina

arouse [ə'raʊz] *vt* **aroused; arousing 1** AWAKE **:** despertar **2** EXCITE **:** excitar

arrange [ə'reɪndʒ] *vt* **-ranged; -ranging :** arreglar, poner en orden — **arrangement** [ə'reɪndʒmənt] *n* **1** ORDER **:** arreglo *m* **2 ~s** *npl* **:** preparativos *mpl*

array [ə'reɪ] *n* **:** selección *f,* surtido *m*

arrears [ə'rɪrz] *npl* **1 :** atrasos *mpl* **2 be in ~ :** estar atrasado en pagos

arrest [ə'rɛst] *vt* **:** detener — ~ *n* **1 :** arresto *m,* detención *f* **2 under ~ :** detenido

arrive [ə'raɪv] *vi* **-rived; -riving :** llegar — **arrival** [ə'raɪvəl] *n* **:** llegada *f*

arrogance ['ærəgən*t*s] *n* **:** arrogancia *f* — **arrogant** ['ærəgənt] *adj* **:** arrogante

arrow ['æro] *n* **:** flecha *f*

arsenal ['ɑrsənəl] *n* **:** arsenal *m*

arsenic ['ɑrsənɪk] *n* **:** arsénico *m*

arson ['ɑrsən] *n* **:** incendio *m* premeditado

art ['ɑrt] *n* **1 :** arte *m* **2 ~s** *npl* **:** letras *fpl* (en educación) **3 fine ~s :** bellas artes *fpl*

artefact *Brit* → **artifact**

artery ['ɑrt̬əri] *n, pl* **-teries :** arteria *f*

artful ['ɑrtfəl] *adj* **:** astuto, taimado

arthritis [ɑr'θraɪt̬əs] *n, pl* **-tides** [ɑr'θrɪt̬ə,di:z] **:** artritis *f* — **arthritic** [ɑr'θrɪt̬ɪk] *adj* **:** artrítico

artichoke ['ɑrt̬ə,tʃo:k] *n* **:** alcachofa *f*

article ['ɑrtɪkəl] *n* **:** artículo *m*

articulate [ɑr'tɪkjə,leɪt] *vt* **-lated; -lating :** articular — ~ [ɑr'tɪkjələt] *adj* **be ~ :** expresarse bien

artifact *or Brit* **artefact** ['ɑrt̬ə,fækt] *n* **:** artefacto *m*

artificial [,ɑrt̬ə'fɪʃəl] *adj* **:** artificial

artillery [ɑr'tɪləri] *n, pl* **-leries :** artillería *f*

artisan ['ɑrt̬əzən, -sən] *n* **:** artesano *m,* **-na** *f*

artist ['ɑrt̬ɪst] *n* **:** artista *mf* — **artistic** [ɑr'tɪstɪk] *adj* **:** artístico

as ['æz] *adv* **1 :** tan, tanto **2 ~ much :** tanto como **3 ~ tall ~ :** tan alto como **4 ~ well :** también — ~ *conj* **1** WHILE **:** mientras **2** (*referring to manner*) **:** como **3** SINCE **:** ya que **4** THOUGH **:** por más que — ~ *prep* **1 :** de **2** LIKE **:** como — ~ *pron* **:** que

asbestos [æz'bɛstəs, æs-] *n* **:** asbesto *m,* amianto *m*

ascend [ə'sɛnd] *vi* **:** ascender, subir — *vt* **:** subir (a) — **ascent** [ə'sɛnt] *n* **:** ascensión *f,* subida *f*

ascertain [,æsər'teɪn] *vt* **:** averiguar, determinar

ascribe [ə'skraɪb] *vt* **-cribed; -cribing :** atribuir

as for *prep* **:** en cuanto a

ash[1] ['æʃ] *n* **:** ceniza *f*

ash[2] *n* **:** fresno *m* (árbol)

ashamed [ə'ʃeɪmd] *adj* **:** avergonzado, apenado *Lat*

ashore [ə'ʃor] *adv* **1 :** en tierra **2 go ~ :** desembarcar

ashtray ['æʃ,treɪ] *n* **:** cenicero *m*

Asian ['eɪʒən, -ʃən] *adj* **:** asiático

aside [ə'saɪd] *adv* **1 :** a un lado **2** APART **:** aparte **3 set ~ :** guardar — **aside from** *prep* **1** BESIDES **:** además de **2** EXCEPT **:** aparte de, menos

as if *conj* **:** como si

ask ['æsk] *vt* **1 :** preguntar **2** REQUEST **:** pedir **3** INVITE **:** invitar — *vi* **:** preguntar

askance [ə'skæn*t*s] *adv* **look ~ :** mirar de soslayo

askew [ə'skju:] *adj* **:** torcido, ladeado

asleep [ə'sli:p] *adj* **1 :** dormido **2 fall ~ :** dormirse, quedarse dormido

as of *prep* **:** desde, a partir de

asparagus [ə'spærəgəs] *n* **:** espárrago *m*

aspect ['æ,spɛkt] *n* **:** aspecto *m*

asphalt ['æs,fɔlt] *n* **:** asfalto *m*

asphyxiate [æ'sfɪksi,eɪt] *v* **-ated; -ating** *vt* **:** asfixiar — **asphyxiation** [æ,sfɪksi'eɪʃən] *n* **:** asfixia *f*

aspire [ə'spaɪr] *vi* **-pired; -piring :** aspirar — **aspiration** [,æspə'reɪʃən] *n* **:** aspiración *f*

aspirin ['æsprən, 'æspə-] *n, pl* **aspirin** *or* **aspirins :** aspirina *f*

ass ['æs] *n* **1 :** asno *m* **2** IDIOT **:** imbécil *mf,* idiota *mf*

assail [ə'seɪl] *vt* **:** atacar, asaltar — **assailant** [ə'seɪlənt] *n* **:** asaltante *mf,* atacante *mf*

assassin [ə'sæsən] *n* **:** asesino *m,* **-na** *f* — **assassinate** [ə'sæsən,eɪt] *vt* **-nated; -nating :** asesinar — **assassination** [ə,sæsən'eɪʃən] *n* **:** asesinato *m*

assault [ə'sɔlt] *n* **1 :** ataque *m,* asalto *m* **2 :** agresión *f* (contra algn) — ~ *vt* **:** atacar, asaltar

assemble [ə'sɛmbəl] *v* **-bled; -bling** *vt* **1** GATHER **:** reunir, juntar **2** CONSTRUCT **:** montar — *vi* **:** reunirse — **assembly** [ə'sɛmbli] *n, pl* **-blies 1** MEETING **:** reunión *f,* asamblea *f* **2** CONSTRUCTING **:** montaje *m*

assent [ə'sɛnt] *vi* **:** asentir, consentir — ~ *n* **:** asentimiento *m*

assert [ə'sərt] *vt* **1 :** afirmar **2 ~ oneself :** hacerse valer — **assertion** [ə'sərʃən] *n* **:** afirmación *f* — **assertive** [ə'sərt̬ɪv] *adj* **:** firme, enérgico

assess [ə'sɛs] *vt* **:** evaluar, valorar — **assessment** [ə'sɛsmənt] *n* **:** evaluación *f,* valoración *f*

asset ['æ,sɛt] *n* **1 :** ventaja *f,* recurso *m* **2 ~s** *npl* **:** bienes *mpl,* activo *m*

assiduous [ə'sɪdʒʊəs] *adj* **:** asiduo

assign [ə'saɪn] *vt* **1** APPOINT **:** designar, nombrar **2** ALLOT **:** asignar — **assignment** [ə'saɪnmənt] *n* **1** TASK **:** misión *f* **2** HOMEWORK **:** tarea *f* **3** ASSIGNING **:** asignación *f*

assimilate [ə'sɪmə,leɪt] *vt* **-lated; -lating :** asimilar

assist [ə'sɪst] *vt* **:** ayudar — **assistance** [ə'sɪstən*t*s] *n* **:** ayuda *f* — **assistant** [ə'sɪstənt] *n* **:** ayudante *mf*

associate [ə'so:ʃi,eɪt, -si-] *v* **-ated; -ating** *vt* **:** asociar — *vi* **:** asociarse — ~ [ə'so:ʃiət, -siət] *n* **:** asociado *m,* **-da** *f;* socio *m,* **-cia** *f* — **association** [ə,so:ʃi'eɪʃən, -si-] *n* **:** asociación *f*

as soon as *conj* **:** tan pronto como

assorted [ə'sɔrt̬əd] *adj* **:** surtido — **assortment** [ə'sɔrtmənt] *n* **:** surtido *m,* variedad *f*

assume [ə'su:m] *vt* **-sumed; -suming 1** SUPPOSE **:** suponer **2** UNDERTAKE **:** asumir **3** TAKE ON **:** adquirir, tomar — **assumption** [ə'sʌmpʃən] *n* **:** suposición *f*

assure [ə'ʃʊr] *vt* **-sured; -suring :** asegurar — **assurance** [ə'ʃʊrən*t*s] *n* **1** CERTAINTY **:** certeza *f,* garantía *f* **2** CONFIDENCE **:** confianza *f,* seguridad *f* (de sí mismo)

asterisk ['æstə,rɪsk] *n* **:** asterisco *m*

asthma ['æzmə] *n* **:** asma *m*

as though → **as if**

as to *prep* **:** sobre, acerca de

astonish [ə'stɑnɪʃ] *vt* **:** asombrar — **astonishing** [ə'stɑnɪʃɪŋ] *adj* **:** asombroso — **astonishment** [ə'stɑnɪʃmənt] *n* **:** asombro *m*

astound [ə'staʊnd] *vt* **:** asombrar, pasmar — **astounding** [ə'staʊndɪŋ] *adj* **:** asombroso, pasmoso

astray [ə'streɪ] *adv* **1 go ~ :** extraviarse **2 lead ~ :** llevar por mal camino

astrology [ə'strɑlədʒi] *n* **:** astrología *f*

astronaut ['æstrə,nɔt] *n* **:** astronauta *mf*

astronomy [ə'strɑnəmi] *n, pl* **-mies :** astronomía *f* — **astronomer** [ə'strɑnəmər] *n* **:** astrónomo *m,* **-ma** *f* — **astronomical** [,æstrə'nɑmɪkəl] *adj* **:** astronómico

astute [ə'stu:t, -'stju:t] *adj* **:** astuto, sagaz — **astuteness** [ə'stu:tnəs, -'stju:t-] *n* **:** astucia *f*

as well as *conj* **:** tanto como — ~ *prep* **:** además de, aparte de

asylum [ə'saɪləm] *n* **1 :** asilo *m* **2 insane ~ :** manicomio *m*

at ['æt] *prep* **1 :** a **2 ~ home :** en casa **3 ~ night :** en la noche, por la noche **4 ~ two o'clock :** a las dos **5 be angry ~ :** estar enojado con **6 laugh ~ :** reírse de — **at all** *adv* **not ~ :** en absoluto, nada

ate → **eat**

atheist ['eɪθiɪst] *n* **:** ateo *m,* atea *f* — **atheism** *n* ['eɪθi,ɪzəm] **:** ateísmo *m*

athlete ['æθ,li:t] *n* **:** atleta *mf* — **athletic** [æθ'lɛt̬ɪk] *adj* **:** atlético — **athletics** [æθ'lɛt̬ɪks] *ns & pl* **:** atletismo *m*

atlas ['ætləs] *n* **:** atlas *m*

atmosphere ['ætmə,sfɪr] *n* **1 :** atmósfera *f* **2** AMBIENCE **:** ambiente *m* — **atmospheric** [,ætmə'sfɪrɪk, -'sfɛr-] *adj* **:** atmosférico

atom ['æt̬əm] *n* **:** átomo *m* — **atomic** [ə'tɑmɪk] *adj* **:** atómico

atomizer ['æt̬ə,maɪzər] *n* **:** atomizador *m*

atone [ə'to:n] *vt* **atoned; atoning ~ for :** expiar

atrocity [ə'trɑsət̬i] *n, pl* **-ties :** atrocidad *f* — **atrocious** [ə'tro:ʃəs] *adj* **:** atroz

atrophy ['ætrəfi] *vi* **-phied; -phying :** atrofiarse

attach [ə'tætʃ] *vt* **1 :** sujetar, atar **2 :** adjuntar (un documento, etc.) **3 ~ importance to :** atribuir importancia a **4 become ~ed to s.o. :** encariñarse con algn — **attachment** [ə'tætʃmənt] *n* **1** ACCESSORY **:** accesorio *m* **2** FONDNESS **:** cariño *m*

attack [ə'tæk] *v* **:** atacar — ~ *n* **:** ataque *m* — **attacker** [ə'tækər] *n* **:** agresor *m,* **-sora** *f*

attain [ə'teɪn] *vt* **:** lograr, alcanzar — **attainment** [ə'teɪnmənt] *n* **:** logro *m*

attempt [ə'tɛmpt] *vt* **:** intentar — ~ *n* **:** intento *m*

attend [ə'tɛnd] *vt* **:** asistir a — vi **1 :** asistir **2 ~ to :** ocuparse de — **attendance** [ə'tɛndən*t*s] *n* **1 :** asistencia *f* **2** TURNOUT **:** concurrencia *f* — **attendant** *n* **:** encargado *m,* **-da** *f;* asistente *mf*

attention [ə'tɛntʃən] *n* **1 :** atención *f* **2 pay ~ :** prestar atención, hacer caso — **attentive** [ə'tɛntɪv] *adj* **:** atento

attest [ə'tɛst] *vt* **:** atestiguar

attic ['æt̬ɪk] *n* **:** desván *m*

attire [ə'taɪr] *n* **:** atavío *m*

attitude ['æt̬ə,tu:d, -,tju:d] *n* **1 :** actitud *f* **2** POSTURE **:** postura *f*

attorney [ə'tərni] *n, pl* **-neys :** abogado *m,* **-da** *f*

attract [ə'trækt] *vt* **:** atraer — **attraction** [ə'trækʃən] *n* **1 :** atracción *f* **2** APPEAL **:** atractivo *m* — **attractive** [ə'træktɪv] *adj* **:** atractivo, atrayente

attribute ['ætrə,bju:t] *n* **:** atributo *m* — ~ [ə'trɪ,bju:t] *vt* **-tributed; -tributing :** atribuir, imputar

auburn ['ɔbərn] *adj* **:** castaño rojizo

auction ['ɔkʃən] *n* **:** subasta *f* — ~ *vt or* **~ off :** subastar

audacious [ɔ'deɪʃəs] *adj* **:** audaz — **audacity** [ɔ'dæsət̬i] *n, pl* **-ties :** audacia *f,* atrevimiento *m*

audible ['ɔdəbəl] *adj* **:** audible

audience ['ɔdiən*t*s] *n* **1** INTERVIEW **:** audiencia *f* **2** PUBLIC **:** público *m*

audiovisual [,ɔdio'vɪʒʊəl] *adj* **:** audiovisual

audition [ɔ'dɪʃən] *n* **:** audición *f*

auditor ['ɔdət̬ər] *n* **1 :** auditor *m,* **-tora** *f* (de finanzas) **2** STUDENT **:** oyente *mf*

auditorium [,ɔdə'toriəm] *n, pl* **-riums** *or* **-ria** [-riæ] **:** auditorio *m*

augment [ɔg'mɛnt] *vt* **:** aumentar

augur ['ɔgər] *vi* **~ well :** ser de buen agüero

August ['ɔgəst] *n* **:** agosto *m*

aunt ['ænt, 'ɑnt] *n* **:** tía *f*

aura ['ɔrə] *n* **:** aura *f*

auspices ['ɔspəsəz, -ˌsiːz] *npl* : auspicios *mpl*

auspicious [ɔ'spɪʃəs] *adj* : propicio, prometedor

austere [ɔ'stɪr] *adj* : austero — **austerity** [ɔ'stɛrət̬i] *n, pl* **-ties** : austeridad *f*

Australian [ɔ'streɪljən] *adj* : australiano

authentic [ə'θɛntɪk, ɔ-] *adj* : auténtico

author ['ɔθər] *n* : autor *m*, -tora *f*

authority [ə'θɔrət̬i, ɔ-] *n, pl* **-ties** : autoridad *f* — **authoritarian** [ɔˌθɔrə'tɛriən, ə-] *adj* : autoritario — **authoritative** [ə'θɔrəˌteɪt̬ɪv, ɔ-] *adj* **1** RELIABLE : autorizado **2** DICTATORIAL : autoritario — **authorization** [ˌɔθərə'zeɪʃən] *n* : autorización *f* — **authorize** ['ɔθəˌraɪz] *vt* **-rized; -rizing** : autorizar

autobiography [ˌɔt̬obaɪ'ɑgrəfi] *n, pl* **-phies** : autobiografía *f* — **autobiographical** [ˌɔt̬oˌbaɪə'græfɪkəl] *adj* : autobiográfico

autograph ['ɔt̬əˌgræf] *n* : autógrafo *m* — ~ *vt* : autografiar

automatic [ˌɔt̬ə'mæt̬ɪk] *adj* : automático — **automate** ['ɔt̬əˌmeɪt] *vt* **-mated; -mating** : automatizar — **automation** [ˌɔt̬ə'meɪʃən] *n* : automatización *f*

automobile [ˌɔt̬əmo'biːl, -'moːˌbiːl] *n* : automóvil *m*

autonomy [ɔ'tɑnəmi] *n, pl* **-mies** : autonomía *f* — **autonomous** [ɔ'tɑnəməs] *adj* : autónomo

autopsy ['ɔˌtɑpsi, -təp-] *n, pl* **-sies** : autopsia *f*

autumn ['ɔt̬əm] *n* : otoño *m*

auxiliary [ɔg'zɪljəri, -'zɪləri] *adj* : auxiliar — ~ *n, pl* **-ries** : auxiliar *mf*

avail [ə'veɪl] *vt* ~ **oneself of** : aprovecharse de — ~ *n* **to no** ~ : en vano — **available** [ə'veɪləbəl] *adj* : disponible — **availability** [əˌveɪlə'bɪlət̬i] *n, pl* **-ties** : disponibilidad *f*

avalanche ['ævəˌlæntʃ] *n* : avalancha *f*

avarice ['ævərəs] *n* : avaricia *f*

avenge [ə'vɛndʒ] *vt* **avenged; avenging** : vengar

avenue ['ævəˌnuː, -ˌnjuː] *n* **1** : avenida *f* **2** MEANS : vía *f*

average ['ævrɪdʒ, 'ævə-] *n* : promedio *m* — ~ *adj* **1** MEAN : medio **2** ORDINARY : regular, ordinario — ~ *vt* **-aged; -aging 1** : hacer un promedio de **2** *or* ~ **out** : calcular el promedio de

averse [ə'vərs] *adj* **be** ~ **to** : sentir aversión por — **aversion** [ə'vərʒən] *n* : aversión *f*

avert [ə'vərt] *vt* **1** AVOID : evitar, prevenir **2** ~ **one's eyes** : apartar los ojos

aviation [ˌeɪvi'eɪʃən] *n* : aviación *f* — **aviator** ['eɪviˌeɪt̬ər] *n* : aviador *m*, -dora *f*

avid ['ævɪd] *adj* : ávido — **avidly** *adv* : con avidez

avocado [ˌævə'kɑdo, ˌɑvə-] *n, pl* **-dos** : aguacate *m*

avoid [ə'vɔɪd] *vt* : evitar — **avoidable** [ə'vɔɪdəbəl] *adj* : evitable

await [ə'weɪt] *vt* : esperar

awake [ə'weɪk] *v* **awoke** [ə'woːk]; **awoken** [ə'woːkən] *or* **awaked; awaking** : despertar — ~ *adj* : despierto — **awaken** [ə'weɪkən] *v* → **awake**

award [ə'wɔrd] *vt* **1** : otorgar, conceder (un premio, etc.) **2** : adjudicar (daños y perjuicios) — ~ *n* **1** PRIZE : premio *m* **2** : adjudicación *f*

aware [ə'wær] *adj* **be** ~ **of** : estar consciente de — **awareness** [ə'wærnəs] *n* : conciencia *f*

away [ə'weɪ] *adv* **1** (*referring to distance*) : de aquí, de distancia **2 far** ~ : lejos **3 give** ~ : regalar **4 go** ~ : irse **5 right** ~ : en seguida **6 take** ~ : quitar — ~ *adj* **1** ABSENT : ausente **2** ~ **game** : partido *m* fuera de casa

awe ['ɔ] *n* : temor *m* reverencial — **awesome** ['ɔsəm] *adj* : imponente, formidable

awful ['ɔfəl] *adj* **1** : terrible, espantoso **2 an** ~ **lot** : muchísimo — **awfully** ['ɔfəli] *adv* : terriblemente

awhile [ə'hwaɪl] *adv* : un rato

awkward ['ɔkwərd] *adj* **1** CLUMSY : torpe **2** EMBARRASSING : embarazoso, delicado **3** DIFFICULT : difícil — **awkwardly** *adv* **1** : con dificultad **2** CLUMSILY : de manera torpe

awning ['ɔnɪŋ] *n* : toldo *m*

awry [ə'raɪ] *adj* **1** ASKEW : torcido **2 go** ~ : salir mal

ax *or* **axe** ['æks] *n* : hacha *f*

axiom ['æksiəm] *n* : axioma *m*

axis ['æksɪs] *n, pl* **axes** [-ˌsiːz] : eje *m*

axle ['æksəl] *n* : eje *m*

B

b ['biː] *n, pl* **b's** *or* **bs** ['biːz] : b, segunda letra del alfabeto inglés

babble ['bæbəl] *vi* **-bled; -bling 1** : balbucear **2** MURMUR : murmurar — ~ *n* : balbuceo *m* (de bebé), murmullo *m* (de voces, de un arroyo)

baboon [bæ'buːn] *n* : babuino *m*

baby ['beɪbi] *n, pl* **-bies** : bebé *m;* niño *m*, -ña *f* — **baby** *vt* **-bied; -bying** : mimar, consentir — **babyish** ['beɪbiɪʃ] *adj* : infantil — **baby–sit** ['beɪbiˌsɪt] *vi* **-sat** [-ˌsæt]; **-sitting** : cuidar a los niños

bachelor ['bætʃələr] *n* **1** : soltero *m* **2** GRADUATE : licenciado *m*, -da *f*

back ['bæk] *n* **1** : espalda *f* **2** REVERSE : reverso *m*, dorso *m*, revés *m* **3** REAR : fondo *m*, parte *f* trasera **4** : defensa *mf* (en deportes) — ~ *adv* **1** : atrás **2 be** ~ : estar de vuelta **3 go** ~ : volver **4 two years** ~ : hace dos años — ~ *adj* **1** REAR : de atrás, trasero **2** OVERDUE : atrasado — ~ *vt* **1** SUPPORT : apoyar **2** *or* ~ **up** : darle marcha atrás a (un vehículo) — *vi* **1** ~ **down** : volverse atrás **2** ~ **up** : retroceder — **backache** ['bækˌeɪk] *n* : dolor *m* de espalda — **backbone** ['bækˌboːn] *n* : columna *f* vertebral — **backfire** ['bækˌfaɪr] *vi* **-fired; -firing** : petardear — **background** ['bækˌgraʊnd] *n* **1** : fondo *m* (de un cuadro, etc.), antecedentes *mpl* (de una situación) **2** EXPERIENCE : formación *f* — **backhand** ['bækˌhænd] *adv* : de revés, con el revés — **backhanded** ['bækˌhændəd] *adj* : indirecto — **backing** ['bækɪŋ] *n* : apoyo *m*, respaldo *m* — **backlash** ['bækˌlæʃ] *n* : reacción *f* violenta — **backlog** ['bækˌlɔg] *n* : atrasos *mpl* — **backpack** ['bækˌpæk] *n* : mochila *f* — **backstage** [ˌbæk'steɪdʒ, 'bækˌ-] *adv & adj* : entre bastidores — **backtrack** ['bækˌtræk] *vi* : dar marcha atrás — **backup** ['bækˌʌp] *n* **1** SUPPORT : respaldo *m*, apoyo *m* **2** : copia *f* de seguridad (para computadoras) — **backward** ['bækwərd] *or* **backwards** [-wərdz] *adv* **1** : hacia atrás **2 do it** ~ : hacerlo al revés **3 fall** ~ : caer de espaldas **4 bend over** ~**s** : hacer todo lo posible — **backward** *adj* **1** : hacia atrás **2** RETARDED : retrasado **3** SHY : tímido **4** UNDERDEVELOPED : atrasado

bacon ['beɪkən] *n* : tocino *m*, tocineta *f Lat*, bacon *m Spain*

bacteria [bæk'tɪriə] : bacterias *fpl*

bad ['bæd] *adj* **worse** ['wərs]; **worst** ['wərst] **1** : malo **2** ROTTEN : podrido **3** SEVERE : grave **4 from** ~ **to worse** : de mal en peor **5 too** ~**!** : ¡qué lástima! — ~ *adv* → **badly**

badge ['bædʒ] *n* : insignia *f*, chapa *f*

badger ['bædʒər] *n* : tejón *m* — ~ *vt* : acosar

badly ['bædli] *adv* **1** : mal **2** SEVERELY : gravemente **3 want** ~ : desear mucho

baffle ['bæfəl] *vi* **-fled; -fling** : desconcertar

bag ['bæg] *n* **1** : bolsa *f*, saco *m* **2** HANDBAG : bolso *m*, cartera *f Lat* **3** SUITCASE : maleta *f* — ~ *vt* **bagged; bagging** : ensacar, poner en una bolsa

baggage ['bægɪdʒ] *n* : equipaje *m*

baggy ['bægi] *adj* **-gier; -est** : holgado

bail ['beɪl] *n* : fianza *f* — ~ *vt* **1** : achicar (agua de un bote) **2** ~ **out** RELEASE : poner en libertad bajo fianza **3** ~ **out** EXTRICATE : sacar de apuros

bailiff ['beɪləf] *n* : alguacil *mf*

bait ['beɪt] *vt* **1** : cebar **2** HARASS : acosar — ~ *n* : cebo *m*, carnada *f*

bake ['beɪk] *v* **baked; baking** *vt* : cocer al horno — *vi* : cocerse (al horno) — **baker** ['beɪkər] *n* : panadero *m*, -ra *f* — **bakery** ['beɪkəri] *n, pl* **-ries** : panadería *f*

balance ['bælənts] *n* **1** SCALES : balanza *f* **2** COUNTERBALANCE : contrapeso *m* **3** EQUILIBRIUM : equilibrio *m* **4** REMAINDER : resto *m* **5** *or* **bank** ~ : saldo *m* — ~ *v* **-anced; -ancing** *vt* **1** : hacer el balance de (una cuenta) **2** EQUALIZE : equilibrar **3** WEIGH : sopesar — *vi* **1** : sostenerse en equilibrio **2** : cuadrar (dícese de una cuenta)

balcony ['bælkəni] *n, pl* **-nies 1** : balcón *m* **2** : galería *f* (de un teatro)

bald ['bɔld] *adj* **1** : calvo **2** WORN : pelado **3 the** ~ **truth** : la pura verdad

bale *n* : bala *f*, fardo *m*

baleful ['beɪlfəl] *adj* : siniestro

balk ['bɔk] *vi* ~ **at** : resistarse a

ball ['bɔl] *n* **1** : pelota *f*, bola *f*, balón *m* **2** DANCE : baile *m* **3** ~ **of string** : ovillo *m* de cuerda

ballad ['bæləd] *n* : balada *f*

ballast *n* : lastre *m*

ball bearing *n* : cojinete *m* de bola

ballerina [ˌbælə'riːnə] *n* : bailarina *f*

ballet [bæ'leɪ, 'bæˌleɪ] *n* : ballet *m*

ballistic [bə'lɪstɪk] *adj* : balístico

balloon *n* : globo *m*

ballot *n* **1** : papeleta *f* (de voto) **2** VOTING : votación *f*

ballpoint pen ['bɔlˌpɔɪnt] *n* : bolígrafo *m*

ballroom ['bɔlˌruːm, -ˌrʊm] *n* : sala *f* de baile

balm ['bɑm, 'bɑlm] *n* : bálsamo *m* — **balmy** ['bɑmi, 'bɑl-] *adj* **balmier; -est** : templado, agradable

baloney [bə'loːni] *n* NONSENSE : tonterías *fpl*

bamboo [bæm'buː] *n* : bambú *m*

bamboozle [bæm'buːzəl] *vt* **-zled; -zling** : engañar, embaucar

ban ['bæn] *vt* **banned; banning** : prohibir — ~ *n* : prohibición *f*

banal [bə'nɑl, bə'næl, 'beɪnəl] *adj* : banal

banana [bə'nænə] *n* : plátano *m*, banana *f Lat*, banano *m Lat*

band ['bænd] *n* **1** STRIP : banda *f* **2** GROUP : banda *f*, grupo *m*, conjunto *m* — ~ *vi* ~ **together** : unirse, juntarse

bandage ['bændɪdʒ] *n* : vendaje *m*, venda *f* — ~ *vt* **-daged; -daging** : vendar

bandit ['bændət] *n* : bandido *m*, -da *f*

bandy ['bændi] *vt* **-died; -dying** ~ **about** : circular, repetir

bang ['bæŋ] *vt* **1** STRIKE : golpear **2** SLAM : cerrar de un golpe — *vi* **1** SLAM : cerrarse de un golpe **2** ~ **on** : golpear — ~ *n* **1** BLOW : golpe *m* **2** NOISE : estrépito *m* **3** SLAM : portazo *m*

bangle ['bæŋgəl] *n* : brazalete *m*, pulsera *f*

bangs ['bæŋz] *npl* : flequillo *m*

banish ['bænɪʃ] *vt* : desterrar

banister ['bænəstər] *n* : pasamanos *m*, barandal *m*

bank ['bæŋk] *n* **1** : banco *m* **2** : orilla *f*, ribera *f* (de un río) **3** EMBANKMENT : terraplén *m* — ~ *vt* : depositar — *vi* **1** : ladearse (dícese de un avión) **2** : tener una cuenta (en un banco) **3** ~ **on** : contar con — **banker** ['bæŋkər] *n* : banquero *m*, -ra *f* — **banking** ['bæŋkɪŋ] *n* : banca *f*

bankrupt ['bæŋˌkrʌpt] *adj* : en bancarrota, en quiebra — **bankruptcy** ['bæŋˌkrʌptsi] *n, pl* **-cies** : quiebra *f*, bancarrota *f*

banner ['bænər] *n* : bandera *f*, pancarta *f*

banquet ['bæŋkwət] *n* : banquete *m*

banter ['bæntər] *n* : bromas *fpl* — ~ *vi* : hacer bromas

baptize [bæp'taɪz, 'bæpˌtaɪz] *vt* **-tized; -tizing** : bautizar — **baptism** ['bæpˌtɪzəm] *n* : bautismo *m*

bar ['bɑr] *n* **1** : barra *f* **2** BARRIER : barrera *f*, obstáculo *m* **3** COUNTER : mostrador *m*, barra *f* **4** TAVERN : bar *m* **5 behind** ~**s** : entre rejas **6** ~ **of soap** : pastilla *f* de jabón — ~ *vt* **barred; barring 1** OBSTRUCT : obstruir, bloquear **2** EXCLUDE : excluir **3** PROHIBIT : prohibir — ~ *prep* **1** : excepto **2** ~ **none** : sin excepción

barbarian [bɑr'bæriən] *n* : bárbaro *m*, -ra *f*

barbecue ['bɑrbɪˌkjuː] *vt* **-cued; -cuing** : asar a la parrilla — ~ *n* : barbacoa *f*

barbed wire ['bɑrbd'waɪr] *n* : alambre *m* de púas

barber ['bɑrbər] *n* : barbero *m*, -ra *f*

bare ['bær] *adj* **1** : desnudo **2** EMPTY : vacío **3** MINIMUM : mero, esencial — **barefaced** ['bærˌfeɪst] *adj* : descarado — **barefoot** ['bærˌfʊt] *or* **barefooted** [-ˌfʊt̬əd] *adv & adj* : descalzo — **barely** ['bærli] *adv* : apenas, por poco

bargain ['bɑrgən] *n* **1** AGREEMENT : acuerdo *m* **2** BUY : ganga *f* — ~ *vi* **1** : regatear, negociar **2** ~ **for** : contar con

barge ['bɑrdʒ] *n* : barcaza *f* — ~ *vi* **barged; barging** ~ **in** : entrometerse, interrumpir

baritone ['bærəˌtoːn] *n* : barítono *m*

bark[1] ['bɑrk] *vi* : ladrar — ~ *n* : ladrido *m* (de un perro)

bark[2] *n* : corteza *f* (de un árbol)

barley ['bɑrli] *n* : cebada *f*

barn ['bɑrn] *n* : granero *m* — **barnyard** ['bɑrnˌjɑrd] *n* : corral *m*

barometer [bə'rɑmət̬ər] *n* : barómetro *m*

baron ['bærən] *n* : barón *m* — **baroness** ['bærənɪs, -nəs, -ˌnɛs] *n* : baronesa *f*

barracks ['bærəks] *ns & pl* : cuartel *m*

barrage [bə'rɑʒ, -'rɑdʒ] *n* **1** : descarga *f* (de artillería) **2** : aluvión *m* (de preguntas, etc.)

barrel ['bærəl] *n* **1** : barril *m*, tonel *m* **2** : cañón *m* (de un arma de fuego)

barren ['bærən] *adj* : estéril

barricade ['bærəˌkeɪd, ˌbærə'-] *vt* **-caded; -cading** : cerrar con barricadas — ~ *n* : barricada *f*

barrier ['bæriər] *n* : barrera *f*

barring ['bɑrɪŋ] *prep* : salvo

barrio ['bɑrio, 'bær-] *n* : barrio *m*

bartender ['bɑrˌtɛndər] *n* : camarero *m*, -ra *f*

barter ['bɑrt̬ər] *vt* : cambiar, trocar — ~ *n* : trueque *m*

base ['beɪs] *n, pl* **bases** : base *f* — ~ *vt* **based; basing** : basar, fundamentar — ~ *adj* **baser; basest** : vil

baseball ['beɪsˌbɔl] *n* : beisbol *m*, béisbol *m*

basement ['beɪsmənt] *n* : sótano *m*

bash ['bæʃ] *vt* : golpear violentamente — ~ *n* **1** BLOW : golpe *m* **2** PARTY: fiesta *f*

bashful ['bæʃfəl] *adj* : tímido, vergonzoso

basic ['beɪsɪk] *adj* : básico, fundamental — **basically** ['beɪsɪkli] *adv* : fundamentalmente

basil ['beɪzəl, 'bæzəl] *n* : albahaca *f*

basin ['beɪsən] *n* **1** WASHBOWL : palangana *f*, lavabo *m* **2** : cuenca *f* (de un río)

basis ['beɪsəs] *n, pl* **bases** [-ˌsiːz] : base *f*

bask ['bæsk] *vi* ~ **in the sun** : tostarse al sol

basket ['bæskət] *n* : cesta *f*, cesto *m* — **basketball** ['bæskətˌbɔl] *n* : baloncesto *m*, basquetbol *m Lat*

bass[1] ['bæs] *n, pl* **bass** *or* **basses** : róbalo *m* (pesca)

bass[2] ['beɪs] *n* : bajo *m* (tono, voz, instrumento)

bassoon [bə'suːn, bæ-] *n* : fagot *m*

bastard ['bæstərd] *n* : bastardo *m*, -da *f*

baste ['beɪst] *vt* **basted; basting 1** STITCH : hilvanar **2** : bañar (carne)

bat[1] ['bæt] *n* : murciélago *m* (animal)

bat[2] *n* : bate *m* — ~ *vt* **batted; batting** : batear

batch ['bætʃ] *n* : hornada *f* (de pasteles, etc.), lote *m* (de mercancías), montón *m* (de trabajo), grupo *m* (de personas)

bath ['bæθ, 'bɑθ] *n, pl* **baths** ['bæðz, 'bæθs, 'bɑðz, 'bɑθs] **1** : baño *m* **2** BATHROOM : baño *m*, cuarto *m* de baño **3 take a** ~ : bañarse — **bathe** ['beɪð] *v* **bathed; bathing** *vt* : bañar, lavar — *vi* : bañarse — **bathrobe** ['bæθˌroːb] *n* : bata *f* (de baño) — **bathroom** ['bæθˌruːm, -ˌrʊm] *n* : baño *m*, cuarto *m* de baño — **bathtub** ['bæθˌtʌb] *n* : bañera *f*, tina *f* (de baño)

baton [bə'tɑn] *n* : batuta *f*

battalion [bə'tæljən] *n* : batallón *m*

batter ['bæt̬ər] *vt* **1** BEAT : golpear **2** MISTREAT : maltratar — ~ *n* **1** : masa *f* para rebozar **2** HITTER : bateador *m*, -dora *f*

battery ['bæt̬əri] *n, pl* **-teries** : batería *f*, pila *f* (de electricidad)

battle ['bæt̬əl] *n* **1** : batalla *f* **2** STRUGGLE : lucha *f* — ~ *vi* **-tled; -tling** : luchar — **battlefield** ['bæt̬əlˌfiːld] *n* : campo *m* de batalla — **battleship** ['bæt̬əlˌʃɪp] *n* : acorazado *m*

bawl ['bɔl] *vi* : llorar a gritos

bay[1] ['beɪ] *n* INLET : bahía *f*

bay[2] *n or* ~ **leaf** : laurel *m*

bay[3] *vi* : aullar — ~ *n* : aullido *m*

bayonet [ˌbeɪə'nɛt, 'beɪəˌnɛt] *n* : bayoneta *f*

bay window *n* : ventana *f* en saliente

bazaar [bə'zɑr] *n* **1** : bazar *m* **2** SALE : venta *f* benéfica

be ['biː] *v* **was** ['wəz, 'wɑz], **were** ['wər]; **been** ['bɪn]; **being; am** ['æm], **is** ['ɪz], **are** ['ɑr] *vi* **1** : ser **2** (*expressing location*) : estar **3** (*expressing existence*) : ser, existir **4** (*expressing a state of being*) : estar, tener — *v impers* **1** (*indicating time*) : ser **2** (*indicating a condition*) : hacer, estar — *v aux* **1** (*expressing occurrence*) : ser **2** (*expressing possibility*) : poderse **3** (*expressing obligation*) : deber **4** (*expressing progression*) : estar

beach ['biːtʃ] *n* : playa *f*

beacon ['biːkən] *n* : faro *m*

bead ['biːd] *n* **1** : cuenta *f* **2** DROP : gota *f* **3** ~**s** *npl* NECKLACE : collar *m*

beak ['biːk] *n* : pico *m*

beam ['biːm] *n* **1** : viga *f* (de madera, etc.) **2** RAY : rayo *m* — ~ *vi* SHINE : brillar — *vt* BROADCAST : transmitir, emitir

bean ['biːn] *n* **1** : habichuela *f*, frijol *m* **2 coffee** ~ : grano *m* **3 string** ~ : judía *f*

bear[1] ['bær] *n, pl* **bears** *or* **bear** : oso *m*, osa *f*

bear[2] *v* **bore** ['bor]; **borne** ['bɔrn]; **bearing** *vt* **1** CARRY : portar **2** ENDURE : soportar — *vi* ~ **right/left** : doble a la derecha/a la izquierda — **bearable** ['bærəbəl] *adj* : soportable

beard ['bɪrd] *n* : barba *f*

bearer ['bærər] *n* : portador *m*, -dora *f*

bearing ['bærɪŋ] *n* **1** MANNER : comportamiento *m* **2** SIGNIFICANCE : relacíon *f*, importancia *f* **3 get one's** ~**s** : orientarse

beast ['biːst] *n* : bestia *f*

beat ['biːt] *v* **beat; beaten** ['biːtən] *or* **beat; beating** *vt* **1** HIT : golpear **2** : batir (huevos, etc.) **3** DEFEAT : derrotar — *vi* : latir (dícese del corazón) — ~ *n* **1** : golpe *m* **2** : latido *m* (del corazón) **3** RHYTHM : ritmo *m*, tiempo *m* — **beating** ['biːtɪŋ] *n* **1** : paliza *f* **2** DEFEAT : derrota *f*

beauty ['bjuːt̬i] *n, pl* **-ties** : belleza *f* — **beautiful** ['bjuːt̬ɪfəl] *adj* : hermoso, lindo — **beautifully** ['bjuːt̬ɪfəli] *adv* WONDERFULLY : maravillosamente — **beautify** ['bjuːt̬ɪˌfaɪ] *vt* **-fied; -fying** : embellecer

beaver ['biːvər] *n* : castor *m*

because [bɪ'kʌz, -'kɔz] *conj* : porque — **because of** *prep* : por, a causa de, debido a

beckon ['bɛkən] *vt* : llamar, hacer señas a — *vi* : hacer una seña

become [bɪ'kʌm] *v* **-came** [-'keɪm]; **-come; -coming** *vi* : hacerse, ponerse — *vt* SUIT : favorecer — **becoming** [bɪ'kʌmɪŋ] *adj* **1** SUITABLE : apropiado **2** FLATTERING : favorecedor

bed ['bɛd] *n* **1** : cama *f* **2** : cauce *m* (de un río), fondo *m* (del mar) **3** : macizo *m* (de flores) **4 go to** ~ : irse a la cama — **bedclothes** ['bɛdˌkloːz, -ˌkloːðz] *npl* : ropa *f* de cama

bedlam ['bɛdləm] *n* : confusión *f*, caos *m*

bedraggled [bɪ'drægəld] *adj* : desaliñado, sucio

bedridden ['bɛdˌrɪdən] *adj* : postrado en cama

bedroom ['bɛdˌruːm, -ˌrʊm] *n* : dormitorio *m*, recámara *f Lat*

bedspread ['bɛdˌsprɛd] *n* : colcha *f*

bedtime ['bɛdˌtaɪm] *n* : hora *f* de acostarse

bee ['biː] *n* : abeja *f*

beech ['biːtʃ] *n, pl* **beeches** *or* **beech** : haya *f*

beef ['biːf] *n* : carne *f* de vaca, carne *f* de res *Lat* — **beefsteak** ['biːfˌsteɪk] *n* : bistec *m*

beehive ['biːˌhaɪv] *n* : colmena *f*

beeline ['biːˌlaɪn] *n* **make a** ~ **for** : irse derecho a

beep ['biːp] *n* : pitido *m* — ~ *v* : pitar

beer ['bɪr] *n* : cerveza *f*

beet ['bi:t] *n* : remolacha *f*
beetle ['bi:ṱəl] *n* : escarabajo *m*
before [bɪ'for] *adv* **1** : antes **2 the month ~** : el mes anterior — **~** *prep* **1** (*in space*) : delante de, ante **2** (*in time*) : antes de — **~** *conj* : antes de que — **beforehand** [bɪ'for,hænd] *adv* : antes
befriend [bɪ'frɛnd] *vt* : hacerse amigo de
beg ['bɛg] *v* **begged; begging** *vt* **1** : pedir, mendigar **2** ENTREAT : suplicar — *vi* : mendigar, pedir limosna — **beggar** ['bɛgər] *n* : mendigo *m*, -ga *f*
begin [bɪ'gɪn] *v* **-gan** [-'gæn]; **-gun** [-'gʌn]; **-ginning** : empezar, comenzar — **beginner** [bɪ'gɪnər] *n* : principiante *mf* — **beginning** [bɪ'gɪnɪŋ] *n* : principio *m*, comienzo *m*
begrudge [bɪ'grʌdʒ] *vt* **-grudged; -grudging 1** : dar de mala gana **2** ENVY : envidiar
behalf [bɪ'hæf, -'haf] *n* **on ~ of** : de parte de, en nombre de
behave [bɪ'heɪv] *vi* **-haved; -having** : comportarse, portarse — **behavior** [bɪ'heɪvjər] *n* : comportamiento *m*, conducta *f*
behind [bɪ'haɪnd] *adv* **1** : detrás **2 fall ~** : atrasarse — **~** *prep* **1** : atrás de, detrás de **2 be ~ schedule** : ir retrasado **3 her friends are ~ her** : tiene el apoyo de sus amigos
behold [bɪ'ho:ld] *vt* **-held; -holding** : contemplar
beige ['beɪʒ] *adj & nm* : beige
being ['bi:ɪŋ] *n* **1** : ser *m* **2 come into ~** : nacer
belated [bɪ'leɪṱəd] *adj* : tardío
belch ['bɛltʃ] *vi* : eructar — **~** *n* : eructo *m*
Belgian ['bɛldʒən] *adj* : belga
belie [bɪ'laɪ] *vt* **-lied; -lying** : contradecir, desmentir
belief [bə'li:f] *n* **1** TRUST : confianza *f* **2** CONVICTION : creencia *f*, convicción *f* **3** FAITH : fe *f* — **believable** [bə'li:vəbəl] *adj* : creíble — **believe** [bə'li:v] *v* **-lieved; -lieving** : creer — **believer** [bə'li:vər] *n* : creyente *mf*
belittle [bɪ'lɪṱəl] *vt* **-littled; -littling** : menospreciar
Belizean [bə'li:ziən] *adj* : beliceño *m*, -ña *f*
bell ['bɛl] *n* **1** : campana *f* **2** : timbre *m* (de teléfono, de la puerta, etc.)
belligerent [bə'lɪdʒərənt] *adj* : beligerante
bellow ['bɛ,lo:] *vi* : bramar, mugir — *vt* or **~ out** : gritar
bellows ['bɛ,lo:z] *ns & pl* : fuelle *m*
belly ['bɛli] *n, pl* **-lies** : vientre *m*
belong [bɪ'lɔŋ] *vi* **1 ~ to** : pertenecer a, ser propiedad de **2 ~ to** : ser miembro de (un club, etc.) **3 where does it ~** : ¿dónde va? — **belongings** [bɪ'lɔŋɪŋz] *npl* : pertenencias *fpl*, efectos *mpl* personales
beloved [bɪ'lʌvəd, -'lʌvd] *adj* : querido, amado — **~** *n* : querido *m*, -da *f*
below [bɪ'lo:] *adv* : abajo — **~** *prep* **1** : abajo de, debajo de **2 ~ average** : por debajo del promedio **3 ~ zero** : bajo cero
belt ['bɛlt] *n* **1** : cinturón *m* **2** BAND, STRAP : cinta *f*, correa *f* **3** AREA : frente *m*, zona *f* — **~** *vt* **1** : ceñir con un cinturón **2** THRASH : darle una paliza a
bench ['bɛntʃ] *n* **1** : banco *m* **2** WORKBENCH : mesa *f* de trabajo **3** COURT : tribunal *m*
bend ['bɛnd] *v* **bent** ['bɛnt]; **bending** *vt* : doblar, torcer — *vi* **1** : torcerse **2 ~ over** : inclinarse — **~** *n* : curva *f*, ángulo *m*
beneath [bɪ'ni:θ] *adv* : abajo, debajo — **~** *prep* : bajo, debajo de
benediction [,bɛnə'dɪkʃən] *n* : bendición *f*
benefactor ['bɛnə,fæktər] *n* : benefactor *m*, -tora *f*
benefit ['bɛnəfɪt] *n* **1** ADVANTAGE : ventaja *f*, provecho *m* **2** AID : asistencia *f*, beneficio *m* — **~** *vt* : beneficiar — *vi* : beneficiarse — **beneficial** [,bɛnə'fɪʃəl] *adj* : beneficioso — **beneficiary** [,bɛnə'fɪʃi,ɛri, -'fɪʃəri] *n, pl* **-ries** : beneficiario *m*, -ria *f*
benevolent [bə'nɛvələnt] *adj* : benévolo
benign [bɪ'naɪn] *adj* **1** KIND : benévolo, amable **2** : benigno (en medicina)
bent ['bɛnt] *adj* **1** : encorvado **2 be ~ on** : estar empeñado en — **~** *n* : aptitud *f*, inclinación *f*
bequeath [bɪ'kwi:θ, -'kwi:ð] *vt* : legar — **bequest** [bɪ'kwɛst] *n* : legado *m*
berate [bɪ'reɪt] *vt* **-rated; -rating** : reprender, regañar
bereaved [bɪ'ri:vd] *adj* : desconsolado, a luto
beret [bə'reɪ] *n* : boina *f*
berry ['bɛri] *n, pl* **-ries** : baya *f*
berserk [bər'sərk, -'zərk] *adj* **1** : enloquecido **2 go ~** : volverse loco
berth ['bərθ] *n* **1** MOORING : atracadero *m* **2** BUNK : litera *f*
beseech [bɪ'si:tʃ] *vt* **-sought** [-'sɔt] *or* **-seeched; -seeching** : suplicar, implorar
beset [bɪ'sɛt] *vt* **-set; -setting 1** HARASS : acosar **2** SURROUND : rodear
beside [bɪ'saɪd] *prep* **1** : al lado de, junto a **2 be ~ oneself** : estar fuera de sí — **besides** [bɪ'saɪdz] *adv* : además — **~** *prep* **1** : además de **2** EXCEPT : excepto
besiege [bɪ'si:dʒ] *vt* **-sieged; -sieging** : asediar
best ['bɛst] *adj* (*superlative of* **good**) : mejor — **~** *adv* (*superlative of* **well**) : mejor — **~** *n* **1 at ~** : a lo más **2 do one's ~** : hacer todo lo posible **3 the ~** : lo mejor — **best man** *n* : padrino *m* (de boda)
bestow [bɪ'sto:] *vt* : otorgar, conceder
bet ['bɛt] *n* : apuesta *f* — **~** *v* **bet; betting** *vt* : apostar — *vi* **~ on sth** : apostarle a algo
betray [bɪ'treɪ] *vt* : traicionar — **betrayal** [bɪ'treɪəl] *n* : traición *f*
better ['bɛṱər] *adj* (*comparative of* **good**) **1** : mejor **2 get ~** : mejorar — **~** *adv* (*comparative of* **well**) **1** : mejor **2 all the ~** : tanto mejor — **~** *n* **1 the ~** : el mejor, la mejor **2 get the ~ of** : vencer a — **~** *vt* **1** IMPROVE : mejorar **2** SURPASS : superar
between [bɪ'twi:n] *prep* : entre — **~** *adv* or **in ~** : en medio
beverage ['bɛvrɪdʒ, 'bɛvə-] *n* : bebida *f*
beware [bɪ'wær] *vi* **~ of** : tener cuidado con
bewilder [bɪ'wɪldər] *vt* : desconcertar — **bewilderment** [bɪ'wɪldərmənt] *n* : desconcierto *m*
bewitch [bɪ'wɪtʃ] *vt* : hechizar, encantar
beyond [bi'jɑnd] *adv* : más allá, más lejos (en el espacio), más adelante (en el tiempo) — **~** *prep* : más allá de
bias ['baɪəs] *n* **1** PREJUDICE : prejuicio *m* **2** TENDENCY : inclinación *f*, tendencia *f* — **biased** ['baɪəst] *adj* : parcial
bib ['bɪb] *n* : babero *m* (para niños)
Bible ['baɪbəl] *n* : Biblia *f* — **biblical** ['bɪblɪkəl] *adj* : bíblico
bibliography [,bɪbli'ɑgrəfi] *n, pl* **-phies** : bibliografía *f*
bicarbonate of soda [,baɪ'kɑrbənət, ,neɪt] *n* : bicarbonato *m* de soda
biceps ['baɪ,sɛps] *ns & pl* : bíceps *m*
bicker ['bɪkər] *vi* : reñir
bicycle ['baɪsɪkəl, -,sɪ-] *n* : bicicleta *f* — **~** *vi* **-cled; -cling** : ir en bicicleta
bid ['bɪd] *vt* **bade** ['bæd, 'beɪd] *or* **bid; bidden** ['bɪdən] *or* **bid; bidding 1** OFFER : ofrecer **2 ~ farewell** : decir adiós — **~** *n* **1** OFFER : oferta *f* **2** ATTEMPT : intento *m*, tentativa *f*
bide ['baɪd] *vt* **bode** ['bo:d] *or* **bided; bided; biding ~ one's time** : esperar el momento oportuno
bifocals ['baɪ,fo:kəlz] *npl* : anteojos *mpl* bifocales
big ['bɪg] *adj* **bigger; biggest** : grande
bigamy ['bɪgəmi] *n* : bigamía *f*
bigot ['bɪgət] *n* : intolerante *mf* — **bigotry** ['bɪgətri] *n, pl* **-tries** : intolerancia *f*, fanatismo *m*
bike ['baɪk] *n* **1** BICYCLE : bici *f fam* **2** MOTORCYCLE : moto *f*
bikini [bə'ki:ni] *n* : bikini *m*
bile ['baɪl] *n* : bilis *f*
bilingual [baɪ'lɪŋgwəl] *adj* : bilingüe
bill ['bɪl] *n* **1** BEAK : pico *m* **2** INVOICE : cuenta *f*, factura *f* **3** BANKNOTE : billete *m* **4** LAW : proyecto *m* de ley, ley *f* — **~** *vt* : pasarle la cuenta a — **billboard** ['bɪl,bord] *n* : cartelera *f* — **billfold** ['bɪl,fo:ld] *n* : billetera *f*, cartera *f*
billiards ['bɪljərdz] *n* : billar *m*
billion ['bɪljən] *n, pl* **billions** *or* **billion** : mil millones *mpl*
billow ['bɪlo] *vi* : ondular, hincharse
billy goat ['bɪli,go:t] *n* : macho *m* cabrío
bin ['bɪn] *n* : cubo *m*, cajón *m*
binary ['baɪnəri, -,nɛri] *adj* : binario *m*
bind ['baɪnd] *vt* **bound** ['baʊnd]; **binding 1** TIE : atar **2** OBLIGATE : obligar **3** UNITE : unir **4** BANDAGE : vendar **5** : encuadernar (un libro) — **binder** ['baɪndər] *n* FOLDER : carpeta *f* — **binding** ['baɪndɪŋ] *n* : encuadernación *f* (de libros)
binge ['bɪndʒ] *n* : juerga *f fam*
bingo ['bɪŋ,go:] *n, pl* **-gos** : bingo *m*
binoculars [bə'nɑkjələrz, baɪ-] *npl* : binoculares *mpl*, gemelos *mpl*
biochemistry [,baɪo'kɛmɪstri] *n* : bioquímica *f*
biography [baɪ'ɑgrəfi, bi:-] *n, pl* **-phies** : biografía *f* — **biographer** [baɪ'ɑgrəfər] *n* : biógrafo *m*, -fa *f* — **biographical** [,baɪə'græfɪkəl] *adj* : biográfico
biology [baɪ'ɑlədʒi] *n* : biología *f* — **biological** [-dʒɪkəl] *adj* : biológico — **biologist** [baɪ'ɑlədʒɪst] *n* : biólogo *m*, -ga *f*
birch ['bərtʃ] *n* : abedul *m*
bird ['bərd] *n* : pájaro *m* (pequeño), ave *f* (grande)
birth ['bərθ] *n* **1** : nacimiento *m*, parto *m* **2 give ~ to** : dar a luz a — **birthday** ['bərθ,deɪ] *n* : cumpleaños *m* — **birthmark** ['bərθ,mark] *n* : mancha *f* de nacimiento — **birthplace** ['bərθ,pleɪs] *n* : lugar *m* de nacimiento — **birthrate** ['bərθ,reɪt] *n* : índice *m* de natalidad
biscuit ['bɪskət] *n* : bizcocho *m*
bisect ['baɪ,sɛkt, ,baɪ'-] *vt* : bisecar
bisexual [,baɪ'sɛkʃəwəl, -'sɛkʃəl] *adj* : bisexual
bishop ['bɪʃəp] *n* : obispo *m*
bison ['baɪzən, -sən] *ns & pl* : bisonte *m*
bit[1] ['bɪt] *n* : bocado *m* (de una brida)
bit[2] **1** : trozo *m*, pedazo *m* **2** : bit *m* (de información) **3 a ~** : un poco
bitch ['bɪtʃ] *n* : perra *f* — **~** *vi* COMPLAIN : quejarse, reclamar
bite ['baɪt] *v* **bit** ['bɪt]; **bitten** ['bɪtən]; **biting** *vt* **1** : morder **2** STING : picar — *vi* : morder — *n* **1** : picadura *f* (de un insecto), mordedura *f* (de un animal) **2** SNACK : bocado *m* — **biting** *adj* **1** PENETRATING : cortante, penetrante **2** CAUSTIC : mordaz
bitter ['bɪṱər] *adj* **1** : amargo **2 it's ~ cold** : hace un frío glacial **3 to the ~ end** : hasta el final — **bitterness** ['bɪṱərnəs] *n* : amargura *f*
bizarre [bə'zɑr] *adj* : extraño
black ['blæk] *adj* : negro — **~** *n* **1** : negro *m* (color) **2** : negro *m*, -gra *f* (persona) — **black–and–blue** [,blækən'blu:] *adj* : amoratado — **blackberry** ['blæk,bɛri] *n, pl* **-ries** : mora *f* — **blackbird** ['blæk,bərd] *n* : mirlo *m* — **blackboard** ['blæk,bord] *n* : pizarra *f*, pizarrón *m Lat* — **blacken** ['blækən] *vt* : ennegrecer — **blackmail** ['blæk,meɪl] *n* : chantaje *m* — **~** *vt* : chantajear — **black market** *n* : mercado *m* negro — **blackout** ['blæk,aʊt] *n* **1** : apagón *m* (de poder eléctrico) **2** FAINT : desmayo *m* — **blacksmith** ['blæk,smɪθ] *n* : herrero *m* — **blacktop** ['blæk,tɑp] *n* : asfalto *m*
bladder ['blædər] *n* : vejiga *f*
blade ['bleɪd] *n* **1** : hoja *f* (de un cuchillo), cuchilla *f* (de un patín) **2** : pala *f* (de un remo, una hélice, etc.) **3 ~ of grass** : brizna *f* (de hierba)
blame ['bleɪm] *vt* **blamed; blaming** : culpar, echar la culpa a — **~** *n* : culpa *f* — **blameless** ['bleɪmləs] *adj* : inocente
bland ['blænd] *adj* : soso, insulso
blank ['blæŋk] *adj* **1** : en blanco (dícese de un papel), liso (dícese de una pared) **2** EMPTY : vacío — **~** *n* : espacio *m* en blanco
blanket ['blæŋkət] *n* **1** : manta *f*, cobija *f Lat* **2 ~ of snow** : manto *m* de nieve — **~** *vt* : cubrir
blare ['blær] *vi* **blared; blaring** : resonar
blasphemy ['blæsfəmi] *n, pl* **-mies** : blasfemia *f*
blast ['blæst] *n* **1** GUST : ráfaga *f* **2** EXPLOSION : explosión *f* **3** : toque *m* (de trompeta, etc.) — **~** *vt* BLOW UP : volar — **blast-off** ['blæst,ɔf] *n* : despegue *m*
blatant ['bleɪtənt] *adj* : descarado
blaze ['bleɪz] *n* **1** FIRE : fuego *m* **2** BRIGHTNESS : resplandor *m*, brillantez *f* **3 ~ of anger** : arranque *m* de cólera — **~** *v* **blazed; blazing** *vi* : arder, brillar — *vt* **~ a trail** : abrir un camino
blazer ['bleɪzər] *n* : chaqueta *f* deportiva
bleach ['bli:tʃ] *vt* : blanquear, decolorar — **~** *n* : lejía *f*, blanqueador *m Lat*
bleachers ['bli:tʃərz] *ns & pl* : gradas *fpl*
bleak ['bli:k] *adj* **1** DESOLATE : desolado **2** GLOOMY : triste, sombrío
bleary–eyed ['blɪri,aɪd] *adj* : con los ojos nublados
bleat ['bli:t] *vi* : balar — **~** *n* : balido *m*
bleed ['bli:d] *v* **bled** ['blɛd]; **bleeding** : sangrar
blemish ['blɛmɪʃ] *vt* : manchar, marcar — **~** *n* : mancha *f*, marca *f*
blend ['blɛnd] *vt* : mezclar, combinar — **~** *n* : mezcla *f*, combinación *f* — **blender** ['blɛndər] *n* : licuadora *f*
bless ['blɛs] *vt* **blessed** ['blɛst]; **blessing** : bendecir — **blessed** ['blɛsəd] *or* **blest** ['blɛst] *adj* : bendito — **blessing** ['blɛsɪŋ] *n* : bendición *f*
blew → **blow**
blind ['blaɪnd] *adj* : ciego — **~** *vt* **1** : cegar, dejar ciego **2** DAZZLE : deslumbrar — **~** *n* **1** : persiana *f* (para una ventana) **2 the ~** : los ciegos — **blindfold** ['blaɪnd,fo:ld] *vt* : vendar los ojos — **~** *n* : venda *f* (para los ojos) — **blindly** ['blaɪndli] *adv* : ciegamente — **blindness** ['blaɪndnəs] *n* : ceguera *f*
blink ['blɪŋk] *vi* **1** : parpadear **2** FLICKER : brillar intermitentemente — **~** *n* : parpadeo *m* — **blinker** ['blɪŋkər] *n* : intermitente *m*, direccional *f Lat*
bliss ['blɪs] *n* : dicha *f*, felicidad *f* (absoluta) — **blissful** ['blɪsfəl] *adj* : feliz
blister ['blɪstər] *n* : ampolla *f* — **~** *vi* : ampollarse
blitz ['blɪts] *n* : bombardeo *m* aéreo
blizzard ['blɪzərd] *n* : ventisca *f* (de nieve)
bloated ['blo:ṱəd] *adj* : hinchado
blob ['blɑb] *n* **1** DROP : gota *f* **2** SPOT : mancha *f*
block ['blɑk] *n* **1** : bloque *m* **2** OBSTRUCTION : obstrucción *f* **3** : manzana *f*, cuadra *f Lat* (de edificios) **4** *or* **building ~** : cubo *m* de construcción — **~** *vt* : obstruir, bloquear — **blockade** [blɑ'keɪd] *n* : bloqueo *m* — **blockage** ['blɑkɪdʒ] *n* : obstrucción *f*
blond *or* **blonde** ['blɑnd] *adj* : rubio — **~** *n* : rubio *m*, -bia *f*
blood ['blʌd] *n* : sangre *f* — **bloodhound** ['blʌd,haʊnd] *n* : sabueso *m* — **blood pressure** *n* : tensión *f* (arterial) — **bloodshed** ['blʌd,ʃɛd] *n* : derramamiento *m* de sangre — **bloodshot** ['blʌd,ʃɑt] *adj* : inyectado de sangre — **bloodstained** ['blʌd,steɪnd] *adj* : manchado de sangre — **bloodstream** ['blʌd,stri:m] *n* : sangre *f*, torrente *m* sanguíneo — **bloody** ['blʌdi] *adj* **bloodier; -est** : ensangrentado, sangriento
bloom ['blu:m] *n* **1** : flor *f* **2 in full ~** : en plena floración — **~** *vi* : florecer
blossom ['blɑsəm] *n* : flor *f* — **~** *vi* : florecer
blot ['blɑt] *n* **1** : borrón *m* (de tinta, etc.) **2** BLEMISH : mancha *f* — **~** *vt* **blotted; blotting 1** : emborronar **2** DRY : secar
blotch ['blɑtʃ] *n* : mancha *f*, borrón *m* — **blotchy** ['blɑtʃi] *adj* **blotchier; -est** : lleno de manchas
blouse ['blaʊs, 'blaʊz] *n* : blusa *f*
blow ['blo:] *v* **blew** ['blu:]; **blown** ['blo:n]; **blowing** *vi* **1** : soplar **2** SOUND : sonar **3** *or* **~ out** : fundirse (dícese de un fusible eléctrico), reventarse (dícese de una llanta) — *vt* **1** : soplar **2** SOUND : tocar, sonar **3** BUNGLE : echar a perder — **~** *n* : golpe *m* — **blowout** ['blo:,aʊt] *n* : reventón *m* — **blow up** *vi* : estallar, hacer explosión — *vt* **1** EXPLODE : volar **2** INFLATE : inflar
blubber ['blʌbər] *n* : esperma *f* de ballena
bludgeon ['blʌdʒən] *vt* : aporrear
blue ['blu:] *adj* **bluer; bluest 1** : azul **2** MELANCHOLY : triste — **~** *n* : azul *m* — **blueberry** ['blu:,bɛri] *n, pl* **-ries** : arándano *m* — **bluebird** ['blu:,bərd] *n* : azulejo *m* — **blue cheese** *n* : queso *m* azul — **blueprint** ['blu:,prɪnt] *n* PLAN : proyecto *m* — **blues** ['blu:z] *npl* **1** SADNESS : tristeza *f* **2** : blues *m* (en música)
bluff ['blʌf] *vi* : hacer un farol — **~** *n* : farol *m*
blunder ['blʌndər] *vi* : meter la pata *fam* — **~** *n* : metedura *f* de pata *fam*
blunt ['blʌnt] *adj* **1** DULL : desafilado **2** DIRECT : directo, franco
blur ['blər] *n* : imágen *f* borrosa — **~** *vt* **blurred; blurring** : hacer borroso
blurb ['blərb] *n* : nota *f* publicitaria
blurt ['blərt] *vt or* **~ out** : espetar
blush ['blʌʃ] *n* : rubor *m* — **~** *vi* : ruborizarse
blustery ['blʌstəri] *adj* : borrascoso, tempestuoso
boar ['bor] *n* : cerdo *m* macho
board ['bord] *n* **1** PLANK : tabla *f*, tablón *m* **2** COMMITTEE : junta *f*, consejo *m* **3** : tablero *m* (de juegos) **4 room and ~** : comida y alojamiento — **~** *vt* **1** : subir a bordo de (una nave, un avión, etc.), subir a (un tren) **2** LODGE : hospedar **3 ~ up** : cerrar con tablas — **boarder** ['bordər] *n* : huésped *mf*
boast ['bo:st] *n* : jactancia *f* — **~** *vi* : alardear, jactarse — **boastful** ['bo:stfəl] *adj* : jactancioso
boat ['bo:t] *n* : barco *m* (grande), barca *f* (pequeña)
bob ['bɑb] *vi* **bobbed; bobbing** *or* **~ up and down** : subir y bajar
bobbin ['bɑbən] *n* : bobina *f*, carrete *m*
bobby pin ['bɑbi,pɪn] *n* : horquilla *f*
body ['bɑdi] *n, pl* **bodies 1** : cuerpo *m* **2** CORPSE : cadáver *m* **3** : carrocería (de un automóvil, etc.) **4** COLLECTION : conjunto *m* **5 ~ of water** : masa *f* de agua — **bodily** *adj* : corporal — **bodyguard** ['bɑdi,gɑrd] *n* : guardaespaldas *mf*
bog ['bɑg, 'bɔg] *n* : ciénaga *f* — **~** *vt* **bogged; bogging** *or* **~ down** : empantanarse
bogus ['bo:gəs] *adj* : falso
boil ['bɔɪl] *v* : hervir — **boiler** ['bɔɪlər] *n* : caldera *f*
bold ['bo:ld] *adj* **1** DARING : audaz **2** IMPUDENT : descarado — **boldness** ['bo:ldnəs] *n* : audacia *f*
Bolivian [bə'lɪviən] *adj* : boliviano *m*, -na *f*
bologna [bə'lo:ni] *n* : salchicha *f* ahumada
bolster ['bo:lstər] *vt* **-stered; -stering** *or* **~ up** : reforzar
bolt ['bo:lt] *n* **1** LOCK : cerrojo *m* **2** SCREW : tornillo *m* **3 ~ of lightning** : relámpago *m*, rayo *m* — **~** *vt* **1** FASTEN : atornillar **2** LOCK : echar el cerrojo a — *vi* FLEE : salir corriendo
bomb ['bɑm] *n* : bomba *f* — **~** *vt* : bombardear — **bombard** [bɑm'bɑrd, bəm-] *vt* : bombardear — **bombardment** [bɑm'bɑrdmənt] *n* : bombardeo *m* — **bomber** ['bɑmər] *n* : bombardero *m*
bond ['bɑnd] *n* **1** TIE : vínculo *m*, lazo *m* **2** SURETY : fianza *f* **3** : bono *m* (en finanzas) — **~** *vi* STICK : adherirse
bondage ['bɑndɪdʒ] *n* : esclavitud *f*
bone ['bo:n] *n* : hueso *m* — **~** *vt* **boned; boning** : deshuesar
bonfire ['bɑn,faɪr] *n* : hoguera *f*
bonus ['bo:nəs] *n* **1** PAY : prima *f* **2** BENEFIT : beneficio *m* adicional
bony ['bo:ni] *adj* **bonier; -est 1** : huesudo **2** : lleno de espinas (dícese de pescados)
boo ['bu:] *n, pl* **boos** : abucheo *m* — **~** *vt* : abuchear
book ['bʊk] *n* **1** : libro *m* **2** NOTEBOOK : libreta *f*, cuaderno *m* — **~** *vt* : reservar — **bookcase** ['bʊk,keɪs] *n* : estantería *f* — **bookkeeping** ['bʊk,ki:pɪŋ] *n* : teneduría *f* de libros, contabilidad *f* — **booklet** ['bʊklət] *n* : folleto *m* — **bookmark** ['bʊk,mɑrk] *n* : marcador *m* de libros — **bookseller** ['bʊk,sɛlər] *n* : librero *m*, -ra *f* — **bookshelf** ['bʊk,ʃɛlf] *n, pl* **-shelves** : estante *m* — **bookstore** ['bʊk,stor] *n* : librería *f*
boom ['bu:m] *vi* **1** : tronar, resonar **2** PROSPER : estar en auge, prosperar — **~** *n* **1** : bramido *m*, estruendo *m* **2** : auge *m* (económico)
boon ['bu:n] *n* : ayuda *f*, beneficio *m*
boost ['bu:st] *vt* **1** LIFT : levantar **2** INCREASE

: aumentar — ~ n 1 INCREASE : aumento m 2 ENCOURAGEMENT : estímulo m

boot ['bu:t] n : bota f, botín m — ~ vt 1 : dar una patada a 2 or ~ up : cargar (un ordenador)

booth ['bu:θ] n, pl **booths** ['bu:ðz, 'bu:θs] : cabina f (de teléfono, de votar), caseta f (de información)

booty ['bu:t̬i] n, pl **-ties** : botín m

booze ['bu:z] n : trago m, bebida f (alcohólica)

border ['bɔrdər] n 1 EDGE : borde m, orilla f 2 TRIM : ribete m 3 FRONTIER : frontera f

bore¹ ['bor] vt **bored; boring** DRILL : taladrar

bore² vt TIRE : aburrir — ~ n : pesado m, -da f fam f (persona), lata f fam (cosa, situación) — **boredom** ['bordəm] n : aburrimiento m — **boring** ['borɪŋ] adj : aburrido, pesado

born ['bɔrn] adj 1 : nacido 2 **be ~** : nacer

borough ['bəro] n : distrito m municipal

borrow ['bɑro] vt : pedir prestado, tomar prestado

Bosnian ['bɑzniən, 'bɔz-] adj : bosnio m, -nia f

bosom ['bʊzəm, 'bu:-] n BREAST : pecho m, seno m — ~ adj **~ friend** : amigo m íntimo

boss ['bɔs] n : jefe m, -fa f; patrón m, -trona f — ~ vt SUPERVISE : dirigir — **bossy** ['bɔsi] adj **bossier; -est** : autoritario

botany ['bɑtəni] n : botánica f — **botanical** [bə'tænɪkəl] adj : botánico

botch ['bɑtʃ] vt : hacer una chapuza de, estropear

both ['bo:θ] adj : ambos, los dos, las dos — ~ pron : ambos m, -bas f; los dos, las dos

bother ['bɑðər] vt 1 TROUBLE : preocupar 2 PESTER : molestar, fastidiar — vi **~ to** : molestarse en — ~ n : molestia f

bottle ['bɑtəl] n 1 : botella f, frasco m 2 or **baby ~** : biberón m — ~ vt **bottled; bottling** : embotellar — **bottleneck** ['bɑtəl,nɛk] n : embotellamiento m

bottom ['bɑt̬əm] n 1 : fondo m (de una caja, del mar, etc.), pie m (de una escalera, una montaña, etc.), final m (de una lista) 2 BUTTOCKS : nalgas fpl, trasero m — ~ adj : más bajo, inferior, de abajo — **bottomless** ['bɑt̬əmləs] adj : sin fondo

bough ['baʊ] n : rama f

bought → **buy**

bouillon ['bu:,jɑn; 'bʊl,jɑn, -jən] n : caldo m

boulder ['bo:ldər] n : canto m rodado

boulevard ['bʊlə,vɑrd, 'bu:-] n : bulevar m

bounce ['baʊnts] v **bounced; bouncing** vt : hacer rebotar — vi : rebotar — ~ n : rebote m

bound¹ ['baʊnd] adj **be ~ for** : ir rumbo a

bound² adj 1 OBLIGED : obligado 2 DETERMINED : decidido 3 **be ~ to** : tener que

bound³ n **out of ~s** : (en) zona prohibida — **boundary** ['baʊndri, -dəri] n, pl **-aries** : límite m — **boundless** ['baʊndləs] adj : sin límites

bouquet [bo:'keɪ, bu:-] n : ramo m

bourgeois ['bʊrʒ,wɑ, bʊrʒ'wɑ] adj : burgués

bout ['baʊt] n 1 : combate m (en deportes) 2 : ataque m (de una enfermedad) 3 : período m (de actividad)

bow¹ ['baʊ] vi : inclinarse — vt **~ one's head** : inclinar la cabeza — ~ ['baʊ] n : reverencia f, inclinación f

bow² ['bo:] n 1 : arco m 2 **tie a ~** : hacer un lazo

bow³ ['baʊ] n : proa f (de un barco)

bowels ['baʊəls] npl 1 : intestinos mpl 2 DEPTHS : entrañas fpl

bowl¹ ['bo:l] n : tazón m, cuenco m

bowl² vi : jugar a los bolos — **bowling** ['bo:lɪŋ] n : bolos mpl

box¹ ['bɑks] vi FIGHT : boxear — **boxer** ['bɑksər] n : boxeador m, -dora f — **boxing** ['bɑksɪŋ] n : boxeo m

box² n 1 : caja f, cajón m 2 : palco m (en el teatro) — ~ vt : empaquetar — **box office** n : taquilla f, boletería f Lat

boy ['bɔɪ] n : niño m, chico m

boycott ['bɔɪ,kɑt] vt : boicotear — ~ n : boicot m

boyfriend ['bɔɪ,frɛnd] n : novio m

bra ['brɑ] → **brassiere**

brace ['breɪs] n 1 SUPPORT : abrazadera f 2 **~s** npl : aparatos mpl (para dientes) — ~ vi **~ oneself for** : prepararse para

bracelet ['breɪslət] n : brazalete m

bracket ['brækət] n 1 SUPPORT : soporte m 2 : corchete m (marca de puntuación) 3 CATEGORY : categoría f — ~ vt 1 : poner entre corchetes 2 CATEGORIZE : catalogar

brag ['bræg] vi **bragged; bragging** : jactarse

braid ['breɪd] vt : trenzar — ~ n : trenza f

braille ['breɪl] n : braille m

brain ['breɪn] n 1 : cerebro m 2 **~s** npl : inteligencia f — **brainstorm** ['breɪn,stɔrm] n : idea f genial — **brainwash** ['breɪn,wɔʃ, -,wɑʃ] vt : lavar el cerebro — **brainy** ['breɪni] adj **brainier; -est** : inteligente, listo

brake ['breɪk] n : freno m — ~ v **braked; braking** : frenar

bramble ['bræmbəl] n : zarza f

bran ['bræn] n : salvado m

branch ['bræntʃ] n 1 : rama f (de una planta) 2 DIVISION : ramal m (de un camino, etc.), sucursal f (de una empresa), agencia f (del gobierno) — ~ vi or **~ off** : ramificarse, bifurcarse

brand ['brænd] n 1 : marca f (de ganado) 2 or **~ name** : marca f de fábrica — ~ vt 1 : marcar (ganado) 2 LABEL : tachar, tildar

brandish ['brændɪʃ] vt : blandir

brand-new ['brænd'nu:, -'nju:] adj : flamante

brandy ['brændi] n, pl **-dies** : brandy m, coñac m

brass ['bræs] n 1 : latón m 2 : metales mpl (de una orquesta)

brassiere [brə'zɪr, brɑ-] n : sostén m, brasier m Lat

brat ['bræt] n : mocoso m, -sa f fam

bravado [brə'vɑdo] n, pl **-does** or **-dos** : bravuconadas fpl

brave ['breɪv] adj **braver; bravest** : valiente, valeroso — ~ vt **braved; braving** : afrontar, hacer frente a — ~ n : guerrero m indio — **bravery** ['breɪvəri] n : valor m, valentía f

brawl ['brɔl] n : pelea f, reyerta f

brawn ['brɔn] n : músculos mpl — **brawny** ['brɔni] adj **brawnier; -est** : musculoso

bray ['breɪ] vi : rebuznar

brazen ['breɪzən] adj : descarado

Brazilian [brə'zɪljən] adj : brasileño m, -ña f

breach ['bri:tʃ] n 1 VIOLATION : infracción f, violación f 2 GAP : brecha f

bread ['brɛd] n 1 : pan m 2 **~ crumbs** : migajas fpl

breadth ['brɛtθ] n : anchura f

break ['breɪk] v **broke** ['bro:k]; **broken** ['bro:kən]; **breaking** vt 1 : romper, quebrar 2 VIOLATE : infringir, violar 3 INTERRUPT : interrumpir 4 SURPASS : batir (un récord, etc.) 5 **~ a habit** : quitarse una costumbre 6 **~ the news** : dar la noticia — vi 1 : romperse, quebrarse 2 **~ away** : escapar 3 **~ down** : estropearse (dícese de una máquina), fallar (dícese de un sistema, etc.) 4 **~ into** : entrar en 5 **~ off** : interrumpirse 6 **~ out of** : escaparse de 7 **~ up** SEPARATE : separarse — ~ n 1 : ruptura f, fractura f 2 GAP : interrupción f, claro m (entre las nubes) 3 **lucky ~** : golpe m de suerte 4 **take a ~** : tomar(se) un descanso — **breakable** ['breɪkəbəl] adj : quebradizo, frágil — **breakdown** ['breɪk,daʊn] n 1 : avería f (de máquinas), interrupción f (de comunicaciones), fracaso m (de negociaciones) 2 or **nervous ~** : crisis f nerviosa

breakfast ['brɛkfəst] n : desayuno m

breast ['brɛst] n 1 : seno m (de una mujer) 2 CHEST : pecho m — **breast-feed** ['brɛst,fi:d] vt **-fed** [-,fɛd]; **-feeding** : amamantar

breath ['brɛθ] n : aliento m, respiración f — **breathe** ['bri:ð] v **breathed; breathing** : respirar — **breathless** ['brɛθləs] adj : sin aliento, jadeante — **breathtaking** ['brɛθ,teɪkɪŋ] adj : impresionante

breed ['bri:d] v **bred** ['brɛd]; **breeding** vt 1 : criar (animales) 2 ENGENDER : engendrar, producir — vi : reproducirse — ~ n 1 : raza f 2 CLASS : clase f, tipo m

breeze ['bri:z] n : brisa f — **breezy** ['bri:zi] adj **breezier; -est** 1 WINDY : ventoso 2 NONCHALANT : despreocupado

brevity ['brɛvət̬i] n, pl **-ties** : brevedad f

brew ['bru:] vt : hacer (cerveza, etc.), preparar (té) — vi 1 : fabricar cerveza 2 : amenazar (dícese de una tormenta) — **brewery** ['bru:əri, 'brʊri] n, pl **-eries** : cervecería f

bribe ['braɪb] n : soborno m — ~ vt **bribed; bribing** : sobornar — **bribery** ['braɪbəri] n, pl **-eries** : soborno m

brick ['brɪk] n : ladrillo m — **bricklayer** ['brɪk,leɪər] n : albañil mf

bride ['braɪd] n : novia f — **bridal** ['braɪdəl] adj : nupcial, de novia — **bridegroom** ['braɪd,gru:m] n : novio m — **bridesmaid** ['braɪdz,meɪd] n : dama f de honor

bridge ['brɪdʒ] n 1 : puente m 2 : caballete m (de la nariz) 3 : bridge m (juego de naipes) — ~ vt **bridged; bridging** 1 : tender un puente sobre 2 **~ the gap** : salvar las diferencias

bridle ['braɪdəl] n : brida f — ~ vt **-dled; -dling** : embridar

brief ['bri:f] adj : breve — ~ n 1 : resumen m, sumario m 2 **~s** npl UNDERPANTS : calzoncillos mpl — ~ vt : dar órdenes a, instruir — **briefcase** ['bri:f,keɪs] n : portafolio m, maletín m — **briefly** ['bri:fli] adv : brevemente

bright ['braɪt] adj 1 : brillante, claro 2 CHEERFUL : alegre, animado 3 INTELLIGENT : listo, inteligente — **brighten** ['braɪtən] vi 1 : hacerse más brillante 2 or **~ up** : animarse, alegrarse — vt 1 ILLUMINATE : iluminar 2 ENLIVEN : alegrar, animar

brilliant ['brɪljənt] adj : brillante — **brilliance** ['brɪljənts] n 1 BRIGHTNESS : resplandor m, brillantez f 2 INTELLIGENCE : inteligencia f

brim ['brɪm] n 1 : borde m (de una taza, etc.) 2 : ala f (de un sombrero) — ~ vi **brimmed; brimming** or **~ over** : desbordarse, rebosar

brine ['braɪn] n : salmuera f

bring ['brɪŋ] vt **brought** ['brɔt]; **bringing** 1 : traer 2 **~ about** : ocasionar 3 **~ around** PERSUADE : convencer 4 **~ back** : devolver 5 **~ down** : derribar 6 **~ on** CAUSE : provocar 7 **~ out** : sacar 8 **~ to an end** : terminar (con) 9 **~ up** REAR : criar 10 **~ up** MENTION : sacar

brink ['brɪŋk] n : borde m

brisk ['brɪsk] adj 1 FAST : rápido 2 LIVELY : enérgico

bristle ['brɪsəl] n : cerda f (de un animal), pelo m (de una planta) — ~ vi **-tled; -tling** : erizarse

British ['brɪt̬ɪʃ] adj : británico

brittle ['brɪtəl] adj **-tler; -tlest** : frágil, quebradizo

broach ['bro:tʃ] vt : abordar

broad ['brɔd] adj 1 WIDE : ancho 2 GENERAL : general 3 **in ~ daylight** : en pleno día

broadcast ['brɔd,kæst] vt **-cast; -casting** : emitir — ~ n : emisión f

broaden ['brɔdən] vt : ampliar, ensanchar — vi : ensancharse — **broadly** ['brɔdli] adv : en general — **broad-minded** ['brɔd'maɪndəd] adj : de miras amplias, tolerante

broccoli ['brɑkəli] n : brócoli m, brécol m

brochure [bro'ʃʊr] n : folleto m

broil ['brɔɪl] vt : asar a la parrilla

broke ['bro:k] → **break** — ~ adj : pelado fam — **broken** ['bro:kən] adj : roto, quebrado — **brokenhearted** [,bro:kən'hɑrt̬əd] adj : desconsolado, con el corazón destrozado

broker ['bro:kər] n : corredor m, -dora f

bronchitis [brɑn'kaɪt̬əs, brɑŋ-] n : bronquitis f

bronze ['brɑnz] n : bronce m

brooch ['bro:tʃ, 'bru:tʃ] n : broche m

brood ['bru:d] n : nidada f (de pájaros), camada f (de mamíferos) — ~ vi 1 INCUBATE : empollar 2 **~ about** : dar vueltas a, pensar demasiado en

brook ['brʊk] n : arroyo m

broom ['bru:m, 'brʊm] n : escoba f — **broomstick** ['bru:m,stɪk, 'brʊm-] n : palo m de escoba

broth ['brɔθ] n, pl **broths** ['brɔθs, 'brɔðz] : caldo m

brothel ['brɑθəl, 'brɔ-] n : burdel m

brother ['brʌðər] n : hermano m — **brotherhood** ['brʌðər,hʊd] n : fraternidad f — **brother-in-law** ['brʌðərɪn,lɔ] n, pl **brothers-in-law**: cuñado m — **brotherly** ['brʌðərli] adj : fraternal

brought → **bring**

brow ['braʊ] n 1 EYEBROW : ceja f 2 FOREHEAD : frente f 3 : cima f (de una colina)

brown ['braʊn] adj : marrón, castaño (dícese del pelo), moreno (dícese de la piel) — ~ n : marrón m — ~ vt : dorar (en cocinar)

browse ['braʊz] vi **browsed; browsing** : mirar, echar un vistazo

bruise ['bru:z] vt **bruised; bruising** 1 : contusionar, magullar (a una persona) 2 : machucar (frutas) — ~ n : cardenal m, magulladura f

brunch ['brʌntʃ] n : brunch m

brunet or **brunette** [bru:'nɛt] adj : moreno — ~ n : moreno m, -na f

brunt ['brʌnt] n **bear the ~ of** : aguantar el mayor impacto de

brush ['brʌʃ] n 1 : cepillo m, pincel m (de artista), brocha f (de pintor) 2 UNDERBRUSH : maleza f — ~ vt 1 : cepillar 2 GRAZE : rozar 3 **~ aside** : rechazar 4 **~ off** DISREGARD : hacer caso omiso de — vi **~ up on** : repasar — **brush-off** ['brʌʃ,ɔf] n **give the ~ to** : dar calabazas a

brusque ['brʌsk] adj : brusco

brutal ['bru:t̬əl] adj : brutal — **brutality** [bru:'tælət̬i] n, pl **-ties** : brutalidad f

brute ['bru:t] adj : bruto — ~ n : bestia f; bruto m, -ta f

bubble ['bʌbəl] n : burbuja f — ~ vi **-bled; -bling** : burbujear

buck ['bʌk] n, pl **buck** or **bucks** 1 : animal m macho, ciervo m (macho) 2 DOLLAR : dólar m — ~ vi 1 : corcovear (dícese de un caballo) 2 **~ up** : animarse, levantar el ánimo — vt OPPOSE : oponerse a, ir en contra de

bucket ['bʌkət] n : cubo m

buckle ['bʌkəl] n : hebilla f — ~ v **-led; -ling** vt 1 FASTEN : abrochar 2 BEND : combar, torcer — vi 1 : combarse, torcerse 2 : doblarse (dícese de las rodillas)

bud ['bʌd] n 1 : brote m 2 or **flower ~** : capullo m — ~ vi **budded; budding** : brotar, hacer brotes

Buddhism ['bu:,dɪzəm, 'bʊ-] n : budismo m — **Buddhist** ['bu:dɪst, 'bʊ-] adj : budista — ~ n : budista mf

buddy ['bʌdi] n, pl **-dies** : compañero m, -ra f

budge ['bʌdʒ] vi **budged; budging** 1 MOVE : moverse 2 YIELD : ceder

budget ['bʌdʒət] n : presupuesto m — ~ vi : presupuestar — **budgetary** ['bʌdʒə,tɛri] adj : presupuestario

buff ['bʌf] n 1 : beige m, color m de ante 2 ENTHUSIAST : aficionado m, -da f — ~ adj : beige — ~ vt POLISH : pulir

buffalo ['bʌfə,lo:] n, pl **-lo** or **-loes** : búfalo m

buffet [,bʌ'feɪ, ,bu:-] n 1 : bufé m (comida) 2 SIDEBOARD : aparador m

bug ['bʌg] n 1 INSECT : bicho m, insecto m 2 FLAW : defecto m 3 GERM : microbio m 4 MICROPHONE : micrófono m (oculto) — ~ vt **bugged; bugging** 1 PESTER : fastidiar, molestar 2 : ocultar micrófonos en (una habitación, etc.)

buggy ['bʌgi] n, pl **-gies** 1 CARRIAGE : calesa f 2 or **baby ~** : cochecito m (para niños)

bugle ['bju:gəl] n : clarín m, corneta f

build ['bɪld] v **built** ['bɪlt]; **building** vt 1 : construir 2 DEVELOP : desarrollar — vi 1 or **~ up** INTENSIFY : aumentar, intensificar 2 or **~ up** ACCUMULATE : acumularse — ~ n PHYSIQUE : físico m, complexión f — **builder** ['bɪldər] n : constructor m, -tora f — **building** ['bɪldɪŋ] n 1 STRUCTURE : edificio m 2 CONSTRUCTION : construcción f — **built-in** ['bɪlt'ɪn] adj : empotrado

bulb ['bʌlb] n 1 : bulbo m (de una planta) 2 LIGHTBULB : bombilla f

bulge ['bʌldʒ] vi **bulged; bulging** : sobresalir — ~ n : bulto m, protuberancia f

bulk ['bʌlk] n 1 VOLUME : volumen m, bulto m 2 **in ~** : en grandes cantidades — **bulky** ['bʌlki] adj **bulkier; -est** : voluminoso

bull ['bʊl] n 1 : toro m 2 MALE : macho m

bulldog ['bʊl,dɔg] n : bulldog m

bulldozer ['bʊl,do:zər] n : bulldozer m

bullet ['bʊlət] n : bala f

bulletin ['bʊlətən, -lət̬ən] n : boletín m — **bulletin board** n : tablón m de anuncios

bulletproof ['bʊlət,pru:f] adj : a prueba de balas

bullfight ['bʊl,faɪt] n : corrida f (de toros) — **bullfighter** ['bʊl,faɪt̬ər] n : torero m, -ra f; matador m

bullion ['bʊljən] n : oro m en lingotes, plata f en lingotes

bull's-eye ['bʊlz,aɪ] n, pl **bull's-eyes** : diana f

bully ['bʊli] n, pl **-lies** : matón m — ~ vt **-lied; -lying** : intimidar

bum ['bʌm] n : vagabundo m, -da f

bumblebee ['bʌmbəl,bi:] n : abejorro m

bump ['bʌmp] n 1 BULGE : bulto m, protuberancia f 2 IMPACT : golpe m 3 JOLT : sacudida f — ~ vt : chocar contra — vi **~ into** MEET : encontrarse con — **bumper** ['bʌmpər] n : parachoques mpl — ~ adj : extraordinario, récord — **bumpy** ['bʌmpi] adj **bumpier; -est** 1 : desigual, lleno de baches (dícese de un camino) 2 **a ~ flight** : un vuelo agitado

bun ['bʌn] n : bollo m

bunch ['bʌntʃ] n : grupo m (de personas), racimo m (de frutas, etc.), ramo m (de flores), manojo m (de llaves) — ~ vi or **~ up** : amontarse, agruparse

bundle ['bʌndəl] n 1 : lío m, bulto m, atado m, haz m (de palos) 2 PARCEL : paquete m 3 **~ of nerves** : manojo m de nervios — ~ vt **-dled; -dling** or **~ up** : liar, atar

bungalow ['bʌŋgə,lo:] n : casa f de un solo piso

bungle ['bʌŋgəl] vt **-gled; -gling** : echar a perder

bunion ['bʌnjən] n : juanete m

bunk ['bʌŋk] n or **bunk bed** : litera f

bunny ['bʌni] n, pl **-nies** : conejo m, -ja f

buoy ['bu:i, 'bɔɪ] n : boya f — ~ vt or **~ up** HEARTEN : animar, levantar el ánimo a — **buoyant** ['bɔɪənt, 'bu:jənt] adj 1 : boyante, flotante 2 LIGHTHEARTED : alegre, optimista

burden ['bərdən] n : carga f — ~ vt **~ s.o. with** : cargar a algn con — **burdensome** ['bərdənsəm] adj : oneroso

bureau ['bjʊro] n 1 : cómoda f (mueble) 2 : departamento m (del gobierno) 3 AGENCY : agencia f — **bureaucracy** [bjʊ'rɑkrəsi] n, pl **-cies** : burocracia f — **bureaucrat** ['bjʊrə,kræt] n : burócrata mf — **bureaucratic** [,bjʊrə'kræt̬ɪk] adj : burocrático

burglar ['bərglər] n : ladrón m, -drona f — **burglarize** ['bərglə,raɪz] vt **-ized; -izing** : robar — **burglary** ['bərgləri] n, pl **-glaries** : robo m

burgundy ['bərgəndi] n, pl **-dies** : borgoña m, vino m de Borgoña

burial ['bɛriəl] n : entierro m

burly ['bərli] adj **-lier; -liest** : fornido

burn ['bərn] v **burned** ['bərnd, 'bərnt] or **burnt** ['bərnt]; **burning** vt 1 : quemar 2 or **~ down** : incendiar 3 **~ up** : consumir — vi 1 : arder (dícese de un fuego), quemarse (dícese de la comida, etc.) 2 : estar encendido (dícese de una luz) 3 **~ out** : apagarse — ~ n : quemadura f — **burner** ['bərnər] n : quemador m

burnish ['bərnɪʃ] vt : pulir

burp ['bərp] vi : eructar — ~ n : eructo m

burro ['bəro, 'bʊr-] n, pl **-os** : burro m

burrow ['bəro] n : madriguera f — ~ vi 1 : cavar 2 **~ into** : hurgar en

bursar ['bərsər] n : tesorero m, -ra f

burst ['bərst] v **burst** or **bursted; bursting** vi : reventarse — vt : reventar — ~ n 1 EXPLOSION : estallido m, explosión f 2 OUTBURST : arranque m, arrebato m 3 **~ of laughter** : carcajada f

bury ['bɛri] vt **buried; burying** 1 INTER : enterrar 2 HIDE : esconder

bus ['bʌs] n, pl **buses** or **busses** : autobús m, bus m — ~ v **bused** or **bussed** ['bʌst]; **busing** or **bussing** ['bʌsɪŋ] vt : transportar en autobús — vi : viajar en autobús

bush ['bʊʃ] n SHRUB : arbusto m, mata f

bushel ['bʊʃəl] n : medida f de áridos igual a 35.24 litros

bushy ['bʊʃi] adj **bushier; -est** : poblado, espeso

busily ['bɪzəli] adv : afanosamente

business ['bɪznəs, -nəz] n **1** COMMERCE : negocios mpl, comercio m **2** COMPANY : empresa f, negocio m **3 it's none of your ~** : no es asunto tuyo — **businessman** ['bɪznəs,mæn, -nəz-] n, pl **-men** [-mən, -,mɛn] : empresario m, hombre m de negocios — **businesswoman** ['bɪznəs,wʊmən, -nəz-] n, pl **-women** [-,wɪmən] : empresaria f, mujer f de negocios

bust[1] ['bʌst] vt BREAK : romper

bust[2] n **1** : busto m (en la escultura) **2** BREASTS : pecho m, senos mpl

bustle ['bʌsəl] vi **-tled; -tling** or ~ **about** : ir y venir, ajetrearse — ~ n or **hustle and** ~ : bullicio m, ajetreo m

busy ['bɪzi] adj **busier; -est 1** : ocupado **2** BUSTLING : concurrido

but ['bʌt] conj **1** : pero **2 not one ~ two** : no uno sino dos — ~ prep : excepto, menos

butcher ['bʊtʃər] n : carnicero m, -ra f — ~ vt **1** : matar **2** BOTCH : hacer una carnicería de

butler ['bʌtlər] n : mayordomo m

butt ['bʌt] vt : embestir (con los cuernos), darle un cabezazo a — vi ~ **in** : interrumpir — ~ n **1** BUTTING : embestida f (de cuernos) **2** TARGET : blanco m **3** : extremo m, culata f (de un rifle), colilla f (de un cigarillo)

butter ['bʌṭər] n : mantequilla f — ~ vt : untar con mantequilla

buttercup ['bʌṭər,kʌp] n : ranúnculo m

butterfly ['bʌṭər,flaɪ] n, pl **-flies** : mariposa f

buttocks ['bʌṭəks, -,taks] npl : nalgas fpl

button ['bʌtən] n : botón m — ~ vt : abotonar — vi or ~ **up** : abotonarse — **buttonhole** ['bʌtən,ho:l] n : ojal m — ~ vt **-holed; -holing** : acorralar

buy ['baɪ] vt **bought** ['bɔt]; **buying** : comprar — ~ n : compra f — **buyer** ['baɪər] n : comprador m, -dora f

buzz ['bʌz] vi : zumbar — ~ n : zumbido m

buzzard ['bʌzərd] n : buitre m

buzzer ['bʌzər] n : timbre m

by ['baɪ] prep **1** NEAR : cerca de **2** VIA : por **3** PAST : por, por delante de **4** DURING : de, durante **5** (in expressions of time) : para **6** (indicating cause or agent) : por, de, a — ~ adv **1** ~ **and** ~ : poco después **2** ~ **and large** : en general **3 go** ~ : pasar **4 stop** ~ : pasar por casa

bygone ['baɪ,gɔn] adj : pasado — ~ n **let ~s be ~s** : lo pasado, pasado está

bypass ['baɪ,pæs] n : carretera f de circunvalación — ~ vt : evitar

by–product ['baɪ,pradəkt] n : subproducto m

bystander ['baɪ,stændər] n : espectador m, -dora f

byte ['baɪt] n : byte m, octeto m

byword ['baɪ,wərd] n **be a ~ for** : estar sinónimo de

C

c ['si:] n, pl **c's** or **cs** : c, tercera letra del alfabeto inglés

cab ['kæb] n **1** : taxi m **2** : cabina f (de un camión, etc.)

cabbage ['kæbɪdʒ] n : col f, repollo m

cabin ['kæbən] n **1** : cabaña f **2** : cabina f (de un avión, etc.), camarote m (de un barco)

cabinet ['kæbnət] n **1** CUPBOARD : armario m **2** : gabinete m (del gobierno) **3** or **medicine** ~ : botiquín m

cable ['keɪbəl] n : cable m — **cable television** n : televisión f por cable

cackle ['kækəl] vi **-led; -ling 1** CLUCK : cacarear **2** LAUGH : reírse a carcajadas

cactus ['kæktəs] n, pl **cacti** [-,taɪ] or **-tuses** : cactus m

cadence ['keɪdənts] n : cadencia f, ritmo m

cadet [kə'dɛt] n : cadete mf

café [kæ'feɪ, kə-] n : café m, cafetería f — **cafeteria** [,kæfə'tɪriə] n : restaurante m autoservicio, cantina f

caffeine [kæ'fi:n] n : cafeína f

cage ['keɪdʒ] n : jaula f — ~ vt **caged; caging** : enjaular

cajole [kə'dʒo:l] vt **-joled; -joling** : engatusar

cake ['keɪk] n **1** : pastel m, torta f **2** : pastilla f (de jabón) **3 take the** ~ : ser el colmo — **caked** ['keɪkt] adj ~ **with** : cubierto de

calamity [kə'læməṭi] n, pl **-ties** : calamidad f

calcium ['kælsiəm] n : calcio m

calculate ['kælkjə,leɪt] v **-lated; -lating** : calcular — **calculating** ['kælkjə,leɪṭɪŋ] adj : calculador — **calculation** [,kælkjə'leɪʃən] n : cálculo m — **calculator** ['kælkjə,leɪṭər] n : calculadora f

calendar ['kæləndər] n : calendario m

calf[1] ['kæf, 'kaf] n, pl **calves** ['kævz, 'kavz] **1** : becerro m, -rra f; ternero m, -ra f (de vacunos) **2** : cría f (de otros mamíferos)

calf[2] n, pl **calves** : pantorrilla f (de la pierna)

caliber or **calibre** ['kæləbər] n : calibre m

call ['kɔl] vi **1** : llamar **2** VISIT : pasar, hacer (una) visita **3** ~ **for** : requerir — vt **1** : llamar **2** ~ **off** : cancelar — ~ n **1** : llamada f **2** SHOUT : grito m **3** VISIT : visita f **4** DEMAND : petición f — **calling** ['kɔlɪŋ] n : vocación f

callous ['kæləs] adj : insensible, cruel

calm ['kam, 'kalm] n : calma f, tranquilidad f — ~ vt : calmar — vi or ~ **down** : calmarse — ~ adj : tranquilo, en calma — **calmly** ['kamli, 'kalm-] adv : con calma

calorie ['kæləri] n : caloría f

came → **come**

camel ['kæməl] n : camello m

camera ['kæmrə, 'kæmərə] n : cámara f

camouflage ['kæmə,flaʒ, -,fladʒ] n : camuflaje m — ~ vt **-flaged; -flaging** : camuflar

camp ['kæmp] n **1** : campamento m **2** FACTION : bando m — ~ vi : acampar, ir de camping

campaign [kæm'peɪn] n : campaña f — ~ vi : hacer (una) campaña

camping ['kæmpɪŋ] n : camping m

campus ['kæmpəs] n : ciudad f universitaria

can[1] ['kæn] v aux, past **could** ['kʊd]; present s & pl **can 1** (expressing possibility or permission) : poder **2** (expressing knowledge or ability) : saber **3 that cannot be!** : ¡no puede ser!

can[2] ['kæn] n : lata f — ~ vt **canned; canning** : enlatar

Canadian [kə'neɪdiən] adj : canadiense

canal [kə'næl] n : canal m

canary [kə'nɛri] n, pl **-naries** : canario m

cancel ['kæntsəl] vt **-celed** or **-celled; -celing** or **-celling** : cancelar — **cancellation** [,kæntsə'leɪʃən] n : cancelación f

cancer ['kæntsər] n : cáncer m — **cancerous** ['kæntsərəs] adj : canceroso

candelabra [,kændə'labrə, -'læ-] n, pl **-bra** or **-bras** : candelabro m

candid ['kændɪd] adj : franco

candidate ['kændə,deɪt, -dət] n : candidato m, -ta f — **candidacy** ['kændədəsi] n, pl **-cies** : candidatura f

candle ['kændəl] n : vela f — **candlestick** ['kændəl,stɪk] n : candelero m

candor or Brit **candour** ['kændər] n : franqueza f

candy ['kændi] n, pl **-dies** : dulce m, caramelo m

cane ['keɪn] n **1** : bastón m (para andar), vara f (para castigar) **2** REED : caña f, mimbre m — ~ vt **caned; caning 1** : tapizar con mimbre **2** FLOG : azotar

canine ['keɪ,naɪn] n or ~ **tooth** : colmillo m, diente m canino — ~ adj : canino

canister ['kænəstər] n : lata f, bote m Spain

cannibal ['kænəbəl] n : caníbal mf

cannon ['kænən] n, pl **-nons** or **-non** : cañón m

cannot (can not) ['kæn,at, kə'nat] → **can**[1]

canny ['kæni] adj **cannier; -est** : astuto

canoe [kə'nu:] n : canoa f, piragua f — ~ vt **-noed; -noeing** : ir en canoa

canon ['kænən] n : canon m — **canonize** ['kænə,naɪz] vt **-ized; -izing** : canonizar

can opener n : abrelatas m

canopy ['kænəpi] n, pl **-pies** : dosel m

can't ['kænt, 'kant] (contraction of **can not**) → **can**[1]

cantaloupe ['kæntəl,o:p] n : melón m, cantalupo m

cantankerous [kæn'tæŋkərəs] adj : irritable, irascible

canteen [kæn'ti:n] n **1** FLASK : cantimplora f **2** CAFETERIA : cantina f

canter ['kæntər] vi : ir a medio galope — ~ n : medio galope m

canvas ['kænvəs] n **1** : lona f (tela) **2** : lienzo m (de pintar)

canvass ['kænvəs] vt **1** : solicitar votos de, hacer campaña entre **2** POLL : sondear — ~ n **1** : solicitación f (de votos) **2** POLL : sondeo m

canyon ['kænjən] n : cañón m

cap n **1** : gorra f, gorro m **2** TOP : tapa f, tapón m (de botellas) **3** LIMIT : tope m — ~ ['kæp] vt **capped; capping 1** COVER : tapar, cubrir **2** OUTDO : superar

capable ['keɪpəbəl] adj : capaz, competente — **capability** [,keɪpə'bɪləṭi] n, pl **-ties** : capacidad f

capacity [kə'pæsəṭi] n, pl **-ties 1** : capacidad f **2** ROLE : calidad f

cape[1] ['keɪp] n : cabo m (en geografía)

cape[2] n CLOAK : capa f

caper[1] ['keɪpər] n : alcaparra f

caper[2] n PRANK : broma f, travesura f

capital ['kæpəṭəl] adj **1** : capital **2** : mayúsculo (dícese de las letras) — ~ n **1** or ~ **city** : capital f **2** WEALTH : capital m **3** or ~ **letter** : mayúscula f — **capitalism** ['kæpəṭəl,ɪzəm] n : capitalismo m — **capitalist** ['kæpəṭəlɪst] or **capitalistic** [,kæpəṭəl'ɪstɪk] adj : capitalista — **capitalize** ['kæpəṭəl,aɪz] vt **-ized; -izing 1** FINANCE : capitalizar **2** : escribir con mayúscula — vi ~ **on** : sacar partido de

capitol ['kæpəṭəl] n : capitolio m

capitulate [kə'pɪtʃə,leɪt] vi **-lated; -lating** : capitular

capsize ['kæp,saɪz, kæp'saɪz] v **-sized; -sizing** vt : hacer volcar — vi : zozobrar, volcar(se)

capsule ['kæpsəl, -,su:l] n : cápsula f

captain ['kæptən] n : capitán m, -tana f

caption ['kæpʃən] n **1** : leyenda f (al pie de una ilustración) **2** SUBTITLE : subtítulo m

captivate ['kæptə,veɪt] vt **-vated; -vating** : cautivar, encantar

captive ['kæptɪv] adj : cautivo — ~ n : cautivo m, -va f — **captivity** [kæp'tɪvəṭi] n : cautiverio m

capture ['kæpʃər] n : captura f, apresamiento m — ~ vt **-tured; -turing 1** SEIZE : capturar, apresar **2** ~ **one's interest** : captar el interés de uno

car ['kar] n **1** : automóvil m, coche m, carro m Lat **2** or **railroad** ~ : vagón m

carafe [kə'ræf, -'raf] n : garrafa f

caramel ['karməl; 'kærəməl, -,mɛl] n : caramelo m, azúcar f quemada

carat ['kærət] n : quilate m

caravan ['kærə,væn] n : caravana f

carbohydrate [,karbo'haɪ,dreɪt, -drət] n : carbohidrato m, hidrato m de carbono

carbon ['karbən] n : carbono m — **carbon copy** n : copia f, duplicado m

carburetor ['karbə,reɪṭər, -bjə-] n : carburador m

carcass ['karkəs] n : cuerpo m (de un animal muerto)

card ['kard] n **1** : tarjeta f **2** or **playing** ~ : carta f, naipe m — **cardboard** ['kard,bord] n : cartón m

cardiac ['kardi,æk] adj : cardíaco

cardigan ['kardɪgən] n : cárdigan m

cardinal ['kardənəl] n : cardenal m — ~ adj : cardinal, fundamental

care ['kær] n **1** : cuidado m **2** WORRY : preocupación **3 take ~ of** : cuidar (de) — ~ vi **cared; caring 1** : preocuparse, inquietarse **2** ~ **for** TEND : cuidar (de), atender **3** ~ **for** LIKE : querer **4 I don't** ~ : no me importa

career [kə'rɪr] n : carrera f — ~ vi : ir a toda velocidad

carefree ['kær,fri:, ,kær'-] adj : despreocupado

careful ['kærfəl] adj : cuidadoso — **carefully** ['kærfəli] adv : con cuidado, cuidadosamente — **careless** ['kærləs] adj : descuidado — **carelessness** ['kærləsnəs] n : descuido m

caress [kə'rɛs] n : caricia f — ~ vt : acariciar

cargo ['kar,go:] n, pl **-goes** or **-gos** : cargamento m, carga f

caricature ['kærɪkə,tʃʊr] n : caricatura f — ~ vt **-tured; -turing** : caricaturizar

caring ['kærɪŋ] adj : solícito, afectuoso

carnage ['karnɪdʒ] n : matanza f, carnicería f

carnal ['karnəl] adj : carnal

carnation [kar'neɪʃən] n : clavel m

carnival ['karnəvəl] n : carnaval m

carol ['kærəl] n : villancico m

carp ['karp] vi ~ **at** : quejarse de

carpenter ['karpəntər] n : carpintero m, -ra f — **carpentry** ['karpəntri] n : carpintería f

carpet ['karpət] n : alfombra f

carriage ['kærɪdʒ] n **1** : transporte m (de mercancías) **2** BEARING : porte m **3** or **baby** ~ : cochecito m **4** or **horse–drawn** ~ : carruaje m, coche m

carrier ['kæriər] n **1** : transportista mf, empresa f de transportes **2** : portador m, -dora f (de una enfermedad)

carrot ['kærət] n : zanahoria f

carry ['kæri] v **-ried; -rying** vt **1** : llevar **2** TRANSPORT : transportar **3** STOCK : vender **4** ENTAIL : acarrear, implicar **5** ~ **oneself** : portarse — vi : oírse (dícese de sonidos) — **carry away** vt **get carried away** : exaltarse, entusiasmarse — **carry on** vt CONDUCT : realizar — vi **1** : portarse inapropiadamente **2** CONTINUE : seguir, continuar — **carry out** vt **1** PERFORM : llevar a cabo, realizar **2** FULFILL : cumplir

cart ['kart] n : carreta f, carro m — ~ vt or ~ **around** : acarrear

cartilage ['karṭəlɪdʒ] n : cartílago m

carton ['kartən] n : caja f (de cartón)

cartoon [kar'tu:n] n **1** : caricatura f **2** COMIC STRIP : historieta f **3** or **animated** ~ : dibujos mpl animados

cartridge ['kartrɪdʒ] n : cartucho m

carve ['karv] vt **carved; carving 1** : tallar, esculpir **2** : trinchar (carne)

case n **1** : caso m **2** BOX : caja f **3 in any ~** : en todo caso **4 in ~ of** : en caso de **5 just in ~** : por si acaso

cash ['kæʃ] n : efectivo m, dinero m en efectivo — ~ vt : convertir en efectivo, cobrar

cashew ['kæ,ʃu:, kə'ʃu:] n : anacardo m

cashier [kæ'ʃɪr] n : cajero m, -ra f

cashmere ['kæʒ,mɪr, 'kæʃ-] n : cachemira f

cash register n : caja f registradora

casino [kə'si:,no:] n, pl **-nos** : casino m

cask ['kæsk] n : barril m

casket ['kæskət] n : ataúd m

casserole ['kæsə,ro:l] n **1** or ~ **dish** : cazuela f **2** : guiso m (comida)

cassette [kə'sɛt, kæ-] n : cassette mf

cast ['kæst] vt **cast; casting 1** THROW : arrojar, lanzar **2** : depositar (un voto) **3** : repartir (papeles dramáticos) **4** MOLD : fundir — ~ n **1** : elenco m, reparto m (de actores) **2** or **plaster** ~ : molde m de yeso, escayola f

castanets [,kæstə'nɛts] npl : castañuelas fpl

castaway ['kæstə,weɪ] n : náufrago m, -ga f

cast iron n : hierro m fundido

castle ['kæsəl] n **1** : castillo m **2** : torre f (en ajedrez)

castrate ['kæs,treɪt] vt **-trated; -trating** : castrar

casual ['kæʒʊəl] adj **1** CHANCE : casual, fortuito **2** INDIFFERENT : despreocupado **3** INFORMAL : informal — **casually** ['kæʒʊəli, 'kæʒəli] adv **1** : de manera despreocupada **2** INFORMALLY : informalmente

casualty ['kæʒʊəlti, 'kæʒəl-] n, pl **-ties 1** : accidente m **2** VICTIM : víctima f; herido m, -da f **3 casualties** npl : bajas fpl (militares)

cat ['kæt] n : gato m, -ta f

catalog or **catalogue** ['kæṭə,lɔg] n : catálogo m — ~ vt **-loged** or **-logued; -loging** or **-loguing** : catalogar

catapult ['kæṭə,pʌlt, -,pʊlt] n : catapulta f

cataract ['kæṭə,rækt] n : catarata f

catastrophe [kə'tæstrə,fi:] n : catástrofe f — **catastrophic** [,kæṭə'strafɪk] adj : catastrófico

catch ['kætʃ, 'kɛtʃ] v **caught** ['kɔt]; **catching** vt **1** CAPTURE, TRAP : capturar, atrapar **2** SURPRISE : sorprender **3** GRASP : agarrar, captar **4** SNAG : enganchar **5** : tomar (un tren, etc.) **6** ~ **a cold** : resfriarse — vi **1** SNAG : engancharse **2** ~ **fire** : prender fuego — **catching** ['kætʃɪŋ, 'kɛ-] adj : contagioso — **catchy** ['kætʃi, 'kɛ-] adj **catchier; -est** : pegadizo, pegajoso Lat

category ['kæṭə,gori] n, pl **-ries** : categoría f — **categorical** [,kæṭə'gɔrɪkəl] adj : categórico

cater ['keɪṭər] vi **1** : proveer comida **2** ~ **to** : atender a — **caterer** ['keɪṭərər] n : proveedor m, -dora f de comida

caterpillar ['kæṭər,pɪlər] n : oruga f

catfish ['kæt,fɪʃ] n : bagre m

cathedral [kə'θi:drəl] n : catedral f

catholic ['kæθlɪk] adj **1** : universal **2 Catholic** : católico — **catholicism** [kə'θalə,sɪzəm] n : catolicismo m

cattle ['kæṭəl] npl : ganado m (vacuno)

caught → **catch**

cauldron ['kɔldrən] n : caldera f

cauliflower ['kalɪ,flaʊər, 'kɔ-] n : coliflor f

cause ['kɔz] n **1** : causa f **2** REASON : motivo m — ~ vt **caused; causing** : causar

caustic ['kɔstɪk] adj : cáustico

caution ['kɔʃən] n **1** WARNING : advertencia f **2** CARE : precaución f, cautela f — ~ vt : advertir — **cautious** ['kɔʃəs] adj : cauteloso, precavido — **cautiously** ['kɔʃəsli] adv : con precaución

cavalier [,kævə'lɪr] adj : arrogante, desdeñoso

cavalry ['kævəlri] n, pl **-ries** : caballería f

cave ['keɪv] n : cueva f — ~ vi **caved; caving** or ~ **in** : hundirse

cavern ['kævərn] n : caverna f

cavity ['kævəṭi] n, pl **-ties 1** : cavidad f **2** : caries f (dental)

cavort [kə'vɔrt] vi : brincar

CD [,si:'di:] n : CD m, disco m compacto

cease ['si:s] v **ceased; ceasing** vt : dejar de — vi : cesar — **cease–fire** ['si:s'faɪr] n : alto m el fuego — **ceaseless** ['si:sləs] adj : incesante

cedar ['si:dər] n : cedro m

ceiling ['si:lɪŋ] n : techo m

celebrate ['sɛlə,breɪt] v **-brated; -brating** vt : celebrar — vi : divertirse — **celebrated** ['sɛlə,breɪṭəd] adj : célebre — **celebration** [,sɛlə'breɪʃən] n **1** : celebración f **2** FESTIVITY : fiesta f — **celebrity** [sə'lɛbrəṭi] n, pl **-ties** : celebridad f

celery ['sɛləri] n, pl **-eries** : apio m

cell ['sɛl] n **1** : célula f **2** : celda f (en una cárcel, etc.)

cellar ['sɛlər] n **1** BASEMENT : sótano m **2** : bodega f (de vinos)

cello ['tʃɛ,lo:] n, pl **-los** : violoncelo m

cellular ['sɛljələr] adj : celular

cement [sɪ'mɛnt] n : cemento m — ~ vt : cementar

cemetery ['sɛmə,tɛri] n, pl **-teries** : cementerio m

censor ['sɛntsər] vt : censurar — **censorship** ['sɛntsər,ʃɪp] n : censura f — **censure** ['sɛntʃər] n : censura f — ~ vt **-sured; -suring** : censurar, criticar

census ['sɛntsəs] n : censo m

cent ['sɛnt] n : centavo m

centennial [sɛn'tɛniəl] n : centenario m

center or Brit **centre** ['sɛntər] n : centro m — ~ v **centered** or Brit **centred; centering** or Brit **centring** vt : centrar — vi ~ **on** : centrarse en

centigrade [ˈsɛntəˌgreɪd, ˈsɑn-] *adj* : centígrado

centimeter [ˈsɛntəˌmiːt̬ər, ˈsɑn-] *n* : centímetro *m*

centipede [ˈsɛntəˌpiːd] *n* : ciempiés *m*

central [ˈsɛntrəl] *adj* **1** : central **2 a ~ location** : un lugar céntrico — **centralize** [ˈsɛntrəˌlaɪz] *vt* **-ized; -izing** : centralizar

centre [ˈsɛntər] → **center**

century [ˈsɛntʃəri] *n, pl* **-ries** : siglo *m*

ceramics [səˈræmɪks] *npl* : cerámica *f*

cereal [ˈsɪriəl] *n* : cereal *m*

ceremony [ˈsɛrəˌmoːni] *n, pl* **-nies** : ceremonia *f* — **ceremonial** [ˌsɛrəˈmoːniəl] *adj* : ceremonial

certain [ˈsərtən] *adj* **1** : cierto **2 be ~ of** : estar seguro de **3 for ~** : seguro, con toda seguridad **4 make ~ of** : asegurarse de — **certainly** [ˈsərtənli] *adv* : desde luego, por supuesto — **certainty** [ˈsərtənti] *n, pl* **-ties** : certeza *f*, seguridad *f*

certify [ˈsərt̬əˌfaɪ] *vt* **-fied; -fying** : certificar — **certificate** [sərˈtɪfɪkət] *n* : certificado *m*, partida *f*, acta *f*

chafe [ˈtʃeɪf] *v* **chafed; chafing** *vi* : rozarse — *vt* : rozar

chain [ˈtʃeɪn] *n* **1** : cadena *f* **2 ~ of events** : serie *f* de acontecimientos — **~** *vt* : encadenar

chair [ˈtʃɛr] *n* **1** : silla *f* **2** : cátedra *f* (en una universidad) — **~** *vt* : presidir — **chairman** [ˈtʃɛrmən] *n, pl* **-men** [-mən, -ˌmɛn] : presidente *m* — **chairperson** [ˈtʃɛrˌpərsən] *n* : presidente *m*, -ta *f*

chalk [ˈtʃɔk] *n* : tiza *f*, gis *m Lat*

challenge [ˈtʃælɪndʒ] *vt* **-lenged; -lenging 1** DISPUTE : disputar, poner en duda **2** DARE : desafiar — **~** *n* : reto *m*, desafío *m* — **challenging** [ˈtʃælɪndʒɪŋ] *adj* : estimulante

chamber [ˈtʃeɪmbər] *n* : cámara *f* — **chambermaid** [ˈtʃeɪmbərˌmeɪd] *n* : camarera *f*

champagne [ʃæmˈpeɪn] *n* : champaña *m*, champán *m*

champion [ˈtʃæmpiən] *n* : campeón *m*, -peona *f* — **~** *vt* : defender — **championship** [ˈtʃæmpiənˌʃɪp] *n* : campeonato *m*

chance [ˈtʃænts] *n* **1** LUCK : azar *m*, suerte *f* **2** OPPORTUNITY : oportunidad *f* **3** LIKELIHOOD : probabilidad *f* **4 by ~** : por casualidad **5 take a ~** : arriesgarse — **~** *vt* **chanced; chancing** RISK : arriesgar — **~** *adj* : fortuito

chandelier [ˌʃændəˈlɪr] *n* : araña *f* (de luces)

change [ˈtʃeɪndʒ] *v* **changed; changing** *vt* **1** : cambiar **2** SWITCH : cambiar de — *vi* **1** : cambiar **2** *or* **~ clothes** : cambiarse (de ropa) — **~** *n* : cambio *m* — **changeable** [ˈtʃeɪndʒəbəl] *adj* : cambiable

channel [ˈtʃænəl] *n* **1** : canal *m* **2** : cauce *m* (de un río) **3** MEANS : vía *f*, medio *m*

chant [ˈtʃænt] *v* : cantar — **~** *n* : canto *m*

chaos [ˈkeɪˌɑs] *n* : caos *m* — **chaotic** [keɪˈɑtɪk] *adj* : caótico

chap¹ [ˈtʃæp] *vi* **chapped; chapping** : agrietarse

chap² *n* : tipo *m fam*

chapel [ˈtʃæpəl] *n* : capilla *f*

chaperon *or* **chaperone** [ˈʃæpəˌroːn] *n* : acompañante *mf*

chaplain [ˈtʃæplɪn] *n* : capellán *m*

chapter [ˈtʃæptər] *n* : capítulo *m*

char [ˈtʃɑr] *vt* **charred; charring** : carbonizar

character [ˈkærɪktər] *n* **1** : carácter *m* **2** : personaje *m* (en una novela, etc.) — **characteristic** [ˌkærɪktəˈrɪstɪk] *adj* : característico — **~** *n* : característica *f* — **characterize** [ˈkærɪktəˌraɪz] *vt* **-ized; -izing** : caracterizar

charcoal [ˈtʃɑrˌkoːl] *n* : carbón *m*

charge [ˈtʃɑrdʒ] *n* **1** : carga *f* (eléctrica) **2** COST : precio *m* **3** BURDEN : carga *f*, peso *m* **4** ACCUSATION : cargo *m*, acusación *f* **5 in ~ of** : encargado de **6 take ~ of** : hacerse cargo de — **~** *v* **charged; charging** *vt* **1** : cargar **2** ENTRUST : encargar **3** COMMAND : ordenar, mandar **4** ACCUSE : acusar — *vi* **1** : cargar **2 ~ too much** : cobrar demasiado

charisma [kəˈrɪzmə] *n* : carisma *m* — **charismatic** [ˌkærəzˈmæt̬ɪk] *adj* : carismático

charity [ˈtʃærət̬i] *n, pl* **-ties 1** : organización *f* benéfica **2** GOODWILL : caridad *f*

charlatan [ˈʃɑrlətən] *n* : charlatán *m*, -tana *f*

charm [ˈtʃɑrm] *n* **1** : encanto *m* **2** SPELL : hechizo *m* — **~** *vt* : encantar, cautivar — **charming** [ˈtʃɑrmɪŋ] *adj* : encantador

chart [ˈtʃɑrt] *n* **1** MAP : carta *f* **2** DIAGRAM : gráfico *m*, tabla *f* — **~** *vt* : trazar un mapa de

charter [ˈtʃɑrt̬ər] *n* : carta *f* — **~** *vt* : alquilar, fletar

chase [ˈtʃeɪs] *n* : persecución *f* — **~** *vt* **chased; chasing 1** PURSUE : perseguir **2** *or* **~ away** : ahuyentar

chasm [ˈkæzəm] *n* : abismo *m*

chaste [ˈtʃeɪst] *adj* **chaster; -est** : casto — **chastity** [ˈtʃæstət̬i] *n* : castidad *f*

chat [ˈtʃæt] *vi* **chatted; chatting** : charlar — **~** *n* : charla *f* — **chatter** [ˈtʃæt̬ər] *vi* **1** : parlotear *fam* **2** : castañetear (dícese de los dientes) — **~** *n* : parloteo *m*, cháchara *f* — **chatterbox** [ˈtʃæt̬ərˌbɑks] *n* : parlanchín *m*, -china *f* — **chatty** [ˈtʃæt̬i] *adj* **chattier; chattiest 1** : parlanchín **2** INFORMAL : familiar

chauffeur [ˈʃoːfər, ʃoˈfər] *n* : chofer *mf*

chauvinist [ˈʃoːvənɪst] *or* **chauvinistic** [ˌʃoːvəˈnɪstɪk] *adj* : chauvinista, patriotero

cheap [ˈtʃiːp] *adj* **1** INEXPENSIVE : barato **2** SHODDY : de baja calidad — **~** *adv* : barato — **cheapen** [ˈtʃiːpən] *vt* : rebajar — **cheaply** [ˈtʃiːpli] *adv* : barato, a precio bajo

cheat [ˈtʃiːt] *vt* : defraudar, estafar — *vi* **1** : hacer trampa(s) **2 ~ on s.o.** : engañar a algn — **~** *or* **cheater** [ˈtʃiːt̬ər] *n* : tramposo *m*, -sa *f*

check [ˈtʃɛk] *n* **1** RESTRAINT : freno *m* **2** INSPECTION : inspección *f*, comprobación *f* **3** DRAFT : cheque *m* **4** BILL : cuenta *f* **5** : jaque *m* (en ajedrez) **6** : tela *f* a cuadros — **~** *vt* **1** RESTRAIN : frenar, contener **2** INSPECT : revisar **3** VERIFY : comprobar **4** : dar jaque (en ajedrez) **5 ~ in** : enregistrarse (en un hotel) **6 ~ out** : irse (de un hotel) **7 ~ out** VERIFY : verificar, comprobar

checkers [ˈtʃɛkərz] *n* : damas *fpl*

checkmate [ˈtʃɛkˌmeɪt] *n* : jaque *m* mate

checkpoint [ˈtʃɛkˌpɔɪnt] *n* : puesto *m* de control

checkup [ˈtʃɛkˌʌp] *n* : chequeo *m*, examen *m* médico

cheek [ˈtʃiːk] *n* : mejilla *f*

cheer [ˈtʃɪr] *n* **1** CHEERFULNESS : alegría *f* **2** APPLAUSE : aclamación *f* **3 ~s!** : ¡salud! — **~** *vt* **1** GLADDEN : alegrar **2** APPLAUD, SHOUT : aclamar, aplaudir — **cheerful** [ˈtʃɪrfəl] *adj* : alegre

cheese [ˈtʃiːz] *n* : queso *m*

cheetah [ˈtʃiːt̬ə] *n* : guepardo *m*

chef [ˈʃɛf] *n* : chef *m*

chemical [ˈkɛmɪkəl] *adj* : químico — **~** *n* : sustancia *f* química — **chemist** [ˈkɛmɪst] *n* : químico *m*, -ca *f* — **chemistry** [ˈkɛmɪstri] *n, pl* **-tries** : química *f*

cheque [ˈtʃɛk] *Brit* → **check**

cherish [ˈtʃɛrɪʃ] *vt* **1** : querer, apreciar **2** HARBOR : abrigar (un recuerdo, una esperanza, etc.)

cherry [ˈtʃɛri] *n, pl* **-ries** : cereza *f*

chess [ˈtʃɛs] *n* : ajedrez *m*

chest [ˈtʃɛst] *n* **1** BOX : cofre *m* **2** : pecho *m* (del cuerpo) **3** *or* **~ of drawers** : cómoda *f*

chestnut [ˈtʃɛsˌnʌt] *n* : castaña *f*

chew [ˈtʃuː] *vt* : masticar, mascar — **chewing gum** *n* : chicle *m*

chic [ˈʃiːk] *adj* : elegante

chick [ˈtʃɪk] *n* : polluelo *m*, -la *f* — **chicken** [ˈtʃɪkən] *n* : pollo *m* — **chicken pox** *n* : varicela *f*

chicory [ˈtʃɪkəri] *n, pl* **-ries 1** : endivia *f* (para ensaladas) **2** : achicoria *f* (aditivo de café)

chief [ˈtʃiːf] *adj* : principal — **~** *n* : jefe *m*, -fa *f* — **chiefly** [ˈtʃiːfli] *adv* : principalmente

child [ˈtʃaɪld] *n, pl* **children** [ˈtʃɪldrən] **1** : niño *m*, -ña *f* **2** OFFSPRING : hijo *m*, -ja *f* — **childbirth** [ˈtʃaɪldˌbərθ] *n* : parto *m* — **childhood** [ˈtʃaɪldˌhʊd] *n* : infancia *f*, niñez *f* — **childish** [ˈtʃaɪldɪʃ] *adj* : infantil — **childlike** [ˈtʃaɪldˌlaɪk] *adj* : infantil, inocente — **childproof** [ˈtʃaɪldˌpruːf] *adj* : a prueba de niños

Chilean [ˈtʃɪliən, tʃɪˈleɪən] *adj* : chileno

chili *or* **chile** *or* **chilli** [ˈtʃɪli] *n, pl* **chilies** *or* **chiles** *or* **chillies 1** *or* **~ pepper** : chile *m* **2** : chile *m* con carne

chill [ˈtʃɪl] *n* **1** CHILLINESS : frío *m* **2 catch a ~** : resfriarse **3 there's a ~ in the air** : hace fresco — **~** *adj* : frío — **~** *v* : enfriar — **chilly** [ˈtʃɪli] *adj* **chillier; -est** : fresco, frío

chime [ˈtʃaɪm] *vi* **chimed; chiming** : repicar, sonar — **~** *n* : carillón *m*

chimney [ˈtʃɪmni] *n, pl* **-neys** : chimenea *f*

chimpanzee [ˌtʃɪmˌpænˈziː, ʃɪm-; tʃɪmˈpænzi, ʃɪm-] *n* : chimpancé *m*

chin [ˈtʃɪn] *n* : barbilla *f*

china [ˈtʃaɪnə] *n* : porcelana *f*, loza *f*

Chinese [tʃaɪˈniːz, -ˈniːs] *adj* : chino — **~** *n* : chino *m* (idioma)

chink [ˈtʃɪŋk] *n* : grieta *f*

chip [ˈtʃɪp] *n* **1** : astilla *f* (de madera o vidrio), lasca *f* (de piedra) **2** : ficha *f* (de póker, etc.) **3** NICK : desportilladura *f* **4** *or* **computer ~** : chip *m* **5** → **potato chips** — **~** *v* **chipped; chipping** *vt* : desportillar — *vi* **1** : desportillarse **2 ~ in** : contribuir

chipmunk [ˈtʃɪpˌmʌŋk] *n* : ardilla *f* listada

chiropodist [kəˈrɑpədɪst, ʃə-] *n* : podólogo *m*, -ga *f*

chiropractor [ˈkaɪrəˌpræktər] *n* : quiropráctico *m*, -ca *f*

chirp [ˈtʃərp] *vi* : piar, gorjear

chisel [ˈtʃɪzəl] *n* : cincel *m* (para piedras, etc.), formón *m*, escoplo *m* (para madera) — **~** *vt* **-eled** *or* **-elled; -eling** *or* **-elling** : cincelar, tallar

chit [ˈtʃɪt] *n* : nota *f*

chitchat [ˈtʃɪtˌtʃæt] *n* : cháchara *f fam*

chivalrous [ˈʃɪvəlrəs] *adj* : caballeroso — **chivalry** [ˈʃɪvəlri] *n, pl* **-ries** : caballerosidad *f*

chive [ˈtʃaɪv] *n* : cebollino *m*

chlorine [ˈklorˌiːn] *n* : cloro *m*

chock–full [ˈtʃɑkˈfʊl, ˈtʃʌk-] *adj* : repleto, atestado

chocolate [ˈtʃɑkələt, ˈtʃɔk-] *n* : chocolate *m*

choice [ˈtʃɔɪs] *n* **1** : elección *f*, selección *f* **2** PREFERENCE : preferencia *f* — **~** *adj* **choicer; -est** : selecto

choir [ˈkwaɪr] *n* : coro *m*

choke [ˈtʃoːk] *v* **choked; choking** *vt* **1** : asfixiar, estrangular **2** BLOCK : atascar — *vi* : asfixiarse, atragantarse (con comida) — **~** *n* : estárter *m* (de un motor)

choose [ˈtʃuːz] *v* **chose** [ˈtʃoːz]; **chosen** [ˈtʃoːzən]; **choosing** *vt* **1** SELECT : escoger, elegir **2** DECIDE : decidir — *vi* : escoger — **choosy** *or* **choosey** [ˈtʃuːzi] *adj* **choosier; -est** : exigente

chop [ˈtʃɑp] *vt* **chopped; chopping 1** : cortar, picar (carne, etc.) **2 ~ down** : talar — **~** *n* : chuleta *f* (de cerdo, etc.) — **choppy** [ˈtʃɑpi] *adj* **-pier; -est** : picado, agitado

chopsticks [ˈtʃɑpˌstɪks] *npl* : palillos *mpl*

chord [ˈkɔrd] *n* : acorde *m* (en música)

chore [ˈtʃor] *n* **1** : tarea *f* **2 household ~s** : faenas *fpl* domésticas

choreography [ˌkoriˈɑgrəfi] *n, pl* **-phies** : coreografía *f*

chortle [ˈtʃɔrt̬əl] *vi* **-tled; -tling** : reírse (con satisfacción o júbilo)

chorus [ˈkorəs] *n* **1** : coro *m* (grupo de personas) **2** REFRAIN : estribillo *m*

chose, chosen → **choose**

christen [ˈkrɪsən] *vt* : bautizar — **christening** [ˈkrɪsənɪŋ] *n* : bautizo *m*

Christian [ˈkrɪstʃən] *n* : cristiano *m*, -na *f* — **~** *adj* : cristiano — **Christianity** [ˌkrɪstʃiˈænət̬i, ˌkrɪsˈtʃæ-] *n* : cristianismo *m*

Christmas [ˈkrɪsməs] *n* : Navidad *f*

chrome [ˈkroːm] *n* : cromo *m*

chronic [ˈkrɑnɪk] *adj* : crónico

chronicle [ˈkrɑnɪkəl] *n* : crónica *f*

chronology [krəˈnɑlədʒi] *n, pl* **-gies** : cronología *f* — **chronological** [ˌkrɑnəlˈɑdʒɪkəl] *adj* : cronológico

chrysanthemum [krɪˈsæntθəməm] *n* : crisantemo *m*

chubby [ˈtʃʌbi] *adj* **-bier; -est** : regordete *fam*, rechoncho *fam*

chuck [ˈtʃʌk] *vt* : tirar, arrojar

chuckle [ˈtʃʌkəl] *vi* **-led; -ling** : reírse (entre dientes) — **~** *n* : risa *f* ahogada

chum [ˈtʃʌm] *n* : amigo *m*, -ga *f*; compinche *mf fam* — **chummy** [ˈtʃʌmi] *adj* **-mier; -est** : muy amigable

chunk [ˈtʃʌŋk] *n* : trozo *m*, pedazo *m*

church [ˈtʃərtʃ] *n* : iglesia *f*

churn [ˈtʃərn] *n* : mantequera *f* — **~** *vt* **1** : agitar **2 ~ out** : producir en grandes cantidades

chute [ˈʃuːt] *n* **1** : vertedor *m* **2** SLIDE : tobogán *m*

cider [ˈsaɪdər] *n* : sidra *f*

cigar [sɪˈgɑr] *n* : puro *m* — **cigarette** [ˌsɪgəˈrɛt, ˈsɪgəˌrɛt] *n* : cigarrillo *m*, cigarro *m*

cinch [ˈsɪntʃ] *n* **it's a ~** : es pan comido

cinema [ˈsɪnəmə] *n* : cine *m*

cinnamon [ˈsɪnəmən] *n* : canela *f*

cipher [ˈsaɪfər] *n* **1** ZERO : cero *m* **2** CODE : cifra *f*

circa [ˈsərkə] *prep* : hacia

circle [ˈsərkəl] *n* : círculo *m* — **~** *v* **-cled; -cling** *vt* **1** : dar vueltas alrededor de **2** : trazar un círculo alrededor de (un número, etc.) — *vi* : dar vueltas

circuit [ˈsərkət] *n* : circuito *m* — **circuitous** [ˌsərˈkjuːət̬əs] *adj* : tortuoso

circular [ˈsərkjələr] *adj* : circular — **~** *n* LEAFLET : circular *f*

circulate [ˈsərkjəˌleɪt] *v* **-lated; -lating** *vt* : hacer circular — *vi* : circular — **circulation** [ˌsərkjəˈleɪʃən] *n* **1** : circulación *f* **2** : tirada *f* (de una publicación)

circumcise [ˈsərkəmˌsaɪz] *vt* **-cised; -cising** : circuncidar — **circumcision** [ˌsərkəmˈsɪʒən, ˈsərkəmˌ-] *n* : circuncisión *f*

circumference [sərˈkʌmpfrənts] *n* : circunferencia *f*

circumspect [ˈsərkəmˌspɛkt] *adj* : circunspecto, prudente

circumstance [ˈsərkəmˌstænts] *n* **1** : circunstancia *f* **2 under no ~s** : bajo ningún concepto

circus [ˈsərkəs] *n* : circo *m*

cistern [ˈsɪstərn] *n* : cisterna *f*

cite [ˈsaɪt] *vt* **cited; citing** : citar — **citation** [saɪˈteɪʃən] *n* : citación *f*

citizen [ˈsɪt̬əzən] *n* : ciudadano *m*, -na *f* — **citizenship** [ˈsɪt̬əzənˌʃɪp] *n* : ciudadanía *f*

citrus [ˈsɪtrəs] *n, pl* **-rus** *or* **-ruses** *or* **~ fruit** : cítrico *m*

city [ˈsɪt̬i] *n, pl* **cities** : ciudad *f*

civic [ˈsɪvɪk] *adj* : cívico — **civics** [ˈsɪvɪks] *ns & pl* : civismo *m*

civil [ˈsɪvəl] *adj* : civil — **civilian** [səˈvɪljən] *n* : civil *mf* — **civility** [səˈvɪlət̬i] *n, pl* **-ties** : cortesía *f* — **civilization** [ˌsɪvələˈzeɪʃən] *n* : civilización *f* — **civilize** [ˈsɪvəˌlaɪz] *vt* **-lized; -lizing** : civilizar

clad [ˈklæd] *adj* **~ in** : vestido de

claim [ˈkleɪm] *vt* **1** DEMAND : reclamar **2** MAINTAIN : afirmar, sostener **3 ~ responsibility** : atribuirse la responsabilidad — **~** *n* **1** DEMAND : demanda *f*, reclamación *f* **2** ASSERTION : afirmación *f*

clam [ˈklæm] *n* : almeja *f*

clamber [ˈklæmbər] *vi* : trepar (con torpeza)

clammy [ˈklæmi] *adj* **-mier; -est** : húmedo y algo frío

clamor [ˈklæmər] *n* : clamor *m* — **~** *vi* : clamar

clamp [ˈklæmp] *n* : abrazadera *f* — **~** *vt* : sujetar con abrazaderas — *vi* **~ down on** : reprimir

clan [ˈklæn] *n* : clan *m*

clandestine [klænˈdɛstɪn] *adj* : clandestino

clang [ˈklæŋ] *n* : ruido *m* metálico

clap [ˈklæp] *v* **clapped; clapping** *vt* **1** : aplaudir **2 ~ one's hands** : dar palmadas — *vi* : aplaudir — **~** *n* : palmada *f*

clarify [ˈklærəˌfaɪ] *vt* **-fied; -fying** : aclarar — **clarification** [ˌklærəfəˈkeɪʃən] *n* : clarificación *f*

clarinet [ˌklærəˈnɛt] *n* : clarinete *m*

clarity [ˈklærət̬i] *n* : claridad *f*

clash [ˈklæʃ] *vi* **1** : chocar, enfrentarse **2** CONFLICT : estar en conflicto — **~** *n* **1** CRASH : choque *m* **2** CONFLICT : conflicto *m*

clasp [ˈklæsp] *n* : broche *m*, cierre *m* — **~** *vt* **1** : abrazar (a una persona), agarrar (una cosa) **2** FASTEN : abrochar

class [ˈklæs] *n* : clase *f*

classic [ˈklæsɪk] *or* **classical** [ˈklæsɪkəl] *adj* : clásico — **classic** *n* : clásico *m*

classify [ˈklæsəˌfaɪ] *vt* **-fied; -fying** : clasificar — **classification** [ˌklæsəfəˈkeɪʃən] *n* : clasificación *f* — **classified** [ˈklæsəˌfaɪd] *adj* RESTRICTED : secreto

classmate [ˈklæsˌmeɪt] *n* : compañero *m*, -ra *f* de clase

classroom [ˈklæsˌruːm] *n* : aula *f*, salón *m* de clase

clatter [ˈklæt̬ər] *vi* : hacer ruido — **~** *n* : estrépito *m*

clause [ˈklɔz] *n* : cláusula *f*

claustrophobia [ˌklɔstrəˈfoːbiə] *n* : claustrofobia *f*

claw [ˈklɔ] *n* : garra *f*, uña *f* (de un gato), pinza *f* (de un crustáceo) — **~** *v* : arañar

clay [ˈkleɪ] *n* : arcilla *f*

clean [ˈkliːn] *adj* **1** : limpio **2** UNADULTERATED : puro **3** SPOTLESS : impecable — **~** *vt* : limpiar — **~** *adv* : limpio — **cleaner** [ˈkliːnər] *n* **1** : limpiador *m*, -dora *f* **2** DRY CLEANER : tintorería *f* — **cleanliness** [ˈklɛnlinəs] *n* : limpieza *f* — **cleanse** [ˈklɛnz] *vt* **cleansed; cleansing** : limpiar, purificar

clear [ˈklɪr] *adj* **1** : claro **2** TRANSPARENT : transparente **3** UNOBSTRUCTED : despejado, libre — **~** *vt* **1** : despejar (una superficie), desatascar (un tubo, etc.) **2** EXONERATE : absolver **3** : saltar por encima de (un obstáculo) **4 ~ the table** : levantar la mesa **5 ~ up** RESOLVE : aclarar, resolver — *vi* **1 ~ up** BRIGHTEN : despejarse (dícese del tiempo, etc.) **2 ~ up** VANISH : desaparecer (dícese de una infección, etc.) — **~** *adv* **1 make oneself ~** : explicarse **2 stand ~!** : ¡aléjate! — **clearance** [ˈklɪrənts] *n* **1** SPACE : espacio *m* (libre) **2** AUTHORIZATION : autorización *f* **3 ~ sale** : liquidación *f* — **clearing** [ˈklɪrɪŋ] *n* : claro *m* — **clearly** [ˈklɪrli] *adv* **1** DISTINCTLY : claramente **2** OBVIOUSLY : obviamente

cleaver [ˈkliːvər] *n* : cuchillo *m* de carnicero

clef [ˈklɛf] *n* : clave *f*

cleft [ˈklɛft] *n* : hendidura *f*, grieta *f*

clement [ˈklɛmənt] *adj* : clemente — **clemency** [ˈklɛməntsi] *n* : clemencia *f*

clench [ˈklɛntʃ] *vt* : apretar

clergy [ˈklərdʒi] *n, pl* **-gies** : clero *m* — **clergyman** [ˈklərdʒimən] *n, pl* **-men** [-mən, -ˌmɛn] : clérigo *m* — **clerical** [ˈklɛrɪkəl] *adj* **1** : clerical **2 ~ work** : trabajo *m* de oficina

clerk [ˈklərk, *Brit* ˈklɑrk] *n* **1** : oficinista *mf*; empleado *m*, -da *f* de oficina **2** SALESPERSON : dependiente *m*, -ta *f*

clever [ˈklɛvər] *adj* **1** SKILLFUL : ingenioso, hábil **2** SMART : listo, inteligente — **cleverly** [ˈklɛvərli] *adv* : ingeniosamente — **cleverness** [ˈklɛvərnəs] *n* **1** SKILL : ingenio *m* **2** INTELLIGENCE : inteligencia *f*

cliché [kliˈʃeɪ] *n* : cliché *m*

click [ˈklɪk] *vt* : chasquear — *vi* **1** : chasquear **2** GET ALONG : llevarse bien — **~** *n* : chasquido *m*

client [ˈklaɪənt] *n* : cliente *m*, -ta *f* — **clientele** [ˌklaɪənˈtɛl, ˌkliː-] *n* : clientela *f*

cliff [ˈklɪf] *n* : acantilado *m*

climate [ˈklaɪmət] *n* : clima *m*

climax [ˈklaɪˌmæks] *n* : clímax *m*, punto *m* culminante

climb [ˈklaɪm] *vt* : escalar, subir a, trepar a — *vi* **1** RISE : subir **2** *or* **~ up** : subirse, treparse — **~** *n* : subida *f*

clinch [ˈklɪntʃ] *vt* : cerrar (un acuerdo, etc.)

cling [ˈklɪŋ] *vi* **clung** [ˈklʌŋ]; **clinging** : adherirse, pegarse

clinic [ˈklɪnɪk] *n* : clínica *f* — **clinical** [ˈklɪnɪkəl] *adj* : clínico

clink [ˈklɪŋk] *vi* : tintinear

clip [ˈklɪp] *vt* **clipped; clipping 1** CUT : cortar, recortar **2** FASTEN : sujetar (con un clip) — **~** *n* **1** FASTENER : clip *m* **2 at a good ~** : a buen trote **3** → **paper clip** — **clippers** [ˈklɪpərz] *npl* **1** : maquinilla *f* para cortar el pelo **2** *or* **nail ~** : cortaúñas *m*

cloak [ˈkloːk] *n* : capa *f*

clock [ˈklɑk] **1** : reloj *m* (de pared) **2 around the ~** : las veinticuatro horas — **clockwise** [ˈklɑkˌwaɪz] *adv & adj* : en el sentido de las agujas del reloj — **clockwork** ['klɑk,wərk] *n* **1** : mecanismo *m* de relojería **2** **like ~** : con precisión

clog ['klɑg] *n* : zueco *m* — **~** *v* **clogged; clogging** *vt* : atascar, obstruir — *vi or* **~ up** : atascarse

cloister ['klɔɪstər] *n* : claustro *m*

close[1] ['klo:z] *v* **closed; closing** *vt* : cerrar — *vi* **1** : cerrarse **2** TERMINATE : terminar **3** **~ in** : acercarse — **~** *n* : final *m*

close[2] ['klo:s] *adj* **closer; closest** **1** NEAR : cercano, próximo **2** INTIMATE : íntimo **3** STRICT : estricto **4** STUFFY : sofocante **5 a ~ game** : un juego reñido — **~** *adv* : cerca, de cerca — **closely** ['klo:sli] *adv* : cerca, de cerca — **closeness** ['klo:snəs] *n* **1** NEARNESS : cercanía *f* **2** INTIMACY : intimidad *f*

closet ['klɑzət] *n* : armario *m*, clóset *m Lat*

closure ['klo:ʒər] *n* : cierre *m*

clot ['klɑt] *n* : coágulo *m* — **~** *v* **clotted; clotting** *vt* : coagular, cuajar — *vi* : coagularse

cloth ['klɔθ] *n, pl* **cloths** ['klɔðz, 'klɔθs] **1** FABRIC : tela *f* **2** RAG : trapo *m*

clothe ['klo:ð] *vt* **clothed** *or* **clad** ['klæd]; **clothing** : vestir — **clothes** ['klo:z, 'klo:ðz] *npl* **1** : ropa *f* **2** **put on one's ~** : vestirse — **clothespin** ['klo:z,pɪn] *n* : pinza *f* (para la ropa) — **clothing** ['klo:ðɪŋ] *n* : ropa *f*

cloud ['klaʊd] *n* : nube *f* — **~** *vt* : nublar — *vi or* **~ over** : nublarse — **cloudy** ['klaʊdi] *adj* **cloudier; -est** : nublado

clout ['klaʊt] *n* **1** BLOW : golpe *m*, tortazo *m fam* **2** INFLUENCE : influencia *f*

clove ['klo:v] *n* **1** : clavo *m* **2** : diente *m* (de ajo)

clover ['klo:vər] *n* : trébol *m*

clown ['klaʊn] *n* : payaso *m*, -sa *f* — **~** *or* **~ around** *vi* : payasear

cloying ['klɔɪɪŋ] *adj* : empalagoso

club ['klʌb] *n* **1** : garrote *m*, porra *f* **2** ASSOCIATION : club *m* **3 ~s** *mpl* : tréboles *mpl* (en los naipes) — **~** *vt* **clubbed; clubbing** : aporrear

cluck ['klʌk] *vi* : cloquear

clue ['klu:] *n* **1** : pista *f*, indicio *m* **2 I haven't got a ~** : no tengo la menor idea

clump ['klʌmp] *n* : grupo *m* (de arbustos)

clumsy ['klʌmzi] *adj* **-sier; -est** : torpe — **clumsiness** ['klʌmzinəs] *n* : torpeza *f*

cluster ['klʌstər] *n* : grupo *m*, racimo *m* (de uvas, etc.) — **~** *vi* : agruparse

clutch ['klʌtʃ] *vt* : agarrar, asir — *vi* **~ at** : tratar de agarrarse de — **~** *n* : embrague *m*, clutch *m Lat* (de un automóvil)

clutter ['klʌṭər] *vt* : llenar desordenadamente — **~** *n* : desorden *m*, revoltijo *m*

coach ['ko:tʃ] *n* **1** CARRIAGE : carruaje *m*, carroza *f* **2** : vagón *m* de pasajeros (de un tren) **3** BUS : autobús *m* **4** : pasaje *m* aéreo de segunda clase **5** TRAINER : entrenador *m*, -dora *f* — *vt* : entrenar (un atleta), dar clases particulares a (un alumno)

coagulate [ko'ægjə,leɪt] *v* **-lated; -lating** *vt* : coagular — *vi* : coagularse

coal ['ko:l] *n* : carbón *m*

coalition [,ko:ə'lɪʃən] *n* : coalición *f*

coarse ['kors] *adj* **coarser; -est** **1** : tosco, basto **2** CRUDE, VULGAR : grosero, ordinario — **coarseness** ['korsnəs] *n* : aspereza *f*, tosquedad *f*

coast ['ko:st] *n* : costa *f* — **~** *vi* : ir en punto muerto (dícese de un automóvil), deslizarse (dícese de una bicicleta) — **coastal** ['ko:stəl] *adj* : costero

coaster ['ko:stər] *n* : posavasos *m*

coast guard *n* : guardacostas *mpl*

coastline ['ko:st,laɪn] *n* : litoral *m*

coat ['ko:t] *n* **1** : abrigo *m* **2** : pelaje *m* (de un animal) **3** : mano *f* (de pintura) — **~** *vt* : cubrir, revestir — **coating** ['ko:ṭɪŋ] *n* : capa *f* — **coat of arms** *n* : escudo *m* de armas

coax ['ko:ks] *vt* : engatusar

cob ['kɑb] → **corncob**

cobblestone ['kɑbəl,sto:n] *n* : adoquín *m*

cobweb ['kɑb,wɛb] *n* : telaraña *f*

cocaine [ko:'keɪn, 'ko:,keɪn] *n* : cocaína *f*

cock ['kɑk] *n* **1** ROOSTER : gallo *m* **2** FAUCET : grifo *m* **3** : martillo *m* (de un arma de fuego) — **~** *vt* **1** : amartillar (un arma de fuego) **2 ~ one's head** : ladear la cabeza — **cockeyed** ['kɑk,aɪd] *adj* **1** ASKEW : ladeado **2** ABSURD : absurdo

cockpit ['kɑk,pɪt] *n* : cabina *f*

cockroach ['kɑk,ro:tʃ] *n* : cucaracha *f*

cocktail ['kɑk,teɪl] *n* : coctel *m*, cóctel *m*

cocky ['kɑki] *adj* **cockier; -est** : engreído, arrogante

cocoa ['ko:,ko:] *n* **1** : cacao *m* **2** : chocolate *m* (bebida)

coconut ['ko:kə,nʌt] *n* : coco *m*

cocoon [kə'ku:n] *n* : capullo *m*

cod ['kɑd] *ns & pl* : bacalao *m*

coddle ['kɑdəl] *vt* **-dled; -dling** : mimar

code ['ko:d] *n* : código *m*

coeducational [,ko:,ɛdʒə'keɪʃənəl] *adj* : mixto

coerce [ko'ərs] *vt* **-erced; -ercing** : coaccionar, forzar — **coercion** [ko'ərʒən, -ʃən] *n* : coacción *f*

coffee ['kɔfi] *n* : café *m* — **coffeepot** ['kɔfi,pɑt] *n* : cafetera *f*

coffer ['kɔfər] *n* : cofre *m*

coffin ['kɔfən] *n* : ataúd *m*, féretro *m*

cog ['kɑg] *n* : diente *m* (de una rueda)

cogent ['ko:dʒənt] *adj* : convincente, persuasivo

cognac ['ko:n,jæk] *n* : coñac *m*

cogwheel ['kɑg,hwi:l] *n* : rueda *f* dentada

coherent [ko'hɪrənt] *adj* : coherente

coil ['kɔɪl] *vt* : enrollar — *vi* : enrollarse — **~** *n* **1** ROLL : rollo *m* **2** : tirabuzón *m* (de pelo), espiral *f* (de humo)

coin ['kɔɪn] *n* : moneda *f* — **~** *vt* : acuñar

coincide [,ko:ɪn'saɪd, 'ko:ɪn,saɪd] *vi* **-cided; -ciding** : coincidir — **coincidence** [ko'ɪntsədənts] *n* : coincidencia *f*, casualidad *f* — **coincidental** [ko,ɪntsə'dɛntəl] *adj* : casual, fortuito

coke ['ko:k] *n* : coque *m* (combustible)

colander ['kʌləndər, 'kɑ-] *n* : colador *m*

cold ['ko:ld] *adj* **1** : frío **2 be ~** : tener frío **3 it's ~ today** : hace frío hoy — **~** *n* **1** : frío *m* **2** : resfriado *m* (en medicina) **3 catch a ~** : resfriarse

coleslaw ['ko:l,slɔ] *n* : ensalada *f* de col

colic ['kɑlɪk] *n* : cólico *m*

collaborate [kə'læbə,reɪt] *vi* **-rated; -rating** : colaborar — **collaboration** [kə,læbə'reɪʃən] *n* : colaboración *f* — **collaborator** [kə'læbə,reɪṭər] *n* : colaborador *m*, -dora *f*

collapse [kə'læps] *vi* **-lapsed; -lapsing** **1** : derrumbarse, hundirse **2** : sufrir un colapso (físico o mental) — **~** *n* **1** FALL : derrumbamiento *m* **2** BREAKDOWN : colapso *m* — **collapsible** [kə'læpsəbəl] *adj* : plegable

collar ['kɑlər] *n* : cuello *m* (de camisa, etc.), collar *m* (para animales) — **collarbone** ['kɑlər,bo:n] *n* : clavícula *f*

colleague ['kɑ,li:g] *n* : colega *mf*

collect [kə'lɛkt] *vt* **1** GATHER : reunir **2** : coleccionar, juntar (timbres, etc.) **3** : recaudar (fondos, etc.) — *vi* **1** ACCUMULATE : acumularse, juntarse **2** CONGREGATE : congregarse, reunirse — **~** *adv* **call ~** : llamar a cobro revertido, llamar por cobrar *Lat* — **collection** [kə'lɛkʃən] *n* **1** : colección *f* **2** : colecta *f* (de contribuciones) — **collective** [kə'lɛktɪv] *adj* : colectivo — **collector** [kə'lɛktər] *n* **1** : coleccionista *mf* **2** : cobrador *m*, -dora *f* (de deudas)

college ['kɑlɪdʒ] *n* **1** : instituto *m* (a nivel universitario) **2** : colegio *m* (electoral, etc.)

collide [kə'laɪd] *vi* **-lided; -liding** : chocar, colisionar — **collision** [kə'lɪʒən] *n* : choque *m*, colisión *f*

colloquial [kə'lo:kwiəl] *adj* : coloquial, familiar

cologne [kə'lo:n] *n* : colonia *f*

Colombian [kə'lʌmbiən] *adj* : colombiano

colon[1] ['ko:lən] *n, pl* **colons** *or* **cola** [-lə] : colon *m* (en anatomía)

colon[2] *n, pl* **colons** : dos puntos *mpl* (signo de puntuación)

colonel ['kərnəl] *n* : coronel *m*

colony ['kɑləni] *n, pl* **-nies** : colonia *f* — **colonial** [kə'lo:niəl] *adj* : colonial — **colonize** ['kɑlə,naɪz] *vt* **-nized; -nizing** : colonizar

color *or Brit* **colour** ['kʌlər] *n* : color *m* — **~** *vt* : colorear, pintar — *vi* BLUSH : sonrojarse — **color–blind** *or Brit* **colour-blind** ['kʌlər,blaɪnd] *adj* : daltónico — **colored** *or Brit* **coloured** ['kʌlərd] *adj* : de color — **colorful** *or Brit* **colourful** ['kʌlərfəl] *adj* **1** : de vivos colores **2** PICTURESQUE : pintoresco — **colorless** *or Brit* **colourless** ['kʌlərləs] *adj* : incoloro

colossal [kə'lɑsəl] *adj* : colosal

colt ['ko:lt] *n* : potro *m*

column ['kɑləm] *n* : columna *f* — **columnist** ['kɑləmnɪst, -ləmɪst] *n* : columnista *mf*

coma ['ko:mə] *n* : coma *m*

comb ['ko:m] *n* **1** : peine *m* **2** : cresta *f* (de un gallo) — **~** *vt* : peinar

combat ['kɑm,bæt] *n* : combate *m* — **~** [kəm'bæt, 'kɑm,bæt] *vt* **-bated** *or* **-batted; -bating** *or* **-batting** : combatir — **combatant** [kəm'bætənt] *n* : combatiente *mf*

combine [kəm'baɪn] *v* **-bined; -bining** *vt* : combinar — *vi* : combinarse — **~** ['kɑm,baɪn] *n* HARVESTER : cosechadora *f* — **combination** [,kɑmbə'neɪʃən] *n* : combinación *f*

combustion [kəm'bʌstʃən] *n* : combustión *f*

come ['kʌm] *vi* **came** ['keɪm]; **come; coming** **1** : venir **2** ARRIVE : llegar **3 ~ about** : suceder **4 ~ back** : regresar, volver **5 ~ from** : venir de, provenir de **6 ~ in** : entrar **7 ~ out** : salir **8 ~ to** REVIVE : volver en sí **9 ~ on!** : ¡ándale! **10 ~ up** OCCUR : surgir **11 how ~?** : ¿por qué? — **comeback** ['kʌm,bæk] *n* **1** RETURN : retorno *m* **2** RETORT : réplica *f*

comedy ['kɑmədi] *n, pl* **-dies** : comedia *f* — **comedian** [kə'mi:diən] *n* : cómico *m*, -ca *f*

comet ['kɑmət] *n* : cometa *m*

comfort ['kʌmpfərt] *vt* : consolar — **~** *n* **1** : comodidad *f* **2** SOLACE : consuelo *m* — **comfortable** ['kʌmpfərṭəbəl, 'kʌmpftə-] *adj* : cómodo

comic ['kɑmɪk] *or* **comical** ['kɑmɪkəl] *adj* : cómico — **~** *n* **1** COMEDIAN : cómico *m*, -ca *f* **2** *or* **~ book** : revista *f* de historietas, cómic *m* — **comic strip** *n* : tira *f* cómica, historieta *f*

coming ['kʌmɪŋ] *adj* : próximo, que viene

comma ['kɑmə] *n* : coma *f*

command [kə'mænd] *vt* **1** ORDER : ordenar, mandar **2** : estar al mando de (un barco, etc.) **3 ~ respect** : inspirar (el) respeto — *vi* : dar órdenes — **~** *n* **1** ORDER : orden *f* **2** LEADERSHIP : mando *m* **3** MASTERY : maestría *f*, dominio *m* — **commander** [kə'mændər] *n* : comandante *mf* — **commandment** [kə'mændmənt] *n* : mandamiento *m*

commemorate [kə'mɛmə,reɪt] *vt* **-rated; -rating** : conmemorar — **commemoration** [kə,mɛmə'reɪʃən] *n* : conmemoración *f*

commence [kə'mɛnts] *v* **-menced; -mencing** : comenzar, empezar — **commencement** [kə'mɛntsmənt] *n* **1** BEGINNING : comienzo *m* **2** GRADUATION : ceremonia *f* de graduación

commend [kə'mɛnd] *vt* **1** ENTRUST : encomendar **2** PRAISE : alabar — **commendable** [kə'mɛndəbəl] *adj* : loable

comment ['kɑ,mɛnt] *n* : comentario *m*, observación *f* — **~** *vi* : hacer comentarios — **commentary** ['kɑmən,tɛri] *n, pl* **-taries** : comentario *m* — **commentator** ['kɑmən,teɪṭər] *n* : comentarista *mf*

commerce ['kɑmərs] *n* : comercio *m* — **commercial** [kə'mərʃəl] *adj* : comercial — **~** *n* : anuncio *m*, aviso *m Lat* — **commercialize** [kə'mərʃə,laɪz] *vt* **-ized; -izing** : comercializar

commiserate [kə'mɪzə,reɪt] *vi* **-ated; -ating** : compadecerse

commission [kə'mɪʃən] *n* : comisión *f* — **~** *vt* : encargar (una obra de arte) — **commissioner** [kə'mɪʃənər] *n* : comisario *m*, -ria *f*

commit [kə'mɪt] *vt* **-mitted; -mitting** **1** ENTRUST : confiar **2** : cometer (un crimen) **3** : internar (a algn en un hospital) **4 ~ oneself** : comprometerse **5 ~ to memory** : aprender de memoria — **commitment** [kə'mɪtmənt] *n* : compromiso *m*

committee [kə'mɪṭi] *n* : comité *m*, comisión *f*

commodity [kə'mɑdəṭi] *n, pl* **-ties** : artículo *m* de comercio, producto *m*

common ['kɑmən] *adj* **1** : común **2** ORDINARY : ordinario, común y corriente — **~** *n* **in ~** : en común — **commonly** ['kɑmənli] *adv* : comúnmente — **commonplace** ['kɑmən,pleɪs] *adj* : común, banal — **common sense** *n* : sentido *m* común

commotion [kə'mo:ʃən] *n* : alboroto *m*, jaleo *m*

commune[1] ['kɑ,mju:n, kə'mju:n] *n* : comuna *f* — **communal** [kə'mju:nəl] *adj* : comunal

commune[2] [kə'mju:n] *vi* **-muned; -muning** **~ with** : comunicarse con

communicate [kə'mju:nə,keɪt] *v* **-cated; -cating** *vt* : comunicar — *vi* : comunicarse — **communicable** [kə'mju:nɪkəbəl] *adj* : transmisible — **communication** [kə,mju:nə'keɪʃən] *n* : comunicación *f* — **communicative** [kə'mju:nɪ,keɪṭɪv, -kəṭɪv] *adj* : comunicativo

communion [kə'mju:njən] *n* : comunión *f*

Communism ['kɑmjə,nɪzəm] *n* : comunismo *m* — **Communist** ['kɑmjə,nɪst] *adj* : comunista — **~** *n* : comunista *mf*

community [kə'mju:nəṭi] *n, pl* **-ties** : comunidad *f*

commute [kə'mju:t] *v* **-muted; -muting** *vt* : conmutar, reducir (una sentencia) — *vi* : viajar de la residencia al trabajo

compact [kəm'pækt, 'kɑm,pækt] *adj* : compacto — **~** ['kɑm,pækt] *n* **1** *or* **~ car** : auto *m* compacto **2** *or* **powder ~** : polvera *f* — **compact disc** ['kɑm,pækt'dɪsk] *n* : disco *m* compacto

companion [kəm'pænjən] *n* : compañero *m*, -ra *f* — **companionship** [kəm'pænjən,ʃɪp] *n* : compañerismo *m*

company ['kʌmpəni] *n, pl* **-nies** **1** : compañía *f* **2** GUESTS : visita *f*

compare [kəm'pær] *v* **-pared; -paring** *vt* : comparar — *vi* **~ with** : poderse comparar con — **comparable** ['kɑmpərəbəl] *adj* : comparable — **comparative** [kəm'pærəṭɪv] *adj* : comparativo, relativo — **comparison** [kəm'pærəsən] *n* : comparación *f*

compartment [kəm'pɑrtmənt] *n* : compartimento *m*

compass ['kʌmpəs, 'kɑm-] *n* **1** : compás *m* **2 points of the ~** : puntos *mpl* cardinales

compassion [kəm'pæʃən] *n* : compasión *f* — **compassionate** [kəm'pæʃənət] *adj* : compasivo

compatible [kəm'pæṭəbəl] *adj* : compatible, afín — **compatibility** [kəm,pæṭə'bɪləṭi] *n* : compatibilidad *f*

compel [kəm'pɛl] *vt* **-pelled; -pelling** : obligar — **compelling** [kəm'pɛlɪŋ] *adj* : convincente

compensate ['kɑmpən,seɪt] *v* **-sated; -sating** *vi* **~ for** : compensar — *vt* : indemnizar, compensar — **compensation** [,kɑmpən'seɪʃən] *n* : compensación *f*, indemnización *f*

compete [kəm'pi:t] *vi* **-peted; -peting** : competir — **competent** ['kɑmpəṭənt] *adj* : competente — **competition** [,kɑmpə'tɪʃən] *n* **1** : competencia *f* **2** CONTEST : concurso *m* — **competitor** [kəm'pɛṭəṭər] *n* : competidor *m*, -dora *f*

compile [kəm'paɪl] *vt* **-piled; -piling** : compilar, recopilar

complacency [kəm'pleɪsəntsi] *n* : satisfacción *f* consigo mismo — **complacent** [kəm'pleɪsənt] *adj* : satisfecho de sí mismo

complain [kəm'pleɪn] *vi* : quejarse — **complaint** [kəm'pleɪnt] *n* **1** : queja *f* **2** AILMENT : enfermedad *f*

complement ['kɑmpləmənt] *n* : complemento *m* — **~** ['kɑmplə,mɛnt] *vt* : complementar — **complementary** [,kɑmplə'mɛntəri] *adj* : complementario

complete [kəm'pli:t] *adj* **-pleter; -est** **1** WHOLE : completo, entero **2** FINISHED : terminado **3** TOTAL : total — **~** *vt* **-pleted; -pleting** : completar — **completion** [kəm'pli:ʃən] *n* : conclusión *f*

complex [kɑm'plɛks, kəm-; 'kɑm,plɛks] *adj* : complejo — **~** ['kɑm,plɛks] *n* : complejo *m*

complexion [kəm'plɛkʃən] *n* : cutis *m*, tez *f*

complexity [kəm'plɛksəṭi, kɑm-] *n, pl* **-ties** : complejidad *f*

compliance [kəm'plaɪənts] *n* **1** : acatamiento *m* **2 in ~ with** : conforme a — **compliant** [kəm'plaɪənt] *adj* : sumiso

complicate ['kɑmplə,keɪt] *vt* **-cated; -cating** : complicar — **complicated** ['kɑmplə,keɪṭəd] *adj* : complicado — **complication** [,kɑmplə'keɪʃən] *n* : complicación *f*

compliment ['kɑmpləmənt] *n* **1** : cumplido *m* **2 ~s** *npl* : saludos *mpl* — **~** ['kɑmplə,mɛnt] *vt* : felicitar — **complimentary** [,kɑmplə'mɛntəri] *adj* **1** FLATTERING : halagador, halagüeño **2** FREE : de cortesía, gratis

comply [kəm'plaɪ] *vi* **-plied; -plying** **~ with** : cumplir, obedecer

component [kəm'po:nənt, 'kɑm,po:-] *n* : componente *m*

compose [kəm'po:z] *vt* **-posed; -posing** **1** : componer **2 ~ oneself** : serenarse — **composer** [kəm'po:zər] *n* : compositor *m*, -tora *f* — **composition** [,kɑmpə'zɪʃən] *n* **1** : composición *f* **2** ESSAY : ensayo *m* — **composure** [kəm'po:ʒər] *n* : calma *f*

compound[1] [kɑm'paʊnd, kəm-; 'kɑm,paʊnd] *vt* **1** COMPOSE : componer **2** : agravar (un problema, etc.) — **~** ['kɑm,paʊnd; kɑm'paʊnd, kəm-] *adj* : compuesto — **~** ['kɑm,paʊnd] *n* : compuesto *m*

compound[2] ['kɑm,paʊnd] *n* ENCLOSURE : recinto *m*

comprehend [,kɑmprɪ'hɛnd] *vt* : comprender — **comprehension** [,kɑmprɪ'hɛntʃən] *n* : comprensión *f* — **comprehensive** [,kɑmprɪ'hɛntsɪv] *adj* **1** INCLUSIVE : inclusivo **2** BROAD : amplio

compress [kəm'prɛs] *vt* : comprimir — **compression** [kəm'prɛʃən] *n* : compresión *f*

comprise [kəm'praɪz] *vt* **-prised; -prising** : comprender

compromise ['kɑmprə,maɪz] *n* : acuerdo *m*, arreglo *m* — **~** *v* **-mised; -mising** *vi* : llegar a un acuerdo — *vt* : comprometer

compulsion [kəm'pʌlʃən] *n* **1** COERCION : coacción *f* **2** URGE : impulso *m* — **compulsive** [kəm'pʌlsɪv] *adj* : compulsivo — **compulsory** [kəm'pʌlsəri] *adj* : obligatorio

compute [kəm'pju:t] *vt* **-puted; -puting** : computar — **computer** [kəm'pju:ṭər] *n* : computadora *f*, computador *m*, ordenador *m Spain* — **computerize** [kəm'pju:ṭə,raɪz] *vt* **-ized; -izing** : informatizar

comrade ['kɑm,ræd] *n* : camarada *mf*

con ['kɑn] *vt* **conned; conning** : estafar — **~** *n* **1** SWINDLE : estafa *f* **2 the pros and ~s** : los pros y los contras

concave [kɑn'keɪv, 'kɑn,keɪv] *adj* : cóncavo

conceal [kən'si:l] *vt* : ocultar

concede [kən'si:d] *vt* **-ceded; -ceding** : conceder, admitir

conceit [kən'si:t] *n* : vanidad *f* — **conceited** [kən'si:ṭəd] *adj* : engreído

conceive [kən'si:v] *v* **-ceived; -ceiving** *vt* : concebir — *vi* **~ of** : concebir — **conceivable** [kən'si:vəbəl] *adj* : concebible

concentrate ['kɑntsən,treɪt] *v* **-trated; -trating** *vt* : concentrar — *vi* : concentrarse — **concentration** [,kɑntsən'treɪʃən] *n* : concentración *f*

concept ['kɑn,sɛpt] *n* : concepto *m* — **conception** [kən'sɛpʃən] *n* : concepción *f*

concern [kən'sərn] *vt* **1** : concernir **2 ~ oneself about** : preocuparse por — **~** *n* **1** AFFAIR : asunto *m* **2** WORRY : preocupación *f* **3** BUSINESS : negocio *m* — **concerned** [kən'sərnd] *adj* **1** ANXIOUS : ansioso **2 as far as I'm ~** : en cuanto a mí — **concerning** [kən'sərnɪŋ] *prep* : con respecto a

concert ['kɑn,sərt] *n* : concierto *m* — **concerted** [kən'sərṭəd] *adj* : concertado

concession [kən'sɛʃən] *n* : concesión *f*

concise [kən'saɪs] *adj* : conciso

conclude [kən'klu:d] *v* **-cluded; -cluding** : concluir — **conclusion** [kən'klu:ʒən] *n* : conclusión *f* — **conclusive** [kən'klu:sɪv] *adj* : concluyente

concoct [kən'kɑkt, kɑn-] *vt* **1** PREPARE : confeccionar **2** DEVISE : inventarse, tramar — **concoction** [kən'kakʃən] n : mezcla f, brebaje m

concourse ['kan,kors] n : vestíbulo m, salón m

concrete [kan'kriːt, 'kan,kriːt] adj : concreto — ~ ['kan,kriːt, kan'kriːt] n : hormigón m, concreto m Lat

concur [kən'kər] vi **concurred; concurring** AGREE : estar de acuerdo

concussion [kən'kʌʃən] n : conmoción f cerebral

condemn [kən'dɛm] vt : condenar — **condemnation** [,kan,dɛm'neɪʃən] n : condenación f

condense [kən'dɛnts] v **-densed; -densing** vt : condensar — vi : condensarse — **condensation** [,kan,dɛn'seɪʃən, -dən-] n : condensación f

condescending [,kandi'sɛndɪŋ] adj : condescendiente

condiment ['kandəmənt] n : condimento m

condition [kən'dɪʃən] n 1 : condición f 2 **in good** ~ : en buen estado — **conditional** [kən'dɪʃənəl] adj : condicional

condolences [kən'doːləntsəz] npl : pésame m

condom ['kandəm] n : condón m

condominium [,kandə'mɪniəm] n, pl **-ums** : condominio m Lat

condone [kən'doːn] vt **-doned; -doning** : aprobar

conducive [kən'duːsɪv, -'djuː-] adj : propicio, favorable

conduct ['kan,dʌkt] n : conducta f — ~ [kən'dʌkt] vt 1 DIRECT, GUIDE : conducir, dirigir 2 CARRY OUT : llevar a cabo 3 ~ **oneself** : conducirse, comportarse — **conductor** [kən'dʌktər] n : revisor m, -sora f (en un tren); cobrador m, -dora f (en un autobús); director m, -tora f (de una orquesta)

cone ['koːn] n 1 : cono m 2 or **ice-cream** ~ : cucurucho m, barquillo m Lat

confection [kən'fɛkʃən] n : dulce m

confederation [kən,fɛdə'reɪʃən] n : confederación f

confer [kən'fər] v **-ferred; -ferring** vt : conferir, otorgar — vi ~ **with** : consultar — **conference** ['kanfrənts, -fərənts] n : conferencia f

confess [kən'fɛs] vt : confesar — vi 1 : confesarse 2 ~ **to** : confesar, admitir — **confession** [kən'fɛʃən] n : confesión f

confetti [kən'fɛţi] n : confeti m

confide [kən'faɪd] v **-fided; -fiding** : confiar — **confidence** ['kanfədənts] n 1 TRUST : confianza f 2 SELF-ASSURANCE : confianza f en sí mismo 3 SECRET : confidencia f — **confident** ['kanfədənt] adj 1 SURE : seguro 2 SELF-ASSURED : confiado, seguro de sí mismo — **confidential** [,kanfə'dɛntʃəl] adj : confidencial

confine [kən'faɪn] vt **-fined; -fining** 1 LIMIT : confinar, limitar 2 IMPRISON : encerrar — **confines** ['kan,faɪnz] npl : confines mpl

confirm [kən'fərm] vt : confirmar — **confirmation** [,kanfər'meɪʃən] n : confirmación f — **confirmed** adj : inveterado

confiscate ['kanfə,skeɪt] vt **-cated; -cating** : confiscar

conflict ['kan,flɪkt] n : conflicto m — ~ [kən'flɪkt] vi : estar en conflicto, oponerse

conform [kən'fɔrm] vi 1 COMPLY : ajustarse 2 ~ **with** : corresponder a — **conformity** [kən'fɔrməţi] n, pl **-ties** : conformidad f

confound [kən'faʊnd, kan-] vt : confundir, desconcertar

confront [kən'frʌnt] vt : afrontar, encarar — **confrontation** [,kanfrən'teɪʃən] n : confrontación f

confuse [kən'fjuːz] vt **-fused; -fusing** : confundir — **confusing** [kən'fjuːzɪŋ] adj : confuso, desconcertante — **confusion** [kən'fjuːʒən] n : confusión f, desconcierto m

congeal [kən'dʒiːl] vi : coagularse

congenial [kən'dʒiːniəl] adj : agradable

congested [kən'dʒɛstəd] adj : congestionado — **congestion** [kən'dʒɛstʃən] n : congestión f

congratulate [kən'grædʒə,leɪt, -'grætʃə-] vt **-lated; -lating** : felicitar — **congratulations** [kən,grædʒə'leɪʃən, -,grætʃə-] npl : felicitaciones fpl

congregate ['kaŋgrɪ,geɪt] vi **-gated; -gating** : congregarse — **congregation** [,kaŋgrɪ'geɪʃən] n : feligreses mpl (en religión)

congress ['kaŋgrəs] n : congreso m — **congressional** [kən'grɛʃənəl, kan-] adj : del congreso — **congressman** ['kaŋgrəsmən] n, pl **-men** [-mən, -,mɛn] : congresista mf

conjecture [kən'dʒɛktʃər] n : conjetura f, presunción f — ~ v **-tured; -turing** vt : conjeturar — vi : hacer conjeturas

conjugal ['kandʒɪgəl, kən'dʒuː-] adj : conyugal

conjugate ['kandʒə,geɪt] vt **-gated; -gating** : conjugar — **conjugation** [,kandʒə'geɪʃən] n : conjugación f

conjunction [kən'dʒʌŋkʃən] n 1 : conjunción f 2 **in** ~ **with** : en combinación con

conjure [kan'dʒər, 'kʌn-] v **-jured; -juring** : hacer juegos de manos — vt or ~ **up** : evocar

connect [kə'nɛkt] vi : conectarse — vt 1 JOIN : conectar, juntar 2 ASSOCIATE : asociar — **connection** [kə'nɛkʃən] n 1

: conexión f 2 : enlace m (con un tren, etc.) 3 ~ **s** npl : relaciones fpl (personas)

connoisseur [,kanə'sər, -'sʊr] n : conocedor m, -dora f

connote [kə'noːt] vt **-noted; -noting** : connotar, implicar

conquer ['kaŋkər] vt : conquistar — **conqueror** ['kaŋkərər] n : conquistador m, -dora f (en un conquest) — **conquest** ['kan,kwɛst, 'kaŋ-] n : conquista f

conscience ['kantʃənts] n : conciencia f — **conscientious** [,kantʃi'ɛntʃəs] adj : concienzudo

conscious ['kantʃəs] adj 1 AWARE : consciente 2 INTENTIONAL : intencional — **consciously** adv : deliberadamente — **consciousness** ['kantʃəsnəs] n 1 AWARENESS : consciencia f 2 **lose** ~ : perder el conocimiento

consecrate ['kantsə,kreɪt] vt **-crated; -crating** : consagrar — **consecration** [,kantsə'kreɪʃən] n : consagración f

consecutive [kən'sɛkjəţɪv] adj : consecutivo, sucesivo

consensus [kən'sɛntsəs] n : consenso m

consent [kən'sɛnt] vi : consentir — ~ n : consentimiento m

consequence ['kantsə,kwɛnts, -kwənts] n 1 : consecuencia f 2 **of no** ~ : sin importancia — **consequent** ['kantsə,kwant, -kwɛnt] adj : consiguiente — **consequently** ['kantsə,kwantli, -,kwɛnt] adv : por consiguiente

conserve [kən'sərv] vt **-served; -serving** : conservar, preservar — **conservation** [,kantsər'veɪʃən] n : conservación f — **conservative** [kən'sərvəţɪv] adj 1 : conservador 2 CAUTIOUS : moderado, prudente — ~ n : conservador m, -dora f — **conservatory** [kən'sərvə,tori] n, pl **-ries** : conservatorio m

consider [kən'sɪdər] vt 1 : considerar 2 **all things considered** : teniéndolo todo en cuenta — **considerable** [kən'sɪdərəbəl] adj : considerable — **considerate** [kən'sɪdərət] adj : considerado — **consideration** [kən,sɪdə'reɪʃən] n 1 : consideración f 2 **take into** ~ : tener en cuenta — **considering** [kən'sɪdərɪŋ] prep : teniendo en cuenta

consign [kən'saɪn] vt 1 : relegar 2 SEND : enviar — **consignment** [kən'saɪnmənt] n : envío m

consist [kən'sɪst] vi 1 ~ **in** : consistir en 2 ~ **of** : constar de, componerse de — **consistency** [kən'sɪstəntsi] n, pl **-cies** 1 TEXTURE : consistencia f 2 COHERENCE : coherencia f 3 UNIFORMITY : regularidad f — **consistent** [kən'sɪstənt] adj 1 UNCHANGING : constante, regular 2 ~ **with** : consecuente con

console [kən'soːl] vt **-soled; -soling** : consolar — **consolation** [,kantsə'leɪʃən] n 1 : consuelo m 2 ~ **prize** : premio m de consolación

consolidate [kən'salə,deɪt] vt **-dated; -dating** : consolidar — **consolidation** [kən,salə'deɪʃən] n : consolidación f

consonant ['kantsənənt] n : consonante f

conspicuous [kən'spɪkjuəs] adj 1 OBVIOUS : visible, evidente 2 STRIKING : llamativo — **conspicuously** [kən'spɪkjuəsli] adv : de manera llamativa

conspire [kən'spaɪr] vi **-spired; -spiring** : conspirar — **conspiracy** [kən'spɪrəsi] n, pl **-cies** : conspiración f

constant ['kantstənt] adj : constante — **constantly** ['kantstəntli] adv : constantemente

constellation [,kantstə'leɪʃən] n : constelación f

constipated ['kantstə,peɪtəd] adj : estreñido — **constipation** [,kantstə'peɪʃən] n : estreñimiento m

constituent [kən'stɪtʃuənt] n 1 COMPONENT : componente m 2 VOTER : elector m, -tora f; votante mf

constitute ['kantstə,tuːt, -,tjuːt] vt **-tuted; -tuting** : constituir — **constitution** [,kantstə'tuːʃən, -,tjuː-] n : constitución f — **constitutional** [,kantstə'tuːʃənəl, -,tjuː-] adj : constitucional

constraint [kən'streɪnt] n : restricción f, limitación f

construct [kən'strʌkt] vt : construir — **construction** [kən'strʌkʃən] n : construcción f — **constructive** [kən'strʌktɪv] adj : constructivo

construe [kən'struː] vt **-strued; -struing** : interpretar

consul ['kantsəl] n : cónsul mf — **consulate** ['kantsələt] n : consulado m

consult [kən'sʌlt] v : consultar — **consultant** [kən'sʌltənt] n : asesor m, -sora f; consultor m, -tora f — **consultation** [,kantsəl'teɪʃən] n : consulta f

consume [kən'suːm] vt **-sumed; -suming** : consumir — **consumer** [kən'suːmər] n : consumidor m, -dora f — **consumption** [kən'sʌmpʃən] n : consumo m

contact ['kan,tækt] n : contacto m — ~ ['kan,tækt, kən-] vt : ponerse en contacto con — **contact lens** ['kan,tækt'lɛnz] : lente mf (de contacto)

contagious [kən'teɪdʒəs] adj : contagioso

contain [kən'teɪn] vt 1 : contener 2 ~ **one-**

self : contenerse — **container** [kən'teɪnər] n : recipiente m, envase m

contaminate [kən'tæmə,neɪt] vt **-nated; -nating** : contaminar — **contamination** [kən,tæmə'neɪʃən] n : contaminación f

contemplate ['kantəm,pleɪt] v **-plated; -plating** vt 1 : contemplar 2 CONSIDER : considerar, pensar en — vi : reflexionar — **contemplation** [,kantəm'pleɪʃən] n : contemplación f

contemporary [kən'tɛmpə,rɛri] adj : contemporáneo — ~ n, pl **-raries** : contemporáneo m, -nea f

contempt [kən'tɛmpt] n : desprecio m — **contemptible** [kən'tɛmptəbəl] adj : despreciable — **contemptuous** [kən'tɛmptʃuəs] adj : desdeñoso

contend [kən'tɛnd] vi 1 COMPETE : contender, competir 2 ~ **with** : enfrentarse a — vt : sostener, afirmar — **contender** [kən'tɛndər] n : contendiente mf

content¹ ['kan,tɛnt] n 1 : contenido m 2 **table of** ~ **s** : índice m de materias

content² [kən'tɛnt] adj : contento — ~ vt ~ **oneself with** : contentarse con — **contented** [kən'tɛntəd] adj : satisfecho, contento

contention [kən'tɛntʃən] n 1 DISPUTE : disputa f 2 OPINION : argumento m, opinión f

contentment [kən'tɛntmənt] n : satisfacción f

contest [kən'tɛst] vt : disputar — ~ ['kan,tɛst] n 1 STRUGGLE : contienda f 2 COMPETITION : concurso m, competencia f — **contestant** [kən'tɛstənt] n : concursante mf, contendiente mf

context ['kan,tɛkst] n : contexto m

continent ['kantənənt] n : continente m — **continental** [,kantən'ɛntəl] adj : continental

contingency [kən'tɪndʒəntsi] n, pl **-cies** : contingencia f

continue [kən'tɪnjuː] v **-tinued; -tinuing** vt 1 : continuar — **continual** [kən'tɪnjuəl] adj : continuo, constante — **continuation** [kən,tɪnjuː'eɪʃən] n : continuación f — **continuity** [,kantən'uːəţi, -'juː-] n, pl **-ties** : continuidad f — **continuous** [kən'tɪnjuəs] adj : continuo

contort [kən'tɔrt] vt : retorcer — **contortion** [kən'tɔrʃən] n : contorsión f

contour ['kan,tʊr] n 1 : contorno m 2 or ~ **line** : curva f de nivel

contraband ['kantrə,bænd] n : contrabando m

contraception [,kantrə'sɛpʃən] n : anticoncepción f — **contraceptive** [,kantrə'sɛptɪv] adj : anticonceptivo — ~ n : anticonceptivo m

contract [kən'trækt] n : contrato m — ~ [kən'trækt] vt : contraer — vi : contraerse — **contraction** [kən'trækʃən] n : contracción f — **contractor** ['kan,træktər, kən'træk-] n : contratista mf

contradiction [,kantrə'dɪkʃən] n : contradicción f — **contradict** [,kantrə'dɪkt] vt : contradecir — **contradictory** [,kantrə'dɪktəri] adj : contradictorio

contraption [kən'træpʃən] n : artilugio m, artefacto m

contrary [kən'trɛri] n, pl **-traries** 1 : contrario 2 **on the** ~ : al contrario — ~ ['kan,trɛri] adj 1 : contrario, opuesto 2 ~ **to** : en contra de

contrast [kən'træst] v : contrastar — ~ ['kan,træst] n : contraste m

contribute [kən'trɪbjət] v **-uted; -uting** vt : contribuir — **contribution** [,kantrə'bjuːʃən] n : contribución f — **contributor** [kən'trɪbjəţər] n 1 : contribuyente mf 2 : colaborador m, -dora f (en periodismo)

contrite [kən'traɪt, 'kan,traɪt] adj : arrepentido

contrive [kən'traɪv] vt **-trived; -triving** 1 DEVISE : idear 2 ~ **to do sth** : lograr hacer algo

control [kən'troːl] vt **-trolled; -trolling** : controlar — ~ n 1 : control m 2 ~ **s** npl : mandos mpl

controversy ['kantrə,vərsi] n, pl **-sies** : controversia f — **controversial** [,kantrə'vərʃəl, -siəl] adj : polémico

convalescence [,kanvə'lɛsənts] n : convalecencia f — **convalescent** [,kanvə'lɛsənt] adj : convaleciente — ~ n : convaleciente mf

convene [kən'viːn] v **-vened; -vening** vt : convocar — vi : reunirse

convenience [kən'viːnjənts] n : conveniencia f, comodidad f — **convenient** [kən'viːnjənt] adj : conveniente

convent ['kanvənt, -vɛnt] n : convento m

convention [kən'vɛntʃən] n : convención f — **conventional** [kən'vɛntʃənəl] adj : convencional

converge [kən'vərdʒ] vi **-verged; -verging** : converger, convergir

converse¹ ['kan,vərs] vi **-versed; -versing** : conversar — **conversation** [,kanvər'seɪʃən] n : conversación f — **conversational** [,kanvər'seɪʃənəl] adj : familiar

converse² ['kan,vərs, kan-] adj : contrario, opuesto — **conversely** [kən'vərsli, 'kan,vərs-] adv : a la inversa

conversion [kən'vərʒən] n : conversión f —

convert [kən'vərt] vt : convertir — vi : convertirse — **convertible** [kən'vərtəbəl] adj : convertible — ~ n : descapotable m, convertible m Lat

convex [kan'vɛks, 'kan-, kən'-] adj : convexo

convey [kən'veɪ] vt 1 TRANSPORT : llevar, transportar 2 TRANSMIT : comunicar

convict [kən'vɪkt] vt : declarar culpable a — ~ ['kan,vɪkt] n : presidiario m, -ria f — **conviction** [kən'vɪkʃən] n 1 : condena f (de un acusado) 2 BELIEF : convicción f

convince [kən'vɪnts] vt **-vinced; -vincing** : convencer — **convincing** [kən'vɪntsɪŋ] adj : convincente

convoke [kən'voːk] vt **-voked; -voking** : convocar

convoluted ['kanvə,luːţəd] adj : complicado

convulsion [kən'vʌlʃən] n : convulsión f — **convulsive** [kən'vʌlsɪv] adj : convulsivo

cook ['kʊk] n : cocinero m, -ra f — vi : cocinar, guisar — vt : preparar (comida) — **cookbook** ['kʊk,bʊk] n : libro m de cocina

cookie or **cooky** ['kʊki] n, pl **-ies** : galleta f (dulce)

cooking n : cocina f

cool ['kuːl] adj 1 : fresco 2 CALM : tranquilo 3 UNFRIENDLY : frío — ~ vt : enfriar — vi : enfriarse — ~ n 1 : fresco m 2 COMPOSURE : calma f — **cooler** ['kuːlər] n : nevera f portátil — **coolness** ['kuːlnəs] n : frescura f

coop ['kuːp, 'kʊp] n : gallinero m — ~ vt or ~ **up** : encerrar

cooperate [ko'apə,reɪt] vi **-ated; -ating** : cooperar — **cooperation** [ko,apə'reɪʃən] n : cooperación f — **cooperative** [ko'apərəţɪv, -apə,reɪţɪv] adj : cooperativo

coordinate [ko'ɔrdə,neɪt] v **-nated; -nating** vt : coordinar — **coordination** [ko,ɔrdən-'eɪʃən] n : coordinación f

cop ['kap] n 1 : poli mf fam 2 **the** ~ **s** : la poli fam

cope ['koːp] vi **coped; coping** 1 : arreglárselas 2 ~ **with** : hacer frente a, poder con

copier ['kapiər] n : fotocopiadora f

copious ['koːpiəs] adj : copioso

copper ['kapər] n : cobre m

copy ['kapi] n, pl **copies** 1 : copia f 2 : ejemplar m (de un libro), número m (de una revista) — ~ vt **copied; copying** 1 DUPLICATE : hacer una copia de 2 IMITATE : copiar — **copyright** ['kapi,raɪt] n : derechos mpl de autor

coral ['kɔrəl] n : coral m

cord ['kɔrd] n 1 : cuerda f 2 or **electric** ~ : cable m (eléctrico)

cordial ['kɔrdʒəl] adj : cordial

corduroy ['kɔrdə,rɔɪ] n : pana f

core ['kɔr] n 1 : corazón m (de una fruta) 2 CENTER : núcleo m, centro m

cork ['kɔrk] n : corcho m — **corkscrew** ['kɔrk,skruː] n : sacacorchos m

corn ['kɔrn] n 1 : grano m 2 or **Indian** ~ : maíz m 3 : callo m (del pie) — **corncob** ['kɔrn,kab] n : mazorca f

corner ['kɔrnər] n 1 : ángulo m, rincón m (en una habitación), esquina f (de una intersección) — ~ vt 1 TRAP : acorralar 2 MONOPOLIZE : acaparar (un mercado) — **cornerstone** ['kɔrnər,stoːn] n : piedra f angular

cornmeal ['kɔrn,miːl] n : harina f de maíz — **cornstarch** ['kɔrn,startʃ] n : maicena f

corny ['kɔrni] adj : cursi, sentimental

coronary ['kɔrə,nɛri] n, pl **-naries** : trombosis f coronaria

coronation [,kɔrə'neɪʃən] n : coronación f

corporal ['kɔrpərəl] n : cabo m

corporation [,kɔrpə'reɪʃən] n : sociedad f anónima, compañía f — **corporate** ['kɔrpərət] adj : corporativo

corps ['kɔr] n, pl **corps** ['kɔrz] : cuerpo m

corpse ['kɔrps] n : cadáver m

corpulent ['kɔrpjələnt] adj : obeso, gordo

corpuscle ['kɔr,pʌsəl] n : glóbulo m

corral [kə'ræl] n : corral m — ~ vt **-ralled; -ralling** : acorralar

correct [kə'rɛkt] vt : corregir — ~ adj : correcto — **correction** [kə'rɛkʃən] n : corrección f

correlation [,kɔrə'leɪʃən] n : correlación f

correspond [,kɔrə'spand] vi 1 WRITE : corresponderse 2 ~ **to** : corresponder a — **correspondence** [,kɔrə'spandənts] n : correspondencia f

corridor ['kɔrədər, -,dɔr] n : pasillo m

corroborate [kə'rabə,reɪt] vt **-rated; -rating** : corroborar

corrode [kə'roːd] v **-roded; -roding** vt : corroer — vi : corroerse — **corrosion** [kə'roːʒən] n : corrosión f — **corrosive** [kə'roːsɪv] adj : corrosivo

corrugated ['kɔrə,geɪţəd] adj : ondulado

corrupt [kə'rʌpt] vt : corromper — ~ adj : corrupto, corrompido — **corruption** [kə'rʌpʃən] n : corrupción f

corset ['kɔrsət] n : corsé m

cosmetic [kaz'mɛţɪk] n : cosmético m — ~ adj : cosmético

cosmic ['kazmɪk] adj : cósmico

cosmopolitan [,kazmə'palətən] adj : cosmopolita

cosmos ['kɑzməs, -ˌmo:s, -ˌmɑs] *n* : cosmos *m*

cost ['kɔst] *n* : costo *m*, coste *m* — ~ *vi* **cost; costing 1** : costar **2 how much does it ~?** : ¿cuánto cuesta?, ¿cuánto vale?

Costa Rican [ˌkɔstə'ri:kən] *adj* : costarricense

costly ['kɔstli] *adj* : costoso

costume ['kɑsˌtu:m, -ˌtju:m] *n* **1** OUTFIT : traje *m* **2** DISGUISE : disfraz *m*

cot ['kɑt] *n* : catre *m*

cottage ['kɑt̬ɪdʒ] *n* : casita *f* (de campo) — **cottage cheese** *n* : requesón *m*

cotton ['kɑtən] *n* : algodón *m*

couch ['kaʊtʃ] *n* : sofá *m*

cough ['kɔf] *vi* : toser — ~ *n* : tos *f*

could ['kʊd] → **can**[1]

council ['kaʊntsəl] *n* **1** : concejo *m* **2** *or* **city ~** : ayuntamiento *m* — **councillor** *or* **councilor** ['kaʊntsələr] *n* : concejal *m*, -jala *f*

counsel *n* **1** ADVICE : consejo *m* **2** LAWYER : abogado *m*, -da *f* — ~ ['kaʊntsəl] *vt* **-seled** *or* **-selled; -seling** *or* **-selling** : aconsejar — **counselor** *or* **counsellor** ['kaʊntsələr] *n* : consejero *m*, -ra *f*

count[1] ['kaʊnt] *vt* : contar — *vi* **1** : contar **2 ~ on** : contar con **3 that doesn't ~** : eso no vale — ~ *n* **1** : recuento *m* **2 keep ~ of** : llevar la cuenta de

count[2] *n* : conde *m* (noble)

counter[1] ['kaʊntər] *n* **1** : mostrador *m* (de un negocio) **2** TOKEN : ficha *f* (de un juego)

counter[2] *vt* : oponerse a — *vi* : contraatacar — ~ *adv* **~ to** : contrario a — **counteract** [ˌkaʊntər'ækt] *vt* : contrarrestar — **counterattack** ['kaʊntərəˌtæk] *n* : contraataque *m* — **counterbalance** [ˌkaʊntər'bæləntʃs] *n* : contrapeso *m* — **counterclockwise** [ˌkaʊntər'klɑkˌwaɪz] *adv & adj* : en sentido opuesto a las agujas del reloj — **counterfeit** ['kaʊntərˌfɪt] *vt* : falsificar — ~ *adj* : falsificado — ~ *n* : falsificación *f* — **counterpart** ['kaʊntərˌpɑrt] *n* : homólogo *m* (de una persona), equivalente *m* (de una cosa) — **counterproductive** [ˌkaʊntərprə'dʌktɪv] *adj* : contraproducente

countess ['kaʊntɪs] *n* : condesa *f*

countless ['kaʊntləs] *adj* : incontable, innumerable

country ['kʌntri] *n, pl* **-tries 1** NATION : país *m* **2** COUNTRYSIDE : campo *m* — ~ *adj* : campestre, rural — **countryman** ['kʌntrimən] *n, pl* **-men** [-mən, -ˌmɛn] *or* **fellow ~** : compatriota *mf* — **countryside** ['kʌntriˌsaɪd] *n* : campo *m*, campiña *f*

county ['kaʊnti] *n, pl* **-ties** : condado *m*

coup ['ku:] *n, pl* **coups** ['ku:z] *or* **~ d'etat** : golpe *m* (de estado)

couple ['kʌpəl] *n* **1** : pareja *f* (de personas) **2 a ~ of** : un par de — ~ *vt* **-pled; -pling** : acoplar, unir

coupon ['ku:ˌpɑn, 'kju:-] *n* : cupón *m*

courage ['kərɪdʒ] *n* : valor *m* — **courageous** [kə'reɪdʒəs] *adj* : valiente

courier ['kʊriər, 'kəriər] *n* : mensajero *m*, -ra *f*

course ['kors] *n* **1** : curso *m* **2** : plato *m* (de una cena) **3** *or* **golf ~** : campo *m* de golf **4 in the ~ of** : en el transcurso de **5 of ~** : desde luego, por supuesto

court ['kort] *n* **1** : corte *f* (de un rey, etc.) **2** : cancha *f*, pista *f* (en deportes) **3** TRIBUNAL : corte *f*, tribunal *m* — ~ *vt* : cortejar

courteous ['kərt̬iəs] *adj* : cortés — **courtesy** ['kərt̬əsi] *n, pl* **-sies** : cortesía *f*

courthouse ['kortˌhaʊs] *n* : palacio *m* de justicia, juzgado *m* — **courtroom** ['kortˌru:m] *n* : sala *f* (de un tribunal)

courtship ['kortˌʃɪp] *n* : cortejo *m*, noviazgo *m*

courtyard ['kortˌjɑrd] *n* : patio *m*

cousin ['kʌzən] *n* : primo *m*, -ma *f*

cove ['ko:v] *n* : ensenada *f*, cala *f*

covenant ['kʌvənənt] *n* : pacto *m*, convenio *m*

cover ['kʌvər] *vt* **1** : cubrir **2** *or* **~ up** : encubrir, ocultar **3** TREAT : tratar — ~ *n* **1** : cubierta *f* **2** SHELTER : abrigo *m*, refugio *m* **3** LID : tapa *f* **4** : cubierta *f* (de un libro), portada *f* (de una revista) **5 ~s** *npl* BEDCLOTHES : mantas *fpl*, cobijas *fpl Lat* **6 take ~** : ponerse a cubierto **7 under ~ of** : al amparo de — **coverage** ['kʌvərɪdʒ] *n* : cobertura *f* — **covert** ['ko:ˌvərt, 'kʌvərt] *adj* : encubierto — **cover–up** ['kʌvərˌʌp] *n* : encubrimiento *m*

covet ['kʌvət] *vt* : codiciar — **covetous** ['kʌvət̬əs] *adj* : codicioso

cow ['kaʊ] *n* : vaca *f* — ~ *vt* : intimidar, acobardar

coward ['kaʊərd] *n* : cobarde *mf* — **cowardice** ['kaʊərdɪs] *n* : cobardía *f* — **cowardly** ['kaʊərdli] *adj* : cobarde

cowboy ['kaʊˌbɔɪ] *n* : vaquero *m*

cower ['kaʊər] *vi* : encogerse (de miedo)

coy ['kɔɪ] *adj* : tímido y coqueto

coyote [kaɪ'o:t̬i, 'kaɪˌo:t] *n, pl* **coyotes** *or* **coyote** : coyote *m*

cozy ['ko:zi] *adj* **-zier; -est** : acogedor

crab ['kræb] *n* : cangrejo *m*, jaiba *f Lat*

crack ['kræk] *vt* **1** SPLIT : rajar, partir **2** : cascar (nueces, huevos) **3** : chasquear (un látigo, etc.) **4 ~ down on** : tomar medidas enérgicas contra — *vi* **1** SPLIT : rajarse, agrietarse **2** : chasquear (dícese de un látigo) **3 ~ up** : sufrir una crisis nerviosa — ~ *n* **1** CRACKING : chasquido *m*, crujido *m* **2** CREVICE : raja *f*, grieta *f* **3 have a ~ at** : intentar

cracker ['krækər] *n* : galleta *f* (de soda, etc.)

crackle ['krækəl] *vi* **-led; -ling** : crepitar, chisporrotear — ~ *n* : crujido *m*, chisporroteo *m*

cradle ['kreɪdəl] *n* : cuna *f* — ~ *vt* **-dled; -dling** : acunar

craft ['kræft] *n* **1** TRADE : oficio *m* **2** CUNNING : astucia *f* **3** → **craftsmanship 4** *pl usually* **craft** BOAT : embarcación *f* — **craftsman** ['kræftsmən] *n, pl* **-men** [-mən, -ˌmɛn] : artesano *m*, -na *f* — **craftsmanship** ['kræftsmənˌʃɪp] *n* : artesanía *f*, destreza *f* — **crafty** ['kræfti] *adj* **craftier; -est** : astuto, taimado

crag ['kræg] *n* : peñasco *m*

cram ['kræm] *v* **crammed; cramming** *vt* **1** STUFF : embutir **2 ~ with** : atiborrar de — *vi* : estudiar a última hora

cramp ['kræmp] *n* **1** : calambre *m*, espasmo *m* (de los músculos) **2 ~s** *npl* : retortijones *mpl*

cranberry ['krænˌbɛri] *n, pl* **-berries** : arándano *m* (rojo y agrio)

crane ['kreɪn] *n* **1** : grulla *f* (ave) **2** : grúa *f* (máquina) — ~ *vt* **craned; craning** : estirar (el cuello)

crank ['kræŋk] *n* **1** : manivela *f* **2** ECCENTRIC : excéntrico *m*, -ca *f* — **cranky** ['kræŋki] *adj* **crankier; -est** : malhumorado

crash ['kræʃ] *vi* **1** : caerse con estrépito **2** COLLIDE : estrellarse, chocar — *vt* : estrellar — ~ *n* **1** DIN : estrépito *m* **2** COLLISION : choque *m*

crass ['kræs] *adj* : burdo, grosero

crate ['kreɪt] *n* : cajón *m* (de madera)

crater ['kreɪt̬ər] *n* : cráter *m*

crave ['kreɪv] *vt* **craved; craving** : ansiar — **craving** ['kreɪvɪŋ] *n* : ansia *f*

crawl ['krɔl] *vi* : arrastrarse, gatear (dícese de un bebé) — ~ *n* **at a ~** : a paso lento

crayon ['kreɪˌɑn, -ən] *n* : lápiz *m* de cera

craze ['kreɪz] *n* : moda *f* pasajera, manía *f*

crazy ['kreɪzi] *adj* **-zier; -est 1** : loco **2 go ~** : volverse loco — **craziness** ['kreɪzinəs] *n* : locura *f*

creak ['kri:k] *vi* : chirriar, crujir — ~ *n* : chirrido *m*, crujido *m*

cream ['kri:m] *n* : crema *f*, nata *f Spain* — **cream cheese** *n* : queso *m* crema — **creamy** ['kri:mi] *adj* **creamier; -est** : cremoso

crease ['kri:s] *n* : pliegue *m*, raya *f* (del pantalón) — ~ *vt* **creased; creasing** : plegar, poner una raya en (el pantalón)

create [kri'eɪt] *vt* **-ated; -ating** : crear — **creation** [kri'eɪʃən] *n* : creación *f* — **creative** [kri'eɪt̬ɪv] *adj* : creativo — **creator** [kri'eɪt̬ər] *n* : creador *m*, -dora *f*

creature ['kri:tʃər] *n* : criatura *f*, animal *m*

credence ['kri:dənts] *n* **lend ~ to** : dar crédito a

credentials [krɪ'dɛntʃəlz] *npl* : credenciales *fpl*

credible ['krɛdəbəl] *adj* : creíble — **credibility** [ˌkrɛdə'bɪlət̬i] *n* : credibilidad *f*

credit ['krɛdɪt] *n* **1** : crédito *m* **2** RECOGNITION : reconocimiento *m* **3 be a ~ to** : ser el orgullo de — ~ *vt* **1** BELIEVE : creer **2** : abonar (en una cuenta) **3 ~ s.o. with sth** : atribuir algo a algn — **credit card** *n* : tarjeta *f* de crédito

credulous ['krɛdʒələs] *adj* : crédulo

creed ['kri:d] *n* : credo *m*

creek ['kri:k, 'krɪk] *n* : arroyo *m*, riachuelo *m*

creep ['kri:p] *vi* **crept** ['krɛpt]; **creeping 1** CRAWL : arrastrarse **2** SLINK : ir a hurtadillas — ~ *n* **1** CRAWL : paso *m* lento **2 the ~s** : escalofríos *mpl* — **creeping** *adj* **~ plant** : planta *f* trepadora

cremate ['kri:ˌmeɪt] *vt* **-mated; -mating** : incinerar

crescent ['krɛsənt] *n* : media luna *f*

cress ['krɛs] *n* : berro *m*

crest ['krɛst] *n* : cresta *f* — **crestfallen** ['krɛstˌfɔlən] *adj* : alicaído

crevice ['krɛvɪs] *n* : grieta *f*

crew ['kru:] *n* **1** : tripulación *f* (de una nave) **2** TEAM : equipo *m*

crib ['krɪb] *n* : cuna *f* (de un bebé)

cricket ['krɪkət] *n* **1** : grillo *m* (insecto) **2** : críquet *m* (juego)

crime ['kraɪm] *n* : crimen *m* — **criminal** ['krɪmənəl] *adj* : criminal — ~ *n* : criminal *mf*

crimp ['krɪmp] *vt* : rizar

crimson ['krɪmzən] *n* : carmesí *m*

cringe ['krɪndʒ] *vi* **cringed; cringing** : encogerse

crinkle ['krɪŋkəl] *vt* **-kled; -kling** : arrugar

cripple ['krɪpəl] *vt* **-pled; -pling 1** DISABLE : lisiar, dejar inválido **2** INCAPACITATE : inutilizar, paralizar

crisis ['kraɪsɪs] *n, pl* **crises** [-ˌsi:z] : crisis *f*

crisp ['krɪsp] *adj* **1** CRUNCHY : crujiente **2** : frío y vigorizante (dícese del aire) — **crispy** ['krɪspi] *adj* **crispier; -est** : crujiente

crisscross ['krɪsˌkrɔs] *vt* : entrecruzar

criterion [kraɪ'tɪriən] *n, pl* **-ria** [-iə] : criterio *m*

critic ['krɪt̬ɪk] *n* : crítico *m*, -ca *f* — **critical** ['krɪt̬ɪkəl] *adj* : crítico — **criticism** ['krɪt̬əˌsɪzəm] *n* : crítica *f* — **criticize** ['krɪt̬əˌsaɪz] *vt* **-cized; -cizing** : criticar

croak ['kro:k] *vi* : croar

crock ['krɑk] *n* : vasija *f* de barro — **crockery** ['krɑkəri] *n* : vajilla *f*, loza *f*

crocodile ['krɑkəˌdaɪl] *n* : cocodrilo *m*

crony ['kro:ni] *n, pl* **-nies** : amigote *m fam*

crook ['krʊk] *n* **1** STAFF : cayado *m* **2** THIEF : ratero *m*, -ra *f*; ladrón *m*, -drona *f* **3** BEND : pliegue *m* — **crooked** ['krʊkəd] *adj* **1** BENT : torcido, chueco *Lat* **2** DISHONEST : deshonesto

crop ['krɑp] *n* **1** WHIP : fusta *f* **2** HARVEST : cosecha *f* **3** : cultivo *m* (de maíz, tabaco, etc.) — ~ *v* **cropped; cropping** *vt* TRIM : recortar, cortar — *vi* **~ up** : surgir

cross ['krɔs] *n* **1** : cruz *f* **2** HYBRID : cruce *m* — ~ *vt* **1** : cruzar, atravesar **2** CROSSBREED : cruzar **3** *or* **~ out** : tachar — ~ *adj* **1** : que atraviesa **2** ANGRY : enojado — **crossbreed** ['krɔsˌbri:d] *vt* **-bred** [-bred]; **-breeding** : cruzar — **cross–examine** *vt* : interrogar — **cross–eyed** ['krɔsˌaɪd] *adj* : bizco — **cross fire** *n* : fuego *m* cruzado — **crossing** ['krɔsɪŋ] *n* **1** INTERSECTION : cruce *m*, paso *m* **2** VOYAGE : travesía *f* (del mar) — **cross–reference** [ˌkrɔs'rɛfrənts, -'rɛfərənts] *n* : referencia *f* — **crossroads** ['krɔsˌro:dz] *n* : cruce *m* — **cross section** *n* **1** : corte *m* transversal **2** SAMPLE : muestra *f* representativa — **crosswalk** ['krɔsˌwɔk] *n* : cruce *m* peatonal, paso *m* de peatones — **crossword puzzle** ['krɔsˌwərd] *n* : crucigrama *m*

crotch ['krɑtʃ] *n* : entrepierna *f*

crouch ['kraʊtʃ] *vi* : agacharse

crouton ['kru:ˌtɑn] *n* : crutón *m*

crow ['kro:] *n* : cuervo *m* — ~ *vi* **crowed** *or Brit* **crew; crowing** : cacarear

crowbar ['kro:ˌbɑr] *n* : palanca *f*

crowd ['kraʊd] *vi* : amontonarse — *vt* : atestar, llenar — ~ *n* : multitud *f*, muchedumbre *f*

crown ['kraʊn] *n* **1** : corona *f* **2** : cima *f* (de una colina) — ~ *vt* : coronar

crucial ['kru:ʃəl] *adj* : crucial

crucify ['kru:səˌfaɪ] *vt* **-fied; -fying** : crucificar — **crucifix** ['kru:səˌfɪks] *n* : crucifijo *m* — **crucifixion** [ˌkru:sə'fɪkʃən] *n* : crucifixión *f*

crude ['kru:d] *adj* **cruder; -est 1** RAW : crudo **2** VULGAR : grosero **3** ROUGH : tosco, rudo

cruel ['kru:əl] *adj* **-eler** *or* **-eller; -elest** *or* **-ellest** : cruel — **cruelty** ['kru:əlti] *n, pl* **-ties** : crueldad *f*

cruet ['kru:ɪt] *n* : vinagrera *f*

cruise ['kru:z] *vi* **cruised; cruising 1** : hacer un crucero **2** : ir a velocidad de crucero — ~ *n* : crucero *m* — **cruiser** ['kru:zər] *n* **1** WARSHIP : crucero *m* **2** : patrulla *f* (de policía)

crumb ['krʌm] *n* : miga *f*, migaja *f*

crumble ['krʌmbəl] *v* **-bled; -bling** *vt* : desmenuzar — *vi* : desmenuzarse, desmoronarse

crumple ['krʌmpəl] *vt* **-pled; -pling** : arrugar

crunch ['krʌntʃ] *vt* : ronzar (con los dientes), hacer crujir (con los pies, etc.) — **crunchy** ['krʌntʃi] *adj* **crunchier; -est** : crujiente

crusade [kru:'seɪd] *n* : cruzada *f*

crush ['krʌʃ] *vt* : aplastar, apachurrar *Lat* — ~ *n* **have a ~ on** : estar chiflado por

crust ['krʌst] *n* : corteza *f*

crutch ['krʌtʃ] *n* : muleta *f*

crux ['krʌks, 'krʊks] *n* : quid *m*

cry ['kraɪ] *vi* **cried; crying 1** SHOUT : gritar **2** WEEP : llorar — ~ *n, pl* **cries** : grito *m*

crypt ['krɪpt] *n* : cripta *f*

crystal ['krɪstəl] *n* : cristal *m*

cub ['kʌb] *n* : cachorro *m*, -rra *f*

Cuban ['kju:bən] *adj* : cubano

cube ['kju:b] *n* : cubo *m* — **cubic** ['kju:bɪk] *adj* : cúbico

cubicle ['kju:bɪkəl] *n* : cubículo *m*

cuckoo ['ku:ˌku:, 'kʊ-] *n* : cuco *m*, cuclillo *m*

cucumber ['kju:ˌkʌmbər] *n* : pepino *m*

cuddle ['kʌdəl] *v* **-dled; -dling** *vi* : acurrucarse, abrazarse — *vt* : abrazar

cudgel ['kʌdʒəl] *n* : porra *f* — ~ *vt* **-geled** *or* **-gelled; -geling** *or* **-gelling** : aporrear

cue[1] ['kju:] *n* SIGNAL : señal *f*

cue[2] *n* : taco *m* (de billar)

cuff[1] ['kʌf] **1** : puño *m* (de una camisa) **2 ~s** *npl* → **handcuffs**

cuff[2] *vt* : bofetear — ~ *n* SLAP : bofetada *f*

cuisine [kwɪ'zi:n] *n* : cocina *f*

culinary ['kʌləˌnɛri, 'kju:lə-] *adj* : culinario

cull ['kʌl] *vt* : seleccionar, entresacar

culminate ['kʌlməˌneɪt] *vi* **-nated; -nating** : culminar — **culmination** [ˌkʌlmə'neɪʃən] *n* : culminación *f*

culprit ['kʌlprɪt] *n* : culpable *mf*

cult ['kʌlt] *n* : culto *m*

cultivate ['kʌltəˌveɪt] *vt* **-vated; -vating** : cultivar — **cultivation** [ˌkʌltə'veɪʃən] *n* : cultivo *m*

culture ['kʌltʃər] *n* **1** : cultura *f* **2** : cultivo *m* (en biología) — **cultural** ['kʌltʃərəl] *adj* : cultural — **cultured** ['kʌltʃərd] *adj* : culto

cumbersome ['kʌmbərsəm] *adj* : torpe (y pesado), difícil de manejar

cumulative ['kju:mjələt̬ɪv, -ˌleɪt̬ɪv] *adj* : acumulativo

cunning ['kʌnɪŋ] *adj* : astuto, taimado — ~ *n* : astucia *f*

cup ['kʌp] *n* **1** : taza *f* **2** TROPHY : copa *f*

cupboard ['kʌbərd] *n* : alacena *f*, armario *m*

curator ['kjʊrˌeɪt̬ər, kjʊ'reɪt̬ər] *n* : conservador *m*, -dora *f*; director *m*, -tora *f*

curb ['kərb] *n* **1** RESTRAINT : freno *m* **2** : borde *m* de la acera — ~ *vt* : refrenar

curdle ['kərdəl] *v* **-dled; -dling** *vi* : cuajarse — *vt* : cuajar

cure ['kjʊr] *n* : cura *f*, remedio *m* — ~ *vt* **cured; curing** : curar

curfew ['kərˌfju:] *n* : toque *m* de queda

curious ['kjʊriəs] *adj* : curioso — **curio** ['kjʊriˌo:] *n, pl* **-rios** : curiosidad *f* — **curiosity** [ˌkjʊri'ɑsət̬i] *n, pl* **-ties** : curiosidad *f*

curl ['kərl] *vt* **1** : rizar **2** COIL : enrollar, enroscar — *vi* **1** : rizarse **2 ~ up** : acurrucarse — ~ *n* : rizo *m* — **curler** ['kərlər] *n* : rulo *m* — **curly** ['kərli] *adj* **curlier; -est** : rizado

currant ['kərənt] *n* **1** : grosella *f* (fruta) **2** RAISIN : pasa *f* de Corinto

currency ['kərəntsi] *n, pl* **-cies 1** MONEY : moneda *f* **2 gain ~** : ganar aceptación

current ['kərənt] *adj* **1** PRESENT : actual **2** PREVALENT : corriente — ~ *n* : corriente *f*

curriculum [kə'rɪkjələm] *n, pl* **-la** [-lə] : plan *m* de estudios

curry ['kəri] *n, pl* **-ries** : curry *m*

curse ['kərs] *n* : maldición *f* — ~ *v* **cursed; cursing** : maldecir

cursor ['kərsər] *n* : cursor *m*

cursory ['kərsəri] *adj* : superficial

curt ['kərt] *adj* : corto, seco

curtail [kər'teɪl] *vt* : acortar

curtain ['kərtən] *n* : cortina *f* (de una ventana), telón *m* (en un teatro)

curtsy ['kərtsi] *vi* **-sied** *or* **-seyed; -sying** *or* **-seying** : hacer una reverencia — ~ *n* : reverencia *f*

curve ['kərv] *v* **curved; curving** *vi* : hacer una curva — *vt* : encorvar — ~ *n* : curva *f*

cushion ['kʊʃən] *n* : cojín *m* — ~ *vt* : amortiguar

custard ['kʌstərd] *n* : natillas *fpl*

custody ['kʌstədi] *n, pl* **-dies 1** : custodia *f* **2 be in ~** : estar detenido — **custodian** [ˌkʌ'sto:diən] *n* : custodio *m*, -dia *f*; guardián, -diana *f*

custom ['kʌstəm] *n* : costumbre *f* — **customary** ['kʌstəˌmɛri] *adj* : habitual, acostumbrado — **customer** ['kʌstəmər] *n* : cliente *m*, -ta *f* — **customs** ['kʌstəmz] *npl* : aduana *f*

cut ['kʌt] *v* **cut; cutting** *vt* **1** : cortar **2** REDUCE : reducir, rebajar **3 ~ oneself** : cortarse **4 ~ up** : cortar en pedazos — *vi* **1** : cortar **2 ~ in** : interrumpir — ~ *n* **1** : corte *m* **2** REDUCTION : rebaja *f*, reducción *f*

cute ['kju:t] *adj* **cuter; -est** : mono *fam*, lindo

cutlery ['kʌtləri] *n* : cubiertos *mpl*

cutlet ['kʌtlət] *n* : chuleta *f*

cutting ['kʌt̬ɪŋ] *adj* : cortante, mordaz

cyanide ['saɪəˌnaɪd, -nɪd] *n* : cianuro *m*

cycle ['saɪkəl] *n* **1** : ciclo *m* **2** BICYCLE : bicicleta *f* — ~ *vi* **-cled; -cling** : ir en bicicleta — **cyclic** ['saɪklɪk, 'sɪ-] *or* **cyclical** [-klɪkəl] *adj* : cíclico — **cyclist** ['saɪklɪst] *n* : ciclista *mf*

cyclone ['saɪˌklo:n] *n* : ciclón *m*

cylinder ['sɪləndər] *n* : cilindro *m* — **cylindrical** [sə'lɪndrɪkəl] *adj* : cilíndrico

cymbal ['sɪmbəl] *n* : platillo *m*, címbalo *m*

cynic ['sɪnɪk] *n* : cínico *m*, -ca *f* — **cynical** ['sɪnɪkəl] *adj* : cínico — **cynicism** ['sɪnəˌsɪzəm] *n* : cinismo *m*

cypress ['saɪprəs] *n* : ciprés *m*

cyst ['sɪst] *n* : quiste *m*

czar ['zɑr, 'sɑr] *n* : zar *m*

Czech ['tʃɛk] *adj* : checo — ~ *n* : checo *m* (idioma)

D

d ['di:] *n, pl* **d's** *or* **ds** ['di:z] : d *f*, cuarta letra del alfabeto inglés

dab ['dæb] *n* : toque *m* — ~ *vt* **dabbed; dabbing** : dar toques ligeros a, aplicar suavemente

dabble ['dæbəl] *vi* **-bled; -bling ~ in** : interesarse superficialmente en — **dabbler** *n* : aficionado *m*, -da *f*

dad ['dæd] *n* : papá *m fam* — **daddy** ['dædi] *n, pl* **-dies** : papá *m fam*

daffodil ['dæfəˌdɪl] *n* : narciso *m*

dagger ['dægər] *n* : daga *f*, puñal *m*

daily ['deɪli] *adj* : diario — ~ *adv* : diariamente

dainty ['deɪnti] *adj* **-tier; -est** : delicado

dairy ['dɛri] *n, pl* **-ies 1** : lechería *f* (tienda) **2** *or* **~ farm** : granja *f* lechera

daisy [ˈdeɪzi] *n, pl* **-sies** : margarita *f*

dam [ˈdæm] *n* : presa *f* — **~** *vt* **dammed; damming** : represar

damage [ˈdæmɪdʒ] *n* **1** : daño *m,* perjuicio *m* **2 ~s** *npl* : daños y perjuicios *mpl* — **~** *vt* **-aged; -aging** : dañar

damn [ˈdæm] *vt* **1** CONDEMN : condenar **2** CURSE : maldecir — **~** *n* **not give a ~** : no importarse un comino *fam* — **~** *or* **damned** [ˈdæmd] *adj* : maldito *fam*

damp [ˈdæmp] *adj* : húmedo — **dampen** [ˈdæmpən] *vt* **1** MOISTEN : humedecer **2** DISCOURAGE : desalentar, desanimar — **dampness** [ˈdæmpnəs] *n* : humedad *f*

dance [ˈdænts] *v* **danced; dancing** : bailar — **~** *n* : baile *m* — **dancer** [ˈdæntsər] *n* : bailarín *m,* -rina *f*

dandelion [ˈdændəlˌaɪən] *n* : diente *m* de león

dandruff [ˈdændrəf] *n* : caspa *f*

dandy [ˈdændi] *adj* **-dier; -est** : de primera, excelente

danger [ˈdeɪndʒər] *n* : peligro *m* — **dangerous** [ˈdeɪndʒərəs] *adj* : peligroso

dangle [ˈdæŋgəl] *v* **-gled; -gling** *vi* HANG : colgar, pender — *vt* : hacer oscilar

Danish [ˈdeɪnɪʃ] *adj* : danés — **~** *n* : danés *m* (idioma)

dank [ˈdæŋk] *adj* : frío y húmedo

dare [ˈdær] *v* **dared; daring** *vt* : desafiar — *vi* : osar — **~** *n* : desafío *m* — **daredevil** [ˈdærˌdɛvəl] *n* : persona *f* temeraria — **daring** [ˈdærɪŋ] *adj* : atrevido, audaz — **~** *n* : audacia *f*

dark [ˈdɑrk] *adj* **1** : oscuro **2** : moreno (dícese del pelo o de la piel) **3** GLOOMY : sombrío **4 get ~** : hacerse de noche — **darken** [ˈdɑrkən] *vt* : oscurecer — *vi* : oscurecerse — **darkness** [ˈdɑrknəs] *n* : oscuridad *f*

darling [ˈdɑrlɪŋ] *n* BELOVED : querido *m,* -da *f* — **~** *adj* : querido

darn [ˈdɑrn] *vt* : zurcir — **~** *adj* : maldito *fam*

dart [ˈdɑrt] *n* **1** : dardo *m* **2 ~s** *npl* : juego *m* de dardos — **~** *vi* : precipitarse

dash [ˈdæʃ] *vt* **1** SMASH : romper **2** HURL : lanzar **3 ~ off** : hacer (algo) rápidamente — *vi* : lanzarse, irse corriendo — **~** *n* **1** : guión *m* largo (signo de puntuación) **2** PINCH : poquito *m,* pizca *f* **3** RACE : carrera *f* — **dashboard** [ˈdæʃˌbord] *n* : tablero *m* de instrumentos — **dashing** [ˈdæʃɪŋ] *adj* : gallardo, apuesto

data [ˈdeɪt̬ə, ˈdæ-, ˈdɑ-] *ns & pl* : datos *mpl* — **database** [ˈdeɪt̬əˌbeɪs, ˈdæ-, ˈdɑ-] *n* : base *f* de datos

date[1] [ˈdeɪt] *n* : dátil *m* (fruta)

date[2] *n* **1** : fecha *f* **2** APPOINTMENT : cita *f* — **~** *v* **dated; dating** *vt* **1** : fechar (una carta, etc.) **2** : salir con (algn) — *vi* **~ from** : datar de — **dated** [ˈdeɪt̬əd] *adj* : pasado de moda

daub [ˈdɔb] *vt* : embadurnar

daughter [ˈdɔt̬ər] *n* : hija *f* — **daughter–in–law** [ˈdɔt̬ərɪnˌlɔ] *n, pl* **daughters–in–law** : nuera *f*

daunt [ˈdɔnt] *vt* : intimidar

dawdle [ˈdɔdəl] *vi* **-dled; -dling** : entretenerse, perder tiempo

dawn [ˈdɔn] *vi* **1** : amanecer **2 it ~ed on him that** : cayó en la cuenta de que — **~** *n* : amanecer *m*

day [ˈdeɪ] *n* **1** : día *m* **2** *or* **working ~** : jornada *f* **3 the ~ before** : el día anterior **4 the ~ before yesterday** : anteayer **5 the ~ after** : el día siguiente **6 the ~ after tomorrow** : pasada mañana — **daybreak** [ˈdeɪˌbreɪk] *n* : amanecer *m* — **daydream** [ˈdeɪˌdriːm] *n* : ensueño *m* — **~** *vi* : soñar despierto — **daylight** [ˈdeɪˌlaɪt] *n* : luz *f* del día — **daytime** [ˈdeɪˌtaɪm] *n* : día *m*

daze [ˈdeɪz] *vt* **dazed; dazing** : aturdir — **~** *n* **in a ~** : aturdido

dazzle [ˈdæzəl] *vt* **-zled; -zling** : deslumbrar

dead [ˈdɛd] *adj* **1** LIFELESS : muerto **2** NUMB : entumecido — **~** *n* **1 in the ~ of night** : en plena noche **2 the ~** : los muertos — **~** *adv* ABSOLUTELY : absolutamente — **deaden** [ˈdɛdən] *vt* **1** : atenuar (dolores) **2** MUFFLE : amortiguar — **dead end** [ˈdɛdˈɛnd] *n* : callejón *m* sin salida — **deadline** [ˈdɛdˌlaɪn] *n* : fecha *f* límite — **deadlock** [ˈdɛdˌlɑk] *n* : punto *m* muerto — **deadly** [ˈdɛdli] *adj* **-lier; -est 1** : mortal, letal **2** ACCURATE : certero, preciso

deaf [ˈdɛf] *adj* : sordo — **deafen** [ˈdɛfən] *vt* : ensordecer — **deafness** [ˈdɛfnəs] *n* : sordera *f*

deal [ˈdiːl] *n* **1** TRANSACTION : trato *m,* transacción *f* **2** : reparto *m* (de naipes) **3 a good ~** : mucho — **~** *v* **dealt; dealing** *vt* **1** : dar **2** : repartir, dar (naipes) **3 ~ a blow** : asestar un golpe — *vi* **1** : dar, repartir (en juegos de naipes) **2 ~ in** : comerciar en **3 ~ with** CONCERN : tratar de **4 ~ with s.o.** : tratar con algn — **dealer** [ˈdiːlər] *n* : comerciante *mf* — **dealings** *npl* : trato *m,* relaciones *fpl*

dean [ˈdiːn] *n* : decano *m,* -na *f*

dear [ˈdɪr] *adj* : querido — **~** *n* : querido *m,* -da *f* — **dearly** [ˈdɪrli] *adv* **1** : mucho **2 pay ~** : pagar caro

death [ˈdɛθ] *n* : muerte *f*

debar [diˈbɑr] *vt* : excluir

debate [diˈbeɪt] *n* : debate *m,* discusión *f* — **~** *vt* **-bated; -bating** : debatir, discutir

debit [ˈdɛbɪt] *vt* : adeudar, cargar — **~** *n* : débito *m,* debe *m*

debris [dəˈbriː, deɪ-; ˈdeɪˌbriː] *n, pl* **-bris** [-ˈbriːz, -ˌbriːz] : escombros *mpl*

debt [ˈdɛt] *n* : deuda *f* — **debtor** [ˈdɛt̬ər] *n* : deudor *m,* -dora *f*

debunk [diˈbʌŋk] *vt* : desmentir

debut [deɪˈbjuː, ˈdeɪˌbjuː] *n* : debut *m* — **~** *vi* : debutar

decade [ˈdɛˌkeɪd, dɛˈkeɪd] *n* : década *f*

decadence [ˈdɛkədənts] *n* : decadencia *f* — **decadent** [ˈdɛkədənt] *adj* : decadente

decal [ˈdiːˌkæl, diˈkæl] *n* : calcomanía *f*

decanter [diˈkæntər] *n* : licorera *f*

decapitate [diˈkæpəˌteɪt] *vt* **-tated; -tating** : decapitar

decay [diˈkeɪ] *vi* **1** DECOMPOSE : descomponerse **2** DETERIORATE : deteriorarse **3** : cariarse (dícese de los dientes) — **~** *n* **1** : descomposición *f* **2** : deterioro *m* (de un edificio, etc.) **3** : caries *f* (de los dientes)

deceased [diˈsiːst] *adj* : difunto — **~** *n* **the ~** : el difunto, la difunta

deceive [diˈsiːv] *vt* **-ceived; -ceiving** : engañar — **deceit** [diˈsiːt] *n* : engaño *m* — **deceitful** [diˈsiːtfəl] *adj* : engañoso

December [diˈsɛmbər] *n* : diciembre *m*

decent [ˈdiːsənt] *adj* **1** : decente **2** KIND : bueno, amable — **decency** [ˈdiːsəntsi] *n, pl* **-cies** : decencia *f*

deception [diˈsɛpʃən] *n* : engaño *m* — **deceptive** [diˈsɛptɪv] *adj* : engañoso

decide [diˈsaɪd] *v* **-cided; -ciding** *vt* : decidir — *vi* : decidirse — **decided** [diˈsaɪdəd] *adj* **1** UNQUESTIONABLE : indudable **2** RESOLUTE : decidido — **decidedly** [diˈsaɪdədli] *adv* **1** DEFINITELY : decididamente **2** RESOLUTELY : con decisión

decimal [ˈdɛsəməl] *adj* : decimal — **~** *n* : número *m* decimal — **decimal point** *n* : coma *f* decimal

decipher [diˈsaɪfər] *vt* : descifrar

decision [dɪˈsɪʒən] *n* : decisión *f* — **decisive** [dɪˈsaɪsɪv] *adj* **1** RESOLUTE : decidido **2** CONCLUSIVE : decisivo

deck [ˈdɛk] *n* **1** : cubierta *f* (de un barco) **2** *or* **~ of cards** : baraja *f* (de naipes) **3** TERRACE : entarimado *m*

declare [diˈklær] *vt* **-clared; -claring** : declarar — **declaration** [ˌdɛkləˈreɪʃən] *n* : declaración *f*

decline [diˈklaɪn] *v* **-clined; -clining** *vt* REFUSE : declinar, rehusar — *vi* DECREASE : disminuir — **~** *n* **1** DETERIORATION : decadencia *f,* deterioro *m* **2** DECREASE : disminución *f*

decode [diˈkoːd] *vt* **-coded; -coding** : descodificar

decompose [ˌdiːkəmˈpoːz] *vt* **-posed; -posing** : descomponer — *vi* : descomponerse

decongestant [ˌdiːkənˈdʒɛstənt] *n* : descongestionante *m*

decorate [ˈdɛkəˌreɪt] *vt* **-rated; -rating** : decorar — **decor** *or* **décor** [deɪˈkɔr, ˈdeɪˌkɔr] *n* : decoración *f* — **decoration** [ˌdɛkəˈreɪʃən] *n* : decoración *f* — **decorator** [ˈdɛkəˌreɪt̬ər] *n* : decorador *m,* -dora *f*

decoy [ˈdiːˌkɔɪ, diˈ-] *n* : señuelo *m*

decrease [diˈkriːs] *v* **-creased; -creasing** : disminuir — **~** [ˈdiːˌkriːs] *n* : disminución *f*

decree [diˈkriː] *n* : decreto *m* — **~** *vt* **-creed; -creeing** : decretar

decrepit [diˈkrɛpɪt] *adj* **1** FEEBLE : decrépito **2** DILAPIDATED : ruinoso

dedicate [ˈdɛdɪˌkeɪt] *vt* **-cated; -cating 1** : dedicar **2 ~ oneself to** : consagrarse a — **dedication** [ˌdɛdɪˈkeɪʃən] *n* **1** DEVOTION : dedicación *f* **2** INSCRIPTION : dedicatoria *f*

deduce [diˈduːs, -ˈdjuːs] *vt* **-duced; -ducing** : deducir — **deduct** [diˈdʌkt] *vt* : deducir — **deduction** [diˈdʌkʃən] *n* : deducción *f*

deed [ˈdiːd] *n* : acción *f,* hecho *m*

deem [ˈdiːm] *vt* : considerar, juzgar

deep [ˈdiːp] *adj* : hondo, profundo — **~** *adv* **1** DEEPLY : profundamente **2 ~ down** : en el fondo **3 dig ~** : cavar hondo — **deepen** [ˈdiːpən] *vt* : ahondar — *vi* : hacerse más profundo — **deeply** [ˈdiːpli] *adv* : hondo, profundamente

deer [ˈdɪr] *ns & pl* : ciervo *m*

deface [diˈfeɪs] *vt* **-faced; -facing** : desfigurar

default [diˈfɔlt, ˈdiːˌfɔlt] *n* **by ~** : en rebeldía — **~** *vi* **1 ~ on** : no pagar (una deuda) **2** : no presentarse (en deportes)

defeat [diˈfiːt] *vt* **1** BEAT : vencer, derrotar **2** FRUSTRATE : frustrar — **~** *n* : derrota *f*

defect [ˈdiːˌfɛkt, diˈfɛkt] *n* : defecto *m* — **~** [diˈfɛkt] *vi* : desertar — **defective** [diˈfɛktɪv] *adj* : defectuoso

defend [diˈfɛnd] *vt* : defender — **defendant** [diˈfɛndənt] *n* : acusado *m,* -da *f* — **defense** *or Brit* **defence** [diˈfɛnts, ˈdiːˌfɛnts] *n* : defensa *f* — **defenseless** *or Brit* **defenceless** *adj* : indefenso — **defensive** [diˈfɛntsɪv] *adj* : defensivo — **~** *n* **on the ~** : a la defensiva

defer [diˈfər] *v* **-ferred; -ferring** *vt* : diferir, aplazar — *vi* **~ to** : deferir a — **deference** [ˈdɛfərənts] *n* : deferencia *f* — **deferential** [ˌdɛfəˈrɛntʃəl] *adj* : deferente

defiance [diˈfaɪənts] *n* **1** : desafío *m* **2 in ~ of** : a despecho de — **defiant** [diˈfaɪənt] *adj* : desafiante

deficiency [diˈfɪʃəntsi] *n, pl* **-cies** : deficiencia *f* — **deficient** [diˈfɪʃənt] *adj* : deficiente

deficit [ˈdɛfəsɪt] *n* : déficit *m*

defile [diˈfaɪl] *vt* **-filed; -filing 1** DIRTY : ensuciar **2** DESECRATE : profanar

define [diˈfaɪn] *vt* **-fined; -fining** : definir — **definite** [ˈdɛfənɪt] *adj* **1** : definido **2** CERTAIN : seguro, incuestionable — **definition** [ˌdɛfəˈnɪʃən] *n* : definición *f* — **definitive** [diˈfɪnət̬ɪv] *adj* : definitivo

deflate [diˈfleɪt] *v* **-flated; -flating** *vt* : desinflar (una llanta, etc.) — *vi* : desinflarse

deflect [diˈflɛkt] *vt* : desviar — *vi* : desviarse

deform [diˈfɔrm] *vt* : deformar — **deformity** [diˈfɔrmət̬i] *n, pl* **-ties** : deformidad *f*

defraud [diˈfrɔd] *vt* : defraudar

defrost [diˈfrɔst] *vt* : descongelar — *vi* : descongelarse

deft [ˈdɛft] *adj* : hábil, diestro

defy [diˈfaɪ] *vt* **-fied; -fying 1** CHALLENGE : desafiar **2** RESIST : resistir

degenerate [diˈdʒɛnəˌreɪt] *vi* : degenerar — **~** [diˈdʒɛnərət] *adj* : degenerado

degrade [diˈgreɪd] *vt* **-graded; -grading** : degradar — **degrading** *adj* : degradante

degree [diˈgriː] *n* **1** : grado *m* **2** *or* **academic ~** : título *m*

dehydrate [diˈhaɪˌdreɪt] *vt* **-drated; -drating** : deshidratar

deign [ˈdeɪn] *vi* **~ to** : dignarse (a)

deity [ˈdiːət̬i, ˈdeɪ-] *n, pl* **-ties** : deidad *f*

dejected [diˈdʒɛktəd] *adj* : abatido — **dejection** [diˈdʒɛkʃən] *n* : abatimiento *m*

delay [diˈleɪ] *n* : retraso *m* — **~** *vt* **1** POSTPONE : aplazar **2** HOLD UP : retrasar — *vi* : demorar

delectable [diˈlɛktəbəl] *adj* : delicioso

delegate [ˈdɛlɪgət, -ˌgeɪt] *n* : delegado *m,* -da *f* — **~** [ˈdɛlɪˌgeɪt] *v* **-gated; -gating** : delegar — **delegation** [ˌdɛlɪˈgeɪʃən] *n* : delegación *f*

delete [diˈliːt] *vt* **-leted; -leting** : borrar

deliberate [dɪˈlɪbəˌreɪt] *v* **-ated; -ating** *vt* : deliberar sobre — *vi* : deliberar — **~** [dɪˈlɪbərət] *adj* : deliberado — **deliberately** [dɪˈlɪbərətli] *adv* INTENTIONALLY : a propósito — **deliberation** [dɪˌlɪbəˈreɪʃən] *n* : deliberación *f*

delicacy [ˈdɛlɪkəsi] *n, pl* **-cies 1** : delicadeza *f* **2** FOOD : manjar *m,* exquisitez *f* — **delicate** [ˈdɛlɪkət] *adj* : delicado

delicatessen [ˌdɛlɪkəˈtɛsən] *n* : charcutería *f*

delicious [diˈlɪʃəs] *adj* : delicioso

delight [dɪˈlaɪt] *n* : placer *m,* deleite *m* — **~** *vt* : deleitar, encantar — *vi* **~ in** : deleitarse con — **delightful** [dɪˈlaɪtfəl] *adj* : delicioso, encantador

delinquent [diˈlɪŋkwənt] *adj* : delincuente — **~** *n* : delincuente *mf*

delirious [diˈlɪriəs] *adj* : delirante — **delirium** [diˈlɪriəm] *n* : delirio *m*

deliver [diˈlɪvər] *vt* **1** DISTRIBUTE : entregar, repartir **2** FREE : liberar **3** : asistir en el parto de (un niño) **4** : pronunciar (un discurso, etc.) **5** DEAL : asestar (un golpe, etc.) — **delivery** [diˈlɪvəri] *n, pl* **-eries 1** DISTRIBUTION : entrega *f,* reparto *m* **2** LIBERATION : liberación *f* **3** CHILDBIRTH : parto *m,* alumbramiento *m*

delude [diˈluːd] *vt* **-luded; -luding 1** : engañar **2 ~ oneself** : engañarse

deluge [ˈdɛlˌjuːdʒ, -juːʒ] *n* : diluvio *m*

delusion [diˈluːʒən] *n* : ilusión *f*

deluxe [diˈlʌks, -ˈlʊks] *adj* : de lujo

delve [ˈdɛlv] *vi* **delved; delving 1** : escarbar **2 ~ into** PROBE : investigar

demand [diˈmænd] *n* **1** REQUEST : petición *f* **2** CLAIM : reclamación *f,* exigencia *f* **3** → **supply** — **~** *vt* : exigir — **demanding** *adj* : exigente

demean [diˈmiːn] *vt* **~ oneself** : rebajarse

demeanor [diˈmiːnər] *n* : comportamiento *m*

demented [diˈmɛntəd] *adj* : demente, loco

demise [dɪˈmaɪz] *n* : fallecimiento *m*

democracy [diˈmɑkrəsi] *n, pl* **-cies** : democracia *f* — **democrat** [ˈdɛməˌkræt] *n* : demócrata *mf* — **democratic** [ˌdɛməˈkræt̬ɪk] *adj* : democrático

demolish [diˈmɑlɪʃ] *vt* : demoler — **demolition** [ˌdɛməˈlɪʃən, ˌdiː-] *n* : demolición *f*

demon [ˈdiːmən] *n* : demonio *m*

demonstrate [ˈdɛmənˌstreɪt] *v* **-strated; -strating** *vt* : demostrar — *vi* RALLY : manifestarse — **demonstration** [ˌdɛmənˈstreɪʃən] *n* **1** : demostración *f* **2** RALLY : manifestación *f*

demoralize [diˈmɔrəˌlaɪz] *vt* **-ized; -izing** : desmoralizar

demote [diˈmoːt] *vt* **-moted; -moting** : bajar de categoría

demure [diˈmjʊr] *adj* : recatado

den [ˈdɛn] *n* LAIR : guarida *f*

denial [diˈnaɪəl] *n* **1** : negación *f,* rechazo *m* **2** REFUSAL : denegación *f*

denim [ˈdɛnəm] *n* : tela *f* vaquera, mezclilla *f Lat*

denomination [dɪˌnɑməˈneɪʃən] *n* **1** : confesión *f* (religiosa) **2** : valor *m* (de una moneda)

denounce [diˈnaʊnts] *vt* **-nounced; -nouncing** : denunciar

dense [ˈdɛnts] *adj* **denser; -est 1** THICK : denso **2** STUPID : estúpido — **density** [ˈdɛntsət̬i] *n, pl* **-ties** : densidad *f*

dent [ˈdɛnt] *vt* : abollar — **~** *n* : abolladura *f*

dental [ˈdɛntəl] *adj* : dental — **dental floss** *n* : hilo *m* dental — **dentist** [ˈdɛntɪst] *n* : dentista *mf* — **dentures** [ˈdɛntʃərz] *npl* : dentadura *f* postiza

deny [diˈnaɪ] *vt* **-nied; -nying 1** : negar **2** REFUSE : denegar

deodorant [diˈoːdərənt] *n* : desodorante *m*

depart [diˈpɑrt] *vi* **1** : salir **2 ~ from** : apartarse de (la verdad, etc.)

department [diˈpɑrtmənt] *n* : sección *f* (de una tienda, etc.), departamento *m* (de una empresa, etc.), ministerio *m* (del gobierno) — **department store** *n* : grandes almacenes *mpl*

departure [diˈpɑrtʃər] *n* **1** : salida *f* **2** DEVIATION : desviación *f*

depend [diˈpɛnd] *vi* **1 ~ on** : depender de **2 ~ on s.o.** : contar con algn **3 that ~s** : eso depende — **dependable** [diˈpɛndəbəl] *adj* : digno de confianza — **dependence** [diˈpɛndənts] *n* : dependencia *f* — **dependent** [diˈpɛndənt] *adj* : dependiente

depict [diˈpɪkt] *vt* **1** PORTRAY : representar **2** DESCRIBE : describir

deplete [diˈpliːt] *vt* **-pleted; -pleting** : agotar, reducir

deplore [diˈplor] *vt* **-plored; -ploring** : deplorar, lamentar — **deplorable** [diˈplorəbəl] *adj* : lamentable

deploy [diˈplɔɪ] *vt* : desplegar

deport [diˈport] *vt* : deportar, expulsar (de un país) — **deportation** [ˌdiˌporˈteɪʃən] *n* : deportación *f*

depose [diˈpoːz] *vt* **-posed; -posing** : deponer

deposit [diˈpɑzət] *vt* **-ited; -iting** : depositar — **~** *n* **1** : depósito *m* **2** DOWN PAYMENT : entrega *f* inicial

depot [*in sense 1 usu* ˈdɛˌpoː, *2 usu* ˈdiː-] *n* **1** WAREHOUSE : almacén *m,* depósito *m* **2** STATION : terminal *mf*

depreciate [diˈpriːʃiˌeɪt] *vi* **-ated; -ating** : depreciarse — **depreciation** [diˌpriːʃiˈeɪʃən] *n* : depreciación *f*

depress [diˈprɛs] *vt* **1** : deprimir **2** PRESS : apretar — **depressed** [diˈprɛst] *adj* : abatido, deprimido — **depressing** [diˈprɛsɪŋ] *adj* : deprimente — **depression** [diˈprɛʃən] *n* : depresión *f*

deprive [diˈpraɪv] *vt* **-prived; -priving** : privar

depth [ˈdɛpθ] *n, pl* **depths** [ˈdɛpθs, ˈdɛps] **1** : profundidad *f* **2 in the ~s of night** : en lo más profundo de la noche

deputy [ˈdɛpjut̬i] *n, pl* **-ties** : suplente *mf;* sustituto *m,* -ta *f*

derail [diˈreɪl] *vt* : hacer descarrilar

deranged [diˈreɪndʒd] *adj* : trastornado

derelict [ˈdɛrəˌlɪkt] *adj* : abandonado

deride [diˈraɪd] *vt* **-rided; -riding** : burlarse de — **derision** [diˈrɪʒən] *n* : mofa *f*

derive [diˈraɪv] *vi* **-rived; -riving** : derivar — **derivation** [ˌdɛrəˈveɪʃən] *n* : derivación *f*

derogatory [diˈrɑgəˌtori] *adj* : despectivo

descend [diˈsɛnd] *v* : descender, bajar — **descendant** [diˈsɛndənt] *n* : descendiente *mf* — **descent** [diˈsɛnt] *n* **1** : descenso *m* **2** LINEAGE : descendencia *f*

describe [diˈskraɪb] *vt* **-scribed; -scribing** : describir — **description** [diˈskrɪpʃən] *n* : descripción *f* — **descriptive** [diˈskrɪptɪv] *adj* : descriptivo

desecrate [ˈdɛsɪˌkreɪt] *vt* **-crated; -crating** : profanar

desert [ˈdɛzərt] *n* : desierto *m* — **~** *adj* **~ island** : isla *f* desierta — **~** [diˈzərt] *vt* : abandonar — *vi* : desertar — **deserter** [diˈzərt̬ər] *n* : desertor *m,* -tora *f*

deserve [diˈzərv] *vt* **-served; -serving** : merecer

design [diˈzaɪn] *vt* **1** DEVISE : diseñar **2** PLAN : proyectar — **~** *n* **1** : diseño *m* **2** PLAN : plan *m,* proyecto *m*

designate [ˈdɛzɪgˌneɪt] *vt* **-nated; -nating** : nombrar, designar

designer [diˈzaɪnər] *n* : diseñador *m,* -dora *f*

desire [diˈzaɪr] *vt* **-sired; -siring** : desear — **~** *n* : deseo *m* — **desirable** [diˈzaɪrəbəl] *adj* : deseable

desk [ˈdɛsk] *n* : escritorio *m,* pupitre *m* (en la escuela)

desolate [ˈdɛsələt, -zə-] *adj* : desolado

despair [diˈspær] *vi* : desesperar — **~** *n* : desesperación *f*

desperate [ˈdɛspərət] *adj* : desesperado — **desperation** [ˌdɛspəˈreɪʃən] *n* : desesperación *f*

despise [diˈspaɪz] *vt* **-spised; -spising** : despreciar — **despicable** [diˈspɪkəbəl, ˈdɛspɪ-] *adj* : despreciable

despite [dəˈspaɪt] *prep* : a pesar de

despondent [diˈspɑndənt] *adj* : desanimado

dessert [diˈzərt] *n* : postre *m*

destination [ˌdɛstəˈneɪʃən] *n* : destino *m* — **destined** [ˈdɛstənd] *adj* **1** : destinado **2 ~ for** : con destino a — **destiny** [ˈdɛstəni] *n, pl* **-nies** : destino *m*

destitute [ˈdɛstəˌtuːt, -ˌtjuːt] *adj* : indigente

destroy [diˈstrɔɪ] *vt* : destruir — **destruction** [diˈstrʌkʃən] *n* : destrucción *f* — **destructive** [diˈstrʌktɪv] *adj* : destructivo

detach [dɪ'tætʃ] *vt* : separar — **detached** [dɪ'tætʃt] *adj* **1** : separado **2** IMPARTIAL : objetivo

detail [dɪ'teɪl, 'di:ˌteɪl] *n* **1** : detalle *m* **2 go into ~** : entrar en detalles — **~** *vt* : detallar — **detailed** *adj* : detallado

detain [dɪ'teɪn] *vt* **1** : detener (un prisionero) **2** DELAY : entretener

detect [dɪ'tɛkt] *vt* : detectar — **detection** [dɪ'tɛkʃən] *n* : detección *f*, descubrimiento *m* — **detective** [dɪ'tɛktɪv] *n* : detective *mf*

detention [dɪ'tɛntʃən] *n* : detención *m*

deter [dɪ'tər] *vt* **-terred; -terring** : disuadir

detergent [dɪ'tərdʒənt] *n* : detergente *m*

deteriorate [dɪ'tɪriəˌreɪt] *vi* **-rated; -rating** : deteriorarse — **deterioration** [dɪˌtɪriə'reɪʃən] *n* : deterioro *m*

determine [dɪ'tərmən] *vt* **-mined; -mining** : determinar — **determined** [dɪ'tərmənd] *adj* RESOLUTE : decidido — **determination** [dɪˌtərmə'neɪʃən] *n* : determinación *f*

deterrent [dɪ'tərənt] *n* : medida *f* disuasiva

detest [dɪ'tɛst] *vt* : detestar — **detestable** [dɪ'tɛstəbəl] *adj* : odioso

detonate ['dɛtənˌeɪt] *v* **-nated; -nating** *vt* : hacer detonar — *vi* EXPLODE : detonar, estallar — **detonation** [ˌdɛtə'neɪʃən, 'dɛtə-] *n* : detonación *f*

detour ['di:ˌtʊr, dɪ'tʊr] *n* **1** : desviación *f* **2 make a ~** : dar un rodeo — **~** *vi* : desviarse

detract [dɪ'trækt] *vi* **~ from** : aminorar, restar importancia a

detrimental [ˌdɛtrə'mɛntəl] *adj* : perjudicial

devalue [di'vælˌju:] *vt* **-ued; -uing** : devaluar

devastate ['dɛvəˌsteɪt] *vt* **-tated; -tating** : devastar — **devastating** *adj* : devastador — **devastation** [ˌdɛvə'steɪʃən] *n* : devastación *f*

develop [dɪ'vɛləp] *vt* **1** : desarrollar **2 ~ an illness** : contraer una enfermedad — *vi* **1** GROW : desarrollarse **2** HAPPEN : aparecer — **development** [dɪ'vɛləpmənt] *n* : desarrollo *m*

deviate ['di:viˌeɪt] *v* **-ated; -ating** *vi* : desviarse — **deviation** [ˌdi:vi'eɪʃən] *n* : desviación *f*

device [dɪ'vaɪs] *n* : dispositivo *m*, mecanismo *m*

devil ['dɛvəl] *n* : diablo *m*, demonio *m* — **devilish** ['dɛvəlɪʃ] *adj* : diabólico

devious ['di:viəs] *adj* **1** CRAFTY : taimado **2** WINDING : tortuoso

devise [dɪ'vaɪz] *vt* **-vised; -vising** : idear, concebir

devoid [dɪ'vɔɪd] *adj* **~ of** : desprovisto de

devote [dɪ'vo:t] *vt* **-voted; -voting** : consagrar, dedicar — **devoted** [dɪ'vo:ṭəd] *adj* : leal — **devotee** [ˌdɛvə'ti:, -'teɪ] *n* : devoto *m*, -ta *f* — **devotion** [dɪ'vo:ʃən] *n* **1** : devoción *f*, dedicación *f* **2** : oración *f* (en religión)

devour [dɪ'vaʊər] *vt* : devorar

devout [dɪ'vaʊt] *adj* : devoto

dew ['du:, 'dju:] *n* : rocío *m*

dexterity [dɛk'stɛrəṭi] *n, pl* **-ties** : destreza *f*

diabetes [ˌdaɪə'bi:ṭi:z] *n* : diabetes *f* — **diabetic** [ˌdaɪə'bɛṭɪk] *adj* : diabético — **~** *n* : diabético *m*, -ca *f*

diabolic [ˌdaɪə'bɑlɪk] *or* **diabolical** [-lɪkəl] *adj* : diabólico

diagnosis [ˌdaɪɪg'no:sɪs] *n, pl* **-noses** [-'no:ˌsi:z] : diagnóstico *m* — **diagnose** ['daɪɪgˌno:s, ˌdaɪɪg'no:s] *vt* **-nosed; -nosing** : diagnosticar — **diagnostic** [ˌdaɪɪg'nɑstɪk] *adj* : diagnóstico

diagonal [daɪ'ægənəl] *adj* : diagonal, en diagonal — **~** *n* : diagonal *f*

diagram ['daɪəˌgræm] *n* : diagrama *m*

dial ['daɪl] *n* : esfera *f* (de un reloj), dial *m* (de un radio, etc.) — **~** *v* **dialed** *or* **dialled; dialing** *or* **dialling** : marcar

dialect ['daɪəˌlɛkt] *n* : dialecto *m*

dialogue ['daɪə ˌlɔg] *n* : diálogo *m*

diameter [daɪ'æməṭər] *n* : diámetro *m*

diamond ['daɪmənd, 'daɪə-] *n* **1** : diamante *m* **2** : rombo *m* (forma) **3** *or* **baseball ~** : cuadro *m*, diamante *m*

diaper ['daɪpər, 'daɪə-] *n* : pañal *m*

diaphragm ['daɪəˌfræm] *n* : diafragma *m*

diarrhea [ˌdaɪə'ri:ə] *n* : diarrea *f*

diary ['daɪəri] *n, pl* **-ries**: diario *m*

dice ['daɪs] *ns & pl* : dados *mpl* (juego)

dictate ['dɪkˌteɪt, dɪk'teɪt] *vt* **-tated; -tating** : dictar — **dictation** [dɪk'teɪʃən] *n* : dictado *m* — **dictator** ['dɪkˌteɪṭər] *n* : dictador *m*, -dora *f* — **dictatorship** [dɪk'teɪṭərˌʃɪp, 'dɪk,-] *n* : dictadura *f*

dictionary ['dɪkʃəˌnɛri] *n, pl* **-naries** : diccionario *m*

did → **do**

die[1] ['daɪ] *vi* **died** ['daɪd]; **dying** ['daɪɪŋ] **1** : morir **2 ~ down** : amainar, disminuir **3 ~ out** : extinguirse **4 be dying for** : morirse por

die[2] ['daɪ] *n* **1** *pl* **dice** ['daɪs] : dado *m* (para jugar) **2** *pl* **dies** ['daɪz] MOLD : molde *m*

diesel ['di:zəl, -səl] *n* : diesel *m*

diet ['daɪət] *n* **1** FOOD : alimentación *f* **2 go on a ~** : ponerse a régimen — **~** *vi* : estar a régimen

differ ['dɪfər] *vi* **-ferred; -ferring 1** : diferir, ser distinto **2** DISAGREE : no estar de acuerdo — **difference** ['dɪfrənts, 'dɪfərənts] *n* : diferencia *f* — **different** ['dɪfrənt, 'dɪfərənt] *adj* : distinto, diferente — **differentiate** [ˌdɪfə'rɛntʃiˌeɪt] *v* **-ated; -ating** *vt* : diferenciar — *vi* : distinguir — **differently** ['dɪfrəntli, 'dɪfərənt-] *adv* : de otra manera

difficult ['dɪfɪˌkʌlt] *adj* : difícil — **difficulty** ['dɪfɪˌkʌlti] *n, pl* **-ties** : dificultad *f*

diffident ['dɪfədənt] *adj* : tímido, que falta confianza

dig ['dɪg] *v* **dug** ['dʌg]; **digging** *vt* **1** : cavar **2 ~ up** : desenterrar — *vi* : cavar — **~** *n* **1** GIBE : pulla *f* **2** EXCAVATION : excavación *f*

digest ['daɪˌdʒɛst] *n* : resumen *m* — **~** [daɪ'dʒɛst] *vt* **1** : digerir **2** SUMMARIZE : resumir — **digestible** [daɪ'dʒɛstəbəl, dɪ-] *adj* : digerible — **digestion** [daɪ'dʒɛstʃən, dɪ-] *n* : digestión *f* — **digestive** [daɪ'dʒɛstɪv, dɪ-] *adj* : digestivo

digit ['dɪdʒət] *n* **1** NUMERAL : dígito *m*, número *m* **2** FINGER, TOE : dedo *m* — **digital** ['dɪdʒəṭəl] *adj* : digital

dignity ['dɪgnəṭi] *n, pl* **-ties** : dignidad *f* — **dignified** ['dɪgnəˌfaɪd] *adj* : digno, decoroso

digress [daɪ'grɛs, də-] *vi* : desviarse del tema, divagar — **digression** [daɪ'grɛʃən, də-] *n* : digresión *f*

dike ['daɪk] *n* : dique *m*

dilapidated [də'læpəˌdeɪṭəd] *adj* : ruinoso

dilate [daɪ'leɪt, 'daɪˌleɪt] *v* **-lated; -lating** *vt* : dilatar — *vi* : dilatarse

dilemma [dɪ'lɛmə] *n* : dilema *m*

diligence ['dɪlədʒənts] *n* : diligencia *f* — **diligent** ['dɪlədʒənt] *adj* : diligente

dilute [daɪ'lu:t, də-] *vt* **-luted; -luting** : diluir

dim ['dɪm] *v* **dimmed; dimming** *vt* : atenuar — *vi* : irse atenuando — **~** *adj* **dimmer; dimmest 1** DARK : oscuro **2** FAINT : débil, tenue

dime ['daɪm] *n* : moneda *f* de diez centavos

dimension [də'mɛntʃən, daɪ-] *n* : dimensión *f*

diminish [də'mɪnɪʃ] *v* : disminuir

diminutive [də'mɪnjʊṭɪv] *adj* : diminuto

dimple ['dɪmpəl] *n* : hoyuelo *m*

din ['dɪn] *n* : estrépito *m*

dine ['daɪn] *vi* **dined; dining** : cenar — **diner** ['daɪnər] *n* **1** : comensal *mf* (persona) **2** : cafetería *f* (restaurante)

dingy ['dɪndʒi] *adj* **-gier; -est** : sucio, deslucido

dinner ['dɪnər] *n* : cena *f*, comida *f*

dinosaur ['daɪnəˌsɔr] *n* : dinosaurio *m*

dint ['dɪnt] *n* **by ~ of** : a fuerza de

dip ['dɪp] *v* **dipped; dipping** *vt* : mojar — *vi* : bajar, descender — **~** *n* **1** DROP : descenso *m*, caída *f* **2** SWIM : chapuzón *m* **3** SAUCE : salsa *f*

diploma [də'plo:mə] *n, pl* **-mas** : diploma *m*

diplomacy [də'plo:məsi] *n* : diplomacia *f* — **diplomat** ['dɪpləˌmæt] *n* : diplomático *m*, -ca *f* — **diplomatic** [ˌdɪplə'mæṭɪk] *adj* : diplomático

dire ['daɪr] *adj* **direr; direst 1** : grave, terrible **2** EXTREME : extremo

direct [də'rɛkt, daɪ-] *vt* **1** : dirigir **2** ORDER : mandar — **~** *adj* **1** STRAIGHT : directo **2** FRANK : franco — **~** *adv* : directamente — **direct current** *n* : corriente *f* continua — **direction** [də'rɛkʃən, daɪ-] *n* **1** : dirección *f* **2 ask ~s** : pedir indicaciones — **directly** [də'rɛktli, daɪ-] *adv* **1** STRAIGHT : directamente **2** IMMEDIATELY : en seguida — **director** [də'rɛktər, daɪ-] *n* **1** : director *m*, -tora *f* **2 board of ~s** : directorio *m* — **directory** [də'rɛktəri, daɪ-] *n, pl* **-ries** : guía *f* (telefónica)

dirt ['dərt] *n* **1** : suciedad *f* **2** SOIL : tierra *f* — **dirty** ['dərṭi] *adj* **dirtier; -est 1** : sucio **2** INDECENT : obsceno, cochino *fam*

disability [ˌdɪsə'bɪləṭi] *n, pl* **-ties** : minusvalía *f*, invalidez *f* — **disable** [dɪs'eɪbəl] *vt* **-abled; -abling** : incapacitar — **disabled** [dɪs'eɪbəld] *adj* : minusválido

disadvantage [ˌdɪsəd'væntɪdʒ] *n* : desventaja *f*

disagree [ˌdɪsə'gri:] *vi* **1** : no estar de acuerdo (con algn) **2** CONFLICT : no coincidir — **disagreeable** [ˌdɪsə'gri:əbəl] *adj* : desagradable — **disagreement** [ˌdɪsə'gri:mənt] *n* **1** : desacuerdo *m* **2** ARGUMENT : discusión *f*

disappear [ˌdɪsə'pɪr] *vi* : desaparecer — **disappearance** [ˌdɪsə'pɪrənts] *n* : desaparición *f*

disappoint [ˌdɪsə'pɔɪnt] *vt* : decepcionar, desilusionar — **disappointment** [ˌdɪsə'pɔɪntmənt] *n* : decepción *f*, desilusión *f*

disapprove [ˌdɪsə'pru:v] *vi* **-proved; -proving ~ of** : desaprobar — **disapproval** [ˌdɪsə'pru:vəl] *n* : desaprobación *f*

disarm [dɪs'ɑrm] *vt* : desarmar — **disarmament** [dɪs'ɑrməmənt] *n* : desarme *m*

disarray [ˌdɪsə'reɪ] *n* : desorden *m*

disaster [dɪ'zæstər] *n* : desastre *m* — **disastrous** [dɪ'zæstrəs] *adj* : desastroso

disbelief [ˌdɪsbɪ'li:f] *n* : incredulidad *f*

disc → **disk**

discard [dɪs'kɑrd, 'dɪsˌkɑrd] *vt* : desechar, deshacerse de

discern [dɪ'sərn, -'zərn] *vt* : percibir, discernir — **discernible** [dɪ'sərnəbəl, -'zər-] *adj* : perceptible

discharge [dɪs'tʃɑrdʒ, 'dɪsˌ-] *vt* **-charged; -charging 1** UNLOAD : descargar **2** RELEASE : liberar, poner en libertad **3** DISMISS : despedir **4** CARRY OUT : cumplir con (una obligación) — **~** ['dɪsˌtʃɑrdʒ, dɪs'-] *n* **1** : descarga *f* (de electricidad), emisión *f* (de humo, etc.) **2** DISMISSAL : despido *m* **3** RELEASE : alta *f* (de un paciente), puesta *f* en libertad (de un preso) **4** : supuración *f* (en medicina)

disciple [dɪ'saɪpəl] *n* : discípulo *m*, -la *f*

discipline ['dɪsəplən] *n* **1** : disciplina *f* **2** PUNISHMENT : castigo *m* — **~** *vt* **-plined; -plining 1** CONTROL : disciplinar **2** PUNISH : castigar

disclaim [dɪs'kleɪm] *vt* : negar

disclose [dɪs'klo:z] *vt* **-closed; -closing** : revelar — **disclosure** [dɪs'klo:ʒər] *n* : revelación *f*

discomfort [dɪs'kʌmfərt] *n* **1** : incomodidad *f* **2** PAIN : malestar *m* **3** UNEASINESS : inquietud *f*

disconcert [ˌdɪskən'sərt] *vt* : desconcertar

disconnect [ˌdɪskə'nɛkt] *vt* : desconectar

disconsolate [dɪs'kɑntsələt] *adj* : desconsolado

discontented [ˌdɪskən'tɛntəd] *adj* : descontento

discontinue [ˌdɪskən'tɪnˌju:] *vt* **-ued; -uing** : suspender, descontinuar

discount ['dɪsˌkaʊnt, dɪs'-] *n* : descuento *m*, rebaja *f* — **~** *vt* **1** : descontar (precios) **2** DISREGARD : descartar

discourage [dɪs'kərɪdʒ] *vt* **-aged; -aging** : desalentar, desanimar — **discouragement** [dɪs'kərɪdʒmənt] *n* : desánimo *m*, desaliento *m*

discover [dɪs'kʌvər] *vt* : descubrir — **discovery** [dɪs'kʌvəri] *n, pl* **-ries** : descubrimiento *m*

discredit [dɪs'krɛdət] *vt* : desacreditar — **~** *n* : descrédito *m*

discreet [dɪs'kri:t] *adj* : discreto

discrepancy [dɪs'krɛpəntsi] *n, pl* **-cies** : discrepancia *f*

discretion [dɪs'krɛʃən] *n* : discreción *f*

discriminate [dɪs'krɪməˌneɪt] *vi* **-nated; -nating 1 ~ against** : discriminar **2 ~ between** : distinguir entre — **discrimination** [dɪsˌkrɪmə'neɪʃən] *n* **1** PREJUDICE : discriminación *f* **2** DISCERNMENT : discernimiento *m*

discuss [dɪs'kʌs] *vt* : hablar de, discutir — **discussion** [dɪs'kʌʃən] *n* : discusión *f*

disdain [dɪs'deɪn] *n* : desdén *m* — **~** *vt* : desdeñar

disease [dɪ'zi:z] *n* : enfermedad *f* — **diseased** [dɪ'zi:zd] *adj* : enfermo

disembark [ˌdɪsɪm'bɑrk] *vi* : desembarcar

disengage [ˌdɪsɪn'geɪdʒ] *vt* **-gaged; -gaging 1** RELEASE : soltar **2 ~ the clutch** : desembragar

disentangle [ˌdɪsɪn'tæŋgəl] *vt* **-gled; -gling** : desenredar

disfavor [dɪs'feɪvər] *n* : desaprobación *f*

disfigure [dɪs'fɪgjər] *vt* **-ured; -uring** : desfigurar

disgrace [dɪ'skreɪs] *vt* **-graced; -gracing** : deshonrar — **~** *n* **1** DISHONOR : deshonra *f* **2** SHAME : vergüenza *f* — **disgraceful** [dɪ'skreɪsfəl] *adj* : vergonzoso, deshonroso

disgruntled [dɪs'grʌntəld] *adj* : descontento

disguise [dɪ'skaɪz] *vt* **-guised; -guising** : disfrazar — **~** *n* : disfraz *m*

disgust [dɪ'skʌst] *n* : asco *m*, repugnancia *f* — **~** *vt* : asquear — **disgusting** [dɪ'skʌstɪŋ] *adj* : asqueroso

dish ['dɪʃ] *n* **1** : plato *m* **2** *or* **serving ~** : fuente *f* **3 wash the ~es** : lavar los platos — **~** *vt or* **~ up** : servir — **dishcloth** ['dɪʃˌklɔθ] *n* : paño *m* de cocina (para secar), trapo *m* de fregar (para lavar)

dishearten [dɪs'hɑrtən] *vt* : desanimar

disheveled *or* **dishevelled** [dɪ'ʃɛvəld] *adj* : desaliñado, despeinado (dícese del pelo)

dishonest [dɪ'sɑnəst] *adj* : deshonesto — **dishonesty** [dɪ'sɑnəsti] *n, pl* **-ties** : falta *f* de honradez

dishonor [dɪ'sɑnər] *n* : deshonra *f* — **~** *vt* : deshonrar — **dishonorable** [dɪ'sɑnərəbəl] *adj* : deshonroso

dishwasher ['dɪʃˌwɔʃər] *n* : lavaplatos *m*, lavavajillas *m*

disillusion [ˌdɪsə'lu:ʒən] *vt* : desilusionar — **disillusionment** [ˌdɪsə'lu:ʒənmənt] *n* : desilusión *f*

disinfect [ˌdɪsɪn'fɛkt] *vt* : desinfectar — **disinfectant** [ˌdɪsɪn'fɛktənt] *n* : desinfectante *m*

disintegrate [dɪs'ɪntəˌgreɪt] *vi* **-grated; -grating** : desintegrarse

disinterested [dɪs'ɪntərəstəd, -ˌrɛs-] *adj* : desinteresado

disk *or* **disc** ['dɪsk] *n* : disco *m*

dislike [dɪs'laɪk] *n* : aversión *f*, antipatía *f* — **~** *vt* **-liked; -liking 1** : tener aversión a **2 I ~ dancing** : no me gusta bailar

dislocate ['dɪsloˌkeɪt, dɪs'lo:-] *vt* **-cated; -cating** : dislocar

dislodge [dɪs'lɑdʒ] *vt* **-lodged; -lodging** : sacar, desalojar

disloyal [dɪs'lɔɪəl] *adj* : desleal — **disloyalty** [dɪs'lɔɪəlti] *n, pl* **-ties** : deslealtad *f*

dismal ['dɪzməl] *adj* : sombrío, deprimente

dismantle [dɪs'mæntəl] *vt* **-tled; -tling** : desmontar, desarmar

dismay [dɪs'meɪ] *vt* : consternar — **~** *n* : consternación *f*

dismiss [dɪs'mɪs] *vt* **1** DISCHARGE : despedir, destituir **2** REJECT : descartar, rechazar — **dismissal** [dɪs'mɪsəl] *n* **1** : despido *m* (de un empleado), destitución *f* (de un funcionario) **2** REJECTION : rechazo *m*

dismount [dɪs'maʊnt] *vi* : desmontar

disobey [ˌdɪsə'beɪ] *v* : desobedecer — **disobedience** [ˌdɪsə'bi:diənts] *n* : desobediencia *f* — **disobedient** [-ənt] *adj* : desobediente

disorder [dɪs'ɔrdər] *n* **1** : desorden *m* **2** AILMENT : afección *f*, problema *m* — **disorderly** [dɪs'ɔrdərli] *adj* : desordenado

disorganize [dɪs'ɔrgəˌnaɪz] *vt* **-nized; -nizing** : desorganizar

disown [dɪs'o:n] *vt* : renegar de

disparage [dɪs'pærɪdʒ] *vt* **-aged; -aging** : menospreciar

dispassionate [dɪs'pæʃənət] *adj* : desapasionado

dispatch [dɪs'pætʃ] *vt* : despachar, enviar

dispel [dɪs'pɛl] *vt* **-pelled; -pelling** : disipar

dispensation [ˌdɪspɛn'seɪʃən] *n* EXEMPTION : exención *m*, dispensa *f*

dispense [dɪs'pɛnts] *v* **-pensed; -pensing** *vt* : repartir, distribuir — *vi* **~ with** : prescindir de

disperse [dɪs'pərs] *v* **-persed; -persing** *vt* : dispersar — *vi* : dispersarse

displace [dɪs'pleɪs] *vt* **-placed; -placing 1** : desplazar **2** REPLACE : reemplazar

display [dɪs'pleɪ] *vt* **1** EXHIBIT : exponer, exhibir **2 ~ anger** : manifestar la ira — **~** *n* : muestra *f*, exposición *f*

displease [dɪs'pli:z] *vt* **-pleased; -pleasing** : desagradar — **displeasure** [dɪs'plɛʒər] *n* : desagrado *m*

dispose [dɪs'po:z] *v* **-posed; -posing** *vt* : disponer — *vi* **~ of** : deshacerse de — **disposable** [dɪs'po:zəbəl] *adj* : desechable — **disposal** [dɪs'po:zəl] *n* **1** REMOVAL : eliminación *f* **2 have at one's ~** : tener a su disposición — **disposition** [ˌdɪspə'zɪʃən] *n* **1** ARRANGEMENT : disposición *f* **2** TEMPERAMENT : temperamento *m*, carácter *m*

disprove [dɪs'pru:v] *vt* **-proved; -proving** : refutar

dispute [dɪs'pju:t] *v* **-puted; -puting** *vt* QUESTION : cuestionar — *vi* ARGUE : discutir — **~** *n* : disputa *f*, conflicto *m*

disqualification [dɪsˌkwɑləfə'keɪʃən] *n* : descalificación *f* — **disqualify** [dɪs'kwɑləˌfaɪ] *vt* **-fied; -fying** : descalificar

disregard [ˌdɪsrɪ'gɑrd] *vt* : ignorar, hacer caso omiso de — **~** *n* : indiferencia *f*

disrepair [ˌdɪsrɪ'pær] *n* : mal estado *m*

disreputable [dɪs'rɛpjʊṭəbəl] *adj* : de mala fama

disrespect [ˌdɪsrɪ'spɛkt] *n* : falta *f* de respeto — **disrespectful** [ˌdɪsrɪ'spɛktfəl] *adj* : irrespetuoso

disrupt [dɪs'rʌpt] *vt* : trastornar, perturbar — **disruption** [dɪs'rʌpʃən] *n* : trastorno *m*

dissatisfaction [dɪsˌsæṭəs'fækʃən] *n* : descontento *m* — **dissatisfied** [dɪs'sæṭəsˌfaɪd] *adj* : descontento

dissect [dɪ'sɛkt] *vt* : disecar

disseminate [dɪ'sɛməˌneɪt] *vt* **-nated; -nating** : diseminar, difundir

dissent [dɪ'sɛnt] *vi* : disentir — **~** *n* : disentimiento *m*

dissertation [ˌdɪsər'teɪʃən] THESIS : tesis *f*

disservice [dɪs'sərvɪs] *n* **do a ~ to** : no hacer justicia a

dissident ['dɪsədənt] *n* : disidente *mf*

dissimilar [dɪ'sɪmələr] *adj* : distinto

dissipate ['dɪsəˌpeɪt] *vt* **-pated; -pating 1** DISPEL : disipar **2** SQUANDER : desperdiciar

dissolve [dɪ'zɑlv] *v* **-solved; -solving** *vt* : disolver — *vi* : disolverse

dissuade [dɪ'sweɪd] *vt* **-suaded; -suading** : disuadir

distance ['dɪstənts] *n* **1** : distancia *f* **2 in the ~** : a lo lejos — **distant** ['dɪstənt] *adj* : distante

distaste [dɪs'teɪst] *n* : desagrado *m* — **distasteful** [dɪs'teɪstfəl] *adj* : desagradable

distend [dɪs'tɛnd] *vt* : dilatar — *vi* : dilatarse

distill [dɪ'stɪl] *or Brit* **distil** *vt* **-tilled; -tilling** : destilar

distinct [dɪ'stɪŋkt] *adj* **1** DIFFERENT : distinto **2** CLEAR : claro — **distinction** [dɪ'stɪŋkʃən] *n* : distinción *f* — **distinctive** [dɪ'stɪŋktɪv] *adj* : distintivo

distinguish [dɪs'tɪŋgwɪʃ] *vt* : distinguir — **distinguished** [dɪs'tɪŋgwɪʃt] *adj* : distinguido

distort [dɪ'stɔrt] *vt* : deformar, distorsionar — **distortion** [dɪ'stɔrʃən] *n* : deformación *f*

distract [dɪ'strækt] *vt* : distraer — **distraction** [dɪ'strækʃən] *n* : distracción *f*

distraught [dɪ'strɔt] *adj* : muy afligido

distress [dɪ'strɛs] *n* **1** : angustia *f*, aflicción *f* **2 in ~** : en peligro — **~** *vt* : afligir — **distressing** [dɪ'strɛsɪŋ] *adj* : penoso

distribute [dɪ'strɪˌbju:t, -bjʊt] *vt* **-uted; -uting** : distribuir, repartir — **distribution** [ˌdɪstrə'bju:ʃən] *n* : distribución *f* — **distributor** [dɪ'strɪbjʊṭər] *n* : distribuidor *m*, -dora *f*

district ['dɪsˌtrɪkt] *n* **1** REGION : región *f*, zona *f*, barrio *m* (de una ciudad) **2** : distrito *m* (zona política)

distrust [dɪsˈtrʌst] *n* : desconfianza *f* — ~ *vt* : desconfiar de

disturb [dɪˈstərb] *vt* **1** BOTHER : molestar, perturbar **2** WORRY : inquietar — **disturbance** [dɪˈstərbənts] *n* **1** COMMOTION : alboroto *m*, disturbio *m* **2** INTERRUPTION : interrupción *f*

disuse [dɪsˈjuːs] *n* **fall into ~** : caer en desuso

ditch [ˈdɪtʃ] *n* : zanja *f*, cuneta *f* — ~ *vt* DISCARD : deshacerse de, botar

ditto [ˈdɪˌtoː] *n, pl* **-tos 1** : ídem *m* **2 ~ marks** : comillas *fpl*

dive [ˈdaɪv] *vi* **dived** *or* **dove** [ˈdoːv]; **dived; diving 1** : zambullirse, tirarse al agua **2** DESCEND : bajar en picada (dícese de un avión, etc.) — ~ *n* **1** : zambullida *f*, clavado *m Lat* **2** DESCENT : descenso *m* en picada — **diver** [ˈdaɪvər] *n* : saltador *m*, -dora *f*

diverge [dəˈvərdʒ, daɪ-] *vi* **-verged; -verging** : divergir

diverse [daɪˈvərs, də-, ˈdaɪˌvərs] *adj* : diverso — **diversify** [daɪˈvərsəˌfaɪ, də-] *v* **-fied; -fying** *vt* : diversificar — *vi* : diversificarse

diversion [daɪˈvərʒən, də-] *n* **1** : desviación *f* **2** AMUSEMENT : diversión *f*, distracción *f*

diversity [daɪˈvərsəti, də-] *n, pl* **-ties** : diversidad *f*

divert [dəˈvərt, daɪ-] *vt* **1** : desviar **2** DISTRACT : distraer **3** AMUSE : divertir

divide [dəˈvaɪd] *v* **-vided; -viding** *vt* : dividir — *vi* : dividirse

dividend [ˈdɪvəˌdɛnd, -dənd] *n* : dividendo *m*

divine [dəˈvaɪn] *adj* **-viner; -est** : divino — **divinity** [dəˈvɪnəti] *n, pl* **-ties** : divinidad *f*

division [dɪˈvɪʒən] *n* : división *f*

divorce [dəˈvors] *n* : divorcio *m* — ~ *v* **-vorced; -vorcing** *vt* : divorciar — *vi* : divorciarse — **divorcée** [dɪˌvorˈseɪ, -ˈsiː; -ˈvorˌ-] *n* : divorciada *f*

divulge [dəˈvʌldʒ, daɪ-] *vt* **-vulged; -vulging** : revelar, divulgar

dizzy [ˈdɪzi] *adj* **dizzier; -est 1** : mareado **2 a ~ speed** : una velocidad vertiginosa — **dizziness** [ˈdɪzinəs] *n* : mareo *m*, vértigo *m*

DNA [ˌdiːˌɛnˈeɪ] *n* : AND *m*

do [ˈduː] *v* **did** [ˈdɪd]; **done** [ˈdʌn]; **doing; does** [ˈdʌz] *vt* **1** : hacer **2** PREPARE : preparar — *vi* **1** BEHAVE : hacer **2** FARE : estar, ir, andar **3** SUFFICE : ser suficiente **4 ~ away with** : abolir, eliminar **5 how are you doing?** : ¿cómo estás? — *v aux* **1** (*used in interrogative sentences*) **do you know her?** : ¿la conoces? **2** (*used in negative statements*) **I don't know** : yo no se **3** (*used as a substitute verb to avoid repetition*) **do you speak English? yes, I do** : ¿habla inglés? sí

dock [ˈdɑk] *n* : muelle *m* — ~ *vt* : descontar dinero de (un sueldo) — *vi* ANCHOR : fondear, atracar

doctor [ˈdɑktər] *n* **1** : doctor *m*, -tora *f* (en derecho, etc.) **2** PHYSICIAN : médico *m*, -ca; doctor *m*, -tora *f* — ~ *vt* ALTER : alterar, falsificar

doctrine [ˈdɑktrɪn] *n* : doctrina *f*

document [ˈdɑkjʊmənt] *n* : documento *m* — ~ [ˈdɑkjʊˌmɛnt] *vt* : documentar — **documentary** [ˌdɑkjʊˈmɛntəri] *n, pl* **-ries** : documental *m*

dodge [ˈdɑdʒ] *n* : artimaña *f*, truco *m* — ~ *v* **dodged; dodging** *vt* : esquivar, eludir — *vi* : echarse a un lado

doe [ˈdoː] *n, pl* **does** *or* **doe** : gama *f*, cierva *f*

does → **do**

dog [ˈdɔg, ˈdɑg] *n* : perro *m*, -rra *f* — ~ *vt* **dogged; dogging** : perseguir — **dogged** [ˈdɔgəd] *adj* : tenaz

dogma [ˈdɔgmə] *n* : dogma *m* — **dogmatic** [dɔgˈmætɪk] *adj* : dogmático

doily [ˈdɔɪli] *n, pl* **-lies** : tapete *m*

doings [ˈduːɪŋz] *npl* : actividades *fpl*

doldrums [ˈdoːldrəmz, ˈdɑl-] *npl* **be in the ~** : estar abatido

dole [ˈdoːl] *n* : subsidio *m* de desempleo — ~ *vt* **doled; doling** *or* **~ out** : repartir

doleful [ˈdoːlfəl] *adj* : triste, lúgubre

doll [ˈdɑl, ˈdɔl] *n* : muñeco *m*, -ca *f*

dollar [ˈdɑlər] *n* : dólar *m*

dolphin [ˈdɑlfən, ˈdɔl-] *n* : delfín *m*

domain [doˈmeɪn, də-] *n* **1** TERRITORY : dominio *m* **2** FIELD : campo *m*, esfera *f*

dome [ˈdoːm] *n* : cúpula *f*

domestic [dəˈmɛstɪk] *adj* **1** : doméstico **2** INTERNAL : nacional — ~ *n* SERVANT : empleado *m* doméstico, empleada *f* doméstica — **domesticate** [dəˈmɛstɪˌkeɪt] *vt* **-cated; -cating** : domesticar

domination [ˌdɑməˈneɪʃən] *n* : dominación *f* — **dominant** [ˈdɑmənənt] *adj* : dominante — **dominate** [ˈdɑməˌneɪt] *v* **-nated; -nating** : dominar — **domineer** [ˌdɑməˈnɪr] *vi* : dominar, tiranizar

dominos [ˈdɑməˌnoːz] *n* : dominó *m* (juego)

donate [ˈdoːˌneɪt, doː-] *vt* **-nated; -nating** : donar, hacer un donativo de — **donation** [doːˈneɪʃən] *n* : donativo *m*

done [ˈdʌn] → **do** — ~ *adj* **1** FINISHED : terminado, hecho **2** COOKED : cocido

donkey [ˈdɑŋki, ˈdʌŋ-] *n, pl* **-keys** : burro *m*

donor [ˈdoːnər] *n* : donante *mf*

don't [ˈdoːnt] (*contraction of* **do not**) → **do**

doodle [ˈduːdəl] *v* **-dled; -dling** : garabatear — ~ *n* : garabato *m*

doom [ˈduːm] *n* : perdición *f*, fatalidad *f* — ~ *vt* : condenar

door [ˈdor] *n* **1** : puerta *f* **2** ENTRANCE : entrada *f* — **doorbell** [ˈdorˌbɛl] *n* : timbre *m* — **doorknob** [ˈdorˌnɑb] *n* : pomo *m* — **doorman** [ˈdormən] *n, pl* **-men** [-mən, -ˌmɛn] : portero *m* — **doormat** [ˈdorˌmæt] *n* : felpudo *m* — **doorstep** [ˈdorˌstɛp] *n* : umbral *m* — **doorway** [ˈdorˌweɪ] *n* : entrada *f*, portal *m*

dope [ˈdoːp] *n* **1** DRUG : droga *f* **2** IDIOT : idiota *mf* — ~ *vt* **doped; doping** : drogar

dormant [ˈdɔrmənt] *adj* : inactivo, latente

dormitory [ˈdɔrməˌtori] *n, pl* **-ries** : dormitorio *m*

dose [ˈdoːs] *n* : dosis *f* — **dosage** [ˈdoːsɪdʒ] *n* : dosis *f*

dot [ˈdɑt] *n* **1** : punto *m* **2 on the ~** : en punto

dote [ˈdoːt] *vi* **doted; doting ~ on** : adorar

double [ˈdʌbəl] *adj* : doble — ~ *v* **-bled; -bling** *vt* : doblar — *vi* : doblarse — ~ *adv* : (el) doble — ~ *n* : doble *mf* — **double bass** *n* : contrabajo *m* — **double–cross** [ˌdʌbəlˈkrɔs] *vt* : traicionar — **doubly** [ˈdʌbli] *adv* : doblemente

doubt [ˈdaʊt] *vt* **1** : dudar **2** DISTRUST : desconfiar de, dudar de — ~ *n* : duda *f* — **doubtful** [ˈdaʊtfəl] *adj* : dudoso — **doubtless** [ˈdaʊtləs] *adv* : sin duda

dough [ˈdoː] *n* : masa *f* — **doughnut** [ˈdoːˌnʌt] *n* : rosquilla *f*, dona *f Lat*

douse [ˈdaʊs, ˈdaʊz] *vt* **doused; dousing 1** DRENCH : empapar, mojar **2** EXTINGUISH : apagar

dove[1] [ˈdoːv] → **dive**

dove[2] [ˈdʌv] *n* : paloma *f*

dowdy [ˈdaʊdi] *adj* **dowdier; -est** : poco elegante

down [ˈdaʊn] *adv* **1** DOWNWARD : hacia abajo **2 come/go ~** : bajar **3 ~ here** : aquí abajo **4 fall ~** : caer **5 lie ~** : acostarse **6 sit ~** : sentarse — ~ *prep* **1** ALONG : a lo largo de **2** THROUGH : a través de **3 ~ the hill** : cuesta abajo — ~ *adj* **1** DESCENDING : de bajada **2** DOWNCAST : abatido — ~ *n* : plumón *m* — **downcast** [ˈdaʊnˌkæst] *adj* : triste, abatido — **downfall** [ˈdaʊnˌfɔl] *n* : ruina *f* — **downhearted** [ˈdaʊnˌhɑrtəd] *adj* : desanimado — **downhill** [ˈdaʊnˈhɪl] *adv & adj* : cuesta abajo — **down payment** *n* : entrega *f* inicial — **downpour** [ˈdaʊnˌpor] *n* : chaparrón *m* — **downright** [ˈdaʊnˌraɪt] *adv* : absolutamente — ~ *adj* : absoluto, categórico — **downstairs** [ˈdaʊnˈstærz] *adv* : abajo — ~ [ˈdaʊnˌstærz] *adj* : de abajo — **downstream** [ˈdaʊnˈstriːm] *adv* : río abajo — **down–to–earth** [ˌdaʊntuˈərθ] *adj* : realista — **downtown** [ˌdaʊnˈtaʊn, ˈdaʊnˌtaʊn] *n* : centro *m* (de la ciudad) — ~ [ˌdaʊnˈtaʊn] *adv* : al centro, en el centro — ~ *adj* : del centro — **downward** [ˈdaʊnwərd] *or* **downwards** [-wərdz] *adv & adj* : hacia abajo

dowry [ˈdaʊri] *n, pl* **-ries** : dote *f*

doze [ˈdoːz] *vi* **dozed; dozing** : dormitar

dozen [ˈdʌzən] *n, pl* **dozens** *or* **dozen** : docena *f*

drab [ˈdræb] *adj* **drabber; drabbest** : monótono, apagado

draft [ˈdræft, ˈdraft] *n* **1** : corriente *f* de aire **2** *or* **rough ~** : borrador *m* **3** : conscripción *f* (militar) **4** *or* **~ beer** : cerveza *f* de barril — ~ *vt* **1** SKETCH : hacer el borrador de **2** CONSCRIPT : reclutar — **drafty** [ˈdræfti] *adj* **draftier; -est** : con corrientes de aire

drag [ˈdræg] *v* **dragged; dragging** *vt* **1** : arrastrar **2** DREDGE : dragar — *vi* : arrastrar(se) — ~ *n* **1** RESISTANCE : resistencia *f* (aerodinámica) **2** BORE : pesadez *f*, plomo *m fam*

dragon [ˈdrægən] *n* : dragón *m* — **dragonfly** [ˈdrægənˌflaɪ] *n, pl* **-flies** : libélula *f*

drain [ˈdreɪn] *vt* **1** EMPTY : vaciar, drenar **2** EXHAUST : agotar — *vi* **1** : escurrir(se) (se dice de los platos) **2** *or* **~ away** : desaparecer poco a poco — ~ *n* **1** : desagüe *m* **2** SEWER : alcantarilla *f* **3** DEPLETION : agotamiento *m* — **drainage** [ˈdreɪnɪdʒ] *n* : drenaje *m* — **drainpipe** [ˈdreɪnˌpaɪp] *n* : tubo *m* de desagüe

drama [ˈdrɑmə, ˈdræ-] *n* : drama *m* — **dramatic** [drəˈmætɪk] *adj* : dramático — **dramatist** [ˈdræmətɪst, ˈdrɑ-] *n* : dramaturgo *m*, -ga *f* — **dramatize** [ˈdræməˌtaɪz, ˈdrɑ-] *vt* **-tized; -tizing** : dramatizar

drank → **drink**

drape [ˈdreɪp] *vt* **draped; draping 1** COVER : cubrir (con tela) **2** HANG : drapear — **drapes** *npl* CURTAINS : cortinas *fpl*

drastic [ˈdræstɪk] *adj* : drástico

draught [ˈdræft, ˈdraft] → **draft**

draw [ˈdrɔ] *v* **drew** [ˈdruː]; **drawn** [ˈdrɔn]; **drawing** *vt* **1** PULL : tirar de **2** ATTRACT : atraer **3** SKETCH : dibujar, trazar **4** : sacar (una espada, etc.) **5 ~ a conclusion** : llegar a una conclusión **6 ~ up** DRAFT : redactar — *vi* **1** SKETCH : dibujar **2 ~ near** : acercarse — ~ *n* **1** DRAWING : sorteo *m* **2** TIE : empate *m* **3** ATTRACTION : atracción *f* — **drawback** [ˈdrɔˌbæk] *n* : desventaja *f* — **drawer** [ˈdrɔr, ˈdrɔər] *n* : gaveta *f*, cajón *m* (en un mueble) — **drawing** [ˈdrɔɪŋ] *n* **1** LOTTERY : sorteo *m* **2** SKETCH : dibujo *m*

drawl [ˈdrɔl] *n* : habla *f* lenta y con vocales prolongadas

dread [ˈdrɛd] *vt* : temer — ~ *n* : pavor *m*, temor *m* — **dreadful** [ˈdrɛdfəl] *adj* : espantoso, terrible

dream [ˈdriːm] *n* : sueño *m* — ~ *v* **dreamed** [ˈdrɛmpt, ˈdriːmd] *or* **dreamt** [ˈdrɛmpt]; **dreaming** *vi* : soñar — *vt* **1** : soñar **2 ~ up** : idear — **dreamer** [ˈdriːmər] *n* : soñador *m*, -dora *f* — **dreamy** [ˈdriːmi] *adj* **dreamier; -est** : soñador

dreary [ˈdrɪri] *adj* **-rier; -est** : sombrío, deprimente

dredge [ˈdrɛdʒ] *vt* **dredged; dredging** : dragar — ~ *n* : draga *f*

dregs [ˈdrɛgz] *npl* : heces *fpl*

drench [ˈdrɛntʃ] *vt* : empapar

dress [ˈdrɛs] *vt* **1** : vestir **2** : preparar (pollo o pescado), aliñar (ensalada) — *vi* **1** : vestirse **2 ~ up** : ponerse elegante — ~ *n* **1** CLOTHING : ropa *f* **2** : vestido *m* (de mujer) — **dresser** [ˈdrɛsər] *n* : cómoda *f* con espejo — **dressing** [ˈdrɛsɪŋ] *n* **1** : aliño *m* (de ensalada), relleno *m* (de pollo) **2** BANDAGE : vendaje *m* — **dressmaker** [ˈdrɛsˌmeɪkər] *n* : modista *mf* — **dressy** [ˈdrɛsi] *adj* **dressier; -est** : elegante

drew → **draw**

dribble [ˈdrɪbəl] *vi* **-bled; -bling 1** DRIP : gotear **2** DROOL : babear **3** : driblar (en basquetbol) — ~ *n* **1** TRICKLE : goteo *m*, hilo *m* **2** DROOL : baba *f*

drier, driest → **dry**

drift [ˈdrɪft] *n* **1** MOVEMENT : movimiento *m* **2** HEAP : montón *m* (de arena, etc.), ventisquero *m* (de nieve) **3** MEANING : sentido *m* — ~ *vi* **1** : ir a la deriva **2** ACCUMULATE : amontonarse

drill [ˈdrɪl] *n* **1** : taladro *m* **2** : ejercicio *m* (en educación), simulacro *m* (de incendio, etc.) — ~ *vt* **1** : perforar, taladrar **2** TRAIN : instruir por repetición — *vi* **~ for** : perforar en busca de

drink [ˈdrɪŋk] *v* **drank** [ˈdræŋk]; **drunk** [ˈdrʌŋk] *or* **drank; drinking** : beber — ~ *n* : bebida *f*

drip [ˈdrɪp] *vi* **dripped; dripping** : gotear — ~ *n* **1** DROP : gota *f* **2** DRIPPING : goteo *m*

drive [ˈdraɪv] *v* **drove** [ˈdroːv]; **driven** [ˈdrɪvən]; **driving** *vt* **1** : manejar **2** IMPEL : impulsar **3 ~ crazy** : volver loco **4 ~ s.o. to (do sth)** : llevar a algn a (hacer algo) — *vi* : manejar, conducir — ~ *n* **1** : paseo *m* (en coche) **2** CAMPAIGN : campaña *f* **3** VIGOR : energía *f* **4** NEED : instinto *m*

drivel [ˈdrɪvəl] *n* : tonterías *fpl*

driver [ˈdraɪvər] *n* : conductor *m*, -tora *f*; chofer *m*

driveway [ˈdraɪvˌweɪ] *n* : camino *m* de entrada

drizzle [ˈdrɪzəl] *n* : llovizna *f* — ~ *vi* **-zled; -zling** : lloviznar

drone [ˈdroːn] *n* **1** BEE : zángano *m* **2** HUM : zumbido *m* — ~ *vi* **droned; droning 1** BUZZ : zumbar **2** *or* **~ on** : hablar con monotonía

drool [ˈdruːl] *vi* : babear — ~ *n* : baba *f*

droop [ˈdruːp] *vi* : inclinarse (dícese de la cabeza), encorvarse (dícese de los escombros), marchitarse (dícese de las flores)

drop [ˈdrɑp] *n* **1** : gota *f* (de líquido) **2** DECLINE, FALL : caída *f* — ~ *v* **dropped; dropping** *vt* **1** : dejar caer **2** LOWER : bajar **3** ABANDON : abandonar, dejar **4 ~ off** LEAVE : dejar — *vi* **1** FALL : caer(se) **2** DECREASE : bajar, descender **3 ~ by** *or* **~ in** : pasar

drought [ˈdraʊt] *n* : sequía *f*

drove → **drive**

droves [ˈdroːvz] *n* **in ~** : en manada

drown [ˈdraʊn] *vt* : ahogar — *vi* : ahogarse

drowsy [ˈdraʊzi] *adj* **drowsier; -est** : somnoliento

drudgery [ˈdrʌdʒəri] *n, pl* **-eries** : trabajo *m* pesado

drug [ˈdrʌg] *n* **1** MEDICATION : medicamento *m* **2** NARCOTIC : droga *f*, estupefaciente *m* — ~ *vt* **drugged; drugging** : drogar — **drugstore** [ˈdrʌgˌstor] *n* : farmacia *f*

drum [ˈdrʌm] *n* **1** : tambor *m* **2** *or* **oil ~** : bidón *m* (de petróleo) — ~ *v* **drummed; drumming** *vi* : tocar el tambor — *vt* : tamborilear con (los dedos, etc.) — **drumstick** [ˈdrʌmˌstɪk] *n* **1** : palillo *m* (de tambor) **2** : muslo *m* (de pollo)

drunk [ˈdrʌŋk] → **drink** — ~ *adj* : borracho — ~ *or* **drunkard** [ˈdrʌŋkərd] *n* : borracho *m*, -cha *f* — **drunken** [ˈdrʌŋkən] *adj* : borracho, ebrio

dry [ˈdraɪ] *adj* **drier; driest** : seco — ~ *v* **dried; drying** *vt* : secar — *vi* : secarse — **dry–clean** [ˈdraɪˌkliːn] *vt* : limpiar en seco — **dry cleaner** *n* : tintorería *f* (servicio) — **dry cleaning** *n* : limpieza *f* en seco — **dryer** [ˈdraɪər] *n* : secadora *f* — **dryness** [ˈdraɪnəs] *n* : sequedad *f*, aridez *f*

dual [ˈduːəl, ˈdjuː-] *adj* : doble

dub [ˈdʌb] *vt* **dubbed; dubbing 1** CALL : apodar **2** : doblar (una película)

dubious [ˈduːbiəs, ˈdjuː-] *adj* **1** UNCERTAIN : dudoso **2** QUESTIONABLE : sospechoso

duchess [ˈdʌtʃəs] *n* : duquesa *f*

duck [ˈdʌk] *n, pl* **duck** *or* **ducks** : pato *m*, -ta *f* — ~ *vt* **1** LOWER : agachar, bajar **2** EVADE : eludir, esquivar — *vi* : agacharse — **duckling** [ˈdʌklɪŋ] *n* : patito *m*, -ta *f*

duct [ˈdʌkt] *n* : conducto *m*

due [ˈduː, ˈdjuː] *adj* **1** PAYABLE : pagadero **2** APPROPRIATE : debido, apropiado **3** EXPECTED : esperado **4 ~ to** : debido a — ~ *n* **1 give s.o. their ~** : hacer justicia a algn **2 ~s** *npl* : cuota *f* — ~ *adv* **~ east** : justo al este

duel [ˈduːəl, ˈdjuː-] *n* : duelo *m*

duet [duˈɛt, dju-] *n* : dúo *m*

dug → **dig**

duke [ˈduːk, ˈdjuːk] *n* : duque *m*

dull [ˈdʌl] *adj* **1** STUPID : torpe **2** BLUNT : desafilado **3** BORING : aburrido **4** LACKLUSTER : apagado — ~ *vt* : entorpecer (los sentidos), aliviar (el dolor)

dumb [ˈdʌm] *adj* **1** MUTE : mudo **2** STUPID : estúpido

dumbfound *or* **dumfound** [ˌdʌmˈfaʊnd] *vt* : dejar sin habla

dummy [ˈdʌmi] *n, pl* **-mies 1** SHAM : imitación *f* **2** MANNEQUIN : maniquí *m* **3** IDIOT : tonto *m*, -ta *f*

dump [ˈdʌmp] *vt* : descargar, verter — ~ *n* **1** : vertedero *m*, tiradero *m Lat* **2 down in the ~s** : triste, deprimido

dumpling [ˈdʌmplɪŋ] *n* : bola *f* de masa hervida

dumpy [ˈdʌmpi] *adj* **dumpier; -est** : regordete

dunce [ˈdʌnts] *n* : burro *m*, -rra *f fam*

dune [ˈduːn, ˈdjuːn] *n* : duna *f*

dung [ˈdʌŋ] *n* **1** : excrementos *mpl* **2** MANURE : estiércol *m*

dungarees [ˌdʌŋgəˈriːz] *npl* JEANS : vaqueros *mpl*, jeans *mpl*

dungeon [ˈdʌndʒən] *n* : calabozo *m*

dunk [ˈdʌŋk] *vt* : mojar

duo [ˈduːoː, ˈdjuː-] *n, pl* **duos** : dúo *m*

dupe [ˈduːp, djuːp] *vt* **duped; duping** : engañar — ~ *n* : inocentón *m*, -tona *f*

duplex [ˈduːˌplɛks, ˈdjuː-] *n* : casa *f* de dos viviendas, dúplex *m*

duplicate [ˈduːplɪkət, ˈdjuː-] *adj* : duplicado — ~ [ˈduːplɪˌkeɪt, ˈdjuː-] *vt* **-cated; -cating** : duplicar, hacer copias de — ~ [ˈduːplɪkət, ˈdjuː-] *n* : duplicado *m*, copia *f*

durable [ˈdʊrəbəl, ˈdjʊr-] *adj* : duradero

duration [dʊˈreɪʃən, djʊ-] *n* : duración *f*

duress [dʊˈrɛs, djʊ-] *n* : coacción *f*

during [ˈdʊrɪŋ, ˈdjʊr-] *prep* : durante

dusk [ˈdʌsk] *n* : anochecer *m*, crepúsculo *m*

dust [ˈdʌst] *n* : polvo *m* — ~ *vt* **1** : quitar el polvo a **2** SPRINKLE : espolvorear — **dustpan** [ˈdʌstˌpæn] *n* : recogedor *m* — **dusty** [ˈdʌsti] *adj* **dustier; -est** : polvoriento

Dutch [ˈdʌtʃ] *adj* : holandés — ~ *n* **1** : holandés *m* (idioma) **2 the ~** : los holandeses

duty [ˈduːti, ˈdjuː-] *n, pl* **-ties 1** OBLIGATION : deber *m* **2** TAX : impuesto *m* **3 on ~** : de servicio — **dutiful** [ˈduːtɪfəl, ˈdjuː-] *adj* : obediente

dwarf [ˈdwɔrf] *n, pl* **dwarfs** [ˈdwɔrfs] *or* **dwarves** [ˈdwɔrvz] : enano *m*, -na *f* — ~ *vt* : hacer parecer pequeño

dwell [ˈdwɛl] *vi* **dwelled** *or* **dwelt** [ˈdwɛlt]; **dwelling 1** RESIDE : morar, vivir **2 ~ on** : pensar demasiado en — **dweller** [ˈdwɛlər] *n* : habitante *mf* — **dwelling** [ˈdwɛlɪŋ] *n* : morada *f*, vivienda *f*

dwindle [ˈdwɪndəl] *vi* **-dled; -dling** : disminuir

dye [ˈdaɪ] *n* : tinte *m* — ~ *vt* **dyed; dyeing** : teñir

dying → **die**[1]

dynamic [daɪˈnæmɪk] *adj* : dinámico

dynamite [ˈdaɪnəˌmaɪt] *n* : dinamita *f*

dynamo [ˈdaɪnəˌmoː] *n, pl* **-mos** : dínamo *m*

dynasty [ˈdaɪnəsti, -ˌnæs-] *n, pl* **-ties** : dinastía *f*

dysentery [ˈdɪsənˌtɛri] *n, pl* **-teries** : disentería *f*

E

e [ˈiː] *n, pl* **e's** *or* **es** [ˈiːz] : e *f*, quinta letra del alfabeto inglés

each [ˈiːtʃ] *adj* : cada — ~ *pron* **1** : cada uno *m*, cada una *f* **2 ~ other** : el uno al otro **3 they hate ~ other** : se odian — ~ *adv* : cada uno, por persona

eager [ˈiːgər] *adj* **1** ENTHUSIASTIC : entusiasta **2** IMPATIENT : impaciente — **eagerness** [ˈiːgərnəs] *n* : entusiasmo *m*, impaciencia *f*

eagle [ˈiːgəl] *n* : águila *f*

ear [ˈɪr] *n* **1** : oreja *f* **2 ~ of corn** : mazorca *f*, choclo *m Lat* — **eardrum** [ˈɪrˌdrʌm] *n* : tímpano *m*

earl [ˈərl] *n* : conde *m*

earlobe [ˈɪrˌloːb] *n* : lóbulo *m* de la oreja

early [ˈərli] *adv* **earlier; -est 1** : temprano **2 as ~ as possible** : lo más pronto posible **3 ten minutes ~** : diez minutos de adelanto — ~ *adj* **earlier; -est 1** FIRST

: primero 2 ANCIENT : primitivo, antiguo 3 **an ~ death** : una muerte prematura 4 **be ~** : llegar temprano 5 **in the ~ spring** : a principios de la primavera

earmark ['ɪr,mɑrk] *vt* : destinar

earn ['ərn] *vt* 1 : ganar 2 DESERVE : merecer

earnest ['ərnəst] *adj* : serio — ~ *n* **in ~** : en serio

earnings ['ərnɪŋz] *npl* 1 WAGES : ingresos *mpl* 2 PROFITS : ganancias *fpl*

earphone ['ɪr,fo:n] *n* : audífono *m*

earring ['ɪr,rɪŋ] *n* : pendiente *m*, arete *m Lat*

earshot ['ɪr,ʃɑt] *n* **within ~** : al alcance del oído

earth ['ərθ] *n* : tierra *f* — **earthenware** ['ərθən ,wær, -ðən-] *n* : loza *f* — **earthly** ['ərθli] *adj* : terrenal — **earthquake** ['ərθ-,kweɪk] *n* : terremoto *m* — **earthworm** ['ərθ,wərm] *n* : lombriz *f* (de tierra) — **earthy** ['ərθi] *adj* **earthier; -est** 1 : terroso 2 COARSE, CRUDE : grosero

ease ['i:z] *n* 1 FACILITY : facilidad *f* 2 COMFORT : comodidad *f* 3 **feel at ~** : sentir cómodo — ~ *v* **eased; easing** *vt* 1 ALLEVIATE : aliviar, calmar 2 FACILITATE : facilitar — *vi* 1 : calmarse 2 **~ up** : disminuir

easel ['i:zəl] *n* : caballete *m*

easily ['i:zəli] *adv* 1 : fácilmente, con facilidad 2 UNQUESTIONABLY : con mucho, de lejos *Lat*

east ['i:st] *adv* : al este — ~ *adj* : este, del este — ~ *n* 1 : este *m* 2 **the East** : el Oriente

Easter ['i:stər] *n* : Pascua *f*

easterly ['i:stərli] *adv & adj* : del este

eastern ['i:stərn] *adj* 1 : del este 2 **Eastern** : oriental, del este

easy ['i:zi] *adj* **easier; -est** 1 : fácil 2 RELAXED : relajado — **easygoing** [,i:zi'go:ɪŋ] *adj* : tolerante, relajado

eat ['i:t] *v* **ate** ['eɪt]; **eaten** ['i:tən]; **eating** *vt* : comer — *vi* 1 : comer 2 **~ into** CORRODE : corroer 3 **~ into** DEPLETE : comerse — **eatable** ['i:təbəl] *adj* : comestible

eaves ['i:vz] *npl* : alero *m* — **eavesdrop** ['i:vz,drɑp] *vi* **-dropped; -dropping** : escuchar a escondidas

ebb ['ɛb] *n* : reflujo *m* — ~ *vi* 1 : bajar (dícese de la marea) 2 DECLINE : decaer

ebony ['ɛbəni] *n, pl* **-nies** : ébano *m*

eccentric [ɪk'sentrɪk] *adj* : excéntrico — ~ *n* : excéntrico *m*, -ca *f* — **eccentricity** [,ɛk-,sen'trɪsəţi] *n, pl* **-ties** : excentricidad *f*

echo ['ɛ,ko:] *n, pl* **echoes** : eco *m* — ~ *v* **echoed; echoing** *vt* : repetir — *vi* : hacer eco, resonar

eclipse [ɪ'klɪps] *n* : eclipse *m* — ~ *vt* **eclipsed; eclipsing** : eclipsar

ecology [i'kɑlədʒi, ɛ-] *n, pl* **-gies** : ecología *f* — **ecological** *adj* [,i:kə'lɑdʒɪkəl, ,ɛkə-] : ecológico

economy [i'kɑnəmi] *n, pl* **-mies** : economía *f* — **economic** [,i:kə'nɑmɪk, ,ɛkə-] *or* **economical** [,i:kə'nɑmɪkəl, ,ɛkə-] *adj* : económico — **economics** [,i:kə'nɑmɪks, ,ɛkə-] *n* : economía *f* — **economist** [i-'kɑnəmɪst] *n* : economista *mf* — **economize** [i'kɑnə,maɪz] *v* **-mized; -mizing** : economizar

ecstasy ['ɛkstəsi] *n, pl* **-sies** : éxtasis *m* — **ecstatic** [ɛk'stæţɪk, ɪk-] *adj* : extático

Ecuadoran [,ɛkwə'dorən] *or* **Ecuadorean** *or* **Ecuadorian** [,ɛkwə'doriən] *adj* : ecuatoriano

edge ['ɛdʒ] *n* 1 BORDER : borde *m* 2 : filo *m* (de un cuchillo) 3 ADVANTAGE : ventaja *f* — ~ *v* **edged; edging** *vt* : bordear, ribetear — *vi* : avanzar poco a poco — **edgewise** ['ɛdʒ,waɪz] *adv* : de lado — **edgy** ['ɛdʒi] *adj* **edgier; -est** : nervioso

edible ['ɛdəbəl] *adj* : comestible

edit ['ɛdɪt] *vt* 1 : editar, redactar, corregir 2 **~ out** : suprimir, cortar — **edition** [ɪ'dɪʃən] *n* : edición *f* — **editor** ['ɛdɪţər] *n* : director *m*, -tora *f* (de un periódico); redactor *m*, -tora *f* (de un libro) — **editorial** [,ɛdɪ'toriəl] *n* : editorial *m*

educate ['ɛdʒə,keɪt] *vt* **-cated; -cating** 1 TEACH : educar, instruir 2 INFORM : informar — **education** [,ɛdʒə'keɪʃən] *n* : educación *f* — **educational** [,ɛdʒə'keɪʃənəl] *adj* 1 : educativo, instructivo 2 TEACHING : docente — **educator** ['ɛdʒə,keɪţər] *n* : educador *m*, -dora *f*

eel ['i:l] *n* : anguila *f*

eerie ['ɪri] *adj* **-rier; -est** : extraño e inquietante, misterioso

effect [ɪ'fɛkt] *n* 1 : efecto *m* 2 **go into ~** : entrar en vigor — ~ *vt* : efectuar, llevar a cabo — **effective** [ɪ'fɛktɪv] *adj* 1 : eficaz 2 ACTUAL : efectivo, vigente — **effectiveness** [ɪ'fɛktɪvnəs] *n* : eficacia *f*

effeminate [ə'fɛmənət] *adj* : afeminado

effervescent [,ɛfər'vɛsənt] *adj* : efervescente

efficient [ɪ'fɪʃənt] *adj* : eficiente — **efficiency** [ɪ'fɪʃəntsi] *n, pl* **-cies** : eficiencia *f*

effort ['ɛfərt] *n* 1 : esfuerzo *m* 2 **it's not worth the ~** : no vale la pena — **effortless** ['ɛfərtləs] *adj* : fácil, sin esfuerzo

egg ['ɛg] *n* : huevo *m* — ~ *vt* **~ on** : incitar — **eggplant** ['ɛg,plænt] *n* : berenjena *f* — **eggshell** ['ɛg,ʃɛl] *n* : cascarón *m*

ego ['i:,go:] *n, pl* **egos** 1 SELF : ego *m*, yo *m* 2 SELF-ESTEEM : amor *m* propio — **egotism** ['i:gə,tɪzəm] *n* : egotismo *m* — **egotist** ['i:gətɪst] *n* : egotista *mf* — **egotistic** [,i:gə-'tɪstɪk] *or* **egotistical** [-'tɪstɪkəl] *adj* : egotista

eiderdown ['aɪdər,daʊn] *n* 1 DOWN : plumón *m* 2 COMFORTER : edredón *m*

eight ['eɪt] *n* : ocho *m* — ~ *adj* : ocho — **eight hundred** *n* : ochocientos *m*

eighteen [eɪt'ti:n] *n* : dieciocho *m* — ~ *adj* : dieciocho — **eighteenth** [eɪt'ti:nθ] *adj* : decimoctavo — ~ *n* 1 : decimoctavo *m*, -va *f* (en una serie) 2 : dieciochoavo *m*, dieciochoava parte *f*

eighth ['eɪtθ] *n* 1 : octavo *m*, -va *f* (en una serie) 2 : octavo *m*, octava parte *f* — ~ *adj* : octavo

eighty ['eɪţi] *n, pl* **eighties** : ochenta *m* — ~ *adj* : ochenta

either ['i:ðər, 'aɪ-] *adj* 1 : cualquiera (de los dos) 2 (*in negative constructions*) : ninguno (de los dos) 3 EACH : cada — ~ *pron* 1 : cualquiera *mf* (de los dos) 2 (*in negative constructions*) : ninguno *m*, -na *f* (de los dos) 3 *or* **~ one** : algún *m*, alguna *f* — ~ *conj* 1 : o 2 (*in negative constructions*) : ni

eject [i'dʒɛkt] *vt* : expulsar, expeler

eke ['i:k] *vt* **eked; eking** *or* **~ out** : ganar a duras penas

elaborate [i'læbərət] *adj* 1 DETAILED : detallado 2 COMPLEX : complicado — ~ [i'læbə,reɪt] *v* **-rated; -rating** *vt* : elaborar — *vi* : entrar en detalles

elapse [i'læps] *vi* **elapsed; elapsing** : transcurrir

elastic [i'læstɪk] *adj* : elástico — ~ *n* 1 : elástico *m* 2 RUBBER BAND : goma *f* (elástica) — **elasticity** [i,læs'tɪsəţi, ,i:,læs-] *n, pl* **-ties** : elasticidad *f*

elated [i'leɪţəd] *adj* : regocijado

elbow ['ɛl,bo:] *n* : codo *m*

elder ['ɛldər] *adj* : mayor — ~ *n* 1 : mayor *mf* 2 : anciano *m*, -na *f* (de un tribu, etc.) — **elderly** ['ɛldərli] *adj* : mayor, anciano

elect [i'lɛkt] *vt* : elegir — ~ *adj* : electo — **election** [i'lɛkʃən] *n* : elección *f* — **electoral** [i'lɛktərəl] *adj* : electoral — **electorate** [i'lɛktərət] *n* : electorado *m*

electricity [i,lɛk'trɪsəţi] *n, pl* **-ties** : electricidad *f* — **electric** [i'lɛktrɪk] *or* **electrical** [-trɪkəl] *adj* : eléctrico — **electrician** [i,lɛk'trɪʃən] *n* : electricista *mf* — **electrify** [i'lɛktrə,faɪ] *vt* **-fied; -fying** : electrificar — **electrocute** [i'lɛktrə,kju:t] *vt* **-cuted; -cuting** : electrocutar

electron [i'lɛk,trɑn] *n* : electrón *m* — **electronic** [i,lɛk'trɑnɪk] *adj* : electrónico — **electronic mail** *n* : correo *m* electrónico — **electronics** [i,lɛk'trɑnɪks] *n* : electrónica *f*

elegant ['ɛlɪgənt] *adj* : elegante — **elegance** ['ɛlɪgənts] *n* : elegancia *f*

element ['ɛləmənt] *n* 1 : elemento *m* 2 **~s** *npl* BASICS : elementos *mpl*, rudimentos *mpl* — **elementary** [,ɛlə'mentri] *adj* : elemental — **elementary school** *n* : escuela *f* primaria

elephant ['ɛləfənt] *n* : elefante *m*, -ta *f*

elevate ['ɛlə,veɪt] *vt* **-vated; -vating** : elevar — **elevator** ['ɛlə,veɪţər] *n* : ascensor *m*

eleven [ɪ'lɛvən] *n* : once *m* — ~ *adj* : once — **eleventh** [ɪ'lɛvəntθ] *adj* : undécimo — ~ *n* 1 : undécimo *m*, -ma *f* (en una serie) 2 : onceavo *m*, onceava parte *f*

elf ['ɛlf] *n, pl* **elves** ['ɛlvz] : duende *m*

elicit [ɪ'lɪsət] *vt* : provocar

eligible ['ɛlədʒəbəl] *adj* : elegible

eliminate [ɪ'lɪmə,neɪt] *vt* **-nated; -nating** : eliminar — **elimination** [ɪ,lɪmə'neɪʃən] *n* : eliminación *f*

elite [eɪ'li:t, i-] *n* : elite *f*

elk ['ɛlk] *n* : alce *m* (de Europa), uapití *m* (de América)

elliptical [ɪ'lɪptɪkəl, ɛ-] *or* **elliptic** [-tɪk] *adj* : elíptico

elm ['ɛlm] *n* : olmo *m*

elongate [i'lɔŋ,geɪt] *vt* **-gated; -gating** : alargar

elope [i'lo:p] *vi* **eloped; eloping** : fugarse — **elopement** [i'lo:pmənt] *n* : fuga *f*

eloquence ['ɛləkwənts] *n* : elocuencia *f* — **eloquent** ['ɛləkwənt] *adj* : elocuente

else ['ɛls] *adv* 1 **how ~ ?** : ¿de qué otro modo? 2 **where ~ ?** : ¿en qué otro sitio? 3 **or ~** : si no, de lo contrario — ~ *adj* 1 **everyone ~** : todos los demás 2 **nobody ~** : ningún otro, nadie más 3 **nothing ~** : nada más 4 **what ~ ?** : ¿qué más? — **elsewhere** ['ɛls,hwɛr] *adv* : en otra parte

elude [i'lu:d] *vt* **eluded; eluding** : eludir, esquivar — **elusive** [i'lu:sɪv] *adj* : esquivo

elves → **elf**

emaciated [i'meɪʃi,eɪţəd] *adj* : esquálido, demacrado

E-mail ['i:,meɪl] → **electronic mail**

emanate ['ɛmə,neɪt] *vi* **-nated; -nating** : emanar

emancipate [i'mæntsə,peɪt] *vt* **-pated; -pating** : emancipar — **emancipation** [i,mæntsə'peɪʃən] *n* : emancipación *f*

embalm [ɪm'bɑm, ɛm-, -'bɑlm] *vt* : embalsamar

embankment [ɪm'bæŋkmənt, ɛm-] *n* : terraplén *m*, dique *m* (de un río)

embargo [ɪm'bɑrgo, ɛm-] *n, pl* **-goes** : embargo *m*

embark [ɪm'bɑrk, ɛm-] *vt* : embarcar — *vi* 1 : embarcarse 2 **~ upon** : emprender — **embarkation** [,ɛm,bɑr'keɪʃən] *n* : embarque *m*, embarco *m*

embarrass [ɪm'bærəs, ɛm-] *vt* : avergonzar — **embarrassing** [ɪm'bærəsɪŋ, ɛm-] *adj* : embarazoso — **embarrassment** [ɪm-'bærəsmənt, ɛm-] *n* : vergüenza *f*

embassy ['ɛmbəsi] *n, pl* **-sies** : embajada *f*

embed [ɪm'bɛd, ɛm-] *vt* **-bedded; -bedding** : incrustar, enterrar

embellish [ɪm'bɛlɪʃ, ɛm-] *vt* : adornar, embellecer — **embellishment** [ɪm'bɛlɪʃmənt, ɛm-] *n* : adorno *m*

embers ['ɛmbərz] *npl* : ascuas *fpl*

embezzle [ɪm'bɛzəl, ɛm-] *vt* **-zled; -zling** : desfalcar, malversar — **embezzlement** [ɪm'bɛzəlmənt, ɛm-] *n* : desfalco *m*, malversación *f*

emblem ['ɛmbləm] *n* : emblema *m*

embody [ɪm'bɑdi, ɛm-] *vt* **-bodied; -bodying** : encarnar, personificar

emboss [ɪm'bɑs, ɛm-, -'bɔs] *vt* : repujar, grabar en relieve

embrace [ɪm'breɪs, ɛm-] *v* **-braced; -bracing** *vt* : abrazar — *vi* : abrazarse — ~ *n* : abrazo *m*

embroider [ɪm'brɔɪdər, ɛm-] *vt* : bordar — **embroidery** [ɪm'brɔɪdəri, ɛm-] *n, pl* **-deries** : bordado *m*

embryo ['ɛmbri,o:] *n, pl* **embryos** : embrión *m*

emerald ['ɛmrəld, 'ɛmə-] *n* : esmeralda *f*

emerge [i'mərdʒ] *vi* **emerged; emerging** : salir, aparecer — **emergence** [i'mərdʒənts] *n* : aparición *f*

emergency [i'mərdʒəntsi] *n, pl* **-cies** 1 : emergencia *f* 2 **~ exit** : salida *f* de emergencia 3 **~ room** : sala *f* de urgencias, sala *f* de guardia

emery ['ɛməri] *n, pl* **-eries** 1 : esmeril *m* 2 **~ board** : lima *f* de uñas

emigrant ['ɛmɪgrənt] *n* : emigrante *mf* — **emigrate** ['ɛmə,greɪt] *vi* **-grated; -grating** : emigrar — **emigration** [,ɛmə'greɪʃən] *n* : emigración *f*

eminence ['ɛmənənts] *n* : eminencia *f* — **eminent** ['ɛmənənt] *adj* : eminente

emission [i'mɪʃən] *n* : emisión *f* — **emit** [i'mɪt] *vt* **emitted; emitting** : emitir

emotion [i'mo:ʃən] *n* : emoción *f* — **emotional** [i'mo:ʃənəl] *adj* 1 : emocional 2 MOVING : emotivo

emperor ['ɛmpərər] *n* : emperador *m*

emphasis ['ɛmfəsɪs] *n, pl* **-phases** [-,si:z] : énfasis *m* — **emphasize** ['ɛmfə,saɪz] *vt* **-sized; -sizing** : subrayar, hacer hincapié en — **emphatic** [ɪm'fæţɪk, ɛm-] *adj* : enérgico, categórico

empire ['ɛm,paɪr] *n* : imperio *m*

employ [ɪm'plɔɪ, ɛm-] *vt* : emplear — **employee** [ɪm,plɔɪ'i:, ɛm-, -'plɔɪ,i:] *n* : empleado *m*, -da *f* — **employer** [ɪm'plɔɪər, ɛm-] *n* : patrón *m*, -trona *f*; empleador *m*, -dora *f* — **employment** [ɪm'plɔɪmənt, ɛm-] *n* : trabajo *m*, empleo *m*

empower [ɪm'paʊər, ɛm-] *vt* : autorizar

empress ['ɛmprəs] *n* : emperatriz *f*

empty ['ɛmpti] *adj* **emptier; -est** 1 : vacío 2 MEANINGLESS : vano — ~ *v* **-tied; -tying** *vt* : vaciar — *vi* : vaciarse — **emptiness** ['ɛmptinəs] *n* : vacío *m*

emulate ['ɛmjə,leɪt] *vt* **-lated; -lating** : emular

enable [ɪ'neɪbəl, ɛ-] *vt* **-abled; -abling** : hacer posible, permitar

enact [ɪ'nækt, ɛ-] *vt* 1 : promulgar (un ley o un decreto) 2 PERFORM : representar

enamel [ɪ'næməl] *n* : esmalte *m*

encampment [ɪn'kæmpmənt, ɛn-] *n* : campamento *m*

encase [ɪn'keɪs, ɛn-] *vt* **-cased; -casing** : encerrar, revestir

enchant [ɪn'tʃænt, ɛn-] *vt* : encantar — **enchanting** [ɪn'tʃæntɪŋ, ɛn-] *adj* : encantador — **enchantment** [ɪn'tʃæntmənt, ɛn-] *n* : encanto *m*

encircle [ɪn'sərkəl, ɛn-] *vt* **-cled; -cling** : rodear

enclose [ɪn'klo:z, ɛn-] *vt* **-closed; -closing** 1 SURROUND : encerrar, cercar 2 INCLUDE : adjuntar (a una carta) — **enclosure** [ɪn-'klo:ʒər, ɛn-] *n* 1 AREA : recinto *m* 2 : anexo *m* (con una carta)

encompass [ɪn'kʌmpəs, ɛn-, -'kɑm-] *vt* 1 ENCIRCLE : cercar 2 INCLUDE : abarcar

encore ['ɑn,kor] *n* : bis *m*

encounter [ɪn'kaʊntər, ɛn-] *vt* : encontrar — ~ *n* : encuentro *m*

encourage [ɪn'kərɪdʒ, ɛn-] *vt* **-aged; -aging** 1 : animar, alentar 2 FOSTER : promover, fomentar — **encouragement** [ɪn-'kərɪdʒmənt, ɛn-] *n* 1 : aliento *m* 2 PROMOTION : fomento *m*

encroach [ɪn'kro:tʃ, ɛn-] *vi* **~ on** : invadir, usurpar, quitar (el tiempo)

encyclopedia [ɪn,saɪklə'pi:diə, ɛn-] *n* : enciclopedia *f*

end ['ɛnd] *n* 1 : fin 2 EXTREMITY : extremo *m*, punta *f* 3 **come to an ~** : llegar a su fin 4 **in the ~** : por fin — ~ *vt* : terminar, poner fin a — *vi* : terminar(se)

endanger [ɪn'deɪndʒər, ɛn-] *vt* : poner en peligro

endearing [ɪn'dɪrɪŋ, ɛn-] *adj* : simpático

endeavor *or Brit* **endeavour** [ɪn'dɛvər, ɛn-] *vt* **~ to** : esforzarse por — ~ *n* : esfuerzo *m*

ending ['ɛndɪŋ] *n* : final *m*, desenlace *m*

endive ['ɛn,daɪv, ,ɑn'di:v] *n* : endibia *f*, endivia *f*

endless ['ɛndləs] *adj* 1 INTERMINABLE : interminable 2 INNUMERABLE : innumerable 3 **~ possibilities** : posibilidades *fpl* infinitas

endorse [ɪn'dɔrs, ɛn-] *vt* **-dorsed; -dorsing** 1 SIGN : endosar 2 APPROVE : aprobar — **endorsement** [ɪn'dɔrsmənt, ɛn-] *n* APPROVAL : aprobación *f*

endow [ɪn'daʊ, ɛn-] *vt* : dotar

endure [ɪn'dʊr, ɛn-, -'djʊr] *v* **-dured; -during** *vt* : soportar, aguantar — *vi* LAST : durar — **endurance** [ɪn'dʊrənts, ɛn-, -'djʊr-] *n* : resistencia *f*

enemy ['ɛnəmi] *n, pl* **-mies** : enemigo *m*, -ga *f*

energy ['ɛnərdʒi] *n, pl* **-gies** : energía *f* — **energetic** [,ɛnər'dʒɛţɪk] *adj* : enérgico

enforce [ɪn'fors, ɛn-] *vt* **-forced; -forcing** 1 : hacer cumplir (un ley, etc.) 2 IMPOSE : imponer — **enforced** *adj* : forzoso — **enforcement** [ɪn'forsmənt, ɛn-] *n* : imposición *f* del cumplimiento

engage [ɪn'geɪdʒ, ɛn-] *v* **-gaged; -gaging** *vt* 1 : captar, atraer (la atención, etc.) 2 **~ the clutch** : embragar — *vi* **~ in** : dedicarse a, entrar en — **engagement** [ɪn'geɪdʒmənt, ɛn-] *n* 1 APPOINTMENT : cita *f*, hora *f* 2 BETROTHAL : compromiso *m* — **engaging** [ɪn'geɪdʒɪŋ, ɛn-] *adj* : atractivo

engine ['ɛndʒən] *n* 1 : motor *m* 2 LOCOMOTIVE : locomotora *f* — **engineer** [,ɛndʒə-'nɪr] *n* 1 : ingeniero *m*, -ra *f* 2 : maquinista *mf* (de locomotoras) — ~ *vt* 1 CONSTRUCT : construir 2 CONTRIVE : tramar — **engineering** [,ɛndʒə'nɪrɪŋ] *n* : ingeniería *f*

English ['ɪŋglɪʃ, 'ɪŋlɪʃ] *adj* : inglés — ~ *n* : inglés *m* (idioma) — **Englishman** ['ɪŋ-glɪʃmən, 'ɪŋlɪʃ-] *n* : inglés *m* — **Englishwoman** ['ɪŋglɪʃ,wʊmən, 'ɪŋlɪʃ-] *n* : inglesa *f*

engrave [ɪn'greɪv, ɛn-] *vt* **-graved; -graving** : grabar — **engraving** [ɪn'greɪvɪŋ, ɛn-] *n* : grabado *m*

engross [ɪn'gro:s, ɛn-] *vt* : absorber

engulf [ɪn'gʌlf, ɛn-] *vt* : envolver

enhance [ɪn'hænts, ɛn-] *vt* **-hanced; -hancing** : aumentar, mejorar

enjoy [ɪn'dʒɔɪ, ɛn-] *vt* 1 : disfrutar, gozar de 2 **~ oneself** : divertirse — **enjoyable** [ɪn-'dʒɔɪəbəl, ɛn-] *adj* : agradable — **enjoyment** [ɪn'dʒɔɪmənt, ɛn-] *n* : placer *m*

enlarge [ɪn'lɑrdʒ, ɛn-] *v* **-larged; -larging** *vt* : agrandar, ampliar — *vi* 1 : agrandarse 2 **~ upon** : extenderse sobre — **enlargement** [ɪn'lɑrdʒmənt, ɛn-] *n* : ampliación *f*

enlighten [ɪn'laɪtən, ɛn-] *vt* : aclarar, iluminar

enlist [ɪn'lɪst, ɛn-] *vt* 1 ENROLL : alistar 2 OBTAIN : conseguir — *vi* : alistarse

enliven [ɪn'laɪvən, ɛn-] *vt* : animar

enmity ['ɛnməţi] *n, pl* **-ties** : enemistad *f*

enormous [ɪ'nɔrməs] *adj* : enorme

enough [ɪ'nʌf] *adj* : bastante, suficiente — ~ *adv* : bastante — ~ *pron* 1 : (lo) suficiente, (lo) bastante 2 **it's not ~** : no basta 3 **I've had ~ !** : ¡estoy harto!

enquire [ɪn'kwaɪr, ɛn-], **enquiry** ['ɪn,kwaɪri, 'ɛn-, -kwəri; ɪn'kwaɪri, ɛn'-] → **inquire, inquiry**

enrage [ɪn'reɪdʒ, ɛn-] *vt* **-raged; -raging** : enfurecer

enrich [ɪn'rɪtʃ, ɛn-] *vt* : enriquecer

enroll *or* **enrol** [ɪn'ro:l, ɛn-] *v* **-rolled; -rolling** *vt* : matricular, inscribir — *vi* : matricularse, inscribirse

ensemble [ɑn'sɑmbəl] *n* : conjunto *m*

ensign ['ɛntsən, 'ɛn,saɪn] *n* 1 FLAG : enseña *f* 2 : alférez *mf* (de fragata)

enslave [ɪn'sleɪv, ɛn-] *vt* **-slaved; -slaving** : esclavizar

ensue [ɪn'su:, ɛn-] *vi* **-sued; -suing** : seguir, resultar

ensure [ɪn'ʃʊr, ɛn-] *vt* **-sured; -suring** : asegurar

entail [ɪn'teɪl, ɛn-] *vt* : suponer, conllevar

entangle [ɪn'tæŋgəl, ɛn-] *vt* **-gled; -gling** : enredar — **entanglement** [ɪn-'tæŋgəlmənt, ɛn-] *n* : enredo *m*

enter ['ɛntər] *vt* 1 : entrar en 2 RECORD : inscribir — *vi* 1 : entrar 2 **~ into** : firmar (un acuerdo), entablar (negociaciones, etc.)

enterprise ['ɛntər,praɪz] *n* 1 : empresa *f* 2 INITIATIVE : iniciativa *f* — **enterprising** ['ɛntər,praɪzɪŋ] *adj* : emprendedor

entertain [,ɛntər'teɪn] *vt* 1 AMUSE : entretener, divertir 2 CONSIDER : considerar 3 **~ guests** : recibir invitados — **entertainment** [,ɛntər'teɪnmənt] *n* : entretenimiento *m*, diversión *f*

enthrall *or* **enthral** [ɪn'θrɔl, ɛn-] *vt* **-thralled; -thralling** : cautivar, embelesar

enthusiasm [ɪn'θu:zi,æzəm, ɛn-, -'θju:-] *n* : entusiasmo *m* — **enthusiast** [ɪn'θu:zi,æst, ɛn-, -'θju:-, -əst] *n* : entusiasta *mf* — **enthusiastic** [ɪn,θu:zi'æstɪk, ɛn-, -,θju:-] *adj* : entusiasta

entice [ɪn'taɪs, ɛn-] *vt* **-ticed; -ticing** : atraer, tentar

entire [ɪn'taɪr, ɛn-] *adj* : entero, completo — **entirely** [ɪn'taɪrli, ɛn-] *adv* : completa-

mente — **entirety** [ɪn'taɪrt̬i, ɛn-, -'taɪrət̬i] *n, pl* **-ties** : totalidad *f*
entitle [ɪn'taɪt̬əl, ɛn-] *vt* **-tled; -tling 1** NAME : titular **2** AUTHORIZE : dar derecho a — **entitlement** [ɪn'taɪt̬əlmənt, ɛn-] *n* : derecho *m*
entity ['ɛntət̬i] *n, pl* **-ties** : entidad *f*
entrails ['ɛnˌtreɪlz, -trəlz] *npl* : entrañas *fpl,* vísceras *fpl*
entrance[1] [ɪn'trænts, ɛn-] *vt* **-tranced; -trancing** : encantar, fascinar
entrance[2] ['ɛntrənts] *n* : entrada *f* — **entrant** ['ɛntrənt] *n* : participante *mf*
entreat [ɪn'tri:t, ɛn-] *vt* : suplicar
entrée *or* **entree** ['ɑnˌtreɪ, ˌɑn'-] *n* : plato *m* principal
entrepreneur [ˌɑntrəprə'nər, -'njʊr] *n* : empresario *m,* -ria *f*
entrust [ɪn'trʌst, ɛn-] *vt* : confiar
entry ['ɛntri] *n, pl* **-tries 1** ENTRANCE : entrada *f* **2** NOTATION : entrada *f,* anotación *f*
enumerate [ɪ'nu:məˌreɪt, ɛ-, -'nju:-] *vt* **-ated; -ating** : enumerar
enunciate [i'nʌntsiˌeɪt, ɛ-] *vt* **-ated; -ating 1** STATE : enunciar **2** PRONOUNCE : articular
envelop [ɪn'vɛləp, ɛn-] *vt* : envolver — **envelope** ['ɛnvəˌlo:p, 'ɑn-] *n* : sobre *m*
envious ['ɛnviəs] *adj* : envidioso — **enviously** *adv* : con envidia
environment [ɪn'vaɪrənmənt, ɛn-, -'vaɪərn-] *n* : medio *m* ambiente — **environmental** [ɪnˌvaɪrən'mɛntəl, ɛn-, -ˌvaɪərn-] *adj* : ambiental — **environmentalist** [ɪnˌvaɪrən'mɛntəlɪst, ɛn-, -ˌvaɪərn-] *n* : ecologista *mf*
envision [ɪn'vɪʒən, ɛn-] *vt* : prever, imaginar
envoy ['ɛnˌvɔɪ, 'ɑn-] *n* : enviado *m,* -da *f*
envy ['ɛnvi] *n, pl* **envies** : envidia *f* — **~** *vt* **-vied; -vying** : envidiar
enzyme ['ɛnˌzaɪm] *n* : enzima *f*
epic ['ɛpɪk] *adj* : épico — **~** *n* : epopeya *f*
epidemic [ˌɛpə'dɛmɪk] *n* : epidemia *f* — **~** *adj* : epidémico
epilepsy ['ɛpəˌlɛpsi] *n, pl* **-sies** : epilepsia *f* — **epileptic** [ˌɛpə'lɛptɪk] *adj* : epiléptico — **~** *n* : epiléptico *m,* -ca *f*
episode ['ɛpəˌso:d] *n* : episodio *m*
epitaph ['ɛpəˌtæf] *n* : epitafio *m*
epitome [ɪ'pɪt̬əmi] *n* : personificación *f* — **epitomize** [ɪ'pɪt̬əˌmaɪz] *vt* **-mized; -mizing** : ser la personificación de, personificar
epoch ['ɛpək, 'ɛˌpɑk, 'i:ˌpɑk] *n* : época *f*
equal ['i:kwəl] *adj* **1** SAME : igual **2 be ~ to** : estar a la altura de (una tarea, etc.) — **~** *n* : igual *mf* — **~** *vt* **equaled** *or* **equalled; equaling** *or* **equalling 1** : igualar **2** : ser igual a (en matemáticas) — **equality** [ɪ'kwɑlət̬i] *n, pl* **-ties** : igualdad *f* — **equalize** ['i:kwəˌlaɪz] *vt* **-ized; -izing** : igualar — **equally** ['i:kwəli] *adv* **1** : igualmente **2 ~ important** : igual de importante
equate [ɪ'kweɪt] *vt* **equated; equating ~ with** : equiparar con — **equation** [ɪ'kweɪʒən] *n* : ecuación *f*
equator [ɪ'kweɪt̬ər] *n* : ecuador *m*
equilibrium [ˌi:kwə'lɪbriəm, ˌɛ-] *n, pl* **-riums** *or* **-ria** [-briə] : equilibrio *m*
equinox ['i:kwəˌnɑks, 'ɛ-] *n* : equinoccio *m*
equip [ɪ'kwɪp] *vt* **equipped; equipping** : equipar — **equipment** [ɪ'kwɪpmənt] *n* : equipo *m*
equity ['ɛkwət̬i] *n, pl* **-ties 1** FAIRNESS : equidad *f* **2 equities** *npl* STOCKS : acciones *fpl* ordinarias
equivalent [ɪ'kwɪvələnt] *adj* : equivalente — **~** *n* : equivalente *m*
era ['ɪrə, 'ɛrə, 'i:rə] *n* : era *f,* época *f*
eradicate [ɪ'rædəˌkeɪt] *vt* **-cated; -cating** : erradicar
erase [ɪ'reɪs] *vt* **erased; erasing** : borrar — **eraser** [ɪ'reɪsər] *n* : goma *f* de borrar, borrador *m*
erect [ɪ'rɛkt] *adj* : erguido — **~** *vt* : erigir, levantar — **erection** [ɪ'rɛkʃən] *n* **1** BUILDING : construcción *f* **2** : erección *f* (en fisiología)
erode [ɪ'ro:d] *vt* **eroded; eroding** : erosionar (el suelo), corroer (metales) — **erosion** [ɪ'ro:ʒən] *n* : erosión *f,* corrosión *f*
erotic [ɪ'rɑt̬ɪk] *adj* : erótico
err ['ɛr, 'ər] *vi* : equivocarse, errar
errand ['ɛrənd] *n* : mandado *m,* recado *m Spain*
erratic [ɪ'ræt̬ɪk] *adj* : errático, irregular
error ['ɛrər] *n* : error *m* — **erroneous** [ɪ'ro:niəs, ɛ-] *adj* : erróneo
erupt [ɪ'rʌpt] *vi* **1** : hacer erupción (dícese de un volcán) **2** : estallar (dícese de la cólera, la violencia, etc.) — **eruption** [ɪ'rʌpʃən] *n* : erupción *f*
escalate ['ɛskəˌleɪt] *vi* **-lated; -lating** : intensificarse
escalator ['ɛskəˌleɪt̬ər] *n* : escalera *f* mecánica
escapade ['ɛskəˌpeɪd] *n* : aventura *f*
escape [ɪ'skeɪp, ɛ-] *v* **-caped; -caping** *vt* : escapar a, evitar — *vi* : escaparse, fugarse — **~** *n* **1** : fuga *f* **2 ~ from reality** : evasión *f* de la realidad — **escapee** [ɪˌskeɪ'pi:, ˌɛ-] *n* : fugitivo *m,* -va *f*
escort ['ɛsˌkɔrt] *n* **1** GUARD : escolta *f* **2** COMPANION : acompañante *mf* — **~** [ɪ'skɔrt, ɛ-] *vt* **1** : escoltar **2** ACCOMPANY : acompañar
Eskimo ['ɛskəˌmo:] *adj* : esquimal
especially [ɪ'spɛʃəli] *adv* : especialmente
espionage ['ɛspiəˌnɑʒ, -ˌnɑdʒ] *n* : espionaje *m*
espresso [ɛ'sprɛˌso:] *n, pl* **-sos** : café *m* exprés
essay ['ɛˌseɪ] *n* : ensayo *m* (literario), composición *f* (académica)
essence ['ɛsənts] *n* : esencia *f* — **essential** [ɪ'sɛntʃəl] *adj* : esencial — **~** *n* **1** : elemento *m* esencial **2 the ~s** : lo indispensable
establish [ɪ'stæblɪʃ, ɛ-] *vt* : establecer — **establishment** [ɪ'stæblɪʃmənt, ɛ-] *n* : establecimiento *m*
estate [ɪ'steɪt, ɛ-] *n* **1** POSSESSIONS : bienes *mpl* **2** LAND, PROPERTY : finca *f*
esteem [ɪ'sti:m, ɛ-] *n* : estima *f* — **~** *vt* : estimar
esthetic [ɛs'θɛt̬ɪk] → **aesthetic**
estimate ['ɛstəˌmeɪt] *vt* **-mated; -mating** : calcular, estimar — **~** ['ɛstəmət] *n* **1** : cálculo *m* (aproximado) **2** *or* **~ of costs** : presupuesto *m* — **estimation** [ˌɛstə'meɪʃən] *n* **1** JUDGMENT : juicio *m* **2** ESTEEM : estima *f*
estuary ['ɛstʃʊˌwɛri] *n, pl* **-aries** : estuario *m,* ría *f*
eternal [ɪ'tərnəl, i:-] *adj* : eterno — **eternity** [ɪ'tərnət̬i, i:-] *n, pl* **-ties** : eternidad *f*
ether ['i:θər] *n* : éter *m*
ethical ['ɛθɪkəl] *adj* : ético — **ethics** ['ɛθɪks] *ns & pl* : ética *f,* moralidad *f*
ethnic ['ɛθnɪk] *adj* : étnico
etiquette ['ɛt̬ɪkət, -ˌkɛt] *n* : etiqueta *f*
Eucharist ['ju:kərɪst] *n* : Eucaristía *f*
eulogy ['ju:lədʒi] *n, pl* **-gies** : elogio *m,* panegírico *m*
euphemism ['ju:fəˌmɪzəm] *n* : eufemismo *m*
euphoria [jʊ'foriə] *n* : euforia *f*
European [ˌjʊrə'pi:ən, -pi:n] *adj* : europeo
evacuate [ɪ'vækjʊˌeɪt] *vt* **-ated; -ating** : evacuar — **evacuation** [ɪˌvækjʊ'eɪʃən] *n* : evacuación *f*
evade [ɪ'veɪd] *vt* **evaded; evading** : evadir, eludir
evaluate [ɪ'væljʊˌeɪt] *vt* **-ated; -ating** : evaluar
evaporate [ɪ'væpəˌreɪt] *vi* **-rated; -rating** : evaporarse
evasion [ɪ'veɪʒən] *n* : evasión *f* — **evasive** [ɪ'veɪsɪv] *adj* : evasivo
eve ['i:v] *n* : víspera *f*
even ['i:vən] *adj* **1** REGULAR, STEADY : regular, constante **2** LEVEL : plano, llano **3** SMOOTH : liso **4** EQUAL : igual **5 ~ number** : número *m* par **6 get ~ with** : desquitarse con — **~** *adv* **1** : hasta, incluso **2 ~ better** : aún mejor, todavía mejor **3 ~ if** : aunque **4 ~ so** : aun así — **~** *vt* : igualar — *vi or* **out** : nivelarse
evening ['i:vnɪŋ] *n* : tarde *f,* noche *f*
event [ɪ'vɛnt] *n* **1** : acontecimiento *m,* suceso *m* **2** : prueba *f* (en deportes) **3 in the ~ of** : en caso de — **eventful** [ɪ'vɛntfəl] *adj* : lleno de incidentes
eventual [ɪ'vɛntʃʊəl] *adj* : final — **eventuality** [ɪˌvɛntʃʊ'ælət̬i] *n, pl* **-ties** : eventualidad *f* — **eventually** [ɪ'vɛntʃʊəli] *adv* : al fin, finalmente
ever ['ɛvər] *adv* **1** ALWAYS : siempre **2 ~ since** : desde entonces **3 hardly ~** : casi nunca **4 have you ~ done it?** : ¿lo has hecho alguna vez?
evergreen ['ɛvərˌgri:n] *n* : planta *f* de hoja perenne
everlasting [ˌɛvər'læstɪŋ] *adj* : eterno
every ['ɛvri] *adj* **1** EACH : cada **2 ~ month** : todos los meses **3 ~ other day** : cada dos días — **everybody** ['ɛvriˌbʌdi, -ˌbɑ-] *pron* : todos *mpl,* -das *fpl;* todo el mundo — **everyday** [ˌɛvri'deɪ, 'ɛvri,-] *adj* : cotidiano, de todos los días — **everyone** ['ɛvriˌwʌn] → **everybody** — **everything** ['ɛvriˌθɪŋ] *pron* : todo — **everywhere** ['ɛvriˌhwer] *adv* : en todas partes, por todas partes
evict [ɪ'vɪkt] *vt* : desahuciar, desalojar — **eviction** [ɪ'vɪkʃən] *n* : desahucio *m*
evidence ['ɛvədənts] *n* **1** PROOF : pruebas *fpl* **2** TESTIMONY : testimonio *m,* declaración *f* — **evident** ['ɛvədənt] *adj* : evidente — **evidently** ['ɛvədəntli, ˌɛvɪ'dɛntli] *adv* **1** OBVIOUSLY : obviamente **2** APPARENTLY : evidentemente, al parecer
evil ['i:vəl, -vɪl] *adj* **eviler** *or* **eviller; evilest** *or* **evillest** : malvado, malo — **~** *n* : mal *m,* maldad *f*
evoke [ɪ'vo:k] *vt* **evoked; evoking** : evocar
evolution [ˌɛvə'lu:ʃən, ˌi:-] *n* : evolución *f,* desarrollo *m* — **evolve** [ɪ'vɑlv] *vi* **evolved; evolving** : evolucionar, desarrollarse
exact [ɪg'zækt, ɛg-] *adj* : exacto, preciso — **~** *vt* : exigir — **exacting** [ɪg'zæktɪŋ, ɛg-] *adj* : exigente — **exactly** [ɪg'zæktli, ɛg-] *adv* : exactamente
exaggerate [ɪg'zædʒəˌreɪt, ɛg-] *v* **-ated; -ating** : exagerar — **exaggeration** [ɪgˌzædʒə'reɪʃən, ɛg-] *n* : exageración *f*
examine [ɪg'zæmən, ɛg-] *vt* **-ined; -ining 1** : examinar **2** INSPECT : revisar **3** QUESTION : interrogar — **exam** [ɪg'zæm, ɛg-] *n* : examen *m* — **examination** [ɪgˌzæmə'neɪʃən, ɛg-] *n* : examen *m*
example [ɪg'zæmpəl, ɛg-] *n* : ejemplo *m*
exasperate [ɪg'zæspəˌreɪt, ɛg-] *vt* **-ated; -ating** : exasperar — **exasperation** [ɪgˌzæspə'reɪʃən, ɛg-] *n* : exasperación *f*
excavate ['ɛkskəˌveɪt] *vt* **-vated; -vating** : excavar — **excavation** [ˌɛkskə'veɪʃən] *n* : excavación *f*
exceed [ɪk'si:d, ɛk-] *vt* : exceder, sobrepasar — **exceedingly** [ɪk'si:dɪŋli, ɛk-] *adv* : extremadamente
excel [ɪk'sɛl, ɛk-] *v* **-celled; -celling** *vi* : sobresalir — *vt* SURPASS : superar — **excellence** ['ɛksələnts] *n* : excelencia *f* — **excellent** ['ɛksələnt] *adj* : excelente
except [ɪk'sɛpt] *prep or* **~ for** : excepto, menos, salvo — **~** *vt* : exceptuar — **exception** [ɪk'sɛpʃən] *n* : excepción *f* — **exceptional** [ɪk'sɛpʃənəl] *adj* : excepcional
excerpt ['ɛkˌsərpt, 'ɛgˌzərpt] *n* : extracto *m*
excess [ɪk'sɛs, 'ɛkˌsɛs] *n* : exceso *m* — **~** ['ɛkˌsɛs, ɪk'sɛs] *adj* : excesivo, de sobra — **excessive** [ɪk'sɛsɪv, ɛk-] *adj* : excesivo
exchange [ɪks'tʃeɪndʒ, ɛks-; 'ɛksˌtʃeɪndʒ] *n* **1** : intercambio *m* **2** : cambio *m* (en finanzas) — **~** *vt* **-changed; -changing** : cambiar, intercambiar
excise [ɪk'saɪz, ɛk-] *n* **~ tax** : impuesto *m* interno, impuesto *m* sobre el consumo
excite [ɪk'saɪt, ɛk-] *vt* **-cited; -citing** : excitar, emocionar — **excited** [ɪk'saɪt̬əd, ɛk-] *adj* : excitado, entusiasmado — **excitement** [ɪk'saɪtmənt, ɛk-] *n* : entusiasmo *m,* emoción *f*
exclaim [ɪks'kleɪm, ɛk-] *v* : exclamar — **exclamation** [ˌɛksklə'meɪʃən] *n* : exclamación *f* — **exclamation point** *n* : signo *m* de admiración
exclude [ɪks'klu:d, ɛks-] *vt* **-cluded; -cluding** : excluir — **excluding** [ɪks'klu:dɪŋ, ɛks-] *prep* : excepto, con excepción de — **exclusion** [ɪks'klu:ʒən, ɛks-] *n* : exclusión *f* — **exclusive** [ɪks'klu:sɪv, ɛks-] *adj* : exclusivo
excrement ['ɛkskrəmənt] *n* : excremento *m*
excruciating [ɪk'skru:ʃiˌeɪt̬ɪŋ, ɛk-] *adj* : insoportable, atroz
excursion [ɪk'skərʒən, ɛk-] *n* : excursión *f*
excuse [ɪk'skju:z, ɛk-] *vt* **-cused; -cusing 1** : perdonar **2 ~ me** : perdóne, perdón — **~** [ɪk'skju:s, ɛk-] *n* : excusa *f*
execute ['ɛksɪˌkju:t] *vt* **-cuted; -cuting** : ejecutar — **execution** [ˌɛksɪ'kju:ʃən] *n* : ejecución *f* — **executioner** [ˌɛksɪ'kju:ʃənər] *n* : verdugo *m*
executive [ɪg'zɛkjət̬ɪv, ɛg-] *adj* : ejecutivo — **~** *n* **1** MANAGER : ejecutivo *m,* -va *f* **2** *or* **~ branch** : poder *m* ejecutivo
exemplify [ɪg'zɛmpləˌfaɪ, ɛg-] *vt* **-fied; -fying** : ejemplificar — **exemplary** [ɪg'zɛmpləri, ɛg-] *adj* : ejemplar
exempt [ɪg'zɛmpt, ɛg-] *adj* : exento — **~** *vt* : dispensar — **exemption** [ɪg'zɛmpʃən, ɛg-] *n* : exención *f*
exercise ['ɛksərˌsaɪz] *n* : ejercicio *m* — **~** *v* **-cised; -cising** *vt* USE : ejercer, hacer uso de — *vi* : hacer ejercicio
exert [ɪg'zərt, ɛg-] *vt* **1** : ejercer **2 ~ oneself** : esforzarse — **exertion** [ɪg'zərʃən, ɛg-] *n* : esfuerzo *m*
exhale [ɛks'heɪl] *v* **-haled; -haling** : exhalar
exhaust [ɪg'zɔst, ɛg-] *vt* : agotar — **~** *n* **1** *or* **~ fumes** : gases *mpl* de escape **2** *or* **~ pipe** : tubo *m* de escape — **exhaustion** [ɪg'zɔstʃən, ɛg-] *n* : agotamiento *m* — **exhaustive** [ɪg'zɔstɪv, ɛg-] *adj* : exhaustivo
exhibit [ɪg'zɪbət, ɛg-] *vt* **1** DISPLAY : exponer **2** SHOW : mostrar — **~** *n* **1** : objeto *m* expuesto **2** EXHIBITION : exposición *f* — **exhibition** [ˌɛksə'bɪʃən] *n* : exposición *f*
exhilarate [ɪg'zɪləˌreɪt, ɛg-] *vt* **-rated; -rating** : alegrar — **exhilaration** [ɪgˌzɪlə'reɪʃən, ɛg-] *n* : regocijo *m*
exile ['ɛgˌzaɪl, 'ɛkˌsaɪl] *n* **1** : exilio *m* **2** OUTCAST : exiliado *m,* -da *f* — **~** *vt* **exiled; exiling** : exiliar
exist [ɪg'zɪst, ɛg-] *vi* : existir — **existence** [ɪg'zɪstənts, ɛg-] *n* : existencia *f* — **existing** *adj* : existente
exit ['ɛgzət, 'ɛksət] *n* : salida *f* — **~** *vi* : salir
exodus ['ɛksədəs] *n* : éxodo *m*
exonerate [ɪg'zɑnəˌreɪt, ɛg-] *vt* **-ated; -ating** : exonerar, disculpar
exorbitant [ɪg'zɔrbət̬ənt, ɛg-] *adj* : exorbitante, excesivo
exotic [ɪg'zɑt̬ɪk, ɛg-] *adj* : exótico
expand [ɪk'spænd, ɛk-] *vt* **1** : ampliar, extender **2** : dilatar (metales, etc.) — *vi* **1** : ampliarse, extenderse **2** : dilatarse (dícese de metales, etc.) — **expanse** [ɪk'spænts, ɛk-] *n* : extensión *f* — **expansion** [ɪk'spæntʃən, ɛk-] *n* : expansión *f*
expatriate [ɛks'peɪtriət, -ˌeɪt] *n* : expatriado *m,* -da *f* — **~** *adj* : expatriado
expect [ɪk'spɛkt, ɛk-] *vt* **1** : esperar **2** REQUIRE : contar con — *vi* **be expecting** : estar embarazada — **expectancy** [ɪk'spɛktəntsi, ɛk-] *n, pl* **-cies** : esperanza *f* — **expectant** [ɪk'spɛktənt, ɛk-] *adj* **1** : expectante **2 ~ mother** : futura madre *f* — **expectation** [ˌɛkˌspɛk'teɪʃən] *n* : esperanza *f*
expedient [ɪk'spi:diənt, ɛk-] *adj* : conveniente — **~** *n* : expediente *m,* recurso *m*
expedition [ˌɛkspə'dɪʃən] *n* : expedición *f*
expel [ɪk'spɛl, ɛk-] *vt* **-pelled; -pelling** : expulsar (a una persona), expeler (humo, etc.)
expend [ɪk'spɛnd, ɛk-] *vt* : gastar — **expendable** [ɪk'spɛndəbəl, ɛk-] *adj* : prescindible — **expenditure** [ɪk'spɛndɪtʃər, ɛk-, -ˌtʃʊr] *n* : gasto *m* — **expense** [ɪk'spɛnts, ɛk-] *n* **1** : gasto *m* **2 ~s** *npl* : gastos *mpl,* expensas *fpl* **3 at the ~ of** : a expensas de — **expensive** [ɪk'spɛntsɪv, ɛk-] *adj* : caro
experience [ɪk'spɪriənts, ɛk-] *n* : experiencia *f* — **~** *vt* **-enced; -encing** : experimentar — **experienced** [ɪk'spɪriəntst, ɛk-] *adj* : experimentado — **experiment** [ɪk'spɛrəmənt, ɛk-, -'spɪr-] *n* : experimento *m* — **~** *vi* : experimentar — **experimental** [ɪkˌspɛrə'mɛntəl, ɛk-, -ˌspɪr-] *adj* : experimental
expert ['ɛkˌspərt, ɪk'spərt] *adj* : experto — **~** ['ɛkˌspərt] *n* : experto *m,* -ta *f* — **expertise** [ˌɛkspər'ti:z] *n* : pericia *f,* competencia *f*
expire [ɪk'spaɪr, ɛk-] *vi* **-pired; -piring 1** : caducar, vencer **2** DIE : expirar, morir — **expiration** [ˌɛkspə'reɪʃən] *n* : vencimiento *m,* caducidad *f*
explain [ɪk'spleɪn, ɛk-] *vt* : explicar — **explanation** [ˌɛksplə'neɪʃən] *n* : explicación *f* — **explanatory** [ɪk'splænəˌtori, ɛk-] *adj* : explicativo
explicit [ɪk'splɪsət, ɛk-] *adj* : explícito
explode [ɪk'splo:d, ɛk-] *v* **-ploded; -ploding** *vt* : hacer explotar — *vi* : explotar, estallar
exploit ['ɛkˌsplɔɪt] *n* : hazaña *f,* proeza *f* — **~** [ɪk'splɔɪt, ɛk-] *vt* : explotar — **exploitation** [ˌɛkˌsplɔɪ'teɪʃən] *n* : explotación *f*
exploration [ˌɛksplə'reɪʃən] *n* : exploración *f* — **explore** [ɪk'splor, ɛk-] *vt* **-plored; -ploring** : explorar — **explorer** [ɪk'splorər, ɛk-] *n* : explorador *m,* -dora *f*
explosion [ɪk'splo:ʒən, ɛk-] *n* : explosión *f* — **explosive** [ɪk'splo:sɪv, ɛk-] *adj* : explosivo — **~** *n* : explosivo *m*
export [ɛk'sport, 'ɛkˌsport] *vt* : exportar — **~** ['ɛkˌsport] *n* : exportación *f*
expose [ɪk'spo:z, ɛk-] *vt* **-posed; -posing 1** : exponer **2** REVEAL : descubrir, revelar — **exposed** [ɪk'spo:zd, ɛk-] *adj* : expuesto, al descubierto — **exposure** [ɪk'spo:ʒər, ɛk-] *n* : exposición *f*
express [ɪk'sprɛs, ɛk-] *adj* **1** SPECIFIC : expreso, específico **2** FAST : expreso, rápido — **~** *adv* : por correo urgente — **~** *n or* **~ train** : expreso *m* — **~** *vt* : expresar — **expression** [ɪk'sprɛʃən, ɛk-] *n* : expresión *f* — **expressive** [ɪk'sprɛsɪv, ɛk-] *adj* : expresivo — **expressly** [ɪk'sprɛsli, ɛk-] *adv* : expresamente — **expressway** [ɪk'sprɛsˌweɪ, ɛk-] *n* : autopista *f*
expulsion [ɪk'spʌlʃən, ɛk-] *n* : expulsión *f*
exquisite [ɛk'skwɪzət, 'ɛkˌskwɪ-] *adj* : exquisito
extend [ɪk'stɛnd, ɛk-] *vt* **1** STRETCH : extender **2** LENGTHEN : prolongar **3** ENLARGE : ampliar **4 ~ one's hand** : tender la mano — *vi* : extenderse — **extension** [ɪk'stɛntʃən, ɛk-] *n* **1** : extensión *f* **2** LENGTHENING : prolongación *f* **3** ANNEX : ampliación *f,* anexo *m* **4 ~ cord** : alargador *m* — **extensive** [ɪk'stɛntsɪv, ɛk-] *adj* : extenso — **extent** [ɪk'stɛnt, ɛk-] *n* **1** SIZE : extensión *f* **2** DEGREE : alcance *m,* grado *m* **3 to a certain ~** : hasta cierto punto
extenuating [ɪk'stɛnjəˌweɪt̬ɪŋ, ɛk-] *adj* **~ circumstances** : circunstancias *fpl* atenuantes
exterior [ɛk'stɪriər] *adj* : exterior — **~** *n* : exterior *m*
exterminate [ɪk'stərməˌneɪt, ɛk-] *vt* **-nated; -nating** : exterminar — **extermination** [ɪkˌstərmə'neɪʃən, ɛk-] *n* : exterminación *f*
external [ɪk'stərnəl, ɛk-] *adj* : externo — **externally** [ɪk'stərnəli, ɛk-] *adv* : exteriormente
extinct [ɪk'stɪŋkt, ɛk-] *adj* : extinto — **extinction** [ɪk'stɪŋkʃən, ɛk-] *n* : extinción *f*
extinguish [ɪk'stɪŋgwɪʃ, ɛk-] *vt* : extinguir, apagar — **extinguisher** [ɪk'stɪŋgwɪʃər, ɛk-] *n* : extintor *m*
extol [ɪk'sto:l, ɛk-] *vt* **-tolled; -tolling** : ensalzar, alabar
extort [ɪk'stɔrt, ɛk-] *vt* : arrancar (algo a algn) por la fuerza — **extortion** [ɪk'stɔrʃən, ɛk-] *n* : extorsión *f*
extra ['ɛkstrə] *adj* : suplementario, de más — **~** *n* : extra *m* — **~** *adv* **1** : extra, más **2 ~ special** : super especial
extract [ɪk'strækt, ɛk-] *vt* : extraer, sacar — **~** ['ɛkˌstrækt] *n* : extracto *m* — **extraction** [ɪk'strækʃən, ɛk-] *n* : extracción *f*
extracurricular [ˌɛkstrəkə'rɪkjələr] *adj* : extracurricular
extradite ['ɛkstrəˌdaɪt] *vt* **-dited; -diting** : extraditar
extraordinary [ɪk'strɔrdənˌɛri, ˌɛkstrə'ɔrd-] *adj* : extraordinario
extraterrestrial [ˌɛkstrətə'rɛstriəl] *adj* : extraterrestre — **~** *n* : extraterrestre *mf*
extravagant [ɪk'strævɪgənt, ɛk-] *adj* **1** WASTEFUL : despilfarrador, derrochador **2** EXAGGERATED : extravagante, exagerado — **extravagance** [ɪk'strævɪgənts, ɛk-] *n* **1** WASTEFULNESS : derroche *m,* despilfarro *m* **2** LUXURY : lujo *m* **3** EXAGGERATION : extravagancia *f*
extreme [ɪk'stri:m, ɛk-] *adj* : extremo — **~** *n* : extremo *m* — **extremely** [ɪk'stri:mli, ɛk-] *adv* : extremadamente — **extremity** [ɪk'strɛmət̬i, ɛk-] *n, pl* **-ties** : extremidad *f*
extricate ['ɛkstrəˌkeɪt] *vt* **-cated; -cating** : librar, (lograr) sacar
extrovert ['ɛkstrəˌvərt] *n* : extrovertido *m,*

-da *f* — **extroverted** ['ɛkstrə,vərt̬əd] *adj* : extrovertido

exuberant [ɪg'zu:bərənt, ɛg-] *adj* **1** JOYOUS : eufórico **2** LUSH : exuberante — **exuberance** [ɪg'zu:bərənts, ɛg-] *n* **1** JOYOUSNESS : euforia *f* **2** VIGOR : exuberancia *f*

exult [ɪg'zʌlt, ɛg-] *vi* : exultar

eye ['aɪ] *n* **1** : ojo *m* **2** VISION : visión *f*, vista *f* **3** GLANCE : mirada *f* — **~** *vt* **eyed; eyeing** *or* **eying** : mirar — **eyeball** ['aɪ,bɔl] *n* : globo *m* ocular — **eyebrow** ['aɪ,braʊ] *n* : ceja *f* — **eyeglasses** ['aɪ,glæsəz] *npl* : anteojos *mpl*, lentes *mpl* — **eyelash** ['aɪ,læʃ] *n* : pestaña *f* — **eyelid** ['aɪ,lɪd] *n* : párpado *m* — **eyesight** ['aɪ,saɪt] *n* : vista *f*, visión *f* — **eyesore** ['aɪ,sor] *n* : monstruosidad *f* — **eyewitness** ['aɪ'wɪtnəs] *n* : testigo *mf* ocular

F

f ['ɛf] *n, pl* **f's** *or* **fs** ['ɛfs] : f, sexta letra del alfabeto inglés

fable ['feɪbəl] *n* : fábula *f*

fabric ['fæbrɪk] *n* : tela *f*, tejido *m*

fabulous ['fæbjələs] *adj* : fabuloso

facade [fə'sɑd] *n* : fachada *f*

face ['feɪs] *n* **1** : cara *f*, rostro *m* (de una persona) **2** APPEARANCE : fisonomía *f*, aspecto *m* **3** : cara *f* (de una moneda), fachada *f* (de un edificio) **4 ~ value** : valor *m* nominal **5 in the ~ of** : en medio de, ante **6 lose ~** : desprestigiarse **7 make ~s** : hacer muecas — **~** *v* **faced; facing** *vt* **1** : estar frente a **2** CONFRONT : enfrentarse a **3** OVERLOOK : dar a — *vi* **~ to the north** : mirar hacia el norte — **facedown** ['feɪs,daʊn] *adv* : boca abajo — **faceless** ['feɪsləs] *adj* : anónimo — **face–lift** ['feɪs,lɪft] *n* : estiramiento *m* facial

facet ['fæsət] *n* : faceta *f*

face–to–face *adv & adj* : cara a cara

facial ['feɪʃəl] *adj* : de la cara, facial — **~** *n* : limpieza *f* de cutis

facetious [fə'si:ʃəs] *adj* : gracioso, burlón

facility [fə'sɪlət̬i] *n, pl* **-ties 1** EASE : facilidad *f* **2** CENTER : centro *m* **3 facilities** *npl* : comodidades *fpl*, servicios *mpl*

facsimile [fæk'sɪməli] *n* : facsímile *m*, facsímil *m*

fact ['fækt] *n* **1** : hecho *m* **2 in ~** : en realidad, de hecho

faction ['fækʃən] *n* : facción *m*, bando *m*

factor ['fæktər] *n* : factor *m*

factory ['fæktəri] *n, pl* **-ries** : fábrica *f*

factual ['fæktʃʊəl] *adj* : basado en hechos

faculty ['fækəlti] *n, pl* **-ties** : facultad *f*

fad ['fæd] *n* : moda *f* pasajera, manía *f*

fade ['feɪd] *v* **faded; fading** *vi* **1** WITHER : marchitarse **2** DISCOLOR : desteñirse, decolorarse **3** DIM : apagarse **4** VANISH : desvanecerse — *vt* : desteñir

fail ['feɪl] *vi* **1** : fracasar (dícese de una empresa, un matrimonio, etc.) **2** BREAK DOWN : fallar **3 ~ in** : faltar a, no cumplir con **4** FLUNK : suspender *Spain*, ser reprobado *Lat* **5 ~ to do sth** : no hacer algo — *vt* **1** DISAPPOINT : fallar **2** FLUNK : suspender *Spain*, reprobar *Lat* — **~** *n* **without ~** : sin falta — **failing** ['feɪlɪŋ] *n* : defecto *m* — **failure** ['feɪljər] *n* **1** : fracaso *m* **2** BREAKDOWN : falla *f*

faint ['feɪnt] *adj* **1** WEAK : débil **2** INDISTINCT : tenue, indistinto **3 feel ~** : estar mareado — **~** *vi* : desmayarse — **~** *n* : desmayo *m* — **fainthearted** ['feɪnt'hɑrt̬əd] *adj* : cobarde, pusilánime — **faintly** ['feɪntli] *adv* **1** WEAKLY : débilmente **2** SLIGHTLY : ligeramente, levemente

fair[1] ['fær] *n* : feria *f*

fair[2] *adj* **1** BEAUTIFUL : bello, hermoso **2** : bueno (dícese del tiempo) **3** JUST : justo **4** : rubio (dícese del pelo), blanco (dícese de la tez) **5** ADEQUATE : adecuado — **~** *adv* **play ~** : jugar limpio — **fairly** ['færli] *adv* **1** JUSTLY : justamente **2** QUITE : bastante — **fairness** ['færnəs] *n* : justicia *f*

fairy ['færi] *n, pl* **fairies 1** : hada *f* **2 ~ tale** : cuento *m* de hadas

faith ['feɪθ] *n, pl* **faiths** ['feɪθs, 'feɪðz] : fe *f* — **faithful** ['feɪθfəl] *adj* : fiel — **faithfully** *adv* : fielmente — **faithfulness** ['feɪθfəlnəs] *n* : fidelidad *f*

fake ['feɪk] *v* **faked; faking** *vt* **1** FALSIFY : falsificar, falsear **2** FEIGN : fingir — *vi* PRETEND : fingir — **~** *adj* : falso — **~** *n* **1** IMITATION : falsificación *f* **2** IMPOSTOR : impostor *m*, -tora *f*

falcon ['fælkən, 'fɔl-] *n* : halcón *m*

fall ['fɔl] *vi* **fell** ['fɛl]; **fallen** ['fɔlən]; **falling 1** : caer, bajar (dícese de los precios), descender (dícese de la temperatura) **2 ~ asleep** : dormirse **3 ~ back** : retirarse **4 ~ back on** : recurrir a **5 ~ down** : caerse **6 ~ in love** : enamorarse **7 ~ out** QUARREL : pelearse **8 ~ through** : fracasar — **~** *n* **1** : caída *f*, bajada *f* (de precios), descenso *m* (de temperatura) **2** AUTUMN : otoño *m* **3 ~s** *npl* WATERFALL : cascada *f*, catarata *f*

fallacy ['fæləsi] *n, pl* **-cies** : concepto *m* erróneo

fallible ['fæləbəl] *adj* : falible

fallow ['fælo] *adj* **lie ~** : estar en barbecho

false ['fɔls] *adj* **falser; falsest 1** : falso **2 ~ alarm** : falsa alarma *f* **3 ~ teeth** : dentadura *f* postiza — **falsehood** ['fɔls,hʊd] *n* : mentira — **falseness** ['fɔlsnəs] *n* : falsedad *f* — **falsify** ['fɔlsə,faɪ] *vt* **-fied; fying** : falsificar, falsear

falter ['fɔltər] *vi* **-tered; -tering 1** STUMBLE : tambalearse **2** WAVER : vacilar

fame ['feɪm] *n* : fama *f*

familiar [fə'mɪljər] *adj* **1** : familiar **2 be ~ with** : estar familiarizado con — **familiarity** [fə,mɪli'ærət̬i, -,mɪl'jær-] *n, pl* **-ties** : familiaridad *f* — **familiarize** [fə'mɪljə,raɪz] *vt* **-ized; -izing ~ oneself** : familiarizarse

family ['fæmli, 'fæmə-] *n, pl* **-lies** : familia *f*

famine ['fæmən] *n* : hambre *f*, hambruna *f*

famished ['fæmɪʃt] *adj* : famélico

famous ['feɪməs] *adj* : famoso

fan ['fæn] *n* **1** : ventilador *m*, abanico *m* **2** : aficionado *m*, -da *f* (a un pasatiempo); admirador *m*, -dora *f* (de una persona) — **~** *vt* **fanned; fanning** : abanicar (a una persona), avivar (un fuego)

fanatic [fə'næt̬ɪk] *or* **fanatical** [-t̬ɪkəl] *adj* : fanático — **~** *n* : fanático *m*, -ca *f* — **fanaticism** [fə'næt̬ə,sɪzəm] *n* : fanatismo *m*

fancy ['fænt̬si] *vt* **-cied; -cying 1** IMAGINE : imaginarse **2** DESIRE : apetecerle (algo a uno) — **~** *adj* **-cier; -est 1** ELABORATE : elaborado **2** LUXURIOUS : lujoso, elegante — **~** *n, pl* **-cies 1** WHIM : capricho *m* **2** IMAGINATION : imaginación *f* **3 take a ~ to** : aficionarse a (una cosa), tomar cariño a (una persona) — **fanciful** ['fænt̬sɪfəl] *adj* **1** CAPRICIOUS : caprichoso **2** IMAGINATIVE : imaginativo

fanfare ['fæn,fær] *n* : fanfarria *f*

fang ['fæŋ] *n* : colmillo *m* (de un animal), diente *m* (de una serpiente)

fantasy ['fæntəsi] *n, pl* **-sies** : fantasía *f* — **fantasize** ['fæntə,saɪz] *vi* **-sized; -sizing** : fantasear — **fantastic** [fæn'tæstɪk] *adj* : fantástico

far ['fɑr] *adv* **farther** ['fɑrðər] *or* **further** ['fər-]; **farthest** *or* **furthest** [-ðəst] **1** : lejos **2** MUCH : muy, mucho **3 as ~ as** : hasta (un lugar), con respecto a (un tema) **4 by ~** : con mucho **5 ~ and wide** : por todas partes **6 ~ away** : a lo lejos **7 ~ from it!** : ¡todo lo contrario! **8 so ~** : hasta ahora, todavía — **~** *adj* **farther** *or* **further; farthest** *or* **furthest 1** REMOTE : lejano **2** EXTREME : extremo — **faraway** ['fɑrə,weɪ] *adj* : remoto, lejano

farce ['fɑrs] *n* : farsa *f*

fare ['fær] *vi* **fared; faring** : irle a uno — **~** *n* **1** : precio *m* del pasaje **2** FOOD : comida *f*

farewell [fær'wɛl] *n* : despedida *f* — **~** *adj* : de despedida

far–fetched ['fɑr'fɛtʃt] *adj* : improbable, exagerado

farm ['fɑrm] *n* : granja *f*, hacienda *f* — **~** *vt* : cultivar (la tierra), criar (animales) — *vi* : ser agricultor — **farmer** ['fɑrmər] *n* : agricultor *m*, -tora *f*; granjero *m*, -jera *f* — **farmhand** ['fɑrm,hænd] *n* : peón *m* — **farmhouse** ['fɑrm,haʊs] *n* : granja *f*, casa *f* de hacienda — **farming** ['fɑrmɪŋ] *n* : agricultura *f*, cultivo *m* (de plantas), crianza *f* (de animales) — **farmyard** ['fɑrm,jɑrd] *n* : corral *m*

far–off ['fɑr,ɔf, -'ɔf] *adj* : lejano

far–reaching ['fɑr'ri:tʃɪŋ] *adj* : de gran alcance

farsighted ['fɑr,saɪt̬əd] *adj* **1** : hipermétrope **2** PRUDENT : previsor

farther ['fɑrðər] *adv* **1** : más lejos **2** MORE : más — *adj* : más lejano — **farthest** *adv* **1** : lo más lejos **2** MOST : más — *adj* : más lejano

fascinate ['fæsən,eɪt] *vt* **-nated; -nating** : fascinar — **fascination** [,fæsən'eɪʃən] *n* : fascinación *f*

fascism ['fæʃ,ɪzəm] *n* : fascismo *m* — **fascist** ['fæʃɪst] *adj* : fascista — **~** *n* : fascista *mf*

fashion ['fæʃən] *n* **1** MANNER : manera *f* **2** STYLE : moda *f* **3 out of ~** : pasada de moda — **fashionable** ['fæʃənəbəl] *adj* : de moda

fast[1] ['fæst] *vi* : ayunar — **~** *n* : ayuno *m*

fast[2] *adj* **1** SWIFT : rápido **2** SECURE : firme, seguro **3** : adelantado (dícese de un reloj) **4 ~ friends** : amigos *mpl* leales — **~** *adv* **1** SECURELY : firmemente **2** SWIFTLY : rápidamente **3 ~ asleep** : profundamente dormido

fasten ['fæsən] *vt* : sujetar (papeles, etc.), abrochar (una blusa, etc.), cerrar (una maleta, etc.) — *vi* : abrocharse, cerrar — **fastener** ['fæsənər] *n* : cierre *m*

fat ['fæt] *adj* **fatter; fattest 1** : gordo **2** THICK : grueso — **~** *n* : grasa *f*

fatal ['feɪt̬əl] *adj* **1** : mortal **2** FATEFUL : fatal, fatídico — **fatality** [feɪ'tæləti, fə-] *n, pl* **-ties** : víctima *f* mortal

fate ['feɪt] *n* **1** : destino *m* **2** LOT : suerte *f* — **fateful** ['feɪtfəl] *adj* : fatídico

father ['fɑðər] *n* : padre *m* — **~** *vt* : engendrar — **fatherhood** ['fɑðər,hʊd] *n* : paternidad *f* — **father–in–law** ['fɑðərɪn,lɔ] *n, pl* **fathers–in–law** : suegro *m* — **fatherly** ['fɑðərli] *adj* : paternal

fathom ['fæðəm] *vt* : comprender

fatigue [fə'ti:g] *n* : fatiga *f* — **~** *vt* **-tigued; -tiguing** : fatigar

fatten ['fætən] *vt* : engordar — **fattening** *adj* : que engorda

fatty ['fæt̬i] *adj* **fattier; -est** : graso

faucet ['fɔsət] *n* : llave *f Lat*, grifo *m Spain*

fault ['fɔlt] *n* **1** FLAW : defecto *m* **2** RESPONSIBILITY : culpa *f* **3** : falla *f* (geológica) — *vt* : encontrar defectos a — **faultless** ['fɔltləs] *adj* : impecable — **faulty** ['fɔlti] *adj* **faultier; -est** : defectuoso

fauna ['fɔnə] *n* : fauna *f*

favor *or Brit* **favour** ['feɪvər] *n* **1** : favor *m* **2 in ~ of** : a favor de — **~** *vt* **1** : favorecer **2** SUPPORT : estar a favor de **3** PREFER : preferir — **favorable** *or Brit* **favourable** ['feɪvərəbəl] *adj* : favorable — **favorite** *or Brit* **favourite** ['feɪvərət] *n* : favorito *m*, -ta *f* — **~** *adj* : favorito — **favoritism** *or Brit* **favouritism** ['feɪvərə,tɪzəm] *n* : favoritismo *m*

fawn[1] ['fɔn] *vi* **~ over** : adular

fawn[2] *n* : cervato *m*

fax ['fæks] *n* : fax *m* — **~** *vt* : faxear, enviar por fax

fear ['fɪr] *v* : temer — **~** *n* **1** : miedo *m*, temor *m* **2 for ~ of** : por temor a — **fearful** ['fɪrfəl] *adj* **1** FRIGHTENING : espantoso **2** AFRAID : temeroso

feasible ['fi:zəbəl] *adj* : viable, factible

feast ['fi:st] *n* **1** BANQUET : banquete *m*, festín *m* **2** FESTIVAL : fiesta *f* — **~** *vi* **1** : banquetear **2 ~ upon** : darse un festín de

feat ['fi:t] *n* : hazaña *f*

feather ['fɛðər] *n* : pluma *f*

feature ['fi:tʃər] *n* **1** : rasgo *m* (de la cara) **2** CHARACTERISTIC : característica *f* **3** : artículo *m* (en un periódico) **4 ~ film** : largometraje *m* — *v* **-tured; -turing** *vt* **1** PRESENT : presentar **2** EMPHASIZE : destacar — *vi* : figurar

February ['fɛbjʊ,ɛri, 'fɛbʊ-, 'fɛbrʊ-] *n* : febrero *m*

feces ['fi:,si:z] *npl* : excremento *mpl*

federal ['fɛdrəl, -dərəl] *adj* : federal — **federation** [,fɛdə'reɪʃən] *n* : federación *f*

fed up *adj* : harto

fee ['fi:] *n* **1** : honorarios *mpl* **2 entrance ~** : entrada *f*

feeble ['fi:bəl] *adj* **-bler; -blest 1** : débil **2 a ~ excuse** : una pobre excusa

feed ['fi:d] *v* **fed** ['fɛd]; **feeding** *vt* **1** : dar de comer a, alimentar **2** SUPPLY : alimentar — *vi* : comer, alimentarse — **~** *n* : pienso *m*

feel ['fi:l] *v* **felt** ['fɛlt]; **feeling** *vt* **1** : sentir (una sensación, etc.) **2** TOUCH : tocar, palpar **3** BELIEVE : creer — *vi* **1** : sentirse (bien, cansado, etc.) **2** SEEM : parecer **3 ~ hot/thirsty** : tener calor/sed **4 ~ like doing** : tener ganas de hacer — **~** *n* : tacto *m*, sensación *f* — **feeling** ['fi:lɪŋ] *n* **1** SENSATION : sensación *f* **2** EMOTION : sentimiento *m* **3** OPINION : opinión *f* **4 hurt s.o.'s ~s** : herir los sentimientos de algn

feet → **foot**

feign ['feɪn] *vt* : fingir

feline ['fi:,laɪn] *adj* : felino — **~** *n* : felino *m*, -na *f*

fell[1] → **fall**

fell[2] ['fɛl] *vt* : talar (un árbol)

fellow ['fɛ,lo:] *n* **1** COMPANION : compañero *m*, -ra *f* **2** MEMBER : socio *m*, -cia *f* **3** MAN : tipo *m* — **fellowship** ['fɛlo,ʃɪp] *n* **1** : compañerismo *m* **2** ASSOCIATION : fraternidad *f* **3** GRANT : beca *f*

felon ['fɛlən] *n* : criminal *mf* — **felony** ['fɛləni] *n, pl* **-nies** : delito *m* grave

felt[1] → **feel**

felt[2] ['fɛlt] *n* : fieltro *m*

female ['fi:,meɪl] *adj* : femenino — **~** *n* **1** : hembra *f* (animal) **2** WOMAN : mujer *f*

feminine ['fɛmənən] *adj* : femenino — **femininity** [,fɛmə'nɪnət̬i] *n* : feminidad *f* — **feminism** ['fɛmə,nɪzəm] *n* : feminismo *m* — **feminist** ['fɛmənɪst] *adj* : feminista — **~** *n* : feminista *mf*

fence ['fɛnts] *n* : cerca *f*, valla *f*, cerco *m Lat* — **~** *v* **fenced; fencing** *vt or* **~ in** : vallar, cercar — *vi* : hacer esgrima — **fencing** ['fɛntsɪŋ] *n* : esgrima *m* (deporte)

fend ['fɛnd] *vt* **~ off** : rechazar (un enemigo), eludir (una pregunta) — *vi* **~ for oneself** : valerse por sí mismo

fender ['fɛndər] *n* : guardabarros *mpl*

fennel ['fɛnəl] *n* : hinojo *m*

ferment [fər'mɛnt] *v* : fermentar — **fermentation** [,fərmən'teɪʃən, -,mɛn-] *n* : fermentación *f*

fern ['fərn] *n* : helecho *m*

ferocious [fə'ro:ʃəs] *adj* : feroz — **ferocity** [fə'rɑsət̬i] *n* : ferocidad *f*

ferret ['fɛrət] *n* : hurón *m* — **~** *vt* **~ out** : descubrir

Ferris wheel ['fɛrɪs] *n* : noria *f*

ferry ['fɛri] *vt* **-ried; -rying** : transportar — **~** *n, pl* **-ries** : ferry *m*

fertile ['fərt̬əl] *adj* : fértil — **fertility** [fər'tɪlət̬i] *n* : fertilidad *f* — **fertilize** ['fərt̬əl,aɪz] *vt* **-ized; -izing** : fecundar (un huevo), abonar (el suelo) — **fertilizer** ['fərt̬əl,aɪzər] *n* : fertilizante *m*, abono *m*

fervent ['fərvənt] *adj* : ferviente — **fervor** *or Brit* **fervour** ['fərvər] *n* : fervor *m*

fester ['fɛstər] *vi* : enconarse

festival ['fɛstəvəl] *n* **1** : fiesta *f* **2 film ~** : festival *m* de cine — **festive** ['fɛstɪv] *adj* : festivo — **festivity** [fɛs'tɪvət̬i] *n, pl* **-ties** : festividad *f*

fetch ['fɛtʃ] *vt* **1** : ir a buscar **2** : venderse por (un precio)

fête ['feɪt, 'fɛt] *n* : fiesta *f*

fetid ['fɛt̬əd] *adj* : fétido

fetish ['fɛt̬ɪʃ] *n* : fetiche *m*

fetters ['fɛt̬ərz] *npl* : grillos *mpl* — **fetter** ['fɛt̬ər] *vt* : encadenar

fetus ['fi:t̬əs] *n* : feto *m*

feud ['fju:d] *n* : enemistad *f* (entre familiares) — **~** *vi* : pelear

feudal ['fju:dəl] *adj* : feudal — **feudalism** ['fju:dəl,ɪzəm] *n* : feudalismo *m*

fever ['fi:vər] *n* : fiebre *f* — **feverish** ['fi:vərɪʃ] *adj* : febril

few ['fju:] *adj* **1** : pocos **2 a ~ times** : varias veces — **~** *pron* **1** : pocos **2 a ~** : algunos, unos cuantos **3 quite a ~** : muchos — **fewer** ['fju:ər] *adj & pron* : menos

fiancé, fiancée [,fi:,ɑn'seɪ, ,fi:'ɑn,seɪ] *n* : prometido *m*, -da *f*; novio *m*, -via *f*

fiasco [fi'æs,ko:] *n, pl* **-coes** : fiasco *m*

fib ['fɪb] *n* : mentirilla *f* — **~** *vi* **fibbed; fibbing** : decir mentirillas

fiber *or* **fibre** ['faɪbər] *n* : fibra *f* — **fiberglass** ['faɪbər,glæs] *n* : fibra *f* de vidrio — **fibrous** ['faɪbrəs] *adj* : fibroso

fickle ['fɪkəl] *adj* : inconstante

fiction ['fɪkʃən] *n* : ficción *f* — **fictional** ['fɪkʃənəl] *or* **fictitious** [fɪk'tɪʃəs] *adj* : ficticio

fiddle ['fɪdəl] *n* : violín *m* — **~** *vi* **-dled; -dling 1** : tocar el violín **2 ~ with** : juguetear con

fidelity [fə'dɛlət̬i, faɪ-] *n, pl* **-ties** : fidelidad *f*

fidget ['fɪdʒət] *vi* **1** : estarse inquieto, moverse **2 ~ with** : juguetear con — **fidgety** ['fɪdʒət̬i] *adj* : inquieto, nervioso

field ['fi:ld] *n* : campo *m* — **~** *vt* : interceptar (una pelota), sortear (una pregunta) — **field glasses** *n* : binoculares *mpl*, gemelos *mpl* — **field trip** *n* : viaje *m* de estudio

fiend ['fi:nd] *n* **1** : demonio *m* **2** FANATIC : fanático *m*, -ca *f* — **fiendish** ['fi:ndɪʃ] *adj* : diabólico

fierce ['fɪrs] *adj* **fiercer; -est 1** : feroz **2** INTENSE : fuerte (dícese del viento), acalorado (dícese de un debate) — **fierceness** ['fɪrsnəs] *n* : ferocidad *f*

fiery ['faɪəri] *adj* **fierier; -est 1** BURNING : llameante **2** SPIRITED : ardiente, fogoso — **fieriness** ['faɪərinəs] *n* : pasión *f*, ardor *m*

fifteen [fɪf'ti:n] *n* : quince *m* — **~** *adj* : quince — **fifteenth** [fɪf'ti:nθ] *adj* : decimoquinto — **~** *n* **1** : decimoquinto *m*, -ta *f* (en una serie) **2** : quinceavo *m* (en matemáticas)

fifth ['fɪfθ] *n* **1** : quinto *m*, -ta *f* (en una serie) **2** : quinto *m* (en matemáticas) — **~** *adj* : quinto

fiftieth ['fɪftiəθ] *adj* : quincuagésimo — **~** *n* **1** : quincuagésimo *m*, -ma *f* (en una serie) **2** : cincuentavo *m* (en matemáticas)

fifty ['fɪfti] *n, pl* **-ties** : cincuenta *m* — **~** *adj* : cincuenta — **fifty–fifty** [,fɪfti'fɪfti] *adv* : a medias, mitad y mitad — **~** *adj* **a ~ chance** : un cincuenta por ciento de posibilidades

fig ['fɪg] *n* : higo *m*

fight ['faɪt] *v* **fought** ['fɔt]; **fighting** *vi* **1** BATTLE : luchar **2** QUARREL : pelear **3 ~ back** : defenderse — *vt* : luchar contra — **~** *n* **1** STRUGGLE : lucha *f* **2** QUARREL : pelea *f* — **fighter** ['faɪt̬ər] *n* **1** : luchador *m*, -dora *f* **2** *or* **~ plane** : avión *m* de caza

figment ['fɪgmənt] *n* **~ of the imagination** : producto *m* de la imaginación

figurative ['fɪgjərət̬ɪv, -gə-] *adj* : figurado

figure ['fɪgjər, -gər] *n* **1** NUMBER : número *m*, cifra *f* **2** PERSON, SHAPE : figura *f* **3 ~ of speech** : figura *f* retórica **4 watch one's ~** : cuidar la línea — **~** *v* **-ured; -uring** *vt* : calcular — *vi* **1** : figurar **2 that ~s!** : ¡no me extraña! — **figurehead** ['fɪgjər,hɛd, -gər] *n* : testaferro *m* — **figure out** *vt* **1** UNDERSTAND : entender **2** RESOLVE : resolver

file[1] ['faɪl] *n* : lima *f* (instrumento) — **~** *vt* **filed; filing** : limar

file[2] *vt* **filed; filing 1** : archivar (documentos) **2 ~ charges** : presentar cargos — **~** *n* : archivo *m*

file[3] *n* LINE : fila *f* — **~** *vi* **~ in/out** : entrar/salir en fila

fill ['fɪl] *vt* **1** : llenar, rellenar **2** : cumplir con (un requisito) **3** : tapar (un agujero), empastar (un diente) — *vi* **1 ~ in for** : reemplazar **2** *or* **~ up** : llenarse — **~** *n* **1 eat one's ~** : comer lo suficiente **2 have one's ~ of** : estar harto de

fillet ['fɪlət, fɪ'leɪ, 'fɪ,leɪ] *n* : filete *m*

filling ['fɪlɪŋ] *n* **1** : relleno *m* **2** : empaste *m* (de dientes) **3 ~ station** → **service station**

filly ['fɪli] *n, pl* **-lies** : potra *f*

film ['fɪlm] *n* : película *f* — **~** *vt* : filmar

filter ['fɪltər] *n* : filtro *m* — **~** *vt* : filtrar

filth ['filθ] *n* : mugre *f* — **filthy** ['filθi] *adj* **filthier; -est 1** : mugriento **2** OBSCENE : obsceno

fin ['fin] *n* : aleta *f*

final ['faɪnəl] *adj* **1** LAST : último **2** DEFINITIVE : definitivo **3** ULTIMATE : final — *n* **1** : final *m* (en deportes) **2** **~s** *npl* : exámenes *mpl* finales — **finalist** ['faɪnəlɪst] *n* : finalista *mf* — **finalize** ['faɪnəlaɪz] *vt* **-ized; -izing** : finalizar — **finally** ['faɪnəli] *adv* : finalmente

finance [fə'næns, 'faɪˌnæns] *n* **1** : finanzas *fpl* **2 ~s** *npl* : recursos *mpl* financieros — *vt* **-nanced; -nancing** : financiar — **financial** [fə'næntʃəl, faɪ-] *adj* : financiero — **financially** [fə'næntʃəli, faɪ-] *adv* : económicamente

find ['faɪnd] *vt* **found** ['faʊnd]; **finding 1** LOCATE : encontrar **2** REALIZE : darse cuenta de **3 ~ guilty** : declarar culpable **4** *or* **~ out** : descubrir — *vi* **~ out** : enterarse — *n* : hallazgo *m* — **finding** ['faɪndɪŋ] *n* **1** FIND : hallazgo *m* **2 ~s** *npl* : conclusiones *fpl*

fine[1] ['faɪn] *n* : multa *f* — **~** *vt* **fined; fining** : multar

fine[2] *adj* **finer; -est 1** DELICATE : fino **2** EXCELLENT : excelente **3** SUBTLE : sutil **4** : bueno (dícese del tiempo) **5 ~ print** : letra *f* menuda **6 it's ~ with me** : me parece bien — *adv* OK : bien — **fine arts** *npl* : bellas artes *fpl* — **finely** ['faɪnli] *adv* **1** EXCELLENTLY : excelentemente **2** PRECISELY : con precisión **3** MINUTELY : fino, menudo

finger ['fɪŋgər] *n* : dedo *m* — **~** *vt* : tocar, toquetear — **fingernail** ['fɪŋgərˌneɪl] *n* : uña *f* — **fingerprint** ['fɪŋgərˌprɪnt] *n* : huella *f* digital — **fingertip** ['fɪŋgərˌtɪp] *n* : punta *f* del dedo

finicky ['fɪnɪki] *adj* : maniático, mañoso *Lat*

finish ['fɪnɪʃ] *v* : acabar, terminar — **~** *n* **1** END : fin *m*, final *m* **2** *or* **~ line** : meta *f* **3** SURFACE : acabado *m*

finite ['faɪˌnaɪt] *adj* : finito

fir ['fər] *n* : abeto *m*

fire ['faɪr] *n* **1** : fuego *m* **2** CONFLAGRATION : incendio *m* **3 catch ~** : incendiarse (dícese de bosques, etc.), prenderse (dícese de fósforos, etc.) **4 on ~** : en llamas **5 open ~ on** : abrir fuego sobre — **~** *vt* **fired; firing 1** DISMISS : despedir **2** SHOOT : disparar — *vi* : disparar — **fire alarm** *n* : alarma *f* contra incendios — **firearm** ['faɪrˌɑrm] *n* : arma *f* de fuego — **firecracker** ['faɪrˌkrækər] *n* : petardo *m* — **fire engine** *n* : carro *m* de bomberos *Lat*, coche *m* de bomberos *Spain* — **fire escape** *n* : escalera *f* de incendios — **fire extinguisher** *n* : extintor *m* (de incendios) — **firefighter** ['faɪrˌfaɪtər] *n* : bombero *m*, -ra *f* — **firefly** ['faɪrˌflaɪ] *n*, *pl* **-flies** : luciérnaga *f* — **firehouse** → **fire station** — **fireman** ['faɪrmən] *n*, *pl* **-men** [-mən, -ˌmɛn] — **firefighter** — **fireplace** ['faɪrˌpleɪs] *n* : hogar *m*, chimenea *f* — **fireproof** ['faɪrˌpruːf] *adj* : ignífugo — **fireside** ['faɪrˌsaɪd] *n* : hogar *m* — **fire station** *n* : estación *f* de bomberos *Lat*, parque *m* de bomberos *Spain* — **firewood** ['faɪrˌwʊd] *n* : leña *f* — **fireworks** ['faɪrˌwərk] *npl* : fuegos *mpl* artificiales

firm[1] ['fərm] *n* : empresa *f*

firm[2] *adj* : firme — **firmly** ['fərmli] *adv* : firmemente — **firmness** ['fərmnəs] *n* : firmeza *f*

first ['fərst] *adj* **1** : primero **2 at ~ sight** : a primera vista **3 for the ~ time** : por primera vez — **~** *adv* **1** : primero **2 ~ and foremost** : ante todo **3 ~ of all** : en primer lugar — **~** *n* **1** : primero *m*, -ra *f* **2 at ~** : al principio — **first aid** *n* : primeros auxilios *mpl* — **first-class** ['fərstˌklæs] *adv* : en primera — *adj* : de primera *f* — **firsthand** ['fərstˈhænd] *adv* : directamente — *adj* : de primera mano — **firstly** ['fərstli] *adv* : en primer lugar — **first name** *n* : nombre *m* de pila — **first-rate** ['fərstˈreɪt] *adj* → **first-class**

fiscal ['fɪskəl] *adj* : fiscal

fish ['fɪʃ] *n*, *pl* **fish** *or* **fishes** : pez *m* (vivo), pescado *m* (para comer) — **~** *vi* **1** : pescar **2 ~ for** SEEK : buscar **3 go ~ing** : ir de pesca — **fisherman** ['fɪʃərmən] *n*, *pl* **-men** [-mən, -ˌmɛn] : pescador *m*, -dora *f* — **fishhook** ['fɪʃˌhʊk] *n* : anzuelo *m* — **fishing** ['fɪʃɪŋ] *n* : pesca *f* — **fishing pole** *n* : caña *f* de pescar — **fish market** *n* : pescadería *f* — **fishy** ['fɪʃi] *adj* **fishier; -est 1** : a pescado (dícese de sabores, etc.) **2** SUSPICIOUS : sospechoso

fist ['fɪst] *n* : puño *m*

fit[1] ['fɪt] *n* **1** : ataque *m* **2 he had a ~** : le dio un ataque

fit[2] *adj* **fitter; fittest 1** SUITABLE : apropiado **2** HEALTHY : en forma **3 be ~ for** : ser apto para — **~** *v* **fitted; fitting** *vt* **1** : encajar en (un hueco, etc.) **2** (*relating to clothing*) : quedar bien a **3** SUIT : ser apropiado para **4** MATCH : coincidir con **5** *or* **~ out** : equipar — *vi* **1** : caber (en una caja, etc.), entrar (en un hueco, etc.) **2** *or* **~ in** BELONG : encajar **3 this dress doesn't ~** : este vestido no me queda bien — **~** *n* **it's a good fit** : me queda bien — **fitful** ['fɪtfəl] *adj* : irregular — **fitness** ['fɪtnəs] *n* **1** HEALTH : salud *f* **2** SUITABILITY : idoneidad *f* — **fitting** ['fɪtɪŋ] *adj* : apropiado — **~** *n* : instalación *f*

five ['faɪv] *adj* : cinco — **~** *n* : cinco *m* — **five hundred** *n* : quinientos *m* — **~** *adj* : quinientos

fix ['fɪks] *vt* **1** ATTACH : fijar, sujetar **2** REPAIR : arreglar **3** PREPARE : preparar — **~** *n* PREDICAMENT : aprieto *m*, apuro *m* — **fixed** ['fɪkst] *adj* : fijo — **fixture** ['fɪkstʃər] *n* : instalación *f*

fizz ['fɪz] *vi* : burbujear — **~** *n* : efervescencia *f*

fizzle ['fɪzəl] *vi* **-zled; -zling** *or* **~ out** : quedar en nada

flabbergasted ['flæbərˌgæstəd] *adj* : estupefacto, pasmado

flabby ['flæbi] *adj* **-bier; -est** : fofo

flaccid ['flæksəd, 'flæsəd] *adj* : fláccido

flag[1] ['flæg] *vi* WEAKEN : flaquear

flag[2] *n* : bandera *f* — **~** *vt* **flagged; flagging** *or* **~ down** : hacer señales de parada a — **flagpole** ['flægˌpoːl] *n* : asta *f*

flagrant ['fleɪgrənt] *adj* : flagrante

flair ['flær] *n* : don *m*, facilidad *f*

flake ['fleɪk] *n* : copo *m* (de nieve), escama *f* (de pintura, de la piel) — **~** *vi* **flaked; flaking** : pelarse

flamboyant [flæm'bɔɪənt] *adj* : extravagante

flame ['fleɪm] *n* **1** : llama *f* **2 burst into ~s** : estallar en llamas **3 go up in ~s** : incendiarse

flamingo [flə'mɪŋgo] *n*, *pl* **-gos** : flamenco *m*

flammable ['flæməbəl] *adj* : inflamable

flank ['flæŋk] *n* : ijada *f* (de un animal), flanco *m* (militar) — **~** *vt* : flanquear

flannel ['flænəl] *n* : franela *f*

flap ['flæp] *n* : solapa *f* (de un sobre, un libro, etc.), tapa *f* (de un recipiente) — **~** *v* **flapped; flapping** *vi* : agitarse — *vt* : batir

flapjack ['flæpˌdʒæk] → **pancake**

flare ['flær] *vi* **flared; flaring 1 ~ up** BLAZE : llamear **2 ~ up** EXPLODE, ERUPT : estallar, explotar — **~** *n* **1** BLAZE : llamarada *f* **2** SIGNAL : (luz *f* de) bengala *f*

flash ['flæʃ] *vi* **1** : brillar, destellar **2 ~ past** : pasar como un rayo **3 ~ a smile** : sonreír — **~** *n* **1** : destello *m* **2 ~ of lightning** : relámpago *m* **3 in a ~** : de repente — **flashlight** ['flæʃˌlaɪt] *n* : linterna *f* — **flashy** ['flæʃi] *adj* **flashier; -est** : ostentoso

flask ['flæsk] *n* : frasco *m*

flat ['flæt] *adj* **flatter; flattest 1** LEVEL : plano, llano **2** DOWNRIGHT : categórico **3** FIXED : fijo **4** MONOTONOUS : monótono **5** : bemol (en la música) **6 ~ tire** : neumático *m* desinflado — **~** *n* **1** : bemol *m* (en la música) **2** *Brit* APARTMENT : apartamento *m*, departamento *m Lat* **3** PUNCTURE : pinchazo *m* — **~** *adv* **1 ~ broke** : pelado **2 in one hour ~** : en una hora justa — **flatly** ['flætli] *adv* : categóricamente — **flat-out** ['flætˈaʊt] *adj* **1** : frenético **2** DOWNRIGHT : categórico — **flatten** ['flætən] *vt* **1** LEVEL : aplanar, allanar **2** KNOCK DOWN : arrasar

flatter ['flætər] *vt* **1** BECOME : favorecer — **flatterer** ['flætərər] *n* : adulador *m*, -dora *f* — **flattering** ['flætərɪŋ] *adj* **1** : halagador **2** BECOMING : favorecedor — **flattery** ['flætəri] *n*, *pl* **-ries** : halagos *mpl*

flaunt ['flɔnt] *vt* : hacer alarde de

flavor *or Brit* **flavour** ['fleɪvər] *n* : gusto *m*, sabor *m* — **~** *vt* : sazonar — **flavorful** *or Brit* **flavourful** ['fleɪvərfəl] *adj* : sabroso — **flavoring** *or Brit* **flavouring** ['fleɪvərɪŋ] *n* : condimento *m*, sazón *f*

flaw ['flɔ] *n* : defecto *m* — **flawless** ['flɔləs] *adj* : perfecto

flax ['flæks] *n* : lino *m*

flea ['fli] *n* : pulga *f*

fleck ['flɛk] *n* **1** PARTICLE : mota *f* **2** SPOT : pinta *f*

flee ['fli] *v* **fled** ['flɛd]; **fleeing** *vi* : huir — *vt* : huir de

fleece ['fli:s] *n* : vellón *m* — **~** *vt* **fleeced; fleecing 1** SHEAR : esquilar **2** DEFRAUD : desplumar

fleet ['flit] *n* : flota *f*

fleeting ['flitɪŋ] *adj* : fugaz

Flemish ['flɛmɪʃ] *adj* : flamenco

flesh ['flɛʃ] *n* **1** : carne *f* **2** PULP : pulpa *f* **3 in the ~** : en persona — **fleshy** ['flɛʃi] *adj* **fleshier; -est 1** : gordo **2** PULPY : carnoso

flew → **fly**

flex ['flɛks] *vt* : flexionar — **flexibility** [ˌflɛksə'bɪləti] *n*, *pl* **-ties** : flexibilidad *f* — **flexible** ['flɛksəbəl] *adj* : flexible

flick ['flɪk] *n* : golpecito *m* — **~** *vt* : dar un golpecito a — *vi* **~ through** : hojear

flicker ['flɪkər] *vi* : parpadear — **~** *n* **1** : parpadeo *m* **2 a ~ of hope** : un rayo de esperanza

flier ['flaɪər] *n* **1** AVIATOR : aviador *m*, -dora *f* **2** *or* **flyer** LEAFLET : folleto *m*, prospecto *m Lat*

flight[1] ['flaɪt] *n* **1** : vuelo *m* **2** TRAJECTORY : trayectoria *f* **3 ~ of stairs** : tramo *m*

flight[2] *n* ESCAPE : huida *f*

flimsy ['flɪmzi] *adj* **flimsier; -est 1** LIGHT : ligero **2** SHAKY : poco sólido **3 a ~ excuse** : una excusa floja

flinch ['flɪntʃ] *vi* **~ from** : encogerse ante

fling ['flɪŋ] *vt* **flung** ['flʌŋ]; **flinging 1** : arrojar **2** *or* **~ open** : abrir de un golpe — **~** *n* **1** AFFAIR : aventura *f* **2 have a ~ at** : intentar

flint ['flɪnt] *n* : pedernal *m*

flip ['flɪp] *v* **flipped; flipping 1** *or* **~ over** : dar la vuelta a **2 ~ a coin** : echarlo a cara o cruz — *vi* **1** *or* **~ over** : volcarse **2 ~ through** : hojear — *n* SOMERSAULT : voltereta *f*

flippant ['flɪpənt] *adj* : ligero, frívolo

flipper ['flɪpər] *n* : aleta *f*

flirt ['flərt] *vi* : coquetear — **~** *n* : coqueto *m*, -ta *f* — **flirtatious** [ˌflərˈteɪʃəs] *adj* : coqueto

flit ['flɪt] *vi* **flitted; flitting** : revolotear

float ['floːt] *n* **1** : flotador *m* **2** : carroza *f* (en un desfile) — **~** *vi* : flotar — *vt* : hacer flotar

flock ['flɑk] *n* : rebaño *m* (de ovejas), bandada *f* (de pájaros) — **~** *vi* : congregarse

flog ['flɑg] *vt* **flogged; flogging** : azotar

flood ['flʌd] *n* **1** : inundación *f*, torrente *m* (de palabras, de lágrimas, etc.) — **~** *vt* : inundar — **floodlight** ['flʌdˌlaɪt] *n* : foco *m*

floor ['flor] *n* **1** : suelo *m*, piso *m Lat* **2** STORY : piso *m* **3** DANCE **~** : pista *f* de baile **4** GROUND **~** : planta *f* baja — **~** *vt* **1** KNOCK DOWN : derribar **2** NONPLUS : desconcertar — **floorboard** ['flor,bord] *n* : tabla *f* del suelo

flop ['flɑp] *vi* **flopped; flopping 1** FLAP : agitarse **2** COLLAPSE : dejarse caer **3** FAIL : fracasar — **~** *n* FAILURE : fracaso *m* — **floppy** ['flɑpi] *adj* **-pier; -est** : flojo, flexible — **floppy disk** *n* : diskette *m*, disquete *m*

flora ['florə] *n* : flora *f* — **floral** ['florəl] *adj* : floral — **florid** ['florɪd] *adj* **1** FLOWERY : florido **2** RUDDY : rojizo — **florist** ['florɪst] *n* : florista *mf*

floss ['flɔs] *n* → **dental floss**

flounder[1] ['flaʊndər] *n*, *pl* **flounder** *or* **flounders** : platija *f*

flounder[2] *vi* **1** *or* **~ about** : resbalarse, revolcarse **2** : titubear (en un discurso)

flour ['flaʊər] *n* : harina *f*

flourish ['flərɪʃ] *vi* : florecer — *vt* BRANDISH : blandir — **~** *n* : floritura *f* — **flourishing** ['flərɪʃɪŋ] *adj* : floreciente

flout ['flaʊt] *vt* : desacatar, burlarse de

flow ['floː] *vi* : fluir, correr — **~** *n* **1** : flujo *m*, circulación *f* **2** : corriente *f* (de información, etc.)

flower ['flaʊər] *n* : flor *f* — **~** *vi* : florecer — **flowered** ['flaʊərd] *adj* : floreado — **flowerpot** ['flaʊərˌpɑt] *n* : maceta *f* — **flowery** ['flaʊəri] *adj* : florido

flown → **fly**

flu ['flu] *n* : gripe *f*

fluctuate ['flʌktʃuˌeɪt] *vi* **-ated; -ating** : fluctuar — **fluctuation** [ˌflʌktʃuˈeɪʃən] *n* : fluctuación *f*

fluency ['fluːəntsi] *n* : fluidez *f* — **fluent** ['fluːənt] *adj* **1** : fluido **2 be ~ in** : hablar con fluidez — **fluently** ['fluːəntli] *adv* : con fluidez

fluff ['flʌf] *n* : pelusa *f* — **fluffy** ['flʌfi] *adj* **fluffier; -est** : de pelusa, velloso

fluid ['fluːɪd] *adj* : fluido — **~** *n* : fluido *m*

flung → **fling**

flunk ['flʌŋk] *vt* : reprobar *Lat*, suspender *Spain* — *vi* : ser reprobado *Lat*, suspender *Spain*

fluorescence [ˌflʊˈrɛsənts, ˌflɔr-] *n* : fluorescencia *f* — **fluorescent** [ˌflʊˈrɛsənt, ˌflɔr-] *adj* : fluorescente

flurry ['fləri] *n*, *pl* **-ries 1** GUST : ráfaga *f* **2** *or* **snow ~** : nevisca *f* **3 ~ of questions** : aluvión *m* de preguntas

flush ['flʌʃ] *vi* BLUSH : ruborizarse, sonrojarse — *vt* **~ the toilet** : tirar de la cadena, jalarle a la cadena *Lat* — **~** *n* BLUSH : rubor *m*, sonrojo *m* — **~** *adj* **~ with** : a nivel con, a ras de — **~** *adv* : al mismo nivel, a ras

fluster ['flʌstər] *vt* : poner nervioso

flute ['fluːt] *n* : flauta *f*

flutter ['flʌtər] *vi* **1** FLIT : revolotear **2** WAVE : ondear **3** *or* **~ about** : ir y venir — **~** *n* **1** : revoloteo *m* (de alas) **2** STIR : revuelo *m*

flux ['flʌks] *n* **be in a state of ~** : cambiar continuamente

fly[1] ['flaɪ] *v* **flew** ['flu]; **flown** ['floːn]; **flying** *vi* **1** : volar **2** TRAVEL : ir en avión **3** WAVE : ondear **4** RUSH : correr **5 ~ by** : pasar volando — *vt* **1** PILOT : pilotar **2** : hacer volar (una cometa), enarbolar (una bandera) — **~** *n*, *pl* **flies** : bragueta *f* (de un pantalón)

fly[2] *n*, *pl* **flies** : mosca *f* (insecto)

flyer → **flier**

flying saucer *n* : platillo *m* volador *Lat*, platillo *m* volante *Spain*

flyswatter ['flaɪˌswɑtər] *n* : matamoscas *m*

foal ['foːl] *n* : potro *m*, -tra *f*

foam ['foːm] *n* : espuma *f* — **~** *vi* : hacer espuma — **foamy** ['foːmi] *adj* **foamier; -est** : espumoso

focus ['foːkəs] *n*, *pl* **-ci** ['foːˌsaɪ, -ˌkaɪ] **1** : foco *m* **2 be in ~** : estar enfocado **3 ~ of attention** : centro *m* de atención — **~** *v* **-cused** *or* **-cussed; -cusing** *or* **-cussing** *vt* **1** : enfocar **2** : centrar (la atención, etc.) — *vi* **~ on** : enfocar (con los ojos), concentrarse en (con la mente)

fodder ['fɑdər] *n* : forraje *m*

foe ['foː] *n* : enemigo *m*, -ga *f*

fog ['fɔg, 'fɑg] *n* : niebla *f* — **~** *v* **fogged; fogging** *vt* : empañar — *vi* : empañarse — **foggy** ['fɔgi, 'fɑ-] *adj* **foggier; -est** : nebuloso — **foghorn** ['fɔgˌhɔrn, 'fɑg-] *n* : sirena *f* de niebla

foil[1] ['fɔɪl] *vt* : frustrar

foil[2] *n* *or* **aluminum ~** : papel *m* de aluminio

fold[1] ['foːld] *n* **1** : redil *m* (para ovejas) **2 return to the ~** : volver al redil

fold[2] *vt* **1** : doblar, plegar **2 ~ one's arms** : cruzar los brazos — *vi* **1** *or* **~ up** : doblarse, plegarse **2** FAIL : fracasar — **~** *n* : pliegue *m* — **folder** ['foːldər] *n* : carpeta *f*

foliage ['foːliɪdʒ, -lɪdʒ] *n* : follaje *m*

folk ['foːk] *n*, *pl* **folk** *or* **folks 1** : gente *f* **2 ~s** *npl* PARENTS : padres *mpl* — **~** *adj* **1** : popular **2 ~ dance** : danza *f* folklórica — **folklore** ['foːkˌlor] *n* : folklore *m*

follow ['fɑlo] *vt* **1** : seguir **2** UNDERSTAND : entender **3 ~ up** : seguir — *vi* **1** : seguir **2** UNDERSTAND : entender **3 ~ up on** : seguir con — **follower** ['fɑloər] *n* : seguidor *m*, -dora *f* — **following** ['fɑloɪŋ] *adj* : siguiente — **~** *n* : seguidores *mpl* — **~** *prep* : después de

folly ['fɑli] *n*, *pl* **-lies** : locura *f*

fond ['fɑnd] *adj* **1** : cariñoso **2 be ~ of sth** : ser aficionado a algo **3 be ~ of s.o.** : tener cariño a algn

fondle ['fɑndəl] *vt* **-dled; -dling** : acariciar

fondness ['fɑndnəs] *n* **1** LOVE : cariño *m* **2** LIKING : afición *f*

food ['fuːd] *n* : comida *f*, alimento *m* — **foodstuffs** ['fuːdˌstʌfs] *npl* : comestibles *mpl*

fool ['fuːl] *n* **1** : idiota *mf* **2** JESTER : bufón *m*, -fona *f* — **~** *vi* **1** JOKE : bromear **2** *or* **~ around** : perder el tiempo — *vt* TRICK : engañar — **foolhardy** ['fuːlˌhɑrdi] *adj* : temerario — **foolish** ['fuːlɪʃ] *adj* : tonto — **foolishness** ['fuːlɪʃnəs] *n* : tontería *f* — **foolproof** ['fuːlˌpruːf] *adj* : infalible

foot ['fʊt] *n*, *pl* **feet** ['fiːt] : pie *m* — **footage** ['fʊtɪdʒ] *n* : secuencias *fpl* (cinemáticas) — **football** ['fʊtˌbɔl] *n* : fútbol *m* americano — **footbridge** ['fʊtˌbrɪdʒ] *n* : pasarela *f*, puente *m* peatonal — **foothills** ['fʊtˌhɪlz] *npl* : estribaciones *fpl* — **foothold** ['fʊtˌhoːld] *n* : punto *m* de apoyo — **footing** ['fʊtɪŋ] *n* **1** BALANCE : equilibrio *m* **2 on equal ~** : en igualdad — **footlights** ['fʊtˌlaɪts] *npl* : candilejas *fpl* — **footnote** ['fʊtˌnoːt] *n* : nota *f* al pie de la página — **footpath** ['fʊtˌpæθ] *n* : sendero *m* — **footprint** ['fʊtˌprɪnt] *n* : huella *f* — **footstep** ['fʊtˌstɛp] *n* : paso *m* — **footstool** ['fʊtˌstuːl] *n* : escabel *m* — **footwear** ['fʊtˌwær] *n* : calzado *m*

for ['for] *prep* **1** (*indicating purpose, etc.*) : para **2** (*indicating motivation, etc.*) : por **3** (*indicating duration*) : durante **4 we walked ~ 3 miles** : andamos 3 millas **5** AS FOR : con respecto a — **~** *conj* : puesto que, porque

forage ['forɪdʒ] *n* : forraje *m* — **~** *vi* **-aged; -aging 1** : forrajear **2 ~ for** : buscar

foray ['forˌeɪ] *n* : incursión *f*

forbid [fər'bɪd] *vt* **-bade** [-'bæd, -'beɪd] *or* **-bad** [-'bæd]; **-bidden** [-'bɪdən]; **-bidding** : prohibir — **forbidding** [fər'bɪdɪŋ] *adj* : intimidante, severo

force ['fors] *n* **1** : fuerza *f* **2 by ~** : por la fuerza **3 in ~** : en vigor, en vigencia **4 armed ~s** : fuerzas *fpl* armadas — **~** *vt* **forced; forcing 1** : forzar **2** OBLIGATE : obligar — **forced** ['forst] *adj* : forzado, forzoso — **forceful** ['forsfəl] *adj* : fuerte, enérgético

forceps ['forsəps, -ˌsɛps] *ns & pl* : fórceps *m*

forcibly ['forsəbli] *adv* : por la fuerza

ford ['ford] *n* : vado *m* — **~** *vt* : vadear

fore ['for] *n* **come to the ~** : empezar a destacarse

forearm ['forˌɑrm] *n* : antebrazo *m*

foreboding [forˈboːdɪŋ] *n* : premonición *f*, presentimiento *m*

forecast ['forˌkæst] *vt* **-cast; -casting** : predecir, pronosticar — **~** *n* : predicción *f*, pronóstico *m*

forefathers ['forˌfɑðərz] *npl* : antepasados *mpl*

forefinger ['forˌfɪŋgər] *n* : índice *m*, dedo *m* índice

forefront ['forˌfrʌnt] *n* **at/in the ~** : a la vanguardia

forego [for'goː] → **forgo**

foregone [for'gɔn] *adj* **~ conclusion** : resultado *m* inevitable

foreground ['forˌgraʊnd] *n* : primer plano *m*

forehead ['for,hɛd, 'forˌhɛd] *n* : frente *f*

foreign ['forən] *adj* **1** : extranjero **2 ~ trade** : comercio *m* exterior — **foreigner** ['forənər] *n* : extranjero *m*, -ra *f*

foreman ['formən] *n*, *pl* **-men** [-mən, -ˌmɛn] : capataz *mf*

foremost ['forˌmoːst] *adj* : principal — **~** *adv* **first and ~** : ante todo

forensic [fə'rɛnsɪk] *adj* : forense

forerunner ['forˌrʌnər] *n* : precursor *m*, -sora *f*

foresee [for'si:] *vt* **-saw; -seen; -seeing** : prever — **foreseeable** [for'si:əbəl] *adj* : previsible
foreshadow [for'ʃædo:] *vt* : presagiar
foresight ['for,saɪt] *n* : previsión *f*
forest ['fɔrəst] *n* : bosque *m* — **forestry** ['fɔrəstri] *n* : silvicultura *f*
foretaste ['for,teɪst] *n* : anticipo *m*
foretell [for'tɛl] *vt* **-told; -telling** : predecir
forethought ['for,θɔt] *n* : reflexión *f* previa
forever [fɔr'ɛvər] *adv* **1** ETERNALLY : para siempre **2** CONTINUALLY : siempre, constantemente
forewarn [for'wɔrn] *vt* : advertir, prevenir
foreword ['forwərd] *n* : prólogo *m*
forfeit ['fɔrfət] *n* **1** PENALTY : pena *f* **2** : prenda *f* (en un juego) — ~ *vt* : perder
forge ['fordʒ] *n* : forja *f* — ~ *v* **forged; forging** *vt* **1** : forjar (metal, etc.) **2** COUNTERFEIT : falsificar — *vi* ~ **ahead** : avanzar, seguir adelante — **forger** ['fordʒər] *n* : falsificador *m*, -dora *f* — **forgery** ['fordʒəri] *n, pl* **-eries** : falsificación *f*
forget [fər'gɛt] *v* **-got** [-'gɑt]; **-gotten** [-'gɑtən] *or* **-got; -getting** *vt* : olvidar, olvidarse de — *vi* **1** : olvidarse **2 I forgot** : se me olvidó — **forgetful** [fər'gɛtfəl] *adj* : olvidadizo
forgive [fər'gɪv] *vt* **-gave** [-'geɪv]; **-given** [-'gɪvən]; **-giving** : perdonar — **forgiveness** [fər'gɪvnəs] *n* : perdón *m*
forgo *or* **forego** [for'go:] *vt* **-went; -gone; -going** : privarse de, renunciar a
fork ['fɔrk] *n* **1** : tenedor *m* **2** PITCHFORK : horca *f* **3** : bifurcación *f* (de un camino, etc.) — *vi* : ramificarse, bifurcarse — *vt* ~ **over** : desembolsar
forlorn [fɔr'lɔrn] *adj* : triste
form ['fɔrm] *n* **1** : forma *f* **2** DOCUMENT : formulario *m* **3** KIND : tipo *m* — ~ *vt* **1** : formar **2** ~ **a habit** : adquirir un hábito — *vi* : formarse
formal ['fɔrməl] *adj* : formal — ~ *n* **1** BALL : baile *m* (formal) **2** *or* ~ **dress** : traje *m* de etiqueta — **formality** [fɔr'mæləṭi] *n, pl* **-ties** : formalidad *f*
format ['fɔr,mæt] *n* : formato *m* — ~ *vt* **-matted; -matting** : formatear
formation [fɔr'meɪʃən] *n* **1** : formación *f* **2** SHAPE : forma *f*
former ['fɔrmər] *adj* **1** PREVIOUS : antiguo, anterior **2** : primero (de dos) — **formerly** ['fɔrmərli] *adv* : anteriormente, antes
formidable ['fɔrmədəbəl, fɔr'mɪdə-] *adj* : formidable
formula ['fɔrmjələ] *n, pl* **-las** *or* **-lae** [-,li:, -,laɪ] **1** : fórmula *f* **2** *or* **baby** ~ : preparado *m* para biberón
forsake [fər'seɪk] *vt* **-sook** [-'sʊk]; **-saken** [-'seɪkən]; **-saking** : abandonar
fort ['fort] *n* : fuerte *m*
forth ['forθ] *adv* **1 and so** ~ : etcétera **2 back and** ~ → **back 3 from this day** ~ : de hoy en adelante — **forthcoming** [forθ-'kʌmɪŋ, 'forθ,-] *adj* **1** COMING : próximo **2** OPEN : comunicativo — **forthright** ['forθ-,raɪt] *adj* : directo, franco
fortieth ['fɔrṭiəθ] *adj* : cuadragésimo — ~ *n* **1** : cuadragésimo *m*, -ma *f* (en una serie) **2** : cuarentavo *m*, cuarentava parte *f*
fortify ['fɔrṭə,faɪ] *vt* **-fied; -fying** : fortificar — **fortification** [,fɔrṭəfə'keɪʃən] *n* : fortificación *f*
fortitude ['fɔrṭə,tu:d, -,tju:d] *n* : fortaleza *f*
fortnight ['fort,naɪt] *n* : quince días *mpl*, quincena *f*
fortress ['fɔrtrəs] *n* : fortaleza *f*
fortunate ['fɔrtʃənət] *adj* : afortunado — **fortunately** ['fɔrtʃənətli] *adv* : afortunadamente — **fortune** ['fɔrtʃən] *n* : fortuna *f* — **fortune-teller** ['fɔrtʃən,tɛlər] *n* : adivino *m*, -na *f*
forty ['fɔrṭi] *n, pl* **forties** : cuarenta *m* — ~ *adj* : cuarenta
forum ['forəm] *n, pl* **-rums** : foro *m*
forward ['fɔrwərd] *adj* **1** : hacia adelante (en dirección), delantero (en posición) **2** BRASH : descarado — ~ *adv* **1** : (hacia) adelante **2 from this day** ~ : de aquí en adelante — ~ *vt* : remitir, enviar — ~ *n* : delantero *m*, -ra *f* (en deportes) — **forwards** ['fɔrwərdz] *adv* → **forward**
fossil ['fɑsəl] *n* : fósil *m*
foster ['fɔstər] *adj* : adoptivo — ~ *vt* : promover, fomentar
fought → **fight**
foul ['faʊl] *adj* **1** REPULSIVE : asqueroso **2** ~ **language** : palabrotas *fpl* **3** ~ **play** : actos *mpl* criminales **4** ~ **weather** : mal tiempo *m* — ~ *n* : falta *f* (en deportes) — ~ *vi* : cometer faltas (en deportes) — *vt* : ensuciar
found[1] ['faʊnd] → **find**
found[2] *vt* : fundar, establecer — **foundation** [faʊn'deɪʃən] *n* **1** : fundación *f* **2** BASIS : fundamento *m* **3** : cimientos *mpl* (de un edificio)
founder[1] ['faʊndər] *n* : fundador *m*, -dora *f*
founder[2] *vi* SINK : hundirse
fountain ['faʊntən] *n* : fuente *f*
four ['for] *n* : cuatro *m* — ~ *adj* : cuatro — **fourfold** ['for,fo:ld, -'fo:ld] *adj* : cuadruple — **four hundred** *adj* : cuatrocientos — ~ *n* : cuatrocientos *m*
fourteen [for'ti:n] *n* : catorce *m* — ~ *adj* : catorce — **fourteenth** [for'ti:nθ] *adj* : decimocuarto — ~ *n* **1** : decimocuarto *m*, -ta *f* (en una serie) **2** : catorceavo *m*, catorceava parte *f*
fourth ['forθ] *n* **1** : cuarto *m*, -ta *f* (en una serie) **2** : cuarto *m*, cuarta parte *f* — ~ *adj* : cuarto
fowl ['faʊl] *n, pl* **fowl** *or* **fowls** : ave *f*
fox ['fɑks] *n, pl* **foxes** : zorro *m*, -ra *f* — ~ *vt* TRICK : engañar — **foxy** ['fɑksi] *adj* **foxier; -est** SHREWD : astuto
foyer ['fɔɪər, 'fɔɪ,jeɪ] *n* : vestíbulo *m*
fraction ['frækʃən] *n* : fracción *f*
fracture ['fræktʃər] *n* : fractura *f* — ~ *vt* **-tured; -turing** : fracturar
fragile ['frædʒəl, -,dʒaɪl] *adj* : frágil
fragment ['frægmənt] *n* : fragmento *m*
fragrant ['freɪgrənt] *adj* : fragante — **fragrance** ['freɪgrənts] *n* : fragancia *f*, aroma *m*
frail ['freɪl] *adj* : débil, delicado
frame ['freɪm] *vt* **framed; framing 1** ENCLOSE : enmarcar **2** COMPOSE, DRAFT : formular **3** INCRIMINATE : incriminar — ~ *n* **1** : armazón *mf* (de un edificio, etc.) **2** : marco *m* (de un cuadro, una puerta, etc.) **3** *or* ~**s** *npl* : montura *f* (para anteojos) **4** ~ **of mind** : estado *m* de ánimo — **framework** ['freɪm,wərk] *n* : armazón *f*
franc ['fræŋk] *n* : franco *m*
frank ['fræŋk] *adj* : franco — **frankly** *adv* : francamente — **frankness** ['fræŋknəs] *n* : franqueza *f*
frantic ['fræntɪk] *adj* : frenético
fraternal [frə'tərnəl] *adj* : fraterno, fraternal — **fraternity** [frə'tərnəṭi] *n, pl* **-ties** : fraternidad *f* — **fraternize** ['fræṭər,naɪz] *vi* **-nized; -nizing** : confraternizar
fraud ['frɔd] *n* **1** DECEIT : fraude *m* **2** IMPOSTOR : impostor *m*, -tora *f* — **fraudulent** ['frɔdʒələnt] *adj* : fraudulento
fraught ['frɔt] *adj* ~ **with** : lleno de, cargado de
fray[1] ['freɪ] *n* **1 join the** ~ : salir a la palestra **2 return to the** ~ : volver a la carga
fray[2] *vt* : crispar (los nervios) — *vi* : deshilacharse
freak ['fri:k] *n* **1** ODDITY : fenómeno *m* **2** ENTHUSIAST : entusiasta *mf* — **freakish** ['fri:kɪʃ] *adj* : anormal
freckle ['frɛkəl] *n* : peca *f*
free ['fri:] *adj* **freer; freest 1** : libre **2** *or* ~ **of charge** : gratuito, gratis **3** LOOSE : suelto — ~ *vt* **freed; freeing 1** : liberar, poner en libertad **2** RELEASE, UNFASTEN : soltar, desatar — ~ *adv or* **for** ~ : gratis — **freedom** ['fri:dəm] *n* : libertad *f* — **freelance** ['fri:,lænts] *adj* : por cuenta propia — **freely** ['fri:li] *adv* **1** : libremente **2** LAVISHLY : con generosidad — **freeway** ['fri:,weɪ] *n* : autopista *f* — **free will** *n* **1** : libre albedrío *m* **2 of one's own** ~ : por su propia voluntad
freeze ['fri:z] *v* **froze** ['fro:z]; **frozen** ['fro:zən]; **freezing** *vi* **1** : congelarse, helarse **2** STOP : quedarse inmóvil — *vt* : helar (agua, etc.), congelar (alimentos, precios, etc.) — **freeze-dry** ['fri:z'draɪ] *vt* **-dried; -drying** : liofilizar — **freezer** ['fri:zər] *n* : congelador *m* — **freezing** ['fri:zɪŋ] *adj* **1** CHILLY : helado **2 it's freezing!** : ¡hace un frío espantoso!
freight ['freɪt] *n* **1** SHIPPING : porte *m*, flete *m Lat* **2** CARGO : carga *f*
French ['frɛntʃ] *adj* : francés — ~ *n* **1** : francés *m* (idioma) **2 the** ~ *npl* : los franceses — **Frenchman** ['frɛntʃmən] *n* : francés *m* — **Frenchwoman** ['frɛntʃ-,wʊmən] *n* : francesa *f* — **french fries** ['frɛntʃ,fraɪz] *npl* : papas *fpl* fritas
frenetic [frɪ'nɛṭɪk] *adj* : frenético
frenzy ['frɛnzi] *n, pl* **-zies** : frenesí *m* — **frenzied** ['frɛnzid] *adj* : frenético
frequent [fri'kwɛnt, 'fri:kwənt] *vt* : frecuentar — ~ ['fri:kwənt] *adj* : frecuente — **frequency** ['fri:kwəntsi] *n, pl* **-cies** : frecuencia *f* — **frequently** *adv* : a menudo, frecuentemente
fresco ['frɛs,ko:] *n, pl* **-coes** : fresco *m*
fresh ['frɛʃ] *adj* **1** : fresco **2** IMPUDENT : descarado **3** CLEAN : limpio **4** NEW : nuevo **5** ~ **water** : agua *m* dulce — **freshen** ['frɛʃən] *vt* : refrescar — *vi* ~ **up** : arreglarse — **freshly** ['frɛʃli] *adv* : recién — **freshman** ['frɛʃmən] *n, pl* **-men** [-mən, -,mɛn] : estudiante *mf* de primer año — **freshness** ['frɛʃnəs] *n* : frescura *f*
fret ['frɛt] *vi* **fretted; fretting** : preocuparse — **fretful** ['frɛtfəl] *adj* : nervioso, irritable
friar ['fraɪər] *n* : fraile *m*
friction ['frɪkʃən] *n* : fricción *f*
Friday ['fraɪ,deɪ, -di] *n* : viernes *m*
friend ['frɛnd] *n* : amigo *m*, -ga *f* — **friendliness** ['frɛndlinəs] *n* : simpatía *f* — **friendly** ['frɛndli] *adj* **-lier; -est** : simpático, amable — **friendship** ['frɛnd,ʃɪp] *n* : amistad *f*
frigate ['frɪgət] *n* : fragata *f*
fright ['fraɪt] *n* : miedo *m*, susto *m* — **frighten** ['fraɪtən] *vt* : asustar, espantar — **frightened** ['fraɪtənd] *adj* **1** : asustado, temeroso **2 be** ~ **of** : tener miedo de — **frightening** ['fraɪtənɪŋ] *adj* : espantoso — **frightful** ['fraɪtfəl] *adj* : espantoso, terrible
frigid ['frɪdʒɪd] *adj* : frío, glacial
frill ['frɪl] *n* **1** RUFFLE : volante *m* **2** LUXURY : lujo *m*
fringe ['frɪndʒ] *n* **1** : fleco *m* **2** EDGE : periferia *f*, margen *m* **3** ~ **benefits** : incentivos *mpl*, extras *mpl*
frisk ['frɪsk] *vt* SEARCH : cachear, registrar — **frisky** ['frɪski] *adj* **friskier; -est** : retozón, juguetón
fritter ['frɪṭər] *n* : buñuelo *m* — ~ *vt or* ~ **away** : malgastar (dinero), desperdiciar (tiempo)
frivolous ['frɪvələs] *adj* : frívolo — **frivolity** [frɪ'vɑləṭi] *n, pl* **-ties** : frivolidad *f*
frizzy ['frɪzi] *adj* **frizzier; -est** : rizado, crespo
fro ['fro:] *adv* **to and** ~ → **to**
frock ['frɑk] *n* : vestido *m*
frog ['frɔg, 'frɑg] *n* **1** : rana *f* **2 have a** ~ **in one's throat** : tener carraspera
frolic ['frɑlɪk] *vi* **-icked; -icking** : retozar
from ['frʌm, 'frɑm] *prep* **1** : de **2** (*indicating a starting point*) : desde **3** (*indicating a cause*) : de, por **4** ~ **now on** : a partir de ahora
front ['frʌnt] *n* **1** : parte *f* delantera **2** : delantera *f* (de un vestido, etc.), fachada *f* (de un edificio), frente *m* (militar) **3 cold** ~ : frente *m* frío **4 in** ~ **of** : delante de, adelante de *Lat* — ~ *vi or* ~ **on** : dar a, estar orientado a — ~ *adj* **1** : delantero, de adelante **2 the** ~ **row** : la primera fila
frontier [,frʌn'tɪr] *n* : frontera *f*
frost ['frɔst] *n* **1** : helada *f* **2** : escarcha *f* (en una superficie) — ~ *vt* ICE : bañar (pasteles) — **frostbite** ['frɔst,baɪt] *n* : congelación *f* — **frosting** ['frɔstɪŋ] *n* ICING : baño *m* — **frosty** ['frɔsti] *adj* **frostier; -est 1** : cubierto de escarcha **2** CHILLY : helado, frío
froth ['frɔθ] *n, pl* **froths** ['frɔθs, 'frɔðz] : espuma *f* — **frothy** ['frɔθi] *adj* **frothier; -est** : espumoso
frown ['fraʊn] *vi* **1** : fruncir el ceño, fruncir el entrecejo **2** ~ **at** : mirar con ceño **3** ~ **upon** : desaprobar — ~ *n* : ceño *m* (fruncido)
froze, frozen → **freeze**
frugal ['fru:gəl] *adj* : frugal
fruit ['fru:t] *n* **1** : fruta *f* **2** PRODUCT, RESULT : fruto *m* — **fruitcake** ['fru:t,keɪk] *n* : pastel *m* de frutas — **fruitful** ['fru:tfəl] *adj* : fructífero — **fruition** [fru'ɪʃən] *n* **come to** ~ : realizarse — **fruitless** ['fru:tləs] *adj* : infructuoso — **fruity** ['fru:ṭi] *adj* **fruitier; -est** : (con sabor) a fruta
frustrate ['frʌs,treɪt] *vt* **-trated; -trating** : frustrar — **frustrating** ['frʌs,treɪṭɪŋ] *adj* : frustrante — **frustration** [,frʌs'treɪʃən] *n* : frustración *f*
fry ['fraɪ] *vt* **fried; frying** : freír — ~ *n, pl* **fries 1 small** ~ : gente *f* de poca monta **2 fries** *npl* → **french fries** — **frying pan** *n* : sartén *mf*
fudge ['fʌdʒ] *n* : dulce *m* blando de chocolate y leche
fuel ['fju:əl] *n* : combustible *m* — ~ *vt* **-eled** *or* **-elled; -eling** *or* **-elling 1** : alimentar (un horno), abastecer de combustible (un avión) **2** STIMULATE : estimular
fugitive ['fju:dʒəṭɪv] *n* : fugitivo *m*, -va *f*
fulfill *or* **fulfil** [fʊl'fɪl] *vt* **-filled; -filling 1** : cumplir con (una obligación), desarrollar (potencial) **2** FILL, MEET : cumplir — **fulfillment** [fʊl'fɪlmənt] *n* **1** ACCOMPLISHMENT : cumplimiento *m* **2** SATISFACTION : satisfacción *f*
full ['fʊl, 'fʌl] *adj* **1** FILLED : lleno **2** COMPLETE : complete, detallado **3** : redondo (dícese de la cara), amplio (dícese de ropa) **4 at** ~ **speed** : a toda velocidad **5 in** ~ **bloom** : en plena flor — ~ *adv* **1** DIRECTLY : de lleno **2 know** ~ **well** : saber muy bien — ~ *n* **1 pay in** ~ : pagar en su totalidad **2 to the** ~ : al máximo — **full-fledged** ['fʊl'flɛdʒd] *adj* : hecho y derecho — **fully** ['fʊli] *adv* **1** COMPLETELY : completamente **2** AT LEAST : al menos, por lo menos
fumble ['fʌmbəl] *vi* **-bled; -bling 1** RUMMAGE : hurgar **2** ~ **with** : manejar con torpeza
fume ['fju:m] *vi* **fumed; fuming 1** SMOKE : echar humo, humear **2** RAGE : estar furioso — **fumes** *npl* : gases *mpl*
fumigate ['fju:mə,geɪt] *vt* **-gated; -gating** : fumigar
fun ['fʌn] *n* **1** AMUSEMENT : diversión *f* **2 have** ~ : divertirse **3 make** ~ **of** : reírse de, burlarse de — ~ *adj* : divertido
function ['fʌŋkʃən] *n* **1** : función *f* **2** GATHERING : recepción *f*, reunión *f* social — ~ *vi* : funcionar — **functional** ['fʌŋkʃənəl] *adj* : funcional
fund ['fʌnd] *n* **1** : fondo *m* **2** ~**s** *npl* RESOURCES : fondos *mpl* — ~ *vt* : financiar
fundamental [,fʌndə'mɛntəl] *adj* : fundamental — **fundamentals** *npl* : fundamentos *mpl*
funeral ['fju:nərəl] *adj* : funeral, fúnebre — ~ *n* : funeral *m*, funerales *mpl* — **funeral home** *or* **funeral parlor** *n* : funeraria *f*
fungus ['fʌŋgəs] *n, pl* **fungi** ['fʌn,dʒaɪ, 'fʌŋ-,gaɪ] : hongo *m*
funnel ['fʌnəl] *n* **1** : embudo *m* **2** SMOKESTACK : chimenea *f*
funny ['fʌni] *adj* **funnier; -est 1** : divertido, gracioso **2** STRANGE : extraño, raro — **funnies** ['fʌniz] *npl* : tiras *fpl* cómicas
fur ['fər] *n* **1** : pelaje *m*, pelo *m* (de un animal) **2** *or* ~ **coat** : (prenda *f* de) piel *f* — ~ *adj* : de piel
furious ['fjʊriəs] *adj* : furioso
furnace ['fərnəs] *n* : horno *m*
furnish ['fərnɪʃ] *vt* **1** SUPPLY : proveer **2** : amueblar (una casa, etc.) — **furnishings** ['fərnɪʃɪŋz] *npl* : muebles *mpl*, mobiliario *m* — **furniture** ['fərnɪtʃər] *n* : muebles *mpl*, mobiliario *m*
furrow ['fəro:] *n* : surco *m*
furry ['fəri] *adj* **furrier; -est** : peludo (dícese de un animal), de peluche (dícese de un juguete, etc.)
further ['fərðər] *adv* **1** FARTHER : más lejos **2** MOREOVER : además **3** MORE : más — ~ *vt* : promover, fomentar — ~ *adj* **1** FARTHER : más lejano **2** ADDITIONAL : adicional, más **3 until** ~ **notice** : hasta nuevo aviso — **furthermore** ['fərðər,mor] *adv* : además — **furthest** ['fərðəst] → **farthest**
furtive ['fərṭɪv] *adj* : furtivo
fury ['fjʊri] *n, pl* **-ries** : furia *f*
fuse[1] *or* **fuze** ['fju:z] *n* : mecha *f* (de una bomba, etc.)
fuse[2] *v* **fused; fusing** *vt* **1** MELT : fundir **2** UNITE : fusionar — *vi* : fundirse, fusionarse — ~ *n* **1** : fusible *m* **2 blow a** ~ : fundir un fusible — **fusion** ['fju:ʒən] *n* : fusión *f*
fuss ['fʌs] *n* **1** : jaleo *m*, alboroto *m* **2 make a** ~ : armar un escándalo — ~ *vi* **1** WORRY : preocuparse **2** COMPLAIN : quejarse — **fussy** ['fʌsi] *adj* **fussier; -est 1** IRRITABLE : irritable **2** ELABORATE : recargado **3** FINICKY : quisquilloso
futile ['fju:ṭəl, 'fju:,taɪl] *adj* : inútil, vano — **futility** [fju'tɪləṭi] *n, pl* **-ties** : inutilidad *f*
future ['fju:tʃər] *adj* : futuro — ~ *n* : futuro *m*
fuze → **fuse**[1]
fuzz ['fʌz] *n* : pelusa *f* — **fuzzy** ['fʌzi] *adj* **fuzzier; -est 1** FURRY : con pelusa, peludo **2** BLURRY : borroso **3** VAGUE : confuso

G

g ['dʒi:] *n, pl* **g's** *or* **gs** ['dʒi:z] : g *f*, séptima letra del alfabeto inglés
gab ['gæb] *vi* **gabbed; gabbing** : charlar, cotorrear *fam* — ~ *n* CHATTER : charla *f*
gable ['geɪbəl] *n* : aguilón *m*
gadget ['gædʒət] *n* : artilugio *m*
gag ['gæg] *v* **gagged; gagging** *vt* : amordazar — *vi* CHOKE : atragantarse — ~ *n* **1** : mordaza *f* **2** JOKE : chiste *m*
gage → **gauge**
gaiety ['geɪəṭi] *n, pl* **-eties** : alegría *f* — **gaily** ['geɪli] *adv* : alegremente
gain ['geɪn] *n* **1** PROFIT : ganancia *f* **2** INCREASE : aumento *m* — ~ *vt* **1** OBTAIN : ganar, adquirir **2** ~ **weight** : aumentar de peso — *vi* **1** PROFIT : beneficiarse **2** : adelantar(se) (dícese de un reloj) — **gainful** ['geɪnfəl] *adj* : lucrativo
gait ['geɪt] *n* : modo *m* de andar
gala ['geɪlə, 'gæ-, 'gɑ-] *n* : fiesta *f*
galaxy ['gæləksi] *n, pl* **-axies** : galaxia *f*
gale ['geɪl] *n* **1** : vendaval *f* **2** ~**s of laughter** : carcajadas *fpl*
gall ['gɔl] *n* **have the** ~ **to** : tener el descaro de
gallant ['gælənt] *adj* **1** BRAVE : valiente **2** CHIVALROUS : galante
gallbladder ['gɔl,blædər] *n* : vesícula *f* biliar
gallery ['gæləri] *n, pl* **-leries** : galería *f*
gallon ['gælən] *n* : galón *m*
gallop ['gæləp] *vi* : galopar — ~ *n* : galope *m*
gallows ['gæ,lo:z] *n, pl* **-lows** *or* **-lowses** [-,lo:zəz] : horca *f*
gallstone ['gɔl,sto:n] *n* : cálculo *m* biliar
galore [gə'lor] *adj* : en abundancia
galoshes [gə'lɑʃəz] *n* : galochas *fpl*, chanclos *mpl*
galvanize ['gælvən,aɪz] *vt* **-nized; -nizing** : galvanizar
gamble ['gæmbəl] *v* **-bled; -bling** *vi* : jugar — *vt* : jugarse — ~ *n* **1** BET : apuesta *f* **2** RISK : riesga *f* — **gambler** ['gæmbələr] *n* : jugador *m*, -dora *f*
game ['geɪm] *n* **1** : juego *m* **2** MATCH : partido *m* **3** *or* ~ **animals** : caza *f* — ~ *adj* READY : listo, dispuesto
gamut ['gæmət] *n* : gama *f*
gang ['gæŋ] *n* : banda *f*, pandilla *f* — ~ *vi* ~ **up on** : unirse contra
gangplank ['gæŋ,plæŋk] *n* : pasarela *f*
gangrene ['gæŋ,gri:n, 'gæn-; gæŋ'-, gæn'-] *n* : gangrena *f*
gangster ['gæŋstər] *n* : gángster *mf*
gangway ['gæŋ,weɪ] *n* → **gangplank**
gap ['gæp] *n* **1** OPENING : espacio *m* **2** IN-

TERVAL : intervalo *m* **3** DISPARITY : brecha *f,* distancia *f* **4** DEFICIENCY : laguna *f*
gape ['geɪp] *vi* **gaped; gaping 1** OPEN : estar abierto **2** STARE : mirar boquiabierto
garage [gə'rɑʒ, -'rɑdʒ] *n* : garaje *m* — **~** *vt* **-raged; -raging** : dejar en un garaje
garb ['gɑrb] *n* : vestido *m*
garbage ['gɑrbɪdʒ] *n* : basura *f* — **garbage can** *n* : cubo *m* de la basura
garble ['gɑrbəl] *vt* **-bled; -bling** : tergiversar — **garbled** ['gɑrbəld] *adj* : confuso, incomprensible
garden ['gɑrdən] *n* : jardín *m* — **~** *vi* : trabajar en el jardín — **gardener** ['gɑrdənər] *n* : jardinero *m,* -ra *f* — **gardening** ['gɑrdənɪŋ] *n* : jardinería *f*
gargle ['gɑrgəl] *vi* **-gled; -gling** : hacer gárgaras
garish ['gærɪʃ] *adj* : chillón
garland ['gɑrlənd] *n* : guirnalda *f*
garlic ['gɑrlɪk] *n* : ajo *m*
garment ['gɑrmənt] *n* : prenda *f*
garnish ['gɑrnɪʃ] *vt* : guarnecer — **~** *n* : adorno *m,* guarnición *f*
garret ['gærət] *n* : buhardilla *f*
garrison ['gærəsən] *n* : guarnición *f*
garrulous ['gærələs] *adj* : charlatán, parlanchín
garter ['gɑrṭər] *n* : liga *f*
gas ['gæs] *n, pl* **gases** ['gæsəz] **1** : gas *m* **2** GASOLINE : gasolina *f* — **~** *v* **gassed; gassing** *vt* : asfixiar con gas — *vi* **~ up** : llenar el tanque con gasolina
gash ['gæʃ] *n* : tajo *m* — **~** *vt* : hacer un tajo en, cortar
gasket ['gæskət] *n* : junta *f*
gasoline ['gæsə,li:n, ,gæsə'-] *n* : gasolina *f*
gasp ['gæsp] *vi* **1** : dar un grito ahogado **2** PANT : jadear — **~** *n* : grito *m* ahogado
gas station *n* : gasolinera *f*
gastric ['gæstrɪk] *adj* : gástrico
gastronomy [gæs'trɑnəmi] *n* : gastronomía *f*
gate ['geɪt] *n* **1** DOOR : puerta *f* **2** BARRIER : barrera *f* — **gateway** ['geɪt,weɪ] *n* : puerta *f*
gather ['gæðər] *vt* **1** ASSEMBLE : reunir **2** COLLECT : recoger **3** CONCLUDE : deducir **4** : fruncir (una tela) **5 ~ speed** : acelerar — *vi* : reunirse (dícese de personas), acumularse (dícese de cosas) — **gathering** ['gæðərɪŋ] *n* : reunión *f*
gaudy ['gɔdi] *adj* **gaudier; -est** : chillón, llamativo
gauge ['geɪdʒ] *n* **1** INDICATOR : indicador *m* **2** CALIBER : calibre *m* — **~** *vt* **gauged; gauging 1** MEASURE : medir **2** ESTIMATE : calcular, evaluar
gaunt ['gɔnt] *adj* : demacrado, descarnado
gauze ['gɔz] *n* : gasa *f*
gave → **give**
gawky ['gɔki] *adj* **gawkier; -est** : desgarbado
gay ['geɪ] *adj* **1** : alegre **2** HOMOSEXUAL : gay, homosexual
gaze ['geɪz] *vi* **gazed; gazing** : mirar (fijamente) — **~** *n* : mirada *f*
gazelle [gə'zɛl] *n* : gacela *f*
gazette [gə'zɛt] *n* : gaceta *f*
gear ['gɪr] *n* **1** EQUIPMENT : equipo *m* **2** POSSESSIONS : efectos *mpl* personales **3** : marcha *f* (de un vehículo) **4** *or* **~ wheel** : rueda *f* dentada — **~** *vt* : orientar, adaptar — *vi* **~ up** : prepararse — **gearshift** ['gɪr,ʃɪft] *n* : palanca *f* de cambio, palanca *f* de velocidades *Lat*
geese → **goose**
gelatin ['dʒɛlətən] *n* : gelatina *f*
gem ['dʒɛm] *n* : gema *f,* piedra *f* preciosa — **gemstone** ['dʒɛm,sto:n] *n* : piedra *f* preciosa
gender ['dʒɛndər] *n* **1** SEX : sexo *m* **2** : género *m* (en la gramática)
gene ['dʒi:n] *n* : gen *m,* gene *m*
genealogy [,dʒi:ni'ɑlədʒi, ,dʒɛ-, -'æ-] *n, pl* **-gies** : genealogía *f*
general ['dʒɛnrəl, 'dʒɛnə-] *adj* : general — **~** *n* **1** : general *mf* (militar) **2 in ~** : en general, por lo general — **generalize** ['dʒɛnrə,laɪz, 'dʒɛnərə-] *v* **-ized; -izing** : generalizar — **generally** ['dʒɛnrəli, 'dʒɛnərə-] *adv* : generalmente, en general — **general practitioner** *n* : médico *m,* -ca *f* de cabecera
generate ['dʒɛnə,reɪt] *vt* **-ated; -ating** : generar — **generation** [,dʒɛnə'reɪʃən] *n* : generación *f* — **generator** ['dʒɛnə,reɪṭər] *n* : generador *m*
generous ['dʒɛnərəs] *adj* **1** : generoso **2** AMPLE : abundante — **generosity** [,dʒɛnə'rɑsəṭi] *n, pl* **-ties** : generosidad *f*
genetic [dʒə'nɛṭɪk] *adj* : genético — **genetics** [dʒə'nɛṭɪks] *n* : genética *f*
genial ['dʒi:niəl] *adj* : afable, simpático
genital ['dʒɛnəṭəl] *adj* : genital — **genitals** ['dʒɛnəṭəlz] *npl* : genitales *mpl*
genius ['dʒi:njəs] *n* : genio *m*
genocide ['dʒɛnə,saɪd] *n* : genocidio *m*
genteel [dʒɛn'ti:l] *adj* : refinado
gentle ['dʒɛntəl] *adj* **-tler; -tlest 1** MILD : suave, dulce **2** LIGHT : ligero **3 a ~ hint** : una indirecta discreta — **gentleman** ['dʒɛntəlmən] *n, pl* **-men** [-mən, -,mɛn] **1** MAN : caballero *m,* señor *m* **2 a perfect ~** : un perfecto caballero — **gentleness** ['dʒɛntəlnəs] *n* : delicadeza *f,* ternura *f*
genuine ['dʒɛnjʊwən] *adj* **1** AUTHENTIC : verdadero, auténtico **2** SINCERE : sincero
geography [dʒi'ɑgrəfi] *n, pl* **-phies** : geografía *f* — **geographic** [,dʒi:ə'græfɪk] *or* **geographical** [-fɪkəl] *adj* : geográfico
geology [dʒi'ɑlədʒi] *n* : geología *f* — **geologic** [,dʒi:ə'lɑdʒɪk] *or* **geological** [-dʒɪkəl] *adj* : geológico
geometry [dʒi'ɑmətri] *n, pl* **-tries** : geometría *f* — **geometric** [,dʒi:ə'mɛtrɪk] *or* **geometrical** [-trɪkəl] *adj* : geométrico
geranium [dʒə'reɪniəm] *n* : geranio *m*
geriatric [,dʒɛri'ætrɪk] *adj* : geriátrico — **geriatrics** [,dʒɛri'ætrɪks] *n* : geriatría *f*
germ ['dʒərm] *n* **1** : germen *m* **2** MICROBE : microbio *m*
German ['dʒərmən] *adj* : alemán — **~** *n* : alemán *m* (idioma)
germinate ['dʒərmə,neɪt] *v* **-nated; -nating** *vi* : germinar — *vt* : hacer germinar
gestation [dʒɛ'steɪʃən] *n* : gestación *f*
gesture ['dʒɛstʃər] *n* : gesto *m* — **~** *vi* **-tured; -turing 1** : hacer gestos **2 ~ to** : hacer señas a
get ['gɛt] *v* **got** ['gɑt]; **got** *or* **gotten** ['gɑtən]; **getting** *vt* **1** OBTAIN : conseguir, obtener **2** RECEIVE : recibir **3** EARN : ganar **4** FETCH : traer **5** CATCH : coger, agarrar *Lat* **6** UNDERSTAND : entender **7** PREPARE : preparar **8 ~ one's hair cut** : cortarse el pelo **9 ~ s.o. to do sth** : lograr que uno haga algo **10 have got** : tener **11 have got to** : tener que — *vi* **1** BECOME : ponerse, hacerse **2** GO, MOVE : ir **3** PROGRESS : avanzar **4 ~ ahead** : progresar **5 ~ at** MEAN : querer decir **6 ~ away** : escaparse **7 ~ away with** : salir impune de **8 ~ back at** : desquitarse con **9 ~ by** : arreglárselas **10 ~ home** : llegar a casa **11 ~ out** : salir **12 ~ over** : reponerse de, consolarse de **13 ~ together** : reunirse **14 ~ up** : levantarse — **getaway** ['gɛṭə,weɪ] *n* : fuga *f,* huida *f* — **get–together** *n* : reunión *f*
geyser ['gaɪzər] *n* : géiser *m*
ghastly ['gæstli] *adj* **-lier; -est** : horrible, espantoso
ghetto ['gɛṭo:] *n, pl* **-tos** *or* **-toes** : gueto *m*
ghost ['go:st] *n* : fantasma *f,* espectro *m* — **ghostly** ['go:stli] *adv* : fantasmal
giant ['dʒaɪənt] *n* : gigante *m,* -ta *f* — **~** *adj* : gigantesco
gibberish ['dʒɪbərɪʃ] *n* : galimatías *m,* jerigonza *f*
gibe ['dʒaɪb] *vi* **gibed; gibing ~ at** : mofarse de — **~** *n* : pulla *f,* mofa *f*
giblets ['dʒɪbləts] *npl* : menudillos *mpl*
giddy ['gɪdi] *adj* **-dier; -est** : mareado, vertiginoso — **giddiness** ['gɪdinəs] *n* : vértigo *m*
gift ['gɪft] *n* **1** PRESENT : regalo *m* **2** TALENT : don *m* — **gifted** ['gɪftəd] *adj* : talentoso, de talento
gigantic [dʒaɪ'gæntɪk] *adj* : gigantesco
giggle ['gɪgəl] *vi* **-gled; -gling** : reírse tontamente — **~** *n* : risa *f* tonta
gild ['gɪld] *vt* **gilded** ['gɪldəd] *or* **gilt** ['gɪlt]; **gilding** : dorar
gill ['gɪl] *n* : agalla *f,* branquia *f*
gilt ['gɪlt] *adj* : dorado
gimmick ['gɪmɪk] *n* : truco *m,* ardid *m*
gin ['dʒɪn] *n* : ginebra *f*
ginger ['dʒɪndʒər] *n* : jengibre *m* — **ginger ale** *n* : refresco *m* de jengibre — **gingerbread** ['dʒɪndʒər,brɛd] *n* : pan *m* de jengibre — **gingerly** ['dʒɪndʒərli] *adv* : con cuidado, cautelosamente
giraffe [dʒə'ræf] *n* : jirafa *f*
girder ['gərdər] *n* : viga *f*
girdle ['gərdəl] *n* CORSET : faja *f*
girl ['gərl] *n* **1** : niña *f,* muchacha *f,* chica *f* — **girlfriend** ['gərl,frɛnd] *n* : novia *f,* amiga *f*
girth ['gərθ] *n* : circunferencia *f*
gist ['dʒɪst] *n* **get the ~ of** : comprender lo esencial de
give ['gɪv] *v* **gave** ['geɪv]; **given** ['gɪvən]; **giving** *vt* **1** : dar **2** INDICATE : señalar **3** PRESENT : presentar **4 ~ away** : regalar **5 ~ back** : devolver **6 ~ out** : repartir **7 ~ up smoking** : dejar de fumar — *vi* **1** YIELD : ceder **2** COLLAPSE : romperse **3 ~ out** : agotarse **4 ~ up** : rendirse — **~** *n* : elasticidad *f* — **given** ['gɪvən] *adj* **1** SPECIFIED : determinado **2** INCLINED : dado, inclinado — **given name** *n* : nombre *m* de pila
glacier ['gleɪʃər] *n* : glaciar *m*
glad ['glæd] *adj* **gladder; gladdest 1** : alegre, contento **2 be ~** : alegrarse **3 ~ to meet you!** : ¡mucho gusto! — **gladden** ['glædən] *vt* : alegrar — **gladly** ['glædli] *adv* : con mucho gusto — **gladness** ['glædnəs] *n* : alegría *f,* gozo *m*
glade ['gleɪd] *n* : claro *m*
glamor *or* **glamour** ['glæmər] *n* : atractivo *m,* encanto *m* — **glamorous** ['glæmərəs] *adj* : atractivo
glance ['glænts] *vi* **glanced; glancing 1 ~ at** : mirar, dar un vistazo a **2 ~ off** : rebotar en — **~** *n* : mirada *f,* vistazo *m*
gland ['glænd] *n* : glándula *f*
glare ['glær] *vi* **glared; glaring 1** : brillar, relumbrar **2 ~ at** : lanzar una mirada feroz a — **~** *n* **1** : luz *f* deslumbrante **2** STARE : mirada *f* feroz — **glaring** ['glærɪŋ] *adj* **1** BRIGHT : deslumbrante **2** FLAGRANT : flagrante
glass ['glæs] *n* **1** : vidrio *m,* cristal *m* **2 a ~ of milk** : un vaso de leche **3 ~es** *npl* SPECTACLES : anteojos *mpl,* lentes *fpl* — **~** *adj* : de vidrio — **glassware** ['glæs,wær] *n* : cristalería *f* — **glassy** ['glæsi] *adj* **glassier; -est 1** : vítreo **2 ~ eyes** : ojos *mpl* vidriosos
glaze ['gleɪz] *vt* **glazed; glazing 1** : poner vidrios a (una ventana, etc.) **2** : vidriar (cerámica) **3** ICE : glasear — **~** *n* **1** : vidriado *m,* barniz *m* (de cerámica) **2** ICING : glaseado *m*
gleam ['gli:m] *n* **1** : destello *m* **2 a ~ of hope** : un rayo de esperanza — **~** *vi* : destellar, relucir
glee ['gli:] *n* : alegría *f* — **gleeful** ['gli:fəl] *adj* : lleno de alegría
glib ['glɪb] *adj* **glibber; glibbest 1** : de mucha labia **2 a ~ reply** : una respuesta simplista — **glibly** ['glɪbli] *adv* : con mucha labia
glide ['glaɪd] *vi* **glided; gliding** : deslizarse (en una superficie), planear (en el aire) — **glider** ['glaɪdər] *n* : planeador *m*
glimmer ['glɪmər] *vi* : brillar con luz trémula — **~** *n* : luz *f* trémula, luz *f* tenue
glimpse ['glɪmps] *vt* **glimpsed; glimpsing** : vislumbrar — **~** *n* : vislumbre
glint ['glɪnt] *vi* : destellar — **~** *n* : destello *m*
glisten ['glɪsən] *vi* : brillar
glitter ['glɪṭər] *vi* : relucir, brillar
gloat ['glo:t] *vi* **~ over** : regodearse con
globe ['glo:b] *n* : globo *m* — **global** ['glo:bəl] *adj* : global, mundial
gloom ['glu:m] *n* **1** DARKNESS : oscuridad *f* **2** SADNESS : tristeza *f* — **gloomy** ['glu:mi] *adj* **gloomier; -est 1** DARK : sombrío, tenebroso **2** DISMAL : deprimente, lúgubre **3** PESSIMISTIC : pesimista
glory ['glori] *n, pl* **-ries** : gloria *f* — **glorify** ['glorə,faɪ] *vt* **-fied; -fying** : glorificar — **glorious** ['gloriəs] *adj* : glorioso, espléndido
gloss ['glɔs, 'glɑs] *n* : lustre *m,* brillo *m* — **~** *vt* **~ over** : minimizar (la importancia de algo)
glossary ['glɔsəri, 'glɑ-] *n, pl* **-ries** : glosario *m*
glossy ['glɔsi, 'glɑ-] *adj* **glossier; -est** : lustroso, brillante
glove ['glʌv] *n* : guante *m*
glow ['glo:] *vi* **1** : brillar, resplandecer **2 ~ with health** : rebosar de salud — **~** *n* : resplandor *m,* brillo *m*
glue ['glu:] *n* : pegamento *m,* cola *f* — **~** *vt* **glued; gluing** *or* **glueing** : pegar
glum ['glʌm] *adj* **glummer; glummest** : sombrío, triste
glut ['glʌt] *n* : superabundancia *f,* exceso *m*
glutton ['glʌtən] *n* : glotón *m,* -tona *f* — **gluttonous** ['glʌtənəs] *adj* : glotón — **gluttony** ['glʌtəni] *n, pl* **-tonies** : glotonería *f*
gnarled ['nɑrld] *adj* : nudoso
gnash ['næʃ] *vt* **~ one's teeth** : hacer rechinar los dientes
gnat ['næt] *n* : jején *m*
gnaw ['nɔ] *vt* : roer
go ['go:] *v* **went** ['wɛnt]; **gone** ['gɔn, 'gɑn]; **going; goes** ['go:z] *vi* **1** : ir **2** LEAVE : irse, salir **3** EXTEND : ir, extenderse **4** SELL : venderse **5** FUNCTION : funcionar, marchar **6** DISAPPEAR : desaparecer **7 ~ back on one's word** : faltar a su palabra **8 ~ crazy** : volverse loco **9 ~ for** LIKE : gustar **10 ~ off** EXPLODE : estallar **11 ~ with** MATCH : armonizar con **12 ~ without** : pasar sin — *v aux* **be going to** : ir a — **~** *n, pl* **goes 1 be on the ~** : no parar **2 have a ~ at** : intentar
goad ['go:d] *vt* : aguijonear (un animal), incitar (a una persona)
goal ['go:l] *n* **1** AIM : meta *m,* objetivo *m* **2** : gol *m* (en deportes) — **goalkeeper** ['go:l,ki:pər] *or* **goalie** ['go:li] *n* : portero *m,* -ra *f;* arquero *m,* -ra *f*
goat ['go:t] *n* : cabra *f*
goatee [go:'ti:] *n* : barbita *f* de chivo
gobble ['gɑbəl] *vt* **-bled; -bling** *or* **~ up** : engullir
goblet ['gɑblət] *n* : copa *f*
goblin ['gɑblən] *n* : duende *m*
god ['gɑd, 'gɔd] *n* **1** : dios *m* **2 God** : Dios *m* — **goddess** ['gɑdəs, 'gɔ-] *n* : diosa *f* — **godchild** ['gɑd,tʃaɪld, 'gɔd-] *n, pl* **-children** : ahijado *m,* -da *f* — **godfather** ['gɑd,fɑðər, 'gɔd-] *n* : padrino *m* — **godmother** ['gɑd,mʌðər, 'gɔd-] *n* : madrina *f* — **godparents** ['gɑd,pærənt, 'gɔd-] *npl* : padrinos *mpl* — **godsend** ['gɑd,sɛnd, 'gɔd-] *n* : bendición *f* (del cielo)
goes → **go**
goggles ['gɑgəlz] *npl* : gafas *fpl* (protectoras), anteojos *mpl*
goings–on [,go:ɪŋz'ɑn, -'ɔn] *npl* : sucesos *mpl*
gold ['go:ld] *n* : oro *m* — **golden** ['go:ldən] *adj* **1** : (hecho) de oro **2** : dorado, de color oro — **goldfish** ['go:ld,fɪʃ] *n* : pez *m* de colores — **goldsmith** ['go:ld,smɪθ] *n* : orfebre *mf*
golf ['gɑlf, 'gɔlf] *n* : golf *m* — **~** *vi* : jugar (al) golf — **golf ball** *n* : pelota *f* de golf — **golf course** *n* : campo *m* de golf — **golfer** ['gɑlfər, 'gɔl-] *n* : golfista *mf*
gone ['gɔn] *adj* **1** : ido, pasado **2** DEAD : muerto **3** LOST : desaparecido
good ['gʊd] *adj* **better** ['bɛṭər]; **best** ['bɛst] **1** : bueno **2** KIND : amable **3 ~ afternoon (evening)** : buenas tardes **4 be ~ at** : tener facilidad para **5 feel ~** : sentirse bien **6 ~ for a cold** : beneficioso para los resfriados **7 have a ~ time** : divertirse **8 ~ morning** : buenos días **9 ~ night** : buenas noches — **~** *n* **1** : bien *m* **2** GOODNESS : bondad *f* **3 ~s** *npl* PROPERTY : bienes *mpl* **4 ~s** *npl* WARES : mercancías *fpl,* mercaderías *fpl* **5 for ~** : para siempre — **~** *adv* : bien — **good–bye** *or* **good–by** [gʊd'baɪ] *n* : adiós *m* — **Good Friday** *n* : Viernes *m* Santo — **good–looking** ['gʊd'lʊkɪŋ] *adj* : bello, guapo — **goodness** ['gʊdnəs] *n* **1** : bondad *f* **2 thank ~!** : ¡gracias a Dios!, ¡menos mal! — **goodwill** [,gʊd'wɪl] *n* : buena voluntad *f* — **goody** ['gʊdi] *n, pl* **goodies** : golosina *f*
gooey ['gu:i] *adj* **gooier; gooiest** : pegajoso
goof *n* ['gu:f] : pifia *f fam* — **~** *vi* **1** *or* **~ up** : cometer un error **2 ~ around** : hacer tonterías
goose ['gu:s] *n, pl* **geese** ['gi:s] : ganso *m,* -sa *f;* oca *f* — **goose bumps** *or* **goose pimples** *npl* : carne *f* de gallina
gopher ['go:fər] *n* : taltuza *f*
gore[1] ['gor] *n* BLOOD : sangre *f*
gore[2] *vt* **gored; goring** : cornear
gorge ['gɔrdʒ] *n* RAVINE : cañon *m* — **~** *vt* **gorged; gorging ~ oneself** : hartarse
gorgeous ['gɔrdʒəs] *adj* : magnífico, espléndido
gorilla [gə'rɪlə] *n* : gorila *m*
gory ['gori] *adj* **gorier; -est** : sangriento
gospel ['gɑspəl] *n* **1** : evangelio *m* **2 the Gospel** : el Evangelio
gossip ['gɑsɪp] *n* **1** : chismoso *m,* -sa *f* (persona) **2** RUMOR : chisme *m* — **~** *vi* : chismear, contar chismes — **gossipy** ['gɑsɪpi] *adj* : chismoso
got → **get**
Gothic ['gɑθɪk] *adj* : gótico
gotten → **get**
gourmet ['gʊr,meɪ, gʊr'meɪ] *n* : gastrónomo *m,* -ma *f*
gout ['gaʊt] *n* : gota *f*
govern ['gʌvərn] *v* : gobernar — **governess** ['gʌvərnəs] *n* : institutriz *f* — **government** ['gʌvərmənt] *n* : gobierno *m* — **governor** ['gʌvənər, 'gʌvərnər] *n* : gobernador *m,* -dora *f*
gown ['gaʊn] *n* **1** : vestido *m* **2** : toga *f* (de magistrados, etc.)
grab ['græb] *v* **grabbed; grabbing** *vt* : agarrar, arrebatar
grace ['greɪs] *n* **1** : gracia *f* **2 say ~** : bendecir la mesa — **~** *vt* **graced; gracing 1** HONOR : honrar **2** ADORN : adornar — **graceful** ['greɪsfəl] *adj* : lleno de gracia, grácil — **gracious** ['greɪʃəs] *adj* : cortés, gentil
grade ['greɪd] *n* **1** QUALITY : calidad *f* **2** RANK : grado *m,* rango *m* (militar) **3** YEAR : grado *m,* año *m* (a la escuela) **4** MARK : nota *f* **5** SLOPE : cuesta *f* — **~** *vt* **graded; grading 1** CLASSIFY : clasificar **2** MARK : calificar (exámenes, etc.) — **grade school** → **elementary school**
gradual ['grædʒʊəl] *adj* : gradual — **gradually** ['grædʒʊəli, 'grædʒəli] *adv* : gradualmente, poco a poco
graduate ['grædʒʊət] *n* : licenciado *m,* -da *f* (de la universidad), bachiller *mf* (de la escuela secundaria) — **~** ['grædʒʊ,eɪt] *v* **-ated; -ating** *vi* : graduarse, licenciarse — *vt* CALIBRATE : graduar — **graduation** [,grædʒʊ'eɪʃən] *n* : graduación *f*
graffiti [grə'fi:ṭi, græ-] *npl* : graffiti *mpl*
graft ['græft] *n* : injerto *m* — **~** *vt* : injertar
grain ['greɪn] *n* **1** : grano *m* **2** CEREALS : cereales *mpl* **3** : veta *f,* vena *f* (de madera)
gram ['græm] *n* : gramo *m*
grammar ['græmər] *n* : gramática *f* — **grammar school** → **elementary school**
grand ['grænd] *adj* **1** : magnífico, espléndido **2** FABULOUS, GREAT : fabuloso, estupendo — **grandchild** ['grænd,tʃaɪld] *n, pl* **-children** : nieto *m,* -ta *f* — **granddaughter** ['grænd,dɔṭər] *n* : nieta *f* — **grandeur** ['grændʒər] *n* : grandiosidad *f* — **grandfather** ['grænd,fɑðər] *n* : abuelo *m* — **grandiose** ['grændi,o:s, ,grændi'-] *adj* : grandioso — **grandmother** ['grænd,mʌðər] *n* : abuela *f* — **grandparents** ['grænd,pærənt] *npl* : abuelos *mpl* — **grandson** ['grænd,sʌn] *n* : nieto *m* — **grandstand** ['grænd,stænd] *n* : tribuna *f*
granite ['grænɪt] *n* : granito *m*
grant ['grænt] *vt* **1** : conceder **2** ADMIT : reconocer, admitir **3 take for granted** : dar (algo) por sentado — **~** *n* **1** SUBSIDY : subvención *f* **2** SCHOLARSHIP : beca *f*
grape ['greɪp] *n* : uva *f*
grapefruit ['greɪp,fru:t] *n* : toronja *f,* pomelo *m*
grapevine ['greɪp,vaɪn] *n* **1** : vid *f,* parra *f* **2 I heard it through the ~** : me lo dijo un pajarito *fam*

graph ['græf] *n* : gráfica *f*, gráfico *m* — **graphic** ['græfɪk] *adj* : gráfico

grapple ['græpəl] *vi* **-pled; -pling** ~ **with** : forcejear con (una persona), luchar con (un problema)

grasp ['græsp] *vt* **1** : agarrar **2** UNDERSTAND : comprender, captar — ~ *n* **1** : agarre *m* **2** UNDERSTANDING : comprensión *f* **3** REACH : alcance *m*

grass ['græs] *n* **1** : hierba *f* (planta) **2** LAWN : césped *m*, pasto *m Lat* — **grasshopper** ['græs,hɑpər] *n* : saltamontes *m* — **grassy** ['græsi] *adj* **grassier; -est** : cubierto de hierba

grate[1] ['greɪt] *v* **grated; -ing** *vt* **1** : rallar (en cocina) **2** ~ **one's teeth** : hacer rechinar los dientes — *vi* RASP : chirriar

grate[2] *n* GRATING : reja *f*, rejilla *f*

grateful ['greɪtfəl] *adj* : agradecido — **gratefully** ['greɪtfəli] *adv* : con agradecimiento — **gratefulness** ['greɪtfəlnəs] *n* : gratitud *f*, agradecimiento *m*

grater ['greɪţər] *n* : rallador *m*

gratify ['græţə,faɪ] *vt* **-fied; -fying 1** PLEASE : complacer **2** SATISFY : satisfacer

grating ['greɪţɪŋ] *n* : reja *f*, rejilla *f*

gratitude ['græţə,tu:d, -,tju:d] *n* : gratitud *f*

gratuitous [grə'tu:əţəs] *adj* : gratuito

grave[1] ['greɪv] *n* : tumba *f*, sepultura *f*

grave[2] *adj* **graver; -est** : grave

gravel ['grævəl] *n* : grava *f*, gravilla *f*

gravestone ['greɪv,sto:n] *n* : lápida *f* — **graveyard** ['greɪv,jɑrd] *n* : cementerio *m*

gravity ['grævəţi] *n, pl* **-ties** : gravedad *f*

gravy ['greɪvi] *n, pl* **-vies** : salsa *f* (preparada con jugo de carne)

gray ['greɪ] *adj* **1** : gris **2** ~ **hair** : pelo *m* canoso — ~ *n* : gris *m* — ~ *vi or* **turn** ~ : encanecer, ponerse gris

graze[1] ['greɪz] *vi* **grazed; grazing** : pastar, pacer

graze[2] *vt* **1** TOUCH : rozar **2** SCRATCH : rasguñarse

grease ['gri:s] *n* : grasa *f* — ~ ['gri:s, 'gri:z] *vt* **greased; greasing** : engrasar — **greasy** ['gri:si, -zi] *adj* **greasier; -est 1** : grasiento **2** OILY : graso, grasoso

great ['greɪt] *adj* **1** : grande **2** FANTASTIC : estupendo, fabuloso — **great–grandchild** [,greɪt'grænd,tʃaɪld] *n, pl* **-children** [-,tʃɪldrən] : bisnieto *m*, -ta *f* — **great–grandfather** [,greɪt'grænd,fɑðər] *n* : bisabuelo *m* — **great–grandmother** [,greɪt'grænd,mʌðər] *n* : bisabuela *f* — **greatly** ['greɪtli] *adv* **1** MUCH : mucho **2** VERY : muy — **greatness** ['greɪtnəs] *n* : grandeza *f*

greed ['gri:d] *n* **1** : codicia *f*, avaricia *f* **2** GLUTTONY : glotonería *f* — **greedily** ['gri:dəli] *adv* : con avaricia — **greedy** ['gri:di] *adj* **greedier; -est 1** : codicioso, avaro **2** GLUTTONOUS : glotón

Greek ['gri:k] *adj* : griego — ~ *n* : griego *m* (idioma)

green ['gri:n] *adj* **1** : verde **2** INEXPERIENCED : novato — ~ *n* **1** : verde *m* (color) **2** ~**s** *npl* : verduras *fpl* — **greenery** ['gri:nəri] *n, pl* **-eries** : vegetación *f* — **greenhouse** ['gri:n,haʊs] *n* : invernadero *m*

greet ['gri:t] *vt* **1** : saludar **2** WELCOME : recibir — **greeting** ['gri:ţɪŋ] *n* **1** : saludo *m* **2** ~**s** *npl* REGARDS : saludos *mpl*, recuerdos *mpl*

gregarious [grɪ'gæriəs] *adj* : sociable

grenade [grə'neɪd] *n* : granada *f*

grew → **grow**

grey → **gray**

greyhound ['greɪ,haʊnd] *n* : galgo *m*

grid ['grɪd] *n* **1** GRATING : rejilla *f* **2** NETWORK : red *f* **3** : cuadriculado *m* (de un mapa)

griddle ['grɪdəl] *n* : plancha *f*

grief ['gri:f] *n* : dolor *m*, pesar *m* — **grievance** ['gri:vənts] *n* : queja *f* — **grieve** ['gri:v] *v* **grieved; grieving** *vt* : entristecer — *vi* ~ **for** : llorar (a), lamentar — **grievous** ['gri:vəs] *adj* : grave, doloroso

grill ['grɪl] *vt* **1** : asar a la parrilla **2** INTERROGATE : interrogar — ~ *n* : parrilla *f* (para cocinar) — **grille** *or* **grill** ['grɪl] GRATING *n* : reja *f*, rejilla *f*

grim ['grɪm] *adj* **grimmer; grimmest 1** STERN : severo **2** GLOOMY : sombrío

grimace ['grɪməs, grɪ'meɪs] *n* : mueca *f* — ~ *vi* **-maced; -macing** : hacer muecas

grime ['graɪm] *n* : mugre *f*, suciedad *f* — **grimy** ['graɪmi] *adj* **grimier; -est** : mugriento, sucio

grin ['grɪn] *vi* **grinned; grinning** : sonreír (abiertamente) — ~ *n* : sonrisa *f* (abierta)

grind ['graɪnd] *v* **ground** ['graʊnd]; **grinding** *vt* **1** : moler (el café, etc.) **2** SHARPEN : afilar **3** ~ **one's teeth** : rechinar los dientes — *vi* : rechinar — ~ *n* **the daily** ~ : la rutina diaria — **grinder** ['graɪndər] *n* : molinillo *m*

grip ['grɪp] *vt* **gripped; gripping 1** : agarrar, asir **2** INTEREST : captar el interés de — ~ *n* **1** GRASP : agarre *m* **2** CONTROL : control *m*, dominio *m* **3** HANDLE : empuñadura *f* **4** **come to** ~**s with** : llegar a entender de

gripe ['graɪp] *vi* **griped; griping** : quejarse — ~ *n* : queja *f*

grisly ['grɪzli] *adj* **-lier; -est** : espeluznante, horrible

gristle ['grɪsəl] *n* : cartílago *m*

grit ['grɪt] *n* **1** : arena *f*, grava *f* **2** GUTS : agallas *fpl fam* **3** ~**s** *npl* : sémola *f* de maíz — ~ *vt* **gritted; gritting** ~ **one's teeth** : acorazarse

groan ['gro:n] *vi* : gemir — ~ *n* : gemido *m*

grocery ['gro:səri, -ʃəri] *n, pl* **-ceries 1** *or* ~ **store** : tienda *f* de comestibles, tienda *f* de abarrotes *Lat* **2** **groceries** *npl* : comestibles *mpl*, abarrotes *mpl Lat* — **grocer** ['gro:sər] *n* : tendero *m*, -ra *f*

groggy ['grɑgi] *adj* **-gier; -est** : atontado, grogui *fam*

groin ['grɔɪn] *n* : ingle *f*

groom ['gru:m, 'grʊm] *n* BRIDEGROOM : novio *m* — ~ *vt* **1** : almohazar (un animal) **2** PREPARE : preparar

groove ['gru:v] *n* : ranura *f*, surco *m*

grope ['gro:p] *vi* **groped; groping 1** : andar a tientas **2** ~ **for** : buscar a tientas

gross ['gro:s] *adj* **1** SERIOUS : grave **2** OBESE : obeso **3** TOTAL : bruto **4** VULGAR : grosero, basto — ~ *n* **1** *or* ~ **income** : ingresos *mpl* brutos **2** *pl* ~ : gruesa *f* (12 docenas) — **grossly** ['gro:sli] *adv* **1** EXTREMELY : enormemente **2** CRUDELY : groseramente

grotesque [gro:'tesk] *adj* : grotesco

grouch ['graʊtʃ] *n* : gruñón *m*, -ñona *f fam* — **grouchy** ['graʊtʃi] *adj* **grouchier; -est** : gruñón *fam*

ground[1] ['graʊnd] → **grind**

ground[2] *n* **1** : suelo *m*, tierra *f* **2** *or* ~**s** LAND : terreno *m* **3** ~**s** REASON : razón *f*, motivos *mpl* **4** ~**s** DREGS : pozo *m* (de café) — ~ *vt* **1** BASE : fundar, basar **2** : conectar a tierra (un aparato eléctrico) **3** : restringir (un avión o un piloto) a la tierra — **groundhog** ['graʊnd,hɔg] *n* : marmota *f* (de América) — **groundless** ['graʊndləs] *adj* : infundado — **groundwork** ['graʊnd,wərk] *n* : trabajo *m* preparatorio

group ['gru:p] *n* : grupo *m* — ~ *vt* : agrupar — *vi or* ~ **together** : agruparse

grove ['gro:v] *n* : arboleda *f*

grovel ['grɑvəl, 'grʌ-] *vi* **-eled** *or* **-elled; -eling** *or* **-elling** : arrastrarse, humillarse

grow ['gro:] *v* **grew** ['gru:]; **grown** ['gro:n]; **growing** *vi* **1** : crecer **2** INCREASE : aumentar **3** BECOME : volverse, ponerse **4** ~ **dark** : oscurecerse **5** ~ **up** : hacerse mayor — *vt* **1** CULTIVATE : cultivar **2** : dejarse crecer (el pelo, etc.) — **grower** ['gro:ər] *n* : cultivador *m*, -dora *f*

growl ['graʊl] *vi* : gruñir — ~ *n* : gruñido *m*

grown–up ['gro:n,əp] *adj* : mayor — ~ *n* : persona *f* mayor

growth ['gro:θ] *n* **1** : crecimiento *m* **2** INCREASE : aumento *m* **3** DEVELOPMENT : desarrollo *m* **4** TUMOR : tumor *m*

grub ['grʌb] *n* **1** LARVA : larva *f* **2** FOOD : comida *f*

grubby ['grʌbi] *adj* **grubbier; -est** : mugriento, sucio

grudge ['grʌdʒ] *vt* **grudged; grudging** : dar de mala gana — ~ *n* **hold a** ~ : guardar rencor

grueling *or* **gruelling** ['gru:lɪŋ, 'gru:ə-] *adj* : extenuante, agotador

gruesome ['gru:səm] *adj* : horripilante

gruff ['grʌf] *adj* **1** BRUSQUE : brusco **2** HOARSE : bronco

grumble ['grʌmbəl] *vi* **-bled; -bling** : refunfuñar, rezongar

grumpy ['grʌmpi] *adj* **grumpier; -est** : malhumorado, gruñón *fam*

grunt ['grʌnt] *vi* : gruñir — ~ *n* : gruñido *m*

guarantee [,gærən'ti:] *n* : garantía *f* — ~ *vt* **-teed; -teeing** : garantizar

guard ['gɑrd] *n* **1** : guardia *f* **2** PRECAUTION : protección *f* — ~ *vt* : proteger, vigilar — *vi* ~ **against** : protegerse contra — **guardian** ['gɑrdiən] *n* **1** : tutor *m*, -tora *f* (de niños) **2** PROTECTOR : guardián *m*, -diana *f*

guava ['gwɑvə] *n* : guayaba *f*

guerrilla *or* **guerilla** [gə'rɪlə] *n* **1** : guerrillero *m*, -ra *f* **2** ~ **warfare** : guerra *f* de guerrillas

guess ['gɛs] *vt* **1** : adivinar **2** SUPPOSE : suponer, creer — *vi* ~ **at** : adivinar — ~ *n* : conjetura *f*, suposición *f*

guest ['gɛst] *n* **1** : invitado *m*, -da *f* **2** : huésped *mf* (a un hotel)

guide ['gaɪd] *n* : guía *mf* (persona), guía *f* (libro, etc.) — ~ *vt* **guided; guiding** : guiar — **guidance** ['gaɪdənts] *n* : orientación *f* — **guidebook** ['gaɪd,bʊk] *n* : guía *f* — **guideline** ['gaɪd,laɪn] *n* : pauta *f*, directriz *f*

guild ['gɪld] *n* : gremio *m*

guile ['gaɪl] *n* : astucia *f*

guilt ['gɪlt] *n* : culpa *f*, culpabilidad *f* — **guilty** ['gɪlti] *adj* **guiltier; -est** : culpable

guinea pig ['gɪni-] *n* : conejillo *m* de Indias, cobaya *f*

guise ['gaɪz] *n* : apariencia *f*

guitar [gə'tɑr, gɪ-] *n* : guitarra *f*

gulf ['gʌlf] *n* **1** : golfo *m* **2** ABYSS : abismo *m*

gull ['gʌl] *n* : gaviota *f*

gullet ['gʌlət] *n* **1** THROAT : garganta *f* **2** ESOPHAGUS : esófago *m*

gullible ['gʌləbəl] *adj* : crédulo

gully ['gʌli] *n, pl* **-lies** : barranco *m*

gulp ['gʌlp] *vt or* ~ **down** : tragarse, engullir — *vi* : tragar saliva — ~ *n* : trago *m*

gum[1] ['gʌm] *n* : encía *f* (de la boca)

gum[2] *n* **1** : resina *f* (de plantas) **2** CHEWING GUM : goma *f* de mascar, chicle *m*

gumption ['gʌmpʃən] *n* : iniciativa *f*, agallas *fpl fam*

gun ['gʌn] *n* **1** FIREARM : arma *f* de fuego **2** *or* **spray** ~ : pistola *f* **3** → **cannon, pistol, revolver, rifle** — ~ *vt* **gunned; gunning 1** *or* ~ **down** : matar a tiros, asesinar **2** ~ **the engine** : acelerar (el motor) — **gunboat** ['gʌn,bo:t] *n* : cañonero *m* — **gunfire** ['gʌn,faɪr] *n* : disparos *mpl* — **gunman** ['gʌnmən] *n, pl* **-men** [-mən, -,mɛn] : pistolero *m*, gatillero *m Lat* — **gunpowder** ['gʌn,paʊdər] *n* : pólvora *f* — **gunshot** ['gʌn,ʃɑt] *n* : disparo *m*, tiro *m*

gurgle ['gərgəl] *vi* **-gled; -gling 1** : borbotar, gorgotear **2** : gorjear (dícese de un niño)

gush ['gʌʃ] *vi* **1** SPOUT : salir a chorros **2** ~ **with praise** : deshacerse en elogios

gust ['gʌst] *n* : ráfaga *f*

gusto ['gʌs,to:] *n, pl* **gustoes** : entusiasmo *m*

gusty ['gʌsti] *adj* **gustier; -est** : racheado, ventoso

gut ['gʌt] *n* **1** : intestino *m* **2** ~**s** *npl* INNARDS : tripas *fpl* **3** ~**s** *npl* COURAGE : agallas *fpl fam* — ~ *vt* **gutted; gutting 1** EVISCERATE : destripar (un pollo, etc.), limpiar (un pescado) **2** : destruir el interior de (un edificio)

gutter ['gʌţər] *n* : canaleta *f* (de un techo), cuneta *f* (de una calle)

guy ['gaɪ] *n* : tipo *m fam*

guzzle ['gʌzəl] *vt* **-zled; -zling** : chupar *fam*, tragar

gym ['dʒɪm] *or* **gymnasium** [dʒɪm'neɪziəm, -ʒəm] *n, pl* **-siums** *or* **-sia** [-ziə, -ʒə] : gimnasio *m* — **gymnast** ['dʒɪmnəst, ,næst] *n* : gimnasta *mf* — **gymnastics** [dʒɪm'næstɪks] *ns & pl* : gimnasia *f*

gynecology [,gaɪnə'kɑlədʒi, ,dʒɪnə-] *n* : ginecología *f* — **gynecologist** [,gaɪnə'kɑlədʒɪst, ,dʒɪnə-] *n* : ginecólogo *m*, -ga *f*

gyp ['dʒɪp] *vt* **gypped; gypping** : estafar, timar

Gypsy ['dʒɪpsi] *n, pl* **-sies** : gitano *m*, -na *f*

gyrate ['dʒaɪ,reɪt] *vi* **-rated; -rating** : girar

H

h ['eɪtʃ] *n, pl* **h's** *or* **hs** ['eɪtʃəz] : h *f*, octava letra del alfabeto inglés

habit ['hæbɪt] *n* **1** CUSTOM : hábito *m*, costumbre *f* **2** : hábito *m* (religioso)

habitat ['hæbɪ,tæt] *n* : hábitat *m*

habitual [hə'bɪtʃuəl] *adj* **1** CUSTOMARY : habitual **2** INVETERATE : empedernido

hack[1] ['hæk] *n* **1** : caballo *m* de alquiler **2** *or* ~ **writer** : escritorzuelo *m*, -la *f*

hack[2] *vt* : cortar — *vi or* ~ **into** : piratear (un sistema informático)

hackneyed ['hæknid] *adj* : manido, trillado

hacksaw ['hæk,sɔ] *n* : sierra *f* para metales

had → **have**

haddock ['hædək] *ns & pl* : eglefino *m*

hadn't ['hædənt] (*contraction of* **had not**) → **have**

hag ['hæg] *n* : bruja *f*

haggard ['hægərd] *adj* : demacrado

haggle ['hægəl] *vi* **-gled; -gling** : regatear

hail[1] ['heɪl] *vt* **1** GREET : saludar **2** : llamar (un taxi)

hail[2] *n* : granizo *m* (en meteorología) — ~ *vi* : granizar — **hailstone** ['heɪl,sto:n] *n* : piedra *f* de granizo

hair ['hær] *n* **1** : pelo *m*, cabello *m* **2** : vello *m* (en las piernas, etc.) — **hairbrush** ['hær,brʌʃ] *n* : cepillo *m* (para el pelo) — **haircut** ['hær,kʌt] *n* **1** : corte *m* de pelo **2** **get a** ~ : cortarse el pelo — **hairdo** ['hær,du:] *n, pl* **-dos** : peinado *m* — **hairdresser** ['hær,drɛsər] *n* : peluquero *m*, -ra *f* — **hairless** ['hærləs] *adj* : sin pelo, calvo — **hairpin** ['hær,pɪn] *n* : horquilla *f* — **hair–raising** ['hær,reɪzɪŋ] *adj* : espeluznante — **hairstyle** ['hær,staɪl] → **hairdo** — **hair spray** *n* : laca *f* (para el pelo) — **hairy** ['hæri] *adj* **hairier; -est** : peludo, velludo

hale ['heɪl] *adj* : saludable, robusto

half ['hæf, 'haf] *n, pl* **halves** ['hævz, 'havz] **1** : mitad *f* **2** *or* **halftime** : tiempo *m* (en deportes) **3** **in** ~ : por la mitad — ~ *adj* **1** : medio **2** ~ **an hour** : una media hora — ~ *adv* : medio — **half brother** *n* : medio hermano *m*, hermanastro *m* — **halfhearted** ['hæf'hɑrţəd] *adj* : sin ánimo, poco entusiasta — **half sister** *n* : media hermana *f*, hermanastra *f* — **halfway** ['hæf'weɪ] *adv* : a medio camino — ~ *adj* : medio

halibut ['hæləbət] *ns & pl* : halibut *m*

hall ['hɔl] *n* **1** HALLWAY : corredor *m*, pasillo *m* **2** AUDITORIUM : sala *f* **3** LOBBY : vestíbulo *m* **4** DORMITORY : residencia *f* universitaria

hallmark ['hɔl,mɑrk] *n* : sello *m* (distintivo)

Halloween [,hælə'wi:n, ,hɑ-] *n* : víspera *f* de Todos los Santos

hallucination [hə,lu:sən'eɪʃən] *n* : alucinación *f*

hallway ['hɔl,weɪ] *n* **1** ENTRANCE : entrada *f* **2** CORRIDOR : corredor *m*, pasillo *m*

halo ['heɪ,lo:] *n, pl* **-los** *or* **-loes** : aureola *f*, halo *m*

halt ['hɔlt] *n* **1** **call a** ~ **to** : poner fin a **2** **come to a** ~ : pararse — ~ *vi* : pararse — *vt* : parar

halve ['hæv, 'hav] *vt* **halved; halving 1** DIVIDE : partir por la mitad **2** REDUCE : reducir a la mitad — **halves** → **half**

ham ['hæm] *n* : jamón *m*

hamburger ['hæm,bərgər] *or* **hamburg** [-,bərg] *n* **1** : carne *f* molida **2** *or* ~ **patty** : hamburguesa *f*

hammer ['hæmər] *n* : martillo *m* — ~ *v* : martillar, martillear

hammock ['hæmək] *n* : hamaca *f*

hamper[1] ['hæmpər] *vt* : obstaculizar, dificultar

hamper[2] *n* : cesto *m*, canasta *f* (para ropa sucia)

hamster ['hæmpstər] *n* : hámster *m*

hand ['hænd] *n* **1** : mano *f* **2** : manecilla *f*, aguja *f* (de un reloj, etc.) **3** HANDWRITING : letra *f*, escritura *f* **4** WORKER : obrero *m*, -ra *f* **5** **by** ~ : a mano **6** **lend a** ~ : echar una mano **7** **on** ~ : a mano, disponible **8** **on the other** ~ : por otro lado — ~ *vt* **1** : pasar, dar **2** ~ **out** : distribuir **3** ~ **over** : entregar — **handbag** ['hænd,bæg] *n* : cartera *f Lat*, bolso *m Spain* — **handbook** ['hænd,bʊk] *n* : manual *m* — **handcuffs** ['hænd,kʌfs] *npl* : esposas *fpl* — **handful** ['hænd,fʊl] *n* : puñado *m* — **handgun** ['hænd,gʌn] *n* : pistola *f*, revólver *m*

handicap ['hændi,kæp] *n* **1** : minusvalía *f* (física) **2** : hándicap *m* (en deportes) — ~ *vt* **-capped; -capping 1** : asignar un handicap a (en deportes) **2** HAMPER : obstaculizar — **handicapped** ['hændi,kæpt] *adj* : minusválido

handicrafts ['hændi,kræfts] *npl* : artesanía(s) *f(pl)*

handiwork ['hændi,wərk] *n* : trabajo *m* (manual)

handkerchief ['hæŋkərtʃəf, -,tʃi:f] *n, pl* **-chiefs** : pañuelo *m*

handle ['hændəl] *n* : asa *m* (de una taza, etc.), mango *m* (de un utensilio), pomo *m* (de una puerta), tirador *m* (de un cajón) — ~ *vt* **-dled; -dling 1** TOUCH : tocar **2** MANAGE : tratar, manejar — **handlebars** ['hændəl,bɑrz] *npl* : manillar *m*, manubrio *m Lat*

handmade ['hænd,meɪd] *adj* : hecho a mano

handout ['hænd,aʊt] *n* **1** ALMS : dádiva *f*, limosna *f* **2** LEAFLET : folleto *m*

handrail ['hænd,reɪl] *n* : pasamanos *m*

handshake ['hænd,ʃeɪk] *n* : apretón *m* de manos

handsome ['hæntsəm] *adj* **-somer; -est 1** ATTRACTIVE : apuesto, guapo **2** GENEROUS : generoso **3** SIZABLE : considerable

handwriting ['hænd,raɪţɪŋ] *n* : letra *f*, escritura *f* — **handwritten** ['hænd,rɪtən] *adj* : escrito a mano

handy ['hændi] *adj* **handier; -est 1** NEARBY : a mano **2** USEFUL : práctico, útil **3** DEFT : habilidoso — **handyman** ['hændimən] *n, pl* **-men** [-mən, -,mɛn] : hombre *m* habilidoso

hang ['hæŋ] *v* **hung** ['hʌŋ]; **hanging** *vt* **1** : colgar **2** (*past tense often* **hanged**) EXECUTE : ahorcar **3** ~ **one's head** : bajar la cabeza — *vi* **1** : colgar, pender **2** : caer (dícese de la ropa, etc.) **3** ~ **up on s.o.** : colgar a algn — ~ *n* **1** DRAPE : caída *f* **2** **get the** ~ **of** : agarrar la onda de

hangar ['hæŋər, 'hæŋgər] *n* : hangar *m*

hanger ['hæŋər] *n* : percha *f*, gancho *m* (para ropa) *Lat*

hangover ['hæŋ,o:vər] *n* : resaca *f*

hanker ['hæŋkər] *vi* ~ **for** : tener ansias de — **hankering** ['hæŋkərɪŋ] *n* : ansia *f*, anhelo *m*

haphazard [hæp'hæzərd] *adj* : casual, fortuito

happen ['hæpən] *vi* **1** : pasar, suceder, ocurrir **2** ~ **to do sth** : hacer algo por casualidad **3** **it so happens that…** : da la casualidad de que… — **happening** ['hæpənɪŋ] *n* : suceso *m*, acontecimiento *m*

happy ['hæpi] *adj* **-pier; -est 1** : feliz **2** **be** ~ : alegrarse **3** **be** ~ **with** : estar contento con **4** **be** ~ **to do sth** : hacer algo con mucho gusto — **happily** ['hæpəli] *adv* : alegremente — **happiness** ['hæpinəs] *n* : felicidad *f* — **happy–go–lucky** ['hæpigo:'lʌki] *adj* : despreocupado

harass [hə'ræs, 'hærəs] *vt* : acosar — **harassment** [hə'ræsmənt, 'hærəsmənt] *n* : acoso *m*

harbor *or Brit* **harbour** ['hɑrbər] *n* : puerto *m* — *vt* **1** SHELTER : albergar **2** ~ **a grudge against** : guardar rencor a

hard ['hɑrd] *adj* **1** : duro **2** DIFFICULT : difícil **3** **be a** ~ **worker** : ser muy trabajador **4** ~ **liquor** : bebidas *fpl* fuertes **5** ~ **water** : agua *f* dura — ~ *adv* **1** FORCEFULLY : fuerte **2** **work** ~ : trabajar duro **3** **take sth** ~ : tomarse algo muy mal — **harden**

['hɑrdən] *vt* : endurecer — **hardheaded** [ˌhɑrd'hɛdəd] *adj* : testarudo, terco — **hard–hearted** [ˌhɑrd'hɑrṭəd] *adj* : duro de corazón — **hardly** ['hɑrdli] *adv* **1** : apenas **2** ~ **ever** : casi nunca — **hardness** ['hɑrdnəs] *n* **1** : dureza *f* **2** DIFFICULTY : dificultad *f* — **hardship** ['hɑrdˌʃɪp] *n* : dificultad *f* — **hardware** ['hɑrdˌwær] *n* **1** : ferretería *f* **2** : hardware *m* (en informática) — **hardworking** ['hɑrd'wərkɪŋ] *adj* : trabajador

hardy ['hɑrdi] *adj* **-dier; -est** : fuerte (dícese de personas), resistente (dícese de las plantas)

hare ['hær] *n, pl* **hare** *or* **hares** : liebre *f*

harm ['hɑrm] *n* : daño *m* — ~ *vt* : hacer daño a (una persona), dañar (una cosa), perjudicar (la reputación de algn, etc.) — **harmful** ['hɑrmfəl] *adj* : perjudicial — **harmless** ['hɑrmləs] *adj* : inofensivo

harmonica [hɑr'mɑnɪkə] *n* : armónica *f*

harmony ['hɑrməni] *n, pl* **-nies** : armonía *f* — **harmonious** [hɑr'mo:niəs] *adj* : armonioso — **harmonize** ['hɑrməˌnaɪz] *v* **-nized; -nizing** : armonizar

harness ['hɑrnəs] *n* : arnés *m* — ~ *vt* **1** : enjaezar **2** UTILIZE : utilizar

harp ['hɑrp] *n* : arpa *m* — ~ *vi* ~ **on** : insistir sobre

harpoon [hɑr'pu:n] *n* : arpón *m*

harpsichord ['hɑrpsɪˌkɔrd] *n* : clavicémbalo *m*

harsh ['hɑrʃ] *adj* **1** ROUGH : áspero **2** SEVERE : duro, severo **3** : fuerte (dícese de una luz), discordante (dícese de sonidos) — **harshness** ['hɑrʃnəs] *n* : severidad *f*

harvest ['hɑrvəst] *n* : cosecha *f* — ~ *v* : cosechar

has → **have**

hash ['hæʃ] *vt* **1** CHOP : picar **2** ~ **over** DISCUSS : discutir — ~ *n* : picadillo *m* (comida)

hasn't ['hæzənt] (*contraction of* **has not**) → **has**

hassle ['hæsəl] *n* : problemas *mpl,* lío *m* — ~ *vt* **-sled; -sling** : fastidiar

haste ['heɪst] *n* **1** : prisa *f,* apuro *m Lat* **2** **make** ~ : darse prisa, apurarse *Lat* — **hasten** ['heɪsən] *vt* : acelerar — *vi* : apresurarse, apurarse *Lat* — **hasty** ['heɪsti] *adj* **hastier; -est** : precipitado

hat ['hæt] *n* : sombrero *m*

hatch ['hætʃ] *n* : escotilla *f* — ~ *vt* **1** : empollar (huevos) **2** CONCOCT : tramar — *vi* : salir del cascarón

hatchet ['hætʃət] *n* : hacha *f*

hate ['heɪt] *n* : odio *m* — ~ *vt* **hated; hating** : odiar, aborrecer — **hateful** ['heɪtfəl] *adj* : odioso, aborrecible — **hatred** ['heɪtrəd] *n* : odio *m*

haughty ['hɔṭi] *adj* **-tier; -est** : altanero, altivo

haul ['hɔl] *vt* : arrastrar, jalar *Lat* — ~ *n* **1** CATCH : redada *f* (de peces) **2** LOOT : botín *m* **3 a long** ~ : un trayecto largo

haunch ['hɔntʃ] *n* : cadera *f* (de una persona), anca *f* (de un animal)

haunt ['hɔnt] *vt* **1** : frecuentar, rondar **2** TROUBLE : inquietar — ~ *n* : sitio *m* predilecto — **haunted** ['hɔntəd] *adj* : embrujado

have ['hæv, *in sense 3 as an auxiliary verb usu* 'hæf] *v* **had** ['hæd]; **having; has** ['hæz, *in sense 3 as an auxiliary verb usu* 'hæs] *vt* **1** : tener **2** CONSUME : comer, tomar **3** ALLOW : permitir **4** : dar (una fiesta, etc.), convocar (una reunión) **5** ~ **one's hair cut** : cortarse el pelo **6** ~ **sth done** : mandar hacer algo — *v aux* **1** : haber **2** ~ **just done sth** : acabar de hacer algo **4 you've finished, haven't you?** : has terminado, ¿no?

haven ['heɪvən] *n* : refugio *m*

havoc ['hævək] *n* : estragos *mpl*

hawk[1] ['hɔk] *n* : halcón *m*

hawk[2] *vt* : pregonar (mercancías)

hay ['heɪ] *n* : heno *m* — **hay fever** *n* : fiebre *f* del heno — **haystack** ['heɪˌstæk] *n* : almiar *m* — **haywire** ['heɪˌwaɪr] *adj* **go** ~ : estropearse

hazard ['hæzərd] *n* : peligro *m,* riesgo *m* — ~ *vt* : arriesgar, aventurar — **hazardous** ['hæzərdəs] *adj* : arriesgado, peligroso

haze ['heɪz] *n* : bruma *f,* neblina *f*

hazel ['heɪzəl] *n* : color *m* avellana — **hazelnut** ['heɪzəlˌnʌt] *n* : avellana *f*

hazy ['heɪzi] *adj* **hazier; -est** : nebuloso

he ['hi:] *pron* : él

head ['hɛd] *n* **1** : cabeza *f* **2** END, TOP : cabeza *f* (de un clavo, etc.), cabecera *f* (de una mesa) **3** LEADER : jefe *m,* -fa *f* **4 be out of one's** ~ : estar loco **5 come to a** ~ : llegar a un punto crítico **6** ~**s or tails** : cara o cruz **7 per** ~ : por cabeza — ~ *adj* MAIN : principal — ~ *vt* : encabezar — *vi* : dirigirse — **headache** ['hɛdˌeɪk] *n* : dolor *m* de cabeza — **headband** ['hɛdˌbænd] *n* : cinta *f* del pelo — **headdress** ['hɛdˌdrɛs] *n* : tocado *m* — **headfirst** ['hɛd'fərst] *adv* : de cabeza — **heading** ['hɛdɪŋ] *n* : encabezamiento *m,* título *m* — **headland** ['hɛdlənd, -ˌlænd] *n* : cabo *m* — **headlight** ['hɛdˌlaɪt] *n* : faro *m* — **headline** ['hɛdˌlaɪn] *n* : titular *m* — **headlong** ['hɛd'lɔŋ] *adv* **1** HEADFIRST : de cabeza **2** HASTILY : precipitadamente — **headmaster** ['hɛdˌmæstər] *n* : director *m* — **headmistress** ['hɛdˌmɪstrəs, -'mɪs-] *n* : directora *f* — **head–on** ['hɛd'ɑn, -'ɔn] *adv & adj* : de frente — **headphones** ['hɛdˌfo:nz] *npl* : auriculares *mpl,* audífonos *mpl Lat* — **headquarters** ['hɛdˌkwɔrṭərz] *ns & pl* : oficina *f* central (de una compañía), cuartel *m* general (de los militares) — **head start** *n* : ventaja *f* — **headstrong** ['hɛdˌstrɔŋ] *adj* : testarudo, obstinado — **headwaiter** ['hɛd'weɪṭər] *n* : jefe *m,* -fa *f* de comedor — **headway** ['hɛdˌweɪ] *n* **1** : progreso *m* **2 make** ~ : avanzar — **heady** ['hɛdi] *adj* **headier; -est** : embriagador

heal ['hi:l] *vt* : curar — *vi* : cicatrizar

health ['hɛlθ] *n* : salud *f* — **healthy** ['hɛlθi] *adj* **healthier; -est** : sano, saludable

heap ['hi:p] *n* : montón *m* — ~ *vt* : amontonar

hear ['hɪr] *v* **heard** ['hərd]; **hearing** *vt* : oír — *vi* **1** : oír **2** ~ **about** : enterarse de **3** ~ **from** : tener noticias de — **hearing** ['hɪrɪŋ] *n* **1** : oído *m* **2** : vista *f* (en un tribunal) — **hearing aid** *n* : audífono *m* — **hearsay** ['hɪrˌseɪ] *n* : rumores *mpl*

hearse ['hərs] *n* : coche *m* fúnebre

heart ['hɑrt] *n* **1** : corazón *m* **2 at** ~ : en el fondo **3 by** ~ : de memoria **4 lose** ~ : descorazonarse **5 take** ~ : animarse — **heartache** ['hɑrṭˌeɪk] *n* : pena *f,* dolor *m* — **heart attack** *n* : infarto *m,* ataque *m* al corazón — **heartbeat** ['hɑrtˌbi:t] *n* : latido *m* (del corazón) — **heartbreak** ['hɑrtˌbreɪk] *n* : congoja *f,* angustia *f* — **heartbroken** ['hɑrtˌbro:kən] *adj* : desconsolado — **heartburn** ['hɑrtˌbərn] *n* : acidez *f* estomacal

hearth ['hɑrθ] *n* : hogar *m*

heartily ['hɑrṭəli] *adv* : de buena gana

heartless ['hɑrtləs] *adj* : de mal corazón, cruel

hearty ['hɑrṭi] *adj* **heartier; -est** **1** : cordial, caluroso **2** : abundante (dícese de una comida)

heat ['hi:t] *vt* : calentar — *vi* or ~ **up** : calentarse — ~ *n* **1** : calor *m* **2** HEATING : calefacción *f* — **heated** ['hi:ṭəd] *adj* : acalorado — **heater** ['hi:ṭər] *n* : calentador *m*

heath ['hi:θ] *n* : brezal *m*

heathen ['hi:ðən] *adj* : pagano — ~ *n, pl* **-thens** *or* **-then** : pagano *m,* -na *f*

heather ['hɛðər] *n* : brezo *m*

heave ['hi:v] *v* **heaved** *or* **hove** ['ho:v]; **heaving** *vt* **1** LIFT : levantar (con esfuerzo) **2** HURL : lanzar, tirar **3** ~ **a sigh** : suspirar — ~ *vi or* ~ **up** : levantarse

heaven ['hɛvən] *n* : cielo *m* — **heavenly** ['hɛvənli] *adj* **1** : celestial **2** ~ **body** : cuerpo *m* celeste

heavy ['hɛvi] *adj* **heavier; -est** **1** : pesado **2** INTENSE : fuerte **3** ~ **sigh** : suspiro *m* profundo **4** ~ **traffic** : tráfico *m* denso — **heavily** ['hɛvəli] *adv* **1** : pesadamente **2** EXCESSIVELY : mucho — **heaviness** ['hɛvinəs] *n* : peso *m,* pesadez *f* — **heavyweight** ['hɛviˌweɪt] *n* : peso *m* pesado

Hebrew ['hi:ˌbru:] *adj* : hebreo — ~ *n* : hebreo *m* (idioma)

heckle ['hɛkəl] *vt* **-led; -ling** : interrumpir (a un orador) con preguntas molestas

hectic ['hɛktɪk] *adj* : agitado, ajetreado

he'd ['hi:d] (*contraction of* **he had** *or* **he would**) → **have, would**

hedge ['hɛdʒ] *n* : seto *m* vivo — ~ *v* **hedged; hedging** *vt* ~ **one's bets** : cubrirse — *vi* : contestar con evasivas — **hedgehog** ['hɛdʒˌhɔg, -ˌhɑg] *n* : erizo *m*

heed ['hi:d] *vt* : prestar atención a, hacer caso de — ~ *n* **take** ~ : tener cuidado — **heedless** ['hi:dləs] *adj* **be** ~ **of** : hacer caso omiso de

heel ['hi:l] *n* : talón *m* (del pie), tacón *m* (de un zapato)

hefty ['hɛfti] *adj* **heftier; -est** : robusto y pesado

heifer ['hɛfər] *n* : novilla *f*

height ['haɪt] *n* **1** : estatura *f* (de una persona), altura *f* (de un objeto) **2** PEAK : cumbre *f* **3 the** ~ **of folly** : el colmo de la locura **4 what is your** ~ **?** : ¿cuánto mides? — **heighten** ['haɪtən] *vt* : aumentar, intensificar

heir ['ær] *n* : heredero *m,* -ra *f* — **heiress** ['ærəs] *n* : heredera *f* — **heirloom** ['ærˌlu:m] *n* : reliquia *f* de familia

held → **hold**

helicopter ['hɛləˌkɑptər] *n* : helicóptero *m*

hell ['hɛl] *n* : infierno *m* — **hellish** ['hɛlɪʃ] *adj* : infernal

he'll ['hi:l, 'hɪl] (*contraction of* **he shall** *or* **he will**) → **shall, will**

hello [hə'lo:, hɛ-] *interj* : ¡hola!

helm ['hɛlm] *n* : timón *m*

helmet ['hɛlmət] *n* : casco *m*

help ['hɛlp] *vt* **1** : ayudar **2** ~ **oneself** : servirse **3 I can't** ~ **it** : no lo puedo remediar — ~ *n* **1** : ayuda *f* **2** STAFF : personal *m* **3 help!** : ¡socorro!, ¡auxilio! — **helper** ['hɛlpər] *n* : ayudante *mf* — **helpful** ['hɛlpfəl] *adj* **1** OBLIGING : servicial, amable **2** USEFUL : útil — **helping** ['hɛlpɪŋ] *n* : porción *f* — **helpless** ['hɛlpləs] *adj* **1** POWERLESS : incapaz **2** DEFENSELESS : indefenso

hem ['hɛm] *n* : dobladillo *m* — ~ *vt* **hemmed; hemming** ~ **in** : encerrar

hemisphere ['hɛməˌsfɪr] *n* : hemisferio *m*

hemorrhage ['hɛmərɪdʒ] *n* : hemorragia *f*

hemorrhoids ['hɛməˌrɔɪdz, 'hɛmˌrɔɪdz] *npl* : hemorroides *fpl,* almorranas *fpl*

hemp ['hɛmp] *n* : cáñamo *m*

hen ['hɛn] *n* : gallina *f*

hence ['hɛnts] *adv* **1** : de aquí, de ahí **2** THEREFORE : por lo tanto **3 ten years** ~ : de aquí a 10 años — **henceforth** ['hɛntsˌforθ, ˌhɛnts'-] *adv* : de ahora en adelante

henpeck ['hɛnˌpɛk] *vt* : dominar (al marido)

hepatitis [ˌhɛpə'taɪṭəs] *n, pl* **-titides** [-'tɪṭəˌdi:z] : hepatitis *f*

her ['hər] *adj* : su, sus — ~ ['hər, ər] *pron* **1** (*used as direct object*) : la **2** (*used as indirect object*) : le, se **3** (*used as object of a preposition*) : ella

herald ['hɛrəld] *vt* : anunciar

herb ['ərb, 'hərb] *n* : hierba *f*

herd ['hərd] *n* : manada *f* — ~ *vt* : conducir (en manada) — *vi or* ~ **together** : reunir

here ['hɪr] *adv* **1** : aquí, acá **2** ~ **you are!** : ¡toma! — **hereabouts** ['hɪrəˌbaʊts] *or* **hereabout** [-ˌbaʊt] *adv* : por aquí (cerca) — **hereafter** [hɪr'æftər] *adv* : en el futuro — **hereby** [hɪr'baɪ] *adv* : por este medio

hereditary [hə'rɛdəˌtɛri] *adj* : hereditario — **heredity** [hə'rɛdəṭi] *n* : herencia *f*

heresy ['hɛrəsi] *n, pl* **-sies** : herejía *f*

herewith [hɪr'wɪθ] *adv* : adjunto

heritage ['hɛrəṭɪdʒ] *n* **1** : herencia *f* **2** : patrimonio *m* (nacional)

hermit ['hərmət] *n* : ermitaño *m,* -ña *f*

hernia ['hərniə] *n, pl* **-nias** *or* **-niae** [-niˌi:, -niˌaɪ] : hernia *f*

hero ['hi:ˌro:, 'hɪrˌo:] *n, pl* **-roes** : héroe *m* — **heroic** [hɪ'ro:ɪk] *adj* : heroico — **heroine** ['hɛroən] *n* : heroína *f* — **heroism** ['hɛroˌɪzəm] *n* : heroísmo *m*

heron ['hɛrən] *n* : garza *f*

herring ['hɛrɪŋ] *n, pl* **-ring** *or* **-rings** : arenque *m*

hers ['hərz] *pron* **1** : (el) suyo, (la) suya, (los) suyos, (las) suyas **2 some friends of** ~ : unos amigos suyos, unos amigos de ella — **herself** [hər'sɛlf] *pron* **1** (*used reflexively*) : se **2** (*used emphatically*) : ella misma

he's ['hi:z] (*contraction of* **he is** *or* **he has**) → **be, have**

hesitant ['hɛzəṭənt] *adj* : titubeante, vacilante — **hesitate** ['hɛzəˌteɪt] *vi* **-tated; -tating** : vacilar, titubear — **hesitation** [ˌhɛzə'teɪʃən] *n* : vacilación *f,* titubeo *m*

heterosexual [ˌhɛṭəro'sɛkʃʊəl] *adj* : heterosexual — ~ *n* : heterosexual *mf*

hexagon ['hɛksəˌgɑn] *n* : hexágono *m*

hey ['heɪ] *interj* : ¡eh!, ¡oye!

heyday ['heɪˌdeɪ] *n* : auge *m,* apogeo *m*

hi ['haɪ] *interj* : ¡hola!

hibernate ['haɪbərˌneɪt] *vi* **-nated; -nating** : hibernar

hiccup ['hɪkəp] *n* **have the** ~**s** : tener hipo — ~ *vi* **-cuped; -cuping** : tener hipo

hide[1] ['haɪd] *n* : piel *f,* cuero *m*

hide[2] *v* **hid** ['hɪd]; **hidden** ['hɪdən] *or* **hid; hiding** *vt* **1** : esconder **2** : ocultar (motivos, etc.) — *vi* : esconderse — **hide–and–seek** ['haɪdəndsi:k] *n* : escondite *m,* escondidas *fpl Lat*

hideous ['hɪdiəs] *adj* : horrible, espantoso

hideout ['haɪdˌaʊt] *n* : escondite *m,* guarida *f*

hierarchy ['haɪəˌrɑrki] *n, pl* **-chies** : jerarquía *f* — **hierarchical** [ˌhaɪə'rɑrkɪkəl] *adj* : jerárquico

high ['haɪ] *adj* **1** : alto **2** INTOXICATED : borracho, drogado **3 a** ~ **voice** : una voz aguda **4 it's two feet** ~ : tiene dos pies de alto **5** ~ **winds** : fuertes vientos *mpl* — ~ *adv* : alto — ~ *n* : récord *m,* máximo *m* — **higher** ['haɪər] *adj* **1** : superior **2** ~ **education** : enseñanza *f* superior — **highlight** ['haɪˌlaɪt] *n* : punto *m* culminante — **highly** ['haɪli] *adv* **1** VERY : muy, sumamente **2** **think** ~ **of** : tener en mucho a — **Highness** ['haɪnəs] *n* **His/Her** ~ : Su Alteza *f* — **high school** *n* : escuela *f* superior, escuela *f* secundaria — **high–strung** [ˌhaɪ'strʌŋ] *adj* : nervioso, excitable — **highway** ['haɪˌweɪ] *n* : carretera *f*

hijack ['haɪˌdʒæk] *vt* : secuestrar — **hijacker** ['haɪˌdʒækər] *n* : secuestrador *m,* -dora *f* — **hijacking** *n* : secuestro *m*

hike ['haɪk] *v* **hiked; hiking** *vi* : ir de caminata — *vt or* ~ **up** RAISE : subir — ~ *n* : caminata *f,* excursión *f* — **hiker** ['haɪkər] *n* : excursionista *mf*

hilarious [hɪ'læriəs, haɪ'-] *adj* : muy divertido — **hilarity** [hɪ'lærəṭi, haɪ-] *n* : hilaridad *f*

hill ['hɪl] *n* **1** : colina *f,* cerro *m* **2** SLOPE : cuesta *f* — **hillside** ['hɪlˌsaɪd] *n* : ladera *f,* cuesta *f* — **hilly** ['hɪli] *adj* **hillier; -est** : accidentado

hilt ['hɪlt] *n* : puño *m*

him ['hɪm, əm] *pron* **1** (*used as direct object*) : lo **2** (*used as indirect object*) : le, se **3** (*used as object of a preposition*) : él — **himself** [hɪm'sɛlf] *pron* **1** (*used reflexively*) : se **2** (*used emphatically*) : él mismo

hind ['haɪnd] *adj* : trasero, posterior

hinder ['hɪndər] *vt* : dificultar, estorbar — **hindrance** ['hɪndrənts] *n* : obstáculo *m*

hindsight ['haɪndˌsaɪt] *n* **in** ~ : en retrospectiva

Hindu ['hɪnˌdu:] *adj* : hindú

hinge ['hɪndʒ] *n* : bisagra *f,* gozne *m* — ~ *vi* **hinged; hinging** ~ **on** : depender de

hint ['hɪnt] *n* **1** : indirecta *f* **2** TIP : consejo *m* **3** TRACE : asomo *m,* toque *m* — ~ *vt* : dar a entender — *vi* ~ **at** : insinuar

hip ['hɪp] *n* : cadera *f*

hippopotamus [ˌhɪpə'pɑṭəməs] *n, pl* **-muses** *or* **-mi** [-ˌmaɪ] : hipopótamo *m*

hire ['haɪr] *n* **1** : alquiler *m* **2 for** ~ : se alquila — ~ *vt* **hired; hiring** **1** EMPLOY : contratar, emplear **2** RENT : alquilar

his ['hɪz, ɪz] *adj* : su, sus, de él — ~ *pron* **1** : (el) suyo, (la) suya, (los) suyos, (las) suyas **2 some friends of** ~ : unos amigos suyos, unos amigos de él

Hispanic [hɪ'spænɪk] *adj* : hispano, hispánico

hiss ['hɪs] *vi* : silbar — *n* : silbido *m*

history ['hɪstəri] *n, pl* **-ries** **1** : historia *f* **2** BACKGROUND : historial *m* — **historian** [hɪ'stɔriən] *n* : historiador *m,* -dora *f* — **historic** [hɪ'stɔrɪk] *or* **historical** [-ɪkəl] *adj* : histórico

hit ['hɪt] *v* **hit; hitting** *vt* **1** : golpear, pegar **2** : dar (con un proyectil) **3** AFFECT : afectar **4** REACH : alcanzar **5 the car** ~ **a tree** : el coche chocó contra un árbol — *vi* : pegar — ~ *n* **1** : golpe *m* **2** SUCCESS : éxito *m*

hitch ['hɪtʃ] *vt* **1** ATTACH : enganchar **2** *or* ~ **up** RAISE : subirse **3** ~ **a ride** : hacer autostop — ~ *n* PROBLEM : problema *m* — **hitchhike** ['hɪtʃˌhaɪk] *vi* **-hiked; -hiking** : hacer autostop — **hitchhiker** ['hɪtʃˌhaɪkər] *n* : autostopista *mf*

hitherto ['hɪðərˌtu:, ˌhɪðər'-] *adv* : hasta ahora

HIV [ˌeɪtʃˌaɪ'vi:] *n* : VIH *m,* virus *m* del sida

hive ['haɪv] *n* : colmena *f*

hives ['haɪvz] *ns & pl* : urticaria *f*

hoard ['hord] *n* : tesoro *m* (de dinero), reserva *f* (de provisiones) — ~ *vt* : acumular

hoarse ['hors] *adj* **hoarser; -est** : ronco

hoax ['ho:ks] *n* : engaño *m*

hobble ['hɑbəl] *vi* **-bled; -bling** : cojear

hobby ['hɑbi] *n, pl* **-bies** : pasatiempo *m*

hobo ['hoˌbo:] *n, pl* **-boes** : vagabundo *m,* -da *f*

hockey ['hɑki] *n* : hockey *m*

hoe ['ho:] *n* : azada *f* — ~ *vt* **hoed; hoeing** : azadonar

hog ['hɔg, 'hɑg] *n* : cerdo *m* — ~ *vt* **hogged; hogging** MONOPOLIZE : acaparar

hoist ['hɔɪst] *vt* **1** : izar (una vela, etc.) **2** LIFT : levantar — ~ *n* : grúa *f*

hold[1] ['ho:ld] *n* : bodega *f* (en un barco o un avión)

hold[2] *v* **held** ['hɛld]; **holding** *vt* **1** GRIP : agarrar **2** POSSESS : tener **3** SUPPORT : sostener **4** : celebrar (una reunión, etc.), mantener (una conversación) **5** CONTAIN : contener **6** CONSIDER : considerar **7** *or* ~ **back** : detener **8** ~ **hands** : agarrarse de la mano **9** ~ **up** ROB : atracar **10** ~ **up** DELAY : retrasar — *vi* **1** LAST : durar, continuar **2** APPLY : ser válido — ~ *n* **1** GRIP : agarre *m* **2 get** ~ **of** : conseguir **3 get** ~ **of oneself** : controlarse — **holder** ['ho:ldər] *n* : tenedor *m,* -dora *f* — **holdup** ['ho:ldˌʌp] *n* **1** ROBBERY : atraco *m* **2** DELAY: retraso *m,* demora *f*

hole ['ho:l] *n* : agujero *m,* hoyo *m*

holiday ['hɑləˌdeɪ] *n* **1** : día *m* feriado, fiesta *f* **2** *Brit* VACATION : vacaciones *fpl*

holiness ['ho:linəs] *n* : santidad *f*

holler ['hɑlər] *vi* : gritar — ~ *n* : grito *m*

hollow ['hɑˌlo:] *n* **1** : hueco *m* **2** VALLEY : hondonada *f* — ~ *adj* **-lower; -est** **1** : hueco **2** FALSE : vacío, falso — ~ *vt or* ~ **out** : ahuecar

holly ['hɑli] *n, pl* **-lies** : acebo *m*

holocaust ['hɑləˌkɔst, 'ho:-, 'hɔ-] *n* : holocausto *m*

holster ['ho:lstər] *n* : pistolera *f*

holy ['ho:li] *adj* **-lier; -est** : santo, sagrado

homage ['ɑmɪdʒ, 'hɑ-] *n* : homenaje *m*

home ['ho:m] *n* **1** : casa *f* **2** FAMILY : hogar *m* **3** INSTITUTION : residencia *f,* asilo *m* **4 at** ~ **and abroad** : dentro y fuera del país — ~ *adv* **go** ~ : ir a casa — **homeland** ['ho:mˌlænd] *n* : patria *f* — **homeless** ['ho:mləs] *adj* : sin hogar — **homely** ['ho:mli] *adj* **-lier; -est** **1** DOMESTIC : casero **2** UGLY : feo — **homemade** ['ho:m'meɪd] *adj* : casero, hecho en casa — **homemaker** ['ho:mˌmeɪkər] *n* : ama *f* de casa — **home run** *n* : jonrón *m* — **homesick** ['ho:mˌsɪk] *adj* **be** ~ : echar de menos a la familia — **homeward** ['ho:mwərd] *adj* : de vuelta, de regreso — **homework** ['ho:mˌwərk] *n* : tarea *f,* deberes *mpl* — **homey** ['ho:mi] *adj* **homier; -est** : hogareño, acogedor

homicide ['hɑməˌsaɪd, 'ho:-] *n* : homicidio *m*

homogeneous [ˌho:mə'dʒi:niəs, -njəs] *adj* : homogéneo

homosexual [ˌho:mə'sɛkʃʊəl] *adj* : homosexual — ~ *n* : homosexual *mf* — **homosexuality** [ˌho:məˌsɛkʃʊ'æləṭi] *n* : homosexualidad *f*

honest ['ɑnəst] *adj* **1** : honrado **2** FRANK : sincero — **honestly** *adv* : sinceramente — **honesty** ['ɑnəsti] *n, pl* **-ties** : honradez *f*

honey ['hʌni] *n, pl* **-eys** : miel *f* — **honey-**

comb ['hʌni,ko:m] n : panal m — **honeymoon** ['hʌni,mu:n] n : luna f de miel

honk ['hɑŋk, 'hɔŋk] vi : tocar la bocina — **~** n : bocinazo m

honor or Brit **honour** ['ɑnər] n : honor m — **~** vt **1** : honrar **2** : aceptar (un cheque, etc.), cumplir con (una promesa) — **honorable** or Brit **honourable** ['ɑnərəbəl] adj : honorable, honroso — **honorary** ['ɑnə,reri] adj : honorario

hood ['hʊd] n **1** : capucha f (de un abrigo, etc.) **2** : capó m (de un automóvil)

hoodlum ['hʊdləm, 'hu:d-] n : matón m

hoodwink ['hʊd,wɪŋk] vt : engañar

hoof ['hʊf, 'hu:f] n, pl **hooves** ['hʊvz, 'hu:vz] or **hoofs** : pezuña f (de una vaca, etc.), casco m (de un caballo)

hook ['hʊk] n **1** : gancho m **2** or **~ and eye** : corchete m **3** → **fishhook 4 off the ~** : descolgado — **~** vt : enganchar — vi : engancharse

hoop ['hu:p] n : aro m

hooray [hʊ'reɪ] → **hurrah**

hoot ['hu:t] vi **1** : ulular (dícese de un búho) **2 ~ with laughter** : reírse a carcajadas — **~** n **1** : ululato m (de un búho) **2 I don't give a ~** : me importa un comino

hop[1] ['hɑp] vi **hopped; hopping** : saltar a la pata coja — **~** n : salto m a la pata coja

hop[2] n **~s** : lúpulo m (planta)

hope ['ho:p] v **hoped; hoping** vi : esperar — vt : esperar que — **~** n : esperanza f — **hopeful** ['ho:pfəl] adj : esperanzado — **hopefully** adv **1** : con esperanza **2 ~ it will help** : se espera que ayude — **hopeless** ['ho:pləs] adj : desesperado — **hopelessly** ['ho:pləsli] adv : desesperadamente

horde ['hord] n : horda f

horizon [hə'raɪzən] n : horizonte m — **horizontal** [,hɔrə'zɑntəl] adj : horizontal

hormone ['hɔr,mo:n] n : hormona f

horn ['hɔrn] n **1** : cuerno m (de un animal) **2** : trompa f (instrumento musical) **3** : bocina f, claxon m (de un vehículo)

hornet ['hɔrnət] n : avispón m

horoscope ['hɔrə,sko:p] n : horóscopo m

horror ['hɔrər] n : horror m — **horrendous** [hɔ'rendəs] adj : horrendo — **horrible** ['hɔrəbəl] adj : horrible — **horrid** ['hɔrɪd] adj : horroroso, horrible — **horrify** ['hɔrə,faɪ] vt **-fied; -fying** : horrorizar

hors d'oeuvre [ɔr'dərv] n, pl **hors d'oeuvres** [-'dərvz] : entremés m

horse ['hɔrs] n : caballo m — **horseback** ['hɔrs,bæk] n **on ~** : a caballo — **horsefly** ['hɔrs,flaɪ] n, pl **-flies** : tábano m — **horseman** ['hɔrsmən] n, pl **-men** [-mən, -,men] : jinete m — **horseplay** ['hɔrs,pleɪ] n : payasadas fpl — **horsepower** ['hɔrs,paʊər] n : caballo m de fuerza — **horseradish** ['hɔrs,rædɪʃ] n : rábano m picante — **horseshoe** ['hɔrs,ʃu:] n : herradura f — **horsewoman** ['hɔrs,wʊmən] n, pl **-women** [-,wɪmən] : jinete f

horticulture ['hɔrṭə,kʌltʃər] n : horticultura f

hose ['ho:z] n **1** pl **hoses** : manguera f, manga f **2 hose** pl STOCKINGS : medias fpl — **~** vt **hosed; hosing** : regar (con manguera) — **hosiery** ['ho:ʒəri, 'ho:zə-] n : calcetería f

hospice ['hɑspəs] n : hospicio m

hospital ['hɑs,pɪṭəl] n : hospital m — **hospitable** [hɑ'spɪṭəbəl, 'hɑs,pɪ-] adj : hospitalario — **hospitality** [,hɑspə'tæləṭi] n, pl **-ties** : hospitalidad f — **hospitalize** ['hɑs,pɪṭəl,aɪz] vt **-ized; -izing** : hospitalizar

host[1] ['ho:st] n **a ~ of** : toda una serie de

host[2] n **1** : anfitrión m, -triona f **2** : presentador m, -dora f (de televisión, etc.) — **~** vt : presentar (un programa de televisión, etc.)

host[3] n EUCHARIST : hostia f, Eucaristía f

hostage ['hɑstɪdʒ] n : rehén m

hostel ['hɑstəl] n or **youth ~** : albergue m juvenil

hostess ['ho:stɪs] n : anfitriona f

hostile ['hɑstəl, -,taɪl] adj : hostil — **hostility** [hɑs'tɪləṭi] n, pl **-ties** : hostilidad f

hot ['hɑt] adj **hotter; hottest 1** : caliente, caluroso (dícese del tiempo), cálido (dícese del clima) **2** SPICY : picante **3 feel ~** : tener calor **4 have a ~ temper** : tener mal genio **5 ~ news** : noticias fpl de última hora **6 it's ~ today** : hace calor

hot dog n : perro m caliente

hotel [ho:'tel] n : hotel m

hotheaded ['hɑt'hedəd] adj : exaltado

hound ['haʊnd] n : perro m (de caza) — **~** vt : acosar, perseguir

hour ['aʊər] n : hora f — **hourglass** ['aʊər,glæs] n : reloj m de arena — **hourly** ['aʊərli] adv & adj : cada hora, por hora

house ['haʊs] n, pl **houses** ['haʊzəz, -səz] **1** : casa f **2** : cámara f (del gobierno) **3 publishing ~** : editorial f — **~** ['haʊz] vt **housed; housing** : albergar — **houseboat** ['haʊs,bo:t] n : casa f flotante — **housefly** ['haʊs,flaɪ] n, pl **-flies** : mosca f común — **household** ['haʊs,ho:ld] adj **1** : doméstico **2 ~ name** : nombre m muy conocido — **~** n : casa f — **housekeeper** ['haʊs,ki:pər] n : ama f de llaves — **housekeeping** ['haʊs,ki:pɪŋ] n : gobierno m de la casa — **housewarming** ['haʊs,wɔrmɪŋ] n : fiesta f de estreno de una casa — **housewife** ['haʊs,waɪf] n, pl **-wives** : ama f de casa — **housework** ['haʊs,wərk] n : faenas fpl domésticas — **housing** ['haʊzɪŋ] n **1** : viviendas fpl **2** CASE : caja f protectora

hove → **heave**

hovel ['hʌvəl, 'hɑ-] n : casucha f, tugurio m

hover ['hʌvər, 'hɑ-] vi **1** : cernerse **2 ~ about** : rondar

how ['haʊ] adv **1** : cómo **2** (used in exclamations) : qué **3 ~ are you?** : ¿cómo está Ud.? **4 ~ come** : por qué **5 ~ much** : cuánto **6 ~ do you do?** : mucho gusto **7 ~ old are you?** : ¿cuántos años tienes? — **~** conj : como

however [haʊ'evər] conj **1** : de cualquier manera que **2 ~ you like** : como quieras — **~** adv **1** NEVERTHELESS : sin embargo, no obstante **2 ~ difficult it is** : por difícil que sea **3 ~ hard I try** : por más que me esfuerce

howl ['haʊl] vi : aullar — **~** n : aullido m

hub ['hʌb] n **1** CENTER : centro m **2** : cubo m (de una rueda)

hubbub ['hʌ,bʌb] n : alboroto m, jaleo m

hubcap ['hʌb,kæp] n : tapacubos m

huddle ['hʌdəl] vi **-dled; -dling** or **~ together** : apiñarse

hue ['hju:] n : color m, tono m

huff ['hʌf] n **be in a ~** : estar enojado

hug ['hʌg] vt **hugged; hugging** : abrazar — **~** n : abrazo m

huge ['hju:dʒ] adj **huger; hugest** : inmenso, enorme

hull ['hʌl] n : casco m (de un barco, etc.)

hum ['hʌm] v **hummed; humming** vi **1** : tararear **2** BUZZ : zumbar — vt : tararear (una melodía) — **~** n : zumbido m

human ['hju:mən, 'ju:-] adj : humano — **~** n : (ser m) humano m — **humane** [hju:'meɪn, ju:-] adj : humano, humanitario — **humanitarian** [hju:,mænə'teriən, ju:-] adj : humanitario — **humanity** [hju:'mænəṭi, ju:-] n, pl **-ties** : humanidad f

humble ['hʌmbəl] vt **-bled; -bling 1** : humillar **2 ~ oneself** : humillarse — **~** adj **-bler; -blest** : humilde

humdrum ['hʌm,drʌm] adj : monótono, rutinario

humid ['hju:məd, 'ju:-] adj : húmedo — **humidity** [hju:'mɪdəṭi, ju:-] n, pl **-ties** : humedad f

humiliate [hju:'mɪli,eɪt, ju:-] vt **-ated; -ating** : humillar — **humiliating** [hju:'mɪli,eɪṭɪŋ, ju:-] adj : humillante — **humiliation** [hju:,mɪli'eɪʃən, ju:-] n : humillación f — **humility** [hju:'mɪləṭi, ju:-] n : humildad f

humor or Brit **humour** ['hju:mər, 'ju:-] n : humor m — **~** vt : seguir la corriente a, complacer — **humorous** ['hju:mərəs, 'ju:-] adj : humorístico, cómico

hump ['hʌmp] n : joroba f

hunch ['hʌntʃ] vi or **~ over** : encorvarse — **~** n : presentimiento m

hundred ['hʌndrəd] adj : cien, ciento — **~** n, pl **-dreds** or **-dred** : ciento m — **hundredth** ['hʌndrədθ] adj : centésimo — **~** n **1** : centésimo m, -ma f (en una serie) **2** : centésimo m (en matemáticas)

hung → **hang**

Hungarian [hʌŋ'gæriən] adj : húngaro — **~** n : húngaro m (idioma)

hunger ['hʌŋgər] n : hambre m — **~** vi **1** : tener hambre **2 ~ for** : ansiar, anhelar — **hungry** ['hʌŋgri] adj **-grier; -est 1** : hambriento **2 be ~** : tener hambre

hunk ['hʌŋk] n : pedazo m (grande)

hunt ['hʌnt] vt **1** : cazar **2 ~ for** : buscar — **~** n **1** : caza f, cacería f **2** SEARCH : búsqueda f, busca f — **hunter** ['hʌntər] n : cazador m, -dora f — **hunting** ['hʌntɪŋ] n **1** : caza f **2 go ~** : ir de caza

hurdle ['hərdəl] n **1** : valla f (en deportes) **2** OBSTACLE : obstáculo m

hurl ['hərl] vt : lanzar, arrojar

hurrah [hʊ'rɑ, -'rɔ] interj : ¡hurra!

hurricane ['hərə,keɪn] n : huracán m

hurry ['həri] n : prisa f, apuro f Lat — v **-ried; -rying** vi : darse prisa, apurarse Lat — vt : apurar, dar prisa a — **hurried** ['hərid] adj : apresurado — **hurriedly** ['hərədli] adv : apresuradamente, de prisa

hurt ['hərt] v **hurt; hurting** vt **1** INJURE : hacer daño a, lastimar **2** OFFEND : ofender, herir — vi **1** : doler **2 my foot ~s** : me duele el pie — **~** n **1** INJURY : herida f **2** DISTRESS : dolor m, pena f — **hurtful** ['hərtfəl] adj : hiriente, doloroso

hurtle ['hərṭəl] vi **-tled; -tling** : lanzarse, precipitarse

husband ['hʌzbənd] n : esposo m, marido m

hush ['hʌʃ] vt : hacer callar, acallar — **~** n : silencio m

husk ['hʌsk] n : cáscara f

husky[1] ['hʌski] adj **-kier; -est** HOARSE : ronco

husky[2] n, pl **-kies** : perro m, -rra f esquimal

husky[3] adj BURLY : fornido

hustle ['hʌsəl] v **-tled; -tling** vt : dar prisa a, apurar Lat — vi : darse prisa, apurarse Lat — **~** n **~ and bustle** : ajetreo m, bullicio m

hut ['hʌt] n : cabaña f

hutch ['hʌtʃ] n or **rabbit ~** : conejera f

hyacinth ['haɪə,sɪnθ] n : jacinto m

hybrid ['haɪbrɪd] n : híbrido m — **~** adj : híbrido

hydrant ['haɪdrənt] n or **fire ~** : boca f de incendios

hydraulic [haɪ'drɔlɪk] adj : hidráulico

hydroelectric [,haɪdroɪ'lektrɪk] adj : hidroeléctrico

hydrogen ['haɪdrədʒən] n : hidrógeno m

hyena [haɪ'i:nə] n : hiena f

hygiene ['haɪ,dʒi:n] n : higiene f — **hygienic** [haɪ'dʒenɪk, -'dʒi:-; ,haɪdʒi'enɪk] adj : higiénico

hymn ['hɪm] n : himno m

hyperactive [,haɪpər'æktɪv] adj : hiperactivo

hyphen ['haɪfən] n : guión m

hypnosis [hɪp'no:sɪs] n, pl **-noses** [-,si:z] : hipnosis f — **hypnotic** [hɪp'nɑṭɪk] adj : hipnótico — **hypnotism** ['hɪpnə,tɪzəm] n : hipnotismo m — **hypnotize** ['hɪpnə,taɪz] vt **-tized; -tizing** : hipnotizar

hypochondriac [,haɪpə'kɑndri,æk] n : hipocondríaco m, -ca f

hypocrisy [hɪp'ɑkrəsi] n, pl **-sies** : hipocresía f — **hypocrite** ['hɪpə,krɪt] n : hipócrita mf — **hypocritical** [,hɪpə'krɪṭɪkəl] adj : hipócrita

hypothesis [haɪ'pɑθəsɪs] n, pl **-eses** [-,si:z] : hipótesis f — **hypothetical** [,haɪpə'θeṭɪkəl] adj : hipotético

hysteria [hɪs'teriə, -'tɪr-] n : histeria f, histerismo m — **hysterical** [hɪs'terɪkəl] adj : histérico

I

i ['aɪ] n, pl **i's** or **is** ['aɪz] : i f, novena letra del alfabeto inglés

I ['aɪ] pron : yo

ice ['aɪs] n : hielo m — **~** v **iced; icing** vt **1** FREEZE : congelar **2** CHILL : enfriar **3** : bañar (pasteles, etc.) — **~** vi or **~ up** : helarse, congelarse — **iceberg** ['aɪs,bərg] n : iceberg m — **icebox** ['aɪs,bɑks] → **refrigerator** — **ice–cold** ['aɪs'ko:ld] adj : helado — **ice cream** n : helado m — **ice cube** n : cubito m de hielo — **ice–skate** ['aɪs,skeɪt] vi **-skated; -skating** : patinar — **ice skate** n : patín m de cuchilla — **icicle** ['aɪ,sɪkəl] n : carámbano m — **icing** ['aɪsɪŋ] n : baño m

icon ['aɪ,kɑn, -kən] n : icono m

icy ['aɪsi] adj **icier; -est 1** : cubierto de hielo (dícese de pavimento, etc.) **2** FREEZING : helado

I'd ['aɪd] (contraction of **I should** or **I would**) → **should, would**

idea [aɪ'di:ə] n : idea f

ideal [aɪ'di:əl] adj : ideal — **~** n : ideal m — **idealist** [aɪ'di:əlɪst] n : idealista mf — **idealistic** [aɪ,di:ə'lɪstɪk] adj : idealista — **idealize** [aɪ'di:ə,laɪz] vt **-ized; -izing** : idealizar

identity [aɪ'denṭəṭi] n, pl **-ties** : identidad f — **identical** [aɪ'dentɪkəl] adj : idéntico — **identify** [aɪ'denṭə,faɪ] v **-fied; -fying** vt : identificar — vi **~ with** : identificarse con — **identification** [aɪ,denṭəfə'keɪʃən] n **1** : identificación f **2 ~ card** : carnet m, carné m

ideology [,aɪdi'ɑləʤi, ,ɪ-] n, pl **-gies** : ideología f — **ideological** [,aɪdiə'lɑdʒɪkəl, ,ɪ-] adj : ideológico

idiocy ['ɪdiəsi] n, pl **-cies** : idiotez f

idiom ['ɪdiəm] n EXPRESSION : modismo m — **idiomatic** [,ɪdiə'mæṭɪk] adj : idiomático

idiosyncrasy [,ɪdio'sɪŋkrəsi] n, pl **-sies** : idiosincrasia f

idiot ['ɪdiət] n : idiota mf — **idiotic** [,ɪdi'ɑṭɪk] adj : idiota

idle ['aɪdəl] adj **idler; idlest 1** LAZY : haragán, holgazán **2** INACTIVE : parado (dícese de una máquina) **3** UNEMPLOYED : desocupado **4** VAIN : frívolo, vano **5 out of ~ curiosity** : por pura curiosidad — **~** v **idled; idling** vi : andar al ralentí (dícese de un motor) — vt **~ away the hours** : pasar el rato — **idleness** ['aɪdəlnəs] n : ociosidad f

idol ['aɪdəl] n : ídolo m — **idolize** ['aɪdəl,aɪz] vt **-ized; -izing** : idolatrar

idyllic [aɪ'dɪlɪk] adj : idílico

if ['ɪf] conj **1** : si **2** THOUGH : aunque, si bien **3 ~ so** : si es así

igloo ['ɪ,glu:] n, pl **-loos** : iglú m

ignite [ɪg'naɪt] v **-nited; -niting** vt : encender — vi : encenderse — **ignition** [ɪg'nɪʃən] n **1** : ignición f **2** or **~ switch** : encendido m

ignore [ɪg'nor] vt **-nored; -noring** : ignorar, no hacer caso de — **ignorance** ['ɪgnərənts] n : ignorancia f — **ignorant** ['ɪgnərənt] adj **1** : ignorante **2 be ~ of** : desconocer, ignorar

ilk ['ɪlk] n : tipo m, clase f

ill ['ɪl] adj **worse** ['wərs]; **worst** ['wərst] **1** SICK : enfermo **2** BAD : malo — adv **worse; worst** : mal — **ill–advised** [,ɪləd'vaɪzd, -əd-] adj : imprudente — **ill at ease** adj : incómodo

I'll ['aɪl] (contraction of **I shall** or **I will**) → **shall, will**

illegal [ɪl'li:gəl] adj : ilegal

illegible [ɪl'ledʒəbəl] adj : ilegible

illegitimate [,ɪlɪ'dʒɪṭəmət] adj : ilegítimo — **illegitimacy** [,ɪlɪ'dʒɪṭəməsi] n : ilegitimidad f

illicit [ɪl'lɪsət] adj : ilícito

illiterate [ɪl'lɪṭərət] adj : analfabeto — **illiteracy** [ɪl'lɪṭərəsi] n, pl **-cies** : analfabetismo m

ill–mannered [,ɪl'mænərd] adj : descortés, maleducado

ill–natured [,ɪl'neɪtʃərd] adj : de mal genio

illness ['ɪlnəs] n : enfermedad f

illogical [ɪl'lɑdʒɪkəl] adj : ilógico

ill–treat [,ɪl'tri:t] vt : maltratar

illuminate [ɪ'lu:mə,neɪt] vt **-nated; -nating** : iluminar — **illumination** [ɪ,lu:mə'neɪʃən] n : iluminación f

illusion [ɪ'lu:ʒən] n : ilusión f — **illusory** [ɪ'lu:səri, -zəri] adj : ilusorio

illustrate ['ɪləs,treɪt] v **-trated; -trating** : ilustrar — **illustration** [,ɪlə'streɪʃən] n **1** : ilustración f **2** EXAMPLE : ejemplo m — **illustrative** [ɪ'lʌstrəṭɪv, 'ɪlə,streɪṭɪv] adj : ilustrativo

illustrious [ɪ'lʌstriəs] adj : ilustre, glorioso

ill will n : animadversión f, mala voluntad f

I'm ['aɪm] (contraction of **I am**) → **be**

image ['ɪmɪdʒ] n : imagen f — **imaginary** [ɪ'mædʒə,neri] adj : imaginario — **imagination** [ɪ,mædʒə'neɪʃən] n : imaginación f — **imaginative** [ɪ'mædʒənəṭɪv, -ə,neɪṭɪv] adj : imaginativo — **imagine** [ɪ'mædʒən] vt **-ined; -ining** : imaginar(se)

imbalance [ɪm'bælənts] n : desequilibrio m

imbecile ['ɪmbəsəl, -,sɪl] n : imbécil mf

imbue [ɪm'bju:] vt **-bued; -buing** : imbuir

imitation [,ɪmə'teɪʃən] n : imitación f — **~** adj : de imitación, artificial — **imitate** ['ɪmə,teɪt] vt **-tated; -tating** : imitar, remedar — **imitator** ['ɪmə,teɪṭər] n : imitador m, -dora f

immaculate [ɪ'mækjələt] adj : inmaculado

immaterial [,ɪmə'tɪriəl] adj : irrelevante, sin importancia

immature [,ɪmə'tʊr, -'tjʊr, -'tʊr] adj : inmaduro — **immaturity** [,ɪmə'tʊrəṭi, -'tjʊr-, -'tʊr-] n, pl **-ties** : inmadurez f

immediate [ɪ'mi:diət] adj : inmediato — **immediately** [ɪ'mi:diətli] adv : inmediatamente

immense [ɪ'ments] adj : inmenso — **immensity** [ɪ'mentsəṭi] n, pl **-ties** : inmensidad f

immerse [ɪ'mərs] vt **-mersed; -mersing** : sumergir — **immersion** [ɪ'mərʒən] n : inmersión f

immigrate ['ɪmə,greɪt] vi **-grated; -grating** : inmigrar — **immigrant** ['ɪmɪgrənt] n : inmigrante mf — **immigration** [,ɪmə'greɪʃən] n : inmigración f

imminent ['ɪmənənt] adj : inminente — **imminence** ['ɪmənənts] n : inminencia f

immobile [ɪm'o:bəl] adj : inmóvil — **immobilize** [ɪm'o:bə,laɪz] vt **-lized; -lizing** : inmovilizar

immoral [ɪ'mɔrəl] adj : inmoral — **immorality** [,ɪmɔ'ræləṭi, ,ɪmə-] n, pl **-ties** : inmoralidad f

immortal [ɪ'mɔrtəl] adj : inmortal — **~** n : inmortal mf — **immortality** [,ɪ,mɔr'tæləṭi] n : inmortalidad f

immune [ɪ'mju:n] adj : inmune — **immunity** [ɪ'mju:nəṭi] n, pl **-ties** : inmunidad f — **immunization** [,ɪmjʊnə'zeɪʃən] n : inmunización f — **immunize** ['ɪmjʊ,naɪz] vt **-nized; -nizing** : inmunizar

imp ['ɪmp] n RASCAL : diablillo m

impact ['ɪm,pækt] n : impacto m

impair [ɪm'pær] vt : dañar, perjudicar

impart [ɪm'pɑrt] vt : impartir (información), conferir (una calidad, etc.)

impartial [ɪm'pɑrʃəl] adj : imparcial — **impartiality** [ɪm,pɑrʃi'æləṭi] n, pl **-ties** : imparcialidad f

impassable [ɪm'pæsəbəl] adj : intransitable

impasse ['ɪm,pæs] n : impasse m

impassioned [ɪm'pæʃənd] adj : apasionado

impassive [ɪm'pæsɪv] adj : impasible

impatience [ɪm'peɪʃənts] n : impaciencia f — **impatient** [ɪm'peɪʃənt] adj : impaciente — **impatiently** [ɪm'peɪʃəntli] adv : con impaciencia

impeccable [ɪm'pekəbəl] adj : impecable

impede [ɪm'pi:d] vt **-peded; -peding** : dificultar — **impediment** [ɪm'pedəmənt] n : impedimento m, obstáculo m

impel [ɪm'pel] vt **-pelled; -pelling** : impeler

impending [ɪm'pendɪŋ] adj : inminente

impenetrable [ɪm'penətrəbəl] adj : impenetrable

imperative [ɪm'perəṭɪv] adj **1** COMMANDING : imperativo **2** NECESSARY : imprescindible — **~** n : imperativo m

imperceptible [,ɪmpər'septəbəl] adj : imperceptible

imperfection [ɪm,pər'fekʃən] n : imperfección f — **imperfect** [ɪm'pərfɪkt] adj : imperfecto — **~** n or **~ tense** : imperfecto m

imperial [ɪm'pɪriəl] adj : imperial — **imperialism** [ɪm'pɪriə,lɪzəm] n : imperialismo m — **imperious** [ɪm'pɪriəs] adj : imperioso

impersonal [ɪmˈpərsənəl] *adj* : impersonal
impersonate [ɪmˈpərsənˌeɪt] *vt* **-ated; -ating** : hacerse pasar por, imitar — **impersonation** [ɪmˌpərsənˈeɪʃən] *n* : imitación *f* — **impersonator** [ɪmˈpərsənˌeɪt̬ər] *n* : imitador *m*, -dora *f*
impertinent [ɪmˈpərtənənt] *adj* : impertinente — **impertinence** [ɪmˈpərtənənts] *n* : impertinencia *f*
impervious [ɪmˈpərviəs] *adj* ~ **to** : impermeable a
impetuous [ɪmˈpɛtʃʊəs] *adj* : impetuoso, impulsivo
impetus [ˈɪmpət̬əs] *n* : ímpetu *m*, impulso *m*
impinge [ɪmˈpɪndʒ] *vi* **-pinged; -pinging** ~ **on** : afectara, incidir en
impish [ˈɪmpɪʃ] *adj* : pícaro, travieso
implant [ɪmˈplænt] *vt* : implantar
implausible [ɪmˈplɔzəbəl] *adj* : inverosímil
implement [ˈɪmpləmənt] *n* : instrumento *m*, implemento *m Lat* — ~ [ˈɪmpləˌmɛnt] *vt* : poner en práctica
implicate [ˈɪmpləˌkeɪt] *vt* **-cated; -cating** : implicar — **implication** [ˌɪmpləˈkeɪʃən] *n* **1** INVOLVEMENT : implicación *f* **2** CONSEQUENCE : consecuencia *f* **3 by** ~ : de forma indirecta
implicit [ɪmˈplɪsət] *adj* **1** : implícito **2** UNQUESTIONING : absoluto, incondicional
implore [ɪmˈplor] *vt* **-plored; -ploring** : implorar, suplicar
imply [ɪmˈplaɪ] *vt* **-plied; -plying 1** HINT : insinuar **2** ENTAIL : implicar
impolite [ˌɪmpəˈlaɪt] *adj* : descortés, maleducado
import [ɪmˈport] *vt* : importar (mercancías) — **important** [ɪmˈpɔrtənt] *adj* : importante — **importance** [ɪmˈportənts] *n* : importancia *f* — **importation** [ˌɪmˌporˈteɪʃən] *n* : importación *f* — **importer** [ɪmˈport̬ər] *n* : importador *m*, -dora *f*
impose [ɪmˈpoːz] *v* **-posed; -posing** *vt* : imponer — *vi* ~ **on** : importunar, molestar — **imposing** [ɪmˈpoːzɪŋ] *adj* : imponente — **imposition** [ˌɪmpəˈzɪʃən] *n* **1** ENFORCEMENT : imposición *f* **2 be an** ~ **on** : molestar
impossible [ɪmˈpɑsəbəl] *adj* : imposible — **impossibility** [ɪmˌpɑsəˈbɪlət̬i] *n, pl* **-ties** : imposibilidad *f*
impostor *or* **imposter** [ɪmˈpɑstər] *n* : impostor *m*, -tora *f*
impotent [ˈɪmpətənt] *adj* : impotente — **impotence** [ˈɪmpətənts] *n* : impotencia *f*
impound [ɪmˈpaʊnd] *vt* : incautar, embargar
impoverished [ɪmˈpɑvərɪʃt] *adj* : empobrecido
impracticable [ɪmˈpræktɪkəbəl] *adj* : impracticable
impractical [ɪmˈpræktɪkəl] *adj* : poco práctico
imprecise [ˌɪmprɪˈsaɪs] *adj* : impreciso — **imprecision** [ˌɪmprɪˈsɪʒən] *n* : imprecisión *f*
impregnable [ɪmˈprɛgnəbəl] *adj* : impenetrable
impregnate [ɪmˈprɛgˌneɪt] *vt* **-nated; -nating 1** : impregnar **2** FERTILIZE : fecundar
impress [ɪmˈprɛs] *vt* **1** : causar una buena impresión a **2** AFFECT : impresionar **3** ~ **sth on s.o.** : recalcar algo a algn — *vi* : impresionar — **impression** [ɪmˈprɛʃən] *n* : impresión *f* — **impressionable** [ɪmˈprɛʃənəbəl] *adj* : impresionable — **impressive** [ɪmˈprɛsɪv] *adj* : impresionante
imprint [ɪmˈprɪnt, ˈɪm-] *vt* : imprimir — ~ [ˈɪmˌprɪnt] *n* MARK : impresión *f*, huella *f*
imprison [ɪmˈprɪzən] *vt* : encarcelar — **imprisonment** [ɪmˈprɪzənmənt] *n* : encarcelamiento *m*
improbable [ɪmˈprɑbəbəl] *adj* : improbable — **improbability** [ɪmˌprɑbəˈbɪlət̬i] *n, pl* **-ties** : improbabilidad *f*
impromptu [ɪmˈprɑmpˌtuː, -ˌtjuː] *adj* : improvisado
improper [ɪmˈprɑpər] *adj* **1** UNSEEMLY : indecoroso **2** INCORRECT : impropio — **impropriety** [ˌɪmprəˈpraɪət̬i] *n, pl* **-eties** : inconveniencia *f*
improve [ɪmˈpruːv] *v* **-proved; -proving** : mejorar — **improvement** [ɪmˈpruːvmənt] *n* : mejora *f*
improvise [ˈɪmprəˌvaɪz] *v* **-vised; -vising** : improvisar — **improvisation** [ɪmˌprɑvəˈzeɪʃən, ˌɪmprəvə-] *n* : improvisación *f*
impudent [ˈɪmpjədənt] *adj* : insolente — **impudence** [ˈɪmpjədənts] *n* : insolencia *f*
impulse [ˈɪmˌpʌls] *n* **1** : impulso *m* **2 on** ~ : sin reflexionar — **impulsive** [ɪmˈpʌlsɪv] *adj* : impulsivo — **impulsiveness** [ɪmˈpʌlsɪvnəs] *n* : impulsividad *f*
impunity [ɪmˈpjuːnət̬i] *n* **1** : impunidad *f* **2 with** ~ : impunemente
impure [ɪmˈpjʊr] *adj* : impuro — **impurity** [ɪmˈpjʊrət̬i] *n, pl* **-ties** : impureza *f*
in [ˈɪn] *prep* **1** : en **2** DURING : por, en *Lat* **3** WITHIN : dentro de **4 dressed** ~ **red** : vestido de rojo **5** ~ **the rain** : bajo la lluvia **6** ~ **the sun** : al sol **7** ~ **this way** : de esta manera **8 the best** ~ **the world** : el mejor del mundo **9 written** ~ **ink/French** : escrito con tinta/en francés — *adv* **1** INSIDE : dentro, adentro **2 be** ~ : estar (en casa) **3 be** ~ **on** : participar en **4 come in!** : ¡entre!, ¡pase! **5 he's** ~ **for a shock** : se va a llevar un shock — ~ *adj* : de moda
inability [ˌɪnəˈbɪlət̬i] *n, pl* **-ties** : incapacidad *f*
inaccessible [ˌɪnɪkˈsɛsəbəl] *adj* : inaccesible
inaccurate [ɪnˈækjərət] *n* : inexacto
inactive [ɪnˈæktɪv] *n* : inactivo — **inactivity** [ˌɪnˌækˈtɪvət̬i] *n, pl* **-ties** : inactividad *f*
inadequate [ɪnˈædɪkwət] *adj* : insuficiente
inadvertently [ˌɪnədˈvərtəntli] *adv* : sin querer
inadvisable [ˌɪnædˈvaɪzəbəl] *adj* : desaconsejable
inane [ɪˈneɪn] *adj* **inaner; -est** : estúpido, tonto
inanimate [ɪnˈænəmət] *adj* : inanimado
inapplicable [ɪnˈæplɪkəbəl, ˌɪnəˈplɪkəbəl] *adj* : inaplicable
inappropriate [ˌɪnəˈproːpriət] *adj* : impropio, inoportuno
inarticulate [ˌɪnɑrˈtɪkjələt] *adj* : incapaz de expresarse
inasmuch as [ˌɪnæzˈmʌtʃæz] *conj* : ya que, puesto que
inattentive [ˌɪnəˈtɛntɪv] *adj* : poco atento
inaudible [ɪnˈɔdəbəl] *adj* : inaudible
inaugural [ɪˈnɔgjərəl, -gərəl] *adj* **1** : inaugural **2** ~ **address** : discurso *m* de investidura — **inaugurate** [ɪˈnɔgjəˌreɪt, -gə-] *vt* **-rated; -rating 1** : investir (a un presidente, etc.) **2** BEGIN : inaugurar — **inauguration** [ɪˌnɔgjəˈreɪʃən, -gə-] *n* : investidura *f* (de una persona), inauguración *f* (de un edificio, etc.)
inborn [ˈɪnˌbɔrn] *adj* : innato
inbred [ˈɪnˌbrɛd] *adj* INNATE : innato
incalculable [ɪnˈkælkjələbəl] *adj* : incalculable
incapable [ɪnˈkeɪpəbəl] *adj* : incapaz — **incapacitate** [ˌɪnkəˈpæsəˌteɪt] *vt* **-tated; -tating** : incapacitar — **incapacity** [ˌɪnkəˈpæsət̬i] *n, pl* **-ties** : incapacidad *f*
incarcerate [ɪnˈkɑrsəˌreɪt] *vt* **-ated; -ating** : encarcelar
incarnate [ɪnˈkɑrnət, -ˌneɪt] *adj* : encarnado — **incarnation** [ˌɪnˌkɑrˈneɪʃən] *n* : encarnación *f*
incendiary [ɪnˈsɛndiˌɛri] *adj* : incendiario
incense[1] [ˈɪnˌsɛnts] *n* : incienso *m*
incense[2] [ɪnˈsɛnts] *vt* **-censed; -censing** : indignar, enfurecer
incentive [ɪnˈsɛntɪv] *n* : incentivo *m*
inception [ɪnˈsɛpʃən] *n* : comienzo *m*, principio *m*
incessant [ɪnˈsɛsənt] *adj* : incesante
incest [ˈɪnˌsɛst] *n* : incesto *m* — **incestuous** [ɪnˈsɛstʃʊəs] *adj* : incestuoso
inch [ˈɪntʃ] *n* : pulgada *f* — ~ *v* : avanzar poco a poco
incident [ˈɪntsədənt] *n* : incidente *m* — **incidence** [ˈɪntsədənts] *n* : índice *m* (de crímenes, etc.) — **incidental** [ˌɪntsəˈdɛntəl] *adj* **1** MINOR : incidental **2** CHANCE : casual — **incidentally** [ˌɪntsəˈdɛntəli, -ˈdɛntli] *adv* : a propósito
incinerate [ɪnˈsɪnəˌreɪt] *vt* **-ated; -ating** : incinerar — **incinerator** [ɪnˈsɪnəˌreɪt̬ər] *n* : incinerador *m*
incision [ɪnˈsɪʒən] *n* : incisión *f*
incite [ɪnˈsaɪt] *vt* **-cited; -citing** : incitar, instigar
incline [ɪnˈklaɪn] *v* **-clined; -clining** *vt* **1** BEND : inclinar **2 be** ~**ed to** : inclinarse a, tender a — ~ *vi* : inclinarse — ~ [ˈɪnˌklaɪn] *n* : pendiente *f* — **inclination** [ˌɪnkləˈneɪʃən] *n* **1** : inclinación *f* **2** DESIRE : deseo *m*, ganas *fpl*
include [ɪnˈkluːd] *vt* **-cluded; -cluding** : incluir — **inclusion** [ɪnˈkluːʒən] *n* : inclusión *f* — **inclusive** [ɪnˈkluːsɪv] *adj* : inclusivo
incognito [ˌɪnˌkɑgˈniːt̬o, ɪnˈkɑgnəˌtoː] *adv & adj* : de incógnito
incoherent [ˌɪnkoˈhɪrənt, -ˈhɛr-] *adj* : incoherente — **incoherence** [ˌɪnkoˈhɪrənts, -ˈhɛr-] *n* : incoherencia *f*
income [ˈɪnˌkʌm] *n* : ingresos *mpl* — **income tax** *n* : impuesto *m* sobre la renta
incomparable [ɪnˈkɑmpərəbəl] *adj* : incomparable
incompatible [ˌɪnkəmˈpæt̬əbəl] *adj* : incompatible
incompetent [ɪnˈkɑmpət̬ənt] *adj* : incompetente — **incompetence** [ɪnˈkɑmpət̬ənts] *n* : incompetencia *f*
incomplete [ˌɪnkəmˈpliːt] *adj* : incompleto
incomprehensible [ˌɪnˌkɑmpriˈhɛntsəbəl] *adj* : incomprensible
inconceivable [ˌɪnkənˈsiːvəbəl] *adj* : inconcebible
inconclusive [ˌɪnkənˈkluːsɪv] *adj* : no concluyente
incongruous [ɪnˈkɑŋgruəs] *adj* : incongruente
inconsiderate [ˌɪnkənˈsɪdərət] *adj* : desconsiderado
inconsistent [ˌɪnkənˈsɪstənt] *adj* **1** : inconsecuente **2 be** ~ **with** : no concordar con — **inconsistency** [ˌɪnkənˈsɪstəntsi] *n, pl* **-cies** : inconsecuencia *f*
inconspicuous [ˌɪnkənˈspɪkjʊəs] *adj* : que no llama la atención
inconvenient [ˌɪnkənˈviːnjənt] *adj* : incómodo, inconveniente — **inconvenience** [ˌɪnkənˈviːnjənts] *n* **1** BOTHER : incomodidad *f*, molestia *f* **2** DRAWBACK : inconveniente *m* — ~ *vt* **-nienced; -niencing** *vt* : importunar, molestar
incorporate [ɪnˈkɔrpəˌreɪt] *vt* **-rated; -rating** : incorporar
incorrect [ˌɪnkəˈrɛkt] *adj* : incorrecto
increase [ˈɪnˌkriːs, ɪnˈkriːs] *n* : aumento *m* — ~ [ɪnˈkriːs, ˈɪnˌkriːs] *v* **-creased; -creasing** : aumentar — **increasingly** [ɪnˈkriːsɪŋli] *adv* : cada vez más
incredible [ɪnˈkrɛdəbəl] *adj* : increíble
incredulous [ɪnˈkrɛdʒələs] *adj* : incrédulo
incriminate [ɪnˈkrɪməˌneɪt] *vt* **-nated; -nating** : incriminar
incubator [ˈɪŋkjʊˌbeɪt̬ər, ˈɪn-] *n* : incubadora *f*
incumbent [ɪnˈkʌmbənt] *n* : titular *mf*
incur [ɪnˈkər] *vt* **incurred; incurring** : provocar (al enojo, etc.), incurrir en (gastos)
incurable [ɪnˈkjʊrəbəl] *adj* : incurable
indebted [ɪnˈdɛt̬əd] *adj* **1** : endeudado **2 be** ~ **to s.o.** : estar en deuda con algn
indecent [ɪnˈdiːsənt] *adj* : indecente — **indecency** [ɪnˈdiːsəntsi] *n, pl* **-cies** : indecencia *f*
indecisive [ˌɪndɪˈsaɪsɪv] *adj* : indeciso
indeed [ɪnˈdiːd] *adv* **1** TRULY : verdaderamente, sin duda **2** IN FACT : en efecto **3** ~? : ¿de veras?
indefinite [ɪnˈdɛfənət] *adj* **1** : indefinido **2** VAGUE : impreciso — **indefinitely** [ɪnˈdɛfənətli] *adv* : indefinidamente
indelible [ɪnˈdɛləbəl] *adj* : indeleble
indent [ɪnˈdɛnt] *vt* : sangrar (un párrafo) — **indentation** [ˌɪnˌdɛnˈteɪʃən] *n* DENT, NOTCH : mella *f*
independent [ˌɪndəˈpɛndənt] *adj* : independiente — **independence** [ˌɪndəˈpɛndənts] *n* : independencia *f*
indescribable [ˌɪndɪˈskraɪbəbəl] *adj* : indescriptible
indestructible [ˌɪndɪˈstrʌktəbəl] *adj* : indestructible
index [ˈɪnˌdɛks] *n, pl* **-dexes** *or* **-dices** [ˈɪndəˌsiːz] : índice *m* — ~ *vt* : incluir en un índice — **index finger** *n* : dedo *m* índice
Indian [ˈɪndiən] *adj* : indio *m*, -dia *f*
indication [ˌɪndəˈkeɪʃən] *n* : indicio *m*, señal *f* — **indicate** [ˈɪndəˌkeɪt] *vt* **-cated; -cating** : indicar — **indicative** [ɪnˈdɪkət̬ɪv] *adj* : indicativo — **indicator** [ˈɪndəˌkeɪt̬ər] *n* : indicador *m*
indict [ɪnˈdaɪt] *vt* : acusar (de un crimen) — **indictment** [ɪnˈdaɪtmənt] *n* : acusación *f*
indifferent [ɪnˈdɪfrənt, -ˈdɪfə-] *adj* **1** : indiferente **2** MEDIOCRE : mediocre — **indifference** [ɪnˈdɪfrənts, -ˈdɪfə-] *n* : indiferencia *f*
indigenous [ɪnˈdɪdʒənəs] *adj* : indígena
indigestion [ˌɪndaɪˈdʒɛstʃən, -dɪ-] *n* : indigestión *f* — **indigestible** [ˌɪndaɪˈdʒɛstəbəl, -dɪ-] *adj* : indigesto
indignation [ˌɪndɪgˈneɪʃən] *n* : indignación *f* — **indignant** [ɪnˈdɪgnənt] *adj* : indignado — **indignity** [ɪnˈdɪgnət̬i] *n, pl* **-ties** : indignidad *f*
indigo [ˈɪndɪˌgoː] *n, pl* **-gos** *or* **-goes** : añil *m*
indirect [ˌɪndəˈrɛkt, -daɪ-] *adj* : indirecto
indiscreet [ˌɪndɪˈskriːt] *adj* : indiscreto — **indiscretion** [ˌɪndɪˈskrɛʃən] *n* : indiscreción *f*
indiscriminate [ˌɪndɪˈskrɪmənət] *adj* : indiscriminado
indispensable [ˌɪndɪˈspɛntsəbəl] *adj* : indispensable, imprescindible
indisputable [ˌɪndɪˈspjuːt̬əbəl, ɪnˈdɪspjʊt̬ə-] *adj* : indiscutible
indistinct [ˌɪndɪˈstɪŋkt] *adj* : indistinto
individual [ˌɪndəˈvɪdʒʊəl] *adj* **1** : individual **2** PARTICULAR : particular — ~ *n* : individuo *m* — **individuality** [ˌɪndəˌvɪdʒʊˈælət̬i] *n, pl* **-ties** : individualidad *f* — **individually** [ˌɪndəˈvɪdʒʊəli, -dʒəli] *adv* : individualmente
indoctrinate [ɪnˈdɑktrəˌneɪt] *vt* **-nated; -nating** : adoctrinar — **indoctrination** [ɪnˌdɑktrəˈneɪʃən] *n* : adoctrinamiento *m*
indoor [ˈɪnˈdor] *adj* **1** : (de) interior **2** ~ **plant** : planta *f* de interior **3** ~ **pool** : piscina *f* cubierta **4** ~ **sports** : deportes *mpl* bajo techo — **indoors** [ˈɪnˈdorz] *adv* : adentro, dentro
induce [ɪnˈduːs, -ˈdjuːs] *vt* **-duced; -ducing 1** : inducir **2** CAUSE : provocar — **inducement** [ɪnˈduːsmənt, -ˈdjuːs-] *n* : incentivo *m*
indulge [ɪnˈdʌldʒ] *v* **-dulged; -dulging** *vt* **1** GRATIFY : satisfacer **2** PAMPER : consentir — *vi* ~ **in** : permitirse — **indulgence** [ɪnˈdʌldʒənts] *n* **1** : indulgencia *f* **2** SATISFYING : satisfacción *f* — **indulgent** [ɪnˈdʌldʒənt] *adj* : indulgente
industry [ˈɪndəstri] *n, pl* **-tries 1** : industria *f* **2** DILIGENCE : diligencia *f* — **industrial** [ɪnˈdʌstriəl] *adj* : industrial — **industrialize** [ɪnˈdʌstriəˌlaɪz] *vt* **-ized; -izing** : industrializar — **industrious** [ɪnˈdʌstriəs] *adj* : diligente, trabajador
inebriated [ɪˈniːbriˌeɪt̬əd] *adj* : ebrio, embriagado
inedible [ɪˈnɛdəbəl] *adj* : no comestible
ineffective [ˌɪnɪˈfɛktɪv] *adj* **1** : ineficaz **2** INCOMPETENT : incompetente — **ineffectual** [ˌɪnɪˈfɛktʃʊəl] *adj* : inútil, ineficaz
inefficient [ˌɪnɪˈfɪʃənt] *adj* **1** : ineficiente **2** INCOMPETENT : incompetente — **inefficiency** [ˌɪnɪˈfɪʃəntsi] *n, pl* **-cies** : ineficiencia *f*
ineligible [ɪˈnɛlədʒəbəl] *adj* : inelegible
inept [ɪˈnɛpt] *adj* **1** : inepto **2** ~ **at** : incapaz para
inequality [ˌɪnɪˈkwɑlət̬i] *n, pl* **-ties** : desigualdad *f*
inert [ɪˈnərt] *adj* : inerte — **inertia** [ɪˈnərʃə] *n* : inercia *f*
inescapable [ˌɪnɪˈskeɪpəbəl] *adj* : ineludible
inevitable [ɪˈnɛvət̬əbəl] *adj* : inevitable — **inevitably** [-bli] *adv* : inevitablemente
inexcusable [ˌɪnɪkˈskjuːzəbəl] *adj* : inexcusable
inexpensive [ˌɪnɪkˈspɛntsɪv] *adj* : barato, económico
inexperienced [ˌɪnɪkˈspɪriəntst] *adj* : inexperto
inexplicable [ˌɪnɪkˈsplɪkəbəl] *adj* : inexplicable
infallible [ɪnˈfæləbəl] *adj* : infalible
infamous [ˈɪnfəməs] *adj* : infame
infancy [ˈɪnfəntsi] *n, pl* **-cies** : infancia *f* — **infant** [ˈɪnfənt] *n* : bebé *m*; niño *m*, -ña *f* — **infantile** [ˈɪnfənˌtaɪl, -təl, -ˌtiːl] *adj* : infantil
infantry [ˈɪnfəntri] *n, pl* **-tries** : infantería *f*
infatuated [ɪnˈfætʃʊˌeɪt̬əd] *adj* **be** ~ **with** : estar encaprichado con — **infatuation** [ɪnˌfætʃʊˈeɪʃən] *n* : encaprichamiento *m*
infect [ɪnˈfɛkt] *vt* : infectar — **infection** [ɪnˈfɛkʃən] *n* : infección *f* — **infectious** [ɪnˈfɛkʃəs] *adj* : contagioso
infer [ɪnˈfər] *vt* **inferred; inferring** : deducir, inferir — **inference** [ˈɪnfərənts] *n* : deducción *f*
inferior [ɪnˈfɪriər] *adj* : inferior — ~ *n* : inferior *mf* — **inferiority** [ɪnˌfɪriˈɔrət̬i] *n, pl* **-ties** : inferioridad *f*
infernal [ɪnˈfərnəl] *adj* : infernal — **inferno** [ɪnˈfərˌnoː] *n, pl* **-nos** : infierno *m*
infertile [ɪnˈfərt̬əl, -ˌtaɪl] *adj* : estéril — **infertility** [ˌɪnfərˈtɪlət̬i] *n* : esterilidad *f*
infest [ɪnˈfɛst] *vt* : infestar
infidelity [ˌɪnfəˈdɛlət̬i, -faɪ-] *n, pl* **-ties** : infidelidad *f*
infiltrate [ɪnˈfɪlˌtreɪt, ˈɪnfɪl-] *v* **-trated; -trating** *vt* : infiltrar — *vi* : infiltrarse
infinite [ˈɪnfənət] *adj* : infinito
infinitive [ɪnˈfɪnət̬ɪv] *n* : infinitivo *m*
infinity [ɪnˈfɪnət̬i] *n, pl* **-ties 1** : infinito *m* **2 an** ~ **of** : una infinidad de
infirm [ɪnˈfərm] *adj* : enfermizo, endeble — **infirmary** [ɪnˈfərməri] *n, pl* **-ries** : enfermería *f* — **infirmity** [ɪnˈfərmət̬i] *n, pl* **-ties 1** FRAILTY : endeblez *f* **2** AILMENT : enfermedad *f*
inflame [ɪnˈfleɪm] *vt* **-flamed; -flaming** : inflamar — **inflammable** [ɪnˈflæməbəl] *adj* : inflamable — **inflammation** [ˌɪnfləˈmeɪʃən] *n* : inflamación *f* — **inflammatory** [ɪnˈflæməˌtori] *adj* : inflamatorio
inflate [ɪnˈfleɪt] *vt* **-flated; -flating** : inflar — **inflation** [ɪnˈfleɪʃən] *n* : inflación *f* — **inflationary** [ɪnˈfleɪʃəˌnɛri] *adj* : inflacionario, inflacionista
inflexible [ɪnˈflɛksɪbəl] *adj* : inflexible
inflict [ɪnˈflɪkt] *vt* : infligir
influence [ˈɪnˌfluːənts, ɪnˈfluːənts] *n* **1** : influencia *f* **2 under the** ~ : embriagado — ~ *vt* **-enced; -encing** : influir en, influenciar — **influential** [ˌɪnfluˈɛntʃəl] *adj* : influyente
influenza [ˌɪnfluˈɛnzə] *n* : gripe *f*, influenza *f*
influx [ˈɪnˌflʌks] *n* : afluencia *f*
inform [ɪnˈfɔrm] *vt* **1** : informar **2 keep me** ~**ed** : manténme al corriente — *vi* ~ **on** : delatar, denunciar
informal [ɪnˈfɔrməl] *adj* **1** : informal **2** : familiar (dícese del lenguaje) — **informality** [ˌɪnfɔrˈmælət̬i, -fər-] *n, pl* **-ties** : falta *f* de ceremonia — **informally** [ɪnˈfɔrməli] *adv* : de manera informal
information [ˌɪnfərˈmeɪʃən] *n* : información *f* — **informative** [ɪnˈfɔrmət̬ɪv] *adj* : informativo — **informer** [ɪnˈfɔrmər] *n* : informante *mf*
infrared [ˌɪnfrəˈrɛd] *adj* : infrarrojo
infrastructure [ˈɪnfrəˌstrʌktʃər] *n* : infraestructura *f*
infrequent [ɪnˈfriːkwənt] *adj* : infrequente — **infrequently** [ɪnˈfriːkwəntli] *adv* : raramente
infringe [ɪnˈfrɪndʒ] *v* **-fringed; -fringing** *vt* : infringir — *vi* ~ **on** : violar — **infringement** [ɪnˈfrɪndʒmənt] *n* : violación *f*
infuriate [ɪnˈfjʊriˌeɪt] *vt* **-ated; -ating** : enfurecer, poner furioso — **infuriating** [ɪnˈfjʊriˌeɪt̬ɪŋ] *adj* : exasperante
infuse [ɪnˈfjuːz] *vt* **-fused; -fusing** : infundir — **infusion** [ɪnˈfjuːʒən] *n* : infusión *f*
ingenious [ɪnˈdʒiːnjəs] *adj* : ingenioso — **ingenuity** [ˌɪndʒəˈnuːət̬i, -ˈnjuː-] *n, pl* **-ities** : ingenio
ingenuous [ɪnˈdʒɛnjʊəs] *adj* : ingenuo
ingest [ɪnˈdʒɛst] *vt* : ingerir
ingot [ˈɪŋgət] *n* : lingote *m*
ingrained [ɪnˈgreɪnd] *adj* : arraigado
ingratiate [ɪnˈgreɪʃiˌeɪt] *vt* **-ated; -ating** ~ **oneself with** : congraciarse con
ingratitude [ɪnˈgræt̬əˌtuːd, -ˌtjuːd] *n* : ingratitud *f*
ingredient [ɪnˈgriːdiənt] *n* : ingrediente *m*
ingrown [ˈɪnˌgroːn] *adj* ~ **nail** : uña *f* encarnada
inhabit [ɪnˈhæbət] *vt* : habitar — **inhabitant** [ɪnˈhæbət̬ənt] *n* : habitante *mf*
inhale [ɪnˈheɪl] *v* **-haled; -haling** *vt* : inhalar, aspirar — *vi* : inspirar
inherent [ɪnˈhɪrənt, -ˈhɛr-] *adj* : inherente — **inherently** [ɪnˈhɪrəntli, -ˈhɛr-] *adv* : intrínsecamente

inherit [ɪnˈhɛrət] *vt* : heredar — **inheritance** [ɪnˈhɛrət̬ənts] *n* : herencia *f*
inhibit [ɪnˈhɪbət] *vt* IMPEDE : inhibir — **inhibition** [ˌɪnhəˈbɪʃən, ˌɪnə-] *n* : inhibición *f*
inhuman [ɪnˈhjuːmən, -juː-] *adj* : inhumano — **inhumane** [ˌɪnhjuˈmeɪn, -ju-] *adj* : inhumano — **inhumanity** [ˌɪnhjuˈmænət̬i, -ju-] *n, pl* **-ties** : inhumanidad *f*
initial [ɪˈnɪʃəl] *adj* : inicial — *n* : inicial *f* — *vt* **-tialed** *or* **-tialled; -tialing** *or* **-tialling** : poner las iniciales a
initiate [ɪˈnɪʃiˌeɪt] *vt* **-ated; -ating 1** BEGIN : iniciar **2 ~ s.o. into sth** : iniciar a algn en algo — **initiation** [ɪˌnɪʃiˈeɪʃən] *n* : iniciación *f* — **initiative** [ɪˈnɪʃət̬ɪv] *n* : iniciativa *f*
inject [ɪnˈdʒɛkt] *vt* : inyectar — **injection** [ɪnˈdʒɛkʃən] *n* : inyección *f*
injure [ˈɪndʒər] *vt* **-jured; -juring 1** : herir **2 ~ oneself** : hacerse daño — **injurious** [ɪnˈdʒʊriəs] *adj* : perjudicial — **injury** [ˈɪndʒəri] *n, pl* **-ries 1** : herida *f* **2** HARM : perjuicio *m*
injustice [ɪnˈdʒʌstəs] *n* : injusticia *f*
ink [ˈɪŋk] *n* : tinta *f* — **inkwell** [ˈɪŋkˌwɛl] *n* : tintero *m*
inland [ˈɪnˌlænd, -lənd] *adj* : interior — **~** *adv* : hacia el interior, tierra adentro
in–laws [ˈɪnˌlɔz] *npl* : suegros *mpl*
inlet [ˈɪnˌlɛt, -lət] *n* : ensenada *f*, cala *f*
inmate [ˈɪnˌmeɪt] *n* **1** PATIENT : paciente *mf* **2** PRISONER : preso *m*, -sa *f*
inn [ˈɪn] *n* : posada *f*, hostería *f*
innards [ˈɪnərdz] *npl* : entrañas *fpl*, tripas *fpl fam*
innate [ɪˈneɪt] *adj* : innato
inner [ˈɪnər] *adj* : interior, interno — **innermost** [ˈɪnərˌmoːst] *adj* : más íntimo, más profundo
inning [ˈɪnɪŋ] *n* : entrada *f*
innocent [ˈɪnəsənt] *adj* : inocente — **~** *n* : inocente *mf* — **innocence** [ˈɪnəsənts] *n* : inocencia *f*
innocuous [ɪˈnɑkjəwəs] *adj* : inocuo
innovate [ˈɪnəˌveɪt] *vi* **-vated; -vating** : innovar — **innovation** [ˌɪnəˈveɪʃən] *n* : innovación *f* — **innovative** [ˈɪnəˌveɪt̬ɪv] *adj* : innovador — **innovator** [ˈɪnəˌveɪt̬ər] *n* : innovador *m*, -dora *f*
innuendo [ˌɪnjʊˈɛndo] *n, pl* **-dos** *or* **-does** : insinuación *f*, indirecta *f*
innumerable [ɪˈnuːmərəbəl, -ˈnjuː-] *adj* : innumerable
inoculate [ɪˈnɑkjəˌleɪt] *vt* **-lated; -lating** : inocular — **inoculation** [ɪˌnɑkjəˈleɪʃən] *n* : inoculación *f*
inoffensive [ˌɪnəˈfɛntsɪv] *adj* : inofensivo
inpatient [ˈɪnˌpeɪʃənt] *n* : paciente *mf* hospitalizado
input [ˈɪnˌpʊt] *n* **1** : contribución *f* **2** : entrada *f* (de datos) — **~** *vt* **-putted** *or* **-put; -putting** : entrar (datos, etc.)
inquire [ɪnˈkwaɪr] *v* **-quired; -quiring** *vt* : preguntar — *vi* **1 ~ about** : informarse sobre **2 ~ into** : investigar — **inquiry** [ˈɪnˌkwaɪri, ɪnˈkwaɪri; ˈɪnkwəri, ˈɪŋ-] *n, pl* **-ries 1** QUESTION : pregunta *f* **2** INVESTIGATION : investigación *f* — **inquisition** [ˌɪnkwəˈzɪʃən, ˌɪŋ-] *n* : inquisición *f* — **inquisitive** [ɪnˈkwɪzət̬ɪv] *adj* : curioso
insane [ɪnˈseɪn] *adj* : loco — **insanity** [ɪnˈsænət̬i] *n, pl* **-ties** : locura *f*
insatiable [ɪnˈseɪʃəbəl] *adj* : insaciable
inscribe [ɪnˈskraɪb] *vt* **-scribed; -scribing** : inscribir — **inscription** [ɪnˈskrɪpʃən] *n* : inscripción *f*
inscrutable [ɪnˈskruːt̬əbəl] *adj* : inescrutable
insect [ˈɪnˌsɛkt] *n* : insecto *m* — **insecticide** [ɪnˈsɛktəˌsaɪd] *n* : insecticida *m*
insecure [ˌɪnsɪˈkjʊr] *adj* : inseguro, poco seguro — **insecurity** [ˌɪnsɪˈkjʊrət̬i] *n, pl* **-ties** : inseguridad *f*
insensitive [ɪnˈsɛntsət̬ɪv] *adj* : insensible — **insensitivity** [ɪnˌsɛntsəˈtɪvət̬i] *n, pl* **-ties** : insensibilidad *f*
inseparable [ɪnˈsɛpərəbəl] *adj* : inseparable
insert [ɪnˈsərt] *vt* : insertar (texto), introducir (una moneda, etc.)
inside [ɪnˈsaɪd, ˈɪnˌsaɪd] *n* **1** : interior *m* **2 ~ out** : al revés — *adv* : dentro, adentro — **~** *adj* : interior — **~** *prep* **1** *or* **~ of** : dentro de **2 ~ an hour** : en menos de una hora
insidious [ɪnˈsɪdiəs] *adj* : insidioso
insight [ˈɪnˌsaɪt] *n* : perspicacia *f*
insignia [ɪnˈsɪgniə] *or* **insigne** [-ˌniː] *n, pl* **-nia** *or* **-nias** : insignia *f*, enseña *f*
insignificant [ˌɪnsɪgˈnɪfɪkənt] *adj* : insignificante
insincere [ˌɪnsɪnˈsɪr] *adj* : insincero
insinuate [ɪnˈsɪnjʊˌeɪt] *vt* **-ated; -ating** : insinuar — **insinuation** [ɪnˌsɪnjʊˈeɪʃən] *n* : insinuación *f*
insipid [ɪnˈsɪpəd] *adj* : insípido
insist [ɪnˈsɪst] *v* : insistir — **insistent** [ɪnˈsɪstənt] *adj* : insistente
insofar as [ˌɪnsoˈfɑræz] *conj* : en la medida en que
insole [ˈɪnˌsoːl] *n* : plantilla *f*
insolent [ˈɪntsələnt] *adj* : insolente — **insolence** [ˈɪntsələnts] *n* : insolencia *f*
insolvent [ɪnˈsɑlvənt] *adj* : insolvente
insomnia [ɪnˈsɑmniə] *n* : insomnio *m*
inspect [ɪnˈspɛkt] *vt* : inspeccionar, revisar — **inspection** [ɪnˈspɛkʃən] *n* : inspección *f* — **inspector** [ɪnˈspɛktər] *n* : inspector *m*, -tora *f*
inspire [ɪnˈspaɪr] *vt* **-spired; -spiring** : inspirar — **inspiration** [ˌɪntspəˈreɪʃən] *n* : inspiración *f* — **inspirational** [ˌɪntspəˈreɪʃənəl] *adj* : inspirador
instability [ˌɪntstəˈbɪlət̬i] *n, pl* **-ties** : inestabilidad *f*
install [ɪnˈstɔl] *vt* **-stalled; -stalling** : instalar — **installation** [ˌɪntstəˈleɪʃən] *n* : instalación *f* — **installment** [ɪnˈstɔlmənt] *n* **1** PAYMENT : plazo *m*, cuota *f* **2** : entrega *f* (de una publicación o telenovela)
instance [ˈɪntstənts] *n* **1** : ejemplo *m* **2 for ~** : por ejemplo **3 in this ~** : en este caso
instant [ˈɪntstənt] *n* : instante *m* — **~** *adj* **1** IMMEDIATE : inmediato **2 ~ coffee** : café *m* instantáneo — **instantaneous** [ˌɪntstənˈteɪniəs] *adj* : instantáneo — **instantly** [ˈɪntstəntli] *adv* : al instante, instantáneamente
instead [ɪnˈstɛd] *adv* **1** : en cambio **2 I went ~** : fui en su lugar — **instead of** *prep* : en vez de, en lugar de
instep [ˈɪnˌstɛp] *n* : empeine *m*
instigate [ˈɪntstəˌgeɪt] *vt* **-gated; -gating** : instigar a — **instigation** [ˌɪntstəˈgeɪʃən] *n* : instigación *f* — **instigator** [ˈɪntstəˌgeɪt̬ər] *n* : instigador *m*, -dora *f*
instill [ɪnˈstɪl] *or Brit* **instil** *vt* **-stilled; -stilling** : inculcar, infundir
instinct [ˈɪnˌstɪŋkt] *n* : instinto *m* — **instinctive** [ɪnˈstɪŋktɪv] *or* **instinctual** [ɪnˈstɪŋktʃʊəl] *adj* : instintivo
institute [ˈɪntstəˌtuːt, -ˌtjuːt] *vt* **-tuted; -tuting 1** : instituir **2** INITIATE : iniciar — **~** *n* : instituto *m* — **institution** [ˌɪntstəˈtuːʃən, -ˈtjuː-] *n* : institución *f*
instruct [ɪnˈstrʌkt] *vt* **1** : instruir **2** COMMAND : mandar — **instruction** [ɪnˈstrʌkʃən] *n* : instrucción *f* — **instructor** [ɪnˈstrʌktər] *n* : instructor *m*, -tora *f*
instrument [ˈɪntstrəmənt] *n* : instrumento *m* — **instrumental** [ˌɪntstrəˈmɛntəl] *adj* **1** : instrumental **2 be ~ in** : jugar un papel fundamental en
insubordinate [ˌɪnsəˈbɔrdənət] *adj* : insubordinado — **insubordination** [ˌɪnsəˌbɔrdənˈeɪʃən] *n* : insubordinación *f*
insufferable [ɪnˈsʌfərəbəl] *adj* : insoportable
insufficient [ˌɪnsəˈfɪʃənt] *adj* : insuficiente
insular [ˈɪntsʊlər, -sjʊ-] *adj* **1** : insular **2** NARROW-MINDED : estrecho de miras
insulate [ˈɪntsəˌleɪt] *vt* **-lated; -lating** : aislar — **insulation** [ˌɪntsəˈleɪʃən] *n* : aislamiento *m*
insulin [ˈɪntsələn] *n* : insulina *f*
insult [ɪnˈsʌlt] *vt* : insultar — **~** [ˈɪnˌsʌlt] *n* : insulto *m* — **insulting** [ɪnˈsʌltɪŋ] *adj* : insultante, ofensivo
insure [ɪnˈʃʊr] *vt* **-sured; -suring** : asegurar — **insurance** [ɪnˈʃʊrənts, ˈɪnˌʃʊr-] *n* : seguro *m*
insurmountable [ˌɪnsərˈmaʊntəbəl] *adj* : insuperable
intact [ɪnˈtækt] *adj* : intacto
intake [ˈɪnˌteɪk] *n* : consumo *m* (de alimentos), entrada *f* (de aire, etc.)
intangible [ɪnˈtændʒəbəl] *adj* : intangible
integral [ˈɪntɪgrəl] *adj* : integral
integrate [ˈɪntəˌgreɪt] *v* **-grated; -grating** *vt* : integrar — *vi* : integrarse
integrity [ɪnˈtɛgrət̬i] *n* : integridad *f*
intellect [ˈɪntəlˌɛkt] *n* : intelecto *m* — **intellectual** [ˌɪntəˈlɛktʃʊəl] *adj* : intelectual — **~** *n* : intelectual *mf* — **intelligence** [ɪnˈtɛlədʒənts] *n* : inteligencia *f* — **intelligent** [ɪnˈtɛlədʒənt] *adj* : inteligente — **intelligible** [ɪnˈtɛlədʒəbəl] *adj* : inteligible
intend [ɪnˈtɛnd] *vt* **1 be ~ed for** : ser para **2 ~ to do** : pensar hacer, tener la intención de hacer — **intended** [ɪnˈtɛndəd] *adj* : intencionado, deliberado
intense [ɪnˈtɛnts] *adj* : intenso — **intensely** [ɪnˈtɛntsli] *adv* : sumamente, profundamente — **intensify** [ɪnˈtɛntsəˌfaɪ] *v* **-fied; -fying** *vt* : intensificar — *vi* : intensificarse — **intensity** [ɪnˈtɛntsət̬i] *n, pl* **-ties** : intensidad *f* — **intensive** [ɪnˈtɛntsɪv] *adj* : intensivo
intent [ɪnˈtɛnt] *n* : intención *f* — **~** *adj* **1** : atento, concentrado **2 ~ on doing** : resuelto a hacer — **intention** [ɪnˈtɛntʃən] *n* : intención *f* — **intentional** [ɪnˈtɛntʃənəl] *adj* : intencional, deliberado — **intently** [ɪnˈtɛntli] *adv* : atentamente, fijamente
interact [ˌɪntərˈækt] *vi* **1** : interactuar **2 ~ with** : relacionarse con — **interaction** [ˌɪntərˈækʃən] *n* : interacción *f* — **interactive** [ˌɪntərˈæktɪv] *adj* : interactivo
intercede [ˌɪntərˈsiːd] *vi* **-ceded; -ceding** : interceder
intercept [ˌɪntərˈsɛpt] *vt* : interceptar
interchange [ˌɪntərˈtʃeɪndʒ] *vt* **-changed; -changing** : intercambiar — **~** [ˈɪntərˌtʃeɪndʒ] *n* **1** : intercambio *m* **2** JUNCTION : enlace *m* — **interchangeable** [ˌɪntərˈtʃeɪndʒəbəl] *adj* : intercambiable
intercourse [ˈɪntərˌkors] *n* : relaciones *fpl* (sexuales)
interest [ˈɪntrəst, -təˌrɛst] *n* : interés *m* — **~** *vt* : interesar — **interested** [-əd] *adj* : interesado — **interesting** [ˈɪntrəstɪŋ, -təˌrɛstɪŋ] *adj* : interesante
interface [ˈɪntərˌfeɪs] *n* : interfaz *mf* (de una computadora)
interfere [ˌɪntərˈfɪr] *vi* **-fered; -fering 1 ~ in** : entrometerse en, interferir en **2 ~ with** DISRUPT : afectar (una actividad, etc.) — **interference** [ˌɪntərˈfɪrənts] *n* **1** : interferencia *f* **2** : intromisión *f* (en el radio, etc.)
interim [ˈɪntərəm] *n* **1** : interín *m* **2 in the ~** : mientras tanto — **~** *adj* : interino, provisional
interior [ɪnˈtɪriər] *adj* : interior — **~** *n* : interior *m*
interjection [ˌɪntərˈdʒɛkʃən] *n* : interjección *f*
interlock [ˌɪntərˈlɑk] *vt* : engranar
interloper [ˌɪntərˈloːpər] *n* : intruso *m*, -sa *f*
interlude [ˈɪntərˌluːd] *n* **1** : intervalo *m* **2** : interludio *m* (en música, etc.)
intermediate [ˌɪntərˈmiːdiət] *adj* : intermedio — **intermediary** [ˌɪntərˈmiːdiˌɛri] *n, pl* **-aries** : intermediario *m*, -ria *f*
interminable [ɪnˈtərmənəbəl] *adj* : interminable
intermission [ˌɪntərˈmɪʃən] *n* : intervalo *m*, intermedio *m*
intermittent [ˌɪntərˈmɪtənt] *adj* : intermitente
intern[1] [ˈɪnˌtərn, ɪnˈtərn] *vt* : confinar
intern[2] [ˈɪnˌtərn] *vi* : hacer las prácticas — **~** *n* : interno *m*, -na *f*
internal [ɪnˈtərnəl] *adj* : interno
international [ˌɪntərˈnæʃənəl] *adj* : internacional
interpret [ɪnˈtərprət] *vt* : interpretar — **interpretation** [ɪnˌtərprəˈteɪʃən] *n* : interpretación *f* — **interpreter** [ɪnˈtərprət̬ər] *n* : intérprete *mf*
interrogate [ɪnˈtɛrəˌgeɪt] *vt* **-gated; -gating** : interrogar — **interrogation** [ɪnˌtɛrəˈgeɪʃən] *n* QUESTIONING : interrogatorio *m* — **interrogative** [ˌɪntəˈrɑgət̬ɪv] *adj* : interrogativo
interrupt [ˌɪntəˈrʌpt] *v* : interrumpir — **interruption** [ˌɪntəˈrʌpʃən] *n* : interrupción *f*
intersect [ˌɪntərˈsɛkt] *vt* : cruzar (dícese de calles), cortar (dícese de líneas) — *vi* : cruzarse, cortarse — **intersection** [ˌɪntərˈsɛkʃən] *n* : cruce *m*, intersección *f*
intersperse [ˌɪntərˈspərs] *vt* **-spersed; -spersing** : intercalar
interstate [ˌɪntərˈsteɪt] *n or* **~ highway** : carretera *f* interestatal
intertwine [ˌɪntərˈtwaɪn] *vi* **-twined; -twining** : entrelazarse
interval [ˈɪntərvəl] *n* : intervalo *m*
intervene [ˌɪntərˈviːn] *vi* **-vened; -vening 1** : intervenir **2** ELAPSE : transcurrir, pasar — **intervention** [ˌɪntərˈvɛntʃən] *n* : intervención *f*
interview [ˈɪntərˌvjuː] *n* : entrevista *f* — **~** *vt* : entrevistar — **interviewer** [ˈɪntərˌvjuːər] *n* : entrevistador *m*, -dora *f*
intestine [ɪnˈtɛstən] *n* : intestino *m* — **intestinal** [ɪnˈtɛstənəl] *adj* : intestinal
intimate[1] [ˈɪntəˌmeɪt] *vt* **-mated; -mating** : insinuar, dar a entender
intimate[2] [ˈɪntəmət] *adj* : íntimo — **intimacy** [ˈɪntəməsi] *n, pl* **-cies** : intimidad *f*
intimidate [ɪnˈtɪməˌdeɪt] *vt* **-dated; -dating** : intimidar — **intimidation** [ɪnˌtɪməˈdeɪʃən] *n* : intimidación *f*
into [ˈɪnˌtuː] *prep* **1** : en, a **2 bump ~** : darse contra **3** (*used in mathematics*) **3 ~ 12** : 12 dividido por 3
intolerable [ɪnˈtɑlərəbəl] *adj* : intolerable — **intolerance** [ɪnˈtɑlərənts] *n* : intolerancia *f* — **intolerant** [ɪnˈtɑlərənt] *adj* : intolerante
intoxicate [ɪnˈtɑksəˌkeɪt] *vt* **-cated; -cating** : embriagar — **intoxicated** [ɪnˈtɑksəˌkeɪt̬əd] *adj* **1** : embriagado **2 ~ with** : ebrio de
intransitive [ɪnˈtræntsət̬ɪv, -ˈtrænzə-] *adj* : intransitivo
intravenous [ˌɪntrəˈviːnəs] *adj* : intravenoso
intrepid [ɪnˈtrɛpəd] *adj* : intrépido
intricate [ˈɪntrɪkət] *adj* : complicado, intrincado — **intricacy** [ˈɪntrɪkəsi] *n, pl* **-cies** : complejidad *f*
intrigue [ˈɪnˌtriːg, ɪnˈtriːg] *n* : intriga *f* — **~** [ɪnˈtriːg] *v* **-trigued; -triguing** : intrigar — **intriguing** [ɪnˈtriːgɪŋ] *adj* : intrigante
intrinsic [ɪnˈtrɪnzɪk, -ˈtrɪntsɪk] *adj* : intrínseco
introduce [ˌɪntrəˈduːs, -ˈdjuːs] *vt* **-duced; -ducing 1** : introducir **2** : presentar (a una persona) — **introduction** [ˌɪntrəˈdʌkʃən] *n* **1** : introducción *f* **2** : presentación *f* (de una persona) — **introductory** [ˌɪntrəˈdʌktəri] *adj* : introductorio
introvert [ˈɪntrəˌvərt] *n* : introvertido *m*, -da *f* — **introverted** [ˈɪntrəˌvərt̬əd] *adj* : introvertido
intrude [ɪnˈtruːd] *vi* **-truded; -truding 1** : entrometerse **2 ~ on s.o.** : molestar a algn — **intruder** [ɪnˈtruːdər] *n* : intruso *m*, -sa *f* — **intrusion** [ɪnˈtruːʒən] *n* : intrusión *f* — **intrusive** [ɪnˈtruːsɪv] *adj* : intruso
intuition [ˌɪntʊˈɪʃən, -tjʊ-] *n* : intuición *f* — **intuitive** [ɪnˈtuːət̬ɪv, -ˈtjuː-] *adj* : intuitivo
inundate [ˈɪnənˌdeɪt] *vt* **-dated; -dating** : inundar
invade [ɪnˈveɪd] *vt* **-vaded; -vading** : invadir
invalid[1] [ɪnˈvæləd] *adj* : inválido
invalid[2] [ˈɪnvələd] *n* : inválido *m*, -da *f*
invaluable [ɪnˈvæljəbəl, -ˈvæljʊə-] *adj* : inestimable, invalorable *Lat*
invariable [ɪnˈværiəbəl] *adj* : invariable
invasion [ɪnˈveɪʒən] *n* : invasión *f*
invent [ɪnˈvɛnt] *vt* : inventar — **invention** [ɪnˈvɛntʃən] *n* : invención *f* — **inventive** [ɪnˈvɛntɪv] *adj* : inventivo — **inventor** [ɪnˈvɛntər] *n* : inventor *m*, -tora *f*
inventory [ˈɪnvənˌtori] *n, pl* **-ries** : inventario *m*
invert [ɪnˈvərt] *vt* : invertir
invertebrate [ɪnˈvərt̬əbrət, -ˌbreɪt] *adj* : invertebrado — **~** *n* : invertebrado *m*
invest [ɪnˈvɛst] *vt* : invertir
investigate [ɪnˈvɛstəˌgeɪt] *v* **-gated; -gating** : investigar — **investigation** [ɪnˌvɛstəˈgeɪʃən] *n* : investigación *f* — **investigator** [ɪnˈvɛstəˌgeɪt̬ər] *n* : investigador *m*, -dora *f*
investment [ɪnˈvɛstmənt] *n* : inversión *f* — **investor** [ɪnˈvɛstər] *n* : inversor *m*, -sora *f*
inveterate [ɪnˈvɛt̬ərət] *adj* : inveterado
invigorating [ɪnˈvɪgəˌreɪt̬ɪŋ] *adj* : vigorizante
invincible [ɪnˈvɪntsəbəl] *adj* : invencible
invisible [ɪnˈvɪzəbəl] *adj* : invisible
invitation [ˌɪnvəˈteɪʃən] *n* : invitación *f* — **invite** [ɪnˈvaɪt] *vt* **-vited; -viting 1** : invitar **2** SEEK : buscar (problemas, etc.) — **inviting** [ɪnˈvaɪt̬ɪŋ] *adj* : atrayente
invoice [ˈɪnˌvɔɪs] *n* : factura *f*
invoke [ɪnˈvoːk] *vt* **-voked; -voking** : invocar
involuntary [ɪnˈvɑlənˌtɛri] *adj* : involuntario
involve [ɪnˈvɑlv] *vt* **-volved; -volving 1** CONCERN : concernir, afectar **2** ENTAIL : suponer — **involved** [ɪnˈvɑlvd] *adj* **1** COMPLEX : complicado **2** CONCERNED : afectado — **involvement** [ɪnˈvɑlvmənt] *n* : participación *f*
invulnerable [ɪnˈvʌlnərəbəl] *adj* : invulnerable
inward [ˈɪnwərd] *adj* INNER : interior, interno — **~** *or* **inwards** [-wərdz] *adv* : hacia adentro, hacia el interior
iodine [ˈaɪəˌdaɪn, -dən] *n* : yodo *m*, tintura *f* de yodo
ion [ˈaɪən, ˈaɪˌɑn] *n* : ion *m*
iota [aɪˈoːt̬ə] *n* : pizca *f*, ápice *m*
IOU [ˌaɪˌoˈjuː] *n* : pagaré *m*, vale *m*
Iranian [ɪˈreɪniən, -ˈræ-, -ˈrɑ-; aɪ-] *adj* : iraní
Iraqi [ɪˈrɑki, -ˈræk-] *adj* : iraquí
ire [ˈaɪr] *n* : ira *f* — **irate** [aɪˈreɪt] *adj* : furioso
iris [ˈaɪrəs] *n, pl* **irises** *or* **irides** [ˈaɪrəˌdiːz, ˈɪr-] **1** : iris *m* (del ojo) **2** : lirio *m* (planta)
Irish [ˈaɪrɪʃ] *adj* : irlandés
irksome [ˈərksəm] *adj* : irritante, fastidioso
iron [ˈaɪərn] *n* **1** : hierro *m*, fierro *m Lat* (metal) **2** : plancha *f* (para la ropa) — **~** *v* : planchar
ironic [aɪˈrɑnɪk] *or* **ironical** [-nɪkəl] *adj* : irónico
ironing board *n* : tabla *f* (de planchar)
irony [ˈaɪrəni] *n, pl* **-nies** : ironía *f*
irrational [ɪˈræʃənəl] *adj* : irracional
irreconcilable [ɪˌrɛkənˈsaɪləbəl] *adj* : irreconciliable
irrefutable [ˌɪrɪˈfjuːt̬əbəl, ɪˈrɛfjə-] *adj* : irrefutable
irregular [ɪˈrɛgjələr] *adj* : irregular — **irregularity** [ɪˌrɛgjəˈlærət̬i] *n, pl* **-ties** : irregularidad *f*
irrelevant [ɪˈrɛləvənt] *adj* : irrelevante
irreparable [ɪˈrɛpərəbəl] *adj* : irreparable
irreplaceable [ˌɪrɪˈpleɪsəbəl] *adj* : irreemplazable
irresistible [ˌɪrɪˈzɪstəbəl] *adj* : irresistible
irresolute [ɪˈrɛzəˌluːt] *adj* : irresoluto
irrespective of [ˌɪrɪˈspɛktɪvəv] *prep* : sin tener en cuenta
irresponsible [ˌɪrɪˈspɑntsəbəl] *adj* : irresponsable — **irresponsibility** [ˌɪrɪˌspɑntsəˈbɪlət̬i] *n, pl* **-ties** : irresponsabilidad *f*
irreverent [ɪˈrɛvərənt] *adj* : irreverente
irreversible [ˌɪrɪˈvərsəbəl] *adj* : irreversible, irrevocable
irrigate [ˈɪrəˌgeɪt] *vt* **-gated; -gating** : irrigar, regar — **irrigation** [ˌɪrəˈgeɪʃən] *n* : irrigación *f*, riego *m*
irritate [ˈɪrəˌteɪt] *vt* **-tated; -tating** : irritar — **irritable** [ˈɪrət̬əbəl] *adj* : irritable — **irritably** [ˈɪrət̬əbli] *adv* : con irritación — **irritating** [ˈɪrəˌteɪt̬ɪŋ] *adj* : irritante — **irritation** [ˌɪrəˈteɪʃən] *n* : irritación *f*
is → **be**
Islam [ɪsˈlɑm, ɪz-, -ˈlæm; ˈɪsˌlɑm, ˈɪz-, -ˌlæm] *n* : el Islam — **Islamic** [ɪsˈlɑmɪk, ɪz-, -ˈlæ-] *adj* : islámico
island [ˈaɪlənd] *n* : isla *f* — **isle** [ˈaɪl] *n* : isla *f*
isolate [ˈaɪsəˌleɪt] *vt* **-lated; -lating** : aislar — **isolation** [ˌaɪsəˈleɪʃən] *n* : aislamiento *m*
Israeli [ɪzˈreɪli] *adj* : israelí
issue [ˈɪˌʃuː] *n* **1** MATTER : asunto *m*, cuestión *f* **2** : número *m* (de una revista, etc.) **3 make an ~ of** : insistir demasiado sobre **4 take ~ with** : disentir de — **~** *v* **-sued; -suing** *vi* **~ from** : surgir de — *vt* **1** : emitir (sellos, etc.), distribuir (provisiones, etc.) **2** PUBLISH : publicar
isthmus [ˈɪsməs] *n* : istmo *m*
it [ˈɪt] *pron* **1** (*as subject*) : él, ella **2** (*as indirect object*) : le, se **3** (*as direct object*) : lo, la **4** (*as object of a preposition*) : él, ella **5 it's raining** : está lloviendo **6 it's 8 o'clock** : son las ocho **7 it's hot out** : hace calor **8 ~ is necessary** : es necesario **9 who is ~?** : ¿quién es? **10 it's me** : soy yo
Italian [ɪˈtæliən, aɪ-] *adj* : italiano — **~** *n* : italiano *m* (idioma)

italics [ɪ'tælɪks, aɪ-] *n* : cursiva *f*
itch ['ɪtʃ] *vi* **1** : picar **2 be ~ing to** : morirse por — **~** *n* : picazón *f* — **itchy** ['ɪtʃi] *adj* **itchier; -est** : que pica
it'd ['ɪt̬əd] (*contraction of* **it had** *or* **it would**) → **have, would**
item ['aɪt̬əm] *n* **1** : artículo *m* **2** : punto *m* (en una agenda) **3 ~ of clothing** : prenda *f* de vestir **4 news ~** : noticia *f* — **itemize** ['aɪt̬ə,maɪz] *vt* **-ized; -izing** : detallar, enumerar
itinerant [aɪ'tɪnərənt] *adj* : ambulante
itinerary [aɪ'tɪnə,rɛri] *n, pl* **-aries** : itinerario *m*
it'll ['ɪt̬əl] (*contraction of* **it shall** *or* **it will**) → **shall, will**
its ['ɪts] *adj* : su, sus
it's ['ɪts] (*contraction of* **it is** *or* **it has**) → **be, have**
itself [ɪt'sɛlf] *pron* **1** (*used reflexively*) : se **2** (*used for emphasis*) : (él) mismo, (ella) misma, sí (mismo) **3 by ~** : solo
I've ['aɪv] (*contraction of* **I have**) → **have**
ivory ['aɪvəri] *n, pl* **-ries** : marfil *m*
ivy ['aɪvi] *n, pl* **ivies** : hiedra *f*

J

j ['dʒeɪ] *n, pl* **j's** *or* **js** ['dʒeɪz] : j *f*, décima letra del alfabeto inglés
jab ['dʒæb] *vt* **jabbed; jabbing 1** PIERCE : pinchar **2** POKE : golpear (con la punta de algo) — **~** *n* **1** PRICK : pinchazo *m* **2** POKE : golpe *m* abrupto
jabber ['dʒæbər] *vi* : farfullar
jack ['dʒæk] *n* **1** : gato *m* (mecanismo) **2** : sota *f* (de naipes) — **~** *vt or* **~ up 1** : levantar (con un gato) **2** INCREASE : subir
jackal ['dʒækəl] *n* : chacal *m*
jackass ['dʒæk,æs] *n* : asno *m*, burro *m*
jacket ['dʒækət] *n* **1** : chaqueta *f* **2** : sobrecubierta *f* (de un libro), carátula *f* (de un disco)
jackhammer ['dʒæk,hæmər] *n* : martillo *m* neumático
jackknife ['dʒæk,naɪf] *n* : navaja *f* — **~** *vi* **-knifed; -knifing** : plegarse (dícese de un camión)
jack–o'–lantern ['dʒækə,læntərn] *n* : linterna *f* hecha de una calabaza
jackpot ['dʒæk,pɑt] *n* : premio *m* gordo
jaded ['dʒeɪdəd] *adj* **1** TIRED : agotado **2** BORED : hastiado
jagged ['dʒægəd] *adj* : dentado
jail ['dʒeɪl] *n* : cárcel *f* — **~** *vt* : encarcelar — **jailer** *or* **jailor** ['dʒeɪlər] *n* : carcelero *m*, -ra *f*
jalapeño [,hɑlə'peɪnjo, ,hæ-, -'pi:no] *n* : jalapeño *m Lat*
jam[1] ['dʒæm] *v* **jammed; jamming** *vt* **1** CRAM : apiñar, embutir **2** BLOCK : atascar, atorar — *vi* : atascarse, atrancarse — **~** *n* **1** *or* **traffic ~** : embotellamiento *m* (de tráfico) **2** FIX : lío *m*, aprieto *m*
jam[2] *n* PRESERVES : mermelada *f*
jangle ['dʒæŋgəl] *v* **-gled; -gling** *vi* : hacer un ruido metálico — *vt* : hacer sonar — **~** *n* : ruido *m* metálico
janitor ['dʒænət̬ər] *n* : portero *m*, -ra *f*; conserje *mf*
January ['dʒænju,ɛri] *n* : enero *m*
Japanese [,dʒæpə'ni:z, -'ni:s] *adj* : japonés — **~** *n* : japonés *m* (idioma)
jar[1] ['dʒɑr] *v* **jarred; jarring** *vi* **1** GRATE : chirriar **2** CLASH : desentonar **3 ~ on** IRRITATE : crispar, enervar (a algn) — *vt* JOLT : sacudir — **~** *n* : sacudida *f*
jar[2] *n* : tarro *m*
jargon ['dʒɑrgən] *n* : jerga *f*
jaundice ['dʒɔndɪs] *n* : ictericia *f*
jaunt ['dʒɔnt] *n* : excursión *f*
jaunty ['dʒɔnti] *adj* **-tier; -est** : garboso, desenvuelto
jaw ['dʒɔ] *n* : mandíbula *f* (de una persona), quijada *f* (de un animal) — **jawbone** ['dʒɔ-,bo:n] *n* : mandíbula *f*, quijada *f*
jay ['dʒeɪ] *n* : arrendajo *m*
jazz ['dʒæz] *n* : jazz *m* — **~** *vt or* **~ up** : animar, alegrar — **jazzy** ['dʒæzi] *adj* **jazzier; -est** FLASHY : llamativo
jealous ['dʒɛləs] *adj* : celoso — **jealousy** ['dʒɛləsi] *n* : celos *mpl*, envidia *f*
jeans ['dʒi:nz] *npl* : jeans *mpl*, vaqueros *mpl*
jeer ['dʒɪr] *vt* **1** BOO : abuchear **2** MOCK : mofarse de — *vi* **~ at** : mofarse de — **~** *n* : mofa *f*
jell ['dʒɛl] *vi* : cuajar
jelly ['dʒɛli] *n, pl* **-lies** : jalea *f* — **jellyfish** ['dʒɛli,fɪʃ] *n* : medusa *f*
jeopardy ['dʒɛpərdi] *n* : peligro *m*, riesgo *m* — **jeopardize** ['dʒɛpər,daɪz] *vt* **-dized; -dizing** : arriesgar, poner en peligro
jerk ['dʒərk] *n* **1** JOLT : sacudida *f* brusca **2** FOOL : idiota *mf* — **~** *vt* : sacudir — *vi* JOLT : dar sacudidas
jersey ['dʒərzi] *n, pl* **-seys** : jersey *m*
jest ['dʒɛst] *n* : broma *f* — **~** *vi* : bromear — **jester** ['dʒɛstər] *n* : bufón *m*
Jesus ['dʒi:zəs, -zəz] *n* : Jesús *m*
jet ['dʒɛt] *n* **1** STREAM : chorro *m* **2** *or* **~ airplane** : avión *m* a reacción, reactor *m* — **jet–propelled** *adj* : a reacción
jettison ['dʒɛt̬əsən] *vt* **1** : echar al mar **2** DISCARD : deshacerse de
jetty ['dʒɛt̬i] *n, pl* **-ties** : desembarcadero *m*, muelle *m*
jewel ['dʒu:əl] *n* **1** : joya *f* **2** GEM : piedra *f* preciosa — **jeweler** *or* **jeweller** ['dʒu:ələr] *n* : joyero *m*, -ra *f* — **jewelry** ['dʒu:əlri] *n* : joyas *fpl*, alhajas *fpl*
Jewish ['dʒu:ɪʃ] *adj* : judío
jibe ['dʒaɪb] *vi* **jibed; jibing** AGREE : concordar
jiffy ['dʒɪfi] *n, pl* **-fies** : santiamén *m*, segundo *m*
jig ['dʒɪg] *n* : giga *f*
jiggle ['dʒɪgəl] *vt* **-gled; -gling** : sacudir, zarandear — **~** *n* : sacudida *f*
jigsaw ['dʒɪg,sɔ] *n* **1** : sierra *f* de vaivén **2** *or* **~ puzzle** : rompecabezas *m*
jilt ['dʒɪlt] *vt* : dejar plantado
jingle ['dʒɪŋgəl] *v* **-gled; -gling** *vi* : tintinear — *vt* : hacer sonar — **~** *n* TINKLE : tintineo *m*
jinx ['dʒɪŋks] *n* CURSE : maldición *f*
jitters ['dʒɪt̬ərz] *npl* **have the ~** : estar nervioso — **jittery** ['dʒɪt̬əri] *adj* : nervioso
job ['dʒɑb] *n* **1** EMPLOYMENT : empleo *m*, trabajo *m* **2** TASK : trabajo *m*
jockey ['dʒɑki] *n, pl* **-eys** : jockey *mf*
jog ['dʒɑg] *v* **jogged; jogging** *vt* **~ s.o.'s memory** : refrescar la memoria a algn — *vi* : hacer footing — **jogging** *n* : footing *m*
join ['dʒɔɪn] *vt* **1** UNITE : unir, juntar **2** MEET : reunirse con **3** : hacerse socio de (una organización, etc.) — *vi* **1** *or* **~ together** : unirse **2** : hacerse socio (de una organización, etc.)
joint ['dʒɔɪnt] *n* **1** : articulación *f* (en anatomía) **2** JUNCTURE : juntura *f*, unión *f* — **~** *adj* : conjunto — **jointly** ['dʒɔɪntli] *adv* : conjuntamente
joke ['dʒo:k] *n* : chiste *m*, broma *f* — **~** *vi* **joked; joking** : bromear — **joker** ['dʒo:kər] *n* **1** : bromista *mf* **2** : comodín *m* (en los naipes)
jolly ['dʒɑli] *adj* **-lier; -est** : alegre, jovial
jolt ['dʒo:lt] *vt* : sacudir — **~** *n* **1** : sacudida *f* brusca **2** SHOCK : golpe *m* (emocional)
jostle ['dʒɑsəl] *v* **-tled; -tling** *vt* : empujar, dar empujones — *vi* : empujarse
jot ['dʒɑt] *vt* **jotted; jotting** *or* **~ down** : anotar, apuntar
journal ['dʒərnəl] *n* **1** DIARY : diario *m* **2** PERIODICAL : revista *f* — **journalism** ['dʒərnəl,ɪzəm] *n* : periodismo *m* — **journalist** ['dʒərnəlɪst] *n* : periodista *mf*
journey ['dʒərni] *n, pl* **-neys** : viaje *m* — **~** *vi* **-neyed; -neying** : viajar
jovial ['dʒo:viəl] *adj* : jovial
joy ['dʒɔɪ] *n* : alegría *f* — **joyful** ['dʒɔɪfəl] *adj* : alegre, feliz — **joyous** ['dʒɔɪəs] *adj* : jubiloso, alegre
jubilant ['dʒu:bələnt] *adj* : jubiloso — **jubilee** ['dʒu:bə,li:] *n* : aniversario *m* especial
Judaism ['dʒu:də,ɪzəm, 'dʒu:di-, 'dʒu:deɪ-] *n* : judaísmo *m*
judge ['dʒʌdʒ] *vt* **judged; judging** : juzgar — **~** *n* : juez *mf* — **judgment** *or* **judgement** ['dʒʌdʒmənt] *n* **1** RULING : fallo *m*, sentencia *f* **2** VIEW : juicio *m*
judicial [dʒʊ'dɪʃəl] *adj* : judicial — **judicious** [dʒʊ'dɪʃəs] *adj* : juicioso
jug ['dʒʌg] *n* : jarra *f*
juggle ['dʒʌgəl] *vi* **-gled; -gling** : hacer juegos malabares — **juggler** ['dʒʌgələr] *n* : malabarista *mf*
jugular vein ['dʒʌgjʊlər-] *n* : vena *f* yugular
juice ['dʒu:s] *n* : jugo *m* — **juicy** ['dʒu:si] *adj* **juicier; -est** : jugoso
jukebox ['dʒu:k,bɑks] *n* : máquina *f* de discos
July [dʒʊ'laɪ] *n* : julio *m*
jumble ['dʒʌmbəl] *vt* **-bled; -bling** : mezclar — **~** *n* : revoltijo *m*
jumbo ['dʒʌm,bo:] *adj* : gigante
jump ['dʒʌmp] *vi* **1** LEAP : saltar **2** START : sobresaltarse **3** RISE : subir de un golpe **4 ~ at** : no dejar escapar (una oportunidad, etc.) — *vt* : saltar — **~** *n* **1** LEAP : salto *m* **2** INCREASE : aumento *m* — **jumper** ['dʒʌmpər] *n* **1** : saltador *m*, -dora *f* (en deportes) **2** : jumper *m* (vestido) — **jumpy** ['dʒʌmpi] *adj* **jumpier; -est** : nervioso
junction ['dʒʌŋkʃən] *n* **1** JOINING : unión *f* **2** : cruce *m* (de calles), empalme *m* (de un ferrocarril) — **juncture** ['dʒʌŋktʃər] *n* : coyuntura *f*
June ['dʒu:n] *n* : junio *m*
jungle ['dʒʌŋgəl] *n* : selva *f*
junior ['dʒu:njər] *adj* **1** YOUNGER : más joven **2** SUBORDINATE : subalterno — **~** *n* **1** : persona *f* de menor edad **2** SUBORDINATE : subalterno *m*, -na *f* **3** : estudiante *mf* de penúltimo año
junk ['dʒʌŋk] *n* : trastos *mpl* (viejos) — **~** *vt* : echar a la basura
junta ['hʊntə, 'dʒʌn-, 'hʌn-] *n* : junta *f* (militar)
jurisdiction [,dʒʊrəs'dɪkʃən] *n* : jurisdicción *f*
jury ['dʒʊri] *n, pl* **-ries** : jurado *m* — **juror** ['dʒʊrər] *n* : jurado *mf*
just ['dʒʌst] *adj* : justo — **~** *adv* **1** BARELY : apenas **2** EXACTLY : exactamente **3** ONLY : sólo, solamente **4 ~ now** : ahora mismo **5 she has ~ left** : acaba de salir **6 we were ~ leaving** : justo íbamos a salir
justice ['dʒʌstɪs] *n* **1** : justicia *f* **2** JUDGE : juez *mf*
justify ['dʒʌstə,faɪ] *vt* **-fied; -fying** : justificar — **justification** [,dʒʌstəfə'keɪʃən] *n* : justificación *f*
jut ['dʒʌt] *vi* **jutted; jutting** *or* **~ out** : sobresalir
juvenile ['dʒu:və,naɪl, -vənəl] *adj* **1** YOUNG : joven **2** CHILDISH : infantil — **~** *n* : menor *mf*
juxtapose ['dʒʌkstə,po:z] *vt* **-posed; -posing** : yuxtaponer

K

k ['keɪ] *n, pl* **k's** *or* **ks** ['keɪz] : k *f*, undécima letra del alfabeto inglés
kaleidoscope [kə'laɪdə,sko:p] *n* : calidoscopio *m*
kangaroo [,kæŋgə'ru:] *n, pl* **-roos** : canguro *m*
karat ['kærət] *n* : quilate *m*
karate [kə'rɑt̬i] *n* : karate *m*
keel ['ki:l] *n* : quilla *f* — **~** *vi or* **~ over** : volcarse (dícese de un barco), desplomarse (dícese de una persona)
keen ['ki:n] *adj* **1** SHARP : afilado **2** PENETRATING : cortante, penetrante **3** ENTHUSIASTIC : entusiasta **4 ~ eyesight** : visión *f* aguda
keep ['ki:p] *v* **kept** ['kɛpt]; **keeping** *vt* **1** : guardar **2** : cumplir (una promesa), acudir a (una cita) **3** DETAIN : hacer quedar, detener **4** PREVENT : impedir **5 ~ up** : mantener — *vi* **1** REMAIN : mantenerse **2** LAST : conservarse **3** *or* **~ on** CONTINUE : no dejar — **~** *n* **1 earn one's ~** : ganarse el pan **2 for ~s** : para siempre — **keeper** ['ki:pər] *n* : guarda *mf* — **keeping** ['ki:pɪŋ] *n* **1** CARE : cuidado *m* **2 in ~ with** : de acuerdo con — **keepsake** ['ki:p,seɪk] *n* : recuerdo *m*
keg ['kɛg] *n* : barril *m*
kennel ['kɛnəl] *n* : caseta *f* para perros, perrera *f*
kept → **keep**
kerchief ['kərtʃəf, -,tʃi:f] *n* : pañuelo *m*
kernel ['kərnəl] *n* **1** : almendra *f* **2** CORE : meollo *m*
kerosene *or* **kerosine** ['kɛrə,si:n, ,kɛrə'-] *n* : queroseno *m*
ketchup ['kɛtʃəp, 'kæ-] *n* : salsa *f* de tomate
kettle ['kɛt̬əl] *n* : hervidor *m*, tetera *f* (para hervir)
key ['ki:] *n* **1** : llave *f* **2** : tecla *f* (de un piano o una máquina) — **~** *vt* **be keyed up** : estar nervioso — **~** *adj* : clave — **keyboard** ['ki:,bord] *n* : teclado *m* — **keyhole** ['ki:,ho:l] *n* : ojo *m* (de la cerradura) — **keynote** ['ki:,no:t] *n* : tónica *f* — **key ring** *n* : llavero *m*
khaki ['kæki, 'kɑ-] *adj* : caqui
kick ['kɪk] *vt* **1** : dar una patada a **2 ~ out** : echar a patadas — *vi* **1** : dar patadas (dícese de una persona), cocear (dícese de un animal) **2** RECOIL : dar un culatazo — **~** *n* **1** : patada *f*, coz *f* (de un animal) **2** RECOIL : culatazo *m* **3** PLEASURE, THRILL : placer *m*
kid ['kɪd] *n* **1** GOAT : chivo *m*, -va *f*; cabrito *m* **2** CHILD : niño *m*, -ña *f* — **~** *v* **kidded; kidding** *vi or* **~ around** : bromear — *vt* TEASE : tomar el pelo a — **kidnap** ['kɪd-,næp] *vt* **-napped** *or* **-naped** [-,næpt]; **-napping** *or* **-naping** [-,næpɪŋ] : secuestrar, raptar
kidney ['kɪdni] *n, pl* **-neys** : riñón *m*
kidney bean *n* : frijol *m*
kill ['kɪl] *vt* **1** : matar **2** DESTROY : acabar con **3 ~ time** : matar el tiempo — **~** *n* **1** KILLING : matanza *f* **2** PREY : presa *f* — **killer** ['kɪlər] *n* : asesino *m*, -na *f* — **killing** ['kɪlɪŋ] *n* **1** : matanza *f* **2** MURDER : asesinato *m*
kiln ['kɪl, 'kɪln] *n* : horno *m*
kilo ['ki:,lo:] *n, pl* **-los** : kilo *m* — **kilogram** ['kɪlə,græm, 'ki:-] *n* : kilogramo *m* — **kilometer** [kɪ'lɑmət̬ər, 'kɪlə,mi:-] *n* : kilómetro *m* — **kilowatt** ['kɪlə,wɑt] *n* : kilovatio *m*
kin ['kɪn] *n* : parientes *mpl*
kind ['kaɪnd] *n* : tipo *m*, clase *f* — **~** *adj* : amable
kindergarten ['kɪndər,gɑrtən, -dən] *n* : jardín *m* infantil, jardín *m* de niños *Lat*
kindhearted [,kaɪnd'hɑrt̬əd] *adj* : de buen corazón
kindle ['kɪndəl] *vt* **-dled; -dling 1** : encender (un fuego) **2** AROUSE : despertar
kindly ['kaɪndli] *adj* **-lier; -est** : bondadoso, amable — **~** *adv* **1** : amablemente **2 take ~ to** : aceptar de buena gana **3 we ~ ask you not smoke** : les rogamos que no fumen — **kindness** ['kaɪndnəs] *n* : bondad *f* — **kind of** *adv* SOMEWHAT : un tanto, algo
kindred ['kɪndrəd] *adj* **1** : emparentado **2 ~ spirit** : alma *f* gemela
king ['kɪŋ] *n* : rey *m* — **kingdom** ['kɪŋdəm] *n* : reino *m*
kink ['kɪŋk] *n* **1** TWIST : vuelta *f*, curva *f* **2** FLAW : problema *m*
kinship ['kɪn,ʃɪp] *n* : parentesco *m*
kiss ['kɪs] *vt* : besar — *vi* : besarse — **~** *n* : beso *m*
kit ['kɪt] *n* **1** : juego *m*, kit *m* **2 first–aid ~** : botiquín *m* **3 tool ~** : caja *f* de herramientas
kitchen ['kɪtʃən] *n* : cocina *f*
kite ['kaɪt] *n* : cometa *f*, papalote *m Lat*
kitten ['kɪtən] *n* : gatito *m*, -ta *f* — **kitty** ['kɪt̬i] *n, pl* **-ties** FUND : fondo *m* común
knack ['næk] *n* : maña *f*, facilidad *f*
knapsack ['næp,sæk] *n* : mochila *f*
knead ['ni:d] *vt* **1** : amasar, sobar **2** MASSAGE : masajear
knee ['ni:] *n* : rodilla *f* — **kneecap** ['ni:,kæp] *n* : rótula *f*
kneel ['ni:l] *vi* **knelt** ['nɛlt] *or* **kneeled** ['ni:ld]; **kneeling** : arrodillarse
knew → **know**
knickknack ['nɪk,næk] *n* : chuchería *f*
knife ['naɪf] *n, pl* **knives** ['naɪvz] : cuchillo *m* — **~** *vt* **knifed** ['naɪft]; **knifing** : acuchillar
knight ['naɪt] *n* **1** : caballero *m* **2** : caballo *m* (en ajedrez) — **knighthood** ['naɪt,hʊd] *n* : título *m* de Sir
knit ['nɪt] *v* **knit** *or* **knitted** ['nɪt̬əd]; **knitting** *v* : tejer — **~** *n* : prenda *f* tejida
knob ['nɑb] *n* : tirador *m*, botón *m*, perilla *f Lat*
knock ['nɑk] *vt* **1** : golpear **2** CRITICIZE : criticar **3 ~ down** : derribar, echar al suelo — *vi* **1** : dar un golpe, llamar (a la puerta) **2** COLLIDE : darse, chocar — **~** *n* : golpe *m*, llamada *f* (a la puerta)
knot ['nɑt] *n* : nudo *m* — **~** *vt* **knotted; knotting** : anudar — **knotty** ['nɑt̬i] *adj* **-tier; -est 1** : nudoso **2** : enredado (dícese de un problema)
know ['no:] *v* **knew** ['nu:, 'nju:]; **known** ['no:n]; **knowing** *vt* **1** : saber **2** : conocer (a una persona, un lugar) **3 ~ how to** : saber — *vi* : saber — **knowing** ['no:ɪŋ] *adj* : cómplice — **knowingly** ['no:ɪŋli] *adv* **1** : de manera cómplice **2** DELIBERATELY : a sabiendas — **know–it–all** ['no:ɪt̬,ɔl] *n* : sabelotodo *mf fam* — **knowledge** ['nɑlɪdʒ] *n* **1** : conocimiento *m* **2** LEARNING : conocimientos *mpl*, saber *m* — **knowledgeable** ['nɑlɪdʒəbəl] *adj* : informado, entendido
knuckle ['nʌkəl] *n* : nudillo *m*
Koran [kə'rɑn, -'ræn] *n* **the Koran** : el Corán *m*
Korean [kə'ri:ən] *adj* : coreano *m*, -na *f* — **~** *n* : coreano *m* (idioma)
kosher ['ko:ʃər] *adj* : aprobado por la ley judía

L

l ['ɛl] *n, pl* **l's** *or* **ls** ['ɛlz] : l *f*, duodécima letra del alfabeto inglés
lab ['læb] → **laboratory**
label ['leɪbəl] *n* **1** TAG : etiqueta *f* **2** BRAND : marca *f* — **~** *vt* **-beled** *or* **-belled; -beling** *or* **-belling** : etiquetar
labor ['leɪbər] *n* **1** : trabajo *m* **2** WORKERS : mano *f* de obra **3 in ~** : de parto — **~** *vi* **1** : trabajar **2** STRUGGLE : avanzar penosamente — *vt* BELABOR : insistir en (un punto)
laboratory ['læbrə,tori, lə'bɔrə-] *n, pl* **-ries** : laboratorio *m*
laborer ['leɪbərər] *n* : trabajador *m*, -dora *f*
laborious [lə'boriəs] *adj* : laborioso
lace ['leɪs] *n* **1** : encaje *m* **2** SHOELACE : cordón *m* (de zapatos), agujeta *f Lat* — **~** *vt* **laced; lacing 1** TIE : atar **2 be laced with** : echar licor a (una bebida, etc.)
lacerate ['læsə,reɪt] *vt* **-ated; -ating** : lacerar
lack ['læk] *vt* : carecer de, no tener — *vi* **be lacking** : faltar — **~** *n* : falta *f*, carencia *f*
lackadaisical [,lækə'deɪzɪkəl] *adj* : apático, indolente
lackluster ['læk,lʌstər] *adj* : sin brillo, apagado
laconic [lə'kɑnɪk] *adj* : lacónico
lacquer ['lækər] *n* : laca *f*
lacrosse [lə'krɔs] *n* : lacrosse *f*
lacy ['leɪsi] *adj* **lacier; -est** : como de encaje
lad ['læd] *n* : muchacho *m*, niño *m*
ladder ['lædər] *n* : escalera *f*
laden ['leɪdən] *adj* : cargado
ladle ['leɪdəl] *n* : cucharón *m* — **~** *vt* **-dled; -dling** : servir con cucharón
lady ['leɪdi] *n, pl* **-dies** : señora *f*, dama *f* —

ladybug ['leɪdiˌbʌg] *n* : mariquita *f* — **ladylike** ['leɪdiˌlaɪk] *adj* : elegante, como señora
lag ['læg] *n* **1** DELAY : retraso *m* **2** INTERVAL : intervalo *m* — ~ *vi* **lagged; lagging** : quedarse atrás, rezagarse
lager ['lɑgər] *n* : cerveza *f* rubia
lagoon [lə'gu:n] *n* : laguna *f*
laid *pp* → **lay**[1]
lain *pp* → **lie**[1]
lair ['lær] *n* : guarida *f*
lake ['leɪk] *n* : lago *m*
lamb ['læm] *n* : cordero *m*
lame ['leɪm] *adj* **lamer; lamest 1** : cojo, renco **2 a ~ excuse** : una excusa poco convincente
lament [lə'mɛnt] *vt* **1** MOURN : llorar **2** DEPLORE : lamentar — ~ *n* : lamento *m* — **lamentable** ['læməntəbəl, lə'mɛntə-] *adj* : lamentable
laminate ['læməˌneɪt] *vt* **-nated; -nating** : laminar
lamp ['læmp] *n* : lámpara *f* — **lamppost** ['læmpˌpo:st] *n* : farol *m* — **lampshade** ['læmpˌʃeɪd] *n* : pantalla *f*
lance ['lænts] *n* : lanza *f* — ~ *vt* **lanced; lancing** : abrir con lanceta (en medecina)
land ['lænd] *n* **1** : tierra *f* **2** COUNTRY : país *m* **3** *or* **plot of ~** : terreno *m* — ~ *vt* **1** : desembarcar (pasajeros de un barco), hacer aterrizar (un avión) **2** CATCH : sacar (un pez) del agua **3** SECURE : conseguir (empleo, etc.) — *vi* **1** : aterrizar (dícese de un avión) **2** FALL : caer — **landing** ['lændɪŋ] *n* **1** : aterrizaje *m* (de aviones) **2** : desembarco *m* (de barcos) **3** : descanso *m* (de una escalera) — **landlady** ['lændˌleɪdi] *n, pl* **-dies** : casera *f* — **landlord** ['lændˌlɔrd] *n* : casero *m* — **landmark** ['lændˌmɑrk] *n* **1** : punto *m* de referencia **2** MONUMENT : monumento *m* histórico — **landowner** ['lændˌo:nər] *n* : hacendado *m*, -da *f*; terrateniente *mf* — **landscape** ['lændˌskeɪp] *n* : paisaje *m* — ~ *vt* **-scaped; -scaping** : ajardinar — **landslide** ['lændˌslaɪd] *n* **1** : desprendimiento *m* de tierras **2** *or* **~ victory** : victoria *f* arrolladora
lane ['leɪn] *n* **1** : carril *m* (de una carretera) **2** PATH, ROAD : camino *m*
language ['læŋgwɪdʒ] *n* **1** : idioma *m*, lengua *f* **2** SPEECH : lenguaje *m*
languid ['læŋgwɪd] *adj* : lánguido — **languish** ['læŋgwɪʃ] *vi* : languidecer
lanky ['læŋki] *adj* **lankier; -est** : delgado, larguirucho *fam*
lantern ['læntərn] *n* : linterna *f*
lap ['læp] *n* **1** : regazo *m* (de una persona) **2** : vuelta *f* (en deportes) — ~ *v* **lapped; lapping** *vt or* **~ up** : beber a lengüetadas — *vi* **~ against** : lamer
lapel [lə'pɛl] *n* : solapa *f*
lapse ['læps] *n* **1** : lapsus *m*, falla *f* (de memoria, etc.) **2** INTERVAL : lapso *m*, intervalo *m* — ~ *vi* **lapsed; lapsing 1** EXPIRE : caducar **2** ELAPSE : transcurrir, pasar **3 ~ into** : caer en
laptop ['læpˌtɑp] *adj* : portátil
larceny ['lɑrsəni] *n, pl* **-nies** : robo *m*
lard ['lɑrd] *n* : manteca *f* de cerdo
large ['lɑrdʒ] *adj* **larger; largest 1** : grande **2 at ~** : en libertad **3 by and ~** : por lo general — **largely** ['lɑrdʒli] *adv* : en gran parte
lark ['lɑrk] *n* **1** : alondra *f* (pájaro) **2 for a ~** : por divertirse
larva ['lɑrvə] *n, pl* **-vae** [-ˌvi:, -ˌvaɪ] : larva *f*
larynx ['lærɪŋks] *n, pl* **-rynges** [lə'rɪnˌdʒi:z] *or* **-ynxes** ['lærɪŋksəz] : laringe *f* — **laryngitis** [ˌlærən'dʒaɪt̬əs] *n* : laringitis *f*
lasagna [lə'zɑnjə] *n* : lasaña *f*
laser ['leɪzər] *n* : láser *m*
lash ['læʃ] *vt* **1** WHIP : azotar **2** BIND : amarrar — *vi* **~ out at** : arremeter contra — ~ *n* **1** BLOW : latigazo *m* (con un látigo) **2** EYELASH : pestaña *f*
lass ['læs] *or* **lassie** ['læsi] *n* : muchacha *f*, chica *f*
lasso ['læˌso:, læ'su:] *n, pl* **-sos** *or* **-soes** : lazo *m*
last ['læst] *vi* : durar — ~ *n* **1** : último *m*, -ma *f* **2 at ~** : por fin, finalmente — ~ *adv* **1** : por última vez, en último lugar **2 arrive ~** : llegar el último — ~ *adj* **1** : último **2 ~ year** : el año pasado — **lastly** ['læstli] *adv* : por último, finalmente
latch ['lætʃ] *n* : picaporte *m*, pestillo *m*
late ['leɪt] *adj* **later; latest 1** : tarde **2** : avanzado (dícese de la hora) **3** DECEASED : difunto **4** RECENT : reciente — ~ *adv* **later; latest** : tarde — **lately** ['leɪtli] *adv* : recientemente, últimamente — **lateness** ['leɪtnəs] *n* **1** : retraso *m* **2** : lo avanzado (de la hora)
latent ['leɪtənt] *adj* : latente
lateral ['læt̬ərəl] *adj* : lateral
latest ['leɪtəst] *n* **at the ~** : a más tardar
lathe ['leɪð] *n* : torno *m*
lather ['læðər] *n* : espuma *f* — ~ *vt* : enjabonar — *vi* : hacer espuma
Latin–American [ˌlætɪnə'mɛrɪkən] *adj* : latinoamericano
latitude ['læt̬əˌtu:d, -ˌtju:d] *n* : latitud *f*
latter ['læt̬ər] *adj* **1** : último **2** SECOND : segundo — ~ *pron* **the ~** : éste, ésta, éstos *pl*, éstas *pl*
lattice ['læt̬əs] *n* : enrejado *m*
laugh ['læf] *vi* : reír(se) — ~ *n* : risa *f* — **laughable** ['læfəbəl] *adj* : risible, ridículo — **laughter** ['læftər] *n* : risa *f*, risas *fpl*
launch ['lɔntʃ] *vt* : lanzar — ~ *n* : lanzamiento *m*
launder ['lɔndər] *vt* **1** : lavar y planchar (ropa) **2** : blanquear, lavar (dinero) — **laundry** ['lɔndri] *n, pl* **-dries 1** : ropa *f* sucia **2** : lavandería *f* (servicio) **3 do the ~** : lavar la ropa
lava ['lɑvə, 'læ-] *n* : lava *f*
lavatory ['lævəˌtori] *n, pl* **-ries** BATHROOM : baño *m*, cuarto *m* de baño
lavender ['lævəndər] *n* : lavanda *f*
lavish ['lævɪʃ] *adj* **1** EXTRAVAGANT : pródigo **2** ABUNDANT : abundante **3** LUXURIOUS : lujoso — ~ *vt* : prodigar
law ['lɔ] *n* **1** : ley *f* **2** : derecho *m* (profesión, etc.) **3 practice ~** : ejercer la abogacía — **lawful** ['lɔfəl] *adj* : legal, legítimo
lawn ['lɔn] *n* : césped *m* — **lawn mower** *n* : cortadora *f* de césped
lawsuit ['lɔˌsu:t] *n* : pleito *m*
lawyer ['lɔɪər, 'lɔjər] *n* : abogado *m*, -da *f*
lax ['læks] *adj* : poco estricto, relajado
laxative ['læksət̬ɪv] *n* : laxante *m*
lay[1] ['leɪ] *vt* **laid** ['leɪd]; **laying 1** PLACE, PUT : poner, colocar **2 ~ eggs** : poner huevos **3 ~ off** : despedir (un empleado) **4 ~ out** PRESENT : presentar, exponer **5 ~ out** DESIGN : diseñar (el trazado de)
lay[2] *pp* → **lie**[1]
lay[3] *adj* **1** SECULAR : laico **2** NONPROFESSIONAL : lego, profano
layer ['leɪər] *n* : capa *f*
layman ['leɪmən] *n, pl* **-men** : lego *m*, laico *m* (en religión)
layout ['leɪˌaʊt] *n* ARRANGEMENT : disposición *f*
lazy ['leɪzi] *adj* **-zier; -est** : perezoso — **laziness** ['leɪzinəs] *n* : pereza *f*
lead[1] ['li:d] *vt* **led** ['lɛd]; **leading 1** GUIDE : conducir **2** DIRECT : dirigir **3** HEAD : encabezar, ir al frente de — *vi* : llevar, conducir (a algo) — ~ *n* **1** : delantera *f* **2 follow s.o.'s ~** : seguir el ejemplo de algn
lead[2] ['lɛd] *n* **1** : plomo *m* (metal) **2** GRAPHITE : mina *f* — **leaden** ['lɛdən] *adj* **1** : de plomo **2** HEAVY : pesado
leader ['li:dər] *n* : jefe *m*, -fa *f* — **leadership** ['li:dərˌʃɪp] *n* : mando *m*, dirección *f*
leaf ['li:f] *n, pl* **leaves** ['li:vz] **1** : hoja *f* **2 turn over a new ~** : hacer borrón y cuenta nueva — ~ *vi* **~ through** : hojear (un libro, etc.) — **leaflet** ['li:flət] *n* : folleto *m*
league ['li:g] *n* **1** : liga *f* **2 be in ~ with** : estar confabulado con
leak ['li:k] *vt* **1** : dejar escapar (un líquido o un gas) **2** : filtrar (información) — *vi* **1** : gotear, escaparse (dícese de un líquido o un gas) **2** : filtrarse (dícese de información) — ~ *n* **1** : agujero *m* (de un cubo, etc.), gotera *f* (de un techo) **2** : fuga *f*, escape *m* (de un líquido o un gas) **3** : filtración *f* (de información) — **leaky** ['li:ki] *adj* **leakier; -est** : que hace agua
lean[1] ['li:n] *v* **leaned** *or Brit* **leant** ['lɛnt]; **leaning** *vi* **1** BEND : inclinarse **2 ~ against** : apoyarse contra — *vt* : apoyar
lean[2] *adj* **1** THIN : delgado **2** : sin grasa (dícese de la carne)
leaning ['li:nɪŋ] *n* : inclinación *f*
leanness ['li:nnəs] *n* : delgadez *f* (de una persona), lo magro (de la carne)
leap ['li:p] *vi* **leapt** *or* **leaped** ['li:pt, 'lɛpt]; **leaping** : saltar, brincar — ~ *n* : salto *m*, brinco *m* — **leap year** *n* : año *m* bisiesto
learn ['lərn] *v* **learned** ['lərnd, 'lərnt]; **learning** : aprender — **learned** ['lərnəd] *adj* : sabio, erudito — **learner** ['lərnər] *n* : principiante *mf*, estudiante *mf* — **learning** ['lərnɪŋ] *n* : erudición *f*, saber *m*
lease ['li:s] *n* : contrato *m* de arrendamiento — ~ *vt* **leased; leasing** : arrendar
leash ['li:ʃ] *n* : correa *f*
least ['li:st] *adj* **1** : menor **2** SLIGHTEST : más mínimo — ~ *n* **1 at ~** : por lo menos **2 the ~** : lo menos **3 to say the ~** : por no decir más — ~ *adv* : menos
leather ['lɛðər] *n* : cuero *m*
leave ['li:v] *v* **left** ['lɛft]; **leaving** *vt* **1** : dejar **2** : salir(se) de (un lugar) **3 ~ out** : omitir — *vi* DEPART : irse — ~ *n* **1** *or* **~ of absence** : permiso *m*, licencia *f* **2 take one's ~** : despedirse
leaves → **leaf**
lecture ['lɛktʃər] *n* **1** TALK : conferencia *f* **2** REPRIMAND : sermón *m*, reprimenda *f* — ~ *v* **-tured; -turing** *vt* : sermonear — *vi* : dar clase, dar una conferencia
led *pp* → **lead**[1]
ledge ['lɛdʒ] *n* : antepecho *m* (de una ventana), saliente *m* (de una montaña)
leech ['li:tʃ] *n* : sanguijuela *f*
leek ['li:k] *n* : puerro *m*
leer ['lɪr] *vi* : lanzar una mirada lascivia — ~ *n* : mirada *f* lasciva
leery ['lɪri] *adj* : receloso
leeway ['li:ˌweɪ] *n* : libertad *f* de acción, margen *m*
left[1] → **leave**
left[2] ['lɛft] *adj* : izquierdo — ~ *adv* : a la izquierda — ~ *n* : izquierda *f* — **left–handed** ['lɛft'hændəd] *adj* : zurdo
leftovers ['lɛftˌo:vərz] *npl* : restos *mpl*, sobras *fpl*
leg ['lɛg] *n* **1** : pierna *f* (de una persona, de ropa), pata *f* (de un animal, de muebles) **2** : etapa *f* (de un viaje)
legacy ['lɛgəsi] *n, pl* **-cies** : legado *m*
legal ['li:gəl] *adj* **1** LAWFUL : legítimo, legal **2** JUDICIAL : legal, jurídico — **legality** [lɪ'gælət̬i] *n, pl* **-ties** : legalidad *f* — **legalize** ['li:gəˌlaɪz] *vt* **-ized; -izing** : legalizar
legend ['lɛdʒənd] *n* : leyenda *f* — **legendary** ['lɛdʒənˌdɛri] *adj* : legendario
legible ['lɛdʒəbəl] *adj* : legible
legion ['li:dʒən] *n* : legión *f*
legislate ['lɛdʒəsˌleɪt] *vi* **-lated; -lating** : legislar — **legislation** [ˌlɛdʒəs'leɪʃən] *n* : legislación *f* — **legislative** ['lɛdʒəsˌleɪt̬ɪv] *adj* : legislativo, legislador — **legislature** ['lɛdʒəsˌleɪtʃər] *n* : asamblea *f* legislativa
legitimate [lɪ'dʒɪt̬əmət] *adj* : legítimo — **legitimacy** [lɪ'dʒɪt̬əməsi] *n* : legitimidad *f*
leisure ['li:ʒər, 'lɛ-] *n* **1** : ocio *m*, tiempo *m* libre **2 at your ~** : cuando te venga bien — **leisurely** ['li:ʒərli, 'lɛ-] *adj & adv* : lento, sin prisas
lemon ['lɛmən] *n* : limón *m* — **lemonade** [ˌlɛmə'neɪd] *n* : limonada *f*
lend ['lɛnd] *vt* **lent** ['lɛnt]; **lending** : prestar
length ['lɛŋkθ] *n* **1** : largo *m* **2** DURATION : duración *f* **3 at ~** FINALLY : por fin **4 at ~** : EXTENSIVELY : extensamente **5 go to any ~s** : hacer todo lo posible — **lengthen** ['lɛŋkθən] *vt* **1** : alargar **2** PROLONG : prolongar — *vi* : alargarse — **lengthways** ['lɛŋkθˌweɪz] *or* **lengthwise** ['lɛŋkθˌwaɪz] *adv* : a lo largo — **lengthy** ['lɛŋkθi] *adj* **lengthier; -est** : largo
lenient ['li:niənt] *adj* : indulgente — **leniency** ['li:niəntsi] *n, pl* **-cies** : indulgencia *f*
lens ['lɛnz] *n* **1** : cristalino *m* (del ojo) **2** : lente *mf* (de un instrumento) **3** → **contact lens**
Lent ['lɛnt] *n* : Cuaresma *f*
lentil ['lɛntəl] *n* : lenteja *f*
leopard ['lɛpərd] *n* : leopardo *m*
leotard ['li:əˌtɑrd] *n* : leotardo *m*, malla *f*
lesbian ['lɛzbiən] *n* : lesbiana *f*
less ['lɛs] *adv* (*comparative of* **little**) : menos — ~ *adj* (*comparative of* **little**) : menos — ~ *pron* : menos — ~ *prep* MINUS : menos — **lessen** ['lɛsən] *v* : disminuir — **lesser** ['lɛsər] *adj* : menor
lesson ['lɛsən] *n* **1** CLASS : clase *f*, curso *m* **2 learn one's ~** : aprender la lección
lest ['lɛst] *conj* **~ we forget** : para que no olvidemos
let ['lɛt] *vt* **let; letting 1** ALLOW : dejar, permitir **2** RENT : alquilar **3 ~'s go!** : ¡vamos!, ¡vámonos! **4 ~ down** DISAPPOINT : fallar **5 ~ in** : dejar entrar **6 ~ off** FORGIVE : perdonar **7 ~ up** ABATE : amainar, disminuir
letdown ['lɛtˌdaʊn] *n* : chasco *m*, decepción *f*
lethal ['li:θəl] *adj* : letal
lethargic [lɪ'θɑrdʒɪk] *adj* : letárgico
let's ['lɛts] (*contraction of* **let us**) → **let**
letter ['lɛt̬ər] *n* **1** : carta *f* **2** : letra *f* (del alfabeto)
lettuce ['lɛt̬əs] *n* : lechuga *f*
letup ['lɛtˌəp] *n* : pausa *f*, descanso *m*
leukemia [lu:'ki:miə] *n* : leucemia *f*
level ['lɛvəl] *n* **1** : nivel *m* **2 be on the ~** : ser honrado — ~ *vt* **-eled** *or* **-elled; -eling** *or* **-elling 1** : nivelar **2** AIM : apuntar **3** RAZE : arrasar — ~ *adj* **1** FLAT : llano, plano **2** : nivel (de altura) — **levelheaded** ['lɛvəl'hɛdəd] *adj* : sensato, equilibrado
lever ['lɛvər, 'li:-] *n* : palanca *f* — **leverage** ['lɛvərɪdʒ, 'li:-] *n* **1** : apalancamiento *m* (en física) **2** INFLUENCE : influencia *f*
levity ['lɛvət̬i] *n* : ligereza *f*
levy ['lɛvi] *n, pl* **levies** : impuesto *m* — ~ *vt* **levied; levying** : imponer, exigir (un impuesto)
lewd ['lu:d] *adj* : lascivo
lexicon ['lɛksɪˌkɑn] *n, pl* **-ica** [-kə] *or* **-icons** : léxico *m*, lexicón *m*
liable ['laɪəbəl] *adj* **1** : responsable **2** LIKELY : probable **3** SUSCEPTIBLE : propenso — **liability** [ˌlaɪə'bɪlət̬i] *n, pl* **-ties 1** RESPONSIBILITY : responsabilidad *f* **2** DRAWBACK : desventaja *f* **3 liabilities** *npl* DEBTS : deudas *fpl*, pasivo *m*
liaison ['li:əˌzɑn, li'eɪ-] *n* **1** : enlace *m* **2** AFFAIR : amorío *m*
liar ['laɪər] *n* : mentiroso *m*, -sa *f*
libel ['laɪbəl] *n* : libelo *m*, difamación *f* — ~ *vt* **-beled** *or* **-belled; -beling** *or* **-belling** : difamar
liberal ['lɪbrəl, 'lɪbərəl] *adj* : liberal — ~ *n* : liberal *mf*
liberate ['lɪbəˌreɪt] *vt* **-ated; -ating** : liberar — **liberation** [ˌlɪbə'reɪʃən] *n* : liberación *f*
liberty ['lɪbərt̬i] *n, pl* **-ties** : libertad *f*
library ['laɪˌbrɛri] *n, pl* **-braries** : biblioteca *f* — **librarian** [laɪ'brɛriən] *n* : bibliotecario *m*, -ria *f*
lice → **louse**
license *or* **licence** ['laɪsənts] *n* **1** PERMIT : licencia *f* **2** FREEDOM : libertad *f* **3** AUTHORIZATION : permiso *m* — ~ *vt* **licensed; licensing** : autorizar
lick ['lɪk] *vt* **1** : lamer **2** DEFEAT : dar una paliza a *fam* — ~ *n* : lamida *f*
licorice ['lɪkərɪʃ, -rəs] *n* : regaliz *m*
lid ['lɪd] *n* **1** : tapa *f* **2** EYELID : párpado *m*
lie[1] ['laɪ] *vi* **lay** ['leɪ]; **lain** ['leɪn]; **lying** ['laɪɪŋ] **1** *or* **~ down** : acostarse, echarse **2** BE : estar, encontrarse
lie[2] *vi* **lied; lying** ['laɪɪŋ] : mentir — ~ *n* : mentira *f*
lieutenant [lu:'tɛnənt] *n* : teniente *mf*
life ['laɪf] *n, pl* **lives** ['laɪvz] : vida *f* — **lifeboat** ['laɪfˌbo:t] *n* : bote *m* salvavidas — **lifeguard** ['laɪfˌgɑrd] *n* : socorrista *mf* — **lifeless** ['laɪfləs] *adj* : sin vida — **lifelike** ['laɪfˌlaɪk] *adj* : natural, realista — **lifelong** ['laɪf'lɔŋ] *adj* : de toda la vida — **life preserver** *n* : salvavidas *m* — **lifestyle** ['laɪfˌstaɪl] *n* : estilo *m* de vida — **lifetime** ['laɪfˌtaɪm] *n* : vida *f*
lift ['lɪft] *vt* **1** RAISE : levantar **2** STEAL : robar — *vi* **1** CLEAR UP : despejarse **2** *or* **~ off** : despegar (dícese de un avión, etc.) — ~ *n* **1** LIFTING : levantamiento *m* **2 give s.o. a ~** : llevar en coche a algn — **liftoff** ['lɪftˌɔf] *n* : despegue *m*
light[1] ['laɪt] *n* **1** : luz *f* **2** LAMP : lámpara *f* **3** HEADLIGHT : faro *m* **4 do you have a ~?** : ¿tienes fuego? — ~ *adj* **1** BRIGHT : bien iluminado **2** : claro (dícese de los colores), rubio (dícese del pelo) — ~ *v* **lit** ['lɪt] *or* **lighted; lighting** *vt* **1** : encender (un fuego) **2** ILLUMINATE : iluminar — *vi or* **~ up** : iluminarse — **lightbulb** ['laɪtˌbʌlb] *n* : bombilla *f*, bombillo *m Lat* — **lighten** ['laɪtən] *vt* BRIGHTEN : iluminar — **lighter** ['laɪt̬ər] *n* : encendedor *m* — **lighthouse** ['laɪtˌhaʊs] *n* : faro *m* — **lighting** ['laɪt̬ɪŋ] *n* : alumbrado *m* — **lightning** ['laɪtnɪŋ] *n* : relámpago *m*, rayo *m* — **light–year** ['laɪtˌjɪr] *n* : año *m* luz
light[2] *adj* : ligero — **lighten** ['laɪtən] *vt* : aligerar — **lightly** ['laɪtli] *adv* **1** : suavemente **2 let off ~** : tratar con indulgencia — **lightness** ['laɪtnəs] *n* : ligereza *f* — **lightweight** ['laɪt'weɪt] *adj* : ligero
like[1] ['laɪk] *v* **liked; liking** *vt* **1** : gustarle (a uno) **2** WANT : querer — *vi* **if you ~** : si quieres — **likes** *npl* : preferencias *fpl*, gustos *mpl* — **likable** *or* **likeable** ['laɪkəbəl] *adj* : simpático
like[2] *adj* SIMILAR : parecido — ~ *prep* : como — ~ *conj* **1** AS : como **2** AS IF : como si — **likelihood** ['laɪkliˌhʊd] *n* : probabilidad *f* — **likely** ['laɪkli] *adj* **-lier; -est** : probable — **liken** ['laɪkən] *vt* : comparar — **likeness** ['laɪknəs] *n* : semejanza *f*, parecido *m* — **likewise** ['laɪkˌwaɪz] *adv* **1** : lo mismo **2** ALSO : también
liking ['laɪkɪŋ] *n* : afición *f* (por una cosa), simpatía *f* (por una persona)
lilac ['laɪlək, -ˌlæk, -ˌlɑk] *n* : lila *f*
lily ['lɪli] *n, pl* **lilies** : lirio *m*, azucena *f* — **lily of the valley** *n* : lirio *m* de los valles
lima bean ['laɪmə] *n* : frijol *m* de media luna
limb ['lɪm] *n* **1** : miembro *m* (en anatomía) **2** : rama *f* (de un arból)
limber ['lɪmbər] *vi or* **~ up** : calentarse, hacer ejercicios preliminares — ~ *adj* : ágil
limbo ['lɪmˌbo:] *n, pl* **-bos** : limbo *m*
lime ['laɪm] *n* : lima *f*, limón *m* verde *Lat*
limelight ['laɪmˌlaɪt] *n* **be in the ~** : estar en el candelero
limerick ['lɪmərɪk] *n* : poema *m* jocoso de cinco versos
limestone ['laɪmˌsto:n] *n* : (piedra *f*) caliza *f*
limit ['lɪmət] *n* : límite *m* — ~ *vt* : limitar, restringir — **limitation** [ˌlɪmə'teɪʃən] *n* : limitación *f*, restricción *f* — **limited** ['lɪmət̬əd] *adj* : limitado
limousine ['lɪməˌzi:n, ˌlɪmə'-] *n* : limusina *f*
limp[1] ['lɪmp] *vi* : cojear — ~ *n* : cojera *f*
limp[2] *adj* : flojo, fláccido
line ['laɪn] *n* **1** : línea *f* **2** ROPE : cuerda *f* **3** ROW : fila *f* **4** QUEUE : cola *f* **5** WRINKLE : arruga *f* **6 drop a ~** : mándar unas líneas — ~ *v* **lined; lining** *vt* **1** : forrar (un vestido, etc.), cubrir (las paredes, etc.) **2** MARK : rayar, trazar líneas en **3** BORDER : bordear — *vi* **~ up** : ponerse en fila, hacer cola
lineage ['lɪniɪdʒ] *n* : linaje *m*
linear ['lɪniər] *adj* : lineal
linen ['lɪnən] *n* : lino *m*
liner ['laɪnər] *n* **1** LINING : forro *m* **2** SHIP : buque *m*, transatlántico *m*
lineup ['laɪnˌəp] *n* **1** *or* **police ~** : fila *f* de sospechosos **2** : alineación *f* (en deportes)
linger ['lɪŋgər] *vi* **1** : quedarse, entretenerse **2** PERSIST : persistir
lingerie [ˌlɑndʒə'reɪ, ˌlænʒə'ri:] *n* : ropa *f* íntima femenina, lencería *f*
lingo ['lɪŋgo] *n, pl* **-goes** JARGON : jerga *f*
linguistics [lɪŋ'gwɪstɪks] *n* : lingüística *f* — **linguist** ['lɪŋgwɪst] *n* : lingüista *mf* — **linguistic** [lɪŋ'gwɪstɪk] *adj* : lingüístico
lining ['laɪnɪŋ] *n* : forro *m*
link ['lɪŋk] *n* **1** : eslabón *m* (de una cadena) **2** BOND : lazo *m* **3** CONNECTION : conexión *f* — ~ *vt* : enlazar, conectar — *vi* **~ up** : unirse, conectar
linoleum [lə'no:liəm] *n* : linóleo *m*
lint ['lɪnt] *n* : pelusa *f*
lion ['laɪən] *n* : león *m* — **lioness** ['laɪənɪs] *n* : leona *f*
lip ['lɪp] *n* **1** : labio *m* **2** EDGE : borde *m* — **lipstick** ['lɪpˌstɪk] *n* : lápiz *m* de labios
liqueur [lɪ'kʊr, -'kər, -'kjʊr] *n* : licor *m*

liquid ['lɪkwəd] *adj* : líquido — ~ *n* : líquido *m* — **liquidate** ['lɪkwəˌdeɪt] *vt* **-dated; -dating** : liquidar — **liquidation** [ˌlɪkwə'deɪʃən] *n* : liquidación *f*

liquor ['lɪkər] *n* : bebidas *fpl* alcohólicas

lisp ['lɪsp] *vi* : cecear — ~ *n* : ceceo *m*

list[1] ['lɪst] *n* : lista *f* — ~ *vt* 1 ENUMERATE : hacer una lista de, enumerar 2 INCLUDE : incluir (en una lista)

list[2] *vi* : escorar (dícese de un barco)

listen ['lɪsən] *vi* 1 : escuchar 2 ~ **to** HEED : hacer caso de 3 ~ **to reason** : atender a razones — **listener** ['lɪsənər] *n* : oyente *mf*

listless ['lɪstləs] *adj* : apático

lit ['lɪt] *pp* → **light**

litany ['lɪtəni] *n, pl* **-nies** : letanía *f*

liter ['li:ṭər] *n* : litro *m*

literacy ['lɪṭərəsi] *n* : alfabetismo *m*

literal ['lɪṭərəl] *adj* : literal — **literally** *adv* : literalmente, al pie de la letra

literate ['lɪṭərət] *adj* : alfabetizado

literature ['lɪṭərəˌtʃʊr, -tʃər] *n* : literatura *f* — **literary** ['lɪṭəˌrɛri] *adj* : literario

lithe ['laɪð, 'laɪθ] *adj* : ágil y grácil

litigation [ˌlɪṭə'geɪʃən] *n* : litigio *m*

litre → **liter**

litter ['lɪṭər] *n* 1 RUBBISH : basura *f* 2 : camada *f* (de animales) 3 *or* **kitty** ~ : arena *f* higiénica — ~ *vt* : tirar basura en, ensuciar — *vi* : tirar basura

little ['lɪṭəl] *adj* **littler** *or* **less** ['lɛs] *or* **lesser** ['lɛsər]; **littlest** *or* **least** ['li:st] 1 SMALL : pequeño 2 **a** ~ SOME : un poco de 3 **he speaks** ~ **English** : habla poco inglés — ~ *adv* **less** ['lɛs]; **least** ['li:st] : poco — ~ *pron* 1 : poco *m*, -ca *f* 2 ~ **by** ~ : poco a poco

liturgy ['lɪṭərdʒi] *n, pl* **-gies** : liturgia *f* — **liturgical** [lə'tərdʒɪkəl] *adj* : litúrgico

live ['lɪv] *vi* **lived; living** 1 : vivir 2 RESIDE : residir 3 ~ **on** : vivir de — *vt* : vivir, llevar (una vida) — ~ ['laɪv] *adj* 1 : vivo 2 : con corriente (dícese de cables eléctricos) 3 : en vivo, en directo (dícese de programas de televisión, etc.) — **livelihood** ['laɪvliˌhʊd] *n* : sustento *m*, medio *m* de vida — **lively** ['laɪvli] *adj* **-lier; -est** : animado, alegre — **liven** ['laɪvən] *vt or* ~ **up** : animar — *vi* : animarse

liver ['lɪvər] *n* : hígado *m*

livestock ['laɪvˌstɑk] *n* : ganado *m*

livid ['lɪvəd] *adj* 1 : lívido 2 ENRAGED : furioso

living ['lɪvɪŋ] *adj* : vivo — ~ *n* **make a** ~ : ganarse la vida — **living room** *n* : living *m*, sala *f* (de estar)

lizard ['lɪzərd] *n* : lagarto *m*

llama ['lɑmə, 'jɑ-] *n* : llama *f*

load ['lo:d] *n* 1 CARGO : carga *f* 2 BURDEN : carga *f*, peso *m* 3 ~**s of** : un montón de — ~ *vt* : cargar

loaf[1] ['lo:f] *n, pl* **loaves** ['lo:vz] : pan *m*, barra *f* (de pan)

loaf[2] *vi* : holgazanear — **loafer** ['lo:fər] *n* 1 : holgazán *m*, -zana *f* 2 : mocasín *m* (zapato)

loan ['lo:n] *n* : préstamo *m* — ~ *vt* : prestar

loathe ['lo:ð] *vt* **loathed; loathing** : odiar — **loathsome** ['lo:θsəm, 'lo:ð-] *adj* : odioso

lobby ['lɑbi] *n, pl* **-bies** 1 : vestíbulo *m* 2 *or* **political** ~ : grupo *m* de presión, lobby *m* — ~ *v* **-bied; -bying** *vt* : ejercer presión sobre

lobe ['lo:b] *n* : lóbulo *m*

lobster ['lɑbstər] *n* : langosta *f*

local ['lo:kəl] *adj* : local — ~ *n* **the** ~**s** : los vecinos del lugar — **locale** [lo'kæl] *n* : escenario *m* — **locality** [lo'kæləṭi] *n, pl* **-ties** : localidad *f*

locate ['lo:ˌkeɪt, lo'keɪt] *vt* **-cated; -cating** 1 SITUATE : situar, ubicar 2 FIND : localizar — **location** [lo'keɪʃən] *n* : situación *f*, lugar *m*

lock[1] ['lɑk] *n* : mechón *m* (de pelo)

lock[2] *n* 1 : cerradura *f* (de una puerta, etc.) 2 : esclusa *f* (de un canal) — ~ *vt* 1 : cerrar (con llave) 2 *or* ~ **up** CONFINE : encerrar — *vi* 1 : cerrarse con llave 2 : bloquearse (dícese de una rueda, etc.) — **locker** ['lɑkər] *n* : armario *m* — **locket** ['lɑkət] *n* : medallón *m* — **locksmith** ['lɑkˌsmɪθ] *n* : cerrajero *m*, -ra *f*

locomotive [ˌlo:kə'mo:ṭɪv] *n* : locomotora *f*

locust ['lo:kəst] *n* : langosta *f*, chapulín *m* *Lat*

lodge ['lɑdʒ] *v* **lodged; lodging** *vt* 1 HOUSE : hospedar, alojar 2 FILE : presentar — *vi* : hospedarse, alojarse — ~ *n* : pabellón *m* — **lodger** ['lɑdʒər] *n* : huésped *m*, -peda *f* — **lodging** ['lɑdʒɪŋ] *n* 1 : alojamiento *m* 2 ~**s** *npl* : habitaciones *fpl*

loft ['lɔft] *n* 1 : desván *m* (en una casa) 2 HAYLOFT : pajar *m* — **lofty** ['lɔfti] *adj* **loftier; -est** 1 : noble, elevado 2 HAUGHTY : altanero

log ['lɔg, 'lɑg] *n* 1 : tronco *m*, leño *m* 2 RECORD : diario *m* — ~ *vi* **logged; logging** 1 : talar (árboles) 2 RECORD : registrar, anotar 3 ~ **on** : entrar (en el sistema) 4 ~ **off** : salir (del sistema) — **logger** ['lɔgər, 'lɑ-] *n* : leñador *m*, -dora *f*

logic ['lɑdʒɪk] *n* : lógica *f* — **logical** ['lɑdʒɪkəl] *adj* : lógico — **logistics** [lə'dʒɪstɪks, lo-] *ns & pl* : logística *f*

logo ['lo:ˌgo:] *n, pl* **logos** [-ˌgo:z] : logotipo *m*

loin ['lɔɪn] *n* : lomo *m*

loiter ['lɔɪṭər] *vi* : vagar, holgazanear

lollipop *or* **lollypop** ['lɑliˌpɑp] *n* : pirulí *m*, chupete *m Lat*

lone ['lo:n] *adj* : solitario — **loneliness** ['lo:nlinəs] *n* : soledad *f* — **lonely** ['lo:nli] *adj* **-lier; -est** : solitario, solo — **loner** ['lo:nər] *n* : solitario *m*, -ria *f* — **lonesome** ['lo:nsəm] *adj* : solo, solitario

long[1] ['lɔŋ] *adj* **longer** ['lɔŋgər]; **longest** ['lɔŋgəst] : largo — ~ *adv* 1 : mucho tiempo 2 **all day** ~ : todo el día 3 **as** ~ **as** : mientras 4 **no** ~**er** : ya no 5 **so** ~! : ¡hasta luego!, ¡adiós! — ~ *n* 1 **before** ~ : dentro de poco 2 **the** ~ **and the short** : lo esencial

long[2] *vi* ~ **for** : anhelar, desear

longevity [lɑn'dʒɛvəṭi] *n* : longevidad *f*

longing ['lɔŋɪŋ] *n* : ansia *f*, anhelo *m*

longitude ['lɑndʒəˌtu:d, -ˌtju:d] *n* : longitud *f*

look ['lʊk] *vi* 1 : mirar 2 SEEM : parecer 3 ~ **after** : cuidar (de) 4 ~ **for** EXPECT : esperar 5 ~ **for** SEEK : buscar 6 ~ **into** : investigar 7 ~ **out** : tener cuidado 8 ~ **over** EXAMINE : revisar 9 ~ **up to** : respetar — *vt* : mirar — ~ *n* 1 : mirada *f* 2 APPEARANCE : aspecto *m*, aire *m* — **lookout** ['lʊkˌaʊt] *n* 1 : puesto *m* de observación 2 WATCHMAN : vigía *mf* 3 **be on the** ~ **for** : estar al acecho de

loom[1] ['lu:m] *n* : telar *m*

loom[2] *vi* 1 APPEAR : aparecer, surgir 2 APPROACH : ser inminente

loop ['lu:p] *n* : lazada *f*, lazo *m* — ~ *vt* : hacer lazadas con — **loophole** ['lu:pˌho:l] *n* : escapatoria *f*

loose ['lu:s] *adj* **looser; -est** 1 MOVABLE : flojo, suelto 2 SLACK : flojo 3 ROOMY : holgado 4 APPROXIMATE : libre, aproximado 5 FREE : suelto 6 IMMORAL : relajado — **loosely** ['lu:sli] *adv* 1 : sin apretar 2 ROUGHLY : aproximadamente — **loosen** ['lu:sən] *vt* : aflojar

loot ['lu:t] *n* : botín *m* — ~ *vt* : saquear, robar — **looter** ['lu:ṭər] *n* : saqueador *m*, -dora *f* — **looting** ['lu:ṭɪŋ] *n* : saqueo *m*

lop ['lɑp] *vt* **lopped; lopping** : cortar, podar

lopsided ['lɑpˌsaɪdəd] *adj* : torcido, chueco *Lat*

lord ['lɔrd] *n* 1 : señor *m*, noble *m* 2 **the Lord** : el Señor

lore ['lor] *n* : saber *m* popular, tradición *f*

lose ['lu:z] *v* **lost** ['lɔst]; **losing** ['lu:zɪŋ] *vt* 1 : perder 2 ~ **one's way** : perderse 3 ~ **time** : atrasarse (dícese de un reloj) — *vi* : perder — **loser** ['lu:zər] *n* : perdedor *m*, -dora *f* — **loss** ['lɔs] *n* 1 : pérdida *f* 2 DEFEAT : derrota *f* 3 **be at a** ~ **for words** : no encontrar palabras — **lost** ['lɔst] *adj* 1 : perdido 2 **get** ~ : perderse

lot ['lɑt] *n* 1 FATE : suerte *f* 2 PLOT : solar *m* 3 **a** ~ **of** *or* ~**s of** : mucho, un montón de

lotion ['lo:ʃən] *n* : loción *f*

lottery ['lɑṭəri] *n, pl* **-teries** : lotería *f*

loud ['laʊd] *adj* 1 : alto, fuerte 2 NOISY : ruidoso 3 FLASHY : llamativo — ~ *adv* 1 : fuerte 2 **out** ~ : en voz alta — **loudly** ['laʊdli] *adv* : en voz alta — **loudspeaker** ['laʊdˌspi:kər] *n* : altavoz *m*

lounge ['laʊndʒ] *vi* **lounged; lounging** 1 : repantigarse 2 *or* ~ **about** : holgazanear — ~ *n* : salón *m*

louse ['laʊs] *n, pl* **lice** ['laɪs] : piojo *m* — **lousy** ['laʊzi] *adj* **lousier; -est** 1 : piojoso 2 BAD : pésimo, muy malo

love ['lʌv] *n* 1 : amor *m* 2 **fall in** ~ : enamorarse — ~ *v* **loved; loving** : querer, amar — **lovable** ['lʌvəbəl] *adj* : adorable, amoroso *Lat* — **lovely** ['lʌvli] *adj* **-lier; -est** : lindo, precioso — **lover** ['lʌvər] *n* : amante *mf* — **loving** ['lʌvɪŋ] *adj* : cariñoso

low ['lo:] *adj* **lower** ['lo:ər]; **-est** 1 : bajo 2 SCARCE : escaso 3 DEPRESSED : deprimido — ~ *adv* 1 : bajo 2 **turn the lights down** ~ : bajar las luces — ~ *n* 1 : punto *m* bajo 2 *or* ~ **gear** : primera velocidad *f* — **lower** ['lo:ər] *adj* : inferior, más bajo — ~ *vt* : bajar — **lowly** ['lo:li] *adj* **-lier; -est** : humilde

loyal ['lɔɪəl] *adj* : leal, fiel — **loyalty** ['lɔɪəlti] *n, pl* **-ties** : lealtad *f*

lozenge ['lɑzəndʒ] *n* : pastilla *f*

lubricate ['lu:brɪˌkeɪt] *vt* **-cated; -cating** : lubricar — **lubricant** ['lu:brɪkənt] *n* : lubricante *m* — **lubrication** [ˌlu:brɪ'keɪʃən] *n* : lubricación *f*

lucid ['lu:səd] *adj* : lúcido — **lucidity** [lu:'sɪdəṭi] *n* : lucidez *f*

luck ['lʌk] *n* 1 : suerte *f* 2 **good** ~! : ¡buena suerte! — **luckily** ['lʌkəli] *adv* : afortunadamente — **lucky** ['lʌki] *adj* **luckier; -est** 1 : afortunado 2 ~ **charm** : amuleto *m* (de la suerte)

lucrative ['lu:krəṭɪv] *adj* : lucrativo

ludicrous ['lu:dəkrəs] *adj* : ridículo, absurdo

lug ['lʌg] *vt* **lugged; lugging** : arrastrar

luggage ['lʌgɪdʒ] *n* : equipaje *m*

lukewarm ['lu:k'wɔrm] *adj* : tibio

lull ['lʌl] *vt* 1 CALM : calmar 2 ~ **to sleep** : adormecer — ~ *n* : período *m* de calma, pausa *f*

lullaby ['lʌləˌbaɪ] *n, pl* **-bies** : canción *f* de cuna, nana *f*

lumber ['lʌmbər] *n* : madera *f* — **lumberjack** ['lʌmbərˌdʒæk] *n* : leñador *m*, -dora *f*

luminous ['lu:mənəs] *adj* : luminoso

lump ['lʌmp] *n* 1 CHUNK, PIECE : pedazo *m*, trozo *m* 2 SWELLING : bulto *m* 3 : grumo *m* (en un líquido) — ~ *vt or* ~ **together** : juntar, agrupar — **lumpy** ['lʌmpi] *adj* **lumpier; -est** : grumoso (dícese de una salsa), lleno de bultos (dícese de un colchón)

lunacy ['lu:nəsi] *n, pl* **-cies** : locura *f*

lunar ['lu:nər] *adj* : lunar

lunatic ['lu:nəˌtɪk] *n* : loco *m*, -ca *f*

lunch ['lʌntʃ] *n* : almuerzo *m*, comida *f* — ~ *vi* : almorzar, comer — **luncheon** ['lʌntʃən] *n* : comida *f*, almuerzo *m*

lung ['lʌŋ] *n* : pulmón *m*

lunge ['lʌndʒ] *vi* **lunged; lunging** 1 : lanzarse 2 ~ **at** : arremeter contre

lurch[1] ['lərtʃ] *vi* 1 STAGGER : tambalearse 2 : dar bandazos (dícese de un vehículo)

lurch[2] *n* **leave in a** ~ : dejar en la estacada

lure ['lʊr] *n* 1 BAIT : señuelo *m* 2 ATTRACTION : atractivo *m* — ~ *vt* **lured; luring** : atraer

lurid ['lʊrəd] *adj* 1 GRUESOME : espeluznante 2 SENSATIONAL : sensacionalista 3 GAUDY : chillón

lurk ['lərk] *vi* : estar al acecho

luscious ['lʌʃəs] *adj* : delicioso, exquisito

lush ['lʌʃ] *adj* : exuberante, suntuoso

lust ['lʌst] *n* 1 : lujuria *f* 2 CRAVING : ansia *f*, anhelo *m* — ~ *vi* ~ **after** : desear (a una persona), codiciar (riquezas, etc.)

luster *or* **lustre** ['lʌstər] *n* : lustre *m*

lusty ['lʌsti] *adj* **lustier; -est** : fuerte, vigoroso

luxurious [ˌlʌg'ʒʊriəs, ˌlʌk'ʃʊr-] *adj* : lujoso — **luxury** ['lʌkʃəri, 'lʌgʒə-] *n, pl* **-ries** : lujo *m*

lye ['laɪ] *n* : lejía *f*

lying → **lie**

lynch ['lɪntʃ] *vt* : linchar

lynx ['lɪŋks] *n* : lince *m*

lyric ['lɪrɪk] *or* **lyrical** ['lɪrɪkəl] *adj* : lírico — **lyrics** *npl* : letra *f* (de una canción)

M

m ['ɛm] *n, pl* **m's** *or* **ms** ['ɛmz] : m *f*, decimotercera letra del alfabeto inglés

ma'am ['mæm] → **madam**

macabre [mə'kɑb, -'kɑbər, -'kɑbrə] *adj* : macabro

macaroni [ˌmækə'ro:ni] *n* : macarrones *mpl*

mace ['meɪs] *n* 1 : maza *f* (arma o símbolo) 2 : macis *f* (especia)

machete [mə'ʃɛṭi] *n* : machete *m*

machine [mə'ʃi:n] *n* : máquina *f* — **machinery** [mə'ʃi:nəri] *n, pl* **-eries** 1 : maquinaria *f* 2 WORKS : mecanismo *m* — **machine gun** *n* : ametralladora *f*

mad ['mæd] *adj* **madder; maddest** 1 INSANE : loco 2 FOOLISH : insensato 3 ANGRY : furioso

madam ['mædəm] *n, pl* **mesdames** [meɪ'dɑm] : señora *f*

madden ['mædən] *vt* : enfurecer

made → **make**

madly ['mædli] *adv* : como un loco, locamente — **madman** ['mædˌmæn, -mən] *n, pl* **-men** [-mən, -ˌmɛn] : loco *m* — **madness** ['mædnəs] *n* : locura *f*

Mafia ['mɑfiə] *n* : Mafia *f*

magazine ['mægəˌzi:n] *n* 1 PERIODICAL : revista *f* 2 : recámara *f* (de un arma de fuego)

maggot ['mægət] *n* : gusano *m*

magic ['mædʒɪk] *n* : magia *f* — ~ *or* **magical** ['mædʒɪkəl] *adj* : mágico — **magician** [mə'dʒɪʃən] *n* : mago *m*, -ga *f*

magistrate ['mædʒəˌstreɪt] *n* : magistrado *m*, -da *f*

magnanimous [mæg'nænəməs] *adj* : magnánimo

magnate ['mægˌneɪt, -nət] *n* : magnate *mf*

magnet ['mægnət] *n* : imán *m* — **magnetic** [mæg'nɛṭɪk] *adj* : magnético — **magnetism** ['mægnəˌtɪzəm] *n* : magnetismo *m* — **magnetize** ['mægnəˌtaɪz] *vt* **-tized; -tizing** : magnetizar

magnificent [mæg'nɪfəsənt] *adj* : magnífico — **magnificence** [mæg'nɪfəsənts] *n* : magnificencia *f*

magnify ['mægnəˌfaɪ] *vt* **-fied; -fying** 1 ENLARGE : ampliar 2 EXAGGERATE : exagerar — **magnifying glass** *n* : lupa *f*

magnitude ['mægnəˌtu:d, -ˌtju:d] *n* : magnitud *f*

magnolia [mæg'no:ljə] *n* : magnolia *f*

mahogany [mə'hɑgəni] *n, pl* **-nies** : caoba *f*

maid ['meɪd] *n* : sirvienta *f*, criada *f*, muchacha *f* — **maiden** ['meɪdən] *adj* FIRST : inaugural — **maiden name** *n* : nombre *m* de soltera

mail ['meɪl] *n* 1 : correo *m* 2 LETTERS : correspondencia *f* — ~ *vt* : enviar por correo — **mailbox** ['meɪlˌbɑks] *n* : buzón *m* — **mailman** ['meɪlˌmæn, -mən] *n, pl* **-men** [-mən, -ˌmɛn] : cartero *m*

maim ['meɪm] *vt* : mutilar

main ['meɪn] *n* : tubería *f* principal (de agua o gas), cable *m* principal (de un circuito) — ~ *adj* : principal — **mainframe** ['meɪnˌfreɪm] *n* : computadora *f* central — **mainland** ['meɪnˌlænd, -lənd] *n* : continente *m* — **mainly** ['meɪnli] *adv* : principalmente — **mainstay** ['meɪnˌsteɪ] *n* : sostén *m* (principal) — **mainstream** ['meɪnˌstri:m] *n* : corriente *f* principal — ~ *adj* : dominante, convencional

maintain [meɪn'teɪn] *vt* : mantener — **maintenance** ['meɪntənənts] *n* : mantenimiento *m*

maize ['meɪz] *n* : maíz *m*

majestic [mə'dʒɛstɪk] *adj* : majestuoso — **majesty** ['mædʒəsti] *n, pl* **-ties** : majestad *f*

major ['meɪdʒər] *adj* 1 : muy importante, principal 2 : mayor (en música) — ~ *n* 1 : mayor *mf*, comandante *mf* (en las fuerzas armadas) 2 : especialidad *f* (universitaria) — ~ *vi* **-jored; -joring** : especializarse — **majority** [mə'dʒɔrəṭi] *n, pl* **-ties** : mayoría *f*

make ['meɪk] *v* **made** ['meɪd]; **making** *vt* 1 : hacer 2 MANUFACTURE : fabricar 3 CONSTITUTE : constituir 4 PREPARE : preparar 5 RENDER : poner 6 COMPEL : obligar 7 ~ **a decision** : tomar una decisión 8 ~ **a living** : ganar la vida — *vi* 1 ~ **do** : arreglárselas 2 ~ **for** : dirigirse a 3 ~ **good** SUCCEED : tener éxito — ~ *n* BRAND : marca *f* — **make–believe** [ˌmeɪkbə'li:v] *n* : fantasía *f* — ~ *adj* : imaginario — **make out** *vt* 1 : hacer (un cheque, etc.) 2 DISCERN : distinguir 3 UNDERSTAND : comprender — *vi* **how did you** ~? : ¿qué tal te fue? — **maker** ['meɪkər] *n* MANUFACTURER : fabricante *mf* — **makeshift** ['meɪkˌʃɪft] *adj* : improvisado — **makeup** ['meɪkˌʌp] *n* 1 COMPOSITION : composición *f* 2 COSMETICS : maquillaje *m* — **make up** *vt* 1 PREPARE : preparar 2 INVENT : inventar 3 CONSTITUTE : formar — *vi* RECONCILE : hacer las paces

maladjusted [ˌmælə'dʒʌstəd] *adj* : inadaptado

malaria [mə'lɛriə] *n* : malaria *f*, paludismo *m*

male ['meɪl] *n* : macho *m* (de animales o plantas), varón *m* (de personas) — ~ *adj* 1 : macho 2 MASCULINE : masculino

malevolent [mə'lɛvələnt] *adj* : malévolo

malfunction [mæl'fʌŋkʃən] *vi* : funcionar mal — ~ *n* : mal funcionamiento *m*

malice ['mælɪs] *n* : mala intención *f*, rencor *m* — **malicious** [mə'lɪʃəs] *adj* : malicioso

malign [mə'laɪn] *adj* : maligno — ~ *vt* : calumniar

malignant [mə'lɪgnənt] *adj* : maligno

mall ['mɔl] *n or* **shopping** ~ : centro *m* comercial

malleable ['mæliəbəl] *adj* : maleable

mallet ['mælət] *n* : mazo *m*

malnutrition [ˌmælnʊ'trɪʃən, -njʊ-] *n* : desnutrición *f*

malpractice [ˌmæl'præktəs] *n* : mala práctica *f*, negligencia *f*

malt ['mɔlt] *n* : malta *f*

mama *or* **mamma** ['mɑmə] *n* : mamá *f*

mammal ['mæməl] *n* : mamífero *m*

mammogram ['mæməˌgræm] *n* : mamografía *f*

mammoth ['mæməθ] *adj* : gigantesco

man ['mæn] *n, pl* **men** ['mɛn] : hombre *m* — ~ *vt* **manned; manning** : tripular (un barco o avión), encargarse de (un servicio)

manage ['mænɪdʒ] *v* **-aged; -aging** *vt* 1 HANDLE : manejar 2 DIRECT : administrar, dirigir — *vi* COPE : arreglárselas — **manageable** ['mænɪdʒəbəl] *adj* : manejable — **management** ['mænɪdʒmənt] *n* : dirección *f* — **manager** ['mænɪdʒər] *n* : director *m*, -tora *f*; gerente *mf* — **managerial** [ˌmænə'dʒɪriəl] *adj* : directivo

mandarin ['mændərən] *n or* ~ **orange** : mandarina *f*

mandate ['mænˌdeɪt] *n* : mandato *m* — **mandatory** ['mændəˌtori] *adj* : obligatorio

mane ['meɪn] *n* : crin *f* (de un caballo), melena *f* (de un león)

maneuver [mə'nu:vər, -'nju:-] *n* : maniobra *f* — ~ *v* **-vered; -vering** : maniobrar

mangle ['mæŋgəl] *vt* **-gled; -gling** : destrozar

mango ['mæŋˌgo:] *n, pl* **-goes** : mango *m*

mangy ['meɪndʒi] *adj* **mangier; -est** : sarnoso

manhandle ['mænˌhændəl] *vi* **-dled; -dling** : maltratar

manhole ['mænˌho:l] *n* : boca *f* de alcantarilla

manhood ['mænˌhʊd] *n* 1 : madurez *f* (de un hombre) 2 VIRILITY : virilidad *f*

mania ['meɪniə, -njə] *n* : manía *f* — **maniac** ['meɪniˌæk] *n* : maníaco *m*, -ca *f*

manicure ['mænəˌkjʊr] *n* : manicura *f* — ~ *vt* **-cured; -curing** : hacer la manicura a

manifest ['mænəˌfɛst] *adj* : manifiesto, patente — ~ *vt* : manifestar — **manifesto** [ˌmænə'fɛsˌto:] *n, pl* **-tos** *or* **-toes** : manifiesto *m*

manipulate [mə'nɪpjəˌleɪt] *vt* **-lated; -lating**

: manipular — **manipulation** [məˌnɪpjəˈleɪʃən] n : manipulación f
mankind [ˈmænˈkaɪnd, ˌkaɪnd] n : género m humano, humanidad f
manly [ˈmænli] adj -lier; -est : viril — **manliness** [ˈmænlinəs] n : virilidad f
man–made [ˈmænˈmeɪd] adj : artificial
mannequin [ˈmænɪkən] n : maniquí m
manner [ˈmænər] n 1 : manera f 2 KIND : clase f 3 ~s npl ETIQUETTE : modales mpl, educación f — **mannerism** [ˈmænəˌrɪzəm] n : peculiaridad f (de una persona)
manoeuvre Brit → **maneuver**
manor [ˈmænər] n : casa f solariega
manpower [ˈmænˌpaʊər] n : mano f de obra
mansion [ˈmæntʃən] n : mansión f
manslaughter [ˈmænˌslɔt̬ər] n : homicidio m sin premeditación
mantel [ˈmæntəl] or **mantelpiece** [ˈmæntəlˌpiːs] n : repisa f de la chimenea
manual [ˈmænjʊəl] adj : manual — ~ n : manual m
manufacture [ˌmænjəˈfæktʃər] n : fabricación f — ~ vt -tured; -turing : fabricar — **manufacturer** [ˌmænjəˈfæktʃərər] n : fabricante mf
manure [məˈnʊr, -ˈnjʊr] n : estiércol m
manuscript [ˈmænjəˌskrɪpt] n : manuscrito m
many [ˈmɛni] adj **more** [ˈmor]; **most** [ˈmoːst] 1 : muchos 2 **as** ~ : tantos 3 **how** ~ : cuántos 4 **too** ~ : demasiados — ~ pron : muchos pl, -chas pl
map [ˈmæp] n : mapa m — ~ vt **mapped; mapping** 1 : trazar el mapa de 2 or ~ **out** : planear, proyectar
maple [ˈmeɪpəl] n : arce m
mar [ˈmɑr] vt **marred; marring** : estropear
marathon [ˈmærəˌθɑn] n : maratón m
marble [ˈmɑrbəl] n 1 : mármol m 2 ~s npl : canicas fpl (para jugar)
march [ˈmɑrtʃ] n : marcha f — ~ vi : marchar, desfilar
March [ˈmɑrtʃ] n : marzo m
mare [ˈmær] n : yegua f
margarine [ˈmɑrdʒərən] n : margarina f
margin [ˈmɑrdʒən] n : margen m — **marginal** [ˈmɑrdʒənəl] adj : marginal
marigold [ˈmærəˌgoːld] n : caléndula f
marijuana [ˌmærəˈhwɑnə] n : marihuana f
marinate [ˈmærəˌneɪt] vt -nated; -nating : marinar
marine [məˈriːn] adj : marino — ~ n : soldado m de marina
marionette [ˌmæriəˈnɛt] n : marioneta f
marital [ˈmærət̬əl] adj 1 : matrimonial 2 ~ **status** : estado m civil
maritime [ˈmærəˌtaɪm] adj : marítimo
mark [ˈmɑrk] n 1 : marca f 2 STAIN : mancha f 3 IMPRINT : huella f 4 TARGET : blanco m 5 GRADE : nota f — ~ vt 1 : marcar 2 STAIN : manchar 3 POINT OUT : señalar 4 : calificar (un examen, etc.) 5 COMMEMORATE : conmemorar 6 CARACTERIZE : caracterizar 7 ~ **off** : delimitar — **marked** [ˈmɑrkt] adj : marcado, notable — **markedly** [ˈmɑrkədli] adv : notablemente — **marker** [ˈmɑrkər] n : marcador m
market [ˈmɑrkət] n : mercado m — ~ vt : vender, comercializar — **marketable** [ˈmɑrkət̬əbəl] adj : vendible — **marketplace** [ˈmɑrkətˌpleɪs] n : mercado m
marksman [ˈmɑrksmən] n, pl -men [-mən, -ˌmɛn] : tirador m — **marksmanship** [ˈmɑrksmənˌʃɪp] n : puntería f
marmalade [ˈmɑrməˌleɪd] n : mermelada f
maroon¹ [məˈruːn] vt : abandonar, aislar
maroon² n : rojo m oscuro
marquee [mɑrˈkiː] n CANOPY : marquesina f
marriage [ˈmærɪdʒ] n 1 : matrimonio m 2 WEDDING : casamiento m, boda f — **married** [ˈmærid] adj 1 : casado 2 **get** ~ : casarse
marrow [ˈmæroː] n : médula f, tuétano m
marry [ˈmæri] v -ried; -rying vt 1 : casar 2 WED : casarse con — vi : casarse
Mars [ˈmɑrz] n : Marte m
marsh [ˈmɑrʃ] n 1 : pantano m 2 or **salt** ~ : marisma f
marshal [ˈmɑrʃəl] n : mariscal m (en el ejército); jefe m, -fa f (de policía, de bomberos, etc.) — ~ vt -shaled or -shalled; -shaling or -shalling : poner en orden (los pensamientos, etc.), reunir (las tropas)
marshmallow [ˈmɑrʃˌmɛloː, -ˌmæloː] n : malvavisco m
marshy [ˈmɑrʃi] adj **marshier; -est** : pantanoso
mart [ˈmɑrt] n : mercado m
martial [ˈmɑrʃəl] adj : marcial
martyr [ˈmɑrt̬ər] n : mártir mf — ~ vt : martirizar
marvel [ˈmɑrvəl] n : maravilla f — ~ vi -veled or -velled; -veling or -velling : maravillarse — **marvelous** [ˈmɑrvələs] or **marvellous** adj : maravilloso
mascara [mæsˈkærə] n : rímel m
mascot [ˈmæsˌkɑt, -kət] n : mascota f
masculine [ˈmæskjələn] adj : masculino — **masculinity** [ˌmæskjəˈlɪnət̬i] n : masculinidad f
mash [ˈmæʃ] vt 1 CRUSH : aplastar, majar 2 PUREE : hacer puré de — **mashed potatoes** npl : puré m de patatas, puré m de papas Lat
mask [ˈmæsk] n : máscara f — ~ vt : enmascarar
masochism [ˈmæsəˌkɪzəm, ˈmæzə-] n : masoquismo m — **masochist** [ˈmæsəˌkɪst, ˈmæzə-] n : masoquista mf — **masochistic** [ˌmæsəˈkɪstɪk, ˌmæzə-] adj : masoquista
mason [ˈmeɪsən] n : albañil mf — **masonry** [ˈmeɪsənri] n, pl -ries : albañilería f
masquerade [ˌmæskəˈreɪd] n : mascarada f — ~ vi -aded; -ading ~ **as** : disfrazarse de, hacerse pasar por
mass [ˈmæs] n 1 : masa f 2 MULTITUDE : cantidad f 3 **the** ~**es** : las masas
Mass [ˈmæs] n : misa f
massacre [ˈmæsɪkər] n : masacre f — ~ vt -cred; -cring : masacrar
massage [məˈsɑʒ, -ˈsɑdʒ] n : masaje m — ~ vt -saged; -saging : dar masaje a, masajear — **masseur** [mæˈsər] n : masajista m — **masseuse** [mæˈsəz, -ˈsərz, -ˈsuːz] n : masajista f
massive [ˈmæsɪv] adj 1 BULKY, SOLID : macizo 2 HUGE : enorme, masivo
mast [ˈmæst] n : mástil m
master [ˈmæstər] n 1 : amo m, señor m (de la casa) 2 EXPERT : maestro m, -tra f 3 ~'s **degree** : maestría f — ~ vt : dominar — **masterful** [ˈmæstərfəl] adj : magistral — **masterpiece** [ˈmæstərˌpiːs] n : obra f maestra — **mastery** [ˈmæstəri] n : maestría f
masturbate [ˈmæstərˌbeɪt] v -bated; -bating vi : masturbarse — **masturbation** [ˌmæstərˈbeɪʃən] n : masturbación f
mat [ˈmæt] n 1 DOORMAT : felpudo m 2 RUG : estera f
matador [ˈmæt̬əˌdɔr] n : matador m
match [ˈmætʃ] n 1 EQUAL : igual mf 2 : fósforo m, cerilla f (para encender) 3 GAME : partido m, combate m (en boxeo) 4 **be a good** ~ : hacer buena pareja — ~ vt 1 or ~ **up** : emparejar 2 EQUAL : igualar 3 : combinar con, hacer juego con (ropa, colores, etc.) — vi : concordar, coincidir
mate [ˈmeɪt] n 1 COMPANION : compañero m, -ra f; amigo m, -ga f 2 : macho m, hembra f (de animales) — ~ vi **mated; mating** : aparearse
material [məˈtɪriəl] adj 1 : material 2 IMPORTANT : importante — ~ n 1 : material m 2 CLOTH : tela f, tejido m — **materialistic** [məˌtɪriəˈlɪstɪk] adj : materialista — **materialize** [məˈtɪriəˌlaɪz] vi -ized; -izing : aparecer
maternal [məˈtərnəl] adj : maternal — **maternity** [məˈtərnət̬i] n, pl -ties : maternidad f — ~ adj 1 : de maternidad 2 ~ **clothes** : ropa f de futura mamá
math [ˈmæθ] → **mathematics**
mathematics [ˌmæθəˈmæt̬ɪks] ns & pl : matemáticas fpl — **mathematical** [ˌmæθəˈmæt̬ɪkəl] adj : matemático — **mathematician** [ˌmæθəməˈtɪʃən] n : matemático m, -ca f
matinee or **matinée** [ˌmætənˈeɪ] n : matiné(e) f, función f de tarde
matrimony [ˈmætrəˌmoːni] n : matrimonio m — **matrimonial** [ˌmætrəˈmoːniəl] adj : matrimonial
matrix [ˈmeɪtrɪks] n, pl -trices [ˈmeɪtrəˌsiːz, ˈmæ-] or -trixes [ˈmeɪtrɪksəz] : matriz f
matte [ˈmæt] adj : mate
matter [ˈmæt̬ər] n 1 SUBSTANCE : materia f 2 QUESTION : asunto m, cuestión f 3 **as a** ~ **of fact** : en efecto, en realidad 4 **for that** ~ : de hecho 5 **to make** ~**s worse** : para colmo de males 6 **what's the** ~? : ¿qué pasa? — ~ vi : importar
mattress [ˈmætrəs] n : colchón m
mature [məˈtʊr, -ˈtjʊr, -ˈtʃʊr] adj -turer; -est : maduro — ~ vi -tured; -turing : madurar — **maturity** [məˈtʊrət̬i, -ˈtjʊr-, -ˈtʃʊr-] n : madurez f
maul [ˈmɔl] vt : maltratar, aporrear
mauve [ˈmoːv, ˈmɔv] n : malva m
maxim [ˈmæksəm] n : máxima f
maximum [ˈmæksəməm] n, pl -ma [ˈmæksəmə] or -mums : máximo m — ~ adj : máximo — **maximize** [ˈmæksəˌmaɪz] vt -mized; -mizing : llevar al máximo
may [ˈmeɪ] v aux, past **might** [ˈmaɪt]; present s & pl **may** 1 : poder 2 **come what** ~ : pase lo que pase 3 **it** ~ **happen** : puede pasar 4 ~ **the best man win** : que gane el mejor
May [ˈmeɪ] n : mayo m
maybe [ˈmeɪbi] adv : quizás, tal vez
mayhem [ˈmeɪˌhɛm, ˈmeɪəm] n : alboroto m
mayonnaise [ˈmeɪəˌneɪz] n : mayonesa f
mayor [ˈmeɪər, ˈmɛr] n : alcalde m, -desa f
maze [ˈmeɪz] n : laberinto m
me [ˈmiː] pron 1 : me 2 **for** ~ : para mí 3 **give it to** ~! : ¡dámelo! 4 **it's** ~ : soy yo 5 **with** ~ : conmigo
meadow [ˈmɛdoː] n : prado m, pradera f
meager [ˈmiːgər] or **meagre** adj : escaso
meal [ˈmiːl] n 1 : comida f 2 : harina f (de maíz, etc.) — **mealtime** [ˈmiːlˌtaɪm] n : hora f de comer
mean¹ [ˈmiːn] vt **meant** [ˈmɛnt]; **meaning** 1 SIGNIFY : querer decir 2 INTEND : querer, tener la intención de 3 **be meant for** : estar destinado a 4 **he didn't** ~ **it** : no lo dijo en serio
mean² adj 1 UNKIND : malo 2 STINGY : mezquino, tacaño 3 HUMBLE : humilde
mean³ adj AVERAGE : medio — ~ n : promedio m
meander [miˈændər] vi -dered; -dering 1 WIND : serpentear 2 WANDER : vagar
meaning [ˈmiːnɪŋ] n : significado m, sentido m — **meaningful** [ˈmiːnɪŋfəl] adj : significativo — **meaningless** [ˈmiːnɪŋləs] adj : sin sentido
meanness [ˈmiːnnəs] n 1 UNKINDNESS : maldad f 2 STINGINESS : mezquindad f
means [ˈmiːnz] n 1 : medio m 2 **by all** ~ : por supuesto 3 **by** ~ **of** : por medio de 4 **by no** ~ : de ninguna manera
meantime [ˈmiːnˌtaɪm] n 1 : interín m 2 **in the** ~ : mientras tanto — ~ adv → **meanwhile**
meanwhile [ˈmiːnˌhwaɪl] adv : mientras tanto — ~ n → **meantime**
measles [ˈmiːzəlz] npl : sarampión m
measly [ˈmiːzli] adj -slier; -est : miserable, misero
measure [ˈmɛʒər, ˈmeɪ-] n : medida f — ~ v -sured; -suring : medir — **measurable** [ˈmɛʒərəbəl, ˈmeɪ-] adj : mensurable — **measurement** [ˈmɛʒərmənt, ˈmeɪ-] n : medida f — **measure up** vi ~ **to** : estar a la altura de
meat [ˈmiːt] n : carne f — **meatball** [ˈmiːtˌbɔl] n : albóndiga f — **meaty** [ˈmiːt̬i] adj **meatier; -est** 1 : carnoso 2 SUBSTANTIAL : sustancioso
mechanic [mɪˈkænɪk] n : mecánico m, -ca f — **mechanical** [mɪˈkænɪkəl] adj : mecánico — **mechanics** [mɪˈkænɪks] ns & pl 1 : mecánica f 2 WORKINGS : mecanismo m — **mechanism** [ˈmɛkəˌnɪzəm] n : mecanismo m — **mechanize** [ˈmɛkəˌnaɪz] vt -nized; -nizing : mecanizar
medal [ˈmɛdəl] n : medalla f — **medallion** [məˈdæljən] n : medallón m
meddle [ˈmɛdəl] vi -dled; -dling : entrometerse
media [ˈmiːdiə] or **mass** ~ npl : medios mpl de comunicación
median [ˈmiːdiən] adj : medio
mediate [ˈmiːdiˌeɪt] vi -ated; -ating : mediar — **mediation** [ˌmiːdiˈeɪʃən] n : mediación f — **mediator** [ˈmiːdiˌeɪt̬ər] n : mediador m, -dora f
medical [ˈmɛdɪkəl] adj : médico — **medicated** [ˈmɛdəˌkeɪt̬əd] adj : medicinal — **medication** [ˌmɛdəˈkeɪʃən] n : medicamento m — **medicinal** [məˈdɪsənəl] adj : medicinal — **medicine** [ˈmɛdəsən] n 1 : medicina f 2 MEDICATION : medicina f, medicamento m
medieval or **mediaeval** [mɪˈdiːvəl, ˌmiː-, ˌmɛ-, -diˈiːvəl] adj : medieval
mediocre [ˌmiːdiˈoːkər] adj : mediocre — **mediocrity** [ˌmiːdiˈɑkrət̬i] n, pl -ties : mediocridad f
meditate [ˈmɛdəˌteɪt] vi -tated; -tating : meditar — **meditation** [ˌmɛdəˈteɪʃən] n : meditación f
medium [ˈmiːdiəm] n, pl -diums or -dia [ˈmiːdiə] 1 MEANS : medio m 2 MEAN : punto m medio, término m medio 3 → **media** — ~ adj : mediano
medley [ˈmɛdli] n, pl -leys 1 : mezcla f 2 : popurrí m (de canciones)
meek [ˈmiːk] adj : dócil
meet [ˈmiːt] v **met** [ˈmɛt]; **meeting** vt 1 ENCOUNTER : encontrarse con 2 SATISFY : satisfacer 3 **pleased to** ~ **you** : encantado de conocerlo — vi 1 : encontrarse 2 ASSEMBLE : reunirse 3 BE INTRODUCED : conocerse — ~ n : encuentro m — **meeting** [ˈmiːt̬ɪŋ] n : reunión f
megabyte [ˈmɛgəˌbaɪt] n : megabyte m
megaphone [ˈmɛgəˌfoːn] n : megáfono m
melancholy [ˈmɛlənˌkɑli] n, pl -cholies : melancolía f — ~ adj : melancólico, triste
mellow [ˈmɛloː] adj 1 : suave, dulce 2 CALM : apacible 3 : maduro (dícese de frutas), añejo (dícese de vinos) — ~ vt : suavizar, endulzar — vi : suavizarse
melody [ˈmɛlədi] n, pl -dies : melodía f
melon [ˈmɛlən] n : melón m
melt [ˈmɛlt] vi : derretirse, fundirse — vt : derretir
member [ˈmɛmbər] n : miembro m — **membership** [ˈmɛmbərˌʃɪp] n 1 : calidad f de miembro 2 MEMBERS : miembros mpl
membrane [ˈmɛmˌbreɪn] n : membrana f
memory [ˈmɛmri, ˈmɛmə-] n, pl -ries 1 : memoria f 2 RECOLLECTION : recuerdo m — **memento** [mɪˈmɛnˌtoː] n, pl -tos or -toes : recuerdo m — **memo** [ˈmɛmoː] n, pl **memos** or **memorandum** [ˌmɛməˈrændəm] n, pl -dums or -da [-də] : memorándum m — **memoirs** [ˈmɛmˌwɑrz] npl : memorias fpl — **memorable** [ˈmɛmərəbəl] adj : memorable — **memorial** [məˈmoriəl] adj : conmemorativo — ~ n : monumento m (conmemorativo) — **memorize** [ˈmɛməˌraɪz] vt -rized; -rizing : aprender de memoria
men → **man**
menace [ˈmɛnəs] n : amenaza f — ~ vt -aced; -acing : amenazar — **menacing** [ˈmɛnəsɪŋ] adj : amenazador
mend [ˈmɛnd] vt 1 : reparar, arreglar 2 DARN : zurcir — vi HEAL : curarse
menial [ˈmiːniəl] adj : servil, bajo
meningitis [ˌmɛnənˈdʒaɪt̬əs] n, pl -gitides [-ˈdʒɪt̬əˌdiːz] : meningitis f
menopause [ˈmɛnəˌpɔz] n : menopausia f
menstruate [ˈmɛntstrʊˌeɪt] vi -ated; -ating : menstruar — **menstruation** [ˌmɛntstrʊˈeɪʃən] n : menstruación f
mental [ˈmɛntəl] adj : mental — **mentality** [mɛnˈtælət̬i] n, pl -ties : mentalidad f
mention [ˈmɛntʃən] n : mención f — **mention** vt 1 : mencionar 2 **don't** ~ **it!** : ¡de nada!, ¡no hay de qué!
menu [ˈmɛnˌjuː] n : menú m
meow [miˈaʊ] n : maullido m, miau m — ~ vi : maullar
mercenary [ˈmərsənˌɛri] n, pl -naries : mercenario m, -ria f — ~ adj : mercenario
merchant [ˈmərtʃənt] n : comerciante mf — **merchandise** [ˈmərtʃənˌdaɪz, -ˌdaɪs] n : mercancía f, mercadería f
merciful [ˈmərsɪfəl] adj : misericordioso, compasivo — **merciless** [ˈmərsɪləs] adj : despiadado
mercury [ˈmərkjəri] n, pl -ries : mercurio m
Mercury n : Mercurio m
mercy [ˈmərsi] n, pl -cies 1 : misericordia f, compasión f 2 **at the** ~ **of** : a merced de
mere [ˈmɪr] adj, superlative **merest** : mero, simple — **merely** [ˈmɪrli] adv : simplemente
merge [ˈmərdʒ] v **merged; merging** vi : unirse, fusionarse (dícese de las compañías), confluir (dícese de los ríos, las calles, etc.) — vt : unir, fusionar, combinar — **merger** [ˈmərdʒər] n : unión f, fusión f
merit [ˈmɛrət] n : mérito m — ~ vt : merecer
mermaid [ˈmərˌmeɪd] n : sirena f
merry [ˈmɛri] adj -rier; -est : alegre — **merry–go–round** [ˈmɛrigoˌraʊnd] n : tiovivo m
mesa [ˈmeɪsə] n : mesa f
mesh [ˈmɛʃ] n : malla f
mesmerize [ˈmɛzməˌraɪz] vt -ized; -izing : hipnotizar
mess [ˈmɛs] n 1 : desorden m 2 MUDDLE : lío m 3 : rancho m (militar) — ~ vt 1 or ~ **up** SOIL : ensuciar 2 ~ **up** DISARRANGE : desordenar 3 ~ **up** BUNGLE : echar a perder — vi 1 ~ **around** PUTTER : entretenerse 2 ~ **with** PROVOKE : meterse con
message [ˈmɛsɪdʒ] n : mensaje m — **messenger** [ˈmɛsəndʒər] n : mensajero m, -ra f
messy [ˈmɛsi] adj **messier; -est** : desordenado, sucio
met → **meet**
metabolism [məˈtæbəˌlɪzəm] n : metabolismo m
metal [ˈmɛt̬əl] n : metal m — **metallic** [məˈtælɪk] adj : metálico
metamorphosis [ˌmɛt̬əˈmɔrfəsɪs] n, pl -phoses [-ˌsiːz] : metamorfosis f
metaphor [ˈmɛt̬əˌfɔr, -fər] n : metáfora f
meteor [ˈmiːt̬iər, -t̬iˌɔr] n : meteoro m — **meteorological** [ˌmiːt̬iˌɔrəˈlɑdʒɪkəl] adj : meteorológico — **meteorologist** [ˌmiːt̬iəˈrɑlədʒɪst] n : meteorólogo m, -ga f — **meteorology** [ˌmiːt̬iəˈrɑlədʒi] n : meteorología f
meter or Brit **metre** [ˈmiːt̬ər] n 1 : metro m 2 : contador m (de electricidad, etc.)
method [ˈmɛθəd] n : método m — **methodical** [məˈθɑdɪkəl] adj : metódico
meticulous [məˈtɪkjələs] adj : meticuloso
metric [ˈmɛtrɪk] or **metrical** [-trɪkəl] adj : métrico
metropolis [məˈtrɑpələs] n : metrópoli f — **metropolitan** [ˌmɛtrəˈpɑlətən] adj : metropolitano
Mexican [ˈmɛksɪkən] adj : mexicano
mice → **mouse**
microbe [ˈmaɪˌkroːb] n : microbio m
microfilm [ˈmaɪkroˌfɪlm] n : microfilm m
microphone [ˈmaɪkrəˌfoːn] n : micrófono m
microscope [ˈmaɪkrəˌskoːp] n : microscopio m — **microscopic** [ˌmaɪkrəˈskɑpɪk] adj : microscópico
microwave [ˈmaɪkrəˌweɪv] n or ~ **oven** : microondas m
mid [ˈmɪd] adj 1 ~ **morning** : a media mañana 2 **in** ~**-August** : a mediados de agosto 3 **she is in her mid thirties** : tiene alrededor de 35 años — **midair** [ˈmɪdˈær] n **in** ~ : en el aire — **midday** [ˈmɪdˈdeɪ] n : mediodía m
middle [ˈmɪdəl] adj : de en medio, del medio — ~ n 1 : medio m, centro m 2 **in the** ~ **of** : en medio de (un espacio), a mitad de (una actividad) 3 **in the** ~ **of the month** : a mediados del mes — **middle–aged** [ˌmɪdəlˈeɪdʒd] adj : de mediana edad — **Middle Ages** npl : Edad f Media — **middle class** n : clase f media — **middleman** [ˈmɪdəlˌmæn] n, pl -men [-mən, -ˌmɛn] : intermediario m, -ria f
midget [ˈmɪdʒət] n : enano m, -na f
midnight [ˈmɪdˌnaɪt] n : medianoche f
midriff [ˈmɪdˌrɪf] n : diafragma m
midst [ˈmɪdst] n 1 **in the** ~ **of** : en medio de 2 **in our** ~ : entre nosotros
midsummer [ˈmɪdˈsʌmər, -ˌsʌ-] n : pleno verano m
midway [ˈmɪdˌweɪ] adv : a mitad de camino, a medio camino
midwife [ˈmɪdˌwaɪf] n, pl -wives [-ˌwaɪvz] : comadrona f

midwinter ['mɪd'wɪntər, -ˌwɪn-] *n* : pleno invierno *m*
miff ['mɪf] *vt* : ofender
might¹ ['maɪt] (*used to express permission or possibility or as a polite alternative to* **may**) → **may**
might² *n* : fuerza *f,* poder *m* — **mighty** ['maɪt̬i] *adj* **mightier; -est 1** : fuerte, poderoso **2** GREAT : enorme — ~ *adv* : muy
migraine ['maɪˌgreɪn] *n* : jaqueca *f,* migraña *f*
migrate ['maɪˌgreɪt] *vi* **-grated; -grating** : emigrar — **migrant** ['maɪgrənt] *n* : trabajador *m,* -dora *f* ambulante
mild ['maɪld] *adj* **1** GENTLE : suave **2** LIGHT : leve **3 a ~ climate** : una clima templada
mildew ['mɪlˌduː, -ˌdjuː] *n* : moho *m*
mildly ['maɪldli] *adv* : ligeramente, suavemente — **mildness** ['maɪldnəs] *n* : apacibilidad *f* (de personas), suavedad *f* (de sabores, etc.)
mile ['maɪl] *n* : milla *f* — **mileage** ['maɪlɪdʒ] *n* : distancia *f* recorrida (en millas), kilometraje *m* — **milestone** ['maɪlˌstoːn] *n* : hito *m*
military ['mɪləˌteri] *adj* : militar — ~ *n* **the ~** : las fuerzas armadas — **militant** ['mɪlətənt] *adj* : militante — ~ *n* : militante *mf* — **militia** [mə'lɪʃə] *n* : milicia *f*
milk ['mɪlk] *n* : leche *f* — ~ *vt* **1** : ordeñar (una vaca, etc.) **2** EXPLOIT : explotar — **milky** ['mɪlki] *adj* **milkier; -est** : lechoso — **Milky Way** *n* **the ~** : la Vía Láctea
mill ['mɪl] *n* **1** : molino *m* **2** FACTORY : fábrica *f* **3** GRINDER : molinillo *m* — ~ *vt* : moler — *vi or* **~ about** : arremolinarse
millennium [mə'lɛniəm] *n, pl* **-nia** [-niə] *or* **-niums** : milenio *m*
miller ['mɪlər] *n* : molinero *m,* -ra *f*
milligram ['mɪləˌgræm] *n* : miligramo *m* — **millimeter** *or Brit* **millimetre** ['mɪləˌmiːt̬ər] *n* : milímetro *m*
million ['mɪljən] *n, pl* **millions** *or* **million 1** : millón *m* **2 a ~ people** : un millón de personas — ~ *adj* **a ~** : un millón de — **millionaire** [ˌmɪljə'nær, 'mɪljəˌnær] *n* : millonario *m,* -ria *f* — **millionth** ['mɪljənθ] *adj* : millonésimo
mime ['maɪm] *n* **1** : mimo *mf* **2** PANTOMIME : pantomima *f* — ~ *v* **mimed; miming** *vt* : imitar — *vi* : hacer la mímica — **mimic** ['mɪmɪk] *vt* **-icked; -icking** : imitar, remedar — ~ *n* : imitador *m,* -dora *f* — **mimicry** ['mɪmɪkri] *n, pl* **-ries** : imitación *f*
mince ['mɪnts] *v* **minced; mincing** *vt* **1** : picar, moler **2 not to ~ one's words** : no tener pelos en la lengua
mind ['maɪnd] *n* **1** : mente *f* **2** INTELLECT : capacidad *f* intelectual **3** OPINION : opinión *f* **4** REASON : razón *f* **5 have a ~ to** : tener intención de — ~ *vt* **1** TEND : cuidar **2** OBEY : obedecer **3** WATCH : tener cuidado con **4 I don't ~ the heat** : no me molesta el calor — *vi* **1** OBEY : obedecer **2 I don't ~** : no me importa, me es igual — **mindful** ['maɪndfəl] *adj* : atento — **mindless** ['maɪndləs] *adj* **1** SENSELESS : estúpido, sin sentido **2** DULL : aburrido
mine¹ ['maɪn] *pron* **1** : (el) mío, (la) mía, (los) míos, (las) mías **2 a friend of ~** : un amigo mío
mine² *n* : mina *f* — ~ *vt* **mined; mining 1** : extraer (oro, etc.) **2** : minar (con artefactos explosivos) — **minefield** ['maɪnˌfiːld] *n* : campo *m* de minas — **miner** ['maɪnər] *n* : minero *m,* -ra *f*
mineral ['mɪnərəl] *n* : mineral *m*
mingle ['mɪŋgəl] *v* **-gled; -gling** *vt* : mezclar — *vi* **1** : mezclarse **2** : circular (a una fiesta, etc.)
miniature ['mɪniəˌtʃʊr, 'mɪnɪˌtʃʊr, -tʃər] *n* : miniatura *f* — ~ *adj* : en miniatura
minimal ['mɪnəməl] *adj* : mínimo — **minimize** ['mɪnəˌmaɪz] *vt* **-mized; -mizing** : minimizar — **minimum** ['mɪnəməm] *adj* : mínimo — ~ *n, pl* **-ma** ['mɪnəmə] *or* **-mums** : mínimo *m*
mining ['maɪnɪŋ] *n* : minería *f*
minister ['mɪnəstər] *n* **1** : pastor *m,* -tora *f* (de una iglesia) **2** : ministro *m,* -tra *f* (en política) — ~ *vi* **~ to** : cuidar (de), atender a — **ministerial** [ˌmɪnə'striəl] *adj* : ministerial — **ministry** ['mɪnəstri] *n, pl* **-tries** : ministerio *m*
mink ['mɪŋk] *n, pl* **mink** *or* **minks** : visón *m*
minnow ['mɪnoː] *n, pl* **-nows** : pececillo *m* de agua dulce
minor ['maɪnər] *adj* **1** : menor **2** INSIGNIFICANT : sin importancia — ~ *n* **1** : menor *mf* (de edad) **2** : asignatura *f* secundaria (de estudios) — **minority** [mə'nɔrət̬i, maɪ-] *n, pl* **-ties** : minoría *f*
mint¹ ['mɪnt] *n* **1** : menta *f* (planta) **2** : pastilla *f* de menta (dulce)
mint² *n* **1 the U.S. Mint** : la casa de la moneda de los EE.UU. **2 be worth a ~** : valer un dineral — ~ *vt* : acuñar — ~ *adj* **in ~ condition** : como nuevo
minus ['maɪnəs] *prep* **1** : menos **2** WITHOUT : sin — ~ *n or* **~ sign** : signo *m* de menos
minuscule ['mɪnəsˌkjuːl, mɪ'nʌs-] *adj* : minúsculo
minute¹ [maɪ'nuːt, mɪ-, -'njuːt] *n* **1** : minuto *m* **2** MOMENT : momento *m* **3 ~s** *npl* : actas *fpl* (de una reunión)
minute² ['mɪnət] *adj* **-nuter; -est 1** TINY : diminuto, minúsculo **2** DETAILED : minucioso
miracle ['mɪrɪkəl] *n* : milagro *m* — **miraculous** [mə'rækjələs] *adj* : milagroso
mirage [mɪ'rɑʒ, 'mɪrˌɑʒ] *n* : espejismo *m*
mire ['maɪr] *n* : lodo *m,* fango *m*
mirror ['mɪrər] *n* : espejo *m* — ~ *vt* : reflejar
mirth ['mərθ] *n* : alegría *f,* risas *fpl*
misapprehension [ˌmɪsˌæprə'hɛntʃən] *n* : malentendido *m*
misbehave [ˌmɪsbi'heɪv] *vi* **-haved; -having** : portarse mal — **misbehavior** [ˌmɪsbi'heɪvjər] *n* : mala conducta *f*
miscalculate [mɪs'kælkjəˌleɪt] *v* **-lated; -lating** : calcular mal
miscarriage [ˌmɪs'kærɪdʒ, 'mɪsˌkærɪdʒ] *n* **1** : aborto *m* **2 ~ of justice** : error *m* judicial
miscellaneous [ˌmɪsə'leɪniəs] *adj* : diverso, vario
mischief ['mɪstʃəf] *n* : travesuras *fpl* — **mischievous** ['mɪstʃəvəs] *adj* : travieso
misconception [ˌmɪskən'sɛpʃən] *n* : concepto *m* erróneo
misconduct [mɪs'kɑndəkt] *n* : mala conducta *f*
misdeed [mɪs'diːd] *n* : fechoría *f*
misdemeanor [ˌmɪsdɪ'miːnər] *n* : delito *m* menor
miser ['maɪzər] *n* : avaro *m,* -ra *f;* tacaño *m,* -ña *f*
miserable ['mɪzərəbəl] *adj* **1** UNHAPPY : triste **2** WRETCHED : miserable **3 ~ weather** : tiempo *m* malo
miserly ['maɪzərli] *adj* : mezquino
misery ['mɪzəri] *n, pl* **-eries 1** : sufrimiento *m* **2** WRETCHEDNESS : miseria *f*
misfire [mɪs'faɪr] *vi* **-fired; -firing** : fallar
misfit ['mɪsˌfɪt, mɪs'fɪt] *n* : inadaptado *m,* -da *f*
misfortune [mɪs'fɔrtʃən] *n* : desgracia *f*
misgiving [mɪs'gɪvɪŋ] *n* : duda *f*
misguided [mɪs'gaɪdəd] *adj* : descaminado, equivocado
mishap ['mɪsˌhæp] *n* : contratiempo *m*
misinform [ˌmɪsɪn'fɔrm] *vt* : informar mal
misinterpret [ˌmɪsɪn'tərprət] *vt* : interpretar mal
misjudge [mɪs'dʒʌdʒ] *vt* **-judged; -judging** : juzgar mal
mislay [mɪs'leɪ] *vt* **-laid** [-leɪd]; **-laying** : extraviar, perder
mislead [mɪs'liːd] *vt* **-led** [-'lɛd]; **-leading** : engañar — **misleading** [mɪs'liːdɪŋ] *adj* : engañoso
misnomer [mɪs'noːmər] *n* : nombre *m* inapropiado
misplace [mɪs'pleɪs] *vt* **-placed; -placing** : extraviar, perder
misprint ['mɪsˌprɪnt, mɪs'-] *n* : errata *f,* error *m* de imprenta
miss ['mɪs] *vt* **1** : errar, faltar **2** OVERLOOK : pasar por alto **3** : perder (una oportunidad, un vuelo, etc.) **4** AVOID : evitar **5** OMIT : saltarse **6 I ~ you** : te echo de menos — ~ *n* **1** : fallo *m* (de un tiro, etc.) **2** FAILURE : fracaso *m*
Miss ['mɪs] *n* : señorita *f*
missile ['mɪsəl] *n* **1** : misil *m* **2** PROJECTILE : proyectil *m*
missing ['mɪsɪŋ] *adj* : perdido, desaparecido
mission ['mɪʃən] *n* : misión *f* — **missionary** ['mɪʃəˌneri] *n, pl* **-aries** : misionero *m,* -ra *f*
misspell [mɪs'spɛl] *vt* : escribir mal
mist ['mɪst] *n* : neblina *f,* bruma *f*
mistake [mɪ'steɪk] *vt* **mistook** [-'stʊk]; **mistaken** [-'steɪkən]; **-taking 1** MISINTERPRET : entender mal **2** CONFUSE : confundir — ~ *n* **1** : error *m* **2 make a ~** : equivocarse — **mistaken** [mɪ'steɪkən] *adj* : equivocado
mister ['mɪstər] *n* : señor *m*
mistletoe ['mɪsəlˌtoː] *n* : muérdago *m*
mistreat [mɪs'triːt] *vt* : maltratar
mistress ['mɪstrəs] *n* **1** : dueña *f,* señora *f* (de una casa) **2** LOVER : amante *f*
mistrust [mɪs'trʌst] *n* : desconfianza *f* — ~ *vt* : desconfiar de
misty ['mɪsti] *adj* **mistier; -est** : neblinoso, nebuloso
misunderstand [ˌmɪsˌʌndər'stænd] *vt* **-stood; -standing** : entender mal — **misunderstanding** [ˌmɪsˌʌndər'stændɪŋ] *n* : malentendido *m*
misuse [mɪs'juːz] *vt* **-used; -using 1** : emplear mal **2** MISTREAT : maltratar — ~ [mɪs'juːs] *n* : mal empleo *m,* abuso *m*
mitigate ['mɪt̬əˌgeɪt] *vt* **-gated; -gating** : mitigar
mitt ['mɪt] *n* : manopla *f,* guante *m* (de béisbol) — **mitten** ['mɪtən] *n* : manopla *f,* mitón *m*
mix ['mɪks] *vt* **1** : mezclar **2 ~ up** : confundir — *vi* : mezclarse — ~ *n* : mezcla *f* — **mixture** ['mɪkstʃər] *n* : mezcla *f* — **mix–up** ['mɪksˌʌp] *n* : confusión *f,* lío *m fam*
moan ['moːn] *n* : gemido *m* — ~ *vi* : gemir
mob ['mɑb] *n* : muchedumbre *f* — ~ *vt* **mobbed; mobbing** : acosar
mobile ['moːbəl, -ˌbiːl, -ˌbaɪl] *adj* : móvil — ~ ['moˌbiːl] *n* : móvil *m* — **mobile home** *n* : caravana *f* — **mobility** [mo'bɪlət̬i] *n* : movilidad *f* — **mobilize** ['moːbəˌlaɪz] *vt* **-lized; -lizing** : movilizar
moccasin ['mɑkəsən] *n* : mocasín *m*
mock ['mɑk, 'mɔk] *vt* : burlarse de, mofarse de — ~ *adj* : falso — **mockery** ['mɑkəri, 'mɔ-] *n, pl* **-eries** : burla *f* — **mock–up** ['mɑkˌʌp] *n* : maqueta *f*
mode ['moːd] *n* **1** : modo *m* **2** FASHION : moda *f*
model ['mɑdəl] *n* **1** : modelo *m* **2** MOCK-UP : maqueta *f* **3** : modelo *mf* (persona) — ~ *v* **-eled** *or* **-elled; -eling** *or* **-elling** *vt* **1** SHAPE : modelar **2** WEAR : lucir — *vi* : trabajar de modelo — ~ *adj* : modelo
modem ['moːdəm, -ˌdɛm] *n* : módem *m*
moderate ['mɑdərət] *adj* : moderado — ~ *n* : moderado *m,* -da *f* — ~ ['mɑdəˌreɪt] *v* **-ated; -ating** *vt* : moderar — *vi* : moderarse — **moderation** [ˌmɑdə'reɪʃən] *n* : moderación *f* — **moderator** ['mɑdəˌreɪt̬ər] *n* : moderador *m,* -dora *f*
modern ['mɑdərn] *adj* : moderno — **modernize** ['mɑdərˌnaɪz] *vt* **-ized; -izing** : modernizar
modest ['mɑdəst] *adj* : modesto — **modesty** ['mɑdəsti] *n* : modestia *f*
modify ['mɑdəˌfaɪ] *vt* **-fied; -fying** : modificar
moist ['mɔɪst] *adj* : húmedo — **moisten** ['mɔɪsən] *vt* : humedecer — **moisture** ['mɔɪstʃər] *n* : humedad *f* — **moisturizer** ['mɔɪtʃəˌraɪzər] *n* : crema *f* hidratante
molar ['moːlər] *n* : muela *f*
molasses [mə'læsəz] *n* : melaza *f*
mold¹ ['moːld] *n* FORM : molde *m* — ~ *vt* : moldear, formar
mold² *n* FUNGUS : moho *m* — **moldy** ['moːldi] *adj* **moldier; -est** : mohoso
mole¹ ['moːl] *n* : lunar *m* (en la piel)
mole² *n* : topo *m* (animal)
molecule ['mɑlɪˌkjuːl] *n* : molécula *f*
molest [mə'lɛst] *vt* **1** HARASS : importunar **2** : abusar (sexualmente)
molten ['moːltən] *adj* : fundido
mom ['mɑm, 'mʌm] *n* : mamá *f*
moment ['moːmənt] *n* : momento *m* — **momentarily** [ˌmoːmən'terəli] *adv* **1** : momentáneamente **2** SOON : dentro de poco, pronto — **momentary** ['moːmənˌteri] *adj* : momentáneo
momentous [mo'mɛntəs] *adj* : muy importante
momentum [mo'mɛntəm] *n, pl* **-ta** [-tə] *or* **-tums 1** : momento *m* (en física) **2** IMPETUS : ímpetu *m*
monarch ['mɑˌnɑrk, -nərk] *n* : monarca *mf* — **monarchy** ['mɑˌnɑrki, -nər-] *n, pl* **-chies** : monarquía *f*
monastery ['mɑnəˌsteri] *n, pl* **-teries** : monasterio *m*
Monday ['mʌnˌdeɪ, -di] *n* : lunes *m*
money ['mʌni] *n, pl* **-eys** *or* **-ies** ['mʌniz] : dinero *m* — **monetary** ['mɑnəˌteri, 'mʌnə-] *adj* : monetario — **money order** *n* : giro *m* postal
mongrel ['mɑŋgrəl, 'mʌŋ-] *n* : perro *m* mestizo
monitor ['mɑnət̬ər] *n* : monitor *m* (de una computadora, etc.) — ~ *vt* : controlar
monk ['mʌŋk] *n* : monje *m*
monkey ['mʌŋki] *n, pl* **-keys** : mono *m,* -na *f* — **monkey wrench** *n* : llave *f* inglesa
monogram ['mɑnəˌgræm] *n* : monograma *m*
monologue ['mɑnəˌlɔg] *n* : monólogo *m*
monopoly [mə'nɑpəli] *n, pl* **-lies** : monopolio *m* — **monopolize** [mə'nɑpəˌlaɪz] *vt* **-lized; -lizing** : monopolizar
monotonous [mə'nɑtənəs] *adj* : monótono — **monotony** [mə'nɑtəni] *n* : monotonía *f*
monster ['mɑntstər] *n* : monstruo *m* — **monstrosity** [mɑn'strɑsət̬i] *n, pl* **-ties** : monstruosidad *f* — **monstrous** ['mɑntstrəs] *adj* **1** : monstruoso **2** HUGE : gigantesco
month ['mʌnθ] *n* : mes *m* — **monthly** ['mʌnθli] *adv* : mensualmente — ~ *adj* : mensual
monument ['mɑnjəmənt] *n* : monumento *m* — **monumental** [ˌmɑnjə'mɛntəl] *adj* : monumental
moo ['muː] *vi* : mugir — ~ *n* : mugido *m*
mood ['muːd] *n* : humor *m* — **moody** ['muːdi] *adj* **moodier; -est 1** GLOOMY : melancólico, deprimido **2** IRRITABLE : malhumorado **3** TEMPERAMENTAL : de humor variable
moon ['muːn] *n* : luna *f* — **moonlight** ['muːnˌlaɪt] *n* : luz *f* de la luna
moor¹ ['mʊr, 'mɔr] *n* : brezal *m,* páramo *m*
moor² *vt* : amarrar — **mooring** ['mʊrɪŋ, 'mɔr-] *n* DOCK : atracadero *m*
moose ['muːs] *ns & pl* : alce *m*
moot ['muːt] *adj* : discutible
mop ['mɑp] *n* **1** : trapeador *m Lat,* fregona *f Spain* **2** *or* **~ of hair** : pelambrera *f* — ~ *vt* **mopped; mopping** : trapear *Lat,* pasar la fregona a *Spain*
mope ['moːp] *vi* **moped; moping** : andar deprimido
moped ['moːˌpɛd] *n* : ciclomotor *m*
moral ['mɔrəl] *adj* : moral — ~ *n* **1** : moraleja *f* (de un cuento, etc.) **2 ~s** *npl* : moral *f,* moralidad *f* — **morale** [mə'ræl] *n* : moral *f* — **morality** [mə'rælət̬i] *n, pl* **-ties** : moralidad *f*
morbid ['mɔrbɪd] *adj* : morboso
more ['mor] *adj* : más — ~ *adv* **1** : más **2 ~ and ~** : cada vez más **3 ~ or less** : más o menos **4 once ~** : una vez más — ~ *n* : más *m* — ~ *pron* : más — **moreover** [mor'oːvər] *adv* : además
morgue ['mɔrg] *n* : depósito *m* de cadáveres
morning ['mɔrnɪŋ] *n* **1** : mañana *f* **2 good ~!** : ¡buenos días! **3 in the ~** : por la mañana
moron ['morˌɑn] *n* : estúpido *m,* -da *f;* imbécil *mf*
morose [mə'roːs] *adj* : malhumorado
morphine ['mɔrˌfiːn] *n* : morfina *f*
morsel ['mɔrsəl] *n* **1** BITE : bocado *m* **2** FRAGMENT : pedazo *m*
mortal ['mɔrt̬əl] *adj* : mortal — ~ *n* : mortal *mf* — **mortality** [mɔr'tælət̬i] *n* : mortalidad *f*
mortar ['mɔrt̬ər] *n* : mortero *m*
mortgage ['mɔrgɪdʒ] *n* : hipoteca *f* — ~ *vt* **-gaged; -gaging** : hipotecar
mortify ['mɔrt̬əˌfaɪ] *vt* **-fied; -fying 1** : mortificar **2** HUMILIATE : avergonzar
mosaic [mo'zeɪɪk] *n* : mosaico *m*
Moslem ['mɑzləm] → **Muslim**
mosque ['mɑsk] *n* : mezquita *f*
mosquito [mə'skiːt̬o] *n, pl* **-toes** : mosquito *m,* zancudo *m Lat*
moss ['mɔs] *n* : musgo *m*
most ['moːst] *adj* **1** : la mayoría de, la mayor parte de **2 (the) ~** : más — ~ *adv* : más — ~ *n* : más *m,* máximo *m* — ~ *pron* : la mayoría, la mayor parte — **mostly** ['moːstli] *adv* **1** MAINLY : en su mayor parte, principalmente **2** USUALLY : normalmente
motel [mo'tɛl] *n* : motel *m*
moth ['mɔθ] *n* : palomilla *f,* polilla *f*
mother ['mʌðər] *n* : madre *f* — ~ *vt* **1** : cuidar de **2** SPOIL : mimar — **motherhood** ['mʌðərˌhʊd] *n* : maternidad *f* — **mother–in–law** ['mʌðərɪnˌlɔ] *n, pl* **mothers–in–law** : suegra *f* — **motherly** ['mʌðərli] *adj* : maternal — **mother–of–pearl** [ˌmʌðərəv'pərl] *n* : nácar *m*
motif [mo'tiːf] *n* : motivo *m*
motion ['moːʃən] *n* **1** : movimiento *m* **2** PROPOSAL : moción *f* **3 set in ~** : poner en marcha — ~ *vi* **~ to s.o.** : hacer una señal a algn — **motionless** ['moːʃənləs] *adj* : inmóvil — **motion picture** *n* : película *f*
motive ['moːt̬ɪv] *n* : motivo *m* — **motivate** ['moːt̬əˌveɪt] *vt* **-vated; -vating** : motivar — **motivation** [ˌmoːt̬ə'veɪʃən] *n* : motivación *f*
motor ['moːt̬ər] *n* : motor *m* — **motorbike** ['moːt̬ərˌbaɪk] *n* : motocicleta *f* (pequeña), moto *f* — **motorboat** ['moːt̬ərˌboːt] *n* : lancha *f* motora — **motorcycle** ['moːt̬ərˌsaɪkəl] *n* : motocicleta *f* — **motorcyclist** ['moːt̬ərˌsaɪkəlɪst] *n* : motociclista *mf* — **motorist** ['moːt̬ərɪst] *n* : automovilista *mf,* motorista *mf Lat*
motto ['mɑt̬oː] *n, pl* **-toes** : lema *m*
mould ['moːld] → **mold**
mound ['maʊnd] *n* **1** PILE : montón *m* **2** HILL : montículo *m*
mount¹ ['maʊnt] *n* **1** HORSE : montura *f* **2** SUPPORT : soporte *m* — ~ *vt* : montar (un caballo, etc.), subir (una escalera) — *vi* INCREASE : aumentar
mount² *n* HILL : monte *m* — **mountain** ['maʊntən] *n* : montaña *f* — **mountainous** ['maʊntənəs] *adj* : montañoso
mourn ['morn] *vt* : llorar (por) — *vi* : lamentarse — **mourner** ['mornər] *n* : doliente *mf* — **mournful** ['mornfəl] *adj* : triste — **mourning** ['mornɪŋ] *n* : luto *m*
mouse ['maʊs] *n, pl* **mice** ['maɪs] : ratón *m* — **mousetrap** ['maʊsˌtræp] *n* : ratonera *f*
moustache ['mʌˌstæʃ, mə'stæʃ] → **mustache**
mouth ['maʊθ] *n* : boca *f* (de una persona o un animal), desembocadura *f* (de un río) — **mouthful** ['maʊθˌfʊl] *n* : bocado *m* — **mouthpiece** ['maʊθˌpiːs] *n* : boquilla *f* (de un instrumento musical)
move ['muːv] *v* **moved; moving** *vi* **1** GO : ir **2** RELOCATE : mudarse **3** STIR : moverse **4** ACT : tomar medidas — *vt* **1** : mover **2** AFFECT : conmover **3** TRANSPORT : transportar, trasladar **4** PROPOSE : proponer — ~ *n* **1** MOVEMENT : movimiento *m* **2** RELOCATION : mudanza *f* **3** STEP : medida *f* — **movable** ['muːvəbəl] *or* **moveable** *adj* : movible, móvil — **movement** ['muːvmənt] *n* : movimiento *m*
movie ['muːvi] *n* **1** : película *f* **2 ~s** *npl* : cine *m*
mow ['moː] *vt* **mowed; mowed** *or* **mown** ['moːn]; **mowing** : cortar (la hierba) — **mower** ['moːər] → **lawn mower**
Mr. ['mɪstər] *n, pl* **Messrs.** ['mɛsərz] : señor *m*
Mrs. ['mɪsəz, -səs, *esp South* 'mɪzəz, -zəs] *n, pl* **Mesdames** [meɪ'dæm, -'dɛm] : señora *f*
Ms. ['mɪz] *n* : señora *f,* señorita *f*
much ['mʌtʃ] *adj* **more; most** : mucho — ~ *adv* **more** ['mor]; **most** ['moːst] **1** : mucho **2 as ~ as** : tanto como **3 how ~?** : ¿cuánto? **4 too ~** : demasiado — ~ *pron* : mucho, -cha
muck ['mʌk] *n* **1** DIRT : mugre *f,* suciedad *f* **2** MANURE : estiércol *m*
mucus ['mjuːkəs] *n* : mucosidad *f*
mud ['mʌd] *n* : barro *m,* lodo *m*

muddle [ˈmʌdəl] *v* **-dled; -dling** *vt* **1** CONFUSE : confundir **2** JUMBLE : desordenar — *vi* **~ through** : arreglárselas — **~** *n* : confusión *f,* lío *m fam*
muddy [ˈmʌdi] *adj* **-dier; -est** : fangoso, lleno de barro
muffin [ˈmʌfən] *n* : mollete *m*
muffle [ˈmʌfəl] *vt* **-fled; -fling** : amortiguar (un sonido) — **muffler** [ˈmʌflər] *n* **1** SCARF : bufanda *f* **2** : silenciador *m,* mofle *m Lat* (de un automóvil)
mug [ˈmʌg] *n* CUP : tazón *m* — **~** *vt* : asaltar, atracar — **mugger** [ˈmʌgər] *n* : atracador *m,* -dora *f*
muggy [ˈmʌgi] *adj* **-gier; -est** : bochornoso
mule [ˈmju:l] *n* : mula *f*
mull [ˈmʌl] *vt or* **~ over** : reflexionar sobre
multicolored [ˌmʌltiˈkʌlərd, ˌmʌltaɪ-] *adj* : multicolor
multimedia [ˌmʌltiˈmi:diə, ˌmʌltaɪ-] *adj* : multimedia
multinational [ˌmʌltiˈnæʃənəl, ˌmʌltaɪ-] *adj* : multinacional
multiple [ˈmʌltəpəl] *adj* : múltiple — **~** *n* : múltiplo *m* — **multiplication** [ˌmʌltəpləˈkeɪʃən] *n* : multiplicación *f* — **multiply** [ˈmʌltəˌplaɪ] *v* **-plied; -plying** *vt* : multiplicar — *vi* : multiplicarse
multitude [ˈmʌltəˌtu:d, -ˌtju:d] *n* : multitud *f*
mum [ˈmʌm] *adj* **keep ~** : guardar silencio
mumble [ˈmʌmbəl] *v* **-bled; -bling** *vt* : mascullar — *vi* : hablar entre dientes
mummy [ˈmʌmi] *n, pl* **-mies** : momia *f*
mumps [ˈmʌmps] *ns & pl* : paperas *fpl*
munch [ˈmʌntʃ] *v* : mascar, masticar
mundane [ˌmʌnˈdeɪn, ˈmʌnˌ-] *adj* : rutinario, ordinario
municipal [mjʊˈnɪsəpəl] *adj* : municipal — **municipality** [mjʊˌnɪsəˈpæləṭi] *n, pl* **-ties** : municipio *m*
munitions [mjʊˈnɪʃənz] *npl* : municiónes *fpl*
mural [ˈmjʊrəl] *n* : mural *m*
murder [ˈmərdər] *n* : asesinato *m,* homicidio *m* — **~** *vt* : asesinar, matar — *vi* : matar — **murderer** [ˈmərdərər] *n* : asesino *m,* -na *f;* homicida *mf* — **murderous** [ˈmərdərəs] *adj* : asesino, homicida
murky [ˈmərki] *adj* **-kier; -est** : turbio, oscuro
murmur [ˈmərmər] *n* : murmullo *m* — **murmur** *v* : murmurar
muscle [ˈmʌsəl] *n* : músculo *m* — **~** *vi* **-cled; -cling** *or* **~ in** : meterse por la fuerza en — **muscular** [ˈmʌskjələr] *adj* **1** : muscular **2** STRONG : musculoso
muse[1] [ˈmju:z] *n* : musa *f*
muse[2] *vi* **mused; musing** : meditar
museum [mjʊˈzi:əm] *n* : museo *m*
mushroom [ˈmʌʃˌru:m, -ˌrʊm] *n* **1** : hongo *m,* seta *f* **2** : champiñón *m* (en la cocina) — **~** *vi* GROW : crecer rápidamente, multiplicarse
mushy [ˈmʌʃi] *adj* **mushier; -est** **1** SOFT : blando **2** MAWKISH : sensiblero
music [ˈmju:zɪk] *n* : música *f* — **musical** [ˈmju:zɪkəl] *adj* : musical — **~** *n* : comedia *f* musical — **musician** [mjʊˈzɪʃən] *n* : músico *m,* -ca *f*
Muslim [ˈmʌzləm, ˈmʊs-, ˈmʊz-] *adj* : musulmán — **~** *n* : musulmán *m,* -mana *f*
muslin [ˈmʌzlən] *n* : muselina *f*
mussel [ˈmʌsəl] *n* : mejillón *m*
must [ˈmʌst] *v aux* **1** : deber, tener que **2 you ~ come** : tienes que venir **3 you ~ be tired** : debes (de) estar cansado — **~** *n* : necesidad *f*
mustache [ˈmʌˌstæʃ, mʌˈstæʃ] *n* : bigote *m,* bigotes *mpl*
mustang [ˈmʌˌstæŋ] *n* : mustang *m*
mustard [ˈmʌstərd] *n* : mostaza *f*
muster [ˈmʌstər] *vt* **1** : reunir **2** *or* **~ up** : armarse de, cobrar (valor, fuerzas, etc.)
musty [ˈmʌsti] *adj* **mustier; -est** : que huele a cerrado
mute [ˈmju:t] *adj* **muter; mutest** : mudo — **~** *n* : mudo *m,* -da *f*
mutilate [ˈmju:ṭəˌleɪt] *vt* **-lated; -lating** : mutilar
mutiny [ˈmju:təni] *n, pl* **-nies** : motín *m* — **~** *vi* **-nied; -nying** : amotinarse
mutter [ˈmʌṭər] *vi* : murmurar
mutton [ˈmʌtən] *n* : carne *f* de carnero
mutual [ˈmju:tʃʊəl] *adj* **1** : mutuo **2** COMMON : común — **mutually** [ˈmju:tʃʊəli, -tʃəli] *adv* : mutuamente
muzzle [ˈmʌzəl] *n* **1** SNOUT : hocico *m* **2** : bozal *m* (para un perro, etc.) **3** : boca *f* (de un arma de fuego) — **~** *vt* **-zled; -zling** : poner un bozal a (un animal)
my [ˈmaɪ] *adj* : mi
myopia [maɪˈo:piə] *n* : miopía *f* — **myopic** [maɪˈo:pɪk, -ˈɑ-] *adj* : miope
myself [maɪˈsɛlf] *pron* **1** (*reflexive*) : me **2** (*emphatic*) : yo mismo **3 by ~** : solo
mystery [ˈmɪstəri] *n, pl* **-teries** : misterio *m* — **mysterious** [mɪˈstɪriəs] *adj* : misterioso
mystic [ˈmɪstɪk] *adj or* **mystical** [ˈmɪstɪkəl] : místico
mystify [ˈmɪstəˌfaɪ] *vt* **-fied; -fying** : dejar perplejo, confundir
mystique [mɪˈsti:k] *n* : aura *f* de misterio
myth [ˈmɪθ] *n* : mito *m* — **mythical** [ˈmɪθɪkəl] *adj* : mítico

N

n [ˈɛn] *n, pl* **n's** *or* **ns** [ˈɛnz] : n *f,* decimocuarta letra del alfabeto inglés
nab [ˈnæb] *vt* **nabbed; nabbing** **1** ARREST : pescar *fam* **2** GRAB : agarrar
nag [ˈnæg] *v* **nagged; nagging** *vi* COMPLAIN : quejarse — *vt* **1** ANNOY : fastidiar, dar la lata a **2** SCOLD : regañar — **nagging** *adj* : persistente
nail [ˈneɪl] *n* **1** : clavo *m* **2** : uña *f* (de un dedo) — **~** *vt or* **~ down** : clavar — **nail file** *n* : lima *f* de uñas
naive *or* **naïve** [nɑˈi:v] *adj* **-iver; -est** : ingenuo — **naïveté** [ˌnɑˌi:vəˈteɪ, nɑˈi:vəˌ-] *n* : ingenuidad *f*
naked [ˈneɪkəd] *adj* **1** : desnudo **2 the ~ truth** : la pura verdad **3 to the ~ eye** : a simple vista
name [ˈneɪm] *n* **1** : nombre *m* **2** REPUTATION : fama *f* **3 what is your ~?** : ¿cómo se llama? **4 → first name, surname** — **~** *vt* **named; naming** **1** : poner nombre a **2** APPOINT : nombrar **3 ~ a price** : fijar un precio — **nameless** [ˈneɪmləs] *adj* : anónimo — **namely** [ˈneɪmli] *adv* : a saber — **namesake** [ˈneɪmˌseɪk] *n* : tocayo *m,* -ya *f*
nap[1] [ˈnæp] *vi* **napped; napping** : echarse una siesta — **~** *n* : siesta *f*
nap[2] *n* : pelo *m* (de una tela)
nape [ˈneɪp, ˈnæp] *n or* **~ of the neck** : nuca *f*
napkin [ˈnæpkən] *n* **1** : servilleta *f* **2 → sanitary napkin**
narcotic [nɑrˈkɑṭɪk] *n* : narcótico *m,* estupefaciente *m*
narrate [ˈnærˌeɪt] *vt* **-rated; -rating** : narrar — **narration** [næˈreɪʃən] *n* : narración *f* — **narrative** [ˈnærəṭɪv] *n* : narración *f* — **narrator** [ˈnærˌeɪṭər] *n* : narrador *m,* -dora *f*
narrow [ˈnærˌo:] *adj* **1** : estrecho, angosto **2** RESTRICTED : limitado — **~** *vi* : estrecharse — *vt* **1** : estrechar **2** *or* **~ down** : limitar — **narrowly** [ˈnæroli] *adv* : por poco — **narrow–minded** [ˌnæroˈmaɪndəd] *adj* : de miras estrechas
nasal [ˈneɪzəl] *adj* : nasal
nasty [ˈnæsti] *adj* **-tier; -est** **1** MEAN : malo, cruel **2** UNPLEASANT : desagradable **3** REPUGNANT : asqueroso — **nastiness** [ˈnæstinəs] *n* : maldad *f*
nation [ˈneɪʃən] *n* : nación *f* — **national** [ˈnæʃənəl] *adj* : nacional — **nationalism** [ˈnæʃənəˌlɪzəm] *n* : nacionalismo *m* — **nationality** [ˌnæʃəˈnæləṭi] *n, pl* **-ties** : nacionalidad *f* — **nationalize** [ˈnæʃənəˌlaɪz] *vt* **-ized; -izing** : nacionalizar — **nationwide** [ˈneɪʃənˈwaɪd] *adj* : por todo el país
native [ˈneɪṭɪv] *adj* **1** : natal (dícese de un país, etc.) **2** INNATE : innato **3 ~ language** : lengua *f* materna — **~** *n* **1** : nativo *m,* -va *f* **2 be a ~ of** : ser natural de — **Native American** : indio *m* americano, india *f* americana — **nativity** [nəˈtɪvəṭi, neɪ-] *n, pl* **-ties the Nativity** : la Navidad
nature [ˈneɪtʃər] *n* **1** : naturaleza *f* **2** KIND : índole *f,* clase *f* **3** DISPOSITION : carácter *m,* natural *m* — **natural** [ˈnætʃərəl] *adj* : natural — **naturalize** [ˈnætʃərəˌlaɪz] *vt* **-ized; -izing** : naturalizar — **naturally** [ˈnætʃərəli] *adv* : naturalmente
naught [ˈnɔt] *n* **1** NOTHING : nada *f* **2** ZERO : cero *m*
naughty [ˈnɔṭi] *adj* **-tier; -est** **1** : travieso, pícaro **2** RISQUÉ : picante
nausea [ˈnɔziə, ˈnɔʃə] *n* : náuseas *fpl* — **nauseating** *adj* : nauseabundo — **nauseous** [ˈnɔʃəs, -ziəs] *adj* **1 feel ~** : sentir náuseas **2** SICKENING : nauseabundo
nautical [ˈnɔṭɪkəl] *adj* : náutico
naval [ˈneɪvəl] *adj* : naval
nave [ˈneɪv] *n* : nave *f* (de una iglesia)
navel [ˈneɪvəl] *n* : ombligo *m*
navigate [ˈnævəˌgeɪt] *v* **-gated; -gating** *vi* : navegar — *vt* **1** : gobernar (un barco), pilotar (un avión) **2** : navegar por (un río, etc.) — **navigable** [ˈnævɪgəbəl] *adj* : navegable — **navigation** [ˌnævəˈgeɪʃən] *n* : navegación *f* — **navigator** [ˈnævəˌgeɪṭər] *n* : navegante *mf*
navy [ˈneɪvi] *n, pl* **-vies** **1** : marina *f* de guerra **2** *or* **~ blue** : azul *m* marino
near [ˈnɪr] *adv* : cerca — **~** *prep* : cerca de — **~** *adj* : cercano, próximo — **~** *vt* : acercarse a — **nearby** [nɪrˈbaɪ, ˈnɪrˌbaɪ] *adv* : cerca — **~** *adj* : cercano — **nearly** [ˈnɪrli] *adv* : casi — **nearsighted** [ˈnɪrˌsaɪṭəd] *adj* : miope, corto de vista
neat [ˈni:t] *adj* **1** TIDY : muy arreglado **2** CLEVER : hábil, ingenioso — **neatly** [ˈni:tli] *adv* **1** : ordenadamente **2** CLEVERLY : hábilmente — **neatness** [ˈni:tnəs] *n* : pulcritud *f,* orden *m*
nebulous [ˈnɛbjʊləs] *adj* : nebuloso
necessary [ˈnɛsəˌsɛri] *adj* : necesario — **necessarily** [ˌnɛsəˈsɛrəli] *adv* : necesariamente — **necessitate** [nɪˈsɛsəˌteɪt] *vt* **-tated; -tating** : exigir, requerir — **necessity** [nɪˈsɛsəṭi] *n, pl* **-ties** **1** : necesidad *f* **2 necessities** *npl* : cosas *fpl* indispensables
neck [ˈnɛk] *n* **1** : cuello *m* (de una persona o una botella), pescuezo *m* (de un animal) **2** COLLAR : cuello *m* — **necklace** [ˈnɛkləs] *n* : collar *m* — **necktie** [ˈnɛkˌtaɪ] *n* : corbata *f*
nectar [ˈnɛktər] *n* : néctar *m*
nectarine [ˌnɛktəˈri:n] *n* : nectarina *f*
need [ˈni:d] *n* **1** : necesidad *f* **2 if ~ be** : si hace falta — **~** *vt* **1** : necesitar, exigir **2 ~ to** : tener que — *v aux* : tener que
needle [ˈni:dəl] *n* : aguja *f* — **~** *vt* **-dled; -dling** : pinchar
needless [ˈni:dləs] *adj* **1** : innecesario **2 ~ to say** : de más está decir
needlework [ˈni:dəlˌwərk] *n* : bordado *m*
needn't [ˈni:dənt] (*contraction of* **need not**) **→ need**
needy [ˈni:di] **needier; -est** *adj* : necesitado
negative [ˈnɛgəṭɪv] *adj* : negativo — **~** *n* **1** : negación *f* (en gramática) **2** : negativo *m* (en fotografía)
neglect [nɪˈglɛkt] *vt* : descuidar — **~** *n* : descuido *m,* abandono *m*
negligee [ˌnɛgləˈʒeɪ] *n* : negligé *m*
negligence [ˈnɛglɪdʒənts] *n* : negligencia *f,* descuido *m* — **negligent** [ˈnɛglɪdʒənt] *adj* : negligente, descuidado
negligible [ˈnɛglɪdʒəbəl] *adj* : insignificante
negotiate [nɪˈgo:ʃiˌeɪt] *v* **-ated; -ating** : negociar — **negotiable** [nɪˈgo:ʃəbəl, -ʃiə-] *adj* : negociable — **negotiation** [nɪˌgo:ʃiˈeɪʃən, -siˈeɪ-] *n* : negociación *f* — **negotiator** [nɪˈgo:ʃiˌeɪṭər, -siˌeɪ-] *n* : negociador *m,* -dora *f*
Negro [ˈni:ˌgro:] *n, pl* **-groes** *sometimes considered offensive* : negro *m,* -gra *f*
neigh [ˈneɪ] *vi* : relinchar — **~** *n* : relincho *m*
neighbor *or Brit* **neighbour** [ˈneɪbər] *n* : vecino *m,* -na *f* — **neighborhood** *or Brit* **neighbourhood** [ˈneɪbərˌhʊd] *n* **1** : barrio *m,* vecindario *m* **2 in the ~ of** : alrededor de — **neighborly** *or Brit* **neighbourly** [ˈneɪbərli] *adv* : amable
neither [ˈni:ðər, ˈnaɪ-] *conj* **1 ~...nor** : ni...ni **2 ~ am/do I** : yo tampoco — **~** *pron* : ninguno, -na — **~** *adj* : ninguno (de los dos)
neon [ˈni:ˌɑn] *n* : neón *m*
nephew [ˈnɛˌfju:, *chiefly British* ˈnɛˌvju:] *n* : sobrino *m*
Neptune [ˈnɛpˌtu:n, -ˌtju:n] *n* : Neptuno *m*
nerve [ˈnərv] *n* **1** : nervio *m* **2** COURAGE : coraje *m* **3** GALL : descaro *m* **4 ~s** *npl* JITTERS : nervios *mpl* — **nervous** [ˈnərvəs] *adj* : nervioso — **nervousness** [ˈnərvəsnəs] *n* : nerviosismo *m* — **nervy** [ˈnərvi] *adj* **nervier; -est** : descarado
nest [ˈnɛst] *n* : nido *m* — **~** *vi* : anidar
nestle [ˈnɛsəl] *vi* **-tled; -tling** : acurrucarse
net[1] [ˈnɛt] *n* : red *f* — **~** *vt* **netted; netting** : pescar, atrapar (con una red)
net[2] *adj* : neto — **~** *vt* **netted; netting** YIELD : producir neto
nettle [ˈnɛṭəl] *n* : ortiga *f*
network [ˈnɛtˌwərk] *n* : red *f*
neurology [nʊˈrɑlədʒi, njʊ-] *n* : neurología *f*
neurosis [nʊˈro:sɪs, njʊ-] *n, pl* **-roses** [-ˌsi:z] : neurosis *f* — **neurotic** [nʊˈrɑṭɪk, njʊ-] *adj* : neurótico
neuter [ˈnu:ṭər, ˈnju:-] *adj* : neutro — **~** *vt* : castrar
neutral [ˈnu:trəl, ˈnju:-] *n* : punto *m* muerto (de un automóvil) — **~** *adj* **1** : neutral **2** : neutro (en electrotecnia o química) — **neutrality** [nu:ˈtræləṭi:, nju:-] *n* : neutralidad *f* — **neutralize** [ˈnu:trəˌlaɪz, ˈnju:-] *vt* **-ized; -izing** : neutralizar
neutron [ˈnu:ˌtrɑn, ˈnju:-] *n* : neutrón *m*
never [ˈnɛvər] *adv* **1** : nunca, jamás **2** NOT : no **3 ~ again** : nunca más **4 ~ mind** : no importa — **nevermore** [ˌnɛvərˈmor] *adv* : nunca jamás — **nevertheless** [ˌnɛvərðəˈlɛs] *adv* : sin embargo, no obstante
new [ˈnu:, ˈnju:] *adj* : nuevo — **newborn** [ˈnu:ˌbɔrn, ˈnju:-] *adj* : recién nacido — **newcomer** [ˈnu:ˌkʌmər, ˈnju:-] *n* : recién llegado *m,* -da *f* — **newly** [ˈnu:li, ˈnju:-] *adv* : recién, recientemente — **newlywed** [ˈnu:liˌwɛd, ˈnju:-] *n* : recién casado *m,* -da *f* — **news** [ˈnu:z, ˈnju:z] *n* : noticias *fpl* — **newscast** [ˈnu:zˌkæst, ˈnju:z-] *n* : noticiario *m,* noticiero *m Lat* — **newscaster** [ˈnu:zˌkæstər, ˈnju:z-] *n* : presentador *m,* -dora *f* (de un noticiario) — **newsletter** [ˈnu:zˌlɛṭər, ˈnju:z-] *n* : boletín *m* informativo — **newspaper** [ˈnu:zˌpeɪpər, ˈnju:z-] *n* : periódico *m,* diario *m* — **newsstand** [ˈnu:zˌstænd, ˈnju:z-] *n* : puesto *m* de periódicos
newt [ˈnu:t, ˈnju:t] *n* : tritón *m*
New Year's Day *n* : día *m* del Año Nuevo
next [ˈnɛkst] *adj* **1** : próximo **2** FOLLOWING : siguiente — **~** *adv* **1** : la próxima vez **2** AFTERWARD : después, luego **3** NOW : ahora — **next–door** [ˈnɛkstˈdor] *adj* : de al lado — **next to** *adv* ALMOST : casi — **~** *prep* BESIDE : al lado de
nib [ˈnɪb] *n* : plumilla *f*
nibble [ˈnɪbəl] *vt* **-bled; -bling** : mordisquear
Nicaraguan [ˌnɪkəˈrɑgwən] *adj* : nicaragüense
nice [ˈnaɪs] *adj* **nicer; nicest** **1** PLEASANT : agradable, bueno **2** KIND : amable — **nicely** [ˈnaɪsli] *adv* **1** WELL : bien **2** KINDLY : amablemente — **niceness** [ˈnaɪsnəs] *n* : amabilidad *f* — **niceties** [ˈnaɪsəṭiz] *npl* : detalles *mpl,* sutilezas *fpl*
niche [ˈnɪtʃ] *n* **1** : nicho *m* **2 find one's ~** : hacerse su hueco
nick [ˈnɪk] *n* **1** : corte *m* pequeño, muesca *f* **2 in the ~ of time** : justo a tiempo — **~** *vt* : hacer una muesca en
nickel [ˈnɪkəl] *n* **1** : níquel *m* (metal) **2** : moneda *f* de cinco centavos
nickname [ˈnɪkˌneɪm] *n* : apodo *m,* sobrenombre *m* — **~** *vt* **-named; -naming** : apodar
nicotine [ˈnɪkəˌti:n] *n* : nicotina *f*
niece [ˈni:s] *n* : sobrina *f*
niggling [ˈnɪgəlɪŋ] *adj* **1** PETTY : insignificante **2** PERSISTENT : constante
night [ˈnaɪt] *n* **1** : noche *f* **2 at ~** : de noche **3 last ~** : anoche **4 tomorrow ~** : mañana por la noche — **nightclub** [ˈnaɪtˌklʌb] *n* : club *m* nocturno — **nightfall** [ˈnaɪtˌfɔl] *n* : anochecer *m* — **nightgown** [ˈnaɪtˌgaʊn] *n* : camisón *m* (de noche) — **nightly** [ˈnaɪt] *adj* : de todas las noches — **~** *adv* : cada noche — **nightmare** [ˈnaɪtˌmær] *n* : pesadilla *f* — **nighttime** [ˈnaɪtˌtaɪm] *n* : noche *f*
nil [ˈnɪl] *n* NOTHING : nada *f*
nimble [ˈnɪmbəl] *adj* **-bler; -blest** : ágil
nine [ˈnaɪn] *adj* : nueve — **~** *n* : nueve *m* — **nine hundred** *adj* : novecientos — **~** *n* : novecientos *m* — **nineteen** [naɪnˈti:n] *adj* : diecinueve — **~** *n* : diecinueve *m* — **nineteenth** [naɪnˈti:nθ] *adj* : decimonoveno, decimonono — **~** *n* **1** : decimonoveno *m,* -na *f;* decimonono *m,* -na *f* (en una serie) **2** : diecinueveavo *m* (en matemáticas) — **ninetieth** [ˈnaɪnṭiəθ] *adj* : nonagésimo — **~** *n* **1** : nonagésimo *m,* -ma *f* (en una serie) **2** : noventavo *m* (en matemáticas) — **ninety** [ˈnaɪnṭi] *adj* : noventa — **~** *n, pl* **-ties** : noventa *m* — **ninth** [ˈnaɪnθ] *adj* : noveno — **~** *n* **1** : noveno *m,* -na *f* (en una serie) **2** : noveno *m* (en matemáticas)
nip [ˈnɪp] *vt* **nipped; nipping** **1** PINCH : pellizcar **2** BITE : mordisquear **3 ~ in the bud** : cortar de raíz — **~** *n* **1** PINCH : pellizco *m* **2** NIBBLE : mordisco *m*
nipple [ˈnɪpəl] *n* **1** : pezón *m* (de una mujer) **2** : tetilla *f* (de un hombre o un biberón)
nitrogen [ˈnaɪtrədʒən] *n* : nitrógen *m*
nitwit [ˈnɪtˌwɪt] *n* : idiota *mf*
no [ˈno:] *adv* : no — **~** *adj* **1** : ninguno **2 I have ~ money** : no tengo dinero **3 it's ~ trouble** : no es ningún problema **4 ~ smoking** : prohibido fumar — **~** *n, pl* **noes** *or* **nos** [ˈno:z] : no *m*
noble [ˈno:bəl] *adj* **-bler; -blest** : noble — **~** *n* : noble *mf* — **nobility** [noˈbɪləṭi] *n* : nobleza *f*
nobody [ˈno:bədi, -ˌbɑdi] *pron* : nadie
nocturnal [nɑkˈtərnəl] *adj* : nocturno
nod [ˈnɑd] *v* **nodded; nodding** *vi* **1** *or* **~ yes** : asentir con la cabeza **2 ~ off** : dormirse — *vt* **~ one's head** : asentir con la cabeza — **~** *n* : señal *m* con la cabeza
noes → no
noise [ˈnɔɪz] *n* : ruido *m* — **noisily** [ˈnɔɪzəli] *adv* : ruidosamente — **noisy** [ˈnɔɪzi] *adj* **noisier; -est** : ruidoso
nomad [ˈnoˌmæd] *n* : nómada *mf* — **nomadic** [noˈmædɪk] *adj* : nómada
nominal [ˈnɑmənəl] *adj* : nominal
nominate [ˈnɑməˌneɪt] *vt* **-nated; -nating** **1** : proponer, postular *Lat* **2** APPOINT : nombrar — **nomination** [ˌnɑməˈneɪʃən] *n* **1** : propuesta *f,* postulación *f Lat* **2** APPOINTMENT : nombramiento *m*
nonalcoholic [ˌnɑnˌælkəˈhɔlɪk] *adj* : no alcohólico
nonchalant [ˌnɑnʃəˈlɑnt] *adj* : despreocupado
noncommissioned officer [ˌnɑnkəˈmɪʃənd] *n* : suboficial *mf*
noncommittal [ˌnɑnkəˈmɪṭəl] *adj* : evasivo
nondescript [ˌnɑndɪˈskrɪpt] *adj* : anodino, soso
none [ˈnʌn] *pron* **1** : ninguno, ninguna **2 there are ~ left** : no hay más — **~** *adv* **1 be ~ the worse** : no sufrir daño alguno **2 ~ too happy** : nada contento **3 ~ too soon** : a buena hora
nonentity [ˌnɑnˈɛntəṭi] *n, pl* **-ties** : persona *f* insignificante
nonetheless [ˌnʌnðəˈlɛs] *adv* : sin embargo, no obstante
nonexistent [ˌnɑnɪgˈzɪstənt] *adj* : inexistente
nonfat [ˌnɑnˈfæt] *adj* : sin grasa
nonfiction [ˌnɑnˈfɪkʃən] *n* : no ficción *f*
nonprofit [ˌnɑnˈprɑfət] *adj* : sin fines lucrativos
nonsense [ˈnɑnˌsɛnts, ˈnɑntsənts] *n* : tonterías *fpl,* disparates *mpl* — **nonsensical** [nɑnˈsɛntsɪkəl] *adj* : absurdo
nonsmoker [ˌnɑnˈsmo:kər] *n* : no fumador *m,* -dora *f*
nonstop [ˌnɑnˈstɑp] *adj* : directo — **~** *adv* : sin parar
noodle [ˈnu:dəl] *n* : fideo *m*
nook [ˈnʊk] *n* : rincón *m*
noon [ˈnu:n] *n* : mediodía *m*
no one *pron* : nadie

noose ['nu:s] *n* **1** : dogal *m,* soga *f* **2** LASSO : lazo *m*
nor ['nɔr] *conj* **1 neither...~** : ni…ni **2 ~ I** : yo tampoco
norm ['nɔrm] *n* **1** : norma *f* **2 the ~** : lo normal — **normal** ['nɔrməl] *adj* : normal — **normality** [nɔr'mæləṭi] *n* : normalidad *f* — **normally** *adv* : normalmente
north ['nɔrθ] *adv* : al norte — **~** *adj* : norte, del norte — **~** *n* **1** : norte *m* **2 the North** : el Norte — **North American** *adj* : norteamericano — **northeast** [nɔrθ'i:st] *adv* : hacia el nordeste — **~** *adj* : nordeste, del nordeste — **~** *n* : nordeste *m,* noreste *m* — **northeastern** [nɔrθ'i:stərn] *adj* : nordeste, del nordeste — **northerly** ['nɔrðərli] *adj* : del norte — **northern** ['nɔrðərn] *adj* : del norte, norteño — **northwest** [ˌnɔrθ'wɛst] *adv* : hacia el noroeste — **~** *adj* : noroeste, del noroeste — **~** *n* : noroeste *m* — **northwestern** [ˌnɔrθ'wɛstərn] *adj* : noroeste, del noroeste
Norwegian [nɔr'wi:dʒən] *adj* : noruego
nose ['no:z] *n* **1** : nariz *f* (de una persona), hocico *m* (de un animal) **2 blow one's ~** : sonarse las narices — **~** *vi* **nosed; nosing** *or* **~ around** : meter las narices — **nosebleed** ['no:zˌbli:d] *n* : hemorragia *f* nasal — **nosedive** ['no:zˌdaɪv] *n* : descenso *m* en picada
nostalgia [nɑ'stældʒə, nə-] *n* : nostalgia *f* — **nostalgic** [nɑ'stældʒɪk, nə-] *adj* : nostálgico
nostril ['nɑstrəl] *n* : ventana *f* de la nariz
nosy *or* **nosey** ['no:zi] *adj* **nosier; -est** : entrometido
not ['nɑt] *adv* **1** : no **2 he's ~ tired** : no esta cansado **3 I hope ~** : espero que no **4 ~ ... anything** : no…nada
notable ['no:ṭəbəl] *adj* : notable — **~** *n* : personaje *m* — **notably** ['no:ṭəbli] *adv* : notablemente
notary public ['no:ṭəri-] *n, pl* **notaries public** *or* **notary publics** : notario *m,* -ria *f*
notation [no'teɪʃən] *n* : anotación *f*
notch ['nɑtʃ] *n* : muesca *f,* corte *m* — **~** *vt* : hacer un corte en
note ['no:t] *vt* **noted; noting 1** NOTICE : observar, notar **2** RECORD : anotar — **~** *n* **1** : nota *f* **2 of ~** : destacado **3 take ~ of** : prestar atención a **4 take ~s** : apuntar — **notebook** ['no:tˌbʊk] *n* : libreta *f,* cuaderno *m* — **noted** ['no:ṭəd] *adj* : renombrado, célebre — **noteworthy** ['no:tˌwərði] *adj* : notable
nothing ['nʌθɪŋ] *pron* **1** : nada **2 be ~ but** : no ser más que **3 for ~** FREE : gratis — **~** *n* **1** ZERO : zero *m* **2** TRIFLE : nimiedad *f*
notice ['no:ṭɪs] *n* **1** SIGN : letrero *m,* aviso *m* **2 at a moment's ~** : sin previo aviso **3 be given one's ~** : ser despedido **4 take ~ of** : prestar atención a — **~** *vt* **-ticed; -ticing** : notar — **noticeable** ['no:ṭɪsəbəl] *adj* : perceptible, evidente
notify ['no:ṭəˌfaɪ] *vt* **-fied; -fying** : notificar, avisar — **notification** [ˌno:ṭəfə'keɪʃən] *n* : notificación *f,* aviso *m*
notion ['no:ʃən] *n* **1** : noción *f,* idea *f* **2 ~s** *npl* : artículos *mpl* de mercería
notorious [no'to:riəs] *adj* : de mala fama — **notoriety** [ˌno:ṭə'raɪəṭi] *n* : mala fama *f,* notoriedad *f*
notwithstanding [ˌnɑtwɪθ'stændɪŋ, -wɪð-] *prep* : a pesar de, no obstante — **~** *adv* : sin embargo — **~** *conj* : a pesar de que
nougat ['nu:gət] *n* : turrón *m*
nought ['nɔt, 'nɑt] → **naught**
noun ['naʊn] *n* : nombre *m,* sustantivo *m*
nourish ['nərɪʃ] *vt* : nutrir — **nourishing** ['nərɪʃɪŋ] *adj* : nutritivo — **nourishment** ['nərɪʃmənt] *n* : alimento *m*
novel ['nɑvəl] *adj* : original, novedoso — **~** *n* : novela *f* — **novelist** ['nɑvəlɪst] *n* : novelista *mf* — **novelty** ['nɑvəlṭi] *n, pl* **-ties** : novedad *f*
November [no'vɛmbər] *n* : noviembre *m*
novice ['nɑvɪs] *n* : novato *m,* -ta *f;* principiante *mf*
now ['naʊ] *adv* **1** : ahora **2** THEN : entonces **3 from ~ on** : de ahora en adelante **4 ~ and then** : de vez en cuando **5 right ~** : ahora mismo — **~** *conj or* **~ that** : ahora que, ya que — **~** *n* **1 a year from ~** : dentro de un año **2 by ~** : ya **3 until ~** : hasta ahora — **nowadays** ['naʊəˌdeɪz] *adv* : hoy en día
nowhere ['no:ˌhwɛr] *adv* **1** (*indicating location*) : por ninguna parte, por ningún lado **2** (*indicating motion*) : a ninguna parte, a ningún lado **3 I'm ~ near finished** : aún me falta mucho para terminar **4 it's ~ near here** : queda bastante lejos de aquí — **~** *n* : ninguna parte *f*
nozzle ['nɑzəl] *n* : boca *f* (de una manguera, etc.)
nuance ['nu:ˌɑnts, 'nju:-] *n* : matiz *m*
nucleus ['nu:kliəs, 'nju:-] *n, pl* **-clei** [-kliˌaɪ] : núcleo *m* — **nuclear** ['nu:kliər, 'nju:-] *adj* : nuclear
nude ['nu:d, 'nju:d] *adj* **nuder; nudest** : desnudo — **~** *n* : desnudo *m*
nudge ['nʌdʒ] *vt* **nudged; nudging** : dar un codazo a — **~** *n* : toque *m* (con el codo)
nudity ['nu:dəṭi, 'nju:-] *n* : desnudez *f*
nugget ['nʌgət] *n* : pepita *f* (de oro, etc.)
nuisance ['nu:sənts, 'nju:-] *n* **1** ANNOYANCE : fastidio *m,* molestia *f* **2** PEST : pesado *m,* -da *f fam*
null ['nʌl] *adj* **~ and void** : nulo y sin efecto
numb ['nʌm] *adj* **1** : entumecido, dormido **2 ~ with fear** : paralizado de miedo — **~** *vt* : entumecer, adormecer
number ['nʌmbər] *n* **1** : número *m* **2 a ~ of** : varios — **~** *vt* **1** : numerar **2** INCLUDE : contar, incluir **3** TOTAL : ascender a
numeral ['nu:mərəl, 'nju:-] *n* : número *m* — **numeric** [nʊ'mɛrɪk, njʊ-] *or* **numerical** [nʊ'mɛrɪkəl, njʊ-] *adj* : numérico — **numerous** ['nu:mərəs, 'nju:-] *adj* : numeroso
nun ['nʌn] *n* : monja *f*
nuptial ['nʌpʃəl] *adj* : nupcial
nurse ['nərs] *n* **1** : enfermero *m,* -ra *f* **2** → **nursemaid** — **~** *vt* **nursed; nursing 1** : cuidar (de), atender **2** SUCKLE : amamantar — **nursemaid** ['nərsˌmeɪd] *n* : niñera *f* — **nursery** ['nərsəri] *n, pl* **-eries 1** : cuarto *m* de los niños **2** *or* **day ~** : guardería *f* **3** : vivero *m* (de plantas) — **nursing home** *n* : asilo *m* de ancianos
nurture ['nərtʃər] *vt* **-tured; -turing 1** NOURISH : nutrir **2** EDUCATE : criar, educar **3** FOSTER : alimentar
nut ['nʌt] *n* **1** : nuez *f* **2** LUNATIC : loco *m,* -ca *f* **3** ENTHUSIAST : fanático *m,* -ca *f* **4 ~s and bolts** : tuercas y tornillos — **nutcracker** ['nʌtˌkrækər] *n* : cascanueces *m*
nutmeg ['nʌtˌmɛg] *n* : nuez *f* moscada
nutrient ['nu:triənt, 'nju:-] *n* : nutriente *m*
nutrition [nʊ'trɪʃən, njʊ-] *n* : nutrición *f* — **nutritional** [nʊ'trɪʃənəl, njʊ-] *adj* : nutritivo — **nutritious** [nʊ'trɪʃəs, njʊ-] *adj* : nutritivo
nuts ['nʌts] *adj* : loco
nutshell ['nʌtˌʃɛl] *n* **1** : cáscara *f* de nuez **2 in a ~** : en pocas palabras
nutty ['nʌṭi] *adj* **-tier; -tiest** : loco
nuzzle ['nʌzəl] *v* **-zled; -zling** *vi* : acurrucarse — *vt* : acariciar con el hocico
nylon ['naɪˌlɑn] *n* **1** : nilón *m* **2 ~s** *npl* : medias *fpl* de nilón
nymph ['nɪmpf] *n* : ninfa *f*

O

o ['o:] *n, pl* **o's** *or* **os** ['o:z] **1** : o *f,* decimoquinta letra del alfabeto inglés **2** ZERO : cero *m*
O ['o:] → **oh**
oaf ['o:f] *n* : zoquete *m*
oak ['o:k] *n, pl* **oaks** *or* **oak** : roble *m*
oar ['or] *n* : remo *m*
oasis [o'eɪsɪs] *n, pl* **oases** [-ˌsi:z] : oasis *m*
oath ['o:θ] *n, pl* **oaths** ['o:ðz, 'o:θs] **1** : juramento *m* **2** SWEARWORD : palabrota *f*
oats ['o:ts] *npl* : avena *f* — **oatmeal** ['o:tˌmi:l] *n* : harina *f* de avena
obedient [o'bi:diənt] *adj* : obediente — **obedience** [o'bi:diənts] *n* : obediencia *f*
obese [o'bi:s] *adj* : obeso — **obesity** [o'bi:səṭi] *n* : obesidad *f*
obey [o'beɪ] *v* **obeyed; obeying** : obedecer
obituary [ə'bɪtʃuˌɛri] *n, pl* **-aries** : obituario *m*
object ['ɑbdʒɪkt] *n* **1** : objeto *m* **2** AIM : objetivo *m* **3** : complemento *m* (en gramática) — **~** [əb'dʒɛkt] *vt* : objetar — *vi* **~ to** : oponerse a — **objection** [əb'dʒɛkʃən] *n* : objeción *f* — **objectionable** [əb'dʒɛkʃənəbəl] *adj* : desagradable — **objective** [əb'dʒɛktɪv] *adj* : objetivo — **~** *n* : objetivo *m*
oblige [ə'blaɪdʒ] *vt* **obliged; obliging 1** : obligar **2 be much ~d** : estar muy agradecido **3 ~ s.o.** : hacer un favor a algn — **obligation** [ˌɑblə'geɪʃən] *n* : obligación *f* — **obligatory** [ə'blɪgəˌtori] *adj* : obligatorio — **obliging** [ə'blaɪdʒɪŋ] *adj* : atento, servicial
oblique [o'bli:k] *adj* **1** SLANTING : oblicuo **2** INDIRECT : indirecto
obliterate [ə'blɪṭəˌreɪt] *vt* **-ated; -ating 1** ERASE : borrar **2** DESTROY : arrasar
oblivion [ə'blɪviən] *n* : olvido *m* — **oblivious** [ə'blɪviəs] *adj* : inconsciente
oblong ['ɑˌblɔŋ] *adj* : oblongo — **~** *n* : rectángulo *m*
obnoxious [ɑb'nɑkʃəs, əb-] *adj* : odioso
oboe ['o:ˌbo:] *n* : oboe *m*
obscene [ɑb'si:n, əb-] *adj* : obsceno — **obscenity** [ɑb'sɛnəṭi, əb-] *n, pl* **-ties** : obscenidad *f*
obscurity [ɑb'skjʊrəṭi, əb-] *n, pl* **-ties** : oscuridad *f* — **obscure** [ɑb'skjʊr, əb-] *adj* : oscuro — **~** *vt* **-scured; -scuring 1** DARKEN : oscurecer **2** HIDE : ocultar
observe [əb'zərv] *v* **-served; -serving** *vt* : observar — *vi* WATCH : mirar — **observance** [əb'zərvənts] *n* **1** : observancia *f* **2 religious ~s** : prácticas *fpl* religiosas — **observant** [əb'zərvənt] *adj* : observador — **observation** [ˌɑbsər'veɪʃən, -zər-] *n* : observación *f* — **observatory** [əb'zərvəˌtori] *n, pl* **-ries** : observatorio *m*
obsess [əb'sɛs] *vt* : obsesionar — **obsession** [ɑb'sɛʃən, əb-] *n* : obsesión *f* — **obsessive** [ɑb'sɛsɪv, əb-] *adj* : obsesivo
obsolete [ˌɑbsə'li:t, 'ɑbsəˌ-] *adj* : obsoleto, desusado
obstacle ['ɑbstɪkəl] *n* : obstáculo *m*
obstetrics [əb'stɛtrɪks] *n* : obstetricia *f*
obstinate ['ɑbstənət] *adj* : obstinado
obstruct [əb'strʌkt] *vt* **1** BLOCK : obstruir **2** HINDER : obstaculizar — **obstruction** [əb'strʌkʃən] *n* : obstrucción *f*
obtain [əb'teɪn] *vt* : obtener, conseguir — **obtainable** [əb'teɪnəbəl] *adj* : asequible
obtrusive [əb'tru:sɪv] *adj* : entrometido (dícese de las personas), demasiado prominente (dícese de las cosas)
obtuse [ɑb'tu:s, əb-, -'tju:s] *adj* : obtuso
obvious ['ɑbviəs] *adj* : obvio, evidente — **obviously** ['ɑbviəsli] *adv* **1** CLEARLY : obviamente **2** OF COURSE : claro, por supuesto
occasion [ə'keɪʒən] *n* **1** : ocasión *f* **2 on ~** : de vez en cuando — **~** *vt* : ocasionar — **occasional** [ə'keɪʒənəl] *adj* : poco frecuente, ocasional — **occasionally** [ə'keɪʒənəli] *adv* : de vez en cuando
occult [ə'kʌlt, 'ɑˌkʌlt] *adj* : oculto
occupy ['ɑkjəˌpaɪ] *vt* **-pied; -pying 1** : ocupar **2 ~ oneself** : entretenerse — **occupancy** ['ɑkjəpəntsi] *n, pl* **-cies** : ocupación *f* — **occupant** ['ɑkjəpənt] *n* : ocupante *mf* — **occupation** [ˌɑkjə'peɪʃən] *n* : ocupación *f* — **occupational** [ˌɑkjə'peɪʃənəl] *adj* : profesional
occur [ə'kər] *vi* **occurred; occurring 1** : ocurrir **2** APPEAR : encontrarse **3 ~ to s.o.** : occurirse a algn — **occurrence** [ə'kərənts] *n* **1** EVENT : acontecimiento *m,* suceso *m* **2** INCIDENCE : incidencia *f*
ocean ['o:ʃən] *n* : océano *m*
ocher *or* **ochre** ['o:kər] *n* : ocre *m*
o'clock [ə'klɑk] *adv* **1 at 6 ~** : a las seis **2 it's one ~** : es la una **3 it's ten ~** : son las diez
octagon ['ɑktəˌgɑn] *n* : octágono *m* — **octagonal** [ɑk'tægənəl] *adj* : octagonal
octave ['ɑktɪv] *n* : octava *f*
October [ɑk'to:bər] *n* : octubre *m*
octopus ['ɑktəˌpʊs, -pəs] *n, pl* **-puses** *or* **-pi** [-ˌpaɪ] : pulpo *m*
oculist ['ɑkjəlɪst] *n* : oculista *mf*
odd ['ɑd] *adj* **1** STRANGE : extraño, raro **2** : sin pareja (dícese de un calcetín, etc.) **3 forty ~ years** : cuarenta y tantos años **4 ~ jobs** : algunos trabajos *mpl* **5 ~ number** : número *m* impar — **oddity** ['ɑdəṭi] *n, pl* **-ties** : rareza *f* — **oddly** ['ɑdli] *adv* : de manera extraña — **odds** ['ɑdz] *npl* **1** CHANCES : probabilidades *fpl* **2 at ~** : en desacuerdo **3 five to one ~** : cinco contra uno (en apuestas) — **odds and ends** *npl* : cosas *fpl* sueltas
ode ['o:d] *n* : oda *f*
odious ['o:diəs] *adj* : odioso
odor *or Brit* **odour** ['o:dər] *n* : olor *m* — **odorless** *or Brit* **odourless** ['o:dərləs] *adj* : inodoro
of ['ʌv, 'ɑv] *prep* **1** : de **2 five minutes ~ ten** : las diez menos cinco **3 the eighth ~ April** : el ocho de abril
off ['ɔf] *adv* **1 be ~** LEAVE : irse **2 cut ~** : cortar **3 day ~** : día *m* de descanso **4 fall ~** : caerse **5 doze ~** : dormirse **6 far ~** : lejos **7 ~ and on** : de vez en cuando **8 shut ~** : apagar **9 ten miles ~** : a diez millas de aquí — **~** *prep* **1** : de **2 be ~ duty** : estar libre **3 ~ center** : descentrado — **~** *adj* **1** CANCELED : cancelado **2** OUT : apagado **3 an ~ chance** : una posibilidad remota
offend [ə'fɛnd] *vt* : ofender — **offender** [ə'fɛndər] *n* : delincuente *mf* — **offense** *or* **offence** [ə'fɛnts, 'ɔˌfɛnts] *n* **1** AFFRONT : afrenta *f* **2** ASSAULT : ataque *m* **3** : ofensiva *f* (en deportes) **4** CRIME : delito *m* **5 take ~** : ofenderse — **offensive** [ə'fɛntsɪv, 'ɔˌfɛnt-] *adj* : ofensivo — **~** *n* : ofensiva *f*
offer ['ɔfər] *vt* : ofrecer — **~** *n* : oferta *f* — **offering** ['ɔfərɪŋ] *n* : ofrenda *f*
offhand ['ɔf'hænd] *adv* : de improviso, en este momento — **~** *adj* : improvisado
office ['ɔfəs] *n* **1** : oficina *f* **2** POSITION : cargo *m* **3 run for ~** : presentarse como candidato — **officer** ['ɔfəsər] *n* **1** : oficial *mf* **2** *or* **police ~** : agente *mf* (de policía) — **official** [ə'fɪʃəl] *n* : funcionario *m,* -ria *f* — **~** *adj* : oficial
offing ['ɔfɪŋ] *n* **in the ~** : en perspectiva
offset ['ɔfˌsɛt] *vt* **-set; -setting** : compensar
offshore ['ɔf'ʃor] *adv* : a una distancia de la costa
offspring ['ɔfˌsprɪŋ] *ns & pl* : prole *f,* progenie *f*
often ['ɔfən, 'ɔftən] *adv* **1** : muchas veces, a menudo, con frecuencia **2 every so ~** : de vez en cuando
ogle ['o:gəl] *vt* **ogled; ogling** : comerse con los ojos
ogre ['o:gər] *n* : ogro *m*
oh ['o:] *interj* **1** : ¡oh!, ¡ah! **2 ~ no!** : ¡ay no! **3 ~ really?** : ¿de veras?
oil ['ɔɪl] *n* **1** : aceite *m* **2** PETROLEUM : petróleo *m* **3** *or* **~ painting** : óleo *m* — **~** *vt* : lubricar — **oilskin** ['ɔɪlˌskɪn] *n* : hule *m* — **oily** ['ɔɪli] *adj* **oilier; -est** : aceitoso, grasiento
ointment ['ɔɪntmənt] *n* : ungüento *m,* pomada *f*
OK *or* **okay** [ˌo:'keɪ] *adv* **1** : muy bien **2 ~!** : ¡de acuerdo!, ¡bueno! — **~** *adj* **1** ALL RIGHT : bien **2 it's ~ with me** : por mí no hay problema — **~** *n* : visto *m* bueno — **~** [ˌo:'keɪ] *vt* **OK'd** *or* **okayed** [ˌo:'keɪd]; **OK'ing** *or* **okaying** : dar el visto bueno a
okra ['o:krə, *South also* -kri] *n* : quingombó *m*
old ['o:ld] *adj* **1** : viejo **2** FORMER : antiguo **3 any ~** : cualquier **4 be ten years ~** : tener diez años (de edad) **5 ~ age** : vejez *f* **6 ~ man** : anciano *m* **7 ~ woman** : anciana *f* — **~** *n* **the ~** : los viejos, los ancianos — **old–fashioned** ['o:ld'fæʃənd] *adj* : anticuado
olive ['ɑlɪv, -ləv] *n* **1** : aceituna *f* (fruta) **2** *or* **~ green** : verde *m* oliva
Olympic [o'lɪmpɪk] *adj* : olímpico — **Olympics** [o'lɪmpɪks] *npl* **the ~** : las Olimpiadas, las Olimpíadas
omelet *or* **omelette** ['ɑmlət, 'ɑmə-] *n* : omelette *mf Lat,* tortilla *f* francesa *Spain*
omen ['o:mən] *n* : agüero *m* — **ominous** ['ɑmənəs] *adj* : ominoso, de mal agüero
omit [o'mɪt] *vt* **omitted; omitting** : omitir — **omission** [o'mɪʃən] *n* : omisión *f*
omnipotent [ɑm'nɪpəṭənt] *adj* : omnipotente
on ['ɑn, 'ɔn] *prep* **1** : en **2** ABOUT : sobre **3 ~ foot** : a pie **4 ~ Monday** : el lunes **5 ~ the right** : a la derecha **6 ~ vacation** : de vacaciones **7 talk ~ the phone** : hablar por teléfono — **~** *adv* **1 and so ~** : etcétera **2 from that moment ~** : a partir de ese momento **3 keep ~** : seguir **4 later ~** : más tarde **5 ~ and ~** : sin parar **6 put ~** : ponerse (ropa), poner (música, etc.) **7 turn ~** : encender (una luz, etc.), abrir (una llave) — **~** *adj* **1** : encendido (dícese de luces, etc.), abierto (dícese de llaves) **2 be ~ to** : estar enterado de
once ['wʌnts] *adv* **1** : una vez **2** FORMERLY : antes — **~** *n* **1 at ~** TOGETHER : al mismo tiempo **2 at ~** IMMEDIATELY : inmediatamente — **~** *conj* : una vez que
oncoming ['ɑnˌkʌmɪŋ, 'ɔn-] *adj* : que viene
one ['wʌn] *adj* **1** : un, uno **2** ONLY : único **3** *or* **~ and the same** : el mismo — **~** *n* **1** : uno *m* (número) **2 ~ by ~** : uno a uno — **~** *pron* **1** : uno, una **2 ~ another** : el uno al otro **3 ~ never knows** : nunca se sabe **4 that ~** : aquél, aquella **5 which ~?** : ¿cuál? — **oneself** [ˌwʌn'sɛlf] *pron* **1** (*used reflexively*) : se **2** (*used after prepositions*) : sí mismo, sí misma **3** (*used emphatically*) : uno mismo, una misma **4 by ~** : solo — **one–sided** ['wʌn'saɪdəd] *adj* **1** UNEQUAL : desigual **2** BIASED : parcial — **one–way** ['wʌn'weɪ] *adj* **1** : de sentido único (dícese de una calle) **2 ~ ticket** : boleto *m* de ida
ongoing ['ɑnˌgo:ɪŋ] *adj* : en curso, corrinte
onion ['ʌnjən] *n* : cebolla *f*
only ['o:nli] *adj* : único — **~** *adv* **1** : sólo, solamente **2 if ~** : ojalá, por lo menos — **~** *conj* BUT : pero
onset ['ɑnˌsɛt] *n* : comienzo *m,* llegada *f*
onslaught ['ɑnˌslɔt, 'ɔn-] *n* : ataque *m,* arremetida *f*
onto ['ɑnˌtu:, 'ɔn-] *prep* : sobre
onus ['o:nəs] *n* : responsabilidad *f*
onward ['ɑnwərd, 'ɔn-] *adv & adj* : hacia adelante
onyx ['ɑnɪks] *n* : ónix *m*
ooze ['u:z] *v* **oozed; oozing** : rezumar
opal ['o:pəl] *n* : ópalo *m*
opaque [o'peɪk] *adj* : opaco
open ['o:pən] *adj* **1** : abierto **2** AVAILABLE : vacante, libre **3 an ~ question** : una cuestión pendiente — **~** *vt* : abrir — *vi* **1** : abrirse **2** BEGIN : comenzar — **~** *n* **in the ~ 1** OUTDOORS : al aire libre **2** KNOWN : sacado a la luz — **open–air** ['o:pən'ær] *adj* : al aire libre — **opener** ['o:pənər] *n* **1** : abridor *m* **2** *or* **bottle ~** : abrebotellas *m* **3** *or* **can ~** : abrelatas *m* — **opening** ['o:pənɪŋ] *n* **1** : abertura *f* **2** BEGINNING : comienzo *m,* apertura *f* **3** OPPORTUNITY : opportunidad *f* — **openly** ['o:pənli] *adv* : abiertamente
opera ['ɑprə, 'ɑpərə] *n* : ópera *f*
operate ['ɑpəˌreɪt] *v* **-ated; -ating** *vi* **1** FUNCTION : funcionar **2 ~ on s.o.** : operar a algn — *vt* **1** : hacer funcionar (una máquina) **2** MANAGE : dirigir, manejar — **operation** [ˌɑpə'reɪʃən] *n* **1** : operación *f* **2** FUNCTIONING : funcionamiento *m* — **operational** [ˌɑpə'reɪʃənəl] *adj* : operacional — **operative** ['ɑpərəṭɪv, -ˌreɪ-] *adj* : en vigor — **operator** ['ɑpəˌreɪṭər] *n* **1** : operador *m,* -dora *f* **2** *or* **machine ~** : operario *m,* -ria *f*
opinion [ə'pɪnjən] *n* : opinión *f* — **opinionated** [ə'pɪnjəˌneɪṭəd] *adj* : dogmático
opium ['o:piəm] *n* : opio *m*
opossum [ə'pɑsəm] *n* : zarigüeya *f,* oposum *m*
opponent [ə'po:nənt] *n* : adversario *m,* -ria *f;* contrincante *mf* (en deportes)
opportunity [ˌɑpər'tu:nəṭi, -'tju:-] *n, pl* **-ties** : oportunidad *f* — **opportune** [ˌɑpər'tu:n,

-tju:n] *adj* : oportuno — **opportunist** [,apər'tu:nist, -tju:-] *n* : oportunista *mf*

oppose [ə'po:z] *vt* **-posed; -posing** : oponerse a — **opposed** *adj* **~ to** : en contra de

opposite ['apəzət] *adj* **1** FACING : de enfrente **2** CONTRARY : opuesto — **~** *n* **the ~** : lo contrario, lo opuesto — **~** *adv* : enfrente — **~** *prep* : enfrente de, frente a — **opposition** [,apə'zɪʃən] *n* **1** : oposición *f* **2 in ~ to** : en contra de

oppress [ə'pres] *vt* : oprimir — **oppression** [ə'preʃən] *n* : opresión *f* — **oppressive** [ə'presɪv] *adj* **1** : opresivo **2** STIFLING : agobiante — **oppressor** [ə'presər] *n* : opresor *m*, -sora *f*

opt ['apt] *vi* **~ for** : optar por

optic ['aptɪk] *or* **optical** [-tɪkəl] *adj* : óptico — **optician** [ap'tɪʃən] *n* : óptico *m*, -ca *f*

optimism ['aptə,mɪzəm] *n* : optimismo *m* — **optimist** ['aptəmɪst] *n* : optimista *mf* — **optimistic** [,aptə'mɪstɪk] *adj* : optimista

optimum ['aptəməm] *n, pl* **-ma** [-mə] : lo óptimo, lo ideal

option ['apʃən] *n* **1** : opción *f* **2 have no ~** : no tener más remedio — **optional** ['apʃənəl] *adj* : facultativo, opcional

opulence ['apjələns] *n* : opulencia *f* — **opulent** ['apjələnt] *adj* : opulento

or ['ɔr] *conj* **1** (*indicating an alternative*) : o (u *before* o- *or* ho-) **2** (*following a negative*) : ni **3 ~ else** : si no

oracle ['ɔrəkəl] *n* : oráculo *m*

oral ['ɔrəl] *adj* : oral

orange ['ɔrɪndʒ] *n* **1** : naranja *f* (fruta) **2** : naranja *m* (color)

orator ['ɔrətər] *n* : orador *m*, -dora *f*

orbit ['ɔrbət] *n* : órbita *f* — **~** *vt* : girar alrededor de — *vi* : orbitar

orchard ['ɔrtʃərd] *n* : huerto *m*

orchestra ['ɔrkəstrə] *n* : orquesta *f*

orchid ['ɔrkɪd] *n* : orquídea *f*

ordain [ɔr'deɪn] *vt* **1** : ordenar (un sacerdote, etc.) **2** DECREE : decretar

ordeal [ɔr'di:l, 'ɔr,di:l] *n* : prueba *f* dura

order ['ɔrdər] *vt* **1** : ordenar **2** : pedir (mercancías, etc.) — *vi* : hacer un pedido — *n* **1** ARRANGEMENT : orden *m* **2** COMMAND : orden *f* **3** REQUEST : pedido *m* **4** : orden *f* (religiosa) **5 in ~ that** : para que **6 in ~ to** : para **7 out of ~** : averiado, descompuesto *Lat* — **orderly** ['ɔrdərli] *adj* : ordenado — *n, pl* **-lies 1** : ordenanza *m* (en el ejército) **2** : camillero *m* (en un hospital)

ordinary ['ɔrdən,eri] *adj* **1** : normal, corriente **2** MEDIOCRE : ordinario — **ordinarily** [,ɔrdən'erəli] *adv* : generalmente

ore ['ɔr] *n* : mena *f*

oregano [ə'regə,no:] *n* : orégano *m*

organ ['ɔrgən] *n* : órgano *m* — **organic** [ɔr'gænɪk] *adj* : orgánico — **organism** ['ɔrgə,nɪzəm] *n* : organismo *m* — **organist** ['ɔrgənɪst] *n* : organista *mf* — **organize** ['ɔrgə,naɪz] *vt* **-nized; -nizing** : organizar — **organization** [,ɔrgənə'zeɪʃən] *n* : organización *f* — **organizer** ['ɔrgə,naɪzər] *n* : organizador *m*, -dora *f*

orgasm ['ɔr,gæzəm] *n* : orgasmo *m*

orgy ['ɔrdʒi] *n, pl* **-gies** : orgía *f*

Orient ['ɔri,ent] *n* **the ~** : el Oriente — **orient** ['ɔri,ent] *vt* : orientar — **oriental** [,ɔri'entəl] *adj* : del Oriente, oriental — **orientation** [,ɔriən'teɪʃən] *n* : orientación *f*

orifice ['ɔrəfəs] *n* : orificio *m*

origin ['ɔrədʒən] *n* : origen *m* — **original** [ə'rɪdʒənəl] *n* : original *m* — *adj* : original — **originality** [ə,rɪdʒə'næləti] *n* : originalidad *f* — **originally** [ə'rɪdʒənəli] *adv* : originariamente — **originate** [ə'rɪdʒə,neɪt] *v* **-nated; -nating** *vt* : originar — *vi* **1** : originarse **2 ~ from** : provenir de — **originator** [ə'rɪdʒə,neɪtər] *n* : creador *m*, -dora *f*

ornament ['ɔrnəmənt] *n* : adorno *m* — **~** *vt* : adornar — **ornamental** [,ɔrnə'mentəl] *adj* : ornamental, de adorno — **ornate** [ɔr'neɪt] *adj* : elaborado, adornado

ornithology [,ɔrnə'θɑlədʒi] *n, pl* **-gies** : ornitología *f*

orphan ['ɔrfən] *n* : huérfano *m*, -na *f* — **~** *vt* : dejar huérfano — **orphanage** ['ɔrfənɪdʒ] *n* : orfelinato *m*, orfanato *m*

orthodox ['ɔrθə,dɑks] *adj* : ortodoxo — **orthodoxy** ['ɔrθə,dɑksi] *n, pl* **-doxies** : ortodoxia *f*

orthopedic [,ɔrθə'pi:dɪk] *adj* : ortopédico

oscillation [,ɑsə'leɪʃən] *n* : oscilación *f* — **oscillate** ['ɑsə,leɪt] *vi* **-lated; -lating** : oscilar

ostensible [ɑ'stentsəbəl] *adj* : aparente, ostensible

ostentation [,ɑstən'teɪʃən] *n* : ostentación *f* — **ostentatious** [,ɑstən'teɪʃəs] *adj* : ostentoso

osteopath ['ɑstiə,pæθ] *n* : osteópata *f*

ostracism ['ɑstrə,sɪzəm] *n* : ostracismo *m* — **ostracize** ['ɑstrə,saɪz] *vt* **-cized; -cizing** : aislar

ostrich ['ɑstrɪtʃ, 'ɑs-] *n* : avestruz *m*

other ['ʌðər] *adj* **1** : otro **2 every ~ day** : cada dos días **3 on the ~ hand** : por otra parte, por otro lado — **~** *pron* **1** : otro, otra **2 the ~s** : los otros, los demás, las demás — **other than** *prep* : aparte de, fuera de — **otherwise** ['ʌðər,waɪz] *adv* **1** : eso aparte, por lo demás **2** DIFFERENTLY : de otro modo **3** OR ELSE : si no

otter ['ɑtər] *n* : nutria *f*

ought ['ɔt] *v aux* **1** : deber **2 you ~ to have done it** : deberías haberlo hecho

ounce ['aʊnts] *n* : onza *f*

our ['ɑr, 'aʊr] *adj* : nuestro, (la) nuestra, (los) nuestros, (las) nuestras **2 a friend of ~** : un amigo nuestro — **ours** ['ɑʊrz, 'arz] *pron* **1** : (el) nuestro, (la) nuestra, (los) nuestros, (las) nuestras — **ourselves** [ɑr'selvz, aʊr-] *pron* **1** (*used reflexively*) : nos **2** (*used after prepositions*) : nosotros, nosotras **3** (*used for emphasis*) : nosotros mismos, nosotras mismas

oust ['aʊst] *vt* : desbancar

out ['aʊt] *adv* **1** OUTSIDE : fuera, afuera **2 cry ~** : gritar **3 eat ~** : comer afuera **4 go ~** : salir **5 look ~** : mirar para afuera **6 run ~ of** : agotar **7 turn ~** : apagar (una luz) **8 take ~** REMOVE : sacar — **~** *prep* → **out of** — **~** *adj* **1** ABSENT : ausente **2** UNFASHIONABLE : fuera de moda **3** EXTINGUISHED : apagado **4 the sun is ~** : hace sol

outboard motor ['aʊt,bɔrd] *n* : motor *m* fuera de borde

outbreak ['aʊt,breɪk] *n* : brote *m* (de una enfermedad), comienzo *m* (de guerra)

outburst ['aʊt,bərst] *n* : arranque *m*, arrebato *m*

outcast ['aʊt,kæst] *n* : paria *mf*

outcome ['aʊt,kʌm] *n* : resultado *m*

outcry ['aʊt,kraɪ] *n, pl* **-cries** : protesta *f*

outdated [,aʊt'deɪtəd] *adj* : anticuado

outdo [,aʊt'du:] *vt* **-did** [-'dɪd]; **-done** [-'dʌn]; **-doing; -does** [-'dʌz] : superar

outdoor ['aʊt,dɔr] *adj* : al aire libre — **outdoors** [,aʊt'dɔrz] *adv* : al aire libre

outer ['aʊtər] *adj* : exterior — **outer space** *n* : espacio *m* exterior

outfit ['aʊt,fɪt] *n* **1** EQUIPMENT : equipo *m* **2** CLOTHES : conjunto *m* — **~** *vt* **-fitted; -fitting** EQUIP : equipar

outgoing ['aʊt,go:ɪŋ] *adj* **1** SOCIABLE : extrovertido **2** : mail : correo *m* (para enviar) **3 ~ president** : presidente *m*, -ta *f* saliente

outgrow [,aʊt'gro:] *vt* **-grew** [-'gru:]; **-grown** [-'gro:n]; **-growing** : crecer más que

outing ['aʊtɪŋ] *n* : excursión *f*

outlandish [aʊt'lændɪʃ] *adj* : estrafalario

outlast [aʊt'læst] *vt* : durar más que

outlaw ['aʊt,lɔ] *n* : forajido *m*, -da *f* — **~** *vt* : declarar ilegal

outlay ['aʊt,leɪ] *n* : desembolso *m*

outlet ['aʊt,let, -lət] *n* **1** EXIT : salida *f* **2** RELEASE : desahogo *m* **3** *or* **electrical ~** : toma *f* de corriente **4** *or* **retail ~** : tienda *f* al por menor

outline ['aʊt,laɪn] *n* **1** CONTOUR : contorno *m* **2** SKETCH : bosquejo *m*, boceto *m* **3** SUMMARY : esquema *m* — **~** *vt* **-lined; -lining 1** SKETCH : bosquejar **2** EXPLAIN : delinear, esbozar

outlive [aʊt'lɪv] *vt* **-lived; -living** : sobrevivir a

outlook ['aʊt,lʊk] *n* **1** PROSPECTS : perspectivas *fpl* **2** VIEWPOINT : punto *m* de vista

outlying ['aʊt,laɪɪŋ] *adj* : alejado, distante

outmoded [,aʊt'mo:dəd] *adj* : pasado de moda, anticuado

outnumber [,aʊt'nʌmbər] *vt* : superar en número a

out of *prep* **1** FROM : de **2** THROUGH : por **3** WITHOUT : sin **4 ~ curiosity** : por curiosidad **5 ~ control** : fuera de control **6 one ~ four** : uno de cada cuatro — **out-of-date** [,aʊtəv'deɪt] *adj* : anticuado — **out-of-door** [,aʊtəv'dɔr] *or* **out-of-doors** [-'dɔrz] *adj* → **outdoor**

outpatient ['aʊt,peɪʃənt] *n* : paciente *m* externo

outpost ['aʊt,po:st] *n* : puesto *m* avanzado

output ['aʊt,pʊt] *n* **1** : producción *f*, rendimiento *m* **2** : salida *f* (informática) — **~** *vt* **-putted** *or* **-put; -putting** : producir

outrage ['aʊt,reɪdʒ] *n* **1** : atrocidad *f*, escándalo *m* **2** ANGER : ira *f*, indignación *f* — **~** *vt* **-raged; -raging** : ultrajar — **outrageous** [,aʊt'reɪdʒəs] *adj* : escandaloso

outright [,aʊt'raɪt] *adv* **1** COMPLETELY : por completo **2** INSTANTLY : en el acto — ['aʊt,raɪt] *adj* : completo, absoluto

outset ['aʊt,set] *n* : comienzo *m*, principio *m*

outside [,aʊt'saɪd, 'aʊt,-] *n* **1** : exterior *m* **2 from the ~** : desde fuera, desde afuera — **~** *adj* **1** : exterior, externo **2 an ~ chance** : una posibilidad remota — **~** *adv* : fuera, afuera — **~** *prep* *or* **~ of** : fuera de — **outsider** [aʊt'saɪdər] *n* : forastero *m*, -ra *f*

outskirts ['aʊt,skərts] *npl* : afueras *fpl*, alrededores *mpl*

outspoken [,aʊt'spo:kən] *adj* : franco, directo

outstanding [,aʊt'stændɪŋ] *adj* **1** UNPAID : pendiente **2** EXCELLENT : excepcional

outstretched [,aʊt'stretʃt] *adj* : extendido

outstrip [,aʊt'strɪp] *vt* **-stripped** *or* **-strip** [-'strɪp]; **-stripping** : aventajar

outward ['aʊtwərd] *adj* **1** : hacia afuera **2** EXTERNAL : externo, external — **~** *or* **outwards** [-wərdz] *adv* : hacia afuera — **outwardly** ['aʊtwərdli] *adv* APPARENTLY : aparentemente

outweigh [aʊt'weɪ] *vt* : pesar más que

outwit [aʊt'wɪt] *vt* **-witted; -witting** : ser más listo que

oval ['o:vəl] *n* : óvalo *m* — **~** *adj* : ovalado

ovary ['o:vəri] *n, pl* **-ries** : ovario *m*

ovation [o:'veɪʃən] *n* : ovación *f*

oven ['ʌvən] *n* : horno *m*

over ['o:vər] *adv* **1** ABOVE : por encima **2** AGAIN : otra vez, de nuevo **3** MORE : más **4 all ~** : por todas partes **5 ask ~** : invitar **6 cross ~** : cruzar **7 fall ~** : caerse **8 and ~** : una y otra vez **9 ~ here** : aquí **10 ~ there** : allí — **~** *prep* **1** ABOVE, UPON : encima de, sobre **2** ACROSS : por encima de, sobre **3** DURING : en, durante **4 fight ~** : pelearse por **5 ~ $5** : más de $5 **6 ~ the phone** : por teléfono — **~** *adj* : terminado, acabado

overall [,o:vər'ɔl] *adv* GENERALLY : en general — *adj* : total, en conjunto — **overalls** ['o:vər,ɔlz] *npl* : overol *m Lat*

overbearing [,o:vər'bærɪŋ] *adj* : dominante, imperioso

overboard ['o:vər,bɔrd] *adv* **fall ~** : caer al agua

overburden [,o:vər'bərdən] *vt* : sobrecargar

overcast ['o:vər,kæst] *adj* : nublado

overcharge [,o:vər'tʃɑrdʒ] *vt* **-charged; -charging** : cobrar demasiado

overcoat ['o:vər,ko:t] *n* : abrigo *m*

overcome [,o:vər'kʌm] *v* **-came** [-'keɪm]; **-come; -coming 1** CONQUER : vencer **2** OVERWHELM : agobiar — *vi* : vencer

overcook [,o:vər'kʊk] *vt* : cocer demasiado

overcrowded [,o:vər'kraʊdəd] *adj* : abarrotado de gente

overdo [,o:vər'du:] *vt* **-did** [-'dɪd]; **-done** [-'dʌn]; **-doing; -does** [-'dʌz] **1** : hacer demasiado **2** EXAGGERATE : exagerar **3** → **overcook**

overdose ['o:vər,do:s] *n* : sobredosis *f*

overdraw [,o:vər'drɔ] *vt* **-drew** [-'dru:]; **-drawn** [-'drɔn]; **-drawing** : girar en descubierto — **overdraft** ['o:vər,dræft] *n* : sobregiro *m*, descubierto *m*

overdue [,o:vər'du:] *adj* : fuera de plazo (dícese de pagos, libros, etc.)

overeat [,o:vər'i:t] *vi* **-ate** [-'eɪt]; **-eaten** [-'eɪtən]; **-eating** : comer demasiado

overestimate [,o:vər'estə,meɪt] *vt* **-mated; -mating** : sobreestimar

overflow [,o:vər'flo:] *vt* : desbordar — *vi* : desbordarse — **~** [,o:vər,flo:] *n* : desbordamiento *m* (de un río)

overgrown [,o:vər'gro:n] *adj* : cubierto de malas hierbas, etc.)

overhand [,o:vər'hænd] *adv* : por encima de la cabeza

overhang [,o:vər'hæŋ] *v* **-hung** [-'hʌŋ]; **-hanging** : sobresalir

overhaul [,o:vər'hɔl] *vt* : revisar (un motor, etc.)

overhead [,o:vər'hed] *adv* : por encima — **~** ['o:vər,hed] *adj* : de arriba — **~** ['o:vər,hed] *n* : gastos *mpl* generales

overhear [,o:vər'hɪr] *vt* **-heard; -hearing** : oír por casualidad

overheat [,o:vər'hi:t] *vt* : calentar demasiado — *vi* : recalentarse

overjoyed [,o:vər'dʒɔɪd] *adj* : encantado

overland ['o:vər,lænd, -lənd] *adv & adj* : por tierra

overlap [,o:vər'læp] *v* **-lapped; -lapping** *vt* : traslapar — *vi* : traslaparse

overload [,o:vər'lo:d] *vt* : sobrecargar

overlook [,o:vər'lʊk] *vt* **1** : dar a (un jardín, el mar, etc.) **2** MISS : pasar por alto

overly ['o:vərli] *adv* : demasiado

overnight [,o:vər'naɪt] *adv* **1** : por la noche **2** SUDDENLY : de la noche a la mañana — **~** *adj* **1** : de noche **2** SUDDEN : repentino

overpass ['o:vər,pæs] *n* : paso *m* elevado

overpopulated [,o:vər'pɑpjə,leɪtəd] *adj* : superpoblado

overpower [,o:vər'paʊər] *vt* **1** SUBDUE : dominar **2** OVERWHELM : agobiar, abrumar

overrated [,o:vər'reɪtəd] *adj* : sobreestimado

override [,o:vər'raɪd] *vt* **-rode** [-'ro:d]; **-ridden** [-'rɪdən]; **-riding 1** : predominar sobre **2** : anular (una decisión, etc.)

overrule [,o:vər'ru:l] *vt* **-ruled; -ruling** : anular (una decisión), rechazar (una protesta)

overrun [,o:vər'rʌn] *vt* **-ran** [-'ræn]; **-running 1** INVADE : invadir **2** EXCEED : exceder

overseas [,o:vər'si:z] *adv* : en el extranjero — ['o:vər,si:z] *adj* : extranjero, exterior

oversee [,o:vər'si:] *vt* **-saw** [-'sɔ]; **-seen** [-'si:n]; **-seeing** : supervisar

overshadow [,o:vər'ʃæ,do:] *vt* : eclipsar

oversight ['o:vər,saɪt] *n* : descuido *m*

oversleep [,o:vər'sli:p] *vi* **-slept** [-'slept]; **-sleeping** : quedarse dormido

overstep [,o:vər'step] *vt* **-stepped; -stepping** : sobrepasar

overt ['o:vərt, o:'vərt] *adj* : manifiesto

overtake [,o:vər'teɪk] *vt* **-took** [-'tʊk]; **-taken** [-'teɪkən]; **-taking 1** PASS : adelantar **2** SURPASS : superar

overthrow [,o:vər'θro:] *vt* **-threw** [-'θru:]; **-thrown** [-'θro:n]; **-throwing** : derrocar

overtime ['o:vər,taɪm] *n* **1** : horas *fpl* extras (de trabajo) **2** : prórroga *f* (en deportes)

overtone ['o:vər,to:n] *n* SUGGESTION : tinte *m*, insinuación *f*

overture ['o:vər,tʃʊr, -tʃər] *n* : obertura *f* (en música)

overturn [,o:vər'tərn] *vt* **1** : dar la vuelta a **2** NULLIFY : anular — *vi* : volcar

overweight [,o:vər'weɪt] *adj* : demasiado gordo

overwhelm [,o:vər'hwelm] *vt* **1** : abrumar, agobiar **2** : aplastar (a un enemigo) — **overwhelming** [,o:vər'hwelmɪŋ] *adj* : abrumador, apabullante

overwork [,o:vər'wərk] *vt* : hacer trabajar demasiado — *vi* : trabajar demasiado

overwrought [,o:vər'rɔt] *adj* : alterado, sobreexitado

owe ['o:] *vt* **owed; owing** : deber — **owing to** *prep* : debido a

owl ['aʊl] *n* : búho *m*

own ['o:n] *adj* : propio — **~** *vt* : poseer, tener — *vi* : trabajar demasiado **1 my (your, his/her/their, our) ~** : el mío, la mía; el tuyo, la tuya; el suyo, la suya; el nuestro, la nuestra **2 be on one's ~** : estar solo **3 to each his ~** : cada uno a lo suyo — **owner** ['o:nər] *n* : propietario *m*, -ria *f* — **ownership** ['o:nər,ʃɪp] *n* : propiedad *f*

ox ['ɑks] *n, pl* **oxen** ['ɑksən] : buey *m*

oxygen ['ɑksɪdʒən] *n* : oxígeno *m*

oyster ['ɔɪstər] *n* : ostra *f*

ozone ['o:,zo:n] *n* : ozono *m*

P

p ['pi:] *n, pl* **p's** *or* **ps** ['pi:z] : p *f*, decimosexta letra del alfabeto inglés

pace ['peɪs] *n* **1** STEP : paso *m* **2** RATE : ritmo *m* **3 keep ~ with** : andar al mismo paso que — **~** *vi* **paced; pacing** *or* **~ up and down** : caminar de arriba para abajo

pacify ['pæsə,faɪ] *vt* **-fied; -fying** : apaciguar — **pacifier** ['pæsə,faɪər] *n* : chupete *m* — **pacifist** ['pæsəfɪst] *n* : pacifista *mf*

pack ['pæk] *n* **1** BUNDLE : fardo *m* **2** BACKPACK : mochila *f* **3** PACKAGE : paquete *m* **4** : baraja *f* (de naipes) **5** : manada *f* (de lobos, etc.), jauría *f* (de perros) — **~** *vt* **1** PACKAGE : empaquetar **2** FILL : llenar **3** : hacer (una maleta) — : hacer las maletas — **package** ['pækɪdʒ] *vt* **-aged; -aging** : empaquetar — **~** *n* : paquete *m* — **packet** ['pækət] *n* : paquete *m*

pact ['pækt] *n* : pacto *m*, acuerdo *m*

pad ['pæd] *n* **1** CUSHION : almohadilla *f* **2** TABLET : bloc *m* (de papel) **3** *or* **ink ~** : tampón *m* **4 launching ~** : plataforma *f* (de lanzamiento) — **~** *vt* **padded; padding** : rellenar — **padding** ['pædɪŋ] *n* **1** : relleno *m* **2** : paja *f* (en un discurso, etc.)

paddle ['pædəl] *n* **1** : canalete *m* (de una canoa) **2** : paleta *f* (en deportes) — **~** *vt* **-dled; -dling** : hacer avanzar (una canoa) con canalete

padlock ['pæd,lɑk] *n* : candado *m* — **~** *vt* : cerrar con candado

pagan ['peɪgən] *n* : pagano *m*, -na *f* — *adj* : pagano

page[1] ['peɪdʒ] *vt* **paged; paging** : llamar por altavoz

page[2] *n* : página *f* (de un libro, etc.)

pageant ['pædʒənt] *n* : espectáculo *m* — **pageantry** ['pædʒəntri] *n* : pompa *f*, boato *m*

paid → **pay**

pail ['peɪl] *n* : cubo *m Spain*, cubeta *f Lat*

pain ['peɪn] *n* **1** : dolor *m* **2** : pena *f* (mental) **3 ~s** *npl* EFFORT : esfuerzos *mpl* — **~** *vt* : doler — **painful** ['peɪnfəl] *adj* : doloroso — **painkiller** ['peɪn,kɪlər] *n* : analgésico *m* — **painless** ['peɪnləs] *adj* : indoloro, sin dolor — **painstaking** ['peɪn,steɪkɪŋ] *adj* : meticuloso, esmerado

paint ['peɪnt] *v* : pintar — **~** *n* : pintura *f* — **paintbrush** ['peɪnt,brʌʃ] *n* : pincel *m* (de un artista), brocha *f* (para pintar casas, etc.) — **painter** ['peɪntər] *n* : pintor *m*, -tora *f* — **painting** ['peɪntɪŋ] *n* : pintura *f*

pair ['pær] *n* **1** : par *m* **2** COUPLE : pareja *f* — **~** *vt* : emparejar

pajamas [pə'dʒɑməz, -'dʒæ-] *npl* : pijama *m*, piyama *mf Lat*

Pakistani [,pækɪ'stæni, ,pɑkɪ'stɑni] *adj* : paquistaní

pal ['pæl] *n* : amigo *m*, -ga *f*

palace ['pæləs] *n* : palacio *m*

palate ['pælət] *n* : paladar *m* — **palatable** ['pælətəbəl] *adj* : sabroso

pale ['peɪl] *adj* **paler; palest 1** PALLID : pálido **2** : claro (dícese de los colores, etc.) — **~** *vi* **paled; paling** : palidecer — **paleness** ['peɪlnəs] *n* : palidez *f*

Palestinian [,pælə'stɪniən] *adj* : palestino

palette ['pælət] *n* : paleta *f*

pallbearer ['pɔl,bærər] *n* : portador *m*, -dora *f* del féretro

pallid ['pæləd] *adj* : pálido — **pallor** ['pælər] *n* : palidez *f*

palm[1] ['pɑm, 'pɑlm] *n* : palma *f* (de la mano)

palm[2] *or* **~ tree** : palmera *f* — **Palm Sunday** *n* : Domingo *m* de Ramos

palpitate ['pælpə,teɪt] *vi* **-tated; -tating** : palpitar — **palpitation** [,pælpə'teɪʃən] *n* : palpitación *f*

paltry ['pɔltri] *adj* **-trier; -est** : mísero, mezquino

pamper ['pæmpər] *vt* : mimar

pamphlet ['pæmpflət] *n* : panfleto *m*, folleto *m*

pan ['pæn] *n* **1** SAUCEPAN : cacerola *f* **2** FRYING PAN : sartén *mf* — ~ *vt* **panned; panning** CRITICIZE : poner por los suelos

pancake ['pæn,keɪk] *n* : crepe *mf*, panqueque *m Lat*

panda ['pændə] *n* : panda *mf*

pandemonium [,pændə'mo:niəm] *n* : pandemonio *m*

pander ['pændər] *vi* ~ **to** : complacer a

pane ['peɪn] *n* : cristal *m*, vidrio *m*

panel ['pænəl] *n* **1** : panel *m* **2** GROUP : jurado *m* **3** *or* **instrument** ~ : tablero *m* (de instrumentos) — ~ *vt* **-eled** *or* **-elled; -eling** *or* **-elling** : adornar con paneles — **paneling** ['pænəlɪŋ] *n* : paneles *mpl*

pang ['pæŋ] *n* : punzada *f*

panic ['pænɪk] *n* : pánico *m* — ~ *v* **-icked; -icking** *vt* : llenar del pánico — *vi* : ser presa del pánico — **panicky** ['pænɪki] *adj* : presa de pánico

panorama [,pænə'ræmə, -'rɑ-] *n* : panorama *m* — **panoramic** [,pænə'ræmɪk, -'rɑ-] *adj* : panorámico

pansy ['pænzi] *n, pl* **-sies** : pensamiento *m*

pant ['pænt] *vi* : jadear, resoplar

panther ['pænθər] *n* : pantera *f*

panties ['pæntiz] *npl* : bragas *fpl Spain*, calzones *mpl Lat*

pantomime ['pæntə,maɪm] *n* : pantomima *f*

pantry ['pæntri] *n, pl* **-tries** : despensa *f*

pants ['pænts] *npl* TROUSERS : pantalón *m*, pantalones *mpl*

papa ['pɑpə] *n* : papá *m fam*

papal ['peɪpəl] *adj* : papal

papaya [pə'paɪə] *n* : papaya *f*

paper ['peɪpər] *n* **1** : papel *m* **2** DOCUMENT : documento *m* **3** NEWSPAPER : periódico *m* — ~ *vt* WALLPAPER : empapelar — ~ *adj* : de papel — **paperback** ['peɪpər,bæk] *n* : libro *m* en rústica — **paper clip** *n* : clip *m*, sujetapapeles *m* — **paperweight** ['peɪpər,weɪt] *n* : pisapapeles *m* — **paperwork** ['peɪpər,wərk] *n* : papeleo *m*

paprika [pə'pri:kə, pæ-] *n* : pimentón *m*

par ['pɑr] *n* **1** : par *m* (en golf) **2 below** ~ : debajo de la par **3 on a** ~ **with** : al nivel de

parable ['pærəbəl] *n* : parábola *f*

parachute ['pærə,ʃu:t] *n* : paracaídas *m* — ~ *vi* **-chuted; -chuting** : lanzarse en paracaídas

parade [pə'reɪd] *n* **1** : desfile *m* **2** DISPLAY : alarde *m* — ~ *v* **-raded; -rading** *vi* MARCH : desfilar — *vt* DISPLAY : hacer alarde de

paradise ['pærə,daɪs, -,daɪz] *n* : paraíso *m*

paradox ['pærə,dɑks] *n* : paradoja *f* — **paradoxical** [,pærə'dɑksɪkəl] *adj* : paradójico

paraffin ['pærəfən] *n* : parafina *f*

paragraph ['pærə,græf] *n* : párrafo *m*

Paraguayan [,pærə'gwaɪən, -'gweɪ-] *adj* : paraguayo

parakeet ['pærə,ki:t] *n* : periquito *m*

parallel ['pærə,lɛl, -ləl] *adj* : paralelo — ~ *n* **1** : paralelo *m* (en geografía) **2** SIMILARITY : paralelismo *m*, semejanza *f* — ~ *vt* : ser paralelo a

paralysis [pə'ræləsəs] *n, pl* **-yses** [-,si:z] : parálisis *f* — **paralyze** *or Brit* **paralise** ['pærə,laɪz] *vt* **-lyzed** *or Brit* **-lised; -lyzing** *or Brit* **-lising** : paralizar

parameter [pə'ræməṭər] *n* : parámetro *m*

paramount ['pærə,maʊnt] *adj* **of** ~ **importance** : de suma importancia

paranoia [,pærə'nɔɪə] *n* : paranoia *f* — **paranoid** ['pærə,nɔɪd] *adj* : paranoico

paraphernalia [,pærəfə'neɪljə, -fər-] *ns & pl* : parafernalia *f*

paraphrase ['pærə,freɪz] *n* : paráfrasis *f* — ~ *vt* **-phrased; -phrasing** : parafrasear

paraplegic [,pærə'pli:dʒɪk] *n* : parapléjico *m*, -ca *f*

parasite ['pærə,saɪt] *n* : parásito *m*

paratrooper ['pærə,tru:pər] *n* : paracaidista *mf* (militar)

parcel ['pɑrsəl] *n* : paquete *m*

parch ['pɑrtʃ] *vt* : resecar

parchment ['pɑrtʃmənt] *n* : pergamino *m*

pardon ['pɑrdən] *n* **1** : perdón *m* **2** REPRIEVE : indulto *m* **3 I beg your** ~ : perdone Ud., disculpe Ud. *Lat* — ~ *vt* **1** : perdonar **2** REPRIEVE : indultar (a un delincuente)

parent ['pærənt] *n* **1** : madre *f*, padre *m* **2** ~**s** *npl* : padres *mpl* — **parental** [pə'rɛntəl] *adj* : de los padres

parenthesis [pə'rɛnθəsɪs] *n, pl* **-theses** [-,si:z] : paréntesis *m*

parish ['pærɪʃ] *n* : parroquia *f* — **parishioner** [pə'rɪʃənər] *n* : feligrés *m*, -gresa *f*

parity ['pærəṭi] *n, pl* **-ties** : igualdad *f*

park ['pɑrk] *n* : parque *m* — ~ *v* : estacionar, parquear *Lat*

parka ['pɑrkə] *n* : parka *f*

parking ['pɑrkɪŋ] *n* : estacionamiento *m*

parliament ['pɑrləmənt, 'pɑrljə-] *n* : parlamento *m* — **parliamentary** [,pɑrlə'mɛntəri, ,pɑrljə-] *adj* : parlamentario

parlor *or Brit* **parlour** ['pɑrlər] *n* : salón *m*

parochial [pə'ro:kiəl] *adj* **1** : parroquial **2** PROVINCIAL : de miras estrechas

parody ['pærədi] *n, pl* **-dies** : parodia *f* — ~ *vt* **-died; -dying** : parodiar

parole [pə'ro:l] *n* : libertad *f* condicional

parrot ['pærət] *n* : loro *m*, papagayo *m*

parry ['pæri] *vt* **-ried; -rying 1** : parar (un golpe) **2** EVADE : eludir (una pregunta, etc.)

parsley ['pɑrsli] *n* : perejil *m*

parsnip ['pɑrsnɪp] *n* : chirivía *f*

parson ['pɑrsən] *n* : clérigo *m*

part ['pɑrt] *n* **1** : parte *f* **2** PIECE : pieza *f* **3** ROLE : papel *m* **4** : raya *f* (del pelo) — ~ *vi* **1** *or* ~ **company** : separarse **2** ~ **with** : deshacerse de — *vt* SEPARATE : separar

partake [pɑr'teɪk, pər-] *vi* **-took; -taken; -taking** ~ **in** : participar en

partial ['pɑrʃəl] *adj* **1** : parcial **2 be** ~ **to** : ser aficionado a

participate [pər'tɪsə,peɪt, pɑr-] *vi* **-pated; -pating** : participar — **participant** [pər'tɪsəpənt, pɑr-] *n* : participante *mf*

participle ['pɑrṭə,sɪpəl] *n* : participio *m*

particle ['pɑrṭɪkəl] *n* : partícula *f*

particular [pər'tɪkjələr] *adj* **1** : particular **2** FUSSY : exigente — ~ *n* **1 in** ~ : en particular, en especial **2** ~**s** *npl* DETAILS : detalles *mpl* — **particularly** [pər'tɪkjələrli] *adv* : especialmente

partisan ['pɑrṭəzən, -sən] *n* : partidario *m*, -ria *f*

partition [pər'tɪʃən, pɑr-] *n* **1** DISTRIBUTION : partición *f* **2** DIVIDER : tabique *m* — ~ *vt* : dividir

partly ['pɑrtli] *adv* : en parte

partner ['pɑrtnər] *n* **1** : pareja *f* (en un juego, etc.) **2** *or* **business** ~ : socio *m*, -cia *f* — **partnership** ['pɑrtnər,ʃɪp] *n* : asociación *f*

party ['pɑrṭi] *n, pl* **-ties 1** : partido *m* (político) **2** GATHERING : fiesta *f* **3** GROUP : grupo *m*

pass ['pæs] *vi* **1** : pasar **2** CEASE : pasarse **3** : aprobar (en un examen) **4** *or* ~ **away** DIE : morir **5** ~ **for** : pasar por **6** ~ **out** FAINT : desmayarse — *vt* **1** : pasar **2** *or* ~ **in front of** : pasar por **3** OVERTAKE : adelantar **4** : aprobar (un examen, una ley, etc.) **5** ~ **down** : transmitir — ~ *n* **1** PERMIT : pase *m*, permiso *m* **2** : pase *m* (en deportes) **3** *or* **mountain** ~ : paso *m* de montaña — **passable** ['pæsəbəl] *adj* **1** ADEQUATE : adecuado **2** : transitable (dícese de un camino, etc.) — **passage** ['pæsɪdʒ] *n* **1** : paso *m* **2** CORRIDOR : pasillo *m* (dentro de un edificio), pasaje *m* (entre edificios) **3** VOYAGE : travesía *f* (por el mar) — **passageway** ['pæsɪdʒ,weɪ] *n* : pasillo *m*, corredor *m*

passenger ['pæsəndʒər] *n* : pasajero *m*, -ra *f*

passerby [,pæsər'baɪ, 'pæsər,-] *n, pl* **passersby** : transeúnte *mf*

passion ['pæʃən] *n* : pasión *f* — **passionate** ['pæʃənət] *adj* : apasionado

passive ['pæsɪv] *adj* : pasivo

Passover ['pæs,o:vər] *n* : Pascua *f* (en el judaísmo)

passport ['pæs,port] *n* : pasaporte *m*

password ['pæs,wərd] *n* : contraseña *f*

past ['pæst] *adj* **1** : pasado **2** FORMER : anterior **3 the** ~ **few months** : los últimos meses — ~ *prep* **1** IN FRONT OF : por delante de **2** BEYOND : más allá de **3 half** ~ **two** : las dos y media — ~ *n* : pasado *m* — ~ *adv* : por delante

pasta ['pɑstə, 'pæs-] *n* : pasta *f*

paste ['peɪst] *n* **1** : pasta *f* **2** GLUE : engrudo *m* — ~ *vt* **pasted; pasting** : pegar

pastel [pæ'stɛl] *n* : pastel *m* — ~ *adj* : pastel

pasteurize ['pæstʃə,raɪz, 'pæstjə-] *vt* **-ized; -izing** : pasteurizar

pastime ['pæs,taɪm] *n* : pasatiempo *m*

pastor ['pæstər] *n* : pastor *m*, -tora *f*

pastry ['peɪstri] *n, pl* **-ries** : pasteles *mpl*

pasture ['pæstʃər] *n* : pasto *m*

pasty ['peɪsti] *adj* **pastier; -est 1** DOUGHY : pastoso **2** PALLID : pálido

pat ['pæt] *n* **1** : palmadita *f* **2 a** ~ **of butter** : una porción de mantequilla — ~ *vt* **patted; patting** : dar palmaditas a — ~ *adv* **have down** ~ : saberse de memoria — ~ *adj* GLIB : fácil

patch ['pætʃ] *n* **1** : parche *m*, remiendo *m* (para la ropa) **2** SPOT : mancha *f*, trozo *m* **3** PLOT : parcela *f* (de tierra) — ~ *vt* **1** MEND : remender **2** ~ **up** : arreglar — **patchy** ['pætʃi] *adj* **patchier; -est 1** : desigual **2** INCOMPLETE : parcial, incompleto

patent ['pætənt] *adj* **1** *or* **patented** ['pætəntəd] : patentado **2** ['pætənt, 'peɪt-] OBVIOUS : patente, evidente — ~ ['pætənt] *n* : patente *f* — ~ ['pætənt] *vt* : patentar

paternal [pə'tərnəl] *adj* **1** FATHERLY : paternal **2** ~ **grandmother** : abuela *f* paterna — **paternity** [pə'tərnəṭi] *n* : paternidad *f*

path ['pæθ, 'pɑθ] *n* **1** TRACK, TRAIL : camino *m*, sendero *m* **2** COURSE : trayectoria *f*

pathetic [pə'θɛṭɪk] *adj* : patético

pathology [pə'θɑlədʒi] *n, pl* **-gies** : patología *f*

pathway ['pæθ,weɪ] *n* : camino *m*, sendero *m*

patience ['peɪʃənts] *n* : paciencia *f* — **patient** ['peɪʃənt] *adj* : paciente — ~ *n* : paciente *mf* — **patiently** *adv* : con paciencia

patio ['pæṭi,o:] *n, pl* **-tios** : patio *m*

patriot ['peɪtriət] *n* : patriota *mf* — **patriotic** [,peɪtri'ɑṭɪk] *adj* : patriótico

patrol [pə'tro:l] *n* : patrulla *f* — ~ *v* **-trolled; -trolling** : patrullar

patron ['peɪtrən] *n* **1** SPONSOR : patrocinador *m*, -dora *f* **2** CUSTOMER : cliente *m*, -ta *f* — **patronage** ['peɪtrənɪdʒ, 'pæ-] *n* **1** SPONSORSHIP : patrocinio *m* **2** CLIENTELE : clientela *f* — **patronize** ['peɪtrə,naɪz, 'pæ-] *vt* **-ized; -izing 1** : ser cliente de (una tienda, etc.) **2** : tratar (a algn) con condescencia

patter ['pæṭər] *n* : tamborileo *m* (de la lluvia), correteo *m* (de los pies)

pattern ['pæṭərn] *n* **1** MODEL : modelo *m* **2** DESIGN : diseño *m* **3** STANDARD : pauta *f*, modo *m* **4** : patrón *m* (en costura) — ~ *vt* : basar (en un modelo)

paunch ['pɔntʃ] *n* : panza *f*

pause ['pɔz] *n* : pausa *f* — ~ *vi* **paused; pausing** : hacer una pausa

pave ['peɪv] *vt* **paved; paving** : pavimentar — **pavement** ['peɪvmənt] *n* : pavimento *m*

pavilion [pə'vɪljən] *n* : pabellón *m*

paw ['pɔ] *n* **1** : pata *f* **2** : garra *f* (de un gato) — ~ *vt* : tocar con la pata

pawn[1] ['pɔn] *n* : peón *m* (en ajedrez)

pawn[2] *vt* : empeñar — **pawnbroker** ['pɔn,bro:kər] *n* : prestamista *mf* — **pawnshop** ['pɔn,ʃɑp] *n* : casa *f* de empeños

pay ['peɪ] *v* **paid** ['peɪd]; **paying** *vt* **1** : pagar **2** ~ **attention** : prestar atención **3** ~ **back** : devolver **4** ~ **one's respects** : presentar uno sus respetos **5** ~ **a visit** : hacer una visita — *vi* **1** : pagar **2 crime doesn't** ~ : no hay crimen sin castigo — ~ *n* : paga *f* — **payable** ['peɪəbəl] *adj* : pagadero — **paycheck** ['peɪ,tʃɛk] *n* : cheque *m* del sueldo — **payment** ['peɪmənt] *n* **1** : pago *m* **2** INSTALLMENT : plazo *m*, cuota *f Lat* — **payroll** *n* : nómina *f*

PC [,pi:'si:] *n, pl* **PCs** *or* **PC's** : PC *mf*, computadora *f* personal

pea ['pi:] *n* : guisante *m*, arveja *f Lat*

peace ['pi:s] *n* : paz *f* — **peaceful** ['pi:sfəl] *adj* **1** : pacífico **2** CALM : tranquilo

peach ['pi:tʃ] *n* : melocotón *m*, durazno *m Lat*

peacock ['pi:,kɑk] *n* : pavo *m* real

peak ['pi:k] *n* **1** SUMMIT : cumbre *f*, cima *f*, pico *m* (de una montaña) **2** APEX : nivel *m* máximo — ~ *adj* : máximo — ~ *vi* : alcanzar su nivel máximo

peal ['pi:l] *n* **1** : repique *m* **2** ~**s of laughter** : carcajadas *fpl*

peanut ['pi:,nʌt] *n* : cacajuete *m*, maní *m Lat*

pear ['pær] *n* : pera *f*

pearl ['pərl] *n* : perla *f*

peasant ['pɛzənt] *n* : campesino *m*, -na *f*

peat ['pi:t] *n* : turba *f*

pebble ['pɛbəl] *n* : guijarro *m*

pecan [pɪ'kɑn, -'kæn, 'pi:,kæn] *n* : pacana *f*, nuez *f Lat*

peck ['pɛk] *vt* : picar, picotear — ~ *n* **1** : picotazo *m* (de un pájaro) **2** KISS : besito

peculiar [pɪ'kju:ljər] *adj* **1** DISTINCTIVE : peculiar, característico **2** STRANGE : extraño, raro — **peculiarity** [pɪ,kju:l'jærəṭi, -,kju:li'ær-] *n, pl* **-ties 1** : peculiaridad *f* **2** ODDITY : rareza *f*

pedal ['pɛdəl] *n* : pedal *m* — ~ *vi* **-aled** *or* **-alled; -aling** *or* **-alling** : pedalear

pedantic [pɪ'dæntɪk] *adj* : pedante

peddle ['pɛdəl] *vt* **-dled; -dling** : vender en las calles — **peddler** ['pɛdlər] *n* : vendedor *m*, -dora *f* ambulante

pedestal ['pɛdəstəl] *n* : pedestal *m*

pedestrian [pə'dɛstriən] *n* : peatón *m*, -tona *f* — ~ *adj* ~ **crossing** : paso *m* de peatones

pediatrics [,pi:di'ætrɪks] *ns & pl* : pediatría *f* — **pediatrician** [,pi:diə'trɪʃən] *n* : pediatra *mf*

pedigree ['pɛdə,gri:] *n* : pedigrí *m* (de un animal), linaje *m* (de una persona)

peek ['pi:k] *vi* : mirar a hurtadillas — ~ *n* : miradita *f* (furtiva)

peel ['pi:l] *vt* : pelar (fruta, etc.) — *vi* : pelarse (dícese de la piel), desconcharse (dícese de la pintura) — ~ *n* : piel *f*, cáscara *f*

peep[1] ['pi:p] *vi* CHEEP : piar — ~ *n* : pío *m* (de un pajarito)

peep[2] *vi* **1** PEEK : mirar a hurtadillas **2** *or* ~ **out** : asomar — ~ *n* GLANCE : mirada *f* (furtiva)

peer[1] ['pɪr] *n* : par *mf*

peer[2] *vi* : mirar (con atención)

peeve ['pi:v] *vt* : irritar — **peevish** ['pi:vɪʃ] *adj* : malhumorado

peg ['pɛg] *n* **1** : clavija *f* **2** HOOK : gancho *m*

pelican ['pɛlɪkən] *n* : pelícano *m*

pellet ['pɛlət] *n* **1** : bolita *f* **2** SHOT : perdigón *m*

pelt[1] ['pɛlt] *n* : piel *f* (de un animal)

pelt[2] *vt* : lanzar (algo a algn)

pelvis ['pɛlvɪs] *n, pl* **-vises** *or* **-ves** ['pɛl,vi:z] : pelvis *f* — **pelvic** ['pɛlvɪk] *adj* : pélvico

pen[1] ['pɛn] *vt* **penned; penning** ENCLOSE : encerrar — ~ *n* : corral *m*, redil *m*

pen[2] *n* **1** *or* **ballpoint** ~ : bolígrafo *m* **2** *or* **fountain** ~ : pluma *f*

penal ['pi:nəl] *adj* : penal — **penalize** ['pi:nəl,aɪz, 'pɛn-] *vt* **-ized; -izing** : penalizar — **penalty** ['pɛnəlti] *n, pl* **-ties 1** : pena *f*, castigo *m* **2** : penalty *m* (en deportes)

penance ['pɛnənts] *n* : penitencia *f*

pencil ['pɛntsəl] *n* : lápiz *m* — **pencil sharpener** *n* : sacapuntas *m*

pendant ['pɛndənt] *n* : colgante *m*

pending ['pɛndɪŋ] *adj* : pendiente — ~ *prep* : en espera de

penetrate ['pɛnə,treɪt] *v* **-trated; -trating** : penetrar — **penetrating** ['pɛnə,treɪṭɪŋ] *adj* : penetrante — **penetration** [,pɛnə'treɪʃən] *n* : penetración *f*

penguin ['pɛŋgwɪn, 'pɛn-] *n* : pingüino *m*

penicillin [,pɛnə'sɪlən] *n* : penicilina *f*

peninsula [pə'nɪntsələ, -'nɪntʃulə] *n* : península *f*

penis ['pi:nəs] *n, pl* **-nes** [-,ni:z] *or* **-nises** : pene *m*

penitentiary [,pɛnə'tɛntʃəri] *n, pl* **-ries** : penitenciaría *f*

pen name *n* : seudónimo *m*

pennant ['pɛnənt] *n* : banderín *m*

penny ['pɛni] *n, pl* **-nies** *or* **pence** ['pɛnts] : centavo *m* (de los Estados Unidos), penique *m* (del Reino Unido) — **penniless** ['pɛniləs] *adj* : sin un centavo

pension ['pɛntʃən] *n* : pensión *m*, jubilación *f*

pensive ['pɛntsɪv] *adj* : pensativo

pentagon ['pɛntə,gɑn] *n* : pentágono *m*

penthouse ['pɛnt,haʊs] *n* : ático *m*

pent–up ['pɛnt,ʌp] *adj* : reprimado

people ['pi:pəl] *ns & pl* **1 people** *npl* : gente *f*, personas *fpl* **2** *pl* ~**s** : pueblo *m*

pep ['pɛp] *n* : energía *f*, vigor *m* — ~ *vt or* ~ **up** : animar

pepper ['pɛpər] *n* **1** : pimienta *f* (condimento) **2** : pimiento *m* (fruta) — **peppermint** ['pɛpər,mɪnt] *n* : menta *f*

per ['pər] *prep* **1** : por **2** ACCORDING TO : según **3** ~ **day** : al día **4 miles** ~ **hour** : millas *fpl* por hora

perceive [pər'si:v] *vt* **-ceived; -ceiving** : percibir

percent [pər'sɛnt] *adv* : por ciento — **percentage** [pər'sɛntɪdʒ] *n* : porcentaje *m*

perception [pər'sɛpʃən] *n* : percepción *f* — **perceptive** [pər'sɛptɪv] *adj* : perspicaz

perch[1] ['pərtʃ] *n* : percha *f* (para los pájaros) — ~ *vi* : posarse

perch[2] *n* : perca *f* (pez)

percolate ['pərkə,leɪt] *vi* **-lated; -lating** : filtrarse — **percolator** ['pərkə,leɪṭər] *n* : cafetera *f* de filtro

percussion [pər'kʌʃən] *n* : percusión *f*

perennial [pə'rɛniəl] *adj* : perenne — ~ *n* : planta *f* perenne

perfect ['pərfɪkt] *adj* : perfecto — ~ [pər'fɛkt] *vt* : perfeccionar — **perfection** [pər'fɛkʃən] *n* : perfección *f* — **perfectionist** [pər'fɛkʃənɪst] *n* : perfeccionista *mf*

perforate ['pərfə,reɪt] *vt* **-rated; -rating** : perforar

perform [pər'fɔrm] *vt* **1** CARRY OUT : realizar, hacer **2** : representar (una obra teatral), interpretar (una obra musical) — *vi* **1** FUNCTION : funcionar **2** ACT : actuar — **performance** [pər'fɔrmənts] *n* **1** : realización *f* **2** INTERPRETATION : interpretación *f* **3** PRESENTATION : representación *f* — **performer** [pər'fɔrmər] *n* : actor *m*, -triz *f*; intérprete *mf* (de música)

perfume ['pər,fju:m, pər'-] *n* : perfume *m*

perhaps [pər'hæps] *adv* : tal vez, quizá, quizás

peril ['pɛrəl] *n* : peligro *m* — **perilous** ['pɛrələs] *adj* : peligroso

perimeter [pə'rɪməṭər] *n* : perímetro *m*

period ['pɪriəd] *n* **1** : período *m* (de tiempo) **2** : punto *m* (en puntuación) **3** ERA : época *f* — **periodic** [,pɪri'ɑdɪk] *adj* : periódico — **periodical** [,pɪri'ɑdɪkəl] *n* : revista *f*

peripheral [pə'rɪfərəl] *adj* : periférico

perish ['pɛrɪʃ] *vi* : perecer — **perishable** ['pɛrɪʃəbəl] *adj* : perecedero — **perishables** ['pɛrɪʃəbəlz] *npl* : productos *mpl* perecederos

perjury ['pərdʒəri] *n* : perjurio *m*

perk ['pərk] *vi* ~ **up** : animarse, reanimarse — ~ *n* : extra *m* — **perky** ['pərki] *adj* **perkier; -est** : alegre

permanence ['pərmənənts] *n* : permanencia *f* — **permanent** ['pərmənənt] *adj* : permanente — ~ *n* : permanente *f*

permeate ['pərmi,eɪt] *v* **-ated; -ating** : penetrar

permission [pər'mɪʃən] *n* : permiso *m* — **permissible** [pər'mɪsəbəl] *adj* : permisible — **permissive** [pər'mɪsɪv] *adj* : permisivo — **permit** [pər'mɪt] *vt* **-mitted; -mitting** : permitir — ~ ['pər,mɪt, pər'-] *n* : permiso *m*

peroxide [pə'rɑk,saɪd] *n* : peróxido *m*

perpendicular [,pərpən'dɪkjələr] *adj* : perpendicular

perpetrate ['pərpə,treɪt] *vt* **-trated; -trating** : cometer — **perpetrator** ['pərpə,treɪṭər] *n* : autor *m*, -tora *f* (de un delito)

perpetual [pər'pɛtʃuəl] *adj* : perpetuo

perplex [pər'plɛks] *vt* : dejar perplejo — **perplexing** [pər'plɛksɪŋ] *adj* : desconcertante — **perplexity** [pər'plɛksəṭi] *n, pl* **-ties** : perplejidad *f*

persecute [ˈpərsɪˌkjuːt] *vt* **-cuted; -cuting** : perseguir — **persecution** [ˌpərsɪˈkjuːʃən] *n* : persecución *f*
persevere [ˌpərsəˈvɪr] *vi* **-vered; -vering** : perseverar — **perseverance** [ˌpərsəˈvɪrənts] *n* : perseverancia *f*
persist [pərˈsɪst] *vi* : persistir — **persistence** [pərˈsɪstənts] *n* : persistencia *f* — **persistent** [pərˈsɪstənt] *adj* : persistente
person [ˈpərsən] *n* : persona *f* — **personal** [ˈpərsənəl] *adj* : personal — **personality** [ˌpərsənˈæləṭi] *n, pl* **-ties** : personalidad *f* — **personally** [ˈpərsənəli] *adv* : personalmente, en persona — **personnel** [ˌpərsənˈɛl] *n* : personal *m*
perspective [pərˈspɛktɪv] *n* : perspectiva *f*
perspiration [ˌpərspəˈreɪʃən] *n* : transpiración *f* — **perspire** [pərˈspaɪr] *vi* **-spired; -spiring** : transpirar
persuade [pərˈsweɪd] *vt* **-suaded; -suading** : persuadir — **persuasion** [pərˈsweɪʒən] *n* : persuasión *f*
pertain [pərˈteɪn] *vi* ~ **to** : estar relacionado con — **pertinent** [ˈpərtənənt] *adj* : pertinente
perturb [pərˈtərb] *vt* : perturbar
Peruvian [pəˈruːviən] *adj* : peruano
pervade [pərˈveɪd] *vt* **-vaded; -vading** : penetrar — **pervasive** [pərˈveɪsɪv, -zɪv] *adj* : penetrante
perverse [pərˈvərs] *adj* **1** CORRUPT : perverso **2** STUBBORN : obstinado — **pervert** [ˈpərˌvərt] *n* : pervertido *m*, -da *f*
peso [ˈpeɪˌsoː] *n, pl* **-sos** : peso *m*
pessimism [ˈpɛsəˌmɪzəm] *n* : pesimismo *m* — **pessimist** [ˈpɛsəmɪst] *n* : pesimista *mf* — **pessimistic** [ˌpɛsəˈmɪstɪk] *adj* : pesimista
pest [ˈpɛst] *n* **1** : insecto *m* nocivo, animal *m* nocivo **2** : peste *f fam* (persona)
pester [ˈpɛstər] *vt* **-tered; -tering** : molestar
pesticide [ˈpɛstəˌsaɪd] *n* : pesticida *m*
pet [ˈpɛt] *n* **1** : animal *m* doméstico **2** FAVORITE : favorito *m*, -ta *f* — ~ *vt* **petted; petting** : acariciar
petal [ˈpɛṭəl] *n* : pétalo *m*
petite [pəˈtiːt] *adj* : chiquita
petition [pəˈtɪʃən] *n* : petición *f* — ~ *vt* : dirigir una petición a
petrify [ˈpɛtrəˌfaɪ] *vt* **-fied; -fying** : petrificar
petroleum [pəˈtroːliəm] *n* : petróleo *m*
petticoat [ˈpɛṭiˌkoːt] *n* : enagua *f*, fondo *m Lat*
petty [ˈpɛṭi] *adj* **-tier; -est** **1** UNIMPORTANT : insignificante, nimio **2** MEAN : mezquino — **pettiness** [ˈpɛṭinəs] *n* : mezquindad *f*
petulant [ˈpɛtʃələnt] *adj* : irritable, de mal genio
pew [ˈpjuː] *n* : banco *m* (de iglesia)
pewter [ˈpjuːṭər] *n* : peltre *m*
phallic [ˈfælɪk] *adj* : fálico
phantom [ˈfæntəm] *n* : fantasma *m*
pharmacy [ˈfɑrməsi] *n, pl* **-cies** : farmacia *f* — **pharmacist** [ˈfɑrməsɪst] *n* : farmacéutico *m*, -ca *f*
phase [ˈfeɪz] *n* : fase *f* — ~ *vt* **phased; phasing** **1** ~ **in** : introducir progresivamente **2** ~ **out** : retirar progresivamente
phenomenon [fɪˈnɑməˌnɑn, -nən] *n, pl* **-na** [-nə] *or* **-nons** : fenómeno *m* — **phenomenal** [fɪˈnɑmənəl] *adj* : fenomenal
philanthropy [fəˈlænθrəpi] *n, pl* **-pies** : filantropía *f* — **philanthropist** [fəˈlænθrəpɪst] *n* : filántropo *m*, -pa *f*
philosophy [fəˈlɑsəfi] *n, pl* **-phies** : filosofía *f* — **philosopher** [fəˈlɑsəfər] *n* : filósofo *m*, -fa *f*
phlegm [ˈflɛm] *n* : flema *f*
phobia [ˈfoːbiə] *n* : fobia *f*
phone [ˈfoːn] → **telephone**
phonetic [fəˈnɛṭɪk] *adj* : fonético
phony *or* **phoney** [ˈfoːni] *adj* **-nier; -est** : falso — ~ *n, pl* **-nies** : farsante *mf*
phosphorus [ˈfɑsfərəs] *n* : fósforo *m*
photo [ˈfoːṭoː] *n, pl* **-tos** : foto *f* — **photocopier** [ˈfoːṭoˌkɑpiər] *n* : fotocopiadora *f* — **photocopy** [ˈfoːṭoˌkɑpi] *n, pl* **-copies** : fotocopia *f* — ~ *vt* **-copied; -copying** : fotocopiar — **photograph** [ˈfoːṭəˌgræf] *n* : fotografía *f*, foto *f* — ~ *vt* : fotografiar — **photographer** [fəˈtɑgrəfər] *n* : fotógrafo *m*, -fa *f* — **photographic** [ˌfoːṭəˈgræfɪk] *adj* : fotográfico — **photography** [fəˈtɑgrəfi] *n* : fotografía *f*
phrase [ˈfreɪz] *n* : frase *f* — ~ *vt* **phrased; phrasing** : expresar
physical [ˈfɪzɪkəl] *adj* : físico — ~ *n* : reconocimiento *m* médico
physician [fəˈzɪʃən] *n* : médico *m*, -ca *f*
physics [ˈfɪzɪks] *ns & pl* : física *f* — **physicist** [ˈfɪzəsɪst] *n* : físico *m*, -ca *f*
physiology [ˌfɪziˈɑlədʒi] *n* : fisiología *f*
physique [fəˈziːk] *n* : físico *m*
piano [piˈænoː] *n, pl* **-anos** : piano *m* — **pianist** [piˈænɪst, ˈpiːənɪst] *n* : pianista *mf*
pick [ˈpɪk] *vt* **1** CHOOSE : escoger **2** GATHER : recoger **3** REMOVE : quitar (poco a poco) **4** ~ **a fight** : buscar camorra — *vi* **1** ~ **and choose** : ser exigente **2** ~ **on** : meterse con — ~ *n* **1** CHOICE : selección *f* **2** *or* **pickax** [ˈpɪkˌæks] : pico *m* **3 the** ~ **of** : lo mejor de
picket [ˈpɪkət] *n* **1** STAKE : estaca *f* **2** *or* ~ **line** : piquete *m* — ~ *v* : piquetear
pickle [ˈpɪkəl] *n* **1** : pepinillo *m* (encurtido) **2** JAM : lío *m fam*, apuro *m* — ~ *vt* **-led; -ling** : encurtir
pickpocket [ˈpɪkˌpɑkət] *n* : carterista *mf*
pickup [ˈpɪkˌəp] *n* **1** IMPROVEMENT : mejora *f* **2** *or* ~ **truck** : camioneta *f* — **pick up** *vt* **1** LIFT : levantar **2** TIDY : arreglar, ordenar — *vi* IMPROVE : mejorar
picnic [ˈpɪkˌnɪk] *n* : picnic *m* — ~ *vi* **-nicked; -nicking** : ir de picnic
picture [ˈpɪktʃər] *n* **1** PAINTING : cuadro *m* **2** DRAWING : dibujo *m* **3** PHOTO : fotografía *f* **4** IMAGE : imagen *f* **5** MOVIE : película *f* — ~ *vt* **-tured; -turing** **1** DEPICT : representar **2** IMAGINE : imaginarse — **picturesque** [ˌpɪktʃəˈrɛsk] *adj* : pintoresco
pie [ˈpaɪ] *n* : pastel *m* (con fruta o carne), empanada *f* (con carne)
piece [ˈpiːs] *n* **1** : pieza *f* **2** FRAGMENT : trozo *m*, pedazo *m* **3 a** ~ **of advice** : un consejo — ~ *vt* **pieced; piecing** *or* ~ **together** : juntar, componer — **piecemeal** [ˈpiːsˌmiːl] *adv* : poco a poco — ~ *adj* : poco sistemático
pier [ˈpɪr] *n* : muelle *m*
pierce [ˈpɪrs] *vt* **pierced; piercing** : perforar — **piercing** *adj* : penetrante
piety [ˈpaɪəṭi] *n, pl* **-eties** : piedad *f*
pig [ˈpɪg] *n* : cerdo *m*, -da *f*; puerco *m*, -ca *f*
pigeon [ˈpɪdʒən] *n* : paloma *f* — **pigeonhole** [ˈpɪdʒənˌhoːl] *n* : casilla *f*
piggyback [ˈpɪgiˌbæk] *adv & adj* : a cuestas
pigment [ˈpɪgmənt] *n* : pigmento *m*
pigpen [ˈpɪgˌpɛn] *n* : pocilga *f*
pigtail [ˈpɪgˌteɪl] *n* : coleta *f*, trenza *f*
pile[1] [ˈpaɪl] *n* HEAP : montón *m*, pila *f* — ~ *v* **piled; piling** *vt* : amontonar, apilar — *vi* ~ **up** : amontonarse, acumularse
pile[2] *n* NAP : pelo *m* (de telas)
pilfer [ˈpɪlfər] *vt* : robar, hurtar
pilgrim [ˈpɪlgrəm] *n* : peregrino *m*, -na *f* — **pilgrimage** [ˈpɪlgrəmɪdʒ] *n* : peregrinación *f*
pill [ˈpɪl] *n* : pastilla *f*, píldora *f*
pillage [ˈpɪlɪdʒ] *n* : saqueo *m* — ~ *vt* **-laged; -laging** : saquear
pillar [ˈpɪlər] *n* : pilar *m*, columna *f*
pillow [ˈpɪˌloː] *n* : almohada *f* — **pillowcase** [ˈpɪloːˌkeɪs] *n* : funda *f* (de almohada)
pilot [ˈpaɪlət] *n* : piloto *mf* — ~ *vt* : pilotar, pilotear — **pilot light** *n* : piloto *m*
pimp [ˈpɪmp] *n* : proxeneta *m*
pimple [ˈpɪmpəl] *n* : grano *m*
pin [ˈpɪn] *n* **1** : alfiler *m* **2** BROOCH : broche *m* **3** *or* **bowling** ~ : bolo *m* — ~ *vt* **pinned; pinning** **1** FASTEN : prender, sujetar (con alfileres) **2** *or* ~ **down** : inmovilizar
pincers [ˈpɪntsərz] *npl* : tenazas *fpl*
pinch [ˈpɪntʃ] *vt* **1** : pellizcar **2** STEAL : robar — *vi* : apretar — ~ *n* **1** : pellizco *m* **2** BIT : pizca *f* **3 in a** ~ : en caso necesario
pine[1] [ˈpaɪn] *n* : pino *m* (árbol)
pine[2] *vi* **pined; pining** **1** LANGUISH : languidecer **2** ~ **for** : suspirar por
pineapple [ˈpaɪnˌæpəl] *n* : piña *f*, ananás *m*
pink [ˈpɪŋk] *n* : rosa *m*, rosado *m* — ~ *adj* : rosa, rosado
pinnacle [ˈpɪnɪkəl] *n* : pináculo *m*
pinpoint [ˈpɪnˌpɔɪnt] *vt* : localizar, precisar
pint [ˈpaɪnt] *n* : pinta *f*
pioneer [ˌpaɪəˈnɪr] *n* : pionero *m*, -ra *f*
pious [ˈpaɪəs] *adj* : piadoso
pipe [ˈpaɪp] *n* **1** : tubo *m*, caño *m* **2** : pipa *f* (para fumar) — **pipeline** [ˈpaɪpˌlaɪn] *n* **1** : conducto *m*, oleoducto *m* (para petróleo)
piquant [ˈpiːkənt, ˈpɪkwənt] *adj* : picante
pique [ˈpiːk] *n* : resentimiento *m*
pirate [ˈpaɪrət] *n* : pirata *mf*
pistachio [pəˈstæʃiˌoː, -ˈstɑ-] *n, pl* **-chios** : pistacho *m*
pistol [ˈpɪstəl] *n* : pistola *f*
piston [ˈpɪstən] *n* : pistón *m*
pit [ˈpɪt] *n* **1** HOLE : hoyo *m*, fosa *f* **2** MINE : mina *f* **3** : hueso *m* (de una fruta) **4** ~ **of the stomach** : boca *f* del estómago — ~ *vt* **pitted; pitting** **1** : marcar de hoyos **2** : deshuesar (una fruta) **3** ~ **against** : enfrentar a
pitch [ˈpɪtʃ] *vt* **1** : armar (una tienda) **2** THROW : lanzar — *vi* **1** *or* ~ **forward** : caerse **2** LURCH : cabecear (dícese de un barco o un avión) — ~ *n* **1** DEGREE, LEVEL : grado *m*, punto *m* **2** TONE : tono *m* **3** THROW : lanzamiento *m* **4** *or* **sales** ~ : presentación *f* (de un vendedor)
pitcher [ˈpɪtʃər] *n* **1** JUG : jarro *m* **2** : lanzador *m*, -dora *f* (en béisbol, etc.)
pitchfork [ˈpɪtʃˌfɔrk] *n* : horquilla *f*, horca *f*
pitfall [ˈpɪtˌfɔl] *n* : riesgo *m*, dificultad *f*
pith [ˈpɪθ] *n* **1** : médula *f* (de un hueso, etc.) **2** CORE : meollo *m* — **pithy** [ˈpɪθi] *adj* **pithier; -est** : conciso y sustancioso
pity [ˈpɪṭi] *n, pl* **pities** **1** COMPASSION : compasión *f* **2 what a** ~! : ¡qué lástima! — ~ *vt* **pitied; pitying** : compadecerse de — **pitiful** [ˈpɪṭɪfəl] *adj* : lastimoso — **pitiless** [ˈpɪṭɪləs] *adj* : despiadado
pivot [ˈpɪvət] *n* : pivote *m* — ~ *vi* **1** : girar sobre un eje **2** ~ **on** : depender de
pizza [ˈpiːtsə] *n* : pizza *f*
placard [ˈplækərd, -ˌkɑrd] *n* POSTER : cartel *m*, póster *m*
placate [ˈpleɪˌkeɪt, ˈplæ-] *vt* **-cated; -cating** : apaciguar
place [ˈpleɪs] *n* **1** : sitio *m*, lugar *m* **2** SEAT : asiento *m* **3** POSITION : puesto *m* **4** ROLE : papel *m* **5 take** ~ : tener lugar **6 take the** ~ **of** : sustituir a — ~ *vt* **placed; placing** **1** PUT, SET : poner, colocar **2** IDENTIFY : identificar, recordar **3** ~ **an order** : hacer un pedido — **placement** [ˈpleɪsmənt] *n* : colocación *f*
placid [ˈplæsəd] *adj* : plácido, tranquilo
plagiarism [ˈpleɪdʒəˌrɪzəm] *n* : plagio *m* — **plagiarize** [ˈpleɪdʒəˌraɪz] *vt* **-rized; -rizing** : plagiar
plague [ˈpleɪg] *n* **1** : plaga *f* (de insectos, etc.) **2** : peste *f* (en medicina)
plaid [ˈplæd] *n* : tela *f* escocesa — ~ *adj* : escocés
plain [ˈpleɪn] *adj* **1** SIMPLE : sencillo **2** CLEAR : claro, evidente **3** CANDID : franco **4** HOMELY : poco atractivo **5 in** ~ **sight** : a la vista (de todos) — ~ *n* : llanura *f*, planicie *f* — **plainly** [ˈpleɪnli] *adv* **1** CLEARLY : claramente **2** FRANKLY : francamente **3** SIMPLY : sencillamente
plaintiff [ˈpleɪntɪf] *n* : demandante *mf*
plan [ˈplæn] *n* **1** : plan *m*, proyecto *m* **2** DIAGRAM : plano *m* — ~ *v* **planned; planning** *vt* **1** : planear, proyectar **2** INTEND : tener planeado — *vi* : hacer planes
plane[1] [ˈpleɪn] *n* **1** LEVEL : plano *m*, nivel *m* **2** AIRPLANE : avión *m*
plane[2] *n or* **carpenter's** ~ : cepillo *m*
planet [ˈplænət] *n* : planeta *f*
plank [ˈplæŋk] *n* : tabla *f*
planning [ˈplænɪŋ] *n* : planificación *f*
plant [ˈplænt] *vt* : plantar (flores, árboles), sembrar (semillas) — ~ *n* **1** : planta *f* **2** FACTORY : fábrica *f*
plantain [ˈplæntən] *n* : plátano *m* (grande)
plantation [plænˈteɪʃən] *n* : plantación *f*
plaque [ˈplæk] *n* : placa *f*
plaster [ˈplæstər] *n* : yeso *m* — ~ *vt* **1** : enyesar **2** COVER : cubrir — **plaster cast** *n* : escayola *f*
plastic [ˈplæstɪk] *adj* **1** : de plástico **2** FLEXIBLE : plástico, flexible **3** ~ **surgery** : cirugía *f* plástica — ~ *n* : plástico *m*
plate [ˈpleɪt] *n* **1** SHEET : placa *f* **2** DISH : plato *m* **3** ILLUSTRATION : lámina *f* — ~ *vt* **plated; plating** : chapar (en metal)
plateau [plæˈtoː] *n, pl* **-teaus** *or* **-teaux** [-ˈtoːz] : meseta *f*
platform [ˈplætˌfɔrm] *n* **1** : plataforma *f* **2** : andén *m* (de una estación de ferrocarril) **3** *or* **political** ~ : programa *m* electoral
platinum [ˈplætənəm] *n* : platino *m*
platitude [ˈplæṭəˌtuːd, -ˌtjuːd] *n* : lugar *m* común
platoon [pləˈtuːn] *n* : sección *f* (en el ejército)
platter [ˈplæṭər] *n* : fuente *f*
plausible [ˈplɔzəbəl] *adj* : creíble, verosímil
play [ˈpleɪ] *n* **1** : juego *m* **2** DRAMA : obra *f* de teatro — ~ *vi* **1** : jugar **2** ~ **in a band** : tocar en un grupo — *vt* **1** : jugar (deportes, etc.), jugar a (juegos) **2** : tocar (música o un instrumento) **3** ~ **the role of** : representar el papel de — **player** [ˈpleɪər] *n* **1** : jugador *m*, -dora *f* **2** ACTOR : actor *m*, actriz *f* **3** MUSICIAN : músico *m*, -ca *f* — **playful** [ˈpleɪfəl] *adj* : juguetón — **playground** [ˈpleɪˌgraʊnd] *n* : patio *m* de recreo — **playing card** *n* : naipe *m*, carta *f* — **playmate** [ˈpleɪˌmeɪt] *n* : compañero *m*, -ra *f* de juego — **play-off** [ˈpleɪˌɔf] *n* : desempate *m* — **playpen** [ˈpleɪˌpɛn] *n* : corral *m* (para niños) — **plaything** [ˈpleɪˌθɪŋ] *n* : juguete *m* — **playwright** [ˈpleɪˌraɪt] *n* : dramaturgo *m*, -ga *f*
plea [ˈpliː] *n* **1** : acto *m* de declararse (en derecho) **2** APPEAL : ruego *m*, súplica *f* — **plead** [ˈpliːd] *v* **pleaded** *or* **pled** [ˈplɛd]; **pleading** *vi* **1** ~ **for** : suplicar **2** ~ **guilty** : declararse culpable **3** ~ **not guilty** : negar la acusación — *vt* **1** : alegar, pretextar **2** ~ **a case** : defender un caso
pleasant [ˈplɛzənt] *adj* : agradable, grato — **please** [ˈpliːz] *v* **pleased; pleasing** *vt* **1** GRATIFY : complacer **2** SATISFY : satisfacer — *vi* **1** : agradar **2 do as you** ~ : haz lo que quieras — ~ *adv* : por favor — **pleased** [ˈpliːzd] *adj* : contento — **pleasing** [ˈpliːzɪŋ] *adj* : agradable — **pleasure** [ˈplɛʒər] *n* : placer *m*, gusto *m*
pleat [ˈpliːt] *vt* : plisar — ~ *n* : pliegue *m*
pledge [ˈplɛdʒ] *n* **1** SECURITY : prenda *f* **2** PROMISE : promesa *f* — ~ *vt* **pledged; pledging** **1** PAWN : empeñar **2** PROMISE : prometer
plenty [ˈplɛnti] *n* **1** : abundancia *f* **2** ~ **of time** : tiempo *m* de sobra — **plentiful** [ˈplɛntɪfəl] *adj* : abundante
pliable [ˈplaɪəbəl] *adj* : flexible
pliers [ˈplaɪərz] *npl* : alicates *mpl*
plight [ˈplaɪt] *n* : situación *f* difícil
plod [ˈplɑd] *vi* **plodded; plodding** **1** : caminar con paso pesado **2** DRUDGE : trabajar laboriosamente
plot [ˈplɑt] *n* **1** LOT : parcela *f* **2** : argumento *m* (de una novela, etc.) **3** CONSPIRACY : complot *m*, intriga *f* — ~ *v* **plotted; plotting** *vt* : tramar (un plan), trazar (una gráfica, etc.) — *vi* CONSPIRE : conspirar
plow *or* **plough** [ˈplaʊ] *n* **1** : arado *m* **2** → **snowplow** — ~ *v* : arar
ploy [ˈplɔɪ] *n* : estratagema *f*
pluck [ˈplʌk] *vt* **1** : arrancar **2** : desplumar (un pollo, etc.) **3** : recoger (flores) **4** ~ **one's eyebrows** : depilarse las cejas
plug [ˈplʌg] *n* **1** STOPPER : tapón *m* **2** : enchufe *m* (eléctrico) — ~ *vt* **plugged; plugging** **1** BLOCK : tapar **2** ADVERTISE : dar publicidad a **3** ~ **in** : enchufar
plum [ˈplʌm] *n* : ciruela *f*
plumb [ˈplʌm] *adj* : a plomo, vertical — **plumber** [ˈplʌmər] *n* : fontanero *m*, -ra *f*; plomero *m*, -ra *f Lat* — **plumbing** [ˈplʌmɪŋ] *n* **1** : fontanería *f*, plomería *f Lat* **2** PIPES : cañerías *fpl*
plume [ˈpluːm] *n* : pluma *f*
plummet [ˈplʌmət] *vi* : caer en picado
plump [ˈplʌmp] *adj* : rechoncho *fam*
plunder [ˈplʌndər] *vi* : saquear, robar — ~ *n* : botín *m*
plunge [ˈplʌndʒ] *v* **plunged; plunging** *vt* **1** IMMERSE : sumergir **2** THRUST : hundir — *vi* **1** : zambullirse (en el agua) **2** DESCEND : descender en picada — ~ *n* **1** DIVE : zambullida *f* **2** DROP : descenso *m* abrupto
plural [ˈplʊrəl] *adj* : plural — ~ *n* : plural *m*
plus [ˈplʌs] *adj* : positivo — ~ *n* **1** *or* ~ **sign** : signo *m* (de) más **2** ADVANTAGE : ventaja *f* — ~ *prep* : más — ~ *conj* : y, además
plush [ˈplʌʃ] *n* : felpa *f* — ~ *adj* **1** : de felpa **2** LUXURIOUS : lujoso
plutonium [pluːˈtoːniəm] *n* : plutonio *m*
ply [ˈplaɪ] *vt* **plied; plying** **1** : ejercer (un oficio) **2** ~ **with questions** : acosar con preguntas
plywood [ˈplaɪˌwʊd] *n* : contrachapado *m*
pneumatic [nʊˈmæṭɪk, njʊ-] *adj* : neumático
pneumonia [nʊˈmoːnjə, njʊ-] *n* : pulmonía *f*
poach[1] [ˈpoːtʃ] *vt* : cocer a fuego lento
poach[2] *vt or* ~ **game** : cazar ilegalmente — **poacher** [ˈpoːtʃər] *n* : cazador *m* furtivo, cazadora *f* furtiva
pocket [ˈpɑkət] *n* : bolsillo *m* — ~ *vt* : meterse en el bolsillo — **pocketbook** [ˈpɑkətˌbʊk] *n* : cartera *f*, bolsa *f Lat* — **pocketknife** [ˈpɑkətˌnaɪf] *n, pl* **-knives** : navaja *f*
pod [ˈpɑd] *n* : vaina *f*
poem [ˈpoːəm] *n* : poema *m* — **poet** [ˈpoːət] *n* : poeta *mf* — **poetic** [poˈɛṭɪk] *or* **poetical** [-ṭɪkəl] *adj* : poético — **poetry** [ˈpoːətri] *n* : poesía *f*
poignant [ˈpɔɪnjənt] *adj* : conmovedor
point [ˈpɔɪnt] *n* **1** : punto *m* **2** PURPOSE : sentido *m* **3** TIP : punta *f* **4** FEATURE : cualidad *f* **5 be beside the** ~ : no venir al caso **6 there's no** ~ **...** : no sirve de nada... — ~ *vt* **1** AIM : apuntar **2** *or* ~ **out** : señalar, indicar — *vi* **1** ~ **at** : señalar (con el dedo) — **point–blank** [ˈpɔɪntˈblæŋk] *adv* : a quemarropa — **pointer** [ˈpɔɪntər] *n* **1** NEEDLE : aguja *f* **2** : perro *m* de muestra **3** TIP : consejo *m* — **pointless** [ˈpɔɪntləs] *adj* : inútil — **point of view** *n* : perspectiva *f*, punto *m* de vista
poise [ˈpɔɪz] *n* **1** : elegancia *f* **2** COMPOSURE : aplomo *m*
poison [ˈpɔɪzən] *n* : veneno *m* — ~ *vt* : envenenar — **poisonous** [ˈpɔɪzənəs] *adj* : venenoso (dícese de una culebra, etc.), tóxico (dícese de una sustancia)
poke [ˈpoːk] *vt* **poked; poking** **1** JAB : golpear (con la punta de algo), dar **2** THRUST : introducir, asomar — ~ *n* : golpe *m* abrupto (con la punta de algo)
poker[1] [ˈpoːkər] *n* : atizador *m* (para el fuego)
poker[2] *n* : póquer *m* (juego de naipes)
polar [ˈpoːlər] *adj* : polar — **polar bear** *n* : oso *m* blanco — **polarize** [ˈpoːləˌraɪz] *vt* **-ized; -izing** : polarizar
pole[1] [ˈpoːl] *n* : palo *m*, poste *m*
pole[2] *n* : polo *m* (en geografía)
police [pəˈliːs] *vt* **-liced; -licing** : mantener el orden en — ~ *ns & pl* **the** ~ : la policía — **policeman** [pəˈliːsmən] *n, pl* **-men** [-mən, -ˌmɛn] : policía *m* — **police officer** *n* : policía *mf*, agente *mf* de policía — **policewoman** [pəˈliːsˌwʊmən] *n, pl* **-women** [-ˌwɪmən] : (mujer *f*) policía *f*
policy [ˈpɑləsi] *n, pl* **-cies** **1** : política *f* **2** *or* **insurance** ~ : póliza *f* de seguros
polio [ˈpoːliˌoː] *or* **poliomyelitis** [ˌpoːliˌoːˌmaɪəˈlaɪṭəs] *n* : polio *f*, poliomielitis *f*
polish [ˈpɑlɪʃ] *vt* **1** : pulir **2** : limpiar (zapatos), encerar (un suelo) — ~ *n* **1** LUSTER : brillo *m*, lustre *m* **2** : betún *m* (para zapatos), cera *f* (para suelos y muebles), esmalte *m* (para las uñas)
Polish [ˈpoːlɪʃ] *adj* : polaco — ~ *n* : polaco *m* (idioma)
polite [pəˈlaɪt] *adj* **-liter; -est** : cortés — **politeness** [pəˈlaɪtnəs] *n* : cortesía *f*
political [pəˈlɪṭɪkəl] *adj* : político — **politician** [ˌpɑləˈtɪʃən] *n* : político *m*, -ca *f* — **politics** [ˈpɑləˌtɪks] *ns & pl* : política *f*
polka [ˈpoːlkə, ˈpoːkə] *n* : polka *f* — **polka dot** [ˈpoːkəˌdɑt] *n* : lunar *m*
poll [ˈpoːl] *n* **1** : encuesta *f*, sondeo *m* **2 the** ~**s** : las urnas — ~ *vt* **1** : obtener (votos) **2** CANVASS : encuestar, sondear
pollen [ˈpɑlən] *n* : polen *m*
pollute [pəˈluːt] *vt* **-luted; -luting** : contaminar — **pollution** [pəˈluːʃən] *n* : contaminación *f*
polyester [ˈpɑliˌɛstər, ˌpɑliˈ-] *n* : poliéster *m*
polygon [ˈpɑliˌgɑn] *n* : polígono *m*

pomegranate ['pɑmə,grænət, 'pɑm,grænət] *n* : granada *f*

pomp ['pɑmp] *n* : pompa *f* — **pompous** ['pɑmpəs] *adj* : pomposo

pond ['pɑnd] *n* : charca *f* (natural), estanque *m* (artificial)

ponder ['pɑndər] *vt* : considerar — *vi* **~ over** : reflexionar sobre

pony ['po:ni] *n, pl* **-nies** : poni *m* — **ponytail** ['po:ni,teɪl] *n* : cola *f* de caballo

poodle ['pu:dəl] *n* : caniche *m*

pool ['pu:l] *n* **1** PUDDLE : charco *m* **2** : fondo *m* común (de recursos) **3** BILLIARDS : billar *m* **4** *or* **swimming ~** : piscina *f* — **~** *vt* : hacer un fondo común de

poor ['pʊr, 'por] *adj* **1** : pobre **2** INFERIOR : malo **3 the ~** : los pobres — **poorly** ['pʊrli, 'por-] *adv* : mal

pop[1] ['pɑp] *v* **popped; popping** *vt* **1** : hacer reventar **2 ~ sth into** : meter algo en — *vi* **1** BURST : reventarse, estallar **2 ~ in** : entrar (un momento) **3 ~ out** : saltar (dícese de los ojos) **4 ~ up** APPEAR : aparecer — **~** *n* **1** : ruido *m* seco **2** → **soda pop**

pop[2] *n or* **~ music** : música *f* popular

popcorn ['pɑp,korn] *n* : palomitas *fpl*

pope ['po:p] *n* : papa *m*

poplar ['pɑplər] *n* : álamo *m*

poppy ['pɑpi] *n, pl* **-pies** : amapola *f*

popular ['pɑpjələr] *adj* : popular — **popularity** [,pɑpjə'lærət̬i] *n* : popularidad *f* — **popularize** ['pɑpjələ,raɪz] *vt* **-ized; -izing** : popularizar

populate ['pɑpjə,leɪt] *vt* **-lated; -lating** : poblar — **population** [,pɑpjə'leɪʃən] *n* : población *f*

porcelain ['porsələn] *n* : porcelana *f*

porch ['portʃ] *n* : porche *m*

porcupine ['pɔrkjə,paɪn] *n* : puerco *m* espín

pore[1] ['por] *vi* **pored; poring ~ over** : estudiar esmeradamente

pore[2] *n* : poro *m*

pork ['pork] *n* : carne *f* de cerdo

pornography [pɔr'nɑgrəfi] *n* : pornografía *f* — **pornographic** [,pɔrnə'græfɪk] *adj* : pornográfico

porous ['porəs] *adj* : poroso

porpoise ['pɔrpəs] *n* : marsopa *f*

porridge ['pɔrɪdʒ] *n* : avena *f* (cocida), gachas *fpl* (de avena)

port[1] ['port] *n* HARBOR : puerto *m*

port[2] *n or* **~ side** : babor *m*

port[3] *n* : oporto *m* (vino)

portable ['port̬əbəl] *adj* : portátil

portent ['pɔr,tɛnt] *n* : presagio *m*

porter ['port̬ər] *n* : maletero *m*, mozo *m* (de estación)

portfolio [port'fo:li,o] *n, pl* **-lios** : cartera *f*

porthole ['port,ho:l] *n* : portilla *f*

portion ['porʃən] *n* : porción *f*

portrait ['portrət, -,treɪt] *n* : retrato *m*

portray [por'treɪ] *vt* **1** : representar, retratar **2** : interpretar (un personaje)

Portuguese [,portʃə'gi:z, -'gi:s] *adj* : portugués — **~** *n* : portugués *m* (idioma)

pose ['po:z] *v* **posed; posing** *vt* : plantear (una pregunta, etc.), representar (una amenaza) — *vi* **1** : posar **2 ~ as** : hacerse pasar por — **~** *n* : pose *f*

posh ['pɑʃ] *adj* : elegante, de lujo

position [pə'zɪʃən] *n* **1** : posición *f* **2** JOB : puesto *m* — **~** *vt* : colocar, situar

positive ['pɑzət̬ɪv] *adj* **1** : positivo **2** CERTAIN : seguro

possess [pə'zɛs] *vt* : poseer — **possession** [pə'zɛʃən] *n* **1** : posesión *f* **2 ~s** *npl* BELONGINGS : bienes *mpl* — **possessive** [pə'zɛsɪv] *adj* : posesivo

possible ['pɑsəbəl] *adj* : posible — **possibility** [,pɑsə'bɪlət̬i] *n, pl* **-ties** : posibilidad *f* — **possibly** ['pɑsəbli] *adv* : posiblemente

post[1] ['po:st] *n* POLE : poste *m*, palo *m*

post[2] *n* POSITION : puesto *m*

post[3] *n* MAIL : cartas *fpl* — **~** *vt* **1** : echar al correo **2 keep ~ed** : tener al corriente — **postage** ['po:stɪdʒ] *n* : franqueo *m* — **postal** ['po:stəl] *adj* : postal — **postcard** ['po:st,kɑrd] *n* : tarjeta *f* postal

poster ['po:stər] *n* : cartel *m*

posterity [pɑ'stɛrət̬i] *n* : posteridad *f*

posthumous ['pɑstʃəməs] *adj* : póstumo

postman ['po:stmən, -,mæn] → **mailman** — **post office** *n* : oficina *f* de correos

postpone [,po:st'po:n] *vt* **-poned; -poning** : aplazar — **postponement** [,po:st'po:nmənt] *n* : aplazamiento *m*

postscript ['po:st,skrɪpt] *n* : posdata *f*

posture ['pɑstʃər] *n* : postura *f*

postwar [,po:st'wɔr] *adj* : de (la) posguerra

pot ['pɑt] *n* **1** : olla *f* (de cocina) **2** FLOWERPOT : maceta *f* **3 ~s and pans** : cacharros *mpl*

potassium [pə'tæsiəm] *n* : potasio *m*

potato [pə'teɪt̬o] *n, pl* **-toes** : patata *f*, papa *f Lat*

potent ['po:tənt] *adj* **1** POWERFUL : poderoso **2** EFFECTIVE : eficaz

potential [pə'tɛntʃəl] *adj* : potencial — **~** *n* : potencial *m*

pothole ['pɑt,ho:l] *n* : bache *m*

potion ['po:ʃən] *n* : poción *f*

pottery ['pɑt̬əri] *n, pl* **-teries** : cerámica *f*

pouch ['paʊtʃ] *n* **1** BAG : bolsa *f* pequeña **2** : bolsa *f* (de un animal)

poultry ['po:ltri] *n* : aves *fpl* de corral

pounce ['paʊnts] *vi* **pounced; pouncing** : abalanzarse

pound[1] ['paʊnd] *n* : libra *f* (unidad de dinero o de peso)

pound[2] *n or* **dog ~** : perrera *f*

pound[3] *vt* **1** CRUSH : machacar **2** HIT : golpear — *vi* : palpitar (dícese del corazón)

pour ['por] *vt* : verter — *vi* **1** FLOW : fluir, salir **2 it's ~ing** : está lloviendo a cántaros

pout ['paʊt] *vi* : hacer pucheros — **~** *n* : puchero *m*

poverty ['pɑvərt̬i] *n* : pobreza *f*

powder ['paʊdər] *vt* **1** : empolvar **2** CRUSH : pulverizar — **~** *n* **1** : polvo *m* **2** *or* **face ~** : polvos *mpl* — **powdery** ['paʊdəri] *adj* : polvoriento

power ['paʊər] *n* **1** CONTROL : poder *m* **2** ABILITY : capacidad *f* **3** STRENGTH : fuerza *f* **4** : potencia *f* (política) **5** ENERGY : energía *f* **6** ELECTRICITY : electricidad *f* — **~** *vt* : impulsar — **powerful** ['paʊərfəl] *adj* : poderoso — **powerless** ['paʊərləs] *adj* : impotente

practical ['præktɪkəl] *adj* : práctico — **practically** ['præktɪkli] *adv* : casi, prácticamente

practice *or* **practise** ['præktəs] *v* **-ticed** *or* **-tised; -ticing** *or* **-tising** *vt* **1** : practicar **2** : ejercer (una profesión) — *vi* : practicar — **practice** *n* **1** : práctica *f* **2** CUSTOM : costumbre *f* **3** : ejercicio *m* (de una profesión) **4 be out of ~** : no estar en forma — **practitioner** [præk'tɪʃənər] *n* **1** : profesional *mf* **2 general ~** : médico *m*, -ca *f* de medicina general

pragmatic [præg'mætɪk] *adj* : pragmático

prairie ['prɛri] *n* : pradera *f*

praise ['preɪz] *vt* **praised; praising** : elogiar, alabar — **~** *n* : elogio *m*, alabanza *f* — **praiseworthy** ['preɪz,wərði] *adj* : loable

prance ['prænts] *vi* **pranced; prancing** : hacer cabriolas

prank ['præŋk] *n* : travesura *f*

prawn ['prɔn] *n* : gamba *f*

pray ['preɪ] *vi* **1** : rezar **2 ~ for** : rogar — **prayer** ['prɛr] *n* : oración *f*

preach ['pri:tʃ] *v* : predicar — **preacher** ['pri:tʃər] *n* MINISTER : pastor *m*, -tora *f*

precarious [pri'kæriəs] *adj* : precario

precaution [pri'kɔʃən] *n* : precaución *f*

precede [pri'si:d] *vt* **-ceded; -ceding** : preceder a — **precedence** ['prɛsədənts, pri'si:dənts] *n* : precedencia *f* — **precedent** ['prɛsədənt] *n* : precedente *m*

precinct ['pri:,sɪŋkt] *n* **1** DISTRICT : distrito *m* **2 ~s** *npl* : recinto *m*

precious ['prɛʃəs] *adj* : precioso

precipice ['prɛsəpəs] *n* : precipicio *m*

precipitate [pri'sɪpə,teɪt] *vt* **-tated; -tating** : precipitar — **precipitation** [pri,sɪpə'teɪʃən] *n* **1** HASTE : precipitación *f* **2** : precipitaciones *fpl* (en meteorología)

precise [pri'saɪs] *adj* : preciso — **precisely** *adv* : precisamente — **precision** [pri'sɪʒən] *n* : precisión *f*

preclude [pri'klu:d] *vt* **-cluded; -cluding 1** PREVENT : impedir **2** EXCLUDE : excluir

precocious [pri'ko:ʃəs] *adj* : precoz

preconceived [,pri:kən'si:v] *adj* : preconcebido

predator ['prɛdət̬ər] *n* : depredador *m*

predecessor ['prɛdə,sɛsər, 'pri:-] *n* : antecesor *m*, -sora *f*; predecesor *m*, -sora *f*

predicament [pri'dɪkəmənt] *n* : apuro *m*

predict [pri'dɪkt] *vt* : pronosticar, predecir — **predictable** [pri'dɪktəbəl] *adj* : previsible — **prediction** [pri'dɪkʃən] *n* : pronóstico *m*, predicción *f*

predispose [,pri:dɪ'spo:z] *vt* **-posed; -posing** : predisponer

predominant [pri'dɑmənənt] *adj* : predominante

preeminent [pri'ɛmənənt] *adj* : preeminente

preempt [pri'ɛmpt] *vt* : adelantarse a (un ataque, etc.)

preen ['pri:n] *vt* **1** : arreglarse (las plumas) **2 ~ oneself** : acicalarse

prefabricated [,pri:'fæbrə,keɪt̬əd] *adj* : prefabricado

preface ['prɛfəs] *n* : prefacio *m*, prólogo *m*

prefer [pri'fər] *vt* **-ferred; -ferring** : preferir — **preferable** ['prɛfərəbəl] *adj* : preferible — **preference** ['prɛfrənts, 'prɛfər-] *n* : preferencia *f* — **preferential** [,prɛfə'rɛntʃəl] *adj* : preferente

prefix ['pri:,fɪks] *n* : prefijo *m*

pregnancy ['prɛgnəntsi] *n, pl* **-cies** : embarazo *m* — **pregnant** ['prɛgnənt] *adj* : embarazada

prehistoric [,pri:hɪs'tɔrɪk] *or* **prehistorical** [-ɪkəl] *adj* : prehistórico

prejudice ['prɛdʒədəs] *n* **1** BIAS : prejuicio *m* **2** HARM : perjuicio *m* — **~** *vt* **-diced; -dicing 1** BIAS : predisponer **2** HARM : perjudicar — **prejudiced** ['prɛdʒədəst] *adj* : parcial

preliminary [pri'lɪmə,nɛri] *adj* : preliminar

prelude ['prɛl,ju:d, 'prɛl,ju:d; 'preɪ,lu:d, 'pri:-] *n* : preludio *m*

premarital [,pri:'mærət̬əl] *adj* : prematrimonial

premature [,pri:mə'tʊr, -'tjʊr, -'tʃʊr] *adj* : prematuro

premeditated [pri'mɛdə,teɪt̬əd] *adj* : premeditado

premier [pri'mɪr, -'mjɪr; 'pri:miər] *adj* : principal — **~** *n* PRIME MINISTER : primer ministro *m*, primera ministra *f*

premiere [pri'mjɛr, -'mɪr] *n* : estreno *m*

premise ['prɛmɪs] *n* **1** : premisa *f* (de un argumento) **2 ~s** *npl* : recinto *m*, local *m*

premium ['pri:miəm] *n* **1** : premio *m* **2** *or* **insurance ~** : prima *f* (de seguro)

preoccupied [pri'ɑkjə,paɪd] *adj* : preocupado

prepare [pri'pær] *v* **-pared; -paring** *vt* : preparar — *vi* : prepararse — **preparation** [,prɛpə'reɪʃən] *n* **1** : preparación *f* **2 ~s** *npl* ARRANGEMENTS : preparativos *mpl* — **preparatory** [pri'pærə,tori] *adj* : preparatorio

prepay [,pri:'peɪ] *vt* **-paid; -paying** : pagar por adelantado

preposition [,prɛpə'zɪʃən] *n* : preposición *f*

preposterous [pri'pɑstərəs] *adj* : absurdo, ridículo

prerequisite [pri'rɛkwəzət] *n* : requisito *m* previo

prerogative [pri'rɑgət̬ɪv] *n* : prerrogativa *f*

prescribe [pri'skraɪb] *vt* **-scribed; -scribing 1** : prescribir **2** : recetar (en medicina) — **prescription** [pri'skrɪpʃən] *n* : receta *f*

presence ['prɛzənts] *n* : presencia *f*

present[1] ['prɛzənt] *adj* **1** CURRENT : actual **2 be ~ at** : estar presente en — **~** *n* **1** : presente *m* **2 at ~** : actualmente

present[2] ['prɛzənt] *n* GIFT : regalo *m* — **~** [pri'zɛnt] *vt* **1** INTRODUCE : presentar **2** GIVE : entregar — **presentation** [,pri:,zɛn'teɪʃən, ,prɛzən-] *n* **1** : presentación *f* **2** *or* **~ ceremony** : ceremonia *f* de entrega

presently ['prɛzəntli] *adv* **1** SOON : dentro de poco **2** NOW : actualmente

preserve [pri'zərv] *vt* **-served; -serving 1** : conservar **2** MAINTAIN : mantener — **~** *n* **1** JAM : confitura *f* **2** *or* **game ~** : coto *m* de caza — **preservation** [,prɛzər'veɪʃən] *n* : preservación *f*, conservación *f* — **preservative** [pri'zərvət̬ɪv] *n* : conservante *m*

president ['prɛzədənt] *n* : presidente *m*, -ta *f* — **presidency** ['prɛzədəntsi] *n, pl* **-cies** : presidencia *f* — **presidential** [,prɛzə'dɛntʃəl] *adj* : presidencial

press ['prɛs] *n* : prensa *f* — **~** *vt* **1** : apretar **2** IRON : planchar — *vi* **1** : apretar **2** URGE : presionar — **pressing** ['prɛsɪŋ] *adj* : urgente — **pressure** ['prɛʃər] *n* : presión *f* — **~** *vt* **-sured; -suring** : presionar, apremiar

prestige [prɛ'sti:ʒ, -'sti:dʒ] *n* : prestigio *m* — **prestigious** [prɛ'stɪdʒəs] *adj* : prestigioso

presume [pri'zu:m] *vt* **-sumed; -suming** : presumir — **presumably** [pri'zu:məbli] *adv* : es de suponer, supuestamente — **presumption** [pri'zʌmpʃən] *n* : presunción *f* — **presumptuous** [pri'zʌmptʃʊəs] *adj* : presuntuoso

pretend [pri'tɛnd] *vt* **1** CLAIM : pretender **2** FEIGN : fingir — *vi* : fingir — **pretense** *or* **pretence** ['pri:,tɛnts, pri'tɛnts] *n* **1** CLAIM : pretensión *f* **2 under false ~s** : con pretextos falsos — **pretentious** [pri'tɛntʃəs] *adj* : pretencioso

pretext ['pri:,tɛkst] *n* : pretexto *m*

pretty ['prɪt̬i] *adj* **-tier; -est** : lindo, bonito — **~** *adv* FAIRLY : bastante

pretzel ['prɛtsəl] *n* : galleta *f* salada

prevail [pri'veɪl] *vi* **1** TRIUMPH : prevalecer **2** PREDOMINATE : predominar **3 ~ upon** : persuadir — **prevalent** ['prɛvələnt] *adj* : extendido

prevent [pri'vɛnt] *vt* : impedir — **prevention** [pri'vɛntʃən] *n* : prevención *f* — **preventive** [pri'vɛntɪv] *adj* : preventivo

preview ['pri:,vju] *n* : preestreno *m*

previous ['pri:viəs] *adj* : previo, anterior — **previously** ['pri:viəsli] *adv* : anteriormente

prey ['preɪ] *n, pl* **preys** : presa *f* — **prey on** *vt* **1** : alimentarse de **2 ~ on one's mind** : atormentar a algn

price ['praɪs] *n* : precio *m* — **~** *vt* **priced; pricing** : poner un precio a — **priceless** ['praɪsləs] *adj* : inestimable

prick ['prɪk] *n* : pinchazo *m* — **~** *vt* **1** : pinchar **2 ~ up one's ears** : levantar las orejas — **prickly** ['prɪkəli] *adj* : espinoso

pride ['praɪd] *n* : orgullo *m* — **~** *vt* **prided; priding ~ oneself on** : enorgullecerse de

priest ['pri:st] *n* : sacerdote *m* — **priesthood** ['pri:st,hʊd] *n* : sacerdocio *m*

prim ['prɪm] *adj* **primmer; primmest** : remilgado

primary ['praɪ,mɛri, 'praɪməri] *adj* **1** FIRST : primario **2** PRINCIPAL : principal — **primarily** [praɪ'mɛrəli] *adv* : principalmente

prime[1] ['praɪm] *vt* **primed; priming 1** : cebar (un arma de fuego, etc.) **2** PREPARE : preparar

prime[2] *n* **the ~ of one's life** : la flor de la vida — **~** *adj* **1** MAIN : principal, primero **2** EXCELLENT : excelente — **prime minister** *n* : primer ministro *m*, primera ministra *f*

primer[1] ['praɪmər] *n* : base *f* (de pintura)

primer[2] ['prɪmər] *n* READER : cartilla *f*

primitive ['prɪmət̬ɪv] *adj* : primitivo

primrose ['prɪm,ro:z] *n* : primavera *f*

prince ['prɪnts] *n* : príncipe *m* — **princess** ['prɪntsəs, 'prɪn,sɛs] *n* : princesa *f*

principal ['prɪntsəpəl] *adj* : principal — **~** *n* : director *m*, -tora *f* (de un colegio)

principle ['prɪntsəpəl] *n* : principio *m*

print ['prɪnt] *n* **1** MARK : huella *f* **2** LETTERING : letra *f* **3** ENGRAVING : grabado *m* **4** : estampado *m* (de tela) **5** : copia *f* (en fotografía) **6 out of ~** : agotado — **~** *vt* : imprimir (libros, etc.) — *vi* : escribir con letra de molde — **printer** ['prɪntər] *n* **1** : impresor *m*, -sora *f* (persona) **2** : impresora *f* (máquina) — **printing** ['prɪntɪŋ] *n* **1** : impresión *f* **2** : imprenta *f* (profesión) **3** LETTERING : letras *fpl* de molde

prior ['praɪər] *adj* **1** : previo **2 ~ to** : antes de — **priority** [praɪ'ɔrət̬i] *n, pl* **-ties** : prioridad *f*

prison ['prɪzən] *n* : prisión *f*, cárcel *f* — **prisoner** ['prɪzənər] *n* **1** : preso *m*, -sa *f* **2 ~ of war** : prisionero *m*, -ra *f* de guerra

privacy ['praɪvəsi] *n, pl* **-cies** : intimidad *f* — **private** ['praɪvət] *adj* **1** : privado **2** SECRET : secreto — **~** *n* : soldado *m* raso — **privately** ['praɪvətli] *adv* : en privado

privilege ['prɪvlɪdʒ, 'prɪvə-] *n* : privilegio *m* — **privileged** ['prɪvlɪdʒd, 'prɪvə-] *adj* : privilegiado

prize ['praɪz] *n* : premio *m* — **~** *adj* : premiado — **~** *vt* **prized; prizing** : valorar, apreciar — **prizefighter** ['praɪz,faɪt̬ər] *n* : boxeador *m*, -dora *f* profesional — **prizewinning** ['praɪz,wɪnɪŋ] *adj* : premiado

pro ['pro:] *n* **1** → **professional 2 the ~s and cons** : los pros y los contras

probability [,prɑbə'bɪlət̬i] *n, pl* **-ties** : probabilidad *f* — **probable** ['prɑbəbəl] *adj* : probable — **probably** [-bli] *adv* : probablemente

probation [pro'beɪʃən] *n* **1** : período *m* de prueba (de un empleado, etc.) **2** : libertad *f* condicional (de un preso)

probe ['pro:b] *n* **1** : sonda *f* (en medicina, etc.) **2** INVESTIGATION : investigación *f* — **~** *vt* **probed; probing 1** : sondar **2** INVESTIGATE : investigar

problem ['prɑbləm] *n* : problema *m*

procedure [prə'si:dʒər] *n* : procedimiento *m*

proceed [pro'si:d] *vi* **1** ACT : proceder **2** CONTINUE : continuar **3** ADVANCE : avanzar — **proceedings** [pro'si:dɪŋz] *npl* **1** EVENTS : actos *mpl* **2** : proceso *m* (en derecho) — **proceeds** ['pro:,si:dz] *npl* : ganancias *fpl*

process ['prɑ,sɛs, 'pro:-] *n, pl* **-cesses** ['prɑ,sɛsəz, 'pro:-, -səsəz, -sə,si:z] **1** : proceso *m* **2 in the ~ of** : en vías de — **~** *vt* : procesar — **procession** [prə'sɛʃən] *n* : desfile *m*

proclaim [pro'kleɪm] *vt* : proclamar — **proclamation** [,prɑklə'meɪʃən] *n* : proclamación *f*

procrastinate [prə'kræstə,neɪt] *vi* **-nated; -nating** : demorar, aplazar

procure [prə'kjʊr] *vt* **-cured; -curing** : obtener

prod ['prɑd] *vt* **prodded; prodding** : pinchar, aguijonear

prodigal ['prɑdɪgəl] *adj* : pródigo

prodigy ['prɑdədʒi] *n, pl* **-gies** : prodigio *m*

produce [prə'du:s, -'dju:s] *vt* **-duced; -ducing 1** : producir **2** CAUSE : causar **3** SHOW : presentar, mostrar **4** : poner en escena (una obra de teatro) — **~** ['prɑ,du:s, 'pro:-, -,dju:s] *n* : productos *mpl* agrícolas — **producer** [prə'du:sər, -'dju:-] *n* : productor *m*, -tora *f* — **product** ['prɑ,dʌkt] *n* : producto *m* — **productive** [prə'dʌktɪv] *adj* : productivo

profane [pro'feɪn] *adj* **1** : profano **2** IRREVERENT : blasfemo — **profanity** [pro'fænət̬i] *n, pl* **-ties** : blasfemia *f*

profess [prə'fɛs] *vt* : profesar — **profession** [prə'fɛʃən] *n* : profesión *f* — **professional** [prə'fɛʃənəl] *adj* : profesional — **~** *n* : profesional *mf* — **professor** [prə'fɛsər] *n* : profesor *m*, -sora *f*

proficiency [prə'fɪʃəntsi] *n* : competencia *f* — **proficient** [prə'fɪʃənt] *adj* : competente

profile ['pro:,faɪl] *n* **1** : perfil *m* **2 keep a low ~** : no llamar la atención

profit ['prɑfət] *n* : beneficio *m*, ganancia *f* — **~** *vi* : sacar provecho (de), beneficiarse (de) — **profitable** ['prɑfət̬əbəl] *adj* : provechoso

profound [prə'faʊnd] *adj* : profundo

profuse [prə'fju:s] *adj* : profuso — **profusion** [prə'fju:ʒən] *n* : profusión *f*

prognosis [prɑg'no:sɪs] *n, pl* **-noses** [-,si:z] : pronóstico *m*

program ['pro:,græm, -grəm] *n* : programa *m* — **~** *vt* **-grammed** *or* **-gramed; -gramming** *or* **-graming** : programar

progress ['prɑgrəs, -,grɛs] *n* **1** : progreso *m* **2** ADVANCE : avance *m* — **~** [prə'grɛs] *vi* : progresar, avanzar — **progressive** [prə'grɛsɪv] *adj* **1** : progresista (dícese de la política, etc.) **2** INCREASING : progresiva

prohibit [pro'hɪbət] *vt* : prohibir — **prohibition** [,pro:ə'bɪʃən, ,pro:hə-] *n* : prohibición *f*

project ['prɑ,dʒɛkt, -dʒɪkt] *n* : proyecto *m* — **~** [prə'dʒɛkt] *vt* : proyectar — *vi* PROTRUDE : sobresalir — **projectile** [prə'dʒɛktəl, -,taɪl] *n* : proyectil *m* — **projection** [prə'dʒɛkʃən] *n* **1** : proyección *f* **2** PROTRUSION : saliente *m* — **projector** [prə'dʒɛktər] *n* : proyector *m*

proliferate [prə'lɪfə,reɪt] *vi* **-ated; -ating** : proliferar — **proliferation** [prə,lɪfə'reɪʃən] *n* : proliferación *f* — **prolific** [prə'lɪfɪk] *adj* : prolífico

prologue ['pro;lɔg] *n* : prólogo *m*
prolong [prə'lɔŋ] *vt* : prolongar
prom ['prɑm] *n* : baile *m* formal (en un colegio)
prominent ['prɑmənənt] *adj* : prominente — **prominence** ['prɑmənənts] *n* 1 : prominencia *f* 2 IMPORTANCE : eminencia *f*
promiscuous [prə'mɪskjuəs] *adj* : promiscuo
promise ['prɑməs] *n* : promesa *f* — ~ *v* **-ised; -ising** : prometer — **promising** ['prɑməsɪŋ] *adj* : prometedor
promote [prə'mo:t] *vt* **-moted; -moting** 1 : ascender (a un alumno o un empleado) 2 FURTHER : promover, fomentar 3 ADVERTISE : promocionar — **promoter** [prə'mo:t̬ər] *n* : promotor *m*, -tora *f*; empresario *m*, -ria *f* (en deportes) — **promotion** [prə'mo:ʃən] *n* 1 : ascenso *m* (de un alumno o un empleado) 2 ADVERTISING : publicidad *f*, propaganda *f*
prompt ['prɑmpt] *vt* 1 INCITE : provocar (una cosa), inducir (a una persona) 2 : apuntar (a un actor, etc.) — ~ *adj* 1 : rápido 2 PUNCTUAL : puntual
prone ['pro:n] *adj* 1 : boca abajo, decúbito prono 2 **be ~ to** : ser propenso a
prong ['prɔŋ] *n* : punta *f*, diente *m*
pronoun ['pro:ˌnaun] *n* : pronombre *m*
pronounce [prə'naunts] *vt* **-nounced; -nouncing** : pronunciar — **pronouncement** [prə'nauntsmənt] *n* : declaración *f* — **pronunciation** [prəˌnʌntsi'eɪʃən] *n* : pronunciación *f*
proof ['pruːf] *n* : prueba *f* — ~ *adj* ~ **against** : a prueba de — **proofread** ['pruːf̩ˌriːd] *vt* **-read; -reading** : corregir
prop ['prɑp] *n* 1 SUPPORT : puntal *m*, apoyo *m* 2 : accesorio *m* (en teatro) — ~ *vt* **propped; propping** 1 ~ **against** : apoyar contra 2 ~ **up** SUPPORT : apoyar
propaganda [ˌprɑpə'gændə, ˌpro:-] *n* : propaganda *f*
propagate ['prɑpəˌgeɪt] *v* **-gated; -gating** *vt* : propagar — *vi* : propagarse
propel [prə'pel] *vt* **-pelled; -pelling** : propulsar — **propeller** [prə'pelər] *n* : hélice *f*
propensity [prə'pentsət̬i] *n, pl* **-ties** : propensión *f*
proper ['prɑpər] *adj* 1 SUITABLE : apropiado 2 REAL : verdadero 3 CORRECT : correcto 4 GENTEEL : cortés 5 ~ **name** : nombre *m* propio — **properly** ['prɑpərli] *adv* : correctamente
property ['prɑpərt̬i] *n, pl* **-ties** 1 : propiedad *f* 2 BUILDING : inmueble *m* 3 LAND, LOT : parcela *f*
prophet ['prɑfət] *n* : profeta *m*, profetisa *f* — **prophecy** ['prɑfəsi] *n, pl* **-cies** : profecía *f* — **prophesy** ['prɑfəˌsaɪ] *vt* **-sied; -sying** *vt* : profetizar — *vi* : hacer profecías — **prophetic** [prə'fɛt̬ɪk] *adj* : profético
proportion [prə'porʃən] *n* 1 : proporción *f* 2 SHARE : parte *f* — **proportional** [prə'porʃənəl] *adj* : proporcional — **proportionate** [prə'porʃənət] *adj* : proporcional
proposal [prə'po:zəl] *n* : propuesta *f*
propose [prə'po:z] *v* **-posed; -posing** *vt* 1 SUGGEST : proponer 2 ~ **to do sth** : pensar hacer algo — *vi* : proponer matrimonio — **proposition** [ˌprɑpə'zɪʃən] *n* : proposición *f*
proprietor [prə'praɪət̬ər] *n* : propietario *m*, -ria *f*
propriety [prə'praɪət̬i] *n, pl* **-eties** : decencia *f*, decoro *m*
propulsion [prə'pʌlʃən] *n* : propulsión *f*
prose ['pro:z] *n* : prosa *f*
prosecute ['prɑsɪˌkjuːt] *vt* **-cuted; -cuting** : procesar — **prosecution** [ˌprɑsɪ'kjuːʃən] *n* 1 : procesamiento *m* 2 **the** ~ : la acusación — **prosecutor** ['prɑsɪˌkjuːt̬ər] *n* : acusador *m*, -dora *f*
prospect ['prɑˌspɛkt] *n* 1 : perspectiva *f* 2 POSSIBILITY : posibilidad *f* — **prospective** [prə'spɛktɪv, 'prɑˌspɛk-] *adj* : futuro, posible
prosper ['prɑspər] *vi* : prosperar — **prosperity** [prɑ'spɛrət̬i] *n* : prosperidad *f* — **prosperous** ['prɑspərəs] *adj* : próspero
prostitute ['prɑstəˌtuːt, -ˌtjuːt] *n* : prostituta *f* — **prostitution** [ˌprɑstə'tuːʃən, -'tjuː-] *n* : prostitución *f*
prostrate ['prɑˌstreɪt] *adj* : postrado
protagonist [pro'tægənɪst] *n* : protagonista *mf*
protect [prə'tɛkt] *vt* : proteger — **protection** [prə'tɛkʃən] *n* : protección *f* — **protective** [prə'tɛktɪv] *adj* : protector — **protector** [prə'tɛkt̬ər] *n* : protector *m*, -tora *f*
protégé ['pro:t̬əˌʒeɪ] *n* : protegido *m*, -da *f*
protein ['pro:ˌtiːn] *n* : proteína *f*
protest ['pro:ˌtɛst] *n* : protesta *f* — ~ [pro'tɛst] *vt* : protestar — *vi* ~ **against** : protestar contra — **Protestant** ['prɑt̬əstənt] *n* : protestante *mf* — **protester** *or* **protestor** ['pro:ˌtɛstər, prə'-] *n* : manifestante *mf*
protocol ['pro:t̬əˌkɔl] *n* : protocolo *m*
prototype ['pro:t̬əˌtaɪp] *n* : prototipo *m*
protract [pro'trækt] *vt* : prolongar
protrude [pro'truːd] *vi* **-truded; -truding** : sobresalir
proud ['praud] *adj* : orgulloso

prove ['pruːv] *v* **proved; proved** *or* **proven** ['pruːvən]; **proving** *vt* : probar — *vi* : resultar
proverb ['prɑˌvərb] *n* : proverbio *m*, refrán *m* — **proverbial** [prə'vərbiəl] *adj* : proverbial
provide [prə'vaɪd] *v* **-vided; -viding** *vt* : proveer — *vi* ~ **for** SUPPORT : mantener — **provided** [prə'vaɪdəd] *or* ~ **that** *conj* : con tal (de) que, siempre que — **providence** ['prɑvədənts] *n* : providencia *f*
province ['prɑvɪnts] *n* 1 : provincia *f* 2 SPHERE : campo *m*, competencia *f* — **provincial** [prə'vɪntʃəl] *adj* : provinciano
provision [prə'vɪʒən] *n* 1 : provisión *f*, suministro *m* 2 STIPULATION : condición *f* 3 ~**s** *npl* : víveres *mpl* — **provisional** [prə'vɪʒənəl] *adj* : provisional — **proviso** [prə'vaɪˌzo:] *n, pl* **-sos** *or* **-soes** : condición *f*
provoke [prə'vo:k] *vt* **-voked; -voking** : provocar — **provocation** [ˌprɑvə'keɪʃən] *n* : provocación *f* — **provocative** [prə'vɑkət̬ɪv] *adj* : provocador, provocativo
prow ['prau] *n* : proa *f*
prowess ['prauəs] *n* 1 BRAVERY : valor *m* 2 SKILL : habilidad *f*
prowl ['praul] *vi* : merodear, rondar — *vt* : merodear por — **prowler** ['praulər] *n* : merodeador *m*, -dora *f*
proximity [prɑk'sɪmət̬i] *n* : proximidad *f*
proxy ['prɑksi] *n, pl* **proxies by** ~ : por poder
prude ['pruːd] *n* : mojigato *m*, -ta *f*
prudence ['pruːdənts] *n* : prudencia *f* — **prudent** ['pruːdənt] *adj* : prudente
prune[1] ['pruːn] *n* : ciruela *f* pasa
prune[2] *vt* **pruned; pruning** : podar (arbustos, etc.)
pry ['praɪ] *v* **pried; prying** *vi* ~ **into** : entrometerse en — *vt* *or* ~ **open** : abrir (a la fuerza)
psalm ['sɑm, 'sɑlm] *n* : salmo *m*
pseudonym ['suːdəˌnɪm] *n* : seudónimo *m*
psychiatry [sə'kaɪətri, saɪ-] *n* : psiquiatría *f* — **psychiatric** [ˌsaɪki'ætrɪk] *adj* : psiquiátrico — **psychiatrist** [sə'kaɪətrɪst, saɪ-] *n* : psiquiatra *mf*
psychic ['saɪkɪk] *adj* : psíquico
psychoanalysis [ˌsaɪkoə'næləsɪs] *n, pl* **-yses** : psicoanálisis *m* — **psychoanalyst** [ˌsaɪko'ænəlɪst] *n* : psicoanalista *mf* — **psychoanalyze** [ˌsaɪko'ænəlˌaɪz] *vt* **-lyzed; -lyzing** : psicoanalizar
psychology [saɪ'kɑlədʒi] *n, pl* **-gies** : psicología *f* — **psychological** [ˌsaɪkə'lɑdʒɪkəl] *adj* : psicológico — **psychologist** [saɪ'kɑlədʒɪst] *n* : psicólogo *m*, -ga *f*
psychopath ['saɪkəˌpæθ] *n* : psicópata *mf*
psychotherapy [ˌsaɪko'θerəpi] *n, pl* **-pies** : psicoterapia *f*
psychotic [saɪ'kɑt̬ɪk] *adj* : psicótico
puberty ['pjuːbərt̬i] *n* : pubertad *f*
pubic ['pjuːbɪk] *adj* : púbico
public ['pʌblɪk] *adj* : público — ~ *n* : público *m* — **publication** [ˌpʌblə'keɪʃən] *n* : publicación *f* — **publicity** [pʌ'blɪsət̬i] *n* : publicidad *f* — **publicize** ['pʌbləˌsaɪz] *vt* **-cized; -cizing** : publicitar, divulgar
publish ['pʌblɪʃ] *vt* : publicar — **publisher** ['pʌblɪʃər] *n* 1 : editor *m*, -tora *f* (persona) 2 : casa *f* editorial (negocio)
pucker ['pʌkər] *vt* : fruncir, arrugar — *vi* : arrugarse
pudding ['pudɪŋ] *n* : budín *m*, pudín *m*
puddle ['pʌdəl] *n* : charco *m*
pudgy ['pʌdʒi] *adj* **pudgier; -est** : rechoncho *fam*
Puerto Rican [ˌpwertə'riːkən, ˌportə-] *adj* : puertorriqueño
puff ['pʌf] *vi* 1 BLOW : soplar 2 PANT : resoplar 3 ~ **up** SWELL : hincharse — *vt* ~ **out** : hinchar — ~ *n* 1 : bocanada *f* (de humo) 2 : chupada *f* (a un cigarrillo) 3 *or* **cream** ~ : pastelito *m* de crema 4 *or* **powder** ~ : borla *f* — **puffy** ['pʌfi] *adj* **puffier; -est** : hinchado
pull ['pul] *vt* 1 : tirar de 2 EXTRACT : sacar 3 TEAR : desgarrarse (un músculo, etc.) 4 ~ **off** REMOVE : quitar 5 ~ **oneself together** : calmarse 6 ~ **up** : levantar, subir — *vi* 1 : tirar 2 ~ **through** RECOVER : reponerse 3 ~ **together** COOPERATE : reunir 4 ~ **up** STOP : parar — ~ *n* 1 : tirón *m* 2 INFLUENCE : influencia *f* — **pulley** ['puli] *n, pl* **-leys** : polea *f* — **pullover** ['pulˌoːvər] *n* : suéter *m*
pulp ['pʌlp] *n* 1 : pulpa *f* (de frutas, etc.) 2 *or* **wood** ~ : pasta *f* de papel
pulpit ['pulˌpɪt, 'pʌl-] *n* : púlpito *m*
pulsate ['pʌlˌseɪt] *vi* **-sated; -sating** : palpitar — **pulse** ['pʌls] *n* : pulso *m*
pulverize ['pʌlvəˌraɪz] *vt* **-ized; -izing** : pulverizar
pummel ['pʌməl] *vt* **-meled; -meling** : aporrear
pump[1] ['pʌmp] *n* : bomba *f* — ~ *vt* 1 : bombear 2 ~ **up** : inflar
pump[2] *n* SHOE : zapato *m* de tacón
pumpernickel ['pʌmpərˌnɪkəl] *n* : pan *m* negro de centeno
pumpkin ['pʌmpkɪn, 'pʌŋkɪn] *n* : calabaza *f*, zapallo *m* *Lat*
pun ['pʌn] *n* : juego *m* de palabras — ~ *vi* **punned; punning** : hacer juegos de palabras
punch[1] ['pʌntʃ] *vt* 1 : dar un puñetazo a 2

PERFORATE : perforar (papeles, etc.), picar (un boleto) — ~ *n* 1 : golpe *m*, puñetazo *m* 2 *or* **paper** ~ : perforadora *f*
punch[2] *n* : ponche *m* (bebida)
punctual ['pʌŋktʃuəl] *adj* : puntual — **punctuality** [ˌpʌŋktʃu'ælət̬i] *n* : puntualidad *f*
punctuate ['pʌŋktʃuˌeɪt] *vt* **-ated; -ating** : puntuar — **punctuation** [ˌpʌŋktʃu'eɪʃən] *n* : puntuación *f*
puncture ['pʌŋktʃər] *n* : pinchazo *m*, ponchadura *f Lat* — ~ *vt* **-tured; -turing** : pinchar, ponchar *Lat*
pungent ['pʌndʒənt] *adj* : acre
punish ['pʌnɪʃ] *vt* : castigar — **punishment** ['pʌnɪʃmənt] *n* : castigo *m* — **punitive** ['pjuːnət̬ɪv] *adj* : punitivo
puny ['pjuːni] *adj* **-nier; -est** : enclenque
pup ['pʌp] *n* : cachorro *m*, -rra *f* (de un perro); cría *f* (de otros animales)
pupil[1] ['pjuːpəl] *n* : alumno *m*, -na *f* (de colegio)
pupil[2] *n* : pupila *f* (del ojo)
puppet ['pʌpət] *n* : títere *m*
puppy ['pʌpi] *n, pl* **-pies** : cachorro *m*, -rra *f*
purchase ['pərtʃəs] *vt* **-chased; -chasing** : comprar — ~ *n* : compra *f*
pure ['pjur] *adj* **purer; purest** : puro
puree ['pjuˌreɪ, -'riː] *n* : puré *m*
purely ['pjurli] *adv* : puramente
purgatory ['pərgəˌtori] *n, pl* **-ries** : purgatorio *m* — **purge** ['pərdʒ] *vt* **purged; purging** : purgar — ~ *n* : purga *f*
purify ['pjurəˌfaɪ] *vt* **-fied; -fying** : purificar — **purification** [ˌpjurəfə'keɪʃən] *n* : purificación *f*
puritanical [ˌpjurə'tænɪkəl] *adj* : puritano
purity ['pjurət̬i] *n* : pureza *f*
purple ['pərpəl] *n* : morado *m*
purport [pər'port] *vi* ~ **to be** : pretender ser
purpose ['pərpəs] *n* 1 : propósito *m* 2 RESOLUTION : determinación *f* 3 **on** ~ : a propósito — **purposeful** ['pərpəsfəl] *adj* : resuelto — **purposely** ['pərpəsli] *adv* : a propósito
purr ['pər] *n* : ronroneo *m* — ~ *vi* : ronronear
purse ['pərs] *n* 1 *or* **change** ~ : monedero *m* 2 HANDBAG : cartera *f*, bolso *m* Spain, bolsa *f Lat* — ~ *vt* **pursed; pursing** : fruncir
pursue [pər'suː] *vt* **-sued; -suing** 1 CHASE : perseguir 2 SEEK : buscar — **pursuer** [pər'suːər] *n* : perseguidor *m*, -dora *f* — **pursuit** [pər'suːt] *n* 1 CHASE : persecución *f* 2 SEARCH : búsqueda *f* 3 OCCUPATION : actividad *f*
pus ['pʌs] *n* : pus *m*
push ['puʃ] *vt* 1 SHOVE : empujar 2 PRESS : apretar 3 URGE : presionar 4 ~ **around** BULLY : mangonear — *vi* 1 : empujar 2 ~ **for** : presionar para — ~ *n* 1 SHOVE : empujón *m* 2 DRIVE : dinamismo *m* 3 EFFORT : esfuerzo *m* — **pushy** ['puʃi] *adj* **pushier; -est** : mandón, prepotente
pussy ['pusi] *n, pl* **pussies** : gatito *m*, -ta *f*; minino *m*, -na *f*
put ['put] *vt* **put; putting** *vt* 1 : poner 2 INSERT : meter 3 EXPRESS : decir 4 ~ **one's mind to** : proponerse hacer algo — ~ **up with** : aguantar — **put away** *vt* 1 STORE : guardar 2 *or* ~ **aside** : dejar a un lado — **put down** *vt* 1 SUPPRESS : sofocar 2 ATTRIBUTE : atribuir — **put off** *vt* DEFER : aplazar, posponer — **put on** *vt* 1 ASSUME : adoptar 2 PRESENT : presentar (una obra de teatro, etc.) 3 WEAR : ponerse — **put out** *vt* INCONVENIENCE : incomodar — **put up** *vt* 1 BUILD : construir 2 LODGE : alojar 3 PROVIDE : poner (dinero)
putrefy ['pjuːtrəˌfaɪ] *vi* **-fied; -fying** : pudrirse
putty ['pʌt̬i] *n, pl* **-ties** : masilla *f*
puzzle ['pʌzəl] *v* **-zled; -zling** *vt* : confundir, dejar perplejo — *vi* ~ **over** : tratar de descifrar — ~ *n* 1 : rompecabezas *m* 2 MYSTERY : enigma *m*
pylon ['paɪˌlɑn, -lən] *n* : pilón *m*
pyramid ['pɪrəˌmɪd] *n* : pirámide *f*
python ['paɪˌθɑn, -θən] *n* : pitón *f*

Q

q ['kjuː] *n, pl* **q's** *or* **qs** ['kjuːz] : q *f*, decimoséptima letra del alfabeto inglés
quack[1] ['kwæk] *vi* : graznar (dícese del pato) — ~ *n* : graznido *m*
quack[2] *n* CHARLATAN : charlatán *m*, -tana *f*
quadruple [kwɑ'druːpəl, -'drʌ-; 'kwɑdrə-] *v* **-pled; -pling** *vt* : cuadruplicar — *vi* : cuadruplicarse
quagmire ['kwægˌmaɪr, 'kwɑg-] *n* : atolladero *m*
quail ['kweɪl] *n, pl* **quail** *or* **quails** : codorniz *f*
quaint ['kweɪnt] *adj* 1 ODD : curioso 2 PICTURESQUE : pintoresco

quake ['kweɪk] *vi* **quaked; quaking** : temblar — ~ *n* → **earthquake**
qualify ['kwɑləˌfaɪ] *v* **-fied; -fying** *vt* 1 LIMIT : matizar 2 : calificar (en gramática) 3 EQUIP : habilitar — *vi* 1 : titularse (de abogado, etc.) 2 : clasificarse (en deportes) — **qualification** [ˌkwɑləfə'keɪʃən] *n* 1 REQUIREMENT : requisito *m* 2 ~**s** *npl* ABILITY : capacidad *f* 3 **without** ~ : sin reservas — **qualified** ['kwɑləˌfaɪd] *adj* : capacitado
quality ['kwɑlət̬i] *n, pl* **-ties** 1 : calidad *f* 2 PROPERTY : cualidad *f*
qualm ['kwɑm, 'kwɑlm, 'kwɔm] *n* 1 DOUBT : duda *f* 2 **have no** ~**s about** : no tener ningún escrúpulo en
quandary ['kwɑndri] *n, pl* **-ries** : dilema *m*
quantity ['kwɑntət̬i] *n, pl* **-ties** : cantidad *f*
quarantine ['kwɔrənˌtiːn] *n* : cuarentena *f* — ~ *vt* **-tined; -tining** : poner en cuarentena
quarrel ['kwɔrəl] *n* : pelea *f*, riña *f* — ~ *vi* **-reled** *or* **-relled; -reling** *or* **-relling** : pelearse, reñir — **quarrelsome** ['kwɔrəlsəm] *adj* : pendenciero
quarry[1] ['kwɔri] *n, pl* **quarries** PREY : presa *f*
quarry[2] *n, pl* **quarries** EXCAVATION : cantera *f*
quart ['kwɔrt] *n* : cuarto *m* de galón
quarter ['kwɔrt̬ər] *n* 1 : cuarto *m* (en matemáticas) 2 : moneda *f* de 25 centavos 3 DISTRICT : barrio *m* 4 ~ **after three** : las tres y cuarto 5 ~**s** *npl* LODGING : alojamiento *m* — ~ *vt* 1 : dividir en cuatro partes 2 : acuartelar (tropas) — **quarterly** ['kwɔrt̬ərli] *adv* : cada tres meses — ~ *adj* : trimestral — ~ *n, pl* **-lies** : publicación *f* trimestral
quartet [kwɔr'tɛt] *n* : cuarteto *m*
quartz ['kwɔrts] *n* : cuarzo *m*
quash ['kwɑʃ, 'kwɔʃ] *vt* 1 ANNUL : anular 2 SUPPRESS : aplastar, sofocar
quaver ['kweɪvər] *vi* : temblar
quay ['kiː, 'keɪ, 'kweɪ] *n* : muelle *m*
queasy ['kwiːzi] *adj* **-sier; -est** : mareado
queen ['kwiːn] *n* : reina *f*
queer ['kwɪr] *adj* ODD : extraño
quell ['kwel] *vt* SUPPRESS : sofocar, aplastar
quench ['kwentʃ] *vt* 1 EXTINGUISH : apagar 2 ~ **one's thirst** : quitar la sed
query ['kwɪri, 'kwer-] *n, pl* **-ries** : pregunta *f* — ~ *vt* **-ried; -rying** 1 ASK : preguntar 2 QUESTION : cuestionar
quest ['kwest] *n* : búsqueda *f*
question ['kwestʃən] *n* 1 QUERY : pregunta *f* 2 ISSUE : cuestión *f* 3 **be out of the** ~ : ser indiscutible 4 **call into** ~ : poner en duda 5 **without** ~ : sin duda — ~ *vt* 1 ASK : preguntar 2 DOUBT : cuestionar 3 INTERROGATE : interrogar — *vi* : preguntar — **questionable** ['kwestʃənəbəl] *adj* : discutible — **question mark** *n* : signo *m* de interrogación — **questionnaire** [ˌkwestʃə'nær] *n* : cuestionario *m*
queue ['kjuː] *n* : cola *f* — ~ *vi* **queued; queuing** *or* **queueing** : hacer cola
quibble ['kwɪbəl] *vi* **-bled; -bling** : discutir, quejarse por nimiedades
quick ['kwɪk] *adj* 1 : rápido 2 CLEVER : agudo — ~ **to the** ~ : en lo vivo — ~ *adv* : rápidamente — **quicken** ['kwɪkən] *vt* : acelerar — **quickly** ['kwɪkli] *adv* : rápidamente — **quicksand** ['kwɪkˌsænd] *n* : arena *f* movediza — **quick-tempered** ['kwɪk'tempərd] *adj* : irascible — **quick-witted** ['kwɪk'wɪt̬əd] *adj* : agudo
quiet ['kwaɪət] *n* 1 : silencio *m* 2 CALM : tranquilidad *f* — ~ *adj* 1 : silencioso 2 CALM : tranquilo 3 RESERVED : callado 4 : discreto (dícese de colores, etc.) — ~ *vt* 1 SILENCE : hacer callar 2 CALM : calmar — *vi or* ~ **down** : calmarse — **quietly** *adv* 1 : silenciosamente 2 CALMLY : tranquilamente
quilt ['kwɪlt] *n* : edredón *m*
quintet [kwɪn'tet] *n* : quinteto *m*
quip ['kwɪp] *n* : ocurrencia *f*, salida *f* — ~ *vt* **quipped; quipping** : decir bromeando
quirk ['kwərk] *n* : peculiaridad *f*
quit ['kwɪt] *v* **quit; quitting** *vt* 1 LEAVE : dejar, abandonar 2 ~ **doing** : dejar de hacer — *vi* 1 STOP : parar 2 RESIGN : dimitir, renunciar
quite ['kwaɪt] *adv* 1 COMPLETELY : completamente 2 RATHER : bastante
quits ['kwɪts] *adj* **call it** ~ : quedar en paz
quiver ['kwɪvər] *vi* : temblar
quiz ['kwɪz] *n, pl* **quizzes** TEST : prueba *f* — ~ *vt* **quizzed; quizzing** : interrogar
quota ['kwoːt̬ə] *n* : cuota *f*, cupo *m*
quotation [kwo'teɪʃən] *n* 1 : cita *f* 2 ESTIMATE : presupuesto *m* — **quotation marks** *npl* : comillas *fpl* — **quote** ['kwoːt] *v* **quoted; quoting** *vt* 1 CITE : citar 2 : cotizar (en finanzas) — ~ *n* 1 → **quotation** 2 ~**s** *npl* → **quotation marks**
quotient ['kwoːʃənt] *n* : cociente *m*

R

r ['ɑr] *n, pl* **r's** *or* **rs** ['ɑrz] : r *f*, decimoctava letra del alfabeto inglés
rabbi ['ræˌbaɪ] *n* : rabino *m*, -na *f*
rabbit ['ræbət] *n, pl* **-bit** *or* **-bits** : conejo *m*, -ja *f*
rabble ['ræbəl] *n* : chusma *f*, populacho *m*
rabies ['reɪbi:z] *ns & pl* : rabia *f* — **rabid** ['ræbɪd] *adj* **1** : rabioso **2** FANATIC : fanático
raccoon [ræ'ku:n] *n, pl* **-coon** *or* **-coons** : mapache *m*
race[1] ['reɪs] *n* **1** : raza *f* **2 human ~** : género *m* humano
race[2] *n* : carrera *f* (competitiva) — **~** *vi* **raced; racing 1** : correr (en una carrera) **2** RUSH : ir corriendo — **racehorse** ['reɪsˌhors] *n* : caballo *m* de carreras — **racetrack** ['reɪsˌtræk] *n* : pista *f* (de carreras)
racial ['reɪʃəl] *adj* : racial — **racism** ['reɪˌsɪzəm] *n* : racismo *m* — **racist** ['reɪsɪst] *n* : racista *mf*
rack ['ræk] *n* **1** SHELF : estante *m* **2 luggage ~** : portaequipajes *m* — **~** *vt* **1 ~ed with** : atormentado por **2 ~ one's brains** : devanarse los sesos
racket[1] ['rækət] *n* : raqueta *f* (en deportes)
racket[2] *n* **1** DIN : alboroto *m*, bulla *f* **2** SWINDLE : estafa *f*
racy ['reɪsi] *adj* **racier; -est** : subido de tono, picante
radar ['reɪˌdɑr] *n* : radar *m*
radiant ['reɪdiənt] *adj* : radiante — **radiance** ['reɪdiənts] *n* : resplandor *m* — **radiate** ['reɪdiˌeɪt] *v* **-ated; -ating** *vt* : irradiar — *vi* **1** : irradiar **2** *or* **~ out** : extenderse (desde un centro) — **radiation** [ˌreɪdi'eɪʃən] *n* : radiación *f* — **radiator** ['reɪdiˌeɪţər] *n* : radiador *m*
radical ['rædɪkəl] *adj* : radical — **~** *n* : radical *mf*
radii → **radius**
radio ['reɪdiˌo:] *n, pl* **-dios** : radio *mf* (aparato), radio *f* (medio) — **~** *vt* : transmitir por radio — **radioactive** ['reɪdio'æktɪv] *adj* : radioactivo, radiactivo
radish ['rædɪʃ] *n* : rábano *m*
radius ['reɪdiəs] *n, pl* **radii** [-diˌaɪ] : radio *m*
raffle ['ræfəl] *vt* **-fled; -fling** : rifar — **~** *n* : rifa *f*
raft ['ræft] *n* : balsa *f*
rafter ['ræftər] *n* : cabrio *m*
rag ['ræg] *n* **1** : trapo *m* **2 ~s** *npl* TATTERS : harapos *mpl*, andrajos *mpl*
rage ['reɪdʒ] *n* **1** : cólera *f*, rabia *f* **2 be all the ~** : hacer furor — **~** *vi* **raged; raging 1** : estar furioso **2** : bramar (dícese del viento, etc.)
ragged ['rægəd] *adj* **1** UNEVEN : irregular **2** TATTERED : andrajoso, harapiento
raid ['reɪd] *n* **1** : invasión *f* (militar) **2** : asalto *m* (por delincuentes), redada *f* (por la policía) — **~** *vt* **1** INVADE : invadir **2** ROB : asaltar **3** : hacer una redada en (dícese de la policía) — **raider** ['reɪdər] *n* ATTACKER : asaltante *mf*
rail[1] ['reɪl] *vi* **~ at s.o.** : recriminar a algn
rail[2] *n* **1** BAR : barra *f* **2** HANDRAIL : pasamanos *m* **3** TRACK : riel *m* **4 by ~** : por ferrocarril — **railing** ['reɪlɪŋ] *n* **1** : baranda *f* (de un balcón), pasamanos *m* (de una escalera) **2** RAILS : reja *f* — **railroad** ['reɪlˌro:d] *n* : ferrocarril *m* — **railway** ['reɪlˌweɪ] → **railroad**
rain ['reɪn] *n* : lluvia *f* — **~** *vi* : llover — **rainbow** ['reɪnˌbo:] *n* : arco *m* iris — **raincoat** ['reɪnˌko:t] *n* : impermeable *m* — **rainfall** ['reɪnˌfɔl] *n* : precipitación *f* — **rainy** ['reɪni] *adj* **rainier; -est** : lluvioso
raise ['reɪz] *vt* **raised; raising 1** : levantar **2** COLLECT : recaudar **3** REAR : criar **4** GROW : cultivar **5** INCREASE : aumentar **6** : sacar (objeciones, etc.) — **~** *n* : aumento *m*
raisin ['reɪzən] *n* : pasa *f*
rake ['reɪk] *n* : rastrillo *m* — **~** *vt* **raked; raking** : rastrillar
rally ['ræli] *v* **-lied; -lying** *vi* **1** : unirse, reunirse **2** RECOVER : recuperarse — *vt* : conseguir (apoyo), unir a (la gente) — **~** *n, pl* **-lies** : reunión *f*, mitin *m*
ram *n* ['ræm] : carnero *m* (animal) — **~** *vt* **rammed; ramming 1** CRAM : meter con fuerza **2** *or* **~ into** : chocar contra
RAM ['ræm] *n* : RAM *f*
ramble ['ræmbəl] *vi* **-bled; -bling 1** WANDER : pasear **2** *or* **~ on** : divagar — **~** *n* : paseo *m*, excursión *f*
ramp ['ræmp] *n* : rampa *f*
rampage ['ræmˌpeɪdʒ, ræm'peɪdʒ] *vi* **-paged; -paging** : andar arrasando todo — **~** ['ræmˌpeɪdʒ] *n* : frenesí *m* (de violencia)
rampant ['ræmpənt] *adj* : desenfrenado
rampart ['ræmˌpɑrt] *n* : muralla *f*
ramshackle ['ræmˌʃækəl] *adj* : destartalado
ran → **run**
ranch ['ræntʃ] *n* : hacienda *f* — **rancher** ['ræntʃər] *n* : hacendado *m*, -da *f*
rancid ['ræntsɪd] *adj* : rancio
rancor ['ræŋkər] *n* : rencor *m*
random ['rændəm] *adj* **1** : aleatorio **2 at ~** : al azar
rang → **ring**
range ['reɪndʒ] *n* **1** GRASSLAND : pradera *f* **2** STOVE : cocina *f* **3** VARIETY : gama *f* **4** SCOPE : amplitud *f* **5** *or* **mountain ~** : cordillera *f* — **~** *vi* **ranged; ranging 1** EXTEND : extenderse **2 ~ from…to…** : variar entre…y… — **ranger** ['reɪndʒər] *n or* **forest ~** : guardabosque *mf*
rank[1] ['ræŋk] *adj* **1** SMELLY : fétido **2** OUTRIGHT : completo
rank[2] *n* **1** ROW : fila *f* **2** : rango *m* (militar) **3 ~s** *npl* : soldados *mpl* rasos **4 the ~ and file** : las bases — **~** *vt* RATE : clasificar — *vi* : clasificarse
rankle ['ræŋkəl] *vi* **-kled; -kling** : causar rencor, doler
ransack ['rænˌsæk] *vt* **1** SEARCH : registrar **2** LOOT : saquear
ransom ['ræntsəm] *n* : rescate *m* — **~** *vt* : rescatar
rant ['rænt] *vi or* **~ and rave** : despotricar
rap[1] ['ræp] *n* KNOCK : golpecito *m* — **~** *v* **rapped; rapping** : golpear
rap[2] *n or* **~ music** : rap *m*
rapacious [rə'peɪʃəs] *adj* : rapaz
rape ['reɪp] *vt* **raped; raping** : violar — **~** *n* : violación *f*
rapid ['ræpɪd] *adj* : rápido — **rapids** ['ræpɪdz] *npl* : rápidos *mpl*
rapist ['reɪpɪst] *n* : violador *m*, -dora *f*
rapport [ræ'pɔr] *n* **have a good ~** : entenderse bien
rapt ['ræpt] *adj* : absorto, embelesado
rapture ['ræptʃər] *n* : éxtasis *m*
rare ['rær] *adj* **rarer; rarest 1** FINE : excepcional **2** UNCOMMON : raro **3** : poco cocido (dícese de la carne) — **rarely** ['rærli] *adv* : raramente — **rarity** ['rærəţi] *n, pl* **-ties** : rareza *f*
rascal ['ræskəl] *n* : pillo *m*, -lla *f*; pícaro *m*, -ra *f*
rash[1] ['ræʃ] *adj* : imprudente, precipitado
rash[2] *n* : sarpullido *m*, erupción *f*
rasp ['ræsp] *vt* SCRAPE : raspar — **~** *n* : escofina *f*
raspberry ['ræzˌbɛri] *n, pl* **-ries** : frambuesa *f*
rat ['ræt] *n* : rata *f*
rate ['reɪt] *n* **1** PACE : velocidad *f*, ritmo *m* **2** : tipo *m*, tasa *m* (de interés, etc.) **3** PRICE : tarifa *f* **4 at any ~** : de todos modos **5 birth ~** : índice *m* de natalidad — **~** *vt* **rated; rating 1** REGARD : considerar **2** DESERVE : merecer
rather ['ræðər, 'rʌ-, 'rɑ-] *adv* **1** FAIRLY : bastante **2 I'd ~…** : prefiero… **3 or ~** : o mejor dicho
ratify ['ræţəˌfaɪ] *vt* **-fied; -fying** : ratificar — **ratification** [ˌræţəfə'keɪʃən] *n* : ratificación *f*
rating ['reɪţɪŋ] *n* **1** : clasificación *f* **2 ~s** *npl* : índice *m* de audiencia
ratio ['reɪʃio] *n, pl* **-tios** : proporción *f*
ration ['ræʃən, 'reɪʃən] *n* **1** : ración *f* **2 ~s** *npl* PROVISIONS : víveres *mpl* — **~** *vt* **rationed; rationing** : racionar
rational ['ræʃənəl] *adj* : racional — **rationale** [ˌræʃə'næl] *n* : lógica *f*, razones *fpl* — **rationalize** ['ræʃənəˌlaɪz] *vt* **-ized; -izing** : racionalizar
rattle ['ræţəl] *v* **-tled; -tling** *vi* : traquetear — *vt* **1** SHAKE : agitar **2** UPSET : desconcertar **3 ~ off** : decir de corrido — **~** *n* **1** : traqueteo *m* **2** *or* **baby's ~** : sonajero *m* — **rattlesnake** ['ræţəlˌsneɪk] *n* : serpiente *f* de cascabel
raucous ['rɔkəs] *adj* **1** HOARSE : ronco **2** BOISTEROUS : bullicioso
ravage ['rævɪdʒ] *vt* **-aged; -aging** : estragar, asolar — **ravages** ['rævɪdʒəz] *npl* : estragos *mpl*
rave ['reɪv] *vi* **raved; raving 1** : delirar **2 ~ about** : hablar con entusiasmo sobre
raven ['reɪvən] *n* : cuervo *m*
ravenous ['rævənəs] *adj* **1** HUNGRY : hambriento **2** VORACIOUS : voraz
ravine [rə'vi:n] *n* : barranco *m*
ravishing ['rævɪʃɪŋ] *adj* : encantador
raw ['rɔ] *adj* **rawer; rawest 1** UNCOOKED : crudo **2** INEXPERIENCED : inexperto **3** CHAFED : en carne viva **4** : frío y húmedo (dícese del tiempo) **5 ~ deal** : trato *m* injusto **6 ~ materials** : materias *fpl* primas
ray ['reɪ] *n* : rayo *m*
rayon ['reɪˌɑn] *n* : rayón *m*
raze ['reɪz] *vt* **razed; razing** : arrasar
razor ['reɪzər] *n* : maquinilla *f* de afeitar — **razor blade** *n* : hoja *f* de afeitar
reach ['ri:tʃ] *vt* **1** : alcanzar **2** *or* **~ out** : extender **3** : llegar a (un acuerdo, un límite, etc.) **4** CONTACT : contactar — *vi* **1** : extenderse **2 ~ for** : tratar de agarrar — **~** *n* **1** : alcance *m* **2 within ~** : al alcance
react [ri'ækt] *vi* : reaccionar — **reaction** [ri'ækʃən] *n* : reacción *f* — **reactionary** [ri'ækʃəˌnɛri] *adj* : reaccionario — **~** *n, pl* **-ries** : reaccionario *m*, -ria *f* — **reactor** [ri'æktər] *n* : reactor *m*
read ['ri:d] *v* **read** ['rɛd]; **reading** *vt* **1** : leer **2** INTERPRET : interpretar **3** SAY : decir **4** INDICATE : marcar — *vi* **1** : leer **2 it ~s as follows** : dice lo siguiente — **readable** ['ri:dəbəl] *adj* : legible — **reader** ['ri:dər] *n* : lector *m*, -tora *f*
readily ['rɛdəli] *adv* **1** WILLINGLY : de buena gana **2** EASILY : fácilmente
reading ['ri:dɪŋ] *n* : lectura *f*
readjust [ˌri:ə'dʒʌst] *vt* : reajustar — *vi* : volverse a adaptar
ready ['rɛdi] *adj* **readier; -est 1** : listo, preparado **2** WILLING : dispuesto **3** AVAILABLE : disponible **4 get ~** : prepararse — **~** *vt* **readied; readying** : preparar
real ['ri:l] *adj* **1** : verdadero, real **2** GENUINE : auténtico — **~** *adv* VERY : muy — **real estate** *n* : propiedad *f* inmobiliaria, bienes *mpl* raices — **realism** ['ri:əˌlɪzəm] *n* : realismo *m* — **realist** ['ri:əlɪst] *n* : realista *mf* — **realistic** [ˌri:ə'lɪstɪk] *adj* : realista — **reality** [ri'æləţi] *n, pl* **-ties** : realidad *f*
realize ['ri:əˌlaɪz] *vt* **-ized; -izing 1** : darse cuenta de **2** ACHIEVE : realizar — **realization** [ˌri:ələ'zeɪʃən] *n* **1** : comprensión *f* **2** FULFILLMENT : realización *f*
really ['rɪli, 'ri:-] *adv* : verdaderamente
realm ['rɛlm] *n* **1** KINGDOM : reino *m* **2** SPHERE : esfera *f*
ream ['ri:m] *n* : resma *f* (de papel)
reap ['ri:p] *v* : cosechar
reappear [ˌri:ə'pɪr] *vi* : reaparecer
rear[1] ['rɪr] *vt* **1** RAISE : levantar **2** : criar (niños, etc.) — *vi or* **~ up** : encabritarse
rear[2] *n* **1** BACK : parte *f* de atrás **2** BUTTOCKS : trasero *m fam* — **~** *adj* : trasero, posterior
rearrange [ˌri:ə'reɪndʒ] *vt* **-ranged; -ranging** : reorganizar, cambiar
reason ['ri:zən] *n* : razón *f* — **~** *vt* THINK : pensar — *vi* : razonar — **reasonable** ['ri:zənəbəl] *adj* : razonable — **reasoning** ['ri:zənɪŋ] *n* : razonamiento *m*
reassure [ˌri:ə'ʃur] *vt* **-sured; -suring** : tranquilizar — **reassurance** [ˌri:ə'ʃurənts] *n* : (palabras *fpl* de) consuelo *m*
rebate ['ri:ˌbeɪt] *n* : reembolso *m*
rebel ['rɛbəl] *n* : rebelde *mf* — **~** [rɪ'bɛl] *vi* **-belled; -belling** : rebelarse — **rebellion** [rɪ'bɛljən] *n* : rebelión *f* — **rebellious** [rɪ'bɛljəs] *adj* : rebelde
rebirth [ˌri:'bərθ] *n* : renacimiento *m*
rebound ['ri:ˌbaund, ˌri:'baund] *vi* : rebotar — **~** ['ri:ˌbaund] *n* : rebote *m*
rebuff [ri'bʌf] *vt* : rechazar — **~** *n* : desaire *m*
rebuild [ˌri:'bɪld] *vt* **-built; -building** : reconstruir
rebuke [ri'bju:k] *vt* **-buked; -buking** : reprender — **~** *n* : reprimenda *f*
rebut [ri'bʌt] *vt* **-butted; -butting** : rebatir — **rebuttal** [ri'bʌţəl] *n* : refutación *f*
recall [ri'kɔl] *vt* **1** : llamar (al servicio, etc.) **2** REMEMBER : recordar **3** REVOKE : revocar — **~** [ri'kɔl, 'ri:ˌkɔl] *n* **1** : retirada *f* **2** MEMORY : memoria *f*
recant [ri'kænt] *vi* : retractarse
recapitulate [ˌri:kə'pɪtʃəˌleɪt] *v* **-lated; -lating** : recapitular
recapture [ˌri:'kæptʃər] *vt* **-tured; -turing 1** : recobrar **2** RELIVE : revivir
recede [ri'si:d] *vi* **-ceded; -ceding** : retirarse
receipt [ri'si:t] *n* **1** : recibo *m* **2 ~s** *npl* : ingresos *mpl*
receive [ri'si:v] *vt* **-ceived; -ceiving** : recibir — **receiver** [ri'si:vər] *n* **1** : receptor *m* (de radio, etc.) **2** *or* **telephone ~** : auricular *m*
recent ['ri:sənt] *adj* : reciente — **recently** [-li] *adv* : recientemente
receptacle [ri'sɛptɪkəl] *n* : receptáculo *m*, recipiente *m*
reception [ri'sɛpʃən] *n* : recepción *f* — **receptionist** [ri'sɛpʃənɪst] *n* : recepcionista *mf* — **receptive** [ri'sɛptɪv] *adj* : receptivo
recess ['ri:ˌsɛs, rɪ'sɛs] *n* **1** ALCOVE : hueco *m* **2** : recreo *m* (escolar) **3** ADJOURNMENT : suspensión *f* de actividades *Spain*, receso *m Lat* — **recession** [ri'sɛʃən] *n* : recesión *f*
recharge [ˌri:'tʃɑrdʒ] *vt* **-charged; -charging** : recargar — **rechargeable** [ˌri:'tʃɑrdʒəbəl] *adj* : recargable
recipe ['rɛsəˌpi:] *n* : receta *f*
recipient [ri'sɪpiənt] *n* : recipiente *mf*
reciprocal [ri'sɪprəkəl] *adj* : recíproco
recite [ri'saɪt] *vt* **-cited; -citing 1** : recitar (un poema, etc.) **2** LIST : enumerar — **recital** [ri'saɪţəl] *n* : recital *m*
reckless ['rɛkləs] *adj* : imprudente — **recklessness** ['rɛkləsnəs] *n* : imprudencia *f*
reckon ['rɛkən] *vt* **1** COMPUTE : calcular **2** CONSIDER : considerar — **reckoning** ['rɛkənɪŋ] *n* : cálculos *mpl*
reclaim [ri'kleɪm] *vt* **1** : reclamar **2** RECOVER : recuperar
recline [ri'klaɪn] *vi* **-clined; -clining** : reclinarse — **reclining** *adj* : reclinable (dícese de un asiento, etc.)
recluse ['rɛˌklu:s, ri'klu:s] *n* : solitario *m*, -ria *f*
recognition [ˌrɛkɪg'nɪʃən] *n* : reconocimiento *m* — **recognizable** ['rɛkɪgˌnaɪzəbəl] *adj* : reconocible — **recognize** ['rɛkɪgˌnaɪz] *vt* **-nized; -nizing** : reconocer
recoil [ri'kɔɪl] *vi* : retroceder — **~** ['ri:ˌkɔɪl, ri'-] *n* : culatazo *m* (de un arma de fuego)
recollect [ˌrɛkə'lɛkt] *v* : recordar — **recollection** [ˌrɛkə'lɛkʃən] *n* : recuerdo *m*
recommend [ˌrɛkə'mɛnd] *vt* : recomendar — **recommendation** [ˌrɛkəmən'deɪʃən] *n* : recomendación *f*
reconcile ['rɛkənˌsaɪl] *v* **-ciled; -ciling** *vt* **1** : reconciliar (personas), conciliar (datos, etc.) **2 ~ oneself to** : resignarse a — *vi* MAKE UP : reconciliarse — **reconciliation** [ˌrɛkənˌsɪli'eɪʃən] *n* : reconciliación *f*
reconnaissance [ri'kɑnəzənts, -sənts] *n* : reconocimiento *m* (militar)
reconsider [ˌri:kən'sɪdər] *vt* : reconsiderar
reconstruct [ˌri:kən'strʌkt] *vt* : reconstruir
record [ri'kɔrd] *vt* **1** WRITE DOWN : anotar, apuntar **2** REGISTER : registrar **3** : grabar (música, etc.) — **~** ['rɛkərd] *n* **1** DOCUMENT : documento *m* **2** REGISTER : registro *m* **3** HISTORY : historial *m* **4** : disco *m* (de música, etc.) **5 criminal ~** : antecedentes *mpl* penales **6 world ~** : récord *m* mundial — **recorder** [ri'kɔrdər] *n* **1** : flauta *f* dulce **2** *or* **tape ~** : grabadora *f* — **recording** [-ɪŋ] *n* : disco *m* — **record player** *n* : tocadiscos *m*
recount[1] [ri'kaunt] *vt* NARRATE : narrar, relatar
recount[2] ['ri:ˌkaunt, ˌri'-] *vt* : volver a contar (votos, etc.) **~** — *n* : recuento *m*
recourse ['ri:ˌkors, ri'-] *n* **1** : recurso *m* **2 have ~ to** : recurrir a
recover [ri'kʌvər] *vt* : recobrar — *vi* RECUPERATE : recuperarse — **recovery** [ri'kʌvəri] *n, pl* **-eries** : recuperación *f*
recreation [ˌrɛkri'eɪʃən] *n* : recreo *m* — **recreational** [ˌrɛkri'eɪʃənəl] *adj* : de recreo
recruit [ri'kru:t] *vt* : reclutar — **~** *n* : recluta *mf* — **recruitment** [ri'kru:tmənt] *n* : reclutamiento *m*
rectangle ['rɛkˌtæŋgəl] *n* : rectángulo *m* — **rectangular** [rɛk'tæŋgjələr] *adj* : rectangular
rectify ['rɛktəˌfaɪ] *vt* **-fied; -fying** : rectificar
rector ['rɛktər] *n* **1** : párroco *m* (clérigo) **2** : rector *m*, -tora *f* (de una universidad) — **rectory** ['rɛktəri] *n, pl* **-ries** : rectoría *f*
rectum ['rɛktəm] *n, pl* **-tums** *or* **-ta** [-tə] : recto *m*
recuperate [ri'ku:pəˌreɪt, -'kju:-] *v* **-ated; -ating** *vt* : recuperar — *vi* : recuperarse — **recuperation** [riˌku:pə'reɪʃən, -ˌkju:-] *n* : recuperación *f*
recur [ri'kər] *vi* **-curred; -curring** : repetirse — **recurrence** [ri'kərənts] *n* : repetición *f* — **recurrent** [ri'kərənt] *adj* : que se repite
recycle [ri'saɪkəl] *vt* **-cled; -cling** : reciclar
red ['rɛd] *adj* : rojo — **~** *n* : rojo *m* — **redden** ['rɛdən] *vt* : enrojecer — *vi* : enrojecerse — **reddish** ['rɛdɪʃ] *adj* : rojizo
redecorate [ˌri:'dɛkəˌreɪt] *vt* **-rated; -rating** : pintar de nuevo
redeem [ri'di:m] *vt* **1** SAVE : salvar, rescatar **2** : desempeñar (de un monte de piedad) **3** : canjear (cupones, etc.) — **redemption** [ri'dɛmpʃən] *n* : redención *f*
red–handed ['rɛd'hændəd] *adv or adj* : con las manos en la masa
redhead ['rɛdˌhɛd] *n* : pelirrojo *m*, -ja *f*
red–hot ['rɛd'hɑt] *adj* : al rojo vivo
redness ['rɛdnəs] *n* : rojez *f*
redo [ˌri:'du:] *vt* **-did** [-'dɪd]; **-done** [-'dʌn]; **-doing** : hacer de nuevo
redouble [ri'dʌbəl] *vt* **-bled; -bling** : redoblar
red tape *n* : papeleo *m*
reduce [ri'du:s, -'dju:s] *v* **-duced; -ducing** *vt* : reducir — *vi* SLIM : adelgazar — **reduction** [ri'dʌkʃən] *n* : reducción *f*
redundant [ri'dʌndənt] *adj* : redundante
reed ['ri:d] *n* **1** : caña *f* **2** : lengüeta *f* (de un instrumento)
reef ['ri:f] *n* : arrecife *m*
reek ['ri:k] *vi* : apestar
reel ['ri:l] *n* : carrete *m* (de hilo, etc.) — **~** *vt* **1 ~ in** : enrollar (un sedal), sacar (un pez) del agua **2 ~ off** : enumerar — *vi* **1** SPIN : dar vueltas **2** STAGGER : tambalearse
reestablish [ˌri:ɪ'stæblɪʃ] *vt* : restablecer
refer [ri'fər] *v* **-ferred; -ferring** *vt* **1** DIRECT : enviar, mandar **2** SUBMIT : remitir — *vi* **~ to 1** MENTION : referirse a **2** CONSULT : consultar
referee [ˌrɛfə'ri:] *n* : árbitro *m*, -tra *f* — **~** *v* **-eed; -eeing** : arbitrar
reference ['rɛfrənts, 'rɛfə-] *n* **1** : referencia *f* **2** CONSULTATION : consulta *f* **3** *or* **~ book** : libro *m* de consulta **4 in ~ to** : con referencia a
refill [ˌri:'fɪl] *vt* : rellenar — **~** ['ri:ˌfɪl] *n* : recambio *m*
refine [ri'faɪn] *vt* **-fined; -fining** : refinar — **refined** [ri'faɪnd] *adj* : refinado — **refinement** [ri'faɪnmənt] *n* : refinamiento *m* — **refinery** [ri'faɪnəri] *n, pl* **-eries** : refinería *f*
reflect [ri'flɛkt] *vt* : reflejar — *vi* **1** : reflejarse **2 ~ badly on** : desacreditar **3 ~ upon** : reflexionar sobre — **reflection** [ri'flɛkʃən] *n* **1** : reflexión *f* **2** IMAGE : reflejo *m* — **reflector** [ri'flɛktər] *n* : reflector *m*
reflex ['ri:ˌflɛks] *n* : reflejo *m*
reflexive [ri'flɛksɪv] *adj* : reflexivo
reform [ri'fɔrm] *vt* : reformar — *vi* : reformarse — **~** *n* : reforma *f* — **reformer** [ri'fɔrmər] *n* : reformador *m*, -dora *f*
refrain[1] [ri'freɪn] *vi* **~ from** : abstenerse de
refrain[2] *n* : estribillo *m* (en música)
refresh [ri'frɛʃ] *vt* : refrescar — **refreshments** [ri'frɛʃmənts] *npl* : refrigerio *m*

refrigerate [rɪˈfrɪdʒəˌreɪt] *vt* **-ated; -ating** : refrigerar — **refrigeration** [rɪˌfrɪdʒəˈreɪʃən] *n* : refrigeración *f* — **refrigerator** [rɪˈfrɪdʒəˌreɪtər] *n* : nevera *f*, refrigerador *m Lat*, frigorífico *m Spain*
refuel [riːˈfjuːəl] *v* **-eled** *or* **-elled; -eling** *or* **-elling** *vt* : llenar de carburante — *vi* : repostar
refuge [ˈrɛˌfjuːdʒ] *n* : refugio *m* — **refugee** [ˌrɛfjʊˈdʒiː] *n* : refugiado *m*, -da *f*
refund [rɪˈfʌnd, ˈriːˌfʌnd] *vt* : reembolsar — ~ [ˈriːˌfʌnd] *n* : reembolso *m*
refurbish [riˈfərbɪʃ] *vt* : renovar, restaurar
refuse[1] [rɪˈfjuːz] *v* **-fused; -fusing** *vt* **1** : rehusar, rechazar **2 ~ to do sth** : negarse a hacer algo — *vi* : negarse — **refusal** [rɪˈfjuːzəl] *n* : negativa *f*
refuse[2] [ˈrɛˌfjuːs, -ˌfjuːz] *n* : residuos *mpl*, desperdicios *mpl*
refute [rɪˈfjuːt] *vt* **-futed; -futing** : refutar
regain [riːˈgeɪn] *vt* : recuperar, recobrar
regal [ˈriːgəl] *adj* : regio, majestuoso — **regalia** [rɪˈgeɪljə] *n* : ropaje *m*, insignias *fpl*
regard [rɪˈgɑrd] *n* **1** : consideración *f* **2** ESTEEM : estima *f* **3 in this ~** : en este sentido **4 ~s** *npl* : saludos *mpl* **5 with ~ to** : respecto a — ~ *vt* **1** : mirar (con recelo, etc.) **2** HEED : tener en cuenta **3** ESTEEM : estimar **4 as ~s** : en lo que se refiere a **5 ~ as** : considerar — **regarding** [rɪˈgɑrdɪŋ] *prep* : respecto a — **regardless** [rɪˈgɑrdləs] *adv* : a pesar de todo — **regardless of** *prep* **1** : sin tener en cuenta **2** IN SPITE OF : a pesar de
regent [ˈriːdʒənt] *n* : regente *mf*
regime [reɪˈʒiːm, rɪ-] *n* : régimen *m* — **regimen** [ˈrɛdʒəmən] *n* : régimen *m*
regiment [ˈrɛdʒəmənt] *n* : regimiento *m*
region [ˈriːdʒən] *n* : región *f* — **regional** [ˈriːdʒənəl] *adj* : regional
register [ˈrɛdʒəstər] *n* : registro *m* — ~ *vt* **1** : registrar (a personas), matricular (vehículos) **2** SHOW : marcar, manifestar **3** : certificar (correo) — *vi* ENROLL : inscribirse, matricularse — **registrar** [ˈrɛdʒəˌstrɑr] *n* : registrador *m*, -dora *f* oficial — **registration** [ˌrɛdʒəˈstreɪʃən] *n* **1** : inscripción *f*, matriculación *f* **2** *or* **~ number** : número *m* de matrícula — **registry** [ˈrɛdʒəstri] *n, pl* **-tries** : registro *m*
regret [rɪˈgrɛt] *vt* **-gretted; -gretting** : lamentar — ~ *n* **1** REMORSE : arrepentimiento *m* **2** SORROW : pesar *m* — **regrettable** [rɪˈgrɛt̬əbəl] *adj* : lamentable
regular [ˈrɛgjələr] *adj* **1** : regular **2** CUSTOMARY : habitual — ~ *n* : cliente *mf* habitual — **regularity** [ˌrɛgjəˈlærət̬i] *n, pl* **-ties** : regularidad *f* — **regularly** [ˈrɛgjələrli] *adv* : regularmente — **regulate** [ˈrɛgjəˌleɪt] *vt* **-lated; -lating** : regular — **regulation** [ˌrɛgjəˈleɪʃən] *n* **1** CONTROL : regulación *f* **2** RULE : regla *f*
rehabilitate [ˌriːhəˈbɪləˌteɪt, ˌriːə-] *vt* **-tated; -tating** : rehabilitar — **rehabilitation** [ˌriːhəˌbɪləˈteɪʃən, ˌriːə-] *n* : rehabilitación *f*
rehearse [rɪˈhərs] *v* **-hearsed; -hearsing** : ensayar — **rehearsal** [rɪˈhərsəl] *n* : ensayo *m*
reign [ˈreɪn] *n* : reinado *m* — ~ *vi* : reinar
reimburse [ˌriːəmˈbərs] *vt* **-bursed; -bursing** : reembolsar — **reimbursement** [ˌriːəmˈbərsmənt] *n* : reembolso *m*
rein [ˈreɪn] *n* : rienda *f*
reincarnation [ˌriːɪnˌkɑrˈneɪʃən] *n* : reencarnación *f*
reindeer [ˈreɪnˌdɪr] *n* : reno *m*
reinforce [ˌriːənˈfors] *vt* **-forced; -forcing** : reforzar — **reinforcement** [ˌriːənˈforsmənt] *n* : refuerzo *m*
reinstate [ˌriːənˈsteɪt] *vt* **-stated; -stating 1** : restablecer **2** : restituir (a algn en su cargo)
reiterate [riˈɪt̬əˌreɪt] *vt* **-ated; -ating** : reiterar
reject [rɪˈdʒɛkt] *vt* : rechazar — **rejection** [rɪˈdʒɛkʃən] *n* : rechazo *m*
rejoice [rɪˈdʒɔɪs] *vi* **-joiced; -joicing** : regocijarse
rejuvenate [rɪˈdʒuːvəˌneɪt] *vt* **-nated; -nating** : rejuvenecer
rekindle [ˌriːˈkɪndəl] *vt* **-dled; -dling** : reavivar
relapse [ˈriːˌlæps, rɪˈlæps] *n* : recaída *f* — ~ [rɪˈlæps] *vi* **-lapsed; -lapsing** : recaer
relate [rɪˈleɪt] *v* **-lated; -lating** *vt* **1** TELL : relatar **2** ASSOCIATE : relacionar — *vi* **~ to 1** CONCERN : estar relacionado con **2** UNDERSTAND : identificarse con **3** : relacionarse con (socialmente) — **related** [rɪˈleɪt̬əd] *adj* **~ to** : emparentado con — **relation** [rɪˈleɪʃən] *n* **1** CONNECTION : relación *f* **2** RELATIVE : pariente *mf* **3 in ~ to** : en relación con **4 ~s** *npl* : relaciones *fpl* — **relationship** [rɪˈleɪʃənˌʃɪp] *n* **1** : relación *f* **2** KINSHIP : parentesco *m* — **relative** [ˈrɛlət̬ɪv] *n* : pariente *mf* — ~ *adj* : relativo — **relatively** *adv* : relativamente
relax [rɪˈlæks] *vt* : relajar — *vi* : relajarse — **relaxation** [ˌriːˌlækˈseɪʃən] *n* **1** : relajación *f* **2** RECREATION : esparcimiento *m*
relay [ˈriːˌleɪ] *n* **1** : relevo *m* **2** *or* **~ race** : carrera *f* de relevos — ~ [ˈriːˌleɪ, rɪˈleɪ] *vt* **-layed; -laying** : transmitir
release [rɪˈliːs] *vt* **-leased; -leasing 1** FREE : liberar, poner en libertad **2** : soltar (un freno, etc.) **3** EMIT : despedir **4** : sacar (un libro, etc.), estrenar (una película) — ~ *n* **1** : liberación *f* **2** : estreno *m* (de una película), publicación *f* (de un libro) **3** : fuga *f* (de gases)
relegate [ˈrɛləˌgeɪt] *vt* **-gated; -gating** : relegar
relent [rɪˈlɛnt] *vi* : ceder — **relentless** [rɪˈlɛntləs] *adj* : implacable
relevant [ˈrɛləvənt] *adj* : pertinente — **relevance** [ˈrɛləvənts] *n* : pertinencia *f*
reliable [rɪˈlaɪəbəl] *adj* : fiable (dícese de personas), fidedigno (dícese de información, etc.) — **reliability** [rɪˌlaɪəˈbɪlət̬i] *n, pl* **-ties** : fiabilidad *f* (de una cosa), responsabilidad *f* (de una persona) — **reliance** [rɪˈlaɪənts] *n* **1** : dependencia *f* **2** TRUST : confianza *f* — **reliant** [rɪˈlaɪənt] *adj* : dependente
relic [ˈrɛlɪk] *n* : reliquia *f*
relief [rɪˈliːf] *n* **1** : alivio *m* **2** AID : ayuda *f* **3** : relieve *m* (en la escultura) **4** REPLACEMENT : relevo *m* — **relieve** [rɪˈliːv] *vt* **-lieved; -lieving 1** : aliviar **2** REPLACE : relevar (a algn) **3 ~ s.o. of** : liberar a algn de
religion [rɪˈlɪdʒən] *n* : religión *f* — **religious** [rɪˈlɪdʒəs] *adj* : religioso
relinquish [rɪˈlɪŋkwɪʃ, -ˈlɪn-] *vt* : renunciar a, abandonar
relish [ˈrɛlɪʃ] *n* **1** : salsa *f* (condimento) **2 with ~** : con gusto — ~ *vt* : saborear
relocate [ˌriːˈloːˌkeɪt, ˌriːloˈkeɪt] *vt* **-cated; -cating** : trasladar — *vi* : trasladarse — **relocation** [ˌriːloˈkeɪʃən] *n* : traslado *m*
reluctance [rɪˈlʌktənts] *n* : reticencia *f*, desgana *f* — **reluctant** [rɪˈlʌktənt] *adj* : reacio, reticente — **reluctantly** [rɪˈlʌktəntli] *adv* : a regañadientes
rely [rɪˈlaɪ] *vi* **-lied; -lying ~ on 1** DEPEND ON : depender de **2** TRUST : confiar (en)
remain [rɪˈmeɪn] *vi* **1** : quedar **2** STAY : quedarse **3** CONTINUE : seguir, continuar — **remainder** [rɪˈmeɪndər] *n* : resto *m* — **remains** [rɪˈmeɪnz] *npl* : restos *mpl*
remark [rɪˈmɑrk] *n* : comentario *m*, observación *f* — ~ *vt* : observar — *vi* **~ on** : observar — **remarkable** [rɪˈmɑrkəbəl] *adj* : extraordinario, notable
remedy [ˈrɛmədi] *n, pl* **-dies** : remedio *m* — ~ *vt* **-died; -dying** : remediar — **remedial** [rɪˈmiːdiəl] *adj* : correctivo
remember [rɪˈmɛmbər] *vt* **1** : acordarse de, recordar **2 ~ to** : acordarse de — *vi* : acordarse, recordar — **remembrance** [rɪˈmɛmbrənts] *n* : recuerdo *m*
remind [rɪˈmaɪnd] *vt* : recordar — **reminder** [rɪˈmaɪndər] *n* : recordatorio *m*
reminiscence [ˌrɛməˈnɪsənts] *n* : recuerdo *m*, reminiscencia *f* — **reminisce** [ˌrɛməˈnɪs] *vi* **-nisced; -niscing** : rememorar los viejos tiempos — **reminiscent** [ˌrɛməˈnɪsənt] *adj* **be ~ of** : recordar
remiss [rɪˈmɪs] *adj* : negligente, remiso
remit [rɪˈmɪt] *vt* **-mitted; -mitting 1** PARDON : perdonar **2** : enviar (dinero) — **remission** [rɪˈmɪʃən] *n* : remisión *f*
remnant [ˈrɛmnənt] *n* **1** : resto *m* **2** TRACE : vestigio *m*
remorse [rɪˈmɔrs] *n* : remordimiento *m* — **remorseful** [rɪˈmɔrsfəl] *adj* : arrepentido
remote [rɪˈmoːt] *adj* **-moter; -est 1** : remoto **2** ALOOF : distante **3 ~ from** : apartado de, alejado de — **remote control** *n* : control *m* remoto — **remotely** [rɪˈmoːtli] *adv* SLIGHTLY : remotamente
remove [rɪˈmuːv] *vt* **-moved; -moving 1** : quitar (una tapa, etc.), quitarse (ropa) **2** EXTRACT : sacar **3** DISMISS : destituir **4** ELIMINATE : eliminar — **removable** [rɪˈmuːvəbəl] *adj* : separable, de quita y pon — **removal** [rɪˈmuːvəl] *n* **1** : eliminación *f* **2** EXTRACTION : extracción *f*
remunerate [rɪˈmjuːnəˌreɪt] *vt* **-ated; -ating** : remunerar
render [ˈrɛndər] *vt* **1** : rendir (homenaje), prestar (ayuda) **2** MAKE : hacer **3** TRANSLATE : traducir
rendezvous [ˈrɑndɪˌvuː, -deɪ-] *ns & pl* : cita *f*
rendition [rɛnˈdɪʃən] *n* : interpretación *f*
renegade [ˈrɛnɪˌgeɪd] *n* : renegado *m*, -da *f*
renew [rɪˈnuː, -ˈnjuː] *vt* **1** : renovar **2** RESUME : reanudar — **renewal** [rɪˈnuːəl, -ˈnjuː-] *n* : renovación *f*
renounce [rɪˈnaʊnts] *vt* **-nounced; -nouncing** : renunciar a
renovate [ˈrɛnəˌveɪt] *vt* **-vated; -vating** : renovar — **renovation** [ˌrɛnəˈveɪʃən] *n* : renovación *f*
renown [rɪˈnaʊn] *n* : renombre *m* — **renowned** [rɪˈnaʊnd] *adj* : célebre, renombrado
rent [ˈrɛnt] *n* **1** : alquiler *m*, arrendamiento *m*, renta *f* **2 for ~** : se alquila — ~ *vt* : alquilar — **rental** [ˈrɛntəl] *n* : alquiler *m* — ~ *adj* : de alquiler — **renter** [ˈrɛntər] *n* : arrendatario *m*, -ria *f*
renunciation [rɪˌnʌntsiˈeɪʃən] *n* : renuncia *f*
reopen [ˌriˈoːpən] *vt* : volver a abrir
reorganize [ˌriˈɔrgənˌaɪz] *vt* **-nized; -nizing** : reorganizar — **reorganization** [ˌriːˌɔrgənəˈzeɪʃən] *n* : reorganización *f*
repair [rɪˈpær] *vt* : reparar, arreglar — ~ *n* **1** : reparación *f*, arreglo *m* **2 in bad ~** : en mal estado
repay [riˈpeɪ] *vt* **-paid; -paying 1** : devolver (dinero), pagar (una deuda) **2** : corresponder a (un favor, etc.)
repeal [rɪˈpiːl] *vt* : abrogar, revocar — ~ *n* : abrogación *f*, revocación *f*
repeat [rɪˈpiːt] *vt* : repetir — ~ *n* : repetición *f* — **repeatedly** [rɪˈpiːt̬ədli] *adv* : repetidas veces
repel [rɪˈpɛl] *vt* **-pelled; -pelling** : repeler — **repellent** [rɪˈpɛlənt] *n* : repelente *m*
repent [rɪˈpɛnt] *vi* : arrepentirse — **repentance** [rɪˈpɛntənts] *n* : arrepentimiento *m*
repercussion [ˌriːpərˈkʌʃən, ˌrɛpər-] *n* : repercusión *f*
repertoire [ˈrɛpərˌtwɑr] *n* : repertorio *m*
repetition [ˌrɛpəˈtɪʃən] *n* : repetición *f* — **repetitious** [ˌrɛpəˈtɪʃəs] *adj* : repetitivo — **repetitive** [rɪˈpɛt̬ət̬ɪv] *adj* : repetitivo
replace [rɪˈpleɪs] *vt* **-placed; -placing 1** : reponer **2** SUBSTITUTE : reemplazar, sustituir **3** EXCHANGE : cambiar — **replacement** [rɪˈpleɪsmənt] *n* **1** : sustitución *f* **2** : sustituto *m*, -ta *f* (persona) **3** *or* **~ part** : repuesto *m*
replenish [rɪˈplɛnɪʃ] *vt* **1** : reponer **2** REFILL : rellenar
replete [rɪˈpliːt] *adj* **~ with** : repleto de
replica [ˈrɛplɪkə] *n* : réplica *f*
reply [rɪˈplaɪ] *vi* **-plied; -plying** : contestar, responder — ~ *n, pl* **-plies** : respuesta *f*
report [rɪˈport] *n* **1** : informe *m* **2** RUMOR : rumor *m* **3** *or* **news ~** : reportaje *m* **4 weather ~** : boletín *m* meteorológico — ~ *vt* **1** RELATE : anunciar **2 ~ a crime** : denunciar un delito **3** *or* **~ on** : informar sobre — *vi* **1** : informar **2 ~ for duty** : presentarse — **report card** *n* : boletín *m* de calificaciones — **reportedly** [rɪˈportədli] *adv* : según se dice — **reporter** [rɪˈport̬ər] *n* : periodista *mf*; reportero *m*, -ra *f*
repose [rɪˈpoːz] *vi* **-posed; -posing** : reposar — ~ *n* : reposo *m*
reprehensible [ˌrɛprɪˈhɛntsəbəl] *adj* : reprensible
represent [ˌrɛprɪˈzɛnt] *vt* **1** : representar **2** PORTRAY : presentar — **representation** [ˌrɛprɪˌzɛnˈteɪʃən, -zən-] *n* : representación *f* — **representative** [ˌrɛprɪˈzɛnt̬ət̬ɪv] *adj* : representativo — ~ *n* : representante *mf*
repress [rɪˈprɛs] *vt* : reprimir — **repression** [rɪˈprɛʃən] *n* : represión *f*
reprieve [rɪˈpriːv] *n* : indulto *m*
reprimand [ˈrɛprəˌmænd] *n* : reprimenda *f* — ~ *vt* : reprender
reprint [riˈprɪnt] *vt* : reimprimir — ~ [ˈriːˌprɪnt, riˈprɪnt] *n* : reedición *f*
reprisal [rɪˈpraɪzəl] *n* : represalia *f*
reproach [rɪˈproːtʃ] *n* **1** : reproche *m* **2 beyond ~** : irreprochable — ~ *vt* : reprochar — **reproachful** [rɪˈproːtʃfəl] *adj* : de reproche
reproduce [ˌriːprəˈduːs, -ˈdjuːs] *v* **-duced; -ducing** *vt* : reproducir — *vi* : reproducirse — **reproduction** [ˌriːprəˈdʌkʃən] *n* : reproducción *f* — **reproductive** [ˌriːprəˈdʌktɪv] *adj* : reproductor
reproof [rɪˈpruːf] *n* : reprobación *f*
reptile [ˈrɛpˌtaɪl] *n* : reptil *m*
republic [rɪˈpʌblɪk] *n* : república *f* — **republican** [rɪˈpʌblɪkən] *n* : republicano *m*, -na *f* — ~ *adj* : republicano
repudiate [rɪˈpjuːdiˌeɪt] *vt* **-ated; -ating** : repudiar
repugnant [rɪˈpʌgnənt] *adj* : repugnante, asqueroso — **repugnance** [rɪˈpʌgnənts] *n* : repugnancia *f*
repulse [rɪˈpʌls] *vt* **-pulsed; -pulsing** : repeler, rechazar — **repulsive** [rɪˈpʌlsɪv] *adj* : repulsivo
reputation [ˌrɛpjəˈteɪʃən] *n* : reputación *f* — **reputable** [ˈrɛpjət̬əbəl] *adj* : de confianza, acreditado — **reputed** [rɪˈpjuːt̬əd] *adj* : supuesto
request [rɪˈkwɛst] *n* : petición *f* — ~ *vt* : pedir
requiem [ˈrɛkwiəm, ˈreɪ-] *n* : réquiem *m*
require [rɪˈkwaɪr] *vt* **-quired; -quiring 1** CALL FOR : requerir **2** NEED : necesitar — **requirement** [rɪˈkwaɪrmənt] *n* **1** NEED : necesidad *f* **2** DEMAND : requisito *m* — **requisite** [ˈrɛkwəzɪt] *adj* : necesario
resale [ˈriːˌseɪl, ˌriːˈseɪl] *n* : reventa *f*
rescind [rɪˈsɪnd] *vt* : rescindir (un contrato), revocar (una ley, etc.)
rescue [ˈrɛsˌkjuː] *vt* **-cued; -cuing** : rescatar, salvar — ~ *n* : rescate *m* — **rescuer** [ˈrɛskjuər] *n* : salvador *m*, -dora *f*
research [rɪˈsərtʃ, ˈriːˌsərtʃ] *n* : investigación *f* — ~ *vt* : investigar — **researcher** [rɪˈsərtʃər, ˈriːˌ-] *n* : investigador *m*, -dora *f*
resemble [rɪˈzɛmbəl] *vt* **-sembled; -sembling** : parecerse a — **resemblance** [rɪˈzɛmbləntss] *n* : parecido *m*
resent [rɪˈzɛnt] *vt* : resentirse de, ofenderse por — **resentful** [rɪˈzɛntfəl] *adj* : resentido — **resentment** [rɪˈzɛntmənt] *n* : resentimiento *m*
reserve [rɪˈzərv] *vt* **-served; -serving** : reservar — ~ *n* **1** : reserva *f* **2 ~s** *npl* : reservas *fpl* (militares) — **reservation** [ˌrɛzərˈveɪʃən] *n* : reserva *f* — **reserved** [rɪˈzərvd] *adj* : reservado — **reservoir** [ˈrɛzərˌvwɑr, -ˌvwɔr, -ˌvɔr] *n* : embalse *m*
reset [ˌriːˈsɛt] *vt* **-set; -setting** : volver a poner (un reloj, etc.)
residence [ˈrɛzədənts] *n* : residencia *f* — **reside** [rɪˈzaɪd] *vi* **-sided; -siding** : residir — **resident** [ˈrɛzədənt] *adj* : residente — ~ *n* : residente *mf* — **residential** [ˌrɛzəˈdɛntʃəl] *adj* : residencial
residue [ˈrɛzəˌduː, -ˌdjuː] *n* : residuo *m*
resign [rɪˈzaɪn] *vt* **1** QUIT : dimitir **2 ~ oneself to** : resignarse a — **resignation** [ˌrɛzɪgˈneɪʃən] *n* **1** : dimisión *f* **2** ACCEPTANCE : resignación *f*
resilient [rɪˈzɪljənt] *adj* **1** : resistente (dícese de personas) **2** ELASTIC : elástico — **resilience** [rɪˈzɪljənts] *n* **1** : resistencia *f* **2** ELASTICITY : elasticidad *f*
resin [ˈrɛzən] *n* : resina *f*
resist [rɪˈzɪst] *vt* : resistir — *vi* : resistirse — **resistance** [rɪˈzɪstənts] *n* : resistencia *f* — **resistant** [rɪˈzɪstənt] *adj* : resistente
resolve [rɪˈzɑlv] *vt* **-solved; -solving** : resolver — ~ *n* : resolución *f* — **resolution** [ˌrɛzəˈluːʃən] *n* **1** : resolución *f* **2** DECISION, INTENTION : propósito *m* — **resolute** [ˈrɛzəˌluːt] *adj* : resuelto
resonance [ˈrɛzənənts] *n* : resonancia *f* — **resonant** [ˈrɛzənənt] *adj* : resonante
resort [rɪˈzɔrt] *n* **1** RECOURSE : recurso *m* **2** *or* **tourist ~** : centro *m* turístico — ~ *vi* **~ to** : recurrir a
resounding [rɪˈzaʊndɪŋ] *adj* **1** RESONANT : resonante **2** ABSOLUTE : rotundo
resource [ˈriːˌsors, rɪˈsors] *n* : recurso *m* — **resourceful** [rɪˈsorsfəl, -ˈzors-] *adj* : ingenioso
respect [rɪˈspɛkt] *n* **1** ESTEEM : respeto *m* **2 in some ~s** : en algún sentido **3 pay one's ~s** : presentar uno sus respetos **4 with ~ to** : (con) respecto a — ~ *vt* : respetar — **respectable** [rɪˈspɛktəbəl] *adj* : respetable — **respectful** [rɪˈspɛktfəl] *adj* : respetuoso — **respective** [rɪˈspɛktɪv] *adj* : respectivo — **respectively** *adv* : respectivamente
respiration [ˌrɛspəˈreɪʃən] *n* : respiración *f* — **respiratory** [ˈrɛspərəˌtori, rɪˈspaɪrə-] *adj* : respiratorio
respite [ˈrɛspɪt, rɪˈspaɪt] *n* : respiro *m*
response [rɪˈspɑnts] *n* : respuesta *f* — **respond** [rɪˈspɑnd] *vi* : responder — **responsibility** [rɪˌspɑntsəˈbɪlət̬i] *n, pl* **-ties** : responsabilidad *f* — **responsible** [rɪˈspɑntsəbəl] *adj* : responsable — **responsive** [rɪˈspɑntsɪv] *adj* : sensible, receptivo
rest[1] [ˈrɛst] *n* **1** : descanso *m* **2** SUPPORT : apoyo *m* **3** : silencio *m* (en música) — ~ *vi* **1** : descansar **2** LEAN : apoyarse **3 ~ on** DEPEND ON : depender de — *vt* **1** RELAX : descansar **2** LEAN : apoyar
rest[2] *n* REMAINDER : resto *m*
restaurant [ˈrɛstəˌrɑnt, -rənt] *n* : restaurante *m*
restful [ˈrɛstfəl] *adj* : tranquilo, apacible
restitution [ˌrɛstəˈtuːʃən, -ˈtjuː-] *n* : restitución *f*
restless [ˈrɛstləs] *adj* : inquieto, agitado
restore [rɪˈstor] *vt* **-stored; -storing 1** RETURN : devolver **2** REESTABLISH : restablecer **3** REPAIR : restaurar — **restoration** [ˌrɛstəˈreɪʃən] *n* **1** : restablecimiento *m* **2** REPAIR : restauración *f*
restrain [rɪˈstreɪn] *vt* **1** : contener **2 ~ oneself** : contenerse — **restrained** [rɪˈstreɪnd] *adj* : comedido, moderado — **restraint** [rɪˈstreɪnt] *n* **1** : restricción *f* **2** SELF-CONTROL : moderación *f*, control *m* de sí mismo
restriction [rɪˈstrɪkʃən] *n* : restricción *f* — **restrict** [rɪˈstrɪkt] *vt* : restringir — **restricted** [rɪˈstrɪktəd] *adj* : restringido — **restrictive** [rɪˈstrɪktɪv] *adj* : restrictivo
result [rɪˈzʌlt] *vi* : resultar — ~ *n* **1** : resultado *m* **2 as a ~ of** : como consecuencia de
resume [rɪˈzuːm] *v* **-sumed; -suming** *vt* : reanudar — *vi* : reanudarse
résumé *or* **resume** *or* **resumé** [ˈrɛzəˌmeɪ, ˌrɛzəˈ-] *n* : currículum *m* (vitae)
resumption [rɪˈzʌmpʃən] *n* : reanudación *f*
resurgence [rɪˈsərdʒənts] *n* : resurgimiento *m*
resurrection [ˌrɛzəˈrɛkʃən] *n* : resurrección *f* — **resurrect** [ˌrɛzəˈrɛkt] *vt* : resucitar
resuscitate [rɪˈsʌsəˌteɪt] *vt* **-tated; -tating** : resucitar
retail [ˈriːˌteɪl] *vt* : vender al por menor — ~ *n* : venta *f* al por menor — ~ *adj* : detallista, minorista — ~ *adv* : al detalle, al por menor — **retailer** [ˈriːˌteɪlər] *n* : detallista *mf*, minorista *mf*
retain [rɪˈteɪn] *vt* : retener
retaliate [rɪˈtæliˌeɪt] *vi* **-ated; -ating** : tomar represalias — **retaliation** [rɪˌtæliˈeɪʃən] *n* : represalias *fpl*
retard [rɪˈtɑrd] *vt* : retardar, retrasar — **retarded** [rɪˈtɑrdəd] *adj* : retrasado
retention [rɪˈtɛntʃən] *n* : retención *f*
reticence [ˈrɛt̬əsənts] *n* : reticencia *f* — **reticent** [ˈrɛt̬əsənt] *adj* : reticente
retina [ˈrɛtənə] *n, pl* **-nas** *or* **-nae** [-əni, -ənˌaɪ] : retina *f*
retinue [ˈrɛtənˌuː, -ˌjuː] *n* : séquito *m*
retire [rɪˈtaɪr] *vi* **-tired; -tiring 1** WITHDRAW : retirarse **2** : jubilarse, retirarse (de un trabajo) **3** : acostarse (en la cama) — **retirement** [rɪˈtaɪrmənt] *n* : jubilación *f* — **retiring** [rɪˈtaɪrɪŋ] *adj* SHY : retraído
retort [rɪˈtɔrt] *vt* : replicar — ~ *n* : réplica *f*

retrace [ˌriːˈtreɪs] *vt* **-traced; -tracing ~ one's steps** : volver sobre sus pasos

retract [riˈtrækt] *vt* **1** WITHDRAW : retirar **2** : retraer (garras, etc.) — *vi* : retractarse

retrain [ˌriːˈtreɪn] *vt* : reciclar

retreat [riˈtriːt] *n* **1** : retirada *f* **2** REFUGE : refugio *m* — **~** *vi* : retirarse

retribution [ˌretrəˈbjuːʃən] *n* : castigo *m*

retrieve [riˈtriːv] *vt* **-trieved; -trieving 1** : cobrar, recuperar **2** RESCUE : salvar — **retrieval** [riˈtriːvəl] *n* : recuperación *f* — **retriever** [riˈtriːvər] *n* : perro *m* cobrador

retroactive [ˌretroˈæktɪv] *adj* : retroactivo

retrospect [ˈretrəˌspekt] *n* **in ~** : mirando hacia atrás — **retrospective** [ˌretrəˈspektɪv] *adj* : retrospectivo

return [riˈtərn] *vi* **1** : volver, regresar **2** REAPPEAR : reaparecer — *vt* **1** : devolver **2** YIELD : producir — **~** *n* **1** : regreso *m*, vuelta *f* **2** : devolución *f* (de algo prestado) **3** YIELD : rendimiento *m* **4 in ~ for** : a cambio de **5** *or* **tax ~** : declaración *f* de impuestos — **~** *adj* : de vuelta

reunite [ˌriːjʊˈnaɪt] *vt* **-nited; -niting** : reunir — **reunion** [riˈjuːnjən] *n* : reunión *f*

revamp [ˌriˈvæmp] *vt* : renovar

reveal [riˈviːl] *vt* **1** : revelar **2** SHOW : dejar ver

revel [ˈrevəl] *vi* **-eled** *or* **-elled; -eling** *or* **-elling ~ in** : deleitarse en

revelation [ˌrevəˈleɪʃən] *n* : revelación *f*

revelry [ˈrevəlri] *n, pl* **-ries** : jolgorio *m*, regocijos *mpl*

revenge [riˈvendʒ] *vt* **-venged; -venging** : vengar — **~** *n* **1** : venganza *f* **2 take ~ on** : vengarse de

revenue [ˈrevəˌnuː, -ˌnjuː] *n* : ingresos *mpl*

reverberate [riˈvərbəˌreɪt] *vi* **-ated; -ating** : retumbar, resonar

reverence [ˈrevərənts] *n* : reverencia *f*, veneración *f* — **revere** [riˈvɪr] *vt* **-vered; -vering** : venerar — **reverend** [ˈrevərənd] *adj* : reverendo — **reverent** [ˈrevərənt] *adj* : reverente

reverie [ˈrevəri] *n, pl* **-eries** : ensueño *m*

reverse [riˈvərs] *adj* : inverso, contrario — **~** *v* **-versed; -versing** *vt* **1** : invertir **2** : cambiar (una política), revocar (una decisión) **3** : dar marcha atrás a (un automóvil) — *vi* : invertirse — **~** *n* **1** BACK : dorso *m*, revés *m* **2** *or* **~ gear** : marcha *f* atrás **3 the ~** : lo contrario — **reversible** [riˈvərsəbəl] *adj* : reversible — **reversal** [riˈvərsəl] *n* **1** : inversión *f* **2** CHANGE : cambio *m* total **3** SETBACK : revés *m* — **revert** [riˈvərt] *vi* : revertir

review [riˈvjuː] *n* **1** : revisión *f* **2** OVERVIEW : resumen *m* **3** CRITIQUE : reseña *f*, crítica *f* **4** : repaso *m* (para un examen) — **~** *vt* **1** EXAMINE : examinar **2** : repasar (una lección) **3** CRITIQUE : reseñar — **reviewer** [riˈvjuːər] *n* : crítico *m*, -ca *f*

revile [riˈvaɪl] *vt* **-viled; -viling** : injuriar

revise [riˈvaɪz] *vt* **-vised; -vising 1** : modificar (una política, etc.) **2** : revisar, corregir (una publicación) — **revision** [riˈvɪʒən] *n* : corrección *f*, modificación *f*

revive [riˈvaɪv] *v* **-vived; -viving** *vt* **1** : reanimar, reactivar **2** : resucitar (a una persona) **3** RESTORE : restablecer — *vi* **1** : reanimarse, reactivarse **2** COME TO : volver en sí — **revival** [riˈvaɪvəl] *n* : reanimación *f*, reactivación *f*

revoke [riˈvoːk] *vt* **-voked; -voking** : revocar

revolt [riˈvoːlt] *vi* : rebelarse, sublevarse — *vt* : dar asco a — **~** *n* : revuelta *f*, sublevación *f* — **revolting** [riˈvoːltɪŋ] *adj* : asqueroso

revolution [ˌrevəˈluːʃən] *n* : revolución *f* — **revolutionary** [ˌrevəˈluːʃənˌeri] *adj* : revolucionario — **~** *n, pl* **-aries** : revolucionario *m*, -ria *f* — **revolutionize** [ˌrevəˈluːʃənˌaɪz] *vt* **-ized; -izing** : revolucionar

revolve [riˈvɑlv] *v* **-volved; -volving** *vt* : hacer girar — *vi* : girar

revolver [riˈvɑlvər] *n* : revólver *m*

revue [riˈvjuː] *n* : revista *f* (teatral)

revulsion [riˈvʌlʃən] *n* : repugnancia *f*

reward [riˈwɔrd] *vt* : recompensar — **~** *n* : recompensa *f*

rewrite [ˌriːˈraɪt] *vt* **-wrote; -written; -writing** : volver a escribir

rhetoric [ˈretərɪk] *n* : retórica *f* — **rhetorical** [rɪˈtɔrɪkəl] *adj* : retórico

rheumatism [ˈruːməˌtɪzəm, ˈrʊ-] *n* : reumatismo *m* — **rheumatic** [rʊˈmætɪk] *adj* : reumático

rhino [ˈraɪˌnoː] *n, pl* **-no** *or* **-nos → rhinoceros — rhinoceros** [raɪˈnɑsərəs] *n, pl* **-noceroses** *or* **-noceros** *or* **-noceri** [-ˌraɪ] : rinoceronte *m*

rhubarb [ˈruːˌbɑrb] *n* : ruibarbo *m*

rhyme [ˈraɪm] *n* **1** : rima *f* **2** VERSE : verso *m* (en rima) — **~** *vi* **rhymed; rhyming** : rimar

rhythm [ˈrɪðəm] *n* : ritmo *m* — **rhythmic** [ˈrɪðmɪk] *or* **rhythmical** [-mɪkəl] *adj* : rítmico

rib [ˈrɪb] *n* : costilla *f* — **~** *vt* TEASE : tomar el pelo a

ribbon [ˈrɪbən] *n* : cinta *f*

rice [ˈraɪs] *n* : arroz *m*

rich [ˈrɪtʃ] *adj* **1** : rico **2 ~ foods** : comidas *fpl* pesadas — **riches** [ˈrɪtʃəz] *npl* : riquezas *fpl* — **richness** [ˈrɪtʃnəs] *n* : riqueza *f*

rickety [ˈrɪkəṭi] *adj* : desvencijado, destartalado

ricochet [ˈrɪkəˌʃeɪ, -ˌʃet] *n* : rebote *m* — **~** *vi* **-cheted** [-ˌʃeɪd] *or* **-chetted** [-ˌʃeṭəd]; **-cheting** [-ˌʃeɪɪŋ] *or* **-chetting** [-ˌʃeṭɪŋ] : rebotar

rid [ˈrɪd] *vt* **rid; ridding 1** : librar **2 get ~ of** : deshacerse de — **riddance** [ˈrɪdənts] *n* **good ~!** : ¡adiós y buen viaje!

riddle[1] [ˈrɪdəl] *n* : acertijo *m*, adivinanza *f*

riddle[2] *vt* **-dled; -dling 1** : acribillar **2 riddled with** : lleno de

ride [ˈraɪd] *v* **rode** [ˈroːd]; **ridden** [ˈrɪdən]; **riding** *vt* **1** : montar (a caballo, en bicicleta), ir (en autobús, etc.) **2** TRAVERSE : recorrer — *vi* **1** *or* **~ horseback** : montar a caballo **2** : ir (en auto, etc.) — **~** *n* **1** : paseo *m*, vuelta *f* **2** : aparato *m* (en un parque de diversiones) — **rider** [ˈraɪdər] *n* **1** : jinete *mf* (a caballo) **2** CYCLIST : ciclista *mf*, motociclista *mf*

ridge [ˈrɪdʒ] *n* : cadena *f* (de montañas)

ridiculous [rəˈdɪkjələs] *adj* : ridículo — **ridicule** [ˈrɪdəˌkjuːl] *n* : burlas *fpl* — **~** *vt* **-culed; -culing** : ridiculizar

rife [ˈraɪf] *adj* **1** : extendido **2 be ~ with** : estar plagado de

rifle[1] [ˈraɪfəl] *vi* **-fled; -fling ~ through** : revolver

rifle[2] *n* : rifle *m*, fusil *m*

rift [ˈrɪft] *n* **1** : grieta *f* **2** : ruptura *f* (entre personas)

rig[1] [ˈrɪg] *vt* : amañar (una elección)

rig[2] *vt* **rigged; rigging 1** : aparejar (un barco) **2** EQUIP : equipar **3** *or* **~ out** DRESS : vestir **4** *or* **~ up** CONSTRUCT : construir — **~** *n* **1** : aparejo *m* (de un barco) **2** *or* **oil ~** : plataforma *f* petrolífera — **rigging** [ˈrɪgɪŋ, -gən] *n* : aparejo *m*

right [ˈraɪt] *adj* **1** JUST : bueno, justo **2** CORRECT : correcto **3** APPROPRIATE : apropiado, adecuado **4** STRAIGHT : recto **5 be ~** : tener razón **6 → right–hand** — **~** *n* **1** GOOD : bien *m* **2** ENTITLEMENT : derecho *m* **3 on the ~** : a la derecha **4** *or* **~ side** : derecha *f* — **~** *adv* **1** WELL : bien **2** PRECISELY : justo **3** DIRECTLY : derecho **4** IMMEDIATELY : inmediatamente **5** COMPLETELY : completamente **6** *or* **to the ~** : a la derecha — **~** *vt* **1** STRAIGHTEN : enderezar **2 ~ a wrong** : reparar un daño — **right angle** *n* : ángulo *m* recto — **righteous** [ˈraɪtʃəs] *adj* : recto, honrado — **rightful** [ˈraɪtfəl] *adj* : legítimo — **right–hand** [ˈraɪtˈhænd] *adj* : derecho — **right–handed** [ˈraɪtˈhændəd] *adj* : diestro — **rightly** [ˈraɪtli] *adv* **1** : justamente **2** CORRECTLY : correctamente — **right–wing** [ˈraɪtˈwɪŋ] *adj* : derechista

rigid [ˈrɪdʒɪd] *adj* : rígido

rigor *or Brit* **rigour** [ˈrɪgər] *n* : rigor *m* — **rigorous** [ˈrɪgərəs] *adj* : riguroso

rim [ˈrɪm] *n* **1** EDGE : borde *m* **2** : llanta *f* (de una rueda) **3** : montura *f* (de anteojos)

rind [ˈraɪnd] *n* : corteza *f*

ring[1] [ˈrɪŋ] *v* **rang** [ˈræŋ]; **rung** [ˈrʌŋ]; **ringing** *vi* **1** : sonar (dícese de un timbre, etc.) **2** RESOUND : resonar — *vt* : tocar (un timbre, etc.) — **~** *n* **1** : toque *m* (de un timbre, etc.) **2** CALL : llamada *f* (por teléfono)

ring[2] *n* **1** : anillo *m*, sortija *f* **2** BAND, HOOP : aro *m* **3** CIRCLE : círculo *m* **4** *or* **boxing ~** : cuadrilátero *m* **5** NETWORK : red *f* — **~** *vt* : cercar, rodear — **ringleader** [ˈrɪŋˌliːdər] *n* : cabecilla *mf*

ringlet [ˈrɪŋlət] *n* : rizo *m*, bucle *m*

rink [ˈrɪŋk] *n* : pista *f* (de patinaje)

rinse [ˈrɪnts] *vt* **rinsed; rinsing** : enjuagar — **~** *n* : enjuague *m*

riot [ˈraɪət] *n* : disturbio *m* — **~** *vi* : causar disturbios — **rioter** [ˈraɪəṭər] *n* : alborotador *m*, -dora *f*

rip [ˈrɪp] *v* **ripped; ripping** *vt* **1** : rasgar, desgarrar **2 ~ off** : arrancar — *vi* : rasgarse — **~** *n* : rasgón *m*, desgarrón *m*

ripe [ˈraɪp] *adj* **riper; ripest 1** : maduro **2 ~ for** : listo por — **ripen** [ˈraɪpən] *v* : madurar — **ripeness** [ˈraɪpnəs] *n* : madurez *f*

rip–off [ˈrɪpˌɔf] *n* : timo *m fam*

ripple [ˈrɪpəl] *v* **-pled; -pling** *vi* : rizarse (dícese de agua) — *vt* : rizar — **~** *n* : onda *f*, rizo *m*

rise [ˈraɪz] *vi* **rose** [ˈroːz]; **risen** [ˈrɪzən]; **rising 1** GET UP : levantarse **2** : salir (dícese del sol, etc.) **3** ASCEND : subir **4** INCREASE : aumentar **5 ~ up** REBEL : sublevarse — **~** *n* **1** ASCENT : subida *f* **2** INCREASE : aumento *m* **3** SLOPE : cuesta *f* — **riser** [ˈraɪzər] *n* **1 early ~** : madrugador *m*, -dora *f* **2 late ~** : dormilón *m*, -lona *f*

risk [ˈrɪsk] *n* : riesgo *m* — **~** *vt* : arriesgar — **risky** [ˈrɪski] *adj* **riskier; -est** : arriesgado, riesgoso *Lat*

rite [ˈraɪt] *n* : rito *m* — **ritual** [ˈrɪtʃʊəl] *adj* : ritual — **~** *n* : ritual *m*

rival [ˈraɪvəl] *n* : rival *mf* — **~** *adj* : rival — **~** *vt* **-valed** *or* **-valled; -valing** *or* **-valling** : rivalizar con — **rivalry** [ˈraɪvəlri] *n, pl* **-ries** : rivalidad *f*

river [ˈrɪvər] *n* : río *m*

rivet [ˈrɪvət] *n* : remache *m* — **~** *vt* **1** : remachar **2** FIX : fijar (los ojos, etc.) **3 be ~ed by** : estar fascinado con

roach [ˈroːtʃ] **→ cockroach**

road [ˈroːd] *n* **1** : carretera *f* **2** STREET : calle *f* **3** PATH : camino *m* — **roadblock** [ˈroːdˌblɑk] *n* : control *m* — **roadside** [ˈroːdˌsaɪd] *n* : borde *m* de la carretera — **roadway** [ˈroːdˌweɪ] *n* : carretera *f*

roam [ˈroːm] *vi* : vagar — *vt* : vagar por

roar [ˈror] *vi* **1** : rugir **2 ~ with laughter** : reírse a carcajadas — *vt* : decir a gritos — **~** *n* : rugido *m* (de un animal), estruendo *m* (de un avión, etc.)

roast [ˈroːst] *vt* : asar (carne, etc.), tostar (café, etc.) — *vi* : asarse — **~** *n* : asado *m* — **~** *adj* : asado — **roast beef** *n* : rosbif *m*

rob [ˈrɑb] *v* **robbed; robbing** *vt* **1** : robar **2 ~ of** : privar de — *vi* : robar — **robber** [ˈrɑbər] *n* : ladrón *m*, -drona *f* — **robbery** [ˈrɑbəri] *n, pl* **-beries** : robo *m*

robe [ˈroːb] *n* **1** : toga *f* (de un magistrado, etc.) **2 → bathrobe**

robin [ˈrɑbən] *n* : petirrojo *m*

robot [ˈroːˌbɑt, -bət] *n* : robot *m*

robust [roˈbʌst, ˈroːˌbʌst] *adj* : robusto

rock[1] [ˈrɑk] *vt* **1** : acunar (a un niño), mecer (una cuna) **2** SHAKE : sacudir — *vi* : mecerse — **~** *n* *or* **~ music** : música *f* rock

rock[2] *n* **1** : roca *f* (sustancia) **2** BOULDER : peña *f*, peñasco *m* **3** STONE : piedra *f*

rocket [ˈrɑkət] *n* : cohete *m*

rocking chair *n* : mecedora *f*

rocky [ˈrɑki] *adj* **rockier; -est 1** : rocoso **2** SHAKY : tambaleante

rod [ˈrɑd] *n* **1** : varilla *f* **2** *or* **fishing ~** : caña *f* de pescar

rode → ride

rodent [ˈroːdənt] *n* : roedor *m*

rodeo [ˈroːdiˌoː, roˈdeɪˌoː] *n, pl* **-deos** : rodeo *m*

roe [ˈroː] *n* : hueva *f*

rogue [ˈroːg] *n* : pícaro *m*, -ra *f*

role [ˈroːl] *n* : papel *m*

roll [ˈroːl] *n* **1** : rollo *m* (de película, etc.) **2** LIST : lista *f* **3** : redoble *m* (de un tambor) **4** SWAYING : balanceo *m* **5** BUN : pancito *m Lat*, panecillo *m Spain* — **~** *vt* **1** : hacer rodar **2** *or* **~ out** : estirar (masa) **3 ~ up** : enrollar (papel, etc.), arremangar (una manga) — *vi* **1** : rodar **2** SWAY : balancearse **3 ~ around** : revolcarse **4 ~ over** : darse la vuelta — **roller** [ˈroːlər] *n* **1** : rodillo *m* **2** CURLER : rulo *m* — **roller coaster** [ˈroːlərˌkoːstər] *n* : montaña *f* rusa — **roller–skate** [ˈroːlərˌskeɪt] *vi* **-skated; -skating** : patinar (sobre ruedas) — **roller skate** *n* : patín *m* (de ruedas)

Roman [ˈroːmən] *adj* : romano — **Roman Catholic** *adj* : católico

romance [roˈmænts, ˈroːˌmænts] *n* **1** : novela *f* romántica **2** AFFAIR : romance *m*

Romanian [rʊˈmeɪniən, ro-] *adj* : rumano — **~** *n* : rumano *m* (idioma)

romantic [roˈmæntɪk] *adj* : romántico

romp [ˈrɑmp] *n* : retozo *m* — **~** *vi* : retozar

roof [ˈruːf, ˈrʊf] *n, pl* **roofs** [ˈruːfs, ˈrʊfs; ˈruːvz, ˈrʊvz] **1** : tejado *m*, techo *m* **2 ~ of the mouth** : paladar *m* — **roofing** [ˈruːfɪŋ, ˈrʊfɪŋ] *n* : techumbre *f* — **rooftop** [ˈruːfˌtɑp, ˈrʊf-] *n* : tejado *m*, techo *m*

rook[1] [ˈrʊk] *n* : grajo *m* (ave)

rook[2] *n* : torre *f* (en ajedrez)

rookie [ˈrʊki] *n* : novato *m*, -ta *f*

room [ˈruːm, ˈrʊm] *n* **1** : cuarto *m*, habitación *f* **2** BEDROOM : dormitorio *m* **3** SPACE : espacio *m* **4** OPPORTUNITY : posibilidad *f* — **roommate** [ˈruːmˌmeɪt, ˈrʊm-] *n* : compañero *m*, -ra *f* de cuarto — **roomy** [ˈruːmi, ˈrʊmi] *adj* **roomier; -est** : espacioso

roost [ˈruːst] *n* : percha *f* — **~** *vi* : posarse — **rooster** [ˈruːstər, ˈrʊs-] *n* : gallo *m*

root[1] [ˈruːt, ˈrʊt] *n* : raíz *f* — **~** *vt* **~ out** : extirpar

root[2] *vi* **~ around in** : hurgar en

root[3] *vi* **~ for** SUPPORT : alentar

rope [ˈroːp] *n* : cuerda *f* — **~** *vt* **roped; roping 1** : atar (con cuerda) **2 ~ off** : acordonar

rosary [ˈroːzəri] *n, pl* **-ries** : rosario *m*

rose[1] → rise

rose[2] [ˈroːz] *n* : rosa *f* (flor), rosa *m* (color) — **~** *adj* : rosa — **rosebush** [ˈroːzˌbʊʃ] *n* : rosal *m*

rosemary [ˈroːzˌmeri] *n, pl* **-maries** : romero *m*

Rosh Hashanah [ˌrɑʃhɑˈʃɑnə, ˌroːʃ-] *n* : el Año Nuevo judío

roster [ˈrɑstər] *n* : lista *f*

rostrum [ˈrɑstrəm] *n, pl* **-tra** *or* **-trums** [-trə] : tribuna *f*

rosy [ˈroːzi] *adj* **rosier; -est 1** : sonrosado **2** PROMISING : halagüeno

rot [ˈrɑt] *v* **rotted; rotting** *vi* : pudrirse — *vt* : pudrir — **~** *n* : putrefacción *f*

rotary [ˈroːṭəri] *adj* : rotativo — **~** *n* : rotonda *f*, glorieta *f Spain*

rotate [ˈroːˌteɪt] *v* **-tated; -tating** *vi* : girar — *vt* **1** : girar **2** ALTERNATE : alternar — **rotation** [roˈteɪʃən] *n* : rotación *f*

rote [ˈroːt] *n* **by ~** : de memoria

rotor [ˈroːṭər] *n* : rotor *m*

rotten [ˈrɑtən] *adj* **1** : podrido **2** BAD : malo

rouge [ˈruːʒ, ˈruːdʒ] *n* : colorete *m*

rough [ˈrʌf] *adj* **1** COARSE : áspero **2** RUGGED : accidentado **3** CHOPPY : agitado **4** DIFFICULT : duro **5** FORCEFUL : brusco **6** APPROXIMATE : aproximado **7** UNREFINED : tosco **8 ~ draft** : borrador *m* — **~** *vt* **1 → roughen 2 ~ up** BEAT : dar una paliza a — **roughage** [ˈrʌfɪdʒ] *n* : fibra *f* — **roughen** [ˈrʌfən] *vt* : poner áspero — *vi* : ponerse áspero — **roughly** [ˈrʌfli] *adv* **1** : bruscamente **2** ABOUT : aproximadamente — **roughness** [ˈrʌfnəs] *n* COARSENESS : aspereza *f*

roulette [ruˈlet] *n* : ruleta *f*

round [ˈraʊnd] *adj* : redondo — **~** *adv* **→ around** — **~** *n* **1** : círculo *m* **2** : ronda *f* (de bebidas, negociaciones, etc.) **3** : asalto *m* (en boxeo), vuelta *f* (en juegos) **4 ~ of applause** : aplauso *m* **5 ~s** *npl* : visitas *fpl* (de un médico), rondas *fpl* (de un policía, etc.) — **~** *vt* **1** TURN : doblar **2 ~ off** : redondear **3 ~ off** *or* **~ out** COMPLETE : rematar **4 ~ up** GATHER : reunir (personas), rodear (ganado) — **~** *prep* **→ around** — **roundabout** [ˈraʊndəˌbaʊt] *adj* : indirecto — **round–trip** [ˈraʊndˈtrɪp] *n* : viaje *m* de ida y vuelta — **roundup** [ˈraʊndˌʌp] *n* : rodeo *m* (de animales), redada *f* (de delincuentes, etc.)

rouse [ˈraʊz] *vt* **roused; rousing 1** AWAKEN : despertar **2** EXCITE : excitar

rout [ˈraʊt] *n* : derrota *f* aplastante — **~** *vt* : derrotar

route [ˈruːt, ˈraʊt] *n* **1** : ruta *f* **2** *or* **delivery ~** : recorrido *m*

routine [ruːˈtiːn] *n* : rutina *f* — **~** *adj* : rutinario

rove [ˈroːv] *v* **roved; roving** *vi* : errar, vagar — *vt* : errar por

row[1] [ˈroː] *vt* **1** : llevar a remo **2 ~ a boat** : remar — *vi* : remar

row[2] *n* **1** : fila *f* (de gente o asientos), hilera *f* (de casas, etc.) **2 in a ~** SUCCESSIVELY : seguido

row[3] [ˈraʊ] *n* **1** RACKET : bulla *f* **2** QUARREL : pelea *f*

rowboat [ˈroːˌboːt] *n* : bote *m* de remos

rowdy [ˈraʊdi] *adj* **-dier; -est** : escandaloso, alborotador — **~** *n, pl* **-dies** : alborotador *m*, -dora *f*

royal [ˈrɔɪəl] *adj* : real — **royalty** [ˈrɔɪəlti] *n, pl* **-ties 1** : realeza *f* **2 royalties** *npl* : derechos *mpl* de autor

rub [ˈrʌb] *v* **rubbed; rubbing** *vt* **1** : frotar **2** CHAFE : rozar **3 ~ in** : aplicar frotando — *vi* **1 ~ against** : rozar **2 ~ off** : salir (al frotar) — **~** *n* : frotamiento *m*

rubber [ˈrʌbər] *n* **1** : goma *f*, caucho *m* **2 ~s** *npl* : chanclos *mpl* — **rubber band** *n* : goma *f* (elástica) — **rubber stamp** *n* : sello *m* (de goma) — **rubbery** [ˈrʌbəri] *adj* : gomoso

rubbish [ˈrʌbɪʃ] *n* **1** : basura *f* **2** NONSENSE : tonterías *fpl*

rubble [ˈrʌbəl] *n* : escombros *mpl*

ruby [ˈruːbi] *n, pl* **-bies** : rubí *m*

rudder [ˈrʌdər] *n* : timón *m*

ruddy [ˈrʌdi] *adj* **-dier; -est** : rubicundo

rude [ˈruːd] *adj* **ruder; rudest 1** IMPOLITE : grosero, mal educado **2** ABRUPT : brusco — **rudely** [ˈruːdli] *adv* : groseramente — **rudeness** [ˈruːdnəs] *n* : mala educación *f*

rudiment [ˈruːdəmənt] *n* : rudimento *m* — **rudimentary** [ˌruːdəˈmentəri] *adj* : rudimentario

rue [ˈruː] *vt* **rued; ruing** : lamentar — **rueful** [ˈruːfəl] *adj* : triste, arrepentido

ruffle [ˈrʌfəl] *vt* **-fled; -fling 1** : despeinar (pelo), erizar (plumas) **2** VEX : alterar, contrariar — **~** *n* : volante *m* (de un vestido, etc.)

rug [ˈrʌg] *n* : alfombra *f*, tapete *m*

rugged [ˈrʌgəd] *adj* **1** : escabroso (dícese del terreno), escarpado (dícese de montañas) **2** HARSH : duro **3** STURDY : fuerte

ruin [ˈruːən] *n* : ruina *f* — **~** *vt* : arruinar

rule [ˈruːl] *n* **1** : regla *f* **2** CONTROL : dominio *m* **3 as a ~** : por lo general — **~** *v* **ruled; ruling** *vt* **1** GOVERN : gobernar **2** : fallar (dícese de un juez) **3 ~ out** : descartar — *vi* : gobernar, reinar — **ruler** [ˈruːlər] *n* **1** : gobernante *mf*; soberano *m*, -na *f* **2** : regla *f* (para medir) — **ruling** [ˈruːlɪŋ] *n* VERDICT : fallo *m*

rum [ˈrʌm] *n* : ron *m*

Rumanian [rʊˈmeɪniən] **→ Romanian**

rumble [ˈrʌmbəl] *vi* **-bled; -bling 1** : retumbar **2** : hacer ruidos (dícese del estómago) — **~** *n* : retumbo *m*, estruendo *m*

rummage [ˈrʌmɪdʒ] *vi* **-maged; -maging** : hurgar

rumor [ˈruːmər] *n* : rumor *m* — **~** *vt* **be ~ed** : rumorearse

rump [ˈrʌmp] *n* **1** : grupa *f* (de un animal) **2 ~ steak** : filete *m* de cadera

rumpus [ˈrʌmpəs] *n* : lío *m*, jaleo *m fam*

run [ˈrʌn] *v* **ran** [ˈræn]; **run; running** *vi* **1** : correr **2** FUNCTION : funcionar **3** LAST : durar **4** : desteñir (dícese de colores) **5** EXTEND : correr, extenderse **6** : presentarse (como candidato) **7 ~ away** : huir **8 ~ into** ENCOUNTER : tropezar con **9 ~ into** HIT : chocar contra **10 ~ late** : ir retrasado **11 ~ out of** : quedarse sin **12 ~ over** : atropellar — *vt* **1** : correr **2** OPERATE : hacer funcionar **3** : hacer correr (agua) **4** MANAGE : dirigir **5 ~ a fever** : tener fiebre — **~** *n* **1** : carrera *f* **2** TRIP : viaje *m*, paseo *m* (en coche) **3** SERIES : serie *f* **4 in the long ~** : a la larga **5 in the short ~** : a corto plazo — **runaway** [ˈrʌnəˌweɪ] *n*

: fugitivo *m*, -va *f* — ~ *adj* : fugitivo — **rundown** [ˈrʌnˌdaʊn] *n* : resumen *m* — **run–down** [ˈrʌnˈdaʊn] *adj* **1** : destartalado **2** EXHAUSTED : agotado
rung[1] → **ring**[1]
rung[2] [ˈrʌŋ] *n* : peldaño *m* (de una escalera, etc.)
runner [ˈrʌnər] *n* **1** : corredor *m*, -dora *f* **2** : patín *m* (de un trineo), riel *m* (de un cajón, etc.) — **runner–up** [ˌrʌnərˈʌp] *n, pl* **runners–up** : subcampeón *m*, -peona *f* — **running** [ˈrʌnɪŋ] *adj* **1** FLOWING : corriente **2** CONTINUOUS : continuo **3** CONSECUTIVE : seguido
runt [ˈrʌnt] *n* : animal *m* más pequeño (de una camada)
runway [ˈrʌnˌweɪ] *n* : pista *f* de aterrizaje
rupture [ˈrʌptʃər] *n* : ruptura *f* — ~ *v* **-tured; -turing** *vt* : romper — *vi* : reventar
rural [ˈrʊrəl] *adj* : rural
ruse [ˈruːs, ˈruːz] *n* : ardid *m*
rush[1] [ˈrʌʃ] *n* : junco *m* (planta)
rush[2] *vi* : ir de prisa — *vt* **1** : apresurar, apurar **2** ATTACK : asaltar **3** : llevar rápidamente (al hospital, etc.) — ~ *n* **1** : prisa *f*, apuro *m* **2** : ráfaga *f* (de aire), torrente *m* (de agua) — ~ *adj* : urgente — **rush hour** *n* : hora *f* punta
russet [ˈrʌsət] *n* : color *m* rojizo
Russian [ˈrʌʃən] *adj* : ruso — ~ *n* : ruso *m* (idioma)
rust [ˈrʌst] *n* : herrumbre *f*, óxido *m* — ~ *vi* : oxidarse — *vt* : oxidar
rustic [ˈrʌstɪk] *adj* : rústico
rustle [ˈrʌsəl] *v* **-tled; -tling** *vt* **1** : hacer susurrar **2** : robar (ganado) — *vi* : susurrar — ~ *n* : susurro *m*
rusty [ˈrʌsti] *adj* **rustier; -est** : oxidado
rut [ˈrʌt] *n* **1** : surco *m* **2 be in a ~** : ser esclavo de la rutina
ruthless [ˈruːθləs] *adj* : despiadado, cruel
rye [ˈraɪ] *n* : centeno *m*

S

s [ˈɛs] *n, pl* **s's** *or* **ss** [ˈɛsəz] : s *f*, decimonovena letra del alfabeto inglés
Sabbath [ˈsæbəθ] *n* **1** : sábado *m* (día santo judío) **2** : domingo *m* (día santo cristiano)
sabotage [ˈsæbəˌtɑʒ] *n* : sabotaje *m* — ~ *vt* **-taged; -taging** : sabotear
saccharin [ˈsækərən] *n* : sacarina *f*
sack [ˈsæk] *n* : saco *m* — ~ *vt* **1** FIRE : despedir **2** PLUNDER : saquear
sacrament [ˈsækrəmənt] *n* : sacramento *m*
sacred [ˈseɪkrəd] *adj* : sagrado
sacrifice [ˈsækrəˌfaɪs] *n* : sacrificio *m* — ~ *vt* **-ficed; -ficing** : sacrificar
sacrilege [ˈsækrəlɪdʒ] *n* : sacrilegio *m* — **sacrilegious** [ˌsækrəˈlɪdʒəs, -ˈliː-] *adj* : sacrílego
sad [ˈsæd] *adj* **sadder; saddest** : triste — **sadden** [ˈsædən] *vt* : entristecer
saddle [ˈsædəl] *n* : silla *f* (de montar) — ~ *vt* **-dled; -dling 1** : ensillar (un caballo, etc.) **2 ~ s.o. with sth** : cargar a algn con algo
sadistic [səˈdɪstɪk] *adj* : sádico
sadness [ˈsædnəs] *n* : tristeza *f*
safari [səˈfɑri, -ˈfær-] *n* : safari *m*
safe [ˈseɪf] *adj* **safer; safest 1** : seguro **2** UNHARMED : ileso **3** CAREFUL : prudente **4 ~ and sound** : sano y salvo — ~ *n* : caja *f* fuerte — **safeguard** [ˈseɪfˌgɑrd] *n* : salvaguarda *f* — ~ *vt* : salvaguardar — **safely** [ˈseɪfli] *adv* **1** : sin peligro **2 arrive ~** : llegar sin novedad — **safety** [ˈseɪfti] *n, pl* **-ties** : seguridad *f* — **safety belt** *n* : cinturón *m* de seguridad — **safety pin** *n* : imperdible *m*
saffron [ˈsæfrən] *n* : azafrán *m*
sag [ˈsæg] *vi* **sagged; sagging 1** : combarse **2** GIVE : aflojarse **3** FLAG : flaquear
saga [ˈsɑgə, ˈsæ-] *n* : saga *f*
sage[1] [ˈseɪdʒ] *n* : salvia *f* (planta)
sage[2] *adj* **sager; -est** : sabio — ~ *n* : sabio *m*, -bia *f*
said → **say**
sail [ˈseɪl] *n* **1** : vela *f* (de un barco) **2 go for a ~** : salir a navegar **3 set ~** : zarpar — ~ *vi* : navegar — *vt* : gobernar (un barco), navegar (el mar) — **sailboat** [ˈseɪlˌboːt] *n* : velero *m* — **sailor** [ˈseɪlər] *n* : marinero *m*
saint [ˈseɪnt, *before a name* ˌseɪnt *or* sənt] *n* : santo *m*, -ta *f* — **saintly** [ˈseɪntli] *adj* **saintlier; -est** : santo
sake [ˈseɪk] *n* **1 for goodness' ~!** : ¡por Dios! **2 for the ~ of** : por (el bien de)
salad [ˈsæləd] *n* : ensalada *f*
salamander [ˈsæləˌmændər] *n* : salamandra *f*
salami [səˈlɑmi] *n* : salami *m*
salary [ˈsæləri] *n, pl* **-ries** : sueldo *m*
sale [ˈseɪl] *n* **1** : venta *f* **2 for ~** : se vende **3 on ~** : de rebaja — **salesman** [ˈseɪlzmən] *n, pl* **-men** [-mən, -ˌmɛn] : vendedor *m*, dependiente *m* — **saleswoman** [ˈseɪlzˌwʊmən] *n, pl* **-women** [-ˌwɪmən] : vendedora *f*, dependienta *f*
salient [ˈseɪljənt] *adj* : saliente
saliva [səˈlaɪvə] *n* : saliva *f*
sallow [ˈsæloː] *adj* : amarillento, cetrino
salmon [ˈsæmən] *ns & pl* : salmón *m*
salon [səˈlɑn, ˈsæˌlɑn] *n* → **beauty salon**
saloon [səˈluːn] *n* : bar *m*
salsa [ˈsɔlsə, ˈsɑl-] *n* : salsa *f* mexicana, salsa *f* picante
salt [ˈsɔlt] *n* : sal *f* — ~ *vt* : salar — **saltwater** [ˈsɔltˌwɔt̬ər, -ˌwɑ-] *adj* : de agua salada — **salty** [ˈsɔlti] *adj* **saltier; -est** : salado
salute [səˈluːt] *v* **-luted; -luting** *vt* : saludar — *vi* : hacer un saludo — ~ *n* : saludo *m*
salvage [ˈsælvɪdʒ] *n* : salvamento *m* — ~ *vt* **-vaged; -vaging** : salvar
salvation [sælˈveɪʃən] *n* : salvación *f*
salve [ˈsæv, ˈsav] *n* : ungüento *m*
same [ˈseɪm] *adj* **1** : mismo **2 be the ~ (as)** : ser igual (que) **3 the ~ thing (as)** : la misma cosa (que) — ~ *pron* **1 all the ~** : igual **2 the ~** : lo mismo — ~ *adv* **the ~** : igual
sample [ˈsæmpəl] *n* : muestra *f* — ~ *vt* **-pled; -pling** : probar
sanatorium [ˌsænəˈtoriəm] *n, pl* **-riums** *or* **-ria** [-iə] : sanatorio *m*
sanctify [ˈsæŋktəˌfaɪ] *vt* **-fied; -fying** : santificar
sanction *n* [ˈsæŋkʃən] : sanción *f* — ~ *vt* : sancionar
sanctity [ˈsæŋktət̬i] *n, pl* **-ties** : santidad *f*
sanctuary [ˈsæŋktʃʊˌeri] *n, pl* **-aries** : santuario *m*
sand [ˈsænd] *n* : arena *f* — ~ *vt* : lijar (madera)
sandal [ˈsændəl] *n* : sandalia *f*
sandpaper [ˈsændˌpeɪpər] *n* : papel *m* de lija — ~ *vt* : lijar
sandwich [ˈsændˌwɪtʃ] *n* : sandwich *m*, bocadillo *m Spain* — ~ *vt* **~ between** : meter entre
sandy [ˈsændi] *adj* **sandier; -est** : arenoso
sane [ˈseɪn] *adj* **saner; sanest 1** : cuerdo **2** SENSIBLE : sensato
sang → **sing**
sanitarium [ˌsænəˈteriəm] *n, pl* **-iums** *or* **-ia** [-iə] → **sanatorium**
sanitary [ˈsænəˌteri] *adj* **1** : sanitario **2** HYGIENIC : higiénico — **sanitary napkin** *n* : compresa *f* (higiénica) — **sanitation** [ˌsænəˈteɪʃən] *n* : sanidad *f*
sanity [ˈsænət̬i] *n* : cordura *f*
sank → **sink**
Santa Claus [ˈsæntəˌklɔz] *n* : Papá *m* Noel
sap[1] [ˈsæp] *n* **1** : savia *f* (de una planta) **2** SUCKER : inocentón *m*, -tona *f*
sap[2] *vt* **sapped; sapping** : minar (la fuerza, etc.)
sapphire [ˈsæˌfaɪr] *n* : zafiro *m*
sarcasm [ˈsɑrˌkæzəm] *n* : sarcasmo *m* — **sarcastic** [sɑrˈkæstɪk] *adj* : sarcástico
sardine [sɑrˈdiːn] *n* : sardina *f*
sash [ˈsæʃ] *n* : faja *f* (de un vestido), fajín *m* (de un uniforme)
sat → **sit**
satanic [səˈtænɪk, seɪ-] *adj* : satánico
satchel [ˈsætʃəl] *n* : cartera *f*
satellite [ˈsæt̬əˌlaɪt] *n* : satélite *m*
satin [ˈsætən] *n* : raso *m*
satire [ˈsæˌtaɪr] *n* : sátira *f* — **satiric** [səˈtɪrɪk] *or* **satirical** [-ɪkəl] *adj* : satírico
satisfaction [ˌsæt̬əsˈfækʃən] *n* : satisfacción *f* — **satisfactory** [ˌsæt̬əsˈfæktəri] *adj* : satisfactorio — **satisfy** [ˈsæt̬əsˌfaɪ] *v* **-fied; -fying** *vt* **1** : satisfacer **2** CONVINCE : convencer — **satisfying** *adj* : satisfactorio
saturate [ˈsætʃəˌreɪt] *vt* **-rated; -rating 1** : saturar **2** DRENCH : empapar — **saturation** [ˌsætʃəˈreɪʃən] *n* : saturación *f*
Saturday [ˈsæt̬ərˌdeɪ, -di] *n* : sábado *m*
Saturn [ˈsæt̬ərn] *n* : Saturno *m*
sauce [ˈsɔs] *n* : salsa *f* — **saucepan** [ˈsɔsˌpæn] *n* : cacerola *f* — **saucer** [ˈsɔsər] *n* : platillo *m* — **saucy** [ˈsɔsi] *adj* **saucier; -est** IMPUDENT : descarado
sauna [ˈsɔnə, ˈsaʊnə] *n* : sauna *mf*
saunter [ˈsɔntər, ˈsɑn-] *vi* : pasear
sausage [ˈsɔsɪdʒ] *n* : salchicha *f*
sauté [sɔˈteɪ, soː-] *vt* **-téed** *or* **-téd; -téing** : saltear, sofreír
savage [ˈsævɪdʒ] *adj* : salvaje, feroz — ~ *n* : salvaje *mf* — **savagery** [ˈsævɪdʒri, -dʒəri] *n, pl* **-ries** : ferocidad *f*
save [ˈseɪv] *vt* **saved; saving 1** RESCUE : salvar **2** RESERVE : guardar **3** : ahorrar (dinero, tiempo, etc.) — ~ *prep* EXCEPT : salvo
savior [ˈseɪvjər] *n* : salvador *m*, -dora *f*
savor [ˈseɪvər] *vt* : saborear — **savory** [ˈseɪvəri] *adj* : sabroso
saw[1] → **see**
saw[2] [ˈsɔ] *n* : sierra *f* — ~ *vt* **sawed; sawed** *or* **sawn; sawing** : serrar — **sawdust** [ˈsɔˌdʌst] *n* : serrín *m*, aserrín *m*
saxophone [ˈsæksəˌfoːn] *n* : saxofón *m*
say [ˈseɪ] *v* **said** [ˈsɛd]; **saying; says** [ˈsɛz] *vt* **1** : decir **2** INDICATE : marcar (dícese de relojes, etc.) — *vi* **1** : decir **2 that is to ~** : es decir — ~ *n, pl* **says** [ˈseɪz] **1 have no ~** : no tener ni voz ni voto **2 have one's ~** : dar su opinión — **saying** [ˈseɪɪŋ] *n* : refrán *m*
scab [ˈskæb] *n* **1** : costra *f* (en una herida) **2** STRIKEBREAKER : esquirol *mf*
scaffold [ˈskæfəld, -ˌfoːld] *n* : andamio *m* (en construcción)
scald [ˈskɔld] *vt* : escaldar
scale[1] [ˈskeɪl] *n* : balanza *f* (para pesar)
scale[2] *n* : escama *f* (de un pez, etc.) — ~ *vt* **scaled; scaling** : escamar
scale[3] *vt* **scaled; scaling 1** CLIMB : escalar **2 ~ down** : reducir — ~ *n* : escala *f* (musical, salarial, etc.)
scallion [ˈskæljən] *n* : cebolleta *f*
scallop [ˈskɑləp, ˈskæ-] *n* : vieira *f*
scalp [ˈskælp] *n* : cuero *m* cabelludo
scam [ˈskæm] *n* : estafa *f*, timo *m fam*
scamper [ˈskæmpər] *vi* **~ away** : irse corriendo
scan [ˈskæn] *vt* **scanned; scanning 1** : escandir (versos) **2** EXAMINE : escudriñar **3** SKIM : echar un vistazo a **4** : escanear (en informática)
scandal [ˈskændəl] *n* **1** : escándalo *m* **2** GOSSIP : habladurías *fpl* — **scandalous** [ˈskændələs] *adj* : escandaloso
Scandinavian [ˌskændəˈneɪviən] *adj* : escandinavo
scant [ˈskænt] *adj* : escaso
scapegoat [ˈskeɪpˌgoːt] *n* : chivo *m* expiatorio
scar [ˈskɑr] *n* : cicatriz *f* — ~ *v* **scarred; scarring** *vt* : dejar una cicatriz en — *vi* : cicatrizar
scarce [ˈskɛrs] *adj* **scarcer; -est** : escaso — **scarcely** [ˈskɛrsli] *adv* : apenas — **scarcity** [ˈskɛrsət̬i] *n, pl* **-ties** : escasez *f*
scare [ˈskɛr] *vt* **scared; scaring 1** : asustar **2 be ~d of** : tener miedo a — ~ *n* **1** FRIGHT : susto *m* **2** ALARM : pánico *m* — **scarecrow** [ˈskɛrˌkroː] *n* : espantapájaros *m*, espantajo *m*
scarf [ˈskɑrf] *n, pl* **scarves** [ˈskɑrvz] *or* **scarfs 1** : bufanda *f* **2** KERCHIEF : pañuelo *m*
scarlet [ˈskɑrlət] *adj* : escarlata — **scarlet fever** *n* : escarlatina *f*
scary [ˈskɛri] *adj* **scarier; -est** : que da miedo
scathing [ˈskeɪðɪŋ] *adj* : mordaz
scatter [ˈskæt̬ər] *vt* **1** STREW : esparcir **2** DISPERSE : dispersar — *vi* : dispersarse
scavenger [ˈskævəndʒər] *n* : carroñero *m*, -ra *f* (animal)
scenario [səˈnæriˌoː, -ˈnɑr-] *n, pl* **-ios 1** : guión *m* (cinemático) **2 the worst-case ~** : el peor de los casos
scene [ˈsiːn] *n* **1** : escena *f* **2 behind the ~s** : entre bastidores **3 make a ~** : armar un escándalo — **scenery** [ˈsiːnəri] *n, pl* **-eries 1** : decorado *m* **2** LANDSCAPE : paisaje *m* — **scenic** [ˈsiːnɪk] *adj* : pintoresco
scent [ˈsɛnt] *n* **1** : aroma *m* **2** PERFUME : perfume *m* **3** TRAIL : rastro *m* — **scented** [ˈsɛntəd] *adj* : perfumado
sceptic [ˈskɛptɪk] → **skeptic**
schedule [ˈskɛˌdʒuːl, -dʒəl, *esp Brit* ˈʃɛdˌjuːl] *n* **1** : programa *m* **2** TIMETABLE : horario *m* **3 behind ~** : atrasado, con retraso **4 on ~** : según lo previsto — ~ *vt* **-uled; -uling** : planear, programar
scheme [ˈskiːm] *n* **1** PLAN : plan *m* **2** PLOT : intriga *f* **3** DESIGN : esquema *f* — ~ *vi* **schemed; scheming** : intrigar
schism [ˈsɪzəm, ˈskɪ-] *n* : cisma *m*
schizophrenia [ˌskɪtsəˈfriːniə, ˌskɪzə-, -ˈfrɛ-] *n* : esquizofrenia *f* — **schizophrenic** [ˌskɪtsəˈfrɛnɪk, ˌskɪzə-] *adj* : esquizofrénico
scholar [ˈskɑlər] *n* : erudito *m*, -ta *f* — **scholarly** [ˈskɑlərli] *adj* : erudito — **scholarship** [ˈskɑlərˌʃɪp] *n* **1** : erudición *f* **2** GRANT : beca *f*
school[1] [ˈskuːl] *n* : banco *m* (de peces)
school[2] *n* **1** : escuela *f* **2** COLLEGE : universidad *f* **3** DEPARTMENT : facultad *f* — ~ *vt* : instruir — **schoolboy** [ˈskuːlˌbɔɪ] *n* : colegial *m* — **schoolgirl** [ˈskuːlˌgərl] *n* : colegiala *f* — **schoolteacher** [ˈskuːlˌtiːtʃər] *n* → **teacher**
science [ˈsaɪənts] *n* : ciencia *f* — **scientific** [ˌsaɪənˈtɪfɪk] *adj* : científico — **scientist** [ˈsaɪəntɪst] *n* : científico *m*, -ca *f*
scissors [ˈsɪzərz] *npl* : tijeras *fpl*
scoff [ˈskɑf] *vi* **~ at** : burlarse de, mofarse de
scold [ˈskoːld] *vt* : regañar
scoop [ˈskuːp] *n* **1** : pala *f* **2** : noticia *f* exclusiva (en periodismo) — ~ *vt* **1** : sacar (con pala) **2 ~ out** : ahuecar **3 ~ up** : recoger
scoot [ˈskuːt] *vi* : ir rápidamente — **scooter** [ˈskuːt̬ər] *n* **1** : patinete *m* **2** *or* **motor ~** : escúter *m*
scope [ˈskoːp] *n* **1** RANGE : alcance *m* **2** OPPORTUNITY : posibilidades *fpl*
scorch [ˈskɔrtʃ] *vt* : chamuscar
score [ˈskor] *n, pl* **scores 1** : tanteo *m* (en deportes) **2** RATING : puntuación *f* **3** : partitura *f* (musical) **4** *or pl* **score** TWENTY : veintena *f* **5 keep ~** : llevar la cuenta **6 on that ~** : en ese sentido — ~ *v* **scored; scoring** *vt* **1** : marcar, anotarse *Lat* (un tanto) **2** : sacar (una nota) — *vi* : marcar (en deportes)
scorn [ˈskɔrn] *n* : desdén *m* — ~ *vt* : desdeñar — **scornful** [ˈskɔrnfəl] *adj* : desdeñoso
scorpion [ˈskɔrpiən] *n* : alacrán *m*, escorpión *m*
Scot [ˈskɑt] *n* : escocés *m*, -cesa *f* — **Scotch** [ˈskɑtʃ] *adj* → **Scottish** — ~ *n or* **~ whiskey** : whisky *m* escocés — **Scottish** [ˈskɑt̬ɪʃ] *adj* : escocés
scoundrel [ˈskaʊndrəl] *n* : sinvergüenza *mf*
scour [ˈskaʊər] *vt* **1** SCRUB : fregar **2** SEARCH : registrar
scourge [ˈskərdʒ] *n* : azote *m*
scout [ˈskaʊt] *n* : explorador *m*, -dora *f*
scowl [ˈskaʊl] *vi* : fruncir el ceño — ~ *n* : ceño *m* fruncido
scram [ˈskræm] *vi* **scrammed; scramming** : largarse
scramble [ˈskræmbəl] *v* **-bled; -bling** *vi* **1** CLAMBER : trepar **2 ~ for** : pelearse por — *vt* : mezclar — ~ *n* : rebatiña *f*, pelea *f* — **scrambled eggs** *npl* : huevos *mpl* revueltos
scrap[1] [ˈskræp] *n* **1** PIECE : pedazo *m* **2** *or* **~ metal** : chatarra *f* **3 ~s** *npl* : sobras — ~ *vt* **scrapped; scrapping** : desechar
scrap[2] *n* FIGHT : pelea *f*
scrapbook [ˈskræpˌbʊk] *n* : álbum *m* de recortes
scrape [ˈskreɪp] *v* **scraped; scraping** *vt* **1** : rascar **2** : rasparse (la rodilla, etc.) **3** *or* **~ off** : raspar **4 ~ together** : reunir — *vi* **1** RUB : rozar **2 ~ by** : arreglárselas — ~ *n* **1** : rasguño *m* **2** PREDICAMENT : apuro *m*
scratch [ˈskrætʃ] *vt* **1** CLAW : arañar **2** MARK : rayar **3** : rascarse (la cabeza, etc.) **4 ~ out** : tachar — ~ *n* **1** : arañazo *m* **2** MARK : rayón *m* **3 start from ~** : empezar desde cero
scrawl [ˈskrɔl] *v* : garabatear — ~ *n* : garabato *m*
scrawny [ˈskrɔni] *adj* **scrawnier; -est** : escuálido
scream [ˈskriːm] *vi* : gritar, chillar — ~ *n* : grito *m*, chillido *m*
screech [ˈskriːtʃ] *n* **1** : chillido *m* (de personas) **2** : chirrido *m* (de frenos, etc.) — ~ *vi* **1** : chillar **2** : chirriar (dícese de los frenos, etc.)
screen [ˈskriːn] *n* **1** : pantalla *f* **2** PARTITION : mampara *f* **3** *or* **window ~** : mosquitero *m* — ~ *vt* **1** SHIELD : proteger **2** HIDE : ocultar **3** : seleccionar (candidatos, etc.)
screw [ˈskruː] *n* : tornillo *m* — ~ *vt* **1** : atornillar **2 ~ up** RUIN : fastidiar — **screwdriver** [ˈskruːˌdraɪvər] *n* : destornillador *m*
scribble [ˈskrɪbəl] *v* **-bled; -bling** : garabatear — ~ *n* : garabato *m*
script [ˈskrɪpt] *n* **1** HANDWRITING : escritura *f* **2** : guión *m* (de cine, etc.) — **scripture** [ˈskrɪptʃər] *n* **1** : escritos *mpl* sagrados **2 the Scriptures** *npl* : las Escrituras *fpl*
scroll [ˈskroːl] *n* : rollo *m* (de pergamino, etc.)
scrounge [ˈskraʊndʒ] *v* **scrounged; scrounging** *vt* : gorrear *fam* — *vi* **~ around for sth** : andar buscando algo
scrub[1] [ˈskrʌb] *n* UNDERBRUSH : maleza *f*
scrub[2] *vt* **scrubbed; scrubbing** SCOUR : fregar — ~ *n* : fregado *m*
scruff [ˈskrʌf] *n* **by the ~ of the neck** : por el pescuezo
scruple [ˈskruːpəl] *n* : escrúpulo *m* — **scrupulous** [ˈskruːpjələs] *adj* : escrupuloso
scrutiny [ˈskruːtəni] *n, pl* **-nies** : análisis *m* cuidadoso — **scrutinize** [ˈskruːtənˌaɪz] *vt* **-nized; -nizing** : escudriñar
scuff [ˈskʌf] *vt* : raspar, rayar
scuffle [ˈskʌfəl] *n* : refriega *f*
sculpture [ˈskʌlptʃər] *n* : escultura *f* — **sculpt** [ˈskʌlpt] *v* : esculpir — **sculptor** [ˈskʌlptər] *n* : escultor *m*, -tora *f*
scum [ˈskʌm] *n* **1** FROTH : espuma *f* **2** : escoria *f* (dícese de personas)
scurry [ˈskəri] *vi* **-ried; -rying** : corretear
scuttle[1] [ˈskʌt̬əl] *n* : cubo *m* (para carbón)
scuttle[2] *vt* **-tled; -tling** : hundir (un barco)
scuttle[3] *vi* SCAMPER : corretear
sea [ˈsiː] *n* **1** : mar *mf* **2 at ~** : en el mar — ~ *adj* : del mar — **seafarer** [ˈsiːˌfærər] *n* : marinero *m* — **seafood** [ˈsiːˌfuːd] *n* : mariscos *mpl* — **seagull** [ˈsiːˌgʌl] *n* : gaviota *f*
seal[1] [ˈsiːl] *n* : foca *f* (animal)
seal[2] *n* **1** STAMP : sello *m* **2** CLOSURE : cierre *m* (hermético) — ~ *vt* : sellar
seam [ˈsiːm] *n* **1** : costura *f* **2** VEIN : veta *f*
seaman [ˈsiːmən] *n, pl* **-men** [-mən, -ˌmɛn] : marinero *m*
seamy [ˈsiːmi] *adj* **seamier; -est** : sórdido
seaplane [ˈsiːˌpleɪn] *n* : hidroavión *m*
seaport [ˈsiːˌport] *n* : puerto *m* marítimo
search [ˈsərtʃ] *vt* : registrar — *vi* **~ for** : buscar — ~ *n* **1** : registro *m* **2** HUNT : búsqueda *f* — **searchlight** [ˈsərtʃˌlaɪt] *n* : reflector *m*
seashell [ˈsiːˌʃɛl] *n* : concha *f* (marina) — **seashore** [ˈsiːˌʃor] *n* : orilla *f* del mar — **seasick** [ˈsiːˌsɪk] *adj* **1** : mareado **2 be ~** : marearse — **seasickness** [ˈsiːˌsɪknəs] *n* : mareo *m*
season [ˈsiːzən] *n* **1** : estación *f* (del año) **2** : temporada *f* (en deportes, etc.) — ~ *vt* **1** FLAVOR : sazonar **2** : secar (madera) — **seasonal** [ˈsiːzənəl] *adj* : estacional —

seasoned *adj* EXPERIENCED : veterano — **seasoning** ['si:zənɪŋ] *n* : condimento *m*

seat ['si:t] *n* **1** : asiento *m* **2** : fondillos *mpl* (de un pantalón) **3** BUTTOCKS : trasero *m* **4** CENTER : sede *f* — ~ *vt* **1 be ~ed** : sentarse **2 the bus ~s 30** : el autobús tiene cabida para 30 — **seat belt** *n* : cinturón *m* de seguridad

seaweed ['si:ˌwi:d] *n* : alga *f* marina

secede [sɪ'si:d] *vi* **-ceded; -ceding** : separarse (de una nación, etc.)

secluded [sɪ'klu:dəd] *adj* : aislado — **seclusion** [sɪ'klu:ʒən] *n* : aislamiento *m*

second ['sɛkənd] *adj* : segundo — ~ *or* **secondly** ['sɛkəndli] *adv* : en segundo lugar — ~ *n* **1** : segundo *m*, -da *f* **2** MOMENT : segundo *m* **3 have ~s** : repetir (en una comida) — ~ *vt* : secundar — **secondary** ['sɛkənˌdɛri] *adj* : secundario — **secondhand** ['sɛkənd'hænd] *adj* : de segunda mano — **second-rate** ['sɛkənd'reɪt] *adj* : mediocre

secret ['si:krət] *adj* : secreto — ~ *n* : secreto *m* — **secrecy** ['si:krəsi] *n, pl* **-cies** : secreto *m*

secretary ['sɛkrəˌtɛri] *n, pl* **-taries 1** : secretario *m*, -ria *f* **2** : ministro *m*, -tra *f* (del gobierno)

secretion [sɪ'kri:ʃən] *n* : secreción *f* — **secrete** [sɪ'kri:t] *vt* **-creted; -creting** : secretar

secretive ['si:krət̬ɪv, sɪ'kri:t̬ɪv] *adj* : reservado — **secretly** ['si:krətli] *adv* : en secreto

sect ['sɛkt] *n* : secta *f*

section ['sɛkʃən] *n* : sección *f*, parte *f*

sector ['sɛktər] *n* : sector *m*

secular ['sɛkjələr] *adj* : secular

security [sɪ'kjʊrət̬i] *n, pl* **-ties 1** : seguridad *f* **2** GUARANTEE : garantía *f* **3 securities** *npl* : valores *mpl* — **secure** [sɪ'kjʊr] *adj* **-curer; -est** : seguro — ~ *vt* **-cured; -curing 1** FASTEN : asegurar **2** GET : conseguir

sedan [sɪ'dæn] *n* : sedán *m*

sedate [sɪ'deɪt] *adj* : sosegado

sedative ['sɛdət̬ɪv] *adj* : sedante — ~ *n* : sedante *m*

sedentary ['sɛdənˌtɛri] *adj* : sedentario

sediment ['sɛdəmənt] *n* : sedimento *m*

seduce [sɪ'du:s, -'dju:s] *vt* **-duced; -ducing** : seducir — **seduction** [sɪ'dʌkʃən] *n* : seducción *f* — **seductive** [sɪ'dʌktɪv] *adj* : seductor

see ['si:] *v* **saw** ['sɔ]; **seen** ['si:n]; **seeing** *vt* **1** : ver **2** UNDERSTAND : entender **3** ESCORT : acompañar **4 ~ s.o. off** : despedirse de algn **5 ~ sth through** : llevar algo a cabo **6 ~ you later!** : ¡hasta luego! — *vi* **1** : ver **2** UNDERSTAND : entender **3 let's ~** : vamos a ver **4 ~ to** : ocuparse de

seed ['si:d] *n, pl* **seed** *or* **seeds 1** : semilla *f* **2** SOURCE : germen *m* — **seedy** ['si:di] *adj* **seedier; -est** SQUALID : sórdido

seek ['si:k] *v* **sought** ['sɔt]; **seeking** *vt* **1** *or* **~ out** : buscar **2** REQUEST : pedir **3 ~ to** : tratar de — *vi* SEARCH : buscar

seem ['si:m] *vi* : parecer

seep ['si:p] *vi* : filtrarse

seesaw ['si:ˌsɔ] *n* : balancín *m*

seethe ['si:ð] *vi* **seethed; seething** : rabiar, estar furioso

segment ['sɛgmənt] *n* : segmento *m*

segregate ['sɛgrɪˌgeɪt] *vt* **-gated; -gating** : segregar — **segregation** [ˌsɛgrɪ'geɪʃən] *n* : segregación *f*

seize ['si:z] *v* **seized; seizing** *vt* **1** GRASP : agarrar **2** CAPTURE : tomar **3** : aprovechar (una oportunidad) — *vi or* **~ up** : agarrotarse — **seizure** ['si:ʒər] *n* **1** CAPTURE : toma *f* **2** : ataque *m* (en medicina)

seldom ['sɛldəm] *adv* : pocas veces, raramente

select [sə'lɛkt] *adj* : selecto — ~ *vt* : seleccionar — **selection** [sə'lɛkʃən] *n* : selección *f* — **selective** [sə'lɛktɪv] *adj* : selectivo

self ['sɛlf] *n, pl* **selves** ['sɛlvz] **1** : ser *m* **2 her better ~** : su lado bueno — **self-addressed** [ˌsɛlfə'drɛst] *adj* : con la dirección del remitente — **self-assured** [ˌsɛlfə'ʃʊrd] *adj* : seguro de sí mismo — **self-centered** [ˌsɛlf'sɛntərd] *adj* : egocéntrico — **self-confidence** [ˌsɛlf'kɑnfədənts] *n* : confianza *f* en sí mismo — **self-confident** [ˌsɛlf'kɑnfədənt] *adj* : seguro de sí mismo — **self-conscious** [ˌsɛlf'kɑntʃəs] *adj* : cohibido — **self-control** [ˌsɛlfkən'tro:l] *n* : dominio *m* de sí mismo — **self-defense** [ˌsɛlfdɪ'fɛnts] *n* : defensa *f* propia — **self-employed** [ˌsɛlfɪm'plɔɪd] *adj* : que trabaja por cuenta propia — **self-esteem** [ˌsɛlfɪ'sti:m] *n* : amor *m* propio — **self-evident** [ˌsɛlf'ɛvədənt] *adj* : evidente — **self-help** [ˌsɛlf'hɛlp] *n* : autoayuda *f* — **self-important** [ˌsɛlfɪm'pɔrtənt] *adj* : presumido — **self-interest** [ˌsɛlf'ɪntrəst, -tərəst] *n* : interés *m* personal — **selfish** ['sɛlfɪʃ] *adj* : egoísta — **selfishness** ['sɛlfɪʃnəs] *n* : egoísmo *m* — **selfless** ['sɛlfləs] *adj* : desinteresado — **self-pity** [ˌsɛlf'pɪt̬i] *n, pl* **-ties** : autocompasión *f* — **self-portrait** [ˌsɛlf'pɔrtrət] *n* : autorretrato *m* — **self-respect** [ˌsɛlfrɪ'spɛkt] *n* : amor *m* propio — **self-righteous** [ˌsɛlf'raɪtʃəs] *adj* : santurrón — **self-service** [ˌsɛlf'sərvɪs] *adj* : de autoservicio — **self-sufficient** [ˌsɛlfsə'fɪʃənt] *adj* : autosuficiente — **self-taught** [ˌsɛlf'tɔt] *adj* : autodidacta

sell ['sɛl] *v* **sold** ['so:ld]; **selling** *vt* : vender — *vi* : venderse — **seller** ['sɛlər] *n* : vendedor *m*, -dora *f*

selves → **self**

semantics [sɪ'mæntɪks] *ns & pl* : semántica *f*

semblance ['sɛmblənts] *n* : apariencia *f*

semester [sə'mɛstər] *n* : semestre *m*

semicolon ['sɛmiˌko:lən, 'sɛˌmaɪ-] *n* : punto y coma *m*

semifinal ['sɛmiˌfaɪnəl, 'sɛˌmaɪ-] *n* : semifinal *f*

seminary ['sɛməˌnɛri] *n, pl* **-naries** : seminario *m* — **seminar** ['sɛməˌnɑr] *n* : seminario *m*

senate ['sɛnət] *n* : senado *m* — **senator** ['sɛnət̬ər] *n* : senador *m*, -dora *f*

send ['sɛnd] *vt* **sent** ['sɛnt]; **sending 1** : mandar, enviar **2 ~ away for** : pedir **3 ~ back** : devolver (mercancías, etc.) **4 ~ for** : mandar a buscar — **sender** ['sɛndər] *n* : remitente *mf*

senile ['si:ˌnaɪl] *adj* : senil — **senility** [sɪ'nɪlət̬i] *n* : senilidad *f*

senior ['si:njər] *n* **1** SUPERIOR : superior *m* **2** : estudiante *mf* de último año (en educación) **3** *or* **~ citizen** : persona *f* mayor **4 be s.o.'s ~** : ser mayor que algn — ~ *adj* **1** : superior (en rango) **2** ELDER : mayor — **seniority** [ˌsi:'njɔrət̬i] *n* : antigüedad *f*

sensation [sɛn'seɪʃən] *n* : sensación *f* — **sensational** [sɛn'seɪʃənəl] *adj* : sensacional

sense ['sɛnts] *n* **1** : sentido *m* **2** FEELING : sensación *f* **3** COMMON SENSE : sentido *m* común **4 make ~** : tener sentido — ~ *vt* **sensed; sensing** : sentir — **senseless** ['sɛntsləs] *adj* **1** : sin sentido **2** UNCONSCIOUS : inconsciente — **sensible** ['sɛntsəbəl] *adj* : sensato, práctico — **sensibility** [ˌsɛntsə'bɪlət̬i] *n, pl* **-ties** : sensibilidad *f* — **sensitive** ['sɛntsət̬ɪv] *adj* **1** : sensible **2** TOUCHY : susceptible — **sensitivity** [ˌsɛntsə'tɪvət̬i] *n, pl* **-ties** : sensibilidad *f* — **sensual** ['sɛntʃʊəl] *adj* : sensual — **sensuous** ['sɛntʃʊəs] *adj* : sensual

sent → **send**

sentence ['sɛntənts, -ənz] *n* **1** : frase *f* **2** JUDGMENT : sentencia *f* — ~ *vt* **-tenced; -tencing** : sentenciar

sentiment ['sɛntəmənt] *n* **1** : sentimiento *m* **2** BELIEF : opinión *f* — **sentimental** [ˌsɛntə'mɛntəl] *adj* : sentimental — **sentimentality** [ˌsɛntəˌmɛn'tælət̬i] *n, pl* **-ties** : sentimentalismo *m*

sentry ['sɛntri] *n, pl* **-tries** : centinela *m*

separation [ˌsɛpə'reɪʃən] *n* : separación *f* — **separate** ['sɛpəˌreɪt] *v* **-rated; -rating** *vt* **1** : separar **2** DISTINGUISH : distinguir — *vi* : separarse — ~ ['sɛprət, 'sɛpə-] *adj* **1** : separado **2** DETACHED : aparte **3** DISTINCT : distinto — **separately** ['sɛprətli, 'sɛpə-] *adv* : por separado

September [sɛp'tɛmbər] *n* : septiembre *m*, setiembre *m*

sequel ['si:kwəl] *n* **1** : continuación *f* **2** CONSEQUENCE : secuela *f*

sequence ['si:kwənts] *n* **1** ORDER : orden *m* **2** : secuencia *f* (de números o escenas)

Serb ['sərb] *or* **Serbian** ['sərbiən] *adj* : serbio

serene [sə'ri:n] *adj* : sereno — **serenity** [sə'rɛnət̬i] *n* : serenidad *f*

sergeant ['sɑrdʒənt] *n* : sargento *mf*

serial ['sɪriəl] *adj* : seriado — ~ *n* : serial *m* — **series** ['sɪrˌi:z] *n, pl* **series** : serie *f*

serious ['sɪriəs] *adj* : serio — **seriously** ['sɪriəsli] *adv* **1** : seriamente **2** GRAVELY : gravemente **3 take ~** : tomar en serio

sermon ['sərmən] *n* : sermón *m*

serpent ['sərpənt] *n* : serpiente *f*

servant ['sərvənt] *n* : criado *m*, -da *f*

serve ['sərv] *v* **served; serving** *vi* **1** : servir **2** : sacar (en deportes) **3 ~ as** : servir de — *vt* **1** : servir **2 ~ time** : cumplir una condena — **server** ['sərvər] *n* **1** WAITER : camarero *m*, -ra *f* **2** : servidor *m* (en informática)

service ['sərvəs] *n* **1** : servicio *m* **2** CEREMONY : oficio *m* **3** MAINTENANCE : revisión *f* **4 armed ~s** : fuerzas *fpl* armadas — ~ *vt* **-viced; -vicing** : revisar (un vehículo, etc.) — **serviceman** ['sərvəsˌmæn, -mən] *n, pl* **-men** [-mən, -ˌmɛn] : militar *m* — **service station** *n* : estación *f* de servicio — **serving** ['sərvɪŋ] *n* : porción *f*, ración *f*

session ['sɛʃən] *n* : sesión *f*

set ['sɛt] *n* **1** : juego *m* (de platos, etc.) **2** : set *m* (en tenis, etc.) **3** *or* **stage ~** : decorado *m* **4 television ~** : aparato *m* de televisión — ~ *v* **set; setting** *vt* **1** *or* **~ down** : poner **2** : poner en hora (un reloj) **3** FIX : fijar (una fecha, etc.) **4 ~ fire to** : prender fuego a **5 ~ free** : poner en libertad **6 ~ off** : hacer sonar (una alarma), hacer estallar (una bomba) **7 ~ out to (do sth)** : proponerse (hacer algo) **8 ~ up** ASSEMBLE : montar, armar **9 ~ up** ESTABLISH : establecer — *vi* **1** : cuajarse (dícese de la gelatina, etc.), fraguar (dícese del cemento) **2** : ponerse (dícese del sol, etc.) **3 ~ in** BEGIN : empezar **4 ~ off** *or* **~ out** : salir (de viaje) — ~ *adj* **1** FIXED : fijo **2** READY : listo, preparado — **setback** ['sɛtˌbæk] *n* : revés *m* — **setting** ['sɛt̬ɪŋ] *n* **1** : posición *f* (de un control) **2** MOUNTING : engaste *m* (de joyas) **3** SCENE : escenario *m*

settle ['sɛt̬əl] *v* **settled; settling** *vi* **1** : asentarse (dícese de polvo, colonos, etc.) **2 ~ down** RELAX : calmarse **3 ~ for** : conformarse con **4 ~ in** : instalarse — *vt* **1** DECIDE : fijar, decidir **2** RESOLVE : resolver **3** PAY : pagar **4** CALM : calmar **5** COLONIZE : colonizar — **settlement** ['sɛt̬əlmənt] *n* **1** PAYMENT : pago *m* **2** COLONY : colonia *f*, poblado *m* **3** AGREEMENT : acuerdo *m* — **settler** ['sɛt̬ələr] *n* : colono *m*, -na *f*

seven ['sɛvən] *adj* : siete — ~ *n* : siete *m* — **seven hundred** *adj* : setecientos — ~ *n* : setecientos *m* — **seventeen** [ˌsɛvən'ti:n] *adj* : diecisiete — ~ *n* : diecisiete *m* — **seventeenth** [ˌsɛvən'ti:nθ] *adj* : decimoséptimo — ~ *n* **1** : decimoséptimo *m*, -ma *f* (en una serie) **2** : diecisieteavo *m* (en matemáticas) — **seventh** ['sɛvənθ] *adj* : séptimo — ~ *n* **1** : séptimo *m*, -ma *f* (en una serie) **2** : séptimo *m* (en matemáticas) — **seventieth** ['sɛvəntiəθ] *adj* : septuagésimo — ~ *n* **1** : septuagésimo *m*, -ma *f* (en una serie) **2** : setentavo *m* (en matemáticas) — **seventy** ['sɛvənt̬i] *adj* : setenta — ~ *n, pl* **-ties** : setenta *m*

sever ['sɛvər] *vt* **-ered; -ering** : cortar, romper

several ['sɛvrəl, 'sɛvə-] *adj* : varios — ~ *pron* : varios, varias

severance ['sɛvrənts, sɛvə-] *n* : ruptura *f*

severe [sə'vɪr] *adj* **severer; -est 1** : severo **2** SERIOUS : grave — **severely** *adv* **1** : severamente **2** SERIOUSLY : gravemente — **severity** [sə'vɛrət̬i] *n* **1** : severidad *f* **2** SERIOUSNESS : gravedad *f*

sew ['so:] *v* **sewed; sewn** ['so:n] *or* **sewed; sewing** : coser

sewer ['su:ər] *n* : cloaca *f* — **sewage** ['su:ɪdʒ] *n* : aguas *fpl* negras

sewing ['so:ɪŋ] *n* : costura *f*

sex ['sɛks] *n* **1** : sexo *m* **2** INTERCOURSE : relaciones *fpl* sexuales — **sexism** ['sɛkˌsɪzəm] *n* : sexismo *m* — **sexist** ['sɛksɪst] *adj* : sexista — **sexual** ['sɛkʃʊəl] *adj* : sexual — **sexuality** [ˌsɛkʃʊ'ælət̬i] *n* : sexualidad *f* — **sexy** ['sɛksi] *adj* **sexier; -est** : sexy

shabby ['ʃæbi] *adj* **shabbier; -est 1** WORN : gastado **2** UNFAIR : malo, injusto

shack ['ʃæk] *n* : choza *f*

shackle ['ʃækəl] *n* : grillete *m*

shade ['ʃeɪd] *n* **1** : sombra *f* **2** : tono *m* (de un color) **3** NUANCE : matiz *m* **4** *or* **lampshade** : pantalla *f* **5** *or* **window ~** : persiana *f* — ~ *vt* **shaded; shading** : proteger de la luz — **shadow** ['ʃædo:] *n* : sombra *f* — **shadowy** ['ʃædowi] *adj* INDISTINCT : vago — **shady** ['ʃeɪdi] *adj* **shadier; -est 1** : sombreado **2** DISREPUTABLE : sospechoso

shaft ['ʃæft] *n* **1** : asta *f* (de una flecha, etc.) **2** HANDLE : mango *m* **3** AXLE : eje *m* **4** : rayo *m* (de luz) **5** *or* **mine ~** : pozo *m*

shaggy ['ʃægi] *adj* **shaggier; -est** : peludo

shake ['ʃeɪk] *v* **shook** ['ʃʊk]; **shaken** ['ʃeɪkən]; **shaking** *vt* **1** : sacudir **2** MIX : agitar **3 ~ hands with s.o.** : dar la mano a algn **4 ~ one's head** : negar con la cabeza **5 ~ up** UPSET : afectar — *vi* : temblar — ~ *n* **1** : sacudida *f* **2** → **handshake** — **shaker** ['ʃeɪkər] *n* **1 salt ~** : salero *m* **2 pepper ~** : pimentero *m* — **shaky** ['ʃeɪki] *adj* **shakier; -est 1** : tembloroso **2** UNSTABLE : poco firme

shall ['ʃæl] *v aux, past* **should** ['ʃʊd]; *pres sing & pl* **shall 1** (*expressing volition or futurity*) → **will 2** (*expressing possibility or obligation*) → **should 3 ~ we go?** : ¿nos vamos?

shallow ['ʃælo:] *adj* **1** : poco profundo **2** SUPERFICIAL : superficial

sham ['ʃæm] *n* : farsa *f* — ~ *v* **shammed; shamming** : fingir

shambles ['ʃæmbəlz] *ns & pl* : caos *m*, desorden *m*

shame ['ʃeɪm] *n* **1** : vergüenza *f* **2 what a ~!** : ¡qué lástima! — ~ *vt* **shamed; shaming** : avergonzar — **shameful** ['ʃeɪmfəl] *adj* : vergonzoso — **shameless** ['ʃeɪmləs] *adj* : desvergonzado

shampoo [ʃæm'pu:] *vt* : lavar (el pelo) — ~ *n, pl* **-poos** : champú *m*

shamrock ['ʃæmˌrɑk] *n* : trébol *m*

shan't ['ʃænt] (*contraction of* **shall not**) → **shall**

shape ['ʃeɪp] *v* **shaped; shaping** *vt* **1** : formar **2** DETERMINE : determinar **3 be ~d like** : tener forma de — *vi or* **~ up** : tomar forma — ~ *n* **1** : forma *f* **2 get in ~** : ponerse en forma — **shapeless** ['ʃeɪpləs] *adj* : informe

share ['ʃɛr] *n* **1** : porción *f* **2** : acción *f* (en una compañía) — ~ *v* **shared; sharing** *vt* **1** : compartir **2** DIVIDE : dividir — *vi* : compartir — **shareholder** ['ʃɛrˌho:ldər] *n* : accionista *mf*

shark ['ʃɑrk] *n* : tiburón *m*

sharp ['ʃɑrp] *adj* **1** : afilado **2** POINTY : puntiagudo **3** ACUTE : agudo **4** HARSH : duro, severo **5** CLEAR : nítido **6** : sostenido (en música) **7 a ~ curve** : una curva cerrada — ~ *adv* **at two o'clock ~** : a las dos en punto — ~ *n* : sostenido (en música) — **sharpen** ['ʃɑrpən] *vt* : afilar (un cuchillo, etc.), sacar punta a (un lápiz) — **sharpener** ['ʃɑrpənər] *n* **1** *or* **knife ~** : afilador *m* **2** *or* **pencil ~** : sacapuntas *m* — **sharply** ['ʃɑrpli] *adv* : bruscamente

shatter ['ʃæt̬ər] *vt* **1** : hacer añicos **2** DEVASTATE : destrozar — *vi* : hacerse añicos

shave ['ʃeɪv] *v* **shaved; shaved** *or* **shaven** ['ʃeɪvən]; **shaving** *vt* **1** : afeitar **2** SLICE : cortar — *vi* : afeitarse — ~ *n* : afeitada *f* — **shaver** ['ʃeɪvər] *n* : máquina *f* de afeitar

shawl ['ʃɔl] *n* : chal *m*

she ['ʃi:] *pron* : ella

sheaf ['ʃi:f] *n, pl* **sheaves** ['ʃi:vz] **1** : gavilla *f* **2** : fajo *m* (de papeles)

shear ['ʃɪr] *vt* **sheared; sheared** *or* **shorn** ['ʃorn]; **shearing** : esquilar — **shears** ['ʃɪrz] *npl* : tijeras *fpl* (grandes)

sheath ['ʃi:θ] *n, pl* **sheaths** ['ʃi:ðz, 'ʃi:θs] : funda *f*, vaina *f*

shed[1] ['ʃɛd] *v* **shed; shedding** *vt* **1** : derramar (lágrimas, etc.) **2** : mudar (de piel, etc.), quitarse (ropa) **3 ~ light on** : aclarar

shed[2] *n* : cobertizo *m*

she'd ['ʃi:d] (*contraction of* **she had** *or* **she would**) → **have, would**

sheen ['ʃi:n] *n* : brillo *m*, lustre *m*

sheep ['ʃi:p] *n, pl* **sheep** : oveja *f* — **sheepish** ['ʃi:pɪʃ] *adj* : avergonzado

sheer ['ʃɪr] *adj* **1** THIN : transparente **2** PURE : puro **3** STEEP : escarpado

sheet ['ʃi:t] *n* **1** : sábana *f* (de la cama) **2** : hoja *f* (de papel) **3** : capa *f* (de hielo, etc.) **4** PLATE : placa *f*, lámina *f*

shelf ['ʃɛlf] *n, pl* **shelves** ['ʃɛlvz] : estante *m*

shell ['ʃɛl] *n* **1** : concha *f* **2** : caparazón *m* (de un crustáceo, etc.) **3** : cáscara *f* (de un huevo, etc.) **4** : armazón *mf* (de un edificio, etc.) **5** POD : vaina *f* **6** MISSILE : proyectil *m* — ~ *vt* **1** : pelar (nueces, etc.) **2** BOMBARD : bombardear

she'll ['ʃi:l, 'ʃɪl] (*contraction of* **she shall** *or* **she will**) → **shall, will**

shellfish ['ʃɛlˌfɪʃ] *n* : marisco *m*

shelter ['ʃɛltər] *n* **1** : refugio *m* **2 take ~** : refugiarse — ~ *vt* **1** PROTECT : proteger **2** HARBOR : albergar

shelve ['ʃɛlv] *vt* **shelved; shelving** DEFER : dar carpetazo a

shepherd ['ʃɛpərd] *n* : pastor *m* — ~ *vt* GUIDE : conducir, guiar

sherbet ['ʃərbət] *n* : sorbete *m*

sheriff ['ʃɛrɪf] *n* : sheriff *mf*

sherry ['ʃɛri] *n, pl* **-ries** : jerez *m*

she's ['ʃi:z] (*contraction of* **she is** *or* **she has**) → **be, have**

shield ['ʃi:ld] *n* : escudo *m* — ~ *vt* : proteger

shier, shiest → **shy**

shift ['ʃɪft] *vt* **1** MOVE : mover **2** SWITCH : transferir — *vi* **1** CHANGE : cambiar **2** MOVE : moverse **3** *or* **~ gears** : cambiar de velocidad — ~ *n* **1** CHANGE : cambio *m* **2** : turno *m* (de trabajo) — **shiftless** ['ʃɪftləs] *adj* : holgazán — **shifty** ['ʃɪfti] *adj* **shiftier; -est** : sospechoso

shimmer ['ʃɪmər] *vi* : brillar, relucir

shin ['ʃɪn] *n* : espinilla *f*

shine ['ʃaɪn] *v* **shone** ['ʃo:n] *or* **shined; shining** *vi* : brillar — *vt* **1** : alumbrar (una luz) **2** POLISH : sacar brillo a — ~ *n* : brillo *m*

shingle ['ʃɪŋgəl] *n* : teja *f* plana y delgada (en construcción) — ~ *vt* **-gled; -gling** : techar — **shingles** ['ʃɪŋgəlz] *npl* : herpes *m*

shiny ['ʃaɪni] *adj* **shinier; -est** : brillante

ship ['ʃɪp] *n* **1** : barco *m*, buque *m* **2** → **spaceship** — ~ *vt* **shipped; shipping** : transportar, enviar (por barco) — **shipbuilding** ['ʃɪpˌbɪldɪŋ] *n* : construcción *f* naval — **shipment** ['ʃɪpmənt] *n* : envío *m* — **shipping** ['ʃɪpɪŋ] *n* **1** : transporte *m* **2** SHIPS : barcos *mpl* — **shipshape** ['ʃɪp'ʃeɪp] *adj* : ordenado — **shipwreck** ['ʃɪpˌrɛk] *n* : naufragio *m* — ~ *vt* **be ~ed** : naufragar — **shipyard** ['ʃɪpˌjɑrd] *n* : astillero *m*

shirk ['ʃərk] *vt* : esquivar

shirt ['ʃərt] *n* : camisa *f*

shiver ['ʃɪvər] *vi* : temblar (del frío, etc.) — ~ *n* : escalofrío *m*

shoal ['ʃo:l] *n* : banco *m*

shock ['ʃɑk] *n* **1** IMPACT : choque *m* **2** SURPRISE, UPSET : golpe *m* emocional **3** : shock *m* (en medicina) **4** *or* **electric ~** : descarga *f* (eléctrica) — ~ *vt* : escandalizar — **shock absorber** *n* : amortiguador *m* — **shocking** ['ʃɑkɪŋ] *adj* : escandaloso

shoddy ['ʃɑdi] *adj* **shoddier; -est** : de mala calidad

shoe ['ʃu:] *n* : zapato *m* — ~ *vt* **shod** ['ʃɑd]; **shoeing** : herrar (un caballo) — **shoelace** ['ʃu:ˌleɪs] *n* : cordón *m* (de zapato) — **shoemaker** ['ʃu:ˌmeɪkər] *n* : zapatero *m*, -ra *f*

shone → **shine**

shook → **shake**

shoot ['ʃu:t] *v* **shot** ['ʃɑt]; **shooting** *vt* **1** : disparar **2** : echar (una mirada) **3** PHOTOGRAPH : fotografiar **4** FILM : rodar — *vi* **1** : disparar **2 ~ by** : pasar como una bala — ~ *n* : brote *m*, retoño *m* (de una planta) — **shooting star** *n* : estrella *f* fugaz

shop ['ʃɑp] *n* **1** : tienda *f* **2** WORKSHOP : taller *m* — ~ *vi* **shopped; shopping 1** : hacer compras **2 go shopping** : ir de

compras — **shopkeeper** ['ʃɑpˌki:pər] *n* : tendero *m*, -ra *f* — **shoplift** ['ʃɑpˌlɪft] *vi* : hurtar mercancía (en tiendas) — **shoplifter** ['ʃɑpˌlɪftər] *n* : ladrón *m*, -drona *f* (que roba en tiendas) — **shopper** ['ʃɑpər] *n* : comprador *m*, -dora *f*
shore ['ʃor] *n* : orilla *f*
shorn → **shear**
short ['ʃɔrt] *adj* **1** : corto **2** : bajo (de estatura) **3** CURT : brusco **4 a ~ time ago** : hace poco **5 be ~ of** : estar corto de — **~** *adv* **1 stop ~** : parar en seco **2 fall ~** : quedarse corto — **shortage** ['ʃɔrtɪdʒ] *n* : escasez *f*, carencia *f* — **shortcake** ['ʃɔrtˌkeɪk] *n* : tarta *f* de fruta — **shortcoming** ['ʃɔrtˌkʌmɪŋ] *n* : defecto *m* — **shortcut** ['ʃɔrtˌkʌt] *n* : atajo *m* — **shorten** ['ʃɔrtən] *vt* : acortar — **shorthand** ['ʃɔrtˌhænd] *n* : taquigrafía *f* — **short–lived** ['ʃɔrt'lɪvd, -'laɪvd] *adj* : efímero — **shortly** ['ʃɔrtli] *adv* : dentro de poco — **shortness** ['ʃɔrtnəs] *n* **1** : lo corto (de una cosa), baja estatura *f* (de una persona) **2 ~ of breath** : falta *f* de aliento — **shorts** *npl* : shorts *mpl*, pantalones *mpl* cortos — **shortsighted** ['ʃɔrtˌsaɪṭəd] → **nearsighted**
shot ['ʃɑt] *n* **1** : disparo *m*, tiro *m* **2** : tiro *m* (en deportes) **3** ATTEMPT : intento *m* **4** PHOTOGRAPH : foto *f* **5** INJECTION : inyección *f* **6** : trago *m* (de licor) — **shotgun** ['ʃɑtˌgʌn] *n* : escopeta *f*
should ['ʃʊd] *past of* **shall 1 if she ~ call** : si llama **2 I ~ have gone** : debería haber ido **3 they ~ arrive soon** : deben llegar pronto **4 what ~ we do?** : ¿qué hacemos?
shoulder ['ʃo:ldər] *n* **1** : hombro *m* **2** : arcén *m* (de una carretera) — **~** *vt* : cargar con (la responsabilidad, etc.) — **shoulder blade** *n* : omóplato *m*
shouldn't ['ʃʊdənt] (*contraction of* **should not**) → **should**
shout ['ʃaʊt] *v* : gritar — **~** *n* : grito *m*
shove ['ʃʌv] *v* **shoved; shoving** : empujar — **~** *n* : empujón *m*
shovel ['ʃʌvəl] *n* : pala *f* — **~** *vt* **-veled** *or* **-velled; -veling** *or* **-velling 1** : mover (tierra, etc.) con una pala **2** DIG : cavar (con una pala)
show ['ʃo:] *v* **showed; shown** ['ʃo:n] *or* **showed; showing** *vt* **1** : mostrar **2** TEACH : enseñar **3** PROVE : demostrar **4** ESCORT : acompañar **5** : proyectar (una película), dar (un programa de televisión) **6 ~ off** : hacer alarde de — *vi* **1** : notarse, verse **2 ~ off** : lucirse **3 ~ up** ARRIVE : aparecer — **~** *n* **1** : demostración *f* **2** EXHIBITION : exposición *f* **3** : espectáculo *m* (teatral), programa *m* (de televisión, etc.) — **showdown** ['ʃo:ˌdaʊn] *n* : confrontación *f*
shower ['ʃaʊər] *n* **1** : ducha *f* **2** : chaparrón *m* (en meteorología) **3** PARTY : fiesta *f* — **~** *vt* **1** SPRAY : regar **2 ~ s.o. with** : colmar a algn de — *vi* **1** : ducharse **2** RAIN : llover
showy ['ʃo:i] *adj* **showier; -est** : llamativo, ostentoso
shrank → **shrink**
shrapnel ['ʃræpnəl] *ns & pl* : metralla *f*
shred ['ʃrɛd] *n* **1** : tira *f* (de tela, etc.) **2** IOTA : pizca *f* — **~** *vt* **shredded; shredding 1** : hacer tiras **2** GRATE : rallar
shrewd ['ʃru:d] *adj* : astuto
shriek ['ʃri:k] *vi* : chillar — **~** *n* : chillido *m*, alarido *m*
shrill ['ʃrɪl] *adj* : agudo, estridente
shrimp ['ʃrɪmp] *n* : camarón *m*
shrine ['ʃraɪn] *n* **1** TOMB : sepulcro *m* **2** SANCTUARY : santuario *m*
shrink ['ʃrɪŋk] *v* **shrank** ['ʃræŋk]; **shrunk** ['ʃrʌŋk] *or* **shrunken** ['ʃrʌŋkən]; **shrinking** *vt* : encoger — *vi* **1** : encogerse (dícese de ropa), reducirse (dícese de números, etc.) **2** *or* **~ back** : retroceder
shrivel ['ʃrɪvəl] *vi* **-veled** *or* **-velled; -veling** *or* **-velling** *or* **~ up** : arrugarse, marchitarse
shroud ['ʃraʊd] *n* **1** : sudario *m*, mortaja *f* **2** VEIL : velo *m* — **~** *vt* : envolver
shrub ['ʃrʌb] *n* : arbusto *m*, mata *f*
shrug ['ʃrʌg] *vi* **shrugged; shrugging** : encogerse de hombros
shrunk → **shrink**
shudder ['ʃʌdər] *vi* : estremecerse — **~** *n* : estremecimiento *m*
shuffle ['ʃʌfəl] *v* **-fled; -fling** *vt* : barajar (naipes), revolver (papeles, etc.) — *vi* : caminar arrastrando los pies
shun ['ʃʌn] *vi* **shunned; shunning** : evitar, esquivar
shut ['ʃʌt] *v* **shut; shutting** *vt* **1** CLOSE : cerrar **2 ~ off** → **turn off 3 ~ up** CONFINE : encerrar — *vi* **1** *or* **~ down** : cerrarse **2 ~ up!** : ¡cállate! — **shutter** ['ʃʌṭər] *n* **1** *or* **window ~** : contraventana *f* **2** : obturador *m* (de una cámara)
shuttle ['ʃʌṭəl] *n* **1** : lanzadera *f* (para tejer) **2** *or* **~ bus** : autobús *m* (de corto recorrido) **3** → **space shuttle** — **~** *v* **-tled; -tling** *vt* : transportar — *vi* : ir y venir
shy ['ʃaɪ] *adj* **shier** *or* **shyer** ['ʃaɪər]; **shiest** *or* **shyest** ['ʃaɪəst] : tímido — **~** *vi* **shied; shying** *or* **~ away** : retroceder — **shyness** ['ʃaɪnəs] *n* : timidez *f*
sibling ['sɪblɪŋ] *n* : hermano *m*, hermana *f*
sick ['sɪk] *adj* **1** : enfermo **2 be ~** VOMIT : vomitar **3 be ~ of** : estar harto de **4 feel ~** : tener náuseas — **sicken** ['sɪkən] *vt* DISGUST : dar asco a — **sickening** ['sɪkənɪŋ] *adj* : nauseabundo
sickle ['sɪkəl] *n* : hoz *f*
sickly ['sɪkli] *adj* **sicklier; -est 1** UNHEALTHY : enfermizo **2** → **sickening** — **sickness** ['sɪknəs] *n* : enfermedad *f*
side ['saɪd] *n* **1** : lado *m* **2** : costado *m* (de una persona), ijada *f* (de un animal) **3** : parte *f* (en una disputa, etc.) **4 ~ by ~** : uno al lado de otro **5 take ~s** : tomar partido — **~** *vi* **~ with** : ponerse de parte de — **sideboard** ['saɪdˌbord] *n* : aparador *m* — **sideburns** ['saɪdˌbərnz] *npl* : patillas *fpl* — **side effect** *n* : efecto *m* secundario — **sideline** ['saɪdˌlaɪn] *n* : línea *f* de banda (en deportes) — **sidestep** ['saɪdˌstɛp] *vt* **-stepped; -stepping** : eludir, esquivar — **sidetrack** ['saɪdˌtræk] *vt* **get ~ed** : distraerse — **sidewalk** ['saɪdˌwɔk] *n* : acera *f* — **sideways** ['saɪdˌweɪz] *adj & adv* : de lado — **siding** ['saɪdɪŋ] *n* : revestimiento *m* exterior
siege ['si:dʒ, 'si:ʒ] *n* : sitio *m*
sieve ['sɪv] *n* : tamiz *m*, cedazo *m*
sift ['sɪft] *vt* **1** : cerner, tamizar **2** *or* **~ through** : pasar por el tamiz
sigh ['saɪ] *vi* : suspirar — **~** *n* : suspiro *m*
sight ['saɪt] *n* **1** : vista *f* **2** SPECTACLE : espectáculo *m* **3** : lugar *m* de interés (turístico) **4 catch ~ of** : avistar — **~** *vt* : avistar — **sightseer** ['saɪtˌsi:ər] *n* : turista *mf*
sign ['saɪn] *n* **1** : signo *m* **2** NOTICE : letrero *m* **3** GESTURE : seña *f*, señal *f* — **~** *vt* : firmar (un cheque, etc.) — *vi* **1** : firmar **2 ~ up** ENROLL : inscribirse
signal ['sɪgnəl] *n* : señal *f* — **~** *v* **-naled** *or* **-nalled; -naling** *or* **-nalling** *vt* **1** : hacer señas a **2** INDICATE : señalar — *vi* **1** : hacer señas **2** : señalizar (en un vehículo)
signature ['sɪgnəˌtʃʊr] *n* : firma *f*
significance [sɪg'nɪfɪkənts] *n* **1** : significado *m* **2** IMPORTANCE : importancia *f* — **significant** [sɪg'nɪfɪkənt] *adj* : importante — **signify** ['sɪgnəˌfaɪ] *vt* **-fied; -fying** : significar
sign language *n* : lenguaje *m* gestual — **signpost** ['saɪnˌpo:st] *n* : poste *m* indicador
silence ['saɪlənts] *n* : silencio *m* — **~** *vt* **-lenced; -lencing** : silenciar — **silent** ['saɪlənt] *adj* **1** : silencioso **2** MUM : callado **3** : mudo (dícese de películas y letras)
silhouette [ˌsɪlə'wɛt] *n* : silueta *f* — **~** *vt* **-etted; -etting be ~d against** : perfilarse contra
silicon ['sɪlɪkən, -ˌkɑn] *n* : silicio *m*
silk ['sɪlk] *n* : seda *f* — **silky** ['sɪlki] *adj* **silkier; -est** : sedoso
sill ['sɪl] *n* : alféizar *m* (de una ventana), umbral *m* (de una puerta)
silly ['sɪli] *adj* **sillier; -est** : tonto, estúpido
silt ['sɪlt] *n* : cieno *m*
silver ['sɪlvər] *n* **1** : plata *f* **2** → **silverware** — **~** *adj* : de plata — **silverware** ['sɪlvərˌwær] *n* : plata *f* — **silvery** ['sɪlvəri] *adj* : plateado
similar ['sɪmələr] *adj* : similar, parecido — **similarity** [ˌsɪmə'lærəṭi] *n, pl* **-ties** : semejanza *f*, parecido *m*
simmer ['sɪmər] *v* : hervir a fuego lento
simple ['sɪmpəl] *adj* **simpler; -plest 1** : simple **2** EASY : sencillo — **simplicity** [sɪm'plɪsəṭi] *n* : simplicidad *f*, sencillez *f* — **simplify** ['sɪmpləˌfaɪ] *vt* **-fied; -fying** : simplificar — **simply** ['sɪmpli] *adv* **1** : sencillamente **2** ABSOLUTELY : realmente
simulate ['sɪmjəˌleɪt] *vt* **-lated; -lating** : simular
simultaneous [ˌsaɪməl'teɪniəs] *adj* : simultáneo
sin ['sɪn] *n* : pecado *m* — **~** *vi* **sinned; sinning** : pecar
since ['sɪnts] *adv* **1** *or* **~ then** : desde entonces **2 long ~** : hace mucho — **~** *conj* **1** : desde que **2** BECAUSE : ya que, como **3 it's been years ~...** : hace años que... — **~** *prep* : desde
sincere [sɪn'sɪr] *adj* **-cerer; -est** : sincero — **sincerely** *adv* : sinceramente — **sincerity** [sɪn'sɛrəṭi] *n* : sinceridad *f*
sinful ['sɪnfəl] *adj* : pecador (dícese de las personas), pecaminoso (dícese de las acciones)
sing ['sɪŋ] *v* **sang** ['sæŋ] *or* **sung** ['sʌŋ]; **sung; singing** : cantar
singe ['sɪndʒ] *vt* **singed; singeing** : chamuscar
singer ['sɪŋər] *n* : cantante *mf*
single ['sɪŋgəl] *adj* **1** : solo, único **2** UNMARRIED : soltero **3 every ~ day** : cada día, todos los días — **~** *n* **1** : soltero *m*, -ra *f* **2** *or* **~ room** : habitación *f* individual — **~** *vt* **-gled; -gling ~ out 1** SELECT : escoger **2** DISTINGUISH : señalar — **single–handed** [ˌsɪŋgəl'hændəd] *adj* : sin ayuda, solo
singular ['sɪŋgjələr] *adj* : singular — **~** *n* : singular *m*
sinister ['sɪnəstər] *adj* : siniestro
sink ['sɪŋk] *v* **sank** ['sæŋk] *or* **sunk** ['sʌŋk]; **sunk; sinking** *vi* **1** : hundirse (en un líquido) **2** DROP : bajar, caer — *vt* **1** : hundir **2 ~ sth into** : clavar algo en — **~** *n* **1** *or* **kitchen ~** : fregadero *m* **2** *or* **bathroom ~** : lavabo *m*, lavamanos *m*
sinner ['sɪnər] *n* : pecador *m*, -dora *f*
sip ['sɪp] *v* **sipped; sipping** *vt* : sorber — *vi* : beber a sorbos — **~** *n* : sorbo *m*
siphon ['saɪfən] *n* : sifón *m* — **~** *vt* : sacar con sifón
sir ['sər] *n* **1** (*in titles*) : sir *m* **2** (*as a form of address*) : señor *m* **3 Dear Sir** : Estimado señor
siren ['saɪrən] *n* : sirena *f*
sirloin ['sərˌlɔɪn] *n* : solomillo *m*
sissy ['sɪsi] *n, pl* **-sies** : mariquita *mf fam*
sister ['sɪstər] *n* : hermana *f* — **sister–in–law** ['sɪstərɪnˌlɔ] *n, pl* **sisters–in–law** : cuñada *f*
sit ['sɪt] *v* **sat** ['sæt]; **sitting** *vi* **1** *or* **~ down** : sentarse **2** LIE : estar (ubicado) **3** MEET : estar en sesión **4** *or* **~ up** : incorporarse — *vt* : sentar
site ['saɪt] *n* **1** : sitio *m*, lugar *m* **2** LOT : solar *m*
sitting room → **living room**
sitter ['sɪṭər] *n* → **baby–sitter**
situated ['sɪtʃʊˌeɪṭəd] *adj* : ubicado, situado — **situation** [ˌsɪtʃʊ'eɪʃən] *n* : situación *f*
six ['sɪks] *adj* : seis — **~** *n* : seis *m* — **six hundred** *adj* : seiscientos — **~** *n* : seiscientos *m* — **sixteen** [sɪks'ti:n] *adj* : dieciséis — **~** *n* : dieciséis *m* — **sixteenth** [sɪks'ti:nθ] *adj* : decimosexto — **~** *n* **1** : decimosexto *m*, -ta *f* (en una serie) **2** : dieciseisavo *m*, dieciseisava parte *f* — **sixth** ['sɪksθ, 'sɪkst] *adj* : sexto — **~** *n* **1** : sexto *m*, -ta *f* (en una serie) **2** : sexto *m* (en matemáticas) — **sixtieth** ['sɪkstiəθ] *adj* : sexagésimo — **~** *n* **1** : sexagésimo *m*, -ma *f* (en una serie) **2** : sesentavo *m* (en matemáticas) — **sixty** ['sɪksti] *adj* : sesenta — **~** *n, pl* **-ties** : sesenta *m*
size ['saɪz] *n* **1** : tamaño *m*, talla *f* (de ropa), número *m* (de zapatos) **2** EXTENT : magnitud *f* — **~** *vt* **sized; sizing ~ up** : evaluar — **sizable** *or* **sizeable** ['saɪzəbəl] *adj* : considerable
sizzle ['sɪzəl] *vi* **-zled; -zling** : chisporrotear
skate[1] ['skeɪt] *n* : raya *f* (pez)
skate[2] *n* : patín *m* — **~** *vi* **skated; skating** : patinar — **skateboard** ['skeɪtˌbord] *n* : monopatín *m* — **skater** ['skeɪṭər] *n* : patinador *m*, -dora *f*
skeleton ['skɛlətən] *n* : esqueleto *m*
skeptic ['skɛptɪk] *n* : escéptico *m*, -ca *f* — **skeptical** ['skɛptɪkəl] *adj* : escéptico — **skepticism** ['skɛptəˌsɪzəm] *n* : escepticismo *m*
sketch ['skɛtʃ] *n* **1** : esbozo *m*, bosquejo *m* **2** SKIT : sketch *m* — **~** *vt* : bosquejar — *vi* : hacer bosquejos — **sketchy** ['skɛtʃi] *adj* **sketchier; -est** : incompleto
skewer ['skju:ər] *n* : brocheta *f*, broqueta *f*
ski ['ski:] *n, pl* **skis** : esquí *m* — **~** *vi* **skied; skiing** : esquiar
skid ['skɪd] *n* : derrape *m*, patinazo *m* — **~** *vi* **skidded; skidding** : derrapar, patinar
skier ['ski:ər] *n* : esquiador *m*, -dora *f*
skill ['skɪl] *n* **1** : habilidad *f*, destreza *f* **2** TECHNIQUE : técnica *f* — **skilled** ['skɪld] *adj* : hábil
skillet ['skɪlət] *n* : sartén *mf*
skillful ['skɪlfəl] *adj* : hábil, diestro
skim ['skɪm] *vt* **skimmed; skimming 1** : espumar (sopa, etc.), descremar (leche) **2** : pasar rozando (una superficie) **3** *or* **~ through** : echar un vistazo a — **~** *adj* : descremado
skimp ['skɪmp] *vi* **~ on** : escatimar — **skimpy** ['skɪmpi] *adj* **skimpier; -est 1** : exiguo, escaso **2** : brevísimo (dícese de ropa)
skin ['skɪn] *n* : piel *f* — **~** *vt* **skinned; skinning** : despellejar — **skin diving** *n* : buceo *m*, submarinismo *m* — **skinny** ['skɪni] *adj* **skinnier; -est** : flaco
skip ['skɪp] *v* **skipped; skipping** *vi* : ir brincando — *vt* OMIT : saltarse — **~** *n* : brinco *m*, salto *m*
skipper ['skɪpər] *n* : capitán *m*, -tana *f*
skirmish ['skərmɪʃ] *n* : escaramuza *f*
skirt ['skərt] *n* : falda *f* — **~** *vt* **1** BORDER : bordear **2** EVADE : eludir
skull ['skʌl] *n* : cráneo *m* (de una persona viva), calavera *f* (de un esqueleto)
skunk ['skʌŋk] *n* : mofeta *f*, zorrillo *m Lat*
sky ['skaɪ] *n, pl* **skies** : cielo *m* — **skylight** ['skaɪˌlaɪt] *n* : claraboya *f*, tragaluz *m* — **skyline** ['skaɪˌlaɪn] *n* : horizonte *m* — **skyscraper** ['skaɪˌskreɪpər] *n* : rascacielos *m*
slab ['slæb] *n* : bloque *m* (de piedra, etc.)
slack ['slæk] *adj* **1** LOOSE : flojo **2** CARELESS : descuidado — **~** *n* **1 take up the ~** : tensar (una cuerda, etc.) **2 ~s** *npl* : pantalones *mpl* — **slacken** ['slækən] *vt* : aflojar — *vi* : aflojarse
slain → **slay**
slam ['slæm] *n* : golpe *m*, portazo *m* (de una puerta) — **~** *v* **slammed; slamming** *vt* **1** *or* **~ down** : tirar, plantar **2** *or* **~ shut** : cerrar de golpe **3 ~ the door** : dar un portazo — *vi* **1** : cerrarse de golpe **2 ~ into** : chocar contra
slander ['slændər] *vt* : calumniar, difamar — **~** *n* : calumnia *f*, difamación *f*
slang ['slæŋ] *n* : argot *m*
slant ['slænt] *n* : inclinación *f* — **~** *vi* : inclinarse
slap ['slæp] *vt* **slapped; slapping 1** : dar una bofetada a **2 ~ s.o. on the back** : dar una palmada en la espalda a algn — **~** *n* : bofetada *f*, cachetada *f Lat*
slash ['slæʃ] *vt* **1** : hacer un tajo en **2** : rebajar (precios) drásticamente — **~** *n* : tajo *m*
slat ['slæt] *n* : tablilla *f*
slate ['sleɪt] *n* : pizarra *f*
slaughter ['slɔṭər] *n* : matanza *f* — **~** *vt* **1** : matar (animales) **2** MASSACRE : masacrar — **slaughterhouse** ['slɔṭərˌhaʊs] *n* : matadero *m*
slave ['sleɪv] *n* : esclavo *m*, -va *f* — **~** *vi* **slaved; slaving** : trabajar como un burro — **slavery** ['sleɪvəri] *n* : esclavitud *f*
Slavic ['slɑvɪk, 'slæ-] *adj* : eslavo
slay ['sleɪ] *vt* **slew** ['slu:]; **slain** ['sleɪn]; **slaying** : asesinar
sleazy ['sli:zi] *adj* **sleazier; -est** : sórdido
sled ['slɛd] *n* : trineo *m*
sledgehammer ['slɛdʒˌhæmər] *n* : almádena *f*
sleek ['sli:k] *adj* : liso y brillante
sleep ['sli:p] *n* **1** : sueño *m* **2 go to ~** : dormirse — **~** *vi* **slept** ['slɛpt]; **sleeping** : dormir — **sleeper** ['sli:pər] *n* **be a light ~** : tener el sueño ligero — **sleepless** ['sli:pləs] *adj* **have a ~ night** : pasar la noche en blanco — **sleepwalker** ['sli:pˌwɔkər] *n* : sonámbulo *m*, -la *f* — **sleepy** ['sli:pi] *adj* **sleepier; -est 1** : somnoliento, soñoliento **2 be ~** : tener sueño
sleet ['sli:t] *n* : aguanieve *f* — **~** *vi* : caer aguanieve
sleeve ['sli:v] *n* : manga *f* — **sleeveless** ['sli:vləs] *adj* : sin mangas
sleigh ['sleɪ] *n* : trineo *m*
slender ['slɛndər] *adj* : delgado
slew ['slu:] → **slay**
slice ['slaɪs] *vt* **sliced; slicing** : cortar — **~** *n* : trozo *m*, rebanada *f* (de pan, etc.), tajada *f* (de carne)
slick ['slɪk] *adj* SLIPPERY : resbaladizo, resbaloso *Lat*
slide ['slaɪd] *v* **slid** ['slɪd]; **sliding** ['slaɪdɪŋ] *vi* : deslizarse — *vt* : deslizar — **~** *n* **1** : deslizamiento *m* **2** : tobogán *m* (para niños) **3** : diapositiva *f* (fotográfica) **4** DECLINE : descenso *m*
slier, sliest → **sly**
slight ['slaɪt] *adj* **1** : ligero, leve **2** SLENDER : delgado — **~** *vt* : desairar — **slightly** ['slaɪtli] *adv* : ligeramente, un poco
slim ['slɪm] *adj* **slimmer; slimmest 1** : delgado **2 a ~ chance** : escasas posibilidades *fpl* — **~** *v* **slimmed; slimming** : adelgazar
slime ['slaɪm] *n* **1** : baba *f* (de un caracol, etc.) **2** MUD : limo *m* — **slimy** ['slaɪmi] *adj* **slimier; -est** : viscoso
sling ['slɪŋ] *vt* **slung** ['slʌŋ]; **slinging 1** THROW : lanzar **2** HANG : colgar — **~** *n* **1** : honda *f* **2** : cabestrillo *m* (en medicina) — **slingshot** ['slɪŋˌʃɑt] *n* : tirachinas *m*
slink ['slɪŋk] *vi* **slunk** ['slʌŋk]; **slinking** : andar furtivamente
slip[1] ['slɪp] *v* **slipped; slipping** *vi* **1** SLIDE : resbalarse **2 let sth ~** : dejar escapar algo **3 ~ away** : escabullirse **4 ~ up** : equivocarse — *vt* **1** : deslizar **2 ~ into** : ponerse (una prenda) **3 it slipped my mind** : se me olvidó — **~** *n* **1** MISTAKE : error *m*, desliz *m* **2 ~ of the tongue** : lapsus *m* **3** PETTICOAT : enagua *f*
slip[2] *n* **~ of paper** : papelito *m*
slipper ['slɪpər] *n* : zapatilla *f*, pantufla *f*
slippery ['slɪpəri] *adj* **slipperier; -est** : resbaladizo, resbaloso *Lat*
slit ['slɪt] *n* **1** OPENING : rendija *f* **2** CUT : corte *m*, raja *f* — **~** *vt* **slit; slitting** : cortar
slither ['slɪðər] *vi* : deslizarse
sliver ['slɪvər] *n* : astilla *f*
slogan ['slo:gən] *n* : eslogan *m*
slop ['slɑp] *v* **slopped; slopping** *vt* : derramar — *vi* : derramarse
slope ['slo:p] *vi* **sloped; sloping** : inclinarse — **~** *n* : pendiente *f*, declive *m*
sloppy ['slɑpi] *adj* **sloppier; -est 1** CARELESS : descuidado **2** UNKEMPT : desaliñado
slot ['slɑt] *n* : ranura *f*
sloth ['slɔθ, 'slo:θ] *n* : pereza *f*
slouch ['slaʊtʃ] *vi* : andar con los hombros caídos (en una silla)
slovenly ['slʌvənli, 'slɑv-] *adj* : desaliñado
slow ['slo:] *adj* **1** : lento **2 be ~** : estar atrasado (dícese de un reloj) — **~** *adv* → **slowly** — **~** *vt* : retrasar, retardar — *vi or* **~ down** : ir más despacio — **slowly** ['slo:li] *adv* : lentamente, despacio — **slowness** ['slo:nəs] *n* : lentitud *f*
sludge ['slʌdʒ] *n* SEWAGE : aguas *fpl* negras
slug[1] ['slʌg] *n* **1** : babosa *f* (molusco) **2** BULLET : bala *f* **3** TOKEN : ficha *f*
slug[2] *vt* **slugged; slugging** : pegar un porrazo a
sluggish ['slʌgɪʃ] *adj* : lento
slum ['slʌm] *n* : barrio *m* bajo
slumber ['slʌmbər] *vi* : dormir — **~** *n* : sueño *m*
slump ['slʌmp] *vi* **1** DROP : bajar **2** COLLAPSE : dejarse caer **3** → **slouch** — **~** *n* : bajón *m*
slung → **sling**
slunk → **slink**
slur[1] ['slər] *n* ASPERSION : calumnia *f*, difamación *f*

slur[2] *vt* **slurred; slurring** : arrastrar (las palabras)
slurp ['slərp] *v* : beber haciendo ruido — ~ *n* : sorbo *m* (ruidoso)
slush ['slʌʃ] *n* : nieve *f* medio derretida
sly ['slaɪ] *adj* **slier** ['slaɪər]; **sliest** ['slaɪəst] **1** : astuto, taimado **2 on the ~** : a escondidas
smack[1] ['smæk] *vi* **~ of** : oler a
smack[2] *vt* **1** : pegar una bofetada a **2** KISS : besar **3 ~ one's lips** : relamerse — ~ *n* : **1** SLAP : bofetada *f* **2** KISS : beso *m* — ~ *adv* : justo, exactamente
small ['smɔl] *adj* : pequeño, chico — **smallpox** ['smɔlˌpɑks] *n* : viruela *f*
smart ['smɑrt] *adj* **1** : listo, inteligente **2** STYLISH : elegante — ~ *vi* STING : escocer — **smartly** ['smɑrtli] *adv* : elegantemente
smash ['smæʃ] *n* **1** BLOW : golpe *m* **2** COLLISION : choque *m* **3** BANG, CRASH : estrépito *m* — ~ *vt* **1** BREAK : romper **2** DESTROY : aplastar — *vi* **1** SHATTER : hacerse pedazos **2 ~ into** : estrellarse contra
smattering ['smæt̬ərɪŋ] *n* : nociones *fpl*
smear ['smɪr] *n* : mancha *f* — ~ *vt* **1** : embadurnar (de pinta, etc.), untar (de aceite, etc.) **2** SMUDGE : manchar
smell ['smɛl] *v* **smelled** *or* **smelt** ['smɛlt]; **smelling** : oler — ~ *n* **1** : (sentido *m* del) olfato *m* **2** ODOR : olor *m* — **smelly** ['smɛli] *adj* **smellier; -est** : maloliente
smelt ['smɛlt] *vt* : fundir
smile ['smaɪl] *vi* **smiled; smiling** : sonreír — ~ *n* : sonrisa *f*
smirk ['smərk] *vi* : sonreír con suficiencia — ~ *n* : sonrisa *f* satisfecha
smitten ['smɪtən] *adj* **be ~ with** : estar enamorado de
smith ['smɪθ] → **blacksmith**
smock ['smɑk] *n* : blusón *m*, bata *f*
smog ['smɑg, 'smɔg] *n* : smog *m*
smoke ['smo:k] *n* : humo *m* — ~ *v* **smoked; smoking** *vi* **1** : humear (dícese de fuegos, etc.) **2** : fumar (dícese de personas) — *vt* **1** : ahumar (carne, etc.) **2** : fumar (cigarillos) — **smoker** ['smo:kər] *n* : fumador *m*, -dora *f* — **smokestack** ['smo:kˌstæk] *n* : chimenea *f* — **smoky** ['smo:ki] *adj* **smokier; -est 1** : lleno de humo **2** : a humo (dícese de sabores, etc.)
smolder ['smo:ldər] *vi* : arder (sin llama)
smooth ['smu:ð] *adj* **1** : liso (dícese de superficies), suave (dícese de movimientos), tranquilo (dícese del mar) **2** : sin grumos (dícese de salsas, etc.) — ~ *vt* : alisar — **smoothly** ['smu:ðli] *adv* : suavemente — **smoothness** ['smu:ðnəs] *n* : suavidad *f*
smother ['smʌðər] *vt* : asfixiar (a algn), sofocar (llamas, etc.)
smudge ['smʌdʒ] *v* **smudged; smudging** *vt* : emborronar — *vi* : correrse — ~ *n* : mancha *f*, borrón *m*
smug ['smʌg] *adj* **smugger; smuggest** : suficiente
smuggle ['smʌgəl] *vt* **-gled; -gling** : pasar de contrabando — **smuggler** ['smʌgələr] *n* : contrabandista *mf*
snack ['snæk] *n* : refrigerio *m*, tentempié *m fam*
snag ['snæg] *n* : problema *m* — ~ *v* **snagged; snagging** *vt* : enganchar — *vi* : engancharse
snail ['sneɪl] *n* : caracol *m*
snake ['sneɪk] *n* : culebra *f*, serpiente *f*
snap ['snæp] *v* **snapped; snapping** *vi* **1** BREAK : romperse **2** : intentar morder (dícese de un perro, etc.) **3 ~ at** : contestar bruscamente a — *vt* **1** BREAK : romper **2 ~ one's fingers** : chasquear los dedos **3 ~ open/shut** : abrir/cerrar de golpe — ~ *n* **1** : chasquido *m* **2** FASTENER : broche *m* (de presión) **3 be a ~** : ser facilísimo — **snappy** ['snæpi] *adj* **snappier; -est 1** FAST : rápido **2** STYLISH : elegante — **snapshot** ['snæpˌʃɑt] *n* : instantánea *f*
snare ['snær] *n* : trampa *f* — ~ *vt* **snared; snaring** : atrapar
snarl[1] ['snɑrl] *vi* TANGLE : enmarañar, enredar — ~ *n* : enredo *m*, maraña *f*
snarl[2] *vi* GROWL : gruñir — *n* : gruñido *m*
snatch ['snætʃ] *vt* : arrebatar
sneak ['sni:k] *vi* : ir a hurtadillas — *vt* : hacer furtivamente — ~ *n* : soplón *m*, -plona *f fam* — **sneakers** ['sni:kərz] *npl* : tenis *mpl*, zapatillas *fpl* — **sneaky** ['sni:ki] *adj* **sneakier; -est** : solapado
sneer ['snɪr] *vi* : sonreír con desprecio — ~ *n* : sonrisa *f* de desprecio
sneeze ['sni:z] *vi* **sneezed; sneezing** : estornudar — ~ *n* : estornudo *m*
snide ['snaɪd] *adj* : sarcástico
sniff ['snɪf] *vi* : oler — *vt* **1** : oler **2** → **sniffle** — ~ *n* : aspiración *f* por la nariz — **sniffle** ['snɪfəl] *vi* **-fled; -fling** : sorberse la nariz — **sniffles** ['snɪfəlz] *npl* **have the ~** : estar resfriado
snip ['snɪp] *n* : tijeretada *f* — ~ *vt* **snipped; snipping** : cortar (con tijeras)
snivel ['snɪvəl] *vi* **-veled** *or* **-velled; -veling** *or* **-velling** : lloriquear
snob ['snɑb] *n* : esnob *mf* — **snobbish** ['snɑbɪʃ] *adj* : esnob
snoop ['snu:p] *vi* : husmear — ~ *n* : fisgón *m*, -gona *f*
snooze ['snu:z] *vi* **snoozed; snoozing** : dormitar — ~ *n* : siestecita *f*, siestita *f*
snore ['snor] *vi* **snored; snoring** : roncar — ~ *n* : ronquido *m*
snort ['snɔrt] *vi* : bufar — ~ *n* : bufido *m*
snout ['snaʊt] *n* : hocico *m*, morro *m*
snow ['sno:] *n* : nieve *f* — ~ *vi* : nevar — **snowfall** ['sno:ˌfɔl] *n* : nevada *f* — **snowflake** ['sno:ˌfleɪk] *n* : copo *m* de nieve — **snowman** ['sno:ˌmæn] *n* : muñeco *m* de nieve — **snowplow** ['sno:ˌplaʊ] *n* : quitanieves *m* — **snowshoe** ['sno:ˌʃu:] *n* : raqueta *f* (para nieve) — **snowstorm** ['sno:ˌstɔrm] *n* : tormenta *f* de nieve — **snowy** ['sno:i] *adj* **snowier; -est 1 a ~ day** : un día nevoso **2 ~ mountains** : montañas *fpl* nevadas
snub ['snʌb] *vt* **snubbed; snubbing** : desairar — ~ *n* : desaire *m*
snuff ['snʌf] *vt or* **~ out** : apagar
snug ['snʌg] *adj* **snugger; snuggest 1** : cómodo **2** TIGHT : ajustado — **snuggle** ['snʌgəl] *vi* **-gled; -gling** : acurrucarse
so ['so:] *adv* **1** LIKEWISE : también **2** THUS : así **3** THEREFORE : por lo tanto **4** *or* **~ much** : tanto **5** *or* **~ very** : tan **6 and ~ on** : etcétera **7 I think ~** : creo que sí **8 I told you ~** : te lo dije — ~ *conj* **1** THEREFORE : así que **2** *or* **~ that** : para que **3 ~ what?** : ¿y qué? — ~ *adj* TRUE : cierto — ~ *pron* **or ~** : más o menos
soak ['so:k] *vi* : estar en remojo — *vt* **1** : poner en remojo **2 ~ up** : absorber — ~ *n* : remojo *m*
soap ['so:p] *n* : jabón *m* — ~ *vt or* **~ up** : enjabonar — **soapy** ['so:pi] **soapier; -est** *adj* : jabonoso
soar ['sor] *vi* **1** : planear **2** SKYROCKET : dispararse
sob ['sɑb] *vi* **sobbed; sobbing** : sollozar — ~ *n* : sollozo *m*
sober ['so:bər] *adj* **1** : sobrio **2** SERIOUS : serio — **sobriety** [sə'braɪət̬i, so-] *n* **1** : sobriedad *f* **2** SERIOUSNESS : seriedad *f*
so–called ['so:'kɔld] *adj* : supuesto, presunto
soccer ['sɑkər] *n* : futbol *m*, fútbol *m*
social ['so:ʃəl] *adj* : social — ~ *n* : reunión *f* social — **sociable** ['so:ʃəbəl] *adj* : sociable — **socialism** ['so:ʃəˌlɪzəm] *n* : socialismo *m* — **socialist** ['so:ʃəlɪst] *n* : socialista *mf* — ~ *adj* : socialista — **socialize** ['so:ʃəˌlaɪz] *v* **-ized; -izing** *vt* : socializar — *vi* **~ with** : alternar con — **society** [sə'saɪət̬i] *n, pl* **-eties** : sociedad *f* — **sociology** [ˌso:si'ɑlədʒi] *n* : sociología *f*
sock[1] ['sɑk] *n, pl* **socks** *or* **sox** ['sɑks] : calcetín *m*
sock[2] *vt* : pegar, golpear — ~ *n* PUNCH : puñetazo *m*
socket ['sɑkət] *n* **1** *or* **electric ~** : enchufe *m*, toma *f* de corriente **2** *or* **eye ~** : órbita *f*, cuenca *f* **3** : glena *f* (de una articulación)
soda ['so:də] *n* **1** *or* **~ pop** : refresco *m*, gaseosa *f* **2** *or* **~ water** : soda *f*
sodium ['so:diəm] *n* : sodio *m*
sofa ['so:fə] *n* : sofá *m*
soft ['sɔft] *adj* **1** : blando **2** SMOOTH : suave — **softball** ['sɔftˌbɔl] *n* : softbol *m* — **soft drink** *n* : refresco *m* — **soften** ['sɔfən] *vt* **1** : ablandar **2** EASE, SMOOTH : suavizar — *vi* **1** : ablandarse **2** EASE : suavizarse — **softly** ['sɔftli] *adv* : suavemente — **software** ['sɔftˌwær] *n* : software *m*
soggy ['sɑgi] *adj* **soggier; -est** : empapado
soil ['sɔɪl] *vt* : ensuciar — ~ *n* DIRT : tierra *f*
solace ['sɑləs] *n* : consuelo *m*
solar ['so:lər] *adj* : solar
sold → **sell**
solder ['sɑdər, 'sɔ-] *n* : soldadura *f* — ~ *vt* : soldar
soldier ['so:ldʒər] *n* : soldado *mf*
sole[1] ['so:l] *n* : lenguado *m* (pez)
sole[2] *n* : planta *f* (del pie), suela *f* (de un zapato)
sole[3] *adj* : único — **solely** ['so:li] *adv* : únicamente, sólo
solemn ['sɑləm] *adj* : solemne — **solemnity** [sə'lɛmnət̬i] *n, pl* **-ties** : solemnidad *f*
solicit [sə'lɪsət] *vt* : solicitar
solid ['sɑləd] *adj* **1** : sólido **2** UNBROKEN : continuo **3 ~ gold** : oro *m* macizo **4 two ~ hours** : dos horas seguidas — ~ *n* : sólido *m* — **solidarity** [ˌsɑlə'dærət̬i] *n* : solidaridad *f* — **solidify** [sə'lɪdəˌfaɪ] *v* **-fied; -fying** *vt* : solidificar — *vi* : solidificarse — **solidity** [sə'lɪdət̬i] *n, pl* **-ties** : solidez *f*
solitary ['sɑləˌtɛri] *adj* : solitario — **solitude** ['sɑləˌtu:d, -ˌtju:d] *n* : soledad *f*
solo ['so:ˌlo:] *n, pl* **solos** : solo *m* — **soloist** ['so:loɪst] *n* : solista *mf*
solution [sə'lu:ʃən] *n* : solución *f* — **soluble** ['sɑljəbəl] *adj* : soluble — **solve** ['sɑlv] *vt* **solved; solving** : resolver — **solvent** ['sɑlvənt] *n* : solvente *m*
somber ['sɑmbər] *adj* : sombrío
some ['sʌm] *adj* **1** (*of unspecified identity*) : un **2** (*of an unspecified amount*) : algo de, un poco de **3** (*of an unspecified number*) : unos **4** CERTAIN : algunos **5 that was ~ game!** : ¡fue un partidazo! — ~ *pron* **1** SEVERAL : algunos, unos **2** PART : un poco, algo — ~ *adv* **~ twenty people** : unas veinte personas — **somebody** ['sʌmbədi, -ˌbɑdi] *pron* : alguien — **someday** ['sʌmˌdeɪ] *adv* : algún día — **somehow** ['sʌmˌhaʊ] *adv* **1** : de algún modo **2 ~ or other** : de alguna manera u otra — **someone** ['sʌmˌwʌn] *pron* : alguien
somersault ['sʌmərˌsɔlt] *n* : voltereta *f*, salto *m* mortal
something ['sʌmθɪŋ] *pron* **1** : algo **2 ~ else** : otra cosa — **sometime** ['sʌmˌtaɪm] *adv* **1** : algún día, en algún momento **2 ~ next month** : (durante) el mes que viene — **sometimes** ['sʌmˌtaɪmz] *adv* : a veces — **somewhat** ['sʌmˌhwʌt, -ˌhwɑt] *adv* : algo — **somewhere** ['sʌmˌhwɛr] *adv* **1** : en alguna parte, en algún lado **2 ~ around** : alrededor de **3 ~ else** → **elsewhere**
son ['sʌn] *n* : hijo *m*
song ['sɔŋ] *n* : canción *f*
son–in–law ['sʌnɪnˌlɔ] *n, pl* **sons–in–law** : yerno *m*
sonnet ['sɑnət] *n* : soneto *m*
soon ['su:n] *adv* **1** : pronto **2** SHORTLY : dentro de poco **3 as ~ as** : en cuanto **4 as ~ as possible** : lo más pronto posible **5 ~ after** : poco después **6 ~er or later** : tarde o temprano **7 the ~er the better** : cuanto antes mejor
soot ['sʊt, 'su:t, 'sʌt] *n* : hollín *m*
soothe ['su:ð] *vt* **soothed; soothing 1** CALM : calmar **2** RELIEVE : aliviar
sop ['sɑp] *vt* **sopped; sopping ~ up** : absorber
sophistication [səˌfɪstə'keɪʃən] *n* : sofisticación *f* — **sophisticated** [sə'fɪstəˌkeɪt̬əd] *adj* : sofisticado
sophomore ['sɑfˌmor, 'sɑfəˌmor] *n* : estudiante *mf* de segundo año
soprano [sə'præˌno:] *n, pl* **-nos** : soprano *mf*
sorcerer ['sɔrsərər] *n* : hechicero *m*, brujo *m* — **sorcery** ['sɔrsəri] *n* : hechicería *f*, brujería *f*
sordid ['sɔrdɪd] *adj* : sórdido
sore ['sor] *adj* **sorer; sorest 1** : dolorido **2** ANGRY : enfadado **3 ~ throat** : dolor *m* de garganta **4 I have a ~ throat** : me duele la garganta — ~ *n* : llaga *f* — **sorely** ['sorli] *adv* : muchísimo — **soreness** ['sornəs] *n* : dolor *m*
sorrow ['sɑrˌo:] *n* : pesar *m*, pena *f* — **sorry** ['sɑri] *adj* **sorrier; -est 1** PITIFUL : lamentable **2 feel ~ for** : compadecer **3 I'm ~** : lo siento
sort ['sɔrt] *n* **1** : tipo *m*, clase *f* **2 a ~ of** : una especie de — ~ *vt* : clasificar — **sort of** *adv* **1** SOMEWHAT : algo **2** MORE OR LESS : más o menos
SOS [ˌɛsˌo:'ɛs] *n* : SOS *m*
so–so ['so:'so:] *adj & adv* : así así *fam*
soufflé [su:'fleɪ] *n* : suflé *m*
sought → **seek**
soul ['so:l] *n* : alma *f*
sound[1] ['saʊnd] *adj* **1** HEALTHY : sano **2** FIRM : sólido **3** SENSIBLE : lógico **4 a ~ sleep** : un sueño profundo **5 safe and ~** : sano y salvo
sound[2] *n* : sonido *m* — *vt* : hacer sonar, tocar (una trompeta, etc.) — *vi* **1** : sonar **2** SEEM : parecer
sound[3] *n* CHANNEL : brazo *m* de mar — ~ *vt* **1** : sondar (en navegación) **2** *or* **~ out** : sondear
soundly ['saʊndli] *adv* **1** SOLIDLY : sólidamente **2** DEEPLY : profundamente
soundproof ['saʊndˌpru:f] *adj* : insonorizado
soup ['su:p] *n* : sopa *f*
sour ['saʊər] *adj* **1** : agrio **2 ~ milk** : leche *f* cortada — ~ *vt* : agriar
source ['sors] *n* : fuente *f*, origen *m*
south ['saʊθ] *adv* : al sur — ~ *adj* : (del) sur — ~ *n* : sur *m* — **South African** *adj* : sudafricano — **South American** *adj* : sudamericano — **southeast** [saʊθ'i:st] *adv* : hacia el sureste — ~ *adj* : (del) sureste — ~ *n* : sureste *m*, sudeste *m* — **southeastern** [saʊθ'i:stərn] *adj* → **southeast** — **southerly** ['sʌðərli] *adv & adj* : del sur — **southern** ['sʌðərn] *adj* : del sur, meridional — **southwest** [saʊθ'wɛst] *adv* : hacia el suroeste — ~ *adj* : (del) suroeste — ~ *n* : suroeste *m*, sudoeste *m* — **southwestern** [saʊθ'wɛstərn] *adj* → **southwest**
souvenir [ˌsu:və'nɪr, 'su:vəˌ-] *n* : recuerdo *m*
sovereign ['sɑvərən] *n* : soberano *m*, -na *f* — ~ *adj* : soberano — **sovereignty** ['sɑvərənti] *n, pl* **-ties** : soberanía *f*
Soviet ['so:viˌɛt, 'sɑ-, -viət] *adj* : soviético
sow[1] ['saʊ] *n* : cerda *f*
sow[2] ['so:] *vt* **sowed; sown** ['so:n] *or* **sowed; sowing** : sembrar
sox → **sock**
soybean ['sɔɪˌbi:n] *n* : soya *f*, soja *f*
spa ['spɑ] *n* : balneario *m*
space ['speɪs] *n* **1** : espacio *m* **2** ROOM, SPOT : sitio *m*, lugar *m* — ~ *vt* **spaced; spacing** : espaciar — **spaceship** ['speɪsˌʃɪp] *n* : nave *f* espacial — **space shuttle** *n* : transbordador *m* espacial — **spacious** ['speɪʃəs] *adj* : espacioso, amplio
spade[1] ['speɪd] *n* SHOVEL : pala *f*
spade[2] *n* : pica *f* (naipe)
spaghetti [spə'gɛt̬i] *n* : espaguetis *mpl*
span ['spæn] *n* **1** PERIOD : espacio *m* **2** : luz *f* (entre dos soportes) — ~ *vt* **spanned; spanning 1** : abarcar (un período) **2** CROSS : extenderse sobre
Spaniard ['spænjərd] *n* : español *m*, -ñola *f*
spaniel ['spænjəl] *n* : spaniel *m*
Spanish ['spænɪʃ] *adj* : español — ~ *n* : español *m* (idioma)
spank ['spæŋk] *vt* : dar palmadas a (en las nalgas)
spar ['spɑr] *vi* **sparred; sparring** : entrenarse (en boxeo)
spare ['spær] *vt* **spared; sparing 1** PARDON : perdonar **2** SAVE : ahorrar **3 can you ~ a dollar?** : ¿me das un dólar? **4 I can't ~ the time** : no tengo tiempo **5 ~ no expense** : no reparar en gastos **6 to ~** : de sobra — ~ *adj* **1** : de repuesto **2** EXCESS : de más **3** LEAN : delgado — ~ *n or* **~ part** : repuesto *m* — **spare time** *n* : tiempo *m* libre — **sparing** ['spærɪŋ] *adj* : parco, económico
spark ['spɑrk] *n* : chispa *f* — ~ *vi* : chispear, echar chispas — *vt* : despertar (interés), provocar (crítica) — **sparkle** ['spɑrkəl] *vi* **-kled; -kling** : destellar, centellear — ~ *n* : destello *m*, centelleo *m* — **spark plug** *n* : bujía *f*
sparrow ['spæro:] *n* : gorrión *m*
sparse ['spɑrs] *adj* **sparser; -est** : escaso
spasm ['spæzəm] *n* : espasmo *m*
spat[1] → **spit**
spat[2] *n* QUARREL : disputa *f*, pelea *f*
spatter ['spæt̬ər] *vt* : salpicar
spawn ['spɔn] *vi* : desovar — *vt* : engendrar, producir — ~ *n* : hueva *f*
speak ['spi:k] *v* **spoke** ['spo:k]; **spoken** ['spo:kən]; **speaking** *vi* **1** : hablar **2 ~ out against** : denunciar **3 ~ up** : hablar más alto **4 ~ up for** : defender — *vt* **1** : decir **2** : hablar (un idioma) — **speaker** ['spi:kər] *n* **1** ORATOR : orador *m*, -dora *f* **2** : hablante *mf* (de un idioma) **3** LOUDSPEAKER : altavoz *m*
spear ['spɪr] *n* : lanza *f* — **spearhead** ['spɪrˌhɛd] *n* : punta *f* de lanza — ~ *vt* : encabezar — **spearmint** ['spɪrmɪnt] *n* : menta *f* verde
special ['spɛʃəl] *adj* : especial — **specialist** ['spɛʃəlɪst] *n* : especialista *mf* — **specialization** [ˌspɛʃələ'zeɪʃən] *n* : especialización *f* — **specialize** ['spɛʃəˌlaɪz] *vi* **-ized; -izing** : especializarse — **specially** *adv* : especialmente — **specialty** ['spɛʃəlt̬i] *n, pl* **-ties** : especialidad *f*
species ['spi:ˌʃi:z, -ˌsi:z] *ns & pl* : especie *f*
specify ['spɛsəˌfaɪ] *vt* **-fied; -fying** : especificar — **specific** [spɪ'sɪfɪk] *adj* : específico — **specifically** [spɪ'sɪfɪkli] *adv* **1** : específicamente **2** EXPLICITLY : expresamente — **specification** [ˌspɛsəfə'keɪʃən] *n* : especificación *f*
specimen ['spɛsəmən] *n* : espécimen *m*
speck ['spɛk] *n* **1** SPOT : mancha *f* **2** BIT : mota *f* — **speckled** ['spɛkəld] *adj* : moteado
spectacle ['spɛktɪkəl] *n* **1** : espectáculo *m* **2 ~s** *npl* GLASSES : gafas *fpl*, lentes *fpl*, anteojos *mpl* — **spectacular** [spɛk'tækjələr] *adj* : espectacular — **spectator** ['spɛkˌteɪt̬ər] *n* : espectador *m*, -dora *f*
specter *or* **spectre** ['spɛktər] *n* : espectro *m*
spectrum ['spɛktrəm] *n, pl* **-tra** [-trə] *or* **-trums 1** : espectro *m* **2** RANGE : gama *f*
speculation [ˌspɛkjə'leɪʃən] *n* : especulación *f*
speech ['spi:tʃ] *n* **1** : habla *f* **2** ADDRESS : discurso *m* — **speechless** ['spi:tʃləs] *adj* : mudo
speed ['spi:d] *n* **1** : rapidez *f* **2** VELOCITY : velocidad *f* — ~ *v* **sped** ['spɛd] *or* **speeded; speeding** *vi* **1** : conducir a exceso de velocidad **2 ~ off** : irse a toda velocidad **3 ~ up** : acelerarse — *vt or* **~ up** : acelerar — **speed limit** *n* : velocidad *f* máxima — **speedometer** [spɪ'dɑmət̬ər] *n* : velocímetro *m* — **speedy** ['spi:di] *adj* **speedier, -est** : rápido
spell[1] ['spɛl] *vt* **1** : escribir (las letras de) **2** *or* **~ out** : deletrear **3** MEAN : significar
spell[2] *n* ENCHANTMENT : hechizo *m*
spell[3] *n* : período *m* (de tiempo)
spellbound ['spɛlˌbaʊnd] *adj* : embelesado
spelling ['spɛlɪŋ] *n* : ortografía *f*
spend ['spɛnd] *vt* **spent** ['spɛnt]; **spending 1** : gastar (dinero) **2** : pasar (las vacaciones, etc.) **3 ~ time on** : dedicar tiempo a
sperm ['spərm] *n, pl* **sperm** *or* **sperms** : esperma *mf*
spew ['spju:] *vt* : vomitar, arrojar (lava, etc.)
sphere ['sfɪr] *n* : esfera *f* — **spherical** ['sfɪrɪkəl, 'sfɛr-] *adj* : esférico
spice ['spaɪs] *n* : especia *f* — ~ *vt* **spiced; spicing** : condimentar, sazonar — **spicy** ['spaɪsi] *adj* **spicier; -est** : picante
spider ['spaɪdər] *n* : araña *f*
spigot ['spɪgət, -kət] *n* : grifo *m Spain*, llave *f Lat*
spike ['spaɪk] *n* **1** : clavo *m* (grande) **2** POINT : punta *f* — **spiky** ['spaɪki] *adj* : puntiagudo
spill ['spɪl] *vt* : derramar — *vi* : derramarse
spin ['spɪn] *v* **spun** ['spʌn]; **spinning** *vi* : girar — *vt* **1** : hilar (lana, etc.) **2** TWIRL : hacer girar — ~ *n* **1** : vuelta *f*, giro *m* **2 go for a ~** : dar una vuelta (en auto)
spinach ['spɪnɪtʃ] *n* : espinacas *fpl*
spinal cord ['spaɪnəl] *n* : médula *f* espinal

spindle ['spɪndəl] *n* : huso *m* (para hilar) — **spindly** ['spɪndli] *adj* : larguirucho *fam*

spine ['spaɪn] *n* **1** : columna *f* vertebral **2** QUILL : púa *f* **3** THORN : espina *f* **4** : lomo *m* (de un libro)

spinster ['spɪntstər] *n* : soltera *f*

spiral ['spaɪrəl] *adj* : de espiral, en espiral — ~ *n* : espiral *f* — ~ *vi* **-raled** *or* **-ralled; -raling** *or* **-ralling** : ir en espiral

spire ['spaɪr] *n* : aguja *f*

spirit ['spɪrət] *n* **1** : espíritu *m* **2 in good ~s** : animado **3 ~s** *npl* : licores *mpl* — **spirited** ['spɪrətəd] *adj* : animado — **spiritual** ['spɪrɪtʃʊəl, -tʃəl] *adj* : espiritual — **spirituality** [ˌspɪrɪtʃʊ'æləṭi] *n, pl* **-ties** : espiritualidad *f*

spit¹ ['spɪt] *n* ROTISSERIE : asador *m*

spit² *v* **spit** *or* **spat** ['spæt]; **spitting** : escupir — *n* SALIVA : saliva *f*

spite ['spaɪt] *n* **1** : rencor *m* **2 in ~ of** : a pesar de — ~ *vt* **spited; spiting** : fastidiar — **spiteful** ['spaɪtfəl] *adj* : rencoroso

spittle ['spɪṭəl] *n* : saliva *f*

splash ['splæʃ] *vt* : salpicar — *vi* **1** : salpicar **2** *or* ~ **about** : chapotear — ~ *n* **1** : salpicadura *f* **2** : mancha *f* (de color, etc.)

splatter ['splæṭər] → **spatter**

spleen ['spli:n] *n* : bazo *m* (órgano)

splendor ['splɛndər] *n* : esplendor *m* — **splendid** ['splɛndəd] *adj* : espléndido

splint ['splɪnt] *n* : tablilla *f*

splinter ['splɪntər] *n* : astilla *f* — *vi* : astillarse

split ['splɪt] *v* **split; splitting** *vt* **1** : partir **2** BURST : reventar **3** *or* ~ **up** : dividir — *vi* **1** : partirse, rajarse **2** *or* ~ **up** : dividirse — ~ *n* **1** CRACK : rajadura *f* **2** *or* ~ **seam** : descosido *m* **3** DIVISION : división *f*

splurge ['splərdʒ] *vi* **splurged; splurging** : derrochar dinero

spoil ['spɔɪl] *vt* **spoiled** *or* **spoilt** ['spɔɪlt]; **spoiling 1** RUIN : estropear **2** PAMPER : consentir, mimar — **spoils** *npl* : botín *m*

spoke¹ ['spo:k] → **speak**

spoke² *n* : rayo *m* (de una rueda)

spoken → **speak**

spokesman ['spo:ksmən] *n, pl* **-men** [-mən, -ˌmɛn] : portavoz *mf* — **spokeswoman** ['spo:ksˌwʊmən] *n, pl* **-women** [-ˌwɪmən] : portavoz *f*

sponge ['spʌndʒ] *n* : esponja *f* — ~ *vt* **sponged; sponging** : limpiar con una esponja — **spongy** ['spʌndʒi] *adj* **spongier; -est** : esponjoso

sponsor ['spɑntsər] *n* : patrocinador *m*, -dora *f* — ~ *vt* : patrocinar — **sponsorship** ['spɑntsərˌʃɪp] *n* : patrocinio *m*

spontaneity [ˌspɑntə'ni:əṭi, -'neɪ-] *n* : espontaneidad *f* — **spontaneous** [spɑn'teɪniəs] *adj* : espontáneo

spooky ['spu:ki] *adj* **spookier; -est** : espeluzante

spool ['spu:l] *n* : carrete *m*

spoon ['spu:n] *n* : cuchara *f* — **spoonful** ['spu:nˌfʊl] *n* : cucharada *f*

sporadic [spə'rædɪk] *adj* : esporádico

spore ['spor] *n* : espora *f*

sport ['sport] *n* **1** : deporte *m* **2 be a good ~** : tener espíritu deportivo — **sportsman** ['sportsmən] *n, pl* **-men** [-mən, -ˌmɛn] : deportista *m* — **sportswoman** ['sportsˌwʊmən] *n, pl* **-women** [-ˌwɪmən] : deportista *f* — **sporty** ['sporṭi] *adj* **sportier; -est** : deportivo

spot ['spɑt] *n* **1** : mancha *f* **2** DOT : punto *m* **3** PLACE : lugar *m*, sitio *m* **4 in a tight ~** : en apuros **5 on the ~** INSTANTLY : en ese mismo momento — ~ *vt* **spotted; spotting 1** STAIN : manchar **2** DETECT, NOTICE : ver, descubrir — **spotless** ['spɑtləs] *adj* : impecable — **spotlight** ['spɑtˌlaɪt] *n* **1** : foco *m*, reflector *m* **2 be in the ~** : ser el centro de atención — **spotty** ['spɑṭi] *adj* **spottier; -est** : irregular

spouse ['spaʊs] *n* : cónyuge *mf*

spout ['spaʊt] *vi* : salir a chorros — ~ *n* **1** : pico *m* (de una jarra, etc.) **2** STREAM : chorro *m*

sprain ['spreɪn] *n* : esguince *m* — ~ *vt* : sufrir un esguince en

sprawl ['sprɔl] *vi* **1** : repantigarse (en un sillón, etc.) **2** EXTEND : extenderse — ~ *n* : extensión *f*

spray¹ ['spreɪ] *n* BOUQUET : ramillete *m*

spray² *n* **1** MIST : rocío *m* **2** *or* **aerosol ~** : spray *m* **3** *or* ~ **bottle** : atomizador *m* — ~ *vt* : rociar (una superficie), pulverizar (un líquido)

spread ['sprɛd] *v* **spread; spreading** *vt* **1** : propagar (enfermedades), difundir (noticias, etc.) **2** *or* ~ **out** : extender **3** : untar (con mantequilla, etc.) — *vi* **1** : propagarse, difundirse **2** *or* ~ **out** : extenderse — ~ *n* **1** : propagación *f*, difusión *f* **2** PASTE : pasta *f* (para untar) — **spreadsheet** ['sprɛdˌʃi:t] *n* : hoja *f* de cálculo

spree ['spri] *n* **go on a ~** : ir de juerga *fam*

sprig ['sprɪg] *n* : ramito *m*

sprightly ['spraɪtli] *adj* **sprightlier; -est** : vivo

spring ['sprɪŋ] *v* **sprang** ['spræŋ] *or* **sprung** ['sprʌŋ]; **sprung; springing** *vi* **1** : saltar **2** ~ **from** : surgir de **3** ~ **up** : surgir — *vt* **1** ACTIVATE : accionar **2** ~ **a leak** : hacer agua **3** ~ **sth on s.o.** : sorprender a algn con algo — ~ *n* **1** : manantial *m* (de aguas) **2** : primavera *f* (estación) **3** LEAP : salto *m* **4** RESILIENCE : elasticidad *f* **5** : resorte *m* (mecanismo) **6** *or* **bedspring** : muelle *m* — **springboard** ['sprɪŋˌbord] *n* : trampolín *m* — **springtime** ['sprɪŋˌtaɪm] *n* : primavera *f* — **springy** ['sprɪŋi] *adj* **springier; -est** : mullido

sprinkle ['sprɪŋkəl] *vt* **-kled; -kling 1** : salpicar, rociar **2** DUST : espolvorear — ~ *n* : llovizna *f* — **sprinkler** ['sprɪŋkələr] *n* : aspersor *m*

sprint ['sprɪnt] *vi* **1** : correr **2** : esprintar (en deportes) — ~ *n* : esprint *m* (en deportes)

sprout ['spraʊt] *vi* : brotar — ~ *n* : brote *m*

spruce¹ ['spru:s] *vt* **spruced; sprucing ~ up** : arreglar

spruce² *n* : pícea *f* (árbol)

spry ['spraɪ] *adj* **sprier** *or* **spryer** ['spraɪər]; **spriest** *or* **spryest** ['spraɪəst] : ágil, activo

spun → **spin**

spur ['spər] *n* **1** : espuela *f* **2** STIMULUS : acicate *m* **3 on the ~ of the moment** : sin pensarlo — ~ *vt* **spurred; spurring** *or* ~ **on 1** : espolear (un caballo) **2** MOTIVATE : motivar

spurn ['spərn] *vt* : desdeñar, rechazar

spurt¹ ['spərt] *vi* : salir a chorros — ~ *n* : chorro *m*

spurt² *n* **1** : arranque *m* (de energía, etc.) **2 work in ~s** : trabajar por rachas

spy ['spaɪ] *v* **spied; spying** *vt* : ver, divisar — *vi* ~ **on s.o.** : espiar a algn — ~ *n* : espía *mf*

squabble ['skwɑbəl] *n* : riña *f*, pelea *f* — ~ *vi* **-bled; -bling** : reñir, pelearse

squad ['skwɑd] *n* : pelotón *m* (militar), brigada *f* (de policías)

squadron ['skwɑdrən] *n* : escuadrón *m* (de soldados), escuadra *f* (de aviones o naves)

squalid ['skwɑlɪd] *adj* : miserable

squall ['skwɔl] *n* : turbión *m*

squalor ['skwɑlər] *n* : miseria *f*

squander ['skwɑndər] *vt* : derrochar (dinero, etc.), desperdiciar (oportunidades, etc.)

square ['skwær] *n* **1** : cuadrado *m* **2** : plaza *f* (de una ciudad) — ~ *adj* **squarer; -est 1** : cuadrado **2** HONEST : justo **3** EVEN : en paz **4 a ~ meal** : una comida decente — ~ *vt* **squared; squaring 1** : elevar al cuadrado (un número) **2** : saldar (una cuenta) — **square root** *n* : raíz *f* cuadrada

squash¹ ['skwɑʃ, 'skwɔʃ] *vt* **1** : aplastar **2** : acallar (protestas, etc.) — ~ *n* : squash *m* (deporte)

squash² *n, pl* **squashes** *or* **squash** : calabaza *f* (vegetal)

squat ['skwɑt] *vi* **squatted; squatting 1** *or* ~ **down** : ponerse en cuclillas **2** : ocupar un lugar sin derecho — ~ *adj* **squatter; squattest** : achaparrado

squawk ['skwɔk] *n* : graznido *m* — ~ *vi* : graznar

squeak ['skwi:k] *vi* **1** : chillar **2** CREAK : chirriar — ~ *n* **1** : chillido *m* **2** CREAK : chirrido *m* — **squeaky** ['skwi:ki] *adj* **squeakier; -est** : chirriante

squeal ['skwi:l] *vi* **1** : chillar (dícese de personas, etc.), chirriar (dícese de frenos, etc.) **2** PROTEST : quejarse — ~ *n* : chillido *m* (de una persona), chirrido *m* (de frenos, etc.)

squeamish ['skwi:mɪʃ] *adj* : impresionable, delicado

squeeze ['skwi:z] *vt* **squeezed; squeezing 1** : apretar **2** : exprimir (frutas, etc.) **3** : extraer (jugo, etc.) — ~ *n* : apretón *m*

squid ['skwɪd] *n, pl* **squid** *or* **squids** : calamar *m*

squint ['skwɪnt] *vi* : entrecerrar los ojos — ~ *n* : estrabismo *m*

squirm ['skwərm] *vi* : retorcerse

squirrel ['skwərəl] *n* : ardilla *f*

squirt ['skwərt] *vt* : lanzar un chorro de — *vi* : salir a chorros — ~ *n* : chorrito *m*

stab ['stæb] *n* **1** : puñalada *f* **2** ~ **of pain** : pinchazo *m* **3 take a ~ at** : intentar — ~ *vt* **stabbed; stabbing 1** KNIFE : apuñalar **2** STICK : clavar

stable ['steɪbəl] *n* **1** : establo *m* (para ganado) **2** *or* **horse ~** : caballeriza *f* — ~ *adj* **-bler; -blest** : estable — **stability** [stə'bɪləṭi] *n, pl* **-ties** : estabilidad *f* — **stabilize** ['steɪbəˌlaɪz] *vt* **-lized; -lizing** : estabilizar

stack ['stæk] *n* : montón *m*, pila *f* — ~ *vt* : amontonar, apilar

stadium ['steɪdiəm] *n, pl* **-dia** *or* **-diums** : estadio *m*

staff ['stæfs, stævz] *n, pl* **staffs** *or* **staves** ['stævz, 'steɪvz] **1** : bastón *m* **2** *pl* **staffs** PERSONNEL : personal *m* **3** *pl* **staffs** : pentagrama *m* (en música) — ~ ['stæf] *vt* : proveer de personal

stag ['stæg] *n, pl* **stags** *or* **stag** : ciervo *m*, venado *m* — ~ *adj* : sólo para hombres — ~ *adv* **go ~** : ir solo

stage ['steɪdʒ] *n* **1** : escenario *m* (de un teatro) **2** PHASE : etapa *f* **3 the ~** : el teatro — ~ *vt* **staged; staging 1** : poner en escena **2** ARRANGE : montar — **stagecoach** ['steɪdʒˌko:tʃ] *n* : diligencia *f*

stagger ['stægər] *vi* : tambalearse — *vt* **1** : escalonar (turnos, etc.) **2 be ~ed by** : quedarse estupefacto por — ~ *n* : tambaleo *m* — **staggering** ['stægərɪŋ] *adj* : asombroso

stagnant ['stægnənt] *adj* : estancado — **stagnate** ['stægˌneɪt] *vi* **-nated; -nating** : estancarse

stain ['steɪn] *vt* **1** : manchar **2** : teñir (madera) — ~ *n* **1** : mancha *f* **2** DYE : tinte *m*, tintura *f* — **stainless steel** ['steɪnləs-] *n* : acero *m* inoxidable

stair ['stær] *n* **1** STEP : escalón *m*, peldaño *m* **2 ~s** *npl* : escalera(s) *f(pl)* — **staircase** ['stærˌkeɪs] *n* : escalera(s) *f(pl)* — **stairway** ['stærˌweɪ] *n* : escalera(s) *f(pl)*

stake ['steɪk] *n* **1** POST : estaca *f* **2** BET : apuesta *f* **3** INTEREST : intereses *mpl* **4 be at ~** : estar en juego — ~ *vt* **staked; staking 1** : estacar **2** BET : jugarse **3 ~ a claim to** : reclamar

stale ['steɪl] *adj* **staler; stalest 1** : duro (dícese del pan) **2** OLD : viejo **3** STUFFY : viciado

stalk¹ ['stɔk] *n* : tallo *m* (de una planta)

stalk² *vt* : acechar — *vi or* ~ **off** : irse con altivez

stall¹ ['stɔl] *n* **1** : compartimiento *m* (de un establo) **2** STAND : puesto *m* — ~ *vt* : parar (un motor) — *vi* : pararse

stall² *vt* DELAY : entretener — *vi* : andar con rodeos

stallion ['stæljən] *n* : caballo *m* semental

stalwart ['stɔlwərt] *adj* **1** STRONG : fornido **2 ~ supporter** : partidario *m* leal

stamina ['stæmənə] *n* : resistencia *f*

stammer ['stæmər] *vi* : tartamudear — ~ *n* : tartamudeo *m*

stamp ['stæmp] *n* **1** SEAL : sello *m* **2** DIE : cuño *m* **3** *or* **postage ~** : sello *m*, estampilla *f Lat*, timbre *m Lat* — ~ *vt* **1** : franquear (una carta) **2** IMPRINT : sellar **3** MINT : acuñar **4 ~ one's foot** : dar una patada (en el suelo)

stampede [stæm'pi:d] *n* : estampida *f* — ~ *vi* **-peded; -peding** : salir en estampida

stance ['stænts] *n* : postura *f*

stand ['stænd] *v* **stood** ['stʊd]; **standing** *vi* **1** : estar de pie, estar parado *Lat* **2** BE : estar **3** CONTINUE : seguir vigente **4** LIE, REST : reposar **5 ~ aside** *or* **~ back** : apartarse **6 ~ out** : sobresalir **7** *or* **~ up** : ponerse de pie, pararse *Lat* — *vt* **1** PLACE : poner, colocar **2** ENDURE : soportar **3 ~ a chance** : tener una posibilidad — **stand by** *vt* **1** : mantener (una promesa, etc.) **2** SUPPORT : apoyar — **stand for** *vt* **1** MEAN : significar **2** PERMIT : permitir — **stand up** *vi* **1 ~ for** : defender **2 ~ up to** : resistir a — ~ *n* **1** RESISTANCE : resistencia *f* **2** STALL : puesto *m* **3** BASE : base *f* **4** POSITION : posición *f* **5 ~s** *npl* : tribuna *f*

standard ['stændərd] *n* **1** : norma *f* **2** BANNER : estandarte *m* **3** CRITERION : criterio *m* **4 ~ of living** : nivel *m* de vida — ~ *adj* : estándar — **standardize** ['stændərˌdaɪz] *vt* **-ized; -izing** : estandarizar

standing ['stændɪŋ] *n* **1** RANK : posición *f* **2** DURATION : duración *f*

standpoint ['stændˌpɔɪnt] *n* : punto *m* de vista

standstill ['stændˌstɪl] *n* **1 be at a ~** : estar paralizado **2 come to a ~** : pararse

stank → **stink**

stanza ['stænzə] *n* : estrofa *f*

staple¹ ['steɪpəl] *n* : producto *m* principal — ~ *adj* : principal, básico

staple² *n* : grapa *f* (para papeles) — ~ *vt* **-pled; -pling** : grapar, engrapar *Lat* — **stapler** ['steɪplər] *n* : grapadora *f*, engrapadora *f Lat*

star ['stɑr] *n* : estrella *f* — ~ *v* **starred; starring** *vt* FEATURE : estar protagonizado por — *vi* ~ **in** : protagonizar

starboard ['stɑrbərd] *n* : estribor *m*

starch ['stɑrtʃ] *vt* : almidonar — ~ *n* **1** : almidón *m* **2** : fécula *f* (comida)

stardom ['stɑrdəm] *n* : estrellato *m*

stare ['stær] *vi* **stared; staring** : mirar fijamente — ~ *n* : mirada *f* fija

starfish ['stɑrˌfɪʃ] *n* : estrella *f* de mar

stark ['stɑrk] *adj* **1** PLAIN : austero **2** HARSH : severo, duro **3** SHARP : marcado — ~ *adv* **1** : completamente **2 ~ naked** : en cueros (vivos)

starlight ['stɑrˌlaɪt] *n* : luz *f* de las estrellas

starling ['stɑrlɪŋ] *n* : estornino *m*

starry ['stɑri] *adj* **starrier; -est** : estrellado

start ['stɑrt] *vi* **1** : empezar, comenzar **2** SET OUT : salir **3** JUMP : sobresaltarse **4** *or* **~ up** : arrancar — *vt* **1** : empezar, comenzar **2** CAUSE : provocar **3** *or* **~ up** ESTABLISH : montar **4** *or* **~ up** : arrancar (un motor, etc.) — ~ *n* **1** : principio *m* **2 get an early ~** : salir temprano **3 give s.o. a ~** : asustar a algn — **starter** ['stɑrṭər] *n* : motor *m* de arranque (de un vehículo)

startle ['stɑrṭəl] *vt* **-tled; -tling** : asustar

starve ['stɑrv] *v* **starved; starving** *vi* : morirse de hambre — *vt* : privar de comida — **starvation** [stɑr'veɪʃən] *n* : inanición *f*, hambre *f*

stash ['stæʃ] *vt* : esconder

state ['steɪt] *n* **1** : estado *m* **2 the States** : los Estados Unidos — ~ *vt* **stated; stating 1** SAY : decir **2** REPORT : exponer — **stately** ['steɪtli] *adj* **statelier; -est** : majestuoso — **statement** ['steɪtmənt] *n* **1** : declaración *f* **2** *or* **bank ~** : estado *m* de cuenta — **statesman** ['steɪtsmən] *n, pl* **-men** [-mən, -ˌmɛn] : estadista *mf*

static ['stæṭɪk] *adj* : estático — ~ *n* : estática *f*

station ['steɪʃən] *n* **1** : estación *f* (de trenes, etc.) **2** RANK : condición *f* (social) **3** : canal *m* (de televisión), emisora *f* (de radio) **4** → **fire station, police station** — *vt* : apostar, estacionar — **stationary** ['steɪʃəˌnɛri] *adj* : estacionario

stationery ['steɪʃəˌnɛri] *n* : papel *m* y sobres *mpl* (para cartas)

station wagon *n* : camioneta *f* (familiar)

statistic [stə'tɪstɪk] *n* : estadística *f* — **statistical** [stə'tɪstɪkəl] *adj* : estadístico

statue ['stæˌtʃu:] *n* : estatua *f*

stature ['stætʃər] *n* : estatura *f*, talla *f*

status ['steɪṭəs, 'stæ-] *n* **1** : situación *f* **2** *or* **social ~** : estatus *m* **3 marital ~** : estado *m* civil

statute ['stæˌtʃu:t] *n* : estatuto *m*

staunch ['stɔntʃ] *adj* : leal

stave ['steɪv] *vt* **staved** *or* **stove** ['sto:v]; **staving 1 ~ in** : romper **2 ~ off** : evitar

staves → **staff**

stay¹ ['steɪ] *vi* **1** REMAIN : quedarse, permanecer **2** LODGE : alojarse **3 ~ awake** : mantenerse despierto **4 ~ in** : quedarse en casa — *vt* : suspender (una ejecución, etc.) — ~ *n* **1** : estancia *f*, estadía *f Lat* **2** SUSPENSION : suspensión *f*

stay² *n* SUPPORT : soporte *m*

stead ['stɛd] *n* **1 in s.o.'s ~** : en lugar de algn **2 stand s.o. in good ~** : ser muy útil a algn — **steadfast** ['stɛdˌfæst] *adj* **1** FIRM : firme **2** LOYAL : leal, fiel — **steadily** ['stɛdəli] *adv* **1** : progresivamente **2** INCESSANTLY : sin parar **3** FIXEDLY : fijamente — **steady** ['stɛdi] *adj* **steadier; -est 1** FIRM, SURE : firme, seguro **2** FIXED : fijo **3** DEPENDABLE : responsable **4** CONSTANT : constante — ~ *vt* **steadied; steadying 1** : mantener firme **2** : calmar (los nervios)

steak ['steɪk] *n* : bistec *m*, filete *m*

steal ['sti:l] *v* **stole** ['sto:l]; **stolen** ['sto:lən]; **stealing** *vt* : robar — *vi* **1** : robar **2 ~ away** : escabullirse

stealth ['stɛlθ] *n* : sigilo *m* — **stealthy** ['stɛlθi] *adj* **stealthier; -est** : furtivo, sigiloso

steam ['sti:m] *n* **1** : vapor *m* **2 let off ~** : desahogarse — ~ *vi* : echar vapor — *vt* **1** : cocer al vapor **2 ~ up** : empañar — **steam engine** *n* : motor *m* de vapor — **steamship** ['sti:mˌʃɪp] *n* : (barco *m* de) vapor *m* — **steamy** ['sti:mi] *adj* **steamier; -est 1** : lleno de vapor **2** PASSIONATE : tórrido

steel ['sti:l] *n* : acero *m* — ~ *vt* ~ **oneself** : armarse de valor — ~ *adj* : de acero

steep¹ ['sti:p] *adj* **1** : empinado **2** CONSIDERABLE : considerable **3** : muy alto (dícese de precios)

steep² *vt* : dejar (té, etc.) en infusión

steeple ['sti:pəl] *n* : aguja *f*, campanario *m*

steer¹ ['stɪr] *n* : buey *m*

steer² *vt* : dirigir (un auto, etc.), pilotear (un barco) — **steering wheel** *n* : volante

stem¹ ['stɛm] *n* : tallo *m* (de una planta), pie *m* (de una copa) — ~ *vi* ~ **from** : provenir de

stem² *vt* **stemmed; stemming** : contener, detener

stench ['stɛntʃ] *n* : hedor *m*, mal olor *m*

stencil ['stɛntsəl] *n* : plantilla *f* (para marcar)

step ['stɛp] *n* **1** : paso *m* **2** RUNG, STAIR : escalón *m* **3 ~ by ~** : paso por paso **4 take ~s** : tomar medidas **5 watch your ~** : mira por dónde caminas — ~ *vi* **stepped; stepping 1** : dar un paso **2 ~ back** : retoceder **3 ~ down** RESIGN : retirarse **4 ~ in** : intervenir **5 ~ out** : salir (por un momento) **6 ~ this way** : pase por aquí — **step up** *vt* INCREASE : aumentar

stepbrother ['stɛpˌbrʌðər] *n* : hermanastro *m* — **stepdaughter** ['stɛpˌdɔṭər] *n* : hijastra *f* — **stepfather** ['stɛpˌfɑðər, -ˌfa-] *n* : padrastro *m*

stepladder ['stɛpˌlædər] *n* : escalera *f* de tijera

stepmother ['stɛpˌmʌðər] *n* : madrastra *f* — **stepsister** ['stɛpˌsɪstər] *n* : hermanastra *f* — **stepson** ['stɛpˌsʌn] *n* : hijastro *m*

stereo ['stɛriˌo:, 'stɪr-] *n, pl* **stereos** : estéreo *m* — ~ *adj* : estéreo

stereotype ['stɛrioˌtaɪp, 'stɪr-] *vt* **-typed; -typing** : estereotipar — ~ *n* : estereotipo *m*

sterile ['stɛrəl] *adj* : estéril — **sterility** [stə'rɪləṭi] *n* : esterilidad *f* — **sterilization** [ˌstɛrələ'zeɪʃən] *n* : esterilización *f* — **sterilize** ['stɛrəˌlaɪz] *vt* **-ized; -izing** : esterilizar

sterling ['stərlɪŋ] *adj* : excelente — **sterling silver** *n* : plata *f* de ley

stern¹ ['stərn] *adj* : severo, adusto

stern² *n* : popa *f*

stethoscope ['stɛθəˌsko:p] *n* : estetoscopio *m*

stew ['stu:, 'stju:] *n* : estofado *m*, guiso *m* — ~ *vt* : estofar, guisar — *vi* **1** : cocer **2** FRET : preocuparse

steward ['stu:ərd, 'stju:-] *n* **1** : administrador *m*, -dora *f* **2** : auxiliar *m* de vuelo (en un avión) **3** : camarero *m* (en un barco) —

— **stewardess** ['stu:ərdəs, 'stju:-] *n* 1 : auxiliar *f* de vuelo, azafata *f* (en un avión) 2 : camarera *f* (en un barco)

stick[1] ['stɪk] *n* 1 : palo *m* 2 TWIG : ramita *f* (suelta) 3 WALKING STICK : bastón *m*

stick[2] *v* **stuck** ['stʌk]; **sticking** *vt* 1 : pegar 2 STAB : clavar 3 PUT : poner 4 **~ out** : sacar (la lengua, etc.) — *vi* 1 : pegarse 2 JAM : atascarse 3 **~ around** : quedarse 4 **~ out** PROTRUDE : sobresalir 5 **~ out** SHOW : asomar 6 **~ up** : sobresalir 7 **~ up for** : defender — **sticker** ['stɪkər] *n* : etiqueta *f* adhesiva — **stickler** ['stɪklər] *n* **be a ~ for** : insistir mucho en — **sticky** ['stɪki] *adj* **stickier; -est** : pegajoso

stiff ['stɪf] *adj* 1 RIGID : rígido, tieso 2 STILTED : forzado 3 STRONG : fuerte 4 DIFFICULT : difícil 5 : entumecido (dícese de músculos) — **stiffen** ['stɪfən] *vt* : fortalecer, hacer más duro — *vi* 1 HARDEN : endurecerse 2 : entumecerse (dícese de músculos) — **stiffness** ['stɪfnəs] *n* : rigidez *f*

stifle ['staɪfəl] *vt* **-fled; -fling** : sofocar

stigmatize ['stɪgməˌtaɪz] *vt* **-tized; -tizing** : estigmatizar

still ['stɪl] *adj* 1 : inmóvil 2 SILENT : callado — **~** *adv* 1 : todavía, aún 2 NEVERTHELESS : de todos modos, aún así 3 **sit ~!** : ¡quédate quieto! — **~** *n* : quietud *f*, calma *f* — **stillborn** ['stɪlˌbɔrn] *adj* : nacido muerto — **stillness** ['stɪlnəs] *n* : calma *f*, silencio *m*

stilt ['stɪlt] *n* : zanco *m* — **stilted** ['stɪltəd] *adj* : forzado

stimulate ['stɪmjəˌleɪt] *vt* **-lated; -lating** : estimular — **stimulant** ['stɪmjələnt] *n* : estimulante *m* — **stimulation** [ˌstɪmjə'leɪʃən] *n* : estimulación *f* — **stimulus** ['stɪmjələs] *n, pl* **-li** [-ˌlaɪ] : estímulo *m*

sting ['stɪŋ] *v* **stung** ['stʌŋ]; **stinging** : picar — **~** *n* : picadura *f* — **stinger** ['stɪŋər] *n* : aguijón *m*

stingy ['stɪndʒi] *adj* **stingier; -est** : tacaño — **stinginess** ['stɪndʒinəs] *n* : tacañería *f*

stink ['stɪŋk] *vi* **stank** ['stæŋk] *or* **stunk** ['stʌŋk]; **stunk; stinking** : apestar, oler mal — **~** *n* : hedor *m*, peste *f fam*

stint ['stɪnt] *vi* **~ on** : escatimar — **~** *n* : período *m*

stipulate ['stɪpjəˌleɪt] *vt* **-lated; -lating** : estipular

stir ['stər] *v* **stirred; stirring** *vt* 1 : remover, revolver 2 MOVE : mover 3 INCITE : incitar 4 *or* **~ up** : despertar (memorias, etc.), provocar (ira, etc.) — *vi* : moverse, agitarse — **~** *n* COMMOTION : revuelo *m*

stirrup ['stərəp, 'stɪr-] *n* : estribo *m*

stitch ['stɪtʃ] *n* 1 : puntada *f* 2 PAIN : punzada *f* (en el costado) — **~** *v* : coser

stock ['stɑk] *n* 1 INVENTORY : existencias *fpl* 2 SECURITIES : acciones *fpl* 3 ANCESTRY : linaje *m*, estirpe *f* 4 BROTH : caldo *m* 5 **out of ~** : agotado 6 **take ~ of** : evaluar — **~** *vt* : surtir, abastecer — *vi* **~ up on** : abastecerse de — **stockbroker** ['stɑkˌbro:kər] *n* : corredor *m*, -dora *f* de bolsa

stocking ['stɑkɪŋ] *n* : media *f*

stock market *n* : bolsa *f* — **stockpile** ['stɑkˌpaɪl] *n* : reservas *fpl* — **~** *vt* **-piled; -piling** : almacenar — **stocky** ['stɑki] *adj* **stockier; -est** : robusto, fornido

stodgy ['stɑdʒi] *adj* **stodgier; -est** 1 DULL : pesado 2 OLD-FASHIONED : anticuado

stoic ['sto:ɪk] *n* : estoico *m*, -ca *f* — **~** *or* **stoical** [-ɪkəl] *adj* : estoico — **stoicism** ['sto:əˌsɪzəm] *n* : estoicismo *m*

stoke ['sto:k] *vt* **stoked; stoking** : echar carbón o leña a

stole[1] ['sto:l] → **steal**

stole[2] *n* : estola *f*

stolen → **steal**

stomach ['stʌmɪk] *n* : estómago *m* — **~** *vt* : aguantar, soportar — **stomachache** ['stʌmɪkˌeɪk] *n* : dolor *m* de estómago

stone ['sto:n] *n* 1 : piedra *f* 2 : hueso *m* (de una fruta) — **~** *vt* **stoned; stoning** : apedrear — **stony** ['sto:ni] *adj* **stonier; -est** 1 : pedregoso 2 **a ~ silence** : un silencio sepulcral

stood → **stand**

stool ['stu:l] *n* : taburete *m*

stoop ['stu:p] *vi* 1 : agacharse 2 **~ to** : rebajarse a — **~** *n* **have a ~** : ser encorvado

stop ['stɑp] *v* **stopped; stopping** *vt* 1 PLUG : tapar 2 PREVENT : impedir 3 HALT : parar, detener 4 CEASE : dejar de — *vi* 1 : detenerse, parar 2 CEASE : cesar, dejar 3 **~ by** : visitar — **~** *n* 1 : parada *f*, alto *m* 2 **come to a ~** : pararse, detenerse 3 **put a ~ to** : poner fin a — **stopgap** ['stɑpˌgæp] *n* : arreglo *m* provisorio — **stoplight** ['stɑpˌlaɪt] *n* : semáforo *m* — **stoppage** ['stɑpɪdʒ] *n or* **work ~** : paro *m* — **stopper** ['stɑpər] *n* : tapón *m*

store ['stor] *vt* **stored; storing** : guardar (comida, etc.), almacenar (datos, mercancías, etc.) — **~** *n* 1 SUPPLY : reserva *f* 2 SHOP : tienda *f* — **storage** ['storɪdʒ] *n* : almacenamiento *m* — **storehouse** ['storˌhaʊs] *n* : almacén *m* — **storekeeper** ['storˌki:pər] *n* : tendero *m*, -ra *f* — **storeroom** ['storˌru:m, -ˌrʊm] *n* : almacén *m*

stork ['stɔrk] *n* : cigüeña *f*

storm ['stɔrm] *n* : tormenta *f*, tempestad *f* — **~** *vi* 1 RAGE : ponerse furioso 2 **~ in/out** : entrar/salir furioso — *vt* ATTACK : asaltar — **stormy** ['stɔrmi] *adj* **stormier; -est** : tormentoso

story[1] ['stori] *n, pl* **stories** 1 TALE : cuento *m* 2 ACCOUNT : historia *f* 3 RUMOR : rumor *m*

story[2] *n* FLOOR : piso *m*, planta *f*

stout ['staʊt] *adj* 1 BRAVE : valiente 2 RESOLUTE : tenaz 3 STURDY : fuerte 4 FAT : corpulento

stove[1] ['sto:v] *n* 1 : estufa *f* (para calentar) 2 RANGE : cocina *f*

stove[2] → **stave**

stow ['sto:] *vt* 1 : guardar 2 LOAD : cargar — *vi* **~ away** : viajar de polizón — **stowaway** ['sto:əˌweɪ] *n* : polizón *m*

straddle ['strædəl] *vt* **-dled; -dling** : sentarse a horcajadas sobre

straggle ['strægəl] *vi* **-gled; -gling** : rezagarse, quedarse atrás — **straggler** ['strægələr] *n* : rezagado *m*, -da *f*

straight ['streɪt] *adj* 1 : recto, derecho 2 : lacio (dícese del pelo) 3 HONEST : franco 4 TIDY : arreglado — **~** *adv* 1 DIRECTLY : derecho 2 EXACTLY : justo 3 CLEARLY : con claridad 4 FRANKLY : con franqueza — **straightaway** ['streɪt'weɪ, -ˌweɪ] *adv* : inmediatamente — **straighten** ['streɪtən] *vt* 1 : enderezar 2 **~ up** : arreglar — **straightforward** [streɪt'fɔrwərd] *adj* 1 FRANK : franco 2 CLEAR : claro, sencillo

strain[1] ['streɪn] *n* 1 LINEAGE : linaje *m* 2 STREAK : veta *f* 3 VARIETY : variedad *f* 4 **~s** *npl* : acordes *mpl* (de música)

strain[2] *vt* 1 : forzar (la vista o la voz) 2 FILTER : colar 3 : tensar (relaciones, etc.) 4 **~ a muscle** : sufrir un esguince 5 **~ oneself** : hacerse daño — *vi* : esforzarse (por) — **~** *n* 1 STRESS : tensión *f* 2 SPRAIN : esguince *m* — **strainer** ['streɪnər] *n* : colador *m*

strait ['streɪt] *n* 1 : estrecho *m* 2 **in dire ~s** : en grandes apuros

strand[1] ['strænd] *vt* **be ~ed** : quedar(se) varado

strand[2] *n* 1 : hebra *f* 2 **a ~ of hair** : un pelo

strange ['streɪndʒ] *adj* **stranger; -est** 1 : extraño, raro 2 UNFAMILIAR : desconocido — **strangely** ['streɪndʒli] *adv* : de manera extraña — **strangeness** ['streɪndʒnəs] *n* 1 : rareza *f* 2 UNFAMILIARITY : lo desconocido — **stranger** ['streɪndʒər] *n* : desconocido *m*, -da *f*

strangle ['stræŋgəl] *vt* **-gled; -gling** : estrangular

strap ['stræp] *n* 1 : correa *f* 2 *or* **shoulder ~** : tirante *m* — **~** *vt* **strapped; strapping** : sujetar con una correa — **strapless** ['stræpləs] *n* : sin tirantes — **strapping** ['stræpɪŋ] *adj* : robusto, fornido

strategy ['strætədʒi] *n, pl* **-gies** : estrategia *f* — **strategic** [strə'ti:dʒɪk] *adj* : estratégico

straw ['strɔ] *n* 1 : paja *f* 2 *or* **drinking ~** : pajita *f* 3 **the last ~** : el colmo

strawberry ['strɔˌbɛri] *n, pl* **-ries** : fresa *f*

stray ['streɪ] *n* : animal *m* perdido — **~** *vi* 1 : perderse, extraviarse 2 : apartarse (de un grupo, etc.) 3 DEVIATE : desviarse — **~** *adj* : perdido

streak ['stri:k] *n* 1 : raya *f* 2 VEIN : veta *f* 3 **~ of luck** : racha *f* de suerte — *vi* **~ by** : pasar como una flecha

stream ['stri:m] *n* 1 : arroyo *m*, riachuelo *m* 2 FLOW : chorro *m*, corriente *f* — **~** *vi* : correr — **streamer** ['stri:mər] *n* 1 PENNANT : banderín *m* 2 : serpentina *f* (de papel) — **streamlined** ['stri:mˌlaɪnd] *adj* 1 : aerodinámico 2 EFFICIENT : eficiente

street ['stri:t] *n* : calle *f* — **streetcar** ['stri:tˌkɑr] *n* : tranvía *m* — **streetlight** ['stri:tˌlaɪt] *n* : farol *m*

strength ['strɛŋkθ] *n* 1 : fuerza *f* 2 FORTITUDE : fortaleza *f* 3 TOUGHNESS : resistencia *f*, solidez *f* 4 INTENSITY : intensidad *f* 5 **~s and weaknesses** : virtudes y defectos — **strengthen** ['strɛŋkθən] *vt* 1 : fortalecer 2 REINFORCE : reforzar 3 INTENSIFY : intensificar

strenuous ['strɛnjuəs] *adj* 1 : enérgico 2 ARDUOUS : duro, riguroso

stress ['strɛs] *n* 1 : tensión *f* 2 EMPHASIS : énfasis *m* 3 : acento *m* (en lingüística) — **~** *vt* 1 EMPHASIZE : enfatizar 2 *or* **~ out** : estresar — **stressful** ['strɛsfəl] *adj* : estresante

stretch ['strɛtʃ] *vt* 1 : estirar (músculos, elástico, etc.) 2 EXTEND : extender 3 **~ the truth** : forzar la verdad — *vi* 1 : estirarse 2 EXTEND : extenderse — **~** *n* 1 : extensión *f* 2 ELASTICITY : elasticidad *f* 3 EXPANSE : tramo *m* 4 : período *m* (de tiempo) — **stretcher** ['strɛtʃər] *n* : camilla *f*

strew ['stru:] *vt* **strewed; strewed** *or* **strewn** ['stru:n]; **strewing** : esparcir (semillas, etc.), desparramar (papeles, etc.)

stricken ['strɪkən] *adj* **~ with** : aquejado de (una enfermedad), afligido por (tristeza, etc.)

strict ['strɪkt] *adj* : estricto — **strictly** *adv* **~ speaking** : en rigor

stride ['straɪd] *vi* **strode** ['stro:d]; **stridden** ['strɪdən]; **striding** : ir dando zancadas — **~** *n* 1 : zancada *f* 2 **make great ~s** : hacer grandes progresos

strident ['straɪdənt] *adj* : estridente

strife ['straɪf] *n* : conflictos *mpl*

strike ['straɪk] *v* **struck** ['strʌk]; **struck; striking** *vt* 1 HIT : golpear 2 *or* **~ against** : chocar contra 3 *or* **~ out** DELETE : tachar 4 : dar (la hora) 5 IMPRESS : impresionar 6 : descubrir (oro o petróleo) 7 **it ~s me as...** : me parece... 8 **~ up** START : entablar — *vi* 1 : golpear 2 ATTACK : atacar 3 : declararse en huelga 4 : sobrevenir (dícese de una enfermedad, etc.) — **~** *n* 1 BLOW : golpe *m* 2 : huelga *f*, paro *m Lat* (de trabajadores) 3 ATTACK : ataque *m* — **strikebreaker** ['straɪkˌbreɪkər] *n* : esquirol *mf* — **striker** ['straɪkər] *n* : huelgista *mf* — **striking** ['straɪkɪŋ] *adj* : notable, llamativo

string ['strɪŋ] *n* 1 : cordel *m* 2 : sarta *f* (de perlas, insultos, etc.), serie *f* (de eventos, etc.) 3 **~s** *npl* : cuerdas *fpl* (en música) — **~** *vt* **strung** ['strʌŋ]; **stringing** 1 : ensartar 2 *or* **~ up** : colgar — **string bean** *n* : habichuela *f* verde

stringent ['strɪndʒənt] *adj* : estricto, severo

strip[1] ['strɪp] *v* **stripped; stripping** *vt* 1 REMOVE : quitar 2 UNDRESS : desnudar 3 **~ s.o. of sth** : despojar a algn de algo — *vi* UNDRESS : desnudarse

strip[2] *n* : tira *f*

stripe ['straɪp] *n* : raya *f*, lista *f* — **striped** ['straɪpt, 'straɪpəd] *adj* : a rayas, rayado

strive ['straɪv] *vi* **strove** ['stro:v]; **striven** ['strɪvən] *or* **strived; striving** 1 **~ for** : luchar por 2 **~ to** : esforzarse por

strode → **stride**

stroke ['stro:k] *vt* **stroked; stroking** : acariciar — **~** *n* 1 : golpe *m* 2 : derrame *m* cerebral (en medicina)

stroll ['stro:l] *vi* : pasearse — **~** *n* : paseo *m* — **stroller** ['stro:lər] *n* : cochecito *m* (para niños)

strong ['strɔŋ] *adj* : fuerte — **stronghold** ['strɔŋˌho:ld] *n* : bastión *m* — **strongly** ['strɔŋli] *adv* 1 DEEPLY : profundamente 2 WHOLEHEARTEDLY : totalmente 3 VIGOROUSLY : enérgicamente

strove → **strive**

struck → **strike**

structure ['strʌktʃər] *n* : estructura *f* — **structural** ['strʌktʃərəl] *adj* : estructural

struggle ['strʌgəl] *vi* **-gled; -gling** 1 : forcejear 2 STRIVE : luchar — **~** *n* : lucha *f*

strum ['strʌm] *vt* **strummed; strumming** : rasguear

strung → **string**

strut ['strʌt] *vi* **strutted; strutting** : pavonearse — **~** *n* : puntal *m* (en construcción)

stub ['stʌb] *n* : colilla *f* (de un cigarrillo), cabo *m* (de un lápiz, etc.), talón *m* (de un cheque) — **~** *vt* **stubbed; stubbing ~ one's toe** : darse en el dedo

stubble ['stʌbəl] *n* : barba *f* de varios días

stubborn ['stʌbərn] *adj* 1 : terco, obstinado 2 PERSISTENT : tenaz

stucco ['stʌko:] *n, pl* **stuccos** *or* **stuccoes** : estuco *m*

stuck → **stick** — **stuck–up** ['stʌk'ʌp] *adj* : engreído, creído *fam*

stud[1] ['stʌd] *n* : semental *m* (animal)

stud[2] *n* 1 NAIL, TACK : tachuela *f*, tachón *m* 2 *or* **~ earring** : arete *m Lat*, pendiente *m Spain* 3 : montante *m* (en construcción)

student ['stu:dənt, 'stju:-] *n* : estudiante *mf*; alumno *m*, -na *f* (de un colegio) — **studio** ['stu:diˌo:, 'stju:-] *n, pl* **studios** : estudio *m* — **study** ['stʌdi] *n, pl* **studies** : estudio *m* — **~** *v* **studied; studying** : estudiar — **studious** ['stu:diəs, 'stju:-] *adj* : estudioso

stuff ['stʌf] *n* 1 : cosas *fpl* 2 MATTER, SUBSTANCE : cosa *f* 3 **know one's ~** : ser experto — **~** *vt* 1 FILL : rellenar 2 CRAM : meter — **stuffing** ['stʌfɪŋ] *n* : relleno *m* — **stuffy** ['stʌfi] *adj* **stuffier; -est** 1 STODGY : pesado, aburrido 2 : tapado (dícese de la nariz) 3 **~ rooms** : salas *fpl* mal ventiladas

stumble ['stʌmbəl] *vi* **-bled; -bling** 1 : tropezar 2 **~ across** *or* **upon** : tropezar con

stump ['stʌmp] *n* 1 : muñón *m* (de una pierna, etc.) 2 *or* **tree ~** : tocón *m* — **~** *vt* : dejar perplejo

stun ['stʌn] *vt* **stunned; stunning** 1 : aturdir (con un golpe) 2 ASTONISH : dejar atónito

stung → **sting**

stunk → **stink**

stunning ['stʌnɪŋ] *adj* 1 : increíble, sensacional 2 STRIKING : imponente

stunt[1] ['stʌnt] *vt* : atrofiar

stunt[2] *n* : proeza *f* (acrobática)

stupendous [stʊ'pɛndəs, stjʊ-] *adj* : estupendo

stupid ['stu:pəd, 'stju:-] *adj* 1 : estúpido 2 SILLY : tonto, bobo — **stupidity** [stʊ'pɪdəti, stjʊ-] *n* : tontería *f*, estupidez *f*

sturdy ['stərdi] *adj* **sturdier; -est** 1 : fuerte, resistente 2 ROBUST : robusto

stutter ['stʌtər] *vi* : tartamudear — **~** *n* : tartamudeo *m*

sty ['staɪ] *n* 1 *pl* **sties** PIGPEN : pocilga *f* 2 *pl* **sties** *or* **styes** : orzuelo *m* (en el ojo)

style ['staɪl] *n* 1 : estilo *m* 2 FASHION : moda *f* 3 **be in ~** : estar de moda — **~** *vt* **styled; styling** : peinar (pelo), diseñar (vestidos, etc.) — **stylish** ['staɪlɪʃ] *adj* : elegante, chic — **stylist** ['staɪlɪst] *n* : estilista *mf*

suave ['swɑv] *adj* : refinado y afable

sub[1] ['sʌb] *vi* **subbed; subbing** → **substitute** — **~** *n* → **substitute**

sub[2] *n* → **submarine**

subconscious [səb'kɑntʃəs] *adj* : subconsciente — **~** *n* : subconsciente *m*

subdivide [ˌsʌbdə'vaɪd, 'sʌbdəˌvaɪd] *vt* **-vided; -viding** : subdividir — **subdivision** ['sʌbdəˌvɪʒən] *n* : subdivisión *f*

subdue [səb'du:, -'dju:] *vt* **-dued; -duing** 1 CONQUER : sojuzgar 2 CONTROL : dominar 3 SOFTEN : atenuar — **subdued** *adj* : apagado

subject ['sʌbdʒɪkt] *n* 1 : sujeto *m* 2 : súbdito *m*, -ta *f* (de un gobierno) 3 TOPIC : tema *m* — **~** *adj* 1 : sometido 2 **~ to** : sujeto a — **~** [səb'dʒɛkt] *vt* **~ to** : someter a — **subjective** [səb'dʒɛktɪv] *adj* : subjetivo

subjunctive [səb'dʒʌŋktɪv] *n* : subjuntivo *m* — **subjunctive** *adj* : subjuntivo

sublime [sə'blaɪm] *adj* : sublime

submarine ['sʌbməˌri:n, ˌsʌbmə'-] *adj* : submarino — **~** *n* : submarino *m*

submerge [səb'mərdʒ] *v* **-merged; -merging** *vt* : sumergir — *vi* : sumergirse

submit [səb'mɪt] *v* **-mitted; -mitting** *vi* 1 YIELD : rendirse 2 **~ to** : someterse a — *vt* : presentar — **submission** [səb'mɪʃən] *n* 1 : sumisión *f* 2 PRESENTATION : presentación *f* — **submissive** [səb'mɪsɪv] *adj* : sumiso

subordinate [sə'bɔrdənət] *adj* : subordinado — **~** *n* : subordinado *m*, -da *f* — **~** [sə'bɔrdənˌeɪt] *vt* **-nated; -nating** : subordinar

subpoena [sə'pi:nə] *n* : citación *f*

subscribe [səb'skraɪb] *vi* **-scribed; -scribing ~ to** : suscribirse a (una revista, etc.), suscribir (una opinión, etc.) — **subscriber** [səb'skraɪbər] *n* : suscriptor *m*, -tora *f* (de una revista, etc.); abonado *m*, -da *f* (de un servicio) — **subscription** [səb'skrɪpʃən] *n* : suscripción *f*

subsequent ['sʌbsɪkwənt, -səˌkwɛnt] *adj* 1 : subsiguiente 2 **~ to** : posterior a — **subsequently** ['sʌbˌkwɛntli, -kwənt-] *adv* : posteriormente

subservient [səb'sərviənt] *adj* : servil

subside [səb'saɪd] *vi* **-sided; -siding** 1 SINK : hundirse 2 : amainar (dícese de tormentas, pasiones, etc.), remitir (dícese de fiebres, etc.)

subsidiary [səb'sɪdiˌɛri] *adj* : secundario — **~** *n, pl* **-ries** : filial *f*

subsidy ['sʌbsədi] *n, pl* **-dies** : subvención *f* — **subsidize** ['sʌbsəˌdaɪz] *vt* **-dized; -dizing** : subvencionar

subsistence [səb'sɪstənts] *n* : subsistencia *f* — **subsist** [səb'sɪst] *vi* : subsistir

substance ['sʌbstənts] *n* : sustancia *f*

substandard [ˌsʌb'stændərd] *adj* : inferior

substantial [səb'stæntʃəl] *adj* 1 CONSIDERABLE : considerable 2 STURDY : sólido 3 : sustancioso (dícese de una comida, etc.) — **substantially** [səb'stæntʃəli] *adv* : considerablemente

substitute ['sʌbstəˌtu:t, -ˌtju:t] *n* : sustituto *m*, -ta *f* (de una persona); sucedáneo *m* (de una cosa) — **~** *vt* **-tuted; -tuting** : sustituir — **substitution** [ˌsʌbstə'tu:ʃən, -'tju:-] *n* : sustitución *f*

subterranean [ˌsʌbtə'reɪniən] *adj* : subterráneo

subtitle ['sʌbˌtaɪtəl] *n* : subtítulo *m*

subtle ['sʌtəl] *adj* **-tler; -tlest** : sutil — **subtlety** ['sʌtəlti] *n, pl* **-ties** : sutileza *f*

subtraction [səb'trækʃən] *n* : resta *f* — **subtract** [səb'trækt] *vt* : restar

suburb ['sʌˌbərb] *n* 1 : barrio *m* residencial, suburbio *m* 2 **the ~s** : las afueras — **suburban** [sə'bərbən] *adj* : de las afueras (de una ciudad)

subversion [səb'vərʒən] *n* : subversión *f* — **subversive** [səb'vərsɪv] *adj* : subversivo

subway ['sʌbˌweɪ] *n* : metro *m*

succeed [sək'si:d] *vt* : suceder a — *vi* : tener éxito (dícese de personas), dar resultado (dícese de planes, etc.) — **success** [sək'sɛs] *n* : éxito *m* — **successful** [sək'sɛsfəl] *adj* : de éxito, exitoso *Lat* — **successfully** *adv* : con éxito

succession [sək'sɛʃən] *n* 1 : sucesión *f* 2 **in ~** : sucesivamente, seguidos — **successive** [sək'sɛsɪv] *adj* : sucesivo — **successor** [sək'sɛsər] *n* : sucesor *m*, -sora *f*

succinct [sək'sɪŋkt, sə'sɪŋkt] *adj* : sucinto

succulent ['sʌkjələnt] *adj* : suculento

succumb [sə'kʌm] *vi* : sucumbir

such ['sʌtʃ] *adj* 1 : tal 2 **~ as** : como 3 **~ a pity!** : ¡qué lástima! — **~** *pron* 1 : tal 2 **and ~** : y cosas por el estilo 3 **as ~** : como tal — **~** *adv* 1 VERY : muy 2 **~ a nice man!** : ¡qué hombre tan simpático! 3 **~ that** : de tal manera que

suck ['sʌk] *vt* 1 *or* **~ on** : chupar 2 *or* **~ up** : sorber (bebidas), aspirar (con una máquina) — **sucker** ['sʌkər] *n* 1 SHOOT : chupón *m* 2 FOOL : imbécil *mf* — **suckle** ['sʌkəl] *vt* **-led; -ling** : amamantar — **suction** ['sʌkʃən] *n* : succión *f*

sudden ['sʌdən] *adj* 1 : repentino 2 **all of a ~** : de repente — **suddenly** ['sʌdənli] *adv* : de repente

suds ['sʌdz] *npl* : espuma *f* (de jabón)

sue ['su:] *vt* **sued; suing** : demandar (por)

suede ['sweɪd] *n* : ante *m*, gamuza *f*

suet ['su:ət] *n* : sebo *m*

suffer ['sʌfər] *vi* : sufrir — *vt* 1 : sufrir 2 BEAR : tolerar — **suffering** ['sʌfərɪŋ] *n* : sufrimiento *m*

suffice [sə'faɪs] vi **-ficed; -ficing** : bastar — **sufficient** [sə'fɪʃənt] adj : suficiente — **sufficiently** [sə'fɪʃəntli] adv : (lo) suficientemente

suffix ['sʌ,fɪks] n : sufijo m

suffocate ['sʌfə,keɪt] v **-cated; -cating** vt : asfixiar — vi : asfixiarse — **suffocation** [,sʌfə'keɪʃən] n : asfixia f

suffrage ['sʌfrɪdʒ] n : sufragio m

sugar ['ʃʊgər] n : azúcar mf — **sugarcane** ['ʃʊgər,keɪn] n : caña f de azúcar — **sugary** ['ʃʊgəri] adj : azucarado

suggestion [səg'dʒɛstʃən, sə-] n **1** : sugerencia f **2** TRACE : indicio m — **suggest** [səg'dʒɛst, sə-] vt **1** : sugerir **2** INDICATE : indicar

suicide ['su:ə,saɪd] n **1** : suicidio m (acto) **2** : suicida mf (persona) — **suicidal** [,su:ə'saɪdəl] adj : suicida

suit ['su:t] n **1** LAWSUIT : pleito m **2** : traje m (ropa) **3** : palo m (de naipes) — **~** vt **1** ADAPT : adaptar **2** BEFIT : ser apropiado para **3 ~ s.o.** : convenir a algn (dícese de fechas, etc.), quedar bien a algn (dícese de ropa) — **suitable** ['su:t̬əbəl] adj : apropiado — **suitcase** ['su:t,keɪs] n : maleta f, valija f Lat

suite ['swi:t, for 2 also 'su:t] n **1** : suite f (de habitaciones) **2** : juego m (de muebles)

suitor ['su:t̬ər] n : pretendiente m

sulfur ['sʌlfər] n : azufre m

sulk ['sʌlk] vi : enfurruñarse fam — **sulky** ['sʌlki] adj **sulkier; -est** : malhumorado

sullen ['sʌlən] adj : hosco

sultry ['sʌltri] adj **sultrier; -est 1** : bochornoso **2** SENSUAL : sensual

sum ['sʌm] n : suma f — **~** vt **summed; summing ~ up** : resumir — **summarize** ['sʌmə,raɪz] v **-rized; -rizing** : resumir — **summary** ['sʌməri] n, pl **-ries** : resumen m

summer ['sʌmər] n : verano m

summit ['sʌmət] n : cumbre f

summon ['sʌmən] vt **1** : llamar (a algn), convocar (una reunión) **2** : citar (en derecho) — **summons** ['sʌmənz] n, pl **summonses** SUBPOENA : citación f

sumptuous ['sʌmptʃʊəs] adj : suntuoso

sun ['sʌn] n : sol m — **sunbathe** ['sʌn,beɪð] vi **-bathed; -bathing** : tomar el sol — **sunbeam** ['sʌn,bi:m] n : rayo m de sol — **sunburn** ['sʌn,bərn] n : quemadura f de sol

Sunday ['sʌn,deɪ, -di] n : domingo m

sundry ['sʌndri] adj : varios, diversos

sunflower ['sʌn,flaʊər] n : girasol m

sung → **sing**

sunglasses ['sʌn,glæsəz] npl : gafas fpl de sol, lentes mpl de sol

sunk → **sink** — **sunken** ['sʌŋkən] adj : hundido

sunlight ['sʌn,laɪt] n : (luz f del) sol m — **sunny** ['sʌni] adj **-nier; -est** : soleado — **sunrise** ['sʌn,raɪz] n : salida f del sol — **sunset** ['sʌn,sɛt] n : puesta f del sol — **sunshine** ['sʌn,ʃaɪn] n : sol m, luz f del sol — **suntan** ['sʌn,tæn] n : bronceado m

super ['su:pər] adj : súper fam

superb [sʊ'pərb] adj : magnífico, espléndido

superficial [,su:pər'fɪʃəl] adj : superficial

superfluous [sʊ'pərfluəs] adj : superfluo

superimpose [,su:pərɪm'po:z] vt **-posed; -posing** : sobreponer

superintendent [,su:pərɪn'tɛndənt] n **1** : superintendente mf (de policía) **2** or **building ~** : portero m, -ra f **3** or **school ~** : director m, -tora f (de un colegio)

superior [sʊ'pɪriər] adj : superior — **~** n : superior m — **superiority** [sʊ,pɪri'ɔrət̬i] n, pl **-ties** : superioridad f

superlative [sʊ'pərlət̬ɪv] adj **1** : superlativo (en gramática) **2** EXCELLENT : excepcional — **~** n : superlativo m

supermarket ['su:pər,mɑrkət] n : supermercado m

supernatural [,su:pər'nætʃərəl] adj : sobrenatural

superpower ['su:pər,paʊər] n : superpotencia f

supersede [,su:pər'si:d] vt **-seded; -seding** : reemplazar, suplantar

supersonic [,su:pər'sɑnɪk] adj : supersónico

superstition [,su:pər'stɪʃən] n : superstición f — **superstitious** [,su:pər'stɪʃəs] adj : supersticioso

supervisor ['su:pər,vaɪzər] n : supervisor m, -sora f — **supervise** ['su:pər,vaɪz] vt **-vised; -vising** : supervisar — **supervision** [,su:pər'vɪʒən] n : supervisión f — **supervisory** [,su:pər'vaɪzəri] adj : de supervisor

supper ['sʌpər] n : cena f, comida f

supplant [sə'plænt] vt : suplantar

supple ['sʌpəl] adj **-pler; -plest** : flexible

supplement ['sʌpləmənt] n : suplemento m — **~** ['sʌplə,mɛnt] vt : complementar — **supplementary** [,sʌplə'mɛntəri] adj : suplementario

supply [sə'plaɪ] vt **-plied; -plying 1** : suministrar **2 ~ with** : proveer de — **~** n, pl **-plies 1** : suministro m, provisión f **2 ~ and demand** : oferta y demanda **3 supplies** npl PROVISIONS : provisiones fpl, víveres mpl — **supplier** [sə'plaɪər] n : proveedor m, -dora f

support [sə'port] vt **1** BACK : apoyar **2** : mantener (una familia, etc.) **3** PROP UP : sostener — **~** n **1** : apoyo m (moral), ayuda f (económica) **2** PROP : soporte m — **supporter** [sə'port̬ər] n : partidario m, -ria f

suppose [sə'po:z] vt **-posed; -posing 1** : suponer **2 be ~d to (do sth)** : tener que (hacer algo) — **supposedly** adv : supuestamente

suppress [sə'prɛs] vt **1** : reprimir **2** : suprimir (noticias, etc.) — **suppression** [sə'prɛʃən] n **1** : represión f **2** : supresión f (de información)

supreme [sʊ'pri:m] adj : supremo — **supremacy** [sʊ'prɛməsi] n, pl **-cies** : supremacía f

sure ['ʃʊr] adj **surer; -est 1** : seguro **2 make ~ that** : asegurarse de que — **~** adv **1** OF COURSE : por supuesto, claro **2 it ~ is hot!** : ¡qué calor! — **surely** ['ʃʊrli] adv : seguramente

surfing ['sərfɪŋ] n : surf m, surfing m

surface ['sərfəs] n : superficie f — **~** v **-faced; -facing** vi : salir a la superficie — vt : revestir

surfeit ['sərfət] n : exceso m

surfing ['sərfɪŋ] n : surf m, surfing m

surge ['sərdʒ] vi **surged; surging 1** SWELL : hincharse (dícese del mar) **2** SWARM : moverse en tropel — **~** n **1** : oleaje m (del mar), oleada f (de gente) **2** INCREASE : aumento m (súbito)

surgeon ['sərdʒən] n : cirujano m, -na f — **surgery** ['sərdʒəri] n, pl **-geries** : cirugía f — **surgical** ['sərdʒɪkəl] adj : quirúrgico

surly ['sərli] adj **surlier; -est** : hosco, arisco

surmount [sər'maʊnt] vt : superar

surname ['sər,neɪm] n : apellido m

surpass [sər'pæs] vt : superar

surplus ['sər,plʌs] n : excedente m

surprise [sə'praɪz, sər-] n **1** : sorpresa f **2 take by ~** : sorprender — **~** vt **-prised; -prising** : sorprender — **surprising** [sə'praɪzɪŋ, sər-] adj : sorprendente

surrender [sə'rɛndər] vt : entregar, rendir — vi : rendirse — **~** n : rendición m (de una ciudad, etc.), entrega f (de posesiones)

surrogate ['sərəgət, -,geɪt] n : sustituto m

surround [sə'raʊnd] vt : rodear — **surroundings** [sə'raʊndɪŋz] npl : ambiente m

surveillance [sər'veɪlənts, -'veɪljənts, -'veɪənts] n : vigilancia f

survey [sər'veɪ] vt **-veyed; -veying 1** : medir (un solar) **2** INSPECT : inspeccionar **3** POLL : sondear — **~** ['sər,veɪ] n, pl **-veys 1** INSPECTION : inspección f **2** : medición f (de un solar) **3** POLL : encuesta f, sondeo m — **surveyor** [sər'veɪər] n : agrimensor m, -sora f

survive [sər'vaɪv] v **-vived; -viving** vi : sobrevivir — vt : sobrevivir a — **survival** [sər'vaɪvəl] n : supervivencia f — **survivor** [sər'vaɪvər] n : superviviente mf

susceptible [sə'sɛptəbəl] adj **~ to** : propenso a — **susceptibility** [sə,sɛptə'bɪlət̬i] n, pl **-ties** : propensión f (a enfermedades, etc.)

suspect ['sʌs,pɛkt, sə'spɛkt] adj : sospechoso — **~** ['sʌs,pɛkt] n : sospechoso m, -sa f — **~** [sə'spɛkt] vt : sospechar (algo), sospechar de (algn)

suspend [sə'spɛnd] vt : suspender — **suspense** [sə'spɛnts] n **1** : incertidumbre m **2** : suspenso m Lat, suspense m Spain (en el cine, etc.) — **suspension** [sə'spɛntʃən] n : suspensión f

suspicion [sə'spɪʃən] n : sospecha f — **suspicious** [sə'spɪʃəs] adj **1** QUESTIONABLE : sospechoso **2** DISTRUSTFUL : suspicaz

sustain [sə'steɪn] vt **1** : sostener **2** SUFFER : sufrir

swagger ['swægər] vi : pavonearse

swallow[1] ['swɑlo:] v : tragar — **~** n : trago m

swallow[2] n : golondrina f (pájaro)

swam → **swim**

swamp ['swɑmp] n : pantano m, ciénaga f — **~** vt : inundar — **swampy** ['swɑmpi] adj **swampier; -est** : pantanoso, cenagoso

swan ['swɑn] n : cisne f

swap ['swɑp] vt **swapped; swapping 1** : intercambiar **2 ~ sth for sth** : cambiar algo por algo **3 ~ sth with s.o.** : cambiar algo a algn — **~** n : cambio m

swarm ['swɔrm] n : enjambre m — **~** vi : enjambrar

swat ['swɑt] vt **swatted; swatting** : aplastar (un insecto)

sway ['sweɪ] n **1** : balanceo m **2** INFLUENCE : influjo m — **~** vi : balancearse — vt : influir en

swear ['swær] v **swore** ['swor]; **sworn** ['sworn]; **swearing** vi **1** : jurar **2** CURSE : decir palabrotas — vt : jurar — **swearword** ['swær,wərd] n : palabrota f

sweat ['swɛt] vi **sweat** or **sweated; sweating** : sudar — **~** n : sudor m — **sweater** ['swɛt̬ər] n : suéter m — **sweatshirt** ['swɛt,ʃərt] n : sudadera f — **sweaty** ['swɛt̬i] adj **sweatier; -est** : sudado

Swedish ['swi:dɪʃ] adj : sueco — **~** n : sueco m (idioma)

sweep ['swi:p] v **swept** ['swɛpt]; **sweeping** vt **1** : barrer **2 ~ aside** : apartar **3 ~ through** : extenderse por — vi : barrer — **~** n **1** : barrido m **2** : movimiento m circular (de la mano, etc.) **3** SCOPE : alcance m — **sweeping** ['swi:pɪŋ] adj **1** WIDE : amplio **2** EXTENSIVE : extenso — **sweepstakes** ['swi:p,steɪks] ns & pl : lotería f

sweet ['swi:t] adj **1** : dulce **2** PLEASANT : agradable — **~** n : dulce m — **sweeten** ['swi:tən] vt : endulzar — **sweetener** ['swi:tənər] n : endulzante m — **sweetheart** ['swi:t,hɑrt] n **1** : novio m, -via f **2** (used as a form of address) : cariño m — **sweetness** ['swi:tnəs] n : dulzura f — **sweet potato** n : batata f, boniato m

swell ['swɛl] vi **swelled; swelled** or **swollen** ['swo:lən, 'swʌl-]; **swelling 1** or **~ up** : hincharse **2** INCREASE : aumentar, crecer — **~** n : oleaje m (del mar) — **swelling** ['swɛlɪŋ] n : hinchazón f

sweltering ['swɛltərɪŋ] adj : sofocante

swept → **sweep**

swerve ['swərv] vi **swerved; swerving** : virar bruscamente

swift ['swɪft] adj : rápido — **swiftly** adv : rápidamente

swig ['swɪg] n : trago m — **~** vi **swigged; swigging** : beber a tragos

swim ['swɪm] vi **swam** ['swæm]; **swum** ['swʌm]; **swimming 1** : nadar **2** REEL : dar vueltas — **~** n **1** : baño m **2 go for a ~** : ir a nadar — **swimmer** ['swɪmər] n : nadador m, -dora f

swindle ['swɪndəl] vt **-dled; -dling** : estafar, timar — **~** n : estafa f, timo m fam

swine ['swaɪn] ns & pl : cerdo m, -da f

swing ['swɪŋ] v **swung** ['swʌŋ]; **swinging** vt **1** : balancear, hacer oscilar **2** MANAGE : arreglar — vi **1** : balancearse, oscilar **2** SWIVEL : girar — **~** n **1** : vaivén m, balanceo m **2** SHIFT : cambio m **3** : columpio m (para niños) **4 in full ~** : en pleno proceso

swipe ['swaɪp] v **swiped; swiping** vt STEAL : birlar fam, robar — vi **~ at** : intentar pegar

swirl ['swərl] vi : arremolinarse — **~** n **1** EDDY : remolino m **2** SPIRAL : espiral f

swish ['swɪʃ] vt : agitar (haciendo un sonido) — vi **1** RUSTLE : hacer frufrú **2 ~ by** : pasar silbando

Swiss ['swɪs] adj : suizo

switch ['swɪtʃ] n **1** WHIP : vara f **2** CHANGE : cambio m **3** : interruptor m, llave f (de la luz, etc.) — **~** vt **1** CHANGE : cambiar de **2** EXCHANGE : intercambiar **3 ~ on** : encender, prender Lat **4 ~ off** : apagar — vi **1** : sacudir (la cola, etc.) **2** CHANGE : cambiar **3** SWAP : intercambiarse — **switchboard** ['swɪtʃ,bord] n : centralita f, conmutador m Lat

swivel ['swɪvəl] vi **-veled** or **-velled; -veling** or **-velling** : girar (sobre un pivote)

swollen → **swell**

swoon ['swu:n] vi : desvanecerse

swoop ['swu:p] vi **~ down on** : abatirse sobre — **~** n : descenso m en picada

sword ['sɔrd] n : espada f

swordfish ['sɔrd,fɪʃ] n : pez m espada

swore, sworn → **swear**

swum → **swim**

swung → **swing**

syllable ['sɪləbəl] n : sílaba f

syllabus ['sɪləbəs] n, pl **-bi** [-,baɪ] or **-buses** : programa m (de estudios)

symbol ['sɪmbəl] n : símbolo m — **symbolic** [sɪm'bɑlɪk] adj : simbólico — **symbolism** ['sɪmbə,lɪzəm] n : simbolismo m — **symbolize** ['sɪmbə,laɪz] vt **-ized; -izing** : simbolizar

symmetry ['sɪmətri] n, pl **-tries** : simetría f — **symmetrical** [sə'mɛtrɪkəl] adj : simétrico

sympathy ['sɪmpəθi] n, pl **-thies 1** COMPASSION : compasión f **2** UNDERSTANDING : comprensión f **3** CONDOLENCES : pésame m **4 sympathies** npl LOYALTY : simpatías fpl — **sympathize** ['sɪmpə,θaɪz] vi **-thized; -thizing 1 ~ with** PITY : compadecerse de **2 ~ with** UNDERSTAND : comprender — **sympathetic** [,sɪmpə'θɛt̬ɪk] adj **1** COMPASSIONATE : compasivo **2** UNDERSTANDING : comprensivo

symphony ['sɪmpfəni] n, pl **-nies** : sinfonía f

symposium [sɪm'po:ziəm] n, pl **-sia** [-ziə] or **-siums** : simposio m

symptom ['sɪmptəm] n : síntoma m — **symptomatic** [,sɪmptə'mæt̬ɪk] adj : sintomático

synagogue ['sɪnə,gɑg, -,gɔg] n : sinagoga f

synchronize ['sɪŋkrə,naɪz, 'sɪn-] vt **-nized; -nizing** : sincronizar

syndrome ['sɪn,dro:m] n : síndrome m

synonym ['sɪnə,nɪm] n : sinónimo m — **synonymous** [sə'nɑnəməs] adj : sinónimo

synopsis [sə'nɑpsɪs] n, pl **-opses** [-,si:z] : sinopsis f

syntax ['sɪn,tæks] n : sintaxis f

synthesis ['sɪnθəsɪs] n, pl **-theses** [-,si:z] : síntesis f — **synthesize** ['sɪnθə,saɪz] vt **-sized; -sizing** : sintetizar — **synthetic** [sɪn'θɛt̬ɪk] adj : sintético

syphilis ['sɪfələs] n : sífilis f

Syrian ['sɪriən] adj : sirio

syringe [sə'rɪndʒ, 'sɪrɪndʒ] n : jeringa f, jeringuilla f

syrup ['sərəp, 'sɪrəp] n : jarabe m

system ['sɪstəm] n **1** : sistema m **2** BODY : organismo m **3 digestive ~** : aparato m digestivo — **systematic** [,sɪstə'mæt̬ɪk] adj : sistemático

T

t ['ti:] n, pl **t's** or **ts** ['ti:z] : t f, vigésima letra del alfabeto inglés

tab ['tæb] n **1** TAG : etiqueta f **2** FLAP : lengüeta f **3** ACCOUNT : cuenta f **4 keep ~s on** : vigilar

table ['teɪbəl] n **1** : mesa f **2** LIST : tabla f **3 ~ of contents** : índice m de materias — **tablecloth** ['teɪbəl,klɔθ] n : mantel m — **tablespoon** ['teɪbəl,spu:n] n **1** : cuchara f grande **2** : cucharada f (cantidad)

tablet ['tæblət] n **1** PAD : bloc m **2** PILL : pastilla f **3** or **stone ~** : lápida f

tabloid ['tæ,blɔɪd] n : tabloide m

taboo [tə'bu:, tæ-] adj : tabú — **~** n : tabú m

tacit ['tæsɪt] adj : tácito

taciturn ['tæsɪ,tərn] adj : taciturno

tack ['tæk] vt **1** : fijar con tachuelas **2 ~ on** ADD : añadir — **~** n **1** : tachuela f **2 change ~** : cambiar de rumbo

tackle ['tækəl] n **1** GEAR : aparejo m **2** : placaje m, tacle m Lat (acción) — **~** vt **-led; -ling 1** : placar, taclear Lat **2** CONFRONT : abordar

tacky ['tæki] adj **tackier; -est 1** : pegajoso **2** GAUDY : de mal gusto

tact ['tækt] n : tacto m — **tactful** ['tæktfəl] adj : diplomático, discreto

tactical ['tæktɪkəl] adj : táctico — **tactic** ['tæktɪk] n : táctica f — **tactics** ['tæktɪks] ns & pl : táctica f

tactless ['tæktləs] adj : indiscreto

tadpole ['tæd,po:l] n : renacuajo m

tag[1] ['tæg] n LABEL : etiqueta f — **~** v **tagged; tagging** vt : etiquetar — vi **~ along with s.o.** : acompañar a algn

tag[2] vt : tocar (en varios juegos)

tail ['teɪl] n **1** : cola f **2 ~s** npl : cruz f (de una moneda) — **~** vt FOLLOW : seguir

tailor ['teɪlər] n : sastre m, -tra f — **~** vt **1** : confeccionar (ropa) **2** ADAPT : adaptar

taint ['teɪnt] vt : contaminar

take ['teɪk] v **took** ['tʊk]; **taken** ['teɪkən]; **taking** vt **1** : tomar **2** BRING : llevar **3** REMOVE : sacar **4** BEAR : soportar, aguantar **5** ACCEPT : aceptar **6 I ~ it that...** : supongo que... **7 ~ a bath** : bañarse **8 ~ a walk** : dar un paseo **9 ~ back** : retirar (palabras, etc.) **10 ~ in** ALTER : achicar **11 ~ in** GRASP : entender **12 ~ in** TRICK : engañar **13 ~ off** REMOVE : quitar, quitarse (ropa) **14 ~ on** : asumir (una responsabilidad, etc.) **15 ~ out** : sacar **16 ~ over** : tomar el poder de **17 ~ place** : tener lugar **18 ~ up** SHORTEN : acortar **19 ~ up** OCCUPY : ocupar — vi **1** : prender (dícese de una vacuna, etc.) **2 ~ off** : despegar (dícese de aviones, etc.) **3 ~ over** : asumir el mando — **~** n **1** PROCEEDS : ingresos mpl **2** : toma f (en el cine) — **takeoff** ['teɪk,ɔf] n : despegue m (de un avión, etc.) — **takeover** ['teɪk,o:vər] n : toma f (de poder, etc.), adquisición f (de una empresa)

talcum powder ['tælkəm] n : polvos mpl de talco

tale ['teɪl] n : cuento m

talent ['tælənt] n : talento m — **talented** ['tæləntəd] adj : talentoso

talk ['tɔk] vi **1** : hablar **2 ~ about** : hablar de **3 ~ to/with** : hablar con — vt **1** SPEAK : hablar **2 ~ over** : hablar de, discutir — **~** n **1** CHAT : conversación f **2** SPEECH : charla f — **talkative** ['tɔkət̬ɪv] adj : hablador

tall ['tɔl] adj **1** : alto **2 how ~ are you?** : ¿cuánto mides?

tally ['tæli] n, pl **-lies** : cuenta f — **~** v **-lied; -lying** vt RECKON : calcular — vi MATCH : concordar, cuadrar

talon ['tælən] n : garra f

tambourine [,tæmbə'ri:n] n : pandereta f

tame ['teɪm] adj **tamer; -est 1** : domesticado **2** DOCILE : manso **3** DULL : insípido, soso — **~** vt **tamed; taming** : domar

tamper ['tæmpər] vi **~ with** : forzar (una cerradura), amañar (documentos, etc.)

tampon ['tæm,pɑn] n : tampón m

tan ['tæn] v **tanned; tanning** vt : curtir (cuero) — vi : broncearse — **~** n **1** SUNTAN : bronceado m **2** : (color m) café m con leche

tang ['tæŋ] n : sabor m fuerte

tangent ['tændʒənt] n : tangente f

tangerine ['tændʒə,ri:n, ,tændʒə'-] n : mandarina f

tangible ['tændʒəbəl] adj : tangible

tangle ['tæŋgəl] v **-gled; -gling** vt : enredar — vi : enredarse — **~** n : enredo m

tango ['tæŋ,go:] n, pl **-gos** : tango m

tank ['tæŋk] n **1** : tanque m, depósito m **2** : tanque m (militar) — **tanker** ['tæŋkər] n **1**

: buque *m* tanque 2 *or* ~ **truck** : camión *m* cisterna

tantalizing ['tæntəˌlaɪzɪŋ] *adj* : tentador

tantrum ['tæntrəm] *n* **throw a** ~ : hacer un berrinche

tap[1] ['tæp] *n* FAUCET : llave *f,* grifo *m Spain* — ~ *vt* **tapped; tapping 1** : sacar (un líquido, etc.), sangrar (un árbol) **2** : intervenir (un teléfono)

tap[2] *vt* **tapped; tapping** STRIKE : tocar, dar un golpecito en — ~ *n* : golpecito *m,* toque *m*

tape ['teɪp] *n* : cinta *f* — ~ *vt* **taped; taping 1** : pegar con cinta **2** RECORD : grabar — **tape measure** *n* : cinta *f* métrica

taper ['teɪpər] *n* : vela *f* (larga) — ~ *vi* **1** NARROW : estrecharse **2** *or* ~ **off** : disminuir

tapestry ['tæpəstri] *n, pl* **-tries** : tapiz *m*

tar ['tɑr] *n* : alquitrán *m* — ~ *vt* **tarred; tarring** : alquitranar

tarantula [tə'ræntʃələ, -'ræntələ] *n* : tarántula *f*

target ['tɑrgət] *n* **1** : blanco *m* **2** GOAL : objetivo *m*

tariff ['tærɪf] *n* : tarifa *f,* arancel *m*

tarnish ['tɑrnɪʃ] *vt* **1** : deslustrar **2** : empañar (una reputación, etc.) — *vi* : deslustrarse

tart[1] ['tɑrt] *adj* SOUR : ácido, agrio

tart[2] *n* : pastel *m*

tartan ['tɑrtən] *n* : tartán *m*

task ['tæsk] *n* : tarea *f*

tassel ['tæsəl] *n* : borla *f*

taste ['teɪst] *v* **tasted; tasting** *vt* TRY : probar — *vi* **1** : saber **2** ~ **like** : saber a — ~ *n* **1** FLAVOR : gusto *m,* sabor *m* **2 have a** ~ **of** : probar **3 in good/bad** ~ : de buen/mal gusto — **tasteful** ['teɪstfəl] *adj* : de buen gusto — **tasteless** ['teɪstləs] *adj* **1** : sin sabor **2** COARSE : de mal gusto — **tasty** ['teɪsti] *adj* **tastier; -est** : sabroso

tatters ['tæt̬ərz] *npl* : harapos *mpl* — **tattered** ['tæt̬ərd] *adj* : harapiento

tattle ['tæt̬əl] *vi* **-tled; -tling** ~ **on s.o.** : acusar a algn

tattoo [tæ'tu:] *vt* : tatuar — ~ *n* : tatuaje *m*

taught → **teach**

taunt ['tɔnt] *n* : pulla *f,* burla *f* — ~ *vt* : mofarse de, burlarse de

taut ['tɔt] *adj* : tirante, tenso

tavern ['tævərn] *n* : taberna *f*

tax ['tæks] *vt* **1** : gravar **2** STRAIN : poner a prueba — ~ *n* **1** : impuesto *m* **2** BURDEN : carga *f* — **taxable** ['tæksəbəl] *adj* : imponible — **taxation** [tæk'seɪʃən] *n* : impuestos *mpl* — **tax–exempt** ['tæksɪg'zɛmpt, -ɛg-] *adj* : libre de impuestos

taxi ['tæksi] *n, pl* **taxis** : taxi *m* — ~ *vi* **taxied; taxiing** *or* **taxying; taxis** *or* **taxies** : rodar por la pista (dícese de un avión)

taxpayer ['tæksˌpeɪər] *n* : contribuyente *mf*

tea ['ti:] *n* : té *m*

teach ['ti:tʃ] *v* **taught** ['tɔt]; **teaching** *vt* : enseñar, dar clases de (una asignatura) — *vi* : dar clases — **teacher** ['ti:tʃər] *n* : profesor *m,* -sora *f;* maestro *m,* -tra *f* (de niños pequeños) — **teaching** ['ti:tʃɪŋ] *n* : enseñanza *f*

teacup ['ti:ˌkʌp] *n* : taza *f* de té

team ['ti:m] *n* : equipo *m* — ~ *vi or* ~ **up** : asociarse — **teammate** ['ti:mˌmeɪt] *n* : compañero *m,* -ra *f* de equipo — **teamwork** ['ti:mˌwərk] *n* : trabajo *m* de equipo

teapot ['ti:ˌpɑt] *n* : tetera *f*

tear[1] ['tær] *v* **tore** ['tor]; **torn** ['torn]; **tearing** *vt* **1** : romper, rasgar **2** ~ **apart** : destrozar **3** ~ **down** : derribar **4** ~ **off** *or* ~ **out** : arrancar **5** ~ **up** : romper (papel, etc.) — *vi* **1** : romperse, rasgarse **2** RUSH : ir a toda velocidad — ~ *n* : desgarro *m,* rasgón *m*

tear[2] ['tɪr] *n* : lágrima *f* — **tearful** ['tɪrfəl] *adj* : lloroso

tease ['ti:z] *vt* **teased; teasing 1** : tomar el pelo a, burlarse de **2** ANNOY : fastidiar

teaspoon ['ti:ˌspu:n] *n* **1** : cucharita *f* **2** : cucharadita *f* (cantidad)

technical ['tɛknɪkəl] *adj* : técnico — **technicality** [ˌtɛknə'kælət̬i] *n, pl* **-ties** : detalle *m* técnico — **technically** [-kli] *adv* : técnicamente — **technician** [tɛk'nɪʃən] *n* : técnico *m,* -ca *f*

technique [tɛk'ni:k] *n* : técnica *f*

technological [ˌtɛknə'lɑdʒɪkəl] *adj* : tecnológico — **technology** [tɛk'nɑlədʒi] *n, pl* **-gies** : tecnología *f*

teddy bear ['tɛdi] *n* : oso *m* de peluche

tedious ['ti:diəs] *adj* : tedioso, aburrido — **tedium** ['ti:diəm] *n* : tedio *m*

tee ['ti:] *n* : tee *m* (en deportes)

teem ['ti:m] *vi* **1** POUR : llover a cántaros **2 be** ~**ing with** : estar repleto de

teenage ['ti:nˌeɪdʒ] *or* **teenaged** [-ˌeɪdʒd] *adj* : adolescente — **teenager** ['ti:nˌeɪdʒər] *n* : adolescente *mf* — **teens** ['ti:nz] *npl* : adolescencia *f*

teepee → **tepee**

teeter ['ti:t̬ər] *vi* : tambalearse

teeth → **tooth** — **teethe** ['ti:ð] *vi* **teethed; teething** : echar los dientes

telecommunication ['tɛləkəˌmju:nə'keɪʃən] *n* : telecomunicación *f*

telegram ['tɛləˌgræm] *n* : telegrama *m*

telegraph ['tɛləˌgræf] *n* : telégrafo *m* — ~ *v* : telegrafiar

telephone ['tɛləˌfo:n] *n* : teléfono *m* — ~ *v* **-phoned; -phoning** : llamar por teléfono

telescope ['tɛləˌsko:p] *n* : telescopio *m*

televise ['tɛləˌvaɪz] *vt* **-vised; -vising** : televisar — **television** ['tɛləˌvɪʒən] *n* : televisión *f*

tell ['tɛl] *v* **told** ['to:ld]; **telling** *vt* **1** : decir **2** RELATE : contar **3** DISTINGUISH : distinguir **4** ~ **s.o. off** : regañar a algn — *vi* **1** : decir **2** KNOW : saber **3** SHOW : tener efecto **4** ~ **on s.o.** : acusar a algn — **teller** ['tɛlər] *n or* **bank** ~ : cajero *m,* -ra *f*

temp ['tɛmp] *n* : empleado *m,* -da *f* temporal

temper ['tɛmpər] *vt* MODERATE : temperar — ~ *n* **1** MOOD : humor *m* **2 have a bad** ~ : tener mal genio **3 lose one's** ~ : perder los estribos — **temperament** ['tɛmpərmənt, -prə-, -pərə-] *n* : temperamento *m* — **temperamental** [ˌtɛmpər'mɛntəl, -prə-, -pərə-] *adj* : temperamental — **temperate** ['tɛmpərət] *adj* **1** : moderado **2** ~ **zone** : zona *f* templada

temperature ['tɛmpərˌtʃʊr, -prə-, -pərə-, -tʃər] *n* **1** : temperatura *f* **2 have a** ~ : tener fiebre

tempest ['tɛmpəst] *n* : tempestad *f*

temple ['tɛmpəl] *n* **1** : templo *m* **2** : sien *f* (en anatomía)

tempo ['tɛmˌpo:] *n, pl* **-pi** [-ˌpi:] *or* **-pos 1** : tempo *m* **2** PACE : ritmo *m*

temporarily [ˌtɛmpə'rɛrəli] *adv* : temporalmente — **temporary** ['tɛmpəˌrɛri] *adj* : temporal

tempt ['tɛmpt] *vt* : tentar — **temptation** [tɛmp'teɪʃən] *n* : tentación *f*

ten ['tɛn] *adj* : diez — ~ *n* : diez *m*

tenacity [tə'næsət̬i] *n* : tenacidad *f* — **tenacious** [tə'neɪʃəs] *adj* : tenaz

tenant ['tɛnənt] *n* : inquilino *m,* -na *f;* arrendatario *m,* -ria *f*

tend[1] ['tɛnd] *vt* MIND : cuidar

tend[2] *vi* ~ **to** : tender a — **tendency** ['tɛndəntsi] *n, pl* **-cies** : tendencia *f*

tender[1] ['tɛndər] *adj* **1** : tierno **2** PAINFUL : dolorido

tender[2] *vt* : presentar — ~ *n* **1** : oferta *f* **2 legal** ~ : moneda *f* de curso legal

tenderloin ['tɛndərˌlɔɪn] *n* : lomo *f* (de cerdo o vaca)

tenderness ['tɛndərnəs] *n* : ternura *f*

tendon ['tɛndən] *n* : tendón *m*

tenet ['tɛnət] *n* : principio *m*

tennis ['tɛnəs] *n* : tenis *m*

tenor ['tɛnər] *n* : tenor *m*

tense[1] ['tɛnts] *n* : tiempo *m* (de un verbo)

tense[2] *v* **tensed; tensing** *vt* : tensar — *vi* : tensarse — ~ *adj* **tenser; tensest** : tenso — **tension** ['tɛntʃən] *n* : tensión *f*

tent ['tɛnt] *n* : tienda *f* de campaña

tentacle ['tɛntɪkəl] *n* : tentáculo *m*

tentative ['tɛntət̬ɪv] *adj* **1** HESITANT : vacilante **2** PROVISIONAL : provisional

tenth ['tɛnθ] *adj* : décimo — ~ *n* **1** : décimo *m,* -ma *f* (en una serie) **2** : décimo *m* (en matemáticas)

tenuous ['tɛnjuəs] *adj* : tenue, endeble

tepid ['tɛpɪd] *adj* : tibio

term ['tərm] *n* **1** WORD : término *m* **2** PERIOD : período *m* **3 be on good** ~**s** : tener buenas relaciones **4 in** ~**s of** : con respecto a — ~ *vt* : calificar de

terminal ['tərmənəl] *adj* : terminal — ~ *n* **1** : terminal *m* **2** *or* **bus** ~ : terminal *f*

terminate ['tərməˌneɪt] *v* **-nated; -nating** *vi* : terminar(se) — *vt* : poner fin a — **termination** [ˌtərmə'neɪʃən] *n* : terminación *f*

termite ['tərˌmaɪt] *n* : termita *f*

terrace ['tɛrəs] *n* : terraza *f*

terrain [tə'reɪn] *n* : terreno *m*

terrestrial [tə'rɛstriəl] *adj* : terrestre

terrible ['tɛrəbəl] *adj* : espantoso, terrible — **terribly** ['tɛrəbli] *adv* : terriblemente

terrier ['tɛriər] *n* : terrier *mf*

terrific [tə'rɪfɪk] *adj* **1** HUGE : tremendo **2** EXCELLENT : estupendo

terrify ['tɛrəˌfaɪ] *vt* **-fied; -fying** : aterrar, aterrorizar — **terrifying** ['tɛrəˌfaɪɪŋ] *adj* : aterrador

territory ['tɛrəˌtori] *n, pl* **-ries** : territorio *m* — **territorial** [ˌtɛrə'toriəl] *adj* : territorial

terror ['tɛrər] *n* : terror *m* — **terrorism** ['tɛrərˌɪzəm] *n* : terrorismo *m* — **terrorist** ['tɛrərɪst] *n* : terrorista *mf* — **terrorize** ['tɛrərˌaɪz] *vt* **-ized; -izing** : aterrorizar

terse ['tərs] *adj* **terser; tersest** : seco, lacónico

test ['tɛst] *n* **1** TRIAL : prueba *f* **2** EXAM : examen *m,* prueba *f* **3** : análisis *m* (en medicina) — ~ *vt* **1** TRY : probar **2** QUIZ : examinar **3** : analizar (la sangre, etc.), examinar (los ojos, etc.)

testament ['tɛstəmənt] *n* **1** WILL : testamento *m* **2 the Old/New Testament** : el Antiguo/Nuevo Testamento

testicle ['tɛstɪkəl] *n* : testículo *m*

testify ['tɛstəˌfaɪ] *v* **-fied; -fying** : testificar

testimony ['tɛstəˌmo:ni] *n, pl* **-nies** : testimonio *m*

test tube *n* : probeta *f,* tubo *m* de ensayo

tetanus ['tɛtənəs] *n* : tétano *m*

tether ['tɛðər] *vt* : atar

text ['tɛkst] *n* : texto *m* — **textbook** ['tɛkstˌbʊk] *n* : libro *m* de texto

textile ['tɛkˌstaɪl, 'tɛkstəl] *n* : textil *m*

texture ['tɛkstʃər] *n* : textura *f*

than ['ðæn] *conj & prep* : que, de (con cantidades)

thank ['θæŋk] *vt* **1** : agradecer, dar (las) gracias a **2** ~ **you!** : ¡gracias! — **thankful** ['θæŋkfəl] *adj* : agradecido — **thankfully** ['θæŋkfəli] *adv* **1** : con agradecimiento **2** FORTUNATELY : gracias a Dios — **thanks** ['θæŋks] *npl* **1** : agradecimiento *m* **2** ~! : ¡gracias!

Thanksgiving [θæŋks'gɪvɪŋ, 'θæŋksˌ-] *n* : día *m* de Acción de Gracias

that ['ðæt] *pron, pl* **those** ['ðo:z] **1** : ése, ésa, eso **2** (*more distant*) : aquél, aquélla, aquello **3 is** ~ **you?** : ¿eres tú? **4 like** ~ : así **5** ~ **is…** : es decir… **6 those who…** : los que… — ~ *conj* : que — ~ *adj, pl* **those 1** : ese, esa **2** (*more distant*) : aquel, aquella **3** ~ **one** : ése, ésa — ~ *adv* : tan

thatched ['θætʃt] *adj* : con techo de paja

thaw ['θɔ] *vt* : descongelar (alimentos), derretir (hielo) — *vi* **1** : descongelarse **2** MELT : derretirse — ~ *n* : deshielo *m*

the [ðə, *before vowel sounds usu* ði:] *art* **1** : el, la, los, las **2** PER : por — ~ *adv* **1** ~ **sooner** ~ **better** : cuanto más pronto, mejor **2 I like this one** ~ **best** : éste es el que más me gusta

theater *or* **theatre** ['θi:ət̬ər] *n* : teatro *m* — **theatrical** [θi'ætrɪkəl] *adj* : teatral

theft ['θɛft] *n* : robo *m,* hurto *m*

their ['ðɛr] *adj* : su, sus, de ellos, de ellas — **theirs** ['ðɛrz] *pron* **1** : (el) suyo, (la) suya, (los) suyos, (las) suyas **2 some friends of** ~ : unos amigos suyos, unos amigos de ellos

them ['ðɛm] *pron* **1** (*used as direct object*) : los, las **2** (*used as indirect object*) : les, se **3** (*used as object of a preposition*) : ellos, ellas

theme ['θi:m] *n* **1** : tema *m* **2** ESSAY : trabajo *m* (escrito)

themselves [ðəm'sɛlvz, ðɛm-] *pron* **1** (*used reflexively*) : se **2** (*used emphatically*) : ellos mismos, ellas mismas **3** (*used after a preposition*) : sí (mismos), sí (mismas)

then ['ðɛn] *adv* **1** : entonces **2** NEXT : luego, después **3** BESIDES : además — ~ *adj* : entonces

thence ['ðɛnts, 'θɛnts] *adv* : de ahí (en adelante)

theology [θi'ɑlədʒi] *n, pl* **-gies** : teología *f* — **theological** [ˌθi:ə'lɑdʒɪkəl] *adj* : teológico

theorem ['θi:ərəm, 'θɪrəm] *n* : teorema *m* — **theoretical** [ˌθi:ə'rɛt̬ɪkəl] *adj* : teórico — **theory** ['θi:əri, 'θɪri] *n, pl* **-ries** : teoría *f*

therapeutic [ˌθɛrə'pju:t̬ɪk] *adj* : terapéutico — **therapist** ['θɛrəpɪst] *n* : terapeuta *mf* — **therapy** ['θɛrəpi] *n, pl* **-pies** : terapia *f*

there ['ðær] *adv* **1** *or* **over** ~ : allí, allá **2** *or* **right** ~ : ahí **3 in** ~ : ahí (dentro) **4** ~, **it's done!** : ¡listo! **5 up/down** ~ : ahí arriba/abajo **6 who's** ~**?** : ¿quién es? — ~ *pron* **1** ~ **is/are** : hay **2** ~ **are three of us** : somos tres — **thereabouts** *or* **thereabout** [ˌðærə'baʊts, -'baʊt; 'ðærəˌ-] *adv* **or** ~ : por ahí — **thereafter** [ðær'æftər] *adv* : después — **thereby** [ðær'baɪ, 'ðærˌbaɪ] *adv* : así — **therefore** ['ðærˌfor] *adv* : por lo tanto

thermal ['θərməl] *adj* : térmico

thermometer [θər'mɑmət̬ər] *n* : termómetro *m*

thermos ['θərməs] *n* : termo *m*

thermostat ['θərməˌstæt] *n* : termostato *m*

thesaurus [θɪ'sɔrəs] *n, pl* **-sauri** [-'sɔrˌaɪ] *or* **-sauruses** [-'sɔrəsəz] : diccionario *m* de sinónimos

these → **this**

thesis ['θi:sɪs] *n, pl* **theses** ['θi:ˌsi:z] : tesis *f*

they ['ðeɪ] *pron* **1** : ellos, ellas **2 where are** ~**?** : ¿dónde están? **3 as** ~ **say** : como dicen — **they'd** ['ðeɪd] (*contraction of* **they had** *or* **they would**) → **have, would** — **they'll** ['ðeɪl, 'ðɛl] (*contraction of* **they shall** *or* **they will**) → **shall, will** — **they're** ['ðɛr] (*contraction of* **they are**) → **be** — **they've** ['ðeɪv] (*contraction of* **they have**) → **have**

thick ['θɪk] *adj* **1** : grueso **2** DENSE : espeso **3 a** ~ **accent** : un acento marcado **4 it's two inches** ~ : tiene dos pulgadas de grosor — ~ *n* **in the** ~ **of** : en medio de — **thicken** ['θɪkən] *vt* : espesar — *vi* : espesarse — **thicket** ['θɪkət] *n* : matorral *m* — **thickness** ['θɪknəs] *n* : grosor *m,* espesor *m*

thief ['θi:f] *n, pl* **thieves** ['θi:vz] : ladrón *m,* -drona *f*

thigh ['θaɪ] *n* : muslo *m*

thimble ['θɪmbəl] *n* : dedal *m*

thin ['θɪn] *adj* **thinner; -est 1** : delgado **2** : ralo (dícese del pelo) **3** WATERY : claro, aguado **4** FINE : fino — ~ *v* **thinned; thinning** *vt* DILUTE : diluir — *vi* : ralear (dícese del pelo)

thing ['θɪŋ] *n* **1** : cosa *f* **2 for one** ~ : en primer lugar **3 how are** ~**s?** : ¿qué tal? **4 it's a good** ~ **that…** : menos mal que… **5 the important** ~ **is…** : lo importante es…

think ['θɪŋk] *v* **thought** ['θɔt]; **thinking** *vt* **1** : pensar **2** BELIEVE : creer **3** ~ **up** : idear — *vi* **1** : pensar **2** ~ **about** *or* ~ **of** CONSIDER : pensar en **3** ~ **of** REMEMBER : acordarse de **4 what do you** ~ **of it?** : ¿qué te parece? — **thinker** ['θɪŋkər] *n* : pensador *m,* -dora *f*

third ['θərd] *adj* : tercero — ~ *or* **thirdly** [-li] *adv* : en tercer lugar — ~ *n* **1** : tercero *m,* -ra *f* (en una serie) **2** : tercero *m* (en matemáticas) — **Third World** *n* : Tercer Mundo *m*

thirst ['θərst] *n* : sed *f* — **thirsty** ['θərsti] *adj* **thirstier; -est 1** : sediento **2 be** ~ : tener sed

thirteen [ˌθər'ti:n] *adj* : trece — ~ *n* : trece *m* — **thirteenth** [ˌθər'ti:nθ] *adj* : décimo tercero — ~ *n* **1** : decimotercero *m,* -ra *f* (en una serie) **2** : treceavo *m* (en matemáticas)

thirty ['θərt̬i] *adj* : treinta — ~ *n, pl* **thirties** : treinta *m* — **thirtieth** ['θərt̬iəθ] *adj* : trigésimo — ~ *n* **1** : trigésimo *m,* -ma *f* (en una serie) **2** : treintavo *m* (en matemáticas)

this ['ðɪs] *pron, pl* **these** ['ði:z] **1** : éste, ésta, esto **2 like** ~ : así — ~ *adj, pl* **these 1** : este, esta **2** ~ **one** : éste, ésta **3** ~ **way** : por aquí — ~ *adv* ~ **big** : así de grande

thistle ['θɪsəl] *n* : cardo *m*

thong ['θɔŋ] *n* **1** : correa *f* **2** SANDAL : chancla *f*

thorn ['θɔrn] *n* : espina *f* — **thorny** ['θɔrni] *adj* : espinoso

thorough ['θəro:] *adj* **1** : meticuloso **2** COMPLETE : completo — **thoroughly** *adv* **1** : a fondo **2** COMPLETELY : completamente — **thoroughbred** ['θəroˌbrɛd] *adj* : de pura sangre — **thoroughfare** ['θəroˌfær] *n* : vía *f* pública

those → **that**

though ['ðo:] *conj* : aunque — ~ *adv* **1** : sin embargo **2 as** ~ : como si

thought ['θɔt] → **think** — ~ *n* **1** : pensamiento *m* **2** IDEA : idea *f* — **thoughtful** ['θɔtfəl] *adj* **1** : pensativo **2** KIND : amable — **thoughtless** ['θɔtləs] *adj* **1** CARELESS : descuidado **2** RUDE : desconsiderado

thousand ['θaʊzənd] *adj* : mil — ~ *n, pl* **-sands** *or* **-sand** : mil *m* — **thousandth** ['θaʊzəntθ] *adj* : milésimo — ~ *n* **1** : milésimo *m,* -ma *f* (en una serie) **2** : milésimo *m* (en matemáticas)

thrash ['θræʃ] *vt* : dar una paliza a — *vi or* ~ **around** : agitarse, revolcarse

thread ['θrɛd] *n* **1** : hilo *m* **2** : rosca *f* (de un tornillo) — ~ *vt* : enhilar (una aguja), ensartar (cuentas) — **threadbare** ['θrɛdˌbær] *adj* : raído

threat ['θrɛt] *n* : amenaza *f* — **threaten** ['θrɛtən] *v* : amenazar — **threatening** ['θrɛtənɪŋ] *adj* : amenazador

three ['θri:] *adj* : tres — ~ *n* : tres *m* — **three hundred** *adj* : trescientos — ~ *n* : trescientos *m*

threshold ['θrɛʃˌho:ld, -ˌo:ld] *n* : umbral *m*

threw → **throw**

thrift ['θrɪft] *n* : frugalidad *f* — **thrifty** ['θrɪfti] *adj* **thriftier; -est** : económico, frugal

thrill ['θrɪl] *vt* : emocionar — ~ *n* : emoción *f* — **thriller** ['θrɪlər] *n* : película *f* de suspense *Spain,* película *f* de suspenso *Lat* — **thrilling** ['θrɪlɪŋ] *adj* : emocionante

thrive ['θraɪv] *vi* **throve** ['θro:v] *or* **thrived; thriven** ['θrɪvən] **1** FLOURISH : florecer **2** PROSPER : prosperar

throat ['θro:t] *n* : garganta *f*

throb ['θrɑb] *vi* **throbbed; throbbing 1** PULSATE : palpitar **2** VIBRATE : vibrar **3** ~ **with pain** : tener un dolor punzante

throes ['θro:z] *npl* **1** PANGS : agonía *f* **2 in the** ~ **of** : en medio de

throne ['θro:n] *n* : trono *m*

throng ['θrɔŋ] *n* : muchedumbre *f,* multitud *f*

throttle ['θrɑtəl] *vt* **-tled; -tling** : estrangular — ~ *n* : válvula *f* reguladora

through ['θru:] *prep* **1** : por, a través de **2** BETWEEN : entre **3** BECAUSE OF : a causa de **4** DURING : durante **5** → **throughout 6 Monday** ~ **Friday** : de lunes a viernes — ~ *adv* **1** : de un lado a otro (en el espacio), de principio a fin (en el tiempo) **2** COMPLETELY : completamente — ~ *adj* **1 be** ~ : haber terminado **2** ~ **traffic** : tráfico *m* de paso — **throughout** [θru:'aʊt] *prep* : por todo (un lugar), a lo largo de (un período de tiempo)

throw ['θro:] *v* **threw** ['θru:]; **thrown** ['θro:n]; **throwing** *vt* **1** : tirar, lanzar **2** : proyectar (una sombra) **3** CONFUSE : desconcertar **4** ~ **a party** : dar una fiesta **5** ~ **away** *or* ~ **out** : tirar, botar *Lat* — *vi* ~ **up** VOMIT : vomitar — ~ *n* : tiro *m,* lanzamiento *m*

thrush ['θrʌʃ] *n* : tordo *m,* zorzal *m*

thrust ['θrʌst] *vt* **thrust; thrusting 1** : empujar (bruscamente) **2** PLUNGE : clavar **3** ~ **upon** : imponer a — ~ *n* **1** : empujón *m* **2** : estocada *f* (en esgrima)

thud ['θʌd] *n* : ruido *m* sordo

thug ['θʌg] *n* : matón *m*

thumb ['θʌm] *n* : (dedo *m*) pulgar *m* — ~ *vt or* ~ **through** : hojear — **thumbnail** ['θʌmˌneɪl] *n* : uña *f* del pulgar — **thumbtack** ['θʌmˌtæk] *n* : tachuela *f,* chinche *f Lat*

thump ['θʌmp] *vt* : golpear — *vi* : latir con fuerza (dícese del corazón) — ~ *n* : ruido *m* sordo

thunder ['θʌndər] *n* : truenos *mpl* — ~ *vi* : tronar — *vt* SHOUT : bramar — **thunderbolt** ['θʌndərˌbo:lt] *n* : rayo *m* — **thunder-**

ous ['θʌndərəs] *adj* : atronador — **thunderstorm** ['θʌndər,stɔrm] *n* : tormenta *f* eléctrica
Thursday ['θərz,deɪ, -di] *n* : jueves *m*
thus ['ðʌs] *adv* **1** : así **2** THEREFORE : por lo tanto
thwart ['θwɔrt] *vt* : frustrar
thyme ['taɪm, 'θaɪm] *n* : tomillo *m*
thyroid ['θaɪ,rɔɪd] *n* : tiroides *mf*
tiara [ti'ærə, -'ɑr-] *n* : diadema *f*
tic ['tɪk] *n* : tic *m* (nervioso)
tick[1] ['tɪk] *n* : garrapata *f* (insecto)
tick[2] *n* **1** : tictac *m* (sonido) **2** CHECK : marca *f* — ~ *vi* : hacer tictac — *vt* **1** *or* ~ **off** CHECK : marcar **2** ~ **off** ANNOY : fastidiar
ticket ['tɪkət] *n* **1** : pasaje *m* (de avión), billete *m Spain* (de tren, avión, etc.), boleto *m Lat* (de tren o autobús) **2** : entrada *f* (al teatro, etc.) **3** FINE : multa *f*
tickle ['tɪkəl] *v* **-led; -ling** *vt* **1** : hacer cosquillas a **2** AMUSE : divertir — *vi* : picar — ~ *n* : cosquilleo *m* — **ticklish** ['tɪkəlɪʃ] *adj* **1** : cosquilloso **2** TRICKY : delicado
tidal wave ['taɪdəl] *n* : maremoto *m*
tidbit ['tɪd,bɪt] *n* MORSEL : golosina *f*
tide ['taɪd] *n* : marea *f* — ~ *vt* **tided; tiding** ~ **over** : ayudar a superar un apuro
tidy ['taɪdi] *adj* **-dier; -est** : ordenado, arreglado — ~ *vt* **-died; -dying** *or* ~ **up** : ordenar, arreglar
tie ['taɪ] *n* **1** : atadura *f*, cordón *m* **2** BOND : lazo *m* **3** : empate *m* (en deportes) **4** NECKTIE : corbata *f* — ~ *v* **tied; tying** *or* **tieing** *vt* **1** : atar, amarrar *Lat* **2** ~ **a knot** : hacer un nudo — *vi* : empatar (en deportes)
tier ['tɪr] *n* : nivel *m*, piso (de un pastel), grada *f* (de un estadio)
tiger ['taɪgər] *n* : tigre *m*
tight ['taɪt] *adj* **1** : apretado **2** SNUG : ajustado, ceñido **3** TAUT : tirante **4** STINGY : agarrado **5** SCARCE : escaso **6 a** ~ **seal** : un cierre hermético **7 a** ~ **spot** : un aprieto — ~ *adv* **closed** ~ : bien cerrado — **tighten** ['taɪtən] *vt* **1** : apretar **2** TENSE : tensar **3** : hacer más estricto (reglas, etc.) — **tightly** ['taɪtli] *adv* : bien, fuerte — **tightrope** ['taɪt,ro:p] *n* : cuerda *f* floja — **tights** ['taɪts] *npl* : leotardo *m*, mallas *fpl*
tile ['taɪl] *n* **1** : azulejo *m*, baldosa *f* (de piso) **2** *or* **roofing** ~ : teja *f* — ~ *vt* **tiled; tiling 1** : revestir de azulejos, embaldosar (un piso) **2** : tejar (un techo)
till[1] ['tɪl] *prep & conj* → **until**
till[2] *vt* : cultivar
till[3] *n* : caja *f* (registradora)
tilt ['tɪlt] *n* **1** : inclinación *f* **2 at full** ~ : a toda velocidad — ~ *vt* : inclinar — *vi* : inclinarse
timber ['tɪmbər] *n* **1** : madera *f* (para construcción) **2** BEAM : viga *f*
timbre ['tæmbər, 'tɪm-] *n* : timbre *m*
time ['taɪm] *n* **1** : tiempo *m* **2** AGE : época *f* **3** : compás *m* (en música) **4 at** ~**s** : a veces **5 at this** ~ : en este momento **6 for the** ~ **being** : por el momento **7 from** ~ **to** ~ : de vez en cuando **8 have a good** ~ : pasarlo bien **9 many** ~**s** : muchas veces **10 on** ~ : a tiempo **11** ~ **after** ~ : una y otra vez **12 what** ~ **is it?** : ¿qué hora es? — ~ *vt* **timed; timing** : tomar el tiempo a (algn), cronometrar (una carrera, etc.) — **timeless** ['taɪmləs] *adj* : eterno — **timely** ['taɪmli] *adj* **-lier; -est** : oportuno — **timer** ['taɪmər] *n* : temporizador *m*, avisador *m* (de cocina) — **times** ['taɪmz] *prep* **3** ~ **4 is 12** : 3 por 4 son 12 — **timetable** ['taɪm,teɪbəl] *n* : horario *m*
timid ['tɪmɪd] *adj* : tímido
tin ['tɪn] *n* **1** : estaño *m* **2** CAN : lata *f*, bote *m Spain* — **tinfoil** ['tɪn,fɔɪl] *n* : papel *m* (de) aluminio
tinge ['tɪndʒ] *vt* **tinged; tingeing** *or* **tinging** ['tɪndʒɪŋ] : matizar — ~ *n* **1** TINT : matiz *m* **2** TOUCH : dejo *m*
tingle ['tɪŋgəl] *vi* **-gled; -gling** : sentir (un) hormigueo — ~ *n* : hormigueo *m*
tinker ['tɪŋkər] *vi* ~ **with** : intentar arreglar (con pequeños ajustes)
tinkle ['tɪŋkəl] *vi* **-kled; -kling** : tintinear — ~ *n* : tintineo *m*
tint ['tɪnt] *n* : tinte *m* — ~ *vt* : teñir
tiny ['taɪni] *adj* **-nier; -est** : diminuto, minúsculo
tip[1] ['tɪp] *v* **tipped; tipping** *vt* **1** TILT : inclinar **2** *or* ~ **over** : volcar — *vi* : inclinarse
tip[2] *n* END : punta *f*
tip[3] *n* ADVICE : consejo *m* — ~ *vt* ~ **off** : avisar
tip[4] *vt* : dar una propina a — ~ *n* GRATUITY : propina *f*
tipsy ['tɪpsi] *adj* **-sier; -est** : achispado
tiptoe ['tɪp,to:] *n* **on** ~ : de puntillas — ~ *vi* **-toed; -toeing** : caminar de puntillas
tip–top ['tɪp'tɑp, -,tɑp] *adj* : excelente
tire[1] ['taɪr] *n* : neumático *m*, llanta *f Lat*
tire[2] *v* **tired; tiring** *vt* : cansar — *vi* : cansarse — **tired** ['taɪrd] *adj* **1** ~ **of** : cansado de, harto de **2** ~ **out** : agotado — **tireless** ['taɪrləs] *adj* : incansable — **tiresome** ['taɪrsəm] *adj* : pesado
tissue ['tɪ,ʃu:] *n* **1** : pañuelo *m* de papel **2** : tejido *m* (en biología)
title ['taɪtəl] *n* : título *m* — ~ *vt* **-tled; -tling** : titular
to ['tu:] *prep* **1** : a **2** TOWARD : hacia **3** IN ORDER TO : para **4** UP TO : hasta **5 a quarter** ~ **seven** : las siete menos cuarto **6 be nice** ~ **them** : trátalos bien **7 ten** ~ **the box** : diez por caja **8 the mate** ~ **this shoe** : el compañero de este zapato **9 two** ~ **four years old** : entre dos y cuatro años de edad **10 want** ~ **do** : querer hacer — ~ *adv* **1 come** ~ : volver en sí **2** ~ **and fro** : de un lado a otro
toad ['to:d] *n* : sapo *m*
toast ['to:st] *vt* **1** : tostar (pan, etc.) **2** : brindar por (una persona) — ~ *n* **1** : pan *m* tostado, tostadas *fpl* **2** DRINK : brindis *m* — **toaster** ['to:stər] *n* : tostador *m*
tobacco [tə'bæko:] *n, pl* **-cos** : tabaco *m*
toboggan [tə'bɑgən] *n* : tobogán *m*
today [tə'deɪ] *adv* : hoy — ~ *n* : hoy *m*
toddler ['tɑdələr] *n* : niño *m* pequeño, niña *f* pequeña (que comienza a caminar)
toe ['to:] *n* : dedo *m* (del pie) — **toenail** ['to:,neɪl] *n* : uña *f* (del pie)
together [tə'geðər] *adv* **1** : juntos **2** ~ **with** : junto con
toil ['tɔɪl] *n* : trabajo *m* duro — ~ *vi* : trabajar duro
toilet ['tɔɪlət] *n* **1** BATHROOM : baño *m*, servicio *m* **2** : inodoro *m* (instalación) — **toilet paper** *n* : papel *m* higiénico — **toiletries** ['tɔɪlətriz] *npl* : artículos *mpl* de tocador
token ['to:kən] *n* **1** SIGN : muestra *f* **2** MEMENTO : recuerdo *m* **3** : ficha *f* (para un tren, etc.)
told → **tell**
tolerable ['tɑlərəbəl] *adj* : tolerable — **tolerance** ['tɑlərənts] *n* : tolerancia *f* — **tolerant** ['tɑlərənt] *adj* : tolerante — **tolerate** ['tɑlə,reɪt] *vt* **-ated; -ating** : tolerar
toll[1] ['to:l] *n* **1** : peaje *m* **2 death** ~ : número *m* de muertos **3 take a** ~ **on** : afectar
toll[2] *vi* RING : tocar, doblar — ~ *n* : tañido *m*
tomato [tə'meɪto, -'mɑ-] *n, pl* **-toes** : tomate *m*
tomb ['tu:m] *n* : tumba *f*, sepulcro *m* — **tombstone** ['tu:m,sto:n] *n* : lápida *f*
tome ['to:m] *n* : tomo *m*
tomorrow [tə'mɑro] *adv* : mañana — ~ *n* : mañana *m*
ton ['tən] *n* : tonelada *f*
tone ['to:n] *n* : tono *m* — ~ *vt* **toned; toning** *or* ~ **down** : atenuar
tongs ['tɑŋz, 'tɔŋz] *npl* : tenazas *fpl*
tongue ['tʌŋ] *n* : lengua *f*
tonic ['tɑnɪk] *n* **1** : tónico *m* **2** *or* ~ **water** : tónica *f*
tonight [tə'naɪt] *adv* : esta noche — ~ *n* : esta noche *f*
tonsil ['tɑntsəl] *n* : amígdala *f*
too ['tu:] *adv* **1** ALSO : también **2** EXCESSIVELY : demasiado
took → **take**
tool ['tu:l] *n* : herramienta *f* — **toolbox** ['tu:l,bɑks] *n* : caja *f* de herramientas
toot ['tu:t] *vt* : sonar (un claxon, etc.) — ~ *n* **1** WHISTLE : pitido *m* **2** HONK : bocinazo *m*
tooth ['tu:θ] *n, pl* **teeth** ['ti:θ] : diente *m* — **toothache** ['tu:θ,eɪk] *n* : dolor *m* de muelas — **toothbrush** ['tu:θ,brʌʃ] *n* : cepillo *m* de dientes — **toothpaste** ['tu:θ,peɪst] *n* : pasta *f* de dientes, pasta *f* dentífrica
top[1] ['tɑp] *n* **1** : parte *f* superior **2** SUMMIT : cima *f*, cumbre *f* **3** COVER : tapa *f*, cubierta *f* **4 on** ~ **of** : encima de — ~ *vt* **topped; topping** COVER : rematar (un edificio, etc.), bañar (un pastel, etc.) **2** SURPASS : superar **3** ~ **off** : llenar — ~ *adj* **1** : de arriba, superior **2** BEST : mejor **3 a** ~ **executive** : un alto ejecutivo
top[2] *n* : trompo *m* (juguete)
topic ['tɑpɪk] *n* : tema *m* — **topical** ['tɑpɪkəl] *adj* : de interés actual
topmost ['tɑp,mo:st] *adj* : más alto
topple ['tɑpəl] *v* **-pled; -pling** *vi* : caerse — *vt* **1** OVERTURN : volcar **2** OVERTHROW : derrocar
torch ['tɔrtʃ] *n* : antorcha *f*
tore → **tear**[1]
torment ['tɔr,mɛnt] *n* : tormento *m* — ~ [tɔr'mɛnt, 'tɔr,-] *vt* : atormentar
torn → **tear**[1]
tornado [tɔr'neɪdo] *n, pl* **-does** *or* **-dos** : tornado *m*
torpedo [tɔr'pi:do] *n, pl* **-does** : torpedo *m* — ~ *vt* : torpedear
torrent ['tɔrənt] *n* : torrente *m*
torrid ['tɔrɪd] *adj* : tórrido
torso ['tɔr,so:] *n, pl* **-sos** *or* **-si** [-,si:] : torso *m*
tortilla [tɔr'ti:jə] *n* : tortilla *f*
tortoise ['tɔrtəs] *n* : tortuga *f* (terrestre) — **tortoiseshell** ['tɔrtəs,ʃɛl] *n* : carey *m*, concha *f*
tortuous ['tɔrtʃuəs] *adj* : tortuoso
torture ['tɔrtʃər] *n* : tortura *f* — ~ *vt* **-tured; -turing** : torturar
toss ['tɔs, 'tɑs] *vt* **1** : tirar, lanzar **2** : mezclar (una ensalada) — *vi* ~ **and turn** : dar vueltas — ~ *n* : lanzamiento *m*
tot ['tɑt] *n* : pequeño *m*, -ña *f*
total ['to:təl] *adj* : total — ~ *n* : total *m* — ~ *vt* **-taled** *or* **-talled; -taling** *or* **-talling 1** : ascender a **2** *or* ~ **up** : totalizar, sumar
totalitarian [to:,tælə'tɛriən] *adj* : totalitario
tote ['to:t] *vt* **toted; toting** : llevar
totter ['tɑtər] *vi* : tambalearse
touch ['tʌtʃ] *vt* **1** : tocar **2** MOVE : conmover **3** AFFECT : afectar **4** ~ **up** : retocar — *vi* : tocarse — ~ *n* **1** : tacto *m* (sentido) **2** HINT : toque *m* **3** BIT : pizca *f* **4 keep in** ~ : mantenerse en contacto **5 lose one's** ~ : perder la habilidad — **touchdown** ['tʌtʃ,daʊn] *n* : touchdown *m* — **touchy** ['tʌtʃi] *adj* **touchier; -est 1** : delicado **2 be** ~ **about** : picarse a la mención de
tough ['tʌf] *adj* **1** : duro **2** STRONG : fuerte **3** STRICT : severo **4** DIFFICULT : difícil — **toughen** ['tʌfən] *vt or* ~ **up** : endurecer — *vi* : endurecerse — **toughness** ['tʌfnəs] *n* : dureza *f*
tour ['tʊr] *n* **1** : viaje *m* (por un país, etc.), visita *f* (a un museo, etc.) **2** : gira *f* (de un equipo, etc.) — ~ *vi* **1** TRAVEL : viajar **2** : hacer una gira (dícese de equipos, etc.) — *vt* : viajar por, recorrer — **tourist** ['tʊrɪst, 'tər-] *n* : turista *mf*
tournament ['tərnəmənt, 'tʊr-] *n* : torneo *m*
tousle ['taʊzəl] *vt* **-sled; -sling** : despeinar
tout ['taʊt] *vt* : promocionar
tow ['to:] *vt* : remolcar — ~ *n* : remolque *m*
toward ['tɔrd, tə'wɔrd] *or* **towards** ['tɔrdz, tə'wɔrdz] *prep* : hacia
towel ['taʊəl] *n* : toalla *f*
tower ['taʊər] *n* : torre *f* — ~ *vi* ~ **over** : descollar sobre — **towering** ['taʊərɪŋ] *adj* : altísimo
town ['taʊn] *n* **1** VILLAGE : pueblo *m* **2** CITY : ciudad *f* — **township** ['taʊn,ʃɪp] *n* : municipio *m*
tow truck ['to:,trʌk] *n* : grúa *f*
toxic ['tɑksɪk] *adj* : tóxico
toy ['tɔɪ] *n* : juguete *m* — ~ *vi* ~ **with** : juguetear con
trace ['treɪs] *n* **1** SIGN : rastro *m*, señal *f* **2** HINT : dejo *m* — ~ *vt* **traced; tracing 1** : calcar (un dibujo, etc.) **2** DRAW : trazar **3** FIND : localizar
track ['træk] *n* **1** : pista *f* **2** PATH : sendero *m* **3** *or* **railroad** ~ : vía *f* (férrea) **4 keep** ~ **of** : llevar la cuenta de — ~ *vt* TRAIL : seguir la pista de
tract[1] ['trækt] *n* **1** EXPANSE : extensión *f* **2** : tracto *m* (en anatomía)
tract[2] *n* PAMPHLET : folleto *m*
traction ['trækʃən] *n* : tracción *f*
tractor ['træktər] *n* **1** : tractor *m* **2** *or* ~ **-trailer** : camión *m* (con remolque)
trade ['treɪd] *n* **1** PROFESSION : oficio *m* **2** COMMERCE : comercio *m* **3** INDUSTRY : industria *f* **4** EXCHANGE : cambio *m* — ~ *v* **traded; trading** *vi* : comerciar — *vt* ~ **sth with s.o.** : cambiar algo a algn — **trademark** ['treɪd,mɑrk] *n* : marca *f* registrada
tradition [trə'dɪʃən] *n* : tradición *f* — **traditional** [trə'dɪʃənəl] *adj* : tradicional
traffic ['træfɪk] *n* : tráfico *m* — ~ *vi* **trafficked; trafficking** ~ **in** : traficar con — **traffic light** *n* : semáforo *m*
tragedy ['trædʒədi] *n, pl* **-dies** : tragedia *f* — **tragic** ['trædʒɪk] *adj* : trágico
trail ['treɪl] *vi* **1** DRAG : arrastrar **2** LAG : rezagarse **3** ~ **off** : apagarse — *vt* **1** DRAG : arrastrar **2** PURSUE : seguir la pista de — ~ *n* **1** : rastro *m*, huellas *fpl* **2** PATH : sendero *m* — **trailer** ['treɪlər] *n* **1** : remolque *m* **2** : caravana *f* (vivienda)
train ['treɪn] *n* **1** : tren *m* **2** : cola *f* (de un vestido) **3** SERIES : serie *f* **4** ~ **of thought** : hilo *m* (de las ideas) — ~ *vt* **1** : adiestrar, entrenar (atletas, etc.) **2** AIM : apuntar — *vi* : prepararse, entrenarse (en deportes, etc.) — **trainer** ['treɪnər] *n* : entrenador *m*, -dora *f*
trait ['treɪt] *n* : rasgo *m*
traitor ['treɪtər] *n* : traidor *m*, -dora *f*
tramp ['træmp] *vi* : caminar (pesadamente) — ~ *n* VAGRANT : vagabundo *m*, -da *f*
trample ['træmpəl] *vt* **-pled; -pling** : pisotear
trampoline [,træmpə'li:n, 'træmpə,-] *n* : trampolín *m*
trance ['trænts] *n* : trance *m*
tranquillity *or* **tranquility** [træŋ'kwɪləti] *n* : tranquilidad *f* — **tranquil** ['træŋkwəl] *adj* : tranquilo — **tranquilize** ['træŋkwə,laɪz] *vt* **-ized; -izing** : tranquilizar — **tranquilizer** ['træŋkwə,laɪzər] *n* : tranquilizante *m*
transaction [træn'zækʃən] *n* : transacción *f*
transatlantic [,træntsət'læntɪk, ,trænz-] *adj* : transatlántico
transcend [træn'sɛnd] *vt* **1** : ir más allá de **2** OVERCOME : superar
transcribe [træn'skraɪb] *vt* **-scribed; -scribing** : transcribir — **transcript** ['træn,skrɪpt] *n* : transcripción *f*
transfer [trænts'fər, 'trænts,fər] *v* **-ferred; -ferring** *vt* **1** : transferir (fondos, etc.) **2** : trasladar (a un empleado, etc.) — *vi* **1** : cambiarse (de escuelas, etc.) **2** : hacer transbordo (entre trenes, etc.) — ~ ['trænts,fər] *n* **1** : transferencia *f* (de fondos, etc.), traslado *m* (de una persona) **2** : boleto *m* (para hacer transbordo) **3** DECAL : calcomanía *f*
transform [trænts'fɔrm] *vt* : transformar — **transformation** [,træntsfər'meɪʃən] *n* : transformación *f*
transfusion [trænts'fju:ʒən] *n* : transfusión *f*
transgression [trænts'grɛʃən, trænz-] *n* : transgresión *f* — **transgress** [trænts'grɛs, trænz-] *vt* : transgredir
transient ['træntʃənt, 'trænsiənt] *adj* : pasajero
transit ['træntsɪt, 'trænzɪt] *n* **1** : tránsito *m* **2** TRANSPORTATION : transporte *m* — **transition** [træn'sɪʃən, -'zɪʃ-] *n* : transición *f* — **transitive** ['træntsətɪv, 'trænzə-] *adj* : transitivo — **transitory** ['træntsə,tori, 'trænzə-] *adj* : transitorio
translate [trænts'leɪt, trænz-; 'trænts,-, 'træns,-] *vt* **-lated; -lating** : traducir — **translation** [trænts'leɪʃən, trænz-] *n* : traducción *f* — **translator** [trænts'leɪtər, trænz-; 'trænts,-, 'træns,-] *n* : traductor *m*, -tora *f*
translucent [trænts'lu:sənt, trænz-] *adj* : translúcido
transmit [trænts'mɪt, trænz-] *vt* **-mitted; -mitting** : transmitir — **transmission** [trænts'mɪʃən, trænz-] *n* : transmisión *f* — **transmitter** [trænts'mɪtər, trænz-; 'trænts,-, 'træns,-] *n* : transmisor *m*
transparent [trænts'pærənt] *adj* : transparente — **transparency** [trænts'pærəntsi] *n, pl* **-cies** : transparencia *f*
transpire [trænts'paɪr] *vi* **-spired; -spiring 1** TURN OUT : resultar **2** HAPPEN : suceder
transplant [trænts'plænt] *vt* : trasplantar — ~ ['trænts,plænt] *n* : trasplante *m*
transport [trænts'port, 'trænts,-] *vt* : transportar — ~ ['trænts,port] *n* : transporte *m* — **transportation** [,træntspər'teɪʃən] *n* : transporte *m*
transpose [trænts'po:z] *vt* **-posed; -posing 1** : trasponer **2** : transportar (en música)
trap ['træp] *n* : trampa *f* — ~ *vt* **trapped; trapping** : atrapar — **trapdoor** ['træp'dor] *n* : trampilla *f*
trapeze [træ'pi:z] *n* : trapecio *m*
trappings ['træpɪŋz] *npl* : adornos *mpl*, atavíos *mpl*
trash ['træʃ] *n* : basura *f*
trauma ['trɔmə, 'traʊ-] *n* : trauma *m* — **traumatic** [trə'mætɪk, trɔ-, traʊ-] *adj* : traumático
travel ['trævəl] *vi* **-eled** *or* **-elled; -eling** *or* **-elling 1** : viajar **2** MOVE : desplazarse — ~ *n* : viajes *mpl* — **traveler** *or* **traveller** ['trævələr] *n* : viajero *m*, -ra *f*
traverse [trə'vərs, træ'vərs, 'trævərs] *vt* **-versed; -versing** : atravesar
travesty ['trævəsti] *n, pl* **-ties** : parodia *f*
trawl ['trɔl] *vi* : pescar (con red de arrastre) — **trawler** ['trɔlər] *n* : barco *m* de pesca
tray ['treɪ] *n* : bandeja *f*
treachery ['trɛtʃəri] *n, pl* **-eries** : traición *f* — **treacherous** ['trɛtʃərəs] *adj* **1** : traidor **2** DANGEROUS : peligroso
tread ['trɛd] *v* **trod** ['trɑd]; **trodden** ['trɑdən] *or* **trod; treading** *vt* **1** *or* ~ **on** : pisar **2** ~ **water** : flotar — *vi* **1** STEP : pisar **2** WALK : caminar — ~ *n* **1** STEP : paso *m* **2** : banda *f* de rodadura (de un neumático) — **treadmill** ['trɛd,mɪl] *n* : rueda *f* de andar
treason ['tri:zən] *n* : traición *f* (a la patria)
treasure ['trɛʒər, 'treɪ-] *n* : tesoro *m* — ~ *vt* **-sured; -suring** : apreciar — **treasurer** ['trɛʒərər, 'treɪ-] *n* : tesorero *m*, -ra *f* — **treasury** ['trɛʒəri, 'treɪ-] *n, pl* **-suries** : erario *m*, tesoro *m*
treat ['tri:t] *vt* **1** : tratar **2** CONSIDER : considerar **3** ~ **s.o. to (dinner, etc.)** : invitar a algn (a cenar, etc.) — ~ *n* **1** : gusto *m*, placer *m* **2 it's my** ~ : invito yo
treatise ['tri:təs] *n* : tratado *m*
treatment ['tri:tmənt] *n* : tratamiento *m*
treaty ['tri:ti] *n, pl* **-ties** : tratado *m*
treble ['trɛbəl] *adj* **1** TRIPLE : triple **2** : de tiple (en música) — ~ *vt* **-bled; -bling** : triplicar — **treble clef** : clave *f* de sol
tree ['tri:] *n* : árbol *m*
trek ['trɛk] *vi* **trekked; trekking** : viajar (con dificultad) — ~ *n* : viaje *m* difícil
trellis ['trɛlɪs] *n* : enrejado *m*
tremble ['trɛmbəl] *vi* **-bled; -bling** : temblar
tremendous [trɪ'mɛndəs] *adj* : tremendo
tremor ['trɛmər] *n* : temblor *m*
trench ['trɛntʃ] *n* **1** : zanja *f* **2** : trinchera *f* (militar)
trend ['trɛnd] *n* **1** : tendencia *f* **2** FASHION : moda *f* — **trendy** ['trɛndi] *adj* **trendier; -est** : de moda
trepidation [,trɛpə'deɪʃən] *n* : inquietud *f*
trespass ['trɛspəs, -,pæs] *vi* : entrar ilegalmente (en propiedad ajena)
trial ['traɪəl] *n* **1** : juicio *m*, proceso *m* **2** TEST : prueba *f* **3** ORDEAL : dura prueba *f* — ~ *adj* : de prueba
triangle ['traɪ,æŋgəl] *n* : triángulo *m* — **triangular** [traɪ'æŋgjələr] *adj* : triangular
tribe ['traɪb] *n* : tribu *f* — **tribal** ['traɪbəl] *adj* : tribal
tribulation [,trɪbjə'leɪʃən] *n* : tribulación *f*
tribunal [traɪ'bju:nəl, trɪ-] *n* : tribunal *m*
tribute ['trɪ,bju:t] *n* : tributo *m* — **tributary** ['trɪbjə,tɛri] *n, pl* **-taries** : afluente *m*
trick ['trɪk] *n* **1** : trampa *f* **2** PRANK : broma *f* **3** KNACK, FEAT : truco *m* **4** : baza *f* (en naipes) — ~ *vt* : engañar — **trickery** ['trɪkəri] *n* : engaño *m*
trickle ['trɪkəl] *vi* **-led; -ling** : gotear — ~ *n* : goteo *m*
tricky ['trɪki] *adj* **trickier; -est 1** SLY : astuto, taimado **2** DIFFICULT : difícil
tricycle ['traɪsəkəl, -,sɪkəl] *n* : triciclo *m*
trifle ['traɪfəl] *n* **1** TRIVIALITY : nimiedad *f* **2**

a ~ : un poco — ~ *vi* **-fled; -fling** ~ **with** : jugar con — **trifling** ['traɪflɪŋ] *adj* : insignificante

trigger ['trɪgər] *n* : gatillo *m* — ~ *vt* : causar, provocar

trill ['trɪl] *n* : trino *m* — ~ *vi* : trinar

trillion ['trɪljən] *n* : billón *m*

trilogy ['trɪləd͡ʒi] *n, pl* **-gies** : trilogía *f*

trim ['trɪm] *vt* **trimmed; trimming 1** : recortar **2** ADORN : adornar — ~ *adj* **trimmer; trimmest 1** SLIM : esbelto **2** NEAT : arreglado — ~ *n* **1** : recorte *m* **2** DECORATION : adornos *mpl* **3 in** ~ : en buena forma — **trimming** ['trɪmɪŋ] *npl* **1** : adornos *mpl* **2** GARNISH : guarnición *f*

Trinity ['trɪnət̬i] *n* : Trinidad *f*

trinket ['trɪŋkət] *n* : chuchería *f*

trio ['tri:,o:] *n, pl* **trios** : trío *m*

trip ['trɪp] *v* **tripped; tripping** *vi* **1** : caminar (a paso ligero) **2** STUMBLE : tropezar **3** ~ **up** : equivocarse — *vt* **1** ACTIVATE : activar **2** ~ **s.o.** : hacer una zancadilla a algn **3** ~ **s.o. up** : hacer equivocar a algn — ~ *n* **1** : viaje *m* **2** STUMBLE : traspié *m*

tripe ['traɪp] *n* **1** : mondongo *m,* callos *mpl* **2** NONSENSE : tonterías *fpl*

triple ['trɪpəl] *vt* **-pled; -pling** : triplicar — ~ *n* : triple *m* — ~ *adj* : triple — **triplet** ['trɪplət] *n* : trillizo *m,* -za *f* — **triplicate** ['trɪplɪkət] *n* : triplicado *m*

tripod ['traɪ,pɑd] *n* : trípode *m*

trite ['traɪt] *adj* **triter; tritest** : trillado

triumph ['traɪəmpf] *n* : triunfo *m* — ~ *vi* : triunfar — **triumphal** [traɪ'ʌmpfəl] *adj* : triunfal — **triumphant** [traɪ'ʌmpfənt] *adj* : triunfante

trivial ['trɪviəl] *adj* : trivial — **trivia** ['trɪviə] *ns & pl* : trivialidades *fpl* — **triviality** [,trɪvi'ælət̬i] *n, pl* **-ties** : trivialidad *f*

trod, trodden → **tread**

trolley ['trɑli] *n, pl* **-leys** : tranvía *m*

trombone [trɑm'bo:n] *n* : trombón *m*

troop ['tru:p] *n* **1** : escuadrón *m* (de caballería), compañía *f* (de soldados) **2** ~**s** *npl* : tropas *fpl* — ~ *vi* ~ **in/out** : entrar/salir en tropel — **trooper** ['tru:pər] *n* **1** : soldado *m* **2** *or* **state** ~ : policía *mf* estatal

trophy ['tro:fi] *n, pl* **-phies** : trofeo *m*

tropic ['trɑpɪk] *n* **1** : trópico *m* **2 the** ~**s** : el trópico — ~ *or* **tropical** [-pɪkəl] *adj* : tropical

trot ['trɑt] *n* : trote *m* — ~ *vi* **trotted; trotting** : trotar

trouble ['trʌbəl] *v* **-bled; -bling** *vt* **1** WORRY : preocupar **2** BOTHER : molestar — *vi* : molestarse — ~ *n* **1** PROBLEMS : problemas *mpl* **2** EFFORT : molestia *f* **3 be in** ~ : estar en apuros **4 get in** ~ : meterse en problemas **5 I had** ~ **doing it** : me costó hacerlo — **troublemaker** ['trʌbəl,meɪkər] *n* : alborotador *m,* -dora *f* — **troublesome** ['trʌbəlsəm] *adj* : problemático

trough ['trɔf] *n, pl* **troughs** ['trɔfs, 'trɔvz] **1** : depresión *f* **2** *or* **feeding** ~ : comedero *m* **3** *or* **drinking** ~ : bebedero *m*

troupe ['tru:p] *n* : compañía *f* (de teatro)

trousers ['traʊzərz] *npl* : pantalón *m,* pantalones *mpl*

trout ['traʊt] *n, pl* **trout** : trucha *f*

trowel ['traʊəl] *n* : paleta *f* (de albañil), desplantador *m* (de jardinero)

truant ['tru:ənt] *n* : alumno *m,* -na *f* que falta a clase

truce ['tru:s] *n* : tregua *f*

truck ['trʌk] *vt* : transportar en camión — ~ *n* **1** : camión *m* **2** CART : carro *m* — **trucker** ['trʌkər] *n* : camionero *m,* -ra *f*

trudge ['trʌd͡ʒ] *vi* **trudged; trudging** : caminar a paso pesado

true ['tru:] *adj* **truer; truest 1** : verdadero **2** LOYAL : fiel **3** GENUINE : auténtico **4 be** ~ : ser cierto, ser verdad

truffle ['trʌfəl] *n* : trufa *f*

truly ['tru:li] *adv* : verdaderamente

trump ['trʌmp] *n* : triunfo *m* (en naipes)

trumpet ['trʌmpət] *n* : trompeta *f*

trunk ['trʌŋk] *n* **1** STEM, TORSO : tronco *m* **2** : trompa *f* (de un elefante) **3** : baúl *m* (equipaje) **4** : maletero *m* (de un auto) **5** ~**s** *npl* : traje *m* de baño (de hombre)

truss ['trʌs] *n* **1** FRAMEWORK : armazón *m* **2** : braguero *m* (en medicina)

trust ['trʌst] *n* **1** CONFIDENCE : confianza *f* **2** HOPE : esperanza *f* **3** CREDIT : crédito *m* **4** : trust *m* (en finanzas) **5 in** ~ : en fideicomiso — ~ *vi* **1** : confiar **2** HOPE : esperar — *vt* **1** : confiar en, fiarse de (en frases negativas) **2** ~ **s.o. with sth** : confiar algo a algn — **trustee** [,trʌs'ti:] *n* : fideicomisario *m,* -ria *f* — **trustworthy** ['trəst,wərði] *adj* : digno de confianza

truth ['tru:θ] *n, pl* **truths** ['tru:ðz, 'tru:θs] : verdad *f* — **truthful** ['tru:θfəl] *adj* : sincero, veraz

try ['traɪ] *v* **tried; trying** *vt* **1** ATTEMPT : tratar (de), intentar **2** : juzgar (un caso, etc.) **3** TEST : poner a prueba **4** *or* ~ **out** : probar **5** ~ **on** : probarse (ropa) — *vi* : hacer un esfuerzo — ~ *n, pl* **tries** : intento *m* — **trying** *adj* **1** ANNOYING : irritante, pesado **2** DIFFICULT : duro — **tryout** ['traɪ,aʊt] *n* : prueba *f*

tsar ['zɑr, 'tsɑr, 'sɑr] → **czar**

T-shirt ['ti:,ʃərt] *n* : camiseta *f*

tub ['tʌb] *n* **1** : cuba *f,* tina *f* **2** CONTAINER : envase *m* **3** BATHTUB : bañera *f*

tuba ['tu:bə, 'tju:-] *n* : tuba *f*

tube ['tu:b, 'tju:b] *n* **1** : tubo *m* **2** *or* **inner** ~ : cámara *f* **3 the** ~ : la tele

tuberculosis [tʊ,bərkjə'lo:sɪs, tjʊ-] *n, pl* **-loses** [-,si:z] : tuberculosis *f*

tubing ['tu:bɪŋ, 'tju:-] *n* : tubería *f* — **tubular** ['tu:bjələr, 'tju:-] *adj* : tubular

tuck ['tʌk] *vt* **1** : meter **2** ~ **away** : guardar **3** ~ **in** : meter por dentro (una blusa, etc.) **4** ~ **s.o. in** : arropar a algn — ~ *n* : jareta *f*

Tuesday ['tu:z,deɪ, 'tju:z-, -di] *n* : martes *m*

tuft ['tʌft] *n* : mechón *m* (de pelo), penacho *m* (de plumas)

tug ['tʌg] *vt* **tugged; tugging** *or* ~ **at** : tirar de, jalar de — ~ *n* : tirón *m,* jalón *m* — **tugboat** ['tʌg,bo:t] *n* : remolcador *m* — **tug-of-war** [,tʌgə'wɔr] *n, pl* **tugs-of-war** : tira y afloja *m*

tuition [tu'ɪʃən, tju:-] *n* **1** : enseñanza *f* **2** *or* ~ **fees** : matrícula *f*

tulip ['tu:lɪp, 'tju:-] *n* : tulipán *m*

tumble ['tʌmbəl] *vi* **-bled; -bling** : caerse — ~ *n* : caída *f* — **tumbler** ['tʌmblər] *n* : vaso *m* (sin pie)

tummy ['tʌmi] *n, pl* **-mies** : barriga *f,* panza *f*

tumor ['tu:mər 'tju:-] *n* : tumor *m*

tumult ['tu:,mʌlt 'tju:-] *n* : tumulto *m* — **tumultuous** [tʊ'mʌltʃʊəs, tju:-] *adj* : tumultuoso

tuna ['tu:nə 'tju:-] *n, pl* **-na** *or* **-nas** : atún *m*

tune ['tu:n, 'tju:n] *n* **1** MELODY : melodía *f* **2** SONG : tonada *f* **3 in** ~ : afinado **4 out of** ~ : desafinado — ~ *v* **tuned; tuning** *vt* : afinar — *vi* ~ **in** : sintonizar — **tuner** ['tu:nər, 'tju:-] *n* **1** : afinador *m,* -dora *f* (de pianos, etc.) **2** : sintonizador *m* (de un receptor)

tunic ['tu:nɪk, 'tju:-] *n* : túnica *f*

tunnel ['tʌnəl] *n* : túnel *m* — ~ *vi* **-neled** *or* **-nelled; -neling** *or* **-nelling** : hacer un túnel

turban ['tərbən] *n* : turbante *m*

turbine ['tərbən, -,baɪn] *n* : turbina *f*

turbulent ['tərbjələnt] *adj* : turbulento — **turbulence** ['tərbjələnts] *n* : turbulencia *f*

turf ['tərf] *n* **1** GRASS : césped *m* **2** SOD : tepe *m*

turgid ['tərd͡ʒɪd] *adj* : ampuloso (dícese de prosa, etc.)

turkey ['tərki] *n, pl* **-keys** : pavo *m*

turmoil ['tər,mɔɪl] *n* : confusión *f*

turn ['tərn] *vt* **1** : hacer girar (una rueda, etc.), volver (la cabeza, una página, etc.) **2** : dar la vuelta a (una esquina) **3** SPRAIN : torcer **4** ~ **down** REFUSE : rechazar **5** ~ **down** LOWER : bajar **6** ~ **in** : entregar **7** ~ **off** : cerrar (una llave), apagar (la luz, etc.) **8** ~ **on** : abrir (una llave), encender, prender *Lat* (la luz, etc.) **9** ~ **out** EXPEL : echar **10** ~ **out** PRODUCE : producir **11** ~ **out** → **turn off 12** *or* ~ **over** FLIP : dar la vuelta a, voltear *Lat* **13** ~ **over** TRANSFER : entregar **14** ~ **s.o.'s stomach** : revolver el estómago a algn **15** ~ **sth into sth** : convertir algo en algo **16** ~ **up** RAISE : subir — *vi* **1** ROTATE : girar, dar vueltas **2** BECOME : ponerse **3** SOUR : agriarse **4** RESORT : recurrir **5** *or* ~ **around** : darse la vuelta, volverse **6** ~ **into** : convertirse en **7** ~ **left** : doblar a la izquierda **8** ~ **out** COME : acudir **9** ~ **out** RESULT : resultar **10** ~ **up** APPEAR : aparecer — ~ *n* **1** : vuelta *f* **2** CHANGE : cambio *m* **3** CURVE : curva *f* **4 do a good** ~ : hacer un favor **5 whose** ~ **is it?** : ¿a quién le toca?

turnip ['tərnəp] *n* : nabo *m*

turnout ['tərn,aʊt] *n* : concurrencia *f* — **turnover** ['tərn,o:vər] *n* **1** : tartaleta *f* (postre) **2** : volumen *m* (de ventas) **3** : movimiento *f* (de personal) — **turnpike** ['tərn,paɪk] *n* : carretera *f* de peaje — **turntable** ['tərn,teɪbəl] *n* : plato *m* giratorio

turpentine ['tərpən,taɪn] *n* : trementina *f*

turquoise ['tər,kɔɪz, -,kwɔɪz] *n* : turquesa *f*

turret ['tərət] *n* **1** : torrecilla *f* **2** : torreta *f* (de un tanque, etc.)

turtle ['tərt̬əl] *n* : tortuga *f* (marina) — **turtleneck** ['tərt̬əl,nek] *n* : cuello *m* de tortuga

tusk ['tʌsk] *n* : colmillo *m*

tussle ['tʌsəl] *n* : pelea *f* — ~ *vi* **-sled; -sling** : pelearse

tutor ['tu:t̬ər, 'tju:-] *n* : profesor *m,* -sora *f* particular — ~ *vt* : dar clases particulares a

tuxedo [,tək'si:,do:] *n, pl* **-dos** *or* **-does** : esmoquin *m,* smoking *m*

TV [,ti:'vi:, 'ti:,vi:] → **television**

twang ['twæŋ] *n* **1** : tañido *m* **2** : acento *m* nasal (de la voz)

tweak ['twi:k] *vt* : pellizcar — ~ *n* : pellizco *m*

tweed ['twi:d] *n* : tweed *m*

tweet ['twi:t] *n* : gorjeo *m,* pío *m* — ~ *vi* : piar

tweezers ['twi:zərz] *npl* : pinzas *fpl*

twelve ['twelv] *adj* : doce — ~ *n* : doce *m* — **twelfth** ['twelfθ] *adj* : duodécimo — ~ *n* **1** : duodécimo *m,* -ma *f* (en una serie) **2** : doceavo *m* (en matemáticas)

twenty ['twʌnti, 'twen-] *adj* : veinte — ~ *n, pl* **-ties** : veinte *m* — **twentieth** ['twʌntiəθ, 'twen-] *adj* : vigésimo — ~ *n* **1** : vigésimo *m,* -ma *f* (en una serie) **2** : veinteavo *m* (en matemáticas)

twice ['twaɪs] *adv* **1** : dos veces **2** ~ **as much/many as** : el doble de (algo), el doble que (algn)

twig ['twɪg] *n* : ramita *f*

twilight ['twaɪ,laɪt] *n* : crepúsculo *m*

twin ['twɪn] *n* : gemelo *m,* -la *f;* mellizo *m,* -za *f* — ~ *adj* : gemelo, mellizo

twine ['twaɪn] *n* : cordel *m,* bramante *m Spain*

twinge ['twɪnd͡ʒ] *n* : punzada *f*

twinkle ['twɪŋkəl] *vi* **-kled; -kling 1** : centellear **2** : brillar (dícese de los ojos) — ~ *n* : centelleo *m,* brillo *m* (de los ojos)

twirl ['twərl] *vt* : girar, dar vueltas a — *vi* : girar, dar vueltas — ~ *n* : giro *m,* vuelta *f*

twist ['twɪst] *vt* **1** : retorcer **2** TURN : girar **3** SPRAIN : torcerse **4** : tergiversar (palabras) — *vi* **1** : retorcerse **2** COIL : enrollarse **3** : serpentear (entre montañas, etc.) — ~ *n* **1** BEND : vuelta *f* **2** TURN : giro *m* **3** ~ **of lemon** : rodajita *f* de limón — **twister** ['twɪstər] → **tornado**

twitch ['twɪtʃ] *vi* : moverse (espasmódicamente) — ~ *n* **nervous** ~ : tic *m* nervioso

two ['tu:] *adj* : dos — ~ *n, pl* **twos** : dos *m* — **twofold** ['tu:,fo:ld] *adj* : doble — ~ ['tu:'fo:ld] *adv* : al doble — **two hundred** *adj* : doscientos — ~ *n* : doscientos *m*

tycoon [taɪ'ku:n] *n* : magnate *mf*

tying → **tie**

type ['taɪp] *n* : tipo *m* — ~ *v* **typed; typing** : escribir a máquina — **typewritten** ['taɪp,rɪtən] *adj* : escrito a máquina — **typewriter** ['taɪp,raɪt̬ər] *n* : máquina *f* de escribir

typhoon [taɪ'fu:n] *n* : tifón *m*

typical ['tɪpɪkəl] *adj* : típico, característico — **typify** ['tɪpə,faɪ] *vt* **-fied; -fying** : tipificar

typist ['taɪpɪst] *n* : mecanógrafo *m,* -fa *f*

typography [taɪ'pɑgrəfi] *n* : tipografía *f*

tyranny ['tɪrəni] *n, pl* **-nies** : tiranía *f* — **tyrant** ['taɪrənt] *n* : tirano *m,* -na *f*

tzar ['zɑr, 'tsɑr, 'sɑr] → **czar**

U

u ['ju:] *n, pl* **u's** *or* **us** ['ju:z] : u *f,* vigésima primera letra del alfabeto inglés

udder ['ʌdər] *n* : ubre *f*

UFO [,ju:,ef'o:, 'ju:,fo:] (*unidentified flying object*) *n, pl* **UFO's** *or* **UFOs** : ovni *m,* OVNI *m*

ugly ['ʌgli] *adj* **uglier; -est** : feo — **ugliness** ['ʌglinəs] *n* : fealdad *f*

ulcer ['ʌlsər] *n* : úlcera *f*

ulterior [,ʌl'tɪriər] *adj* ~ **motive** : segunda intención *f*

ultimate ['ʌltəmət] *adj* **1** FINAL : final, último **2** UTMOST : máximo **3** FUNDAMENTAL : fundamental — **ultimately** ['ʌltəmətli] *adv* **1** FINALLY : por último, finalmente **2** EVENTUALLY : a la larga

ultimatum [,ʌltə'meɪt̬əm, -'mɑ-] *n, pl* **-tums** *or* **-ta** [-t̬ə] : ultimátum *m*

ultraviolet [,ʌltrə'vaɪələt] *adj* : ultravioleta

umbilical cord [,ʌm'bɪlɪkəl] *n* : cordón *m* umbilical

umbrella [,ʌm'brelə] *n* : paraguas *m*

umpire ['ʌm,paɪr] *n* : árbitro *m,* -tra *f* — ~ *vt* **-pired; -piring** : arbitrar

umpteenth [,ʌmp'ti:nθ] *adj* : enésimo

unable [,ʌn'eɪbəl] *adj* **1** : incapaz **2 be** ~ **to** : no poder

unabridged [,ʌnə'brɪd͡ʒd] *adj* : íntegro

unacceptable [,ʌnɪk'septəbəl] *adj* : inaceptable

unaccountable [,ʌnə'kaʊntəd] *adj* : inexplicable

unaccustomed [,ʌnə'kʌstəmd] *adj* **be** ~ **to** : no estar acostumbrado a

unadulterated [,ʌnə'dʌltə,reɪt̬əd] *adj* : puro

unaffected [,ʌnə'fektəd] *adj* **1** : no afectado **2** NATURAL : sin afectación, natural

unafraid [,ʌnə'freɪd] *adj* : sin miedo

unaided [,ʌn'eɪdəd] *adj* : sin ayuda

unanimous [jʊ'nænəməs] *adj* : unánime

unannounced [,ʌnə'naʊnst] *adj* : sin dar aviso

unarmed [,ʌn'ɑrmd] *adj* : desarmado

unassuming [,ʌnə'su:mɪŋ] *adj* : modesto, sin pretensiones

unattached [,ʌnə'tætʃt] *adj* **1** : suelto **2** UNMARRIED : soltero

unattractive [,ʌnə'træktɪv] *adj* : poco atractivo

unauthorized [,ʌn'ɔθə,raɪzd] *adj* : no autorizado

unavailable [,ʌnə'veɪləbəl] *adj* : no disponible

unavoidable [,ʌnə'vɔɪdəbəl] *adj* : inevitable

unaware [,ʌnə'wær] *adj* **1** : inconsciente **2 be** ~ **of** : ignorar — **unawares** [,ʌnə'wærz] *adv* **catch s.o.** ~ : agarrar a algn desprevenido

unbalanced [,ʌn'bæləntst] *adj* : desequilibrado

unbearable [,ʌn'bærəbəl] *adj* : inaguantable, insoportable

unbelievable [,ʌnbə'li:vəbəl] *adj* : increíble

unbending [,ʌn'bendɪŋ] *adj* : inflexible

unbiased [,ʌn'baɪəst] *adj* : imparcial

unborn [,ʌn'bɔrn] *adj* : aún no nacido

unbreakable [,ʌn'breɪkəbəl] *adj* : irrompible

unbridled [,ʌn'braɪdəld] *adj* : desenfrenado

unbroken [,ʌn'bro:kən] *adj* **1** INTACT : intacto **2** CONTINUOUS : continuo

unbutton [,ʌn'bʌtən] *vt* : desabrochar, desabotonar

uncalled-for [,ʌn'kɔld,fɔr] *adj* : inapropiado, innecesario

uncanny [ən'kæni] *adj* **-nier; -est** : extraño, misterioso

unceasing [,ʌn'si:sɪŋ] *adj* : incesante

unceremonious [,ʌn,serə'mo:niəs] *adj* **1** INFORMAL : poco ceremonioso **2** ABRUPT : brusco

uncertain [,ʌn'sərtən] *adj* **1** : incierto **2 in no** ~ **terms** : de forma vehemente — **uncertainty** [,ʌn'sərtənti] *n, pl* **-ties** : incertidumbre *f*

unchanged [,ʌn'tʃeɪnd͡ʒd] *adj* : igual, sin alterar — **unchanging** [,ʌn'tʃeɪd͡ʒɪŋ] *adj* : inmutable

uncivilized [,ʌn'sɪvə,laɪzd] *adj* : incivilizado

uncle ['ʌŋkəl] *n* : tío *m*

unclear [,ʌn'klɪr] *adj* : poco claro

uncomfortable [,ʌn'kʌmpfərt̬əbəl] *adj* **1** : incómodo **2** DISCONCERTING : inquietante, desagradable

uncommon [,ʌn'kɑmən] *adj* : raro

uncompromising [,ʌn'kɑmprə,maɪzɪŋ] *adj* : intransigente

unconcerned [,ʌnkən'sərnd] *adj* : indiferente

unconditional [,ʌnkən'dɪʃənəl] *adj* : incondicional

unconscious [,ʌn'kɑntʃəs] *adj* : inconsciente

unconstitutional [,ʌn,kɑntstə'tu:ʃənəl, -'tju:-] *adj* : inconstitucional

uncontrollable [,ʌnkən'tro:ləbəl] *adj* : incontrolable

unconventional [,ʌnkən'ventʃənəl] *adj* : poco convencional

uncouth [,ʌn'ku:θ] *adj* : grosero

uncover [,ʌn'kʌvər] *vt* **1** : destapar **2** REVEAL : descubrir

undecided [,ʌndɪ'saɪdəd] *adj* : indeciso

undeniable [,ʌndɪ'naɪəbəl] *adj* : innegable

under ['ʌndər] *adv* **1** : debajo **2** LESS : menos **3** *or* ~ **anesthetic** : bajo los efectos de la anestesia — ~ *prep* **1** BELOW, BENEATH : debajo de, abajo de **2** ~ **20 minutes** : menos de 20 minutos **3** ~ **the circumstances** : dadas las circunstancias

underage [,ʌndər'eɪd͡ʒ] *adj* : menor de edad

underclothes ['ʌndər,klo:z, -,klo:ðz] → **underwear**

undercover [,ʌndər'kʌvər] *adj* : secreto

undercurrent ['ʌndər,kərənt] *n* : tendencia *f* oculta

underdeveloped [,ʌndərdɪ'veləpt] *adj* : subdesarrollado

underestimate [,ʌndər'estə,meɪt] *vt* **-mated; -mating** : subestimar

underfoot [,ʌndər'fʊt] *adv* : bajo los pies

undergo [,ʌndər'go:] *vt* **-went** [-'went;]; **-gone** [-'gɔn]; **-going** : sufrir, experimentar

undergraduate [,ʌndər'græd͡ʒʊət] *n* : estudiante *m* universitario, estudiante *f* universitaria

underground [,ʌndər'graʊnd] *adv* **1** : bajo tierra **2 go** ~ : pasar a la clandestinidad — ~ ['ʌndər,graʊnd] *adj* **1** : subterráneo **2** SECRET : secreto, clandestino — ~ ['ʌndər,graʊnd] *n* : movimiento *m* clandestino

undergrowth ['ʌndər'gro:θ] *n* : maleza *f*

underhanded [,ʌndər'hændəd] *adj* SLY : solapado

underline ['ʌndər,laɪn] *vt* **-lined; -lining** : subrayar

underlying [,ʌndər'laɪɪŋ] *adj* : subyacente

undermine [,ʌndər'maɪn] *vt* **-mined; -mining** : socavar, minar

underneath [,ʌndər'ni:θ] *adv* : debajo, abajo — ~ *prep* : debajo de, abajo de *Lat*

underpants ['ʌndər,pænts] *npl* : calzoncillos *mpl,* calzones *mpl Lat*

underpass ['ʌndər,pæs] *n* : paso *m* inferior

underprivileged [,ʌndər'prɪvlɪd͡ʒd] *adj* : desfavorecido

underrate [,ʌndər'reɪt] *vt* **-rated; -rating** : subestimar

undershirt ['ʌndər,ʃərt] *n* : camiseta *f*

understand [,ʌndər'stænd] *v* **-stood** [-'stʊd]; **-standing** : comprender, entender — **understandable** [,ʌndər'stændəbəl] *adj* : comprensible — **understanding** [,ʌndər'stændɪŋ] *adj* : comprensivo, compasivo — ~ *n* **1** : comprensión *f* **2** AGREEMENT : acuerdo *m*

understatement [,ʌndər'steɪtmənt] *n* **that's an** ~ : decir sólo eso es quedarse corto

understudy ['ʌndər,stʌdi] *n, pl* **-dies** : sobresaliente *mf* (en el teatro)

undertake [ˌʌndərˈteɪk] *vt* **-took** [-ˈtʊk]; **-taken** [-ˈteɪkən]; **-taking** : emprender (una tarea), encargarse de (una responsabilidad) — **undertaker** [ˈʌndərˌteɪkər] *n* : director *m*, -tora *f* de una funeraria — **undertaking** [ˈʌndərˌteɪkɪŋ, ˌʌndərˈ-] *n* : empresa *f*, tarea *f*

undertone [ˈʌndərˌto:n] *n* **1** : voz *f* baja **2** SUGGESTION : matiz *m*

undertow [ˈʌndərˌto:] *n* : resaca *f*

underwater [ˌʌndərˈwɔt̬ər, -ˈwɑ-] *adj* : submarino — **~** *adv* : debajo (del agua)

under way [ˌʌndərˈweɪ] *adv* **get ~** : ponerse en marcha

underwear [ˈʌndərˌwær] *n* : ropa *f* interior

underwent → **undergo**

underworld [ˈʌndərˌwərld] *n* **the ~** CRIMINALS : la hampa, los bajos fondos

underwriter [ˈʌndərˌraɪt̬ər, ˌʌndərˈ-] *n* : asegurador *m*, -dora *f*

undesirable [ˌʌndɪˈzaɪrəbəl] *adj* : indeseable

undeveloped [ˌʌndɪˈvɛləpt] *adj* : sin desarrollar

undignified [ˌʌnˈdɪgnəˌfaɪd] *adj* : indecoroso

undisputed [ˌʌndɪˈspju:t̬əd] *adj* : indiscutible

undo [ˌʌnˈdu:] *vt* **-did** [-ˈdɪd]; **-done** [-ˈdʌn]; **-doing 1** UNFASTEN : deshacer, desatar **2** : reparar (daños, etc.)

undoubtedly [ˌʌnˈdaʊt̬ədli] *adv* : indudablemente

undress [ˌʌnˈdrɛs] *vt* : desnudar — *vi* : desnudarse

undue [ˌʌnˈdu:, -ˈdju:] *adj* : indebido, excesivo

undulate [ˈʌndʒəˌleɪt] *vi* **-lated; -lating** : ondular

unduly [ˌʌnˈdu:li, -ˈdju:-] *adv* : excesivamente

undying [ˌʌnˈdaɪɪŋ] *adj* : eterno

unearth [ˌʌnˈərθ] *vt* : desenterrar

unearthly [ˌʌnˈərθli] *adj* **-lier; -est** : sobrenatural, de otro mundo

uneasy [ˌʌnˈi:zi] *adj* **-easier; -est 1** AWKWARD : incómodo **2** WORRIED : inquieto **3** RESTLESS : agitado — **uneasily** [ˌʌnˈi:zəli] *adv* : inquietamente — **uneasiness** [ˌʌnˈi:zinəs] *n* : inquietud *f*

uneducated [ˌʌnˈɛdʒəˌkeɪt̬əd] *adj* : inculto

unemployed [ˌʌnɪmˈplɔɪd] *adj* : desempleado — **unemployment** [ˌʌnɪmˈplɔɪmənt] *n* : desempleo *m*

unerring [ˌʌnˈɛrɪŋ, -ˈər-] *adj* : infalible

unethical [ˌʌnˈɛθɪkəl] *adj* : poco ético

uneven [ˌʌnˈi:vən] *adj* **1** : desigual **2** : impar (dícese de un número)

unexpected [ˌʌnɪkˈspɛktəd] *adj* : inesperado

unfailing [ˌʌnˈfeɪlɪŋ] *adj* **1** CONSTANT : constante **2** INEXHAUSTIBLE : inagotable

unfair [ˌʌnˈfær] *adj* : injusto — **unfairly** [ˌʌnˈfærli] *adv* : injustamente — **unfairness** [ˌʌnˈfærnəs] *n* : injusticia *f*

unfaithful [ˌʌnˈfeɪθfəl] *adj* : infiel — **unfaithfulness** [ˌʌnˈfeɪθfəlnəs] *n* : infidelidad *f*

unfamiliar [ˌʌnfəˈmɪljər] *adj* **1** : desconocido **2 be ~ with** : desconocer

unfasten [ˌʌnˈfæsən] *vt* **1** : desabrochar (ropa, etc.) **2** UNDO : desatar (una cuerda, etc.)

unfavorable [ˌʌnˈfeɪvərəbəl] *adj* : desfavorable

unfeeling [ˌʌnˈfi:lɪŋ] *adj* : insensible

unfinished [ˌʌnˈfɪnɪʃt] *adj* : sin terminar

unfit [ˌʌnˈfɪt] *adj* **1** UNSUITABLE : impropio **2** UNSUITED : no apto, incapaz

unfold [ˌʌnˈfo:ld] *vt* **1** : desplegar, desdoblar **2** REVEAL : revelar (un plan, etc.) — *vi* **1** : extenderse, desplegarse **2** DEVELOP : desarrollarse

unforeseen [ˌʌnforˈsi:n] *adj* : imprevisto

unforgettable [ˌʌnfərˈgɛt̬əbəl] *adj* : inolvidable

unforgivable [ˌʌnfərˈgɪvəbəl] *adj* : imperdonable

unfortunate [ˌʌnˈfɔrtʃənət] *adj* **1** UNLUCKY : desgraciado, desafortunado **2** INAPPROPRIATE : inoportuno — **unfortunately** [ˌʌnˈfɔrtʃənətli] *adv* : desgraciadamente

unfounded [ˌʌnˈfaʊndəd] *adj* : infundado

unfriendly [ˌʌnˈfrɛndli] *adj* **-lier; -est** : poco amistoso

unfurl [ˌʌnˈfərl] *vt* : desplegar

unfurnished [ˌʌnˈfərnɪʃt] *adj* : desamueblado

ungainly [ˌʌnˈgeɪnli] *adj* : desgarbado

ungodly [ˌʌnˈgɑdli, -ˈgɔd-] *adj* **1** : impío **2 an ~ hour** : una hora intempestiva

ungrateful [ˌʌnˈgreɪtfəl] *adj* : desagradecido

unhappy [ˌʌnˈhæpi] *adj* **-pier; -est 1** SAD : infeliz, triste **2** UNFORTUNATE : desafortunado — **unhappily** [ˌʌnˈhæpəli] *adv* **1** SADLY : tristemente **2** UNFORTUNATELY : desgraciadamente — **unhappiness** [ˌʌnˈhæpinəs] *n* : tristeza *f*

unharmed [ˌʌnˈhɑrmd] *adj* : salvo, ileso

unhealthy [ˌʌnˈhɛlθi] *adj* **-thier; -est 1** : malsano **2** SICKLY : enfermizo

unheard–of [ˌʌnˈhərdəv] *adj* : sin precedente, insólito

unhook [ˌʌnˈhʊk] *vt* : desenganchar

unhurt [ˌʌnˈhərt] *adj* : ileso

unicorn [ˈju:nəˌkɔrn] *n* : unicornio *m*

unification [ˌju:nəfəˈkeɪʃən] *n* : unificación *f*

uniform [ˈju:nəˌfɔrm] *adj* : uniforme — **~** *n* : uniforme *m* — **uniformity** [ˌju:nəˈfɔrmət̬i] *n, pl* **-ties** : uniformidad *f*

unify [ˈju:nəˌfaɪ] *vt* **-fied; -fying** : unificar

unilateral [ˌju:nəˈlæt̬ərəl] *adj* : unilateral

unimaginable [ˌʌnɪˈmædʒənəbəl] *adj* : inconcebible

unimportant [ˌʌnɪmˈpɔrtənt] *adj* : insignificante

uninhabited [ˌʌnɪnˈhæbət̬əd] *adj* : deshabitado, despoblado

uninjured [ˌʌnˈɪndʒərd] *adj* : ileso

unintentional [ˌʌnɪnˈtɛntʃənəl] *adj* : involuntario

union [ˈju:njən] *n* **1** : unión *f* **2** *or* **labor ~** : sindicato *m*, gremio *m Lat*

unique [jʊˈni:k] *adj* : único — **uniquely** [jʊˈni:kli] *adv* EXCEPTIONALLY : excepcionalmente

unison [ˈju:nəsən, -zən] *n* **in ~** : al unísono

unit [ˈju:nɪt] *n* **1** : unidad *f* **2** : módulo *m* (de un mobiliario)

unite [jʊˈnaɪt] *v* **united; uniting** *vt* : unir — *vi* : unirse — **unity** [ˈju:nət̬i] *n, pl* **-ties 1** : unidad *f* **2** HARMONY : acuerdo *m*

universe [ˈju:nəˌvərs] *n* : universo *m* — **universal** [ˌju:nəˈvərsəl] *adj* : universal

university [ˌju:nəˈvərsət̬i] *n, pl* **-ties** : universidad *f*

unjust [ˌʌnˈdʒʌst] *adj* : injusto — **unjustified** [ˌʌnˈdʒʌstəˌfaɪd] *adj* : injustificado

unkempt [ˌʌnˈkɛmpt] *adj* **1** : descuidado, desaseado **2** : despeinado (dícese del pelo)

unkind [ˌʌnˈkaɪnd] *adj* : poco amable, cruel — **unkindness** [ˌʌnˈkaɪndnəs] *n* : falta *f* de amabilidad, crueldad *f*

unknown [ˌʌnˈno:n] *adj* : desconocido

unlawful [ˌʌnˈlɔfəl] *adj* : ilegal

unless [ənˈlɛs] *conj* : a menos que, a no ser que

unlike [ˌʌnˈlaɪk] *adj* : diferente — **~** *prep* : a diferencia de — **unlikelihood** [ˌʌnˈlaɪkliˌhʊd] *n* : improbabilidad *f* — **unlikely** [ˌʌnˈlaɪkli] *adj* **-lier; -est** : improbable

unlimited [ˌʌnˈlɪmət̬əd] *adj* : ilimitado

unload [ˌʌnˈlo:d] *v* : descargar

unlock [ˌʌnˈlɑk] *vt* : abrir (con llave)

unlucky [ˌʌnˈlʌki] *adj* **-luckier; -est 1** UNFORTUNATE : desgraciado **2** : de mala suerte (dícese de un número, etc.)

unmarried [ˌʌnˈmærid] *adj* : soltero

unmask [ˌʌnˈmæsk] *vt* : desenmascarar

unmistakable [ˌʌnmɪˈsteɪkəbəl] *adj* : inconfundible

unnatural [ˌʌnˈnætʃərəl] *adj* **1** : anormal **2** AFFECTED : afectado, forzado

unnecessary [ˌʌnˈnɛsəˌsɛri] *adj* : innecesario — **unnecessarily** [-ˌnɛsəˈsɛrəli] *adv* : innecesariamente

unnerving [ˌʌnˈnərvɪŋ] *adj* : desconcertante

unnoticed [ˌʌnˈno:t̬əst] *adj* : inadvertido

unobtainable [ˌʌnəbˈteɪnəbəl] *adj* : inasequible

unobtrusive [ˌʌnəbˈstru:sɪv] *adj* : discreto

unofficial [ˌʌnəˈfɪʃəl] *adj* : no oficial

unorthodox [ˌʌnˈɔrθəˌdɑks] *adj* : poco ortodoxo

unpack [ˌʌnˈpæk] *vt* **1** : desempaquetar, desempacar *Lat* (un paquete, etc.) **2** : deshacer (una maleta) — *vi* : deshacer las maletas

unparalleled [ˌʌnˈpærəˌlɛld] *adj* : sin igual

unpleasant [ˌʌnˈplɛzənt] *adj* : desagradable

unplug [ˌʌnˈplʌg] *vt* **-plugged; -plugging** : desconectar, desenchufar

unpopular [ˌʌnˈpɑpjələr] *adj* : poco popular

unprecedented [ˌʌnˈprɛsəˌdɛntəd] *adj* : sin precedente

unpredictable [ˌʌnprɪˈdɪktəbəl] *adj* : imprevisible

unprepared [ˌʌnprɪˈpærd] *adj* **1** : no preparado **2** UNREADY : desprevenido

unqualified [ˌʌnˈkwɑləˌfaɪd] *adj* **1** : no calificado, sin título **2** COMPLETE : absoluto

unquestionable [ˌʌnˈkwɛstʃənəbəl] *adj* : indiscutible — **unquestioning** [ˌʌnˈkwɛstʃənɪŋ] *adj* : incondicional

unravel [ˌʌnˈrævəl] *v* **-eled** *or* **-elled; -eling** *or* **-elling** *vt* : desenmarañar — *vi* : deshacerse

unreal [ˌʌnˈri:l] *adj* : irreal — **unrealistic** [ˌʌnˌri:əˈlɪstɪk] *adj* : poco realista

unreasonable [ˌʌnˈri:zənəbəl] *adj* **1** : irrazonable **2** EXCESSIVE : excesivo

unrecognizable [ˌʌnˈrɛkəgˌnaɪzəbəl] *adj* : irreconocible

unrelated [ˌʌnrɪˈleɪt̬əd] *adj* : no relacionado

unrelenting [ˌʌnrɪˈlɛntɪŋ] *adj* : implacable

unreliable [ˌʌnrɪˈlaɪəbəl] *adj* : que no es de fiar

unrepentant [ˌʌnrɪˈpɛntənt] *adj* : impenitente

unrest [ˌʌnˈrɛst] *n* **1** : inquietud *f*, malestar *m* **2** *or* **political ~** : disturbios *mpl*

unripe [ˌʌnˈraɪp] *adj* : verde, no maduro

unrivaled *or* **unrivalled** [ˌʌnˈraɪvəld] *adj* : incomparable, sin par

unroll [ˌʌnˈro:l] *vt* : desenrollar — *vi* : desenrollarse

unruly [ˌʌnˈru:li] *adj* : indisciplinado

unsafe [ˌʌnˈseɪf] *adj* : inseguro

unsaid [ˌʌnˈsɛd] *adj* : sin decir

unsanitary [ˌʌnˈsænəˌtɛri] *adj* : antihigiénico

unsatisfactory [ˌʌnˌsæt̬əsˈfæktəri] *adj* : insatisfactorio

unscathed [ˌʌnˈskeɪðd] *adj* : ileso

unscrew [ˌʌnˈskru:] *vt* : destornillar

unscrupulous [ˌʌnˈskru:pjələs] *adj* : sin escrúpulos

unseemly [ˌʌnˈsi:mli] *adj* **-lier; -est** : indecoroso

unseen [ˌʌnˈsi:n] *adj* **1** : no visto **2** UNNOTICED : inadvertido

unselfish [ˌʌnˈsɛlfɪʃ] *adj* : desinteresado

unsettle [ˌʌnˈsɛtəl] *vt* **-tled; -tling** DISTURB : perturbar — **unsettled** [ˌʌnˈsɛtəld] *adj* **1** CHANGEABLE : inestable **2** DISTURBED : agitado, inquieto **3** : variable (dícese del tiempo)

unsightly [ˌʌnˈsaɪtli] *adj* : feo

unskilled [ˌʌnˈskɪld] *adj* : no calificado — **unskillful** [ˌʌnˈskɪlfəl] *adj* : torpe, poco hábil

unsociable [ˌʌnˈso:ʃəbəl] *adj* : poco sociable

unsound [ˌʌnˈsaʊnd] *adj* **1** : defectuoso, erróneo **2 of ~ mind** : demente

unspeakable [ˌʌnˈspi:kəbəl] *adj* **1** : indecible **2** TERRIBLE : atroz

unstable [ˌʌnˈsteɪbəl] *adj* : inestable

unsteady [ˌʌnˈstɛdi] *adj* **1** : inestable **2** SHAKY : tembloroso

unsuccessful [ˌʌnsəkˈsɛsfəl] *adj* **1** : fracasado **2 be ~** : no tener éxito

unsuitable [ˌʌnˈsu:t̬əbəl] *adj* **1** : inadecuado **2** INCONVENIENT : inconveniente

unsure [ˌʌnˈʃʊr] *adj* : inseguro

unsuspecting [ˌʌnsəˈspɛktɪŋ] *adj* : confiado

unsympathetic [ˌʌnˌsɪmpəˈθɛt̬ɪk] *adj* : indiferente

unthinkable [ˌʌnˈθɪŋkəbəl] *adj* : inconcebible

untidy [ˌʌnˈtaɪdi] *adj* : desordenado (dícese de una sala, etc.), desaliñado (dícese de una persona)

untie [ˌʌnˈtaɪ] *vt* **-tied; -tying** *or* **-tieing** : desatar

until [ˌʌnˈtɪl] *prep* : hasta — **~** *conj* : hasta que

untimely [ˌʌnˈtaɪmli] *adj* **1** PREMATURE : prematuro **2** INOPPORTUNE : inoportuno

untold [ˌʌnˈto:ld] *adj* : incalculable

untoward [ˌʌnˈtɔrd, -ˈto:ərd, -təˈwɔrd] *adj* **1** ADVERSE : adverso **2** IMPROPER : indecoroso

untroubled [ˌʌnˈtrʌbəld] *adj* **1** : tranquilo **2 be ~ by** : no estar afectado por

untrue [ˌʌnˈtru:] *adj* : falso

unused [ˌʌnˈju:zd, *in sense 2 usually* -ˈju:st] *adj* **1** NEW : nuevo **2 be ~ to** : no estar acostumbrado a

unusual [ˌʌnˈju:ʒuəl] *adj* : poco común, insólito — **unusually** [ˌʌnˈju:ʒuəl, -ˈju:ʒəli] *adv* : excepcionalmente

unveil [ˌʌnˈveɪl] *vt* : descubrir, revelar

unwanted [ˌʌnˈwɑntəd] *adj* : superfluo (dícese de un objeto), no deseado (dícese de un niño, etc.)

unwarranted [ˌʌnˈwɔrəntəd] *adj* : injustificado

unwelcome [ˌʌnˈwɛlkəm] *adj* : inoportuno, molesto

unwell [ˌʌnˈwɛl] *adj* **be ~** : sentirse mal

unwieldy [ˌʌnˈwi:ldi] *adj* : difícil de manejar

unwilling [ˌʌnˈwɪlɪŋ] *adj* : poco dispuesto — **unwillingly** [ˌʌnˈwɪlɪŋli] *adv* : de mala gana

unwind [ˌʌnˈwaɪnd] *v* **-wound** [-ˈwaʊnd]; **-winding** *vt* : desenrollar — *vi* **1** : desenrollarse **2** RELAX : relajarse

unwise [ˌʌnˈwaɪz] *adj* : imprudente

unworthy [ˌʌnˈwərði] *adj* **be ~ of** : no ser digno de

unwrap [ˌʌnˈræp] *vt* **-wrapped; -wrapping** : desenvolver

up [ˈʌp] *adv* **1** ABOVE : arriba **2** UPWARDS : hacia arriba **3 ten miles farther ~** : diez millas más adelante **4 ~ here/there** : aquí/allí arriba **5 ~ north** : en el norte **6 ~ until** : hasta — **~** *adj* **1** AWAKE : levantado **2** FINISHED : terminado **3 be ~ against** : enfrentarse con **4 be ~ on** : estar al corriente de **5 it's ~ to you** : depende de tí **6 prices are ~** : los precios han aumentado **7 the sun is ~** : ha salido el sol **8 what's ~?** : ¿qué pasa? — **~** *prep* **1 go ~ the river** : ir río arriba **2 go ~ the stairs** : subir la escalera **3 ~ the coast** : a lo largo de la costa — **~** *v* **upped** [ˈʌpt]; **upping; ups** *vt* : aumentar — *vi* **she ~ and left** : agarró y se fue

upbringing [ˈʌpˌbrɪŋɪŋ] *n* : educación *f*

upcoming [ˌʌpˈkʌmɪŋ] *adj* : próximo

update [ˌʌpˈdeɪt] *vt* **-dated; -dating** : poner al día, actualizar — **~** [ˈʌpˌdeɪt] *n* : puesta *f* al día

upgrade [ˈʌpˌgreɪd, ˌʌpˈ-] *vt* **-graded; -grading** : elevar la categoría de (un puesto, etc.), mejorar (una facilidad, etc.)

upheaval [ˌʌpˈhi:vəl] *n* : trastorno *m*

uphill [ˌʌpˈhɪl] *adv* : cuesta arriba — **~** [ˈʌpˌhɪl] *adj* **1** : en subida **2 be an ~ battle** : ser muy difícil

uphold [ˌʌpˈho:ld] *vt* **-held; -holding** : sostener, apoyar

upholstery [ˌʌpˈho:lstəri] *n, pl* **-steries** : tapicería *f*

upkeep [ˈʌpˌki:p] *n* : mantenimiento *m*

upon [əˈpɔn, əˈpɑn] *prep* **1** : en, sobre **2 ~ leaving** : al salir

upper [ˈʌpər] *adj* : superior — **~** *n* : parte *f* superior (del calzado, etc.)

uppercase [ˌʌpərˈkeɪs] *adj* : mayúsculo

upper class *n* : clase *f* alta

upper hand *n* : ventaja *f*, dominio *m*

uppermost [ˈʌpərˌmo:st] *adj* : más alto

upright [ˈʌpˌraɪt] *adj* **1** VERTICAL : vertical **2** ERECT : derecho **3** JUST : recto, honesto — **~** *n* : montante *m*, poste *m*

uprising [ˈʌpˌraɪzɪŋ] *n* : insurrección *f*, revuelta *f*

uproar [ˈʌpˌror] *n* COMMOTION : alboroto *m*

uproot [ˌʌpˈru:t, -ˈrʊt] *vt* : desarraigar

upset [ˌʌpˈsɛt] *vt* **-set; -setting 1** OVERTURN : volcar **2** DISTRESS : alterar, inquietar **3** DISRUPT : trastornar — **~** *adj* **1** DISTRESSED : alterado **2 have an ~ stomach** : estar mal del estómago — **~** [ˈʌpˌsɛt] *n* : trastorno *m*

upshot [ˈʌpˌʃɑt] *n* : resultado *m* final

upside down [ˌʌpˌsaɪdˈdaʊn] *adv* **1** : al revés **2 turn ~** : volver — **upside–down** [ˌʌpˌsaɪdˈdaʊn] *adj* : al revés

upstairs [ˌʌpˈstærz] *adv* : arriba — **~** [ˈʌpˌstærz, ˌʌpˈ-] *adj* : de arriba — **~** [ˈʌpˌstærz, ˌʌpˈ-] *ns & pl* : piso *m* de arriba

upstart [ˈʌpˌstɑrt] *n* : advenedizo *m*, -za *f*

upstream [ˈʌpˌstri:m] *adv* : río arriba

upswing [ˈʌpˌswɪŋ] *n* **be on the ~** : estar mejorándose

up–to–date [ˌʌptəˈdeɪt] *adj* **1** : corriente, al día **2** MODERN : moderno

uptown [ˈʌpˈtaʊn] *adv* : hacia la parte alta de la ciudad, hacia el distrito residencial

upturn [ˈʌpˌtərn] *n* : mejora *f*, auge *m* (económico)

upward [ˈʌpwərd] *or* **upwards** [-wərdz] *adv* : hacia arriba — **upward** *adj* : ascendente, hacia arriba

uranium [jʊˈreɪniəm] *n* : uranio *m*

urban [ˈərbən] *adj* : urbano

urbane [ˌərˈbeɪn] *adj* : urbano, cortés

urge [ˈərdʒ] *vt* **urged; urging 1** PRESS : instar, exhortar **2 ~ on** : animar — **~** *n* : impulso *m*, ganas *fpl* — **urgency** [ˈərdʒəntsi] *n, pl* **-cies** : urgencia *f* — **urgent** [ˈərdʒənt] *adj* **1** : urgente **2 be ~** : urgir

urine [ˈjʊrən] *n* : orina *f* — **urinate** [ˈjʊrəˌneɪt] *vi* **-nated; -nating** : orinar

urn [ˈərn] *n* : urna *f*

Uruguayan [ˌʊrəˈgwaɪən, ˌjʊr-, -ˈgweɪ-] *adj* : uruguayo

us [ˈʌs] *pron* **1** (*as direct or indirect object*) : nos **2** (*as object of a preposition*) : nosotros, nosotras **3 both of ~** : nosotros dos **4 it's ~!** : ¡somos nosotros!

usage [ˈju:sɪdʒ, -zɪdʒ] *n* : uso *m*

use [ˈju:z] *v* **used** [ˈju:zd, *the phrase "used to" is usually* ˈju:stu:]; **using** *vt* **1** : usar **2** CONSUME : consumir, tomar (drogas, etc.) **3 ~ up** : agotar, consumir — *vi* **1 she ~d to dance** : acostumbraba bailar **2 winters ~d to be colder** : los inviernos solían ser más fríos — **~** [ˈju:s] *n* **1** : uso *m* **2 have no ~ for** : no necesitar **3 have the ~ of** : poder usar, tener acceso a **4 it's no ~!** : ¡es inútil! — **used** [ˈju:zd, *in sense 2 usually* ˈju:st] *adj* **1** SECONDHAND : usado **2 be ~ to** : estar acostumbrado a — **useful** [ˈju:sfəl] *adj* : útil, práctico — **usefulness** [ˈju:sfəlnəs] *n* : utilidad *f* — **useless** [ˈju:sləs] *adj* : inútil — **user** [ˈju:zər] *n* : usuario *m*, -ria *f*

usher [ˈʌʃər] *vt* **1** : acompañar, conducir **2 ~ in** : hacer entrar — **~** *n* : acomodador *m*, -dora *f*

usual [ˈju:ʒuəl] *adj* **1** : habitual, usual **2 as ~** : como de costumbre — **usually** [ˈju:ʒuəli, ˈju:ʒəli] *adv* : usualmente

usurp [jʊˈsərp, -ˈzərp] *vt* : usurpar

utensil [jʊˈtɛntsəl] *n* : utensilio *m*

uterus [ˈju:t̬ərəs] *n, pl* **uteri** [-ˌraɪ] : útero *m*, matriz *f*

utility [ju:ˈtɪlət̬i] *n, pl* **-ties 1** : utilidad *f* **2** *or* **public ~** : empresa *f* de servicio público

utilize [ˈju:t̬əlˌaɪz] *vt* **-lized; -lizing** : utilizar

utmost [ˈʌtˌmo:st] *adj* **1** FARTHEST : extremo **2 of the ~ importance** : de suma importancia — **~** *n* **do one's ~** : hacer todo lo posible

utopia [jʊˈto:piə] *n* : utopía *f* — **utopian** [jʊˈto:piən] *adj* : utópico

utter[1] [ˈʌt̬ər] *adj* : absoluto, completo

utter[2] *vt* : decir, pronunciar (palabras) — **utterance** [ˈʌt̬ərənts] *n* : declaración *f*, expresión *f*

utterly [ˈʌt̬ərli] *adv* : completamente, totalmente

V

v [ˈvi:] *n, pl* **v's** *or* **vs** [ˈvi:z] : v *f*, vigésima segunda letra del alfabeto inglés

vacant [ˈveɪkənt] *adj* **1** AVAILABLE : libre **2** UNOCCUPIED : desocupado **3** : vacante (dícese de un puesto) **4** : ausente (dícese de una mirada) — **vacancy** [ˈveɪkəntsi] *n, pl* **-cies 1** : (puesto *m*) vacante *f* **2** : habitación *f* libre (en un hotel, etc.)

vacate ['veɪˌkeɪt] *vt* **-cated; -cating** : desalojar, desocupar

vacation [veɪ'keɪʃən, və-] *n* : vacaciones *fpl*

vaccination [ˌvæksə'neɪʃən] *n* : vacunación *f* — **vaccinate** ['væksəˌneɪt] *vt* **-nated; -nating** : vacunar — **vaccine** [væk'si:n, 'vækˌ-] *n* : vacuna *f*

vacuum ['væˌkju:m, -kjəm] *n, pl* **vacuums** *or* **vacua** : vacío *m* — ~ *vt* : pasar la aspiradora por — **vacuum cleaner** *n* : aspiradora *f*

vagina [və'dʒaɪnə] *n, pl* **-nae** [-ˌni:, -ˌnaɪ] *or* **-nas** : vagina *f*

vagrant ['veɪgrənt] *n* : vagabundo *m*, -da *f*

vague ['veɪg] *adj* **vaguer; -est** : vago, indistinto

vain ['veɪn] *adj* **1** CONCEITED : vanidoso **2 in ~** : en vano

valentine ['vælənˌtaɪn] *n* : tarjeta *f* del día de San Valentín

valiant ['væljənt] *adj* : valiente, valeroso

valid ['væləd] *adj* : válido — **validate** ['væləˌdeɪt] *vt* **-dated; -dating** : validar — **validity** [və'lɪdəṭi, væ-] *n* : validez *f*

valley ['væli] *n, pl* **-leys** : valle *m*

valor ['vælər] *n* : valor *m*, valentía *f*

value ['vælˌju:] *n* : valor *m* — ~ *vt* **-ued; -uing** : valorar — **valuable** ['væljuəbəl, 'væljəbəl] *adj* : valioso — **valuables** *npl* : objetos *mpl* de valor

valve ['vælv] *n* : válvula *f*

vampire ['væmˌpaɪr] *n* : vampiro *m*

van ['væn] *n* : furgoneta *f*, camioneta *f*

vandal ['vændəl] *n* : vándalo *m* — **vandalism** ['vændəlˌɪzəm] *n* : vandalismo *m* — **vandalize** ['vændəlˌaɪz] *vt* : destrozar, destruir

vane ['veɪn] *n or* **weather ~** : veleta *f*

vanguard ['vænˌgɑrd] *n* : vanguardia *f*

vanilla [və'nɪlə, -'nɛ-] *n* : vainilla *f*

vanish ['vænɪʃ] *vi* : desaparecer

vanity ['vænəṭi] *n, pl* **-ties 1** : vanidad *f* **2** *or* **~ table** : tocador *m*

vantage point ['væntɪdʒ] *n* : posición *f* ventajosa

vapor ['veɪpər] *n* : vapor *m*

variable ['vɛriəbəl] *adj* : variable — ~ *n* : variable *f* — **variance** ['vɛriənts] *n* **at ~ with** : en desacuerdo con — **variant** ['vɛriənt] *n* : variante *f* — **variation** [ˌvɛri'eɪʃən] *n* : variación *f* — **varied** ['vɛrid] *adj* : variado — **variegated** ['vɛriəˌgeɪṭəd] *adj* : abigarrado, multicolor — **variety** [və'raɪəṭi] *n, pl* **-ties 1** : variedad *f* **2** ASSORTMENT : surtido *m* **3** SORT : clase *f* — **various** ['vɛriəs] *adj* : varios, diversos

varnish ['vɑrnɪʃ] *n* : barniz *f* — ~ *vt* : barnizar

vary ['vɛri] *v* **varied; varying** : variar

vase ['veɪs, 'veɪz, 'vɑz] *n* **1** : jarrón *m* **2** *or* **flower ~** : florero *m*

vast ['væst] *adj* : vasto, enorme — **vastness** ['væstnəs] *n* : inmensidad *f*

vat ['væt] *n* : cuba *f*

vault[1] ['vɔlt] *vi* LEAP : saltar — ~ *n* : salto *m*

vault[2] *n* **1** DOME : bóveda *f* **2** *or* **bank ~** : cámara *f* acorazada, bóveda *f* de seguridad *Lat* **3** CRYPT : cripta *f*

VCR [ˌvi:ˌsi:'ɑr] (*videocassette recorder*) *n* : video *m*

veal ['vi:l] *n* : (carne *f* de) ternera *f*

veer ['vɪr] *vi* : virar

vegetable ['vɛdʒtəbəl, 'vɛdʒəṭə-] *adj* : vegetal — ~ *n* **1** : vegetal *m* (planta) **2 ~s** *npl* : verduras *fpl* — **vegetarian** [ˌvɛdʒə'tɛriən] *n* : vegetariano *mf* — **vegetation** [ˌvɛdʒə'teɪʃən] *n* : vegetación *f*

vehemence ['vi:əmənts] *n* : vehemencia *f* — **vehement** ['vi:əmənt] *adj* : vehemente

vehicle ['vi:əkəl, 'vi:ˌhɪkəl] *n* : vehículo *m*

veil ['veɪl] *n* : velo *m* — ~ *vt* **1** : cubrir con un velo **2** CONCEAL : velar

vein ['veɪn] *n* **1** : vena *f* **2** : veta *f* (de un mineral, etc.)

velocity [və'lɑsəṭi] *n, pl* **-ties** : velocidad *f*

velvet ['vɛlvət] *n* : terciopelo *m* — **velvety** ['vɛlvəṭi] *adj* : aterciopelado

vending machine ['vɛndɪŋ-] *vt* : máquina *f* expendedora

vendor ['vɛndər] *n* : vendedor *m*, -dora *f*

veneer [və'nɪr] *n* **1** : chapa *f* **2** FACADE : apariencia *f*

venerable ['vɛnərəbəl] *adj* : venerable — **venerate** ['vɛnəˌreɪt] *vt* **-ated; -ating** : venerar — **veneration** [ˌvɛnə'reɪʃən] *n* : veneración *f*

venereal [və'nɪriəl] *adj* : venéreo

venetian blind [və'ni:ʃən-] *n* : persiana *f* veneciana

Venezuelan [ˌvɛnə'zweɪlən, -zʊ'eɪ-] *adj* : venezolano

vengeance ['vɛndʒənts] *n* **1** : venganza *f* **2 take ~ on** : vengarse de — **vengeful** ['vɛndʒfəl] *adj* : vengativo

venison ['vɛnəsən, -zən] *n* : (carne *f* de) venado *m*

venom ['vɛnəm] *n* : veneno *m* — **venomous** ['vɛnəməs] *adj* : venenoso

vent ['vɛnt] *vt* : desahogar — ~ *n* **1** *or* **air ~** : rejilla *f* de ventilación **2** OUTLET : desahogo *m* — **ventilate** ['vɛntəlˌeɪt] *vt* **-lated; -lating** : ventilar — **ventilation** [ˌvɛntəl'eɪʃən] *n* : ventilación *f* — **ventilator** ['vɛntəlˌeɪṭər] *n* : ventilador *m*

ventriloquist [vɛn'trɪləˌkwɪst] *n* : ventrílocuo *m*, -cua *f*

venture ['vɛntʃər] *v* **-tured; -turing** *vt* **1** RISK : arriesgar **2** : aventurar (una opinión, etc.) — *vi* : atreverse — ~ *n or* **business ~** : empresa *f*

venue ['vɛnˌju:] *n* : lugar *m*

Venus ['vi:nəs] *n* : Venus *m*

veranda *or* **verandah** [və'rændə] *n* : veranda *f*

verb ['vərb] *n* : verbo *m* — **verbal** ['vərbəl] *adj* : verbal — **verbatim** [vər'beɪṭəm] *adv* : palabra por palabra — ~ *adj* : literal — **verbose** [vər'bo:s] *adj* : verboso

verdict ['vərdɪkt] *n* **1** : veredicto *m* **2** OPINION : opinión *f*

verge ['vərdʒ] *n* **1** : borde *m* **2 on the ~ of** : a punto de (hacer algo), al borde de (algo) — ~ *vi* **verged; verging ~ on** : rayar en

verify ['vɛrəˌfaɪ] *vt* **-fied; -fying** : verificar — **verification** [ˌvɛrəfə'keɪʃən] *n* : verificación *f*

vermin ['vərmən] *ns & pl* : alimañas *fpl*

vermouth [vər'mu:th] *n* : vermut *m*

versatile ['vərsəṭəl] *adj* : versátil — **versatility** [ˌvərsə'tɪləṭi] *n* : versatilidad *f*

verse ['vərs] *n* **1** LINE : verso *m* **2** POETRY : poesía *f* **3** : versículo *m* (en la Biblia) — **versed** ['vərst] *adj* **be well ~ in** : ser muy versado en

version ['vərʒən] *n* : versión *f*

versus ['vərsəs] *prep* : versus

vertebra ['vərṭəbrə] *n, pl* **-brae** [-ˌbreɪ, -ˌbri:] *or* **-bras** : vértebra *f*

vertical ['vərṭɪkəl] *adj* : vertical — ~ *n* : vertical *f*

vertigo ['vərṭɪˌgo:] *n, pl* **-goes** *or* **-gos** : vértigo *m*

verve ['vərv] *n* : brío *m*

very ['vɛri] *adv* **1** : muy **2 at the ~ least** : por lo menos **3 the ~ same thing** : la misma cosa **4 ~ much** : mucho **5 ~ well** : muy bien — ~ *adj* **verier; -est 1** PRECISE, SAME : mismo **2** MERE : solo, mero **3 the ~ thing** : justo lo que hacía falta

vessel ['vɛsəl] *n* **1** CONTAINER : recipiente *m* **2** SHIP : nave *f*, buque *m* **3** *or* **blood ~** : vaso *m* sanguíneo

vest ['vɛst] *n* **1** : chaleco *m* **2** *Brit* UNDERSHIRT : camiseta *f*

vestibule ['vɛstəˌbju:l] *n* : vestíbulo *m*

vestige ['vɛstɪdʒ] *n* : vestigio *m*

vet ['vɛt] *n* **1** → **veterinarian 2** → **veteran**

veteran ['vɛṭərən, 'vɛtrən] *n* : veterano *m*, -na *f*

veterinarian [ˌvɛṭərə'nɛriən, ˌvɛṭə'nɛr-] *n* : veterinario *m*, -ria *f* — **veterinary** ['vɛṭərəˌnɛri] *adj* : veterinario

veto ['vi:ṭo] *n, pl* **-toes** : veto *m* — ~ *vt* : vetar

vex ['vɛks] *vt* ANNOY : irritar

via ['vaɪə, 'vi:ə] *prep* : por, vía

viable ['vaɪəbəl] *adj* : viable

viaduct ['vaɪəˌdʌkt] *n* : viaducto *m*

vial ['vaɪəl] *n* : frasco *m*

vibrant ['vaɪbrənt] *adj* : vibrante — **vibrate** ['vaɪˌbreɪt] *vi* **-brated; -brating** : vibrar — **vibration** [vaɪ'breɪʃən] *n* : vibración *f*

vicar ['vɪkər] *n* : vicario *m*, -ria *f*

vicarious [vaɪ'kæri:əs, vɪ-] *adj* : indirecto

vice ['vaɪs] *n* : vicio *m*

vice president *n* : vicepresidente *m*, -ta *f*

vice versa [ˌvaɪsɪ'vərsə, ˌvaɪs'vər-] *adv* : viceversa

vicinity [və'sɪnəṭi] *n, pl* **-ties 1** : inmediaciones *fpl* **2 in the ~ of** ABOUT : alrededor de

vicious ['vɪʃəs] *adj* **1** SAVAGE : feroz **2** MALICIOUS : malicioso

victim ['vɪktəm] *n* : víctima *f*

victor ['vɪktər] *n* : vencedor *m*, -dora *f*

victory ['vɪktəri] *n, pl* **-ries** : victoria *f* — **victorious** [vɪk'to:riəs] *adj* : victorioso

video ['vɪdiˌo:] *n* : video *m*, vídeo *m Spain* — ~ *adj* : de video — **videocassette** [ˌvɪdioka'sɛt] *n* : videocasete *m* — **videotape** ['vɪdioˌteɪp] *n* : videocinta *f* — ~ *vt* **-taped; -taping** : videograbar

vie ['vaɪ] *vi* **vied; vying** ['vaɪɪŋ] : competir

Vietnamese [viˌɛtnə'mi:z, -'mi:s] *adj* : vietnamita

view ['vju:] *n* **1** : vista *f* **2** OPINION : opinión *f* **3 come into ~** : aparecer **4 in ~ of** : en vista de (que) — ~ *vt* **1** : ver **2** CONSIDER : considerar — **viewer** ['vju:ər] *n or* **television ~** : televidente *mf* — **viewpoint** ['vju:ˌpɔɪnt] *n* : punto *m* de vista

vigil ['vɪdʒəl] *n* : vela *f* — **vigilance** ['vɪdʒələnts] *n* : vigilancia *f* — **vigilant** ['vɪdʒələnt] *adj* : vigilante

vigor *or Brit* **vigour** ['vɪgər] *n* : vigor *m* — **vigorous** ['vɪgərəs] *adj* **1** : enérgico **2** ROBUST : vigoroso

Viking ['vaɪkɪŋ] *n* : vikingo *m*, -ga *f*

vile ['vaɪl] *adj* **viler; vilest 1** : vil **2** REVOLTING : asqueroso **3** TERRIBLE : horrible

villa ['vɪlə] *n* : casa *f* de campo

village ['vɪlɪdʒ] *n* : pueblo *m* (grande), aldea *f* (pequeña) — **villager** ['vɪlɪdʒər] *n* : vecino *m*, -na *f* (de un pueblo); aldeano *m*, -na *f* (de una aldea)

villain ['vɪlən] *n* : villano *m*, -na *f*

vindicate ['vɪndəˌkeɪt] *vt* **-cated; -cating 1** : vindicar **2** JUSTIFY : justificar

vindictive [vɪn'dɪktɪv] *adj* : vengativo

vine ['vaɪn] *n* **1** : enredadera *f* **2** GRAPEVINE : vid *f*

vinegar ['vɪnɪgər] *n* : vinagre *m*

vineyard ['vɪnjərd] *n* : viña *f*, viñedo *m*

vintage ['vɪntɪdʒ] *n* **1** : cosecha *f* (de vino) **2** ERA : época *f* — ~ *adj* **1** : añejo (dícese de un vino) **2** CLASSIC : de época

vinyl ['vaɪnəl] *n* : vinilo

viola [vi:'o:lə] *n* : viola *f*

violate ['vaɪəˌleɪt] *vt* **-lated; -lating** : violar — **violation** [ˌvaɪə'leɪʃən] *n* : violación *f*

violence ['vaɪlənts, 'vaɪə-] *n* : violencia *f* — **violent** ['vaɪlənt, 'vaɪə-] *adj* : violento

violet ['vaɪlət, 'vaɪə-] *n* : violeta *f* (flor), violeta *m* (color)

violin [ˌvaɪə'lɪn] *n* : violín *m* — **violinist** [ˌvaɪə'lɪnɪst] *n* : violinista *mf* — **violoncello** [ˌvaɪələn'tʃɛlo:, ˌvi:-] → **cello**

VIP [ˌvi:ˌaɪ'pi:] *n, pl* **VIPs** [-'pi:z] : VIP *mf*

viper ['vaɪpər] *n* : víbora *f*

virgin ['vərdʒən] *n* : virgen *mf* — ~ *adj* **1** : virgen (dícese de la lana, etc.) **2** CHASTE : virginal — **virginity** [vər'dʒɪnəṭi] *n* : virginidad *f*

virile ['vɪrəl, -ˌaɪl] *adj* : viril — **virility** [və'rɪləṭi] *n* : virilidad *f*

virtual ['vərtʃuəl] *adj* : virtual — **virtually** ['vərtʃuəli, 'vərtʃəli] *adv* : prácticamente

virtue ['vərˌtʃu:] *n* **1** : virtud *f* **2 by ~ of** : en virtud de

virtuoso [ˌvərtʃʊ'o:so:, -zo:] *n, pl* **-sos** *or* **-si** [-ˌsi:, -ˌzi:] : virtuoso *m*, -sa *f*

virtuous ['vərtʃʊəs] *adj* : virtuoso

virulent ['vɪrələnt, 'vɪrjə-] *adj* : virulento

virus ['vaɪrəs] *n* : virus *m*

visa ['vi:zə, -sə] *n* : visado *m*, visa *f Lat*

vis-à-vis [ˌvi:zə'vi:, -sə-] *prep* : con respecto a

viscous ['vɪskəs] *adj* : viscoso

vise ['vaɪs] *n* : torno *m* de banco

visible ['vɪzəbəl] *adj* **1** : visible **2** NOTICEABLE : evidente — **visibility** [ˌvɪzə'bɪləṭi] *n, pl* **-ties** : visibilidad *f*

vision ['vɪʒən] *n* **1** : visión *f* **2 have ~s of** : imaginarse — **visionary** ['vɪʒəˌnɛri] *adj* : visionario — ~ *n, pl* **-ries** : visionario *m*, -ria *f*

visit ['vɪzət] *vt* : visitar — *vi* **1** : hacer una visita **2 be ~ing** : estar de visita — ~ *n* : visita *f* — **visitor** ['vɪzəṭər] *n* **1** : visitante *mf* **2** GUEST : visita *f*

visor ['vaɪzər] *n* : visera *f*

vista ['vɪstə] *n* : vista *f*

visual ['vɪʒuəl] *adj* : visual — **visualize** ['vɪʒuəˌlaɪz] *vt* **-ized; -izing** : visualizar

vital ['vaɪṭəl] *adj* **1** : vital **2** CRUCIAL : esencial — **vitality** [vaɪ'tæləṭi] *n, pl* **-ties** : vitalidad *f*, energía *f*

vitamin ['vaɪṭəmən] *n* : vitamina *f*

vivacious [və'veɪʃəs, vaɪ-] *adj* : vivaz, animado

vivid ['vɪvəd] *adj* : vivo (dícese de colores), vívido (dícese de sueños, etc.)

vocabulary [vo:'kæbjəˌlɛri] *n, pl* **-laries** : vocabulario *m*

vocal ['vo:kəl] *adj* **1** : vocal **2** OUTSPOKEN : vociferante — **vocal cords** *npl* : cuerdas *fpl* vocales — **vocalist** ['vo:kəlɪst] *n* : cantante *mf*, vocalista *mf*

vocation [vo'keɪʃən] *n* : vocación *f* — **vocational** [vo'keɪʃənəl] *adj* : profesional

vociferous [vo'sɪfərəs] *adj* : vociferante, ruidoso

vodka ['vɑdkə] *n* : vodka *m*

vogue ['vo:g] *n* **1** : moda *f*, boga *f* **2 be in ~** : estar de moda, estar en boga

voice ['vɔɪs] *n* : voz *f* — ~ *vt* **voiced; voicing** : expresar

void ['vɔɪd] *adj* **1** INVALID : nulo **2 ~ of** : falto de — ~ *n* : vacío *m* — ~ *vt* : anular

volatile ['vɑləṭəl] *adj* : volátil — **volatility** [ˌvɑlə'tɪləṭi] *n* : volatilidad *f*

volcano [vɑl'keɪˌno:] *n, pl* **-noes** *or* **-nos** : volcán *m* — **volcanic** [vɑl'kænɪk] *adj* : volcánico

volition [vo'lɪʃən] *n* **of one's own ~** : por voluntad propia

volley ['vɑli] *n, pl* **-leys 1** : descarga *f* (de tiros) **2** : torrente *m* (de insultos, etc.) **3** : volea *f* (en deportes) — **volleyball** ['vɑliˌbɔl] *n* : voleibol *m*

volt ['vo:lt] *n* : voltio *m* — **voltage** ['vo:ltɪdʒ] *n* : voltaje *m*

voluble ['vɑljəbəl] *adj* : locuaz

volume ['vɑljəm, -ju:m] *n* : volumen *m* — **voluminous** [və'lu:mənəs] *adj* : voluminoso

voluntary ['vɑlənˌtɛri] *adj* : voluntario — **volunteer** [ˌvɑlən'tɪr] *n* : voluntario *m*, -ria *f* — ~ *vt* : ofrecer — *vi* — **to** : ofrecerse a

voluptuous [və'lʌptʃʊəs] *adj* : voluptuoso

vomit ['vɑmət] *n* : vómito *m* — ~ *v* : vomitar

voracious [vɔ'reɪʃəs, və-] *adj* : voraz

vote ['vo:t] *n* **1** : voto *m* **2** SUFFRAGE : derecho *m* al voto — ~ *vi* **voted; voting** : votar — **voter** ['vo:ṭər] *n* : votante *mf* — **voting** ['vo:ṭɪŋ] *n* : votación *f*

vouch ['vaʊtʃ] *vi* **~ for** : responder de (algo), responder por (algn) — **voucher** ['vaʊtʃər] *n* : vale *m*

vow ['vaʊ] *n* : voto *m* — ~ *vt* : jurar

vowel ['vaʊəl] *n* : vocal *m*

voyage ['vɔɪɪdʒ] *n* : viaje *m*

vulgar ['vʌlgər] *adj* **1** COMMON : ordinario **2** CRUDE : grosero, vulgar — **vulgarity** [ˌvʌl'gærəṭi] *n, pl* **-ties** : vulgaridad *f*

vulnerable ['vʌlnərəbəl] *adj* : vulnerable — **vulnerability** [ˌvʌlnərə'bɪləṭi] *n, pl* **-ties** : vulnerabilidad *f*

vulture ['vʌltʃər] *n* : buitre *m*

vying → **vie**

W

w ['dʌbəlˌju:] *n, pl* **w's** *or* **ws** [-ˌju:z] : w *f*, vigésima tercera letra del alfabeto inglés

wad ['wɑd] *n* : taco *m* (de papel, etc.), fajo *m* (de billetes)

waddle ['wɑdəl] *vi* **-dled; -dling** : andar como un pato

wade ['weɪd] *v* **waded; wading** *vi* : caminar por el agua — *vt or* **~ across** : vadear

wafer ['weɪfər] *n* : barquillo *m*

waffle ['wɑfəl] *n* : gofre *m Spain*, wafle *m Lat*

waft ['wɑft, 'wæft] *vt* : llevar por el aire — *vi* : flotar

wag ['wæg] *v* **wagged; wagging** *vt* : menear — *vi* : menearse

wage ['weɪdʒ] *n or* **wages** *npl* : salario *m* — ~ *vt* **waged; waging ~ war** : hacer la guerra

wager ['weɪdʒər] *n* : apuesta *f* — ~ *v* : apostar

wagon ['wægən] *n* **1** CART : carrito *m* **2** → **station wagon**

waif ['weɪf] *n* : niño *m* abandonado

wail ['weɪl] *vi* : lamentarse — ~ *n* : lamento *m*

waist ['weɪst] *n* : cintura *f* — **waistline** ['weɪstˌlaɪn] *n* : cintura *f*

wait ['weɪt] *vi* : esperar — *vt* **1** AWAIT : esperar **2 ~ tables** : servir a la mesa — ~ *n* **1** : espera *f* **2 lie in ~** : estar al acecho — **waiter** ['weɪṭər] *n* : camarero *m*, mozo *m Lat* — **waiting room** *n* : sala *f* de espera — **waitress** ['weɪtrəs] *n* : camarera *f*, moza *f Lat*

waive ['weɪv] *vt* **waived; waiving** : renunciar a — **waiver** ['weɪvər] *n* : renuncia *f*

wake[1] ['weɪk] *v* **woke** ['wo:k]; **woken** ['wo:kən] *or* **waked; waking** *vi or* **~ up** : despertarse — *vt* : despertar — ~ *n* : velatorio *m* (de un difunto)

wake[2] *n* **1** : estela *f* (de un barco) **2 in the ~ of** : tras, como consecuencia de

waken ['weɪkən] *vt* : despertar — *vi* : despertarse

walk ['wɔk] *vi* **1** : caminar, andar **2** STROLL : pasear **3 too far to ~** : demasiado lejos para ir a pie — *vt* **1** : caminar por **2** : sacar a pasear (a un perro) — ~ *n* **1** : paseo *m* **2** PATH : camino *m* **3** GAIT : andar *m* — **walker** ['wɔkər] *n* **1** : paseante *mf* **2** HIKER : excursionista *mf* — **walking stick** *n* : bastón *m* — **walkout** ['wɔkˌaʊt] *n* STRIKE : huelga *f* — **walk out** *vi* **1** STRIKE : declararse en huelga **2** LEAVE : salir, irse **3 ~ on** : abandonar

wall ['wɔl] *n* : muro *m* (exterior), pared *f* (interior), muralla *f* (de una ciudad)

wallet ['wɑlət] *n* : billetera *f*, cartera *f*

wallflower ['wɔlˌflaʊər] *n* **be a ~** : comer pavo

wallop ['wɑləp] *vt* : pegar fuerte — ~ *n* : golpe *m* fuerte

wallow ['wɑˌlo:] *vi* : revolcarse

wallpaper ['wɔlˌpeɪpər] *n* : papel *m* pintado — ~ *vt* : empapelar

walnut ['wɔlˌnʌt] *n* : nuez *f*

walrus ['wɔlrəs, 'wɑl-] *n, pl* **-rus** *or* **-ruses** : morsa *f*

waltz ['wɔlts] *n* : vals *m* — ~ *vi* : valsar

wan ['wɑn] *adj* **wanner; -est** : pálido

wand ['wɑnd] *n* : varita *f* (mágica)

wander ['wɑndər] *vi* **1** : vagar, pasear **2** STRAY : divagar — *vt* : pasear por — **wanderer** ['wɑndərər] *n* : vagabundo *m*, -da *f* — **wanderlust** ['wɑndərˌlʌst] *n* : pasión *f* por viajar

wane ['weɪn] *vi* **waned; waning** : menguar — ~ *n* **be on the ~** : estar disminuyendo

want ['wɑnt, 'wɔnt] *vt* **1** DESIRE : querer **2** NEED : necesitar **3** LACK : carecer de — ~ *n* **1** NEED : necesidad *f* **2** LACK : falta *f* **3** DESIRE : deseo *m* — **wanting** ['wɑntɪŋ, 'wɔn-] *adj* **be ~** : carecer

wanton ['wɑntən, 'wɔn-] *adj* **1** LEWD : lascivo **2 ~ cruelty** : crueldad *f* despiadada

war ['wɔr] *n* : guerra *f*

ward ['wɔrd] *n* **1** : sala *f* (de un hospital, etc.) **2** : distrito *m* electoral **3** : pupilo *m*, -la *f* (de un tutor, etc.) — ~ *vt* **~ off** : protegerse contra — **warden** ['wɔrdən] *n* **1** : guardián *m*, -diana *f* **2** *or* **game ~** : guardabosque *mf* **3** *or* **prison ~** : alcaide *m*

wardrobe ['wɔrdˌro:b] *n* **1** CLOSET : armario *m* **2** CLOTHES : vestuario *m*

warehouse ['wærˌhaʊs] *n* : almacén *m*,

bodega *f Lat* — **wares** ['wærz] *npl* : mercancías *fpl*

warfare ['wɔr,fær] *n* : guerra *f*

warily ['wærəli] *adv* : cautelosamente

warlike ['wær,laɪk] *adj* : belicoso

warm ['wɔrm] *adj* **1** : caliente **2** LUKEWARM : tibio **3** CARING : cariñoso **4 I feel ~** : tengo calor **5 ~ clothes** : ropa *f* de abrigo — **~** *vt or* **~ up** : calentar — *vi* **1** *or* **~ up** : calentarse **2 ~ to** : tomar simpatía a (algn), entusiasmarse con (algo) — **warm–blooded** ['wɔrm'blʌdəd] *adj* : de sangre caliente — **warmhearted** ['wɔrm'hɑrṭəd] *adj* : cariñoso — **warmly** ['wɔrmli] *adv* **1** : calurosamente **2 dress ~** : abrigarse — **warmth** ['wɔrmpθ] *n* **1** : calor *m* **2** AFFECTION : cariño *m*, afecto *m*

warn ['wɔrn] *vt* : advertir, avisar— **warning** ['wɔrnɪŋ] *n* : advertencia *f*, aviso *m*

warp ['wɔrp] *vt* **1** : alabear (madera, etc.) **2** DISTORT : deformar — *vi* : alabearse

warrant ['wɔrənt] *n* **1** : autorización *f* **2 arrest ~** : orden *f* judicial — **~** *vt* : justificar — **warranty** ['wɔrənti, ˌwɔrən'ti:] *n, pl* **-ties** : garantía *f*

warrior ['wɔriər] *n* : guerrero *m*, -ra *f*

warship ['wɔr,ʃɪp] *n* : buque *m* de guerra

wart ['wɔrt] *n* : verruga *f*

wartime ['wɔr,taɪm] *n* : tiempo *m* de guerra

wary ['wæri] *adj* **warier; -est** : cauteloso

was → **be**

wash ['wɔʃ, 'wɑʃ] *vt* **1** : lavar(se) **2** CARRY : arrastrar **3 ~ away** : llevarse **4 ~ over** : bañar — *vi* : lavarse — **~** *n* **1** : lavado *m* **2** LAUNDRY : ropa *f* sucia — **washable** ['wɔʃəbəl, 'wɑ-] *adj* : lavable — **washcloth** ['wɔʃ,klɔθ, 'wɑʃ-] *n* : toallita *f* (para lavarse) — **washed–out** ['wɔʃt'aʊt, 'wɑʃt-] *adj* **1** : desvaído (dícese de colores) **2** EXHAUSTED : agotado — **washer** ['wɔʃər, 'wɑ-] *n* **1** → **washing machine 2** : arandela *f* (de una llave, etc.) — **washing machine** *n* : máquina *f* de lavar, lavadora *f* — **washroom** ['wɔʃ,ru:m, 'wɑʃ-, -ˌrʊm] *n* : servicios *mpl* (públicos), baño *m*

wasn't ['wʌzənt] (*contraction of* **was not**) → **be**

wasp ['wɑsp] *n* : avispa *f*

waste ['weɪst] *v* **wasted; wasting** *vt* **1** : desperdiciar, derrochar, malgastar **2 ~ time** : perder tiempo — *vi or* **~ away** : consumirse — **~** *adj* : de desecho — **~** *n* **1** : derroche *m*, desperdicio *m* **2** RUBBISH : desechos *mpl* **3 a ~ of time** : una pérdida de tiempo — **wastebasket** ['weɪst,bæskət] *n* : papelera *f* — **wasteful** ['weɪstfəl] *adj* : derrochador — **wasteland** ['weɪst,lænd, -lənd] *n* : yermo *m*

watch ['wɑtʃ] *vi* **1** : mirar **2** *or* **keep ~** : velar **3 ~ out!** : ¡ten cuidado!, ¡ojo! — *vt* **1**: mirar **2** *or* **~ over** : vigilar, cuidar **3 ~ what you do** : ten cuidado con lo que haces — **~** *n* **1** reloj *m* **2** SURVEILLANCE : vigilancia *f* **3** LOOKOUT : guardia *mf* — **watchdog** ['wɑtʃ,dɔg] *n* : perro *m* guardián — **watchful** ['wɑtʃfəl] *adj* : vigilante — **watchman** ['wɑtʃmən] *n, pl* **-men** [-mən, -ˌmɛn] : vigilante *m*, guarda *m* — **watchword** ['wɑtʃ,wərd] *n* : santo *m* y seña

water ['wɔṭər, 'wɑ-] *n* : agua *f* — **~** *vt* **1** : regar (el jardín, etc.) **2 ~ down** DILUTE : diluir, aguar — *vi* **1** : lagrimar (dícese de los ojos) **2 my mouth is ~ing** : se me hace agua la boca — **watercolor** ['wɔṭər,kʌlər, 'wɑ-] *n* : acuarela *f* — **watercress** ['wɔṭər,krɛs, 'wɑ-] *n* : berro *m* — **waterfall** ['wɔṭər,fɔl, 'wɑ-] *n* : cascada *f*, salto *m* de agua — **water lily** *n* : nenúfar *m* — **waterlogged** ['wɔṭər,lɔgd, 'wɑṭər,lɑgd] *adj* : lleno de agua, empapado — **watermelon** ['wɔṭər,mɛlən, 'wɑ-] *n* : sandía *f* — **waterpower** ['wɔṭər,paʊər, 'wɑ-] *n* : energía *f* hidráulica — **waterproof** ['wɔṭər,pru:f, 'wɑ-] *adj* : impermeable — **watershed** ['wɔṭər,ʃɛd, 'wɑ-] *n* **1** : cuenca *f* (de un río) **2** : momento *m* crítico — **waterskiing** ['wɔṭər,ski:ɪŋ, 'wɑ-] *n* : esquí *m* acuático — **watertight** ['wɔṭər,taɪt, 'wɑ-] *adj* : hermético — **waterway** ['wɔṭər,weɪ, 'wɑ-] *n* : vía *f* navegable — **waterworks** ['wɔṭər,wərks, 'wɑ-] *npl* : central *f* de abastecimiento de agua — **watery** ['wɔṭəri, 'wɑ-] *adj* **1** : acuoso **2** DILUTED : aguado, diluido **3** WASHED-OUT : desvaído (dícese de colores)

watt ['wɑt] *n* : vatio *m* — **wattage** ['wɑṭɪdʒ] *n* : vataje *m*

wave ['weɪv] *v* **waved; waving** *vi* **1** : saludar con la mano **2** : flotar (dícese de una bandera) — *vt* **1** SHAKE : agitar **2** CURL : ondular **3** SIGNAL : hacer señas a (con la mano) — **~** *n* **1** : ola *f* (de agua) **2** CURL : onda *f* **3** : onda *f* (en física) **4** : señal *f* (con la mano) **5** SURGE : oleada *f* — **wavelength** ['weɪv,lɛŋkθ] *n* : longitud *f* de onda

waver ['weɪvər] *vi* : vacilar

wax[1] ['wæks] *vi* : crecer (dícese de la luna)

wax[2] *n* : cera *f* (para pisos, etc.) — **~** *vt* : encerar — **waxy** ['wæksi] *adj* **waxier; -est** : ceroso

way ['weɪ] *n* **1** : camino *m* **2** MEANS : manera *f*, modo *m* **3 by the ~** : a propósito, por cierto **4 by ~ of** : vía, pasando por **5 come a long ~** : hacer grandes progresos **6 get in the ~** : meterse en el camino **7 get one's own ~** : salirse uno con la suya **8 mend one's ~s** : dejar las malas costumbres **9 out of the ~** REMOTE : remoto, recóndito **10 which ~ did he go?** : ¿por dónde fue?

we ['wi:] *pron* : nosotros, nosotras

weak ['wi:k] *adj* **1** : débil **2** DILUTED : aguado **3 a ~ excuse** : una excusa poco convincente — **weaken** ['wi:kən] *vt* : debilitar — *vi* : debilitarse — **weakling** ['wi:klɪŋ] *n* : debilucho *m*, -cha *f* — **weakly** ['wi:kli] *adv* : débilmente — **~** *adj* **weaklier; -est** : enfermizo — **weakness** ['wi:knəs] *n* **1** : debilidad *f* **2** FLAW : flaqueza *f*, punto *m* débil

wealth ['wɛlθ] *n* : riqueza *f* — **wealthy** ['wɛlθi] *adj* **wealthier; -est** : rico

wean ['wi:n] *vt* : destetar

weapon ['wɛpən] *n* : arma *f*

wear ['wær] *v* **wore** ['wor]; **worn** ['worn]; **wearing** *vt* **1** : llevar (ropa, etc.), calzar (zapatos) **2** *or* **~ away** : desgastar **3 ~ oneself out** : agotarse **4 ~ out** : gastar — *vi* **1** LAST : durar **2 ~ off** : desaparecer **3 ~ out** : gastarse — **~** *n* **1** USE : uso *m* **2** CLOTHING : ropa *f* **3 be the worse for ~** : estar deteriorado — **wear and tear** *n* : desgaste *m*

weary ['wɪri] *adj* **-rier; -est** : cansado — **~** *v* **-ried; -rying** *vt* : cansar — *vi* : cansarse — **weariness** ['wɪrinəs] *n* : cansancio *m* — **wearisome** ['wɪrisəm] *adj* : cansado

weasel ['wi:zəl] *n* : comadreja *f*

weather ['wɛðər] *n* : tiempo *m* — **~** *vt* **1** WEAR : erosionar, desgastar **2** ENDURE, OVERCOME : superar — **weather–beaten** ['wɛðər,bi:tən] *adj* : curtido — **weatherman** ['wɛðər,mæn] *n, pl* **-men** [-mən, -ˌmɛn] : meteorólogo *m*, -ga *f* — **weather vane** *n* : veleta *f*

weave ['wi:v] *v* **wove** ['wo:v] *or* **weaved; woven** ['wo:vən] *or* **weaved; weaving** *vt* **1** : tejer (tela) **2** INTERLACE : entretejer **3 ~ one's way** : abrirse camino — *vi* : tejer — **~** *n* : tejido *m* — **weaver** ['wi:vər] *n* : tejedor *m*, -dora *f*

web ['wɛb] *n* **1** : telaraña *f* (de araña) **2** : membrana *f* interdigital (de aves) **3** NETWORK : red *f*

wed ['wɛd] *v* **wedded; wedding** *vt* : casarse con — *vi* : casarse

we'd ['wi:d] (*contraction of* **we had, we should,** *or* **we would**) → **have, should, would**

wedding ['wɛdɪŋ] *n* : boda *f*, casamiento *m*

wedge ['wɛdʒ] *n* **1** : cuña *f* **2** PIECE : porción *f*, trozo *m* — **~** *vt* **wedged; wedging 1** : apretar (con una cuña) **2** CRAM : meter

Wednesday ['wɛnz,deɪ, -di] *n* : miércoles *m*

wee ['wi:] *adj* **1** : pequeñito **2 in the ~ hours** : a las altas horas

weed ['wi:d] *n* : mala hierba *f* — **~** *vt* **1** : desherbar **2 ~ out** : eliminar

week ['wi:k] *n* : semana *f* — **weekday** ['wi:k,deɪ] *n* : día *m* laborable — **weekend** ['wi:k,ɛnd] *n* : fin *m* de semana — **weekly** ['wi:kli] *adv* : semanalmente — **~** *adj* : semanal — **~** *n, pl* **-lies** : semanario *m*

weep ['wi:p] *v* **wept** ['wɛpt]; **weeping** : llorar — **weeping willow** *n* : sauce *m* llorón — **weepy** ['wi:pi] *adj* **weepier; -est** : lloroso

weigh ['weɪ] *vt* **1** : pesar **2** CONSIDER : sopesar **3 ~ down** : sobrecargar (con una carga), abrumar (con preocupaciones, etc.) — *vi* : pesar

weight ['weɪt] *n* **1** : peso *m* **2 gain ~** : engordar **3 lose ~** : adelgazar — **weighty** ['weɪṭi] *adj* **weightier; -est 1** HEAVY : pesado **2** IMPORTANT : importante, de peso

weird ['wɪrd] *adj* **1** : misterioso **2** STRANGE : extraño

welcome ['wɛlkəm] *vt* **-comed; -coming** : dar la bienvenida a, recibir — **~** *adj* **1** : bienvenido **2 you're ~** : de nada — **~** *n* : bienvenida *f*, acojida *f*

weld ['wɛld] *v* : soldar

welfare ['wɛl,fær] *n* **1** WELL-BEING : bienestar *m* **2** AID : asistencia *f* social

well[1] ['wɛl] *adv* **better** ['bɛṭər]; **best** ['bɛst] **1** : bien **2** CONSIDERABLY : bastante **3 as ~** : también **4 as ~ as** : además de — **~** *adj* : bien — **~** *interj* **1** (*used to introduce a remark*) : bueno **2** (*used to express surprise*) : ¡vaya!

well[2] *n* : pozo *m* — **~** *vi or* **~ up** : brotar, manar

we'll ['wi:l, wɪl] (*contraction of* **we shall** *or* **we will**) → **shall, will**

well–being ['wɛl'bi:ɪŋ] *n* : bienestar *m* — **well–bred** ['wɛl'brɛd] *adj* : fino, bien educado — **well–done** ['wɛl'dʌn] *adj* **1** : bien hecho **2** : bien cocido (dícese de la carne, etc.) — **well–known** ['wɛl'no:n] *adj* : famoso, bien conocido — **well–meaning** ['wɛl'mi:nɪŋ] *adj* : bienintencionado — **well–off** ['wɛl'ɔf] *adj* : acomodado — **well–rounded** ['wɛl'raʊndəd] *adj* : completo — **well–to–do** [,wɛltə'du:] *adj* : próspero, adinerado

Welsh ['wɛlʃ] *adj* : galés — **~** *n* **1** : galés *m* (idioma) **2 the ~** : los galeses

went → **go**

wept → **weep**

were → **be**

we're ['wɪr, 'wər, 'wi:ər] (*contraction of* **we are**) → **be**

weren't ['wərənt, 'wərnt] (*contraction of* **were not**) → **be**

west ['wɛst] *adv* : al oeste — **~** *adj* : oeste, del oeste — **~** *n* **1** : oeste *m* **2 the West** : el Oeste, el Occidente — **westerly** ['wɛstərli] *adv & adj* : del oeste — **western** ['wɛstərn] *adj* **1** : del oeste **2 Western** : occidental — **Westerner** ['wɛstərnər] *n* : habitante *mf* del oeste — **westward** ['wɛstwərd] *adv & adj* : hacia el oeste

wet ['wɛt] *adj* **wetter; wettest 1** : mojado **2** RAINY : lluvioso **3 ~ paint** : pintura *f* fresca — **~** *vt* **wet** *or* **wetted; wetting** : mojar, humedecer

we've ['wi:v] (*contraction of* **we have**) → **have**

whack ['hwæk] *vt* : golpear fuertemente — **~** *n* : golpe *m* fuerte

whale ['hweɪl] *n, pl* **whales** *or* **whale** : ballena *f*

wharf ['hwɔrf] *n, pl* **wharves** ['hwɔrvz] : muelle *m*, embarcadero *m*

what ['hwɑt, 'hwʌt] *adj* **1** (*used in questions and exclamations*) : qué **2** WHATEVER : cualquier — **~** *pron* **1** (*used in questions*) : qué **2** (*used in indirect statements*) : lo que, que **3 ~ does it cost?** : ¿cuánto cuesta? **4 ~ for?** : ¿por qué? **5 ~ if** : y si — **whatever** [hwɑṭ'ɛvər, 'hwʌṭ-] *adj* **1** : cualquier **2 there's no chance ~** : no hay ninguna posibilidad **3 nothing ~** : nada en absoluto — **~** *pron* **1** ANYTHING : lo que **2** (*used in questions*) : qué **3 ~ it may be** : sea lo que sea — **whatsoever** [,hwɑtso'ɛvər, 'hwʌṭ-] *adj & pron* → **whatever**

wheat ['hwi:t] *n* : trigo *m*

wheedle ['hwi:dəl] *vt* **-dled; -dling** : engatusar

wheel ['hwi:l] *n* **1** : rueda *f* **2** *or* **steering ~** : volante *m* (de automóviles, etc.), timón *m* (de barcos) — **~** *vt* : empujar (algo sobre ruedas) — *vi or* **~ around** : darse la vuelta — **wheelbarrow** ['hwi:l,bær,o:] *n* : carretilla *f* — **wheelchair** ['hwi:l,tʃær] *n* : silla *f* de ruedas

wheeze ['hwi:z] *vi* **wheezed; wheezing** : resollar — **~** *n* : resuello *m*

when ['hwɛn] *adv* : cuándo — **~** *conj* **1** : cuando **2 the days ~ I clean the house** : los días (en) que limpio la casa — **~** *pron* : cuándo — **whenever** [hwɛn'ɛvər] *adv* : cuando sea — **~** *conj* **1** : cada vez que **2 ~ you like** : cuando quieras

where ['hwɛr] *adv* **1** : dónde **2 ~ are you going?** : ¿adónde vas? — **~** *conj & pron* : donde — **whereabouts** ['hwɛrə,baʊts] *adv* : (por) dónde — **~** *ns & pl* : paradero *m* — **wherever** [hwɛr'ɛvər] *adv* **1** : en cualquier parte **2** WHERE : dónde, adónde — **~** *conj* : dondequiera que

whet ['hwɛt] *vt* **whetted; whetting 1** : afilar **2 ~ the appetite** : estimular el apetito

whether ['hwɛðər] *conj* **1** : si **2 we doubt ~ he'll show up** : dudamos que aparezca **3 ~ you like it or not** : tanto si quieras como si no

which ['hwɪtʃ] *adj* **1** : qué, cuál **2 in ~ case** : en cuyo caso — **~** *pron* **1** (*used in questions*) : cuál **2** (*used in relative clauses*) : que, el (la) cual — **whichever** [hwɪtʃ'ɛvər] *adj* : cualquier — **~** *pron* : el (la) que, cualquiera que

whiff ['hwɪf] *n* **1** PUFF : soplo *m* **2** SMELL : olorcillo *m*

while ['hwaɪl] *n* **1** : rato *m* **2 be worth one's ~** : valer la pena **3 in a ~** : dentro de poco — **~** *conj* **1** : mientras **2** WHEREAS : mientras que **3** ALTHOUGH : aunque — **~** *vt* **whiled; whiling ~ away the time** : matar el tiempo

whim ['hwɪm] *n* : capricho *m*, antojo *m*

whimper ['hwɪmpər] *vi* : lloriquear— **~** *n* : quejido *m*

whimsical ['hwɪmzɪkəl] *adj* : caprichoso, fantasioso

whine ['hwaɪn] *vi* **whined; whining 1** : gimotear **2** COMPLAIN : quejarse — **~** *n* : quejido *m*, gemido *m*

whip ['hwɪp] *v* **whipped; whipping** *vt* **1** : azotar **2** BEAT : batir (huevos, crema, etc.) **3 ~ up** AROUSE : avivar, despertar — *vi* FLAP : agitarse — **~** *n* : látigo *m*

whir ['hwər] *vi* **whirred; whirring** : zumbar — **~** *n* : zumbido *m*

whirl ['hwərl] *vi* **1** : dar vueltas, girar **2** *or* **~ about** : arremolinarse — **~** *n* **1** : giro *m* **2** SWIRL : torbellino *m* — **whirlpool** ['hwərl,pu:l] *n* : remolino *m* — **whirlwind** ['hwərl,wɪnd] *n* : torbellino *m*

whisk ['hwɪsk] *vt* **1** : batir **2 ~ away** : llevarse — **~** *n or* **egg ~** : batidor *m* — **whisk broom** *n* : escobilla *f*

whisker ['hwɪskər] *n* **1** : pelo *m* (de la barba) **2 ~s** *npl* : bigotes *mpl* (de animales)

whiskey *or* **whisky** ['hwɪski] *n, pl* **-keys** *or* **-kies** : whisky *m*

whisper ['hwɪspər] *vi* : cuchichear, susurrar — *vt* : susurrar — **~** *n* : susurro *m*

whistle ['hwɪsəl] *v* **-tled; -tling** *vi* **1** : silbar, chiflar *Lat* **2** : pitar (dícese de un tren, etc.) — *vt* : silbar — **~** *n* **1** : silbido *m*, chiflido *m* (sonido) **2** : silbato *m*, pito *m* (instrumento)

white ['hwaɪt] *adj* **whiter; -est** : blanco — **~** *n* **1** : blanco *m* (color) **2** : clara *f* (de huevos) **3** *or* **~ person** : blanco *m*, -ca *f* — **white–collar** ['hwaɪt'kɑlər] *adj* **1** : de oficina **2 ~ worker** : oficinista *mf* — **whiten** ['hwaɪtən] *vt* : blanquear — **whiteness** ['hwaɪtnəs] *n* : blancura *f* — **whitewash** ['hwaɪt,wɔʃ] *vt* **1** : enjalbegar **2** CONCEAL : encubrir (un escándalo, etc.) — **~** *n* **1** : jalbegue *m*, lechada *f* **2** COVER-UP : encubrimiento *m*

whittle ['hwɪṭəl] *vt* **-tled; -tling 1** : tallar (madera) **2** *or* **~ down** : reducir

whiz *or* **whizz** ['hwɪz] *vi* **whizzed; whizzing 1** BUZZ : zumbar **2 ~ by** : pasar muy rápido — **~** *or* **whizz** *n, pl* **whizzes** : zumbido *m* — **whiz kid** *n* : joven *m* prometedor

who ['hu:] *pron* **1** (*used in direct and indirect questions*) : quién **2** (*used in relative clauses*) : que, quien — **whodunit** [hu:'dʌnɪt] *n* : novela *f* policíaca — **whoever** [hu:'ɛvər] *pron* **1** : quienquiera que, quien **2** (*used in questions*) : quién

whole ['ho:l] *adj* **1** : entero **2** INTACT : intacto **3 a ~ lot** : muchísimo — **~** *n* **1** : todo *m* **2 as a ~** : en conjunto **3 on the ~** : en general — **wholehearted** ['ho:l'hɑrṭəd] *adj* : sincero — **wholesale** ['ho:l,seɪl] *n* : venta *f* al por mayor — **~** *adj* **1** : al por mayor **2 ~ slaughter** : matanza *f* sistemática — **~** *adv* : al por mayor — **wholesaler** ['ho:l,seɪlər] *n* : mayorista *mf* — **wholesome** ['ho:lsəm] *adj* : sano — **whole wheat** *adj* : de trigo integral — **wholly** ['ho:li] *adv* : completamente

whom ['hu:m] *pron* **1** (*used in direct questions*) : a quién **2** (*used in indirect questions*) : de quién, con quién, en quién **3** (*used in relative clauses*) : que, a quien

whooping cough *n* : tos *f* ferina

whore ['hor] *n* : puta *f*

whose ['hu:z] *adj* **1** (*used in questions*) : de quién **2** (*used in relative clauses*) : cuyo — **~** *pron* : de quién

why ['hwaɪ] *adv* : por qué — **~** *n, pl* **whys** : porqué *m* — **~** *conj* : por qué — **~** *interj* (*used to express surprise*) : ¡vaya!, ¡mira!

wick ['wɪk] *n* : mecha *f*

wicked ['wɪkəd] *adj* **1** : malo, malvado **2** MISCHIEVOUS : travieso **3** TERRIBLE : terrible, horrible — **wickedness** ['wɪkədnəs] *n* : maldad *f*

wicker ['wɪkər] *n* : mimbre *m* — **~** *adj* : de mimbre

wide ['waɪd] *adj* **wider; widest 1** : ancho **2** VAST : amplio, extenso **3** *or* **~ of the mark** : desviado — **~** *adv* **1 ~ apart** : muy separados **2 far and ~** : por todas partes **3 ~ open** : abierto de par en par — **wide–awake** ['waɪdə'weɪk] *adj* : (completamente) despierto — **widely** ['waɪdli] *adv* : extensivamente — **widespread** ['waɪd'sprɛd] *adj* : extendido

widow ['wɪ,do:] *n* : viuda *f* — **~** *vt* : dejar viuda — **widower** ['wɪdowər] *n* : viudo *m*

width ['wɪdθ] *n* : ancho *m*, anchura *f*

wield ['wi:ld] *vt* **1** : usar, manejar **2** EXERT : ejercer

wiener ['wi:nər] → **frankfurter**

wife ['waɪf] *n, pl* **wives** ['waɪvz] : esposa *f*, mujer *f*

wig ['wɪg] *n* : peluca *f*

wiggle ['wɪgəl] *v* **-gled; -gling** *vt* : menear, contonear — *vi* : menearse — **~** *n* : meneo *m*

wigwam ['wɪg,wɑm] *n* : wigwam *m*

wild ['waɪld] *adj* **1** : salvaje **2** DESOLATE : agreste **3** UNRULY : desenfrenado **4** RANDOM : al azar **5** FRANTIC : frenético **6** OUTRAGEOUS : extravagante — **~** *adv* **1** → **wildly 2 run ~** : volver al estado silvestre (dícese de las plantas), desmandarse (dícese de los niños) — **wildcat** ['waɪld,kæt] *n* : gato *m* montés — **wilderness** ['wɪldərnəs] *n* : yermo *m*, desierto *m* — **wildfire** ['waɪld,faɪr] *n* **1** : fuego *m* descontrolado **2 spread like ~** : propagarse como un reguero de pólvora — **wildflower** ['waɪld,flaʊər] *n* : flor *f* silvestre — **wildlife** ['waɪld,laɪf] *n* : fauna *f* — **wildly** ['waɪldli] *adv* **1** FRANTICALLY : frenéticamente **2** EXTREMELY : locamente

will[1] ['wɪl] *v past* **would** ['wʊd]; *pres sing & pl* **will** *vi* WISH : querer — *v aux* **1 tomorrow we ~ go shopping** : mañana iremos de compras **2 he ~ get angry over nothing** : se pone furioso por cualquier cosa **3 I ~ go despite them** : iré a pesar de ellos **4 I won't do it** : no lo haré **5 that ~ be the mailman** : eso ha de ser el cartero **6 the couch ~ hold three people** : en el sofá cabrán tres personas **7 accidents ~ happen** : los accidentes ocurrirán **8 you ~ do as I say** : harás lo que digo

will[2] *n* **1** : voluntad *f* **2** TESTAMENT : testamento *m* **3 free ~** : libre albedrío *m* — **willful** *or* **wilful** ['wɪlfəl] *adj* **1** OBSTINATE : terco **2** INTENTIONAL : intencionado — **willing** ['wɪlɪŋ] *adj* **1** : complaciente **2 be ~ to** : estar dispuesto a — **willingly** ['wɪlɪŋli] *adv* : con gusto — **willingness** ['wɪlɪŋnəs] *n* : buena voluntad *f*

willow [ˈwɪˌlo:] *n* : sauce *m*
willpower [ˈwɪlˌpauər] *n* : fuerza *f* de voluntad
wilt [ˈwɪlt] *vi* : marchitarse
wily [ˈwaɪli] *adj* **wilier; -est** : artero, astuto
win [ˈwɪn] *v* **won** [ˈwʌn]; **winning** *vi* : ganar — *vt* **1** : ganar, conseguir **2 ~ over** : ganarse a — **~** *n* : triunfo *m*, victoria *f*
wince [ˈwɪnts] *vi* **winced; wincing** : hacer una mueca de dolor — **~** *n* : mueca *f* de dolor
winch [ˈwɪntʃ] *n* : torno *m*
wind[1] [ˈwɪnd] *n* **1** : viento *m* **2** BREATH : aliento *m* **3** FLATULENCE : flatulencia *f* **4 get ~ of** : enterarse de
wind[2] [ˈwaɪnd] *v* **wound** [ˈwaʊnd]; **winding** *vi* : serpentear — *vt* **1** COIL : enrollar **2 ~ a clock** : dar cuerda a un reloj
windfall [ˈwɪndˌfɔl] *n* : beneficio *m* imprevisto
winding [ˈwaɪndɪŋ] *adj* : tortuoso
wind instrument *n* : instrumento *m* de viento
windmill [ˈwɪndˌmɪl] *n* : molino *m* de viento
window [ˈwɪnˌdo:] *n* : ventana *f* (de un edificio o una computadora), ventanilla *f* (de un vehículo), vitrina *f* (de una tienda) — **windowpane** [ˈwɪnˌdo:ˌpeɪn] *n* : vidrio *m* — **windowsill** [ˈwɪnˌdo:ˌsɪl] *n* : repisa *f* de la ventana
windpipe [ˈwɪndˌpaɪp] *n* : tráquea *f*
windshield [ˈwɪndˌʃi:ld] *n* **1** : parabrisas *m* **2 ~ wiper** : limpiaparabrisas *m*
window–shop [ˈwɪndoˌʃɑp] *vi* **-shopped; -shopping** : mirar las vitrinas
wind up [ˈwaɪndˌʌp] *vt* : terminar, concluir — *vi* : terminar, acabar — **windup** *n* : conclusión *f*
windy [ˈwɪndi] *adj* **windier; -est 1** : ventoso **2 it's ~** : hace viento
wine [ˈwaɪn] *n* : vino *m* — **wine cellar** *n* : bodega *f*
wing [ˈwɪŋ] *n* **1** : ala *f* **2 under s.o.'s ~** : bajo el cargo de algn — **winged** [ˈwɪŋd, ˈwɪŋəd] *adj* : alado
wink [ˈwɪŋk] *vi* : guiñar — **~** *n* **1** : guiño *m* **2 not sleep a ~** : no pegar el ojo
winner [ˈwɪnər] *n* : ganador *m*, -dora *f* — **winning** [ˈwɪnɪŋ] *adj* **1** : ganador **2** CHARMING : encantador — **winnings** [ˈwɪnɪŋz] *npl* : ganancias *fpl*
winter [ˈwɪntər] *n* : invierno *m* — **~** *adj* : invernal, de invierno — **wintergreen** [ˈwɪntərˌgri:n] *n* : gaulteria *f* — **wintertime** [ˈwɪntərˌtaɪm] *n* : invierno *m* — **wintry** [ˈwɪntri] *adj* **wintrier; -est** : invernal, de invierno
wipe [ˈwaɪp] *vt* **wiped; wiping 1** : limpiar **2 ~ away** : enjugar (lágrimas), borrar (una memoria) **3 ~ out** : aniquilar, destruir — **~** *n* : pasada *f* (con un trapo, etc.)
wire [ˈwaɪr] *n* **1** : alambre *m* **2** : cable *m* (eléctrico o telefónico) **3** TELEGRAM : telegrama *m* — **~** *vt* **-wired; wiring 1** : instalar el cableado en (una casa, etc.) **2** BIND : atar con alambre **3** TELEGRAPH : enviar un telegrama a — **wireless** [ˈwaɪrləs] *adj* : inalámbrico — **wiring** [ˈwaɪrɪŋ] *n* : cableado *m* — **wiry** [ˈwaɪri] *adj* **wirier; -est 1** : hirsuto, tieso (dícese del pelo) **2** : esbelto y musculoso (dícese del cuerpo)
wisdom [ˈwɪzdəm] *n* : sabiduría *f* — **wisdom tooth** *n* : muela *f* de juicio
wise [ˈwaɪz] *adj* **wiser; wisest 1** : sabio **2** SENSIBLE : prudente — **wisecrack** [ˈwaɪzˌkræk] *n* : broma *f*, chiste *m* — **wisely** [ˈwaɪzli] *adv* : sabiamente
wish [ˈwɪʃ] *vt* **1** : desear **2 ~ s.o. well** : desear lo mejor a algn — *vi* **1** : pedir (como deseo) **2 as you ~** : como quieras — **~** *n* **1** : deseo *m* **2 best ~es** : muchos recuerdos — **wishbone** [ˈwɪʃˌbo:n] *n* : espoleta *f* — **wishful** [ˈwɪʃfəl] *adj* **1** : deseoso **2 ~ thinking** : ilusiones *fpl*
wishy–washy [ˈwɪʃiˌwɔʃi, -ˌwɑʃi] *adj* : insípido, soso
wisp [ˈwɪsp] *n* **1** : mechón *m* (de pelo) **2** : voluta *f* (de humo)
wistful [ˈwɪstfəl] *adj* : melancólico
wit [ˈwɪt] *n* **1** CLEVERNESS : ingenio *m* **2** HUMOR : agudeza *f* **3 at one's ~'s end** : desesperado **4 scared out of one's ~s** : muerto de miedo
witch [ˈwɪtʃ] *n* : bruja *f* — **witchcraft** [ˈwɪtʃˌkræft] *n* : brujería *f*, hechicería *f*
with [ˈwɪð, ˈwɪθ] *prep* **1** : con **2 I'm going ~ you** : voy contigo **3 it varies ~ the season** : varía según la estación **4 the girl ~ red hair** : la muchacha de pelo rojo **5 ~ all his work, the business failed** : a pesar de su trabajo, el negocio fracasó
withdraw [wɪðˈdrɔ, wɪθ-] *v* **-drew** [-ˈdru:]; **-drawn** [-ˈdrɔn]; **-drawing** *vt* : retirar — *vi* : apartarse — **withdrawal** [wɪðˈdrɔəl, wɪθ-] *n* **1** : retirada *f* **2** : abandono (de drogas, etc.) — **withdrawn** [wɪðˈdrɔn, wɪθ-] *adj* : introvertido
wither [ˈwɪðər] *vi* : marchitarse
withhold [wɪθˈho:ld, wɪð-] *vt* **-held** [-ˈhɛld]; **-holding** : retener (fondos), negar (permiso, etc.)
within [wɪðˈɪn, wɪθ-] *adv* : dentro — **~** *prep* **1** : dentro de **2** (*in expressions of distance*) : a menos de **3** (*in expressions of time*) : dentro de, en menos de **4 ~ reach** : al alcance de la mano
without [wɪðˈaʊt, wɪθ-] *adv* **do ~** : pasar sin algo — **~** *prep* : sin
withstand [wɪθˈstænd, wɪð-] *vt* **-stood** [-ˈstʊd]; **-standing 1** BEAR : aguantar **2** RESIST : resistir
witness [ˈwɪtnəs] *n* **1** : testigo *mf* **2** EVIDENCE : testimonio *m* **3 bear ~** : atestiguar — **~** *vt* **1** SEE : ser testigo de **2** : atestiguar (una firma, etc.)
witticism [ˈwɪt̬əˌsɪzəm] *n* : agudeza *f*, ocurrencia *f*
witty [ˈwɪt̬i] *adj* **-tier; -est** : ingenioso, ocurrente
wives → **wife**
wizard [ˈwɪzərd] *n* **1** : mago *m*, brujo *m* **2 a math ~** : un genio de matemáticas
wizened [ˈwɪzənd, ˈwi:-] *adj* : arrugado
wobble [ˈwɑbəl] *vi* **-bled; -bling 1** : tambalearse **2** : temblar (dícese de la voz, etc.) — **wobbly** [ˈwɑbəli] *adj* : cojo
woe [ˈwo:] *n* **1** : aflicción *f* **2 ~s** *npl* TROUBLES : penas *fpl* — **woeful** [ˈwo:fəl] *adj* : triste
woke, woken → **wake**
wolf [ˈwʊlf] *n, pl* **wolves** [ˈwʊlvz] : lobo *m*, -ba *f* — **~** *vt or* **~ down** : engullir
woman [ˈwʊmən] *n, pl* **women** [ˈwɪmən] : mujer *f* — **womanly** [ˈwʊmənli] *adj* : femenino
womb [ˈwu:m] *n* : útero *m*, matriz *f*
won → **win**
wonder [ˈwʌndər] *n* **1** MARVEL : maravilla *f* **2** AMAZEMENT : asombro *m* — **~** *v* : preguntarse — **wonderful** [ˈwʌndərfəl] *adj* : maravilloso, estupendo
won't [ˈwo:nt] (*contraction of* **will not**) → **will**
woo [ˈwu:] *vt* **1** COURT : cortejar **2** : buscar el apoyo de (clientes, votantes, etc.)
wood [ˈwʊd] *n* **1** : madera *f* (materia) **2** FIREWOOD : leña *f* **3** *or* **~s** *npl* FOREST : bosque *m* — **~** *adj* : de madera — **woodchuck** [ˈwʊdˌtʃʌk] *n* : marmota *f* de América — **wooded** [ˈwʊdəd] *adj* : arbolado, boscoso — **wooden** [ˈwʊdən] *adj* : de madera — **woodpecker** [ˈwʊdˌpɛkər] *n* : pájaro *m* carpintero — **woodshed** [ˈwʊdˌʃɛd] *n* : leñera *f* — **woodwind** [ˈwʊdˌwɪnd] *n* : instrumento *m* de viento de madera — **woodwork** [ˈwʊdˌwərk] *n* : carpintería *f*
wool [ˈwʊl] *n* : lana *f* — **woolen** *or* **woollen** [ˈwʊlən] *adj* : de lana — **~** *n* **1** : lana *f* (tela) **2 ~s** *npl* : prendas *fpl* de lana — **woolly** [ˈwʊli] *adj* **-lier; -est** : lanudo
word [ˈwərd] *n* **1** : palabra *f* **2** NEWS : noticias *fpl* **3 ~s** *npl* : letra *f* (de una canción, etc.) **4 have ~s with** : reñir con **5 just say the ~** : no tienes que decirlo **6 keep one's ~** : cumplir su palabra — **~** *vt* : expresar — **word processing** *n* : procesamiento *m* de textos — **word processor** *n* : procesador *m* de textos — **wordy** [ˈwərdi] *adj* **wordier; -est** : prolijo
wore → **wear**
work [ˈwərk] *n* **1** LABOR : trabajo *m* **2** EMPLOYMENT : trabajo *m*, empleo *m* **3** : obra *f* (de arte, etc.) **4 ~s** *npl* FACTORY : fábrica *f* **5 ~s** *npl* MECHANISM : mecanismo *m* — **~** *v* **worked** [ˈwərkt] *or* **wrought** [ˈrɔt]; **working** *vt* **1** : hacer trabajar (a una persona) **2** : manejar, operar (una máquina, etc.) — *vi* **1** : trabajar **2** FUNCTION : funcionar **3** : surtir efecto (dícese de una droga), resultar (dícese de una idea, etc.) — **worked up** *adj* : nervioso — **worker** [ˈwərkər] *n* : trabajador *m*, -dora *f*; obrero *m*, -ra *f* — **working** [ˈwərkɪŋ] *adj* **1** : que trabaja (dícese de personas), de trabajo (dícese de la ropa, etc.) **2 be in ~ order** : funcionar bien — **working class** *n* : clase *f* obrera — **workingman** [ˈwərkɪŋˌmæn] *n, pl* **-men** [-mən, -ˌmɛn] : obrero *m* — **workman** [ˈwərkmən] *n, pl* **-men** [-mən, -ˌmɛn] **1** : obrero *m* **2** ARTISAN : artesano *m* — **workmanship** [ˈwərkmənˌʃɪp] *n* : artesanía *f*, destreza *f* — **workout** [ˈwərkˌaʊt] *n* : ejercicios *mpl* (físicos) — **work out** *vt* **1** DEVELOP : elaborar **2** SOLVE : resolver — *vi* **1** TURN OUT : resultar **2** SUCCEED : lograr, salir bien **3** EXERCISE : hacer ejercicio — **workshop** [ˈwərkˌʃɑp] *n* : taller *m* — **work up** *vt* **1** EXCITE : ponerse como loco **2** GENERATE : generar
world [ˈwərld] *n* **1** : mundo *m* **2 think the ~ of s.o.** : tener a algn en alta estima — **~** *adj* : mundial, del mundo — **worldly** [ˈwərldli] *adj* : mundano — **worldwide** [ˈwərldˈwaɪd] *adv* : en todo el mundo — **~** *adj* : global, mundial
worm [ˈwərm] *n* **1** : gusano *m*, lombriz *f* **2 ~s** *npl* : lombrices *fpl* (parásitos)
worn → **wear** — **worn–out** [ˈwo:rnˈaʊt] *adj* **1** USED : gastado **2** TIRED : agotado
worry [ˈwəri] *v* **-ried; -rying** *vt* : preocupar, inquietar — *vi* : preocuparse, inquietarse — **~** *n, pl* **-ries** : preocupación *f* — **worried** [ˈwərid] *adj* : preocupado — **worrisome** [ˈwərisəm] *adj* : inquietante
worse [ˈwərs] *adv* (*comparative of* **bad** *or of* **ill**) : peor — **~** *adj* (*comparative of* **bad** *or of* **ill**) **1** : peor **2 from bad to ~** : de mal en peor **3 get ~** : empeorar — **~** *n* **1 the ~** : el (la) peor, lo peor **2 take a turn for the ~** : ponerse peor — **worsen** [ˈwərsən] *v* : empeorar
worship [ˈwərʃəp] *v* **-shiped** *or* **-shipped; -shiping** *or* **-shipping** *vt* : adorar — *vi* : practicar una religión — **~** *n* : adoración *f*, culto *m* — **worshiper** *or* **worshipper** [ˈwərʃəpər] *n* : adorador *m*, -dora *f*
worst [ˈwərst] *adv* (*superlative of* **ill** *or of* **bad** *or* **badly**) : peor — **~** *adj* (*superlative of* **bad** *or of* **ill**) : peor — **~** *n* **the ~** : lo peor, el (la) peor
worth [ˈwərθ] *n* **1** : valor *m* (monetario) **2** MERIT : mérito *m*, valía *f* **3 ten dollars' ~ of gas** : diez dólares de gasolina — **~** *prep* **1 it's ~ $10** : vale $10 **2 it's ~ doing** : vale la pena hacerlo — **worthless** [ˈwərθləs] *adj* **1** : sin valor **2** USELESS : inútil — **worthwhile** [wərθˈhwaɪl] *adj* : que vale la pena — **worthy** [ˈwərði] *adj* **-thier; -est** : digno
would [ˈwʊd] *past of* **will 1 he ~ often take his children to the park** : solía llevar a sus hijos al parque **2 I ~ go if I had the money** : iría yo si tuviera el dinero **3 I ~ rather go alone** : preferiría ir sola **4 she ~ have won if she hadn't tripped** : habría ganado si no hubiera tropezado **5 ~ you kindly help me with this?** : ¿tendría la bondad de ayudarme con esto? — **would–be** [ˈwʊdˈbi:] *adj* **a ~ poet** : un aspirante a poeta — **wouldn't** [ˈwʊdənt] (*contraction of* **would not**) → **would**
wound[1] [ˈwu:nd] *n* : herida *f* — **~** *vt* : herir
wound[2] [ˈwaʊnd] → **wind**
wove, woven → **weave**
wrangle [ˈræŋgəl] *vi* **-gled; -gling** : reñir — **~** *n* : riña *f*, disputa *f*
wrap [ˈræp] *vt* **wrapped; wrapping 1** : envolver **2 ~ up** FINISH : dar fin a — **~** *n* **1** : prenda *f* que envuelve (como un chal) **2** WRAPPER : envoltura *f* — **wrapper** [ˈræpər] *n* : envoltura *f*, envoltorio *m* — **wrapping** [ˈræpɪŋ] *n* : envoltura *f*, envoltorio *m*
wrap [ˈræp] *vt* **wrapped; wrapping 1** : envolver **2 ~ up** FINISH : dar fin a — **~** *n* **1** : prenda *f* que envuelve (como un chal) **2** WRAPPER : envoltura *f* — **wrapper** [ˈræpər] *n* : envoltura *f*, envoltorio *m* — **wrapping** [ˈræpɪŋ] *n* : envoltura *f*, envoltorio *m*
wrath [ˈræθ] *n* : ira *f*, cólera *f* — **wrathful** [ˈræθfəl] *adj* : iracundo
wreath [ˈri:θ] *n, pl* **wreaths** [ˈri:ðz, ˈri:θs] : corona *f* (de flores, etc.)
wreck [ˈrɛk] *n* **1** WRECKAGE : restos *mpl* **2** RUIN : ruina *f*, desastre *m* **3 be a nervous ~** : tener los nervios destrozados — **~** *vt* : destrozar (un automóvil), naufragar (un barco) — **wreckage** [ˈrɛkɪdʒ] *n* : restos *mpl* (de un buque naufragado, etc.), ruinas *fpl* (de un edificio)
wren [ˈrɛn] *n* : chochín *m*
wrench [ˈrɛntʃ] *vt* **1** PULL : arrancar (de un tirón) **2** SPRAIN, TWIST : torcerse — **~** *n* **1** TUG : tirón *m*, jalón *m* **2** SPRAIN : torcedura *f* **3** *or* **monkey ~** : llave *f* inglesa
wrestle [ˈrɛsəl] *vi* **-tled; -tling** : luchar — **wrestler** [ˈrɛsələr] *n* : luchador *m*, -dora *f* — **wrestling** [ˈrɛsəlɪŋ] *n* : lucha *f*
wretch [ˈrɛtʃ] *n* : desgraciado *m*, -da *f* — **wretched** [ˈrɛtʃəd] *adj* **1** : miserable **2 ~ weather** : tiempo *m* espantoso
wriggle [ˈrɪgəl] *vi* **-gled; -gling** : retorcerse, menearse
wring [ˈrɪŋ] *vt* **wrung** [ˈrʌŋ]; **wringing 1** *or* **~ out** : escurrir (el lavado, etc.) **2** TWIST : retorcer **3** EXTRACT : arrancar (información, etc.)
wrinkle [ˈrɪŋkəl] *n* : arruga *f* — **~** *v* **-kled; -kling** *vt* : arrugar — *vi* : arrugarse
wrist [ˈrɪst] *n* : muñeca *f* — **wristwatch** [ˈrɪstˌwɑtʃ] *n* : reloj *m* de pulsera
writ [ˈrɪt] *n* : orden *f* (judicial)
write [ˈraɪt] *v* **wrote** [ˈro:t]; **written** [ˈrɪtən]; **writing** : escribir — **write down** *vt* : apuntar, anotar — **write off** *vt* CANCEL : cancelar — **writer** [ˈraɪt̬ər] *n* : escritor *m*, -tora *f*
writhe [ˈraɪð] *vi* **writhed; writhing** : retorcerse
writing [ˈraɪt̬ɪŋ] *n* : escritura *f*
wrong [ˈrɔŋ] *n* **1** INJUSTICE : injusticia *f*, mal *m* **2** : agravio *m* (en derecho) **3 be in the ~** : haber hecho mal — **~** *adj* **wronger** [ˈrɔŋər]; **wrongest** [ˈrɔŋəst] **1** : malo **2** UNSUITABLE : inadecuado, inapropiado **3** INCORRECT : incorrecto, equivocado **4 be ~** : no tener razón — **~** *adv* : mal, incorrectamente — **~** *vt* **wronged; wronging** : ofender, ser injusto con — **wrongful** [ˈrɔŋfəl] *adj* **1** UNJUST : injusto **2** UNLAWFUL : ilegal — **wrongly** [ˈrɔŋli] *adv* **1** UNJUSTLY : injustamente **2** INCORRECTLY : mal
wrote → **write**
wrought iron [ˈrɔt] *n* : hierro *m* forjado
wrung → **wring**
wry [ˈraɪ] *adj* **wrier** [ˈraɪər]; **wriest** [ˈraɪəst] : irónico, sardónico (dícese del humor)

X

x *n, pl* **x's** *or* **xs** [ˈɛksəz] : x *f*, vigésima cuarta letra del alfabeto inglés
xenophobia [ˌzɛnəˈfo:biə, ˌzi:-] *n* : xenofobia *f*
Xmas [ˈkrɪsməs] *n* : Navidad *f*
X ray [ˈɛksˌreɪ] *n* **1** : rayo *m* X **2** *or* **~ photograph** : radiografía *f* — **x–ray** *vt* : radiografiar
xylophone [ˈzaɪləˌfo:n] *n* : xilófono *m*

Y

y [ˈwaɪ] *n, pl* **y's** *or* **ys** [ˈwaɪz] : y *f*, vigésima quinta letra del alfabeto inglés
yacht [ˈjɑt] *n* : yate *m*
yam [ˈjæm] *n* **1** : ñame *m* **2** SWEET POTATO : batata *f*, boniato *m*
yank [ˈjæŋk] *vt* : tirar de, jalar *Lat* — **~** *n* : tirón *m*, jalón *m Lat*
Yankee [ˈjæŋki] *n* : yanqui *mf*
yap [ˈjæp] *vi* **yapped; yapping** : ladrar — **~** *n* : ladrido *m*
yard [ˈjɑrd] *n* **1** : yarda *f* (medida) **2** COURTYARD : patio *m* **3** : jardín *m* (de una casa) — **yardstick** [ˈjɑrdˌstɪk] *n* **1** : vara *f* (de medir) **2** CRITERION : criterio *m*
yarn [ˈjɑrn] *n* **1** : hilado *m* **2** TALE : historia *f*, cuento *m*
yawn [ˈjɔn] *vi* : bostezar — **~** *n* : bostezo *m*
year [ˈjɪr] *n* **1** : año *m* **2 she's ten ~s old** : tiene diez años **3 I haven't seen them in ~s** : hace siglos que no los veo — **yearbook** [ˈjɪrˌbʊk] *n* : anuario *m* — **yearling** [ˈjɪrlɪŋ, ˈjərlən] *n* : animal *m* menor de dos años — **yearly** [ˈjɪrli] *adv* **1** : anualmente **2 three times ~** : tres veces al año — **~** *adj* : anual
yearn [ˈjərn] *vi* : anhelar — **yearning** [ˈjərnɪŋ] *n* : anhelo *m*, ansia *f*
yeast [ˈji:st] *n* : levadura *f*
yell [ˈjɛl] *vi* : gritar, chillar — *vt* : gritar — **~** *n* : grito *m*, chillido *m*
yellow [ˈjɛlo] *adj* : amarillo — **~** *n* : amarillo *m* — **yellowish** [ˈjɛloɪʃ] *adj* : amarillento
yelp [ˈjɛlp] *n* : gañido *m* — **~** *vi* : dar un gañido
yes [ˈjɛs] *adv* **1** : sí **2 say ~** : decir que sí — **~** *n* : sí *m*
yesterday [ˈjɛstərˌdeɪ, -di] *adv* : ayer — **~** *n* **1** : ayer *m* **2 the day before ~** : anteayer
yet [ˈjɛt] *adv* **1** : aún, todavía **2 has he come ~?** : ¿ya ha venido? **3 not ~** : todavía no **4 ~ more problems** : más problemas aún **5** NEVERTHELESS : sin embargo — **~** *conj* : pero
yield [ˈji:ld] *vt* **1** PRODUCE : producir **2 ~ the right of way** : ceder el paso — *vi* : ceder — **~** *n* : rendimiento *m*, rédito *m* (en finanzas)
yoga [ˈjo:gə] *n* : yoga *m*
yogurt [ˈjo:gərt] *n* : yogur *m*, yogurt *m*
yoke [ˈjo:k] *n* : yugo *m*
yolk [ˈjo:k] *n* : yema *f* (de un huevo)
you [ˈju:] *pron* **1** (*used as subject—familiar*) : tú; vos (*in some Latin American countries*); ustedes *pl*; vosotros, vosotras *pl Spain* **2** (*used as subject—formal*) : usted, ustedes *pl* **3** (*used as indirect object—familiar*) : te, les *pl* (se *before* lo, la, los, las), os *pl Spain* **4** (*used as indirect object—formal*) : lo (*Spain sometimes* le), la; los (*Spain sometimes* les), las *pl* **5** (*used after a preposition—familiar*) : ti; vos (*in some Latin American countries*); ustedes *pl*; vosotros, vosotras *pl Spain* **6** (*used after a preposition—formal*) : usted, ustedes *pl* **7 with ~** (*familiar*) : contigo; con ustedes *pl*; con vosotros, con vosotras *pl Spain* **8 with ~** (*formal*) : con usted, con ustedes *pl* **9 ~ never know** : nunca se sabe — **you'd** [ˈju:d, ˈjʊd] (*contraction of* **you had** *or* **you would**) → **have, would** — **you'll** [ˈju:l, ˈjʊl] (*contraction of* **you shall** *or* **you will**) → **shall, will**
young [ˈjʌŋ] *adj* **younger** [ˈjʌŋgər]; **youngest** [-gəst] **1** : joven **2 my ~er brother** : mi hermano menor **3 she is the ~est** : es la más pequeña **4 the ~** : los jóvenes — **~** *npl* : jóvenes *mfpl* (de los humanos), crías *fpl* (de los animales) — **youngster** [ˈjʌŋkstər] *n* : chico *m*, -ca *f*; joven *mf*
your [ˈjʊr, ˈjo:r, jər] *adj* **1** (*familiar singular*)

: tu **2** (*familiar plural*) su, vuestro *Spain* **3** (*formal*) : su **4 on** ~ **left** : a la izquierda

you're ['jʊr, 'jɔːr, 'jər, 'juːər] (*contraction of* **you are**) → **be**

yours ['jʊrz, 'jɔːrz] *pron* **1** (*belonging to one person—familiar*) : (el) tuyo, (la) tuya, (los) tuyos, (las) tuyas **2** (*belonging to more than one person—familiar*) : (el) suyo, (la) suya, (los) suyos, (las) suyas; (el) vuestro, (la) vuestra, (los) vuestros, (las) vuestras *Spain* **3** (*formal*) : (el) suyo, (la) suya, (los) suyos, (las) suyas

yourself [jər'self] *pron, pl* **yourselves** [-'selvz] **1** (*used reflexively—familiar*) : te, se *pl*, os *pl Spain* **2** (*used reflexively—formal*) : se **3** (*used for emphasis*) : tú

mismo, tú misma; usted mismo, usted misma; ustedes mismos, ustedes mismas *pl*; vosotros mismos, vosotras mismas *pl Spain*

youth ['juːθ] *n, pl* **youths** ['juːðz, 'juːθs] **1** : juventud *f* **2** BOY : joven *m* **3 today's** ~ : los jóvenes de hoy — **youthful** ['juːθfəl] *adj* **1** : juvenil, de juventud **2** YOUNG : joven

you've ['juːv] (*contraction of* **you have**) → **have**

yowl ['jaʊl] *vi* : aullar — ~ *n* : aullido *m*

yucca ['jʌkə] *n* : yuca *f*

Yugoslavian [juːgo'slɑviən] *adj* : yugoslavo

yule ['juːl] *n* CHRISTMAS : Navidad *f* — **yuletide** ['juːl,taɪd] *n* : Navidades *fpl*

Z

z ['ziː] *n, pl* **z's** *or* **zs** : z *f*, vigésima sexta letra del alfabeto inglés

zany ['zeɪni] *adj* **-nier; -est** : alocado, disparatado

zeal ['ziːl] *n* : fervor *m*, celo *m* — **zealous** ['zeləs] *adj* : entusiasta

zebra ['ziːbrə] *n* : cebra *f*

zenith ['ziːnəθ] *n* **1** : cenit *m* (en astronomía) **2** PEAK : apogeo *m*

zero ['ziːro, 'zɪro] *n, pl* **-ros** : cero *m*

zest ['zɛst] *n* **1** : gusto *m* **2** FLAVOR : sazón *f*

zigzag ['zɪg,zæg] *n* : zigzag *m* — ~ *vi* **-zagged; -zagging** : zigzaguear

zinc ['zɪŋk] *n* : cinc *m*, zinc *m*

zip ['zɪp] *v* **zipped; zipping** *vt or* ~ **up** : cerrar la cremallera de, cerrar el cierre de *Lat* — *vi* SPEED : pasarse volando — **zip code** *n* : código *m* postal — **zipper** ['zɪpər] *n* : cremallera *f*, cierre *m Lat*

zodiac ['zo,diæk] *n* : zodíaco *m*

zone ['zoːn] *n* : zona *f*

zoo ['zuː] *n, pl* **zoos** : zoológico *m*, zoo *m* — **zoology** [zo'ɑlədʒi, zu-] *n* : zoología *f*

zoom ['zuːm] *vi* : zumbar, ir volando — ~ *n* **1** : zumbido *m* **2 or** ~ **lens** : zoom *m*

zucchini [zʊ'kiːni] *n, pl* **-ni** *or* **-nis** : calabacín *m*, calabacita *f Lat*

Common Spanish Abbreviations

SPANISH ABBREVIATION AND EXPANSION		ENGLISH EQUIVALENT	
abr.	abril	Apr.	April
A.C., a.C.	antes de Cristo	BC	before Christ
a. de J.C.	antes de Jesucristo	BC	before Christ
admon., admón.	administración	—	administration
a/f	a favor	—	in favor
ago.	agosto	Aug.	August
Apdo.	apartado (de correos)	—	P.O. box
aprox.	aproximadamente	approx.	approximately
Aptdo.	apartado (de correos)	—	P.O. box
Arq.	arquitecto	arch.	architect
A.T.	Antiguo Testamento	O.T.	Old Testament
atte.	atentamente	—	sincerely
atto., atta.	atento, atenta	—	kind, courteous
av., avda.	avenida	ave.	avenue
a/v	a vista	—	on receipt
BID	Banco Interamericano de Desarrollo	IDB	Interamerican Development Bank
Bo	banco	—	bank
BM	Banco Mundial	—	World Bank
c/, C/	calle	st.	street
C	centígrado, Celsius	C	centigrade, Celsius
C.	compañía	Co.	company
CA	corriente alterna	AC	alternating current
cap.	capítulo	ch., chap.	chapter
c/c	cuenta corriente	—	current account, checking account
c.c.	centímetros cúbicos	c.c.	cubic centimeters
CC	corriente continua	DC	direct current
c/d	con descuento	—	with discount
Cd.	ciudad	—	city
CE	Comunidad Europea	EC	European Community
CEE	Comunidad Económica Europea	EEC	European Economic Community
cf.	confróntese	cf.	compare
cg.	centígramo	cg	centigram
CGT	Confederación General de Trabajadores or del Trabajo	—	confederation of workers, workers° union
CI	coeficiente intelectual or de inteligencia	IQ	intelligence quotient
Cía.	compañía	Co.	company
cm.	centímetro	cm	centimeter
Cnel.	coronel	Col.	colonel
col.	columna	col.	column
Col. *Mex*	colonia	—	residential area
Com.	comandante	Cmdr.	commander
comp.	compárese	comp.	compare
Cor.	coronel	Col.	colonel
C.P.	código postal	—	zip code
CSF, c.s.f.	coste, seguro y flete	c.i.f.	cost, insurance, and freight
cta.	cuenta	ac., acct.	account
cte.	corriente	cur.	current
c/u	cada uno, cada una	ea.	each
CV	caballo de vapor	hp	horsepower
D.	Don	—	—
Da., D.ª	Doña	—	—
d.C.	después de Cristo	AD	anno Domini (in the year of our Lord)
dcha.	derecha	—	right
d. de J.C.	después de Jesucristo	AD	anno Domini (in the year of our lord)
dep.	departamento	dept.	department
DF, D.F.	Distrito Federal	—	Federal District
dic.	diciembre	Dec.	December
dir.	director, directora	dir.	director
dir.	dirección	—	address
Dña.	Doña	—	—
do.	domingo	Sun.	Sunday
dpto.	departamento	dept.	department
Dr.	doctor	Dr.	doctor
Dra.	doctora	Dr.	doctor
dto.	descuento	—	discount
E, E.	Este, este	E	East, east
Ed.	editorial	—	publishing house
Ed., ed.	edición	ed.	edition
edif.	edificio	bldg.	building
edo.	estado	st.	state
EEUU, EE.UU.	Estados Unidos	US, U.S.	United States
ej.	por ejemplo	e.g.	for example
E.M.	esclerosis multiple	MS	multiple sclerosis
ene.	enero	Jan.	January
etc.	etcétera	etc.	et cetera
ext.	extensión	ext.	extension
F	Fahrenheit	F	Fahrenheit
f.a.b.	franco a bordo	f.o.b.	free on board
FC	ferrocarril	RR	railroad
feb.	febrero	Feb.	February
FF AA, FF.AA.	Fuerzas Armadas	—	armed forces
FMI	Fondo Monetario Internacional	IMF	International Monetary Fund
g.	gramo	g., gm, gr.	gram
G.P.	giro postal	M.O.	money order
gr.	gramo	g., gm, gr.	gram
Gral.	general	Gen.	general
h.	hora	hr.	hour
Hnos.	hermanos	Bros.	brothers
I + D, I & D, I y D	investigación y desarrollo	R & D	research and development
i.e.	esto es, es decir	i.e.	that is
incl.	inclusive	incl.	inclusive, inclusively
Ing.	ingeniero, ingeniera	eng.	engineer
IPC	indice de precios al consumo	CPI	consumer price index
IVA	impuesto al valor agregado	VAT	value-added tax
izq.	izquierda	l.	left
juev.	jueves	Thurs.	Thursday
jul.	julio	Jul.	July
jun.	junio	Jun.	June
kg.	kilogramo	kg	kilogram
km.	kilómetro	km	kilometer
km/h	kilómetros por hora	kph	kilometers per hour
kv, kV	kilovatio	kw, kW	kilowatt
l.	litro	l, lit.	liter
Lic.	licenciado, licenciada	—	—
Ltda.	limitada	Ltd.	limited
lun.	lunes	Mon.	Monday
m	masculino	m	masculine
m	metro	m	meter
m	minuto	m	minute
mar.	marzo	Mar.	March
mart.	martes	Tues.	Tuesday
mg.	miligramo	mg	milligram
miérc.	miércoles	Wednes.	Wednesday
min	minuto	min.	minute
mm.	milímetro	mm	millimeter
M-N, m/n	moneda nacional	—	national currency
Mons.	monseñor	Msgr.	monsignor
Mtra.	maestra	—	teacher
Mtro.	maestro	—	teacher
N, N.	Norte, norte	N, no.	North, north
n/o	nuestro	—	our
n.º	número	no.	number
N. de (la) R.	nota de (la) redacción	—	editorœs note
NE	nordeste	NE	northeast
NN.UU.	Naciones Unidas	UN	United Nations
NO	noroeste	NW	northwest
nov.	noviembre	Nov.	November
N.T.	Nuevo Testamento	N.T.	New Testament
ntra., ntro.	nuestra, nuestro	—	our
NU	Naciones Unidas	UN	United Nations
núm.	número	num.	number
O, O.	Oeste, oeste	W	West, west
oct.	octubre	Oct.	October
OEA, O.E.A.	Organización de Estados Americanos	OAS	Organization of American States
OMS	Organización Mundial de la Salud	WHO	World Health Organization
ONG	organización no gubernamental	NGO	non-governmental organization
ONU	Organización de las Naciones Unidas	UN	United Nations
OTAN	Organización del Tratado del Atlántico Norte	NATO	North Atlantic Treaty Organization
p.	página	p.	page
P, P.	padre	Fr.	father
pág.	página	pg.	page

SPANISH ABBREVIATION AND EXPANSION		ENGLISH EQUIVALENT		SPANISH ABBREVIATION AND EXPANSION		ENGLISH EQUIVALENT	
pat.	patente	**pat.**	patent	**S.M.**	Su Majestad	**HM**	His Majesty, Her Majesty
PCL	pantalla de cristal líquido	**LCD**	liquid crystal display	**s/n**	sin número	**—**	no (street) number
P.D.	post data	**P.S.**	postscript	**s.n.m.**	sobre el nivel de mar	**a.s.l.**	above sea level
p. ej.	por ejemplo	**e.g.**	for example	**SO**	sudoeste/suroeste	**SW**	southwest
PNB	Producto Nacional Bruto	**GNP**	gross national product	**S.R.C.**	se ruega contestación	**R.S.V.P.**	please reply
pº	paseo	**Ave.**	avenue	**ss.**	siguientes	**—**	the following ones
p.p.	porte pagado	**ppd.**	postpaid	**SS, S.S.**	Su Santidad	**H.H.**	His Holiness
PP, p.p.	por poder, por poderes	**p.p.**	by proxy	**Sta.**	santa	**St.**	Saint
prom.	promedio	**av., avg.**	average	**Sto.**	santo	**St.**	saint
ptas., pts.	pesetas	**—**	—	**t, t.**	tonelada	**t., tn.**	ton
q.e.p.d.	que en paz descanse	**R.I.P.**	may he/she rest in peace	**TAE**	tasa anual efectiva	**APR**	annual percentage rate
R, R/	remite	**—**	sender	**tb.**	también	**—**	also
RAE	Real Academia Española	**—**	—	**tel., Tel.**	teléfono	**tel.**	telephone
ref., ref.ª	referencia	**ref.**	reference	**Tm.**	tonelada métrica	**MT**	metric ton
rep.	república	**rep.**	republic	**Tn.**	tonelada	**t., tn.**	ton
r.p.m.	revoluciones por minuto	**rpm.**	revolutions per minute	**trad.**	traducido	**tr., trans., transl.**	translated
rte.	remite, remitente	**—**	sender	**UE**	Unión Europea	**EU**	European Union
s.	siglo	**c., cent.**	century	**Univ.**	universidad	**Univ., U.**	university
s/	su, sus	**—**	his, her, your, their	**UPC**	unidad procesadora central	**CPU**	central processing unit
S, S.	Sur, sur	**S, so.**	South, south	**Urb.**	urbanización	**—**	residential area
S.	san, santo	**St.**	saint	**v**	versus	**v., vs.**	versus
S.A.	sociedad anónima	**Inc.**	incorporated (company)	**v**	verso	**v., ver., vs.**	verse
sáb.	sábado	**Sat.**	Saturday	**v.**	véase	**vid.**	see
s/c	su cuenta	**—**	your account	**Vda.**	viuda	**—**	widow
SE	sudeste, sureste	**SE**	southeast	**v.g., v.gr.**	verbigracia	**e.g.**	for example
seg.	segundo, segundos	**sec.**	second, seconds	**vier., viern.**	viernes	**Fri.**	Friday
sep., sept.	septiembre	**Sept.**	September	**V.M.**	Vuestra Majestad	**—**	Your Majesty
s.e.u.o.	salvo error u omisión	**—**	errors and omissions excepted	**VºBº, V.ºB.º**	visto bueno	**—**	OK, approved
Sgto.	sargento	**Sgt.**	sergeant	**vol, vol.**	volumen	**vol.**	volume
S.L.	sociedad limitada	**Ltd.**	limited (corporation)	**vra., vro.**	vuestra, vuestro	**—**	your

Common English Abbreviations

ENGLISH ABBREVIATION AND EXPANSION			SPANISH EQUIVALENT
AAA	American Automobile Association	—	—
AD	anno Domini (in the year of our Lord)	d.C., d. de J.C.	después de Cristo, después de Jesucristo
AK	Alaska	—	Alaska
AL, Ala.	Alabama	—	Alabama
Alas.	Alaska	—	Alaska
a.m., AM	ante meridiem	a.m.	ante meridiem (de la mañana)
Am., Amer.	America, American	—	América, americano
amt.	amount	—	cantidad
anon.	anonymous	—	anónimo
ans.	answer	—	respuesta
Apr.	April	abr.	abril
AR	Arkansas	—	Arkansas
Ariz.	Arizona	—	Arizona
Ark.	Arkansas	—	Arkansas
asst.	assistant	ayte.	ayudante
atty.	attorney	—	abogado, -da
Aug.	August	ago.	agosto
ave.	avenue	av., avda.	avenida
AZ	Arizona	—	Arizona
BA	Bachelor of Arts	Lic.	Licenciado, -da en Filosofía y Letras
BA	Bachelor of Arts (degree)	—	Licenciatura en Filosofía y Letras
BC	before Christ	a.C., A.C., a. de J.C.	antes de Cristo, antes de Jesucristo
BCE	before the Christian Era, before the Common Era	—	antes de la era cristiana, antes de la era común
bet.	between	—	entre
bldg.	building	edif.	edificio
blvd.	boulevard	blvar., br.	bulevar
Br., Brit.	Britain, British	—	Gran Bretaña, británico
Bro(s).	brother(s)	Hno(s).	hermano(s)
BS	Bachelor of Science	Lic.	Licenciado, -da en Ciencias
BS	Bachelor of Science (degree)	—	Licenciatura en Ciencias
c	carat	—	quilate
c	cent	—	centavo
c	centimeter	cm.	centímetro
c	century	s.	siglo
c	cup	—	taza
C	Celsius, centigrade	C	Celsius, centígrado
CA, Cal., Calif.	California	—	California
Can., Canad.	Canada, Canadian	—	Canadá, canadiense
cap.	capital	—	capital
cap.	capital	—	mayúscula
Capt.	captain	—	capitán
cent.	century	s.	siglo
CEO	chief executive officer	—	presidente, -ta (de una corporación)
ch., chap.	chapter	cap.	capítulo
CIA	Central Intelligence Agency	—	—
cm	centimeter	cm.	centímetro
Co.	company	C., Cía.	compañía
co.	county	—	condado
CO	Colorado	—	Colorado
c/o	care of	a/c	a cargo de
COD	cash on delivery, collect on delivery	—	(pago) contra reembolso
col.	column	col.	columna
Col., Colo.	Colorado	—	Colorado
Conn.	Connecticut	—	Connecticut
corp.	corporation	—	corporación
CPR	cardiopulmonary resuscitation	RCP	reanimación cardiopulmonar, resucitación cardiopulmonar
ct.	cent	—	centavo
CT	Connecticut	—	Connecticut
D.A.	district attorney	—	fiscal (del distrito)
DC	District of Columbia	—	—
DDS	Doctor of Dental Surgery	—	doctor de cirugía dental

ENGLISH ABBREVIATION AND EXPANSION			SPANISH EQUIVALENT
DE	Delaware	—	Delaware
Dec.	December	dic.	diciembre
Del.	Delaware	—	Delaware
DJ	disc jockey	—	disc-jockey
dept.	department	dep., dpto.	departamento
DMD	Doctor of Dental Medicine	—	doctor de medicina dental
doz.	dozen	—	docena
Dr.	doctor	Dr., Dra.	doctor, doctora
DST	daylight saving time	—	—
DVM	Doctor of Veterinary Medicine	—	doctor de medicina veterinaria
E	East, east	E, E.	Este, este
ea.	each	c/u	cada uno, cada una
e.g.	for example (exempli gratia)	v.g., v.gr.	verbigracia
EMT	emergency medical technician	—	técnico, -ca en urgencias médicas
Eng.	England, English	—	Inglaterra, inglés
esp.	especially	—	especialmente
EST	eastern standard time	—	—
etc.	et cetera	etc.	etcétera
f	false	—	falso
f	female	f	femenino
F	Fahrenheit	F	Fahrenheit
FBI	Federal Bureau of Investigation	—	—
Feb.	February	feb.	febrero
fem.	feminine	—	femenino
FL, Fla.	Florida	—	Florida
Fri.	Friday	vier., viern.	viernes
ft.	feet, foot	—	pie(s)
g	gram	g., gr.	gramo
Ga., GA	Georgia	—	Georgia
gal.	gallon	—	galón
Gen.	general	Gral.	general
gm	gram	g., gr.	gramo
gov.	governor	—	gobernador, -dora
govt.	government	—	gobierno
gr.	gram	g., gr.	gramo
HI	Hawaii	—	Hawai, Hawaii
hr.	hour	h.	hora
HS	high school	—	colegio secundario
ht.	height	—	altura
Ia., IA	Iowa	—	Iowa
ID	Idaho	—	Idaho
i.e.	that is (id est)	i.e.	id est (esto es, es decir)
IL, Ill.	Illinois	—	Illinois
in.	inch	—	pulgada
IN	Indiana	—	Indiana
Inc.	incorporated	S.A.	sociedad anónima
Ind.	Indian, Indiana	—	Indiana
Jan.	January	ene.	enero
Jul.	July	jul.	julio
Jun.	June	jun.	junio
Jr., Jun.	Junior	Jr.	Júnior
Kan., Kans.	Kansas	—	Kansas
kg	kilogram	kg.	kilogramo
km	kilometer	km.	kilómetro
KS	Kansas	—	Kansas
Ky., KY	Kentucky	—	Kentucky
l	liter	l.	litro
l.	left	izq.	izquierda
L	large	G	(talla) grande
La., LA	Louisiana	—	Luisiana, Louisiana
lb.	pound	—	libra
Ltd.	limited	S.L.	sociedad limitada
m	male	m	masculino
m	meter	m	metro
m	mile	—	milla
M	medium	M	(talla) mediana
MA	Massachusetts	—	Massachusetts
Maj.	major	—	mayor
Mar.	March	mar.	marzo
masc.	masculine	—	masculino
Mass.	Massachusetts	—	Massachusetts
Md., MD	Maryland	—	Maryland
M.D.	Doctor of Medicine	—	doctor de medicina
Me., ME	Maine	—	Maine
Mex.	Mexican, Mexico	Méx.	mexicano, México

ENGLISH ABBREVIATION AND EXPANSION		SPANISH EQUIVALENT	
mg	milligram	mg.	miligramo
mi.	mile	—	milla
MI, Mich.	Michigan	—	Michigan
min.	minute	min	minuto
Minn.	Minnesota	—	Minnesota
Miss.	Mississippi	—	Mississippi, Misisipí
ml	mililiter	ml.	mililitro
mm	millimeter	mm.	milímetro
MN	Minnesota	—	Minnesota
mo.	month	—	mes
Mo., MO	Missouri	—	Missouri
Mon.	Monday	lun.	lunes
Mont.	Montana	—	Montana
mpg	miles per gallon	—	millas por galón
mph	miles per hour	—	millas por hora
MS	Mississippi	—	Mississippi, Misisipí
mt.	mount, mountain	—	monte, montaña
MT	Montana	—	Montana
mtn.	mountain	—	montaña
N	North, north	N	Norte, norte
NASA	National Aeronautics and Space Administration	—	—
NC	North Carolina	—	Carolina del Norte, North Carolina
ND, N. Dak.	North Dakota	—	Dakota del Norte, North Dakota
NE	northeast	NE	nordeste
NE, Neb., Nebr.	Nebraska	—	Nebraska
Nev.	Nevada	—	Nevada
NH	New Hampshire	—	New Hampshire
NJ	New Jersey	—	Nueva Jersey, New Jersey
NM, N. Mex.	New Mexico	—	Nuevo México, New Mexico
no.	north	N	norte
no.	number	n.⁰	número
Nov.	November	nov.	noviembre
N.T.	New Testament	N.T.	Nuevo Testamento
NV	Nevada	—	Nevada
NW	northwest	NO	noroeste
NY	New York	NY	Nueva York, New York
O	Ohio	—	Ohio
Oct.	October	oct.	octubre
OH	Ohio	—	Ohio
OK, Okla.	Oklahoma	—	Oklahoma
OR, Ore., Oreg.	Oregon	—	Oregon
O.T.	Old Testament	A.T.	Antiguo Testamento
oz.	ounce, ounces	—	onza, onzas
p.	page	p.	página
Pa., PA	Pennsylvania	—	Pennsylvania, Pensilvania
pat.	patent	pat.	patente
PD	police department	—	departamento de policía
PE	physical education	—	educación física
Penn., Penna.	Pennsylvania	—	Pennsylvania, Pensilvania
pg.	page	pág.	página
PhD	Doctor of Philosophy	—	doctor, -tora (en filosofía)
pkg.	package	—	paquete
p.m., PM	post meridiem	p.m.	post meridiem (de la tarde)
P.O.	post office	—	oficina de correos, correo
pp.	pages	págs.	páginas
PR	Puerto Rico	PR	Puerto Rico
pres.	present	—	presente
pres.	president	—	presidente, -ta
prof.	professor	—	profesor, -sora
P.S.	postscript	P.D.	postdata
P.S.	public school	—	escuela pública
pt.	pint	—	pinta
pt.	point	pto.	punto
PTA	Parent-Teacher Association	—	—
PTO	Parent-Teacher Organization	—	—
q, qt.	quart	—	cuarto de galón
r.	right	dcha.	derecha
rd.	road	c/, C/	calle
RDA	recommended daily allowance	—	consumo diario recomendado
recd.	received	—	recibido
Rev.	reverend	Rdo.	reverendo
RI	Rhode Island	—	Rhode Island
rpm	revolutions per minute	r.p.m.	revoluciones por minuto
RR	railroad	FC	ferrocarril
R.S.V.P.	please reply (répondez sœil vous plaît)	S.R.C.	se ruega contestación
rt.	right	dcha.	derecha
rte.	route	—	ruta
S	small	P	(talla) pequeña
S	South, south	S	Sur, sur
S.A.	South America	—	Sudamérica, América del Sur
Sat.	Saturday	sáb.	sábado
SC	South Carolina	—	Carolina del Sur, South Carolina
SD, S. Dak.	South Dakota	—	Dakota del Sur, South Dakota
SE	southeast	SE	sudeste, sureste
Sept.	September	sep., sept.	septiembre
so.	south	S	sur
sq.	square	—	cuadrado
Sr.	Senior	Sr.	Sénior
Sr.	sister	—	sor
st.	state	—	estado
st.	street	c/, C/	calle
St.	saint	S., Sto., Sta.	santo, santa
Sun.	Sunday	dom.	domingo
SW	southwest	SO	sudoeste, suroeste
t.	teaspoon	—	cucharadita
T, tb., tbsp.	tablespoon	—	cucharada (grande)
Tenn.	Tennessee	—	Tennessee
Tex.	Texas	—	Texas
Thu., Thur., Thurs.	Thursday	juev.	jueves
TM	trademark	—	marca (de un producto)
TN	Tennessee	—	Tennessee
tsp.	teaspoon	—	cucharadita
Tue., Tues.	Tuesday	mart.	martes
TX	Texas	—	Texas
UN	United Nations	NU, NN.UU.	Naciones Unidas
US	United States	EEUU, EE.UU.	Estados Unidos
USA	United States of America	EEUU, EE.UU.	Estados Unidos de América
usu.	usually	—	usualmente
UT	Utah	—	Utah
v.	versus	v	versus
Va., VA	Virginia	—	Virginia
vol.	volume	vol.	volumen
VP	vice president	—	vicepresidente, -ta
vs.	versus	v	versus
Vt., VT	Vermont	—	Vermont
W	West, west	O	Oeste, oeste
WA, Wash.	Washington (estado)	—	Washington
Wed.	Wednesday	miérc.	miércoles
WI, Wis., Wisc.	Wisconsin	—	Wisconsin
wt.	weight	—	peso
WV, W. Va.	West Virginia	—	Virginia del Oeste, West Virginia
WY, Wyo.	Wyoming	—	Wyoming
yd.	yard	—	yarda
yr.	year	—	año

Irregular English Verbs

INFINITIVE	PAST	PAST PARTICIPLE
arise	arose	arisen
awake	awoke	awoken *or* awaked
be	was, were	been
bear	bore	borne
beat	beat	beaten *or* beat
become	became	become
befall	befell	befallen
begin	began	begun
behold	beheld	beheld
bend	bent	bent
beseech	beseeched *or* besought	beseeched *or* besought
beset	beset	beset
bet	bet	bet
bid	bade *or* bid	bidden *or* bid
bind	bound	bound
bite	bit	bitten
bleed	bled	bled
blow	blew	blown
break	broke	broken
breed	bred	bred
bring	brought	brought
build	built	built
burn	burned *or* burnt	burned *or* burnt
burst	burst	burst
buy	bought	bought
can	could	—
cast	cast	cast
catch	caught	caught
choose	chose	chosen
cling	clung	clung
come	came	come
cost	cost	cost
creep	crept	crept
cut	cut	cut
deal	dealt	dealt
dig	dug	dug
do	did	done
draw	drew	drawn
dream	dreamed *or* dreamt	dreamed *or* dreamt
drink	drank	drunk *or* drank
drive	drove	driven
dwell	dwelled *or* dwelt	dwelled *or* dwelt
eat	ate	eaten
fall	fell	fallen
feed	fed	fed
feel	felt	felt
fight	fought	fought
find	found	found
flee	fled	fled
fling	flung	flung
fly	flew	flown
forbid	forbade	forbidden
forecast	forecast	forecast
forego	forewent	foregone
foresee	foresaw	foreseen
foretell	foretold	foretold
forget	forgot	forgotten *or* forgot
forgive	forgave	forgiven
forsake	forsook	forsaken
freeze	froze	frozen
get	got	got *or* gotten
give	gave	given
go	went	gone
grind	ground	ground
grow	grew	grown
hang	hung	hung
have	had	had
hear	heard	heard
hide	hid	hidden *or* hid
hit	hit	hit
hold	held	held
hurt	hurt	hurt
keep	kept	kept
kneel	knelt *or* kneeled	knelt *or* kneeled
know	knew	known
lay	laid	laid
lead	led	led
lean	leaned	leaned
leap	leaped *or* leapt	leaped *or* leapt
learn	learned	learned
leave	left	left
lend	lent	lent
let	let	let
lie	lay	lain
light	lit *or* lighted	lit *or* lighted
lose	lost	lost
make	made	made
may	might	—
mean	meant	meant
meet	met	met
mow	mowed	mowed *or* mown
pay	paid	paid
put	put	put
quit	quit	quit
read	read	read
rend	rent	rent
rid	rid	rid
ride	rode	ridden
ring	rang	rung
rise	rose	risen
run	ran	run
saw	sawed	sawed *or* sawn
say	said	said
see	saw	seen
seek	sought	sought
sell	sold	sold
send	sent	sent
set	set	set
shake	shook	shaken
shall	should	—
shear	sheared	sheared *or* shorn
shed	shed	shed
shine	shone *or* shined	shone *or* shined
shoot	shot	shot
show	showed	shown *or* showed
shrink	shrank *or* shrunk	shrunk *or* shrunken
shut	shut	shut
sing	sang *or* sung	sung
sink	sank *or* sunk	sunk
sit	sat	sat
slay	slew	slain
sleep	slept	slept
slide	slid	slid
sling	slung	slung
smell	smelled *or* smelt	smelled *or* smelt
sow	sowed	sown *or* sowed
speak	spoke	spoken
speed	sped *or* speeded	sped *or* speeded
spell	spelled	spelled
spend	spent	spent
spill	spilled	spilled
spin	spun	spun
spit	spit *or* spat	spit *or* spat
split	split	split
spoil	spoiled	spoiled
spread	spread	spread
spring	sprang *or* sprung	sprung
stand	stood	stood
steal	stole	stolen
stick	stuck	stuck
sting	stung	stung
stink	stank *or* stunk	stunk
stride	strode	stridden
strike	struck	struck
swear	swore	sworn
sweep	swept	swept
swell	swelled	swelled *or* swollen
swim	swam	swum
swing	swung	swung
take	took	taken
teach	taught	taught
tear	tore	torn
tell	told	told
think	thought	thought
throw	threw	thrown
thrust	thrust	thrust
tread	trod	trodden *or* trod
wake	woke	woken *or* waked
waylay	waylaid	waylaid
wear	wore	worn
weave	wove *or* weaved	woven *or* weaved
wed	wedded	wedded
weep	wept	wept
will	would	—
win	won	won
wind	wound	wound
withdraw	withdrew	withdrawn
withhold	withheld	withheld
withstand	withstood	withstood
wring	wrung	wrung
write	wrote	written